Foto: Helmut Zimmermann

Vergleichende Erziehungswissenschaft

Herausforderung – Vermittlung – Praxis

Festschrift für Wolfgang Mitter zum 70. Geburtstag

Comparative Education

Challenges – Intermediation – Practice

Essays in honour of Wolfgang Mitter on the occasion of his 70th birthday

Éducation Comparée

Défis – Médiations – Pratiques

Mélanges offerts à Wolfgang Mitter pour son 70ᵉ anniversaire

Herausgegeben von / Edited by / Edité par

Christoph Kodron, Botho von Kopp, Uwe Lauterbach,
Ulrich Schäfer, Gerlind Schmidt

Band 1 / Volume 1 / Tome 1

Böhlau Verlag 1997

Die Deutsche Bibliothek - CIP-Einheitsaufnahme

Vergleichende Erziehungswissenschaft : Herausforderung - Vermittlung - Praxis ; Festschrift für Wolfgang Mitter zum 70. Geburtstag = Comparative education / hrsg. von Christoph Kodron ... - Köln : Böhlau.
ISBN 3-412-06597-8

Bd. 1. - (1997)

Copyright © 1997 by Deutsches Institut für Internationale Pädagogische Forschung, Frankfurt am Main

Ohne schriftliche Genehmigung des Verlages ist es nicht gestattet, das Werk unter Verwendung mechanischer, elektronischer und anderer Systeme in irgendeiner Weise zu verarbeiten und zu verbreiten. Insbesondere vorbehalten sind die Rechte der Vervielfältigung – auch von Teilen des Werkes – auf photomechanischem oder ähnlichem Wege, der tontechnischen Wiedergabe, des Vortrags, der Funk- und Fernsehsendung, der Speicherung in Datenverarbeitungsanlagen, der Übersetzung und der literarischen oder anderweitigen Bearbeitung. Ausgenommen von diesem Vorbehalt sind die Zusammenfassungen der Aufsätze in Deutsch, Englisch und Französisch auf den Seiten 763 bis 824. Diese dürfen in Datenbanken übernommen werden.

Druck und buchbinderische Verarbeitung:
Deutsches Institut für Internationale Pädagogische Forschung
Frankfurt am Main

Printed in Germany
ISBN 3-412-06597-8

Vorwort

Wolfgang Mitter ist seit 1972 Leiter der Abteilung Allgemeine und Vergleichende Erziehungswissenschaft des Deutschen Instituts für Internationale Pädagogische Forschung, der wir, die Herausgeber dieses Buches, angehören. Mehrfach war er auch Direktor des Forschungskollegiums unseres Instituts. Seit seiner Emeritierung im Herbst 1995 führt er die Abteilung kommissarisch. Außerdem ist er nach wie vor in verschiedenen Gremien und einschlägigen Fachgesellschaften tätig, hält Vorträge vor Fachkollegen und interessierter Öffentlichkeit, verfaßt Beiträge für wissenschaftliche Zeitschriften und Bücher in verschiedenen Sprachen und bereist forschend die Regionen unserer Erde.

Bereits zu seinem 60. Geburtstag erschienen eine Festschrift[1] sowie ein Sammelband mit Aufsätzen von Wolfgang Mitter[2]. Als wir darangingen, ihn auch zu seinem 70. Geburtstag mit einer Festschrift zu ehren, nicht zuletzt um unseren Dank für die Anregungen und Kontakte auszudrücken, die er uns als seinen Mitarbeitern immer wieder vermittelt hat, stellte sich die Frage: Welcher Personenkreis sollte angesprochen werden? Während in der ersten Festschrift ein kleiner Kreis von Beiträgern, gruppiert um die Professorenkollegen aus unserem Institut, zu Worte kam, wollten wir dieses Mal die große Gemeinde derer einladen, die mit Wolfgang Mitter durch seine langjährige Arbeit im In- und Ausland verbunden sind.

Dabei sollten nicht nur die Fachkollegen aus der Vergleichenden Erziehungswissenschaft angesprochen werden, vielmehr legten es Wolfgang Mitters vielfältige Aktivitäten in nationalen und internationalen Organisationen und Gremien nahe, ebenso seine Partner aus dem Bereich der Politik einzubeziehen. Daß der Jubilar – nicht nur in Organisationen wie dem Europarat, der OECD oder der UNESCO – weltweit gewirkt hat und

---

1 Döbrich, Peter / Kopp, Botho von (Hrsg.): Vergleichende Bildungsforschung. Festschrift für Wolfgang Mitter zum 60. Geburtstag. Köln u. a.: Böhlau 1987. (Zeitschrift für internationale erziehungs- und sozialwissenschaftliche Forschung. Sonderheft. 1987)
2 Mitter, Wolfgang: Schule zwischen Reform und Krise. Zur Theorie und Praxis der vergleichenden Bildungsforschung. Gesammelte Aufsätze. Hrsg. von Christoph Führ und Bernard Trouillet. Köln u. a.: Böhlau 1987. (Studien und Dokumentationen zur deutschen Bildungsgeschichte. 36)

wirkt, wird aus dem Kreis der Autoren und Autorinnen deutlich, denn aus allen fünf Kontinenten unseres Erdballs erreichten uns Zusagen und Beiträge.

Diese Festschrift will auch Zeichen setzen: Die Vergleichende Erziehungswissenschaft ist nach wie vor höchst lebendig und produktiv (ungeachtet der bedauerlichen Schließung von Instituten und der Umwidmung von Lehrstühlen); sie ist bereit, die Herausforderungen anzugehen, die sich aus der Internationalisierung von Bildung und Erziehung und den Auswirkungen der neuen Technologien ergeben; sie pflegt einen weltweiten Diskurs, um zukunftsweisende Ansätze zu entwickeln.

Dem internationalen Charakter dieser Disziplin tragen wir dadurch Rechnung, daß wir die Aufsätze durch Zusammenfassungen in allen drei Sprachen des vorliegenden Buches erschlossen haben. Damit wollen wir deutlich machen, daß „Internationalisierung" oder gar „Globalisierung" – die häufig verwendeten, aber bislang kaum begriffenen Schlagworte – mehr bedeuten als eine bloße Reduzierung der weltweiten wissenschaftlichen Kommunikation auf das Medium der englischen Sprache. Auch Wolfgang Mitter hat bei seinen Vorträgen auf internationalen Veranstaltungen stets die sprachliche Vielfalt unserer Welt geachtet.

Viele haben den Gang unserer Arbeit mit Rat und Tat begleitet. Unser besonderer Dank gilt:

- zunächst Oskar Anweiler, einem langjährigen Kollegen und Freund Wolfgang Mitters, dafür, daß er es übernommen hat, den einleitenden Beitrag zu schreiben, und für seinen kontinuierlichen Rat;
- unserer Kollegin Ingrid Plath und unserem Kollegen Christian Alix, die uns als Muttersprachler bei der Betreuung einzelner englischer und französischer Beiträge und der Übersetzung der Zusammenfassungen geholfen haben;
- unserer Kollegin Sigrun Dosek, die die Druckvorlage termingerecht fertigstellte und mit vielen Ideen dazu beitrug, daß das Werk auch äußerlich ansprechend gestaltet ist;
- unseren Kolleginnen Regine Düvel-Small und Eva Hübner, die uns durch Schreib- und Korrekturarbeiten unterstützt haben, die aufgrund des mehrsprachigen Charakters dieses Buches nicht immer einfach waren;
- nicht zuletzt den Autoren, denn wir haben bei unserer Arbeit an den Texten viele wertvolle Anregungen erhalten.

Vorwort

Sicher wird man unter den Autoren manchen Namen vermissen. Dies ist zum Teil unser Verschulden, denn leider haben wir an manche nicht oder erst zu spät gedacht. Andere mußten mit großem Bedauern wegen privater oder beruflicher Belastung absagen oder waren trotz anfänglicher Zusage aufgrund unvorhergesehener anderweitiger Verpflichtungen verhindert, ihren Beitrag termingerecht abzuschließen.

Allen Lesern, ganz besonders Ihnen, lieber Herr Mitter, wünschen wir nun viel Gewinn und Vergnügen bei der Lektüre.

Frankfurt am Main, den 14. September 1997

Christoph Kodron
Botho von Kopp
Uwe Lauterbach
Ulrich Schäfer
Gerlind Schmidt

Preface

Since 1972 Wolfgang Mitter has been the head of the Department of General and Comparative Education at the German Institute for International Educational Research. The editors of this books are research staff in this department. Wolfgang Mitter has also been Director of the Research Council of our institute several times. After becoming an emeritus professor in the autumn of 1995, he has been the acting head of our department. Furthermore he is still active in several bodies and societies relevant to the field, lecturing to the members of the field and the interested public, writing contributions to scholarly journals and books in different languages and travelling through the regions of our globe as researcher.

On the occasion of his sixtieth birthday a *Festschrift* was already published[1] as well as a collection of Wolfgang Mitter's essays[2]. When we decided to honour him again in celebration of his seventieth birthday, not least of all to thank him for his stimulating influence on our work and the contacts he has arranged for us, his colleagues, we asked ourselves: What circle of persons should be approached for contributions? In the first *Festschrift* only a small number of contributors, centred around his fellow professors in the institute, were included. This time we wanted to invite the large community of those persons who have been linked with Wolfgang Mitter throughout his many years of work at home and abroad.

Wolfgang Mitter's various activities in national and international organisations and bodies gave us the idea that not only his colleagues from the field of comparative education should be approached but also his partners from the field of policies. That Wolfgang Mitter has been active world-wide – not only in organisations like the Council of Eu-

---

1 Döbrich, Peter / Kopp, Botho von (eds.): Vergleichende Bildungsforschung. Festschrift für Wolfgang Mitter zum 60. Geburtstag. [Comparative Education. Essays in honour of Wolfgang Mitter on the occasion of his 60th birthday.] Köln et al.: Böhlau 1987. (Zeitschrift für internationale erziehungs- und sozialwissenschaftliche Forschung. Sonderheft. 1987)
2 Mitter, Wolfgang: Schule zwischen Reform und Krise. Zur Theorie und Praxis der vergleichenden Bildungsforschung. Gesammelte Aufsätze. [School between Reform and Crisis. On Theory and Practice of Comparative Education. Collected Essays.] Ed. by Christoph Führ and Bernard Trouillet. Köln et al.: Böhlau 1987. (Studien und Dokumentationen zur deutschen Bildungsgeschichte. 36)

rope, OECD and UNESCO – is clearly visible in the range of authors sending contributions from all five continents of our globe.

But this *Festschrift* also wants to send a signal: Comparative education is now, as it has been, full of live and prolific (despite the closure of institutes and the reallocation of professorial chairs); it is ready to take up the challenges presented by the internationalisation of education and the implications of the new technologies; it is cultivating a world-wide dialogue in order to continue to develop promising future approaches.

We accounted for the international character of this discipline by making all essays accessible by including abstracts in all three languages used in the book. By doing so we wanted to emphasise that „internationalisation" or even „globalisation" – the frequently used but not really comprehended catchphrases – mean more than merely using the medium of English language for world-wide scientific communication. Wolfgang Mitter himself has also respected the linguistic variety of our world in his wide range of contributions to the field.

Many people have accompanied our editorial work by word and deed. The following deserve our special thanks:

- first Oskar Anweiler, a long-standing colleague and friend of Wolfgang Mitter, not only for undertaking to write the introductory essay, but also for his continuous advice;
- our colleagues Ingrid Plath and Christian Alix who, as native speakers, have helped us both in editing individual English and French essays and translating abstracts;
- our colleague Sigrun Dosek who has prepared the book for printing – in time – and whose ideas have contributed to the fact that the book's general appearance is attractive;
- our colleagues Regine Düvel-Small und Eva Hübner who assisted us by doing the typing and correction work which was not an easy task at times because of the polyglot character of the book;
- last but not least the authors themselves because their contributions provided us with valuable and stimulating ideas during the process of editing.

Certainly some names that could have been expected to be among the contributing authors might not be found. On the one hand, this is our fault: Regretfully we just did not think of some of them in time. On the other hand, there were authors who greatly regretted their not being able to participate because of private or professional workloads or others who, despite initially intending to contribute, were not able to complete their articles in time.

Now we wish all readers, but especially you, dear Wolfgang Mitter, intellectually stimulating and enjoyable reading.

Frankfort on the Main, September 14, 1997

Christoph Kodron
Botho von Kopp
Uwe Lauterbach
Ulrich Schäfer
Gerlind Schmidt

Avant-propos

Depuis 1972 Wolfgang Mitter dirige le Département de Sciences de l'Éducation Générales et Comparées de l'Institut Allemand de Recherche Pédagogique Internationale dont nous-mêmes, les éditeurs de cet ouvrage, faisons partie. Il a assuré au cours de cette période plusieurs fois la direction du Conseil de Recherche de notre institut. Depuis son départ à la retraite à l'automne 1995, il a continué toutefois à diriger ce département à titre transitoire. De plus, il poursuit ses activités dans différentes instances et dans des sociétés savantes réputées, ses conférences dans les milieux spécialisés et auprès d'un public intéressé, rédige des contributions pour des revues scientifiques et des livres en différentes langues et parcourt en chercheur les différentes régions du globe.

Déjà, à l'occasion de son soixantième anniversaire, des mélanges[1] et un recueil de ses articles[2] ont été publiés. Lors qu'il s'est agi de lui rendre hommage pour son soixante-dixième anniversaire, entre autres pour lui témoigner notre reconnaissance pour nous avoir autant stimulés et permis d'établir tant de contacts, la question s'est posé à nous de savoir à quel public cet ouvrage devait s'adresser. Alors que lors des premiers mélanges on n'avait fait appel qu'à un petit groupe de contributeurs, presque tous professeurs et collègues de l'Institut, nous souhaitions cette fois-ci solliciter la grande communauté de ceux qui, en Allemagne et à l'étranger, se sentaient liés à Wolfgang Mitter par une longue collaboration.

En l'occurrence il n'était pas uniquement question des collègues experts de l'éducation comparée car les nombreuses activités de Wolfgang Mitter au sein des organismes et des organisations nationaux et internationaux nous incitaient tout autant à avoir recours à ses partenaires de la sphère politique. Le cercle de ceux et de celles qui ont

---

1   Döbrich, Peter / Kopp, Botho von (eds.): Vergleichende Bildungsforschung. Festschrift für Wolfgang Mitter zum 60. Geburtstag. [Recherche en éducation comparée. Mélanges offerts à Wolfgang Mitter pour son 60e anniversaire.] Köln et al.: Böhlau 1987. (Zeitschrift für internationale erziehungs- und sozialwissenschaftliche Forschung. Sonderheft. 1987)
2   Mitter, Wolfgang: Schule zwischen Reform und Krise. Zur Theorie und Praxis der vergleichenden Bildungsforschung. Gesammelte Aufsätze. [École entre réforme et crise. De la théorie et de la pratique de la recherche en éducation comparée. Recueil d'articles.] Ed. par Christoph Führ et Bernard Trouillet. Köln et al.: Böhlau 1987. (Studien und Dokumentationen zur deutschen Bildungsgeschichte. 36)

contribué à cet ouvrage et les nombreux échos qui nous sont parvenus des cinq continents montrent assez clairement que celui à qui ils rendent hommage ne s'est pas contenté d'œuvrer au sein d'organismes tels que le Conseil de l'Europe, l'OCDE et l'UNESCO, mais aussi bien au-delà.

Ces mélanges entendent aussi marquer une étape. L'éducation comparée reste une discipline très vivante et productive (indépendamment de la fermeture regrettable d'instituts et de la transformation de chaires). Elle est prête à relever les défis qui résultent de l'internationalisation de la formation, de l'éducation et des implications des nouvelles technologies. Elle s'attache à mener un débat global afin d'élaborer des approches innovatrices.

Nous tenons à témoigner du caractère international de cette discipline en rendant les articles accessibles par des résumés dans les trois langues de l'ouvrage. Nous entendons ainsi montrer que l'„internationalisation" et même la „mondialisation" – ces termes si souvent employés mais sans qu'on en saisisse jusqu'à maintenant la portée – vont bien au-delà de la réduction d'une communication scientifique mondiale à la simple utilisation de l'anglais. Lors de ses interventions dans les rencontres internationales Wolfgang Mitter, lui-même, a constamment tenu à respecter la diversité linguistique de notre monde.

Nombreux sont ceux qui ont accompagné et entouré de leurs conseils notre travail. Nous tenons à remercier particulièrement

- en premier lieu Oskar Anweiler, très ancien collègue et ami de Wolfgang Mitter, pour la rédaction de l'introduction;
- nos collègues, Ingrid Plath et Christian Alix, qui nous ont assistés en tant que „natifs" dans la rédaction de certains articles anglais et français et dans la traduction des résumés;
- notre collègue, Sigrun Dosek, qui a élaboré dans les meilleurs délais les épreuves et a contribué par ses idées à lui donner une forme agréable;
- nos collègues, Regine Düvel-Small et Eva Hübner, qui nous ont aidés dans la mise sur ordinateur et dans la correction, ce qui n'était pas toujours facile étant donné le caractère plurilingue de l'ouvrage;
- les auteurs, enfin, qui nous ont fait de nombreuses et précieuses suggestions.

Avant-propos

Bien sûr, on regrettera l'absence de tel ou tel auteur. La faute nous en incombe partiellement car certains noms ne nous sont venus à l'esprit que trop tard. D'autres ont dû décliner l'offre à leur grand regret pour des raisons personnelles, par surcharge de travail, ou bien n'ont pu malgré leur accord initial et du fait d'autres obligations remettre leur manuscrit dans les délais imposés.

Nous souhaitons à tous les lecteurs mais aussi spécialement à vous même, Monsieur Mitter, de tirer profit de la lecture de cet ouvrage et d'y trouver grand plaisir.

Francfort-sur-le-Main, le 14 septembre 1997

Christoph Kodron
Botho von Kopp
Uwe Lauterbach
Ulrich Schäfer
Gerlind Schmidt

INHALT / CONTENTS / SOMMAIRE

Band 1 / Volume 1 / Tome 1

Oskar Anweiler — 1
Vergleichende Erziehungswissenschaft und international vergleichende
Bildungsforschung als Herausforderung und Aufgabe

1.
Theoretische und methodische Aspekte der Vergleichenden Erziehungswissenschaft
Theoretical and Methodological Aspects of Comparative Education
Aspects théoriques et méthodologiques de l'éducation comparée

Philip G. Altbach — 15
Research on Higher Education: Global Perspectives

Erwin H. Epstein — 32
Filtering Democracy through Schools:
The Ignored Paradox of Compulsory Education

Mark B. Ginsburg — 46
The Limitations and Possibilities of Comparative
Analysis of Education in Global Context

Detlef Glowka — 52
Überlegungen zu einer „Einführung in die
Vergleichende Erziehungswissenschaft"

Wolfgang Hörner — 65
„Europa" als Herausforderung für die Vergleichende Erziehungswissenschaft –
Reflexionen über die politische Funktion einer pädagogischen Disziplin

Edmund King — 81
A Turning-Point in Comparative Education: Retrospect and Prospect

Richard Koch 91
Gesellschaftliche Steuerung von Berufsbildungssystemen –
Ein Analysekonzept für politikorientierte internationale Vergleiche

Mauro Laeng 105
From Yesterday to Tomorrow: Developments in Comparative Education

Jean-Michel Leclercq 117
Comment envisager et prendre en compte la culture d'un système éducatif?

Vandra L. Masemann 127
Recent Directions in Comparative Education

Heliodor Muszyński 135
Die Pädagogische Studienreise als Instrument
der wissenschaftlichen Erkenntnis

Shin'ichi Suzuki 143
Shifts in Political Regimes and the Geopolitical Reorganization
of Educational Space: Implications for Comparative Education

Juan Carlos Tedesco 152
Le renouveau de l'éducation comparée

Ulrich Teichler 161
Vergleichende Hochschulforschung – Probleme und Perspektiven

Henk Van daele 173
Éducation comparée et éducation internationale: problèmes linguistiques

Anthony R. Welch 182
Things Fall Apart: Dis-Integration, Universities, and the Decline of
Discipline(s). Problematising Comparative Education in an Uncertain Age

Christoph Wulf 192
Mimesis des Anderen – Annäherungen an das Fremde

2.
Bildungspolitik und Vergleichende Erziehungswissenschaft
Educational Policy and Comparative Education
Politique éducative et éducation comparée

Candido Alberto Gomes 209
Comparative Education and Public Policies: A View from the South

Stephen P. Heyneman 219
Educational Cooperation between Nations in the 21st Century

Georg Knauss 234
Von 1988 bis 1996 – Wege zur Weiterentwicklung der gymnasialen Oberstufe

Hermann Müller-Solger 245
Anerkennung, Akkreditierung, Transparenz – Notwendige
Begriffsklärungen für die Europäische Union

Raymond Ryba 262
Developing the European Dimension of Education in Practice:
The Contribution of the Council of Europe's European Dimension
Pedagogical Materials Programme

Rita Süssmuth 272
Politik und Vergleichende Erziehungswissenschaft in gemeinsamer
Verantwortung für eine humane Lerngesellschaft

Michael Vorbeck 282
Bildungsforschung und besonders Vergleichende Erziehungswissenschaft
in Europa – für Europa

3.
Globale Vergleiche und internationale Aspekte des Bildungswesens
Global Comparisons and International Aspects of Education
Comparaisons globales et aspects internationaux de l'éducation

Birgit Brock-Utne Internationalisierung des Bildungswesens – Eine kritische Perspektive	301
Walter Georg Berufliche Bildung zwischen Internationalisierung und nationaler Identität	312
Torsten Husén The „Education Gap"	329
Joachim H. Knoll From Literacy to Functional Literacy	344
Pierre Laderrière Les transformations à l'Est: une leçon pour l'Ouest?	359
Robert F. Lawson Relationships of Political Contexts to Democracy in Education	367
Donatella Palomba L'éducation à la citoyenneté dans l'Europe multiculturelle: une perspective comparative	381
Vlastimil Pařizek The Crisis in Schools and Solutions to the Problem	393
J. J. Smolicz Language Education Policies in Multilingual Settings: Australia and the Philippines	402
Werner Stephan Lehrer und Gesellschaft – Ein internationaler Vergleich	414

Janusz Tomiak 426
Looking Back, Looking Forward: Education in Central-
Eastern Europe on the Eve of the XXIst Century

David N. Wilson 437
The German Dual System of Vocational Education and Training:
A Comparative Study of Influence upon Educational Policy and
Practice in Other Countries

Band 2 / Volume 2 / Tome 2

4.
Länderstudien
Country and Area Studies
Études par pays

Christel Adick Formale und nonformale Grundbildung in Afrika – Komplementarität oder Konkurrenz?	451
Cesar Bîrzea The Use and Abuse of Educational Research: The Case of a Political Manipulation in Romania	468
Günter Brinkmann Lehrerrolle und Lehrerausbildung in den Niederlanden	477
Harold Herman Education and Political Change in the New South Africa	490
Vitalij Grigor'evič Kostomarov Das Bildungswesen in den Nachfolgestaaten der Sowjetunion und die russische Sprache	502
Nikolaj Dmitrievič Nikandrov Die Werteproblematik in Gesellschaft und Bildungswesen der Russischen Föderation	512
Ioannis Pirgiotakis Greek Education: Myths and Realities	524
Jan Průcha Private versus State Schools: A Comparison of Their Quality in the Czech Republic	538

Bernhard Schiff 550
Das Orthodoxe Klassische Gymnasium in Moskau

Witold Tulasiewicz 559
Education for Sale: Recent Developments in the United Kingdom

Makoto Yûki 572
Die rechtliche Struktur der Bildungsverwaltung in Japan

5.
Historische Dimension
Historical Dimension
La dimension historique

Siegfried Baske 583
Die neuhumanistische Phase des Jenkauer Conradinums
im Urteil der deutschen und polnischen Bildungsgeschichte

Wilhelm Ebert 593
Magna Carta for the Status of Teachers: Thirty Years of
the UNESCO-Recommendation for the Status of Teachers

Yaacov Iram 610
The Status of the Humanities in Education

Victor Karady 621
Schulbildung und Religion – Zu den ethnisch-konfessionellen
Strukturmerkmalen der ungarischen Intelligenz in der Zwischenkriegszeit

Michael Kelpanides 642
Universitätsstudium für jedermann? Die Politisierung der
Sozialwissenschaften als bleibendes Erbe der Bildungsexpansion

Marianne Krüger-Potratz 656
Ein Blick in die Geschichte ausländischer Schüler
und Schülerinnen in deutschen Schulen

David Phillips 673
Prolegomena to a History of British Interest in Education in Germany

Hermann Röhrs 688
Gründung und Gestaltung der „Deutschen Sektion" des „Weltbunds für Erneuerung der Erziehung" (1921 bis 1931) – Ein bildungspolitisch bedeutsames Kapitel der internationalen Reformpädagogik

Leo Roth 707
Die Reformation als Zäsur in der deutschen Universitätsentwicklung – Von der Universalität zur Regionalisierung

Mirosław S. Szymański 725
Erziehung zur Demokratie durch die Schülerselbstregierung in der Zweiten Polnischen Republik (1918 bis 1939)

Heinz-Elmar Tenorth 740
Pädagogik und Soziologie

Verzeichnis der Autoren / List of authors / Liste des auteurs 757

Zusammenfassungen 763

Abstracts 785

Résumés 804

Tabula Gratulatoria

Christel Adick, Bochum
Christina Allemann-Ghionda, Bern
Philip G. Altbach, Chestnut Hill
Masaharu Amano, Tôkyô
Oskar Anweiler, Bochum
Siegfried Baske, Berlin
Zoltán Báthory, Budapest
Paul Bélanger, Hamburg
John J. Bergen, Edmonton
Anne-Marie Bergh, Pretoria
Cesar Bîrzea, Bucureşti
Viktor von Blumenthal, Marburg
Werner Boppel, Bonn
László Brezsnyánszky, Debrecen
Günter Brinkmann, Freiburg im Breisgau
Birgit Brock-Utne, Oslo
Bund-Länder-Kommission für Bildungsplanung
und Forschungsförderung, Bonn
Franz Burgstaller, Spittal
Adelheid Busch, Osnabrück
Herbert Chiout, Kassel
Manuel Crespo, Montréal
Erhard Denninger, Königstein
Deutsche UNESCO-Kommission, Bonn
Horst Dichanz, Hagen
Erika Dingeldey, Wiesbaden
Heinz Durner, Unterhaching
Wilhelm Ebert, München
Max A. Eckstein, New York
Ekkehard Eichberg, Hamburg
Erwin H. Epstein, Columbus, Ohio
Peter Fischer-Appelt, Hamburg

Tabula Gratulatoria

Karl Frey, Zürich
Bernd Frommelt, Wiesbaden
E. E. Geißler, Bonn
Walter Georg, Hagen
Mark B. Ginsburg, Pittsburgh
Hans Glöckel, Nürnberg
Detlef Glowka, Münster
Candido Alberto Gomes, Brasília
Ingrid Hamm, Gütersloh
Hans-Hellmut Hansen, Pinneberg
Jan Havránek, Praha
Helmut Heid, Regensburg
Jürgen Helmchen, Dresden
Jürgen Henze, Berlin
Harold Herman, Belville
Stephen P. Heyneman, Washington, D. C.
J. H. Higginson, Canterbury
Walter Hirche, Hannover
Wolfgang Hörner, Leipzig
Hans Arno Horn, Frankfurt am Main
Klaus Hüfner, Berlin
Torsten Husén, Stockholm
International Bureau of Education, Genève
Yaacov Iram, Ramat-Gan
Mykola D. Jarmačenko, Kiïv
Siegfried Jenkner, Hannover
Egon Jüttner, Mannheim
Jürgen J. Justin, Chemnitz
Heide Kallert, Frankfurt am Main
Victor Karady, Paris
Michael Kelpanides, Thessaloniki
Edmund King, Epsom
Wolfgang Klafki, Marburg
K. J. Klauer, Aachen
Aharon F. Kleinberger, Jerusalem
Gisela Knaup, Bochum
Georg Knauss, München

Tabula Gratulatoria

Joachim H. Knoll, Bochum
Richard Koch, Berlin
Werner Korthaase, Berlin
Vitalij Grigor'evič Kostomarov, Moskva
Jiří Kotásek, Praha
Mikolaj Kozakiewicz, Warszawa
Tamas Kozma, Budapest
Richard Krenzer, Frankfurt am Main
Hans Krönner, Berlin
Marianne Krüger-Potratz, Münster
Volker Krumm, Salzburg
Friedrich Kuebart, Bochum
Pierre Laderrière, Paris
Mauro Laeng, Roma
Robert F. Lawson, Columbus, Ohio
Jean-Michel Leclercq, Paris
Erich Leitner, Klagenfurt
Leo Leitner, Wien
Volker Lenhart, Heidelberg
Dieter Lenzen, Berlin
Karl Chr. Lingelbach, Marburg
Sigrid Luchtenberg, Bielefeld
Sabine Manning, Berlin
Vandra L. Masemann, Tallahassee
Klaus-Dieter Mende, Berlin
Verena Metze-Mangold, Frankfurt am Main
Gisela Miller-Kipp, Düsseldorf
Hermann Müller-Solger, Bonn
Heliodor Muszyński, Poznań
Irmela Neu, München
Gerhart Neuner, Zeuthen
Nikolaj Dmitrievič Nikandrov, Moskva
Harold J. Noah, New York
Donatella Palomba, Roma
Giovanni Pampanini, Catania
Vlastimil Pařizek, Praha
Harm Paschen, Bielefeld

Tabula Gratulatoria

Miguel A. Pereyra, Granada
David Phillips, Oxford
Ioannis Pirgiotakis, Rethymnon
Franz Pöggeler, Aachen
Agostino Portera, Verona
Jan Průcha, Praha
Väino Rajangu, Tallinn
Vasilij Grigor'evič Razumovskij, Moskva
Hans-Wolf Rissom, Paris
Christian Rittelmeyer, Göttingen
P. M. Roeder, Hamburg
Hermann Röhrs, Wilhelmsfeld
Leo Roth, Bremen
Raymond Ryba, Manchester
Bernhard Schiff, Walsrode
Miriam Schmida, Ramat-Gan
Hanno Schmitt, Potsdam
Jürgen Schriewer, Berlin
Joachim Schulz-Hardt, Bonn
Wolfgang Seitter, Frankfurt am Main
Ellen Sessar-Karpp, Leipzig
Kaare Skagen, Tromsø
J. J. Smolicz, Adelaide
Stanjo Stanev, Sofija
Wolfgang Steinhöfel, Chemnitz
Arnold Stenzel, Flensburg
Werner Stephan, Saskatoon
Peter Stokes, Newport
Heinz Stübig, Marburg
Rita Süssmuth, Bonn
Shin'ichi Suzuki, Tôkyô
Mirosław S. Szymański, Warszawa
Rumjana Taulova, Sofija
Juan Carlos Tedesco, Genève
Ulrich Teichler, Kassel
Heinz-Elmar Tenorth, Berlin
Helga Thomas, Berlin

Tabula Gratulatoria

Arild Tjeldvoll, Oslo
Marco Todeschini, Milano
Janusz Tomiak, London
Edmund A. van Trotsenburg, Pörtschach
Witold Tulasiewicz, Cambridge
Henk Van daele, Brussel
Michael Vorbeck, Strasbourg
Eliška Walterová, Praha
Anthony R. Welch, Sydney
Marie-Luise Wengert-Köppen, München
Rolf Wernstedt, Hannover
Karl-Friedrich Wessel, Berlin
Ingeborg Willke, Bochum
David N. Wilson, Toronto
Thyge Winther-Jensen, København
Ilse Renate Wompel, Bochum
Christoph Wulf, Berlin
Panos Xochellis, Thessaloniki
Makoto Yûki, Tôkyô

*Vergleichende Erziehungswissenschaft
und international vergleichende
Bildungsforschung als Herausforderung und Aufgabe*

Oskar Anweiler

Das Themenspektrum der Vergleichenden Erziehungswissenschaft (comparative education) ist, wie dieser Wolfgang Mitter zum 70. Geburtstag gewidmete Band auf eindrucksvolle Weise zeigt, breit und vielfältig. Die hier versammelten Beiträge behandeln neben Grundfragen und aktuellen Problemen der Vergleichenden Erziehungswissenschaft verschiedene Einzelthemen, die in den weiteren Umkreis dieser Disziplin gehören.

Zwischen der Stringenz theoretischer Ansprüche an eine wissenschaftliche Disziplin, bei der es auf Methoden-, Definitions- und Abgrenzungsfragen ankommt, und den Erwartungen verschiedener Art, die an ihre Ergebnisse gerichtet werden, besteht oft eine Spannung, die wiederum Gegenstand innerfachlicher Diskussion ist. Das gilt aber nicht nur für die Vergleichende Erziehungswissenschaft, sondern findet sich ähnlich auch bei benachbarten Disziplinen. Wenn man z. B. die Vergleichende Politikwissenschaft ins Auge faßt, so stößt man auf ähnliche Fragestellungen, methodische Probleme und Abläufe der wissenschaftlichen Diskussion wie in der Vergleichenden Erziehungswissenschaft. Es zeigt sich dabei auch, daß für die Vergleichende Erziehungswissenschaft die Nähe zu einer anderen „vergleichenden Disziplin" mindestens ebenso wichtig ist wie ihr Bezug zur sogenannten „Mutterdisziplin", der Erziehungswissenschaft. Das hat primär mit dem Gegenstand und der besonderen Blickrichtung zu tun, die gewöhnlich mit dem Attribut „international" charakterisiert werden, zu dem später das Attribut „interkulturell" hinzukam. Die Existenz verschiedener Kulturen, Völker und Staaten sowie deren Wechselbeziehungen bilden den Ausgangspunkt und die Grundlage aller sich als vergleichend bezeichnenden Geistes- und Sozialwissenschaften.

Wenn im folgenden versucht werden soll, aus der Fülle der in dieser Festschrift versammelten Aufsätze einige allgemeine Fragestellungen und Richtungen auf dem durch Wolfgang Mitter repräsentierten Arbeits- und Forschungsgebiet vorzustellen, so kann dies nur beispielhaft und selektiv geschehen. Nicht alle abgedruckten Beiträge können durch einen entsprechenden Hinweis einbezogen werden. Auch ergänzende Literaturangaben werden auf ein Mindestmaß beschränkt.[1]

Rückblicke und terminologische Klärungen

Die akademische Disziplin „Vergleichende Pädagogik" oder „Vergleichende Erziehungswissenschaft" ist aus einer praktisch und politisch motivierten pädagogischen Auslandskunde hervorgegangen. Das geschah überall dort, wo durch zunehmende internationale Kontakte das Bedürfnis nach genaueren Kenntnissen fremder, oft als Vorbild angesehener Schulen und Universitäten entstanden war (vgl. *Anweiler 1966; Zymek 1975; Brickman 1988*). Das englische Interesse an Deutschland auf diesem Gebiet, das nicht unwesentlich zur Etablierung der comparative education in England beigetragen hat, ist hierfür ebenso ein gutes historisches Beispiel *(PHILLIPS)*, wie der teils nachweisbare, teils nur vermutete Einfluß des deutschen „dualen Systems" der Berufsausbildung auf andere Länder in der Gegenwart *(WILSON)*.

„Lessons from Abroad – How Other Countries Educate Their Children" – eine solche Buchpublikation *(McAdams 1993)* gehört nicht nur zur „Vorgeschichte" der Vergleichenden Erziehungswissenschaft, sondern bildet auch heute noch ihren pragmatischen Kern, manchmal zum Mißvergnügen der strengen Theoretiker. Sogenannte Länderstudien, die Gesamtanalysen eines Bildungssystems unternehmen (z. B. *HERMAN, PIRGIOTAKIKS*) oder einen bestimmten Ausschnitt bzw. Problembereich zum Gegenstand haben (z. B. *BRINKMANN, PRŮCHA*), sind deshalb unverzichtbar. Auf die Spannung zwischen den auf einen – im weitesten Sinne – praktischen Nutzen zielenden wissenschaftlichen Arbeiten und den vor allem auf einen theoretischen Ertrag im Wissenschaftssystem selbst bedachten hat nicht zuletzt Wolfgang *Mitter (1996a)* im Rückblick auf die eigene Tätigkeit hingewiesen. Wie diese Spannung bewältigt werden kann, zeigt der auf Lehrerfahrungen an der Universität beruhende Versuch einer didaktischen Grundlegung des Faches von *GLOWKA*. Darüber hinaus bleibt aber die Frage virulent, welche Forschungsstrategien in international vergleichenden Studien verfolgt werden müssen, will man sich nicht nur im engen Zirkel der Spezialisten bewegen, sondern verschiedene „Abnehmer" erreichen *(KING)*.

---

[1] Die Autoren der Beiträge in diesem Band werden ohne Jahresangaben in Großbuchstaben aufgeführt. Andere Literaturhinweise und Zitate erfolgen mit Angabe des Verfassers und des Erscheinungsjahres. Die Titel sind im Literaturverzeichnis angegeben.

Das war auch ein wichtiges, im Rückblick sogar entscheidendes Motiv der sich in der Bundesrepublik Deutschland Mitte der sechziger Jahre konstituierenden Bildungsforschung. Es ging darum, den engeren Rahmen einer Universitätsdisziplin, nämlich der damaligen Erziehungswissenschaft, zu verlassen und sich durch Kooperation mehrerer wissenschaftlicher Fächer in der Öffentlichkeit als notwendiger, wenn nicht unentbehrlicher Partner einer modernen Bildungspolitik zu präsentieren. Der Anstoß kam von der Soziologie, namentlich von den Schriften Helmut *Schelskys (1957, 1961)*. Aber erst die programmatische Abhandlung Eugen Lembergs, die 1963 unter dem Titel „Von der Erziehungswissenschaft zur Bildungsforschung" erschienen ist (mit dem Untertitel „Das Bildungswesen als gesellschaftliche Institution"), enthielt alle seitdem wiederholten Argumente für die Notwendigkeit einer multidisziplinären und im Idealfall interdisziplinären Analyse von Bildungswesen, Bildungspolitik und Bildungsreform *(Lemberg 1963)*. Lemberg war an der Hochschule (dem nachmaligen Deutschen Institut) für Internationale Pädagogische Forschung in Frankfurt am Main tätig, deren Struktur dem Ziel multidisziplinärer empirischer Forschung entsprechen sollte. Das ebenfalls im Jahre 1963 in Berlin gegründete Institut für Bildungsforschung in der Max-Planck-Gesellschaft hat dann den Begriff der Bildungsforschung popularisiert (vgl. *Becker 1979*). Der Anstoß, der von diesen beiden Instituten ausging, kam auch den Universitäten zugute.

Nach dem damaligen Verständnis sollte Bildungsforschung – auf die knappste Formel gebracht – es mit Struktur- und Entwicklungsproblemen des Bildungswesens (als gesellschaftlicher Institution und nicht bloß als staatlicher Organisation), den dort ablaufenden Lehr- und Lernprozessen, seiner (permanenten) Reform und nicht zuletzt mit den internationalen Zusammenhängen und Entwicklungen zu tun haben. Letzteren widmet sich die vergleichende Bildungsforschung. Bei ihr handelt es sich ebenfalls um ein von mehreren wissenschaftlichen Disziplinen getragenes Forschungs- und Arbeitsgebiet, die ihre jeweiligen fachspezifischen Aspekte einbringen (z. B. Bildungsökonomie, Bildungssoziologie, Bildungsrecht). Die Vergleichende Erziehungswissenschaft als eine pädagogische Disziplin bildet dabei den Kern einer so verstandenen multidisziplinären vergleichenden Bildungsforschung. Es besteht somit auch kein Gegensatz, sondern ein komplementäres Verhältnis zwischen einer in erster Linie an einer Disziplin orientierten Sichtweise – wir sprechen dann von Vergleichender Erziehungswissenschaft – und einer im oben beschriebenen Sinne auf den Gegenstand bezogenen, wofür wir den integrativen Begriff der vergleichenden Bildungsforschung verwenden.

Es bleiben noch einige Bemerkungen zu den mit dem Attribut „international" verknüpften Aufgabenbezeichnungen auf unserem Feld. Dieses Thema begleitet die Entwicklung der Vergleichenden Erziehungswissenschaft in den USA ebenso wie in Deutschland und in anderen Ländern *(VAN DAELE)*. Es leidet an seiner Vieldeutigkeit: „Internationale Bildung und Erziehung" hieß zunächst Erziehung zur internationalen Verständigung – heute einschließlich der Friedenspädagogik –, meint aber auch internationale praktische Bildungshilfe und schließlich die wissenschaftliche Begleitung und Analyse internationaler Projekte der Entwicklungs- und Bildungshilfe. Wie verhält sich dieses komplexe Feld mit seiner theoretischen Unterfütterung zu der „klassischen" Vergleichenden Erziehungswissenschaft? Darüber ist jüngst ein umfassender Überblick erstellt worden *(Wilson 1994)*, und Wolfgang *Mitter (1995)* hat ebenfalls theoretische und praktische Schlußfolgerungen gezogen. Die internationale Orientierung war und ist für die Vergleichende Erziehungswissenschaft konstitutiv. Die zusammenfassende Bezeichnung „International Comparative Education" findet daher mit Recht Zuspruch und Verbreitung (vgl. *Thomas 1990*). In der deutschen Terminologie böte sich hierzu, vom Gegenstand her gedacht, die im Titel dieses Beitrages verwendete Bezeichnung „International vergleichende Bildungsforschung" an.

Die historische Fundierung

Inwiefern stellt die Vergleichende Erziehungswissenschaft eine „Fortsetzung des Studiums der Geschichte in die Gegenwart" dar? Die Formulierung stammt von Isaac L. Kandel, einem „Klassiker" dieser Disziplin *(Kandel 1959, S. 273;* vgl. dazu *Schriewer 1975)*. Das war nicht exklusiv als alleinige theoretische Bestimmung des Charakters der Vergleichenden Erziehungswissenschaft als einer „Zeitgeschichte" von Bildung und Erziehung gemeint, sondern als Hinweis auf die Notwendigkeit, bei allen Gegenwartsanalysen die historische Dimension nicht zu vernachlässigen. Eine ähnliche Auffassung vertrat auch Nicholas Hans, der eigentliche Begründer der *comparative education* als Universitätsdisziplin in England. Die Aufsätze beider erschienen in der Festschrift für Pedro Roselló, den verdienstvollen Leiter des Bureau International d'Éducation in Genf, im Jahre 1959. Die Beiträge lesen sich auch heute noch als eine nicht durch die Zeitumstände überholte Aufgabenbeschreibung und methodische Orientierung einer offenen, nicht auf einen einzigen Zugang festgelegten Vergleichenden Erziehungswissenschaft und Bildungsforschung. Die Spannweite reichte von den traditionellen Geisteswissenschaften über die Soziologie bis zur Statistik und Bildungsplanung. Die Titel seien daher im Wortlaut genannt *(Thoughts on Comparative Education 1959)*:

- The Methodology of Comparative Education (Isaac L. Kandel)
- The Philosophical Approach to Comparative Education (Joseph A. Lauwerys)
- The Historical Approach to Comparative Education (Nicholas Hans)
- Sociology in the Service of Comparative Education (C. Arnold Anderson)
- Pédagogie expérimentale, pédagogie comparée et plans d'études (Robert Dottrens)
- Die Bedeutung der Statistik für die Vergleichende Erziehungswissenschaft (Philip J. Idenburg)
- The Global Approach to Comparative Education (Leo Fernig)
- Utilización de la educación comparada en el planeamiento integral de la educación (Ricardo Díez Hochleitner).

Warum wird hier daran erinnert? Zum einen deshalb, weil die in einer solchen Aufgabenbeschreibung enthaltene Herausforderung an die international vergleichende Bildungsforschung fortbesteht, zum andern, weil auch Wolfgang Mitter den Zusammenhang zwischen den verschiedenen möglichen Zugangsweisen in der Lehre und in der Forschung betont und praktiziert hat. Dabei kamen ihm die methodische Schulung und die Denkweise des Historikers zustatten, der nicht monokausal oder deterministisch historische Erscheinungen und Abläufe erklärt, sondern gegenüber Generalisierungen im Gewand angeblicher „wissenschaftlicher Gesetze" stets skeptisch bleibt.

„Historische Fundierung" bedeutet Bewußtmachung der geschichtlichen Wurzeln der gegenwärtigen Situation, aber auch das – kaum bewußt wahrgenommene – Fortwirken älterer Formen und Strukturen im gesellschaftlichen Zusammenleben. Die jüngste Entwicklung im östlichen Teil Europas, im früheren kommunistischen Machtbereich, hat dies vor aller Augen demonstriert. Der 1989 begonnene Umbruch in Ostmitteleuropa und das Ende der Sowjetunion haben auch im Bildungs- und Erziehungswesen zunächst die Wiederbelebung älterer nationalkultureller Traditionen, dann aber auch die beharrende Kraft der seit 1917 bzw. 1945 entstandenen Lebensgewohnheiten breiter Bevölkerungsschichten deutlich gemacht (vgl. *Anweiler 1996*). So fanden beispielsweise die Ideen der internationalen Reformpädagogik aus dem ersten Drittel des 20. Jahrhunderts, die in diesen Staaten jahrzehntelang verpönt waren, überraschend schnell eine erstaunliche Resonanz. Dabei handelte es sich vor allem um eine spontane Reaktion auf den totalitären Erziehungsanspruch einer Ideologie und Partei, um die Selbsthilfe gesellschaftlicher Gruppen, um das Ziel der Befreiung des einzelnen von staatlicher Allmacht. Die Reformpädagogik bot hierfür, so sahen es die engagierten Eltern und Lehrer, eine ideelle Orientierung wie auch internationale Beispiele der Realisierung. Diese Rezeption historisch älterer, aber für die betreffenden Länder moderner Ideen und Praktiken wurde durch die Hilfe von außen teilweise unterstützt, konnte aber, wie Polen zeigt, an eigene, jetzt wieder aktivierte Beispiele anknüpfen *(SZYMAŃSKI)*.

Man erinnerte sich dabei auch, daß ein gesamteuropäischer Dialog in pädagogischen Fragen trotz der politisch-ideologischen Gegensätze noch bis in die späten dreißiger Jahre am Leben erhalten werden konnte. Der deutschen Reformpädagogik kam dabei gegenüber den östlichen Nachbarn eine wichtige Vermittlungsrolle zu. Allerdings unterlag sie, ähnlich wie in der Sowjetunion, auch bald der politischen Repression oder Anpassungszwängen. Die zentrale Frage, die Carl Heinrich Becker in der Oktobernummer von 1932 der Zeitschrift des Weltbundes für die Erneuerung der Erziehung (New Education Fellowship) „New Era" zu beantworten suchte, hieß: „Gibt es nun wirklich eine einheitliche Menschheit?" Das Thema seines Kongreßbeitrages lautete: „Der soziale Wandel und die Erziehung unter dem Gesichtspunkt der Verschiedenheit der Völker" *(RÖHRS)*. Gibt es auch am Ende des 20. Jahrhunderts ein aktuelleres Thema für die Vergleichende Erziehungswissenschaft?

Die kulturelle, nationale und regionale Differenzierung

Der Auslandspädagogik als einem zwischen praktischen Interessen und wissenschaftlichen Ambitionen angesiedelten Betätigungsfeld lag seit deren Aufkommen im 19. Jahrhundert eine nationalstaatliche Perspektive zugrunde. Diese ist zwar nicht, wie oft behauptet wird, am Ende des 20. Jahrhunderts obsolet geworden, sie kann aber nicht mehr die dominierende sein. Das hat weniger mit methodischen Fragen des Vergleichs in den einschlägigen Disziplinen zu tun, als vielmehr mit dem Wechsel der Perspektiven und mit der unterschiedlichen Gewichtung der Rolle des ehemals souveränen Nationalstaates in der Weltpolitik von heute. Die Bildungssysteme, auch in der Europäischen Union, erscheinen zwar als die letzten Reservate einer unabhängigen, von außen nicht direkt beeinflußten Politik der jeweiligen nationalen Gesetzgebungen und Verwaltungen, aber in Wirklichkeit verläuft ihre Entwicklung längst nicht mehr isoliert. Der europäische Integrationsprozeß eröffnet daher der Vergleichenden Erziehungswissenschaft die Chance, mit ihrem methodischen Rüstzeug zur Klärung grundlegender Fragen, aber auch zur Unterstützung praktischer Vorhaben beizutragen *(HÖRNER)*. Auch der Gedanken- und Erfahrungsaustausch in etablierten Organisationen trägt wesentlich zu der „Internationalisierung" der Bildungspolitik bei. Das kann innerhalb einer institutionell verankerten Kooperation, wie sie der Europarat betreibt, geschehen *(RYBA, VORBECK)*, oder in einem weltweiten Rahmen durch andere internationale Organisationen, in denen auch Bildungsfragen ihren Platz gefunden haben (*HEYNEMAN*).

Die Wechselbeziehungen zwischen endogenen und exogenen Einflußkräften und Faktoren lassen sich besonders bei den „Transformationen" der osteuropäischen Gesellschaften verfolgen *(LADERRIÈRE, TOMIAK)*. Auch für die vergleichende Bildungsforschung stellen diese Entwicklungen eine Herausforderung dar. Es genügt nämlich nicht, allein von außen mit den in anderen Gesellschafts- und Wissenschaftssystemen erworbenen Kenntnissen und Kriterien die Veränderungsprozesse zu beurteilen, sondern es kommt ebenso darauf an, die immanenten Wahrnehmungs- und Erklärungsweisen einzubeziehen, und zwar in ihrer Differenziertheit. Für die notwendigen Kooperationspartner der international vergleichenden Bildungsforschung in den einzelnen Ländern dieser Region ist dies dabei in vielen Fällen nicht nur mit einem fachlichen Nachholbedarf, sondern ebenso mit einem neuen Verhältnis zwischen Wissenschaft und Politik verbunden *(BÎRZEA)*. Vergleichende Studien, die Probleme in den „Transformationsländern" zusammen mit denen in westlich-demokratischen behandeln, wie das z. B. eine Untersuchung der Arbeitsbedingungen der Lehrer zeigt *(STEPHAN)*, sind daher besonders wichtig. Ein weiteres Beispiel für die erhellende Wirkung international vergleichender Analysen dreier ganz verschiedener Gesellschafts- und Bildungssysteme unter demokratietheoretischen Aspekten bietet *LAWSON*. Die „demokratisierende" Rolle der allgemeinen Schulpflicht, die lange Zeit hindurch einfach unterstellt wurde, dürfte bei einer differenzierenden Betrachtung inzwischen ebenfalls zu bezweifeln sein *(EPSTEIN)*.

„Erziehung und die Vielfalt der Kulturen" lautete der Titel der maßgeblich von Wolfgang Mitter gestalteten Konferenz der Comparative Education Society in Europe 1983 in Würzburg *(Mitter / Swift 1985)*. Zu einem verhältnismäßig frühen Zeitpunkt wurde damit von der Vergleichenden Erziehungswissenschaft in Deutschland das später populär gewordene Thema einer interkulturellen und multikulturellen Bildung und Erziehung aufgegriffen. Die von *Mitter (1986)* geforderte und entwickelte, auf kulturtheoretischen Überlegungen beruhende Klarheit der Begriffsbildung konnte sich aber in der Folgezeit auch in der wissenschaftlichen Diskussion, geschweige im öffentlichen Sprachgebrauch, nur teilweise durchsetzen. Die Problematik als solche ist gleichzeitig dringlicher und komplizierter geworden: im Innern der meisten Gesellschaften und Staaten auf der Welt und in dem Verhältnis zwischen den „Kulturen". Wie der Kulturbegriff definiert und in welchem theoretischen oder politischen Zusammenhang er verwendet wird, bleibt weiterhin in der Diskussion. Daß dabei im jeweiligen rechtlichen und politischen Kontext genau unterschieden werden muß, zeigt ein Blick in die Geschichte des Unterrichts für ausländische Schüler im Deutschen Reich *(KRÜGER-POTRATZ)* oder ein Vergleich zweier sich gern als „multikulturell" bezeichnender Gesellschaften, nämlich derjenigen Australiens und der Philippinen *(SMOLICZ)*.

Die gegenwärtige kulturvergleichende Bildungsforschung, wie man diese Richtung bezeichnen könnte, enthält auch eine geisteswissenschaftliche Traditionslinie, für die hier die Namen von Robert Ulich und Friedrich Schneider stehen mögen. Der „kulturalistische Ansatz" in der Vergleichenden Erziehungswissenschaft *(Halls 1971)* konnte sich jedoch seinerzeit gegenüber dem dominant gewordenen soziologischen und ökonomischen nur schwer behaupten. Inzwischen sind die großen Weltkulturen, insbesondere die Unterschiede zwischen der christlich geprägten „Western civilization" und dem Islam ins Rampenlicht der Öffentlichkeit gerückt. Gegenüber Samuel P. Huntingtons pessimistischer Prognose eines möglichen „clash of civilizations" *(Huntington 1993)* verlangte sogar der deutsche Bundespräsident eine „Zivilisation der Verständigung", um einem „globalen Kulturkampf" zu widerstehen *(Herzog 1996, S. 194-207)*. Von einem solchen kann zwar, wenn man das kulturelle Argument in einem primär politisch und ökonomisch motivierten „Verteilungskampf" nüchtern gewichtet, kaum die Rede sein (vgl. *Kondylis 1996*), aber bedeutsam bleibt die Frage trotzdem, weshalb und in welchem Zusammenhang die Rolle der Kultur so stark betont wird. Tritt jetzt ihre Abgrenzungsfunktion gegenüber einer universellen Kulturidee in den Vordergrund? Es liegt auf der Hand, daß dies auch Auswirkungen auf die interkulturell vergleichende Bildungsforschung hat. Ein „Blick aus der südlichen Hemisphäre" *(GOMES)* oder aus einem zerfallenen übernationalen Reich (Sowjetunion) mit der sprachlich-kulturellen Dominanz eines Volkes (der Russen) kann hier einiges zur Klärung beitragen *(KOSTOMAROV)*.

Globale und universelle Perspektiven

Die Entwicklung der Vergleichenden Erziehungswissenschaft im 20. Jahrhundert läßt sich auch als ein Beitrag zur „Internationalisierung" der Pädagogik insgesamt beschreiben (vgl. *Anweiler 1989*). Aus den Bemühungen vieler, Einzelpersonen wie nichtstaatlicher Organisationen, entstand nach dem Zweiten Weltkrieg im Rahmen der Vereinten Nationen die Sonderorganisation für Erziehung und Kultur, die Unesco. Sie war vom Ursprung her und der Idee nach eine westlich-demokratische Einrichtung, die aber einen universellen und globalen Anspruch erhob. Dieser ist jedoch in seinen Zielen und Voraussetzungen inzwischen nicht mehr unumstritten. Das grundsätzliche Problem für die Legitimität einer „Weltpädagogik" resultiert aus der Spannung zwischen dem universellen Geltungsanspruch der Menschenrechte für das Individuum und dem oft als gleichrangig oder sogar als höherrangig eingestuften kollektiven Recht auf kulturelle, nationale oder religiöse „Identität" der betreffenden Gruppe (vgl. *Schmale 1993*). Auch das Ziel einer Erneuerung einer „humanistischen" Bildung und Erziehung *(IRAM)* muß dies in Rechnung stellen.

Trotz des Ost-West-Konflikts zwischen 1947 und 1989 konnte die Unesco als Klammer dienen, da der Nutzen für die Empfängerländer sich mit den Interessen der Geberländer ausbalancieren ließ. Auch die international vergleichende Bildungsforschung konnte von dieser Konstellation in gewissem Umfang profitieren. Globale Programme, vor allem die zur Bekämpfung des weltweiten Analphabetismus, ermöglichten Wissenschaftlern den Zugang zu dieser Problematik und die Begegnung mit fremden Kulturen *(KNOLL)*. Dabei konnte es nicht ausbleiben, daß durch unmittelbare Kontakte auch die Spannung zwischen den als universell gültig verkündeten Zielen und der davon oft himmelweit entfernten Realität praktisch erfahren wurde. Schon die in den entwickelten Industrienationen demokratischen Typs gebräuchlichen Bezeichnungen im Erziehungs- und Bildungsbereich, die in der Literatur der Vergleichenden Erziehungswissenschaft verwendet werden, können in die Irre führen. Wichtiger ist aber natürlich die erfahrene Differenz der Lebensweisen und Kulturen, die nur durch intellektuelle Anstrengung überbrückt werden kann *(ADICK)*.

Auf diesem Hintergrund läßt sich der Beitrag der vergleichenden Bildungsforschung zur Klärung weltweiter Erziehungsprobleme durch einige weitere Überlegungen umreißen. Die „gemeinsame Verantwortung für eine humane Lerngesellschaft", die auf dem Leitbild eines „globalen Denkens und kooperativen Handelns" beruht, proklamiert einen internationalen Rahmen für bildungspolitisches Handeln und pädagogische Verantwortung *(SÜSSMUTH)*. Dem wird kaum jemand widersprechen wollen. Die Vergleichende Erziehungswissenschaft kann diese ideellen und politischen Ziele teilen, aber sie bleibt in erster Linie aufgefordert, die Voraussetzungen und Bedingungen, die Wege und Methoden, die Wirkungen, auch die ungewollten, zu bedenken und zu klären, möglichst sine ira et studio. Diese Differenz von Wissenschaft und Politik gilt es zu beachten.

Ein „World Educational System", von dem manchmal die Rede ist, besteht als ein gedankliches Konstrukt, jedoch nicht in der Realität. Das westliche Modell der Schulpflicht für alle Kinder eines Staates (zumindest als Ziel) oder die äußere Übernahme der grundlegenden Strukturmodelle des Bildungswesens der industrialisierten Staaten durch die Entwicklungsländer bewirken noch keine „Globalisierung" in diesem Bereich. Die

„Bildungslücke", die sich in schulischen Leistungsunterschieden niederschlägt, beruht nur zum Teil auf dem Rückstand des formalen Bildungssystems *(HUSÉN)*. Auch die Trendanalysen über die Teilnahmeraten in formalen Bildungseinrichtungen oder Alphabetisierungskursen – ein konventionelles Mittel vergleichender statistischer Studien – besagen nicht viel über eine Konvergenz der Entwicklung, geschweige denn über inhaltliche Fortschritte.

Ebenso hat die internationale Hochschulforschung, ein stark expandierendes Gebiet der beiden letzten Jahrzehnte *(ALTBACH)*, zwar in erheblichem Maße zu einem klareren Blick auf die Vielfalt der auf der Welt existierenden Hochschultypen beigetragen und damit auch die internationalen Beziehungen verstärkt und erleichtert *(TEICHLER)*, aber ein „Welthochschulsystem" wäre eine Chimäre. Bekanntlich gehen sogar im Rahmen der Europäischen Union mit ihren internen Regelungsmechanismen die Fortschritte bei der Anerkennung der nationalen Diplome und Abschlüsse nur im Schneckentempo voran *(MÜLLER-SOLGER)*. Den klassischen und unverzichtbaren Beitrag der Vergleichenden Erziehungswissenschaft bei der Herausarbeitung der wesentlichen Unterschiede, Ähnlichkeiten und Gemeinsamkeiten auf diesem wichtigen Gebiet hat ebenfalls Wolfgang *Mitter (1996c)* mit einer Vier-Länder-Studie zum Verhältnis von Sekundarabschluß und Hochschulzugang überzeugend demonstriert.

Die in Mode gekommene Rede von der „Globalisierung" scheint der hier geäußerten Skepsis gegenüber „weltgesellschaftlichen" Denkmodellen, die oft auf kapitalismus-kritischen politischen Wertpräferenzen beruhen *(GINSBURG)*, zu widersprechen. Aber nur scheinbar: Die durch die neueste Kommunikationstechnologie weltweit ermöglichte „mediale Homogenisierung" über Sprach- und Kulturgrenzen hinweg schafft beileibe nicht eine „kollektive Weltidentität", sondern bewirkt im Gegenteil kollektive Widerstände aus religiösen oder ethnischen Wurzeln (vgl. *Barloewen 1996*). Insofern bleibt es auch für die Vergleichende Erziehungswissenschaft eine Herausforderung, sich der „geopolitischen Reorganisation" der Weltkarte der Erziehung zu stellen *(SUZUKI)*. „Internationalisierung", erfahren als Vordringen einer anderen, übermächtigen „Marktkultur" *(TULASIEWICZ)*, ist nahezu das Gegenteil dessen, was die Ideenträger der „internationalen Erziehung" und die Vertreter der Vergleichenden Erziehungswissenschaft in unserem Jahrhundert angestrebt hatten *(BROCK-UTNE)*. Die „Annäherung an das Fremde", die Begegnung mit dem Anderen, in unmittelbarem Umgang oder in der kulturellen Welt der Symbole, bleibt daher gerade wegen der technisch-ökonomischen Globalisierung eine stete Herausforderung an Bildung und Erziehung *(WULF)*.

Wolfgang Mitter hat in einem seiner jüngsten Aufsätze das Thema „Universalismus und kultureller Pluralismus in der Vergleichenden Erziehungswissenschaft" auf der Grundlage seiner Erfahrungen auf den verschiedenen internationalen Tätigkeitsfeldern reflektiert und im Unterschied zu der hier angeklungenen, eher skeptischen eine hoffnungsvollere Sicht vertreten: *„Während der Vergleich einerseits die Komplexität universalistischen Denkens und Handelns aufzuzeigen vermag, kann er andererseits zutage fördern, daß das Feld der Ähnlichkeiten sowie Gemeinsamkeiten unterschiedlicher politischer und pädagogischer Kulturen größer ist, als eine ungeprüfte Akzeptanz eines kulturellen Relativismus als Vergleichsbasis vermuten läßt" (Mitter 1996b).* Daraus spricht das Engagement eines Wissenschaftlers, der sich einer – im Wort- und Geschichtssinn – humanistischen Aufgabe verpflichtet weiß. Ohne diesen personalen Antrieb verlöre auch die Vergleichende Erziehungswissenschaft ihre über die Fachgrenzen hinausweisende Bedeutung und Funktion.

Bibliographie

Anweiler, Oskar: Von der pädagogischen Auslandskunde zur Vergleichenden Erziehungswissenschaft. In: Pädagogische Rundschau, 20 (1966) 10, S. 886-896.

Anweiler, Oskar: Die internationale Dimension der Pädagogik. In: Röhrs, Hermann / Scheuerl, Hans (Hrsg.): Richtungsstreit in der Erziehungswissenschaft und pädagogische Verständigung, Frankfurt a. M. u. a.: Lang 1989, S. 83-97.

Anweiler, Oskar: Historische und vergleichende Aspekte der Wandlungen in der Pädagogik und im Bildungswesen Polens, Rußlands und der früheren DDR. In: Bandau, Susanne u. a. (Hrsg.): Schule und Erziehungswissenschaft im Umbruch. Ergebnisse eines deutsch-polnischen Symposiums (= Studien und Dokumentationen zur vergleichenden Bildungsforschung. 69), Köln u. a.: Böhlau 1996, S. 2-13.

Barloewen, Constantin von: Gibt es ein Weltdorf? Die Globalisierung ist nur die Oberfläche der Wirklichkeit. In: Frankfurter Allgemeine Zeitung vom 8. März 1996.

Becker, Helmut: Was ist Bildungsforschung? In: Röhrs, Hermann (Hrsg.): Die Erziehungswissenschaft und die Pluralität ihrer Konzepte, Wiesbaden: Akademische Verlagsgesellschaft 1979, S. 215-226.

Brickman, William W.: History of Comparative Education. In: Postlethwaite, Thomas Neville (Hrsg.): The Encyclopedia of Comparative Education and International Systems of Education, Oxford u. a.: Pergamon Press 1988, S. 3-7.

Halls, William D.: Kultur und Erziehung. Der kulturalistische Ansatz in vergleichenden Studien. In: Bildung und Erziehung, 24 (1971) 6, S. 509-520.

Herzog, Roman: Vision Europa. Antworten auf globale Herausforderungen. 2. Aufl. Hamburg: Hoffmann und Campe 1996.

Huntington, Samuel P.: The Clash of Civilizations? In: Foreign Affairs, 72 (1993) 3, S. 22-49.

Kandel, Isaac L.: The Methodology of Comparative Education. In: International Review of Education, 5 (1959) 3, S. 270-280.

Kondylis, Panajotis: Globale Mobilmachung, Konflikt der Kulturen oder Konflikte ohne Kultur? In: Frankfurter Allgemeine Zeitung vom 13. Juli 1996.
Lemberg, Eugen: Von der Erziehungswissenschaft zur Bildungsforschung. Das Bildungswesen als gesellschaftliche Institution. In: ders. (Hrsg.): Das Bildungswesen als Gegenstand der Forschung (= Veröffentlichungen der Hochschule für Internationale Pädagogische Forschung. 3), Heidelberg: Quelle und Meyer 1963, S. 21-100.
McAdams, Richard P.: Lessons from Abroad. How Other Countries Educate Their Children. Lancaster, Pa.: Technomic Press 1993.
Mitter, Wolfgang: Multikulturelle Erziehung im Spiegel der Vergleichenden Erziehungswissenschaft. Überlegungen zur Begriffsbildung und Thematik. In: Dilger, Bernhard u. a. (Hrsg.): Vergleichende Bildungsforschung. DDR, Osteuropa und interkulturelle Perspektiven. Festschrift für Oskar Anweiler zum 60. Geburtstag, Berlin: Berlin-Verlag Arno Spitz 1986, S. 493-508.
Mitter, Wolfgang: Vergleichende Analyse und internationale Erziehung in der Vergleichenden Erziehungswissenschaft, Oktober 1995 (unveröffentlichtes Vortragsmanuskript).
Mitter, Wolfgang: Rückblick und Ausblick: Internationale Bildungsforschung am Deutschen Institut. Zwei Reden zur Amtsübergabe. In: Zeitschrift für Internationale Erziehungs- und Sozialwissenschaftliche Forschung, 13 (1996a) 1, S. 1-12.
Mitter, Wolfgang: Universalismus und kultureller Pluralismus in der Vergleichenden Erziehungswissenschaft, 1996b (unveröffentlichtes Manuskript).
Mitter, Wolfgang (Hrsg.): Wege zur Hochschulbildung in Europa. Vergleichsstudie zum Verhältnis von Sekundarabschluß und Hochschulzugang in Frankreich, England und Wales, Schweden und Deutschland. Köln u. a.: Böhlau 1996c. (Studien und Dokumentationen zur vergleichenden Bildungsforschung. 70)
Mitter, Wolfgang / Swift, James (Hrsg.): Education and the Diversity of Cultures. The Contribution of Comparative Education. Bd. 1. 2. Köln u. a.: Böhlau 1985. (Bildung und Erziehung. Beiheft. 2)
Schelsky, Helmut: Schule und Erziehung in der industriellen Gesellschaft. Würzburg: Werkbund-Verlag 1957.
Schelsky, Helmut: Anpassung oder Widerstand? Soziologische Bedenken zur Schulreform. Heidelberg: Quelle und Meyer 1961.
Schmale, Wolfgang (Hrsg.): Human Rights and Cultural Diversity. Goldbach: Keip 1993.
Schriewer, Jürgen: „Verlängerung des Studiums der Geschichte der Erziehung in die Gegenwart"? Erkenntnisinteressen und -möglichkeiten der Vergleichenden Erziehungswissenschaft. In: Böhm, Winfried / ders. (Hrsg.): Geschichte der Pädagogik und systematische Erziehungswissenschaft, Stuttgart: Klett-Cotta 1975, S. 109-134.
Thomas, R. Murray (Hrsg.): International Comparative Education. Practices, Issues and Prospects. Oxford u. a.: Pergamon Press 1990.
Thoughts on Comparative Education. Festschrift for Pedro Rosselló. (Themenheft). In: International Review of Education, 5 (1959) 3, S. 257-368.
Wilson, David N.: Comparative and International Education: Fraternal of Siamese Twins? A Preliminary Genealogy of Our Twin Fields. In: Comparative Education Review, 38 (1994) 4, S. 449-486.
Zymek, Bernd: Das Ausland als Argument in der pädagogischen Reformdiskussion. Schulpolitische Selbstrechtfertigung, Auslandspropaganda, internationale Verständigung und Ansätze zu einer vergleichenden Erziehungswissenschaft in der internationalen Berichterstattung deutscher pädagogischer Zeitschriften, 1871-1952. Ratingen u. a.: Henn 1975. (Schriftenreihe zur Geschichte und politischen Bildung. 19)

1.

Theoretische und methodische Aspekte der Vergleichenden Erziehungswissenschaft
Theoretical and Methodological Aspects of Comparative Education
Aspects théoriques et méthodologiques de l'éducation comparée

Looking back to the history of Comparative Education in the past four decades, the interpreter gets aware of changes of paradigms which have been stimulated by developments and trends in the reality of the socioeconomic, political and cultural framework as well as in the continuous debates within the science system. On the other hand these changes should not be only considered as turning-points, but also as incentives of continuity which has always challenged comparative educationists to new ideas and action-oriented suggestions.

Wolfgang Mitter, 1996

Wolfgang Mitter: Challenges to Comparative Education. Between Retrospect and Expectation. Presidential Address delivered to the IXth World Congress of Comparative Education, Sydney, Australia, 2 July, 1996.

Research on Higher Education: Global Perspectives

Philip G. Altbach

Introduction

Universities are central institutions in modern society. They have a long and complex history which affects contemporary reality. Universities have assumed central roles in providing the training needed for knowledge-based societies, and have also emerged as important centers for research, especially in the basic sciences. Universities facilitate social mobility as they educate a growing portion of the population. Several decades ago, Martin *Trow (1972)* looked at the progression of higher education from elite to mass and finally to universal access. In the industrialized nations, at least, mass access has been achieved, and a few countries, most notably the United States and Canada, have moved to semi-universal access, enrolling about half of the relevant age group. Others, notably such Pacific Rim nations as Japan, Korea and Taiwan, educate close to 40 per cent.

As the 21st century approaches, universities face a variety of challenges, many of them stemming from their success. As academic institutions have grown, they have become more complex, have taken on more functions, and have consumed ever greater resources. In many countries, questions are being asked about the funding of higher education as well as about the mission of the university. In almost all countries, limitations have been placed on public spending, and public universities have felt budgetary constraints.

In this complex environment and in an atmosphere of controversy about higher education, there is a great need for expert knowledge and data about all aspects of higher education, and an even greater need for a sophisticated understanding of the nature of academic institutions, their roles, and their key components – students and faculty. It is here that research on higher education is of crucial importance for the future of the university. Clearly, academic institutions must understand themselves if they are to survive and prosper. Similarly, policy makers outside academic institutions, increasingly powerful in shaping future directions for academe through their budgetary and other decisions, need to fully understand the complex realities of higher education. Academic institutions themselves must articulate their multiple roles and purposes, and their responsibilities to increasingly wary and skeptical external constituencies.

This essay looks at the past, present and future of research on higher education.[1] It adopts an international perspective and seeks to help the reader understand the complex web of research relating to higher education. Many have noted that scholars have generally avoided studying themselves or their own institutions – as a result there has been surprisingly little research and analysis concerning higher education until the very recent period. The reasons for the lack of research on higher education have never been carefully studied. Respect for traditional academic values, a reluctance to expose academe to public scrutiny, the lack of a supportive research subculture, and until recently few opportunities for publication all hindered research in the field. Much of the limited data collection was done on an institutional basis, was not published, and did not contribute to the development of a research tradition.

For many countries, analysis concerning higher education is almost entirely absent. For others, it is quite limited. Even for countries which have large research communities and a tradition of analysis in the field of education, the literature on higher education is surprisingly limited. It is clear that the need for data collection and research concerning higher education is substantial. Planning, accountability, governmental involvement in academic life, and the sheer size of many contemporary higher education institutions means that data and analysis are needed so that the decisions are based on accurate information and thoughtful discussion.

Scarcity of Data and Analysis

It is important to examine the reasons for the general paucity of data, research and analysis concerning higher education, because this will tell us about the origin of the field and the nature of interest in it. Few claim that the study of higher education is a full-fledged academic discipline. As a result, the infrastructures that go along with a scientific discipline – academic departments, professorships, and the like – are for the most part missing.[2] In part because higher education has no disciplinary base, it has had

---

1   For an earlier consideration of similar topics, see *Altbach (1985)* and *Klucyczynski (1985)*.
2   *Dressel/Mayhew (1974)* discuss the origin of the field in the United States and deal with the debate about higher education as a discipline. In one of the few other studies of the development of the

no clear academic home. In countries with an Anglo-Saxon academic tradition, such as the United States, Britain, Canada, Australia and some others, where the study of higher education has been incorporated into the research and teaching activities of universities, it has been in schools of education. Higher education is often seen as peripheral to the traditional concerns of schools of education – primary and secondary education and the issues concerned with schools. In only a few countries, and in a limited number of academic institutions within these countries, is higher education an established part of educational studies.

The study of higher education is an interdisciplinary endeavor. This has been a strength and a weakness. It is a strength because researchers in many social science disciplines – including but not limited to sociology, political science, psychology, economics and history – have contributed very significantly to the development of research on higher education. Researchers in the field of educational studies have slowly begun to develop an interest in higher education – curriculum specialists, educational planners and others now work on post-secondary issues. The small number of researchers focusing on higher education has made the emergence of a distinctive field more difficult. In part because it is an interdisciplinary field, higher education research has no established methodology. It borrows from other fields. Again, this is both a strength and a weakness. Interdisciplinarity has contributed to original and quite innovative research. On the other hand, it has hindered the creation of an identifiable research community.

Funding stimulates research, and until recently, there was little money available for research on higher education. There have been some exceptions to this rule, and in these cases, the research base was significantly improved, if only temporarily, since the emphasis was generally short-lived. For example, major reform efforts in Britain (the Robbins Commission) and in Sweden (the U-68 Report) stimulated research *(Robbins 1966)*. The Carnegie Foundation for the Advancement of Teaching in the United States and the Leverhulme Trust in Britain sponsored major studies of higher education in order to understand academic systems in the midst of change and facing considerable challenges.[3] It is significant to note that research funding became available to under-

---

    field, Xu *Yu (1995)* focuses on similar debates in China, where many of the first generation of researchers attempted to establish higher education as a discipline.

3 In the early 1970s, under the leadership of Clark Kerr, the Carnegie Commission on Higher Education sponsored more than 50 volumes which provided an impressive research base for American higher education. At the end of the decade, again under Kerr's leadership, the Carnegie Council on Policy Studies in Higher Education sponsored additional studies and reports. At about the same

stand and presumably to solve pressing problems. For a period of time, governments in Central and Eastern Europe sponsored research on higher education and supported research institutions. Educational research generally has traditionally been underfunded, and higher education received little attention from those providing resources to educational research or from agencies funding research in the social sciences.

There are, within the field of higher education, several areas which have a fairly strong research base and foci of literature. The economics of higher education is an especially central topic in a period when the allocation of resources is of considerable concern. The Institut de Recherche sur l'Économie de l'Éducation in Dijon, France and the Institute for Research on Higher Education at the University of Pennsylvania have both focused attention on economic issues in higher education. Gathering international statistical information relating to higher education has been seen as a priority by UNESCO, which has collected information on statistical trends for several decades.[4] In the United States, the National Center for Educational Statistics of the U.S. Government has recently developed initiatives to ensure accurate international statistics concerning higher education. Comparative studies in higher education are also an identifiable trend in the literature, and researchers in many countries have an interest in comparative studies, in part to provide a basis for comparison for national policy makers.

Two major international analyses of trends have added significantly to current discussions of comparative higher education. The *World Bank*'s *(1994)* recent policy review for higher education included several comparative research studies. This report stimulated a good deal of discussion and controversy, including a volume of critiques *(Buchert/King 1995)*. *UNESCO (1995)* also completed an overview of higher education trends worldwide.

Much of the research and data concerning higher education has not been formally published in standard books and journals and may be considered part of a 'gray literature' that is difficult to access, and which often is not permanently in library or other collections. This data often relates to individual academic institutions and is circulated only within the institution. For the most part, detailed institutional reporting, on such

---

time, the Leverhulme Trust in Britain sponsored a dozen or more studies relating to British higher education in the aftermath of the Robbins Report.

4 UNESCO's *World Education Report, 1993* provides some international statistical information. See also UNESCO's *Statistical Yearbooks* for a range of information relating to education and other cultural developments.

issues as trends in enrollments, student achievement, detailed fiscal arrangements, and the like, have little relevance to a wider audience despite the importance of this information for institutional planning and assessment. In many cases, it is appropriate to maintain confidentiality for some kinds of institutional data. Still, institutional research data has many uses beyond the direct and immediate needs of a specific campus – e. g. comparison or 'benchmarking' of institutional trends – and the potential of this data is almost never exploited. The institutional research community is well organized only in a few countries, and outside of Europe and North America, there are few international links. Outlets for publication and analysis of data based on institutional research are limited. There are no internationally circulated journals that focus on institutional research, and few means of international discussion in this field other than at conferences held in the United States or Europe.

Governmental and other reports are frequently issued only for limited audiences, and there is no effort to disseminate the data more widely. Similarly, many of the studies commissioned by the World Bank are kept confidential and are unavailable to the research community. This serious limitation has kept the data and research base for higher education less widespread than it might otherwise be.

Expansion and the Growth of a Higher Education Research Infrastructure

The field of higher education research has significantly expanded in large part because conditions have created a need for such research and the means to conduct it. The objective circumstances of higher education have changed – expansion of enrollment, staff and budgets, a focus on the research mission of the universities, and a sense that academic institutions are of central importance to modern societies have all increased the attention paid to higher education in most societies. The 'ivory tower' no longer exists. These trends have contributed not only to a larger and more important academic system, but to a need for research and the development of research institutions devoted to higher education.

Several specific elements have contributed to the expansion of interest in higher education research:

– As academic institutions have expanded, they need more information about themselves – enrollment trends, data concerning student achievement, faculty and staff

information, and other research. This data gathering and research is referred to as 'institutional research', and it is focused on a single institution, but may be relevant to a wider audience.[5] Networks of researchers in this field are well organized in North America and Europe, but much less so elsewhere.
- University-based centers or departments focusing on higher education have been established in a small number of countries to educate higher education professionals and researchers. These departments and academic programs, located mainly in academic institutions in Anglo-Saxon countries, have also been the source of a considerable amount of research. University-based centers probably number in the hundreds worldwide. In the United States alone, close to 100 universities have programs in higher education located in schools of education that provide post-baccalaureate degrees.
- Governments require national data and research for purposes of planning for higher education, the allocation of funds, and related purposes. National research institutes have in some cases been established, and funding has been made available for higher education research and data collection.[6]
- State planning and coordinating agencies have been established in many countries, and these organizations sometimes sponsor research and collect statistics to help them in their work. These agencies resulted from the expansion of higher education and the need to have access to relevant information and analysis. In general, they were established in the 1960s or more recently. Not surprisingly, the former 'socialist countries', with their centrally planned economies, established large higher education research agencies to provide the data needed for planning and development, as well as for coordination with other economic and political entities.[7] While the research produced by these types of agencies is generally aimed as providing national data and analyses of specific issues, it is sometimes useful for researchers or policy makers outside of the country.

---

[5] Institutional researchers have organized themselves into several national and regional groups. The Association for Institutional Research in the United States is one of the largest research-oriented organizations in the world. In Europe, the European Association for Institutional Research has recently expanded its focus beyond institutional research to broader higher education issues.

[6] Examples of national organizations focused on higher education research and information are, among many others, the Hochschul-Informations-System (HIS) in Germany, the Research Institute on Higher Education in Russia, and the National Center for Educational Statistics in the United States.

[7] For a detailed discussion of this topic, see *Kluczynski (1985)*.

- University associations in many countries, and to some extent internationally, engage in research. In the United States, the American Council on Education, the National Association of State Universities and Land Grant Colleges, the Council of Graduate Schools, and many others have made research and the dissemination of information part of their missions. The German Hochschulrektorenkonferenz sponsors publications and supports some research. The Association of Indian Universities publishes books and journals and supports some research. On a regional basis, the Association of African Universities and the European Rectors Conference (CRE) disseminate information and occasionally conduct research. The International Association of Universities has promoted research and dissemination at an international level.
- International and regional organizations are among the most important in terms of bringing together specialists on higher education as well as providing fora for discussing higher education issues. UNESCO, established in 1946, has from the beginning been involved with post-secondary education. It has sponsored many conferences, has stimulated research and has published books and reports. UNESCO has also established regional offices that focus on higher education. Such groups as the Association of African Universities, the Association of Francophone Universities (AUPUELF), and others have built regional cooperation.

The perceived need for data and analysis has helped to create a range of organizations and agencies which provide information and analysis. Many of these are recent, reflecting the newness of the field of higher education research. They exist at the institutional, national, regional, and international levels. There is frequently relatively little interaction or cooperation among them. With very few exceptions, the entire infrastructure of higher education research is a post-World War II phenomenon, with the bulk of growth taking place in the aftermath of the expansion of higher education of the 1960s, and again in the 1980s and 1990s, as post-secondary education experienced financial problems and accountability and assessment became central forces.

The Information Infrastructure in Higher Education

As research centers and agencies concerned with higher education administration, coordination and policy have grown, a nexus of publications and other means of communicating the knowledge base in higher education have developed as well. The scope and number of publications is quite impressive. Many countries have journals relating to higher education that are aimed at researchers and other professionals in the field. In most cases, the circulation of these journals is limited, but they provide access to relevant research, current data, and analysis of the field. There are also many publishers who consistently publish books and monographs in the field of higher education. There are a much smaller number of internationally circulated journals and books in the field.

It is not possible, in the context of this essay, to discuss all of the national, regional, and international publications that exist in the field. However, it is useful to focus on selected sources of information. As noted earlier, a large proportion of the research base on higher education is not easily available because it has not been published, or has been issued only as 'gray literature' in limited editions by institutions. This material is generally not included in standard indexes or reference sources. Unfortunately, there is no clearing house for the 'gray literature' in higher education. The ERIC (Educational Resources Information Center) bibliographies and data base, sponsored by the United States Department of Education, is the largest single source of bibliographical information. It includes some 'gray literature'. However, ERIC collects mainly American material, and is only of limited relevance to the rest of the world.

In addition to ERIC, there are several bibliographical sources in higher education. *Contents Pages in Education,* a journal that provides comprehensive coverage of scholarly and research journals in education, including higher education, is an important worldwide resource, although it is limited to publications in English. There are abstracting journals dealing with higher education in Britain and the United States which provide good coverage of their respective countries. However, as pointed out earlier, these publications cover only material published in journals or, in some cases, books.

Important recent additions to the research literature are two encyclopedias that deal with higher education in an international context *(Altbach 1991; Clark / Neave 1992).* These key reference volumes provide not only worldwide coverage of higher education but also provide 'state of the art' essays on key topics in the research literature. They provide a benchmark for the field, and they show that the study of higher education has, in a sense, come of age, resulting in a coherent and reasonably comprehensive body of research. An earlier international encyclopedia, edited by Asa *Knowles (1976),* helped significantly to establish higher education studies as a field of inquiry. There are also several national encyclopedias or handbooks.

The number of research and other journals focusing on higher education has expanded in the past several decades. Indeed, most of the internationally circulated journals in the field were established since the 1960s. Just in the past few years, new journals dealing with assessment, with technology, and with teaching in higher education have been founded, reflecting important new trends in the field. There are several different kinds of periodical publications in the field, reflecting different orientations and perspectives. There are several internationally circulated magazines and newspapers relating to higher education that provide news, commentary, and reporting of research and policy initiatives. The most important of these are the *Chronicle of Higher Education* in the United States, the *Times Higher Education Supplement* in Britain, and *Le Monde d'Éducation* in France. All three publications have significant international circulation and all report on international developments as well as national news. There are also many national periodicals with similar aims – for example *University News* in India, *Das Hochschulwesen* in Germany, *Universitas* in Italy, *Universidades 2000* in Mexico, and others.

There are a small number of internationally circulated research journals in higher education. These publications set the standard internationally for research, and disseminate key scholarship in the field. They are, without exception, published in English and most are edited and published in the United States or Western Europe. *Higher Education, Higher Education Management, Minerva,* and *Higher Education Policy* are the most explicitly international of the journals. Also influential are *Studies in Higher Education* and *Higher Education Review* (Britain), the *Journal of Higher Education, Review of Higher Education,* and *Research in Higher Education* (United States). *Higher Education in Europe* and the *European Journal of Education* focus on higher education from a mainly European perspective.

Hundreds of national journals also exist. In general, these are not circulated outside the country of origin. Some of these journals, such as the *IDE Journal* in Japan, *Universidad Futura* in Mexico, the *Canadian Journal of Higher Education,* and *Change* and *Lingua Franca* in the United States, are among the more important. Others, such as the *Journal of Higher Education* in India and the *South African Journal of Higher Education*, are less well known internationally but publish valuable material. There are approximately 400 journals devoted to higher education in China alone – all but a half-dozen published by individual universities and seldom circulated outside the institution.[8]

---

8 It is also the case that many Chinese higher education journals are officially 'restricted' and cannot be circulated outside of China.

The publication of books dealing with higher education has also significantly increased. Several publishers now specialize on higher education. Examples include Jessica Kingsley Publishers, Pergamon Press, and the Open University Press in Britain, Garland Publishers, Jossey-Bass, and Johns Hopkins University Press in the United States, Tamagawa University Press in Japan, Campus Verlag in Germany, Lemma Publishers in Holland, and others. Research institutions and other organizations also publish books and monographs in the field – among these are the Research Institute on Higher Education at Hiroshima University in Japan, the Russian Research Institute on Higher Education in Moscow, and the American Council on Education in the United States.

There is no question that the literature on higher education has expanded in recent years, and the number of journals and publishers available to publish in the field has grown equally fast. There are still considerable segments of the literature that are not easily available because this material is not formally 'published' but rather issued by specific institutions or government agencies, and often difficult to obtain. More important, there are few ways to easily access existing information. The growth of publications in the field has been dramatic and impressive, reflecting the rising importance of higher education as a field for research.

History and Geography of the Field

Higher education research as an organized field of inquiry is quite new, but scholars and others have been concerned with the nature of teaching, learning and research in post-secondary education for centuries. The Arab scholars who were responsible for the establishment of the Al-Azhar University in Cairo thought about higher education, as did those responsible for the establishment of universities in medieval Europe *(Makdisi 1981)*. In the 19th century, thinkers such as Alexander von Humboldt, who pioneered the reformed German university model which became so important to the emergence of the modern research-oriented university, wrote on higher education *(Ben-David / Zloczower 1962)*. José Ortega y Gasset and John Henry Cardinal Newman were influential thinkers who wrote about higher education and whose ideas were influential. Hastings *Rashdall (1936)* wrote the classic history of higher education in the Middle Ages. Other scholars in history, philosophy and the emerging social sciences, wrote occasionally on higher education. Max Weber, for example, dealt with higher education in the early period of the development of sociology, as did Emile *Durkheim (1977)*. One of the first government-sponsored reports done anywhere on higher education was conducted as part of a reform effort at the University of Calcutta in India in 1911. This document, and several others commissioned to shape higher education policies in colonial areas, influenced the later use of official reports on higher education *(Ashby 1966)*. There is a rich literature in the history of higher education, focusing especially on the history of individual universities. This brief and incomplete discussion indicates that although the research has been scattered and lacking in focus, very influential work of a high standard of quality has been carried out. Thinkers and researchers worked within the confines of their disciplines, with little if any communication across fields of study.

There are close links between the field of higher education and that of science policy studies. The journal *Minerva* straddles both fields and has attempted to link the concerns of researchers in both areas. Others, such as *Technology and Society*, cover this intersection of fields. However, there is little cross-fertilization and only a limited number of researchers pay attention to both fields. Science policy is especially important to higher education now because it seeks to examine research networks that extend beyond the universities – a topic that is of importance to university-industry linkages.

More integrally related to higher education is the community of researchers dealing with planning for college and universities. There are professional organizations in this field, and a small research network.[9] Higher education management has also emerged quite recently as a distinct subspecialty, but in this case there are strong links with higher education research. The Organisation for Economic Co-operation and Development's (OECD) *Higher Education Management* journal provides an international perspective on this topic. Because of the increasing complexity of academic institutions and the growing professionalization of university administration, there is a growing interest in management issues. So far, there seem to be few links between the broader field of management studies and higher education.[10]

Another strand of research relates to international study and international students. The internationalization of higher education has become a topic of considerable interest in many countries. The European Union, through ERASMUS, TEMPUS, and other programs, has fostered international study and scholarly exchange. There are more than one million students studying outside their home countries, and there are major issues relat-

---

9 The Society for College and University Planning in the United States is probably the largest organization in this area. It publishes its own journal and holds professional meetings.
10 One of the few contributions by researchers in management studies is *Cohen / March (1986)*.

ing to policy, orientation and focus of international study.[11] Organizations such as the National Association for Foreign Student Affairs in the United States, the European Association for International Education, and other groups have sponsored research. The Institute of International Education has published a series of studies focusing on international education issues.[12]

Despite some very distinguished work, there was no clearly identified field of higher education studies until the 1960s anywhere in the world. The work was sporadic, written because of the intellectual interests of the researchers or occasionally in response to a policy focus in higher education. The field of higher education research was established in response to the practical needs of an expanding university system, and in the United States, as a means of training a cadre of academic administrators. While researchers in the social science disciplines continued to do research on higher education, the focus of the newly emerging field came from schools of education rather than from the mainstream academic disciplines. At the same time, institutional research offices within universities and government, and other research agencies were established. Often, there were few links between the academic units and other research agencies. A small number of social scientists continued to work on higher education issues, again often in isolation from the emerging field of higher education studies.

The field of higher education displays the same geographical inequality that characterize most scientific disciplines, although probably to a lesser extent than in many fields. The international centers of the field control most of the publications, and the major research paradigms originate in these countries. They play a central role in defining the foci of the field. Other parts of the world are to a considerable extent peripheral in terms of setting research agendas and determining major trends. The location of publications, editorships, and the major databases in the center is a key factor. Although there has been no reliable analysis, it is likely that 75 percent of the world's internationally circulated research and commentary in the field of higher education comes from the United States, Britain and Australia. The research communities in such countries as Japan, France, the Netherlands, and Germany also contribute significantly. A small but growing effort on the Pacific Rim, and to a lesser extent in Latin America are to varying

---

11 For an overview of the issues, see *Altbach / Kelly / Lulat (1985)*.
12 The Institute of International Education (IIE) is an American organization with branch offices in many countries. Its main responsibilities include the administration of exchange programs between the United States and other countries. It has also sponsored research on international exchanges and related topics. See, for example, *Goodwin / Nacht (1991)*.

degrees tied to the centers in the English-speaking nations. The balance is, however, rapidly changing as other countries build up research capacity in higher education.

The field is, however, far from monolithic. There is a small research community publishing in French, especially in the field of economics of higher education, although there is surprisingly little communication between this group and the major research network operating largely in English. Prior to the collapse of the Soviet Union, there was an active research network in Central and Eastern Europe. This network has disappeared. Economic problems and the restructuring of local research institutions have also caused significant disruption, especially in Russia. There are currently some efforts to integrate the research communities in Central and Eastern Europe with the Western European higher education research network.

Future Trends

This discussion suggests a number of future trends in the field of higher education research. The field has, in responding to the needs for data and analysis about rapidly expanding higher education systems worldwide, grown impressively. There is now a nexus of publications, professional and other organizations, and researchers in the field worldwide. While research communities remain nationally based, there is growing international contact and communication. Higher education research is well established, and serves an important role in understanding the complex higher education institutions. Yet, many in government and in academic administration feel that much of the research in higher education, and the analysis reported in major journals in the field, is not relevant to the day-to-day problems faced by managers in post-secondary education. This is probably an inevitable tension in the field, and it is unlikely to be solved. Some of the research produced by higher education scholars is focused on understanding broader issues or in building up the methodological or knowledge base in the field, and is therefore largely irrelevant to the search for immediate solution to problems faced by academic institutions or systems. At the same time, at least some of this work is a necessary underpinning for more applied research. The tension between the two poles in the field is, in many ways, a strength. Those who control funding for research, largely at the applied end of the spectrum, must be more understanding of the need to build a solid knowledge base and methodological rigor in the field. At the same time, there is often an unnecessary distance between university-based researchers and the 'users' of research in academic administration or government agencies.

The following trends may characterize the future development of the field of higher education studies:

- The field will expand dramatically into places where it is either weak or nonexistent at the present time. The most significant growth will probably be in East Asia, where economic conditions are good and higher education is expanding rapidly.
- Although it is difficult to predict, the current centers of research in higher education may to some extent lose some of their dominance, due to financial cutbacks in higher education generally, and to the development of new research communities in other regions, especially on the Pacific Rim.
- Despite these trends, the leadership of the traditional centers in the field will in most likelihood continue – the established publications, research communities and the like will retain their impact.
- There is a growing interest in the process of teaching, learning, and assessment in higher education. Instruction is, after all, the central element of the process of higher education, and is imperfectly understood. In part to improve learning, and in part to provide improved ways to measure the results of higher education, there has been increased interest in the evaluation of teaching, measurement of instructional results, and assessment in general.
- The gulf between institutional research and other research on higher education remains considerable. There is little use of institutional research outside individual universities. The field would benefit from better articulation. Similarly, the tension between basic and applied research in higher education will continue, with some confusion regarding the audiences for research in the field.
- Higher education will continue to be an interdisciplinary field of inquiry – there are few indications that it will emerge as a separate scientific discipline.
- The recognition that academic institutions require a trained cadre of administrators will mean the expansion worldwide of university-based training programs in higher education, and this will result in a larger research community, since many of the faculty members appointed to teaching positions in these programs will also be doing research on higher education.
- Large scale research, either within one country or internationally, will be limited due to lack of funds. Higher education research will see diminishing resources in common with other categories of research in the major industrialized countries – again, growth will be mainly in the newly industrializing countries of the Pacific Rim.

A Future Agenda

The field of higher education studies has a variety of needs that must be addressed if it is to develop further. These include:

- Better balance between the research agenda of higher education researchers on the one hand, and the users on the other. There is a tendency for funding agencies to provide support for research that will provide specific answers to questions of immediate concern. In the long run, this weakens the knowledge base.
- Strengthening of regional and international networks for reporting data and research. It is especially strong at the regional level so that a community of researchers that goes beyond national boundaries may be effectively coordinated and so that the entire field is less dependent on the currently existing centers in the field. Organizations that bring together researchers from different countries also need expanding.
- Inclusion of currently peripheral research communities in the international mainstream.
- Better integration of the institutional research community as well as institutional research into the higher education research system.
- Improvement of links between the higher education research community, now located in faculties of education in universities, in government agencies, or in independent research centers, among each other and with researchers in the social sciences.
- Further strengthening of the interdisciplinary nature of the field – this is already characteristic of some research.
- Linking research in the field with the immediate needs of institutional administrators and policy makers is difficult, but it is nonetheless important.
- Linking the higher education research community to research groups in related fields, including science policy, international education, and comparative education.

Conclusion

Higher education research has developed impressively in the past three decades. The organized infrastructures of a research field have emerged. A community of researchers and scholars is working actively in the field. The geographical spread of the field, although it remains concentrated in a few centers, is quite impressive. Higher education research has contributed significantly to a broader understanding of the university, and especially of the complexities of academe in a period of expansion, as well as to the specific policy needs of academic administrators and political authorities. This is a significant accomplishment, especially for a field which is new and small. Higher education has legitimized itself as a research field within educational studies, and it has gained acceptance among those who are responsible for the leadership of higher education.

In a number of countries, the research community has been significantly strengthened by the establishment of university-based training programs for academic administrators. These programs have contributed significantly to the expansion and legitimization of higher education research. Scholars engage in research and contribute to the literature in the field. Some of the graduates of these programs themselves become researchers in the field, although most go into academic administration or policy making, where they use research results. This trend is likely to expand to other countries, as there is a demonstrated need for professionally educated administrators for large post-secondary institutions and systems.

The research output in the field remains mixed and is hard to characterize. It ranges from what the social scientists would call 'middle range theory' to the most applied data gathering that is relevant to a specific problem at a single university. Social scientists from a number of disciplines have attempted to theorize about the nature of the university, about the dynamic of leadership in higher education, and about the nature of teaching and learning. However, there are few widely agreed upon theories which apply generally to post-secondary institutions. The quality of the research output is also mixed, as is probably inevitable for a field in its early stages of development.

The field of higher education research is poised for change. In the traditional centers, growth has slowed as resources have become limited, although research is still needed. Expansion will be slower in these regions. At the same time, higher education research is gaining importance and legitimacy in parts of the world traditionally underserved. The field has achieved a measure of legitimacy in the academic community, and it is accepted as important by policy makers in national as well as regional and international organizations.

Bibliography

Altbach, Philip G.: Perspectives on Comparative Higher Education. A Survey of Research and Literature. In: idem / Kelly, David (eds.): Higher Education in International Perspective, London: Mansell 1985, pp. 3-54.

Altbach, Philip G. (ed.): International Higher Education. An Encyclopedia. New York: Garland 1991.
Altbach, Philip G. / Kelly, David H. / Lulat, Y. G. M.: Research on Foreign Students and International Study. An Overview and Bibliography. New York: Praeger 1985.
Ashby, Eric: Universities: British, Indian, African. A Study in the Ecology of Higher Education. Cambridge, Mass.: Harvard University Press 1966.
Ben-David, Joseph / Zloczower, Awraham: Universities and Academic Systems in Modern Societies. In: European Journal of Sociology, 3 (1962) 1, pp. 45-84.
Buchert, Lene / King, Kenneth (eds.): Learning from Experience. Policy and Practice in Aid to Higher Education. The Hague: Center for the Study of Education in Developing Countries 1995.
Clark, Burton / Neave, Guy (eds.): The Encyclopedia of Higher Education. Oxford: Pergamon Press 1992.
Cohen, Michael D. / March, James D.: Leadership and Ambiguity: The American College President. Boston, Mass.: Harvard Business School Press 1986.
Dressel, Paul L. / Mayhew, Lewis B.: Higher Education as a Field of Study. San Francisco: Jossey-Bass 1974.
Durkheim, Emile: The Evolution of Educational Thought. London: Routledge and Kegan Paul 1977. [First published in French in 1938 and originally written by Durkheim in 1904/5]
Goodwin, Craufurd D. / Nacht, Michael: Missing the Boat. The Failure to Internationalize American Higher Education. New York: Cambridge University Press 1991.
Klucyczynski, Jan: Research on Higher Education in European Socialist Countries. In: Altbach, Philip G. / Kelly, David (eds.): Higher Education in International Perspective, London: Mansell 1985, pp. 55-88.
Knowles, Asa (ed.): Encyclopedia of Higher Education. San Francisco: Jossey-Bass 1976.
Makdisi, George: The Rise of Colleges. Institutions of Learning in Islam and the West. Edinburgh: Edinburgh University Press 1981.
Rashdall, Hastings: The Universities of Europe in the Middle Ages. Oxford: Clarendon Press 1936.
Robbins, Lord: The University in the Modern World. London: Macmillan 1966.
Salmi, Jamil / Verspoor, Adriaan M. (eds.): Revitalizing Higher Education. Oxford: Pergamon Press 1994.
Trow, Martin: The Expansion and Transformation of Higher Education. In: International Review of Education, 18 (1972) 1, pp. 61-83.
UNESCO (ed.): World Education Report. 1993. Paris: Unesco 1993.
UNESCO (ed.): Policy Paper for Change and Development in Higher Education. Paris: Unesco 1995.
World Bank (ed.): Higher Education: The Lessons of Experience. Washington, D. C.: The World Bank 1994.
Yu, Xu: The Development of Higher Education in China. Buffalo, N. Y., State University of New York, Ph. D. Thesis, 1995.

Filtering Democracy through Schools:
The Ignored Paradox of Compulsory Education

Erwin H. Epstein

Schools as Filters

However important the school may be as a vehicle to institutionalize and perpetuate democracy, it has been largely ignored by contemporary scholars of democratization in developing and formerly socialist countries. Rather, their focus has been almost exclusively on the political consequences of economic reform programs and on external contexts for political change. Consequently, cumulative knowledge about the ability of actors to sustain over time a guarantee of political rights and liberties, a representative form of government, and, more generally, an equitable distribution of power is weak, notwithstanding the crucial importance of this area of research for comprehending democracy's long-term ability to survive.

Pervasive neglect of the school's socializing role by economists and political scientists is clearly displayed by the contents of the many comprehensive studies and compilations that have appeared in recent years. For example, only one among 19 chapters in Kenneth *Bauzon's (1992)* edited volume on development and democratization examines education, and even that chapter *(Mehrangiz / Mennerick 1992)* concentrates merely on school enrollments, ignoring the agency of schools in the *process* of democratization. Martin *Needler (1987)*, in his book on democracy in Latin America, limits his remarks on education to a brief mention of the spread of education after the Prussian victory of France in 1870 *(p. 34)* and of achievements during the early years of the Sandinista regime in Nicaragua *(pp. 83-84)*. Virtually no reference at all is made to education in the nine chapters of Joseph *Tulchin's (1995)* compilation on democracy in Latin America – not even, astonishingly, in a chapter entitled „Building Citizenship: A Balance Between Solidarity and Responsibility" *(Jelin 1995)*. Indeed, Robert *Pinkney (1994, pp. 18-38, 83-99)*, in his comprehensive review of the literature, discerned seven explanatory conditions advanced by social scientists for the development and survival of continuous democracies in developing countries, not one of which included education.

I contend that comprehensive examinations of democratization as a long-term development are perforce incomplete and inadequate when they fail to take careful account of education as a socializing process. I also argue that commonplace assumptions about that process are inadequate to explain the school's agency in democratization, a reason, perhaps, why education has been so much ignored in studies of democracy in transitional states. Finally, I discuss the irony of nations' use of schools to compel democratization, an irony magnified by transitional societies' inclination to use industrialized countries as models.

State Control of Education

Whether out of willfulness or ignorance, the neglect of education by social scientists who study democratization in the developing world is surprising. Policy makers, autocrats included, have long known the power of schools to transform societies. Napoleon believed that education was likely the most important consideration in establishing a nation. As he put it: „*If the child is not taught from infancy that he ought to be a republican or a monarchist, a Catholic or a freethinker, the state will not constitute a nation; it will rest on uncertain and shifting foundations, and it will be constantly exposed to disorder and change*" (quoted in *Kandel 1955-56, p. 10*). Governments wishing to exercise vigorous control over citizens' intellectual development and access to power, wealth, and prestige have often unhesitatingly resorted to the state's police power to prescribe education – its nature, amount, and to whom it is directed. In testimony to schools' effectiveness in the hands of government, John Stuart *Mill (1977, p. 302)* wrote in 1859:

„*A general State education is a mere contrivance for moulding people to be exactly like one another: and as the mould in which it casts them is that which pleases the predominant power in the government, whether this be a monarch, a priesthood, an aristocracy, or the majority of the existing generation, in proportion as it is efficient and successful, it establishes a despotism over the mind, leading by natural tendency to one over the body.*"

Naturally, the imposition of state control in the form of compulsory education has the greatest impact in communities whose life ways most vary from the culture of the imposing government. In such communities, sudden social change produces a temporal vacuum during which familiar cultural norms lack force and become highly susceptible to displacement from deliberate outside imposition. In particular, technologically simple societies and societies confronting abrupt and far-reaching political disruption – such as those experiencing defeat in war; colonialism or decolonialization; and ideological transition, be it to socialism or from communist collapse to liberal democracy – are especially vulnerable to the state's control of collective conscience through the manipulation of schools.

Cultural displacement by means of schools can be paradoxical. Governments ordinarily seek citizens' willing allegiance knowing that it is easier to rule with popular support than by coercive power. Yet virtually all contemporary states use education to coerce allegiances, compelling children to attend school where they are taught 'appropriate' norms and values. Compulsory education is a paradox especially in liberal democracies, whose claim to legitimacy rests on citizens' voluntary participation in the political process. In democratic states, in other words, children often unwillingly learn to participate willingly in the affairs of their nation. This paradox may not be problematic when community cultures are isomorphic with the national culture. When not, however, it can be a festering dilemma.

At the center of the dilemma of compulsory instruction in democratic states is the teaching of myths. Contrary to official rhetoric, all schools teach myths, and this applies in both authoritarian and democratic states. This is partly because reality is elusive and susceptible to interpretation. Subjective reality is the content of education in the absence of systematically derived, empirically based information, and large areas of school subjects are uninformed by empirical knowledge. Yet myths are also taught because schools operate universally not merely to convey objective truths and because they lack objective knowledge, but also because they function to teach particular values and, as mentioned above, allegiance to the state. Values and allegiances, in other words, are too important to be left to the informal socializing devices of the family, community, and other extra-school institutions; instead, they are deliberately conveyed by the school acting in behalf of the state.

Myths are used by schools to elevate the image of the state in children's minds, and in this capacity are essential in cultivating allegiances. Myths, of course, are not neutral; the images they convey are developed as favorable compared to counterparts. Early in this century schoolboys in colonial India and Nigeria memorized the lists of English kings through the wars of succession, and in French Indochina and West Africa they learned the precise locations of the Louvre and Notre Dame in Paris. With independence, the curricula in these nations were modified to transform liberation movement leaders from 'law-breaking insurgents' to national heroes *(Elder 1971)*. Textbooks transmit ideologies, whether in authoritarian or democratic societies *(Anyon 1979)*. In her her study of pre-collegiate United States history textbooks, Linda Salvucci found that texts used in Texas classrooms between 1986 and 1992 fashioned images of Mexico and Mexicans *„that were inconsistent, idiosyncratic, incorrect, and empty ... with the most egregious anti-Mexican stereotypes used in descriptions of the battle of the Alamo"* (Salvucci 1992, p. 59). These images contrasted markedly with these textbooks' agreeable impressions of the United States and its citizens in their relations with Mexico.

In democratic societies, authoritarian rule is a counterpart taught negatively by schools, but in teaching universalistic values schools also convey an unfavorable image of cultural particularism. Paradoxically, schools teach children to reason scientifically, and thus to demystify particularisms – concurrently as it teaches them to embrace favorable myths about the national culture. In so doing, schools mimic on the local level states' condescending or contemptuous behavior toward people whose collective conduct is unfamiliar. As Mircea *Eliade (1982, p. 137)* observes:

„One day ... descendants of those we once colonized ... will say to us: ... 'Your anthropologists never stop insisting on the socioeconomic presuppositions of our religion or our messianic and millenarist movements, thereby implying that our spiritual creations, unlike yours, never rise above material or political determining factors. In other words, we primitives are incapable of attaining the creative freedom of a Dante or a Vergil.' Such a 'demystifying' attitude ought to be arraigned in its turn, on charges of ethnocentrism, of Western 'provincialism', and so, ultimately, be 'demystified' itself."

Western societies have, to be sure, been rather careful to avoid judging the intellectual capabilities of other societies ever since Claude Lévi-Strauss demonstrated the rigorous logic of 'primitive' humanity's myths and rituals. Not so, however, judgment of their moral fiber and that of most societies unlike our own. A reason for this is the need of nations to be nationalistic. Nations are, as Benedict Anderson defines them, imagined political communities – *„imagined, because the members of even the smallest nation will never know most of their fellow-members, meet them, or even hear of them, yet in the minds of each lives the image of their communion"* (Anderson 1991, p. 6). That image is of a community that is both limited and sovereign: limited because 'community' itself implies boundaries and is therefore finite, and sovereign because the community's integrity depends on freedom to govern itself. That a nation is defined by an image means that it is a creation of the mind, not a tangible physical reality, and, as such, is shaped by the needs of its members as well as those of nationals from other states.

In this regard, whatever may be said about industrial societies' patterns of judgment toward developing countries can also be said about nations' – even developing nations' – judgments of their own subcultures. The very act of schooling, including 'democratic' schooling, can fatally disrupt minority communities. Introducing schools both forces a change in the community's social, economic, and cultural environment and sets in motion a socialization process that alters fundamentally children's consciousness of their social and cultural condition and undermines their indigenous identity and sense of community belonging. Consider Laura Rival's account of schooling in Huaorani villages of Ecuador *(Rival 1996, pp. 158-159):*

> *„... As soon as the state grants a school to a village, it appears on the map of Ecuador, and the Huaorani villagers, now formally recognized as Ecuadorian citizens, especially in their parental capacity, are faced with new obligations and administrative formalities. They must vote, get birth and marriage certificates, and own identity cards. Another direct consequence of schooling is the remaking of the social space, with the creation of a public sphere, and the introduction of a new division of labor based on the redefinition of production. ... This new division of labor, explicitly presented as rational and progressive, is reinforced in the teachings dedicated to changing the conceptions of work, production, and gender. Children are taught, for example, that agriculture, the creation of abundance and welfare through hard labor, represents an evolutionary stage superior to that of hunting and that if their parents intensify horticultural production, food will be more nutritious and varied. Schools, with their strong pro-agriculture advocacy, remove children from their natural environment and de-skill them with regard to forest knowledge. ... As the village environment (with its large grassy spaces, its compounds, and its dispersed plantations) differs substantially from the forest environment, and as the children have little exposure to the latter, their knowledge of the primary rain forest and its resources is undermined."*

For the Huaorani, in other words, the school demands a change in villagers' traditional connection with their environment, requiring a fundamental alteration in social relations. The knowledge children learn is *decontextualized,* separated from the group's traditional activities of hunting, gathering, chanting, and the crafting of artifacts. Weaned away from context-specific activities, children change their concept of personal autonomy and collective sharing of natural abundance, and take on a 'modern' identity, fundamentally at variance with that of the traditional group. Concurrently, parents and village elders lose much of their authority as arbiters of culture and sources of normative behavior for their children.

In such societies, myths taught by schools about mainstream society come to displace in children's' consciousness myths about their indigenous past taught in traditional, less formal ways by parents and elders. This process of 'modernization' is an essential part of the program of 'democratization'. Children learn to be citizens of the nation – to participate with others in the polity, vote, obey laws, compete and be productive in the national marketplace, and render allegiance to the state. Yet the very path to democracy – paved in good part by the school – is itself compelled, fraught with danger to the life of the traditional community, and, therefore, ironically undemocratic. To grasp this paradox, it is important to understand the distinctive impact of school socialization in societies that experience abrupt social change.

The Impact of the School under Abrupt Social Change

Nations have at their disposal several means to promote a shared sense of nationality, but none is as important as formal education. Schools teach a common history and language, and they dictate the proper norms and ideas for children to follow. In developing countries, schools often serve to disabuse people of particularistic ways in favor of a secular, national orientation. Before entering school, a child becomes conscious of the political world as mediated by a variety of social groups. Within these, the child learns to accept certain predispositions toward authority and limits of submissiveness and dominance. Somewhat later in development the child learns to distinguish between membership in primary groups and other groups whose members are not in intimate and frequent contact.

How a child learns a sense of nationality depends in good part on whether the norms of behavior and expectations of primary groups are consistent with those of more socially distant, impersonal secondary groups, and with the larger society overall (see *LeVine 1960b*). When these are consistent, primary socialization tends to play a binding role in shaping individuals' national identity *(Levine 1965)*, and the school may be viewed as an extension of the family in achieving that objective. If, however, there is incongruity of norms and values between the larger society and the child's primary groups, the child may find it difficult to generalize from allegiances and behavioral patterns learned within family or tribe to national political objects and symbols.

When such instances are common in a society, the school is often commissioned to perform a resocializing function. This may occur, for example, when children are immigrants or belong to ethnic groups, or when a society experiences abrupt social change such that the congruity between community and society is shattered.

In transitional societies, especially when village life is far removed from the national culture, discontinuities between political values of family and local community on the one hand, and of nation on the other hand, are likely to arise with an influx of schools *(Foster 1962; Nash 1965; Hagstrom 1968)*. The school as an agent of the larger society may force a wedge between home and child by reorienting the child to national political realities that may be incongruous with values of the local community.

However disorienting it may be to children exposed to abrupt change, this resocialization process may be critical to the life of a country struggling to unify ethnicities or urban and rural subcultures, and seeking to define their national character. If there is an incongruity of norms and values between the larger society and a child's primary groups, the child may find it difficult to generalize from allegiances and behavioral patterns learned within family or tribe to national political objects and symbols.

What, then, is the behavioral process at work that places schools at a critical juncture in transitional states' struggle for stability and unified nationhood? Early work on this issue relied on a theory of *stimulus generalization*, which posits that a conditioned response will be elicited not only by the stimulus used in conditioning but also by a variety of similar stimuli *(Murdock 1949; Hull 1950)*. Robert *LeVine (1960b)* reasoned that the fewer the stimulus elements common to the distant political environment and the proximate family environment, the less likely individuals will be to extend their family response patterns to the political sphere of action. As applied to education, stimulus generalization implies that the more pupils are attached to primordial ethnic values and the more ethnically homogeneous they are, the less likely schools will be to succeed in socializing them to nationally oriented allegiances and behaviors *(Nash 1965)*.

My research, however, has cast doubt on the value of stimulus-generalization theory in explaining sense of nationality among schoolchildren in societies experiencing abrupt change. I found that pupils whose families have *fewer* stimulus elements in common with the larger society actually displayed *more* acculturative tendencies. This was shown most clearly in studies I conducted in Peru, Puerto Rico, and St. Lucia.

In Peru, I found that highland schoolchildren living in rural, more ethnically homogeneous Indian areas were on the whole significantly more accepting of the Mestizo (Europeanized) culture taught in schools than were urban pupils *(Epstein 1971, 1982)*. In Puerto Rico, an island whose political status is ambiguous and where dual allegiance to Puerto Rican and U.S. nationality is taught, I showed that public-school children, who were less exposed outside the school to North American patterns of behavior, were more amenable to Americanization than the more Americanized private-school pupils *(Epstein 1967)*. In St. Lucia, an island whose political status has shifted over recent years and where schools stress a St. Lucian indigenous nationality, I reported that schoolchildren living in rural areas displayed a stronger affinity to St. Lucian national symbols than children in the urban centers *(Epstein 1997)*. In all of these studies, contrary to what stimulus-generalization theory would have predicted, a cultural gap between school and home/community actually enhanced the impact of education on the political orientation taught by schools.

To explain these findings, I deduced that the school filters out 'undesirable' aspects of national life and presents a largely favorable picture of the dominant culture. The school actually 'controls' the nature of schoolchildren's exposure to the dominant culture more effectively at the periphery (i. e., in remote, rural, or technologically primitive areas) than at the center, because at the periphery the school is more frequently and to a greater degree the principal representation of the dominant society. Although virtually all schools systematically foster a favorable view of the government and nation, schools at the periphery – being located where sources of conflicting knowledge about the realities of national life are relatively absent – have the effect of turning favorable myths about national life into compelling and credible images. This 'filter-effect' theory holds that, *ceteris paribus*, schoolchildren who are the least assimilated into the national, social, and political mainstream are the most susceptible to patriotic appeals and behavior.

This is not to say that stimulus-generalization theory lacks cogency. It is plausible that stimulus generalization takes on binding explanatory power at a point where the culture of home and community at the periphery is so strong as to offset the acculturating and nationalizing influence of schools. Or, this point may be reached if there is societal ambivalence in regard to national goals, as when a country is in a severe state of indecision or ambiguity over its political status such that it erodes the influence of schools. The weakness, however, of conventional explanations for socialization rooted in stimulus-generalization theory is that they assume a condition of social and political stability when assessing the congruence of norms and values shared by family and nation, and, indeed, under that condition family cultural patterns should transmute to nationally appropriate behaviors and ideals. Yet that condition rarely holds in nations experiencing abrupt change – developing and formerly socialist countries in particular – where the periphery is marked by progressive cultural rupture between the home and the national mainstream.

Compulsory Education in Western Democracies as a Model

Developing and formerly socialist countries are often enthusiastically receptive to educational practices of the industrialized West. These are societies that commonly experience social upheaval, in which traditional ways of doing things are no longer sustainable and new ways have not yet taken root. People living in such a social vacuum can be desperate to adopt stabilizing norms, and inclined to seek outside models whose application they hope will reestablish a condition of equilibrium. Formerly socialist countries in particular have appealed to the industrialized West for assistance in converting to a free-market economy and liberal democracy. As one Polish educator puts it: „*We are trying to fill an empty well with an empty bucket in a very great hurry*" (cited in *Patrick 1996, p. 18*). In this quest for equilibrium, civic educators have become the new missionaries of the West, invited to help plan democratic education in Eastern Europe, Africa, and Latin America *(Tucker 1993; Dalbec 1994; Romero Vargas / Buitrago Buitrago 1994; Sullivan 1994; Remy / Strzemieczny 1996).*

Unfortunately, schools in Western industrialized nations are hardly paragons of democratic practice. In an effort to universalize education and ensure widespread and enlightened participation in the democratic process, Western democracies virtually everywhere have made schooling compulsory for children. Education is used globally to inculcate prescribed cultural norms and values, but in democratic nations it is used to coerce citizens to believe and behave 'democratically'. Western democracies are not the only nations, of course, to have compulsory education. And, to be sure, coercion *per se* – in particular, when it is used in enforcing laws to protect against physical harm to people and property – is not an evil. But when schools are used to impel people to behave in a predetermined way before they have misbehaved or even formed intent to do so is quite another matter. As we have seen, the resort to compulsion by schools in Western democracies is paradoxical, because coercion itself as a device to ensure that all citizens internalize values, albeit 'democratic' ones, is undemocratic.

Resort to compulsory education in Western democracies is no guarantee that democratic values will be taught. Once in school, children, as Barbara *McEwan (1996, p. 96)* observes, *„are told, often in trivial detail, what to wear and not to wear, what they can and cannot do, and even when they may or may not attend to the calls of nature, based on schedules that have more to do with arbitrary time slots than with biological need. Commonly, students are stripped of the ability to make decisions concerning their bodies, their habits, and their behaviors while, by means of embarrassment and coercion, they are bent to the will of another's convenience and standards. We call this educating for democracy"*. When democracy is taught, it is frequently left to civics courses – normally an isolated segment of the overall curriculum – which, unsurprisingly, have little impact *(Levine 1980; Fetters / Brown / Owings 1984; Bricker 1989)*. It is not only that these courses comprise a small portion of overall school time; it is also that every time students step outside – into other courses, often taught with autocratic methods in an authoritarian environment – their perception of the inconsistencies between what they learn in civics and the messages contained in the school's overall environment is unavoidable.

Families and communities in a variety of ways commonly impose curricular content or structure schools to teach undemocratically, often defying laws designed to promote democratic education. For example, many public schools in the United States and elsewhere routinely circumvent legal strictures on school prayer, using the system of compulsory education to induce a majoritarian form of Christianity for all *(Beggs / McQuigg 1965; Muir 1967; Swomley 1968; Laubach 1969)*, what sociologists commonly refer to as 'civil religion' *(Bellah 1975; Moodie 1975; Hammond 1976; McGuire 1981; Beckford 1989)*. Once the state brings children into the system, schools, reflecting majoritarian community norms, regularly inculcate, mostly subtly through routine symbols and habits of language – teachers' small, familiar turns of phrase and constant, often mindless and inconspicuous reminders of national identity, such as displays of the national flag – an association between nationality and the embrace of majoritarian values *(Billig 1995)* to gain what David *Easton* and Jack *Dennis (1967)* refer to as 'diffuse support' – adherence to the system of government regardless of its conduct.

Parents from minority religions in Western democracies are thus often forced to pay taxes in support of alien religious practices, and to choose between sending their children to schools where civil religion is foisted or paying dearly to have their children educated in private schools (in addition to being forced to share in the cost of educating children not their own – that is, children from the majoritarian religion and the very community that is coercively imposing its will). In Germany, Bavarian 'public' schools are suffused with Christian symbols and rituals, with no provision for minority (Jewish and Muslim) children to receive instruction in their own religions *(Simel 1996)*. 'Open' to all, these schools 'invite' minority children to participate in their majoritarian Christian practices. In this way, the authority of the state is invoked by the school to entice minority children and their parents, whose choice in the matter is negligible, to relinquish cherished customs, values, and traditions.

To be sure, a primary aim of compulsory schooling is universal education. Yet education for all need not be compelled; it can be achieved in non-coercive ways, especially by offering free education without regard to religious or ethnic preference; giving parents voice in choosing schools for their children; and conducting public campaigns to persuade people of the importance of schooling. As long as non-coercive means are declined, individuals coerced against their will to attend and participate in schools will carry with them skepticism about the democratic nature of the education they receive – and plausibly doubts about democracy itself.

But the commonplace use of the state's police power to coerce children in the name of democracy to attend schools whose practices are undemocratic and often culturally alien has consequences that extend beyond the industrialized nations. Whether as models of public schooling or as sources for the export of Western religious practices by means of private schools *(Scanlon 1966)*, the inconsistencies and ambiguities relating to Western 'democratic' education are conveyed to developing countries and nations emerging from a socialist past. As these nations 'emerge', they adopt the disabilities – including an entire set of potentially negative consequences attendant with compulsory schooling – as well as the benefits of Western education.

Conclusion

A nation's ability to rule is advanced by having a loyal and obedient citizenry which shares a common set of norms and values. Yet some nations – particularly those in transition – must struggle harder to achieve unity and legitimacy. Being in transition implies purging old ways and adopting new ones, an unavoidably unsettling condition. Nations in transition, therefore, employ state-controlled institutions in the struggle to win the hearts of people and gain social and political equilibrium. The military, for example, is often used to assimilate culturally disparate population segments. But the institution employed most systematically to this end is the school. It is, after all, at the age when people attend school that they are the most impressionable and susceptible to political socialization.

The state's interest in teaching children to be loyal is so compelling that it cannot allow schools merely to teach objective knowledge. Consequently, schools mix myth with facts to ensure that children gain a favorable view of the national culture. However, democratic states also claim as a hallmark that their citizens are freer both to express themselves and to choose what knowledge professed by others to accept. Unfortunately, the democratic aim of ensuring unfettered access to knowledge is undermined by the universal need of nations to gain political legitimacy and social and economic stability.

Schools are caught in the middle; they are expected to convey objective knowledge objectively to satisfy the aims of democracy, yet also to teach national myths that obscure reality but make citizens loyal, and to do so through the undemocratic measure of compulsory attendance. 'Democratic education' is therefore an oxymoron when used to describe schooling especially in transitional states, and most especially in formerly socialist countries struggling to be democratic. The imposition of schools as vehicles by which to filter 'correct' knowledge to children makes 'democratic' education undemocratic, most notably among populations outside the cultural mainstream, at the periphery where children and their parents are the most vulnerable to mystification. The paradox is magnified by the specter of Western democracies purveying their own forms of compelled learning in the name of democracy. That scholars of democracy have largely overlooked the instrumentality of schools has meant the absence of a sorely missing chapter in this genre of scholarship.

Bibliography

Anderson, Benedict: Imagined Communities. Reflections on the Origin and Spread of Nationalism. London: Verso 1991.
Anyon, Jean: Ideology and United States History Textbooks. In: Harvard Educational Review, 49 (1979) 3, pp. 361-386.
Bauzon, Kenneth E. (ed.): Development and Democratization in the Third World. Myths, Hopes, and Realities. Washington, D. C.: Taylor and Francis 1992.
Beckford, James: Religion in Advanced Industrial Society. Boston: Unwin, Hyman 1989.
Beggs, David W. / McQuigg, R. Bruce: America's Schools and Churches. Partners in Conflict. Bloomington: Indiana University Press 1965.
Bellah, Robert N.: The Broken Covenant. American Civil Religion in a Time of Trial. New York: Seabury 1975.

Billig, Michael: Banal Nationalism. Thousand Oaks, Calif.: Sage 1995.
Bricker, David C.: Classroom Life as Civic Education. Individual Achievement and Student Cooperation in Schools. New York: Teachers College Press 1989.
Dalbec, William: South Africa. A Voter Education Success Story. In: Campaigns and Elections, 15 (1994) 7, pp. 27 and 55.
Easton, David / Dennis, Jack: Children in the Political System. New York: McGraw-Hill 1967.
Elder, Joseph W.: The Decolonization of Educational Culture. The Case of India. In: Comparative Education Review, 15 (1971) 2, pp. 288-295.
Eliade, Mircea: Ordeal by Labyrinth. Chicago: University of Chicago Press 1982.
Epstein, Erwin H.: National Identity and the Language Issue in Puerto Rico. In: Comparative Education Review, 11 (1967) 2, pp. 133-143.
Epstein, Erwin H.: Education and *Peruanidad*. „Internal" Colonialism in the Peruvian Highlands. In: Comparative Education Review, 15 (1971) 2, pp. 188-201.
Epstein, Erwin H.: Peasant Consciousness under Peruvian Military Rule. In: Harvard Educational Review, 52 (1982) 3, pp. 280-300.
Epstein, Erwin H.: Sense of Nationality among St. Lucian Schoolchildren. In: Carrión, Juan Manuel (ed.): Ethnicity, Race, and Nationality in the Caribbean, San Juan: University of Puerto Rico, Institute of Caribbean Studies 1997, pp. 338-363.
Fetters, William B. / Brown, George H. / Owings, Jeffrey A.: High School Seniors. A Comparative Study of the Classes of 1972 and 1980. Washington, D. C.: Government Printing Office 1984.
Foster, Philip J.: Ethnicity and the Schools in Ghana. In: Comparative Education Review, 6 (1962) 2, pp. 127-135.
Hagstrom, Warren O.: Deliberate Instruction within Family Units. In: Kazamias, Andreas M. / Epstein, Erwin H. (eds.): Schools in Transition. Essays in Comparative Education, Boston: Allyn and Bacon 1968, pp. 262-279.
Hammond, Phillip: The Sacred in a Secular Age. Toward Revision in the Scientific Study of Religion. Berkeley: University of California Press 1976.
Hull, Clark L.: A Primary Social Science Law. In: Scientific Monthly, 71 (1950), pp. 221-228.
Jelin, Elizabeth: Building Citizenship. A Balance Between Solidarity and Responsibility. In: Tulchin, Joseph S. (ed.) with Bernice Romero: The Consolidation of Democracy in Latin America, Boulder, Colo.: Lynne Rienner 1995, pp. 83-100.
Kandel, Isaac Leon: The Study of Comparative Education. In: The Educational Forum, 20 (1955-56) 1, pp. 5-15.
Laubach, John Herbert: School Prayers. Congress, the Courts, and the Public. Washington, D. C.: Public Affairs Press 1969.
Levine, Arthur: When Dreams and Heroes Died. A Portrait of Today's College Student. San Francisco: Jossey-Bass 1980.
Levine, Donald N.: Ethiopia. Identity, Authority, and Realism. In: Pye, Lucian W. / Verba, Sidney (eds.): Political Culture and Political Development (= Studies in Political Development. 5), Princeton: Princeton University Press 1965, pp. 245-281.
LeVine, Robert A.: The Internalization of Political Values in Stateless Societies. In: Human Organization, 19 (1960a) 2, pp. 51-58.
LeVine, Robert A.: The Role of the Family in Authority Systems. A Cross-Cultural Application of Stimulus-Generalization Theory. In: Behavioral Science, 5 (1960b), pp. 291-296.

McEwan, Barbara: Assaulting the Last Bastions of Authoritarianism. Democratic Education Meets Classroom Discipline. In: Burstyn, Joan N. (ed.): Educating Tomorrow's Valuable Citizen, Albany: State University of New York Press 1996, pp. 93-118.
McGuire, Meredith: Religion. The Social Context. Belmont, Calif.: Wadsworth 1981.
Mehrangiz, Najafizadeh / Mennerick, Lewis A.: Professionals and Third World Public Well-Being. Social Change, Education, and Democratization. In: Bauzon, Kenneth E. (ed.): Development and Democratization in the Third World, Washington, D. C.: Taylor and Francis 1992, pp. 239-252.
Mill, John Stuart: On Liberty. (1859). In: ibid.: Essays on Politics and Society. Ed. by John M. Robson (= Collected Works of John Stuart Mill. 18), Toronto et al.: University of Toronto Press 1977, pp. 213-310.
Moodie, Dunbar: The Rise of Afrikanerdom. Power, Apartheid, and the Afrikaner Civil Religion. Berkeley: University of California Press 1975.
Muir, William K.: Prayer in the Public Schools. Law and Attitude Change. Chicago: University of Chicago Press 1967.
Murdock, George P.: Social Structure. New York: Macmillan 1949.
Nash, Manning.: The Role of Village Schools in the Process of Cultural and Economic Modernization. In: Social and Economic Studies, 14 (1965) 1, pp. 131-145.
Needler, Martin C.: The Problem of Democracy in Latin America. Lexington, Mass.: Heath 1987.
Patrick, John J.: Principles of Democracy for the Education of Citizens in Former Communist Countries of Central and Eastern Europe. In: Remy, Richard C. / Strzemieczny, Jacek (eds.): Building Civic Education for Democracy in Poland, Washington, D. C.: National Council for the Social Studies 1996, pp. 1-22.
Pinkney, Robert: Democracy in the Third World. Boulder, Colo.: Lynne Rienner 1994.
Remy, Richard C. / Strzemieczny, Jacek: Education for Democratic Citizenship in Poland. Activities and Assumptions. In: idem / idem (eds.): Building Civic Education for Democracy in Poland, Washington, D. C.: National Council for the Social Studies 1996, pp. 55-66.
Rival, Laura: Formal Schooling and the Production of Modern Citizens in the Ecuadorian Amazon. In: Levinson, Bradley A. / Foley, Douglas E. / Holland, Dorothy C. (eds.): The Cultural Production of the Educated, Albany: State University of New York Press 1996, pp. 153-168.
Romero Vargas, Germán / Buitrago Buitrago, Edgardo: En Busca de la Democracia. Managua: Programa de Educación Para la Democracia MED/AFT, American Federation of Teachers Educational Foundation 1994.
Salvucci, Linda K.: Getting the Facts Straight. New Views of Mexico and its Peoples in Recently Adopted U.S. History Textbooks in Texas. In: The Public Historian, 14 (1992) 4, pp. 57-69.
Scanlon, David G. (ed.): Church, State, and Education in Africa. New York: Teachers College Press 1966.
Simel, Dana L.: Exclusionary Christian Civil Religion for Jewish and Islamic Students in Bavarian Schools. In: Comparative Education Review, 40 (1996) 1, pp. 28-46.
Sullivan, John D.: Democratization and Business Interests. In: Journal of Democracy, 5 (1994) 4, pp. 146-160.
Swomley, John M.: Religion, the State, and the Schools. New York: Pegasus 1968.
Tucker, Jan L.: Global Lessons from Siberia. In: Social Education, 57 (1993) 3, pp. 101-103.
Tulchin, Joseph S. (ed.) with Bernice Romero: The Consolidation of Democracy in Latin America. Boulder, Colo.: Lynne Rienner 1995.

The Limitations and Possibilities of Comparative Analysis of Education in Global Context

Mark B. Ginsburg

Comparison is a central element of disciplined inquiry or what some term scientific investigation.[1] For example, *Farrell (1986, p. 203)* includes comparative along with systematic and empirical as necessary and sufficient attributes of the scientific method, which he describes as „*not a rigid set of prescriptions but ... a highly flexible and adaptable way to order our perceptions of the external world*". Although not an unproblematic concept *(Farrell 1986; Kohn 1987; Sztompka 1988)*, comparison can be defined as involving a search to identify and explain similarities *and* differences between or among phenomena.

Stating this, though, does not enable us to avoid the dilemma of comparative inquiry – that similar or different 'findings' may stem from 1) 'real' similarities or differences in the phenomena being investigated, 2) similarities or differences in the theoretical assumptions or methodological approaches used by those studying the phenomena, and/or 3) similarities or differences in the way people being studied view their social reality *(Kohn 1987, Sztompka 1988)*. *King (1979, p. 15)* stresses the second and third alternative explanations of observed similarities and differences, when he argues that as comparative education scholars „*we are more scientific if we recognize two inescapably subjective aspects: our own [i.e. scholars'] subjective involvement in the debates about education; and the equally subjective involvement of those policy makers, educators, citizens who are trying to arrive at solutions in other countries*".

Particularly in this period when post-structuralist and post-modernist notions are gaining in popularity among social scientists and educational researchers *(Cherryholmes 1988, Rust 1996)*, it seems important to consider seriously the second and third alternative explanations and not conclude immediately that the observed similarities or dif-

---

[1] Note, however, that in accord with *Popkewitz (1981)* I am employing the term science as not being limited to work done within the positivist (or empirico-analytic) paradigm, but would also include interpretive (or symbolic) and critical as scientific traditions *(Ginsburg et al. 1996)*.

ferences are 'real'. Since comparative analyses have the possibility of shrouding the 'truth' as well as shedding new light on previously ignored or misinterpreted phenomena *(Eckstein 1986)*, we must be cautious to avoid the 'abuses' – exaggeration, overly-emphatic conclusions, decontextualization, and ego-centrism – sometimes found in work in fields such as comparative education *(Noah 1986)*.

With respect to the second alternative explanation, *Farrell (1986, p. 209)* comments that similarity or dissimilarity *„is not something which inheres in the data. It is characteristic of the relationship between the observer and the data, and depends upon the conceptual structures within the mind of the observer"*. With respect to the third alternative explanation, I would note that conclusions about similarities or differences in answers to the question of whether teaching is considered to be a profession are complicated in that the meanings educators and others attach to the terrain 'professionalism' vary across – as well as within – societal contexts *(Ginsburg / Meyenn / Miller 1980; Ginsburg 1987, 1988; Ginsburg et al. 1988)*.

Selecting the appropriate unit(s) of analysis for comparison is also problematic. The dominant approach within comparative education and comparative social sciences is to focus on cross-national or inter-societal comparisons *(Sztompka 1988; Wakeman 1988; Bray/Thomas 1995)*. As *Kohn (1987, p. 725)* observes: *„In many discussions, ... the term 'comparative research' is treated as synonymous with cross-national research, as if the only possible comparisons were international comparisons."* This dominant approach, however, is based at least implicitly on the notion that societies are relatively independent or isolated social formations. But as *Wallerstein (1974-80)* as well as some comparative educationists *(Meyer / Hannan 1979; Altbach 1982; Ginsburg 1991; Arnove 1992)* have argued, it is increasingly more appropriate to consider nation-states as integrated to varying degrees in a World capitalist economic 'system and/or word cultural system'. International or inter-societal relations – militarily, economically, politically, and culturally – obviously predate the contemporary focus on the world systems. However, increasing 'globalization' makes the assumption of the study of independent societal cases even more problematic than it was in the 19th century when Sir Francis Galton identified the problem *„that valid comparison requires mutually independent and isolated cases, and therefore cultural diffusion, cultural contact, culture clash or outright conquest – with their consequent borrowing, imitation, migrations etc. – invalidates the results of comparative studies"* *(Sztompka 1988, p. 213)*.

Sztompka (ibid., p. 214) seeks to address this problem resulting from the increasing globalization[2] of society (and the internationalization of the social sciences) by arguing that we should shift the concern in comparative analysis from one of seeking *„commonalties and uniformities among variety"* to one of searching for *„differences, uniqueness among uniformity."* I do not concur. Acknowledging the existence of a world system does not render a search for similarities less important. That nation-states are integrated in a stratified world economic and/or cultural systems, in which same societies are located at the center and other in the periphery – is not tantamount to establishing uniformity among all societies. As *Peacock / Hoover / Killian (1988)* observe, both convergence and divergence in characteristics of nation-states occur in the world system.[3] Similarities and differences in a society's position in the world system in interaction with similarities and differences in historically derived national (and intra-national) political, economic and cultural factors should be examined as possible explanations of similarities and differences in educational phenomena.

Moreover, we need to move beyond *only* comparing nation-states. That is, we must seek to break out of the *„cast-iron grid that exercises a transcendent despotism over reality..."* as *Young (1976, p. 66)* referred to the nation-state in discussing its limitations as the basic unit of social analysis. In this regard, *Bray's* and *Thomas' (1995, p. 473)* contribution[4] is helpful in that they distinguish among seven different geographical/locational levels:

- world regions/continents
- countries
- states/provinces
- districts
- schools
- classrooms
- individuals

---

2 Note that despite drawing attention to globalization, Sztompka emphasizes nation-states as the unit of analysis.

3 *Meyer / Hannan (1979)* and their colleagues do not place much emphasis on the hierarchical nature of the world system, thus allowing them, like *Sztompka (1988)*, to conceive of the process of integration of nation-states as a process of convergence or homogenization

4 *Bray / Thomas (1995)* also subsume under the geographic/locational dimension what I think would be more appropriately labeled a political economic dimension. This, the incorporate core-periphery and (neo)colonizer/(neo)colonized status under the world regions/continents level. Differentiation along such a political economic dimension also seems appropriate when comparing among units within countries or within states/provinces.

and promote multilevel analyses (see also *Burstein 1988*). They also draw attention to „*non-locational demographic groupings, including ethnicity, religion, age, and gender*" and I would add social class and immigrant or refugee status.

In conclusion, I should note that in pursuing a comparative analysis in education I am not only interested in aiding our understanding *(Eckstein 1986; Noah 1986)* or ill assessing alternative policy or practice options *(King 1979; Holmes 1986)*. I am also interested in shaping strategies for individual and collective action by educational workers, including ourselves. Thus, for me, comparative analyses, for example, of the politics of educators' work[5] and lives *(Ginsburg 1995)* or of the political dimension in teacher education *(Ginsburg / Lindsay 1995)* seek to inform theory, policy, and 'critical praxis' – the joining of critical theory and practice in and outside the educators' work sites *(Ginsburg 1988)*. A concern with critical praxis is important because „*styles of reasoning, definitional categories, and 'accepted' policies and practices in ... education, all legitimate particular social interests and actions – while at the same time they omit other possibilities*" *(Popkewitz 1993, p. 15)*.

The above-discussed limitations to our understanding and policy development efforts deriving from comparative analysis of education also affect our ability to forge successful strategies for action. I want to argue that a necessary component in shaping such strategies is an examination of similarities and differences among educators' experiences in different historical periods and settings, as well as by a comparison of the situations of educators with those of other groups of workers. Based on such comparative analyses we can develop and refine our goals and strategies for action based on struggle in collaboration with other workers and other subordinated groups in educational institutions and within the political economic and cultural contexts of the locality, nation, and the world.

Bibliography

Alger, Chadwick F.: Perceiving, Analysing and Coping with the Local-Global Nexus. In: International Social Science Journal, 40 (1988) 117, pp. 321-340.

---

5   *Ozga / Lawn (1981, p. 67)* comment, „*all workers ... have similar difficulties depending on their level of political development, their class consciousness, the nature of their work under monopoly capitalism or the complexities or contradictions of their class position*".

Altbach, Philip G: Servitude of the Mind? Education, Dependency, and Neocolonialism. In: idem / Arnove, Robert F. / Kelly, Gail P. (eds.): Comparative Education, New York et al.: Macmillan et al. 1982, pp. 469-494.

Arnove, Robert F: Comparative Education and World-Systems. In: Altbach, Philip G. / idem / Kelly, Gail P. (eds.): Comparative Education, New York et al.: Macmillan et al. 1982, pp. 453-468.

Bray, Mark / Thomas, Robert Murray: Levels of Comparison in Educational Studies. Different Insights from Different Literatures and the Value of Multilevel Analyses. In: Harvard Educational Review, 65 (1995) 3, S. 472-490.

Burstein, Leigh: Units of Analysis. In: Keeves, John P. (ed.): Educational Research, Methodology and Measurement, An International Handbook, Oxford et al.: Pergamon Press 1988, pp. 775-781.

Cherryholmes, Cleo H.: Power and Criticism. Poststructural Investigations in Education. New York et al.: Teachers College Press 1988. (Advances in Contemporary Educational Thought Series. 2)

Eckstein, Max A.: The Comparative Mind. In: Altbach, Philip G. / Kelly, Gail P. (eds.): New Approaches to Comparative Education, Chicago et al.: University of Chicago Press 1986, pp. 167-178.

Farrell, Joseph P.: The Necessity of Comparisons in the Study of Education. The Salience of Science and the Problem of Comparability. In: Altbach, Philip G. / Kelly, Gail P. (eds.): New Approaches to Comparative Education, Chicago et al.: University of Chicago Press 1986, pp. 201-214.

Ginsburg, Mark B.: Reproduction, Contradiction and Conceptions of Professionalism. The Case of Preservice Teachers. In: Popkewitz, Thomas S. (ed.): Critical Studies in Teacher Education, New York et al.: Falmer Press 1987, pp. 86-129.

Ginsburg, Mark B.: Contradictions in Teacher Education and Society. A Critical Analysis. London et al.: Falmer Press 1988.

Ginsburg, Mark B.: El proceso de trabajo y la acción politica de los educadores. Un analysis comparado. In: Revista de Educacion, 38 (1990) Extraordinario, pp. 315-346.

Ginsburg, Mark B.: Understanding Educational Reform in Global Context. Economy, Ideology, and the State. New York: Garland 1991. (Reference Books in International Education. 22; Garland Reference Library of Social Science. 663)

Ginsburg, Mark B.: The Politics of Educators' Work and Lives. New York: Garland 1995. (Studies in Education/Politics. 1; Garland Reference Library of Social Science. 915)

Ginsburg, Mark B. et al.: El concepto de professionalismo en el profesorado. Comparación de contextos entre Inglaterra y Estados Unidos. In: Revista de Educación, 36 (1988) 285, pp. 5-31.

Ginsburg, Mark B. et al.: Choices in Conceptualizing Classroom-Anchored Research and Linking it to Policy/Practice to Improve Educational Quality in 'Developing' Countries. In: Research Papers in Education, 11 (1996) 3, pp. 239-254.

Ginsburg, Mark B. / Lindsay, B.: The Political Dimension in Teacher Education. Comparative Perspectives on Policy Formation, Socialization, and Society. London et al.: Falmer Press 1995. (Wisconsin Series on Teacher Education. 5)

Ginsburg, Mark B. / Meyenn, Robert J. / Miller, Henry D. R.: Teachers' Conceptions of Professionalism and Trades Unionism. An Ideological Analysis. In: Woods, Peter (ed.): Teacher Strategies. Explorations in the Sociology of the School, London: Croom Helm 1980, pp. 178-212.

Holmes, Brian: Paradigm Shifts in Comparative Education. In: Altbach, Philip G. / Kelly, Gail P. (eds.): New Approaches to Comparative Education, Chicago et al.: University of Chicago Press 1986, pp. 179-200.

King, Edward James: Other Schools and Ours. 5. ed. New York et al.: Holt, Rinehart, and Winston 1979.
Kohn, Melvin L.: Cross-National Research as an Analytic Strategy. In: American Sociological Review, 52 (1987) 6, pp. 713-731.
Meyer, John W. / Hannan, Michael T. (eds.): National Development and the World System. Educational, Economic, and Political Change, 1950-70. Chicago: University of Chicago Press 1979.
Noah, Harold J.: The Use and Abuse of Comparative Education. In: Altbach, Philip G. / Kelly, Gail P. (eds.): New Approaches to Comparative Education, Chicago et al.: University of Chicago Press 1986, pp. 153-166.
Ozga, Jennifer / Lawn, Martin: Teachers, Professionalism, and Class. A Study of Organized Teachers. London: Falmer Press 1981.
Peacock, Walter Gillis / Hoover, Greg A. / Killian, Charles D.: Divergence and Convergence in International Development. A Decomposition Analysis of Inequality in the World System. In: American Sociological Review, 53 (1988) 6, pp. 838-852.
Popkewitz, Thomas S.: The Study of Schooling. Paradigms and Field-Based Methodologies in Educational Research and Evaluation. In: idem / Tabachnick, B. Robert (eds.): The Study of Schooling, New York: Praeger 1981, pp. 1-26.
Popkewitz, Thomas S. (ed.): Changing Patterns of Power. Social Regulation and Teacher Education Reform. Albany: State University of New York Press 1993.
Rust, Val D.: From Modern to Postmodern Ways of Seeing Social and Educational Change. In: Paulston, Rolland (ed.): Social Cartography, New York: Garland 1996, pp. 19-52.
Sztompka, Piotr: Conceptual Frameworks in Comparative Inquiry: Divergent or Convergent? In: International Sociology, 3 (1988) 3, pp. 207-218.
Wakeman, Frederic E.: Transnational and Comparative Research. In: Items, 42 (1988) 4, pp. 85-89.
Wallerstein, Immanuel: The Modern World System. Vol. 1. 2. New York: Academic Press 1974-80.
Young, Crawford: The Politics of Cultural Pluralism. Madison: University of Wisconsin Press 1976.

Überlegungen zu einer „Einführung in die Vergleichende Erziehungswissenschaft"

Detlef Glowka

Den Anlaß der folgenden Betrachtung bildet das Projekt einer ERASMUS-Gruppe, gemeinsam einen Kurs „Einführung in die Vergleichende Erziehungswissenschaft" zu entwickeln und zu erproben, ihn dabei schrittweise zu verbessern und schließlich zu publizieren. Bei der Gruppe handelt es sich um je einen Hochschullehrer von 13 Universitäten (Dresden, Florenz, Glasgow, Groningen, Kopenhagen, Löwen, London, Madrid, Münster, Oslo, Oulu, Udine, Uppsala), die im Rahmen dieses ERASMUS-Programms noch in anderer Hinsicht kooperieren (Entwicklung weiterer Kurse zur Vergleichenden Erziehungswissenschaft, Studentenaustausch). Der von Winther-Jensen (Kopenhagen) eingebrachte Entwurf erwies sich rasch als konsensfähig; folgende Themenliste wurde als Gerüst des Einführungskurses akzeptiert: 1. What is Comparative Education? 2. Organizations, Institutions and Documentation; 3. „Nation" and „Nation State"; 4. Education and Culture; 5. Educational Systems: Structure and Organizations; 6. Theories of Curriculum in an International Context; 7. Education and the European Idea; 8. Comparative Method.

Mein Mitarbeiter H.-G. Kotthoff und ich haben im Sommersemester 1996 versucht, diesen Entwurf in ein Seminar am Fachbereich Erziehungswissenschaft der Universität Münster umzusetzen. Es soll hier über die dabei gewonnenen Erfahrungen berichtet werden.

Voraussetzungen

Schon eine flüchtige Durchsicht relevanter Bibliographien läßt heute erkennen, daß der der Vergleichenden Erziehungswissenschaft (VE) zurechenbare Literaturbestand umfänglich und vielfältig geworden ist. Jede didaktische Absicht, in dieses weite Feld der VE einzuführen, sieht sich vor die Aufgabe gestellt, besonders geeignete Texte auswählen zu müssen. Einige Werke wie die von *Sadler (1979)*, *Kandel (1933)*, *Hans (1967)* oder *Schneider (1961)* gelten als repräsentativ, doch nicht für den gegenwärtigen Stand der VE, sondern für ihre Geschichte, für Etappen ihrer Herausbildung. Unter den Publikationen der letzten Jahrzehnte genießt wohl kaum eine ein solches Ansehen, daß sie als Lehrbuch der VE gelten könnte. Es gibt eine Reihe von herausragenden Arbeiten zu Teilbereichen der VE, die in diesem Sinne als Standardwerke gelten können, aber sie lassen sich nicht zu einer Gruppe von Grundlagentexten für eine Einführung aneinanderreihen; dafür sind sie zu unterschiedlich hinsichtlich ihres Gegenstandes, ihrer Theorie und ihrer Methodik.

Dabei fehlt es wahrlich nicht an Versuchen, den Stand der VE in repräsentativer Weise zu erfassen und die Struktur der Disziplin und ihre Aufgaben in normsetzender Weise darzustellen. Ansätze dieser Art rücken Methoden- und Theoriefragen in den Mittelpunkt. Ich denke an Publikationen wie etwa jene von *Robinsohn (1970-75), Anweiler / Glowka (1971), Busch u. a. (1974), Holmes (1981), Froese (1983), Schriewer / Holmes (1988)* – dies ist nur eine kleine Auswahl aus der enormen Literatur zu Methodenfragen. In die gleiche Richtung, doch mit anspruchsvollerem Ansatz gehen die Versuche, den Stand der VE zu bilanzieren, um die verworren scheinenden Entwicklungen rückblickend auf den Begriff zu bringen. Hier denke ich insbesondere an die Publikationen von *Kazamias (1977), Altbach / Kelly (1986), Halls (1990)* und *Arnove / Altbach / Kelly (1992)*. Für diese wie für die zuvor genannten Arbeiten scheint mir charakteristisch zu sein, daß sie sich an die Fachwelt – oder genauer gesagt: an den theorie- und methodeninteressierten Teil der Fachwelt – wenden; sie setzen eine detaillierte Kenntnis des Feldes voraus; als Lektüre zur Einführung in das Feld sind sie kaum geeignet. Das gilt auch für ein solches Monumentalwerk der Bilanzierung wie die Enzyklopädie von *Husén / Postlethwaite (1994)*.

Sieht man sich nach Arbeiten um, die eine lehrbuchhafte Einführung in die VE anstreben, bleibt eine weitgehende 'Fehlanzeige' zu vermelden. *Noah / Eckstein (1969)* bilden eine herausragende Ausnahme; *Bereday (1964)* konnte ihnen in gewisser Weise als Vorbild dienen. In deutschsprachiger Form bieten die Arbeiten von *Seidenfaden (1966), Kern (1973), Wittig (1973)* und *Röhrs (1975)* am ehesten eine Darstellung der VE im Stile einer Einführung, doch es ließen sich auch die Gründe benennen, warum sie sich weder international noch national durchsetzen konnten. Mir ist nicht bekannt, ob es in anderen Sprachen lehrbuchhafte Darstellungen der VE gibt. Es ist auffallend, daß in der englischsprachigen Literatur – soweit sich sehen läßt – der Aspekt einer 'Didaktisierung' der VE während der letzten 25 Jahre keine Beachtung gefunden hat. Noch 1970 konnte *Eckstein (1970, S. 279)* konstatieren: „*From the very beginning, some attention has been given to teaching the subject of comparative education.*" Er plädierte dafür, Forschung und Lehre als einen untrennbaren Zusammenhang zu begreifen: „*to be effective as a teacher ... one must be a model of doing ... comparative education*" *(ebd., S. 280).* Einige Jahre zuvor hatten *Noah und Eckstein (1966, S. 511)* die Aufgabe der Lehre auf die Frage zugespitzt: „*How do we teach them to formulate and test fruitful, non-trivial hypotheses about the relationship between education and society, using cross-national and/or cross-cultural data?"* In ihrem genannten Buch *(Noah / Eckstein 1969)* führen sie ihren Ansatz exemplarisch vor. – Warum hat diese didaktische Denkweise in der VE keine Nachfolge gefunden?

Es gibt mit Sicherheit im angelsächsischen Raum – stimuliert durch das Kurssystem an den Universitäten – nicht wenige Beispiele von elaborierten Einführungen in die VE; so hat beispielsweise die Universität Oxford 1996 einen solchen Kurs neu aufgelegt. Wenn es trotzdem keine 'Theorie der Lehre' zum Bereich der VE gibt, so liegt sicherlich einer der Gründe – wie ich vermute: der Hauptgrund – in der Verfassung der VE als einer wissenschaftlichen 'Disziplin'.

Bis in die siebziger Jahre hinein wurde von der VE gern als einer 'jungen Disziplin' gesprochen, die sich in einer 'tiefgreifenden Identitätskrise' befinde; durch methodologische und 'gegenstandstheoretische' Reflexion bzw. Strukturierung des VE-spezifischen Ansatzes sollte für die Disziplin ein klares Profil gewonnen und damit das Schiff gleichsam flott gemacht werden (so z. B. die Einleitung zu *Busch u. a. 1974*). Dies scheint sich seit der Bilanz „State of the Art" *(Kazamias 1977)* geändert zu haben. Die Vielfalt der Gegenstände, der Methoden und der Erklärungsansätze wird inzwischen als normal und als nicht revidierbar angesehen. Wie in der Soziologie, gelte auch für die VE: „*there is no clear center or overall direction ... there are many schools of thought in comparative education, and none has dominance*" (Altbach 1991, S. 493). Fast wörtlich gleichlautend heißt es bei *Arnove / Altbach / Kelly (1992)*: „*This volume illustrates the dynamism and increasing diversity of comparative education ...*" (S. 3); „*the field has no center – rather it is an amalgam of interdisciplinary studies, informed by a number of different theoretical frameworks*" *(S. 21f.).*

Traditionellerweise besteht die Aufgabe einer Einführung darin, den Anfängern die 'Struktur' einer 'Disziplin' zu erschließen. Wie aber muß eine Einführung beschaffen sein, wenn wir statt einer Struktur ein 'Amalgam', statt einer Disziplin ein 'Feld' antreffen? Angesichts dieser Lage mag es als vergebliche Mühe erscheinen, sich für eine didaktische Theorie der Lehre der VE zu engagieren.

Überlegungen zu einer „Einführung in die Vergleichende Erziehungswissenschaft"

In seiner Presidential Address auf dem neunten Weltkongress für Vergleichende Erziehungswissenschaft im Juli 1996 hat Wolfgang *Mitter (1996)* – wie mir scheint: deutlicher als andere vergleichbare Statements – anhand seiner eigenen Biographie hervorgehoben, wie sehr die Paradigmenwechsel der VE mit den epochalen und nationalen Konstellationen kovariieren. Diesem wechselhaften Wehen des Zeitgeistes stellt Mitter zwei Aspekte entgegen: Erstens, wir dürfen nicht 'modisch' werden, denn auch die unmodern gewordenen Ansätze behalten eine fortdauernde Berechtigung (beispielsweise benötigen wir in der VE weiterhin 'Reiseberichte' oder 'Länderstudien', wofür Mitter selbst zahlreiche Beispiele geliefert hat); und zweitens: „*I have repeatedly emphasized the ties of comparative education to the task of humanizing education*" *(ebd., S. 11)* – ein Zug im Denken Mitters, den *García Garrido (1987)* bereits so engagiert gewürdigt hat. Es wird zu prüfen sein, ob von Mitters Position ausgehend sich nicht strukturierende Aspekte für die Anlage einer Einführung gewinnen lassen.

Aus den von uns herangezogenen Bilanzierungen ist noch ein Gedanke nachzutragen – es ist ein optimistischer: Die auf dem Feld der VE eingetretene Unübersichtlichkeit wird positiv genommen: „*The field of comparative education ... is in remarkably good health. It is marked by a considerable degree of intellectual vigor*" *(Altbach 1991, S. 506)*. Oder: „*The fact that the field has not resolved the debates about culture, method, and theory may well be a strength, rather than a weakness and point to the viability of the field and its continued growth*" *(Arnove / Altbach / Kelly 1992, S. 22)*. Damit deutet sich eine weitere Leitlinie für die Anlage von 'Einführungen' an.

Didaktische Aspekte

'Einführungen' haben Konjunktur; manche Verlage legen dafür besondere Reihen auf (z. B. die Wissenschaftliche Buchgesellschaft in Darmstadt oder Litt in Münster). Für die Erziehungswissenschaft gilt dies in besonderem Maße; in Deutschland erscheinen jedes Jahr etwa drei entsprechende Titel. Es liegt offenbar an der unklar gewordenen oder verloren gegangenen Struktur der Wissenschaftsbereiche, daß Autoren oder Herausgeber sich immer wieder zu dem Versuch veranlaßt sehen, den Bestand einer Wissenschaft „neu zu ordnen", „Schneisen zu schlagen", „Übersicht zu schaffen", „Karten anzulegen", „einen Leitfaden zu bieten" usw.; häufig sind es mehr die Arrangements, die dabei variieren, als die eigentlichen Gehalte. Für Studierende ist es nicht unbedingt hilfreich, wenn man ihnen 'zur Einführung' dreißig oder sechzig Buchtitel empfiehlt.

Obgleich diese Literaturgattung durch ihren Bestand deutlich macht, daß 'Einführungen' sich auf ganz unterschiedliche Weise schreiben lassen, zeichnet sich bei einer Durchsicht doch so etwas wie ein Muster ab; bestimmte strukturierende Momente sind offenbar unverzichtbar und tauchen – in Variationen – immer wieder auf. In Anlehnung an diese Erfahrung hielten wir uns bei unserer Einführung an die folgenden sechs Aspekte:

– *Geschichte.* Ohne einen Überblick zur Geschichte der VE würde sich ihr gegenwärtiger Stand kaum begreifen lassen.
– *Untersuchungsgegenstände.* Es muß deutlich werden, womit sich die VE beschäftigt, welchen Sachverhalten und Problemen sie sich überwiegend zuwendet. „*All comparative educationists make comparisons in space*" *(Cowen 1982, S. 165);* auf der Basis von Regionen, von Ländern, 'areas', der 'Welt' und innerhalb eines Zeithorizontes untersuchen sie Sachverhalte und 'Probleme' in der Erstreckung des Speziellen (etwa: Ermittlung von Stundentafeln für einzelne Fächer) bis hin zum Globalen (etwa: der Zusammenhang von Bildung und „Postmoderne"). Anhand der Gegenstände läßt sich verdeutlichen, auf welche Weise sich das Feld in Teilbereiche gliedert.
– *Fragestellungen.* Obgleich jeder Untersuchung eine explizite Fragestellung zugrunde liegt oder liegen sollte (Holmes: problem approach; Noah / Eckstein: Hypothesenprüfung), bleibt sie bisweilen selbst dem Forscher unbewußt; im Rückblick erkennt man deutlicher die forschungsleitenden Annahmen (Modernisierungshypothese, Konflikttheorie, gesellschaftliche Relevanz der Bildung, Steuerbarkeit des Bildungswesens usw.)
– *Methoden.* Methoden konstituieren die Untersuchungsgegenstände, Fragestellungen führen zu neuen Methoden. Die Methodenfrage besitzt für die VE insofern eine besondere Relevanz, als größere Teile des Feldes sich so lesen lassen, als seien sie nicht durch Fragestellungen und spezifische Gegenstände konstituiert, sondern allein durch die vergleichende Methode. Immer wieder stößt man in der VE-Literatur auf die Empfehlung, sich der allgemeinen Rolle des Vergleichs in den Sozialwissenschaften zu vergewissern *(Eckstein 1986).*
– *Standardwerke.* Standardwerke vermitteln Orientierung in einer Wissenschaft – für den Anfänger wie für den Fachmann. Das Vorhandensein konkurrierender Standardwerke oder das Fehlen solcher Leitpublikationen – wie es für die VE weitgehend typisch ist – verstärkt die Unübersichtlichkeit des Feldes. Für Teilbereiche der VE lassen sich solche Leitfiguren sicherlich ausmachen; in Deutschland hat Oskar Anweiler 'Schule gemacht', Noah und Eckstein haben Maßstäbe gesetzt, Holmes hat am

Londoner Institut die Ausbildung einer ganzen Generation von Komparatisten beeinflußt, die heute in Asien an Boden gewinnt.
- *Organisation.* Keine Wissenschaft kommt ohne Organisation aus: Sie benötigt dafür freigestelltes Personal (z. B. Lehrstühle), Ressourcen (z. B. Forschungseinrichtungen, Mittelgeber), Organisationen (z. B. Gesellschaften), Kommunikationsformen (z. B. Zeitschriften, Kongresse). Der Grad ihrer Institutionalisierung indiziert also das Florieren einer Wissenschaft *(Cowen 1990).*

Selbst wenn sich somit die allgemeine Struktur einer Einführung in die VE abzeichnet, sind damit die konkreten Inhalte noch nicht gewonnen bzw. legitimiert. Als weiterführend bietet sich die Fragestellung des adressatenbezogenen Ansatzes der Didaktik an: Wer will bzw. soll etwas zur VE lernen und warum?

Der Lernkontext soll die Anlage der 'Einführung' bestimmen. Bildet der Einführungskurs den Anfang eines elaborierten, umfangreichen Lehrganges, so hat er vor allem auf die anschließenden Studien vorzubereiten; 'Lücken' können leicht toleriert werden, weil sie im weiteren Verlauf ausgleichbar sind. Die Einführung bewährt sich in ihrer Verzahnung mit dem Lehrgang. Anders in unserem Falle: Die 'Einführung' hat – zumindest: auch – die Funktion eines Grundkurses, eines abgeschlossenen Minilehrgangs, weil die Teilnehmer vielleicht oder wahrscheinlich in ihrer weiteren Ausbildung nicht mehr mit der VE in Berührung kommen. Oder soweit ein Anschluß stattfindet, handelt es sich um frei wählbare und in ihren Thematiken weitgehend heterogene Lehrangebote; auf den Umgang mit diesen Lehrangeboten vorzubereiten, sollte eine weitere Funktion unserer Einführung sein.

Warum sollen oder wollen unsere Teilnehmer etwas über die VE erfahren? Die VE als Ausbildungslehrgang oder als Ausbildungselement bietet sich an bei Personen, deren berufliche Tätigkeit mit den internationalen pädagogischen Zusammenhängen zu tun hat. Für unsere Klientel (Lehramtsstudenten) hingegen bildet das VE-Angebot einen Teil ihrer allgemeinen pädagogischen Ausbildung, den sie als Wahlpflichtfach wahrnehmen. Aus dieser Perspektive heraus ist also ein möglicher Bildungseffekt des VE-Kurses zu bedenken. Als mögliche allgemeine Lernziele erscheinen naheliegend:

- das eigene Bildungswesen besser verstehen;
- Kompetenz für den Prozeß der europäischen Integration erwerben;
- die Internationalität pädagogischer Entwicklungen begreifen;
- am Beispiel der VE die erziehungswissenschaftliche Denkweise schulen.

Die Behandlung der einzelnen Themen des Kurses sollte so ausgelegt sein, daß die Erreichung dieser allgemeinen Lernziele gefördert wird. Die Verbundenheit der Themen ergibt sich also aus der didaktischen Absicht des Kurses. Zugleich ist der Diskontinuität des Lernens unserer Studenten Rechnung zu tragen: Jede Seminarsitzung sollte nach Möglichkeit in sich geschlossen sein und einen eigenen Lernertrag ermöglichen.

Die methodische Umsetzung der Konzeption hat uns am meisten Kopfzerbrechen bereitet. Bei einer Vorlesung wäre die inhaltlich-methodische Gestaltung den Lehrenden zugefallen. Hier, als einem Seminar, waren wir auf die Mitarbeit der teilnehmenden Studenten angewiesen, deren Möglichkeiten es realistisch einzuschätzen galt. Unter den gegebenen Bedingungen erfolgt eine Textlektüre nur jeweils von Sitzung zu Sitzung; auf eine von allen Teilnehmern erarbeitete Grundlagenliteratur läßt sich also kaum zurückgreifen. Wir haben versucht, für jedes Thema einen treffenden Text im Umfang von etwa 20 Seiten zu finden (immerhin ist er meistens in einer Fremdsprache zu lesen), der durch Hinweise auf weiterführende Literatur ergänzt wird.

Zugänge

Das oben mitgeteilte Kurskonzept aus acht Themen haben wir in ein Seminarprogramm für zwölf Sitzungen umgewandelt. Statt sie hier einzeln vorzustellen, möchte ich sie zu drei Bereichen zusammenfassen, um den Gehalt unseres Kurses vorzustellen; sie lassen sich folgendermaßen überschreiben: a) Die VE als Wissenschaft; b) Vergleichende Analyse von nationalen Bildungssystemen; c) Vergleichende Analyse von Aspekten nationaler Bildungssysteme – und zwar jeweils begrenzt auf das Europa der Europäischen Union. Damit war das von der VE bearbeitete Feld natürlich drastisch eingeschränkt. Wir waren bemüht, bei passender Gelegenheit auf den weiteren Horizont der VE hinzuweisen: auf die Verhältnisse in Entwicklungs- und Schwellenländern, auf die besondere Bildungssituation in Ländern wie den USA, Rußland, Japan, China, auf areastudies usw. Doch die konsequente Konzentration auf die Mitgliedstaaten der Europäischen Union hielten wir für angebracht, einmal, um den besonderen Bildungsinteressen der angehenden Lehrer zu entsprechen, und zum anderen, um den Kurs in zeitökonomischer Hinsicht handhabbar zu halten.

Die VE als Wissenschaft

Als Einstieg präsentierten wir eine Liste „Themen der VE", um daran zu erörtern, womit sich die VE überhaupt beschäftigt. Begreift man 'Themen' in einem tieferen Sinne – in der Richtung von 'Fragestellungen' –, gelangt die Diskussion rasch zu jenen Aspekten, die in den Periodisierungen und Bilanzierungen der letzten Zeit erörtert werden. Unter den herangezogenen – von den Studenten meist als schwierig empfundenen – Büchern und Aufsätzen wirkt ein so von Humor und Altersweisheit getragener Text wie der von *Noah (1986)* geradezu befreiend. In der Erörterung der Motive für vergleichendes erziehungswissenschaftliches Forschen wurde neben den erkenntnistheoretischen und politischen Interessen auch das von Mitter angeschlagene Motiv der Humanisierung von Bildung angesprochen.

Erst nachdem sich bei den Studenten bereits eine gewisse Kenntnis zu Gegenständen und Fragestellungen entwickelt hatte, lenkten wir die Aufmerksamkeit auf Methodenfragen. Für die Behandlung des quantifizierenden Zuganges liefert das Unternehmen der International Association for the Evaluation of Educational Achievement ein reichhaltiges Material; für den uns ebenso wichtigen historiographisch orientierten Ansatz finden sich gerade in der deutschsprachigen Literatur markante Beispiele *(Röhrs 1975; Froese 1983; Anweiler 1990)*. Dem Thema „Bildung als Reproduktion und Modifikation von Kultur" wurde eine eigene Seminarsitzung eingeräumt (Kulturbegriff, 'internationaler' oder 'interkultureller' Vergleich, Ethnomethodologie). Zur Institutionalisierung der VE erhielten die Studenten eine Liste mit den wichtigsten Daten.

Im Grunde wäre mit den hier angedeuteten Themen das oben angedeutete Pflichtrepertoire einer Einführung bereits weitgehend abgedeckt. Wir haben diese Themen nicht als Block behandelt sondern im Wechsel mit den Themen der zwei anderen Bereiche, die gewissermaßen jene materielle Basis vermitteln sollten, auf der sich Methoden- und Theoriefragen erst sinnvoll erörtern lassen. Die didaktische Schwierigkeit des ersten Abschnitts sahen wir weniger in der Identifikation der relevanten Themen als vielmehr im Auffinden geeigneter Literatur. An Schriften zur Selbstreflexion der VE fehlt es wahrlich nicht, doch Hinweise auf Titel, mit denen sich Anfänger auf diesem Gebiet erfahrungsgemäß ansprechen lassen, würden wir gern entgegennehmen.

Vergleichende Analyse von nationalen Bildungssystemen

Wir versuchten den Studenten zu vermitteln, warum 'die Nation' für lange Zeit die wichtigste Untersuchungseinheit und Bezugsgröße der VE bildete und warum sich dies in unserer Zeit geändert hat und heute die europäische Integration auf der Tagesordnung steht. Bei aller inzwischen gewonnenen kritischen Distanz zum 'Nationalen' bleiben 'Länder' und 'Staaten' wichtige Grundgegebenheiten der Analyse, und sogar die Frage nach dem 'Nationalcharakter', so scheint es, zieht wieder Interesse auf sich. Wir waren bemüht, den Themenbereich vor allem im Hinblick auf die folgenden zwei Aspekte zu akzentuieren: Erstens, Bildungssysteme als Untersuchungsgegenstände müssen historisch gesehen werden; dabei läßt sich die geschichtliche Herausbildung des 'Systemcharakters' eines Bildungswesens gerade aus international vergleichender Sicht aufzeigen *(Müller/Ringer/Simon 1987)*. Zweitens: Die genaue Kenntnis des Bildungswesens einzelner Länder bildet nach wie vor die unverzichtbare Grundlage für solide erziehungswissenschaftliche Vergleiche; Länderstudien bieten eine Vergleichsbasis jedoch nur in dem Maße, wie eine Strukturierung durch Methoden und Theorien in sie eingeht *(Robinsohn 1970-75)*. Das Buch von *Anweiler u. a. (1996)* fanden wir besonders geeignet, um im Seminar einen gewissen Grundbestand an Länderkenntnis zu gewinnen. Wir konzentrierten uns auf die Länder Frankreich, England und Niederlande und auf Deutschland als Bezugsfeld. Eine spezifische, den Vergleich stimulierende Perspektive ergibt sich, wenn die vom 'Ausland' kommende Analyse im 'Inland' rezipiert wird (z. B. *Phillips 1995*) oder wenn die Länderstudien der 'Verbesserung' des eigenen Bildungswesens dienen sollen (z. B. *McAdams 1993*). Dem Verhältnis von Ländervergleich und Systemvergleich hat Mitter, wie überhaupt die deutsche Komparatistik, besondere Aufmerksamkeit gewidmet.

Literatur zu unserem zweiten Themenabschnitt, die auch Studenten zugänglich ist, findet sich ohne Schwierigkeiten (die VE-Literatur ist bekanntlich voll von Länderstudien); ein Problem aber ergibt sich immer wieder daraus, daß eine hinreichende (also Vergleiche fundierende) Länderkenntnis doch einen erheblichen Arbeitsaufwand abfordert, den nur wenige Studenten im Seminar zu erbringen vermögen.

Vergleichende Analyse von Aspekten nationaler Bildungssysteme

Die vergleichende Analyse von 'Ausschnitten' aus Bildungssystemen erwies sich als derjenige Zugang, der nicht nur den Interessen der Studenten am besten entgegenkam, sondern der auch wissenschaftsdidaktisch gesehen im Stand der VE die günstigsten Voraussetzungen findet (z. B. *Thomas 1990; Phillips 1991; Burnes / Welch 1992*). Im Seminar behandelten wir auf dieser Grundlage die folgenden Themen:

- Recht, Leitung und Verwaltung in europäischen Bildungssystemen, insbesondere: Zentralisation und Dezentralisation;
- 'privates' und 'staatliches' Schulwesen in europäischen Ländern;
- die Entwicklung von schulischen Lehrplänen im internationalen Vergleich;
- zur Leistungsfähigkeit von Bildungssystemen im internationalen Vergleich.

Natürlich handelt es sich bei diesen Gegenständen nicht einfach um 'Ausschnitte' aus nationalen Bildungssystemen, sondern um Fragestellungen und um Reformthemen. Insofern läßt sich bei diesen Themen das Methoden- und Theoriespektrum der VE ohne weiteres einbeziehen. Für die Studierenden wirkt der Umstand stimulierend, daß sie in den Themen eigene Bildungserfahrungen wiederfinden und den Zusammenhang mit aktuellen Reformdiskussionen erkennen. Die Liste hätte leicht um Themen ergänzt werden können wie: Strategien der Lehrerausbildung in den Mitgliedstaaten der Europäischen Union, Examina und Zertifikate, Struktur und Entwicklung des Hochschulwesens, Integration und Differenzierung im Sekundarschulwesen, Schuleffektivität u. a. m. Zu diesen Themen mangelt es nicht an geeigneter Literatur. Selten freilich findet man einen Text, der die Sache lehrbuchmäßig behandelt; weiß man als Dozent, daß die Studenten ihre Lektüre zu dem Thema auf etwa zwanzig Seiten beschränken werden, so bleibt jede einzelne Leseempfehlung relativ willkürlich und mit Skrupeln behaftet. Man kann versuchen, die schmal bleibende Textkenntnis der Studenten durch Überblick schaffende Vorträge seitens der Lehrenden und Studierenden auszugleichen. Die Studierenden sind mit dieser Aufgabe rasch überfordert; das Referat müßte eigentlich im engen Kontakt mit dem Lehrenden vorbereitet werden; doch dazu fehlt in der Regel auf beiden Seiten die Zeit.

Schlußbemerkung

Es war die Absicht dieser Betrachtung, die Anlage eines Kurses zur Einführung in die VE unter didaktischen Aspekten zu reflektieren. Ziele, Wege und Grenzen einer Einführung (genauer: unserer Einführung) sollten verdeutlicht werden. Eines unserer Hauptprobleme sahen wir in der Textauswahl. Rückblickend erscheint uns dieses Problem in einem etwas anderen Licht. Es wäre wohl eine didaktisch überzogene Vorstellung, für vorgegebene Themen den optimalen Text zu suchen bzw. sich vorzustellen, er könnte von einem Autor lehrbuchmäßig geschrieben werden. Wichtig ist, die Studenten mit gehaltvollen, also wirklich guten Texten zu konfrontieren und sie daran 'sich abarbeiten' zu lassen. Also nicht nur den Zugang verfolgen: „Das Seminarthema bestimmt den Umgang mit den Texten", sondern auch umgekehrt: „Der Text bestimmt die Thematik des Seminars." Dieser Aspekt erleichtert die inhaltliche Anlage eines Kurses erheblich. Doch unberührt davon bleibt der Appell an die Scientific Community der VE, Fragen der Lehre in den Blick zu nehmen und studentengerechte Texte zu verfassen.

Bibliographie

Altbach, Philip G.: Trends in Comparative Education. In: Comparative Education Review, 35 (1991) 3, S. 491-507.
Altbach, Philip G. / Kelly, Gail P. (Hrsg.): New Approaches to Comparative Education. Chicago u. a.: University of Chicago Press 1986.
Anweiler, Oskar: Wissenschaftliches Interesse und politische Verantwortung: Dimensionen vergleichender Bildungsforschung. Ausgewählte Schriften 1967-1989. Hrsg. von Jürgen Henze, Wolfgang Hörner und Gerhard Schreier. Opladen: Leske und Budrich 1990.
Anweiler, Oskar / Glowka, Detlef (Hrsg.): Vergleichende Erziehungswissenschaft. (Themenheft). In: Bildung und Erziehung, 24 (1971) 6, S. 497-575.
Anweiler, Oskar u. a.: Bildungssysteme in Europa. Entwicklung und Struktur des Bildungswesens in zehn Ländern. 4., völlig. überarb. Aufl. Weinheim u. a.: Beltz 1996.
Arnove, Robert F. / Altbach, Philip G. / Kelly, Gail P. (Hrsg.): Emergent Issues in Education. Comparative Perspectives. Albany: State University of New York Press 1992.
Bereday, George Zygmunt Fijalkowski: Some Methods of Teaching Comparative Education. In: Comparative Education Review, 2 (1958) 1, S. 5-9.
Bereday, George Zygmunt Fijalkowski: Comparative Methods in Education. New York u. a.: Holt, Rinehart, and Winston 1964.
Burns, Robin J. / Welch, Anthony R. (Hrsg.): Contemporary Perspectives in Comparative Education. New York u. a.: Garland 1992. (Reference Books in International Education. 16; Garland Reference Library of Social Science. 703)
Busch, Adelheid u. a. (Hrsg.): Vergleichende Erziehungswissenschaft. Texte zur Methodologie-Diskussion. Pullach: Verlag Dokumentation 1974. (Uni-Taschenbücher. 410)
Cowen, Robert: The Concept of Time in Comparative Education. In: ibid. / Stokes, Peter (Hrsg.): Methodological Issues in Comparative Education, London: London Association of Comparative Educationalists 1982, S. 165-174.
Cowen, Robert: The National and International Impact of Comparative Education. In: Halls, Wilfred Douglas (Hrsg.): Comparative Education. Contemporary Issues and Trends, London u. a.: Kingsley u. a. 1990, S. 321-352.
Cowen, Robert / Stokes, Peter (Hrsg.): Methodological Issues in Comparative Education. London: London Association of Comparative Educationalists 1982.

Döbrich, Peter / Kopp, Botho von (Hrsg.): Vergleichende Bildungsforschung. Festschrift für Wolfgang Mitter zum 60. Geburtstag. Köln u. a.: Böhlau 1987. (Zeitschrift für Internationale Erziehungs- und Sozialwissenschaftliche Forschung. Sonderheft. 1987)

Eckstein, Max A.: On Teaching a „Scientific" Comparative Education. In: Comparative Education Review, 14 (1970) 3, S. 279-282.

Eckstein, Max A.: The Comparative Mind. In: Altbach, Philip G. / Kelly, Gail P. (Hrsg.): New Approaches to Comparative Education, Chicago u. a.: University of Chicago Press 1986, pp. 167-178.

Edwards, Reginald u. a. (Hrsg.): Relevant Methods in Comparative Education. Hamburg: Unesco Institute of Education 1973. (International Studies in Education. 33)

Froese, Leonhard: Ausgewählte Studien zur Vergleichenden Erziehungswissenschaft. Positionen und Probleme. München: Minerva-Publikation 1983. (Marburger Beiträge zur Vergleichenden Erziehungswissenschaft und Bildungsforschung. 19)

García Garrido, José Luis: Wolfgang Mitter's Commitment to the Comparative Education Society in Europe. In: Döbrich, Peter / Kopp, Botho von (Hrsg.): Vergleichende Bildungsforschung, Köln u. a.: Böhlau 1987, S. 5-17.

Halls, Wilfred Douglas (Hrsg.): Comparative Education. Contemporary Issues and Trends. London u. a.: Kingsley u. a. 1990.

Hans, Nicholas: Comparative Education. A Study of Educational Factors and Traditions. 3. ed., revised. London: Routledge and Kegan Paul 1967. (Routledge Paperbacks. 68)

Holmes, Brian: Comparative Education. Some Considerations of Method. London u. a.: Allen and Unwin 1981.

Husén, Torsten / Postlethwaite, Thomas Neville (Hrsg.): The International Encyclopedia of Education. 2. ed. Vol. 1-10. Oxford: Pergamon Press 1994.

Kandel, Isaac Leon: Comparative Education. Boston, Mass. u. a.: Houghton Mifflin 1933.

Kazamias, Andreas (Hrsg.): The State of the Art. Twenty Years of Comparative Education. (Themenheft). In: Comparative Education Review, 21 (1977) 2-3, S. 127-419.

Kern, Peter: Einführung in die Vergleichende Pädagogik. Konzepte, Theorie, Problematik. Darmstadt: Wissenschaftliche Buchgesellschaft 1973.

McAdams, Richard P.: Lessons from Abroad. How Other Countries Educate Their Children. Lancaster: Technomic Publications 1993.

Mitter, Wolfgang: Schule zwischen Reform und Krise. Zur Theorie und Praxis der vergleichenden Bildungsforschung. Gesammelte Aufsätze. Hrsg. von Christoph Führ und Bernard Trouillet. Köln u. a.: Böhlau 1987. (Studien und Dokumentationen zur deutschen Bildungsgeschichte. 36)

Mitter, Wolfgang: Challenges to Comparative Education: Between Retrospect and Expectation. Presidential Address delivered to the IXth World Congress of Comparative Education, Sydney, Australia, 1-6 July, 1996.

Müller, Detlef K. / Ringer, Fritz / Simon, Brian (Hrsg.): The Rise of the Modern Educational System. Structural Change and Social Reproduction 1870-1920. Cambridge: Cambridge University Press 1987.

Noah, Harold J.: The Use and Abuse of Comparative Education. In: Altbach, Philip G. / Kelly, Gail P. (Hrsg.): New Approaches to Comparative Education, Chicago u. a.: University of Chicago Press 1986, pp. 153-166.

Noah, Harold J. / Eckstein, Max A.: A Design for Teaching „Comparative Education". In: Comparative Education Review, 10 (1966) 3, S. 511-513.

Noah, Harold J. / Eckstein, Max A.: Towards a Science of Comparative Education. London: Macmillan 1969.

Phillips, David (Hrsg.): Lessons of Cross-National Comparison in Education. Wallingford: Triangle Books 1991. (Oxford Studies in Comparative Education. 1)

Phillips, David (Hrsg.): Education in Germany. Tradition and Reform in Historical Context. London u. a.: Routledge 1995.

Robinsohn, Saul Benjamin: Erziehungswissenschaft: Vergleichende Erziehungswissenschaft. In: Speck, Josef / Wehle, Gerhard (Hrsg.): Handbuch pädagogischer Grundbegriffe. Bd. 1, München: Kösel 1970, S. 456-492.

Robinsohn, Saul Benjamin (Hrsg.): Schulreform im gesellschaftlichen Prozeß. Ein interkultureller Vergleich. Bd. 1. 2. Stuttgart: Klett 1970-75.

Röhrs, Hermann: Forschungsstrategien in der Vergleichenden Erziehungswissenschaft. Eine Einführung in Probleme der Vergleichenden Erziehungswissenschaft. Weinheim u. a.: Beltz 1975. (Beltz-Studienbuch. 83)

Sadler, Michael: Selections from Michael Sadler. Studies in World Citizenship. Compiled by J. H. Higginson. Liverpool: Dejall and Meyore 1979.

Schneider, Friedrich: Vergleichende Erziehungswissenschaft. Geschichte, Forschung, Lehre. Heidelberg: Quelle und Meyer 1961. (Vergleichende Erziehungswissenschaft und Pädagogik des Auslands. 1)

Schriewer, Jürgen / Holmes, Brian (Hrsg.): Theories and Methods in Comparative Education. Frankfurt a. M. u. a.: Lang 1988. (Komparatistische Bibliothek. 1)

Seidenfaden, Fritz: Der Vergleich in der Pädagogik. Braunschweig: Westermann 1966. (Das pädagogische Forum. 9)

Thomas, Robert Murray (Hrsg.): International Comparative Education. Practices, Issues and Prospects. Oxford u. a.: Pergamon Press 1990.

Wittig, Hans: Vergleichende Pädagogik. Darmstadt: Wissenschaftliche Buchgesellschaft 1973. (Wege der Forschung. 12)

„Europa" als Herausforderung für die
Vergleichende Erziehungswissenschaft –
Reflexionen über die politische Funktion einer pädagogischen Disziplin

Wolfgang Hörner

Zu Thematik

Beim Lesen dieses Titels kann man sich fragen, wie ein Begriff, der auf den ersten Blick lediglich eine geographische Bestimmung darstellt, als „Herausforderung" für eine wissenschaftliche Disziplin verstanden werden kann. Der Sinn der Themenformulierung wird deutlicher, wenn man beispielsweise einen Blick in den Studienplan der Universität Leipzig für den Magisterstudiengang „Erziehungswissenschaft" wirft. Dort ist als Pflichtelement der Baustein „Vergleichende Erziehungswissenschaft unter besonderer Berücksichtigung des europäischen Einigungsprozesses" aufgeführt. „Europa" ist also nicht als bloß geographischer Begriff, sondern als *politischer Prozeß* gemeint. Es ist der Prozeß der europäischen Integration, zu dem die Vergleichende Erziehungswissenschaft in Beziehung treten soll. Das setzt voraus, daß der europäische Einigungsprozeß nicht nur einen politisch gesteuerten Prozeß darstellt, sondern (auch) als ein gesellschaftlicher Bewußtseinsprozeß verstanden wird, der möglicherweise Rückwirkungen auf den Gegenstand der Vergleichenden Erziehungswissenschaft hat.

Inwieweit kann ein so verstandener Prozeß jedoch eine „Herausforderung" für eine wissenschaftliche Disziplin darstellen? Damit ist die zweite Komponente der Themenformulierung angesprochen. Der Begriff „Herausforderung" signalisiert, daß ein Prüfstein für die Grenzen der Leistungsfähigkeit gesetzt wird. Im Bereich des Sports wird dabei suggeriert, daß der Herausgeforderte sich bemüht zu beweisen, daß diese Grenzen noch nicht erreicht sind. Aus dem Bereich des Sports wurde der Begriff der Herausforderung u. a. auch auf die Leistungsfähigkeit von gesellschaftlichen Subsystemen, insbesondere von Wirtschaftssystemen übertragen (z. B. als „japanische Herausforderung").

Bezogen auf die „Leistungsfähigkeit" einer wissenschaftlichen Disziplin setzt eine solche Themenformulierung natürlich voraus, daß konkrete Vorstellungen darüber bestehen, welche „Leistung" man von der betreffenden Disziplin erwarten kann. Damit ist im vorliegenden Zusammenhang die Frage nach dem Selbstverständnis der Vergleichenden Erziehungswissenschaft gestellt. Die Frage nach dem Selbstverständnis muß aber insbesondere die Frage nach ihren möglichen Funktionen einschließen, die für einen solchen Prozeß eine Rolle spielen könnten.

Zum Selbstverständnis der Vergleichenden Erziehungswissenschaft

Zur internationalen Begrifflichkeit

Die Frage nach dem Selbstverständnis der Vergleichenden Erziehungswissenschaft scheint so alt wie die Disziplin selber. Die seit den siebziger Jahren zentrale Frage, ob sich das Fach nach dem Gegenstand (die Bildung „anderswo") oder dem Verfahren (dem Vergleich) konstituiert, schien die deutsche Disziplinbezeichnung zunächst nicht zu tangieren, denn in Deutschland war bis in die sechziger Jahre lediglich strittig, ob „Vergleichende Erziehungswissenschaft" (Friedrich *Schneider 1961*) oder „Vergleichende Pädagogik" (Franz *Hilker 1962*) die zutreffendere Bezeichnung sei. In beiden Fällen verweist das Partizip Präsens „vergleichend" darauf, daß das *Verfahren* als konstitutiv angesehen wird. Dabei deutet die jeweilige Argumentationslinie der beiden gegensätzlichen Positionen darauf hin, daß sich der Streitpunkt letztlich auf ein unterschiedlich weites Verständnis von „Erziehung" zurückführen läßt. Während Hilker einen eher traditionellen engen (deutschen) Begriff von „Erziehung" (abgegrenzt gegenüber Bildung) hat, vertritt Schneider einen eher international erweiterten Erziehungsbegriff, der – in Anlehnung an den weiteren englischen Begriff „education" – über die traditionelle deutsche Abgrenzung von „Bildung" und „Erziehung" hinausgeht. Dieser weitere Begriff von „Erziehung" hat sich für die Kennzeichnung der Gesamtdisziplin „Erziehungswissenschaft" im deutschen Sprachraum durchgesetzt, um die erfahrungswissenschaftliche Dignität des Faches zu unterstreichen und die praktizistischen Konnotationen von „Pädagogik" zu vermeiden – auch wenn vielerorts und gerade in den neukonstituierten Fachbereichen bzw. Fakultäten der neuen Bundesländer zur Bezeichnung der Unterdisziplinen der Erziehungswissenschaft der traditionelle Begriff „Pädagogik" häufig wieder aufgegriffen wurde.[1]

---

1 So z. B. an der Universität Leipzig, wo im Rahmen der „Erziehungswissenschaftlichen Fakultät" alle einzelnen Arbeitsbereiche ein Kompositum von „Pädagogik" aufweisen (z. B. Schulpädagogik, Erwachsenenpädagogik, aber auch Allgemeine Pädagogik und Vergleichende Pädagogik).

Das Nebeneinander von Vergleichender Pädagogik und Vergleichender Erziehungswissenschaft in der deutschen Terminologie wurde noch bereichert durch einen neuen Begriff, der in den sechziger Jahren auch für die Komparatistik von Bedeutung werden sollte: die „Bildungsforschung". Man kann die These wagen, daß ein wichtiges Motiv zur Einführung dieses Begriffs in die deutsche Diskussion durch Eugen *Lemberg (1963)* letztlich ebenfalls in semantischen Unterschieden zwischen der deutschen und der englischen Terminologie begründet ist. Nicht zuletzt die verstärkte Rezeption anglo-amerikanischer Forschung (nicht nur auf der Ebene der Ergebnisse, sondern auch als neues Paradigma eigener Forschungsbemühungen) zu soziologischen, politischen und ökonomischen Aspekten von Bildung und Erziehung („educational research") machte einen neuen deutschen Begriff notwendig, da diese Aspekte weder durch den älteren Begriff „Pädagogik" (mit seinem Doppelaspekt als Theorie und Praxis erzieherischen Handelns), noch durch den strenger erfahrungswissenschaftlich verstandenen Begriff „Erziehungswissenschaft" wiedergegeben werden konnten. Da hier die institutionelle Dimension von Bildung im Vordergrund stand (die unter politischen, ökonomischen und soziologischen Aspekten zu untersuchen war), erschien es naheliegend, von „Bildungsforschung" zu sprechen. Aus der Perspektive der gesellschaftlichen Institutionen war nämlich vor allem der Bildungsaspekt des deutschen Doppelbegriffs „Bildung und Erziehung" von Bedeutung. Die Bezeichnung „Bildungsforschung" folgte also derselben Logik wie die Wiedergabe von „educational policy" mit „Bildungspolitik", „educational economics" mit „Bildungsökonomie" usw. Man versteht den Sinn dieser Komposita von „Bildung" nur, wenn man sie als verkürzte Übersetzungen aus dem Englischen wahrnimmt und keine Residuen neuhumanistischer Bildungstheorie darin sucht, ein Mißverständnis, dem auch renommierte Autoren erlegen sind (vgl. *Luhmann / Schorr 1979, S. 83f.*).

Die Einführung des Begriffs „Bildungsforschung" signalisierte eine Erweiterung des Untersuchungsfeldes und damit einen potentiell pluridisziplinären Zugang zum Phänomen „institutionalisierte Bildung". Bildung wird hier als Prozeß verstanden, der unter mehreren Aspekten Untersuchungsgegenstand werden kann. Damit lag es von Anfang an nahe, Bildungsforschung auch unter vergleichendem Aspekt zu sehen. Sicher ist es kein Zufall, daß die ersten deutschen Institutionen, die einer so verstandenen Bildungsforschung gewidmet waren, dem internationalen Vergleich einen breiten Raum boten. Das gilt sowohl für das Max-Planck-Institut für Bildungsforschung in Berlin, das in der ersten Phase seiner Wirksamkeit eine bedeutende vergleichende Abteilung hatte, als auch für das (seit 1964 so umbenannte) Deutsche Institut für Internationale Pädagogische Forschung, an dem Eugen Lemberg selbst wirkte. Vertreter der Vergleichenden Erziehungswissenschaft, die ihre Disziplin ohnehin gern als eine Integrations- oder Querschnittswissenschaft betrachteten *(Anweiler 1974)*, griffen deshalb den neuen Begriff „Bildungsforschung" bereitwillig auf, und es entstanden auch kleinere Forschungseinheiten, die sich der „vergleichenden Bildungsforschung"[2] widmeten.

Mit dieser neuen Begrifflichkeit schien es möglich, die Spezifik der Vergleichsforschung im Bereich von Bildung und Erziehung adäquat auszudrücken. Einen Nachteil konnte man allenfalls darin sehen, daß durch die Konzentration auf den Begriff „Forschung" der Aspekt der (universitären) Lehre nicht angesprochen war, auch wenn die Vertreter der Vergleichenden Erziehungswissenschaft an den Universitäten und Hochschulen sich dem neuen Begriff gegenüber aufgeschlossen zeigten.

Indes war diese Kontroverse um die Bezeichnung der Disziplin offensichtlich eine spezifisch deutsche Debatte. Im Englischen war die Fachbezeichnung „comparative education" niemals fraglich. Die semantische Breite des englischen Nomens „education" ließ dabei viele Aspekte zu, nicht nur Bildung und Erziehung (verstanden als formale Qualifikation und Charakterbildung), „education" war zugleich die Bezeichnung der wissenschaftlichen Bezugsdisziplin.

Der semantischen und syntaktischen Struktur gemäß bedeutet „comparative education" also zunächst die Betrachtung des Untersuchungsgegenstandes Bildung und Erziehung unter vergleichendem Aspekt, konnte zugleich aber auch als Bezeichnung der wissenschaftlichen Disziplin (education = „Pädagogik") verstanden werden, die mit „komparativen" Mitteln betrieben werden sollte. In beiden Bedeutungsnuancen steckte ein verfahrensbezogenes Disziplinverständnis, das alle deutschen begrifflichen Kontroversen absorbierte.

Die französische Bezeichnung „éducation comparée" kann auf den ersten Blick wie eine Lehnübersetzung aus dem Englischen erscheinen. Die sprachliche Struktur nennt das Untersuchungsobjekt, verbunden aber nicht mit einem qualifizierenden Adjektiv wie im Englischen, sondern mit einem Partizip Perfekt Passiv als Bestimmung des Objekts (dieses ist bereits verglichen worden). Es herrscht demnach ein deutlicher Objektbezug vor, und es wird nicht die wissenschaftliche Disziplin angesprochen (im Französischen ist „éducation" im Gegensatz zum englischen Homonym „education" nicht zugleich Disziplinbezeichnung).

---

2 Z. B. die „Arbeitsstelle für vergleichende Bildungsforschung" in Bochum, an welcher der Autor selbst lange Jahre tätig war.

Die Bezeichnung einer Disziplin ist dagegen im parallel dazu gebräuchlichen Ausdruck „pédagogie comparée" gegeben, der von einigen älteren Autoren bevorzugt wurde *(Vexliard 1967; Debesse/Mialaret 1972)*. Da in diesem sprachlichen Ausdruck ebenfalls die passive Partizipialkonstruktion Anwendung findet, ist die Logik der Disziplinbezeichnung allerdings anders als im Deutschen: nicht das wissenschaftliche Verfahren ist vergleichend bestimmt (aktive Partizipialkonstruktion: „vergleichende Pädagogik"), sondern Theorie und Praxis erzieherischen Handelns (pédagogie) werden zum Objekt des Vergleichs (passive Partizipialkonstruktion, wörtlich: „verglichene Pädagogik").

Die Unterschiede in der Logik der Sprache haben zur Folge, daß der als Reaktion auf die bloße Verfahrensfixiertheit der deutschen Terminologie entstandene methodologische Zweifel, ob eine wissenschaftliche Disziplin nicht besser nach dem Objekt zu definieren sei und nicht nach einer bloßen heuristischen Operation (so *Mitter 1976, S. 318ff.*), sich in dieser Pointierung in den anderen westlichen Sprachen gar nicht stellt. Sowohl im Französischen als auch im Englischen steht das Objekt im Mittelpunkt.[3] Dadurch kann eine enge Festlegung der Disziplin allein auf ein „heuristisches Verfahren" kaum erfolgen.

Tatsächlich steht im englischen Sprachraum „International Education" gleichberechtigt neben „Comparative Education". Gerade Wolfgang Mitter hat in jüngster Zeit im Anschluß an die amerikanische Debatte noch einmal prägnant die beiden gleichermaßen legitimen Interessenperspektiven herausgearbeitet, die in der Bezeichnung der amerikanischen Regionalgesellschaft „Comparative and International Education Society" schon im Namen zum Ausdruck kommen: die Verbindung von vergleichenden Analysen staatlich geprägter oder kulturell abgegrenzter Bildungsphänomene im internationalen oder interkulturellen Vergleich einerseits und der Erziehung zur Völkerverständigung als eine praxisbezogene Dimension der Disziplin andererseits.

Was soll diese Disziplin also leisten?

---

3 Die anderen romanischen Sprachen haben die gleiche Struktur wie das Französische, das Polnische übernimmt die ältere deutsche Begriffsstruktur, aber mit einer adjektivischen, nicht partizipialen Bestimmung „pedagogika porównawcza" (vergleichsbezogene Pädagogik), so daß auch hier der Verfahrensbezug von einem möglichen Objektbezug überlagert wird.

Funktionen des Vergleichs

Versucht man das bisher Angedeutete zu systematisieren, dann kommt man auf die bereits mehrfach beschriebenen vier Funktionen vergleichender Forschung (z. B. *Anweiler/Hörner 1990, S. 680ff.; Hörner 1993, S. 16ff.*), die sich aus der Kreuzung der beiden Gegensatzpaare „theoretisches/praktisches Interesse" und „Besonderheit/Universalität" ergeben.

Schaubild 1:   Funktionen des Vergleichs

	Besonderheit	Universalität
Theoretisches Interesse	idiographisch	experimentell
Praktisches Interesse	melioristisch	evolutionistisch

Die vier Funktionen lassen sich, kurz zusammengefaßt, in folgender Weise voneinander abgrenzen:

1. *Die idiographische Funktion* als die Suche nach dem Besonderen zielt – nach der Methode der klassischen Geschichtswissenschaft – darauf ab, das je Besondere, Einmalige in den untersuchten Phänomenen zu beschreiben und zu erklären. Spätestens seit Michael Sadler (1861–1943) wird eine enge Verbindung des Bildungswesens mit seinem gesellschaftlichen und kulturellen Umfeld gesehen, dessen Erkundung zur Erklärung der Bildungsphänomene unverzichtbar ist.
2. *Die melioristische Funktion* als die Suche nach dem besseren Modell ist das bildungspolitisch-praktische Motiv, das den Vergleich für den Bildungspolitiker attraktiv macht: das Bestreben, positive fremde Erfahrungen zu nutzen, aus den Erfahrungen der anderen zu „lernen". Nun zeigt die Geschichte, daß dies nicht unproblematisch ist, wenn man es unreflektiert tut. Bei dem eben schon erwähnten Michael Sadler wird dieses Problem zum ersten Mal erkenntnistheoretisch reflektiert; wir werden noch darauf zurückkommen.

3. *Die evolutionistische Funktion* als Suche nach dem Entwicklungstrend hat als Ziel nicht das Herausstellen des Besonderen, sondern des allgemeinen Trends, einer gewissen Eigengesetzlichkeit der Entwicklungsdynamik. Dabei läßt sich oft eine bildungspolitische (Neben-)Absicht erkennen: Die Frage nach der eigenen Position auf dieser verborgenen Entwicklungsskala verleiht der herausgearbeiteten Entwicklungsdynamik oft eine „kryptonormative" Funktion; der (vermeintliche) Trend wird zur Richtschnur der eigenen Reformpolitik.
4. *Die experimentelle Funktion* als Suche nach dem Universellen geht in ihrem Kern auf den französischen Soziologen Emile Durkheim zurück. Er entwickelte schon 1885 den Gedanken, daß der Vergleich in den Sozialwissenschaften die Rolle des Experiments in den Naturwissenschaften einnehmen müsse, da die Schaffung künstlicher experimenteller Situationen zur Isolierung von Variablen in den Sozialwissenschaften aus praktischen und ethischen Gründen nicht ohne weiteres möglich sei. Der Vergleich eines Phänomens in unterschiedlichen Kontexten (Variablenkombinationen) ersetzt also die experimentelle Situation, wobei die Auswahl der Vergleichsgegenstände an die Stelle der Isolierung von Variablen tritt. Nach einer bekannten Formulierung von Harold *Noah (1971, S. 508)* muß es bei solchen Untersuchungen möglich sein, Ländernamen durch die Bezeichnungen von Variablen zu ersetzen.

Nun ist es augenscheinlich, daß von diesen vier Funktionen der vergleichenden Forschung die idiographische Funktion am häufigsten anzutreffen ist. Das ist auch nicht verwunderlich, denn die genaue Erforschung eines Gegenstandes im Hinblick auf seine Besonderheit ist gewöhnlich die Voraussetzung für die Aktivierung der anderen Funktionen. Es ist also grundsätzlich möglich, mehrere dieser Funktionen in einer Untersuchung miteinander zu verknüpfen. Diese Verknüpfung erscheint unstrittig im Falle der Verbindung der idiographischen mit der experimentellen Funktion, denn um Ländernamen durch die Bezeichnung von Variablen ersetzen zu können, muß zunächst einmal sehr differenziert untersucht werden, für welche Sachverhalte die Länder stehen können. Lediglich bei der Verknüpfung der idiographischen mit der melioristischen (oder auch der evolutionistischen) Funktion scheint sich ein erkenntnistheoretisches Problem zu stellen: Aus einer einmaligen Konstellation von Umständen erscheint es auf den ersten Blick nicht möglich, allgemeingültige, „universelle" Schlüsse für andere zu ziehen; und idiographische und nomothetische Fragestellungen scheinen sich auszuschließen, da beide Untersuchungstypen unterschiedlichen wissenschaftstheoretischen Grundtypen zuzuordnen sind. Die Suche nach dem je Besonderen in einem national definierten Bildungswesen, verbunden mit der Frage nach dessen Ursachen, kann unmöglich auf den ersten Blick übertragbare Lösungen für praktische Probleme hervorbringen. Dieses erkenntnistheoretische Problem wurde in der Methodologiediskussion der Vergleichenden Erziehungswissenschaft als „Sadler-Dilemma" bezeichnet *(Schriewer 1982, S. 190ff.)*, da das Problem zum ersten Mal bei Michael Sadler bewußt geworden sei.

Nun trifft dieser Zweifel an der praktischen Brauchbarkeit vergleichender Untersuchungen nicht nur die Erziehungswissenschaft, sondern alle mit der historischen Methode operierenden Disziplinen. Nach dieser Logik wäre es z. B. auch nicht möglich, aus der Geschichte zu „lernen", da jedes historische Ereignis aus einer einmaligen Konstellation von Variablen entstanden ist („man kann nicht zweimal in denselben Fluß steigen" sagt Heraklit). Gerade der Strukturalismus in den Humanwissenschaften (und auch in der Geschichtswissenschaft selbst) hat aber diese radikale individualisierende Position in Frage gestellt, indem er gleiche Strukturen innerhalb der Verschiedenheit sucht.

Den logischen Weg dahin kann man in den Bemühungen des Neukantianers Heinrich *Rickert (1926)* sehen, durch die Einführung des neuen Begriffs „Kulturwissenschaften" die herkömmliche Klassifikation der Wissenschaften in idiographische (Geistes-)Wissenschaften und nomothetische (Natur-)Wissenschaften zu transzendieren, die sein Lehrer Windelband bekannt gemacht hatte. Für Rickert gibt es letztlich keine individualisierenden Wissenschaften. Denn auch die erklärenden Wissenschaften – sogar die Geschichte selbst – benötigen zur Erklärung *Begriffe*. Diese sind aber zwangsläufig Abstraktionen, also allgemein. Die Erklärung eines historischen Faktums muß auf eine Vielzahl von begrifflich faßbaren Einflußfaktoren reduziert werden. Dies ist nur möglich durch ein Auswahlprinzip, das historisch bedeutsame, sinntragende Elemente von anderen, zufälligen zu unterscheiden vermag. Es ist die *Relevanz* eines Phänomens für die Erklärung eines anderen. Dieses wertende Auswahlprinzip nennt Rickert „Kultur". Damit scheint auch die Lösung des Sadler-Dilemmas angedeutet. Auch die Analyse der „Einmaligkeit" eines Bildungswesens mit „kulturwissenschaftlichen" Begriffen kann eine Unterscheidung von strukturellen, möglicherweise übertragbaren Elementen einerseits und einmaligen (einfach „anderen") Elementen andererseits ermöglichen – genau wie es in einem solchen Sinne auch möglich sein kann, aus bestimmten historischen „Strukturen" zu „lernen".

Die wissenschaftslogische Auseinandersetzung mit der Kritik an der melioristischen Funktion vergleichender Untersuchungen erscheint deshalb von Interesse, weil der Gedanke, von den anderen zu lernen, nicht nur konstitutiv für die *Entstehung* der Disziplin war, sondern auch von profilierten internationalen Vertretern des Faches bis in die jüngste Zeit als Charakteristikum der Vergleichenden Erziehungswissenschaft aufrechterhalten wurde (z. B. *Van daele 1993, S. 17*). Die grundsätzliche Transfermöglichkeit macht einen großen Teil der politischen Attraktivität der Vergleichenden Bildungsforschung aus.

Vergleichende Erziehungswissenschaft in der Lehre

Zum praktischen Interesse der Vergleichenden Erziehungswissenschaft gehören aber auch ihre möglichen Funktionen in der Lehre.[4]

Hier stünde zunächst eine *„wissenschaftsdidaktische" Funktion* im Vordergrund. Das Erfahrungsfeld für das gesamte erziehungswissenschaftliche Studium kann nicht mehr nur auf das nationale System beschränkt sein, um den Studenten ein differenziertes Bild von erziehungswissenschaftlichen Studien zu vermitteln. Wie für die Forschung selbst, so soll auch für die Wissenschaftspropädeutik der internationale Vergleich dazu dienen, das Spektrum der Variablen zu erweitern, um den Studierenden zu vermitteln, wie man zu abgesicherten Ergebnissen kommt (Ausschluß von Zufallsvariablen).

Wenn man davon ausgeht, daß eine Aufgabe des erziehungswissenschaftlichen Studiums auch darin besteht, bildungspolitische Mündigkeit zu vermitteln, dann kann Vergleichende Erziehungswissenschaft in der Lehre auch eine *bildungspolitische Funktion* haben und dies in einer doppelten Zielrichtung. Zum einen ermöglicht die Erweiterung des Wahrnehmungshorizonts auf eine internationale Dimension dem zukünftigen Lehrer oder außerschulisch tätigen Pädagogen (im weitesten Sinn) eine Relativierung seiner eigenen institutionellen Gegebenheiten. Das heißt, sie ist ein wesentliches Mittel zum Aufbrechen der Selbstverständlichkeit, mit der das eigene Bildungssystem oft als das bestmögliche angesehen wird. Die Beschäftigung mit anderen Bildungssystemen und Bildungswirklichkeiten kann so generell zur Erweiterung des Bewußtseinshorizontes beitragen. Sie kann, philosophisch gesprochen, zur *Kontingenzerfahrung* werden, d. h. zur Erkenntnis, daß das Seiende auch „ganz anders" sein könnte. Diese Kontingent-Setzung, die Relativierung der eigenen Position, kann aber in bildungspolitischer Hinsicht kritisch-innovatives Potential freisetzen, das einer nationalistischen Selbstzufriedenheit entgegenwirkt.

---

4   Die folgenden Ausführungen erweitern die Skizze in *Hörner 1996, S. 14f.*

In umgekehrter bildungspolitischer Zielrichtung kann eine gründlichere Analyse ausländischer Erfahrungen schon auf einer rein idiographischen Ebene dem Studenten eine fundierte kritische Mitsprachemöglichkeit dort geben, wo – in einer sehr alten bildungspolitischen Tradition – oberflächliche Argumentationsmuster mit dem „Ausland" zur Festigung vorgefaßter bildungspolitischer Positionen dienen sollen. Die deutsche Diskussion um das Für und Wider des 13. Schuljahres bietet hierzu in beiden Richtungen einen sehr plastischen Anschauungsunterricht: Befürworter der Schulzeitverkürzung berufen sich gerne auf den großen europäischen Nachbarn Frankreich mit einer formell zwölfjährigen Schulzeit bis zur Hochschulreife, übersehen aber dabei den Umstand, daß statistisch nur eine Minderheit von Schülern die Schule auch in dieser Regelschulzeit absolviert (hohe Wiederholerquote!). Aber auch bei manchen Befürwortern einer Schulzeitdauer von 13 Jahren, die diese Eigenheit des französischen Schulsystems kennen und die für den Erhalt des 13. Schuljahres plädieren, finden sich als Gegenargumente wiederum bisweilen höchst ungenaue Vorstellungen, beispielsweise über die Funktion der Vorbereitungsklassen für den Aufnahmewettbewerb zu den Elitehochschulen, die als bloße Verlängerung der Sekundarschulzeit (auf dann 14 Jahre!) angesehen werden. Dabei wird nicht wahrgenommen, daß sie ihrer Funktion nach bereits ein Äquivalent des universitären Grundstudiums darstellen. Dieses Beispiel zeigt, daß ein mit dem deutschfranzösischen Bildungsvergleich vertrauter Student ohne weiteres in der Lage wäre, die ungenauen Argumente beider Positionen zu relativieren und damit zu einer Versachlichung der Debatte beizutragen.

Nimmt man an, daß das erziehungswissenschaftliche Studium einen – wie auch immer zu definierenden – Praxisbezug hat, dann kann die Beschäftigung mit fremden Bildungsphänomenen auch eine *praktisch-pädagogische Funktion* haben: Sie kann innovative pädagogische Phantasie anregen. Nicht von ungefähr ist die internationale reformpädagogische Bewegung eine wichtige Wurzel der Entstehung der Vergleichenden Erziehungswissenschaft. Eine so verstandene Lehrfunktion läßt sich direkt mit dem genannten Begriff der „International Education" in Verbindung bringen, in dem die Praxisbeziehung eine unmittelbare Rolle spielt.

Eine letzte Funktion schließlich ist erwähnenswert, wenn Vergleichende Erziehungswissenschaft in der Lehre „nutzbar" gemacht werden soll. Man könnte sie die *kulturaufklärerische oder interkulturelle Funktion* nennen. Was ist damit gemeint? Bildung ist ein Schlüsselelement des sozialen und kulturellen Lebens eines Landes. Die Beschäftigung mit dem Phänomen Bildung – zumal in der skizzierten multidisziplinär ausgreifenden Form – kann also dazu dienen, in verdichteter Weise in die Kultur eines fremden Landes einzuführen. Dies kann *einerseits* für künftige Fremdsprachenlehrer von Interesse sein, die in einem Gebiet, das mit ihrem zukünftigen Einsatzfeld besonders eng verknüpft ist, eine Bereicherung ihrer Kenntnisse in der jeweiligen Landeskunde erhalten können. Der Aspekt der Einführung in die „andere" Kultur über die Phänomene Bildung und Erziehung kann aber *andererseits* auch für Lehrer von Migrantenkindern oder Kindern aus Aussiedlungsgebieten im östlichen Mitteleuropa oder der ehemaligen Sowjetunion von Bedeutung sein. In diesem Sinn wird die institutionalisierte Bildung zum Schlüssel für die Gesamtkultur eines Landes.

Bildung und europäische Integration

Versucht man, das Verhältnis des europäischen Integrationsprozesses zum Phänomen Bildung genauer zu beschreiben, so stößt man zunächst auf eine widersprüchliche Situation. Zunächst gehört es zu den Standardformeln „tiefergehender" europapolitischer Reden zu postulieren, daß die Europäische Union nicht nur eine wirtschaftliche Interessengemeinschaft, sondern vor allem eine Kulturgemeinschaft sei. Eine solche Aussage kann einen kulturhistorischen Sinn haben, wenn man darunter eine gemeinsame geistige Grundströmung versteht, die den verschiedenen Nationalkulturen zugrunde liegt. Diese Nationalkulturen lassen sich mit nur wenigen Ausnahmen grob in drei Sprachfamilien zusammenfassen: romanisch, germanisch und slawisch, wobei es einige mehrsprachige Überschneidungsbereiche gibt. Der Begriff „Kultur" hat aber nicht nur im Französischen („culture") eine enge Beziehung zur Bildung. Nach einer bekannten, klassisch gewordenen Definition Adornos läßt sich „Bildung" nämlich fassen als subjektive Aneignung von Kultur. Daraus folgt, daß Europa zwangsläufig nicht nur eine Kultur-, sondern auch eine Bildungsgemeinschaft darstellt.

Ein solches Verständnis erscheint indessen vormodern, da es das Bild des mittelalterlichen fahrenden Scholaren assoziiert, für den das Streben nach Wahrheit keine Landes- und Sprachgrenzen kannte. Spätestens mit der Etablierung der Nationalstaaten und der ihnen eigenen *Bildungssysteme* muß Bildungserwerb aber mit sehr engen Grenzen rechnen. Bildung – unter dem institutionellen Aspekt je partikularer verfaßter Bildungssysteme – scheint also dem angestrebten europäischen Bildungs-/Kulturraum gerade entgegenzustehen. Aber nicht nur das: Da seit dem 19. Jahrhundert das *Berechtigungswesen* das Bildungssystem „systemisch" mit der Wirtschaft verknüpft, droht die Bildung paradoxerweise sogar zu einem Hindernis für die wirtschaftliche Integration zu werden.

Manche Europapolitiker erkannten deshalb früh, daß der gemeinsame Markt mit seiner geplanten Mobilität von Kapital, Waren, Dienstleistungen und Arbeitskräften zwangsläufig eine Rückwirkung auf die Qualifikationsprofile der Arbeitskräfte haben mußte. Deshalb wurde schon im „alten" EWG-Vertrag (Artikel 128) auch die Berufsbildung in den Mitgliedsstaaten zum „europäischen" Thema erklärt. Und die Gemeinschaft suchte ihren Einfluß auf den Bildungsbereich systematisch zu erweitern. Durch ein Urteil des Europäischen Gerichtshofs vom 30. Mai 1989, das sogenannte ERASMUS-Urteil, wurden auch Hochschulbildungsgänge als „Berufsbildung" – und damit als in die Kompetenz der Europäischen Gemeinschaft fallend – definiert (vgl. *Müller-Solger 1990, S. 808ff.*).

Mit dem Unionsvertrag von Maastricht erhielt die Beziehung der Europäischen Union zur Bildungsproblematik eine neue Dimension. Erstmalig wurde (in Artikel 126) neben der Berufsbildung auch die *„Entwicklung einer qualitativ hochstehenden Bildung"* allgemein als Gemeinschaftsaufgabe definiert. Allerdings muß dies – nach dem Wortlaut des Vertragstextes – *„unter strikter Beachtung der Verantwortung der Mitgliedsstaaten für die Lehrinhalte und die Gestaltung des Bildungssystems"* geschehen. Auch alle geplanten Fördermaßnahmen der Union sind *„unter Ausschluß jeglicher Harmonisierung der Rechts- und Verwaltungsvorschriften der Mitgliedsstaaten"* zu realisieren *(Vertrag über die Europäische Union 1992, S. 23)*. Dieselbe stereotype Formel *„unter Ausschluß jeglicher Harmonisierung"* taucht schließlich auch im nächsten Artikel des Vertrages (Artikel 127) auf, der die berufliche Bildung zum Gegenstand hat: Dort wird die Verwirklichung der Ziele des gesamten Berufsbildungsartikels genau dem gleichen „Harmonisierungsverbot" unterworfen. Es erscheint plausibel, wenn berichtet wird, dieser quasi stereotyp in beiden Artikeln auftauchende Passus sei insbesondere unter dem Druck von Vertretern der deutschen Bundesländer eingefügt worden.

Der Eindruck, daß die Ausweitung der Bildungsdimension in dem Vertragswerk zugleich ihre Festschreibung auf den Status quo der Mitgliedsstaaten bedeutet, läßt sich nicht von der Hand weisen. Die „europäische Bildungseinheit" bleibt strikt ideeller Natur. Sie soll sozusagen durch die Verschiedenheit der partikularen Systeme hindurchscheinen.

Die Rolle der Vergleichenden Erziehungswissenschaft

Kann Vergleichende Erziehungswissenschaft in diesem festgeschriebenen Kontext dann überhaupt eine Funktion haben? Ist diese Annahme nicht eine gewaltige Selbstüberschätzung?

Gerade die Erfahrungen mit dem deutschen Föderalismus haben gezeigt, daß trotz allen eifersüchtigen Festhaltens der Länder an ihrer Kulturhoheit der wirtschaftliche Sektor mit seiner Forderung nach Freizügigkeit und Mobilität von Arbeitskräften tatsächlich einen kaum zu unterschätzenden Anpassungsdruck auf die partikularen Bildungssysteme ausübt. Neben der Kulturhoheit steht in Deutschland in der Tat die Kultusministerkonferenz, die im Laufe ihres fast fünfzigjährigen Bestehens trotz aller Schwächen das notwendige Minimum an Gemeinsamkeit erarbeitet und garantiert hat. Insofern ist es sicherlich auch notwendig für die Vergleichende Bildungsforschung, gewissermaßen im Aufgreifen ihrer evolutionistischen Funktion die „Unabwendbarkeit" einer letztlich konvergierenden Entwicklung vorauszusetzen und international angelegte Forschung zu entsprechenden Innovationen im Bildungsbereich zu betreiben. In diesen Zusammenhang läßt sich auch die bildungspolitische Funktion der Vergleichenden Erziehungswissenschaft in der Lehre stellen, die, wie gezeigt, die positive wie die negative Referenz von Reformkonzepten auf ausländische Erfahrungen objektivieren helfen soll. Eine spezifische Funktion der Vergleichenden Erziehungswissenschaft wäre in dieser Perspektive die Analyse und Verstärkung von Innovationen im Bildungswesen, welche die Bildungsgrenzen abbauen helfen.

Zum Abbau von Bildungsgrenzen kann auch eine pragmatische Funktion der Vergleichenden Erziehungswissenschaft beitragen, die sie schon seit längerer Zeit wahrnimmt: die Entwicklung von Kriterien der Beurteilung formaler Leistung im Hinblick auf die Festlegung von Äquivalenzen von Bildungsabschlüssen (vgl. z. B. *Anweiler 1986*). Die Dringlichkeit dieser Aufgabe spitzt sich infolge des genannten faktischen Harmonisierungsdrucks aufgrund der Mobilitätsgarantien im ökonomischen Sektor noch zu. Die gesellschaftliche Erwartung an die Vergleichende Erziehungswissenschaft übersteigt hier deutlich eine bloß idiographische Funktion zugunsten der Bereitstellung von politischem Handlungswissen, beispielsweise indem funktionale Äquivalenzen unterschiedlich zusammengesetzter formaler Qualifikationsnachweise bestimmt werden.

Aber selbst wenn man das Harmonisierungsverbot von Maastricht wörtlich nimmt und nicht an die Assimilationskraft der ökonomischen Fakten glaubt, verbleibt der Vergleichenden Erziehungswissenschaft eine zentrale europapolitische Funktion. Gerade um in der skizzierten dialektischen Weise eine „Einheit in der Vielfalt" aufzeigen zu können, bedarf es fundierter und differenzierter idiographischer Analysen – dies haben auch europapolitisch engagierte Nicht-Komparatisten erkannt und deutlich ausgesprochen (z. B. *Vaniscotte 1996, S. 305*). Diese Analysen sind besonders wertvoll, wenn sie sich nicht nur auf Einzelsysteme beschränken, sondern mehrere Systeme im Hinblick auf ihre Kontraste oder ihre (oft versteckte) Gemeinsamkeit untersuchen. Eine solche Aufgabe übersteigt bei weitem, was Selbstbeschreibungen zu leisten vermögen. Hier ist die objektivierende und vergleichsweise distanzierte komparatistische Außensicht gefordert. Solcherart strukturierte Vergleiche können beispielsweise auch Lehrern, die sich an der „Basis" mit europäischem Schüleraustausch befassen, ganz einfach Hilfestellung dabei geben, die Systeme und die Schulkulturen ihrer Austauschpartner genauer zu verstehen.[5] Generell gilt, daß Pädagogen (im weitesten Sinn) am besten dadurch auf die europäische Vielfalt von Bildung und Erziehung vorbereitet werden, daß man ihnen die genannte Kontingenzerfahrung der vergleichenden Perspektive vermittelt (ähnlich auch *Vaniscotte 1996, S. 305*).

Zur Erkenntnis der tieferen Gemeinsamkeit kann aber auch die Aktivierung der experimentellen Funktion der vergleichenden Forschung beitragen: eine Europäisierung des gesamten erziehungswissenschaftlichen Forschungsfeldes kann dazu beitragen, Regelmäßigkeiten zu entdecken, die für den europäischen Kontext gelten.

Es zeigt sich somit, daß zur Förderung des europäischen Integrationsprozesses alle Funktionen der Vergleichenden Erziehungswissenschaft beitragen können. Es ist gerade die mögliche Multifunktionalität des Vergleichs, die in diesem Prozeß gefragt ist.

Die vorgestellten Gedankengänge haben einen direkten Bezug zu einem bedeutenden Arbeitsanliegen Wolfgang Mitters. Am 4. und 5. November 1991 fand unter seiner Leitung eine Tagung mit dem Thema „Vergleichende Bildungsforschung in der Europäischen Gemeinschaft" statt. In dem auf dieser Tagung erarbeiteten „Memorandum" (an die Adresse der Politik) kann man vor allem unter Punkt 3 wesentliche Kerngedanken

---

5 Der Verfasser denkt hier an ein Schlüsselerlebnis einer polnisch-französischen Lehrerbegegnung (im Hinblick auf einen Schüleraustausch), bei der erst der außenstehende Komparatist die tiefgehenden Mißverständnisse aufklären konnte, die durch eine zwangsläufig an der Oberfläche bleibende wechselseitige Selbstdarstellung entstanden waren. Erst dann wurden den beteiligten Lehrern die tiefer liegenden Gemeinsamkeiten in den Schulkulturen und der gesellschaftlichen Wahrnehmung von „Bildung" deutlich.

der hier vorgetragenen Überlegungen wiederfinden *(Deutsches Institut für Internationale Pädagogische Forschung 1992, S. 21-24)*.

Unter Punkt 7 des Memorandums wird jedoch noch ein weiterer Gesichtspunkt genannt, ohne den diese Überlegungen unvollständig wären: *„Die auf die Europäische Gemeinschaft bezogene Bildungsforschung kann nur dann sinnvoll betrieben werden, wenn sie sich ... für die Probleme öffnet, die sich durch die Entwicklung des 'weiteren Europas' stellen ..."* (ebd., S. 23).

Insbesondere die Vergleichende Erziehungswissenschaft in Deutschland hat sich traditionell sehr darum bemüht, das „gemeinsame europäische Haus" nicht nur in Westeuropa zu suchen – und diese Brückenfunktion zwischen West und Ost läßt sich nicht zuletzt als ein Leitmotiv im Werk Wolfgang Mitters ausmachen.

Versteht man „Europa" in diesem weiteren Sinn, dann kann die Vision eines bayerischen „Schulmannes" aus dem Jahr 1838 fast wie ein Programm „europabezogener Vergleichender Bildungsforschung" klingen (Friedrich Thiersch, zitiert nach *Hilker 1962, S. 32*):

„Wir wollen, daß sich auf den Gebieten der Bildung die europäischen Nationen im tiefsten Wesen als Eine erkennen, aber damit sie dieses tun können, müssen sie sich vor allem ihrer besonderen Natur, ihrer Sitten, ihrer eigenen Gestalt bewußt werden. Erst wenn dieses geschehen, werden sie imstande sein, sich und ihr Wesen von dem Zufälligen zu trennen und sich in einer höheren Einheit als Glieder eines Ganzen zu erkennen, dessen Größe eben in der Mannigfaltigkeit der zur Einheit vermittelten Charaktere besteht."

Bibliographie

Anweiler, Oskar: Konzeptionen der Vergleichenden Pädagogik. In: Busch, Adelheid u. a. (Hrsg.): Vergleichende Erziehungswissenschaft. Texte zur Methodologie-Diskussion (= Uni-Taschenbücher. 410), Pullach: Verlag Dokumentation 1974, S. 19-26.

Anweiler, Oskar: Äquivalenzprobleme bei Bildungsabschlüssen. Anwendungsfelder vergleichender Bildungsforschung. In: Reichert, Erich u. a. (Hrsg.): Berufliche Bildung im Zusammenwirken von Schule und Betrieb. 10 Jahre Berufspädagogik an der Fridericiana, Villingen-Schwenningen: Nekkar-Verlag 1986, S. 1-9.

Anweiler, Oskar / Hörner, Wolfgang: Kriterien- und Methodenprobleme. In: Anweiler, Oskar u. a. (Hrsg.): Vergleich von Bildung und Erziehung in der Bundesrepublik Deutschland und in der DDR,

Köln: Verlag Wissenschaft und Politik 1990, S. 677-685.

Debesse, Maurice / Mialaret, Gaston: Pédagogie comparée. Paris: Presses Universitaires de France 1972. (Traité des sciences pédagogiques. 3)

Deutsches Institut für Internationale Pädagogische Forschung (Hrsg.): Vergleichende Bildungsforschung in der Europäischen Gemeinschaft. Bericht über die Konferenz vom 4. bis 5. November 1991 in Neu-Isenburg. Frankfurt a. M.: DIPF 1992.

Hilker, Franz: Vergleichende Pädagogik. Eine Einführung in ihre Geschichte, Theorie und Praxis. München: Hueber 1962.

Hörner, Wolfgang: Technische Bildung und Schule. Eine Problemanalyse im internationalen Vergleich. Köln u. a.: Böhlau 1993. (Studien und Dokumentationen zur vergleichenden Bildungsforschung. 52)

Hörner, Wolfgang: Einführung: Bildungssysteme in Europa – Überlegungen zu einer vergleichenden Betrachtung. In: Anweiler, Oskar u. a.: Bildungssysteme in Europa. 4. neu überarb. u. erw. Aufl., Weinheim u. a.: Beltz 1996, S. 13-29.

Lemberg, Eugen: Von der Erziehungswissenschaft zur Bildungsforschung. Das Bildungswesen als gesellschaftliche Institution. In: ders. (Hrsg.): Das Bildungswesen als Gegenstand der Forschung (= Veröffentlichungen der Hochschule für Internationale Pädagogische Forschung. 3), Heidelberg: Quelle und Meyer 1963, S. 21-100.

Luhmann, Niklas / Schorr, Karl-Eberhard: Reflexionsprobleme im Erziehungssystem. Stuttgart: Klett-Cotta 1979.

Mitter, Wolfgang: Komparative Forschung in der Erziehungswissenschaft. In: Internationale Zeitschrift für Erziehungswissenschaft, 22 (1976) 3, S. 317-337.

Müller-Solger, Hermann: Bildungspolitische Zusammenarbeit der Europäischen Gemeinschaft in Europa. In: Zeitschrift für Pädagogik, 36 (1990) 6, S. 805-825.

Noah, Harold J.: Zum Begriff des erziehungswissenschaftlichen Vergleichs. In: Bildung und Erziehung, 24 (1971) 6, S. 503-509.

Rickert, Heinrich: Kulturwissenschaft und Naturwissenschaft. Tübingen: Mohr 1926.

Schneider, Friedrich: Vergleichende Erziehungswissenschaft. Geschichte, Forschung, Lehre. Heidelberg: Quelle und Meyer 1961. (Vergleichende Erziehungswissenschaft und Pädagogik des Auslands. 1)

Schriewer, Jürgen: „Erziehung" und „Kultur". Zur Theorie und Methodik Vergleichender Erziehungswissenschaft. In: Brinkmann, Wilhelm / Renner, Karl (Hrsg.): Die Pädagogik und ihre Bereiche, Paderborn u. a.: Schöningh 1982, S. 185-236.

Van daele, Henk: L'éducation comparée. Paris: Presses Universitaires de France 1993. (Que sais-je? 2786)

Vaniscotte, Francine: Les écoles de l'Europe. Systèmes éducatifs et dimension européenne. Paris: Institut National de Recherche Pédagogique 1996.

Vertrag über die Europäische Union, unterzeichnet zu Maastricht am 7. Februar 1992. In: Amtsblatt der Europäischen Gemeinschaften. C, 35 (1992) 191, S. 1-112.

Vexliard, Alexandre: La pédagogie comparée. Méthodes et problèmes. Paris: Presses Universitaires de France 1967.

A Turning-Point in Comparative Education: Retrospect and Prospect

Edmund King

Introduction

It is a pleasure to honour Professor Wolfgang Mitter, as he richly deserves, on the conclusion of so many years of responsibility for the development of Comparative Education in so many capacities – not only as Director of Research in the world-famous Deutsches Institut für Internationale Pädagogische Forschung (DIPF) but also in a wider context – first as Vice-President of the Comparative Education Society in Europe (from 1977), then as its President (1981 onwards), and eventually as President of the World Council of Comparative Education Societies (1988-1996). Professor Mitter has earned warm eulogies for his indefatigable researches and his personal contributions to the academic study of Comparative Education, especially in relation to changes in Eastern Europe; but it is in the context of his wider European and world encouragement of comparative scholarship that I offer this appreciation.

'Encouragement' and 'guidance' are words that spring to the mind when we look back on Wolfgang Mitter's contributions over the decades – first, in fostering notable studies at the DIPF in Frankfurt, but no less during the delicate discussions of policy surrounding the congresses of the World Council of Comparative Education Societies (WCCES). In all academic circles there are prima donnas and factions, and in a world society of members from so many traditions and contexts it is often difficult to reconcile the diversity of interests and priorities. There are also diplomatic difficulties in finding acceptable venues which are also convenient for the gathering-in of colleagues from all over the world. In this regard Wolfgang Mitter's deft but patient management of WCCES affairs and meetings has been remarkably skilful, all the more so because almost three decades of WCCES enlargement have been turbulent across the whole field of education.

Comparative Studies in a Rapidly Evolving Context

Today we hear much about the transformation of education because of technological advance and the globalisation of all human concerns. It is therefore obvious that specialists in Comparative Education must now be deeply involved in problems never even considered by the pioneers in our field; we must also tackle them with concepts and techniques beyond the ken of those pioneers.

Conventional texts in Comparative Education used to speak of pioneers as scholars in previous centuries: Jullien, Diderot, and so on. Later they might name post-1945 giants such as Schneider, Hilker, Kandel, Ulich and Hans. More recently they might name writers or activists such as Bereday, Mallinson, Noah, and others too numerous to list. Each of these scholars provided not merely up-to-date information about rapidly changing educational systems but recommendations for future comparative study. In addition there were compilers of yearbooks and source-books (like Lauwerys, King-Hall, and Altbach), not to speak of editors of journals and an ever-growing number of single-topic articles.

Yet although those post-1945 scholars were so recent that I have known them all personally (indeed Noah and Altbach are still happily alive) the topics they addressed only a few years ago – and the constituency of teachers' colleges and researchers they also addressed – have to all intents and purposes been metamorphosed into history.

Events and scholarship have moved so fast that our bookshelves are unintentionally a record of Comparative Education as it used to be in more slowly moving times. Typically, Nicholas Hans, my immediate predecessor at King's College London, devoted his great scholarship to historical and cultural factors which in his view had firmly shaped national systems of education. His approach influenced many subsequent writers.

Now books, journals and such solid sources of information and discussion are increasingly stated to be outmoded because much contemporary news and questioning is immediately retrievable world-wide on the Internet. Nevertheless books are still published in ever-increasing numbers, and journals multiply. However, many of those distributing information and activating discussion do not work in universities and conventional centres but in agencies like the World Bank, OECD, UNESCO, and even commercial circles. Meanwhile, university departments of Comparative Education are ever fewer in number and of dwindling strength.

Why does Comparative Education (under that name) seem to have declined in academic prestige and public influence when educational decisions with international repercussions must be made? Perhaps because of self-isolation and priestliness. One or two would-be theologians have tried to prescribe what Comparative Education *ought to be*, without reference to actuality. Among realists studying what actually goes on in schools, homes and other places of learning, few clearly recognise (or bother much about) the challenge forcefully presented to *all* existing systems by the rapid advance of industrialisation, communication technologies or the pervasive penetration of new concerns such as democratisation at home and the internationalisation of trade and careers. That is the reason why crucial comparative studies of education and re-education are being made by other specialists – not in 'Comparative Education'. We should all perhaps move together to a new horizon of scholarship and take a fresh look at today's context.

A Biographical Dimension

It is usually instructive to look back over changes in our lifetime. Most of the recent Comparative Education scholars named above were also migrants (sometimes from countries no longer existing) whose own life-experience necessitated a comparative perspective. Nowadays even stay-at-homes are also conscious of being migrants in one way or another – from one region or social class to another, from one national context of concerns to a vastly extended awareness of an unfamiliar world. We are continuously re-engaged in freshly challenging perspectives. We are all comparativists, willy-nilly. Therefore comparative analysis, as such, is no longer an exclusively professional activity for our kind of scholarship; it is, or should be, a critical element in everyone's perceptions. We are learning a new context like another language.

The newness of this concept, and of its challenge to education as a whole, can hardly be overstated. We used to be sure of things, and of everything's place in a contained and predictable universe. I vividly remember my first ride in a friend's motor-car, a very rare treat, at the age of six years. There were children in the elementary school I attended who had never been to the sea, only 40 kilometres away. In a London grammar school where I taught in 1939 there were boys who had never visited the city centre, ten kilometres distant but visible from the school's playing fields. The world is still full of people whose lives are equally circumscribed, although airlines after 1955 brought Australia and Japan within a day's journey. In fact, by 1964 I was teaching in Tokyo one evening and in King's College London on the following morning, reviewing similar topics.

We older people have actually seen men on the moon. Our children already have careers established on satellite communications. Our grandchildren can not imagine a world (or perhaps even a home) without access to the Internet. We are utterly dependent on changes for which there is no prescription in any educational system as we know it – even after all the reforms of post-war years. There are no permanent careers in the industrialised world, partly because there are no permanently valid skills or sufficient knowledge, but also because the daily contacts and data of international commerce are literally ephemeral. Yet where are the Comparative Education texts – especially articles on comparative method – taking account of the living context in which we specialists work and everyone daily makes decisions affecting education?

'Strategic' Comparisons

It might be said that there have indeed been such policy-oriented comparative studies ever since 1945, contrasting (for instance) scientific and technological achievements in the former USSR or in Japan with lower attainments in the USA or Western European countries. Weighty monographs, and the wealth of researches presented in the International Evaluation of Educational Achievement (IEA) from 1967 onwards, could no longer be classified simply as 'library' scholarship for future teachers or postgraduate researchers. They were meant to be goals for action. (Nicholas Hans once said that Comparative Education was „intentionally reformative", and Michael Sadler said much the same as long ago as 1900). There has been a spate of such works in the USA. Ever since the oil and energy crises of the 1960s many European ministers of education have taken to visiting foreign countries so as to discover how to produce more 'skill' back home by energising their school systems – preferably without spending more money or disturbing the familiar hierarchy of scholastic preference. But such 'strategic' globe-trotting, or even copying useful gadgetry from successful neighbours, is political manoeuvring rather than serious analysis.

It is a very good thing that politicians and businessmen should be frightened by their neighbours' educational successes and their own countries' failures. That instils motivation for legislative reform and the disbursement of financial support; but any intention to transform education generically – not only at home and during juvenile stages but lifelong and in preparation for an unforeseeable world – hardly seems to cross politicians' minds. Within educational establishments themselves (schools, higher education, teacher-preparation and retraining) the lack of a comparative perspective and of a realistic commitment to world considerations is usually manifest. That is a sad state of affairs in itself, yet sadder because it prevents recognition that all schooling is *of provisional relevance*. From that follows neglect of the need to train for *lifelong judgement and re-appraisal in unforeseeable circumstances*.

In other words, the essential shortcoming of all traditional education is its failure to educate for responsible uncertainty, with its corollary of willingness to *compare alternatives* and co-operate in their deeper analysis, with decisions and development to follow in due course.

To achieve that, instead of outdated prescriptions for Comparative Education, we need both an updated conceptual framework and new tools for a job without precedent. Part of our conceptual reorientation lies in escaping from a purely pedagogical preoccupation: our 'constituency' today includes not just other academics but a limitless array of participants giving us feedback from their daily experience and re-learning.

I emphasise the paradoxical word 'participants'. Nowadays comparative researches, often having a practical outcome in the reform of education or the continuing re-education of ordinary learners, increasingly undertaken by themselves, may receive valuable feedback from them. These participants in their own education thus become partners in furthering research itself. We are engaged together in continuous comparative investigation. For this enlarged commitment we need new guidelines, and probably new tools.

Finding Modern Guidelines for Comparative Education

Let us turn back once again to reflect on older prescriptions. In the 1950s there was a vogue of 'manpower planning' and 'social engineering'. In the 1960s this kind of scientism was extended to Comparative Education by one writer who imagined (like Marx and Engels more than a century earlier) that we could discover inherent 'laws' of development as a „*deterministic element*" so as to „*predict chain reactions*", and „*provide the scientific basis of planning*", in which „*man's ability directly to control certain processes of social transformation is theoretically as restricted as in, say, a chemical reaction which he sets in motion. ... Indeed he has less power because it is less feasible to control the initial conditions"* (Holmes 1965, pp. 52, 53).

Such notions have been shown to be nonsense not only by Karl *Popper (1971, pp. 9-11, 196, 247, 359, and passim),* who was mistakenly claimed in their support, but by the economic and social upheavals begun by wars in the 1970s. These have been followed by the collapse of the Soviet Union, the disintegration of formerly sovereign states, and most of all by the communications revolution which penetrates every aspect of learning and all careers, as well as by the panorama of personal and political *choices* filling every newspaper and broadcast.

All the educational systems within which we grew up assumed that they were in a real sense self-sufficient and autonomous. They were dominated if not controlled by a state apparatus managed or otherwise constrained by laws, taxation, and officials – primarily to serve a recognisable hierarchy of occupations, social positions and well defined roles, probably for a life-time. It hardly needs saying that the technological revolution which now seems 'natural' to our grandchildren negates every such assumption. On top of the international upheavals mentioned in my last paragraph we must reckon with the consequences of the contraceptive pill, and the emancipation of women and other hitherto underprivileged populations. All these considerations and many others accentuate the challenge of unpredictability and lifelong reappraisal.

Guidelines for comparative studies today exemplify this acceptance of uncertainty – not, of course, in a spirit of despair or indifference but as a conceptual shift. That leads us towards new operational procedures. We find fewer *ex cathedra* pronouncements or one-way communications, and more openness to co-operative feedback from others. Instead of the past's didactic prescriptions, Comparative Education today is *exploratory*, welcoming *participant* investigation.

Procedural Generalities and Specific Tools for Particular Jobs

It is true that I myself have felt obliged to outline analytical frameworks for particular purposes – to help my students *(King 1975)* or to programme the work of a research team *(King 1976, p. 17).* But these were simply hypotheses open to modification or rejection as work proceeded. Every research commitment starts with explicit or implied questions, perhaps questions sequential on each other. There is generally a hypothesis about possible outcomes, either finally or in stages as the work proceeds; but continually throughout any complex investigation 'the problem' under scrutiny may change shape *(Popper 1971, pp. 246-247)*. If so, it will require fresh modes of examination for newly revealed aspects or changes of context which must be taken into account. So on each occasion we need different tools, which we may have to invent *ad hoc* or borrow from other branches of social study.

The most conspicuous example of bringing the techniques of other social studies into Comparative Education is seen in the outstanding work of the International Association for the Evaluation of Educational Achievement (IEA), whose first report in 1967 showed how psychologists, sociologists, statistical experts and others acting together could amass and evaluate empirical evidence never previously brought on a world scale into comparative studies of educational practice and results. Of course there were flaws of judgement and mistaken interpretations – not surprising in a pioneering enterprise from which 'official' Comparative Education specialists at first withheld support; but it is impossible to praise too highly the general merits of successive IEA reports, most notably because they represented a model of empirical methods and field enquiry.

However, large-scale objective compilations of data and school methods – no matter how revealing – may give little or no idea of the 'inside feeling' of those being educated, or of the changing personal and social context in which vital educational choices are made. Are such contexts peculiar to one place or time? Or are generic changes of perception and need taking place? If so, how can an investigation be mounted to reveal what is specific, what is generic, and what demands closer scrutiny to reveal guidelines not only for local and topical decision but for long-term policy?

After taking part in many international discussions in pursuit of answers to such questions, in 1970 I established a Comparative Research Unit at King's College in the University of London, financed by the Social Science Research Council of the United Kingdom and with some assistance from the Council of Europe. Our three-year task was to examine specifically the social and educational consequences of rapidly increasing enrolments between the ages of 16 and 20 in five Western European countries chosen as representing different educational traditions and varying degrees of response to technological and social change.

Needless to say, a vast amount of clarification of our own central points of focus and priorities had to be followed by careful laying of the ground plan of action. There was delicate diplomacy in the cities and institutions we wished to visit, after meticulous preparation (and up-to-the minute translation) of some 12.000 interlocking and confidential questionnaires which we finally succeeded in administering personally on the ground. All this was followed by discussions of responses *in situ* with teachers and students.

We compared different types of school pattern, expectations of outcome, changes in enrolments, and variations between industrial, post-industrial and suburban conditions; but essentially we were looking for significant points of 'newness'. The astonishing and central finding was that in our chosen age-range – in whatever type of institution (traditional or innovative, for 'academic' or vocational studies) – *all students in post-compulsory education were 'new' in vital respects.*

'Vital' is a strong word; but it is justified by the fact that a changed life around the schools permeated and transformed all learning inside them, especially in its expectations and commitments. However, with one exception, no investigator (and certainly no comparative research team) had ever asked students aged 16-20 to contribute their 'inside view' as part of an international perspective for educational policy. We not only invited their views in answering interlocking questionnaires but also welcomed freely written statements at the end of each hour-long period assigned to answering.

Fresh Terminology for New Perceptions

We needed new words to communicate the evolving insights of our research, and to emphasise the significance of its findings as they emerged. In 1970, when we began, nobody had ever used the phrase 'post-compulsory education' in the generic sense of including *all* types of learning and training beyond obligatory attendance (other than academic higher education).

'Post-compulsory' seemed a handy term avoiding the divisive distinctions found everywhere. We had of course to explain its focus and implications to administrators and teachers concerned with this level in Britain and abroad – and, not least, to the respondents themselves in the 16-20 age-range. The novelty of such a generic concept as 'post-compulsory education', applicable to a *level* of learning rather than a particular age or type of school, soon became manifest. The term was welcomed everywhere as a key to new understanding of interlocking educational and social phenomena.

Still more unprecedented was another term we learned to use: 'young adults'. As respondents to us they were not merely observed from outside; they were participant assessors of a situation without precedent, which we were careful to present in its international perspectives. Not only were students at the 16-20 age-level (and sometimes younger) more mature and perceptive in scholastic terms than teachers, administrators and researchers had yet recognised; in non-scholastic respects they were already young men and women, increasingly recognised as such by the world outside. Many already had been in employment (paid or not) and had adult social or sexual experience.

Yet teachers and educational writers continued to call young adults 'children', 'kids', 'youth', or (at best) 'young people'. Many still do in 1997! Despite that, in our published findings the 16-20 population made observations and recommendations which matched expert educational advice. They were often shrewder in educational perceptions than their teachers and administrators. They were still more far-sighted than most prospective employers calling for this or that 'skill' as an outcome of extended schooling.

Our published findings *(King/Moor/Mundy 1974, 1975)* started a crescendo of discussions. The first took place as 'feedback' seminars in the countries where the research was undertaken, from ministerial down to practitioner level. These in turn gave rise to conferences, both national and international. For these, working papers were published by the Council of Europe and UNESCO. Though that was very gratifying, by far the greatest reward was the recognition of common post-compulsory concerns across so many differently organised systems, against different political and cultural backgrounds, and at varying socio-economic levels. During more than two decades since our research reports appeared, a world-wide ferment of concern for post-compulsory education has continued.

A New Departure

This example of purposive and policy-oriented comparative study marked a new departure from traditional modes. It also provided pointers for further comparative investigations and interpretations in traditional fields, not least in preparing a modern workforce and suiting personal requirements. Though focused on a specific theme it acknowledged the interdependence of many considerations and possible solutions. Unlike earlier educational categories, post-compulsory education does not segregate 'general' from 'vocational' interests, or 'higher' from 'continuing' education, but recognises possible links between any of them. There we see pointers for further comparative research and reform, in which the *pivotal* position of post-compulsory education is acknowledged, as OECD has already recommended *(Organisation for Economic Co-operation and Development 1984, p. 1)*.

However, being pivotal entails turning round a good deal else. The changes of our times bring into view the concerns not only of young adults themselves but of the many who return to that level of learning or re-orientation at any time of life, after widely varying realms of experience for which no schooling prepared them. So there are corollaries in distance education, in the continuing education of much older 'returners', in links between professional and non-professional education, and above all in providing for the education of whole populations after political transformation.

In many such instances there is no need to maintain old distinctions between institutional (or even curricular) categories, or age barriers. The world is open to a new horizon of comparative and co-operative studies of education. Only one thing is certain: that Comparative Education will undergo continuous and adaptive evolution if it is to sustain its time-honoured commitment to policy-oriented research relevant to the world around it.

Bibliography

Holmes, Brian: Problems in Education. A Comparative Approach. London: Routledge and Kegan Paul 1965.
King, Edmund: Analytical Frameworks in Comparative Studies of Education. In: Comparative Education, 11 (1975) 1, pp. 85-103.
King, Edmund: Education for Uncertainty. London: King's College 1976.
King, Edmund J. / Moor, Christine H. / Mundy, Jennifer A.: Post-Compulsory Education. A New Analysis in Western Europe. London: Sage 1974.
King, Edmund J. / Moor, Christine H. / Mundy, Jennifer A.: Post-Compulsory Education. 2. The Way Ahead. London: Sage 1975.
Organisation for Economic Co-operation and Development (ed.): Innovation in Education. No. 38. Paris: OECD 1984.
Popper, Karl: Objective Knowledge. An Evolutionary Approach. London: Oxford University Press 1972.

Gesellschaftliche Steuerung von Berufsbildungssystemen – Ein Analysekonzept für politikorientierte internationale Vergleiche

Richard Koch

Internationalisierung berufsbildungspolitischer Problemstellungen als Herausforderung an die vergleichende Berufsbildungsforschung

Mit der Internationalisierung des Problems der Qualifizierung von Arbeitskräften infolge der Globalisierung der Wirtschaft wächst der Bedarf der Berufsbildungspolitik an international vergleichenden Erkenntnissen über die Funktionsweise von Berufsbildungssystemen. Im einzelnen sind vor allem folgende Entwicklungen hervorzuheben:

– *Wirtschaftlicher und politischer Integrationsprozeß in der Europäischen Union.*
Mit fortschreitender Integration können die nationalen Berufsbildungssysteme der Staaten in der Europäischen Union immer weniger aus nur rein nationaler Perspektive weiterentwickelt werden, trotz der prinzipiellen Souveränität der Mitgliedstaaten, Form und Inhalt der beruflichen Bildung zu bestimmen. Die nationale Berufsbildungspolitik benötigt gute Kenntnisse der Funktionslogik und Funktionsprobleme der Berufsbildungssysteme anderer EU-Mitgliedstaaten. Das gleiche gilt für die Mitwirkung an der Berufsbildungspolitik der Gemeinschaft, die ein wechselseitiges Verständnis der jeweiligen nationalen Ausgangssituation voraussetzt.

– *Globaler wirtschaftlicher (Standort-)Wettbewerb.*
Für die Berufsbildungspolitik geht es dabei um die Frage, inwieweit das jeweilige nationale Berufsbildungssystem einen hinreichenden Beitrag zur Bewältigung des wirtschaftlich-technischen Strukturwandels und der damit verbundenen Qualifizierungsprobleme im Vergleich zu den Berufsbildungssystemen der konkurrierenden Volkswirtschaften leisten und wie seine Leistungsfähigkeit und Effizienz verbessert werden kann. Aus Erkenntnissen über Vorzüge und Nachteile von Konzepten anderer Staaten bei der Bewältigung ähnlicher Herausforderungen lassen sich Anregungen für Gestaltungsoptionen der nationalen Berufsbildung ableiten.

– *Berufsbildungshilfe als Hilfe zur Systementwicklung.*
Bei der Berufsbildungshilfe gewinnt der Aspekt der Systementwicklung an Bedeutung, da nur so die Nachhaltigkeit von Maßnahmen auf der Ebene der Durchfüh-

rungspraxis der beruflichen Bildung gesichert werden kann. Nachdem sich die – früher auch in Deutschland verbreitete – Vorstellung als unrealistisch erwiesen hat, man könne Berufsbildungssysteme von Industriestaaten auf Entwicklungsländer übertragen, geht es nunmehr um einen den sozioökonomischen Rahmenbedingungen dieser Länder angemessenen Prozeß der Systementwicklung. Hierfür können international vergleichende Erkenntnisse zur Funktionsweise verschiedener Systemkonfigurationen und zur Effizienz bestimmter Reformmaßnahmen in der Berufsbildung hilfreiche Anregungen geben.

Forschungsstand

Der Forschungsstand der international vergleichenden Berufsbildungsforschung[1] in Deutschland ist durch ein doppeltes Defizit gekennzeichnet. Zu einen besteht ein *"... auffälliges Mißverhältnis zwischen der großen Zahl theoretischer Reflexionen über die Methodologie des Vergleichs und der geringen Zahl real durchgeführter systematischer Vergleichsstudien ..." (Hörner 1993, S. 23).* Zum anderen hat sich die vergleichende Berufsbildungsforschung bislang nur punktuell mit den obengenannten bildungspolitischen Aktionsbereichen befaßt.

Diese Situation dürfte nicht nur an den theoretisch-methodischen sowie forschungspraktischen Problemen der Durchführung komplexer Vergleichsstudien liegen. Bei potentiellen Auftraggebern für solche eher kostspielige Studien scheinen teilweise auch Zweifel an ihrem Nutzen für die Bildungspolitik zu bestehen. Zumindest ist immer wieder das Argument zu hören, die ausländischen Berufsbildungssysteme seien so verschieden vom eigenen, daß man aus Vergleichen keine für bildungspolitische Entscheidungen relevanten Erkenntnisse ziehen könne. Möglicherweise bestehen auch Befürchtungen, der Vergleich der nationalen Berufsbildungssysteme in der EU könne Bestrebungen fördern, die nationalen Berufsbildungssysteme zu harmonisieren. (Jedenfalls hat die EG-Kommission/Europäische Kommission in den letzten zehn bis 15 Jahren zahlreiche Berufsbildungsvergleiche in Auftrag gegeben.)

---

1 Der Forschungsstand der Vergleichenden Erziehungswissenschaft im Bereich der allgemeinen Bildung wird hier nicht betrachtet. Die traditionelle Trennung von Vergleichender Erziehungswissenschaft und vergleichender Berufsbildungsforschung muß angesichts der wachsenden Interdependenzen von allgemeiner und beruflicher Bildung auf der Ebene von Systemvergleichen zunehmend als obsolet angesehen werden *(Mitter 1995, S. 13)*.

Der Nutzen internationaler Berufsbildungsvergleiche ist generell darin zu sehen, daß „... *der 'Umweg' über ausländische Erfahrungen ein vertieftes Verständnis der Ausgangsproblematik in der eigenen Gesellschaft und eine Reformulierung der Problemdefinition, der ihr zugrundeliegenden Theorien und Paradigmen [ermöglicht]"* (Georg 1995, S. 79). Problemlösungsansätze des Auslandes können – trotz ihres spezifischen nationalen Kontextes – auf Möglichkeiten der Bearbeitung inländischer Probleme hinweisen, zu einem Überdenken bisheriger Vorgehensweisen führen oder zumindest Alternativen denkbar machen. Eine bildungspolitisch wesentliche Funktion des Vergleichs in dynamischer Perspektive besteht darin, Vorzüge und Risiken unterschiedlicher institutioneller Konfigurationen bei der Bearbeitung gegenwärtiger oder sich abzeichnender Problemkonstellationen aufzuzeigen.

In der Vergangenheit wurden überwiegend deskriptive Ländermonographien (etwa die vom CEDEFOP herausgegebenen Darstellungen zu den Berufsbildungssystemen der EU-Mitgliedstaaten) und internationale Überblicksdarstellungen zu einzelnen Aspekten der beruflichen Bildung (z. B. *Gordon 1993*) angefertigt. Dadurch wurden zwar der Zugang zu Informationen über die Strukturen ausländischer Berufsbildungssysteme verbessert. Erkenntnisse über deren Funktionsweise konnten daraus nur begrenzt abgeleitet werden.

Systematische Vergleichsstudien, die bildungspolitisch relevante Probleme in analytische Forschungsfragen transformieren und komplexere Sachverhalte der beruflichen Bildung vor dem Hintergrund des jeweiligen sozioökonomischen, kulturellen und politischen Kontextes eines Landes darstellen, wurden bislang nur selten vorgelegt.[2]

Die vergleichende Evaluierung von (Berufs-)Bildungssystemen und von berufsbildungspolitischen Maßnahmen „*als weiterführende Forschungsperspektive*" (*Koch 1991, S. 17*) steckt noch weitgehend in den Anfängen bzw. steht in der Tradition makro-ökonomischer Analysen zur Erklärung von Produktivitätseffekten durch Bildungsinvestitionen.[3]

---

2 Aufgrund ihrer Reflexion von historischen Entwicklungslinien und sozioökonomischen Rahmenbedingungen hervorzuheben sind die vergleichenden arbeits- und bildungssoziologischen Studien von *Lutz* (1976), *Maurice / Sellier / Sylvestre* (1979) und *Drexel (1993a)*.

3 Einen aktuellen Überblick über die internationalen Studien zu diesem Thema geben *Büchtemann / Verdier (1995, S. 12ff.)*. Zu der Frage der Effizienz von Berufsbildungssystemen vgl. auch *Lipsmeier (1989)*.

Die Relevanz der vergleichenden Berufsbildungsforschung für die Bildungspolitik hängt nicht nur von der Fragestellung, sondern auch von der theoretischen und forschungspraktischen Konzeption der Studien ab. Angesichts der geringen Zahl an einschlägigen Studien mangelt es nach wie vor an empirisch erprobten Analysekonzepten für die Durchführung von politikorientierten internationalen Vergleichsstudien.

Methodische Konzepte der Vergleichsforschung

Die einem internationalen Vergleich zugrunde gelegte Interpretation von Andersartigkeit gesellschaftlicher Phänomene in verschiedenen Ländern prägt die bildungspolitischen Schlußfolgerungen vor.

Traditionelle universalistische Ansätze, die dazu tendieren, den meist aus nur wenigen Ländern abgeleiteten „weltweiten Trend" als Richtschnur für eine nationale Reformpolitik anzubieten *(Hörner 1993, S. 9)*, kommen zwar dem Bedürfnis von Politik nach einfachen „Botschaften" entgegen. Der bei diesen Ansätzen unterstellte Determinismus, demzufolge es für eine bestimmte Problemkonstellation immer genau eine optimale Problemlösung gibt, findet in der Realität jedoch keine Entsprechung.

Dem steht ein Ansatz gegenüber, der Unterschiede institutioneller Strukturen von Berufsbildungssystemen als das „geronnene" Ergebnis gesellschaftsspezifischer sozialer Beziehungen interpretiert, die durch einen mehr oder weniger kohärenten kulturellen, sozialen, ökonomischen und politischen Kontext geprägt sind *(cohérence sociétal)*. Das Erkenntnisinteresse des Vergleichs nach diesem sozietalen Ansatz richtet sich darauf, unterschiedliche Logiken von analogen gesellschaftlichen Funktionen und Institutionen aufzuzeigen *(Maurice 1991)*.

Allein aus der Erkenntnis, daß die Unterschiede der verglichenen Berufsbildungssysteme durch einen einzigartigen nationalen Kontext bedingt sind, lassen sich allerdings nur bedingt bildungspolitisch relevante Schlußfolgerungen ziehen. Um der Gefahr einer unverbundenen Paralleldarstellung der länderspezifischen Bedingungen zu entgehen, muß das Vergleichsobjekt in den unterschiedlichen nationalen Kontexten abgegrenzt werden. Hierzu ist eine *„theoretisch begründete Strukturfrage"* erforderlich, *„die sich empirisch in unterschiedlichen nationalen Kontexten je nach konkreten nationalen Bedingungen operationalisieren läßt und als kleinster gemeinsamer Nenner für den Vergleich dienen kann"* *(Drexel 1993a, S. 250f.)*. Zudem muß der sozietale Ansatz um eine dynamische Perspektive erweitert werden *(Drexel 1993b, S. 6f.).* Für die Bildungspolitik sind gerade die Entwicklungsprozesse der betrachteten Berufsbildungssysteme über einen längeren Zeitraum und die Genese von neuen institutionellen Lösungen von Interesse. *„Dann wären ... Bildungssysteme ..., die in einer bloß 'sozietalen' Perspektive kaum etwas miteinander gemein haben, als Ergebnis historischer Prozesse zu verstehen, deren Ausgangspunkt, deren Mechanismen und deren Triebkräfte möglicherweise sehr viel mehr Gemeinsamkeiten aufweisen, die vielleicht – gleichzeitig oder in verschiedenen Augenblicken? – mit identischen Problemlagen konfrontiert waren, auf die dann freilich die jeweiligen Gesellschaften – warum und unter dem Einfluß welcher Zwänge und welcher Kräfte? – mit verschiedenen Lösungen reagierten" (Lutz 1991, S. 104).*

Klassifizierung von Berufsbildungssystemen

Ein in der vergleichenden Berufsbildungsforschung häufiger benutztes Instrument ist die Klassifizierung von Berufsbildungssystemen anhand bestimmter Kriterien. Solche Typologien sollen dazu beitragen, die Vielfalt der Berufsbildungssysteme auf wenige Grundtypen zu reduzieren. Ein erstes Problem hierbei ist die Wahl eines geeigneten Klassifizierungskriteriums. Das in zahlreichen älteren Klassifikationen gewählte statische Kriterium „Lernort" hat für politikorientierte Fragestellungen nur einen begrenzten analytischen Wert, da es die für die Struktur und Entwicklung von Berufsbildungssystemen zentralen gesellschaftlichen Machtkonstellationen ausblendet. *Greinert (1990)* schlägt deshalb die „Rolle des Staates" als ein politisch und zugleich dynamisch strukturiertes Kriterium für die Klassifikation von Berufsbildungssystemen vor. Nach dem Umfang und der Art staatlicher Intervention in die Berufsbildung unterscheidet er als Grundformen von Berufsbildungssystemen: *„Marktmodell", „staatlich gesteuertes Marktmodell"* und *„bürokratisches bzw. Schulmodell".* Als problematisch erweist sich der Versuch, solchen Modellen bestimmte nationale Berufsbildungssysteme zuzuordnen *(Lauterbach 1995).* Dies wird schon daran deutlich, daß in einem Land oft mehrere Teilsysteme der Berufsbildung (z. B. vollschulische Berufsausbildung und Lehre) nebeneinander existieren. Selbst solche Teilsysteme sind Mischtypen, deren konkrete Funktionsweisen empirisch ermittelt werden müssen. Hierzu wird das im folgenden dargestellte Analysekonzept vorgeschlagen.

Gesellschaftliche Steuerung von Berufsbildungssystemen als Analysekonzept für den Berufsbildungsvergleich

Bei Vergleichen der Funktionsweise von Berufsbildungssystemen, die auf bildungspolitische Probleme ausgerichtet sind, steht die Frage im Zentrum, welche Mechanismen und Institutionen die Prozesse im System der beruflichen Bildung steuern. Hierzu gehören so verschiedene Dinge wie z. B. Rahmenbedingungen für die Mitwirkung von privaten Betrieben an der Berufsausbildung, Regelungen für die Lehrerausbildung oder Selektionsmechanismen beim Zugang zur Berufsbildung. Dabei geht es nicht um den deskriptiven Vergleich von formalen Strukturen des Berufsbildungssystems, sondern um die Analyse der – funktionalen oder dysfunktionalen – Wirkungen der jeweiligen Formen gesellschaftlicher Steuerung der beruflichen Bildung. Diese sind meist durch Kombinationen der steuernden Wirkungen folgender Faktoren gekennzeichnet:

- Steuerungswirkungen allgemein befolgter „ungeschriebener" Regeln bzw. Konventionen;[4]
- Steuerungswirkungen institutioneller Strukturen und Mechanismen (z. B. Lehrstellenmarkt);
- Wirkungen staatlicher Steuerungsinstrumente (finanzielle Anreize, gesetzliche Regelungen u. ä.);
- Wirkungen von Steuerungsinstrumenten nicht-staatlicher Akteure (z. B. Prüfungsordnungen der Kammern, tarifvertragliche Regelungen der Sozialparteien).

Die Steuerung der beruflichen Bildung durch staatliche Stellen und nicht-staatliche Akteure wie Kammern oder Sozialparteien erfolgt durch intentionale, zielgerichtete Intervention in die Handlungsbedingungen sozialer Akteure der beruflichen Bildung (z. B. Ausbildungsbetriebe, Schulen, Ausbilder, Lehrer). Diese hier als öffentliche Steuerung bezeichneten Interventionen sind darauf ausgerichtet, andere über-individuelle Formen und Mechanismen der Handlungssteuerung, wie marktvermittelte Handlungszwänge oder traditionelle Werthaltungen, in ihren Wirkungen zu beschränken, zu ergänzen oder zu substituieren *(Böhle / Deiß 1980)*. Die öffentliche Steuerung verfolgt vor allem das Ziel, die Handlungsbedingungen der Anbieter von beruflicher Bildung (Betriebe, Schu-

---

4 Ein Beispiel mit erheblichen Auswirkungen auf die Steuerung des deutschen dualen Ausbildungssystems ist das Konsensprinzip. Die Bundesregierung überläßt nach diesem gesetzlich nicht festgeschriebenen Prinzip in freiwilliger Selbstbeschränkung ihrer Regelungskompetenz die Aushandlung der Eckwerte von Ausbildungsordnungen den Sozialparteien.

len, sonstige Träger) so zu gestalten, daß ein aus wirtschafts- und gesellschaftspolitischer Sicht quantitativ und qualitativ hinreichendes Berufsbildungsangebot zustande kommt.

Durch das Konzept der gesellschaftlichen Steuerung werden nicht nur Interventionen des Staates, sondern auch anderer öffentlicher Akteure erfaßt. Ebenso können über die Steuerungswirkungen öffentlicher Interventionen hinaus auch solche sonstiger gesellschaftlicher Mechanismen analysiert werden. Das Analysekonzept läßt sich deshalb anwenden sowohl auf hoch institutionalisierte Berufsbildungssysteme der Industrienationen als auch auf weniger formalisierte Systeme der beruflichen Bildung in Entwicklungsländern.

Für die vergleichende empirische Analyse von Ausbildungssystemen weist das Konzept der gesellschaftlichen Steuerung vor allem zwei Vorzüge auf: Ein erster Vorzug besteht darin, daß die Steuerungsleistungen von Markt, Staat und Verbänden statt als ordnungspolitisch gegensätzliche Konzepte sich nun in ihren Interdependenz- und Substitutionsbeziehungen betrachten lassen. In den einzelnen nationalen Berufsbildungssystemen werden bestimmte Steuerungsfunktionen (z. B. Abstimmung des Ausbildungsplatzangebots mit der Bildungsnachfrage) durch unterschiedliche Kombinationen der Steuerungsleistungen von Markt, Staat und Verbänden erfüllt. Welche Kombinationen hierbei Vorteile oder Nachteile aufweisen, ist eine bildungspolitisch relevante Frage für den internationalen Vergleich.

Ein zweiter Vorzug ist darin zu sehen, daß strukturtheoretische und handlungstheoretische Perspektiven verknüpfbar werden. Die für bildungspolitische Problemstellungen zentralen Wechselbeziehungen zwischen der Makroebene der institutionellen Strukturen des Ausbildungssystems, der Mesoebene der Interessenvermittlung durch Verbände und der Mikroebene des Handelns der Ausbildungsträger und Ausbildungsnachfrager können in den Mittelpunkt der Analyse gerückt werden. Gerade die in systemtheoretischen Ansätzen vielfach ausgeblendete handlungstheoretische Perspektive erweist sich als notwendig für das Verständnis der Funktionsweise und Entwicklungsdynamik von Berufsbildungssystemen. Für die bildungspolitische Diskussion können auch internationale Vergleiche von Reformplänen und der politischen Interessenauseinandersetzung dazu instruktiv sein.

Projekte des internationaler Berufsbildungsvergleichs, die sich mit Policy-Problemen befassen, müssen demnach die Gesamtheit der für die Fragestellung relevanten Formen,

Akteure und Instrumente der Steuerung von Berufsbildungssystemen betrachten. Diese erfordert *„eine konkrete ... Analyse politischer, sozialer und ökonomischer Institutionen und Handlungsarenen"* *(Gretschmann 1984, S. 197)*.

Formen öffentlicher Steuerung von Berufsbildungssystemen

Die theoretische und bildungspolitische Diskussion darüber, welche Form der Steuerung von Ausbildungssystemen ein quantitativ und qualitativ ausreichendes Ausbildungsangebot am effizientesten gewährleisten kann, blieb in den sechziger und siebziger Jahren, aber teilweise auch noch in der jüngeren Vergangenheit, auf die Dualität der Steuerungsformen „Markt" und „Staat" begrenzt. Seit den achtziger Jahren rückten durch die sozialwissenschaftliche Neokorporatismus-Forschung darüber hinaus die möglichen Steuerungsfunktionen von Verbänden bzw. die der Sozialparteien stärker in das Blickfeld.

Neben Staat und Markt können prinzipiell auch Verbände Leistungen öffentlicher Steuerung erbringen, indem sie mit Funktionen kollektiver Selbststeuerung ausgestattet werden. Im Vordergrund des Interesses der sozialwissenschaftlichen Neokorporatismus-Forschung steht dabei die Frage, wie *„organisierte soziale Gruppen zu bewegen [sind], sich aus Eigeninteresse sozial- und gemeinwohlverträglich selbst zu regulieren"* (Streeck 1994, S. 17), wie also *„Interessenverbände ... im Bereich der Berufsbildungspolitik zu 'privaten Regierungen' werden können, die gegenüber ihren Mitgliedern quasi-öffentliche Autorität ausüben und an der Produktion und Implementation bindender gesellschaftlicher Entscheidungen teilhaben"* (Hilbert / Südmersen / Weber 1990, S. 9; die Autoren stützen sich dabei auf das Konzept „privater Regierungen" von *Schmitter* und *Streeck 1981*).

Die für den Bereich der beruflichen Bildung wichtigsten Formen nicht-etatistischer gesellschaftlicher Selbststeuerung sind nach *Schimank* und *Glagow (1984, S. 14ff.)*:

- Korporatismus: Verbandlich organisierte Interessengemeinschaften handeln (Kompromiß-)Lösungen zu gesellschaftlichen Steuerungsproblemen aus. Kollektive Vereinbarungen zwischen Arbeitgeberverbänden und Gewerkschaften bereiten staatliche Regelungen vor (Beispiel: Ordnungen von beruflichen Bildungsabschlüssen) oder treten an deren Stelle (Beispiel: tarifvertragliche Regelungen zur Umlagefinanzierung).

- Delegation: Staatliche Funktionen werden öffentlich-rechtlichen Körperschaften zur Selbststeuerung übertragen. Das für die Berufsbildung in Deutschland wichtigste Beispiel sind die Kammern als Selbstverwaltungsorgane der Wirtschaft bzw. berufsständischer Vereinigungen.

Die Formen öffentlicher Steuerung von Berufsbildungssystemen können von rein staatlicher Planung über neo-korporatistische Aushandlungsprozesse bis hin zu minimalen Interventionen von Staat oder Verbänden in die Steuerungsmechanismen des Marktes oder durch Tradition gesteuerte Handlungsfelder reichen. Die in einem nationalen Berufsbildungssystem dominierende Steuerungsform ist dessen wesentliches Charakteristikum. So sind z. B. das deutsche duale Ausbildungssystem durch einen dominierenden Einfluß nicht-etatistischer Formen verbandlicher Selbststeuerung und das schulische Ausbildungssystem Frankreichs durch eine Dominanz staatlicher Steuerung geprägt.

Akteure öffentlicher Steuerung

Die Analyse der Interessen und Politikkonzepte der maßgeblichen Akteure in der nationalen Bildungspolitik sowie der institutionellen Formen der Interessenaushandlung ist ein wichtiger Zugang zur Interpretation der Funktionsweise und Entwicklungsdynamik von Berufsbildungssystemen.

Akteure der öffentlichen Steuerung von beruflicher Bildung können sein:

- staatliche Stellen auf nationaler, regionaler und lokaler Ebene;
- Institutionen, denen der Staat bestimmte öffentliche Aufgaben übertragen hat (z. B. in Deutschland den Kammern die Akkreditierung der Ausbildungsbetriebe);
- intermediäre Organisationen, die bestimmte Rechte der Selbstverwaltung wahrnehmen (z. B. Arbeitgeberverbände und Gewerkschaften, die tarifvertragliche Regelungen aushandeln).

In den unterschiedlich gestalteten nationalen Systemen der Berufsbildung ist die Rolle des Staates und anderer Steuerungsakteure verschieden ausgeprägt. Die Kompetenzverteilung und ggf. die Formen der Zusammenarbeit und Abstimmung zwischen diesen Gruppen von Akteuren sind zentrale Merkmale der öffentlichen Steuerung eines nationalen Berufsbildungssystems. Theoretisch kann die Spannbreite der institutionalisierten

Formen von einer überwiegend zentralistischen staatlichen Steuerung bis hin zu einer weitgehend dezentralen Selbstverwaltung durch intermediäre Organisationen reichen. So steht z. B. einer staatlich-zentralistischen Entscheidungsfindung bei der Neuordnung von beruflichen Bildungsabschlüssen in Frankreich ein weitgehend auf die Sozialparteien des betreffenden Wirtschaftszweigs verlagerter Entscheidungsprozeß in Deutschland gegenüber.

Die formale Kompetenzverteilung setzt lediglich den Rahmen für das tatsächliche „Spiel" der Akteure. Eine empirische Analyse der öffentlichen Steuerung von Berufsbildungssystemen kann nicht davon ausgehen, daß die einzelnen Akteure jeweils eine einheitliche Ziel- oder Interessenausrichtung aufweisen. So agiert der Staat durch eine Vielzahl von Stellen, die auf verschiedenen Ebenen an der Steuerung der Berufsbildung beteiligt sind. Ähnliches gilt für nicht-staatliche Akteure (z. B. Sozialparteien), die ihrerseits horizontale und vertikale Untergliederungen aufweisen. Hinzu kommt, daß formale Kompetenzen und faktische Macht vielfach nicht deckungsgleich sind. Für den internationalen Vergleich der Steuerungsformen in der beruflichen Bildung genügt es deshalb z. B. nicht, die formale Verteilung von Stimmen in Entscheidungsgremien zu ermitteln.

Instrumente öffentlicher Steuerung von Berufsbildungssystemen

Die Einflußmöglichkeiten der öffentlichen Akteure werden durch die Art, Reichweite und Wirksamkeit der ihnen gesetzlich zur Verfügung stehenden Steuerungsinstrumente bestimmt. Eine wesentliches Merkmal des jeweiligen nationalen Modells der Systemsteuerung ist, in welchem Umfang bestimmte Instrumente nicht-staatlichen Akteuren für öffentliche Steuerungsfunktionen überlassen sind. Im internationalen Vergleich von Berufsbildungspolitik ist zu ermitteln, wie diese Instrumente faktisch genutzt werden.

Für die detaillierte empirische Analyse der öffentlichen Steuerung eines Berufsbildungssystems kann folgende Typologie von Steuerungsinstrumenten, welche die von *Offe (1975, S. 210ff.)* unterschiedenen Formen öffentlicher Steuerung erweitert, verwendet werden:

1   Steuerung durch Information, Beratung und Appelle
2   Steuerung durch finanzielle Anreize und Abgaben
2.1   Subventionen
2.1.1   Finanzhilfen (fiskalisch, parafiskalisch)

2.1.2 Steuervergünstigungen
2.2 Abgaben
2.2.1 Sanktionen bei „Fehlverhalten"
2.2.2 Steuern
3 Steuerung durch rechtliche Normierung der Berufsausbildung
3.1 Zugangsbedingungen für Nachfrager
3.2 Eignung von Trägern
3.3 Ausbildungsvergütung
3.4 Durchführung der Berufsausbildung (Regelungen zu Qualitätsfaktoren wie Inhalte, Organisation, Personal, Ausstattung)
3.5 Zertifizierung und Anerkennung erworbener Qualifikationen
4 Infrastrukturelle Steuerung
4.1 Investitionen in Ausbildungsinfrastruktur und in Lehrpersonal
4.2 Investitionen in Forschungs- und Planungseinrichtungen
5 Prozedurale Steuerung durch die Einrichtung von Koordinierungs- und Verhandlungssystemen
5.1 zwischen staatlichen Stellen
5.2 zwischen Verbänden
5.3 zwischen staatlichen Stellen und Verbänden

Diese Typologie beschreibt allerdings nicht ein von den nationalen Akteuren der Berufsbildungspolitik beliebig einsetzbares Set von Instrumenten. Die für die Bearbeitung von Problemen der nationalen Berufsbildung zur Verfügung stehenden Instrumente und deren Verwendungsform sind vielmehr durch das nationale Wirtschafts- und Gesellschaftssystem vorgeprägt und müssen mit der gegebenen institutionellen Struktur der beruflichen Bildung kompatibel sein. In einem Ausbildungssystem wie dem deutschen dualen System, das auf dem freiwilligen Ausbildungsplatzangebot privater Betriebe basiert, muß die Steuerung durch rechtliche Normierung zurückhaltender erfolgen als bei staatlich-schulischen Systemen. Der „Mix" und die Reichweite der jeweils eingesetzten Instrumente öffentlicher Steuerung sind letztlich das Resultat von bildungspolitischen Aushandlungsprozessen.

Für internationale Vergleiche kann die dargestellte Typologie genutzt werden, um die im Untersuchungsfeld gegebenen „Profile" öffentlicher Steuerung der beruflichen Bildung zu ermitteln. Solche Profile können z. B. gekennzeichnet sein durch: „weiche" Konzepte der Steuerung, die vor allem auf Information und Anreizen basieren; durch „regelungsorientierte" Steuerungskonzepte, die mit detaillierten Regelungen und finanziellen Sanktionen operieren; durch beteiligungsorientierte Steuerungskonzepte, die sich durch eine breite Einbeziehung von Verbänden in bildungspolitische Entscheidungen auszeichnen; oder durch „dirigistische" Konzepte, bei denen die zentralstaatliche Steuerung dominiert.

Forschungspraktische Umsetzung des Analysekonzeptes

Praktisch erprobt wurde das Konzept der gesellschaftlichen Steuerung von Berufsbildungssystemen in einem vom Autor durchgeführten Vergleich der Reaktions- und Innovationsfähigkeit des deutschen dualen und des französischen schulischen Berufsbildungssystems der neunziger Jahre. Ermittelt wurden die national- und systemspezifischen Funktionslogiken der durch unterschiedliche institutionelle Rahmenbedingungen gekennzeichneten Ausbildungssysteme bei der Steuerung der Kapazität und der Qualität des gesellschaftlichen Angebots an Berufsausbildung. Die differenziert herausgearbeiteten Reaktionsformen und Steuerungsprofile der betrachteten Ausbildungssysteme gegenüber dem sozioökonomischen Wandel können hier im einzelnen nicht dargestellt werden.[5] Hingewiesen werden soll nur auf einige systemspezifische Aspekte:

- Die Gestaltung der Ausbildungskapazität und der Ausbildungsqualität des deutschen dualen Ausbildungssystems wird in starkem Maße durch Steuerungsmechanismen des Lehrstellenmarktes beeinflußt. Das Ausbildungsangebot der Betriebe kann durch öffentliche Steuerung nur beeinflußt, nicht erzwungen werden. Die Ausbildungsfähigkeit und Ausbildungsbereitschaft einer der Ausbildungsplatznachfrage entsprechenden Zahl an Betrieben bildet eine Schranke öffentlicher Interventionen in die Ausbildungsqualität. Die Definition von Mindeststandards der betrieblichen Ausbildungsqualität überläßt der Staat deshalb weitgehend Aushandlungsprozessen zwischen den Sozialparteien.
- Das Ausbildungsplatzangebot der französischen *lycées professionnels* nach Fachrichtungen und Ausbildungsniveaus wird durch staatliche Planungsprozesse festgelegt. Neben Bedarfsabschätzungen fließen hierbei Gesichtspunkte der Auslastung der verfügbaren Ausbildungskapazitäten und der Steuerung der Schülerströme ein. Der von seiten der Sozialparteien geäußerte Bedarf an bestimmten Qualifikationen wird in Entscheidungen der staatlichen Neuordnungspolitik transformiert, die den internen Steuerungsproblemen des Schulsystems (Schaffung von Ausbildungswe-

---

5 Eine ausführliche Darstellung der Ergebnisse der Studie ist in Vorbereitung.

gen, Versorgung bestimmter Zielgruppen mit Ausbildungsplätzen u. ä.) entsprechen.
- Mit diesen systemtypischen Steuerungsformen verbunden sind jeweils spezifische Risiken von Fehlsteuerung. Beim dualen System dominiert das Risiko von „Marktversagen" gegenüber der Ausbildungsplatznachfrage. Dementsprechend waren öffentliche Programme und Maßnahmen in den letzten beiden Jahrzehnten vor allem darauf ausgerichtet, das Gesamtangebot an Lehrstellen zu steigern und Zugangsbarrieren zum Lehrstellenmarkt für marktbenachteiligte Gruppen zu reduzieren. Im Falle des schulischen Ausbildungssystems Frankreichs besteht vor allem das Risiko von „Staatsversagen" sowohl gegenüber der Ausbildungsnachfrage (Fehllenkung) als auch gegenüber dem Arbeitsmarkt (Fehlqualifizierung). Die öffentlichen Programme und Maßnahmen der französischen Berufsbildungspolitik richteten sich in der jüngeren Vergangenheit deshalb insbesondere darauf, die Reaktionsfähigkeit des schulischen Ausbildungssystems gegenüber dem Beschäftigungssystem zu verbessern.

Die durch den deutsch-französischen Vergleich gewonnenen Erkenntnisse können herangezogen werden, um die nationale Debatte über die Zukunft des dualen Systems durch eine weithin vernachlässigte Außensicht zu ergänzen. Aus der Analyse der in Frankreich vorfindbaren institutionellen Arrangements und deren Wirkungen lassen sich Hinweise auf Risiken oder Chancen von bestimmten Optionen der Strukturreform im deutschen Berufsbildungssystem gewinnen.

Bibliographie

Böhle, Fritz / Deiß, Manfred: Arbeitnehmerpolitik und betriebliche Strategien. Zur Institutionalisierung und Wirksamkeit staatlicher und kollektiver Interessendurchsetzung. Frankfurt a. M.: Campus-Verlag 1980.
Büchtemann, Christoph F. / Verdier Eric: Education and Training Regimes. Macro-Institutional Evidence. Santa Monica / Aix-en-Provence 1995 (unveröffentlichtes Typoskript).
Drexel, Ingrid: Das Ende des Facharbeiteraufstiegs? Neue mittlere Bildungs- und Karrierewege in Deutschland und Frankreich – ein Vergleich. Frankfurt a. M. u. a.: Campus-Verlag 1993a.
Drexel, Ingrid: Le segment intermédiaire des systèmes de formation en France et en République fédérale d'Allemagne. Vers un rapprochement? In: Formation Emploi, (1993b) 44, S. 3-22.
Georg, Walter: Probleme vergleichender Berufsbildungsforschung im Kontext neuer Produktionskonzepte. Das Beispiel Japan. In: Dybowski, Gisela u. a. (Hrsg.): Berufsbildung und Organisationsentwicklung, Bremen: Donat 1995, S. 67-84.
Gordon, Jean: Systeme und Verfahren der Zertifizierung von Qualifikationen in der Europäischen Gemeinschaft. Berlin: Europäisches Zentrum für die Förderung der Berufsbildung 1993.

Greinert, Wolf-Dietrich: Systeme beruflicher Bildung im internationalen Vergleich. Versuch einer Klassifizierung. In: Bundesminister für Bildung und Wissenschaft (Hrsg.): Innovative Methoden in der beruflichen Bildung (= Bildung, Wissenschaft international. 1990, 1), Bonn: BMBW 1990, S. 15-19.

Gretschmann, Klaus: Subsidiarität. Zur Ökonomik eines evolutionären Steuerungspotentials. In: Glagow, Manfred (Hrsg): Gesellschaftssteuerung zwischen Korporatismus und Subsidiarität, Bielefeld: AJZ-Verlag 1984, S. 195-221.

Hilbert, Josef / Südmersen, Helmi / Weber, Hajo: Berufsbildungspolitik. Geschichte, Organisation, Neuordnung. Opladen: Leske und Budrich 1990.

Hörner, Wolfgang: Technische Bildung und Schule. Eine Problemanalyse im internationalen Vergleich. Köln u. a.: Böhlau 1993. (Studien und Dokumentationen zur vergleichenden Bildungsforschung. 52)

Koch, Richard: Perspektiven der vergleichenden Berufsbildungsforschung im Kontext des europäischen Integrationsprozesses. In: Berufsbildung in Wissenschaft und Praxis, 20 (1991) 2, S. 14-19.

Lauterbach, Uwe: Vergleichende Berufsbildungsforschung als Bestätigung für Stereotypen? In: ders. u. a. (Hrsg.): Internationales Handbuch der Berufsbildung, Baden-Baden: Nomos-Verlagsgesellschaft 1995, S. VGL26-VGL29.

Lipsmeier, Antonius: Das System der beruflichen Bildung in der Bundesrepublik Deutschland. Seine Vor- und Nachteile im EG-Binnenmarkt. In: Arnold, Rolf / ders. (Hrsg): Betriebspädagogik in nationaler und internationaler Perspektive, Baden-Baden: Nomos-Verlagsgesellschaft 1989, S. 355-367.

Lutz, Burkart: Bildungssystem und Beschäftigungsstruktur in Deutschland und Frankreich. In: Mendius, Hans-Gerhard u. a.: Betrieb, Arbeitsmarkt, Qualifikation. Bd. 1, Frankfurt a. M.: Aspekte-Verlag 1976, S. 83-151.

Maurice, Marc: Methodologische Aspekte internationaler Vergleiche. Zum Ansatz des gesellschaftlichen Effekts. In: Heidenreich, Martin / Schmidt, Gert (Hrsg.): International vergleichende Organisationsforschung, Opladen: Westdeutscher Verlag 1991, S. 82-90.

Maurice, Marc / Sellier, François / Sylvestre, Jean-Jacques: Die Entwicklung der Hierarchie im Industrieunternehmen: Untersuchung eines gesellschaftlichen Effektes. Ein Vergleich Frankreich – Bundesrepublik Deutschland. In: Soziale Welt, 30 (1979) 3, S. 294-327.

Mitter, Wolfgang: Vergleichende Berufsbildungsforschung und Vergleichende Erziehungswissenschaft. In: Lauterbach, Uwe u. a. (Hrsg.): Internationales Handbuch der Berufsbildung, Baden-Baden: Nomos-Verlagsgesellschaft 1995, S. VGL13-VGL17.

Offe, Claus: Berufsbildungsreform. Eine Fallstudie über Reformpolitik. Frankfurt a. M.: Suhrkamp 1975. (edition suhrkamp. 761)

Schimank, Uwe / Glagow, Manfred: Formen politischer Steuerung: Etatismus, Subsidiarität, Delegation und Neokorporatismus. In: Glagow, Manfred (Hrsg.): Gesellschaftssteuerung zwischen Korporatismus und Subsidiarität, Bielefeld: AJZ-Verlag 1984, S. 4-27.

Schmitter, Philippe Charles / Streeck, Wolfgang: The Organization of Business Interests. A Proposal to Study the Associative Action of Business in the Advanced Industrial Societies of Western Europe. Berlin: Wissenschaftszentrum, International Institute of Management 1981. (Discussion paper. 1981, 13)

Streeck, Wolfgang: Staat und Verbände: Neue Fragen. Neue Antworten? In: ders. (Hrsg.): Staat und Verbände (= Politische Vierteljahresschrift. Sonderheft. 25), Opladen: Westdeutscher Verlag 1994, S. 7-34.

From Yesterday to Tomorrow: Developments in Comparative Education

Mauro Laeng

The cybernetic metaphor of the *World Wide Web* puts before us the prospect of communication without boundaries, potentially involving all mankind, collectively as well as individually. As relations between different peoples increase and exchanges multiply, large migratory flows carry millions of people to other countries. Very often, those who share race, language, habits, and customs tend to keep tight links with each other, even within the vast multicultural nations which take them in. This has occurred among Africans, Chinese, and Japanese in the United States of America as well as with Irish, Italians, and, today, Hispanics, who nonetheless maintain a separate identity as Roman Catholics or Latinos within the vast majority of WASP's (White Anglo-Saxon Protestants). Nevertheless, all have been strongly influenced by their host country. According to the „empirical three generations law", the grandchildren of the first immigrants are usually nearly completely assimilated, even if some differences and disparities persist.

This phenomenon is usually observed through the comparison of two cultures, that of origin and that of reception. On a continental scale the problem is more complex. In America there are cultures which share large common traditions, such as the English, the Spanish, and the Portuguese. On the other hand, Europe is a mosaic of nations and languages. Immigrants from countries outside the European Community are confronted by a dozen different groups. (I have tried to disentangle the problem in a recent book, cf. *Laeng 1995*). In Asia there are not only many ethnic groups, but also strong tensions, which make a complete blending difficult, as we can see in Iran, Afghanistan, Pakistan, and India, and in Southeast Asia. The giant China counts at least a score of ethnic groups in its interior, some of them large, such as the Tibetans, Mongolians, and Manchus. Vast areas show a risky particularism, outweighed only for economic and political reasons by the necessity of using vehicular languages. These are no longer commercial pidgins, but widespread international languages.

This situation can only be intensified in the near future. Social classes which are culturally and economically active in the next century will rely on widespread bilingualism or trilingualism. In some European countries (the Netherlands, Switzerland, the

Czechoslovakian region, Hungary), speaking two or more languages, besides one's mother tongue and English, is already common. Meanwhile, English has become the preferred language of scientific and technological communication as well as for all air and sea lines, and is gaining ground in banking and commerce. The mastery of two or more languages is not merely useful; it also triggers chain reactions which can bring people closer to each other.

First Phase: The Forerunners and Global Comparisons

Comparative education studies are born from a rib of the history of education and of educational institutions, adding a new „synchronic" perspective of transversal comparison of the present reality to the traditional „diachronic", or longitudinal perspective. Comparative law and statistics have contributed to the establishment of the discipline. Today it must cope with new problems: on the one side with those of advanced educational research, which shares contributions from psychology and sociology; and on the other side with those of international, interracial, and interreligious policies. It is being transformed from a „quiet" field to a non-neutral ground for dramatic confrontations.

In general, comparative studies in several fields (linguistic, philological, literary, historical, and juridical) have largely preceded educational studies. The comparison of civilisations had long fascinated the Enlighteners, who found in it arguments to relativise the absolutist claims of Eurocentrism, and to affirm a universal vision of man. The Romantics found suggestions for research into what the Germans call the *Geist,* or characteristic, of each people or nation. Georg Wilhelm Friedrich Hegel took his cue, painting vast canvases of historical epochs, even if the traits are slightly forced. The syntheses of Wilhelm Dilthey and Ernst Cassirer, or the comparative portraits of civilisations by Arnold J. Toynbee are freer.

We could say that was a preliminary and introductory phase to comparative studies in general, i. e., the phase of a global confrontation among syntheses of civilisations. Thus, the history of a country or a nation was studied as a „whole" from an „idiographic" point of view. As a consequence, „pedagogy" as such did not emerge, but an entire culture was qualified. An example of this kind was the „Germania" by Publius Cornelius Tacitus, and much later „De l'Allemagne" by Madame de Staël, and more specific the „Rapport sur l'état de l'instruction publique dans quelques pays de l'Allemagne" by Victor Cousin.

Sometimes these are philosophers' reflections on a period of their own country's history, as in the „History of England" by David Hume, and Voltaire's „Histoire de siècle de Louis XIV". Sometimes they are studies by professional writers of historiography, such as Thomas Macaulay and George M. Trevelyan for England, or Adolphe Thiers, Jules Michelet, Henri Lefebvre, Georges Duby for France; or the works of Leopold von Ranke for Germany. Some are the reflection of economists, as in „Modern Capitalism" by Werner Sombart, or of art historians, as in the „History of the Arts in Greece" by Johann Joachim Winckelmann, or „The Civilisation of Renaissance in Italy" by Jakob Burckhardt, and the studies by Bernhard Berenson.

In short, a comparative study of education among the patterns of culture of two or more peoples must carve out a niche for itself from a broader body. The hinterland of comparative studies is endless, and takes contributions from all areas of culture. The study of languages suggested lines of enquires, for example the work about „The Heterogeneity of Language and Its Influence upon the Intellectual Development of Mankind" by Wilhelm von Humboldt. Later, ethnolinguistics and sociolinguistics treated interesting observations in this line, as in Franz Boas's and Bronislaw Malinowski's work, and even more in that of Edward Sapir and Benjamin Whorf. But the very first strictly „technical" approach to comparative education came from Marc Antoine *Jullien* de Paris (1817) and Friedrich *Thiersch* (1838).

New Institutions

After these early forerunners, comparative education did not receive due attention quickly from Italian educationists, with the praiseworthy exception of Aristide Gabelli and Adolfo Pick, but rather from politicians, jurists and statisticians. The first pedagogical research trips from Italy were promoted in the last decades of the 19th century by the ministers of Public Instruction, Ruggero Bonghi and Pasquale Villari. The first deserves to be remembered also for having founded the *Museo dell'Istruzione*, then the *Museo Pedagogico*, which collected the material sent to the international EXPO in Vienna in 1873. The same museum still exists today under the name of *Museo Storico della Didattica*; it has a provisional seat in the Department of Sciences of Education of the Third University of Rome, and it has been directed by myself for the last ten years. It contains valuable collections of documents on education in Europe which straddle two centuries as well as documents on Maria Montessori, and on the activities of the *Ente per le Scuole dei Contadini dell'Agro Romano e delle Paludi Pontine*, where at the beginning of the new century illiteracy and malaria were fought at this same time.

In the last half of the 19th century, several national structures, with international goals, were born in Zurich, Geneva, Paris, London, Berlin, Frankfurt, Brussels and Amsterdam. More recent institutions are the *Fondation Européenne de la Culture*, born in Holland but developed in other European and American countries; UNESCO's *International Institute for Educational Planning* (IIEP) and OECD's *Centre for Educational Research and Innovation* (CERI) in Paris, which promote inquiries into innovation. In this volume we celebrate in particular the activity of the *Deutsches Institut für Internationale Pädagogische Forschung* (DIPF) in Frankfurt am Main, founded by the Land of Hesse and supported by federal financing, which under the direction of Professor Dr. Wolfgang Mitter has long been the centre best informed about the educational reality of Eastern Europe.

We should also mention the *International Association for the Evaluation of Educational Achievement* (IEA), which aims to compare school results world-wide. It has been steered by Thorsten Husén and Neville T. Postlethwaite, with the contribution of Benjamin S. Bloom, Gilbert de Landsheere, Aldo Visalberghi and many others. I myself have been co-ordinator of research for Italy. The organisation has had active centres in Stockholm, Liège, London, New York, Sydney, Vancouver, and Frascati near Rome.

In this century in Italy the *Biblioteca di Documentazione Pedagogica*, founded by Giovanni Calò, then directed by Enzo Petrini, has been especially active in Florence; and the *Centro Europeo dell'Educazione*, which has long been directed by Giovanni Gozzer and then by Aldo Visalberghi, has been active at Villa Falconieri in Frascati. Twenty IRRSAE (*Istituti Regionali di Ricerca Sperimentale Aggiornamento Educativi,* regional institutes, mainly for in-service education of teachers) have worked towards applied goals, as well as the Office for Foreign Relations of Public Instruction directed by Antonio Augenti. Of course, some universities are also active in comparative studies, such as Rome, Milan, Bologna, Florence, Padua, Trent and Cosenza. In Bari, Lecce, and Catania keen attention is paid to Albania and the Maghreb.

Second Phase: Statistics and Documentation

The first phase, philosophically and historically inspired, was followed by a second, concerned with the observation of facts from a descriptive and quantitative standpoint.

The activity of the first international organisations was crucial; they stressed the importance of efficient statistical systems and documentation offices. The project was not easily affordable, given the irreducible differences among the school systems of different countries, and of regions and districts within countries, even as regards raw numerical data, gathered under heterogeneous criteria in various places.

Highly accurate statistics with a detailed disaggregation of data were kept in the old kingdom of Prussia, later absorbed into the second Reich. On the other hand, the international *Institute of Statistics* founded in London in 1885 had the huge task of accounting for all the English-speaking countries in five continents. After the first World War, from 1926 on, the „International Statistical Year-Book" began to be issued regularly by the League of Nations. In Italy the *Istituto Centrale di Statistica (*ISTAT, Central Institute of Statistics*)* was established in 1926 under a law which stipulated that all official data flow to it, with the aim of ensuring unification and standardisation. It publishes its own Yearbook, „Annuario dell'Istruzione in Italia" and several special monographs.

Eventually, the adoption of structured schedules and questionnaires on a world-wide scale, regularly sent to all governments, proposed by the *International Bureau of Education* (IBE) in Geneva since 1925, deserves the merit for starting up the first systematic gathering of data in accordance with common grids. It was a first step towards overcoming the „babel" of codes and criteria, aiming at a conceptual unification. Unfortunately, machine processing of punched cards (aside from commercial purposes) was only at its beginning. The impact of „mechanisation" on research methods was as yet limited; at that time the computer era had not yet begun. Nevertheless, the choices were already in the right direction. Anyway, from 1933 onward, the thematic „Annuaire International d'Éducation" of the same Bureau, edited by Pedro Rosselló, presented the results for over sixty countries, the number of which increased over the years. Especially important was volume VII of 1939, the last one before the war broke out and publication was cancelled for six years. Traditionally the IBE publications like those of other international organisations were issued both in English and in French.

The rest is relatively recent, and I shall refrain from repeating it. The Society of Nations after World War I and Unesco after World War II, have actively fostered cultural co-operation and published international outlines and surveys of research.

Third Phase: Problems of Development and Planning

Contributions with a new slant appeared in the course of years from economic organisations, such as the *Organisation for Economic Co-operation and Development* (OECD). Its first „Education Statistics Yearbook" dates back to 1974. Important OECD monographs are relevant to secondary school and university reforms. Italians recall that in 1970 on the impetus of the OECD, a meeting was convened in Frascati in order to debate the general reform of upper secondary schools (this work has unfortunately been protracted for political reasons up to the present), laying the famous „ten points" as cornerstones for reforms. This is an important example of how comparative studies can influence policies; this actually means that such studies have not been „neutral" or indifferent, but can give decision makers food for thought.

The *European Economic Community* (EEC) in Brussels and the *Council of Europe* (CE) in Strasbourg have also issued large volumes on „L'éducation en Europe" since 1964. Moreover, even organisations which were founded for military defence purposes, such as the *Western European Union* (WEU) and the *North Atlantic Treaty Organisation* (NATO), have assigned a part of their efforts to support scientific research and integration, assistance and mobility of students.

After the first statistic surveys, systematically pursued to follow-up and outline dynamic trends, and the beginning of documentation services, a new phase, contemporary with the establishment of many of these institutions, was constituted by anticipatory projections and forecasts through more or less „futurologic" extrapolations, useful for long range planning. Attention to economic and social forecasting became required as a consequence of the deep modifications that came to pass in the European population, following three big orders of facts, which have posed as many challenges:

1. *External and internal migration* from the 1950s onward, to the industrialised and metropolitan areas of developed countries.
2. The rapid *demographic transition,* which jeopardises all forecast of gradual development in Africa, Asia and Latin America, while in Europe there is a trend to falling birth rates (especially in Italy) and a contemporary prolongation of the average lifespan, so that the aged outnumber the young.
3. *Technological innovations*, which make available more goods and services, giving rise to a consumer mentality and producing big developments but *no jobs,* or at least very few of them. „Robotics" in industry oust many unqualified workers from their

jobs, in turn they cannot be absorbed in the service economy, due to the contemporary development of „Burotics", i. e. office automation. In this way the withdrawal of manpower from agriculture, and its transfer first to industry and later to clerical work has lost its power of compensation, to the detriment of those who are waiting for their first job, with after-effects of demotivation and frustration.

Today we must ponder the conviction that the „epochal" solution to the main problems of mankind will be confronted without further delay with starvation and poverty, and then inequality and ignorance. Great efforts are needed to give substantial support to the poorest countries, without demanding returns in a stingy neo-colonialist manner. The present unbalanced surplus must be reallocated. Any future planning cannot be separated from the guarantee of world peace.

These forces urged us to redesign the profile of training in schools. The „dual" model is typical of German-speaking countries (a sharp split between general academic courses and technical-vocational ones). This has been opposed by the French model of „maximal initial continuity" for all, even if structured in branches. Italy, beginning as a unitary state little more than a century ago, has made tremendous progress, and is now attracted by the latter model, interpreted in an empirical and simplistic way. As a consequence, we now have a rather messy scholastic yield, with a high waste of resources, an increase of dropouts, and maladjustment to the labour-market. As for planning, Italy simply has a lack of planning.

The modified internal equilibrium of the population, resulting from an unrestrainable stream of entering non-Europeans, second only to the historical migrations of the second to the fifth century across the borders of the ancient Roman empire, has led to pressing confrontations, frictions, difficulties in integration and assimilation, especially when the differences are more pronounced, for instance when aggravated by different religions. Interculturalism and international co-operation, assistance to refugees, and the protection of children are becoming of impelling necessity all over the world. Even the „white man's burden" of Victorian times has radically changed.

A big tragedy, which has overshadowed all the above mentioned hardships, has been the rekindling of hotbeds of war, caused after decades and often centuries of rivalries which we wrongly believed had been appeased. These have paradoxically been made worse by facts perceived as positive ones, such as the waning of the colonial dominance and then by the fall of the Soviet Union and its satellites. Substantially deep conflicts are provoked by the intermingled economic, political and religious interests of many different ethnic groups, which carry differences to the point of terrorism, and do not hesitate to employ the most ferocious forms of genocide and slaughter of their so-called „enemies", as in Bosnia and in Ruanda.

These facts of unprecedented gravity confront educators with serious questions. The sense of belonging to a social group has always been considered an irreversible *value*, descending from the tradition of families and religion, which have given substance to patriotism and allegiance. These same values, misinterpreted, have now hurled peoples against peoples with devastating violence. Bertrand Russell once wrote that „nothing has caused as much evil to mankind, as religion and patriotism", when they are not tempered by healthy relativism, which can inspire comprehension and tolerance. Fanaticism is bred in schools as a natural consequence of dogmatism, absolutism, nationalism, and chauvinism.

Comparative education, which compares different cultures, should offer a *forum* where all diversities can be turned to good account. The international organisations exist in a peaceful environment only. The churches will not betray their true mission if they abandon aggressive proselytism and devote themselves to the service of the weakest people, refusing to become *instrumentum regni* of the strongest. After the last wars, reconstruction, material, civil and moral, will require a big effort for decades, and education will be called upon to perform a task more difficult than ever.

The concept of education is broader than that of school. Therefore an association of comparative education such as the *Comparative Education Society in Europe* (CESE) must take note of these transformations, which mark in a real and not merely rhetorical manner the end of our second millennium. The revolution in the labour market and in the world of information must be taken into account. Moreover, the time has come to comprehend in a broader sense other cultures, in Asia, Africa, South America etc., for which the past millenniums have been far more than two. Present challenges and multiculturalism offer CESE a variegated picture which cannot be judged from an outdated point of view with the same yardstick as the comparisons of school systems.

Developments in Italy: From IEA to SICESE

An important turning point for the growth of a comparative attitude in Italy was the participation in the international studies of the *International Association for the Evaluation of Educational Achievement* (IEA) since the end of 1960s on the school outcomes in many subjects at the ages of 10, 14 and 19 (that is at the end of our elementary, middle, and secondary school). The research was carried out under the responsibility of Luigi Meschieri and Aldo Visalberghi. My own job was technical management. More than twenty countries in different continents took part in the comparison for the first time in 1970. The studies have since been repeated and widened.

On that occasion, scientific committees were set up with the co-operation of the best specialists. In Italy something like 4.000 teachers and 32.000 students were involved. The work with educationists, psychologists, and statisticians in universities and at the *Consiglio Nazionale delle Ricerche* (CNR, National Research Council) furthered a fruitful co-operation. IEA carried on its interdisciplinary activity in later years at the *Centro Nazionale per le Tecnologie Educative* (CNITE, National Centre for Educational Technologies) and then at the *Centro Europeo dell'Educazione* (CEDE, European Centre of Education) in Frascati near Rome, both chaired by Aldo Visalberghi with the assistance of myself. IEA testing instruments have been used in the following years to assess the results of experimental schools, and to follow up research on students qualified in secondary schools. Today, the inheritance of IEA should be taken in hand by a new public agency in order to manage a „National System of Evaluation".

For my own part, I believe that the importance of IEA goes beyond that of a noteworthy international survey which has been going on for about thirty years. As I said at the extraordinary Conference held in Garda for the XXVth anniversary of CESE, the introduction of the IEA techniques of comparative evaluation through transversally homogeneous instruments has marked a turning point in the methodology of these studies, launching the phase of a comparative „observational-experimental" pedagogy. It evaluates the reaction of different populations to identical tests, previously elaborated and settled in agreement by scientific committees of different countries, so that a *common basis of reference* is possible. Nothing similar was done before, and very little has been done since.

The same central unit that directed the work of IEA has edited an „International Encyclopedia of Education", followed by another „Encyclopedia of Comparative Education".

At the same time I have been the editor of an Italian „*Enciclopedia Pedagogica*" *(Laeng 1989-1994)* in six volumes, to which nearly 500 authors have contributed. It devotes much space to comparative education and foreign systems.

After that, I have also been editor of another, easier to handle, co-operative work entitled „*Atlante della Pedagogìa" (Laeng 1993)*, which includes a world survey by Sandra Chistolini. At present, a group led by Anna Baldazzi, is working at CEDE in Frascati on a new „European Lexicon of Education", in many languages, beginning with Greek and Latin. Among the contributors are Italians, Germans, French, English and Spanish.

The SICESE *(Sezione Italiano della CESE,* the Italian Section of CESE) nucleus in Italy, founded by CESE members, has good connections with other pedagogical associations; the oldest one is *Associazione Pedagogica Italiana* (ASPEI), apolitical and non-denominational, which dates back to the last century and includes all types and grades of school. More recent are the *Società Italiana di Pedagogia* (SIPED) with a university related layout; furthermore the *Società Italiana di Ricerca Didattica* (SIRD) and the *Centro di Ricerche sulla Storia dell'Educazione* (CIRSE). Good connections are also maintained with the *Association Européenne des Enseignants* (AEDE) and the *Association for Teacher Education in Europe* (ATEE). It is not difficult to recognise the underpinning of particular groups of disciplines in each society. Of course, the teachers of Philosophy, History, Literature, Fine Arts, Foreign Languages, Mathematics, Physics, Biology, Geography etc. all have their own associations, which very often have active relations abroad and participate in exchanges.

Among the more recent initiatives of international co-operation we should also mention the *Centro Mediterraneo di Educazione* (CEME) created in Sicily as a result of an Italo-Arab Colloquium in 1992, and the *Consortium of the Mediterranean Universities* in Bari/Lecce. Particular links of co-operation are planned with Albania. In the last four centuries many Albanians have sought refuge in Italy, and in the south there are areas where an Albanian culture is preserved. New tides of immigrants are now pushed overseas in search for a better life.

Comparative Education Tomorrow

The latest developments in comparative education studies have allowed a critical rethinking of its subjects and methods, and a general reflection of the „epistemological" position in the social sciences and especially within the sciences of education and of training („formazione").

The information which forms the basis of these studies is on the eve of great events. The „net of nets" that by now envelops the whole world makes it possible to communicate in real time at lower and lower cost. Thus, old data bases do not become completely obsolete, but are swallowed up, recycled, and re-employed by broader systems, open to all, on-line. Perhaps in the future a programmed selective casting into oblivion of old bulks will be necessary. Right now, behemoth mass memories can gobble increasing amounts of data. Evolving query-languages are facilitated by the critical work of assigning descriptors which can be criss-crossed to perform a set-intersection inquiry following a Boolean logic. The introductory phase to all studies, which was difficult and time-consuming a few years ago, is now easier: more time and resources are freed for more intelligent work.

The new perspectives of electronic and automatic information have to be considered as something more than merely instrumental media, as they offer opportunities and facilities for new contacts and dialogues. The comparative studies can discover terrific possibilities in the world net. Documentation networks such as ERIC or EUDISED can be revolutionised. Every national society must have its e-mail address, and eventually an Internet site; the fast circulation of data should become a daily habit. Each association should also act as a clearinghouse of information for all others, in conformity to a plan of organised co-operation. Today, it is even easy to draw a synoptic spread-sheet comparing the contemporary evolution of different countries, pointing to relevant indicators. Publishing statistics, which up to now were paced according to a three-year period of latency (one year for the facts, one year for collecting and elaborating the data, one year for publishing and disseminating them), can be speeded up; it is not crazy to imagine having school data available nearly in real time, like those of the stock exchange.

In approaching this goal, many scholars who are looking forward are getting ready. The recent translations into Italian of two fundamental works by *Schriewer / Holmes (1995)* and by *Lê Thành Khôi (1996)* edited by Giovanni Pampanini cast a new light on some problems and on some better standardised methodologies. Both the theoretical background of so-called human sciences, and the instruments of observation and elaboration are up-to-date. Comparative education is no longer an appendix to studies on school legislation or applied statistics; instead it is a strong branch of the sciences of education, which promises better international comprehension and co-operation.

Bibliography

Jullien, Marc Antoine: Esquisse et vues préliminaires d'un ouvrage sur l'éducation comparée. Paris: Colas 1817. [Facsimile reprint: Genève: Bureau International d'Education 1992]
Laeng, Mauro (ed.): Enciclopedia pedagogica. Vol. 1-6. Brescia: Editrice La Scuola 1989-1994.
Laeng, Mauro (ed.): Atlante della pedagogìa. Vol. 1-3. Napoli: Edizioni Tecnodid 1993.
Laeng, Mauro: Identità e contraddizioni d'Europa. Roma: Editrice Studium 1995.
Lê Thân Khôi: L'éducation. Cultures et sociétés. Paris: Publications de la Sorbonne 1991. [Italian translation: L'educazione. Cultura e società. Catania: Latessa 1996]
Schriewer, Jürgen / Holmes, Brian (eds.): Theories and Methods in Comparative Education. Frankfurt a. M. et al.: Lang 1988. (Komparatistische Bibliothek. 1) [Italian translation of the 3rd German edition, 1992: Educazione comparata. Teorie e metodi. Catania: Cooperativa Universitaria Editrice Catanese Magistero 1995]
Thiersch, Friedrich: Über den gegenwärtigen Zustand des öffentlichen Unterrichts in den westlichen Staaten von Deutschland, in Holland, Frankreich und Belgien. Th. 1-3. Stuttgart et al.: Cotta 1838.

Comment envisager et prendre en compte la culture d'un système éducatif ?

Jean-Michel Leclercq

Comme on le rappelle souvent, tout propos relatif à la culture expose aux ambiguïtés et aux déceptions faute de pouvoir prétendre, après tant de tentatives infructueuses, proposer de la notion une définition qui ne suscite pas des réserves à cause de son excessive généralité ou au contraire de son champ d'application trop limité.

Toutefois, si diverses et si problématiques que puissent être les conceptions de la culture, il s'avère qu'elles retiennent toujours deux caractéristiques qui se relient au domaine de l'éducation. D'abord, comme le disait déjà Taylor, en incluant „les savoirs, les croyances, les arts, la morale, les lois, les coutumes et les autres capacités acquises par l'homme" *(Berthier 1996, p. 47)*, elle fixe naturellement des objectifs à l'éducation et les légitimise. Ensuite, comme y a insisté en particulier Parsons, la culture est toujours faite pour être transmise et apprise; même si d'autres interventions sont décisives à cet égard comme celles de la famille ou de la société dans son ensemble, les écoles ont donc aussi un rôle déterminant. On comprend ainsi que dans une société le lien entre sa culture et l'éducation qui s'y trouve dispensée apparaisse toujours comme une évidence presque banale.

On a cependant intérêt à éclaircir les fondements de cette évidence et surtout ses implications si l'on souhaite approfondir la nature et les formes de la relation invoquée notament en ce qui concerne les influences qu'exercent ou subissent ses termes.

L'une de ces implications est que l'éducation donnée dans une société est supposée pratiquement indissociable de sa culture. Or ce que l'on pourrait prendre au premier abord comme une simple variante de l'évidence initiale introduit en fait de nouvelles dimensions et de nouveaux problèmes. Une relation indissociable sous-entend entre ses deux éléments un rapport très étroit à propos duquel on évite difficilement de se demander ce qu'il comporte de sujétion réciproque ou unilatérale. En d'autres termes se pose la question de savoir si l'éducation se trouve totalement soumise à la culture de la société et si toute démarche qui l'oublierait ne ferait pas abstraction d'un des aspects les plus essentiels.

L'éducation comparée devant la culture de la société

C'est bien l'impression que l'on ressent devant les diverses approches envisagées par l'éducation comparée. Beaucoup d'entre elles font une place majeure à la culture de la société quand il s'agit d'expliquer l'organisation et le fonctionnement des systèmes éducatifs. Quant à celles qui entendent constituer l'éducation en champ plus autonome, il est rare qu'elles accomplissent entièrement leur projet.

On le vérific en se reportant aux „modèles d'analyse" ou aux „perspectives" qu'Antonio *Novoa (1995)* identifie en éducation comparée. Dans la perspective „historiciste", il va de soi qu'une place prépondérante est accordée à la culture de la société car, comme le pensait Isaac Leon Kandel, *„L'objectif est de bien cerner les raisons sociales, économiques ou culturelles qui expliquent les formes d'organisation de l'enseignement adoptées par les divers pays"* (ibid., p. 29). Il n'en va guère autrement dans la „perspective socio-historique" où la primauté donnée à l'interprétation historique par Novoa lui-même, Schriewer ou Peyrera conduit à *„privilégier des contextes définis selon l'invisibilité des pratiques discursives qui lui donnent sens"* (ibid., p. 40), c'est-à-dire par certaines des tendances les plus profondes de la culture sociale qui sont ses démarches intellectuelles prédominantes. Même si cette perspective tend à se situer dans l'optique d'un système mondial, elle conduit davantage à mettre en question l'idée de culture nationale qu'à se détacher d'une prise en compte des cultures des sociétés dont les processus de diffusion retiennent alors particulièrement l'attention comme chez Schriewer. Dans les autres „configurations" proposées par Novoa, le recours à la culture de la société comme facteur explicatif de l'organisation ou du fonctionnement du système éducatif ne semble plus s'avérer indispensable. L'objectif généralement affiché est en effet d'appréhender ce système dans des modalités et des processus qui doivent être abordés en eux-mêmes de manière à constituer un objet de connaissance scientifique par lui-même. On est toutefois en droit d'estimer que dans la majorité des cas, la référence à la culture de la société demeure largement implicite ou qu'elle est même réintroduite formellement. Dans les perspectives „positivistes" qu'ont illustrées Noah ou Epstein ou dans les „perspectives de la modernisation" en faveur dans les instances internationales, il ne s'agit pas seulement d'offrir le choix entre les scénarios les plus pertinents mais aussi d'aider à l'adoption de la politique éducative la plus adéquate. Mais, comme le laisse entendre Novoa, comment se décider pour celle-ci en oubliant la „différence des contextes" où celle des cultures ne saurait être mise entre parenthèses. C'est de celle-ci que reste encore bien conscient „l'approche de résolution de problèmes", telle qu'elle a été pratiquée par Holmes cherchant à établir des lois sociologiques qui, selon Epstein, mettent en rapport des *„institutions éducationnelles socio-économiques et politiques"* *(ibid., p. 34)* dans lesquelles se retrouve tout l'impact de la culture de la société. Quant à la dernière perspective envisagée par Novoa, la „perspective critique", de manière assez analogue avec ce qui se passe dans la perspective socio-historique ou celle du système mondial, elle opère moins un revirement qu'un nouvel éclairage en substituant à une culture du consensus une culture du conflit dont il convient de recenser les manifestations notamment par des enquêtes ethnographiques et sociologiques dans les établissements d'enseignement.

Il n'est donc guère douteux que les travaux d'éducation comparée confortent dans l'idée d'un lien intrinsèque et particulièrement fort entre la culture d'une société et son système éducatif. Mais il n'est guère douteux non plus que ces travaux accréditent aussi l'impression d'un modelage du système éducatif par la culture de la société. On ne doit pas non plus oublier, c'est peut être un point trop peu abordé par Novoa, que lorsqu'un certain dynamisme est reconnu au système éducatif, c'est surtout celui de reprendre la culture dominante au plan national ou au plan mondial. Les adeptes de l'école comme lieu de la reproduction sociale ou de la théorie de la dépendance ne se sont pas privés de le souligner. Bref tout se passe comme si un système éducatif n'avait que par procuration une culture qui lui viendrait de la société et qui pour cette raison serait trop anémique ou pas assez originale pour qu'on l'envisage autrement que comme un reflet de celle-ci.

L'autonomie de la culture d'un système éducatif

Il ne manque pourtant pas d'indices pour s'interroger sur le bien fondé de ce point de vue.

On sait bien que les écoles n'échapent pas à l'obligation de transmettre des valeurs ou des connaissances qu'elles ne choisissent pas. Elles appartiennet la plupart du temps à des systèmes nationaux d'éducation qui ont été créés par des États soucieux de faire prévaloir des options politiques ou économiques. Quand celles-ci ont moins de prégnance, comme c'est souvent le cas aujourd'hui, dans la société civile ou les milieux éconimiques des porte-parole ou des groupes de pression formulent des exigences quant aux attitudes ou aux savoirs à inculquer. Toutefois les écoles s'acquittent de cette obligation avec une marge d'autonomie qui n'est pas niable en procédant à des réorientations ou en effectuant des décalages.

C'est ce qui a d'abord conduit à parler d'une culture scolaire considérée souvent comme une dégradation de la „vraie" culture mais également comme une version nécessaire pour que l'éducation remplisse ses fonctions. Or cette version est loin de ne résulter que d'influences subies. A des problèmes qui peuvent bien lui être posés d'ailleurs, elle apporte des réponses élaborées selon des critères et des lignes de force qui lui sont propres. On constate en particulier que les diverses disciplines scolaires ne sont pas calquées sur les divers secteurs de la connaissance „scientifique". Tant par leur découpage que par leur teneur, elles sont des reconstructions parfois méconnaissables de ceux-ci qui observent des codes bien particuliers relatifs à la définition de savoirs scolaires dont on peut contester l'opportunité ou la validité mais pas la spécificité *(Qu'est-ce qu'un programme d'enseignement? 1994)*. Ces élaborations ont leur origine et leur justification dans le souci d'adapter les contenus et les niveaux des enseignements aux besoins des élèves concernés. Mais ils ont aussi leur logique propre qui explique les résistances qu'elles opposent souvent à des remises en question qui seraient pourtant justifiées par la nécessité de réviser les connaissances à offrir ou par des préoccupations d'innovation pédagogique, les sollicitations de la culture de la société étant bien visibles dans les deux cas.

On peut se demander si le même phénomène ne se constate pas à propos des messages que la culture scolaire est chargée de transmettre pour relayer les mots d'ordre émanant d'un supposé consensus culturel ou politique. Par exemple la substitution de mythologies nationales aux connaissances historiques avérées a souvent révélé une capacité de l'école à faire preuve d'un zèle singulier et redoutable. C'est aussi ce qui s'est produit jadis avec la transformation de l'étude de la religion en catéchisme ou plus récemment dans l'univers soviétique, avec l'étude du marxisme devenue la vulgate des cours de matérialisme dialectique. Il y a là de nombreuses instigations à penser que la culture scolaire n'est pas un simple décalque de la culture de la société dont elle peut se démarquer y compris par des surenchères.

Ce sont sans doute les études sur le fonctionnement des premiers cycles intégrés[1] introduits dans le cadre des grandes réformes lancées à partir des années 60 qui ont le mieux mis en évidence le poids de cette culture scolaire et surtout signalé sa capacité de résistance à des évolutions pourtant supposées correspondre à des changements interve-

---

1 Nous pensons bien entendu aux travaux de *Hargreaves (1982)* et de *Forquin (1989)* sur la Comprehensive School britannique, mais aussi à ceux de *Van Haecht (1985)* sur le rénové belge, de *Demailly (1991)* sur le collège français ou de *Ball / Larsson (1989)* sur la Grundskola suédoise.

nus ou souhaités dans la société et sa culture. Les nouvelles structures se révélaient ne pas être l'instrument de démocratisation et d'innovation qu'on avait imaginé parce qu'y survivaient des pratiques inspirées par toute une culture sous-jacente continuant de régir dans un „curriculum caché" les objectifs de la formation, les comportements des enseignants ou les choix réels des responsables administratifs. La culture scolaire rimait ainsi fortement avec tradition et conservatisme. Mais surtout elle affichait sa prégnance en apparaissant comme un ensemble de conceptions et de pratiques qui était géré comme un patrimoine même s'il avait pu se constituer à l'origine par des emprunts à la culture dominante de la société environnante comme les profils de compétence souhaitables et la proportion à prévoir pour chacun d'entre eux.

On doit aussi constater que l'appropriation de ces emprunts n'a pas cessé de s'affirmer dans des dispositifs d'éducation qui fonctionnaient comme des systèmes produisant leurs propres effets en particulier à travers leurs structures pédagogiques.

Comme y insistent les analyses qui soulignent leur rôle comme facteurs de la reproduction sociale, celles-ci répercutent bien soit la volonté de maintenir les clivages sociaux existants soit l'intention plus ou moins réelle de les atténuer. Toutefois, les parallélismes envisageables entre l'organisation sociale et l'organisation pédagogique sont toujours relatifs et il est remarquable à cet égard que dans l'enseignement secondaire de premier cycle, ce ne soit pas seulement la suppression des filières qui donne lieu à des distorsions. Leur maintien en vaut tout autant. Ni le profil ni la fréquentation des filières ne peuvent être rapportées strictement à des catégories sociales bien précises. Le modèle tripartite allemand est loin de correspondre terme à terme aux seules „classes" identifiables dans la société et dans chaque type d'établissement se trouvent représentées les diverses catégories socio-professionnelles même si certaines d'entre elles prédominent. En outre la faveur croissante dont bénéficie le Gymnasium peut s'expliquer tout autant par la volonté de promotion sociale qui anime certaines couches de la population que par l'image de marque du Gymnasium comme lieu où pourraient s'acquérir des connaissances plus larges et plus solides. Il est donc bien visible que joue un effet de système. Sans doute n'élimine-t-il pas les conséquences de la diversification ségrégative adoptée au départ mais il leur donne une autre portée *(Max-Planck-Institut für Bildungsforschung. Arbeitsgruppe Bildungsbericht 1994, pp. 483ss.)*. Il paraissait notamment inévitable que l'existence des trois filières très hiérarchisées pousse à délaisser les moins prestigieuses au profit des autres. Ce mouvement n'est certes pas étranger au souci d'élévation du niveau d'instruction qui anime une partie de la population. Mais il est généré aussi par l'organisation pédagogique dans la mesure où celle-ci en tant que telle, tout en étant fondée sur des orientations précoces et autoritaires, tolérait ou même invitait à des choix plus ambitieux à cause de sa polymorphie. C'est le phénomène inverse qui a joué en France dans les années 50 quand le clivage rigoureux entre le secondaire et le primaire supérieur a commencé à disparaître: l'unicité croissante du dispositif a freiné ou tout au moins perturbé les classes moyennes dans leur recherche d'une instruction plus poussée pour leurs enfants *(Prost 1992)*. Leur élan ne reprendra guère que dans les années 80 quand la pluralité des voies du deuxième cycle du secondaire les stimulera de nouveau à condition d'avoir triomphé de l'étape du collège unique du premier cycle. L'engouement pour le baccalauréat d'enseignement général rappellera celui pour le Gymnasium en Allemagne.

Même en se limitant à ces quelques exemples, on a de bonnes raisons de penser qu'avec la culture attribuable à un système éducatif, on se trouve peut-être devant une sous-culture de la société mais que celle-ci, comme tout sous-système de type parsonien, n'en présente pas moins des caractéristiques dans ses manières de réagir aux situations qu'elle doit affronter et gérer.

Quelle spécificité pour la culture d'un système éducatif?

D'après ces exemples, il est toutefois aussi plausible de considérer qu'on peut adopter dans l'analyse de cette culture des démarches assez différentes dans leur teneur et dans leurs aboutissements. Quand on se concentre sur les effets de système, on reste au niveau de fonctionnements institutionnels ou pédagogiques et des comportements individuels ou collectifs qu'ils suscitent. Au contraire, quand on se consacre à l'examen des répercussions imputables à la culture scolaire sur le déroulement des enseignements, on se propose surtout de dévoiler et de reconstituer un implicite. Dans ce cas la spécificité qu'on vise à mettre en lumière est créditée du fort pouvoir explicatif d'une transcendance. Dans l'autre cas, cette spécificité reste immanente à des stratégies qui ne permettent pas toujours de la déchiffrer clairement et qui la rendent parfois incertaine et en tout cas plus difficile à définir. En d'autres termes on a d'un côté le risque d'une tentation essentialiste qui s'en remettrait volontiers à des intuitions comme „l'esprit" d'un système éducatif et de l'autre le danger d'une simple approche descriptive dans laquelle pourraient être accusées de se cantonner maintes entreprises de sociologie et d'ethnographie de l'éducation.

Une synthèse ou tout au moins un recours simultané aux deux modalités d'analyse semble la seule issue pour éviter de s'en tenir à une interprétation plus suggestive qu'opérante de la culture d'un système éducatif ou à l'ambition d'un inventaire exhaustif de ses manifestations pratiquement irréalisable.

Dans la plupart de leurs champs, les sciences sociales ont procédé à cette conjonction et les sciences de l'éducation n'ont pas été étrangères à ce mouvement en particulier par leur intérêt croissant pour les significations investies dans les conduites des acteurs et des usagers. Il est toutefois probable que pour s'associer à ce mouvement, l'éducation comparée, indispensable pour accéder aux cultures des différents systèmes éducatifs que seule leur confrontation révèle significativement, doit d'abord lever une hypothèque, celle de la conception prédominante de la spécificité de la culture des systèmes éducatifs. Habituée à traiter les systèmes éducatifs comme nationaux, elle est en effet toujours encline à les créditer chacun d'une spécificité très singulière qui serait enracinée dans les traditions d'une histoire ou les valeurs d'une société qui n'auraient pas leurs pareils. Or la possibilité de s'en tenir à un tel point de vue n'a pas cessé de devenir plus problématique. On sait bien d'abord maintenant que toute culture allie l'universel au particulier (*Zahariah 1990*). Par ailleurs, le phénomène de la mondialisation concerne également l'éducation dont les préoccupations et les mises en œuvre ignorent désormais largement les frontières. Comme le souligne Jürgen Schriewer, il faut privilégier les „*analyses globales des interdépendances transnationales*" (cité par *Novoa 1995, p. 37*). Dans cette perspective, la conception à se faire de la culture d'un système éducatif et la manière de l'appréhender se trouvent profondément modifiées. En premier lieu, la spécificité dégagée ne saurait être que relative parce qu'elle est la série des réponses apportées à des enjeux qui finissent par se poser partout et rien ne garantit que les mêmes ne se constatent pas dans plusieurs dispositifs. On a donc toutes les chances d'être en présence moins de principes ou de pratiques dotés d'une originalité absolue que de configurations présentant davantage des différences de degré que des différences de nature. Ensuite l'identification de ces configurations oblige à privilégier des réponses concrètement faites aux enjeux reconnus. C'est une précaution indispensable pour deux raisons. D'abord pour ne pas s'illusionner sur la portée et la prétention de discours continuant d'affirmer la singularité et l'originalité de choix qui sont de plus en plus influencés et ont de plus en plus tendance à s'aligner les uns sur les autres. Ensuite, pour disposer de termes de comparaisons sans lesquels serait impossible l'appréciation de la composition du spectre des solutions retenues qui est la seule démarche véritablement éclairante.

Ainsi c'est à une notion profondément remaniée de la culture d'un système éducatif qu'on devrait se référer. Il faudrait se détacher de tout souci d'exhaustivité car si cette culture peut être définie en principe comme l'ensemble des réponses apportées, en fait de celui-ci on ne saisira toujours qu'une série limitée pour des raisons méthodologiques bien entendu mais aussi pour des raisons par exemple historiques puisque tout incite à penser que selon les époques les questions changent.

Les aspects caractéristiques de la culture d'un système éducatif

C'est aussi pourquoi les caractéristiques de la culture d'un système éducatif gagneraient à être envisagées sous des angles bien différents de ceux qui ont eu tendance à prévaloir jusqu'ici car il faudrait s'intéresser plus à sa forme qu'à son contenu.

On devrait naturellement porter une attention toute particulière au degré de cohérence des solutions intervenant dans un dispositif en s'interrogeant sur leur compatibilité d'après des critères qui eux aussi n'auraient été élaborés qu'après des investigations comparatives. A juste titre, on a toujours bien ressenti qu'un système éducatif manifestait une cohérence liée à l'importance reconnue à certaines valeurs ou à la persistance de certaines pratiques. Mais il faut aussi convenir que cette cohérence est demeurée plus souvent perçue comme un arrière-plan mal accessible que comme repérable dans des éléments tangibles. C'est ceux-ci qu'il faudrait désormais appréhender et exploiter.

L'appréciation de cette cohérence appellerait bien entendu la prise en compte d'une dimension historique car on ne saurait se contenter d'évaluer la compatibilité des choix à un seul moment donné. On se trouve nécessairement en présence de strates de choix dont il importerait d'analyser les relations harmonieuses ou contradictoires qui peuvent être autant de facteurs propices ou néfastes à la congruence des formules en vigueur ou à leur éventuelle modification.

C'est pourquoi on serait aussi conduit à accorder toute l'importance qu'elle mérite à la capacité de changement décelable. C'est un autre aspect fondamental de la culture d'un système éducatif puisqu'il peut le prédisposer à l'immobilisme ou au contraire lui faciliter les évolutions. Ici également, on devrait pouvoir passer d'impressions intuitives à des bilans argumentés. Au lieu d'invoquer la force des traditions pour expliquer des réticences ou des refus, on devrait pouvoir signaler des mécanismes précis de résistance ou de blocage. Et il va sans dire que l'analyse historique pourrait être aussi déterminante sur ce plan que sur les autres.

Il serait vain de vouloir d'avance dresser la liste de tous les aspects qui devraient être investigués selon cette optique. En tentant de le faire, on s'inféoderait encore à une vision donnée d'avance de la culture d'un système éducatif alors que cette vision doit être construite et reconstruite en fonction des problèmes qui se présentent et surtout de ceux qui sont abordables. Or, compte tenu des informations disponibles ou de celles qui peuvent être réunies, tous ne le sont pas. Il faudrait accepter cette limitation qui est sans doute imposée par l'objet de la réflexion. Il n'y a pas de totalité concevable de la culture d'un système éducatif à moins de l'aborder à un niveau de généralité inexploitable. Elle ne se conceptualise et ne s'appréhende qu'à condition de l'accepter comme accessible seulement dans un état fragmentaire et probablement aussi précaire à cause des évolutions qu'elle ne peut manquer de connaître.

On pressent qu'une telle approche pourrait aisément s'appliquer à tous les domaines de la culture dont on devine que l'analyse expose souvent aux mêmes difficultés et aux mêmes ambiguïtés. Il resterait pourtant à se demander si, par ses aspects formels, la culture d'un système éducatif n'est pas précisément d'un type particulier. N'a-t-elle pas et ne doit-elle pas avoir une cohérence plus marquée que d'autres secteurs de la culture? N'a-t-elle pas non plus des rythmes d'évolutions qui lui sont propres et leur mise en évidence ne serait-elle pas nécessaire pour éviter des malentendus liés à la supposition d'un immobilisme irrémédiable des systèmes éducatifs qui peuvent rendre aveugle à des changements en profondeur et se faire se tromper de situation ou de cible?

On se trouve là devant l'éventualité d'un nouvel élargissement du chantier qu'il serait loisible de refuser mais qu'on aurait intérêt à ne pas oublier totalement pour garder présentes à l'esprit toutes ses dimensions possibles.

Bibliographie

Ball, Stephen J. / Larsson, Staffan: The Struggle for Democratic Education, Equality and Participation in Sweden. Lewes: Falmer Press 1989.
Berthier, Patrick: L'ethnographie de l'école. Éloge critique. Paris: Economica 1996.
Demailly, Lise: Le collège: crise, mythes et métiers. Lille: Presses Universitaires de Lille 1991.
Forquin, Jean-Claude: École et culture. Le point de vue des sociologues britanniques. Bruxelles: De Boeck-Wesmael 1989.

Hargreaves, David H.: The Challenge for the Comprehensive School Culture. Curriculum and Community. London: Routledge and Kegan Paul 1982.
Max-Planck-Institut für Bildungsforschung. Arbeitsgruppe Bildungsbericht: Das Bildungswesen in der Bundesrepublik Deutschland. Strukturen und Entwicklungen im Überblick. Vollständ. überarb. u. erw. Neuausg. 19.-28. Taus. Reinbek: Rowohlt Taschenbuch-Verlag 1994. (rororo-Sachbuch. 9193)
Novoa, Antonio: Modèles d'analyse en éducation comparée, le champ et la carte. In: Les sciences de l'éducation, (1995) 2-3, pp. 1-61.
Prost, Antoine: Éducation, société et politiques. Une histoire de l'enseignement en France de 1945 à nos jours. Paris: Editions du Seuil 1992.
Qu'est-ce qu'un programme d'enseignement? Paris: Hachette 1994.
Van Haecht, Anne: L'enseignement rénové, de l'origine à l'éclipse. Bruxelles: Editions de l'Université de Bruxelles 1985.
Zahariah, Mattew: For a Comitted Internationalism in the Comparative Study of Culture. In: Compare, 20 (1990) 1, pp. 83-87.

Recent Directions in Comparative Education

Vandra L. Masemann

Introduction

It is almost self evident to say that the field of comparative and international education has been changing in its nature and scope, not only in this century, but more specifically in very recent times. At the IXth World Congress of Comparative Education in Sydney, Australia, Professor Mitter gave his Presidential Address on this very topic. He used his own biographical experiences as a model to show the various perspectives from which he was able to view these changes over the last forty years. He then traced the major thematic, theoretical, and methodological changes that have occurred over the period of his very active professional life. The main themes he referred to were as follows: East-West conflict and its impacts on education; large-scale educational reforms in Europe and other industrial countries; intercultural education in multicultural societies; the collapse of the communist system and its educational subsystems; the post modern revolt against theories of modernity; the interrelation between universalism and cultural pluralism *(Mitter 1996, pp. 4-6)*.

It is the purpose of this paper to focus attention on the recent developments in comparative education, on events that have affected the field in the more recent years in Professor Mitter's life, namely those years from 1990-1996. This is a fitting time period for two reasons: because it encompasses the time since the World Conference on Education for All in Jomtien, which was a landmark event in comparative education; and because Professor Mitter was during those years Co-President and President of the World Council of Comparative Education Societies. Moreover, the last review of the field published in the Comparative Education Review was in August 1991 *(Altbach 1991)*, and this review continues from there. Since that article gave very scant recognition to the activities of the World Council of Comparative Education Societies, this paper will be an attempt to remedy this lack.

Conferences held during this Period

A list that is by no means comprehensive of some meetings relevant to the interests of comparative educators held in the period under review is as follows: the World Conference on Education for All in Jomtien, in March 1990; the VIIIth World Congress of Comparative Education in Prague in 1992 in the then Czech and Slovak Federated Republic, the IXth World Congress of Comparative Education in Sydney, Australia in 1996, and the regularly scheduled International Conferences of Education of UNESCO in Geneva. Many international, regional, and local meetings were held in conjunction with the International Literacy Year (1990). The meetings of the Comparative Education Society in Europe (CESE) were held in Madrid, Spain in 1990, in Dijon, France in 1992, in Copenhagen, Denmark in 1994, and in 1996 in Athens, Greece. The meetings of the Comparative and International Education Society (CIES) have been held yearly in the United States and other countries: in Anaheim, California (1990); Pittsburgh, Pennsylvania (1991) Annapolis, Maryland (1992); Kingston, Jamaica (1993); San Diego, California (1994); Boston, Massachusetts (1995), Williamsburg, Virginia (1996) and in 1997 in Mexico City. Various national comparative education societies held meetings which attracted a primarily local gathering, and others held symposia to which international speakers were invited (in Tokyo, Beijing, Taipei, and Hong Kong, to name a few locations).

The Role of UNESCO

International agencies that had been active in the Education for All Conference also held follow-up meetings, and regional consultations were held in various countries. The World Council is a member of the Standing Committee of Non-Governmental Organizations that was established after the Jomtien Conference as part of UNESCO's role as the lead agency in follow-up activities. The International Bureau of Education began to publish the „WCCES Bulletin" in its quarterly publication, „Educational Innovation and Information". The Delors Commission was established by UNESCO to create a new vision for education in the future *(Delors et al. 1996),* and it held a series of meetings and consultations in various regions of the world. National commissions of UNESCO were very active in organizing regional input for these consultations.

The Influence of Political Changes

The fall of communism also brought about the infusion of aid money from the West to former Eastern Bloc countries, and meetings that could never have earlier taken place became possible in the field of comparative education. The appearance of all of the Ministers of Education from Eastern European countries together on one stage at the CIES Annual Meeting in Annapolis in 1992 was an unprecedented event.

The dismantling of apartheid led to an increasing interest in South Africa during this period; and panels on South Africa were increasingly common at CIES meetings, for example. However, the shift in aid to Eastern Europe and Russia meant that the rest of Africa was somewhat neglected, both from a financial and academic point of view.

The Expanding Membership of the World Council

The composition of the World Council of Comparative Education Societies underwent an expansion from twenty to thirty member societies during the years 1990-1996. After the CESE meeting in Budapest in 1988, there was increasing interest from Eastern European countries in forming comparative education societies. By 1996, there were comparative education societies admitted to the World Council from Bulgaria, the Czech (and formerly Slovak) Republic, Hungary, and Poland. During this period, the comparative education societies of China-Taipei, Greece, Hong Kong, Israel, and Portugal also joined the World Council. There was a marked growth of activity in comparative education in several countries in Asia; and the Comparative Education Society of Asia held its founding meeting in December, 1996.

Since 1992, the Southern Africa Comparative and History of Education Society has been a member of the World Council; and the Xth World Congress of Comparative Education is scheduled for Cape Town, South Africa in 1998. However, there is not much contact between the World Council and other African comparative education societies, except for the working group GRETAF (Groupe d'Étude sur l'Éducation en Afrique) established by Michel Debeauvais, focusing on follow-up to the World Conference on Education for All, linking some 12 Francophone African countries. This group was formerly within the AFEC (Association Francophone d'Éducation Comparée), the comparative education society of Francophone countries, but is now an independent organization. The World Council now has 30 active member societies, and participants from some 50 countries attended the Sydney Congress.

Journals, Publications and Communication Networks

The role of journals and publications in the field of comparative education has also been very important. *Altbach (1991, pp. 494-495)* refers to the dominant position of journals and publications such as the „International Encyclopedia of Education" published in Great Britain and the United States. At the 1996 World Congress in Sydney, Australia, a meeting of journal editors was held which 20 editors attended. The journals continue to be almost exclusively published in English. Of major concern was an attempt to spread out the publication of papers from future congresses in special issues of a variety of journals. The proceedings of both the Prague Congress and the Sydney Congress are to be published as special issues of the „International Review of Education" by the publisher Kluwer in Amsterdam.[1]

The emerging role of the Internet as a communications tool cannot be overlooked in a review of recent developments. The Comparative Education Discussion Group was established by the Comparative Education Research Centre at the University of Hong Kong in March 1995. It provides a world-wide electronic forum in comparative education[2] and also provides a gopher containing documents in comparative education to which any scholar can add material.[3] The 1996 World Congress in Sydney also used the Internet to a much greater extent than any previous congress. The organizers established a web-site for prospective congress participants and a system for disseminating the papers after the congress for a period of three years.[4] Various Internet groups have also been established to share information and ideas about specific topics of interest to comparative educators. For example, a discussion group was established in 1996 to discuss issues pertaining to the World Bank and the impact of its policies on education *(Klees 1996)*.

---

1 The German Institute for International Educational Research has already published a separate volume of proceedings of the Prague Congress *(Mitter / Schäfer 1993)*.
2 To subscribe, send e-mail to: <majordomo@hkusub.hku.hk> with the message: subscribe compared your e-mail address.
3 The gopher is at <gopher.hku.hk> and the documents should be sent in ASCII format to <cerc@hkusub.hku.hk>.
4 For access to papers, the Congress homepage is at: http//www.usyd.edu.au./su/wccomped/.

Lastly, communication about issues relevant to comparative education has occurred in working groups and networks of researchers and policy makers in various parts of the world. One such group whose members have presented at comparative education meetings and congresses during the period under review is the Northern Research Review and Advisory Group (NORRAG), a network that seeks to improve communications among educators, researchers, and policy makers about education in the South. Similar networks that were founded earlier are the South East Asia Research, Review, and Advisory Group and the Red Latinoamericana de Información y Documentación en Educación (REDUC). The role of such networks is discussed in a recent anthology on the subject *(McGinn 1996)*.

Major Themes in Recent World Congresses

The most recent World Congresses have had a large programme and a great diversity of participants. The VIth World Congress in Rio de Janeiro was the first one held in the southern hemisphere, and the theme was „Education, Crisis and Change". The VIIth World Congress was held in Montreal, Canada with the theme „Development, Communication and Language". These two Congresses, both of which were well attended by participants from several continents, linked the World Council more closely with the comparative education societies in both South and North America (particularly those in Brazil, Canada, and the United States). Moreover, some of the more Eurocentric perspectives of scholars previously active only in Europe began to be broadened. One mechanism which helped to bring about these closer links was the establishment of Workshops (composed of individually submitted papers) in the Brazil and Montreal Congresses in addition to the traditional Commissions (composed of groups of previously submitted papers by scholars already part of a network). The Workshops allowed scholars who had never previously met to meet those with common interests; while the format of the Commissions allowed work to continue between congresses among scholars with closely allied interests.This dual form of organization has persisted to the present.

At the World Congress held in Brazil in 1987, the Commissions focused on various aspects of the educational crisis referred to in the theme of the Congress: international issues in comparative education, comparisons of national policies, the state, women, and education, education and social change, recent trends in pedagogy, new educational technologies, theories and methods in comparative education, and the education of young adults. The Working Groups were somewhat more eclectic, dealing with a wide variety of topics: teaching and research, editing the journals in the field, human rights and education, radical perspectives, women and social conditions, rural education, education and work, management and education, innovation, information services abroad for study in other countries, teacher education, financing of education, social demand for education, intervention and innovation, vocational education, educational change in crisis, educational reform and the national project, privatization, equity issues, educational policies, and comparative pedagogy (*Sociedade Brasileira de Educaçao Comparada / World Council of Comparative Education Societies 1988*).

At the VII World Congress in Montreal in 1989, several of these major themes were continued in the work of the Commissions, notably in those focusing on theory and method in comparative education, women and education, education and young adults, multicultural and intercultural issues, teacher education, and others. The commissions were integrated into the programme of the congress in a format similar to that of the workshops. There was a noticeable number of workshops devoted specifically to language issues, the theme of the Congress. The Congress attracted a very sizeable audience, especially of North Americans who had not attended any of the previous congresses *(Comparative and International Education Society of Canada / World Council of Comparative Education Societies 1989)*.

At the VIIIth Congress in Prague in 1992, the programme had a more „European" appearance again, with a clear distinction between the commissions and workshops. The commissions were more numerous than they had been at previous congresses, and more women and scholars from non-European countries were chairing them. The topics focused on theory and methods, history and historical approaches, literacy and basic education, democracy and development, young adults' education, national policies, women's education, learning and teaching, international issues in education and development, higher education, and teacher education. Thus, the number of commissions had increased to 12 from the five or six in Brazil. The biggest increase, however, came in the number of workshops; the topics are too numerous to list here of the 63 workshops. There was a great diversity of topics and the presenters were from an even greater variety of countries than before *(Czech and Slovak Pedagogical Societies / World Council of Comparative Education Societies 1992)*.

At the IXth Congress in Sydney, Australia, the theme was „Tradition, Modernity, and Post-Modernity in Education". There was great diversity of participants from all areas of the world, and an increase in the number of participants from Asia, and, of course, Australia. There were three varieties of presentations: commissions, submitted panels, and groupings of papers that had been individually submitted. The topics of the commissions were very much continuations of the previous ones, with a few new ones added: theories and theory shift, higher education, Europe, language policies, peace and social justice, literacy and basic education, gender, indigenous education, post compulsory education, Third World education, and teacher education. The panels focused on topics of globalisation, international collaboration, civic education, teacher education, adult education, homeless street children, environmental education, political regimes and education, and transcultural, transnational, and international education. The main area studies panels were on Asia, including a panel on the educational implications of the Kobe earthquake. The paper groupings also focused on global and globalisation issues, as well as postmodernity and post colonialism, teacher education, politics of change, South Africa, Japan, Chinese education, and culturalism and multiculturalism *(Australia and New Zealand Comparative and International Education Society / World Council of Comparative Education Societies 1996).*

Conclusion

The shift in topics of commissions and workshops/panels at the four last World Congresses tends to mirror trends in the study of comparative education itself. Professor Mitter addressed these trends in his Presidential Address in Sydney. The last trend he identified, of the struggle between issues of universalism and cultural diversity, were exemplified very strongly at the Sydney Congress. Issues that are of current interest such as gender, indigenous education, environmentalism, and peace and justice issues were throroughly debated. Issues of transformation in the Third World were the focus of a large Commission and a strong debate.

Interestingly, the very organization of the World Congresses over the years has mirrored the very post-modern concerns that were addressed in the congress. There is no central consensus about what the World Congress should be focusing on or what its organization should be like. There was a great diversity of viewpoints, of topics, and of disciplinary backgrounds. There was some critique of the implications of this kind of fragmentation in terms of dispersing people's intellectual energies away from the struggle for equity and fairness worldwide in education. Other participants were concerned about the fragmentation of the Congress organization itself, and the impossibility of knowing what happened in all of the presentations. On the other hand, there was also no one way of defining comparative education that was being promulgated as the only way, and the richness of the offerings meant that scholars from many different backgrounds could find panels which suited their interests. The major themes that have been the focus of attention in this period of time, from 1991-1996 will no doubt continue to absorb our attention for the foreseeable future.

Bibliography

Altbach, Philip G.: Trends in Comparative Education. In: Comparative Education Review, 35 (1991) 3, pp. 491-507.
Australia and New Zealand Comparative and International Education Society / World Council of Comparative Education Societies (eds.): Program of the IXth World Congress of Comparative Education. Sydney: University of Sydney 1996.
Comparative and International Education Society of Canada / World Council of Comparative Education Societies (eds.): Program of the VIIth World Congress of Comparative Education. Montreal: University of Montreal 1989.
Czech and Slovak Pedagogical Societies / World Council of Comparative Education Societies (eds.): Program of the VIIIth World Congress of Comparative Education. Prague: Charles University 1992.
Delors, Jacques et al.: Learning: The Treasure Within. Report to the UNESCO of the International Commission on Education for the Twenty-First Century. Paris: UNESCO 1996.
Klees, Steve: An Invitation to Join an On-line Discussion Group of World Bank Educational Policy. In: CIES Newsletter, (1996) 112, p. 11.
McGinn, Noel (ed.): Crossing Lines. Research and Policy Networks for Developing Country Education. Westport, Conn.: Praeger 1996.
Mitter, Wolfgang: Challenges to Comparative Education. Between Retrospect and Expectation. Presidential Address delivered to the IXth World Congress of Comparative Education, Sydney, Australia, 1-6 July, 1996.
Mitter, Wolfgang / Schäfer, Ulrich (eds.): Upheaval and Change in Education. Papers presented by Members of the German Institute at the VIIIth World Congress of Comparative Education, „Education, Democracy and Development", Prague, July 8-14, 1992. Frankfurt a. M.: German Institute for International Educational Research 1993.
Sociedade Brasileira de Educação Comparada / World Council of Comparative Education Societies (eds.): Annals of the VIth World Congress of Comparative Education. Rio de Janeiro: SBEC 1988.

Die Pädagogische Studienreise als Instrument der wissenschaftlichen Erkenntnis

Heliodor Muszyński

Meine langjährige Bekanntschaft mit Wolfgang Mitter – aus der inzwischen eine herzliche Freundschaft geworden ist – hat infolge zahlreicher Begegnungen in mein Leben hineingewirkt und mich zu vielfältigen Überlegungen und wissenschaftlichen Untersuchungen inspiriert. Ich habe daraus soviel Gewinn ziehen können, daß ich kaum auszudrücken vermag, wie sehr ich ihm zu Dank verpflichtet bin. Wenn ich mir all diese Jahre der Kontakte und der Zusammenarbeit noch einmal vergegenwärtige, so möchte ich mich besonders auf die Reihe von „pädagogischen" Reisen konzentrieren, die uns gemeinsam durch Polen, mein Heimatland, geführt haben. Diese Reisen trugen nicht nur zur Bereicherung unserer Kenntnis der besuchten Regionen wie auch des ganzen Landes und insbesondere seines Schulwesens bei, sie bedeuteten auch die „Entdeckung" der zahlreichen Vorteile, welche solche Reisen für die wissenschaftliche Erkenntnis haben.

Als ich mit der Organisation jener Fahrt durch Polen mit meinem deutschen Kollegen, die ich für das Jahr 1989 geplant hatte, begann, war mir noch nicht bewußt, was sich daraus ergeben würde. Unter dem Einfluß der ersten „Bestandsaufnahme" entwickelte sich die Idee, dieses Reiseprojekt zu einem ganzen Zyklus auszudehnen. Die begonnenen Überlegungen führten schließlich zum dem Gedanken, unseren Reisen eine klare Forschungsabsicht zugrundezulegen. So entstand eine Konzeption für pädagogische Studienreisen, die als Instrument der Gewinnung wissenschaftlicher Erkenntnisse über das Bildungswesen in dem bereisten Land angelegt sind.

Selbstverständlich waren wir uns bewußt, daß wir uns auf einem wenn auch nicht völlig unbekannten, so doch stark in Vergessenheit geratenen Terrain bewegten. In der pädagogischen Literatur lassen sich viele schöne Beispiele von Tagebüchern und Berichten finden, die über solche Reisen verfaßt wurden und reichhaltige Informationen über bestimmte Länder enthalten. Leider fielen solche „Reiseberichte" später für eine gewisse Zeit bei Fachleuten und beim Publikum „in Ungnade". Hierfür gab es zwei Hauptgründe. Der erste ist in der Entwicklung einer positivistischen Methodologie in den empirischen Wissenschaften zu suchen, der zweite in der Entstehung und Verbreitung der audiovisuellen Massenmedien. Einerseits begann man in der empirischen Wissenschaft solche Forschungen zu schätzen, deren Ergebnisse quantitativ erfaßbar waren und auf deren Grundlage man zu Verallgemeinerungen gelangen konnte. Diejenigen Forschungen, die auf der reflektierenden Beschreibung des jeweils Einmaligen beruhten, galten fortan als unpräzise und dem Erkenntnisgewinn wenig förderlich. Andererseits wurde es den Massenmedien überlassen, den Menschen zu ermöglichen, das Einmalige kennenzulernen. So entstand der Eindruck, in der „richtigen" Wissenschaft sei kein Platz mehr für diese Form des Erkenntnisgewinns.

Die vergangenen Jahre haben jedoch eine „Wiederentdeckung" der qualitativen Methoden mit sich gebracht. Es hat sich erwiesen, daß die Beschreibung und Analyse des jeweils Einmaligen durchaus einen wichtigen Stellenwert in der wissenschaftlichen Forschung einnimmt und keineswegs durch die ausschließlich mit quantitativen Methoden arbeitende empirische Forschung zu ersetzen ist. Gewiß eröffnet die Anwendung qualitativer Methoden nicht den Zugang zu verallgemeinernden Aussagen, es sei denn unter Verlust ihrer wesentlichen Eigenschaften, nämlich der Identifizierung von Individualität und Einzigartigkeit. Die idiographische Forschung und die qualitativen Methoden haben jedoch in der Vergleichenden Erziehungswissenschaft durchaus ihre Berechtigung. Das Prinzip des Holismus, nach dem die erforschte Wirklichkeit als ein in sich geschlossenes Ganzes betrachtet wird, kommt hierbei in besonderer Weise zur Anwendung. Die Bildungssysteme erscheinen in diesem Ansatz als komplexe Netze, innerhalb derer man das Funktionieren der einzelnen Bestandteile nicht verstehen kann, wenn man nicht das Ganze berücksichtigt. Das im Inneren wirkende Netzwerk von Beziehungen steht mit einem größeren Netzwerk von Außenbeziehungen in Verbindung, welche die Gesamtheit der kulturellen, politischen, sozialen und ökonomischen Faktoren beinhalten und nur aus ihrer geschichtlichen Herkunft und Entwicklung zu verstehen sind. Durch die Einsicht in den Gesamtzusammenhang bzw. in die Wechselwirkung der beiden Netzwerke läßt sich beispielsweise erklären, wie sich bestimmte Typen von Bildungseinrichtungen oder Bildungswegen in einem Nationalstaat in ihrem Verhältnis zum Gesamtsystem von einem entsprechenden Vergleichsobjekt in einem anderen Bildungssystem gänzlich unterscheiden.

Es läßt sich daher die These aufstellen, daß – so gesehen – jedes Bildungssystem einzigartig ist: Es funktioniert innerhalb eines einmaligen Gesamtzusammenhangs von Voraussetzungen und spiegelt sowohl die früheren Erfahrungen der jeweiligen Gesellschaft als auch deren Zustand, Zielsetzungen, Perspektiven und Möglichkeiten in der Gegenwart wider. Vor allem jedoch ist jedes Bildungssystem historisch geprägt und wird unter den jeweils gegebenen gesellschaftlichen, politischen, ökonomischen und kulturellen Umständen von lebenden Menschen gestaltet. Dieser Komplex von Merkmalen eines Bildungssystems muß in seiner Einmaligkeit betrachtet werden: ihn zu verstehen ist nur durch das Eindringen in sein inneres Gefüge, seine individuellen Grundlagen, Mechanismen und Bedingtheiten möglich. Hierzu bedarf es einer besonderen Art der Forschung, die sich aber von jener unterscheidet, die in der Methodologie der empirischen Forschung als Fallstudie bezeichnet wird. Die hier gemeinten Analysen überwiegen in der Forschungspraxis, und sie werden nach bestimmten immanenten Vergleichskriterien durchgeführt. Diese Kriterien sind in jedem Falle gesondert zu definieren und ermöglichen den – ebenfalls notwendigen – Zugang zur eigentlichen vergleichenden Forschung. Es wäre jedoch falsch zu erwarten, daß sich mit diesem Ansatz das Wesentliche eines gegebenen Systems erschöpfend erfassen läßt. Das liegt darin begründet, daß jedes Bildungssystem eine eigene, individuelle und unwiederholbare Wahrheit über sich selbst enthält. Zu dieser Wahrheit vorzudringen, ist nur auf dem Wege über eine intensive idiographisch-beschreibende Forschung möglich, deren Ziel nicht in der Suche nach bestimmten Verallgemeinerungen und Regeln besteht, welche die Bildungssysteme unter kategorialem Aspekt betreffen, sondern vor allem im Verstehen des jeweils gegebenen Einzelsystems, seiner Struktur und Gestalt, seiner Funktionsweisen und Wirkungen. Ein Verstehen ist freilich nur dann möglich, wenn man in die Gesamtheit der Bedingungen des gegebenen Systems eindringt – sowohl der gegenwärtigen als auch der vergangenen.

Es erhebt sich nun die Frage, was eigentlich die Substanz dieses „Verstehens" ausmacht und welche Funktion ihm in der wissenschaftlichen Erkenntnis zukommt. Welche Ziele werden dabei eigentlich verfolgt? Zweifellos haben wir es hier mit einem Begriff von Verstehen zu tun, der sich vor allem auf individuelle Erkenntnis bezieht. Dieses Verstehen ist eine Art intellektueller Freude, die man dann erlebt, wenn sich die zunächst „undurchschaubare" Wirklichkeit zu einem geordneten und erfüllten Ganzen entfaltet. Wesentlich sind hierbei zwei Aspekte.

Der erste davon besteht im Zusammentragen von Einzelaspekten der Wirklichkeit, welche sich dann zu einem Gesamtbild zusammenfügen. Wir beginnen unsere Arbeit, indem wir aus dem Zusammenhang gelöste, isolierte Tatsachen, Ereignisse und Erscheinungen mit einander verknüpfen sowie bestimmte Wirkungszusammenhänge und Zeitsequenzen aufspüren. Das „Verstehen" zielt dabei auf die Wahrnehmung der Tatsache, daß die erforschten Einzelerscheinungen nicht isoliert, d. h. spontan und zufällig, auftreten, sondern ganz im Gegenteil bestimmte Verbindungen miteinander eingehen – seien es solche, die für sich bereits Ursachen oder Folgen sind, oder auch solche, welche die Folgen irgendwelcher anderen, allgemeineren und umfassenderen Ursachen darstellen.

Der zweite Aspekt des „Verstehens" ist dagegen rein psychologischer und zugleich soziologischer Natur. Tatsachen und Ereignisse verbleiben danach in einem Erkenntnisvakuum und erscheinen solange isoliert und zufällig, als wir nicht das Handeln der beteiligten Menschen berücksichtigen, das heißt ihre individuellen wie auch gemeinschaftlichen Aktivitäten. Hinter diesen Handlungen verbergen sich menschliche Erfahrungen, Erlebnisse, Hoffnungen, Erwartungen und Bestrebungen, die oft eine lange Geschichte haben. Kurz gesagt, die erforschten Gegenstände erfüllen sich erst dann mit Leben und Bedeutung, wenn wir die dahinterstehenden Menschen einbeziehen, ihre absehbare Zukunft – die manchmal ganze Generationen umfassen kann – und ihre Gegenwart, ihre gemeinsamen wie auch ihre individuellen Erfahrungen, auch in den Fällen, in denen sie sich nur wenig von einander unterscheiden.

Die *verstehende* unterscheidet sich von der *empirischen* Erkenntnis weder bezüglich des den beiden Wegen eigenen Bestrebens, Zusammenhänge zwischen verschiedenen Erscheinungen aufzusuchen, noch durch ihren kausal-konsekutiven Charakter. Grundlegend unterscheidet sie sich von ihr jedoch vor allem dadurch, daß sie diese Zusammenhänge nicht auf dem Wege der empirisch-induktiven Erfahrung erfaßt, d. h. durch ein Verfahren, bei dem das Sammeln einer gewissen Menge von empirisch ermittelten und gewöhnlich standardisierten Daten, die man auf dem Wege statistischer Analyse auswertet und dann einem Verallgemeinerungsprozeß unterzieht, charakteristisch ist. Die „verstehende" Erkenntnis stützt sich vielmehr auf Einzeltatsachen und nichtstandardisierte Verhaltensweisen, die mehr oder weniger hypothetisch betrachtet werden. Daher ist ihr Ziel grundsätzlich ein anderes als das der „empirischen" Erkenntnis. Im Unterschied zu den empirischen Forschungen geht es hier immer um die Herstellung eines ganzen, eines einheitlichen Bildes der erforschten Wirklichkeit, in dem freilich die Einzelheiten noch aufgehoben sind. Der empirisch-induktiv arbeitende Forscher muß sich gewöhnlich all dessen begeben, was sich nicht verallgemeinern läßt. Der „verstehende Humanist" hingegen beschränkt sich nicht auf quantitativ erfaßbare Daten – im Gegenteil: Ihn interessiert der je individuelle Charakter der Ereignisse, Tatsachen und Merkmale sowie die nicht reproduzierbare Natur, welche den menschlichen Schicksalen und Handlungen eigen ist. Der Empiriker strebt unerläßlich danach, die untersuchten Erscheinungen aus ihrem Kontext herauszulösen, während der „verstehende" Forscher nach der umfassenden Rekonstruktion der Zusammenhänge strebt, in die er die untersuchten Erscheinungen stellt und „verstehend" zu erklären sucht.

Natürlich stellt sich beim verstehenden Ansatz in der wissenschaftlichen Forschung unvermeidlich die Frage nach dem Nutzen. Auch in dieser Hinsicht sieht sich die Wissenschaft ununterbrochen dem Einfluß des Positivismus ausgesetzt, dessen einziges Forschungsziel die reine Theorie ist, also das Auffinden allgemeiner Sätze, durch die sich die untersuchten Erscheinungen erklären lassen: In diesem Ansatz ist also die Erklärung Grundlage für Verallgemeinerungen. Nun läßt sich natürlich nicht ausschließen, daß auch eine auf Verstehen ausgerichtete Forschung diesem Ziel dienen kann, ja geradezu dienen soll. Gewiß können auf Einzelfälle gerichtete Untersuchungen in sich viele Elemente enthalten, die Verallgemeinerungen erlauben und zu Grundlagen für Forschungshypothesen werden können, welche solche Verallgemeinerungen wiederum ermöglichen. Insofern leisten auch sie einen Beitrag zur Entwicklung des Paradigmas empirischer Wissenschaft. Dieses ist freilich nicht das einzige Paradigma, es konkurriert vielmehr mit dem auf Verstehen ausgerichteten Paradigma, das ebenfalls vielfältig anwendbar ist und sich keineswegs auf die persönliche Freude oder das Erfolgserlebnis des jeweiligen Forschers beschränkt. Es lassen sich vielmehr zumindest zwei Anwendungsebenen feststellen.

Zum einen führt „verstehende Erkenntnis" zu unschätzbaren Erfahrungen auf den Gebieten des menschlichen Handelns, wo Verallgemeinerungen nur eine partielle Rolle spielen können. Zu denken ist hierbei beispielsweise an massenhaft auftretende Handlungen, wie etwa bei der Einführung gesellschaftlicher Veränderungen und Reformen. Ein und dieselben Initiativen führen bekanntlich in verschiedenen Ländern sehr häufig zu ganz unterschiedlichen Ergebnissen. Daraus läßt sich folgern, daß Reformer im wesentlichen eher zur Suche nach eigenen Lösungen „verurteilt" sind, als daß sie aus allgemeinen Hinweisen der Wissenschaft Nutzen ziehen könnten. Dagegen erweisen sich bei dieser Art von Suche Einzelerfahrungen anderer als unschätzbare Hilfe. Anders ausgedrückt: Die Wirkungen gesellschaftlicher Prozesse scheinen eher einmalig und unwiederholbar zu sein als allgemeinen Regeln zu unterliegen. Auch ist es ergiebiger, sich bei der Suche nach sinnvollen Lösungen auf konkrete Erfahrungen anderer zu berufen als auf theoretisches, empirisch „geprüftes" Wissen. Die Geschichte der Schulreformen bietet uns hierfür zahlreiche Bestätigungen. Schulreformer sind in der Regel in dem Bewußtsein befangen, sie würden neue und einzigartige Wege einschlagen. Die Erfahrungen anderer werden hierbei um so stärker genutzt, je mehr sie der Realität, in der solche Reformen stattfinden, entsprechen. Das bedeutet aber nicht, daß bei der Umsetzung von Reformen nicht auch Wissen genutzt werden kann, das der theoretischen Verallgemeinerung entspringt, was insbesondere dann der Fall ist, wenn sich dieses Wissen in konkrete Handlungsanweisungen umsetzen läßt.

Zum anderen erweist sich die „verstehende" Erkenntnis dann als unendlich wertvoll, wenn wir die gesellschaftliche Funktion der Wissenschaft in Betracht ziehen. Sie soll ja nicht nur den Zielen dienen, welche die Wissenschaftler selbst verwirklichen wollen, sondern auch dazu, jedes Individuum mit elementaren Kenntnissen von der Welt insgesamt auszustatten und auch mit solchen, die es zum besseren Verständnis dieser Welt benötigt. Bei diesem Wissen kommt zweifellos der Art und Weise, wie *andere* ihre Umwelt wahrnehmen, eine besondere Bedeutung zu. Häufig sind unsere Meinungen über die anderen und ihre Motive sowie unsere Sympathien und Vorurteile dadurch entstanden, daß wir einzelne, isolierte Tatsachen oder Haltungen beurteilen, ohne daß wir ihre Ursachen, Quellen und Funktionen kennen.

Bildung und Erziehung sind ein besonders wichtiger Gegenstandsbereich der verstehenden Erkenntnis. Dies beruht darauf, daß Bildungserfahrungen einen universalen Charakter haben und wir durch sie, gleichsam wie durch ein Prisma, viele gesellschaftliche Erscheinungen wahrnehmen und demnach auch verstehen können. Das Bildungswesen ist in dieser Hinsicht ein Kriterium eigener Art, weil sich in ihm einerseits Bedingungen und Faktoren des gesellschaftlichen Lebens widerspiegeln, es andererseits aber auch selbst ein Faktor ist, durch den viele Erscheinungen des gesellschaftlichen Lebens bestimmt werden.

Kehren wir abschließend zum zentralen Gedanken unserer Überlegungen zurück. Sie betreffen die Reise – oder präziser gesagt: das Reisen – als eine Form der wissenschaftlichen Erkenntnis. Ich bezeichne eine solche Reise als „Studienreise", weil dieses Wort am besten ihren einzigartigen Charakter widerspiegelt, der auf die Sammlung verschiedenartiger und auf eine bestimmte Thematik bezogener Informationen ausgerichtet ist. Es geht dabei immer um die Betrachtung einer einzelnen oder mehrerer Erscheinungen in solchen Kontexten, die nicht nur ein Konstatieren, sondern auch ein „Verstehen" ermöglichen. Dieses Verstehen richtet sich seinerseits auf Fragen nach den Voraussetzungen und Funktionen der wahrgenommenen Erscheinungen.

Das Objekt unserer Reisen durch Polen war das Bildungswesen des Landes: sein gegenwärtiger Zustand und die entsprechenden Aufgaben und Probleme, zugleich aber auch seine Möglichkeiten und Perspektiven. Entsprechend den oben erwähnten Erkenntniszielen wollten wir uns aber nicht allein auf die Schul- und Hochschulinstitutionen selbst konzentrieren, sondern zugleich auch ihre Funktionen und Probleme im breiteren gesellschaftlichen Kontext untersuchen. Diese breitere Sichtweise der Probleme des polnischen Bildungswesens sollte durch die Auswahl der besuchten Orte gewährleistet werden. Ebenso sollte eine Erweiterung über die Grenzen des Bildungswesens hinaus bei der Vorbereitung möglicher Kontakte mit Gesprächspartnern zur Bereicherung beitragen.

Die Realisierung des ersten Ziels richtete sich auf die Beobachtung von Institutionen und Erscheinungen im Bildungssystem im Rahmen seiner vielfältigen Verknüpfungen und Bedingungen, vor allem unter Berücksichtigung der in ihm handelnden Personen. Die Suche nach lebendigen Kontakten dagegen beruhte auf der Einsicht, daß passive Erkenntnis eine Barriere darstellt, durch die sich die Beobachtung auf die Perspektive des Außenstehenden – die Außensicht – beschränkt. Es ging also darum, aus der Rolle eines bloßen „Besuchers" die eines „Teilnehmers" und „Mitdiskutierenden" werden zu lassen. In der Praxis bedeutete diese modifizierte Zielstellung, von dem Standard abzuweichen, der wissenschaftlichen Reisen häufig eigen ist. Im einzelnen äußerte sich diese Zielrichtung folgendermaßen:

– Herstellung von Kontakten in einem Feld, das weit über das Bildungswesen hinausreicht;
– Auswahl der Gesprächspartner über die offiziellen und rein informativen Kontakte hinaus;
– Ausweitung des Erkenntnisfeldes auf Gegenstände, die das Bildungswesen nicht mehr unmittelbar betreffen: durch die Einbeziehung der Geschichte der besuchten Regionen, der sozialen und ethnischen Struktur der Bevölkerung, der spezifischen Traditionen und kulturellen Merkmale, der ökonomischen Bedingungen u. ä.;
– Suche nach Gesprächspartnern zum Zweck des Dialogs, der Diskussion und des Erfahrungsaustauschs;
– Verarbeitung isolierter Informationen, welche auf Einzelprobleme oder auf Ausschnitte der Wirklichkeit bezogen sind, zu komplexen Einsichten, die sich zu einem geschlossenen Ganzen verbinden lassen.

Entscheidend bei solchen Reisen ist die Programmgestaltung. Auch die abwechslungsreichsten und aktivsten Formen der Erkenntnis haben keinen großen Nutzen, wenn sie an der Oberflächliche bleibt oder wenn das Objekt zu speziell ist. Ich habe daher meine Programmgestaltung darauf konzentriert, daß die einzelnen Besuchsstationen weder fragmentarische, diffuse oder gar oberflächliche Eindrücke noch ein statisches Bild der Schulverhältnisse in der Region vermittelten. Das Ergebnis unseres Erkenntnisstrebens sollte weniger in einem „faktographischen" als in einem „aufgeklärten" Wissen über das Bildungswesen bestehen. Die Programme mußten meinem deutschen Reise-partner daher gestatten, solche Fragen zu stellen, die weit über die Erfassung des gegenwärtigen Zustands hinausgingen.

Deshalb vereinbarten wir, daß auch Fragen zu folgenden Themen zugelassen wurden, die über die Wechselwirkungen zwischen einzelnen Erscheinungen hinaus interessant waren: Welches sind die Ursachen bestimmter Erscheinungen? Mit welchen besonderen Schwierigkeiten sieht sich das Schulwesen der besuchten Region konfrontiert? Über welche Möglichkeiten und Potenzen zur Überwindung dieser Schwierigkeiten verfügt es? Wie beurteilen die Befragten die Perspektiven der künftigen Schulentwicklung?

Shifts in Political Regimes and the Geopolitical Reorganization of Educational Space: Implications for Comparative Education

Shin'ichi Suzuki

Introduction

Since the collapse of the Berlin Wall in 1989 people have been witnessing a vast growth of nationalism in almost all of the regions within the geopolitical divisions of space, not only from the South to the North but also from the East to the West of the globe. As religious zeal is very often mixed with a sense of cultural and ethnic differences, the new types of statecentrism cause a rather high frequency of civil wars or political violence and terrorism within their societies. This can be taken as a symptom of the absence of leading principles to guide the socio-political reconstruction in the societies concerned. These chaotic situations remind observers of boats drifting without a compass on an ocean of shifting political regimes. Situations of this sort cannot but affect in various ways other societies that are old and mature in the conventional sense. It is hard for anyone to foresee now the political appearance of evolving future societies. Going back to the post-World War II period, peoples were also in the dark then, or in the twilight at best, regarding the future appearances of their societies, because there were two kinds of blueprints which they could fall back onto in reconstructing their societies: the American blueprint and the Soviet Russian. What they suffered from was the hostile coexistence of two distinct political paradigms and fear or anxiety about the possible disaster or the catastrophe caused by the world-wide phenomenon called „cold-war". Under such conditions people did not suffer because they had no clear image of future societies for them, but rather because there was a sharp contrast between two conceptions of future societies for them to choose from. Contrast and strain between two ideals of future society caused tension and anxiety among peoples concerning their synthesization of them into a harmonious unity. What impresses people most today is not this kind of contrast, anxiety or contradiction, but the utter absence of a conception of the future of human society. Peoples nowadays drive nowhere on the plane of political geography without a road map. No one can escape the feeling that the foundation is shaking and few can say in what direction one should go.

Against this sort of background, education should take new types of tasks upon itself. For example, in 1995, the United Nations Year for Tolerance, the experts met at Bandar Seri Begawan in Brunei to discuss at grass-roots level issues of enhancing tolerance in education. There Dr. Valai na Pombejr, as UNESCO representative, disclosed the overt issues of democracy and tolerance in remarks as the following:

„This unique international forum for dialogue and discussion concerning education is an event of great significance and its theme is timely and most appropriate. Every one of us is witnessing and is concerned at the upsurge of intolerance and extremism, the increasing number of manifestations of racial and ethnic hatred and the way in which discrimination and violence have become everyday occurrences. Promotion of tolerance through education is important for mutual respect and is essential to the realization of human rights and the achievement of peace" (Pombejr 1995, p. 3-4).

And Professor Nelly Aleotti *Maia (1995, p. 3-4)* from Brazil, as the Frank Klassen Memorial Lecturer, pointed out the grave consequence of „axiological holes" touching the urgency of finding a sound solution to the relationship required between value education and politics. Referring to Karl *Jaspers (1965)*, Professor *Maia (1995, pp. 4, 8, 14)* analyzed the dialectical structure between truth and power, and disclosed the covert interrelatedness between politics and axiological orientation toward education. However, the reciprocal mediation between the phenomenological situations of violence and intolerance and the philosophical contexts in axiological analyses of present circumstances is not as simple as might be assumed, because the value systems are shifting on their own accord and the constitutional principles are changing rapidly even within the circle of democracy. To emphasize this another citation from one of the presentations made at the Brunei conference appears appropriate:

„The cry for peace everywhere in the world today has become as omnipresent as talk of the weather in social circles and print and broadcast media. This can be attributed to mounting discontent, crime, personal violence, terrorism, confrontation and protest, experiments with drugs and sex and increasing break-up of families and communities happening across continents ... The rising chorus of demands for peace around the world heightens the need for teaching tolerance and peace, and to do it effectively" (Sutaria 1995, p. 1).

It is urgent for all of us comparative educationists to re-define the role of public education against the background of the struggle towards solutions of political disorders and social instability. The author intends to clarify the hidden contexts of „problems in education" from the viewpoint of the shifting geopolitical dimensions of social life.

Shifts as a Result of New Media

The notion of nation-state has become dysfunctional in some domains of comparative and international education. An example is the European Union, where educational space has been totally reorganized into a new dimension in the sense that within a stable geopolitical and geo-administrative structure schooling alone cannot be the ultimate unit of measure for describing the total educational system. Presumably educational space is a geopolitical and geocultural structure that not only emerges within a given human group, old or new, by itself, but also is invented as an institution in the modern sense we observe now. Nowadays educational space can be restructured in the highly civilized corners of the globe by means such as:

– computer-assisted learning and its media;
– international information-processing systems;
– satellite channeling of visual and vocal information;
– computed virtual reality, and
– transferability of mobile learners.

ERASMUS, LINGUA, COMETT, SOCRATES and other programmes related to vocational training and qualifications are illuminating examples of the restructured educational space in Europe. Distance learning not only in Australia but also in Spain, for example, is another illustration of such shifts in educational setting. The Open University and the Universities on Air are also examples and so-called correspondence courses are still reckoned as a working illustration of changing educational space despite their long history. In the Japanese context a life-long learning system has been created in networking all tracks of education and training throughout society as a whole.

On the micro-level of primary and secondary education so-called „intelligent buildings" are growing in number and progressive information technology has enabled practicing teachers to utilize international information through the Internet as contents of instruction and so-called multimedia have been widely adopted in organizing learning-teaching space within schools and class-rooms.

According to the Asahi Evening News the President of the United States decided in 1996 to support the internet approach financially for all primary schools in the U.S. On the other side of the spectrum at the tertiary level, as visible in the U.S., a new federal type of on-line-university has come into being, whose main purposes are a) to broaden access to higher education by fostering the use of advanced technology for the delivery of educational services and b) to provide mechanisms for the formal recognition or certification of learning achieved, regardless of the source *(Pipho 1996)*. A conglomerate type university of this type may prevail. All of these examples of shifts in educational space suggest how far present situations in education have penetrated the new dimension of the steadily growing hyper-information society. Apparently this kind of newly information-loaded education has crossed over the high hurdle of former geocultural and geopolitical boundaries of old nation-states and is running towards a goal on a new horizon.

Problems as a Result of the Centre-Periphery Division

At the advent of the Single European Market, a comparative educationist wrote: „*The removal of economic barriers brings two main consequences for the lives of ordinary people and for the schools that serve them. Work moves across national frontiers and so do workers and their families. Schools have to prepare students to compete in a European labour market with their coevals from other countries. Teachers have to be able to meet the needs of migrant children and young people from many European countries*"*(McLean 1990, p. VII)*. In the concluding chapter he makes the following remark: „*Educational producers and consumers both will find they have much to gain from trans-continental associations of interest. There is need for an attitude of openness, curiosity and anticipation towards these links. In the end, each national educational culture may retain much of its own distinctiveness, which will add to the richness of Europe and to enhanced consumer choice. But distinctiveness will be accompanied by awareness of what rival cultures have to offer and by the universal acceptance of a minimum international currency of rational public knowledge*" *(ibid., pp. 117-118)*.

Here, however, the persistent issue about the latent political relations between national „distinctiveness" and „a minimum international currency of rational public knowledge" arises. The grammarians of modernity assert the common structure of sociopolitical modernity which can be observed in all the processes of modernization fully achieved in the industrialized nation-states. The structure common to all consists of several sets of political strategies whose characteristics can be described as a unity of political and cultural hegemonies.

What are theses strategies? They are the authorization: 1) of national language, 2) of national history, 3) of national geography, 4) of national religion, 5) of national academism, 6) of national fine arts, 7) of national ethos, 8) of national education, 9) of national military force, and 10) of national currency. Some good comparable historical examples can be found in the modern periods since Meiji Restoration of Japan (1868). When Japan expanded its territory into Taiwan and Korea, an influential scholar of Japanese literature from the former Imperial University of Tokyo revealed his concern for the importance of standardized Japanese as national language. Most scholars teaching at the Imperial Universities were sent to European or American universities and they acquired learning that originated in Western culture. What they learnt from the West became the measures by which they observed the current Japanese society, viewing rural or local parts as peripheral to the centre. The Imperial Universities educated the future bureaucrats who served as high officers in the departments of central government or as supervisors in the local governments. They trained the future technologists who later served as leading industrialists. The graduates from the Imperial Universities joined publishing circles, worked as journalists, went into teaching, became business managers, and could enjoy other modern jobs. More often than not they became politicians. Through the skillfully structured school system the Meiji Government invited the gifted not only from the centre but also from the peripheries of the Japanese archipelago to take enlightened modern jobs. Thus, people who educated themselves at higher levels could hold political and cultural positions of influence at the same time. They were not only politically more powerful in the machinery of modern polity than those less educated but also leaders in the area of culture of the time. And how such a scheme works is indicated in the following diagram.

Diagram 1

highly educated

B	A
C	D

centrifugal   centripetal

less educated

Japanese people were regrouped into a new society which was artificially but skillfully planned. A social force was at work by which people driven to the sectors B to D were once again segregated from people in the sector A which occupied the centre of the nation-state. The various authorizations mentioned above effectively supplemented the mental, moral, spiritual, cultural and social processes of centre-periphery division. What must be remembered is that this kind of centralization in modern Japanese society is based on the centre-periphery reorganization model of world order invented by Western societies. In diagram 1 the Western culture would occupy the sector A and the Japanese culture would occupy one of the three sectors from B to D. This can be interpreted as an abstract and structuralist explanation of one-nation = one-language, and one-nation = one-ethnicity principle which was stressed through the whole course of modernization in Japan. Western societies could be assumed to hold the central position in world culture while the rest of the cultures are peripherized and segregated as being inferior. A double centrifugal force is observable. Even in the continent of Europe this double centrifugality can be tested and proved to exist.

If so, is it possible for Europe as a geopolitical and geocultural whole to define the distinctiveness of former states as sub-cultural units of Europe? An opinion poll carried out in the Czech Republic last year indicates a possible answer. When people were asked how much they agree or disagree with the statements in table 1 their responses were ambivalent regarding one point at least, that is, nationality and universality of education.

When Professor Mitter spoke about the future potential of comparative education at a plenary session of the IXth World Congress of Comparative Education Societies in Sydney, he summed up this type of issue as a challenge to paradigm change; the interrelation between universalism and cultural pluralism *(Mitter 1996, p. 6)*. The present author once referred to the dilemma of concurrence of national identity and European identity in present day Europe *(Suzuki 1994, p. 12)*. Several facts observed in the overall trends of local societies suggest that it would not be easy for any member state of the European Union to satisfy both the needs of universalism and multiculturalism. Education must assist in solving the dilemma but it would be still a heavier burden upon education to overcome pluricentrism, anthropocentrism, statecentrism and econocentrism. In essence, a series of authorizations of human behavior and their institutionalization, tightly woven into the matrix of modern society, must be deconstructed through creative new education. This emphasizes once more the urgency of genuine comparisons in studies of education. Comparative education has to sharpen its edge.

Table 1: Attitudes to Other Countries (in %)

Question: How much do you agree or disagree with the following statements?

Statements	Agree	Neither agree nor disagree	Disagree
Foreigners should not be allowed to buy land in the Czech Republic	59	12	29
Czech television should give preference to Czech films and programmes	56	24	20
The Czech Republic should limit the import of foreign goods in order to protect national economy	54	18	28
Czech schools should make much more efforts to teach foreign languages	88	9	3
Regarding foreign problems, like environmental pollution, international bodies (e.g. UN, EU, WHO) should have rights to enforce the solutions	74	15	11
People should support their country even if the country is wrong	34	23	43
The Czech Republic should follow its own interests even if this leads to conflicts with other nations	32	22	46

Source: *Institute of Sociology (1995), Table 1.*

Concluding Remarks: The Feasibility of the Profile Approach in Comparative Studies

Professor *Mitter (1996, pp. 1-3)* started his Presidential Address with a biographical sketch. The present author also started his lecture at the Copenhagen Conference *(Suzuki, 1994, pp. 1-10)* with biographical notes. This coincidence is quite illustrating. The present author defines this as a profile approach.

Admitting that the centre-periphery socialization processes necessarily work within given societies, and admitting that the authorization by the state (the central government) of all cultural activities within a given society is the essential device and scheme invented by the political elites, we clearly can see how inescapable and fundamental it is for us, the researchers, to excavate our socio-cultural and socio-political tombs as it were, in order to find and re-examine the hidden stories of the making of modern academic disciplines. This is the way in which we can protect our unique experiences from distortion and alienation caused by the centre-periphery authorization processes of modern society. In this way, the present author assumes, anyone could ensure that they recover what has been lost in the sociopolitical processes of authorization. An authorized national history, for example, is nothing but an institutionalized discourse on selected materials. It means that something has been rejected, and hence a sample of an authorized history can be seen as a kind of narration in a vacuum from another standpoint.

A subjective discourse on a certain topic can remedy the absence of what should have been described within the authorized narratives and descriptions. Probably it can safely be said that something national is something that rejects or hides anything minor, local, non-standard, that is, in a word, anything peripheral. A profile approach is an approach in which a researcher may discover the depth of his/her or their own motives for 1) a given discipline, 2) problem formulation, 3) paradigm selection and 4) projective reasoning. Through such discoveries, what has been described and projected in actions of the researcher(s) should be relativized against the dynamic contexts of general knowledge. Cultural studies might come closer to this profile approach *(Denzin 1992, p. 71sq.)*, and such a notion or a sense of Diaspora, for example, may lead some comparative educationists to analytical comparisons of the somewhat subjective dimensions of their hidden motives for comparison itself, in the studies of spiritual, moral, physical, social and cultural phenomena of human upbringing.

On the other hand, as was once being maintained, comparison is the way in which any researcher keeps him/herself from being centristic in reasoning and argumentation *(Piaget 1972)*. Therefore it is the next step for the comparative educationists of today to find and elaborate the methods by which it can be ensured that the profile approach is comparative and heuristic in studies of education.

Bibliography

Denzin, Norman K.: Symbolic Interactionism and Cultural Studies. The Politics of Interpretation. Oxford: Blackwell 1992.
Institute of Sociology (ed.): ISSP-95 Survey on National Identity. Prague: The Institute of Sociology 1995.

Jaspers, Karl: Kleine Schule des philosophischen Denkens. München: Piper 1965.

McLean, Martin: Britain and a Single Market Europe. Prospects for a Common School Curriculum. London: Kogan Page et al. 1990. (The Bedford Way Series)

Maia, Nelly Aleotti: Values. An Issue in Education and Politics. The Frank Klassen Lecture given at the 1995 annual meeting of the ECET, Bandar Seri Begawan, Brunei, 3-7 July 1995.

Mitter, Wolfgang: Challenges to Comparative Education. Between Retrospect and Expectation. Presidential Address delivered to the IXth World Congress of Comparative Education, Sydney, Australia, 1-6 July, 1996.

Piaget, Jean: Epistémologie des sciences de l'homme. Paris: Gallimard 1972. (Idées. 260)

Pipho, Chris: Getting Higher Education on-line. In: Phi Delta Kappan, 77 (1996) 7, p. 7.

Pombejr, Valai na: Teaching Tolerance for All. Education Strategies to Promote Global Peace. Paper submitted at the 1995 annual meeting of the ICET, Bandar Seri Begawan, Brunei, 3-7 July, 1995.

Sutaria, Minda C.: Rethinking the School Curriculum to Teach Tolerance and Peace. Paper presented at the ICET World Assembly, Bandar Seri Begawan, 4 July, 1995.

Suzuki, Shin'ichi: Europe: Illumination or Illusion? Lessons from Comparative and International Education. Late Professor Lawerys Memorial Lecture, addressed at the 16th CESE Conference at the University of Copenhagen 1994. [Partly printed in: Winther-Jensen, Thyge (ed.): Challenges to European Education. Cultural Values, National Identities, and Global Responsibilities (= Comparative Studies Series. 6). Frankfurt a. M. et al.: Lang 1996, pp. 447-448.]

Le renouveau de l'éducation comparée

Juan Carlos Tedesco

Introduction

Depuis déjà quelques années, nous assistons à un important renouveau de l'éducation comparée. Les résultats des différents pays en matière d'éducation, l'organisation institutionnelle de cette dernière et les innovations destinées à résoudre les problèmes que posent les changements de nature économique comme ceux de nature politique et culturelle, sont maintenant examinés avec une grande attention, non seulement par les chercheurs en éducation comparée mais également par d'autres spécialistes, par les responsables des décisions politiques et par l'opinion publique en général. A ce sujet, il est intéressant d'examiner l'importance accordée à l'éducation dans les récentes analyses comparatives de la situation économique ou de la gestion d'entreprise. Voir, par exemple *Drucker (1995)* et *Thurow (1996)*. Toutefois, cette comparaison ne s'opère plus sur la base des mêmes catégories et méthodologies que par le passé. Le renouveau de l'éducation comparée est associé à une modification importante tant des thèmes abordés et des instruments méthodologiques utilisés que des acteurs impliqués dans les études comparées.

Une revue rapide des objets d'investigation de l'éducation comparée abordés au cours des dernières décennies permettrait de comprendre que les préoccupations étaient principalement centrées sur la solution des questions d'effectifs, de financement et de résultats de l'apprentissage dans des domaines précis des programmes d'étude, particulièrement en matière de langues, de mathématiques et de sciences. Dans un article publié au début de cette décennie – et qui a provoqué une polémique importante entre les comparatistes – George *Psacharopoulos (1990)* résumait les sept questions auxquelles l'éducation comparée pouvait apporter quelque réponse: un plus large accès à l'enseignement primaire, l'amélioration de la qualité de l'école, l'extension de l'enseignement postprimaire, l'extension de l'enseignement postsecondaire, la formation des compétences, le financement de l'éducation et l'équité nécessaires. A l'époque, la polémique provoquée par cet article se cristallisa essentiellement sur le pragmatisme et l'empirisme de Psacharopoulos, par rapport à l'importance de la théorie et des méthodes qualitatives de recherche défendues par d'autres comparatistes. La liste des problèmes, quant à elle, n'obtint qu'une place secondaire dans le débat.

La caractéristique fondamentale des objets d'investigations traités dans les dernières décennies est qu'ils abordent des questions qui se définissent en fonction de l'insatisfaction ressentie face à la réponse qui est faite aux demandes quantitatives ou qualitatives relativement acceptées par tous: un plus large accès, une distribution plus équitable et des meilleurs résultats sur le plan qualitatif sont des points qui ne sont plus mis en question. Au contraire, actuellement, le questionnement commence à concerner ce qui est attendu et exigé de l'éducation. Pour comprendre ce phénomène il faut accepter le fait que nous vivons un profond processus de transformation sociale qui modifie les fonctions de l'éducation et ses liens avec les autres composantes du tissu social *(Tedesco 1995)*. L'éventail de la recherche en éducation comparée s'est donc élargi de manière significative. Une analyse globale de la littérature récente permettrait d'identifier, au moins, trois grandes catégories dans lesquelles peuvent être regroupés les thèmes qui le constituent

– l'éducation en tant que processus de socialisation,
– l'éducation en tant que processus cognitif, et
– le débat sur les finalités de l'éducation.

L'éducation en tant que processus de socialisation

Un des phénomènes sociaux contemporains les plus importants est l'érosion des bases selon lesquelles se définissent les identités professionnelles, culturelles et politiques de l'individu. Ainsi, par exemple, la rapidité acquise par le changement technologique provoque la disparition de nombreuses charges et fonctions traditionnelles et oblige à une reconversion professionnelle permanente. Les changements politiques ont modifié le sens des identités classiques de „droite" et de „gauche". Dans le domaine culturel, l'exigence d'une reconnaissance des identités ethniques et/ou religieuses ainsi que la construction d'entités économiques et politiques supranationales, affaiblissent les identités nationales traditionnelles. La forte concentration de la production des messages véhiculés par les moyens de communication de masse provoque une diffusion mondiale d'un modèle culturel dominant, érodant les bases des autres traditions culturelles. Les changements de la structure familiale – participation massive de la femme au marché du travail, abaissement constant de l'âge d'accès des enfants aux institutions éducatives, etc. – ont modifié les modèles de la „socialisation primaire" des nouvelles générations.

L'érosion des fondements traditionnels de la socialisation des nouvelles générations provoque l'apparition d'objets d'investigation éducative nouveaux et nombreux. Parmi les plus notables on dénombre: l'analyse des différentes modalités d'articulation entre la famille, l'école et les moyens d'information – spécialement la télévision – en tant qu'agents de socialisation; l'impact de la reconversion professionnelle permanente sur la structure des systèmes formels d'éducation et sur les processus de socialisation eux-mêmes; la relation entre les processus de socialisation et les phénomènes d'exclusion et de marginalisation sociale, tels que la violence, la drogue et d'autres comportements anomiques, ou les manifestations d'individualisme antisolidaire qui caractérisent le comportement de certaines élites; les représentations, préjugés et stéréotypes des enseignants comme des élèves confrontés à la diversité culturelle croissante de nos sociétés. En résumé, l'éducation devra s'occuper mieux et de façon plus approfondie du processus grâce auquel un individu devient membre de la société.

Par le passé, l'importance de ces thèmes allait de pair avec un discours fondé sur des variables essentiellement idéologiques. Maintenant, en revanche, le débat est beaucoup plus large. Les analyses économiques les plus récentes, par exemple, soulignent l'importance que revêtent les niveaux de cohésion sociale, de consensus et de solidarité pour le succès des stratégies de croissance (un exemple récent est *Fukuyama 1995*). Mais sur un plan plus global, la culture a acquis un rôle central dans l'analyse et dans l'anticipation des futurs scénarios sociaux. Samuel R. *Huntington (1993)*, pour qui la source fondamentale des futurs conflits mondiaux ne sera ni idéologique ni économique, mais bien culturelle, a effectué une présentation des plus radicales de cette hypothèse fondée sur la place centrale qu'occupe la culture dans la société. Bien que le postulat de Huntington ait été mis en question sous différents angles, il démontre la pertinence des processus actuels de construction d'identités nouvelles par rapport au développement social. L'éducation comprise au sens large de processus de socialisation est au centre de ce débat qui ouvre à la recherche comparée des perspectives thématiques très importantes.

La comparaison des processus de socialisation entre différentes cultures modifie aussi l'un des objectifs classiques de l'éducation comparée. Alors que par le passé la comparaison s'effectuait dans le but fondamental de connaître „l'autre", aujourd'hui cette comparaison a une très grande importance dans la recherche de la connaissance de soi-même. La diversité culturelle n'est plus exclusivement le propre de territoires différents, mais elle existe au sein de chaque société. C'est-à-dire que, si l'éducation comparée était autrefois une activité fondamentalement inter-nationale, aujourd'hui elle est également une activité intra-nationale. Des phénomènes extrêmes comme la guerre inter-ethnique dans l'Ex-Yougoslavie ou dans des pays africains comme le Rwanda, le Burundi, la Somalie ou le Liberia montrent que ces problèmes sont également prioritaires dans les pays en développement et qu'il faudra consacrer d'autres efforts de recherche à l'analyse du processus de socialisation – y compris à son aspect scolaire – qui a engendré ces phénomènes d'intolérance.

Le développement cognitif

Outre les changements observés dans les fondements du processus de socialisation, nous assistons également à une évolution profonde tant du rôle du savoir dans la société que des théories qui expliquent le développement de l'intelligence. Plusieurs facteurs sont à l'origine de ce phénomène. Premièrement, l'avancement des techniques d'exploration de l'activité cérébrale. Deuxièmement, le développement des nouvelles technologies de l'information et de la communication qui permettent d'intégrer dans les ordinateurs des opérations mentales qui peuvent être effectuées par des machines *(Delacôte 1996)*. Troisièmement, les changements des systèmes de production, qui exigent le développement de compétences tant intellectuelles qu'affectives qui modifient elles-mêmes de façon importante les exigences quant à l'éducation. Le rapport fait à l'UNESCO par la Commission internationale sur l'éducation pour le XXIe siècle fonde l'éducation du futur sur quatre apprentissages essentiels: „apprendre à connaître, *c'est-à-dire acquérir les instruments de la compréhension;* apprendre à faire, *pour pouvoir agir sur son environnement;* apprendre à vivre ensemble, *afin de coopérer avec les autres à toutes les activités humaines;* enfin, apprendre à être, *cheminement essentiel qui participe des trois précédents"* *(Delors et al. 1996)*. Ces quatre apprentissages sont considérés comme la base nécessaire au développement des compétences exigées de l'individu pour lui permettre de s'accomplir dans une société de l'information et des connaissances.

Une des conséquences les plus intéressantes de cette revalorisation des processus cognitifs est la reconnaissance de l'existence de diverses formes d'intelligence, au-delà de l'intelligence logico-mathématique qui dominait les études sur la question en s'inspirant particulièrement des théories de Jean Piaget (voir spécialement *Gardner 1993*). Une participation réelle au système de production et à la société requiert autant de capacités logico-mathématiques que de capacités affectives, de facultés de communiquer et de sens éthique. Les recherches récentes paraissent indiquer que les acquis dans chacune de ces „zones" ne sont pas transférables aux autres et que le développement de chacune d'entre elles répond à des stimuli spécifiques.

La prise de conscience de la diversité cognitive impose une modification des méthodes traditionnelles d'évaluation et de comparaison des résultats de l'apprentissage. Du point de vue cognitif, l'éducation comparée „traditionnelle" mesurait les acquis par l'intermédiaire de tests cernant les résultats de l'apprentissage selon des critères et des variables liés notamment à l'intelligence linguistique ou logico-mathématique. A l'avenir, au contraire, il faudra élaborer des instruments méthodologiques qui permettent d'analyser les différentes formes de développement cognitif. A cet égard, un des domaines les plus polémiques et les plus importants de l'éducation comparée sera précisément le développement d'instruments méthodologiques permettant de mesurer et de comparer de façon adéquate les différents résultats des actes éducatifs. La comparaison internationale n'est pas seule à se heurter à ce défi; il existe également sur le plan national, puisque les sociétés elles-mêmes tendent à se différencier toujours davantage sur les plans culturel et cognitif.

L'importance croissante des facteurs cognitifs et culturels implique également une modification des disciplines qui dominent dans les analyses comparatives. Dans ce sens, la suprématie des théories économiques, particulièrement le capital humain, perd de l'importance. La nécessité d'approches interdisciplinaires se révèle de façon toujours plus intense, en raison de la complexité des phénomènes éducatifs. Dans un article récent, Stephen P. *Heyneman (1995, pp. 625)* analysait avec lucidité les limites des explications économiques de l'éducation et reconnaissait que „*l'économiste de l'éducation doit appréhender la nature de l'enseignement et de la profession enseignante ... Il doit aussi avoir à l'esprit les différences d'âge et de style d'apprentissage individuel entre les apprenants, et le fait que des objectifs pédagogiques différents exigent des ressources différentes. Il doit en outre être capable de faire la distinction entre le nombre d'élèves par classe et le nombre d'élèves par enseignant (ou le taux d'encadrement); entre un savoir et l'application de ce savoir; entre les performances cognitives et les performances affectives; et entre la réussite individuelle (objectif des pays occidentaux) et la réussite du groupe (objectif des pays asiatiques). L'économiste de l'éducation doit être prêt à envisager des produits éducatifs divergents et des conséquences éducatives divergentes*".

La différenciation du développement cognitif et la reconnaissance de la diversité culturelle ont été associées à la transformation institutionnelle de l'éducation. Dans ce sens le phénomène le plus important des dernières années est la tendance vers la décentralisation et vers une plus grande autonomie accordée aux établissements scolaires qui domine actuellement les processus de gestion de l'éducation. De ce point de vue nous serions en train de passer d'une conception de la gestion de l'éducation fondée sur la notion de système à une conception centrée sur l'institution éducative. Ce changement expliquerait l'intérêt manifesté actuellement pour la promotion, l'enregistrement et le transfert des innovations. Différemment du passé, où l'on cherchait à transférer des modèles de systèmes d'éducation, on perçoit à l'heure actuelle un mouvement allant vers la recherche des innovations et l'établissement de réseaux de communication entre les écoles, en lieu et place de structures formelles régies par des liens purement administratifs. Cette tendance – qui a une longue tradition historique dans certains pays industrialisés – se développe depuis peu dans une grande partie des pays en développement. Les conséquences de ce processus sont encore incertaines. Cependant, deux effets sont déjà observables: d'un côté, ce que le Professeur *Mitter (1996)* a qualifié de *„decrease of interests in education systems as embodiments of national history and policy and, consequently, by a growing perception of the micro-level of education, namely of individual schools, communities and social mini-groups, these units subsumed under the term 'grass roots'"*. D'autre part, l'apparition de nouveaux objets de recherche. Le processus de différentiation institutionnelle engendre de nouveaux acteurs, dont le profil n'est pas encore défini, et modifie le comportement des acteurs traditionnels. L'analyse de ces *processus de construction des acteurs de la société* est un autre des défis les plus intéressants pour l'éducation comparée.

Les finalités de l'éducation

Le rythme accéléré du changement socio-économique et la crise dans les domaines traditionnels de la socialisation expliquent le „manque de sens" (voir en particulier *Laïdi 1994*) que de nombreuses études attribuent à la période historique actuelle. Ce manque de sens ne se présente pas seulement comme un problème individuel, il est également social et universel. D'après ces analyses, du temps de la guerre froide les États fragiles et les secteurs dominés avaient un point de référence pour se situer dans le monde et cet accès à l'universel favorisait leur propre cohésion interne. La fin de la guerre froide aurait sonné le glas non seulement du communisme mais également celui de deux siècles d'Illuminisme, c'est-à-dire de prédominance d'un schéma conceptuel, idéologique et politique qui donnait un sens à l'action de tous les acteurs. La rupture de ce schéma conceptuel se reflète dans la difficulté éprouvée à se représenter de quelque façon que ce soit le futur que propose la mondialisation, qui permettrait de s'investir pour des motifs intellectuels et affectifs et d'adhérer à des principes qui vont bien au-delà de la simple nécessité économique. L'incertitude est devenue la référence la plus répandue par rapport au futur et les promesses sociales ou politiques d'un „avenir meilleur" se sont considérablement estompées.

Dans les conditions actuelles, cette *perte de sens* a, pour le moins, trois conséquences majeures:

- le futur et les perspectives de trajectoire – tant individuelle que sociale – sont réduits à un seul dénominateur commun: le critère économique. Cependant l'évolution économique actuelle n'a pas la capacité d'incorporation et de mobilisation que possédait le capitalisme industriel traditionnel. Les nouvelles technologies et la dérégulation économique provoquent des phénomènes d'exclusion sociale toujours plus massifs. En conséquence, la possibilité d'atteindre un niveau approprié de cohésion sociale indispensable au développement durable et de formuler un message socialisateur qui offre une place à chacun va en s'amenuisant;
- la transmission des identités, qu'elles soient culturelles, professionnelles ou politiques prend une tournure régressive. Les difficultés à transmettre le patrimoine culturel du passé selon une ligne de continuité historique dirigée vers l'avenir provoquent la tentation d'un retour à des visions fixes et rigides des identités d'antan, typiquement anti-modernes;
- comme conséquence de ce qui précède, alors que certains secteurs sont totalement capables de prendre part au processus de changement, on observe dans d'autres un renforcement de l'immobilisme et de la méfiance envers toute idée de transformation. Le besoin de transformation est vécu par ces derniers comme une opposition au besoin de transmission de l'identité. Dans ce contexte, la transmission comme la transformation présentent des aspects négatifs: la première est jugée passéiste et la seconde destructrice.

Ce *„manque de sens"* a un impact direct sur l'éducation. De nombreux témoignages indiquent une augmentation croissante des demandes visant à l'incorporation dans les programmes d'études de dimensions qui satisfassent la nécessité d'atteindre des finalités déterminées (formation éthique, religieuse, civique, etc.), ainsi qu'une nouvelle formulation du rôle de l'enseignant, qui renforce son autorité morale et sa fonction de modèle et de guide des nouvelles générations. L'éducation, et plus particulièrement l'école, ne peut accomplir une tâche qui relève de la société dans son ensemble. Cette situation générale ouvre cependant au moins deux lignes d'action pour la théorie de l'éducation et pour la recherche en éducation comparée.

La première de ces lignes a trait au retour à la discussion classique sur les finalités de l'éducation, sur qui assume la responsabilité de former les nouvelles générations et sur l'héritage culturel, les valeurs, la conception de l'homme et de la société que nous désirons transmettre. La dimension philosophique recouvre donc une place d'importance dans la recherche en matière d'éducation. Il est clair qu'il ne s'agit pas de procéder à une réflexion métaphysique, détachée des aspects sociaux, économiques, culturels et politiques. Au contraire, il faut engager une analyse qui doit tirer profit de l'important développement des sciences sociales réalisé au cours des dernières décennies. En conjonction avec ce débat théorico-politique, la deuxième ligne d'action se réfère à l'étude des diverses façons dont les sociétés organisent leurs concertations et leurs accords sur les objectifs et les stratégies en matière d'éducation. Ce n'est pas par hasard que le „manque de sens" s'accompagne actuellement d'une insistance très nette sur le fait que les politiques de l'éducation exigent des accords à long terme entre tous les secteurs de la société. La question du consensus et des accords nationaux en matière d'éducation est devenue une condition indispensable pour garantir la continuité des politiques nationales d'éducation. Les modalités adoptées et les difficultés rencontrées dans l'élaboration de ces consensus constituent des éléments qui permettent d'étudier et de comparer les alternatives distinctes qui sont proposées pour offrir un „*sens*" à l'évolution de la société.

L'étendue de ces thèmes ne se limite pas au cadre des pays industrialisés. Dans ce domaine, il faut se débarrasser d'une assertion implicite qui sous-tend de nombreuses approches de l'éducation comparée et selon laquelle ces débats „philosophiques" sont secondaires face à l'urgence qu'il y a à résoudre les problèmes fondamentaux de l'analphabétisme, de l'accès à l'éducation de base ou de la disponibilité des manuels scolaires. Les dernières années nous ont fourni quelques leçons très pénibles dans ce domaine. En fait, les pays qui ont réussi à résoudre ces problèmes sont ceux qui sont parvenus à un accord social de base fondé sur le principe qui veut que tout projet de société doit offrir une place à chacun.

Conclusion

En résumé, le renouveau de l'éducation comparée implique un élargissement important des thèmes d'étude, la diversification de ses méthodes et l'utilisation d'approches interdisciplinaires. Dans l'allocution qu'il a faite lors du IXe Congrès mondial d'éducation comparée, Wolfgang *Mitter (1996)* analysait l'évolution historique de cette discipline et ses perspectives d'avenir. Sa propre biographie intellectuelle est un exemple de l'évolution des paradigmes de l'éducation comparée. Le débat ouvert sur le futur ne peut – comme le Professeur Mitter l'a démontré dans son discours – se limiter à considérer la question de l'éducation comparée en tant que discipline. Les intérêts corporatistes d'une discipline ne peuvent s'opposer aux intérêts du développement de la connaissance.

Bibliographie

Delacôte, Goéry: Savoir apprendre. Les nouvelles méthodes. Paris: Jacob 1996.
Delors, Jacques et al.: L'éducation; un trésor est caché dedans. Rapport à l'UNESCO de la Commission internationale sur l'éducation pour le vingt et unième siècle. Paris: UNESCO / Jacob 1996. [Version anglaise: Learning: the Treasure within. Report to UNESCO of the International Commission on Education for the Twenty-First Century. Paris: UNESCO 1996]
Drucker, Peter: Managing in a Time of Great Change. New York: Talley 1995.
Fukuyama, Francis: Trust. The Social Virtues and the Creation of Prosperity. London: Hamish Hamilton 1995.
Gardner, Howard: Frames of Mind. The Theory of Multiple Intelligences. New York: Basic Books 1993.
Heyneman, Stephen P.: L'économie de l'éducation: désillusions et espoirs. In: Perspectives, 25 (1995) 4, pp. 611-642.
Huntington, Samuel R.: The Clash of Civilizations? In: Foreign Affairs, 72 (1993) 3, pp. 22-49.
Laïdi, Zakï: Un monde privé de sens. Paris: Fayard 1994.
Mitter, Wolfgang: Challenges to Comparative Education: Between Retrospect and Education. Presidential Address delivered to the IXth World Congress of Comparative Education, Sydney, Australia, 1-6 July, 1996.
Psacharopoulos, George: Comparative Education. From Theory to Practice, or Are You A:\neo.* or B:*.ist? In: Comparative Education Review, 34 (1990) 3, pp. 369-380.
Tedesco, Juan Carlos: El nuevo pacto educativo. Educación, competitividad y ciudadanía en la sociedad moderna. Madrid: Anaya 1995.
Thurow, Lester C.: The Future of Capitalism. How Today's Economic Forces Shape Tomorrow's World. London: Brealey 1996.

Vergleichende Hochschulforschung – Probleme und Perspektiven

Ulrich Teichler

Einleitung

Hochschulforschung – hier verstanden als Forschung, die Fragen der Hochschule zum Gegenstand hat – hat sich in der Vergangenheit zumeist mit größter Selbstverständlichkeit mit einzelnen Nationen befaßt.[1] Gleichgültig, ob es um Reformbestrebungen und deren Wirkungen, die Beziehung von Hochschule und Staat, die Verwaltung der Hochschulen, Curricula, Lehr- und Lernprozesse oder Studium und Leben der Studierenden geht – üblicherweise wird davon ausgegangen, daß das Land die Bezugsebene ist. Deutlich wird dies auch daran, daß fast immer, wenn in methodischen Ausführungen empirischer Studien Fragen der Repräsentativität erörtert werden, das gesamte Hochschulwesen einer Nation das Idealbild ist, gegenüber welchem gegebenenfalls Einschränkungen gerechtfertigt werden. Wenn Hochschulforscher in dieser Weise das Hochschulwesen des eigenen Landes untersuchen, wird es zumeist nicht für notwendig gehalten, näher zu begründen, ob man die Befunde als typisch für dieses Land, für alle industrialisierten Gesellschaften, für die Gesellschaften marktwirtschaftlich-kapitalistischer Prägung oder als universell gültig betrachtet. Demgegenüber galt vergleichende Forschung als etwas Besonderes, das einer eigenen Begründung bedurfte.

Das bedeutet allerdings keineswegs, daß bisher kein Interesse an international vergleichender Forschung bestand. Für lange Zeit hatten vergleichende Studien jedoch fast ausschließlich den Zuschnitt von Sekundärstudien. Oft waren die Analysen mit hochschulpolitischen Empfehlungen verbunden, wobei zumeist inter- und supranationale Agenturen – etwa die UNESCO, die OECD, die Weltbank oder der Europarat – die Studien durchführten oder veranlaßten. Manche dieser Studien waren auch nach Urteil der Hochschulforschung eindrucksvoll, während andere nur Verwunderung darüber auslösten, wie schnell auf der Basis solider Kenntnis allenfalls von wenigen Ländern und wenigen einschlägigen Konzeptionen und eher oberflächlicher Kenntnis anderer Länder

---

1 Zum Stand der Hochschulforschung siehe die Übersichten in *Clark (1984); Research on Higher Education in Europe (1989); Fulton (1992); Teichler (1992, 1994)*.

und anderer Konzeptionen anmaßende Generalisierungen über welt-, europa- oder industriegesellschaftsweite Trends postuliert wurden.

Im Laufe der letzten Jahre ist das Interesse an vergleichenden Analysen zu verschiedenen Hochschulfragen deutlich gewachsen. Impliziter Vergleich prägt stärker als zuvor die Analysen und Diskussionen in den einzelnen Ländern. Die Informationsbasis, die in vergleichenden Sekundärstudien verarbeitet wird, ist reichhaltiger als zuvor. Nicht zuletzt nimmt die Zahl vergleichender Forschungsprojekte, in denen neues Wissen gesammelt wird, deutlich zu. Diese Entwicklungen sind in Europa besonders ausgeprägt *(Neave 1991; Teichler 1992).*

Die Zunahme international vergleichender Hochschulstudien kann nicht ohne weiteres als ein Fortschritt in der Hochschulforschung betrachtet werden. Natürlich ist der Vergleich eine grundlegende Verfahrensweise in den Sozialwissenschaften; natürlich ist er unentbehrlich, wenn makrogesellschaftliche Phänomene untersucht werden, um überhaupt mehr als einen Fall zu haben; natürlich gewinnt die Analyse jedes Themenbereichs in der Hochschulforschung, wenn ihr Kenntnisse aus verschiedenen Ländern zugrunde liegen. Dennoch trifft international vergleichende Forschung häufig auf Zurückhaltung oder sogar Mißtrauen, weil sie als verharrend in kuriosen, minutiösen Details, als wenig fundiert und schnell generalisierend und nicht zuletzt als wenig theoretisch und methodisch reflektiert empfunden wird. Wenn dagegen manche Studien auf der Basis klarer Konzeptionen und Methoden sich ausgewählten Phänomenen international vergleichend zuwenden, wird ihnen sofort vorgeworfen, daß sie sich nicht hinreichend auf die Komplexität des nationalen Kontexts einließen. Schließlich verfallen Debatten über vergleichende Befunde oft in Extreme: chauvinistische Selbstüberheblichkeit, devote Suche nach ausländischen Heilslehren und Warnungen davor, Äpfel mit Birnen zu vergleichen, lösen sich in munterer Folge ab. Chancen und Grenzen des internationalen Vergleichs scheinen auf der Hand zu liegen.

In dieser Lage erscheint es angebracht, eine Zwischenbilanz zu ziehen. Daher hat das Consortium of Higher Education Researchers (CHER) bei seinen Jahrestagungen 1994 in Enschede und 1995 in Rom den Stand und die Perspektiven der vergleichenden Hochschulforschung zur Diskussion gestellt. In diesem Rahmen entstand auch dieser Beitrag.[2]

---

2 Die ausführliche Analyse wurde in *Kehm / Teichler (1996)* veröffentlicht.

Im folgenden wird vor allem gefragt: Was beobachten wir an Leistungen und Mängeln der vergleichenden Hochschulforschung? Und in welchen Richtungen können wir Verbesserungen erwarten? Solche Überlegungen können sich nicht auf die Erörterung theoretischer und methodologischer Grundlagen des Vergleichs in den Geistes- und Sozialwissenschaften beschränken. Vielmehr scheint es erforderlich, daß die besonderen Bedingungen berücksichtigt werden, denen themenorientierte human- und sozialwissenschaftliche Forschung allgemein und die Hochschulforschung im besonderen begegnen. Dabei wird der praktische Kontext der Forschung – z. B. eine vorwiegende Förderung der vergleichenden Forschung in solchen Gebieten durch staatliche und politische Instanzen oder typische Probleme der Zusammenarbeit in internationalen Forschungsteams – nicht als zufälliger Rahmen betrachtet, sondern als Erfahrung, die systematisch bei der Forschungsplanung zu berücksichtigen ist.

Der vergleichende Ansatz in der Hochschulforschung

Zunehmende Aktivitäten der vergleichenden Forscher

Seit einigen Jahren vollzieht sich in der Hochschulforschung verschiedener europäischer Länder eine deutliche Akzentverschiebung: Viele Hochschulforscher sehen heute ihre Kollegen in Europa als ihre wichtigste wissenschaftliche Referenzgruppe, d. h. nicht mehr primär die Kollegen im eigenen Land und auch nicht primär die Kollegen in aller Welt. Dabei trägt der verbesserte Informationsaustausch auf europäischer Ebene – durch Vereinigungen, Konferenzen, Publikationen und zum Teil auch durch Kooperation in vergleichenden Projekten – zur Stärkung dieses Trends bei. Drei Faktoren sind meines Erachtens vor allem zu nennen, die dazu beitragen, daß die europäische Ebene für viele europäische Hochschulforscher solche Bedeutung in der wissenschaftlichen Kommunikation gewonnen hat.

Erstens ist in vielen einzelnen europäischen Ländern die Zahl der Hochschulforscher zu klein, um eine funktionierende wissenschaftliche Referenzgruppe darzustellen. Ein weiterer Rahmen der Kommunikation bietet sich an, um eine gewisse Objektivität und Vielfalt der gegenseitigen Herausforderung zu sichern.

Zweitens ist die gegenseitige Anregung durch internationale Kooperation und Informationsaustausch in den Human- und Sozialwissenschaften eher fruchtbar, wenn die Differenzen der Situation nicht extrem groß sind. In der Hochschulforschung beobachten wir eine gewisse grundlegende Ähnlichkeit der Forschung in Europa im Vergleich zu den USA darin, daß hochschulinterne Prozesse in der Regel in ihrem makrostrukturellen Kontext reflektiert werden.

Drittens hat natürlich die zunehmende „regionale" Kooperation innerhalb Europas das Interesse am innereuropäischen Vergleich erhöht, was immer dann der praktische Zweck sein mag – „benchmarking", gegenseitige Anregung bei der Suche nach Lösungen innerhalb der einzelnen Länder oder Vorklärung für die Schaffung gemeinsamer Lösungen in Europa. Dies hat auch zur Folge, daß – wie später noch behandelt wird – nicht nur Studien zum Vergleich der Hochschulsysteme, sondern auch zur Internationalisierung der Hochschulen an Popularität gewinnen und daß beide Ansätze zuweilen miteinander verknüpft werden.

Methodologische Fragen

Methodologische Fragen der vergleichenden Forschung sind in verschiedenen Bereichen der Human- und Sozialwissenschaften bereits so eingehend behandelt worden, daß eine weitere Beschäftigung mit dieser Thematik kaum neue Einsichten verspricht. Allerdings können wir beobachten, daß eine solche Debatte fortlebt und daß immer wieder weiterführende Konzepte über die Leistungsmöglichkeiten und angemessenen Methodiken des Vergleichs zur Diskussion gestellt werden.

Die Hochschulforschung hat sich nicht sehr ausführlich in methodologische Debatten über Fragen des Vergleichs hineinbegeben. Unter den international bekannten Hochschulforschern hat nur *Altbach* (z. B. *1988, 1991*) wiederholt zu Fragen der Konzepte und des Wissensstands der vergleichenden Hochschulforschung publiziert. Andere Wissenschaftler haben sich gelegentlich zu dieser Thematik geäußert (z. B. *Clark 1984; Goedegebuure / van Vught 1994*); darüber hinaus werden methodologische Fragen des Vergleichs gewöhnlich nur im Rahmen von Ergebnisberichten von vergleichenden Projekten aufgenommen. Die Hochschule ist jedoch häufig Gegenstand in methodologischen Schriften der vergleichenden Erziehungswissenschaften *(Mitter 1992)*, die die Hochschule als einen ihrer Gegenstandsbereiche betrachtet.

Hier ist nicht beabsichtigt, die einschlägigen methodologischen Diskussionen nachzuzeichnen. Vielmehr sollen deren wichtigste Erträge für die Hochschulforschung kurz resümiert werden.

Erstens ist festzustellen, daß international vergleichende Hochschulforschung – d. h. Forschung, die Aspekte des Hochschulwesens in mehr als einer „Kultur", „Gesellschaft" oder „Nation" vergleicht oder die Aspekte in einer Gesellschaft in vergleichender Perspektive betrachtet – sich nicht systematisch von der Forschung unterscheidet, die keine internationalen Vergleiche vornimmt. Die typische Logik des Vergleichs ist universell; wir bringen sie immer zur Geltung, wenn wir Gemeinsamkeiten oder Unterschiede zwischen verschiedenen Einheiten betrachten oder wenn wir erklärende Hypothesen prüfen wollen.

Zweitens können wir feststellen, daß die Erforschung makrogesellschaftlicher Phänomene des Hochschulwesens ohne internationalen Vergleich nicht auskommt. Analysen zum Beispiel über die Beziehung von Hochschule und Staat innerhalb eines Landes bleiben idiosynkratisch, wenn nicht andere Konfigurationen von Hochschulsystemen und andere Charakteristika staatlichen Handels gegenüber den Hochschulen herangezogen werden.

Drittens gewinnt man den Eindruck, daß die meisten theoretisch anspruchsvollen und empirisch gehaltvollen vergleichenden Analysen in der Hochschulforschung von einem semistrukturierten Rahmen von anfänglichen Annahmen ausgehen. Auf diese Weise wird die Stärke konzeptioneller Anleitung der Analyse mit der „Goldminen"-Leistung des Vergleichs – des Antreffens wertvoller nicht erahnter Einsichten – verknüpft.

Die Studien dagegen, die auf klare hypothetische Stringenz Wert legen und einen begrenzten Satz von Variablen im Vergleich kausal-analytisch prüfen wollen, geraten immer in ein doppeltes Problem. Erstens müssen sie die Fülle der Variablen, die zur Erklärung bestimmter Phänomene herangezogen werden, künstlich begrenzen, um die Stringenz ihres Ansatzes zu erhalten; deswegen werden solche Studien in der Regel als naiv im Übergehen der Fülle von kulturellen und sozialen Kontextbedingungen kritisiert. Wird der interpretative Rahmen entsprechend erweitert, so wird deutlich, daß die Qualität der Studie stärker von der interpretativen Virtuosität als von den im engeren Sinne geprüften Variablenzusammenhängen abhängt. Zweitens lassen so angelegte Studien nicht genügend Raum für Überraschungen, d. h. für relevante Phänomene, die bei der Hypothesenbildung nicht antizipiert wurden.

Auch die vergleichenden Studien, die auf Beschreibung und enzyklopädischer Sammlung von Details basieren, können natürlich als sondierende Vorstufen für die Entwicklung von Konzeptionen verstanden werden. Sehr oft verlieren sich solche Studien jedoch im Sammeln von Kuriositäten.

Daher sind solche Ansätze des Vergleichs am vielversprechendsten, bei denen die Wissenschaftler sehr wohl wissen, warum sie sich für bestimmte Probleme interessieren, aber zugleich in der Logik der Studie Raum dafür geben, daß die Befunde den ursprünglichen konzeptionellen Rahmen zerstören und Anregungen für eine neue Konzeptionalisierung erbringen können. So werden Überprüfungen von Annahmen und heuristische Anregung miteinander verbunden.

Viertens muß international vergleichende Forschung zu Hochschulfragen in Betracht ziehen, inwieweit ihre Grundannahme gerechtfertigt ist, daß es einzelne „Hochschulsysteme" gibt, die auf verschiedenen „Nationen", „Gesellschaften" oder „Kulturen" basieren. Die international vergleichende Hochschulforschung kann ihres Gegenstands verlustig gehen, wenn sich eine „Weltgesellschaft" entwickelt oder wenn sich transnationale Kooperation und Mobilität so verbreiten und vertiefen, daß demgegenüber nationale Systeme kaum noch eine Bedeutung haben.

Sicherlich erleben wir in mancher Hinsicht eine Globalisierungstendenz von Bildungsmodellen *(Dierkes / Weiler / Berthoin-Antal 1987)*, aber auch in mancher Hinsicht eine „Beharrlichkeit der Vielfalt" *(Teichler 1990)*. Wir beobachten zugleich Bewegungen in Richtung Internationalisierung und Indegenisierung sowie in Richtung supranationaler Integration und Differenzierung innerhalb einzelner Länder. Wir sind nicht sicher, ob sich eine „Regionalisierung" (Europa, Pazifisches Becken usw.) stärker durchsetzen wird als eine Globalisierung. Wir erleben zunehmend transnationale Aktivitäten im Hochschulwesen, aber wenn supranationale Kooperationen sich zu neuen sozialen Entitäten entwickeln, kann man nicht mehr von „transnational" sprechen. Auch gibt es einige Anzeichen dafür, daß globale Gemeinsamkeiten und Interdependenzen das Konzept nationaler Gesellschaften in der Zukunft ersetzen könnten.

Die These, daß sich die Bedeutung nationaler Hochschulsysteme bereits verflüchtigt, ist sicherlich verfrüht. Bei der Analyse von Strukturen des Hochschulwesens in den letzten zwei Jahrzehnten läßt sich zweifellos feststellen, daß die Entscheidungen zur Gestaltung der Hochschulstrukturen keineswegs durchgängig generellen funktionalen Erfordernissen von Industriegesellschaften folgen, keineswegs durchgängig mit bestimmten gesellschaftspolitischen Richtungsentscheidungen erklärbar sind und auch keineswegs eindeutig idiosynkratische Charakteristika des Hochschulwesens eines jeden Landes reproduzieren. Vielmehr werden heute nach eingehender Analyse der Situation anderer Länder jeweils spezifische Lösungen gewählt, wobei sich insgesamt die internationale Einheitlichkeit nicht deutlich erhöht *(Teichler 1990)*. Auch eine neuere Studie zum Hochschullehrerberuf kommt zu dem Ergebnis, daß deren Einschätzungen der eigenen beruflichen Lage und die Bewertung der Beziehungen von Hochschule und Gesellschaft stärker nach dem Land als nach der Disziplin variieren *(Maassen 1996)*. In jedem Falle ist es jedoch an der Zeit, bei vergleichenden Analysen nicht allein auf die Gemeinsamkeiten und Unterschiede nationaler Hochschulsysteme zu achten, sondern die supranationalen Entwicklungstendenzen genauer zu bestimmen. Auch kann die Analyse transnationaler Kooperation und Mobilität im Hochschulwesen nicht als ein Gegenstand betrachtet werden, der wenig mit dem Vergleich zu tun hat (so argumentieren *Goedegebuure / van Vught 1994*); vielmehr sind transnationale Kooperation und Mobilität immer wichtiger werdende Gegenstände vergleichender Analyse, weil die an internationaler Kooperation und Mobilität beteiligten Personen die Konfrontation unterschiedlicher Hochschulsysteme unmittelbar erleben.

Praktische Probleme der vergleichenden Hochschulforschung

International vergleichende Forschung ist in viel stärkerem Maße als Forschung innerhalb eines einzelnen Landes einer Fülle praktischer Probleme ausgesetzt. Diese können nicht gegenüber grundlegenden Fragen der Theorie und Methoden nur als Koinzidenzien abgetan werden, über die nur kurze buchhalterische Anmerkungen in entsprechenden Abschnitten zur Anlage der Studie innerhalb von Projektberichten zu erfolgen hätten. Sie beeinflussen vielmehr die vergleichende Forschung so sehr, daß sie ebenso als systematische Rahmenbedingungen zur Kenntnis genommen und behandelt werden müssen.

Die *Sprachbarrieren* sind das offenkundigste Problem. Nur selten gelingt es, ein Forschungsdesign für vergleichende Forschung vorzunehmen, bei dem Sprachbarrieren nicht intervenieren. Nicht selten beobachten wir eine solche Einschränkung des Untersuchungsgegenstands, daß oberflächliche Sprachkenntnisse nicht störend sind. Oder Länder werden vor allem nach dem Bekanntheitsgrad der Landessprache ausgewählt. Oder Regionalwissenschaften werden für Länder mit schwer zugänglichen Sprachen und Kulturen etabliert; endemisch für solche Lösungen ist, daß der höhere Aufwand für Sprach- und Feldkenntnisse oft mit geringeren Kenntnissen einschlägiger Theorien und Methoden sowie mit geringen Feldkenntnissen über das eigene Land oder dritte Länder einhergeht. Oder man stützt sich auf ausländische Kooperationspartner, was – wie später noch zu behandeln sein wird – oft zu unzureichender Abstimmung der Projektbeteiligten führt.

Kosten und Aufwand sind bei international vergleichender Forschung ceteris paribus höher als bei der Forschung in der näheren Umgebung. Dies mag dazu führen, daß kleinere Zuschnitte von Forschungsprojekten gerechtfertigt werden. Auch wird die Auswahl der Länder nicht selten unter dem Gesichtspunkt der Kostenminimierung vorgenommen. Gelingt jedoch eine ausreichende Mittelakquisition, so ist ein solches Forschungsprojekt auch einem größeren Erwartungsdruck ausgesetzt, was die Konzeptionen, Methoden und Erträge angeht.

Bei größeren vergleichenden Projekten ist oft die *Gegenstandswahl politisch bestimmt.* Solche Projekte werden in der Regel nur realisiert, wenn auch Staat und Politik überzeugt werden, daß die Thematik förderungswürdig ist. Denn weitgehend unabhängige Forschungsförderungssysteme sind oft im Selbstverständnis und in der finanziellen Größenordnung gegenüber vergleichenden Studien zurückhaltend. So kann es nicht wundern, daß bei der Auswahl der untersuchten Länder nicht selten politische Macht, politische Kooperation oder politische und wirtschaftliche Rivalität eine größere Rolle spielen, als dies sonst von der Konzeption der jeweiligen Studien her zu erklären ist.

In der vergleichenden Forschung fällt es schwer, ausreichende *Feldkenntnisse* zu gewinnen. Erst angesichts der Probleme des Vergleichs wird bewußt, in welchem Maße unser Wissen über den unmittelbar recherchierten Bereich hinausreichen muß, um die untersuchten Phänomene adäquat erfassen zu können. Bei vielen sozialwissenschaftlichen Themen wird in der näheren Umgebung ein Teil solcher Feldkenntnisse nicht systematisch im Forschungsprozeß erworben, sondern vorab unsystematisch aufgegriffen. Bei der Analyse eines anderen Landes müssen solche Feldkenntnisse dagegen zumeist intentional und im Rahmen des jeweiligen Forschungsprojektes erworben werden.

Natürlich bietet es sich an, Barrieren der Feld- und Sprachkenntnisse mit Hilfe von *internationalen Forschungsteams* zu überwinden. Zu bedenken ist allerdings, daß der Vorteil einer breiteren Feldkenntnis zumeist mit der größeren Schwierigkeit erkauft wird, innerhalb eines internationalen Projekts eine Übereinkunft über die Wahl theoretischer Bezugsrahmen, präferierter Methoden und die Relevanz der einzelnen Untersuchungsthemen zu erzielen; darüber hinaus ist die Kommunikation in einem internationalen Team, das auf verschiedene Orte verteilt ist, deutlich erschwert.

Oft wird versucht, eine solche Problematik, wie im folgenden Abschnitt noch näher diskutiert wird, dadurch zu umgehen, daß die Forscher eines Landes den theoretischen und methodischen Rahmen setzen und andere Forscher nur zur Datensammlung und Interpretationshilfe einbeziehen. Dies mag die Konsistenz des Ansatzes zunächst erhöhen, ist aber viel stärker dem Risiko ausgesetzt, daß überraschende und die Konzeption möglicherweise in Frage stellende Befunde gar nicht gewonnen werden. Der Versuch dagegen, ein integriertes internationales Team zu etablieren, erzwingt oft so viele Kompromisse in der Anlage der Studie, daß die besonderen Akzente der einzelnen Forschungsansätze verwässert werden und die Konsistenz des gesamten Projekts möglicherweise erheblich eingeschränkt wird.

Schließlich stellt sich für eine vergleichende sozialwissenschaftliche Forschung die *Problematik der Nähe und des Abstandes der Forschenden zum Gegenstand* noch ernster dar, als dies schon für die Forschung zur näheren Umgebung der Fall ist. So ist international vergleichende Forschung in besonderem Maße einem Ideologieverdacht ausgesetzt. Für manche Studien ist ein „vergleichender Chauvinismus" charakteristisch: Der Vergleich ist so sehr von den in der näheren Umgebung vorherrschenden Werten getragen, daß die Untersuchungen zielstrebig zu dem Ergebnis kommen, daheim sei es doch am besten. Andere Studien erscheinen als Produkt der Xenophilie: Die Wissenschaftler verhalten sich wie Botschafter, die zu lange in ein Land entsandt sind und sich dort assimilieren. Schließlich wird vergleichend tätigen Wissenschaftlern nicht selten vorgehalten, ihren Studien liege eine so hohe Wertschätzung von Internationalität und des Kosmopolitischen zugrunde, daß sie gegenüber ihrer Gesellschaft Wertinseln bildeten. Diese Vorwürfe mögen in vielen Fällen übertrieben sein; berechtigt ist sicherlich die Kritik, daß vergleichende Studien in besonderem Maße für Wertungen anfällig sind, die von den Adressaten der Forschungsberichte nur bedingt nachvollziehbar sind und nur bedingt geteilt werden.

Implikationen für zukünftige Forschung

Das Interesse an vergleichender Forschung ist in den letzten Jahren sehr gestiegen. Die Hochschule gehört zu den Bereichen, in denen Lernen aus den Erfahrungen anderer Länder höchst produktiv ist, universelle Elemente für sehr bedeutsam gehalten werden und wachsende internationale Kooperation als eine allgemein akzeptierte Aufgabe von hoher Priorität gesehen wird. Da vergleichende Forschung ohnehin hohe Ansprüche an Theorie und Methodik stellt, bietet sich für die Hochschulforschung durch das wachsende Interesse am Vergleich wie auch an transnationalen Aktivitäten die Chance, auf dem Weg zu einer unverwechselbaren Identität und zu einer hohen Qualität voranzukommen. Zugleich zeigt sich jedoch, daß vergleichende Forschung vielen Schwierigkeiten ausgesetzt ist.

Vergleichende Forschung zu Hochschulfragen hat selten eine geschlossene theoretische Basis. Nur wenige vergleichende Forschungsprojekte folgen dem Idealbild einer eindeutigen theoretischen Festlegung im Vorfeld und einer eindeutigen hypothetischen Struktur, die in der Untersuchung getestet wird. Die Mehrzahl der Projekte zeichnet sich vielmehr dadurch aus, daß zu Beginn eine Problembestimmung und vorläufige Entscheidung für theoretische und methodische Rückgriffe erfolgt; so werden einerseits Richtungen für die Analyse fixiert, aber zugleich eine heuristische Offenheit für die Verarbeitung überraschender Befunde und somit für die Fortentwicklung des theoretischen Rahmens gesichert.

In sich geschlossene Forschungsdesigns von elaborierter hypothetischer Struktur sind im Bereich der vergleichenden Hochschulforschung auch nicht in großer Zahl zu erwarten. Die nationalen Bedingungen für zu vergleichende Phänomene sind in der Regel zu komplex, um in einer hypothetischen Struktur ausbuchstabiert zu werden; deswegen verfallen Projekte, die diesem Postulat folgen, dem Verdikt allzu großer Simplizität. Hinzu kommt, daß der internationale Vergleich seine größte Stärke darin erweist, konzeptionelle Landkarten durch überraschende Befunde in Frage zu stellen.

Ebenso kommt hinzu, daß vergleichende Hochschulforschung auf viele Probleme praktischer Natur trifft. Die aufwendige vergleichende Forschung hat offenkundig nur Chancen auf ausreichende Finanzierung, wenn sie ein hohes Maß an praktischer Relevanz in Aussicht stellen kann. Sprachbarrieren und Grenzen der Feldkenntnisse führen oft dazu, daß vergleichende Studien in der Qualität nicht mit dem mithalten, was von solchen Studien erwartet wird, die sich nur auf ein Land beziehen. Dies kann im Prinzip am ehesten durch Kooperation zwischen Wissenschaftlern aus verschiedenen Ländern überwunden werden; diese ist aber wiederum besonderen Schwierigkeiten ausgesetzt: mit größerer Wahrscheinlichkeit als innerhalb von nationalen Forschungsverbünden ist mit einer Heterogenität der Lehrmeinungen zu rechnen. Zusätzliche Kosten, unterschiedliche Arbeitsstile und andere Faktoren führen dazu, daß internationale Forschungsteams anfälliger sind als nationale Teams.

Dabei läßt sich nicht eindeutig unterscheiden, welche Probleme der international vergleichenden Hochschulforschung theoretischer und welche forschungspraktischer Natur sind. Vielleicht gewinnt die vergleichende Hochschulforschung gerade dadurch, daß in der Projektplanung diese künstliche Grenze zwischen vermeintlich bedeutsamen theoretischen und vermeintlich akzidentiellen praktischen Problemen überwunden wird und daß bedacht wird, was im Zusammenwirken theoretischer und forschungspraktischer Faktoren die typischen Stärken und Schwächen der vergleichenden Hochschulforschung sind.

Die Einsicht, daß die Probleme in der Realisierung international vergleichender Hochschulforschung groß sind, braucht jedoch nicht zu entmutigen. Die erforderliche Vorgehensweise eines semistrukturierten Forschungsdesigns braucht nicht als Schwäche angesehen zu werden. Die Produktion simpler Analysen auf der Basis klarer Vorstrukturierungen oder die Bereitstellung großer Informationsmengen ohne konzeptionelle Sortierung sind ohnehin keine überzeugenden Alternativen. Wichtig ist die Erfahrung, daß halbstrukturierte Ansätze sich erfolgreich die „Goldminen"-Chance der vergleichenden Forschung zunutze machen.

Darüber hinaus kann man feststellen, daß eine gegenstandsbezogene Forschung, an die hohe Ansprüche theoretischer Qualität und praktischer Relevanz gestellt werden, ohnehin vor die Aufgabe gestellt ist, verschiedene Disziplinen zu verbinden und verschiedene Theorien im Untersuchungsdesign miteinander zu konfrontieren, anstatt sich streng an einzelne Disziplinen, Theorien und Methoden anzulehnen. Nicht nur der vergleichenden Hochschulforschung, sondern der Hochschulforschung allgemein steht es gut an, die Wahl der Disziplinen, Theorien und Methoden in der Durchführung eines Projekts systematisch der Frage zu unterwerfen, was sie jeweils im Vergleich zu anderen Ansätzen leisten.

Bibliographie

Altbach, Philip G.: Comparative Studies in Higher Education. In: Postlethwaite, Thomas Neville (Hrsg.): The Encyclopedia of Comparative Education and National Systems of Education, Oxford: Pergamon Press 1988, S. 66-68.
Altbach, Philip G. (Hrsg.): International Higher Education. An Encyclopedia. Bd. 1. 2. New York u. a.: Garland 1991.
Altbach, Philip G. / Kelly, David H.: Higher Education in International Perspective. A Survey and Bibliography. London: Mansell 1985.

CEPES/UNESCO (Hrsg.): International Directory of Higher Education Research Institutions. Bucharest: UNESCO/CEPES 1981.
Clark, Burton R. (Hrsg.): Perspectives on Higher Education. Eight Disciplinary and Comparative Views. Berkeley: University of California Press 1984.
Clark, Burton R. / Neave, Guy (Hrsg.): The Encyclopedia of Higher Education. Bd. 1-4. Oxford: Pergamon Press 1992.
Dierkes, Meinolf / Weiler, Hans N. / Berthoin-Antal, Ariane (Hrsg.): Comparative Policy Research. Learning from Experience. Aldershot: Gower 1987.
Fulton, Oliver: Higher Education Studies. In: Clark, Burton R. / Neave, Guy (Hrsg.): The Encyclopedia of Higher Education. Bd. 3, Oxford: Pergamon Press 1992, S. 1810-1821.
Goedegebuure, Leo / Vught, Frans van: Comparative Higher Education Policy Studies. In: dies. (Hrsg.): Comparative Policy Studies in Higher Education, Utrecht: Uitgeverij Lemma 1994, S. 1-34.
Kehm, Barbara / Teichler, Ulrich (Hrsg.): Vergleichende Hochschulforschung – eine Zwischenbilanz. Kassel: Wissenschaftliches Zentrum für Berufs- und Hochschulforschung der UniversitätGesamthochschule 1996. (Werkstattberichte. 50)
Leitner, Erich: Die Forschung über die Hochschule. Reflexionen zum 'Field of Study' und das Konzept eines Institutes für vergleichende Bildungs- und Hochschulforschung in Wien. In: Beiträge zur Hochschulforschung, (1995) 2, S. 133-156.
Maassen, Peter: Changing Political Contexts and Their Effects on Quality Assessment of Teaching and Research in European Higher Education. Paper presented to the Academia Workshop on New Challenges to the Academic Profession, Rotterdam 1996.
Mitter, Wolfgang: Comparative Education. In Clark, Burton R. / Neave, Guy (Hrsg.): The Encyclopedia of Higher Education. Bd. 3, Oxford: Pergamon Press 1992, S. 1788-1797.
Neave, Guy: A Changing Europe: Challenges for Higher Education Research. In: Higher Education in Europe, 16 (1991) 3, S. 3-27.
Research on Higher Education in Europe (Themenheft). In: European Journal of Education, 24 (1989) 3, S. 207-315.
Teichler, Ulrich: Europäische Hochschulsysteme. Die Beharrlichkeit vielfältiger Modelle. Frankfurt a. M. u. a.: Campus-Verlag 1990.
Teichler, Ulrich: Research on Higher Education in Europe. Some Aspects of Recent Developments. In: Frackmann, Edgar / Maassen, Peter (Hrsg.): Towards Excellence in European Higher Education. Proceedings. 11th European AIR Forum, Utrecht: Uitgeverij Lemma 1992, S. 37-61.
Teichler, Ulrich: Hochschulforschung – Situation und Perspektiven. In: Das Hochschulwesen, 42 (1994) 4, S. 169-177.

Éducation comparée et éducation internationale:
problèmes linguistiques

Henk Van daele

Éducation comparée et éducation internationale

Le terme „éducation comparée" apparaissait pour la première fois en 1817 avec la publication de „L'Esquisse et vues préliminaires d'un ouvrage sur l'éducation comparée" par Marc-Antoine *Jullien (1817),* dit „de Paris". En publiant cette brochure, malheureusement inachevée, Jullien créa non seulement une nouvelle science, mais la baptisa en outre „éducation comparée", expression qui jusque-là n'existait ni en français, ni dans un autre idiome.

Malgré l'existence de l'éducation comparée depuis près de 175 ans, il est de notre devoir de constater que les spécialistes ne sont pas unanimes en donnant une définition de l'éducation comparée *(Van daele 1993, pp. 16-21).* Les comparatistes discutent aussi de la place de leur champ d'étude parmi les autres sciences de l'éducation, ainsi que de ses méthodes et de ses paradigmes. Comme disait Wolfgang *Mitter (1995, p. 1):* „*Obwohl die Vergleichende Erziehungswissenschaft, wie Jürgen Schriewer 1986 bemerkte, als eine 'in die Jahre' gekommene Disziplin zu betrachten sei, sind die Diskussionen über ihren Standort und ihr Selbstverständnis trotz jahrzehntelanger Ansätze und Bemühungen immer noch in vollem Gange.*"

Récemment une discussion scientifique assez intéressante a redémarré au sujet de la ou des relation(s) entre l'éducation comparée d'une part, et l'éducation internationale de l'autre. Les promoteurs de ce débat actuel sont deux éminents savants nord-américains, Stephen P. *Heyneman (1993)* et David N. *Wilson (1994).* Le fait qu'ils ont déclenché de nouveau cette discussion, et cela pendant leur présidence de la prestigieuse „Comparative and International Education Society" (CIES), a surpris pas mal de collègues.

Surpris, d'abord, parce que la société américaine d'éducation comparée s'appelait jadis „Comparative Education Society" (CES) à quoi on a ajouté l'épithète „International" déjà en 1968. L'exemple américain a été suivi assez vite par la société britannique qui, elle aussi, a changé son nom initial en „British Comparative and International Education Society" (BCIES).

Surpris, encore, parce que durant des décennies pas mal d'auteurs ont essayé de distinguer clairement l'éducation comparée de l'éducation internationale. Une littérature assez abondante à ce sujet est à la disposition des intéressés.

Surpris, en fin de compte, parce que l'UNESCO a adopté en 1974, lors de sa XVIIIe Conférence générale, la „Recommandation sur l'éducation pour la compréhension, la coopération et la paix internationale et l'éducation relative aux droits de l'homme et aux libertés fondamentales". Dans cette recommandation, les diverses connotations de ces termes sont rassemblées en un concept succinct, à savoir „éducation internationale", ou „international education" en anglais; notons en passant que certains auteurs francophones préfèrent l'expression plus univoque „éducation à vocation internationale".

Enfin, on pourrait se demander si, de nos jours, les spécialistes des sciences de l'éducation n'ont pas d'autres chats à fouetter que de s'occuper des relations entre deux champs d'étude limitrophes parmi les sciences de l'éducation. Ne vivons-nous pas dans un monde qui traverse actuellement de profonds changements, et qui exige de nous tous de nouvelles connaissances et de nouvelles compétences? Oublie-t-on les millions d'analphabètes et les nombreuses victimes de l'exclusion sociale (femmes, réfugiés, enfants-travailleurs, chômeurs, migrants, etc.) pour qui des formes adéquates d'enseignement et de formation restent à organiser ou à perfectionner?

Problèmes de langues

Dans la première moitié du vingtième siècle, les termes „éducation comparée" et „éducation internationale" ont souvent été confondus, en anglais comme en français. Dernièrement, certains auteurs anglophones considéraient les „comparatistes" plutôt comme des théoriciens, alors que les „internationalistes" seraient des praticiens.

Wolfgang Mitter vient de souligner que ce point de vue est inhérent à l'approche anglophone. La langue allemande est plus précise: le terme anglais „comparative education" (ainsi que son équivalent français) doit être traduit par „Vergleichende Erziehungswissenschaft" ou *science* de l'éducation comparée; mais le terme anglais „international education" peut être traduit de deux manières: soit „Internationale Erziehung" („éducation internationale"), soit „Internationale Erziehungswissenschaft" („*science* de l'éducation internationale").

Des pionniers allemands de l'éducation comparée, comme Friedrich *Schneider (1931)*, Franz *Hilker (1964)* et Hermann *Röhrs (1975)*, faisaient déjà cette distinction il y a quelques décennies. Mais la plupart des collègues nord-américains semblent encore l'ignorer.

La remarque de Mitter confirme donc la thèse que l'éducation comparée exige de ses adeptes une profonde connaissance de plusieurs langues vivantes.

Education comparée: champ d'étude multilingue

Un spécialiste en éducation comparée est multilingue par nécessité. Nous sommes d'accord avec le polyglotte Américain William Brickman qui a défini les onze compétences qu'un étudiant-comparatiste doit posséder; en ce qui concerne les connaissances linguistiques, *Brickman (1969, p. 559)* précise: „*An ability to read with understanding and fluency the languages which are needed in research. Generally speaking, the student should be able to read well the languages of the country or countries in which he is specializing. If he is concerned with a cross-national study, he should get a reliable reading knowledge of the several languages involved in his study. For observation and research abroad, it is also necessary for the student to be able to speak and understand the foreign language or languages. Sometimes an ability to correspond in a foreign language may be a great asset to research.*"

Il n'est donc pas surprenant que certaines universités exigent explicitement la connaissance de plusieurs langues (européennes) comme condition préalable à l'étude de l'éducation comparée. Ainsi, l'Espagnol *González Hernández (1991, p. 19)* signale que c'était déjà le cas en 1966 à l'université de Barcelone, où les étudiants devaient „*traducir correctamente textos de dos lenguas extranjeras, una de las cuales debe ser inglés o alemán*".

A première vue, cette exigence spécifique imposée aux futurs comparatistes deviendra bientôt presque superflue sur le vieux continent, puisque la *Commission Européenne (1995b, p. 70)* dit clairement: „*Dans la prolongation de la résolution du Conseil des ministres de l'Éducation du 31 mars 1995, il devient nécessaire de permettre à chacun, quel que soit le parcours de formation et d'éducation qu'il emprunte, d'acquérir et de maintenir la capacité de communiquer dans au moins deux langues communautaires autres que sa langue maternelle.*" Remarquons que cette maîtrise de trois langues communautaires est une exigence de l'Union européenne qui va plus loin que les recommandations antérieures de l'UNESCO et du Conseil de l'Europe à ce sujet.

Bien que l'allemand soit la langue parlée par le plus grand nombre d'habitants de l'Union européenne, „*l'évolution de l'enseignement des langues étrangères pendant les deux dernières décennies est marquée par la course spectaculaire de l'anglais*" *(Commission Européenne 1995a, p. 69).* Cette préférence des jeunes pour la langue de Shakespeare est bien connue. Mais les linguistes se font des soucis: „*Ist das Englische eigentlich noch eine einheitliche und eindeutig definierbare Sprache?*" *(Erdmenger 1993, p. 9)* Même pour les traducteurs et les interprètes européens les différences entre le „Queen's English" et l'américain actuel posent parfois des problèmes de vocabulaire, de prononciation et d'orthographe. En plus, il y a des variantes dans les anciennes colonies britanniques, ou dans des secteurs spécifiques tels que le transport aérien ou l'informatique; travailler journellement sur Internet nous paraît la meilleure manière de se déshabituer des règles grammaticales et orthographiques de la langue anglaise.

Pour les comparatistes la connaissance approfondie de plusieurs langues ne suffit même pas. La raison est simple: l'éducation et la formation sont organisées par les États, les communautés, les cantons ou les „Länder". Si la même langue est parlée dans deux ou plusieurs de ces unités, les significations et les connotations des concepts éducatifs peuvent être fort différentes parce que chaque société éducative s'exprime dans son propre jargon. Les exemples abondent, aussi bien pour les langues moins répandues que pour celles qui ont une diffusion internationale.

A titre d'exemple, parmi beaucoup d'autres, signalons que le mot néerlandais „beroepsonderwijs", ou enseignement professionnel, a une autre signification aux Pays-Bas que dans la partie néerlandophone de la Belgique. Il existe aussi pas mal d'expressions et de termes néerlandais relatifs à l'éducation et la formation aux Pays-Bas qui sont inconnus en Flandre, et vice versa.

Ce qui est vrai pour le néerlandais – un idiome qui n'est parlé que par vingt millions d'Européens – l'est encore plus pour l'anglais, langue dominante des spécialistes de l'éducation comparée. Pas mal de termes éducatifs anglais ont un autre sens selon la partie du monde où l'on se trouve: l'ouvrage „A Glossary of Educational Terms: Usage in

Five English-Speaking Countries" de *Walker / Mumford / Steel (1973)* en fournit la preuve. Pour un comparatiste il ne suffit donc pas de „parler" la langue anglaise. Il doit aussi étudier la législation (de préférence dans la langue et avec la terminologie originales!) et le vocabulaire qui est typique pour la structure, la gestion, l'administration, etc., de l'éducation et de la formation de chaque État ou de chaque communauté. Des termes anglais comme „academy", „bachelor", „college", „master" ou „public school" sont représentatifs à cet égard, puisque leur signification peut différer d'un pays à un autre.

Naturellement le même problème existe aussi pour d'autres langues. Un mot français comme „collège" désigne un établissement scolaire différent suivant qu'on est en France, en Suisse romande, en Belgique francophone, au Québec ou dans certains pays africains appartenant à la francité *(Mialaret 1979, pp. 93-95)* ou, comme on le dit maintenant, à la francophonie.

Traduttore, traditore

Afin d'atteindre un plus grand nombre de lecteurs, les non-anglophones ont tendance à traduire ou faire traduire leurs publications dans la langue de Shakespeare. C'est alors que les vraies difficultés commencent. Bien sûr il existe de bons dictionnaires, et on peut aussi consulter les glossaires et les thésaurus plurilingues, comme le „Thésaurus de l'éducation" (*UNESCO 1991*) et le „Thésaurus européen de l'éducation" (*Communautes Europeennes / Conseil de l'Europe 1991*). Mais nous sommes d'avis que deux restrictions s'imposent.

Primo: les noms des écoles, des filières, des diplômes, etc., de chaque pays ou communauté doivent être considérés comme des noms propres dont, par conséquent, la traduction est proscrite. Ces concepts ont des particularités et des connotations propres qui trop souvent se perdent en les traduisant. „Grande école" (France), „public school" (Angleterre et Pays de Galles), „Prytanis" (Grèce), „Laurea" (Italie), voilà quelques exemples de termes impossibles ou difficiles à traduire, pris au hasard dans le „Diccionario Europeo de la Educación" et qui illustrent notre point de vue *(García Garrido 1996)*.

En second lieu, d'autres substantifs, pourtant couramment employés, peuvent créer des malentendus.

Prenons par exemple le descripteur „enseignement obligatoire" dans le „Thésaurus européen de l'éducation" *(Communautes Europeennes / Conseil de l'Europe 1991)* multilingue. Comme traduction anglaise cet ouvrage de référence donne le terme „compulsory education", pour l'espagnol „enseñanza obligatoria", et pour l'allemand „Schulpflicht". Le „Thésaurus de l'éducation" *(UNESCO 1991)* préfère le terme français „scolarité obligatoire", avec comme équivalent anglais „compulsory education" et, pour l'espagnol, „escolaridad obligatoria".

Il va sans dire qu'ici, deux notions ont été confondues: d'une part „enseignement ou instruction obligatoire" („compulsory education", „enseñanza obligatoria", „Unterrichtspflicht"); et d'autre part „scolarité obligatoire" („compulsory schooling", „escolaridad obligatoria", „Schulpflicht"). Pourtant les législations scolaires de la grande majorité des États européens prévoient que l'instruction obligatoire peut être donnée soit dans une école publique ou privée, soit à domicile par quelqu'un de la famille ou par une tierce personne.

En Europe, l'Allemagne fait exception à cette règle: l'obligation scolaire („Schulpflicht") y connaît une longue tradition. Déjà la „Gothaische Schulordnung" de 1642 stipulait explicitement la scolarité obligatoire aussi bien pour les garçons que pour les filles à partir de l'âge de cinq ans, en été comme en hiver *(Dietrich / Klink 1964, p. 55)*.

Education obligatoire et scolarité obligatoire ne sont donc pas synonymes. Mais comme disait Amanda *Petrie (1995, p. 285)*, spécialiste dans cette matière: *„Writers, journalists and academics have frequently made the fundamental mistake of confusing compulsory education with compulsory schooling."* Elle donne plusieurs exemples de cette confusion mais il n'est pas difficile d'allonger sa liste avec des publications plus récentes dont les auteurs mélangent les deux notions. Citons, parmi bien d'autres, un document de l'Unité européenne d'*EURYDICE*, „Dispositions relatives à la scolarité obligatoire" *(1991)* et le livre édité par J. A. *Mangan (1994)*, „A Significant Social Revolution. Cross-Cultural Aspects of the Evolution of Compulsory Education".

Il y a toute une série de concepts éducatifs qui offrent les mêmes difficultés. On constate par exemple que „Education at a Glance / Regards sur l'éducation" de l'*Organisation de Coopération et de Développement Economiques (1995)* emploie les mots „éducation préscolaire" et „early childhood education". „Le Thésaurus de l'éducation" *(UNESCO 1991)* ne mentionne pas „éducation préscolaire" mais préfère les termes „éducation préprimaire" et „pre-primary education". Le „Thésaurus européen de l'éducation" *(Communautes Europeennes / Conseil de l'Europe 1991)* prescrit „éducation préscolaire" et „pre-school education". Cet amalgame inutile de termes jette la confusion dans les esprits.

Bien que ces ouvrages de référence ne soient pas des bibles contenant des prescriptions inviolables, ils ne nous aident pas non plus à atteindre une certaine uniformité dans notre vocabulaire éducatif, vocabulaire trop souvent vague et confus. Et pourtant, la clarté et la précision des termes nous paraissent souhaitables pour la coopération éducative en Europe, pour la reconnaissance réciproque des compétences entre les États, ainsi que pour le développement des sciences de l'éducation.

Suggestion en guise de conclusion

En 1817, Marc-Antoine *Jullien (1817, p. 13)* écrivait: *„Les recherches sur l'anatomie comparée ont fait avancer la science de l'anatomie. De même, les recherches sur l'éducation comparée doivent fournir des moyens nouveaux pour perfectionner la science de l'éducation."* Seulement, les spécialistes en anatomie comparée disposaient au début du 19e siècle d'une langue commune et précise, le latin.

Il est de notre devoir de constater que nous ne disposons pas encore d'une „lingua franca" pour la terminologie internationale de l'éducation et de la formation. Or, pour nous Européens, l'équivalence des termes éducatifs dans nos multiples langues devient de plus en plus une nécessité absolue. Une commission internationale, composée de spécialistes polyglottes en éducation comparée, devrait se mettre à l'œuvre, si possible sous l'égide collective de l'Union européenne, du Conseil de l'Europe, de l'OCDE et de l'UNESCO. Nous croyons que c'est le seul moyen efficace pour atteindre les objectifs visés: la composition d'un glossaire multilingue univoque et l'unification du vocabulaire des sciences de l'éducation.

Parmi les experts chevronnés de cette commission devrait certainement figurer notre collègue Wolfgang Mitter. Nous avons eu la possibilité de suivre son itinéraire scientifique de très près pendant plus de deux décennies. Pendant la période de sa présidence enthousiaste et dévouée de l'„Association d'éducation comparée en Europe / Comparative Education Society in Europe", de 1981 à 1985, nous avons eu l'honneur de collaborer presque journellement avec lui comme secrétaire-trésorier de la CESE. Ses qualités de dirigeant ne passant pas inaperçues, Mitter était appelé à d'autres fonctions importantes. Ceux qui l'ont vu à l'œuvre à la présidence du „Conseil mondial des sociétés d'éducation comparée / World Council of Comparative Education Societies" (CMSEC / WCCES) ont pu apprécier ses dons de médiateur international et d'orateur plurilingue pendant une période difficile.

Si, comme nous le souhaitons, cette commission internationale pour l'unification de la terminologie éducative voit le jour, le professeur Mitter devra certainement y jouer un rôle important.

Bibliographie

Brickman, William Wolfgang: Guidance for Doctoral Students in International Educational History, Comparative Education, and International Education. In: Paedagogica Historica, 9 (1969) 2, pp. 554-562.
Commission européenne (ed.): Les chiffres clés de l'éducation dans l'Union européenne. Luxembourg: Office des publications officielles des Communautés européennes 1995a. [Version anglaise: Key Data on Education in the European Union]
Commission européenne (ed.): Enseigner et apprendre – Vers la société cognitive. Livre blanc sur l'éducation et la formation. Luxembourg: Office des publications officielles des Communautés européennes 1995b. (COM(95)590final) [Version anglaise: Teaching and Learning. Towards the Learning Society. White Paper on Education and Training]
Communautés européennes / Conseil de l'Europe (ed.): Thésaurus européen de l'éducation. Luxembourg: Office des publications officielles des Communautés européennes 1991.
Dietrich, Theo / Klink, Job-Günter (eds.): Zur Geschichte der Volksschule. 1. Bad Heilbrunn: Klinkhardt 1964. (Klinkhardts Pädagogische Quellentexte)
Erdmenger, Manfred: Weltsprache Englisch – die Sprache für Europa? In: Zeitschrift für Internationale Erziehungs- und Sozialwissenschaftliche Forschung, 10 (1993) 1, pp. 1-20.
EURYDICE (ed.): Dispositions relatives à la scolarité obligatoire dans les États membres de la Communauté européenne. Bruxelles: Unité européenne d'EURYDICE 1991.
García Garrido, José Luis et al.: Diccionario Europeo de la educación. Madrid: Dykinson 1996.
González Hernández, Angel: Lecturas de educación comparada. Barcelona: Promociones y Publicaciones Universitarias 1991. (Colección Maior. 3)
Heyneman, Stephen P.: Quantity, Quality and Source. In: Comparative Education Review, 37 (1993) 4, pp. 372-388.
Hilker, Franz: Internationale Pädagogik. In: Bildung und Erziehung, 17 (1964) 5, pp. 317-331.
Jullien, Marc-Antoine: Esquisse et vues préliminaires d'un ouvrage sur l'éducation comparée. Paris: Colas 1817. [Reproduction en fac-similé: Genève: Bureau International d'Education 1992]
Mangan, J. A. (ed.): A Significant Social Revolution. Cross-Cultural Aspects of the Evolution of Compulsory Education. London: Woburn 1994.
Mialaret, Gaston: Vocabulaire de l'éducation. Paris: Presses Universitaires de France 1979.

Mitter, Wolfgang: Vergleichende Analyse und internationale Erziehung in der Vergleichenden Erziehungswissenschaft. Discours prononcé à Heidelberg le 21 octobre 1995 à l'occasion du 80ème anniversaire du professeur Hermann Röhrs.

Organisation de Coopération et de Développement Economiques (ed.): Regards sur l'éducation / Education at a Glance. Paris: OCDE 1995.

Petrie, Amanda: Home Education and the Law within Europe. In: International Review of Education, 41 (1995) 3-4, pp. 285-296.

Röhrs, Hermann: Forschungsstrategien in der Vergleichenden Erziehungswissenschaft. Weinheim et al.: Beltz 1975.

Schneider, Friedrich: Internationale Pädagogik, Auslandspädagogik und Vergleichende Erziehungswissenschaft. In: Internationale Zeitschrift für Erziehungswissenschaft, 1 (1931) 1, pp. 15-39.

UNESCO (ed.): Thésaurus de l'éducation. 5. éd. Paris: UNESCO 1991. (IBEdata.)

Van daele, Henk: L'éducation comparée. Paris: Presses Universitaires de France 1993. (Que sais-je? 2786)

Walker, William George / Mumford, John E. / Steel, Carolyn: A Glossary of Educational Terms. Usage in Five English Speaking Countries. Saint Lucia: University of Queensland Press 1973.

Wilson, David N.: Comparative and International Education: Fraternal or Siamese Twins? A Preliminary Genealogy of Our Twin Fields. In: Comparative Education Review, 30 (1994) 4, pp. 449-486.

Things Fall Apart: Dis-Integration, Universities, and the Decline of Discipline(s). Problematising Comparative Education in an Uncertain Age

Anthony R. Welch

While modernity has arguably been a *leitmotif* of comparative education for much of this century, at least implicitly, the claims of post-modernity upon the field are much more recent, having begun with Val D. *Rust's (1991)* introductory disquisition less than a decade ago. This article sets out to critically evaluate the claims and prospects for a modern and a postmodern comparative education.

As Robert Cowen has pointed out in his recent edited issue of „Comparative Education", there are reasons why comparative education was relatively late in responding to the challenge posed by post-modernity. Having grown up in the full flood of modernist optimism about the use of education for reforming society, and (at least for much of the nineteenth century) as having often been allied to administrators' agendas in relation to educational reforms, it largely developed within the bounds of nineteenth and twentieth century positivist social science, whether based on more inductive or deductive formulations *(Welch 1996b)*. In this sense, it was not remote from the major debates of other examples of social science, in particular the modernist problematic of which competing position within the philosophy of science was to be preferred.

> „... the main theory debate of comparative education – the search for viable and scientific methodologies which so dominated the writings of the 1960s – was a re-emphasis on one of the strongest themes of modernity: that the social sciences would be scientific" (Cowen 1996, p. 152).

It is in this sense that comparative education was, perhaps for much of this century, captive to the so-called 'modernist project': that is, it may, like other social sciences, be associated with the ethos of the Enlightenment, with its passionate faith in rationality, and moral perfectibility. The conventional view of the Enlighteners, that if only the moral sciences could be brought to the same degree of perfection as the physical sciences, as Bacon explicitly and Newton implicitly had vouchsafed, held that the promised-land of the reform of practical philosophy (ethics, politics and the like) was, if not in hand, then at least in view. If, as was generally agreed, the physical sciences had effected a vast improvement in our technology and mastery over our dominion, then as the Philosopher Condorcet asked rhetorically, was it

„not also part of the necessary order of nature that the moral and political sciences should exercise a similar influence upon the motives that direct our feelings and our actions?" (Condorcet 1955, p. 192)

According to the Enlighteners, knowledge of the laws, and probabilities, of human history, for example, would warrant the prediction of humanity's destiny *(ibid., p. 173)*. We may discern in Enlightenment science the continuity of the modernist program of projecting a positivist natural science into all areas of human understanding, moral as much as physical. Had not Condorcet boldly claimed that nature set no limit to the perfectibility of *'les facultés humaines'*, beyond the duration of the earth itself? Furthermore, the progress of rationality and society, it was felt, depended on little more than scientific method, which was by now fully perfected:

„Philosophy has nothing more to guess, no more hypothetical surmizes to make; it is enough to assemble and order the facts, and show the useful truths that can be derived from their totality" (ibid., p. 9).

The Enlighteners, anxious to free man from the bounds of religious dogma and traditional authority, in matters moral and political, just as in matters physical, held that the divorce of reason from authority and moral constraint would presage great gains in the human sciences, as it had already done in the physical sciences. The new scientific values of the revealed religion of Bacon, Galilei, Newton and Descartes involved the renunciation of all traditional notions, and their replacement by 'certain truths' and 'precise ideas'. Descartes' legacy was in *„command[ing] men to shake off the yoke of authority, to recognize none save that which was avowed by reason"* (ibid., p. 122).[1] It is in this sense, as Habermas puts it, that *„the concept of enlightenment functions as a bridge between the idea of scientific progress and the conviction that the sciences also serve the moral perfection of human beings"* (Habermas 1984, p. 147).

---

1   But as *Luckmann (1980?, pp. 4-5)* notes, *„Although social theory tentatively freed itself from the constraints of a traditional religious world view, it accepted a different kind of foreign domination. It was subjugated by the new physical cosmology."*

The corollary of this view was the conviction that false moral and political views are inevitably rooted in specious theories of nature *(Condorcet 1955, p. 163)*. Science took on the function of enlightenment *vis à vis* the constraints of hidebound intellectual tradition and Church dogma. In this way, the progressive rationalization of society was taken one step further, and the claims of science to act as arbiter of rationality in every intellectual nook and cranny further secured. What was not science was mere opinion. Science was the guarantor of progress for mankind. Not only would hygiene and health be vastly improved, leading to an „*eternal life before death*" *(Habermas 1984, p. 148)*, but sexual inequality ended, civil liberties guaranteed, international peace assured and social inequalities reversed. Science was indeed providence for the children of the Enlightenment.

The somewhat contradictory heritage bequeathed by the Enlightenment *(Horkheimer / Adorno 1974)*, is one with which the developing social sciences, including research in comparative education, has grappled ever since, more or less effectually. Part of the ambiguous intellectual baggage that came with this modernist notion of social science had substantial implications for mainstream comparative education. At least three taken-for-granted assertions may be identified:

- the role of science as guaranteeing the highest form of rationality, upon which all forms of investigation in whatever field should be parasitic;
- the nation-state as the conventional unit of analysis; and
- Western culture as epitomizing the highest, most developed form of humanity.

Within comparative education of the twentieth century, the dominance of the first assumption meant that the earlier more cultural and historical styles of research such as those advanced, inter alia, by Nicholas *Hans (1949)*, Isaac *Kandel (1933)*, and Friedrich *Schneider (1947)*, increasingly fell by the wayside, bypassed in the rush to develop one or other form of scientific methodology, upon which rigorous research in comparative education could be based. The nineteen sixties in comparative education represented the apogee of this Methodenstreit (or better perhaps Positivismusstreit) *(Adorno et al. 1976)*, with figures such as *Bereday (1964), Holmes (1965), Noah / Eckstein (1969)*, and *Eckstein / Noah (1969)* each laying succeeding claims to have found the scientific lodestone of comparative research. Equally, and inspired by the same broad set of assumptions, the nineteen sixties was also perhaps the highpoint of modernization theory in comparative education (inter alia *Coombs 1968, McClelland 1961, Inkeles / Smith 1974, Harbison / Myers 1964, 1965)*, with its view that the unilinear progress of 'underdeveloped' states towards the *telos* of modernity could be assured by one or other set of universal structural characteristics and values *(Welch 1985)*.

The dominance of the second modernist taken-for-granted – the continuation of a bias towards the nation-state as the unit of analysis *(Mitter 1992, p. 1789;* also *Mitter 1989)* – was also to some extent arguably a product of history, reflecting the rise of the nation-state in Europe in the nineteenth century and, in turn perhaps, the role of the school in constructing nations *(Coulby / Jones 1996)*. The rise of nationalism had a significant impact not merely upon the history of colonialism (later to become of substantial interest to comparative educators examining cultural dominance, change and continuity) but more specifically on the developing social sciences themselves, including comparative education, where for much of the nineteenth and twentieth centuries, the nation-state ruled as the prime unit of analysis *(Burns / Welch 1992, Introduction)*. For much of the post World War Two era, organizations such as UNESCO, and later the OECD, compiled impressive databases of educational statistics, collected upon national lines, and often employed by researchers in comparative education. Only partly as a result, comparisons were usually conducted at the level of nation-states, without always acknowledging the constructed forms of individual nations; although as *Cowen (1996)* points out, the so-called forces or factors were logically and analytically prior in the work of the more culturally, or historically oriented comparativists, such as Hans and Kandel.

The perpetuation of the Western-centric bias in comparative research was also arguably a product of the modernist motif, in that modernism represented, *inter alia*, a triumph of reason over the traditional ethical bounds of established traditions, as had been intended in the Enlightenment. These included not merely the claims of rationality (in the form of science) over the bounds of established Western religious orthodoxies, but also over the claims of non-Western world views, which were often dismissed as simply primitive or unenlightened. The assumption of Western superiority was common in modernist social sciences, including in other comparative cultural disciplines such as anthropology, at much the same time. Such rigid adherence to the modernist canon left little scope for cultural difference. It dismissed rich and long-standing spiritual traditions such as those of native American peoples and Australian Aboriginals as simply heathenism, and helped license the appalling treatment meted out to long established indigenous communities in Australia, the USA, and Africa, despite a rising tide of revolution in the eighteenth and nineteenth centuries, based at least in part upon notions of universal human rights *(Welch 1996a)*. The all-conquering triple alliance of Christianity, capitalism and science, which, according to figures such as Feyerabend, was behind the technological and economic dominance of Western nations, was also to be found in the pronouncements of Western 'experts' who purveyed their advice throughout what was then called the 'un(der)developed countries'. Thus it may be argued, not merely was the process of modernization alluded to above, unilinear, it also inevitably advanced the *telos* of advanced Western capitalism.

Things Fall Apart: Problematising Comparative Education in an Uncertain Age

The context of *fin de siècle* comparative education, however, is substantially different to that of the 1960s, both economically, and intellectually. Clearly the oil crisis of the 1970s, intermittent recessions, the increasing internationalization of economies, and the financial deregulation, or even abandon, of the late 1980s in many countries are only some of the more important features of a changed social and economic landscape, one which forms a significant part of the altered topography of educational reform in the 1990s. As only one example, economic uncertainties, and the squeeze to do-more-with-less in higher education have clearly had an impact on the institutionalization of comparative education in many parts of the world. Shrinkage is now evident in many traditional centers of comparative research, at least in the established regions such as North America, Europe, the USA and Australia, and it is by no means clear that this process is yet at an end. To be sure, comparative education is not the only example of this trend, with similar patterns evident throughout the range of offerings in departments devoted to the study and teaching of 'educational foundations'. One consequence of this contraction in comparative education has been something of a failure to recruit a newer generation of scholars into the field.

More than this however is required to explain the changed landscape: contemporary comparative education is, like other 'subjects' beset by an increasingly diverse and uncertain context, which is by no means restricted merely to the economic. Economic contractions have also been accompanied by increasing moral and intellectual uncertainties, which are, however, yet to have such a decisive influence upon the practice of comparative research and teaching. (The late Brian Holmes might well have characterized this disjunction as a form of cultural lag.[2])

---

2 Holmes was particularly fond of this feature of the work of the social theorist W. F. Ogburn. See *Ogburn (1923)*.

The end of the twentieth century is in fact witness to a considerable corrosion of what were previously confident intellectual expressions as to the shape and character of 'knowledge'. To what extent does the end of the millennium also herald a millenarian change in the nature of 'knowledge', 'subjects', 'pedagogy', indeed even the idea of certainty and progress which, as was argued above, provided some of the intellectual foundations of comparative education? And how far does this also help us account for the gradual decline in 'foundations', including comparative education? Indeed how secure are these so-called 'foundations'? The challenge to the more traditional framing of educational knowledge has been based in substantial part upon the rejection of foundations, a challenge which in this instance is especially directed at the 'totalizing discourses' such as Marxism (or other such grand theories), or science, which purport to explain the world according to one or other set of overall principles. The world of grand theory, we are told, has been superseded by the (endless, uncharitable and inescapable) world of discourse. In this new world, style, image and an orientation of blasé, ironic detachment have usurped long-standing commitments to social justice and the reform of society, whose genealogy can be traced back to the Enlightenment, at least. Indeed, society itself is called into question, in the postmodern universe where collective action oriented towards any particular social goal is rendered illegitimate, and in which identity is seen as formed and re-formed under the impact of an ever-rising tide of undifferentiated imagery.

To the extent that comparative education has often not been burdened by long-standing and tightly defined disciplinary bounds to the same extent as say, the fields of history or sociology of education, and has displayed an at least intermittent affinity for such multi-disciplinary arenas of activity and research as multiculturalism *(Cowen 1996, p. 167; Coulby 1995)*, it could be argued that the postmodern challenge to the dominance of intellectual 'disciplines' posed less of a threat. Indeed the postmodern promise to centrally situate difference, including cultural diversity, could be seen as providing substantial support for a renewed form of comparative research and teaching, rendering redundant the quest for the holy grail of scientific method.

It is to be much regretted, therefore, that for two reasons, perhaps connected, this has not occurred. Perhaps the first is that the original promise of post-modernity to give voice to silenced minorities has not been fulfilled, indeed largely been overwhelmed by a tendency towards the obscure, and the arcane. Although perhaps less evident in comparative education, it remains true that in general, postmodern posturings have become increasingly characterized by a concentration upon esoteric language games, tropes and the like, overpowering any remaining commitment to the politics of difference. Equally, however, comparativists are at fault in having been slow to explore the potential of earlier post-modernity, in particular its capacity to both site difference at centre stage, and to reject the dominance of Western-centric modes of reasoning. Both of these alternative directions could still provide important correctives to some of the historical biases of comparative education, which although still being significantly challenged *(Lee 1996)*, are nonetheless common.

The swiftly changing contemporary context within which comparative education is being re-fashioned, is also due to some extent to (as yet ill-defined) processes of 'globalisation'.[3] At one level, these may be discerned in the increased use of electronic forms of communication, which denote an increasing (if superficial) ease with which cultural boundaries can be traversed, and penetrated. Such technological developments, however, are but a minor, if significant index of shifting boundaries, intellectual as much as geo-political. At another level, the process encompasses the globalisation of production, finance, media, the labour market, and, to a point, education. In this (more global) sense, globalisation represents more than the extension of global capital but rather „*the increasing tendency for the globe to constitute the effective domain of action and thinking, in relation to a specific issue*" *(Kress 1996, p. 186)*. This is having a substantial impact on the curriculum, as well as on other phenomena. The reconceptualization of subjects along such lines, including comparative education, and of geo-political entities, could represent an opening for subjects such as comparative education, which in a sense have always been multi-disciplinary, or at least had a disciplinary mix (not the same thing). Moreover, it is conceivable that in the current chilly climate in higher education, whereby subjects are increasingly differentiated within the institution in terms of their capacity to add surplus value and hence to attract corporate sponsorship *(Weber 1996)*, the more applied dimensions of comparative education may give it a certain edge, relative to other subjects which cannot so easily market their services.

But there is perhaps a contradiction here. Comparative education is only taught in universities, where traditional framing and patterning of knowledge is still paramount, especially in Europe. And in order to profess comparative education, one goes through a rigorous process whereby one learns to pattern knowledge (itself, as seen above, an increasingly uncertain term), and to parse 'it' in various ways. However, it is not clear

---

3   Giddens' rather twee expression 'action at distance' captures something of the flavour, but hardly does justice to the phenomenon, and its agenda *(Giddens 1994, p. 4)*.

whether such backgrounds and capacities will be as highly prized in the new globalized economies, where increasingly economistic solutions and logics are applied in social and educational research and policies. Will research, consultancies and policy activities now undertaken by those with many years of training in 'comparative education' be done in future by those well outside the university, and without its traditional training and socialization? In an era when both training and research are increasingly moving outside the confines of the university, to be located within specialist research laboratories or units, and within industry, is it inevitable that 'comparative education' will (need to) be undertaken by a wider range of individuals, with specific needs and diverse backgrounds? As Mitter's allusions to Heyneman in his recent presidential address to the recent Sydney World Congress of Comparative Education indicate, this is beginning to happen already, and there are signs that the current trend is to continue *(Mitter 1996, p. 1)*.

Taken together with the emerging trend away from traditional forms of teaching and learning in higher education, and towards virtual pedagogies (sometimes characterized as signifying a move away from the sage on the stage, towards the guide on the side), the impact on the institutionalization of comparative education is quite momentous, and by no means necessarily at an end. That this is happening more broadly in higher education provides little comfort to comparativists. The increasing availability of knowledge and information in electronic form means that knowledge is becoming less localized,[4] while increasing means of electronic communication is altering the pedagogies available, and hence the notion of pedagogical space. Unless comparative education learns to respond creatively to this diverse and swiftly changing context, it runs the risk of becoming increasingly bypassed in the rush towards a globalized, and uncertain future.

Bibliography

Adorno, Theodor W. et al.: The Positivist Dispute in German Sociology. London: Heinemann 1976.
Bereday, George Zygmunt Fijalkowski: Comparative Methods in Education. New York et al.: Holt, Rinehart, and Winston 1964.
Burns, Robin J. / Welch, Anthony R. (eds.): Contemporary Perspectives in Comparative Education. New York et al.: Garland 1992. (Reference Books in International Education. 16; Garland Reference Library of Social Science. 703)

---

4 „*Digital libraries, tele-teaching, teleconferencing, and electronic networking of all sorts profoundly relativise the importance of universities as localised institutions*" *(Weber 1996, p. 29)*.

Condorcet, Antoine Nicolas de: Sketch for an Historical Picture of the Progress of the Human Mind. London: Weidenfeld and Nicholson 1955.
Coombs, Philip Hall: The World Crisis in Education. A Systems Analysis. New York et al.: Oxford University Press 1968.
Coulby, David: Ethnocentrism, Post-Modernity and European Curricular Systems. In: European Journal of Teacher Education, 18 (1995) 2-3, pp. 143-153.
Coulby, David / Jones, Crispin: Post-Modernity, Education and European Identities. In: Comparative Education, 32 (1996) 2, pp. 171-184.
Cowen, Robert: Last Past the Post. Comparative Education, Modernity and Perhaps Post-Modernity. In: Comparative Education, 32 (1996) 2, pp. 151-170.
Eckstein, Max A. / Noah, Harold J.: Scientific Investigations in Comparative Education. London: Collier-Macmillan 1969.
Giddens, Anthony: Beyond Left and Right. The Future of Radical Politics. Oxford: Polity Press 1994.
Habermas, Jürgen: Theory of Communicative Action. Vol. 1. London: Heinemann 1984.
Hans, Nicholas: Comparative Education. A Study of Educational Factors and Traditions. London: Routledge and Kegan Paul 1949.
Harbison, Frederick / Myers, Charles A.: Education, Manpower and Economic Growth. New York: McGraw-Hill 1964.
Harbison, Frederick / Myers, Charles A.: Manpower and Education. New York: McGraw-Hill 1965.
Holmes, Brian: Problems in Education. A Comparative Approach. London: Routledge 1965.
Horkheimer, Max / Adorno, Theodor W.: The Dialectic of Enlightenment. New York: Continuum 1974.
Inkeles, Alex / Smith, David H.: Becoming Modern. Individual Change in Six Developing Countries. London: Heinemann 1974.
Kandel, Isaac Leon: Comparative Education. Boston, Mass. et al.: Houghton Mifflin 1933.
Kress, Gunther: Internationalization and Globalisation. Rethinking a Curriculum of Communication. In: Comparative Education, 32 (1996) 2, pp. 185-196.
Lee, Wing-On: The Cultural Context for Chinese Learners. Conceptions of Learning in the Confucian Tradition. In: Watkins, David / Biggs, John (eds.) The Chinese Learner. Cultural, Psychological and Contextual Influences, Hong Kong: Comparative Education Research Centre (Hong Kong University) and the Australian Council for Educational Research 1996, pp. 25-41.
Luckmann, Thomas: Phenomenology and Sociology. Wollongong, NSW: University of Wollongong 1980(?) (unpublished manuscript.)
McClelland, David Clarence: The Achieving Society. Princeton, N. J. et al.: Van Nostrand 1961.
Mitter, Wolfgang: Pädagogik, vergleichende. In: Lenzen, Dietmar / Rost, Friedrich (eds.): Pädagogische Grundbegriffe. Vol. 2. (= Rowohlts Enzyklopädie. 488), Reinbek: Rowohlt Taschenbuch-Verlag 1989, pp. 1246-1260.
Mitter, Wolfgang: Comparative Education. In: Clark, Burton R. / Neave, Guy (eds.): The Encyclopedia of Higher Education. Vol. 3, Oxford et al.: Pergamon Press 1992, pp. 1788-1797.
Mitter, Wolfgang: Challenges to Comparative Education. Between Retrospect and Expectation. Presidential Address delivered to the IXth World Congress of Comparative Education, Sydney, Australia, 1-6 July, 1996.
Noah, Harold J. / Eckstein, Max A.: Towards a Science of Comparative Education. London: Macmillan 1969.

Ogburn, William Fielding: Social Change with Respect to Culture and Original Nature. London: Allen and Unwin 1923.
Rust, Val D.: Postmodernism and its Comparative Education Implications. In: Comparative Education Review, 35 (1991) 4, pp. 610-626.
Schneider, Friedrich: Triebkräfte der Pädagogik der Völker. Eine Einführung in die vergleichende Erziehungswissenschaft. Salzburg: O. Müller 1947. (Veröffentlichungen des Instituts für Vergleichende Erziehungswissenschaft Salzburg. 1)
Weber, Samuel: The Future Campus: Virtual or Reality. In: The Australian, 18 (1996) 9, pp. 28-30.
Welch, Anthony R.: The Functionalist Tradition in Comparative Education. In: Comparative Education, 21 (1985) 1, pp. 5-19.
Welch, Anthony R.: Aboriginal Education as Internal Colonialism. The Schooling of Indigenous Minorities. In: idem (ed.): Australian Education: Reform or Crisis? Sydney: Allen and Unwin 1996a, pp. 24-53.
Welch, Anthony R.: Tradition, Modernity and Post-Modernity in Comparative Education. Opening Plenary Address delivered to the IXth World Congress of Comparative Education, Sydney, Australia, 1-6 July, 1996b.

Mimesis des Anderen – Annäherungen an das Fremde

Christoph Wulf

Der Andere

In Erziehungs- und Bildungsfragen spielt der Andere eine zentrale Rolle. Insofern Bildung und Erziehung es mit der Annäherung und Verarbeitung zunächst fremder Gegenstände, Zusammenhänge und Personen zu tun haben, ist die Auseinandersetzung mit dem Anderen unerläßlich. Infolge der Globalisierung der Lebenszusammenhänge und der mit der Entstehung der Europäischen Union notwendigen politischen, ökonomischen und kulturellen Anforderungen sind *Bildung und Erziehung zu einer interkulturellen Aufgabe* geworden *(Wulf 1995)*. Um dieser gerecht zu werden, ist die Begegnung und die Auseinandersetzung mit dem Anderen eine Herausforderung für die Bewahrung und Transformation der eigenen Kultur.

Für jeden einzelnen und jede Gruppe, jede Gemeinschaft und jede Kultur ist das Verhältnis zum Anderen konstitutiv. Wie einzelne Menschen und Gemeinschaften keine in sich abgeschlossenen Einheiten darstellen, so verhält es sich auch mit dem Anderen. Der Andere entsteht in einer Relation der Komplementarität zum Eigenen. Mit Hilfe von Grenzziehungen und Ordnungsmustern werden die Differenzen geschaffen, die den Anderen unterscheidbar machen. Wer und warum jemand als Anderer begriffen wird, ist vom historischen und kulturellen Kontext und seinen symbolischen Ordnungen abhängig. Wie Eigenes und Fremdes einander bedingen, so stehen der einzelne und der Andere in Relation. Weder ist der einzelne ohne den Anderen, noch ist der Andere ohne den einzelnen begreifbar. Als Anderer wird zunächst bezeichnet, wer komplementär zum einzelnen ist.

In der europäischen Kultur gibt es viele *Figurationen des Anderen*: den Fremden, den Feind, den Irren, das Kind, das Tier, das andere Geschlecht, das Gespenst, das Böse, das Unheimliche, das Heilige. In diesen Figurationen erfolgt eine Überlagerung zwischen einem konkreten Anderen und dem ganz Anderen. Der konkrete Andere verweist auf das sich der Bestimmung und Festsetzung entziehende radikal Andere. Im Falle Gottes wird die Überlagerung eines personifizierten Anderen durch das ganz Andere besonders deutlich. Doch erfolgen diese Überschneidungen auch in anderen Konstellationen. Indem das radikal Andere den konkreten Anderen überlagert, erhält dessen Repräsentation einen über sie hinaus weisenden Charakter. Jede Figuration des Anderen hat daher eine geschichtlich-konkrete Ausprägung und einen über sie hinaus weisenden Charakter. Dieser Doppelcharakter des Anderen ist eine Folge der symbolischen Ordnung der Sprache.

In anthropologischer Hinsicht ist die Erfahrung des Anderen an die menschliche *Exzentrizität* gebunden, die bewirkt, daß wir in uns *sind* und gleichzeitig uns so zu uns verhalten können, daß wir uns *haben*. Diese Spaltung ermöglicht auch die Komplexität der Figuration des Anderen. Der Andere ist der tragende Grund eines jeden einzelnen. Diese Konstellation ist bei einem neugeborenen Kind gegeben, das erst durch die Zuwendung des Anderen in eine menschliche Existenz kommt. Die Sorge des Anderen bezeichnet nicht nur die Unterstützung der individuellen Eltern, sondern verweist auch auf Aspekte, die zwar in dieser enthalten sind, zugleich jedoch über sie hinausreichen. Dazu gehören die mit der elterlichen Zuwendung zugleich übermittelten kulturellen Schemata, mit denen Gefühle ausgedrückt und erzeugt werden. Das Gleiche gilt für die Sprache, die über das Sprechen der Eltern an die nachwachsende Generation weitergegeben wird. Kulturelle Schemata und Sprache sind Elemente des Anderen, an denen alle Angehörigen einer Kultur Teil haben und die über die Generationenbeziehung dem Neugeborenen vermittelt werden. Für die Individuation des Kindes bedarf es der Vermittlung des Anderen durch Sprache und kulturelle Schemata im Austausch mit anderen Menschen.

Die grundsätzliche Spaltung des Menschen macht es möglich, daß er sich zu sich selbst verhalten kann und muß. Diese Situation ist die Voraussetzung für die Wahrnehmung des Anderen und der damit verbundenen Differenzen. Je nach Aufmerksamkeitsrichtung kann sich der Andere verschieben und sich in wechselnden Figurationen präsentieren. Ermöglicht wird seine Vielgestaltigkeit durch die Plastizität der menschlichen Konstitution. Wer als Anderer bzw. was als Anderes empfunden wird, ist Ergebnis eines Prozesses des Sich-in-Beziehung-Setzens mit einem äußeren oder inneren Gegenüber.

Eine eher paradoxe Verbindung zum Anderen entsteht durch Trennung. Radikale Differenz bewirkt nicht aufhebbare Asymmetrien im Verhältnis von Eigenem und Fremden. Das Andere ist irreduzibel; es gibt keine Brücke zu ihm. Rudolf *Otto (1963)* hat diese Vorstellung vom Anderen in bezug auf Gott als das ganz Andere entwickelt. Diesem wird eine nicht begreifbare Existenz zugeschrieben, die dem Menschen unheimlich und bedrohlich ist und die ihn dennoch fasziniert und anzieht. Auch *Levinas (1995)* hat an diese, sich der Reduktion durch menschliche Assimilation entziehende Vorstellung vom radikal Anderen erinnert. Sie führt dazu, den Anderen in seinen alltäglichen Lebenszusammenhängen wahrzunehmen, ohne dabei der Versuchung zu erliegen, ihn zu kolonialisieren oder zu vereinnahmen.

Der Diskurs über den Anderen macht auf die mit *Egozentrismus, Logozentrismus* und *Ethnozentrismus* einhergehenden Verkürzungen aufmerksam. Trotz entsprechender Zielsetzungen haben die Dynamiken des Egozentrismus den Anderen nicht zum Verschwinden bringen können. Auch wenn es zeitweilig den Anschein hatte, als gelänge eine Entschleierung des Anderen, so hat sich dieser Eindruck nicht bewahrheitet. Mitten im Alltäglichen, Bekannten und Vertrauten werden Dinge, Situationen und Menschen fremd. Die erwartete Sicherheit und Vertrautheit der Lebensbedingungen wird fragwürdig. Zwar hat die Strategie, das Andere durch Verstehen aufzulösen, dazu geführt, daß vieles Fremde zu Bekanntem geworden ist und daß an die Stelle von Verunsicherung und Bedrohung Sicherheit und Vertrautheit getreten sind. Doch ist diese Sicherheit oft nur Schein; hinter ihrem Rücken und an ihren Rändern haben sich Unsicherheit und Gefährdung nicht verringert. Der Gestus des Sich-die-Welt-vertraut-Machens hat die in ihn gesetzten Erwartungen nicht erfüllt. Mit der Zunahme des Bekannten vergrößert sich der Umfang des Unbekannten. Mit Hilfe der Ausweitung des Wissens gelingt es nicht, die Komplexität der Lebenszusammenhänge zu reduzieren. Je mehr das Wissen über Phänomene und Zusammenhänge zunimmt, desto mehr wächst das Nichtwissen. Immer wieder zeigt sich Nichtwissen und verweist den Gestus des Wissens und eines auf ihm basierenden souveränen menschlichen Handelns auf seine Grenzen. Das Andere wird häufig auf dasselbe reduziert, doch wird es dadurch nicht überwunden. Es artikuliert sich im Zentrum und an den Grenzen des Bekannten und fordert seine Berücksichtigung.

Mit der Zunahme des Individualismus wächst die *Egozentrismus. Elias (1976), Foucault (1976)* und *Beck / Vossenkuhl / Ziegler (1995)* haben diese Prozesse der modernen Subjektkonstitution detailliert beschrieben. „Technologien des Selbst" werden dazu verwendet, Subjekte zu bilden *(Martin 1993)*. Viele dieser Strategien orientieren sich an Vorstellungen von einem in sich geschlossenen Selbst, das als subjekthaftes Handlungszentrum unter dem Anspruch steht, ein *eigenes Leben* zu führen und eine eigene Biographie zu entwickeln. Die ungewollten Nebenwirkungen der Entwicklung zu einem sich selbst genügenden Subjekt sind bekannt. Nicht selten scheitert das sich-selbst-setzende Subjekt am Akt der Selbstsetzung. Die erhoffte Selbstbestimmung und das erwartete Glück autonomen Handelns werden von anderen, sich diesen Ansprüchen nicht unterordnenden Kräften konterkariert. Die Ambivalenz europäischer Subjektkonstitution zeigt sich darin, daß der ihr inhärente Egozentrismus einerseits als Überlebens-, Aneignungs- und Machtstrategie, andererseits als Reduktions- und Nivellierungsstrategie dient. Der in der Zentrierung auf die Ich-Kräfte liegende Versuch, den Anderen auf seine Nützlichkeit, seine Funktionalität und seine Verfügbakeit zu reduzieren, scheint gleichzeitig gelungen und gescheitert zu sein. Daraus ergibt sich für den Umgang mit dem Anderen ein neuer Horizont und ein neues Erkenntnis- und Aufgabenfeld.

Der *Logozentrismus* hat dazu geführt, vom Anderen wahrzunehmen und zu verarbeiten, was der Vernunft entspricht. Was vom Anderen nicht vernunftfähig und vernunftförmig ist, gerät nicht in den Blick und wird ausgeschlossen und abgewertet. Wer auf der Seite der Vernunft steht, ist im Recht. Das gilt selbst von der eingeschränkten Vernunft funktionaler Rationalität. Erwachsene haben gegenüber Kindern, Zivilisierte gegenüber Primitiven, Gesunde gegenüber Kranken Recht. Durch den Besitz der Vernunft beanspruchen sie, denen, die über Vorformen oder Fehlformen der Vernunft verfügen, überlegen zu sein. Nietzsche, Freud, Adorno und andere haben die Selbstgefälligkeit der Vernunft der Kritik unterzogen und gezeigt, daß Menschen in vielen Zusammenhängen leben, zu denen die Vernunft nur unzulänglichen Zugang hat. Der Ausdruck des Anderen in Körperinszenierungen bringt sprachlich nicht faßbare Bedeutungsüberschüsse zur Darstellung. Wenn sich der Andere vom universalistischen Charakter der Sprache und der Vernunft unterscheidet, wachsen die Schwierigkeiten, sich ihm anzunähern und ihn zu verstehen.

Nachhaltig hat der *Ethnozentrismus* die Unterwerfung des Anderen betrieben. *Todorov (1985), Greenblatt (1994)* und andere haben die Prozesse der Zerstörung fremder Kulturen analysiert. Am deutlichsten ist sicherlich die Kolonialisierung Lateinamerikas im Namen Christi und der christlichen Könige. Mit der Europäisierung des Kontinents geht die Vernichtung der dortigen Kulturen einher. Bereits beim ersten Kontakt wird Anspruch auf Anpassung und Assimilierung erhoben. Versklavung oder Vernichtung sind die Alternativen. Das Fremde muß so zurecht gestutzt werden, daß es sich in die eigene Ordnung einfügt. Gelingt dies nicht, muß es beseitigt werden, damit es nicht verunsichert oder gar gefährdet. Mit einer ungeheuerlichen Herrschaftsgeste wird das Eigene durchgesetzt, als müsse eine Welt ohne den Anderen geschaffen werden. Mit Hilfe eines machtstrategischen Verstehens wird es möglich, die Ausrottung der Eingeborenenvölker zu betreiben. Die Indios begreift nicht, daß die Spanier sich skrupellos berechnend verhalten und ihre Diskurse zur Täuschung einsetzen: Freundlichkeit meint nicht, was sie vorgibt und Versprechen dienen nicht dazu, etwas zu vereinbaren, sondern nur dazu, den Anderen zu hintergehen. Jede Handlung dient anderen Zielen, als vorgegeben wird. Legitimiert wird dieser Umgang mit den Interessen der Krone, dem Missionsauftrag des Christentums und der Minderwertigkeit der Eingeborenen. Verschwiegen und aus dem eigenen Selbst- und Weltbild ausgegrenzt werden Goldgier und ökonomische Motive. Was den eigenen Interessen nutzt, wird getan. Die Eingeborenen werden nicht als andere Menschen wahrgenommen, so daß moralische Kriterien im Umgang mit ihnen keine Rolle spielen.

Der Andere als Fremder

In der Kulturanthropologie, die sich als Wissenschaft vom Fremden begreift, hat es in den letzten Jahren umfangreiche epistemologische Diskussionen über den Anderen gegeben. Wie läßt sich der Andere denken, begreifen, darstellen? Nachdem man zunächst davon ausgegangen war, man könne ihn erkennen, verstehen und angemessen darstellen, ist in den letzten Jahren diese Gewißheit in Zweifel geraten. Wie läßt sich eine fremde Kultur darstellen, ohne daß die dabei verwendeten Gesichtspunkte und Kriterien dazu führen, ihr Selbstverständnis zu verfehlen? Ist die Repräsentation des Selbstverständnisses einer Gesellschaft auch die adäquate Form ihrer Erforschung? Verfehlt nicht das Selbstverständnis einer Gesellschaft ihre Realität? Was ist diese Realität? Wie läßt sie sich begreifen? Kann objektivierende Forschung und die mit ihr verbundene Vergegenständlichung sie erfassen? Welche Aspekte der Realität bekommt sie in den Blick, welche entgehen ihr und welche verfälscht sie aufgrund ihres Vorgehens? Inwieweit ist das Bild des Anderen, das die Ethnologie entwickelt, nicht ihr eigenes Bild, nicht ihre Konstruktion vom Fremden?

Auch wenn dies nur partiell der Fall ist, stellt sich grundsätzlich die Frage, wie weit sich jede Wissenschaft den Gegenstand schafft, den sie erforscht. In methodologischer Hinsicht steht die *Fallstudie* im Mittelpunkt der ethnologischen Erforschung des Fremden. Mit Hilfe *teilnehmender Beobachtung* werden Informationen erhoben, die nach dem Feldforschungsprozeß *verschriftlicht* werden. Teilnehmende Beobachtung und Verschriftlichung des Anderen in Fallstudien stehen nach wie vor im Zentrum der Kulturanthropologie. Nur besteht heute ein differenziertes Bewußtsein von den mit diesen Bedingungen notwendigerweise gegebenen Verkürzungen in der Erforschung des Anderen. In diesem Arrangement kommt der Andere nur in einer bestimmten Weise in den Blick. Seine Äußerungen werden wie ein Text „gelesen" und anschließend in Form einer Fallstudie verschriftlicht. Das Verstehen und Darstellen des Anderen bewegt sich von der Textstruktur des Anderen zu seiner Darstellung im Text des Ethnologen, dessen Aufgabe darin besteht, eine „dichte Beschreibung" (Geertz 1983) zu erarbeiten. Diese dichte phänomenologische Beschreibung ist an die Voraussetzung gebunden, daß die Verkörperlichungen und Ausdrucksweisen des Anderen nach Art eines „Textes" gelesen werden und daß diese Lektüre in einen neuen, den Anderen repräsentierenden Text übersetzt werden kann. Wird diese Voraussetzung in Frage gestellt, vermindern sich Aussagekraft und Wert der auf diese Weise gewonnenen Erkenntnisse.

Kulturanthropologie ist als hermeneutische Wissenschaft in der Gefahr, *„das Moment der Differenz, des Nicht-Identischen aufzulösen in einen allgemeinen Begriff des Verstehens und eine universale positive Methodologie hermeneutischer Aneignung des passend zugerichteten Fremden" (Berg / Fuchs 1993, S. 20)*. Sie steht in der Spannung zwischen der Einsicht in die Differenz des Anderen und der Versuchung, diese in eine allgemeine Begrifflichkeit aufzulösen. Eine hermeneutisch orientierte Ethnologie bearbeitet die Welt des Anderen mit Hilfe von Lektüre und Interpretation; sie thematisiert aber auch die Beziehung zwischen Anderem und dem Eigenen, zwischen der anderen Kultur und dem ethnologischen Referenzrahmen, und bezieht den Interpreten in die Interpretation ein. Eine hermeneutisch orientierte Kulturanthropologie arbeitet also mit Verfahren der Objektivierung und der Reflexion des Welt- und Selbstbezugs. Letztere kann zu einer Ethnologie des Selbst führen, die die Ethnologie des Anderen um wichtige Erkenntnisse ergänzt

Die Ethnologie hat den Anderen im Schnittpunkt von Kulturanalyse und allgemeiner Theorie des Menschen sowie ethnographischer Übersetzung und Beschreibung konstituiert. *Malinowski (1979)* hatte dazu in der Einführung zu den Argonauten drei einander ergänzende Objektivierungsverfahren vorgeschlagen:

1. die statistische Dokumentation der durch Befragungen und Beobachtungen gewonnenen Daten mit dem Ziel, Gesetzmäßigkeiten und Ordnungsschemata herauszuarbeiten;
2. das systematische und kontinuierliche Festhalten der Beobachtungen des Verhaltens der untersuchten Menschen im Feldtagebuch;
3. die Sammlung typischer Erzählungen, Äußerungen und magischer Formeln.

Diese Verfahren Malinowskis schaffen den *„Anderen als Objekt intimer und systematischer wissenschaftlicher Betrachtung überhaupt erst richtig: 'othering' durch Distanzierung, Kontextualisierung, Eingrenzung (Holismus)" (Berg / Fuchs 1993, S. 35)*. Als Ethnologe erarbeitete Malinowski eine Zusammenfassung der fremden Gesellschaft; als

Außenstehender konnte er ihre Charakteristika auf den Punkt bringen; er wurde zum Übersetzer, Chronisten und Sprecher der anderen Gesellschaft. Noch handelte es sich bei diesen Vorstellungen Malinowskis nicht um einen aktiven Wechselprozeß zwischen dem Anderen und seinem Erforscher. Aktiv und kreativ ist nur der Ethnologe. Die seiner Einstellung und Forschung entsprechende Darstellungs- und Textform ist die Monographie, die nach wie vor *eine* der zentralen Formen der *Vertextlichung, Objektivierung, Repräsentation* der Ethnologie ist. Malinowskis Umgang mit dem Anderen stößt auf die für jede Erkenntnis des Anderen konstitutiven Schwierigkeiten der Gegenstandskonstitution, des paradoxen Verhältnisses zwischen Nähe und Distanz, Partikularem und Allgemeinem, der Doppelrolle des Ethnologen als Feldforscher und als Autor. Diese Schwierigkeiten der Ethnologie im Umgang mit dem Anderen haben in der Folge dazu geführt, Textualität und Diskursivität der Ethnologie zu reflektieren und Experimente mit neuen Repräsentationsformen zu entwickeln.

Zu den wichtigen Beiträgen in der neueren Diskussion über den Anderen und die Möglichkeiten seiner Repräsentation gehören die Schriften von Clifford Geertz, die wesentlich zur hermeneutischen Wende in der Kulturanthropologie beigetragen haben. Nicht mehr die Erforschung des Verhaltens, sondern die Erforschung fremder Lebens- und Weltentwürfe steht im Mittelpunkt. Welchen Sinn und welche Bedeutung schreiben Menschen ihrem Empfinden und Handeln zu und wie können diese Sinn- und Bedeutungszusammenhänge dargestellt werden? Sinn und Bedeutung entstehen durch individuelle Auslegung und kollektives Verstehen zwischen Tradition und Neuinterpretation; sie sind gesellschaftlich konstituiert und sind daher öffentlich. Ins Zentrum rückt die Interpretation der Symbolsysteme, mit denen Menschen in anderen Kulturen ihre Welt und ihr Handeln wahrnehmen und interpretieren. Der Schwerpunkt der Forschung richtet sich weniger auf die individuellen Intentionen und Interpretationen der Handelnden als vielmehr auf den objektiven Sinngehalt ihrer Intentionen und ihres Handelns. Ziel ist die Erforschung der in einer anderen Kultur verfügbaren Werte, Bedeutungen und Handlungsorientierungen. Dazu bedarf es der „dichten Beschreibung" von Handlungen und Gesprächen mit erfahrungsnahen Begriffen.

Bei diesem Verfahren erfolgt eine Konzentration auf den Gehalt des Beschriebenen. Mit Hilfe der Verschriftlichung erfolgt eine Fixierung der Bedeutungsgehalte der mündlichen Rede, nicht jedoch eine Fixierung der Rede als orales Ereignis, bzw. als Sprechakt. Die Transformierung der Rede in einen Text impliziert notwendigerweise eine Distanzierung gegenüber den emotionalen und geistigen Intentionen der sprechenden Menschen. Darüber hinaus erfolgt in der Verschriftlichung eine Ablösung des Gehalts der Rede von den situativen zeit- und ortsgebunden Bedingungen des Sprechens. Durch den Wegfall der körperlichen und szenischen Präsenz der Sprecher entsteht eine Abstraktion ihrer Rede, die deren Gehalt für viele unterschiedliche Adressaten relevant macht. Ethnologie wird zur Ethnographie und wird zum Bemühen, einen Text zu lesen, seine Struktur herauszuarbeiten, seine Bedeutung zu entschlüsseln und die Ergebnisse dieses Prozesses in einen ethnologischen Text zu überführen. Im Mittelpunkt des Interesses steht die Idee, Kultur und soziales Handeln, Institutionen und Traditionen wie einen Text zu lesen und zu interpretieren. Dabei sind Sprachspiele, Metaphern und Metonyme in der Analyse zu berücksichtigen. Interpretiert wird zunächst, was die untersuchten Personen nach Auffassung der Ethnologen sagen. Sodann wird das Ergebnis dieses Prozesses noch einmal einer höherstufigen Interpretation unterzogen, in der Konstruktion, Fiktion und Kritik des Ethnologen eine zentrale Rolle spielen. Im allgemeinen sind die Adressaten des Ethnologen die Mitglieder seiner Kultur.

Für diese schreibt und arbeitet er an der Übersetzung der anderen Kultur. Offen bleibt in diesen Überlegungen, *wie* sich die beschriebenen Prozesse vollziehen. Sicher ist jedoch, daß in Folge dieser Sichtweise ein neues literarisches, methodologisches und epistemologisches Bewußtsein in der Kulturanthropologie entstanden ist, das sich fruchtbar auf die Wissenschaftsentwicklung und ihr Reflexionsniveau auswirkt. Wieweit es Geertz gelungen ist, in seinen Feldstudien seine Ansprüche an Qualität und Art der Annäherung an den Anderen sowie der Repräsentation des Fremden zu realisieren, ist in der Rezeption seiner Arbeiten umstritten.

Hatte sich im Werk Malinowskis eine problematische Aufspaltung von Subjektivität und Objektivität gezeigt und hatte Geertz versucht, dieser Schwierigkeit durch Rückgriff auf den hermeneutischen Zirkel gerecht zu werden, so wurde in der Folge gefordert, man müsse den *Stimmen der Anderen* mehr Raum geben. „The other speaks back" wurde zum Programm einer wichtigen Richtung der Ethnologie. Mit Hilfe eigenen Sprechens sollte der Andere versuchen, sich seine Subjektivität und Repräsentation wieder anzueignen. Dabei reicht das Spektrum *„von den grundsätzlichen politischen Attacken und Appellen Frantz Fanons (1969) über die Dekonstruktion des hegemonialen Diskurses des Westens, der die Anderen fixierte und noch die Kritik daran zu binden droht (Said 1981, Nandy 1983 und andere), bis zur Hinterfragung des autoritativen Bildes der einzelnen Kulturen, das die Ethnologie durchgesetzt hat"* (Berg / Fuchs 1993, S. 67). In zunehmendem Maße melden sich Vertreter einer indigenen Anthropologie zu Worte, deren Arbeiten in epistemologischer Hinsicht jedoch noch häufig in der angelsächsischen Ethnologie verankert sind. Die in den siebziger und achtziger Jahren in den Humanwissenschaften diagnostizierte „Krise" des Subjekts, der schon bald eine „Krise" des Objekts folgte, wirkte sich auch auf diese Versuche aus, den Anderen selbst verstärkt zur Sprache und zu Gehör kommen zu lassen. So konnten diese Ansätze nicht ohne weiteres davon ausgehen, einen privilegierten Zugang zur Kultur des Anderen zu haben. Auch sie mußten sich den Problemen der Gegenstandskonstitution und der Repräsentation des Anderen sowie der Subjektivität und der Kontrolle auf Seiten des Ethnologen stellen.

Mimetische Annäherungen

Unter den Verfahren des Umgangs mit dem Anderen kommt der Mimesis zentrale Bedeutung zu. In der Ethnologie hatte Frazer dies schon sehr früh gesehen. So beginnt er seine Ausführungen über *sympathetische Magie* im *Goldenen Zweig* mit der Unterscheidung zwischen der auf Ähnlichkeit beruhenden „nachahmenden Magie" und der auf dem Gesetz der Berührung beruhenden „Übertragungsmagie", deren Funktion er wie folgt bestimmt: *„Wenn wir die Grundlagen der Ideen im einzelnen untersuchen, auf welchen die Magie beruht, so sehen wir, daß diese sich in zwei Teile gliedern: einmal, daß Gleiches wieder Gleiches hervorbringt, oder daß eine Wirkung ihrer Ursache gleicht; und dann, daß Dinge, die einmal in Beziehung zueinander gestanden haben, fortfahren, aus der Ferne aufeinander zu wirken, nachdem die physische Berührung aufgehoben wurde. Der erste Grundsatz kann das Gesetz der Ähnlichkeit, der zweite das der Berührung oder der direkten Übertragung genannt werden. Aus dem ersten dieser Grundsätze schließt der Magier, daß er allein durch Nachahmung jede Wirkung hervorbringen kann, die er hervorbringen will"* (Frazer 1989, S. 15f.). Im Rahmen der Magie wird mit Hilfe von Mimesis Macht über den Anderen ausgeübt. Voraussetzung für das Gelingen der magischen Handlung ist Ähnlichkeit. Diese Ähnlichkeit stellt die Beziehung sicher, die der Magier zwischen zwei Gegenständen, Situationen oder Menschen herstellt. Sie erlaubt es ihm, mit Hilfe der Abbildung bzw. Repräsentation eines Originals Einfluß auf dieses Original zu gewinnen. Entscheidend für die Wirkungen der Magie ist der Glaube an sie. Allerdings täuscht sich Frazer, wenn er in der Ähnlichkeit eine unerläßliche Bedingung dafür sieht, daß magische Wirkungen mit Hilfe von Mimesis zustande kommen. Nicht die Ähnlichkeit ist entscheidend, sondern die Herstellung einer Beziehung zwischen einer Repräsentation und einem ihr zugrunde liegenden Ausgangspunkt bzw. die Stiftung einer Beziehung zwischen zwei „Welten". Durch den mimetischen Bezug meiner „Welt" zur „Welt" des Anderen erfolgt eine Annäherung an den Anderen.

Taussig (1993) verdeutlicht diese Prozesse am Beispiel von Figurinen der Cuna, eines Volkes im heutigen Panama, unter denen einige im Aussehen und in der Kleidung den weißen Kolonisatoren ähneln. Indem die Cuna durch einen mimetischen Akt Repräsentationen der Weißen in Form von Figurinen schaffen, gelingt es ihnen, die weißen Kolonisatoren zu verkleinern und ihnen ihren bedrohlichen Charakter zu nehmen. Mit Hilfe magischer Verfahren sind sie nun in der Lage, Macht über die als übermächtig erlebten Weißen auszuüben. Die kulturanthropologische Literatur kennt zahlreiche derartige Beispiele. In ihnen findet eine Annäherung an den Anderen dadurch statt, daß eine *Repräsentation* von ihm hergestellt wird. Mit der Schaffung dieser Repräsentation werden Gefühle und Einstellungen dem Anderen gegenüber zum Ausdruck gebracht und dargestellt. Der Andere wird in die eigene Symbolwelt überführt; die Beziehung zu ihm wird verkörperlicht. In der Repräsentation wird etwas sichtbar gemacht, das vorher nicht greifbar war. Die Herstellung einer Repräsentation der Weißen ist daher keine bloße Imitation, sondern ein mimetischer Akt, durch den unter Bezug auf Vorgegebenes Neues entsteht. Der mimetische Akt ist keine bloße Reproduktion, sondern eine kreative Handlung. Die Herstellung dieser Figuration der Weißen ist ein Versuch, mit ihrer Fremdheit umzugehen. Hinter der Hervorbringung dieser Repräsentation stehen Irritation, Verunsicherung und der Wunsch, das Unbekannte und Faszinierende der Weißen durch ihre figurative Darstellung und deren Bezug auf die eigene Symbolwelt zu begrenzen. In dieser Mimesis der Weißen geht es den Cuna weniger darum, die Weißen als Andere in den Motiven ihres Handelns und in den Werten und Symbolisierungen ihrer Kultur zu verstehen, als vielmehr darum, die Bedeutung der Weißen für die Cuna zum Ausdruck zu bringen und darzustellen. Der mimetische Akt der Schaffung dieser Repräsentationen ist eine imaginäre und symbolische In-Besitz-Nahme der Weißen, die aus dem Bedürfnisses nach Klärung der Beziehung zu den Weißen erfolgt.

Mimesis fügt das Fremde in die Logik und Dynamik der eigenen imaginären Welt ein. Dadurch wird das Fremde in eine Repräsentation transformiert. Als Repräsentation wird es noch nicht zum Eigenen; es wird zu einer Figuration, in der sich Fremdes und Eigenes mischen, zu einer Figuration des „*Dazwischen*". Dem Entstehen einer solchen Figuration des „Dazwischen" kommt in der Begegnung mit dem Anderen außerordentliche Bedeutung zu. Eine mit Hilfe von Mimesis geschaffene Repräsentation bietet die Möglichkeit, das Fremde in seiner Ambivalenz als Fremdes und zugleich Bekanntes zu erhalten, statt es festzusetzen und einzugemeinden. Die mimetische Bewegung gleicht einem Tanz zwischen dem Fremden und dem Eigenen. Weder verweilt sie beim Eigenen noch beim Anderen; sie bewegt sich hin und her zwischen beiden. Repräsentationen des Anderen sind kontingent. Sie müssen nicht so sein, wie sie sind; sie können sich auch in anderen Figurationen bilden. Zu welcher Figuration die mimetische Bewegung führt, ist offen und abhängig vom Spiel der Phantasie und dem symbolischen und sozialen Kontext. Keine Form der Repräsentation oder Figuration ist notwendig. Viele differente und heterogene Formen sind denkbar. Welche Figuren getanzt werden, welche Formen des Spiels gewählt werden, ergibt sich in der mimetischen Bewegung. Mimesis des Anderen führt zu ästhetischen Erfahrungen; in ihnen kommt es zu einem Spiel mit dem Unbekannten, zu einer Ausweitung des Eigenen ins Fremde. Mimesis bewirkt eine Anähnlichung an das Fremde. Sie ist sinnlich und kann sich über alle Sinne erstrecken. Mimesis führt nicht zu einem „Hineinfallen" ins Fremde und zu einer Verschmelzung mit ihm. Eine solche Bewegung implizierte die Aufgabe des Eigenen. Sie wäre Angleichung, Mimikry ans Fremde unter Verlust des Eigenen. Mimesis des Fremden beinhaltet Annäherung und Abstand in einem, Verweilen in der Unentschiedenheit des „Dazwischen", Tanz auf der Grenze zwischen Eigenem und Fremdem. Jedes Verweilen auf einer Seite der Grenze wäre Verfehlung, entweder des Eigenen oder des Fremden, und das Ende der mimetischen Bewegung.

Die Mimesis des Anderen vollzieht sich zwischen Skylla und Charybdis, zwischen der Auslieferung ans Fremde unter Verzicht auf das Eigene und der Reduktion des Fremden auf das Eigene. Auf der einen Seite finden sich die verklärten Gesichter projektiver Xenophilie, auf der anderen die schrecklichen Fratzen der Xenophobie. In beiden zeigt sich die Vermeidung von Begegnung und Auseinandersetzung. Im ersten Fall werden Differenzen übersprungen, im zweiten nicht zugelassen. In beiden Fällen wird geopfert: entweder das Eigene oder das Fremde. In keinem Fall entsteht etwas Neues. Xenophilie führt zu keiner Erfahrung des Anderen. Wenn der Andere nicht die in ihn gesetzten Erwartungen und Hoffnungen erfüllt, wird aus der projektiven Zuneigung Ablehnung und Feindschaft, die zu ähnlichen Gefühlen beim Anderen führt. Ein sich wechselseitig verstärkender Zirkel von Feindschaft und Gewalt entsteht, dem mimetische Prozesse zugrunde liegen. Beide Seiten reagieren auf die Feindschaft des Anderen und intensivieren mit ihren Reaktionen das Ausmaß der Gewalt. Erst mit Hilfe von Sündenböcken, auf die die Gesellschaft die ihr inhärente Gewalt projiziert, kann die zerbrochene soziale Ordnung wieder hergestellt werden. Sündenböcke werden identifiziert und zu Opfern gemacht, um die „mimetische Krise" *(Girard 1988)* zu überwinden. Solange diese Mechanismen von den Beteiligten nicht durchschaut werden, wirken sie ungebrochen. Keine Verständigung ist möglich. Projektionen und wechselseitig sich verstärkende Feindbilder verhindern Wahrnehmung, Begegnung und Auseinandersetzung mit dem Anderen.

Die zweite Möglichkeit, den Anderen zu verfehlen, liegt darin, ihn nicht in seiner Differenz zum Eigenen wahrzunehmen. Wie leicht dies geschieht und wie nachhaltig die Folgen des Verdrängens von Differenzen sind, haben *Todorov (1985)* und *Greenblatt (1994)* an der Begegnung zwischen den spanischen Eroberern und den Eingeborenen Lateinamerikas verdeutlicht. Kolumbus nimmt von den Eingeborenen nur das wahr, was er schon vorher von ihnen weiß. Er sieht in ihrer Welt nur Zeichen, die ihn auf Bekanntes verweisen und die er in bezug auf seinen Referenzrahmen liest, einordnet und interpretiert. Dieser Referenzrahmen ist in sich geschlossen, so daß er dem Bett des Prokrustes gleicht, in das alles Fremde so hinein gezwungen wird, daß es in die vorgegebenen Strukturen „paßt". Der Andere wird von den Bilder und Symbolen des Eigenen zugedeckt und in sie eingeschlossen. Was sich nicht einfügt, bleibt außerhalb der Wahrnehmung und der Verarbeitung. Dadurch entsteht keine Bewegung zum Anderen. Staunen und Verwunderung sind die Folge. Man berichtet von der Einmaligkeit und Außergewöhnlichkeit des Gesehenen und vergleicht es mit Traumbildern. Eine solche Beschreibung entrückt das Gesehene: *„Die Verwunderung ist die Erfahrung eines doppelten Versagens, eines Versagens der Worte – es bleibt nur der stammelnde Rückgriff auf alte Ritterlegenden – und eines Versagens der Augen, insofern der Anblick eines Gegenstandes keinerlei Gewähr mehr dafür bietet, daß er auch wirklich existiert"* (Greenblatt 1994, S. 204). Die Verwunderung wird zu einer Hürde, die die Bewegung zum Anderen blockiert und die Erregung intensiviert. Mit der sich aus der Blockade der Bewegung zum Anderen ergebenden Distanz wächst das Begehren, diese Grenze zu überschreiten.

Zwei Wege bieten sich an.

Der eine führt über die Bildung von Repräsentationen des Anderen, über Figurationen, in die das Fremde transformiert wird, so daß ein Umgang mit ihm möglich wird. Zu dieser Form gehören auch Versuche diskursiver Annäherung an den Anderen sowie die in der Verschriftlichung entstehenden sprachlichen Repräsentationen. Wird dieser Weg beschritten, kommt es zu einer Form der Akzeptanz des Anderen, die sich auf den Anderen im Außen und Fremden und den Anderen im Eigenen und Vertrauten erstreckt. In den figurativen, diskursiven und literalen Repräsentationen wird der Andere zum Eigenen und das Eigene zum Anderen.

Der andere Weg betont die unüberwindbare Differenz, die keine Umwandlung des Anderen ermöglicht: *„Die Bewegung verläuft über die Identifikation zur vollkommenen Entfremdung: Einen Augenblick lang kann man sich selbst nicht vom Anderen unterscheiden, aber dann macht man den Anderen zu einem radikal fremden Gegenstand, einem*

Ding, das sich ganz nach Belieben zerstören oder einverleiben läßt" *(Greenblatt 1994, S. 206).* Diesen Weg wählen die spanischen Eroberer. Sie können die Differenz zur Welt der Eingeborenen nicht aushalten. Daher wollen und müssen sie diese Welt in Besitz nehmen. Ihr Traum vom Besitz gilt dem Land, dem Gold, den Körpern und Seelen der Menschen. Doch ihre Besitzergreifung ist nur nach der Zerstörung möglich. Erst infolge der Zerstörung verliert diese Welt ihre Andersheit. Über ihre Trümmer läßt sich unbekümmert verfügen. Sie erst ermöglichen die erstrebte In-Besitz-Nahme der anderen Welt. Für die Spanier sind Zerstörung und Besitznahme Schutz vor der Gefahr, sich an die Eingeborenen zu verlieren. In den wiederholt berichteten fiktiven Geschichten vom Kannibalismus der Indios kommt die Angst der Eroberer davor zum Ausdruck, getötet und verschlungen, aufgelöst und assimiliert zu werden. Der in der Rhetorik dieser Geschichten produzierte Abscheu vor den kannibalischen Eingeborenen ist ein Versuch, Abstand gegenüber der Faszination durch den Anderen zu gewinnen. Die Zerstörung der Eingeborenen schafft nachhaltig Distanz und läßt sich als Selbsterhaltungs- und Überlebensstrategie der Spanier begreifen. Wenn die Eingeborenen vernichtet sind, können sie ihre Andersheit nicht mehr ausdrücken; sie verlieren ihre Bedrohlichkeit. Die Eroberer nehmen, was sie bekommen können, in Besitz und verfügen darüber beliebig: kein Widerstand, keine Auseinandersetzung. Sie begnügen sich nicht mit der Inbesitznahme der Reichtümer und der Frauen; ihr Begehren richtet sich auch darauf, die religiösen Energien der Eingeborenen auf ihre eigenen Symbole umzulenken und so die Imagination der Indios zu unterwerfen und neu zu besetzen. Nicht Öffnung gegenüber dem Fremden und Bereicherung, sondern in Besitznahme und Zerstörung sind die Folge.

Die Annäherung an den Anderen ist stets ambivalent. Sie kann gelingen und zu einer Bereicherung des Eigenen werden. Sie kann aber auch fehlschlagen und zur Zerstörung des Anderen und des Eigenen führen. Die Begegnung mit dem Anderen oszilliert zwischen den Polen des Bestimmten und des Unbestimmten. Wieweit es gelingt, Verunsicherungen durch das Nicht-Identische des Anderen auszuhalten, entscheidet über das Gelingen der Annäherung und des Umgangs mit dem Fremden.

Bibliographie

Augé, Marc: Le sens des autres. Actualité de l'anthropologie. Paris: Fayard 1994.
Baudrillard, Jean / Guillaume, Marc: Figures de l'altérité. Paris: Descartes 1994.
Beck, Ulrich / Vossenkuhl, Wilhelm / Ziegler, Ulf Erdmann: Eigenes Leben. Ausflüge in die unbekannte Gesellschaft, in der wir leben. München: Beck 1995. (Erkundungen. 7)

Berg, Eberhard / Fuchs, Martin (Hrsg.): Kultur, soziale Praxis, Text. Die Krise der ethnographischen Repräsentation. Frankfurt a. M.: Suhrkamp 1993. (Suhrkamp-Taschenbuch Wissenschaft. 1051)
Dieckmann, Bernhard / Wulf, Christoph / Wimmer, Michael (Hrsg.): Violence. Racism, Nationalism, Xenophobia. Münster u. a.: Waxmann 1996.
Elias, Norbert: Über den Prozeß der Zivilisation. Bd. 1. 2. Frankfurt a. M.: Suhrkamp 1976. (Suhrkamp-Taschenbuch Wissenschaft. 158-159)
Fanon, Frantz: Die Verdammten dieser Erde. Reinbek: Rowohlt Taschenbuch-Verlag 1969. (rororo aktuell. 1209-1210)
Foucault, Michel: Überwachen und Strafen. Frankfurt a. M.: Suhrkamp 1976.
Frazer, James George: Der goldene Zweig. Das Geheimnis von Glauben und Sitten der Völker. Reinbek: Rowohlt 1989. (Rowohlts Enzyklopädie. 483)
Gebauer, Gunter / Wulf, Christoph: Mimesis. Kultur – Kunst – Gesellschaft. Reinbek: Rowohlt 1992. (Rowohlts Enzyklopädie. 497)
Geertz, Clifford: Dichte Beschreibung. Beiträge zum Verstehen kultureller Systeme. Frankfurt a. M.: Suhrkamp 1983.
Geertz, Clifford: Die künstlichen Wilden. Anthropologen als Schriftsteller. München u. a.: Hanser 1990.
Girard, René: Der Sündenbock. Zürich: Benziger 1988.
Greenblatt, Stephen: Wunderbare Besitztümer. Die Erfindung des Fremden: Reisende und Entdecker. Berlin: Wagenbach 1994.
Kristeva, Julia: Fremde sind wir uns selbst. Frankfurt a. M.: Suhrkamp 1990. (Edition Suhrkamp. 1604)
Lévinas, Emmanuel: Zwischen uns. Versuche über das Denken an den Anderen. München: Hanser 1995.
Malinowski, Bronislaw: Argonauten des westlichen Pazifik. Ein Bericht über Unternehmungen und Abenteuer der Eingeborenen in den Inselwelten von Melanesisch-Neuguinea. Hrsg. von Fritz Kramer. Frankfurt a. M.: Syndikat 1979.
Martin, Luther H. (Hrsg.): Technologien des Selbst. Frankfurt a. M.: S. Fischer 1993.
Nandy, Ashis: The Intimate Enemy. Loss and Recovery of Self under Colonialism. Delhi: Oxford University Press 1983.
Otto, Rudolf: Das Heilige. Über das Irrationale in der Idee des Göttlichen und sein Verhältnis zum Rationalen. München: Beck 1963.
Ricœur, Paul: Soi-même comme un autre. Paris: Editions du Seuil 1990.
Said, Edward William: Orientalismus. Frankfurt a. M. u. a.: Ullstein 1981.
Schäffter, Ortfried (Hrsg.): Das Fremde. Erfahrungsmöglichkeiten zwischen Faszination und Bedrohung. Opladen: Westdeutscher Verlag 1991.
Simmel, Georg: Der Fremde. In: ders.: Das individuelle Gesetz. Philosophische Exkurse (= Suhrkamp-Taschenbuch Wissenschaft. 660), Frankfurt a. M: Suhrkamp 1987, S. 63-70.
Taussig, Michael: Mimesis and Alterity. A Particular History of the Senses. New York u. a.: Routledge 1993.
Todorov, Tzvetan: Die Eroberung Amerikas. Das Problem des Anderen. Frankfurt a. M.: Suhrkamp 1985. (edition suhrkamp. 1213)
Todorov, Tzvetan: Nous et les autres. Paris: Editions du Seuil 1989.
Waldenfels, Bernhard: Der Stachel des Fremden. Frankfurt a. M.: Suhrkamp 1990. (Suhrkamp-Taschenbuch Wissenschaft. 868)

Wimmer, Michael: Der Andere und die Sprache. Vernunftkritik und Verantwortung. Berlin: Reimer 1988.

Wimmer, Michael: Der Fremde. In: Wulf, Christoph (Hrsg.): Vom Menschen, Weinheim u. a.: Beltz 1996, S. 112-124.

Wimmer, Michael / Wulf, Christoph / Dieckmann, Bernhard (Hrsg.): Das zivilisierte Tier. Zur historischen Anthropologie der Gewalt. Frankfurt a. M.: Fischer Taschenbuch-Verlag 1996. (ZeitSchriften. 12955)

Wulf, Christoph (Hrsg.): Education in Europe. An Intercultural Task. Münster u. a.: Waxmann 1995.

2.

Bildungspolitik und Vergleichende Erziehungswissenschaft
Educational Policy and Comparative Education
Politique éducative et éducation comparée

> *Writing my report on a visiting tour to the educational research centres in the Netherlands, Belgium and France in March 1973, I inserted these functions in my concluding remarks when referring to the function of educational research in the context of political decision-making: „Is there a real chance of achieving substantial co-ordination between policies, science and educational practice? Or is educational research permanently verging upon the dichotomy of being held in high formal esteem and, at the same time, of being restricted to a 'playground' to use up its energies?" It seems to me these questions are relevant to the situation of comparative research also.*
>
> Wolfgang Mitter, 1977

Wolfgang Mitter: Policy-oriented Task of Comparative Education. In: Comparative Education, 13 (1977) 2, pp. 95-100 (here: p. 100).

Comparative Education and Public Policies: A View from the South

Candido Alberto Gomes

Comparative education has a variety of theoretical trends, with a wide array of converging and opposing perspectives. Its implications for the Southern Hemisphere (a somewhat inaccurate designation) are also diverse, leading to many questions in our environment, such as: Is comparative education really necessary? Can comparative education provide effective contributions to the solution of our educational problems? Is comparative education actually useful to us? If the answer is yes, how should comparative education be of interest for the South? This contribution will focus on these questions, at first by means of some theoretical reflections and later by discussing practical experiences in the political arena.

Is Comparative Education of Interest for the South?

In attempting to answer these questions the theoretical change in comparative education is a fundamental matter. The end of the cold war has led to a relativization of the traditional consensus and conflict paradigm in social sciences as well as in comparative education. This means that the frontier between both paradigms is blurring, which may mean a new era of convergence of those paradigms *(Paulston 1977, 1993)*. Functionalism and dependency theories, for instance, have not proved to be able to provide good representations of reality to guide scientific explorers. It seems that, at the threshold of a new millennium, old theories are not longer fulfilling expectations satisfactorily, whilst the new ones have not yet been born. However, some flashes of insight allow us to realize in what education and research make the difference between more and less developed countries as well as their rich and poor citizens. Globalisation has not closed the gap in social and international stratification. On the contrary, this gap may even increase since the quality of work is the wealth of nations *(Reich 1991)*. Finally, it is much more difficult to develop good education and research than to offer abundant natural resources or a greater number of unqualified workers.

Returning to the questions related to comparative education and the Southern Hemisphere within this context of rapid changes, there is not one answer to the above questions. Moreover, each trend may even provide a variety of answers – a warning about prejudice. Numerous works stimulate the transfer, or the imposition, of external solutions to the South, overlooking the fact that educational systems do not travel around the world successfully. Thus, comparative education would merely reinforce cosmopolitanism and dependency in less developed countries. Instead of deepening the roots in the specific environment, it may lead educators, as did their ancestors in the colonial era, to keep their eyes on the horizon, waiting for the ships which would bring the latest fashionable ideas from the Old World. Worse than this, international assistance to the social sector frequently reveals the basic patterns of infrastructure projects. It is often predominantly outward-oriented and does not include enough participation by local populations: In other words, it appears as if the distinction between *Naturwissenschaften* and *Geistwissenschaften* had not been established. As a result, specialists understand reality, but they do not make *Verstehen*, as emphasized by Max *Weber (1968),* one of the crucial features of the sociological method.

These possibilities, in general, result from the fact that some theories essentially present a view from the outside, and remain unrooted in particular societies. 'Traditional societies' are induced to look at themselves not with their own eyes, but from the perspective of 'modern societies'. Nevertheless, this is not a prerogative of certain theories, often labeled conservative. Even the most revolutionary theory would suffer from the same shortcomings, if non-critically imported. The decisive point is: how theories are adopted and applied to a variety of historical and social contexts.

Has comparative education then been able to play a liberating role? That is, instead of inspiring the mere transfer of 'modern' ideas and conceptions, has it been able to effectively help the Southern countries to cope with their problems? Would it not be better for these countries to perform a profound introspection instead of looking for comparative education? In fact, reality is complex and full of contradictions, not symmetrical or monolithic. As in some painted masterpieces, there is a gap between reality and its rational, perfectionist representation. For instance, numerous educators who adopted the reproduction theory in the seventies and even in the eighties. Though they tried to interpret the dynamics of social and educational reality on the basis of contradictions, they emphasized to the conservative role of education so much that they did not leave room for social changes – as if society and education were endlessly self-perpetuating. In contrast, even comparative education aimed at cultural import (or 'cultural imperialism') may have liberating effects. The most serious limitation of modernization is that it works like a mirror: the 'traditional' society tries to change itself through the image of the 'modern' ones. This often means renouncing its own existence, a process so grievous that it may lead to awareness. The multiplicity of intercultural contacts led to deep reflections on the Southern position in the international system as well as on the alternatives to changing it. In the same way that classical liberalism resulted in contradictions and finally led to the construction of concepts like development/underdevelopment, the external contribution has often been a stimulus for transformation. An example is the dependency theory, which could never have been elaborated by Latin Americans in intellectual isolation. The interaction of national and international influences may develop the awareness of the complex process involved in the adaptation of scientific findings to national and regional realities. Therefore, even supposedly conflicting theories, like modernization and dependency, may have intersections: modernity may uncover dependency.

The partial conclusion is that both cultural servility and xenophobia are sterile positions. A less developed country cannot be conceived as a passive entity, without a will of its own. The literature on international economic and educational assistance illustrates this point. Both isolation and alienated cosmopolitanism are treacherous for the international community.

Thus, comparative education that is of interest for us needs to gain significance by means of a process some scholars call 'reduction', based on phenomenology and the sociology of knowledge (e.g. *Ramos 1967; Berger 1976*). It is similar to what was called *Entschränken* by Heidegger *(Biemel 1950)*. Nevertheless, such a process does not lead to some sort of indigenous science. In fact, it distinguishes the immanent and transcendent 'components' of the scientific work from its historical and social context. Those 'components', immediately rooted in their milieu, will hardly be useful in other circumstances. However, the other 'components', in other words, those which are universal to science, can be applied to the specific circumstances of each society. To some extent, this differentiation recalls another one made by Alfred *Weber (1941):* culture, like a folk dance, is inherent to a specific group, whereas civilization, e.g. mathematics, transcends such groups and becomes a part of common human heritage, in principle useful to all groups.

How then would the Southern societies cultivate a comparative education of significance to their specific reality? First of all, they would develop a universal science. Of course, non-transferable intellectual products would not make any sense. For such a development to take place it is necessary to explore the synergy of inward and outward oriented views to study issues which have priority with respect to the reality of the societies. It is worthwhile to remember that comparison rules out isolation and the resultant impoverishment. Poor countries do not need poor science.

Secondly, comparative education which is of interest for us should broaden its focus. Most of our work concerns schooling. As this is more selective in the Southern than in the Northern hemisphere, large sectors of education may be neglected, whilst intellectual efforts are concentrated in a relatively privileged sector. I do not intend to advocate a return to the unrealistic hopes concerning non-formal education, prevalent in the seventies. However, it is necessary to broaden our focus so that the less well-known areas can be investigated.

Thirdly, comparative education which is of interest for us should stimulate the study of cultural and ethnic diversities. International comparisons, encompassing a plurality of national educational systems, have been well-covered in the literature as well as research on ethnic and linguistic groups of the more developed countries. In contrast, despite the vast cultural diversities of the South, these are much less studied. In Brazil, for example, research had to overcome strong ideological biases against these issues. For some decades, since the beginning of our social research, important scholars obscured our ethnical differences and their educational implications. Colonial unitarism should not contaminate comparative education. Therefore, one cannot ignore questions such as the cultural and physical destruction of some groups, like the Native Americans. The contribution of comparative education is surely welcome in this respect.

Fourthly, comparative education largely focuses on macro-level issues like the relation between education and social stratification. This useful stream may be a reflection of some past influences of research, when school and the educational process were assumed to be a 'black box'. Change has displaced such interest: the school and the classroom, where educational processes are studied in loco. To me, it does not appear that comparative education has fully explored this trend of educational research. Although the classical methodologies and social sciences have offered invaluable contributions to comparative education, it needs to turn more frequently to other sciences, such as psychology, as well as new methodologies.

Fifthly, comparative education which is of interest for us has to have some essential features, such as methodological rigor and theoretical consistency. Sometimes fact finding, particularly in large international comparisons, replaces actual science. In the South and in the North one finds such undesirable exceptions in literature.

More or less obvious reflections of a practitioner

Comparative education which is of interest for the needs of the South should:
- strive for or keep its universality, while being rooted in its particular context;
- distinguish 'components' which are immanent from those which are transcendent to their context in international scientific work;
- broaden its focus on other educational processes besides schooling;
- study cultural and ethnic diversities within societies accurately;
- open the 'black box' to focus on the school, the classroom and every other environment in which educational processes occur;
- offer effective contributions to educational policies, both to short and long term goals.

Last but not least, comparative education which is of interest for us should be useful for practitioners. Theoretical questions are attractive no doubt. Nevertheless, the seriousness of the South's problems often leads to another set of questions. Even when comparative education, from a theoretical point of view, plays a liberating role, would it really be useful or would it just be another intellectual ornament? Excellent contributions have been written on how to build bridges between research and public policies as well as educational practice. I have nothing to add except that comparative education must offer its contribution whenever possible. Of course, this does not mean that it will be applicable immediately in the South.

In short, comparative education which is of interest for us has to be balanced on the edge of a knife: To be open to the outside world, avoiding cultural servility; to be rooted in society, avoiding xenophobia; to study schooling without neglecting that it is only one of the educational processes; to devise national unity without obscuring its internal differentiation; to focus on the school's environment without being dogmatic; to be methodologically rigorous, without rigidity; to direct scientific work towards both immediate questions and distant horizons. It is difficult to meet so many demands, as it is usual in science, but it presents a good challenge.

How Useful is Comparative Education?

I would not dare to add a paper on research and public policies to the existing literature. However, I cannot end this article without summarizing some lessons I have learned from my experience as an adviser to the Federal Senate of Brazil. My enthusiasm in a period of re-democratization led me to participate in a national contest for such a position. Once accepted, I, a former university professor, found myself in the middle of a relatively unknown arena (although not much more fragmented or less ethical than the academy). Learning by trial and error, my first lesson was that the rhythm in politics was much faster. A colleague and I were once asked by a young senator to elaborate a complex law proposal. When we asked him for more time, he answered that when the horse is saddled one must be ready to ride on it. After some discussions, we reached a compromise thus enabling the senator not to miss a political opportunity.

The second lesson was the change in my agenda. When I was hired I possessed very well defined areas of academic interest (academic – that is what mattered). However, frequent senators' demands forced me to study educational finance. This field is crucial when a country is going through a fiscal crisis, particularly if an adviser must participate in budgeting, defending the sector. I found myself in a dilemma: I would have to tell everybody that a sociologist could not go beyond his knowledge and skills, or I would have to pull up my sleeves and study a new field in order to discuss matters with experts. I chose the last alternative. As a result, my best client for almost ten years was an unforgettable person. An old, stubborn senator who in his own words had a „true obsession for education". I cannot count the hundreds or thousands of answers I personally gave him in reply to his inquires by phone, by fax or other means. Senator João Calmon had faith in education and trust in research. Now that he is gone I remember the best lesson he taught me: one person alone in an institution such as the Senate can make the difference and turn matters in favor of education if he or she acts persistently. That is why there is such a significant intersection between biography and history.

My third lesson concerns independence and the search for best solutions, essential elements in a legislative house. Feared at first as a famous educator, anthropologist and novelist who would not be inclined to listen to specialists, Senator Darcy Ribeiro turned out to be a young man aged 70. His manner was so open and dynamic that he easily accepted every interesting proposal regardless of political and ideological frontiers. In contrast to some people who become bitter after long years of political exile and who persist insistently on some political conceptions, he learned how to learn and he was always willing to learn.

The primary question I asked myself for some years was whether I actually have managed to build a bridge between research and public policies. Since the answer was, to a large extent, yes, my next question was: How does one do it? Unfortunately, I have not yet found a recipe. Eleven years later I now understand that such a bridge is mostly based on dialogue and personal confidence, similar to the relationship with a health professional or a lawyer. You begin by discussing public policies and you end up by listening to the secrets of political life, like in a confessional ... An important dimension of this trusting relationship is the distance from political parties. If I were politically engaged, I would lose my credibility, which means that objectivity or at least enough distance from the heat of ideologies and politics is required from a scientist. *Science engagée* is not appreciated. Finally, senators have to submit to the polls, whilst the technical staff do not. Though this may seem obvious at first sight, it may sometimes be difficult to recognize in countries thirsty for political participation.

Pragmatism is another praised quality. Many senators were state governors or ministers, experienced managers who coped with difficult situations. Usually the easiest way to meet the demands is superficial pragmatism, disregarding that there is nothing as practical as a good theory. Therefore, besides the above mentioned theoretical grounds, I have good reasons for aligning science's contribution to this circumstance. It would not be good for my reputation if a senator said: „What planet is this guy on? I need to assess concrete solutions."

The main procedures used in this dialogue are short written reports and oral replies to immediate answer consultations. Some of these are often warning about negative implications of bills and amendments. Someone might ask about what returns receive the taxpayers as a result of the advisor's work. I would say that success should rather be measured in terms of damages avoided than in terms of benefits induced.

During this process comparative education helped me enormously. Each World Congress, each Society meeting, each contact held with colleagues was like refreshing water. My comments at times led to such curiosity that some World Council activities were mentioned in Plenary speeches. Since Brazil has, little by little, abandoned its inward-oriented industrialization process, many authorities have expressed a growing concern about the country's position in the international system. This leads to numerous questions on education, equality, and economic competitiveness. Speed, synthesis capacity, and a good scientific network have been some means of survival as an adviser and as a researcher. However, this is not more complex than academy. Perhaps the Senate is even clearer and more objective in its conflicts.

Bridging the Gap between Research and Public Policies:
Lessons Learned by a Practitioner

- Rhythm is much faster in politics and administration. There is no better way to hell than perfectionism.
- Flexibility and pragmatism are essential (of course, no concessions to lack of professionalism).
- Dialogue and personal confidence are cornerstones. Political and ideological engagement negatively affect such a confidence.
- One person alone, aware of research contributions, may make a difference. One swallow does make a summer, but it depends on the swallow.
- Decision-makers are rational. What matters is the kind of rationality and the goals pursued.
- Short written or oral reports are more effective than the most highly praised paper in the academy.

To me the emphasis given to personal relationships sometimes seems like an expression of Brazilian institutional fragility. However, I fell that the technical staff's work has been bureaucratized, although in a small house it depends on warmth and closer personal relations. Not everything is bureaucratic in bureaucracies, since, according to Max Weber *(1968)*, it is an ideal type.

Another important issue in my experience is the rationality of decision-makers. They do frequently seem irrational and incompetent. Nevertheless, I found (and I am by no means the first one to do so) that the question is: With regard to what goals are they irrational and incompetent? In fact, there is a latent or overt conflict between scientific and political rationality. The latter has to submit to all kinds of pressure groups, deadlines, impositions for immediate or delayed actions. The world is not Plato's Republic. Moreover, it is doubtful whether it would be better than the existing one.

Final Remarks

In conclusion to this diverse piece of work, which includes some theoretical considerations and the summary of an experience in progress, I want to make three remarks. First of all, I proved to myself at least that comparative education is useful as a window open to the world. In fact, it provides scientific grounds for public policies even in the midst of hot political arenas. My work would be the poorer if I had not become familiar with this field in an interdependent world. Nevertheless, no miracles should be expected.

Moreover, one of the lessons I learned is that, despite its universality, science needs to be embedded in specific contexts. Science is similar to a light over the rain forest. It exists, but additional effort is necessary before it can reach the soil.

Lastly, for a long time I have been aware that I do not work alone. To choose my way at the crossroads is my responsibility, but I count on the harvest of science. Thus, I depend on the hard work of many visible and, in particular, a crowd of invisible colleagues. According to ancient Romans, *liber ex libris*, i.e. a book results from other books, benefiting from the continuity of human heritage. From my standpoint, this is the main reason for this *Festschrift*. It celebrates Wolfgang Mitter's work which generously seeded so many books, articles, booklets and other kinds of scientific communication: In the North as well as in my South.

Bibliography

Berger, Manfredo: Educaçao e dependência. Porto Alegre: Difel – Universidade Federal do Rio Grande do Sul 1976.
Biemel, Walter: Le concept de monde chez Heidegger. Paris: Alcan 1950.
Paulston, Rolland G.: Social and Educational Change. Conceptual Frameworks. In: Comparative Education Review, 21 (1977) 2-3, pp. 370-395.
Paulston, Rolland G.: Mapping Discourse in Comparative Education Texts. In: Compare, 23 (1993) 3, pp. 101-114.
Ramos, Alberto G.: A reduçao sociológica. Rio de Janeiro: Tempo Brasileiro 1967.

Reich, Robert B.: The Work of Nations. Preparing Ourselves for the 21st Century. New York: Knopf 1991.
Weber, Alfred: Historia de la cultura. Mexico City: Fondo de Cultura Económica 1941.
Weber, Max: Economy and Society. An Outline of Interpretative Sociology. New York: Bedminster 1968.

Educational Cooperation between Nations in the 21st Century[1]

Stephen P. Heyneman

Motivations for Educational Cooperation in the Next Century

Much has changed since the cold war rivalry ended, but one of the most important changes has been with the factors that affect motivation for foreign assistance. Foreign assistance is no longer justified on the basis of competition between East and West. Domestic economic priorities – unemployment, fiscal deficits, trade imbalance – have taken the place of foreign assistance. Over last four years, 16 of 21 donor countries have reduced foreign aid as a proportion of GDP[2] *(World Bank 1996, p. 13)*. The voting public in industrialized countries tends to be older, hence more concerned with issues of pensions, health insurance, and personal safety. Questions have been raised about the effectiveness of development assistance agencies – are they really helping the poor; could NGO's deliver assistance more effectively with less bureaucracy? Would NGOs be more free to operate autonomously from governments with records of corruption and human rights problems? There are also the post conflict circumstances such as drought, civil war, and genocide. Voting publics tend to see these situations as more compelling justifications for foreign aid. Lastly there are the economic problems of the former Soviet Union itself, once a major source of foreign assistance in Africa, Asia and some parts of Latin America. Official development assistance will continue to be driven by humanitarian justifications. Nevertheless, it is safe to suggest that other motivations will play a role as well. Aid will likely be delivered and targeted differently and be lower in magnitude.

Trade and flows of private capital will take an increasingly important role in economic development. But as traditional aid declines, what will happen to education? Much of the international cooperation in education has been developed under the auspices of in-

---

1 The views are those of the author alone and do not necessarily represent the World Bank or any of its affiliated institutions.
2 At the end of the text there is a list explaining the abbreviations used.

ternational aid. Will the decline in aid spell a similar decline in international cooperation in education?

Today there are more countries participating in IEA studies than at any previous time over the last thirty years. Projects include studies of literacy, mathematics and science, but also of civics education, video taping of comparative teaching techniques, and comparative curriculum emphases. Demand is high for joining OECD's cooperative project on educational indicators, including countries with only loose affiliation with OECD itself. Almost every country in Eastern and Central Europe and the former Soviet Union would like access to comparable descriptive information about their educational systems, and so would Malaysia, Mexico, Chile, Brazil, and the People's Republic of China. The APEC has inaugurated new programs of educational cooperation, and NAFTA and the WTO have initiated new studies comparing labor markets. Each of these signals suggest that there are new demands for educational cooperation. What is behind these new demands? At the same time as traditional humanitarian-based assistance is on the decline, international cooperation in education is on the rise. What is behind this apparent anomaly?

Motivation in OECD Countries

Cooperation is on the rise because of necessity:

1. The level of educational expenditures (measured as a proportion of GDP per capita) has probably reached a maximum.
2. The principal educational challenge in the next century will be to raise coverage at pre- and post-compulsory ages, and improve quality at all levels, but without increasing the level of fiscal expenditures.
3. To make major breakthroughs in (2) above, it is essential to increase the level of international information and the international cooperation necessary to obtain it.

A few words about each.

Fiscal Expenditures. The proportion of GDP allocated to education in OECD countries over the last decade has increased slightly in the United States, but has decreased slightly in Canada, Japan, the Netherlands and Austria, with the overall net result of a slight decline on average. There is reason to believe that the range of GDP per capita allocated to education in OECD countries (between 5 and 7%) has reached a maximum.

In OECD countries population pressures do not come from the burden of more children but from its opposite – from the burden of a population living longer and the social pressures on families to support a high percentage age dependency. Economic growth has stabilized from being slightly negative to slightly positive, but nowhere within the OECD countries has growth come close to the double digit level as in some parts of Latin America and Asia. Steady growth of between three and five percent is considered an optimistic scenario for the OECD countries. Combine high age dependency and slow economic growth with national debt, health insurance, and public security, and one can see that as a proportion of overall public resources, education resources are unlikely to increase.

Increasing Demands for Education. On the other hand, the demand for education continues to increase both at the pre-compulsory and at the post-compulsory levels, and in terms of quality, at all levels. Currently, the percentage of public educational investments allocated to pre-compulsory education ranges between four percent (Japan) and eleven percent (France). As more women enter the labor market, in part because two salaries are necessary to pay an increasing tax burden, the level of public investment in pre-compulsory education is likely to increase. The proportion of the age cohort which demands access to higher education has also grown over the last several decades. Differences among countries have narrowed, and by the end of the century it seems likely that the proportion of the relevant age cohort attending post-compulsory education will level off at about 35 or 40 percent, up from less than ten percent in 1968 *(Heyneman 1994)*.

Increasing demand and a stable or declining percentage of a low-growth tax base implies that structural and managerial reforms will be required in an unprecedented fashion. To increase quality and expand coverage at the pre- and post-compulsory levels, the only option will be for OECD countries to diversify resources, allocate current resources more wisely, and retrench, that is, to eliminate or significantly reduce low priority educational functions.[3] But how will these managerial options be identified?

---

3   Many structural and managerial changes are well under way. For instance, private financing now adds 27% to public educational expenditures in the United States, 38% in Germany, and about 20% in Japan. (Source: *United States Department of Education 1994, p. 336.*) One illustration of a 'low priority' function, now under considerable strain is the tradition of having free transportation to and from school in the United States.

How will the effects of these high risk choices be monitored? Against what standard of performance will the reforms be measured?

Increasing Demands for Educational Information. In the history of Comparative and International Education, there has never been a period like the present. The origins of the field lie in the 19th Century, when colorful and literate individuals, like Horace Mann, Matthew Arnold, and Joseph Kay, traveled to different countries and gathered ideas for use in their domestic schools. Today we are in a period where new innovation, legislation, and empirical results are in more demand than at any other time in the history of the field. Comparative and International Education is currently in a 'golden era', reflecting an expansion of political and professional visibility which can be expected to continue into the next century *(Heyneman 1993a).*

But who is asking for this information? The demand is not necessarily from central governments. The roots are often with local school boards, local education authorities, local teacher associations, organizations of businesses and tax-payers who ask for action, ideas and measurement in order to judge the comparative effectiveness of local reform. On the other hand, state and national governments are required to respond to these requests. The demand for information is often non-partisan. The National Governors Association and the Chief State School Officers of the United States, both bipartisan organizations, helped to lay the groundwork for the multitude of reforms in the United States and promoted the legislation, signed by President Clinton in April, 1994 on Educational Goals 2000. Similarly, local concerns constitute the origins of much (though not always non-partisan) domestic education debates in France, the Netherlands, Finland and Great Britain. The result of these domestic pressures for reform are motivated in part by economic pressures and the consequent need for international standards of excellence. In part they are motivated by demands for greater social cohesion and good governance and by the feeling that other countries have solutions deserving of domestic attention. They are also motivated by straight professionalism and the recognition in education, as in health, agriculture or transport, that innovations in supporting managerial excellence can originate from many parts of the world.

Actually, this latter point is quite new. Only a few decades ago, most educational managers – school board presidents, university chancellors, head teachers – would hardly have thought it relevant to learn of managerial innovations from outside their own domestic environments, but much has changed. It is possible to hear Michigan school teachers debating the pros and cons of Japanese or German pedagogical practice; or

British administrators discussing the results of contract schools in California; or German and Canadian university rectors trading information on alternative sources of finance, and techniques for negotiating fees and tuitions with political authorities and students.

Local managerial authorities are no longer likely to reject *ipso facto* new and interesting ideas because of their foreign origins. Nor are they likely to make as much of a distinction between the types of countries considered relevant. British and Chilean voucher experiences are interesting to school authorities in Louisiana; Colombian mechanisms of financing vocational education (SENAI) are of interest in Britain; and US school board democracy is interesting to regional officials in Russia. Russian summer camp vouchers (in Vladimir where youth now have behavior problems similar to those in the west) are interesting to officials in US urban school districts. Schools are bankrupt in both Moscow and Chicago. Local officials do not judge innovation on the basis of its country of origin as they once did, but rather on the likelihood of their local relevance. Local officials will decide whether the ideas are relevant to Chicago or Moscow. What they demand from their governments is information on good ideas, and unless their governments help locate this information quickly and succinctly, local voters may well demand a change in government.

This puts new and very healthy pressures on domestic and international education agencies. Resources for international education studies in the United States with bipartisan support at both federal and local levels is at an all time high. Technologies and techniques continue to improve. International willingness to collaborate continues to increase within Europe, Asia, and the former Soviet Union. Given these tendencies, one can anticipate increasing demand for full membership in the international organizations responsible for carrying out educational comparisons, particularly the IEA, OECD, UNESCO, and APEC.

Motivations in Other Countries

What about the countries traditionally labeled as 'developing' countries – in Africa, Asia, Latin America and the Middle East? What are their motivations for cooperation in the field of education? Have they remained stagnant?

Their motivations for international cooperation in the field of education have also changed. The incorporation of 26 new borrowers into the World Bank and the European

Bank for Reconstruction and Development from the Europe and Central Asia Region, including the Russian Federation, have changed the characteristics of the client. To these new clients the description of being a 'developing' country is interpreted as patronizing. There are many characteristics of OECD countries, such as family breakdown, crime, and domestic violence, which are not worthy of emulation by countries with lower GDPs per capita. Political leaders in these countries may feel that their own cultures and social structures are as 'developed' as those countries with membership in the OECD. Objections to being labeled 'developing' may also be expected from countries in Africa, Asia and Latin America. In fact the term in the future may be eliminated from normal international discourse.

Sensitivity over a label is only a symbol of a wider phenomenon. Many countries have shifted their perspectives as a result of the end of the cold war, the expansion of the European Union, and the inauguration of NAFTA and regional trading agreements in Asia. Lesser industrialized countries that are World Bank borrowers now tend to see their interests as being in competition for trade advantage and labor market niches in services, manufacturing, and agriculture *(Heyneman 1997b)*.

A common vision for educational excellence has emerged from economic interdependence. All education systems must use resources wisely, and treat all students fairly. Additionally, all must provide intellectual challenge universally. Standards for performance of an education system do not differ systematically between Ghana and Georgia (either the state or the country). Educational officials in Africa, Asia, Latin America, the Middle East, and Europe and Central Asia hold similar standards of excellence. As a result, they demand similar innovations and reforms as do educational leaders of the OECD countries. This convergence of needs and interests can be expected to increase.

Convergence does not imply that an emphasis on topics within a mathematics curriculum, or science or language curriculum will be identical. It is not a sign that local culture will cease to be pre-eminent. It does not imply that the purposes of education will cease to be determined by domestic priorities. Commonality of purpose is no sign of an international 'conspiracy'. It is not a sign of imperialism or of paradigmatic determinism. It is simply a fact about education in a world where universal coverage is becoming a reality; a world where every country requires a minimal level of information to manage their enormous public education systems so that these systems might provide the knowledge and cultural experience for which they were designed.

Universal education is a permanent feature of national life and a normal feature of child rearing. But like health, education systems require a considerable amount of information. Whether in high, middle or low income countries, all have common requirements: remuneration, supplies, public safety, faculty pensions, modern equipment, and access to capital markets. Common requirements require common standards of professionalism, common indicators of efficiency, and common demands for innovation. In principle, relevant innovations do not differ between East and West, and rich or poor countries. All countries demand new ideas. In turn, these demands will determine the characteristics of international cooperation in education in the next century, and the nature of the international organizations financed and staffed to service this international cooperation.

But are the international organizations founded after World War II capable of meeting these new demands? And if not, what changes will have to be made? What kinds of staff will they need? What kinds of programs will they be responsible for? Where will they gather their financial resources? It is these questions to which we now turn.

International Institutions

Current international institutions with responsibilities in education have three crippling problems.

First is an *imbalance in mandate*. Some institutions have mandates covering only the wealthier parts of the world – Europe, North America and OECD countries. Other institutions have regional mandates – Africa, Asia or Latin America. Still others have worldwide mandates, but are burdened by weak governance structures of one-vote-per-country which makes it difficult to specialize or maintain professional standards.

The second problem is *institutional duplication*. Much of the professional expertise and infrastructure required for international comparisons are common right across agencies even though those agencies have differing mandates. Despite the fact that these agencies share common sources of finance, staff functions overlap. This illustrates one of the managerial questions now being raised about the United Nations. Tax-payers may recognize there are duplications in function and not feel compelled to continue to finance them.

UNICEF, the World Bank, OECD, EUROSTAT, UNESCO, IEA, the OAU, and SEAMEO all have separate but differing professional capabilities. On the other hand, they have over-lapping data needs. The wealthier countries, such as the United States, tend to target international educational programs through organizations which they believe capable of supplying information on countries relevant to trade and economic interests. This is normal, and from the domestic tax-payers point of view, it is fair. For the most part, the 'countries of interest' have been confined to OECD countries, i. e., to only 26 of the world's economies and education systems. UNESCO, however, covers almost 200 countries. These include China, Russia, Brazil, Indonesia, Nigeria and many economies and education systems which are now deeply interesting to the Americans as well as to other OECD countries. The United States and the United Kingdom are not members of UNESCO, and hence have few avenues to improve the professional coverage and quality of the information coming from those areas of the world even though they now recognize that this information is essential to them.

Similarly Eastern Europe and the former Soviet Union are of high interest to the members of the European Union. But in spite of the efforts to expand OECD's technical assistance, it is fair to say that OECD does not have the same mandate as does UNESCO to monitor and publicize the educational statistics from that important region.

Non-official agencies, such as IEA, which conduct systematic research and evaluation in the field of education are politically visible and increasingly important. Their governance structures are fragile. Moreover, they need a permanent institutional home which will not jeopardize professional autonomy.

The third problem is the *difference in technical and financial capability*. Standards of educational management are increasingly common. Standards in statistics and research necessary to monitor innovation are also common, but the resources necessary to perform these functions are vastly different.

Even where there are technical traditions, such as in Russia and Eastern Europe, the financial crisis makes it impossible for these countries to participate in the international assessments such as those organized by ETS, IEA or the OECD.[4] Financial problems

---

4 There are 130 professionals working in the National Center for Educational Statistics in the United States and only six professionals working in the department of Educational Statistics in Russia. This suggests that the differences in availability and quality of information are not solely attributable to differences in economic resource, but rather in the allocation of available resources in order

make it impossible for them to keep abreast of the new demands for valid and reliable descriptive information required by UNESCO and other international agencies including the IMF, the World Bank, and the regional development banks *(Heyneman 1993b; Gutherie / Hansen 1995; Puryear 1995)*. Similar data quality problems are common too in LAC, in SSA, and in the Middle East.

There is an increasing understanding of professional education standards and the necessity of new ideas on innovations and efficiency, but at the same time, there is a widening gap in the ability of countries to afford this information. The key to understanding the difference between aid in the past and aid in the future is to know that this gap in the ability to afford educational information is an intolerable situation to the industrial economies. It is in their own legitimate interest to have good, up-to-date quality information on education from all over the world. Industrial countries now depend on having valid comparisons and access to the best and most innovative ideas available from anywhere, but they will not be available unless these three problems are solved.

Suggested Solutions

Structural Problems

The institutional situation requires an in-depth review. All agencies involved would need to be consulted. They would need to develop recommendations for changes in the structures and institutional mandates of the international organizations involved in servicing international educational needs. These recommendations should minimize duplication; maintain the necessary regional focus; and suggest areas where statistical programs and functions can be combined.

Financial Problems

Regularity. No professional education system of information can exist if it is *ad hoc*. The world can no longer afford to have data which are so inaccurate that major mistakes in judgment can result from using it. Systems must now be regular and predictable if they are to be professional. But this regularity requires stable financing.

---

to responsibly open up statistical information to parliamentary authorities and to the general public *(Heyneman et al. 1995)*.

Fair Sharing of Financing Responsibility. Even within OECD countries, the burden of responsibility for financing educational statistics and indicators has been very unbalanced. A small number of countries have led the way financially and technically. This is permissible when the product is an experiment to test whether or not it can be accomplished. That has now changed. Educational indicators and assessments will now become regular programs, and therefore, the imbalance in financing cannot be sustained. To match this change, a new agreement to bear the financial costs in an equitable fashion must now be put forth.

Subsidized Financing. Countries in Africa, Asia, Latin America, the Middle East, Eastern and Central Europe and the former Soviet Union need and deserve financial assistance of two kinds. First, they need an increased level of resources through the programs of lending and bilateral programs of technical assistance. These resources are necessary for long-term institution building. For instance they might be used to assist statistics institutes at local, regional and national levels, university faculties or local private education research and development companies.

Second, a grant-based program is required to allow many countries to fully participate in major international projects. Their need for information and technical discussions is just as acute as the OECD countries participating in the same exercises. The rationale for this fund, however, is not solely humanitarian. As in health, agriculture, population or trade, such a fund is an essential ingredient for assuring that the base of educational statistics does not differ widely in quality or coverage despite the fact that countries may be endowed with very different resources.

Staffing Problems

International agencies are not staffed properly to perform new functions. Staffing is biased by national quotas; and staff 'with tenure' are kept without regard to the external demand for their particular skill. No plan to improve and regularize international educational statistics will be effective without a thorough review of how to engage the best people and to have them stay only so far as they remain so.

Career paths of the most technically advanced staff may no longer be limited to domestic experiences. NCES, for instance, will require staff with an intimate understanding of the statistical problems in other environments. Whether one's task is to measure one of the many sub-topics in the science curriculum in Florida or to calculate unit expenditures in Tokyo and Moscow, one needs personal experience working with others addressing similar problems. A period working in an international agency may become a preferred career path for some of the better minds in the profession. This may also make it possible for international agencies to more systematically exploit secondments. Education ministries may inaugurate competitive programs where the best will compete for the opportunity to work in an international agency.

This cannot come too soon for the international agencies themselves. Staff in these agencies are sometimes out of synchronization with their shift in function. They tend to conceive of education problems as analogous to medical models where education systems in the client countries are inefficient and ineffective, i. e. are 'sick' and they themselves are the doctors. It is increasingly common for local officials to reject this style of relationship. They recognize that all countries have systems with similar categories of educational dilemmas. Where is there a system without inefficiency and without some resource constraints?

Staff in international agencies will have to cease functioning as 'scientific judges' and begin functioning as 'scientific advisors'. The difference is subtle but important. No longer will it be acceptable to suggest that there are policy 'lessons' to disseminate or that there are policy 'models' to emulate. Demand-based financing, vouchers, teacher remuneration mechanisms, etc., are all issues of contention on which there are differing sides and points of view. Instead of solutions, staff of international agencies will be expected to provide information on both sides of an issue so that the client may make intelligent choices. This will require more than an attitude change; rather it will require staff equipped with more intellectual rigor and more sophisticated professional experience. This suggests that the expectations for permanent staff in international agencies would have to shift from being experts themselves, to those whose job it is would be to facilitate the in- and out-flow of expertise.

New Functions and Programs

International education agencies will have many new functions in the next century, among them:

- the collection and analysis of a wide variety of educational statistics including unit expenditures, private contributions to both public and private education, and academic achievement across a wide variety of curricular topics and performance objectives. Utility would be regularly monitored in both formal and informal labor markets, as would political participation and political attitudes;
- systematic assessments of educational quality in higher education;
- international monitoring of performance of graduates across national boundaries;
- monitoring of multinational firms which market educational equipment and software, examinations, and accreditation services. There will be 'macro-universities' providing degrees simultaneously in different countries. Businesses will perform new functions in the certification of skills. There will be new roles for the licensing of professionals; new standards for the social sciences, and a spread of new international degrees, such as the international baccalaureate. There will be a new trade in educators and educated people, for instance, international contract teachers in specialized fields. There will also be new challenges to civic behavior and civil rights and new demands for professional standards of civics education and other sensitive curriculum areas.

All these activities will require new functions on the part of international education agencies. They will be called upon to monitor and help regulate the activities of these new corporations in ways similar to international pharmaceutical or other commerce. They may also be called upon to protect minority rights, but at the same time, to insure standards of discourse of the minorities themselves so that they do not endanger civic peace. Educators and public education systems will be increasingly recognized as holding the key to good governance *(Heyneman 1995, 1996, 1997a)*. Hence the role of international agencies in providing information, skills, and a „code of educational conduct" will inevitably increase.

Summary

Decline of the competition between East and West has significantly altered the reasons for international educational cooperation. OECD countries now recognize that national interests are not solely military, nor simply trade. Instead, national interests are intellectual and behavioral, including the degree to which countries can produce, develop and disseminate new skills; and the degree to which citizens know, understand and accept personal obligations and responsibilities as well as rights and privileges. The importance of these interests for large and diverse populations implies that OECD countries will have to dramatically improve the systems of educational delivery.

At the same time as educational demands are increasing, the sources for educational finance are stagnant. The hope for increasing both quality and coverage is to dramatically change the pace of internal reform. This requires better information, not just information about other wealthy countries, and information about all countries.

This new demand implies a significant shift in responsibility for international agencies, their structures, staff, and programs. Educational cooperation in the next century can be expected to dramatically increase in quantity and quality despite declining aid. Thus, the major contact point in the field of education will not be the bilateral aid agency. In fact, many bilateral aid agencies may well disappear. The international responsibility in education will shift to the domestic education ministry, whose technical capacities and professional cadre with international experience will increase dramatically.

It also implies a shift for university education faculties. Instead of segregating international and comparative education into a specialized field, all education faculty whether in administration, pedagogy, economics or psychology will need to be familiar with international innovations, theories and issues. Few university faculties or research institutes can expect to be competitive if educational interests are limited to domestic and parochial experience. Tenure may be granted, not on the basis of empirical publications, but increasingly on the basis of proven effectiveness to educational leaders and managers. This implies that the ideal career path in a major university will have to be more heterogeneous – with periods of time assisting education in another country, in a domestic local education system, and in an international agency, as well teaching and research in a university.

In low income countries, needs and demands for ideas are no less severe than in OECD countries, but they will require new programs of assistance. These will continue to be designed in collaboration with the development banks and international agencies, but they will also require new programs on a grant-making basis. These can be financed though new structures yet to be designed.

The real issue is that cooperation in education is now in the domestic interest of all nations and all regions. It will no longer be a research experiment or a humanitarian gesture. The adjustment to these new functions will be very difficult for the current educational agencies and their staff, however, this adjustment will be good for the field of education.

List of Acronyms and Abbreviations

APEC	Asia Pacific Economic Conference
ETS	Educational Testing Service
EUROSTAT	Statistical Office of the European Communities
GDP	Gross Domestic Product
IEA	International Association for the Evaluation of Educational Achievement
IMF	International Monetary Fund
LAC	Latin America and the Caribbean
NAFTA	North American Free Trade Agreement
NCES	National Center for Educational Statistics
NGO	Non-Governmental Organization
OAU	Organization of African Unity
OECD	Organisation for Economic Co-operation and Development
SEAMEO	South East Asia Ministers of Education Organization
SENAI	Servicio Nacional de Aprendizaje Industrial (National Service for Industrial Learning of Colombia)
SSA	Sub-Saharan Africa
UNESCO	United Nations Education, Scientific and Cultural Organization
UNICEF	United Nations International Children's Education Fund
US	United States of America
WTO	World Trade Organization

Bibliography

Gutherie, James W. / Hansen, Janet S. (eds.): Worldwide Education Statistics. Enhancing UNESCO's Role. Washington, D. C.: Board on International Comparative Studies in Education, National Research Council 1995.

Heyneman, Stephen P.: Comparative Education. Questions of Quantity, Quality and Source. In: Comparative Education Review, 37 (1993a) 4, pp. 372-388.

Heyneman, Stephen P.: Educational Quality and the Crisis of Educational Research. In: International Review of Education, 39 (1993b) 6, pp. 511-517.

Heyneman, Stephen P.: Issues of Education Finance and Management in ECA and OECD Countries. Washington, D. C.: The World Bank 1994. (HRO Working Paper. 26)

Heyneman, Stephen P.: Good Governance in Education. America's Most Precious Export. In: American School Board Journal, 182 (1995) 3, pp. 23-26.

Heyneman, Stephen P.: Education and Economic Transformation. Paper presented at the United States National Academy of Sciences, September 1996 (mimeographed).

Heyneman, Stephen P.: Education and Social Stability in Russia. In: Compare, 27 (1997a) 1, pp. 5-18.

Heyneman, Stephen P.: The Quality of Education in the Middle East and North Africa. In: International Journal of Educational Development, 17 (1997b) (forthcoming).

Heyneman, Stephen P. et al.: Russia: Education in the Transition. Washington, D. C.: The World Bank, ECA Country Department III, Human Resources Division 1995.

Puryear, Jeffrey M.: International Education Statistics and Research. Status and Problems. In: International Journal of Educational Development, 15 (1995) 1, pp. 79-91.

United States Department of Education (ed.): The Condition of Education 1994. Washington, D. C.: U.S. DOE, Office of Educational Research and Improvement 1994.

World Bank (ed.): Global Economic Prospects and the Developing Countries. Washington, D. C.: The World Bank 1996.

Von 1988 bis 1996 – Wege zur Weiterentwicklung der gymnasialen Oberstufe

Georg Knauss

Am 1. Dezember 1995 hat die Ständige Konferenz der Kultusminister der Länder in der Bundesrepublik Deutschland (KMK) „Richtungsentscheidungen zur Weiterentwicklung der Prinzipien der gymnasialen Oberstufe und des Abiturs" *(Ständige Konferenz der Kultusminister der Länder in der Bundesrepublik Deutschland 1995a)* beschlossen, über deren Umsetzung in Form einer für alle 16 Länder verbindlichen Vereinbarung zur Zeit beraten wird. Diese „Richtungsentscheidungen" markieren einen bedeutsamen Schritt in einer immer wiederkehrenden Reformdiskussion, die schon bald nach dem Ende des Zweiten Weltkrieges begonnen hat und sich bis heute wie in Wellen fortbewegt. Es geht dabei um die möglichst sach- und zeitgemäße Vorbereitung begabter junger Menschen auf ein Hochschulstudium und auf die Übernahme verantwortungsvoller Tätigkeiten in Staat, Wirtschaft und Gesellschaft. Wie läßt sich der „Lehrplan des Abendlandes" (Josef Dolch) auf die heutige Zeit übertragen, wie können die neuen Anforderungen einer rasant sich wandelnden Welt so von unseren Schulen aufgenommen werden, daß die junge Generation in die Lage versetzt wird, ihr eigenes Leben und das Fortschreiten der Gesellschaft sinnvoll zu gestalten? Diese beiden Pole – Tradition und Modernität – bestimmen seit Jahrzehnten die Auseinandersetzung um das Gymnasium – einer Schulart, die sich trotz aller Kritik nicht nur wegen der mit ihrem Abschluß verbundenen Berechtigungen noch immer eines besonderen Sozialprestiges erfreut.

Vorangegangene Reformen der gymnasialen Oberstufe

Zur Einordnung unseres Themas sei zunächst in der gebotenen Kürze auf drei vorhergehende „Reformwellen" eingegangen, die sich an den Jahren 1960, 1972 und 1988 festmachen lassen.[1]

---

1 Eine ausführliche Darstellung ist in dem einführenden Bericht der Kultusministerkonferenz zur Vereinbarung zur Neugestaltung der gymnasialen Oberstufe in der Sekundarstufe II enthalten *(Handbuch für die Kultusministerkonferenz 1995, S. 200-206)*.

Der Wiederaufbau der „Höheren Schulen" nach den Zerstörungen des Krieges vollzog sich weitgehend unter Rückgriff auf traditionelle Ziele und Inhalte. Doch schon bald wurde deutlich, daß das überkommene gymnasiale Muster nicht mehr den veränderten Anforderungen entsprach; auch klagten die Hochschulen über die uneinheitliche Vorbildung der Studienanfänger. Es kam zu Gesprächen zwischen der KMK und der Westdeutschen Rektorenkonferenz, die im April 1958 zum sogenannten „Tutzinger Maturitätskatalog" führten, mit dem versucht wurde, das inhaltliche Minimum dessen, was nach Auffassung der Hochschulen bei jedem Studienanfänger vorauszusetzen war, zu definieren. Am 29. Juni 1960 beschloß dann die KMK die sogenannte „Saarbrücker Rahmenvereinbarung", die zum Ziel hatte, den Unterricht auf der Oberstufe des Gymnasiums neu zu ordnen; durch eine Verminderung der Zahl der Pflichtfächer und die Konzentration der Bildungsstoffe sollte eine Vertiefung des Unterrichts ermöglicht und die Erziehung der Schüler zu geistiger Selbständigkeit und Verantwortung gefördert werden.

Die Schulen nahmen die neuen Arbeitsmöglichkeiten bereitwillig auf; viele von ihnen experimentierten mit neuen Organisationsformen, um den Schülern individuellere Schwerpunktbildungen zu eröffnen. Wesentlich für die weitere Reformarbeit wurden aber die vom Schulausschuß der Westdeutschen Rektorenkonferenz im Januar 1969 vorgelegten „Kriterien der Hochschulreife", in denen erstmals zwischen Grundanforderungen in drei großen Aufgabenfeldern und gehobenen Anforderungen in zwei bis drei wissenschaftlichen Fächern unterschieden wurde.

Diese Entwicklungen bildeten die Grundlage für die von der KMK am 7. Juli 1972 beschlossene „Vereinbarung zur Neugestaltung der gymnasialen Oberstufe in der Sekundarstufe II". Danach ist die Grundstruktur der gymnasialen Oberstufe durch folgende Merkmale gekennzeichnet:

– die Gliederung in eine einjährige Einführungs- und eine zweijährige Qualifikationsphase;
– ein System von Grund- und Leistungskursen mit differenzierten Anforderungen;
– die Zuordnung der Fächer zu drei Aufgabenfeldern;
– die Ausgestaltung in einen Pflicht- und einen Wahlbereich zur individuellen Schwerpunktbildung;
– ein Punkt-Credit-System zur Vermittlung der Gesamtqualifikation.

Die Vereinbarung von 1972 veränderte die herkömmliche Struktur der Oberstufe ganz entscheidend. Ausgehend vom Prinzip der Gleichwertigkeit der Fächer und der Differenzierung der Anforderungen setzte sie eine tiefgreifende curriculare Erneuerung in Gang und erweiterte zugleich beträchtlich die Wahlmöglichkeiten der einzelnen Schüler. Das Modell war aber auch offen für die Aufnahme berufsbezogener Fachrichtungen, ohne dafür schon Regelungen im einzelnen vorzusehen.

Die Reform fand jedoch nicht überall Zustimmung. Kritisiert wurden die breiten Möglichkeiten der Fächerwahl und der damit verbundene Verlust der für alle verbindlichen Grundbildung, die Auflösung des Klassenverbands durch das Kurssystem und auch die angebliche Leistungsfeindlichkeit des neuen Bewertungssystems. All dies wurde dadurch verstärkt, daß die Länder den Rahmen der Vereinbarung enger oder weiter auslegten und damit aus der Sicht der Hochschulen eine verläßliche Hochschulreife in Gefahr brachten. Andererseits betrieben manche Länder zielstrebig die Aufnahme berufsbezogener Fachrichtungen in die gymnasiale Oberstufe bzw. die Einrichtung eigener berufsbezogener Bildungsgänge in Form von Fachgymnasien oder doppelqualifizierenden Bildungsgängen, so zum Beispiel in Form den sogenannten Kollegschulen in Nordrhein-Westfalen.

Die Auseinandersetzung um diese kritischen Punkte wurde zwischen den verschiedenen politischen Lagern und den interessierten Verbänden mit zunehmender Erbitterung geführt. Schließlich einigte sich die KMK am 11. April 1988 auf eine Novellierung der Vereinbarung von 1972, mit der einerseits die Wahlmöglichkeiten in der gymnasialen Oberstufe teilweise wieder eingeschränkt wurden, vor allem aber klare Regelungen für die Fachgymnasien bzw. berufsbezogenen Bildungsgänge und die doppelqualifizierenden Bildungsgänge, soweit sie zur allgemeinen Hochschulreife führen, getroffen wurden *(Handbuch für die Kultusministerkonferenz 1995, S. 200ff.)*. Das auf diese Weise neu geregelte Abitur wurde erstmals 1992 abgelegt, ein Land hatte sich die Umsetzung bestimmter Regelungen sogar erst für 1999 ausbedungen.

Anstöße zur und Vorgehensweisen bei der erneuten Reform

Damit ist der Ausgangspunkt für die Darstellung der weiteren Entwicklung erreicht, die im Titel dieses Beitrages bezeichnet ist; der Verfasser hat an ihr in den Jahren von 1989 bis 1995 als Vorsitzender des Schulausschusses der KMK beobachtend und mitgestaltend teilgenommen.

Reformen brauchen erfahrungsgemäß Zeit. Lagen jedoch die Intervalle zwischen den oben geschilderten Reformwellen zwischen 12 und 15 Jahren, so fällt auf, daß der jetzt zu beschreibende Zeitabschnitt nur halb so lang ist. Es kann kein Zweifel daran bestehen, daß der Grund dafür in dem säkularen Ereignis der deutschen Wiedervereinigung liegt. Der Einigungsvertrag vom 31. August 1990 sah zwar vor, daß in den neuen Ländern das Hamburger Abkommen der Ministerpräsidenten der (west-)deutschen Länder und die einschlägigen Vereinbarungen der Kultusministerkonferenz „Basis für die Neugestaltung des Schulwesens" sein sollten.[2] Doch die neuen Länder machten bei ihrer Schulgesetzgebung sogleich von der neu gewonnenen Kulturhoheit Gebrauch. Vier der neuen Länder – Mecklenburg-Vorpommern, Sachsen, Sachsen-Anhalt und Thüringen – entschieden sich im Gegensatz zum Hamburger Abkommen für zwölf Jahre bis zum Abitur und rückten damit nicht nur die gesamte Schulzeit bis zum Erwerb der Hochschulreife, sondern auch die Struktur des Gymnasiums – wo ist im achtjährigen Gymnasium der Ort der Oberstufe? – in den Mittelpunkt der bildungspolitischen Diskussion. In ihrer Haltung wurden sie dabei durch eine allgemeinpolitische Diskussion, die eine Verkürzung der in Deutschland „überlangen Ausbildungszeiten" bis zum Hochschulabschluß forderte, unterstützt; zudem lasse der europäische Vergleich angeblich zwölf Jahre Schulzeit bis zur Hochschulreife als Norm erkennen. Auch in den alten Bundesländern gab es ja – und gibt es noch immer – verschiedene Versuche mit gymnasialen Schnellzügen und anderen Verkürzungsmodellen. Schließlich stellte sich das Problem, wie mit den Abiturzeugnissen aus der ehemaligen DDR und den in der Umbruchssituation nach der Wende in den neuen Ländern erworbenen Zeugnissen umzugehen sei.

Bei den Zeugnissen mit einer Hochschulzugangsberechtigung entschied sich die KMK, wenn auch nicht ohne fachliche Bedenken, in drei Stufen (1990, 1992 und 1994) für eine faktische Anerkennung, auch wenn ihnen nur ein zwölfjähriger Schulbesuch zugrunde lag *(Knauss 1992)*. Über die viel wichtigere Frage aber, ob den Ländern nicht generell eine Verkürzung der gymnasialen Schulzeit auf dem Weg über Schulversuche freigestellt werden sollte, kam es zu keiner Einigung. Bei einer denkwürdigen Plenarsitzung der KMK am 10./11. Dezember 1991 in Dresden widersetzten sich die SPD-geführten Länder einer allgemeinen Verkürzungstendenz; sie befürchteten ganz offensichtlich ei-

---

2 Das sogenannte Hamburger Abkommen zwischen den Ländern in der Bundesrepublik Deutschland, das von den Ministerpräsidenten am 28. 10. 1964 „zur Vereinheitlichung auf dem Gebiet des Schulwesens" geschlossen wurde, legt die Grundstruktur des (allgemeinbildenden) Schulwesens in den Ländern fest. Es wurde 1968 zur Aufnahme der Fachoberschulen ergänzt und 1971 im Hinblick auf die zu unterrichtende erste Fremdsprache geändert. Für die neuen Länder gilt Art. 37 (4) des Einigungsvertrages.

nen Einbruch in die bildungs- und gesellschaftspolitische Errungenschaft des 10. Schuljahres für alle – hier stellt sich wieder die Frage der Dauer und des Ortes der gymnasialen Oberstufe – und eine Verschärfung des Ausleseprozesses auf dem Weg zum Abitur. Eine Entscheidung über „12 oder 13" Jahre wurde daher vertagt. Statt dessen wurde beschlossen, zunächst „die zum Abitur führenden Curricula" in den Ländern durch den Schulausschuß vergleichen zu lassen, um auf diese Weise inhaltliche Aufschlüsse über die Qualität des Abiturs in den Ländern zu erhalten.

In der Zwischenzeit war das Thema der Schulzeitverkürzung – unter dem aber immer nur die Verkürzung der Gymnasialzeit verstanden wurde – auf eine noch höhere politische Ebene gerückt. Bei einer Sitzung der Ministerpräsidentenkonferenz im März 1993 wurde deutlich, daß einige Ministerpräsidenten fest entschlossen waren, aus bildungspolitischen wie aus ökonomischen Gründen die seit langem diskutierte Verkürzung durchzusetzen. Da aber keine Einigung zu erzielen war, wurde die KMK gebeten, die Verkürzung der Schulzeit und die damit zusammenhängenden Fragen zu prüfen und so konkret aufzubereiten, daß die Ministerpräsidentenkonferenz noch im Jahre 1994 abschließend darüber entscheiden könnte.

Dieser Beschluß alarmierte die KMK aufs höchste. Bei aller Anerkennung der unterschiedlichen Länderpositionen zu dem Thema wurde jedoch einmütig festgestellt, daß ökonomische Überlegungen hinter Inhalts- und Qualitätsfragen zurückstehen müßten. Anfang Juli 1993 beschloß die KMK daher zwei Handlungslinien: Zum einen sollten alle Länder anhand eines vorgegebenen Fragenkatalogs ihre Sicht der Auswirkungen einer möglichen Verkürzung auf die verschiedenen Bildungsbereiche darstellen; zum anderen folgte man einem Vorschlag des niedersächsischen Kultusministers Prof. Rolf Wernstedt, die früheren „Tutzinger Gespräche" zu inhaltlichen Fragen der Hochschulreife wieder aufzunehmen. Die erste Tagung sollte in der Evangelischen Akademie in Loccum stattfinden; von daher rührt die Bezeichnung „Loccumer Gespräche" für die vier Tagungen, die danach geplant und durchgeführt wurden.

„Loccum I" fand am 13./14. Oktober 1993 als „internes Gespräch" der Kultusminister statt, zu dem als Referenten Vertreter der Erziehungswissenschaft, der Hochschulrektorenkonferenz und der Arbeitsmarktforschung geladen waren *(Abitur – Hochschulreife – Studierfähigkeit 1993)*. Heftige Diskussionen löste vor allem ein Beitrag des Bielefelder Professors Ludwig Huber aus, der als Voraussetzung der Studierfähigkeit „basale Qualifikationen" benannte, die er in einer aktiven und passiven Beherrschung der eigenen Sprache (Sprachkompetenz), in einer Fremdsprache (aus historischen Gründen Englisch) und in Kenntnissen der elementaren Mathematik sah. Dabei sollten diese basalen Fähigkeiten möglichst schon am Ende der Sekundarstufe I erreicht sein, um in der Oberstufe Raum für individuelle Vertiefungen und Erweiterungen zu gewinnen.

Bei „Loccum II" am 17./18. Februar 1994 in Bonn wurde der Gedankenaustausch der Minister auf informeller Ebene fortgesetzt. Dabei ergab sich, auch unter Rückbezug auf Loccum I, eine erstaunliche Übereinstimmung in inhaltlichen Fragen, die in der danach folgenden Plenarsitzung am 25. Februar 1994 in Bonn wie folgt protokolliert wurde:

„Es bestand Einvernehmen darüber, daß am Konzept der allgemeinen Hochschulreife als schulischer Abschlußqualifikation und Zugangsberechtigung für alle Studiengänge festgehalten wird. Voraussetzung hierfür ist die Festigung einer vertieften allgemeinen Bildung mit einem gemeinsamen Grundbestand von Kenntnissen und Fähigkeiten, die nicht erst in der Oberstufe erworben werden sollen. Dabei kommt für die Ausprägung der Studierfähigkeit dem Erwerb einer fachbezogenen, aber auch fächerübergreifenden Kompetenz in Deutsch, einer Fremdsprache und Mathematik eine besondere Bedeutung zu. Gleichzeitig ist der individuellen Schwerpunktbildung angemessener Raum zu geben. Der Herausbildung von Einstellungen und Verhaltensweisen für das selbständige und fächerübergreifende Lernen sowie der Stärkung der sozialen Kompetenz und der Kooperationsfähigkeit ist mehr Beachtung als bisher zu schenken" (Handbuch für die Kultusministerkonferenz 1995, S. 179-180).

Dies waren wegweisende Formulierungen und zugleich die Grundlage für den Beschluß, „die Prinzipien der gymnasialen Oberstufe und des Abiturs weiterzuentwickeln". Der Schulausschuß wurde mit entsprechenden Vorarbeiten beauftragt; außerdem wurde beschlossen, die anstehenden Fragen mit der Hochschulrektorenkonferenz in einem eigenen Gesprächskreis zu erörtern. Schließlich wurde ein weiteres Loccumer Gespräch zur Weiterentwicklung der Gleichwertigkeit von allgemeiner und beruflicher Bildung in Aussicht genommen.

Diese Beschlußlage ermöglichte der KMK eine gemeinsam getragene Antwort an die Ministerpräsidentenkonferenz. Dabei konnte auch auf die Auswertung zum oben erwähnten Fragenkatalog und auf den durch den Schulausschuß durchgeführten Lehrplanvergleich zurückgegriffen werden.

Die Länderantworten zu dem Fragenkatalog zeigten, wie komplex das Problemfeld ist, das mit der so einfach erscheinenden Streichung des 13. Schuljahres am Gymnasium aufgetan wird. Zahlreiche Auswirkungen sind dabei ebenso auf die Struktur der Schulen im Sekundarbereich I zu erwarten wie auf das Verhältnis von allgemeiner Hochschulreife zu Fachhochschulreife. Im europäischen Vergleich liegt Deutschland, was die Anzahl der Unterrichtsstunden bis zum Abitur angeht, im unteren Drittel: die Verkürzung um ein Schuljahr müßte also eine stundenmäßige Kompensation in den verbleibenden 12 Schuljahren zur Folge haben; ein finanzieller Einspareffekt würde dadurch kaum erreicht (vgl. auch *Döbrich / Huck 1993; Mitter / von Kopp 1994*).

Der mit großem Aufwand durchgeführte Lehrplanvergleich führte zu keinen schlüssigen Ergebnissen für die Entscheidung der Frage: „12 oder 13?" Zwar ist festzustellen, daß das geringere Zeitbudget der zwölfjährigen Bildungsgänge zur Verlagerung und Komprimierung, teilweise auch zum Verzicht auf wichtige Lehrplaninhalte führt. Auswirkungen auf die Qualitätsstandards im Abitur würden sich aber erst aufgrund eines Vergleichs konkreter Prüfungsergebnisse ermitteln lassen. Zur Herstellung von Transparenz durch Maßnahmen einer vergleichenden Evaluation aber führt in Deutschland noch ein weiter Weg.

Bei diesem Stand der Beratungen war offensichtlich die Zeit für eine endgültige Entscheidung über die Dauer der Schulzeit noch nicht reif. Andererseits drängten die vier neuen Länder auf Sicherheit für ihre Abiturienten. Die KMK beschloß daher ebenfalls am 25. Februar 1994, das bestehende Moratorium für die Anerkennung der Abiturzeugnisse dieser vier Länder bis zum Jahre 2000 zu verlängern. Die Verlängerung des Moratoriums sowie die Ergebnisse der verschiedenen Untersuchungen wurden der Ministerpräsidentenkonferenz mitgeteilt, die dies ohne förmlichen Beschluß zur Kenntnis nahm.

Während „Loccum III" mit dem Thema, wie die Gleichwertigkeit von allgemeiner und beruflicher Bildung verbessert werden könnte, vorbereitet und am 27./28. Oktober 1994 in Tutzing durchgeführt wurde – das Ergebnis wurde durch die KMK in einen Beschluß vom 2. Dezember 1994 bestätigt *(Handbuch für die Kultusministerkonferenz 1995, S. 181-182)* –, hatte der Schulausschuß mit Hilfe einer eigens dafür eingesetzten Arbeitsgruppe den Sachstand und die Positionen der Länder in der Oberstufenfrage so weit aufgearbeitet, daß dem Ministerplenum vier „Eckentscheidungen" vorgelegt werden konnten, über die eine Verständigung auf rein fachlicher Ebene nicht möglich erschien:

1. Soll die Grundstruktur der Oberstufe beibehalten, verändert oder gar aufgegeben werden?
2. Welche Auflagen sollen für die Fächer Deutsch, Fremdsprache und Mathematik gelten?
3. Welche Bedingungen werden für die Abiturprüfungsfächer vorgesehen?
4. Soll es Freiräume zur Erprobung fächerübergreifenden Lernens und Arbeitens geben?

Das Plenum verschob jedoch im Dezember 1994 eine sofortige Entscheidung darüber und beschloß statt dessen, über die Loccumer Gespräche und die Vorarbeiten des Schulausschusses hinaus sich noch zusätzlichen Sachverstandes zu versichern und eine breitere öffentliche Diskussion in seine Überlegungen einzubeziehen. Im Februar 1995 wurde daher eine Expertenkommission aus Wissenschaftlern, anderen Fachleuten und Schulpraktikern einberufen, die nach Einholung von Expertisen und der Anhörung von weiteren Fachleuten und Verbandsvertretern ein ausführliches Gutachten zu den verschiedenen Aspekten der Oberstufenreform vorlegen sollte.

Die Rolle der Expertenkommission

Der Vorsitz in der Expertenkommission wurde Professor Dr. Jürgen Baumert, Kiel, übertragen; als eines der weiteren neun Mitglieder wurde Professor Dr. Wolfgang Mitter, Frankfurt am Main, in das Gremium berufen, um gezielt auch Aspekte der internationalen Bildungsentwicklung und der vergleichenden Bildungsforschung einzubringen. Es ist hier nicht der Ort, die Arbeitsweise der Kommission und die Ergebnisse des Gutachtens ausführlich darzustellen (*Ständige Konferenz der Kultusminister der Länder in der Bundesrepublik Deutschland 1995b*; vgl. dazu *Loos 1996*). Es möge die Aussage genügen, daß die Kommission in einem ganz ungewöhnlich intensiven Beratungsverfahren und in kürzest möglicher Zeit ein außerordentlich fakten- und gedankenreiches Gutachten erarbeitet hat. Kern der Aussage ist einerseits, daß sich die Grundstruktur der Oberstufe mit ihrem System von Grund- und Leistungskursen, der Zuordnung der Fächer zu Aufgabenfeldern und der Möglichkeit, Leistungen über ein Punktesystem anzusammeln und nachzuweisen, insgesamt bewährt hat, um die Zielsetzungen der vertieften Allgemeinbildung, der Wissenschaftspropädeutik und der Studierfähigkeit zu erreichen. Andererseits schlägt die Expertenkommission vor, die drei „Sprachen", unter denen sie Deutsch, eine Fremdsprache und Mathematik versteht und die sie für die Welterschließung für unentbehrlich hält, stärker als bisher in der Oberstufe zu verankern. Darüber hinaus werden zahlreiche Anregungen zu einer inhaltlich-didaktischen Weiterentwicklung der gymnasialen Oberstufe gegeben, so vor allem zu einer gezielten Verstärkung des fächerübergreifenden Lernens, mit dem das für die heutige Welt so wichtige vernetzte Denken besser gefördert werden soll. Zentralabitur und dezentrales Abitur, die in den Ländern jeweils tief verwurzelte Traditionen aufweisen, werden als „funktionale Äquivalente" bezeichnet, die allerdings im Interesse der Verläßlichkeit der Zertifikate einer Reihe von vertrauensbildenden Maßnahmen zwischen den Ländern bedürfen.

Welche Rolle spielen in diesem Gutachten Aspekte eines internationalen Vergleichs? Die vorliegende Darstellung hat gezeigt, daß im Laufe der gesamten Oberstufendiskussion nur selten ein Blick auf ausländische Erfahrungen geworfen wurde; am ehesten läßt sich dies für die Differenzierung in Grund- und Leistungskurse sagen, wo seinerzeit auf die englischen O- und A-levels beim Sekundarabschluß (General Certificate of Education) Bezug genommen wurde, und bei den pauschalen, aber problematischen Aussagen zur Schulzeitdauer in Europa bis zum Erwerb einer Hochschulreife. Es ist bemerkenswert, daß in dem Gutachten der Expertenkommission ganz bewußt und ausführlich „Varianten der Oberstufe im internationalen Vergleich" beschrieben und bewertet worden sind. Das Kapitel geht auf eine vergleichende Expertise der studienvorbereitenden Sektoren des Sekundarbereichs II in Frankreich, Schweden sowie England und Wales zurück, die Wolfgang Mitter in die Beratungen eingebracht hat. Zusammenfassend sieht sich die Kommission freilich „*in ihrer Meinung bestärkt, daß konkrete Vorschläge [aus internationalen Vergleichen] nur sinnvoll sind, wenn sie das Geflecht der politischen und rechtlichen, institutionellen und organisatorischen, pädagogisch-professionellen und didaktischen Regelungen und Vorhaben berücksichtigen, die je national das Bildungswesen auszeichnen ...*" (Ständige Konferenz der Kultusminister der Länder in der Bundesrepublik Deutschland 1995b, S. 67-68). Es werden dann „Besonderheiten" hervorgehoben, die als Vorteile, aber auch als Nachteile in den deutschen Wegen zum Universitätsstudium im Vergleich zu denen anderer Bildungssysteme betrachtet werden können.[3]

---

3 Die Expertise zu „Varianten der Oberstufe im internationalen Vergleich" beruht auf einem von Professor Mitter geleiteten Forschungsprojekt am Deutschen Institut für Internationale Pädagogische Forschung in Frankfurt am Main, dessen Ergebnisse inzwischen in ausführlicher Form veröffentlicht worden sind *(Mitter 1996)*.

Die Neuregelung: Stärkung zentraler Fächer und Öffnung

Die Vorschläge der Expertenkommission begegnen in vielen Punkten einem Positionspapier der Hochschulrektorenkonferenz, das zur gleichen Zeit, aber unabhängig davon, der Kultusministerkonferenz zugeleitet wurde. Aus der Sicht der Hochschulen muß alles getan werden, um die Zugangsvoraussetzungen der Abiturienten homogener zu gestalten und vor allem solide Kenntnisse in fünf zentralen Fächern, d. h. über die drei „Sprachen" der Expertenkommission hinaus in Geschichte und in Naturwissenschaften, zu vermitteln.

Sowohl das Gutachten der Expertenkommission wie das Positionspapier der Hochschulrektorenkonferenz wurden bei „Loccum IV" am 26./27. Oktober 1995 in Hamburg, wieder in Form eines internen Meinungsaustausches der KMK, mit den Autoren erörtert. Der daraus resultierende Beschlußentwurf wurde in einem Gespräch der damaligen Präsidentin der KMK, der Hamburger Schulsenatorin Rosemarie Raab, und dem Sprecher der CDU/CSU-geführten Länder, dem bayerischen Kultusminister Hans Zehetmair, weiter beraten und schließlich in einer dramatischen Sitzung der KMK am 1. Dezember 1995 in Mainz in Form der eingangs erwähnten „Richtungsentscheidungen" beschlossen, die für die gymnasiale Oberstufe einerseits eine Festigung und Verstärkung der zentralen Fächer, andererseits aber auch eine Öffnung für neue Entwicklungen vorsehen. Zugleich wurde in der Schulzeitfrage eine Entscheidung in der Weise getroffen, daß die Dauer der Schulzeit bis zum Abitur entsprechend dem Hamburger Abkommen dreizehn Jahre beträgt, bei Nachweis eines (noch zu überprüfenden) Gesamtstundenvolumens von mindestens 265 Wochenstunden für die Sekundarstufe I und für die gymnasiale Oberstufe auch ein nach zwölf Schuljahren erworbenes Abitur anerkannt wird. Eine weitere Konkretisierung der „Richtungsentscheidungen" in zwei strittigen Punkten hat die KMK am 24./25.10.1996 in Dresden beschlossen, so daß die Novellierung der Vereinbarungen von 1972 und 1988 nunmehr endgültig erfolgen kann. Die Neuregelung soll erstmals für Schülerinnen und Schüler gelten, die am 1. 8. 1997, spätestens aber am 1. 8. 1999 in die gymnasiale Oberstufe eintreten.

Reformen, vor allem im Bildungswesen, brauchen Zeit. Hoffen wir, daß die jetzt bevorstehende Reform ihr doppeltes Ziel erreichen und für einige Zeit Bestand haben wird.

Bibliographie

Abitur – Hochschulreife – Studierfähigkeit. Zur Grundlegung eines neuen Maturitätskataloges. Vorträge in einer Tagung der Kultusministerkonferenz in der Evangelischen Akademie Loccum am 13. und 14. Oktober 1993. Rehburg-Loccum: Evangelische Akademie 1993. (Loccumer Protokolle. 1993, 56)

Döbrich, Peter / Huck, Wolfgang: Quantitative Tendenzen der Schulzeit im internationalen Vergleich. Memorandum zu einer aktuellen Debatte in Deutschland. Frankfurt a. M.: Deutsches Institut für Internationale Pädagogische Forschung 1993.

Handbuch für die Kultusministerkonferenz 1995. Bonn: Sekretariat der KMK 1995.

Knauss, Georg: Zur Zulassung von Hochschulzugangsberechtigten aus den neuen Ländern an Hochschulen in der Bundesrepublik Deutschland. In: Schulverwaltung. Ausgabe Bayern, 15 (1992) 4, S. 111-113.

Loos, Barbara: Weiterentwicklung der gymnasialen Oberstufe? Bericht der Expertenkommission und Richtungsentscheidungen der Kultusministerkonferenz. In: Schulverwaltung. Ausgabe Bayern, 19 (1996) 2, S. 61-65.

Mitter, Wolfgang (Hrsg.): Wege zur Hochschulbildung in Europa. Köln u. a.: Böhlau 1996. (Studien und Dokumentationen zur vergleichenden Bildungsforschung. 70)

Mitter, Wolfgang / Kopp, Botho von (Hrsg.): Die Zeitdimension in der Schule als Gegenstand des Bildungsvergleichs. Köln u. a.: Böhlau 1994. (Studien und Dokumentationen zur vergleichenden Bildungsforschung. 61)

Ständige Konferenz der Kultusminister der Länder in der Bundesrepublik Deutschland: Richtungsentscheidungen zur Weiterentwicklung der Prinzipien der gymnasialen Oberstufe und des Abiturs. (Beschluß der Kultusministerkonferenz vom 01. 12. 1995). Bonn: Sekretariat der KMK 1995a.

Ständige Konferenz der Kultusminister der Länder in der Bundesrepublik Deutschland (Hrsg.): Weiterentwicklung der Prinzipien der gymnasialen Oberstufe und des Abiturs. Abschlußbericht der von der Kultusministerkonferenz eingesetzten Expertenkommission. Bonn: Sekretariat der KMK 1995b.

Anerkennung, Akkreditierung, Transparenz –
Notwendige Begriffsklärungen für die Europäische Union

Hermann Müller-Solger

Zwei zentrale Aufgaben der Europäischen Union im Bildungsbereich

Die Aufgaben der EU im Bereich der Bildungspolitik lassen sich in zwei Zielsetzungen zusammenfassen:

1. die Entwicklung einer europäischen Dimension des Bildungswesens für alle Bürger der Union
2. die Erleichterung der Anerkennung von Abschlüssen oder Teilabschlüssen der verschiedenen Bildungswege in der gesamten Europäischen Union.

Die erste Aufgabe zielt auf die innere Entwicklung des Bildungswesens ab, von der Partnerschaft zwischen Bildungseinrichtungen und der Entdeckung Europas durch Austauschmaßnahmen bis hin zu Initiativen zum Abgleich zwischen Geschichtsbüchern oder zur Vorbereitung auf den europäischen Arbeitsmarkt. Die zweite Aufgabe betrifft die Nutzung der Ergebnisse von Bildungsgängen, in erster Linie auf dem Arbeitsmarkt selbst, aber auch in anderen sozialen Zusammenhängen bis hin zur Anrechnung einzelner Bildungsnachweise bei der Fortsetzung einer Ausbildung an einer anderen Bildungseinrichtung im europäischen Ausland.

Die Debatte über diese zweite Aufgabe hat auf vielen Ebenen an Dringlichkeit zugenommen. Zu den Motiven im Hintergrund zählen die wachsende Globalisierung, die zunehmende Mobilität, die Verschärfung des Wettbewerbs auf dem Arbeitsmarkt wie auch der Wille zur Modernisierung der Angebote der Schulen und Hochschulen, der Erstausbildung sowie der allgemeinen und beruflichen Weiterbildung. Die in dieser Debatte verwendeten Begriffe und Zusammenhänge bedürfen sehr dringlich der Klärung. Es ist mir daher eine willkommene Gelegenheit, im Rahmen dieses Beitrags ein durchaus persönliches Exerzitium der Begriffs- und Problemklärung vorzulegen. Anregungen und Hinweise verdanke ich vielen Partnern in dienstlichen und außerdienstlichen Diskussionen sowie zum Teil auch einer frühen wissenschaftlichen Beschäftigung mit diesem

Thema *(Müller-Solger 1974, 1978)*. Die Zusammenschau und die in diesem Beitrag vorgetragenen Schlußfolgerungen liegen naturgemäß ausschließlich in der alleinigen Verantwortung des Autors.[1]

Eine Analogie

Man hat Zeugnisnoten wiederholt mit Banknoten verglichen. Der Einzelne will möglichst viel davon haben und sie möglichst vorteilhaft einsetzen. Der Abnehmer (der Arbeitgeber oder die Bildungseinrichtung) will in bezug auf die Aussagekraft der Zeugnisse sicher sein und nach Möglichkeit den Preis drücken. Eine Art Bundesbank soll den Notenwert sichern. Es gibt Inflationseffekte *(Müller-Solger/Jesinghaus 1977)*, Auf- und Abwertungen[2] und eine immerwährende Spekulation. Es scheint Zeitgenossen zu geben, die sich den Tauschwert von Zertifikaten und Zeugnissen offenbar ebenso gesichert wünschen wie den der Zahlungsmittel, mit festen Preisen im Inland und festen Wechselkursen oder zumindest engen Wechselkursbandbreiten im Ausland. Die europäische Währungsschlange läßt grüßen.

Man muß jedoch nüchtern festhalten: In Zertifikaten geronnene Bildungsleistung ist in keiner Weise ebenso objektivierbar wie die in Geld geronnene Arbeitsleistung. Bildungszertifikate bleiben personengebunden, von individuellem Profil und in erheblichem Maße interpretationsbedürftig. Das Verhältnis zwischen Anbietern und Nachfragern von Zertifikaten und Qualifikationen bleibt seiner Natur nach eher das eines Tauschhandels. Der Vermarktung von Zertifikaten sind Grenzen gesetzt. Zertifikate sind nicht beliebig handelbar und schon gar nicht frei konvertierbar, auch wenn zahlreiche Regelungen für Äquivalenzen geschaffen worden sind *(Bundesministerium für Bildung, Wissenschaft, Forschung und Technologie 1996)*. Ein konsequent meritokratisches System, das sich für die erforderlichen Selektionsprozesse in Wirtschaft und Gesellschaft allein auf noch so perfekte Zeugnisnoten stützen würde, müßte am Abstand zwischen schola und vita scheitern, ebenso am historisch-sozialen Gleichheitsanspruch und an dem grundlegenden Erfordernis, daß ein erhebliches undefiniertes Potential als „Reserve" an Qualifikationen als Grundlage und Motivation für Anpassungen und Innovation

---

[1] Frau Christine Bäumler, cand. päd. an der Universität Bielefeld, bin ich für ihre kritische Hilfe bei der Ausarbeitung dankbar.
[2] In einem Kulturabkommen wurden beispielsweise in den sechziger Jahren spanische Zeugnisse für Zwecke der Hochschulzulassung von Kategorie III (Studienkolleg nötig) nach Kategorie I (Studium ohne weiteres möglich) aufgewertet.

bestehen bleiben muß. Der Einzelne erlebt dies in Zeugnissen nicht zu erfassende Potential als Grundlage für sein Selbstvertrauen und als Hoffnung, bei neuer Chance doch neue Qualifikationen zur Geltung bringen zu können (ich kann mehr als meine Zeugnisse sagen). Für die Gesellschaft und die Volkswirtschaft liegt hierin das Moment der Erhaltung der Dynamik zur Sicherung von Zukunft auch auf neuen Wegen. (Das reale Qualifikationspotential ist mehr als die Summe aller Bildungszertifikate.)

Einige Begriffe

In der Diskussion über Qualifikationsnachweise und deren Nutzung im europäischen Rahmen kommt es oft durch Uneinigkeit bei der Verwendung der Fachtermini zu unnötigen Verwirrungen. Für die weitere Diskussion ist es daher unerläßlich, zu den im folgenden aufgeführten Begriffen soweit wie möglich Klarheit zu schaffen, um Mißverständnissen vorzubeugen und die Diskussion ergebnisorientiert voranzutreiben.

1. *Zertifikat oder Zeugnis:* Sammelbegriff für Prüfungszeugnisse und Diplome. Im Bildungswesen stellt es den Nachweis einer erbrachten Leistung dar. Es wird attestiert, daß der Inhaber des Zertifikats bestimmte Kenntnisse und Verhaltensweisen unter Beweis gestellt hat, die als Voraussetzung für die weitere Teilnahme an Bildungsangeboten oder für die Aufnahme bestimmter Tätigkeiten in der Arbeitswelt interpretiert werden. Zertifikate bedürfen grundsätzlich der schriftlichen Form mit Angabe der zertifizierenden Stelle, des Inhabers des Zertifikats und der zertifizierten Leistung *(Rat der Europäischen Union 1996).*
2. *Diplom:* Berufsbefähigender Bildungsabschluß auf höherem Niveau. Nach den Anerkennungsrichtlinien der EG deckt der Begriff Hochschuldiplome (drei Jahre Studium) und andere postsekundäre Ausbildungsabschlüsse ab. Diese sind weitgehend im Anhang C der Richtlinie von 1992 abschließend aufgezählt (dem Zweck der Richtlinie entsprechend bleibt die Aufzählung auf sogenannte reglementierte Berufe beschränkt) *(Rat der Europäischen Gemeinschaften 1992).*
3. *Prüfungszeugnis:* Jeder Ausbildungsnachweis, bzw. die Verbindung mehrerer Einzelnachweise in einem Dokument. Die zweite Anerkennungsrichtlinie der EG von 1992 verwendet diesen Begriff für Berufsqualifikationen unterhalb des Diplomniveaus.
4. *Befähigungsnachweis:* Die EG-Richtlinie von 1992 verwendet diesen Begriff für Feststellungen von Qualifikationen zur Aufnahme eines Berufs, die keine grundständige Ausbildung voraussetzen.

5. *Anerkennung:* Umfassendster Begriff für die Feststellung der Wertigkeit von Zertifikaten. In der Regel meint der Begriff die staatliche Anerkennung, d. h. die Einräumung bestimmter Rechte durch das staatliche Rechtssystem. Ist diese Ebene nicht gemeint, wird die anerkennende Institution oder auch die Einzelperson ausdrücklich benannt, z. B. Anerkennung durch einen Verband, eine Einrichtung oder auch durch einen einzelnen Lehrgangsleiter oder Arbeitgeber.
6. *Anrechnung:* Berücksichtigung von Teilleistungen im Hinblick auf den Abschluß von Bildungsgängen oder auf die Erfüllung von Qualitätsstandards auf dem Arbeitsmarkt. Dies kann sich auf Bildungsnachweise beziehen, aber auch auf den Nachweis von Berufserfahrung.
7. *Äquivalenz:* Gleichwertigkeit von Bildungsnachweisen aus verschiedenen Bildungssystemen. Diese darf nicht mit Gleichartigkeit verwechselt werden. Basis für die Feststellung von Äquivalenzen sind daher gegenseitiges Vertrauen sowie ein gewisses Maß an Großzügigkeit und Flexibilität *(Bundesministerium für Bildung, Wissenschaft, Forschung und Technologie 1996, S. 9f.).*
8. *Akkreditierung:* Stammt im Bildungskontext aus dem anglo-amerikanischen Sprachgebrauch und verweist auf zweierlei: Zum einen auf die Akkreditierung von Zertifikaten durch Institutionen, z. B. Bildungseinrichtungen oder Prüfungsagenturen (i.d.R. unterhalb der staatlichen Ebene), zum anderen auf die „accreditation of prior learning" (APL) im Hinblick auf den Erwerb von weiterführenden Qualifikationen. Der Unterschied zur „Anrechnung" im deutschen Sprachgebrauch ist damit sehr gering. Es erscheint jedoch zweckmäßig, Akkreditierung als einen stärker institutionalisierten Prozeß zu begreifen (Akkreditierungsverfahren, Akkreditierungsagentur), der über einzelne Anrechnungsentscheidungen hinausgeht.
9. *Credit:* Anrechenbare Einheit im Hinblick auf den Erwerb eines Zertifikats; besonders bekannt aus dem amerikanischen Hochschulwesen. In der Europäischen Union gibt es Bemühungen um die Einführung eines European Credit Transfer System (ECTS).
10. *Transparenz:* Sicherung einer verläßlichen Interpretation von Zertifikaten innerhalb einzelner Bildungssysteme und über solche Systeme hinaus im Hinblick auf ihre Relevanz für Zwecke der Bildungs- oder Berufslaufbahn. Transparenz ist über die Gestaltung der Zeugnisse selbst sowie über begleitende erläuternde Dokumente und Informationsdienste herzustellen.

In dieser Übersicht über die wichtigsten Begriffe aus dem Bereich der Anerkennung von Zeugnissen, in die die Begriffe über die verschiedenen Formen von Prüfungen selbst (z. B. Tests usw.) nicht aufgenommen worden sind, wird erkennbar: Es gibt Unterschiede bei den Begriffen für die Zeugnisse einerseits und den Akt ihrer Bewertung andererseits. Bei den Zeugnissen geht es letztlich um die Einordnung in eine hierarchische Struktur. Wieweit Einvernehmen über eine solche Struktur in Europa besteht, bleibt nach wie vor offen.[3] Für die Bewertung ist hingegen ausschlaggebend, ob sie vom Staat durch die Festlegung von Äquivalenzen oder in anderer Weise garantiert wird oder ob nachgeordnete oder auch nicht-staatliche Stellen einen erheblichen Ermessensspielraum haben, diese Bewertung auch im Lichte eigener Interessen vornehmen zu können. Der Ansatz der Transparenz leistet zwischen beiden eine Art Vermittlung: Der Staat sichert die Rahmenbedingungen für die Verwertung von Zeugnissen, indem er für eine einheitliche Lesbarkeit sorgt. Die Bewertung selbst erfolgt jedoch dezentral und im Rahmen erheblicher Ermessensspielräume *(Gordon 1995)*.

Vor dem Hintergrund der aktuellen Diskussion in der Europäischen Union bedarf darüber hinaus besonders der Begriff der Akkreditierung einer besonderen Erläuterung. Zunächst verbindet man damit die Erinnerung an die Akkreditierung von Botschaftern, ein völkerrechtlich geregelter Vorgang, der einer Person Vertretungsvollmachten zuschreibt. In den bildungspolitischen Sprachgebrauch ist der Begriff am Ende des 19. Jahrhunderts in den USA übernommen worden. Ähnlich wie heute in Europa bestand damals der Bedarf, eine überregionale Mobilität bei der Rekrutierung von Studenten und beim Austausch von Studenten und Absolventen zu sichern. Es entstanden Akkreditierungsvereinigungen auf regionaler Ebene und auf Fachbereichsebene, die sich die Sicherung bestimmter Standards zum Zwecke der wechselseitigen Anerkennung von Studiennachweisen und Abschlüssen zum Ziel setzten. Diese Akkreditierungsvereinigungen stehen insgesamt in einem Wettbewerb zueinander. Seit 1965 sieht das amerikanische Hochschulgesetz vor, daß nur Hochschulen, die einer vom Staat anerkannten Akkreditierungsvereinigung angehören, staatliche Fördermittel erhalten *(Müller-Solger 1979, S. 28f.; El-Khawas 1993)*.

Diese bildungspolitische Verwendung des Begriffs Akkreditierung bezieht sich auf Institutionen und nicht auf Personen. Die hervorragende Studie der OECD aus dem Jahre 1977 über „Selection and Certification in Education and Employment" hält an diesem Sprachgebrauch fest, indem sie definiert *„accreditation: a process or act whereby a government department or specially constituted agency recognises the standing of an educational institution in the light of its ability to satisfy prescribed criteria. Such recognition*

---

3 Die Frage der Geltung der fünf Niveaustufen im Anhang zur Entscheidung des *Rates der Europäischen Gemeinschaften (1985)* ist nach wie vor offen.

usually confers valuable advantages upon the institution and upon its graduates. The term 'formal education' primarily refers to institutions and programmes which have been accredited" (Organisation for Economic Co-operation and Development 1977, S. 8).[4]

Eine neuere Verwendung des Begriffs der Akkreditierung taucht vornehmlich im englischen Sprachgebrauch bei Anbietern von außerschulischer Weiterbildung auf, indem auf die Möglichkeit von *„accreditation of prior learning"* im Kontext des Erwerbs von NVQ's (national vocational qualifications) hingewiesen wird *(National Council for Vocational Qualifications 1990; RSA Examinations Board 1995, S. 12)*. Bei diesem Vorgang werden vorgelegte Zeugnisse oder auch vorangegangene Berufserfahrungen im Hinblick auf ihre Anrechenbarkeit bewertet. Dies kann pauschal geschehen oder durch eine Eignungsprüfung, wie wir sie beispielsweise bei der sogenannten Begabtensonderprüfung für die Hochschulzulassung kennen und wie auch die Anerkennungsrichtlinien der EG sie vorsehen.

Es ist ein großer Unterschied, ob der Begriff der Akkreditierung auf „prior learning" (hinsichtlich von NVQ's) oder, wie dies in Äußerungen der *Europäischen Kommission (1995, S. 59)* neuerdings vorkommt, unmittelbar auf einzelne Befähigungen bezogen wird. Indem die Kommission ankündigt, ein europäisches und europaweit verfügbares Akkreditierungssystem von Einzelqualifikationen („Europäisches System zur Anerkennung von Fähigkeiten") *(Arbault 1996)* einrichten zu wollen, geht sie von der Ebene der institutionellen Akkreditierung vollständig auf die der Examination Boards oder der Testing Services über. Die Vorstellung eines einheitlichen europäischen Systems stellt dieses Angebot überdies in die unmittelbare staatliche Verantwortung. Eine flexible, an den Bedürfnissen der Lernenden wie der Abnehmer von Qualifikationen orientierte Struktur dürfte so, wie noch zu zeigen sein wird, kaum zu erreichen sein.

Einige Zusammenhänge

Man sagt: Wer das Prüfungssystem in der Hand hat, der hat das Bildungswesen in der Hand. Die genannte OECD-Studie formuliert noch grundsätzlicher: *„Credentials and awards make the existence of an educational system possible" (Organisation for Econo-*

---

4 Vgl. auch den folgenden Wörterbucheintrag: *„accreditation: U.S. The grant to an academic institution, by an accrediting body, of status indicating valuation of its course credits and degrees as in accord with the standards set by the accrediting body" (Accreditation 1964).*

mic Co-operation and Development 1977, S. 15). Die Prüfungshoheit hat bestimmende Auswirkungen bis hinein in die Unterrichtsstunden und den dort behandelten Stoff, bis hin zum Verhalten einzelner Lehrer und bis hin zu der Kette von Abhängigkeiten innerhalb der Bildungsverwaltung. Es ist eindeutig: Das Prüfungswesen gehört zum innersten Kern der Gestaltung des Bildungssystems. Man kann es gar als dessen Rückgrat ansehen. Bezogen auf die Europäische Union, um dies hier vorab anzumerken, ist ebenso eindeutig: Nach Artikel 126 und 127 EG-Vertrag bleibt die Gestaltung der allgemeinen wie der beruflichen Bildung den Mitgliedstaaten vorbehalten. Das Recht zum Aufbau eines eigenen Prüfungswesens ist der Union nicht gegeben. Dazu später mehr.

Was für die großen historischen Strukturen des Bildungswesens gilt, gilt selbstverständlich auch für kleinere Zertifikatssysteme außerhalb dieser Strukturen. Nehmen wir die Führerscheinprüfungen. Alles ist hier darauf ausgerichtet, den Nachweis der Befähigung zum Führen eines Kraftfahrzeuges zu erbringen. Hier wird deutlicher als in den verzweigten Großstrukturen des formalen Bildungssystems: Das Schutzinteresse der Öffentlichkeit einerseits und das unmittelbare vitale Interesse des Lernenden andererseits sind die zentralen Ankerpunkte für dieses Prüfungsverfahren. Die Nachfrage ist die treibende Kraft. Die Menschen möchten Auto fahren. Die Prüfung ist darauf ausgerichtet. Ein komplexeres Beispiel ist die Meisterprüfung: Auch hier gibt es Ordnungs- und Sicherheitsbedarf auf der einen Seite und auf der anderen Seite den Antrieb, daß der Lernende, der sich der Prüfung stellt, durch das Ablegen dieser Prüfung die Berechtigung zur selbständigen Führung eines Handwerksbetriebes erlangen kann. Fiele diese Nachfrage weg, würden die Prüfungen sinnlos.

Diese Beispiele machen zweierlei deutlich: Prüfungssysteme müssen von konkreten Bedürfnissen der Bürger ausgehen. Ein bloß formales Höher oder Mehr, vorgegeben von einem abstrakten staatlichen System führt zur Unfruchtbarkeit. (Das Schicksal solcher Systeme vom Mandarinismus und der Scholastik bis zum europäischen öffentlichen Dienst zu verfolgen, wäre eine reizvolle Aufgabe). Prüfungssysteme müssen daneben auch konkreten Interessen der Prüfungsinstitutionen dienen. Hier geht es um die Relevanz und Attraktivität der Prüfungen. Dabei kommt es darauf an, daß die Prüfungsinstitutionen überhaupt in der Lage sind, nach bestimmten Interessen zu handeln. Ein bloßer neutraler Qualifikationsfilter, wie ihn der Staat mit einem dichten Netz von Vorschriften und Kontrollen gewährleisten müßte, läßt letztlich nur ein sehr abstraktes Gerechtigkeitsinteresse zu. Es ist bezeichnend, daß in den Anerkennungsrichtlinien der EG sehr penibel klargestellt wird, daß eine etwaige Eignungsprüfung sich nur auf Qualifikationselemente zu richten und alle sonstigen Interessen auszuschließen habe. Wir stehen hier vor dem Dilemma zwischen abstrakter Gerechtigkeit einerseits und der notwendigen lebendigen Dynamik für den Fortschritt der Qualifikationsinhalte und -formen andererseits.

Wenn Prüfungen keine bestimmten Berechtigungen vermitteln oder wenn sie keine unmittelbaren persönlichen Interessen erfüllen wie Sprach- oder Sportprüfungen, dann werden sie nicht angenommen und laufen leer. Wenn Prüfungen andererseits nicht in einem letztlich von Interessen geleiteten Verwendungszusammenhang stehen, im Bildungswesen oder auf dem Arbeitsmarkt, dann verlieren Prüfungsinstitutionen ihre Funktion; sie werden rituell. Die Aufgabe besteht also darin, zugleich den Motivationen der Anbieter und Nachfrager zu entsprechen und Gerechtigkeit zu sichern. Ein Test für das erstere liegt darin, ob beide bereit sind, für die Durchführung der Prüfung zu bezahlen. Der Test für das zweite liegt vor allem in der Sicherung einer größtmöglichen Transparenz.

Ein problematisches Konzept

„Beurteilen Sie Ihre Fähigkeiten!" ist ein Artikel in der im September 1996 erschienenen fünften Ausgabe von Le Magazine, einem Organ der Öffentlichkeitsarbeit der Generaldirektion XXII der Europäischen Kommission, überschrieben *(Arbault 1996)*. Der Bürger ist im Visier. Seine Motivation zur Qualifikation zu steigern, ist das Ziel. Die Entwicklung der „Wissensgesellschaft" voranzutreiben, ist eine dringliche Aufgabe, der die Europäische Kommission seit dem Weißbuch über Wachstum, Wettbewerb und Beschäftigung aus dem Jahre 1992 bereits vielfache Impulse gegeben hat.

Mit dem Appell aber ist es nicht getan. Welche Prüfung soll der Einzelne denn für sich bestehen? Wo liegt sein Interesse? Welche Institutionen sollen die Prüfungen abnehmen? Wo liegen deren Interessen? Welche Bedeutung soll das Prüfungsergebnis auf dem Arbeitsmarkt oder im Bildungswesen haben? Wer soll diese Geltung gewährleisten?

Das in dem genannten Artikel dargestellte Konzept läßt sich wie folgt zusammenfassen:

– In der Form eines Projekts will die Kommission neue Möglichkeiten für den Nachweis von Qualifikationen entwickeln lassen.

- Neben vorhandene Diplome und Zertifikate soll ein europäisches System zur Anerkennung von Fähigkeiten (European System of Skills Accreditation) in der gesamten Union treten. Dieses wird als ein komplementäres System bezeichnet.
- Ein solches System soll permanent und leicht zugänglich sein. Tests im Internet oder über andere On-line-Dienste sollen diese Zugänglichkeit sichern.
- Ein solches System soll neutral sein: *„Nur die Unparteilichkeit einer Software (ungeachtet ihrer Genauigkeit bei der Bewertung) kann absolute Objektivität bei Bewertung und Anerkennung der Fähigkeiten garantieren."* Das System soll in ganz Europa eine einheitliche (Bewertungs-)Methode anwenden und in allen Gemeinschaftssprachen in identischer Weise verfügbar sein.
- Die Inhalte sollen standardisiert sein und gegenüber nationalen und kulturellen Bezügen neutral. Bestimmte Bereiche dieser Art, die in arbeitsmarktrelevante Einheiten auf verschiedenen Ebenen zerlegt werden könnten, seien bereits identifiziert, und zwar Grundkenntnisse (Mathematik, Naturwissenschaften, Informatik, Geographie, schriftlicher Ausdruck, Fremdsprachen), berufliche Kenntnisse (Marketing, Management und andere Fähigkeiten, die im Industrie- und Dienstleistungsbereich von Bedeutung sind) und schließlich Schlüsselqualifikationen (Logistik, Organisationstechniken, Kommunikation, Entscheidungsfähigkeit und anderes). Neben solchen standardisierten Inhalten sollen auch Inhalte mit nationalen Unterschieden möglich bleiben.
- Die Ergebnisse sollen schließlich in eine „Persönliche Kompetenzkarte" eingetragen werden. Diese soll neben herkömmlichen Zeugnissen eine zusätzliche Bewerbungsunterlage auf dem Arbeitsmarkt werden. Es ist auch denkbar, daß die herkömmlichen Zeugnisse in diesen Qualifikationsausweis aufgenommen werden.

Das Konzept mag manchen stimulieren, auf diesem Wege endlich Qualifikationshürden zu überwinden, die ihm das formale Bildungswesen in den Weg stellt. Doch bei genauerem Hinsehen bleibt ein Eindruck von großer technizistischer Abstraktheit vorherrschend. Es ist ein Zeichen von Realitätsferne, daß besonders drei Fragen nicht beantwortet sind: Worin liegt tatsächlich die Motivation der Bürger, sich weiteren Prüfungen zu unterziehen? (Test: Wären sie bereit, dafür zu bezahlen wie für den Führerschein?) Wer soll die Prüfungen abnehmen und standardisieren und ihren Wert garantieren? Welche Interessen stehen hinter den Prüfungsagenturen? (Test: Wären diese bereit, dafür zu bezahlen?)

Ich verzichte auf eine Erörterung der technischen Aspekte des Konzepts der Kommission. Sind kulturneutrale Inhalte überhaupt denkbar? Wie sind Validität und Reliabilität solcher Prüfungen zu sichern? Wie lange würde es dauern, ein solches System zu entwickeln? Welche (immensen) Kosten wären damit verbunden? Könnte es bei seinem europaweiten Anspruch überhaupt mit der Entwicklung von Angebot und Nachfrage von Qualifikationen Schritt halten? Bei der Beantwortung all dieser Fragen sind offenkundig große Zweifel in bezug auf die Umsetzbarkeit der Vorschläge angebracht.

Wichtiger ist mir die Frage der Systemarchitektur. Es geht letztlich um die Rolle des Staates im Verhältnis zu den Bürgern und zu den Einrichtungen des Bildungswesens und der Wirtschaft, und zwar auch in seiner überstaatlichen Gestalt, d. h. in der Form des Rechtssystems der Europäischen Union *(Greinert 1990; Koch 1995)*. Weder die Europäische Union noch die vereinigte Autorität ihrer Mitgliedstaaten vermag heute ein umfassendes relevantes Prüfungssystem zu begründen. Schon die Sicherung von umfassenden Äquivalenzregelungen, z. B. zwischen Deutschland und Frankreich, will nicht gelingen.[5] Man muß ernsthaft dem Gedanken nahetreten, daß der Staat als Garant für die Feststellung der Qualifizierung des einzelnen in Wirtschaft und Gesellschaft ein Stück weit in den Hintergrund treten muß. Wir müssen einen Qualifikationswettbewerb organisieren, der durch die Motivation der Bürger und durch die Motivation der Qualifikationsanbieter, -prüfer und -nachfrager vorangetrieben wird. Der Staat muß hierzu neue Rahmenbedingungen schaffen. Es ist nützlich, daß die Kommission mit ihrer Initiative neue Impulse für die Diskussion über die Prüfungssysteme gibt. Das vorgestellte Konzept scheint aber leider einem allzu populistischen Motto zu folgen: „Freu Dich, Bürger, Europa erkennt Deine Qualifikation an!" Der Bürger wird nicht wissen, ob er sich wirklich freuen soll und kann. Viel Geld wird aufgewendet werden müssen, um ein solches paralleles Prüfungssystem zu installieren. Der Nutzen wird gering bleiben, nicht zuletzt weil der Bedarf nicht ausreichend geklärt ist.

Eine Mittlerrolle für den Staat: Transparenz

Die Anerkennung von Zeugnissen im Bildungswesen und auf dem Arbeitsmarkt bleibt ein anzustrebendes Ziel. Wo der Staat vor allem aus Gründen des Verbraucherschutzes und der öffentlichen Ordnung den Zugang zu Berufen an den Nachweis bestimmter Qualifikationen geknüpft hat (sog. reglementierte Berufe), soll die Gleichstel-

---

5 Auf der Grundlage eines Abkommens zwischen Deutschland und Frankreich aus dem Jahre 1977 konnten bisher lediglich 22 Prüfungszeugnisse – noch dazu mit anerkannt geringer praktischer Bedeutung – wechselseitig anerkannt werden.

lung von Zeugnissen aus anderen Mitgliedstaaten der EU durch die auf Artikel 57 gestützten Richtlinien zur Anerkennung von Diplomen und Prüfungszeugnissen sichergestellt werden. Auch Artikel 126 EG-Vertrag hat die Anerkennung im Visier, und zwar die akademische Anerkennung von Diplomen und Studienzeiten. Die Tätigkeit der EU bleibt hier jedoch auf die Förderung einer solchen Anerkennung beschränkt. Und schließlich enthalten auch die Bestimmungen in Artikel 123 und 127 EG-Vertrag, die auf die Erleichterung der Anpassung an die industriellen Wandlungsprozesse sowie die berufliche Eingliederung und Wiedereingliederung abzielen, die Vorstellung, daß die Anerkennung von Zertifikaten dabei eine wesentliche Rolle spielt. Anerkennung ist erwünscht. Doch die Einsicht setzt sich mehr und mehr durch, daß sie auf europäischer Ebene mit den Mitteln der Mitgliedstaaten und der Europäischen Union nur mittelbar zu erreichen ist. Die Bildungseinrichtungen oder die Arbeitgeber kommen immer mehr in die Rolle derjenigen, die die Anerkennung aus eigener Autonomie vornehmen. Der Staat muß sich darauf beschränken, die Interessen dieser Abnehmer von Qualifikationen zu steuern,[6] insbesondere durch Wettbewerb, und die Grundlagen für die Anerkennungsentscheidungen zu sichern, insbesondere durch die Transparenz der Diplome und Befähigungsnachweise.

Die Diskussion über diese Fragen ist keineswegs neu. Bereits dem Beschluß des Rates über das sogenannte Entsprechungsverfahren aus dem Jahre 1985 lag die Überzeugung zugrunde, daß objektivierte und vergleichbare Angaben über Befähigungen und damit verbundene Ausbildungen mehr Erfolg versprechen und eher erreichbar sein würden als ein Weg über umfassende Anerkennungsverfahren, für deren Einführung es in der EG überdies nicht einmal eine ausreichende Rechtsgrundlage gab. Das Projekt des Entsprechungsverfahrens war eine wertvolle Schule des kategorialen Vergleichs und des Dialogs. Für die praktische Anwendung aber erwiesen sich die umfangreichen im Amtsblatt der EG abgedruckten Entsprechungslisten als zu abstrakt und auch zu lückenhaft *(Europäische Kommission. Generaldirektion Allgemeine und Berufliche Bildung und Jugend 1996)*.

Nachdem der Rat in einer Entschließung vom 18. 12. 1990 gemahnt hatte, das Entsprechungsverfahren effizienter voranzubringen, schwenkte er in einer Entschließung vom 7. 12. 1992 unter dem Stichwort 'Transparenz der Qualifikationen' auf einen neuen Pfad ein *(Rat der Europäischen Gemeinschaften 1993)*. Dabei nahm er auch auf eine ge-

---

6 *Greinert (1990)* unterscheidet ein Marktmodell, ein bürokratisches oder Schulmodell und ein staatlich gesteuertes Marktmodell. Letzteres gewinnt an Bedeutung.

meinsame Stellungnahme der Arbeitgeber und Arbeitnehmer im Rahmen des Sozialen Dialogs vom 3. 7. 1992 Bezug, in der *„eher eine evolutive Lösung als eine von oben diktierte Einheitslösung"* befürwortet wurde. Gefordert wurde ein pragmatischer Ansatz. Ziel sollte sein, daß Arbeitnehmer ihre Zeugnisse und Angaben über ihren beruflichen Werdegang *„in der gesamten Gemeinschaft klar und in nachvollziehbarer Form zur Geltung bringen können"* und daß Arbeitgeber entsprechend Zugang zu klaren Beschreibungen erhalten. Eine solche mögliche standardisierte Dokumentation von Befähigungsnachweisen wurde individuelles Portfolio genannt.

Das auf diese Entschließung gestützte von 1993 bis 1995 in allen Mitgliedstaaten durchgeführte Projekt zur Erprobung eines individuellen Portfolio mit 1 200 Versuchspersonen zeigte allerdings, daß auch auf diesem Wege die Ziele letztlich nicht erreicht werden konnten *(Handley 1995).* Vordergründig bereiten sprachliche Probleme die größten Schwierigkeiten, letztlich muß der Mangel jedoch in dem Fehlen gemeinsamer Begriffe und gemeinsamer Standards gesehen werden. Dennoch erbrachte diese Arbeit immerhin einen Teilschritt nach vorn, da das erarbeitete Portfolio-Schema weiterhin als Format für Bewerbungen auf der Grundlage des europaweit vermittelten Arbeitsplatzangebots im Rahmen des sogenannten EURES-Verfahrens verwendet wird.

Die zugleich mit dem Portfolio-Ansatz verfolgte Strategie, vergleichbare Beschreibungen der Bildungssysteme zu erarbeiten und eine Vernetzung von nationalen Datenbanken über berufliche Befähigungsnachweise zu erreichen, stellte eine wichtige Ergänzung dar, stieß jedoch ebenfalls bald an Grenzen: Die vom CEDEFOP erarbeiteten Beschreibungen der Bildungssysteme bleiben schwer lesbar, und bei den Datenbanken gab es brauchbare Ansätze nur in Deutschland, Frankreich und dem Vereinigten Königreich. Ein engagierter Kommentar aus dem CEDEFOP erscheint als nicht unbegründet: *„Der Versuch, die Systeme zwar nicht anzugleichen, aber zumindest vergleichbar zu machen, muß als weitgehend gescheitert angesehen werden, woran nicht nur die nicht zu negierenden effektiven Schwierigkeiten, sondern auch die Blockadehaltung einiger Mitgliedstaaten maßgeblich Anteil haben dürfte"* (Sellin 1996, S. 9).

Die Mitgliedstaaten müssen Farbe bekennen. Der mühsame Weg zu mehr Transparenz durch individuelle Portfolios und Referenzzentren muß fortgesetzt werden. Die politische Bedeutung dieser Ausrichtung wird darin deutlich, daß die Transparenz von Befähigungsnachweisen nicht nur eine Bedeutung für die Mobilität von Arbeitnehmern in Europa hat, sondern vielmehr zugleich ein Qualitätssicherungsinstrument erster Ordnung darstellt. Das wird im internationalen Vergleich evident, gilt aber auch im nationalen Kontext. Wer weiß nicht, ein wie heißes Eisen Leistungsvergleiche zwischen den Bundesländern oder zwischen Kammerbezirken oder einzelnen Prüfungsämtern sind? Das Zusammenwachsen Europas stellt uns in großem Maßstab vor eine Herausforderung, die auch auf anderen Ebenen gilt: Der Staat muß Qualifikationstransparenz gewährleisten, dann kann er in deutlich höherem Maße als bisher Prüfungsverantwortung delegieren.

Eine Entwicklungsperspektive: Transparenz und Dezentralisierung

Die Förderung der Anerkennung von Diplomen und Prüfungszeugnissen stellt neben der Entwicklung der europäischen Dimension im Bildungswesen die zentrale bildungspolitische Aufgabe der Europäischen Union dar. Das bleibt festzuhalten. Ebenso ist deutlich: Eine volle Konvertierbarkeit von Zeugnisnoten kann es nicht geben. Für ein eigenes europäisches Prüfungssystem fehlen überdies die Rechtsgrundlagen. Neuere Initiativen der Kommission in diese Richtung müssen daher zu Konflikten führen, die nur neue Blockaden durch die Mitgliedstaaten und Zeitverlust erzeugen können.

Es ist daher ein anderer strategischer Weg einzuschlagen, für den es sowohl bei der Kommission als auch in den Mitgliedstaaten bereits verschiedene Ansätze gibt. Er läuft zusammen in den Begriffen Transparenz und Dezentralisierung. Die Mitgliedstaaten und die Europäische Kommission haben für Transparenz zu sorgen. Transnationale Pilotvorhaben, zur Zeit insbesondere im Rahmen des LEONARDO-Programms, müssen in einem Bottum-up-Ansatz und durchaus inselartig neue Ansätze für die Zertifizierung entwickeln, und zwar sowohl im Hinblick auf die Inhalte als auch im Hinblick auf die Prüfungsmethoden.

Wenn das Prüfungswesen tatsächlich das Rückgrat des Bildungswesens darstellt, dann geht es bei solchen Überlegungen auch um eine Strategie für das Bildungswesen insgesamt, und zwar sowohl im Bereich der Erstausbildung als auch in dem der Weiterbildung. Die Träger der Weiterbildung und der Einrichtungen der Erstausbildung, die Schulen, die Hochschulen und die Betriebe, müssen in ihrer Autonomie gestärkt, aber zugleich in deutlich höherem Maße für ihre Prüfungsergebnisse verantwortlich gemacht werden. Wettbewerb und Transparenz sind hier die Schlüsselbegriffe. Wir kennen die Wirkungen des Wettbewerbs aus dem Bereich der beruflichen Weiterbildung gut. Ein Blick in den anglo-amerikanischen Raum zeigt überdies, daß dieses Prinzip auch für große Erstausbildungssysteme konstitutiv sein kann. Wir kennen ebenso die Wirkungen von Transparenz in bestimmter Weise durch den seit den siebziger Jahren erstellten jährlichen Berufsbildungsbericht des Bundes. Dieser Bericht zwingt immer wieder von neuem dazu, die Bilanz der Ausbildungsangebote in Ordnung zu bringen und sich über Probleme und Fortschritte bei der Entwicklung des Berufsbildungswesens Rechenschaft zu geben.

Der sektorale Ansatz, den die Kommission mit einer Ausschreibung zu Initiativen für die gegenseitige Anerkennung von beruflichen Befähigungsnachweisen 1994 eingeschlagen hat, ist daher grundsätzlich zu begrüßen. Zwar fehlt es noch an einer ausreichenden strategischen Abstimmung mit den Mitgliedstaaten, da ohne diese weiterreichende Lösungen nicht erwartet werden können, doch stellt der sektorale Ansatz, der sich abzeichnet, einen gemeinsamen gangbaren Weg dar. Akkreditierungsverbünde z. B. für den Bereich der Bauindustrie, der Automobilindustrie, des Versicherungswesens oder des Hotel- und Gaststättengewerbes, oder auch für bestimmte transversale Qualifikationen wie z. B. das Fremdsprachenlernen oder den „Computerführerschein" können Anerkennungsfunktionen übernehmen, die der Staat zwar unterstützen, aber nicht garantieren muß. Es ist einerseits durchaus denkbar, daß in einzelnen Sektoren verschiedene Akkreditierungsverbünde im Wettbewerb zueinander stehen. Andererseits kann durch das Zusammenwirken der Sozialpartner und das Eigeninteresse der Sektoren an der Rekrutierung der am besten ausgebildeten Mitarbeiter bereits ein so hoher Qualitätsdruck entstehen, daß es – auf der Grundlage einer großräumigen Erfolgsorientierung – eines kleinräumigen Wettbewerbs gar nicht mehr bedarf.

Akkreditierung kann hierbei durchaus auch die Qualifikation aus Berufserfahrung mit umfassen, so daß auf diesem Wege Portfolio-Lösungen für den Einzelnen entstehen können, wie der Rat der EG sie besonders deutlich 1992 gefordert hat. Rigorose Bemühung um gemeinsame Beschreibungskriterien und verläßliche Netzwerke von Referenzzentren müssen jedoch hinzukommen.[7] Mehrere Mitgliedstaaten müssen hierbei gemeinsam mit der Kommission zusammenwirken. Vielleicht sind die Evaluatorenteams der OECD für Länderexamina im Bildungsbereich dafür denkbare Modelle. Ein europäischer Berufsbildungsbericht könnte diese Bemühungen zusammenfassen.

---

7 Es ist ein noch zu wenig beachteter Schritt in diese Richtung, daß die Bundesregierung mit den Spitzenorganisationen der deutschen Wirtschaft vereinbart hat, daß ab 1996 alle neu erarbeiteten oder modernisierten Ausbildungsordnungen mit einem sog. „Ausbildungsprofil" versehen werden, in dem die Ausbildungsdauer, das berufstypische Arbeitsgebiet und die mit der Ausbildung erworbenen beruflichen Fähigkeiten genau beschrieben werden. Zugleich wird vorgesehen, daß diese Ausbildungsprofile auch in die englische und französische Sprache übersetzt werden.

Ausblick

Das alles braucht Zeit und guten Willen. Beides scheint auf dem hier diskutierten Gebiet rar zu sein. Es muß klar sein: Wir brauchen keine europäischen Einheitssysteme, sondern die Freisetzung der Kräfte der Basis. Die Mitgliedstaaten müssen dazu mehr Flexibilität an den Tag legen, neue Formen der Qualifizierung zulassen und für europäische Entwicklungen offen sein. Die Kommission wiederum muß deutlicher ihre Aufgabe wahrnehmen, Helfer bei der Annäherung der Völker und Mitgliedstaaten in der EU, und das heißt auch bei der Annäherung der Qualifikationsnachweise, zu sein. Sie muß gemeinsam mit den Mitgliedstaaten und in Abstimmung mit den Sozialpartnern neue Lösungen von der Basis her möglich machen und der nicht nur von den Sozialpartnern kritisierten Versuchung widerstehen, „von oben diktierte Einheitslösungen" zu verfolgen.

Nicht zuletzt angesichts der bevorstehenden Erweiterung der Europäischen Union scheint es nötig, daß sich die Mitgliedstaaten und die Kommission darauf besinnen, wozu ihre Gemeinschaft im Bereich der allgemeinen und beruflichen Bildung fähig und notwendig ist. Vier Aufgaben für die Menschen und für Europa lassen sich unterscheiden. Es müssen Möglichkeiten geboten werden, Europa insbesondere durch Austauschmaßnahmen im Rahmen der EU zu entdecken. Durch Informationsaustausch, Forschung, Öffentlichkeitsarbeit und Fachdiskussionen auf EU-Ebene müssen Voraussetzungen dafür geschaffen werden, daß die verschiedenen Bildungssysteme in Europa besser verstanden werden und gemeinsame vorwärtsweisende Konzepte entwickelt werden können. Durch die Förderung von transnationalen Pilotprojekten mit Mitteln der EU sollte gezielt zur Innovation der Bildungssysteme beigetragen werden. Dabei könnte ein europäischer Fonds für Pilotvorhaben im Bildungsbereich eine zentrale Rolle bei der Förderung der Bildungsreform spielen. Und schließlich als viertes sollten durch die Europäische Union die grenzüberschreitende Transparenz und die Anerkennung von Qualifikationen durch die Entwicklung geeigneter Instrumente erleichtert werden. Man geht nicht fehl, diese letzte Aufgabe, die zugleich die schwierigste sein dürfte, als den Schlußstein für das Engagement der Europäischen Union im Bereich von Bildung und Ausbildung anzusehen.

Bibliographie

Accreditation. In: Funk and Wagnalls Standard Dictionary of the English Language. International Edition. Vol. 1, New York: Funk and Wagnalls 1964, S. 10.

Arbault, François: Beurteilen Sie Ihre Fähigkeiten! Das europäische Projekt zur Bewertung und Anerkennung von Kompetenzen. In: Le Magazine, (1996) 5, S. 11.

Bundesministerium für Bildung, Wissenschaft, Forschung und Technologie (Hrsg.): Äquivalenzen im Hochschulbereich. Eine Übersicht. Bonn: BMBF 1996.

El-Khawas, Elaine: Accreditation and Evaluation. Reciprocity and Exchange. In: Conference on Frameworks for European Quality Assessment of Higher Education, Copenhagen 3-4 May 1993, Copenhagen: Danish Center for Quality Assurance and Evaluation of Higher Education 1993, S. 40-49.

Europäische Kommission (Hrsg.): Lehren und Lernen. Auf dem Weg zur kognitiven Gesellschaft. Weißbuch zur allgemeinen und beruflichen Bildung. Luxemburg: Amt für amtliche Veröffentlichungen der Europäischen Gemeinschaften 1995. (KOM(95)590 endg.)

Europäische Kommission. Generaldirektion Allgemeine und Berufliche Bildung und Jugend (Hrsg.): Transparenz und Anerkennung der beruflichen Befähigungsnachweise. Bilanz und Perspektiven. Seminar über die Transparenz der beruflichen Befähigungsnachweise, Rom 14. – 16. 03. 1996. Brüssel: Europäische Kommission 1996.

Gordon, Jean: An Innovative Approach to the Comparison of Qualifications in Europe. The Regional Perspective. In: European Journal of Education, 30 (1995) 3, S. 277-293.

Greinert, Wolf-Dietrich: Systeme beruflicher Bildung im internationalen Vergleich. Versuch einer Klassifizierung. In: Bundesminister für Bildung und Wissenschaft (Hrsg.): Innovative Methoden in der beruflichen Bildung (= Bildung, Wissenschaft international. 1990, 1), Bonn: BMBW 1990, S. 15-19.

Handley, David: Pilotprojekt zu Individualportfolios. Zusammenfassender Abschlußbericht. London, März 1995 (unveröffentlicht).

Koch, Richard: Die Berufsbildungssysteme in Deutschland und Frankreich. Vergleichende Betrachtungen in einem dynamischen Ansatz der Systemanalyse. In: Heitmann, Werner / Greinert, Wolf-Dietrich (Hrsg.): Analyseinstrumente in der Berufsbildungszusammenarbeit (= Diskussionsbeiträge und Materialien zur internationalen Berufsbildungszusammenarbeit. 1), Berlin: Overall-Verlag 1995, S. 262-272.

Müller-Solger, Hermann: Probleme der Hochschulprüfungen in den USA und der Bundesrepublik. In: Mitteilungen des Deutschen Germanistenverbandes, 21 (1974) 2, S. 12-20.

Müller-Solger, Hermann / Jesinghaus, Jürgen: Über die Wahrscheinlichkeit eines Studienplatzerwerbs in Medizin ab WS 1978/79. In: Die Deutsche Universitäts-Zeitung vereinigt mit Hochschul-Dienst, (1977) 10, S. 310-314.

Müller-Solger, Hermann: Vorschläge zur Organisation von Prüfungen im Fernstudium. In: Pädagogische Rundschau, 32 (1978) 12, S. 891-915.

Müller-Solger, Hermann: Amerikanische Hochschulen im Wandel. Weiterbildendes Studium in den USA. Bonn: Bundesminister für Bildung und Wissenschaft 1979.

National Council for Vocational Qualifications (Hrsg.): Accreditation of Prior Learning in the Context of National Vocational Qualifications. London: NCVQ 1990. (NCVQ R-and-D Report. 7)

Organisation for Economic Co-operation and Development (Hrsg.): Selection and Certification in Education and Employment. Paris: OECD 1977.

Rat der Europäischen Gemeinschaften: Entscheidung des Rates vom 16. Juli 1985 über die Entsprechungen der beruflichen Befähigungsnachweise zwischen Mitgliedstaaten der Europäischen Gemeinschaften. In: Amtsblatt der Europäischen Gemeinschaften. L, 28 (1985) 199, S. 56-59.

Rat der Europäischen Gemeinschaften: Richtlinie 92/51/EWG des Rates vom 18. Juni 1992 über eine zweite allgemeine Regelung zur Anerkennung beruflicher Befähigungsnachweise in Ergänzung zur Richtlinie 89/48/EWG. In: Amtsblatt der Europäischen Gemeinschaften. L, 35 (1992) 209, S. 25-45.

Rat der Europäischen Gemeinschaften: Entschließung des Rates vom 3. Dezember 1992 zur Transparenz auf dem Gebiet der Qualifikationen. In: Amtsblatt der Europäischen Gemeinschaften. C, 36 (1993) 49, S. 1-3.

Rat der Europäischen Union: Entschließung des Rates vom 15. Juli 1996 zur Transparenz auf dem Gebiet der Ausbildungs- und Befähigungsnachweise. In: Amtsblatt der Europäischen Gemeinschaften. C, 39 (1996) 224, S. 7-8.

RSA Examinations Board (Hrsg.): National Vocational Qualifications. Coventry: RSA 1995.

Sellin, Burkart: Haben gemeinsame europäische Bildungsstandards eine Chance? Zur Anerkennung bzw. Transparenz von Qualifikationen. Thessaloniki: Europäisches Zentrum für die Förderung der Berufsbildung 1996. (CEDEFOP-Panorama)

Developing the European Dimension of Education in Practice: The Contribution of the Council of Europe's European Dimension Pedagogical Materials Programme

Raymond Ryba

Introduction

Two of the many aspects of Wolfgang Mitter's scholarly interests over the years have been his attachment to the development of a European spirit in the conduct of education in European countries and to the desirability of linking theory to practice. It is to these two particular aspects of his thinking that this contribution is addressed. The subject to be discussed is the Council of Europe's 'European Dimension Pedagogical Materials Programme' (EDPM Programme). This programme, co-ordinated by the author and recently completed, formed a major part of the Council's 'Secondary Education for Europe Project', one of the most ambitious educational projects which it has ever carried out.

The Secondary Education for Europe Project and the Origins of the Programme

Early discussions took place in 1990 concerning the form and content of the Council's 'Secondary Education for Europe Project'. It quickly became evident that the Project would need to answer two sets of pressing questions which concerned the Council at that time: what was the actual state of secondary education in the different countries belonging to the Council; and how could teachers be helped to develop the European dimension of education. This led to the formulation of two axes or dimensions which the Project would seek to develop: first, a 'general' dimension concerned with a survey of secondary education in all the countries who were signatories of the Cultural Convention of the Council; and, second, a more 'specific' dimension, concerned essentially with providing direct support to secondary schools and their teachers in the task of developing the European dimension of education through their curricular and extra-curricular activities.

The planning of both these dimensions was profoundly affected by the rapid enlargement of the Council of Europe's membership which began to take place following the collapse of the Iron Curtain in 1989 and which was followed by a lively interest in participation then shown by all the Central and Eastern European countries. For the 'general' dimension of the Project, this meant that secondary education in some ten additional countries had to be considered. For the 'specific' dimension, with which we are more directly concerned, it meant that the whole conception of what could effectively be done had to be re-thought,

Originally, the intention of the Council had been to create an 'atlas' of the European dimension of education, similar in conception but much more extensive than an atlas of this kind which had already been produced for the then European Community countries by the Francophone Belgian Authorities *(Vandermotten 1989)*. However, by the time the 'Secondary Education for Europe Project' was finally set up in 1991 *(Council of Europe 1991b)* and, more particularly, by the time that the Expert Group which advised on the development of the 'specific' dimension of the Project was formed, at the end of 1991, it had become evident that such a project would not be feasible within the time and resources which the Council could put at its disposal. In these circumstances, the advice of the 'specific' programme's Expert Group, accepted by the Council of Europe in 1992, was that the original intention should be abandoned and replaced by the 'European Dimension Pedagogical Materials Programme' in the form which it has since taken *(Council of Europe 1992, p. 3)*.

Key Elements of the EDPM Programme

Although the 'European Dimension Pedagogical Materials Programme' was re-designed along the lines described above, it remained entirely faithful in other ways to the key founding ideas laid down by the Council for the 'Secondary Education for Europe Project'. Thus, it fully accepted the terms of the Parliamentary Assembly of the Council of Europe's 1989 Recommendation on the European dimension in education *(Council of Europe 1989)*, as well as the Council for Cultural Co-operation's decisions regarding the nature of the Project as a whole *(Council of Europe 1991a, p. 38)*. These stated the intention to „*promote the development of secondary education* for *Europe by promoting education* on *Europe and developing operational strategies to deal with secondary education* in *Europe*". To achieve this, it was further proposed to:

1. give young people the knowledge, skills and attitudes they will need to meet the major challenges of European society;
2. prepare young people for higher education, and for mobility, work and daily life in a multilingual and multicultural Europe;
3. make young people aware of their common cultural heritage and their shared responsibilities as Europeans *(ibid.)*.

The Programme's advisory Expert Group also considered whether the best way to achieve these objectives would be through the production of a European textbook or through the construction of separate autonomous modules or dossiers. It chose the latter for a variety of reasons. The most important of these was the need to find a formula which, while offering support, did not impose any outside structure on the curricular decisions made in so many different ways in so many countries. It was felt that the module or dossier format achieved this better than a book format. This left greater freedom to teachers in each country to utilise or reject different elements of the programme as they saw fit.

Building on this decision, the Programme's Expert Group set out a number of further principles and characteristics which it felt the outcomes of the Programme should meet *(Council of Europe 1992, p. 3)*. It agreed that these outcomes should be:

1. multi-functional in nature;
2. pedagogical, rather than simply referential, in character;
3. capable of being used across the whole curriculum of secondary education, rather than in single subjects, disciplinal areas or levels;
4. adaptable to the great variety of curricular structures to be found in the many European countries in which they would be intended to be used.

It was further agreed that what should be aimed at was the construction of a kind of exemplar bank of dossiers to which new ones could be progressively added and old ones eventually withdrawn or revised as appropriate. The aim should be to provide materials directly usable by teachers in their classrooms, including not only textual information but also essential documents such as maps, pictures, tables, graphs and primary extracts. Related explanatory texts, examples of possible approaches and related pedagogical suggestions should also be included. The approach agreed was one which could complement and enrich existing teaching by adding the possibility of introducing the European dimension into existing programmes. It was also agreed that the material provided should be capable of being used in problem-solving learning approaches. This was seen as important in order to encourage the development of relevant skills and attitudes as well as relevant factual knowledge.

Implementing the Programme

In order to ensure that authors of the Programme's materials would produce results that could truly fit into curricular and teaching arrangements, not only in their own countries but also in others, it was necessary to apply a materials development model which stipulated both relatively common rules of presentation and an international evaluation procedure. Without such a model, materials produced by nationals of particular countries might not be successfully transferable to other countries.

To begin with we asked writers to choose topics within a framework of European dimension fields defined by the Programme's Expert Group. This framework was a broad one. It of course included knowledge of the nature and workings of European institutions, but it went much further. It also sought to comprise themes that could contribute to an understanding of all that was common to the history, culture and values of European countries, including, particularly, the development in Europe of ideas associated with liberty, democracy, human rights and tolerance in human affairs. In addition, it included all that was common in the form of current and future challenges to Europeans in the economic, social and political fields. It was particularly concerned with helping young Europeans to come to terms with the opportunities and responsibilities with which they would be faced in tomorrow's Europe.

Of course, time and resources available to the Programme were too limited to do more than sample the fields in the framework. In fact, the Council was only prepared to develop fourteen dossiers. Full coverage was obviously impossible. On the other hand, it had always been the intention of the Programme to have a pump-priming function rather than a fully inclusive one. It was hoped, incidentally that the exemplar models provided would stimulate interest in the diversity of approaches suggested, ranging from dossiers conceived in largely textual terms through to ones containing many illustrations and diagrams.

Once authors and dossier subjects had been selected, advice on the detailed development of the materials to be included was offered to all the participants *(Ryba 1994)*. In addition, further advice was offered on the more detailed nature and format of Programme dossiers. This was done in order to ensure reasonable communality across the programme as a whole. Contributory authors were asked to construct their dossiers to contain two main sections, comprising, on the one hand, the intended pupil or student resource materials, and, on the other hand, offering surrounding and supporting materials intended for use by teachers.

As regards the resource materials intended for pupils and students, emphasis was placed on selecting items which could be directly useful in the construction of learning exercises and activities. Emphasis was placed on the selection of materials which were copiable into worksheet form or as overhead projection transparencies. Generally, this implied an A4 format of presentation and the use of black and white for most of the material. Coloured material could however be introduced by, for example, the inclusion of colour diapositives. Within these resource materials, emphasis was naturally placed on the provision of a central set of stimulus learning resources which provided useful classroom starting points. However, authors were also encouraged to include supplementary learning resources which allowed learning to be further developed within the context of the central theme.

As regards the surrounding and supporting materials, i.e. those directed more particularly at teachers, it was proposed that these should be formulated as suggestions rather than prescriptions. This was considered very important because, given the variety of settings in which the dossiers were likely to be used, it would not be possible to be sure how individual teachers might best use them. Emphasis was placed on the importance of including an introduction to the theme and contents of each dossier and on explaining how these could contribute to the development of a truly European dimension.

In order to help authors further, a check list was devised to remind them of the main characteristics to be borne in mind:

1. The materials must be *obviously useful* to students and in the development of an important aspect of the European dimension.
2. The materials should be capable of being inserted into *existing programmes* across appropriate parts of the curriculum.
3. The tasks proposed and the themes adopted should be *demonstrably linked to actual problems* and issues of importance throughout Europe and for all its citizens.

4. The themes adopted should be *clearly relevant* to the specific needs of young people growing up in Europe as well as to their future adult lives in the European environment.
5. The materials should be devised in ways capable of being used in „*problem-solving*" and „*active*" approaches to learning.
6. Efforts should be made to devise materials capable of being used across *the whole range of secondary* education, whether general or technical.
7. The material assembled should always have an *international element* in the sense of being:
   a. capable of being used in *different countries* of Europe;
   b. prepared to incorporate relevant data, statistics and a *trans-frontier element* relating to Europe as a whole.
8. The material should be designed to illustrate *diversity* in Europe, as well as *unity*.
9. Care should be taken to ensure that the European dimension was developed in ways that respect legitimate aspects of the local, regional, national and global dimensions.
10. Full details of relevant documentation and references should be included.
11. The material presented should include cartographic, diagrammatic and tabular representations of relevant data at the European level as well as details of relevant European statistics *(Ryba 1994)*.

Generally speaking, all these conditions were conformed with by the authors of dossiers, though, in some cases, variations from them were agreed as appropriate. Inevitably, with authors coming from different countries and cultures and dealing with diverse subjects in different ways, interesting differences in interpretation occurred. These introduce an element of diversity alongside the general unity of the collection.

Evaluating the Programme's Materials

An appropriate evaluation model is important for any curriculum materials development project. In the case of an international development project such as the 'European Dimension Pedagogical Materials Programme', the importance of effective evaluation is obviously even more important. Care needed to be taken to ensure that the materials created would be acceptable not only in the author's country of origin but also in at least a wide variety of other Council of Europe countries.

To achieve international validity, a two stage model of evaluation was instituted. The first stage was concerned with a face evaluation of the detailed proposals received from the Programme's prospective authors. This was mainly carried out through discussion between the individual authors and members of the Programme's Expert Group. In some cases, there was further discussion with members of selected international panels of experts. The purpose of this stage of evaluation was to ensure that the materials would be written and prepared in ways acceptable over a range of countries. Once accepted at this stage, authors were invited to complete their initial manuscripts along the lines agreed.

When the manuscripts had been completed they were submitted to a second stage of evaluation. This was a school-based trialling programme, using a panel of trial schools assembled from different countries and was in fact the main phase of the trialling and evaluation programme. It aimed to be formative in nature as well as summative. Teachers involved in the evaluation were invited both to offer their own opinions on the materials and to actually trial them in their classrooms. They were also asked to suggest additional relevant materials which might usefully be incorporated into final versions of the trial materials.

In general, this process of evaluation worked well and resulted in a number of changes which were incorporated into the final versions of the materials. However, it became clear that the style of materials produced in different countries did not appeal equally in all the other countries. Indeed, in some cases, materials which had been thought excellent in some countries did not appeal in others. This difference of response justified the decision to use a panel of authors from a number of different countries and emphasised the importance of an international basis to the trialling.

The Outcomes of the Programme and Their Implications

Once final adjustments to the authors' manuscripts had been made, completed texts of each of the dossiers were made available in either English or French, the two official languages of the Council. Translation was therefore required into the other of the two official languages. Arrangements for this were made by the Council, ensuring that all the dossiers would be available in both official languages. Further translations into other languages, for which arrangements may be made in different member countries of the Council, are also being encouraged.

In this way, the major outcome of the Programme has been the production of a pilot resource bank of the fourteen modules or dossiers of learning materials listed in Figure 1. These are available in both English and French. It will be evident from the dossier titles listed, in the selected language of their initial presentation to the Council, that the topics offered by the different authors range widely over the relevant fields originally decided upon for the Programme. It will be equally clear that their particular themes can easily be included either in particular subjects across the curriculum or in an interdisciplinary course without upsetting existing curricular arrangements.

Figure 1 Titles and Authors of EDPM Programme Dossiers
 (in original language of submission)

1. Les révolutions industrielles: naissance d'un espace technologique européen, by Marcella Colle-Michel, René Leboutte and Danielle Leclercq.
2. Europeans on the Move, by Andrew Convey.
3. Environmental Damage in Europe – Air Pollution, by Donald MacDonald.
4. Les droits de l'homme en Europe, by F. Audigier and G. Lagelée.
5. Discovery or Encounter: Europe and the Development of its Empires, by H. Skovgaard Nielsen.
6. Orientations pour une présentation de la révolution française dans une perspective européenne, by J.-M. Leclercq et al.
7. A European Economic Database, by Steve Hurd.
8. Greek Drama and its Influence on European Literature and Ideas, by M. Hardy et al.
9. Prévenir la xénophobie, le racisme et l'antisémitisme pour construire une Europe démocratique, plurilingue et pluriculturelle, by M. Perregaux.
10. Citizenship Education, by Ken Fogelman.
11. Les Roms (Tsiganes) en Europe, by M. Cortiade.
12. Conflict in Europe, by Andrew Convey et al.
13. Identity, Solidarity and the Development of a New Europe, by Hartwig Haubrich.
14. Le Chemin de Saint-Jacques: une route paneuropéenne, by Carmen Gonzalez-Munoz and Josefa Reyes Boncasa.

The international nature of the team of authors involved in the Programme is also evident. In fact, in spite of the need to present dossiers initially in either English or French, authors were drawn not only from Britain and France but also from Belgium, Denmark, Germany, Spain and Switzerland, with additional material being suggested from the

Czech Republic, Italy, the Netherlands, Norway and Romania. Regrettably, Central and Eastern European countries were under-represented in the authorship of the initial dossiers but it is hoped that they may come forward with proposals for the future.

An important feature of the dossiers, taken together, is the wide variety of types of learning material which they incorporate. As had always been intended, there is a strong emphasis on materials which can be used in student-centred active learning approaches, particularly suitable for the development of skills and values associated with the European dimension. This, however, does not mean that the inclusion of important factual information has been neglected. Also as intended, the dossiers include a variety of types of resources. Extracts from key original documents characterise much of the textual material provided and striking diagrams, maps and pictures as well as valuable tables of statistics have been included. In one case – the dossier presenting a European economic database – the material is in the form of a computer programme which can be manipulated in a large number of ways.

While the main outcome of the European Dimension Pedagogical Materials Programme has obviously been the construction of a bank of teaching and learning resources, usable in their own right in a wide range of different European countries, it has not been the only one. To begin with, the Programme has already stimulated much discussion concerning the meaning of the European dimension of education. In the past, such discussion has generally started from the theoretical point of view. There have been many attempts to define what it means, but usually without reference to appropriate content. The result has been a great diversity of views but little practical advance *(Mickel 1987, p. 13)*. In the case of this programme, however, the process has been reversed. The starting point has been the assembly of the dossiers, providing examples of what is thought to be appropriate for the European dimension in a variety of different fields. Perhaps this practical approach, concerned more with what the European dimension *contains* rather than what it *is*, may turn out to be a more productive one *(Ryba 1995)*.

Then, as already stated, the dossiers included in the Programme are exemplary in nature. Their authors were 'shooting in the dark' into an area which has so far been relatively little developed. Hopefully, they will have provided useful examples of what might be done by future authors of European dimension materials. Certainly, the guidance to authors and contributors developed by the Programme should be a useful aid in this respect.

Another important outcome has been the number of teachers in many of the Council of Europe countries who have been brought together in various ways by the Programme and who are thus familiar with its objectives and outcomes. In addition to the authors and members of the Programme's expert group, this also includes a sizeable group of teachers which has been involved in one way or another in the Programme's evaluation procedures. It also includes nearly a hundred teachers brought together by two major international seminars held at Donaueschingen, under the joint auspices of the Council of Europe and the Authorities of the Land Baden-Württemberg / Federal Republic of Germany, on the development and utilisation of European dimension curricular materials. These seminars, based on the European Dimension Pedagogical Materials produced by the Programme, proved very successful and point the way to future in-service teacher courses at both the national and international levels *(Ryba 1993)*.

In all these ways, it is to be hoped that the European Pedagogical Materials Programme of the Council of Europe has not only been successful in its own right but also points the way to future work on the European dimension in education both at the National and at the European level.

Bibliography

Council of Europe: Recommendation No. 1111. Strasbourg: Council of Europe 1989.

Council of Europe. Council for Cultural Co-operation: Cultural Fund Budget for 1991. Strasbourg: Council of Europe 1991a.

Council of Europe. Council for Cultural Co-operation: Resolution No. 1, Strasbourg, 5-8 February 1991. Strasbourg: Council of Europe 1991b.

Council of Europe. Council for Cultural Co-operation (ed.): Atlas of the European Dimension: Progress Report. Strasbourg: Council of Europe 1992. (A Secondary Education for Europe; DECS/SE/SEC(92)16)

Mickel, Wolfgang W.: The European Dimension in the Classroom. Justification, Documents and Proposals. Aalkmaar: European Curriculum Network 1987.

Ryba, Raymond: Educational Resources for Teaching about Europe in Schools. Report of the 61st European Teachers' Seminar, October 1993, Donaueschingen. Strasbourg: Council of Europe 1993. (DECS/SE/BS/Donau(93)3)

Ryba, Raymond: European Dimension Pedagogical Materials Programme. Guidelines for Authors and Contributors. Strasbourg: Council of Europe, Council for Cultural Co-operation 1994. (A Secondary Education for Europe; DECS/SE/SEC(94)7)

Ryba, Raymond: Unity in Diversity. The Enigma of the European Dimension in Education. In: Oxford Review of Education, 21 (1995) 1, pp. 25-36.

Vandermotten, Christian et al.: Atlas de la Communauté Européenne. Frameries: Centre Technique de la Communauté Française 1989.

Politik und Vergleichende Erziehungswissenschaft in gemeinsamer Verantwortung für eine humane Lerngesellschaft

Rita Süssmuth

Das Prinzip Verantwortung gilt in Politik und Wissenschaft

Hans Blumenberg hat in einem Essay über den gnostischen Ursprung der Cura-Fabel des Hyginus den narzißtischen Kern dieses Schöpfungsmythos herausgearbeitet. Danach sei die allegorische Figur der Sorge um ihres Spiegelbildes willen über den Fluß gegangen, womit dieser Mythos das anthropologische Phänomen erkläre, daß die nach dem Ebenbild der Sorge geschaffenen Menschen wesensmäßig in Sorge, primär in Selbst-Sorge lebten. Der hedonistisch geprägte Zeitgeist unserer Tage scheint ein beredtes Zeugnis für diese angenommene Daseinskonstante abzulegen. Aristoteles hat uns demgegenüber ergänzend darauf aufmerksam gemacht, daß der Mensch immer auch ein „Zoon politikon" sei, das meint ein je um den anderen Menschen besorgtes Lebewesen. Furcht und Sorge um das eigene Wohl lassen sich via praktische Vernunft sehr wohl in personale und soziale Verantwortung aufheben. Das Prinzip Verantwortung ist somit eine gleichermaßen für wertorientiertes politisches Handeln und vorurteilsfreies wissenschaftliches Forschen verbindliche Sozialnorm. Politik und Wissenschaft als funktionalelitäre Subsysteme einer Gesellschaft stehen darum auch in der Verantwortung, in gemeinsamer Anstrengung die existentiellen Herausforderungen beim Übergang in das 21. Jahrhundert zu bewältigen.

Neue Leitbilder: Globales Denken und kooperatives Handeln

Es sind insbesondere wissenschaftlich-technologische Innovationen selbst, die unser Welt- und Menschenbild verändert haben. Die Raumfahrt hat uns erstmals in der Menschheitsgeschichte mit einer Totalperspektive unserer Erde konfrontiert. An diese neue Aussicht ist zugleich die Einsicht geknüpft, daß wir nur diese eine Erde haben und daß wir selbst es sind, die für den Frieden in der Welt, eine nachhaltige Entwicklung und damit für das Überleben der Menschheit verantwortlich sind. Gleichzeitig haben wir mit den modernen Informations- und Kommunikationstechnologien neue Mittel in die Hand bekommen, um weltweit und interaktiv zu kommunizieren. Wissenschaft und Technik haben die Menschen sowohl räumlich als auch zeitlich in einer nie zuvor erlebbaren Qualität einander näher gebracht. Den Prognosen des US-Ökonomen Robert B. Reich zufolge ist mit dem Aufstieg des „Symbol-Analytikers" der Niedergang der Nationalökonomie verbunden. Darum wird eine auf nationalstaatliche Gruppeninteressen beschränkte Politik zum Anachronismus verurteilt sein. Diese neue globale Verantwortung zwingt Politik und Wissenschaft gleichermaßen zur internationalen Kooperation.

Bildung als transnationale Überlebensfrage

Politik muß im Unterschied zur Wissenschaft darüber hinaus auch mehrheitsfähig sein. Insofern muß sie nicht nur neue Einsichten, sie muß die Menschen auch für ein den neuen Einsichten gemäßes Handeln gewinnen. Globales Denken, wie es in Ökonomie und Ökologie durchgängig praktiziert wird, hat auch in der Bildungspolitik eine Leitbildfunktion wahrzunehmen, denn die Beantwortung der Frage der Delors-Kommission, „What kind of education is needed for what kind of society of tomorrow?", ist keine nationalstaatliche Standortfrage, sondern eine transnationale Überlebensfrage. Erich Hylla, einer der Nestoren der Vergleichenden Erziehungswissenschaft, hat bereits 1928 in seiner bekannten Studie „Die Schule der Demokratie" *(Hylla 1928)* auf den Kausalzusammenhang zwischen der zunehmenden Globalisierung und einem auf Völkerverständigung ausgerichteten Bildungswesen hingewiesen. Daß die Bildung in diesem Prozeß des Strukturwandels eine zentrale Rolle spielen wird, ist international anerkannt: *„Knowledge will be needed in many forms and for many purposes: to preserve the environment, control population growth, assure access by all to science and technology, to reinforce communication capacities and facilitate the free flow of information and to foster social cohesion and democratic participation. Knowledge will be the motive power of progress and change" (IPU / UNESCO 1996).*

Bildungsforschung und Bildungspolitik im Dialog

Die jüngsten Erfahrungen mit der Angleichung der beiden deutschen Bildungssysteme haben gezeigt, wie wichtig in der politischen Praxis ein offener und auf Verstehen setzender Dialog für einen echten Integrationsprozeß ist. Hätte man beispielsweise das gut aufbereitete Wissen der Vergleichenden Erziehungswissenschaft zum Bildungswesen in Osteuropa, wie es unter Leitung von Oskar Anweiler in Bochum und unter Leitung von Wolfgang Mitter in Frankfurt erarbeitet worden ist, politisch genutzt, wären uns viele Friktionen erspart geblieben und das Zusammenwachsen hätte von beiden Seiten als Chance zu einer gemeinsam gestalteten Bildungsreform genutzt werden können. Das gilt cum grano salis auch für das politisch noch zu bauende „europäische Haus". Hier wäre im Interesse einer auf Kooperation ausgerichteten Bildungspolitik zu wünschen, daß gerade die Arbeiten des von Mitter geleiteten Deutschen Instituts für Internationale Pädagogische Forschung in Frankfurt am Main im Vorfeld der bildungspolitischen Entscheidungsfindung angemessen zu Rate gezogen würden. Für den bildungspolitischen Beitrag der Vergleichenden Erziehungswissenschaft zur Herausbildung einer Europäischen Union reicht es nicht aus, daß sie nur Daten sammelt, so wichtig dies auch für Anerkennungsregelungen für eine mobil gewordene Arbeitnehmerschaft oder für die Optimierung des eigenen Qualifikationssystems sein mag. Sie muß sich im Wissen um die Zusammenhänge zwischen Bildung und Erziehung auf der einen und Demokratie und Entwicklung auf der anderen Seite dem politischen Dialog in einer das Risiko und die Mitverantwortung nicht scheuenden Bereitschaft zur praktischen Mitgestaltung stellen.

Auch hier kann Wolfgang Mitter als Vorbild dienen. Ganz in der Tradition des friedenspädagogischen Aufklärers Marc Antoine Jullien de Paris und ganz im pragmatistischen Sinne von John Dewey hat Mitter den Elfenbeinturm der Wissenschaft immer nur als einen Ort des kritischen Weitblicks zum Nutzen der Praxis zu nutzen gewußt, und nie bloß als einen Ort der theoretischen Nabelschau. Umgekehrt muß sich aber die Politik selbstkritisch davor hüten, die Ergebnisse der Vergleichenden Erziehungswissenschaft zu rein opportunistischen Legitimationszwecken zu mißbrauchen. In der Folge führt dies zu bildungspolitischen Wellenbewegungen zwischen Euphorie und Enttäuschung, die dem unverzichtbaren Vertrauen im Dialog zwischen Bildungsforschung und Bildungspolitik schaden. Hier sollte endlich eine Versachlichung der Diskurse und eine Verstetigung der Förderung eintreten. Wenn die politische Realität vielfach so geartet ist, daß primär ökonomische Argumente zur Begründung für bildungspolitische Anstrengungen herhalten müssen, sei es der Sputnik-Schock in den späten fünfziger Jahren oder der Computer-Schock in den achtziger Jahren, dann müßte das ökonomische Interesse an Bildungspolitik und Bildungsforschung beim Umbruch in eine globalisierte „Wissensgesellschaft" *(Drucker 1993)* sprunghaft steigen. Die antizyklischen Bildungs- und Forschungsinvestitionen Japans sprechen für diese These.

Paradigmenwechsel in der internationalen Bildungsforschung

Zu Beginn der Vergleichenden Bildungsforschung standen vom Kriterium der nationalstaatlichen Begrenzung ausgehend bestimmte auslandspädagogische Fragestellungen im Vordergrund. Ziel der komparatistischen Bemühungen war dabei der zweckdienliche Transfer von fremden Bildungselementen zur Optimierung der Effizienz des eigenen Bildungssystems. Heute haben sich die Ansprüche der Politik an die Vergleichende Erziehungswissenschaft erweitert, erstens mit Blick auf einen problemorientierten Methodenpluralismus *(Tippelt 1994)* und zweitens hinsichtlich einer internationalen Kooperationsdimension, womit sie wieder an die friedenspädagogische Tradition des großen Johann Amos Comenius anknüpfen kann. Im Zuge dieses Strukturwandels ist darüber hinaus auch eine Erweiterung des Objektfeldes der vergleichenden Betrachtungen nötig geworden. Konnte Ellen Key an der Schwelle zum 20. Jahrhundert noch ein „Jahrhundert des Kindes" ausrufen, so kann man am Ende dieses Jahrhunderts nicht umhin festzustellen, daß die Zeit der ausschließlichen Fokussierung der Pädagogik auf Kindheit und Jugend vorbei ist. Wir befinden uns heute längst im Übergang zu einer „Lifelong Learning Society". Dafür sprechen mehrere Gründe. Zum einen ist unsere Zeit von einem beschleunigten Wandel des Wissens und der Technologien geprägt, zum anderen leben wir in einer Zeit des demographischen Wandels, zunehmender Divergenz der Wertvorstellungen und einem gestiegenen durchschnittlichen Lebensalter. Das wirkt sich gleichermaßen auf die Arbeits- und Lebenswelt aus, führt zusammengenommen zu einer Pluralisierung der Statuspassagen und Lebensstile und erzwingt ein Umdenken in der Lebenslaufplanung. In der Konsequenz kommt es zu einer völlig neuen zeitlichen und qualitativen Proportionierung der Erstausbildung in Relation zur Weiterbildung. Daß der Mensch zu einem lebensbegleitenden Lernen durchaus fähig ist, das hat die Altersforschung inzwischen hinlänglich nachweisen können, was nicht heißt, daß sich nicht wenige Menschen hiervon zum Teil erheblich überfordert fühlen.

Bei aller Lerneuphorie, so muß aber kritisch angemerkt werden, darf die Forderung nach einem lebensbegleitenden Lernen nicht mit einer entmündigenden Pädagogisierung unserer Gesamtbiographie verwechselt werden. Wenn pädagogisches Handeln darauf abzielt, sich selbst überflüssig zu machen, kann es in der an Bedeutung gewinnenden Erwachsenenbildung nicht darum gehen, die Illusion einer kompensierbaren Unwissenheit im eigenen Verwertungsinteresse zu mißbrauchen, sondern Anleitungen zu einem selbstgesteuerten und eigenverantworteten Lernen anzubieten *(Dohmen 1996, S. 44ff.)*. Mit dieser neuen Situation hat sich auch die Vergleichende Erziehungswissenschaft, die sich in der Vergangenheit mehr mit Schul- und Hochschulvergleichen befaßt hat, auseinanderzusetzen. Im Vergleich zu den 100 Milliarden ECU an jährlichen Aufwendungen für die Erwachsenenbildung in Europa erscheinen die Investitionen in die Vergleichende Erwachsenenbildungsforschung und deren Aktivitäten freilich mehr als nur dürftig *(Hake 1995)*. Andernorts hat der notwendige Umdenkungsprozeß bereits begonnen, wie die Gründung eines „Lifelong Learning Development Office" im Jahre 1990 im berühmten japanischen Ministerium für Internationalen Handel und Industrie zeigt *(Okamoto 1994)*. Die OECD hat für die Bildungsministerkonferenz im Januar 1996 zwischenzeitlich Strategien zur Realisierung eines „Zeitalters des lebenslangen Lernens" vorgelegt *(Dohmen 1996, S. 23 ff.)*, und auch die Europäische Union signalisiert mit einem Europäischen Jahr für lebensbegleitendes Lernen, wo sie ihre bildungspolitischen Zukunftsaufgaben sieht. Im Weißbuch zur allgemeinen und beruflichen Bildung wird von der Kommission analog gefordert, *„die Voraussetzungen zu schaffen, um ein ständiges, das Leben begleitendes Streben nach allgemeiner und beruflicher Bildung zu stimulieren" (Europäische Kommission 1995, S. 7)*.

Dieser Paradigmenwechsel kann nicht dem freien Spiel der Marktkräfte überlassen bleiben. Hier ist die Politik als gestaltgebende und rahmensetzende Instanz gefragt. Beratungsbedarf seitens der Politik gibt es dabei genug, wie die Problem- und Empfehlungskataloge der Europäischen und Internationalen Erwachsenenbildungskonferenzen immer wieder zeigen *(Dokumente 1994; Alheit/Tippelt 1994)*. Aus der Vielzahl transnationaler Fragestellungen, die sich auf die Zukunftsaufgabe der Erwachsenenbildung beziehen – das Spektrum reicht von A wie Alphabetisierung bis Z wie Zielgruppenforschung – sei hier nur auf drei thematische Einzelaspekte näher eingegangen, die sowohl von der Europäischen Kommission als auch von der UNESCO unter dem bildungspolitischen Generalaspekt der Chancengleichheit behandelt werden.

Frauenförderung durch Frauenbildung

Die Umsetzung der frauenpolitischen Forderung nach Gleichberechtigung kann langfristig nur durch eine entsprechende Frauenbildung gesichert werden. Den Angaben der Internationalen Arbeitsorganisation zufolge stellt sich die Situation der Frauen heute weltweit wie folgt dar: Sie stellen die Hälfte der Weltbevölkerung, leisten nahezu zwei Drittel der Arbeit, erhalten ein Zehntel des Welteinkommens und besitzen nur ein Hundertstel des Welteigentums. Frauen haben also eine grenzüberschreitende Gemeinsamkeit: Sie sind die diskriminierte Hälfte der Erdbevölkerung. Frauen erhalten minderwertige und schlechter bezahlte Jobs, sind in Rezessionszeiten von Arbeitslosigkeit betroffen und schaffen nur selten den Aufstieg in Führungspositionen. Zum Geschlecht addieren sich in vielen Ländern noch Hautfarbe, ethnische Abstammung und Religionszugehörigkeit als Stigmata einer mehrfachen Benachteiligung. Wie die Geschichte gezeigt hat, reichen weder die unternehmensethischen Selbstbindungskräfte der freien Marktwirtschaft noch der feministisch induzierte Bewußtseinswandel aus, um dies zu ändern. Hier ist die Politik als Gestaltungsmacht von gesellschaftlichen Verhältnissen gefragt. Wie sich aber immer wieder beim Kampf gegen Benachteiligungen bewahrheitet hat, kommt der Bildung eine Schlüsselrolle im Emanzipationsprozeß zu. Dem jüngsten Weltbildungsbericht der *UNESCO (1996)* zufolge sind Frauen die größte Gruppe von Menschen, denen das in der Präambel zugesicherte „Recht aller auf ungeschmälerte und gleiche Bildungsmöglichkeiten" vorenthalten wird. Konsequenterweise hat die Internationale Konferenz für Bevölkerung und Entwicklung 1994 in Kairo ein Aktionsprogramm verabschiedet, durch das Frauen – insbesondere mit Hilfe von Bildungsmaßnahmen – zu einer gleichberechtigten Teilhabe verholfen werden soll. Die Verbesserung der Startchancen durch eine Intensivierung der schulischen und beruflichen Bildung ist ein wichtiger Schritt für nachfolgende Generationen, und hier gilt es, internationale Erfahrungen im Bereich der Mädchenbildung zu nutzen. Dies hilft freilich den Frauen in ihrer akuten Problemsituation wenig, sich in einem sich verschärfenden Qualifikationswettbewerb einer Lerngesellschaft zu behaupten. Hier ist in erster Linie die Erwachsenenbildung gefragt. Dabei ist immer auch den kultur- und geschlechtsspezifischen Aspekten des Lernens Rechnung zu tragen. Im Weltbildungsbericht der UNESCO wird beklagt, daß umfassende internationale Vergleichsuntersuchungen hierzu fehlen.

Die Vergleichende Erziehungswissenschaft ist aufgefordert, mit entsprechenden Studien erfolgversprechende Reformschritte der Politik vorzubereiten. Die Forderung eines lebensbegleitenden Lernens stellt auch für die meisten Frauen in den Industrieländern im Rahmen ihrer gesamtgesellschaftlichen Benachteiligungen eine nicht leicht zu bewältigende Herausforderung dar. Hier muß der Staat subsidiär tätig werden und die Weiterbildung von Frauen besonders fördern, seien es Wiedereingliederungsangebote für Berufsrückkehrerinnen oder Kinderbetreuungsmöglichkeiten bei berufsbegleitenden Maßnahmen. Auch dazu werden vergleichende Konzeptstudien zu Modellen der zielgruppenspezifischen Erwachsenenbildung benötigt. Dabei geht es nicht nur um eine arbeitsmarktbezogene Anpassungs- und Aufstiegsfortbildung, sondern auch um Angebote, die speziell *von Frauen für Frauen* konzipiert sind und der rollenspezifischen Orientierung in der Gesellschaft wie der Selbstbestimmung ihrer Biographie dienen. Mit wachsendem Bildungspotential legitimiert sich ferner der Anspruch von Frauen, in kompetenter Weise Führungsverantwortung zu übernehmen. Die sich herausbildende Lerngesellschaft wird nicht nur eine neue Lernkultur, sondern auch eine neue Führungskultur einfordern, in welcher das alte Konkurrenzprinzip von einem neuen Kooperationsprinzip abgelöst wird. Hierin sehe ich gerade für Frauen die Chance, ihre Stärken einzubringen und prägend mitzuwirken.

Medienkompetenz in der Informationsgesellschaft

Mit dem Vordringen der neuen Informations- und Kommunikationstechnologien brauchen wir eine pädagogische Begleitung des globalen Übergangs zu einer Informationsgesellschaft. Wissen und Innovationen sind die zukunftsgestaltenden Wertschöpfungsressourcen einer transnational agierenden Dienstleistungsgesellschaft. In der ungebrochen boomenden Medienbranche werden bereits heute jährlich 3,5 Billionen DM umgesetzt. Bei vielen Menschen, die nicht mit Gameboy und Internet aufgewachsen sind, lösen das Tempo und das Ausmaß der Auswirkungen dieser Technologien zum Teil überzogene, aber auch berechtigte Existenz- und Orientierungsängste aus, die von der Politik ernst genommen werden müssen. Treffen die Arbeitsmarktprognosen des Instituts für Arbeitsmarkt- und Berufsforschung in Nürnberg zu, werden bereits im Jahr 2000 zwei von drei Arbeitnehmern ihren Beruf nurmehr mit Computerkenntnissen ausüben können. Dem Bildungswesen, so der Rat für Forschung, Technologie und Innovation, kommt sowohl für die Nutzung der Chancen als auch für die Bewältigung der Probleme der Informationsgesellschaft eine Schlüsselstellung zu. Deutschland hat hierbei einen im internationalen Vergleich nicht unerheblichen Rückstand bezüglich Infrastruktur, Ausstattung und Mediendidaktik aufzuholen. Der Technologierat empfiehlt ausdrücklich, sich die in europäischen Nachbarländern und in Überseestaaten gemachten Erfahrungen zunutze zu machen. Das gilt nicht nur für die schulische Bildung, sondern gerade auch für die Erwachsenenbildung *(Rat für Forschung, Technologie und Innovation 1995)*.

Die Vergleichende Erziehungswissenschaft ist also gerade hier herausgefordert, durch eine Intensivierung des Erfahrungsaustauschs die Lücken im Bereich der medienpädagogischen Weiterbildung zu schließen. Neue Medien sind aber nicht nur Gegenstand vergleichender Studien, im Zuge ihrer vermehrten Nutzung werden sie selbst die Arbeit der Vergleichenden Erziehungswissenschaft gravierend verändern und dazu beitragen, ein fruchtbares Netzwerk der Kommunikation und Kooperation aufzubauen. Des weiteren kann mit Multimedia eine Servicebrücke zum informationssuchenden und beratungsbedürftigen Bürger geschlagen werden. Eine Informationsgesellschaft ist aber nicht notwendigerweise auch zugleich eine informierte Gesellschaft. Über die berufsqualifizierende Anpassung hinaus wird es in der Erwachsenenbildung auch darauf ankommen, die Menschen zu einem verantwortungsbewußten Umgang mit der neuen Vielfalt der Informationen zu befähigen. Bildungsmaßnahmen müssen insbesondere verhindern, daß eine Zweiklassengesellschaft von Wissenden und Unwissenden entsteht. Daran muß auch die Politik originär interessiert sein, da mit einer un- oder desinformierten Gesellschaft letztlich auch der Grundpfeiler unserer Demokratie gefährdet wäre.

Weiterbildung als ganzheitliche Persönlichkeitsbildung

Es ist an der Zeit, die Dualität von beruflicher Qualifizierung und allgemeiner Persönlichkeitsbildung durch einen personalen Bildungsansatz zu überwinden. Die Trennungsideologie, wonach im Betrieb die berufliche Weiterbildung und in der Volkshochschule die allgemeine Persönlichkeitsbildung stattzufinden habe, wird den Anforderungen einer modernen Lerngesellschaft nicht mehr gerecht, worauf auch im Weißbuch der *Europäischen Kommission (1995)* mit Blick auf die geforderten Schlüsselqualifikationen nachdrücklich hingewiesen wird. Ganzheitlich verstandene Erwachsenenbildung geht aber noch einen Schritt weiter und fordert vor dem Hintergrund wachsender Mobilität und zunehmender Migration die Vermittlung einer interkulturellen Bildung. Das macht sowohl die Kultivierung eines offenen Dialogs als auch die Herausarbeitung von konsensualen Zielen notwendig. Hierfür wird wiederum die Zuarbeit der Vergleichenden Erziehungswissenschaft gebraucht. Bildung und Weiterbildung als ein „grundlegendes Menschenrecht" für jedermann zu realisieren, wäre der kleinste gemeinsame Nenner öffentlicher Verantwortung. Ferner geht es um die Vereinbarung internationaler Rahmenregelungen, die die Transparenz und Qualitätskontrolle des Angebots sowie den freien Zugang und die finanzielle Absicherung der Teilnehmer betreffen. Gerade letzteres scheint dringend geboten, da auch in der jüngsten OECD-Studie erneut bestätigt wird, daß die Weiterbildungsteilnahme nach wie vor nach dem „Matthäus-Prinzip" erfolgt. Ganzheitliche Erwachsenenbildung wird letztlich immer auch ethische und politische Fragen mit einschließen. Zusehends läßt sich beim Übergang in die neue Lerngesellschaft ein kulturübergreifendes Dissonanzphänomen, ein Spannungsbogen zwischen Wissensmacht und Orientierungsohnmacht beobachten. Der Historiker Paul Kennedy sieht hier Kräfte am Werk, die *„nichts Geringeres als eine Neu-Erziehung der Menschheit erfordern"* *(Kennedy 1993, S. 431)*. Ein vor kurzem vorgelegtes UNESCO-Dokument spricht darum zu Recht von der Notwendigkeit der gemeinsamen Entwicklung eines *„global set of ethics that would define minimum standards that every community should observe"* und schlägt hierfür fünf Leitprinzipien vor: *„human rights and responsibilities, democracy,* *the protection of minorities, commitment to peaceful conflict resolution, fair negotiation and promotion of equity and justice"* (IPU / UNESCO 1996, S. 8).

Schlußbemerkung

Für die Erwachsenenbildung im neuen Jahrhundert wäre aus der Sicht der Politik zu wünschen, daß sich die Vergleichende Erziehungswissenschaft – vor dem Hintergrund des sich vollziehenden Strukturwandels hin zu einer Lerngesellschaft – wieder auf ihre Reformwurzeln besinnt und daß die Erwachsenenbildung selbst sich über die kompensatorische und komplementäre Qualifizierungsleistung hinaus emanzipatorisch an der Transformation zu einer humanen Wissensgesellschaft beteiligen möge.

Bibliographie

Alheit, Peter / Tippelt, Rudolf: Neue Forschungstendenzen in der europäischen Erwachsenenbildung. In: Benner, Dietrich / Lenzen, Dieter (Hrsg.): Bildung und Erziehung in Europa (= Zeitschrift für Pädagogik. Beiheft. 32), Weinheim u. a.: Beltz 1994, S. 367-383.
Dohmen, Günther: Das lebenslange Lernen. Leitlinien einer modernen Bildungspolitik. Gutachten für das Bundesministerium für Bildung, Wissenschaft, Forschung und Technologie. Bonn: BMBF 1996.
Dokumente. In: Institut für Internationale Zusammenarbeit des Deutschen Volkshochschul-Verbandes (Hrsg.): Erwachsenenbildung und Entwicklung (= Internationale Perspektiven der Erwachsenenbildung. 12), Bonn: IFZ 1994, S. 340-428.
Drucker, Peter F.: Die postkapitalistische Gesellschaft. Düsseldorf u. a.: ECON-Verlag 1993.
Europäische Kommission (Hrsg.): Lehren und Lernen. Auf dem Weg zur kognitiven Gesellschaft. Weißbuch zur allgemeinen und beruflichen Bildung. Luxemburg: Amt für amtliche Veröffentlichungen der Europäischen Gemeinschaften 1995. (KOM(95)590 endg.)
Hake, Barry J.: Erwachsenenbildungsforschung in der Europäischen Union. Tendenzen und Entwicklungen. In: DIE – Zeitschrift für Erwachsenenbildung, (1995) 4, S. 28-30.
Hylla, Erich: Die Schule der Demokratie. Langensalza u. a.: Beltz 1928.
IPU / UNESCO (Hrsg.): On Education, Science, Culture and Communication on the Eve of the 21st Century, Paris, 3-6 June 1996. Final Document.
Kennedy, Paul: In Vorbereitung auf das 21. Jahrhundert. Frankfurt a. M.: S. Fischer 1993.
Okamoto, Kaoru: Lifelong Learning Movement in Japan. Strategies, Practices and Challenges. Tokyo: Ministry of Education, Science and Culture 1994.
Rat für Forschung, Technologie und Innovation (Hrsg.): Informationsgesellschaft. Chancen, Innovationen und Herausforderungen. Feststellungen und Empfehlungen. Bonn: Bundesministerium für Bildung, Wissenschaft, Forschung und Technologie 1995.

Reich, Robert B.: Die neue Weltwirtschaft. Das Ende der nationalen Ökonomie. Frankfurt a. M. u. a.: Ullstein 1993.
Tippelt, Rudolf (Hrsg.): Handbuch Erwachsenenbildung/Weiterbildung. Opladen: Leske und Budrich 1994.
UNESCO (Hrsg.): Weltbildungsbericht 1995. Bonn: UNO-Verlag 1996.

Bildungsforschung und besonders Vergleichende
Erziehungswissenschaft in Europa – für Europa

Michael Vorbeck

Ausgangsbetrachtung

Der 70. Geburtstag von Professor Dr. Wolfgang Mitter, einem der führenden Erziehungswissenschaftler Europas, bietet Anlaß zum Rückblick auf die letzten dreißig Jahre europäischer Zusammenarbeit im Bildungswesen, vor allem im Rahmen des Europarats, und die Rolle Professor Mitters und des Deutschen Instituts für Internationale Pädagogische Forschung (DIPF) in Frankfurt am Main im Dienste der europäischen Erziehungswissenschaft. Ziel des Europarats war es nämlich nie, Bildungssysteme zu vereinheitlichen und in ein Korsett europäischer Richtlinien zu zwängen, sondern vielmehr, Entwicklungen im Bildungswesen der inzwischen 44 an den Arbeiten beteiligten Staaten zu vergleichen, Vor- und Nachteile verschiedener möglicher Lösungen aufzuzeigen und den Ministerien, Hochschulen und Schulen durch die gemeinsame Auswertung geglückter oder mißlungener Reformen dabei zu helfen, voneinander zu lernen. Nach dem Zusammenbruch des Sowjet-Kommunismus 1989 war dieses Bemühen um Vergleichen, Auswerten und gegenseitiges Lernen für die Länder Mittel- und Osteuropas besonders wichtig. Professor Mitter und das DIPF boten und bieten sich aufgrund ihrer einschlägigen Erfahrungen in der Vergleichenden Erziehungswissenschaft und nicht zuletzt auch der besonderen Kenntnisse der mittel- und osteuropäischen Bildungslandschaft hierbei als gleichsam natürliche Partner an.

Bildungsreformen und Bildungsforschung

Die sechziger und siebziger Jahre waren für die meisten damals im Europarat zusamenarbeitenden Staaten von einer raschen Ausweitung des höheren Schulwesens und des Hochschulwesens und – damit einhergehend – von wachsender Nachfrage nach Bildungsplanung, Bildungsökonomie und Bildungsforschung geprägt. Die Wissenschaft sollte die Reformen vorbereiten helfen, begleiten und auswerten, nach Meinung mancher Politiker vor allem ihre Richtigkeit bestätigen. Die Vergleichende Erziehungswissenschaft war stärker als je gefragt, zahlreiche Einrichtungen und Organisationen der Bildungsforschung entstanden oder wurden ausgebaut.

Die Entwicklung in den einzelnen Staaten

Je nach Tradition und Verständnis für die unabhängige Rolle der Forschung finden sich in den Ländern des Europarats unterschiedliche Formen von Einrichtungen der Bildungsforschung. Manche Staaten entschieden sich für die Gründung von Instituten, die dem jeweiligen Ministerium entweder angegliedert oder unterstellt waren oder ihm zumindest nahestanden. Als Beispiele seien genannt: das dänische Institut für Bildungsforschung, das französische Institut National de Recherche Pédagogique, die Staats- oder Landesinstitute in Deutschland (z. B. in Bayern, Baden-Württemberg, Hessen, Nordrhein-Westfalen), das Bundesinstitut für Berufsbildung in Berlin, die Pädagogischen Akademien in Bulgarien, Polen und der ehemaligen Sowjetunion, das griechische Zentrum für Bildungsforschung und Lehrerfortbildung, das spanische Instituto Nacional de Ciencias de la Educación, inzwischen umbenannt in Centro de Investigación y Documentación Educativa sowie die Schweizerische Koordinierungsstelle für Bildungsforschung. Die herkömmlichen erziehungswissenschaftlichen Hochschulinstitute erhielten zusätzliche Aufgaben, neue Institute wurden gegründet (z. B. Institute für Hochschuldidaktik oder Hochschulforschung, die niederländischen Institute für Onderzoek van het (Wetenschappelijk) Onderwijs, die spanischen Institutos de Ciencias de la Educación). An unabhängigen, aber mit öffentlichen Mitteln finanzierten Einrichtungen seien genannt: das von vornherein international ausgerichtete DIPF, das Max-Planck-Institut für Bildungsforschung in Berlin, der Scottish Council for Research in Education (seit 1928 bestehend) und der Northern Ireland Council for Educational Research. In anderen Fällen gab man der Form einer Stiftung oder Gesellschaft den Vorzug: die niederländische Stichting voor het Onderzoek van het Onderwijs, inzwischen umgewandelt in The Netherlands Institute for Educational Research, die National Foundation for Educational Research in England and Wales, das Hochschul-Informations-System als GmbH in Hannover, der deutsche Arbeitskreis für Hochschuldidaktik und die britische Society for Research into Higher Education. Das Handbuch „Educational Research Information Sources", das 1983 unter der Schirmherrschaft des Generalsekretärs des Europarats veröffentlicht wurde, illustriert diese bunte Vielfalt.

Jeder, der Bildung planen und reformieren wollte, hielt sich einen „Hofstaat" von Erziehungswissenschaftlern und bestellte vergleichende Untersuchungen. Dennoch ist nicht sicher, ob die Bildungsforschung jener Jahre, die zweifellos von hoher Qualität war, einen nennenswerten Einfluß auf die Bildungspolitik ausgeübt hat. Eine 1981 von der niederländischen Stichting voor het Onderzoek van het Onderwijs mit dem Europarat zu diesem Thema veranstaltete Tagung hinterließ den Eindruck, daß es mitunter bis zu zehn Jahren dauere, bis Forschungsergebnisse zu den Politikern durchsickern.

Entwicklungen auf europäischer und internationaler Ebene

Der Europarat und sein Rat für kulturelle Zusammenarbeit (CDCC)

Gemäß einer Entschließung zur Bildungsforschung der 4. Plenarsitzung der Europäischen Erziehungsministerkonferenz des Europarats (London 1964) wurde 1965 im Europarat in Straßburg ein Dokumentationszentrum für das Bildungswesen in Europa (das bis 1995 einen weitverbreiteten und sehr beliebten Newsletter herausgab) sowie 1967 ein Referat für Bildungsforschung und -dokumentation (die heutige Sektion Forschung) eingerichtet.

Die Federführung der damals eingeleiteten Arbeiten lag beim Rat für kulturelle Zusammenarbeit (Comité directeur de la Coopération culturelle, CDCC), in dem heute (1997) 44 Staaten vertreten sind. Von 1967 bis 1976 betreute das Referat für Bildungsforschung und -dokumentation zwei Ad-hoc-Ausschüsse des CDCC: einen für Bildungsforschung und einen für Bildungsdokumentation (die beide 1977 im Zuge einer Reform der Europaratsausschüsse aufgelöst wurden). Heute werden die einschlägigen Arbeiten teils vom Bildungsausschuß, teils vom Hochschulausschuß des CDCC überwacht. Seit 1973 spielte Professor Mitter im Ausschuß für Bildungsforschung eine führende Rolle und war zuletzt, bis zur Auflösung 1977, dessen Vorsitzender.

Ziele der Tätigkeit des Europarats im Bereich Bildungsforschung, bei der das DIPF stets ein wichtiger Partner war, waren Information, Koordination und Zusammenarbeit. Es galt:

– die Ergebnisse der Bildungsforschung, also auch der Vergleichenden Erziehungswissenschaft, über die Grenzen Europas hinweg bekanntzumachen;
– engere Kontakte zwischen den einzelnen europäischen Wissenschaftlern anzubahnen, weil diese oft zu sehr auf die USA fixiert waren und zu wenig von der Arbeit ihrer Kollegen in Europa wußten;

- gemeinsame Forschungsarbeiten anzuregen;
- die interessantesten Bildungsreformen gemeinsam auszuwerten.

Im Zuge dieser Arbeiten wurde zu Beginn der siebziger Jahre das European Documentation and Information System for Education (EUDISED) als per Computer abrufbare Datenbank erziehungswissenschaftlicher Untersuchungen entwickelt. 34 Koordinierungsstellen in den einzelnen Ländern schicken Kurzbeschreibungen (Abstracts) der wichtigsten Forschungsarbeiten auf Diskette an die Biblioteca di Documentazione Pedagogica in Florenz, die sie im Auftrag des Europarats in die Datenbank eingibt. Die sprachliche und technische Überprüfung der Beiträge erfolgt durch die National Foundation for Educational Research in England and Wales. Abrufbar ist EUDISED entweder über den Information Retrieval Service der European Space Agency in Frascati oder über die Biblioteca di Documentazione Pedagogica in Florenz (auch auf Internet: Man tippe „http://linux.bdp.fi.it", sodann wähle man „Database consultation" und anschließend „EUDI"). In gedruckter Form erhältlich war EUDISED bis 1993 in Form der Zeitschrift „EUDISED R&D Bulletin"; 1993 trat das „EUDISED-European Educational Research Yearbook" an die Stelle des Bulletins.

Die Beiträge werden mit den Deskriptoren des ebenfalls ab 1970 entwickelten „Europäischen Thesaurus Bildungswesen" (früher EUDISED-Thesaurus) verschlagwortet. Der Thesaurus liegt derzeit in 17 Sprachen vor. Die inzwischen vom Europarat und der Europäischen Kommission gemeinsam herausgegebene Publikation beschränkt sich allerdings auf neun Sprachen; sie ist auch als Magnetband erhältlich. Die anderen Sprachfassungen wurden nur auf nationaler Ebene veröffentlicht. Der Thesaurus enthält über 3 500 hierarchisch gegliederte Schlagwörter und wird seit 1981 gemeinsam mit dem Informationsnetz EURYDICE der Europäischen Kommission in Brüssel fortgeschrieben.

Seit den siebziger Jahren hat der Europarat außerdem regelmäßig erziehungswissenschaftliche Tagungen veranstaltet, bei denen das DIPF und Professor Mitter häufig beteiligt waren. Es gab (als eine Art Fortsetzung des 1977 aufgelösten Ausschusses für Bildungsforschung) gemeinsam mit dem UNESCO-Institut für Pädagogik in Hamburg und später auch der Pariser UNESCO-Zentrale organisierte Konferenzen der Direktoren der Bildungsforschung (deren einer Professor Mitter war), ferner in Zusammenarbeit zwischen dem Europarat und jeweils verschiedenen nationalen Stellen Symposien, Bildungsforschungskolloquien sowie sogenannte Workshops, bei denen es darum ging, gemeinsam den Stand der Bildungsforschung zu aktuellen Themen zu ermitteln. (Eine Liste dieser erziehungswissenschaftlichen Tagungen, deren Unterlagen häufig in Buch-form erschienen, ist im Anhang beigefügt, wobei jeweils die etwaige Beteiligung Professor Mitters vermerkt ist.)

Der Europarat veröffentlichte auch eine Reihe erziehungswissenschaftlicher Berichte und vergleichender Darstellungen (z. B. über Vorschulerziehung, Lehrerbildung, Lehrplanforschung und Evaluierungsmethoden).

Manche Ideen freilich blieben auf dem Papier, so der Wunsch nach Gründung einer Europäischen Stiftung für Bildungsforschung, nach einem Europäischen Austauschprogramm für Erziehungswissenschaftler und nach entsprechenden Fortbildungsstipendien. Auch die Zusammenarbeit der verschiedenen Wissenschaftlerteams über die Ländergrenzen hinweg hat sich nicht in der Weise entwickelt, wie dies 1970 erhofft worden war.

Die Arbeit anderer Organisationen und Einrichtungen

Natürlich war der Europarat nicht die einzige Organisation, die sich mit wissenschaftlichen Untersuchungen zu Bildungsfragen befaßte. Verschiedene andere Organisationen und Einrichtungen seien genannt:

Die Europäische Union

Die Europäische Union in Brüssel besitzt seit 1974 einen Bildungsausschuß und hält seit 1974 regelmäßig Sitzungen des Ministerrats in der Zusammensetzung der Bildungsminister ab. 1975 wurde EURYDICE als Informationsnetz für das Bildungswesen gegründet, und seit 1981 wird der im Europarat entstandene Europäische Thesaurus Bildungswesen benutzt und gemeinsam mit Straßburg weiterentwickelt. Im Rahmen der Arbeit der Kommission und des EURYDICE-Netzes wurden seither zahlreiche vergleichende Studien erstellt. Derzeit wird die Frage nach einer gesonderten Erhebung bildungspolitisch relevanter Forschungsdaten – in Konkurrenz zu EUDISED – erörtert.

Die UNESCO

Die UNESCO hat sich seit ihrer Gründung 1948 weltweit mit vergleichenden Untersuchungen befaßt und – besonders in den Jahren des Kalten Krieges, als der Europarat keinen direkten Zugang zu Mittel- und Osteuropa hatte – häufig mit dem Europarat zusammengearbeitet, um Erziehungswissenschaftler aus Ost und West an einen Tisch zu bringen.

Das Internationale Erziehungsbüro (International Bureau of Education, IBE) der UNESCO in Genf besteht seit 1925 als ein Zentrum für Vergleichende Erziehungswissenschaft und Bildungsinformation aus aller Welt. Das IBE veranstaltet alle zwei Jahre große Konferenzen zu Bildungsfragen. Die 1966 abgehaltene Konferenz beispielsweise empfahl – dem Trend der Zeit folgend – eine verstärkte internationale Zusammenarbeit in der Bildungsforschung. 1973 gab es eine Arbeitsgruppe zur Bildungsforschungspolitik. – Besonders das UNESCO-Institut für Pädagogik in Hamburg war dem Europarat ein wertvoller Partner bei der Ausrichtung der gesamteuropäischen Bildungsforschungskonferenzen und hat ausgezeichnete Arbeit geleistet, was den internationalen Vergleich von Bildungssystemen (und besonders der Erwachsenenbildung) angeht. – Auch das Europäische Zentrum für das Hochschulwesen der UNESCO in Bukarest arbeitet eng mit dem Europarat zusammen, vor allem bei der wissenschaftlichen Untersuchung des Hochschulwesens. – Letztlich sei auch die hervorragende Arbeit des Internationalen Instituts für Bildungsplanung in Paris genannt.

Die OECD

Die OECD, ihr Bildungsausschuß (seit 1970) und ganz besonders ihr 1968 gegründetes Zentrum für Forschung und Innovation im Bildungswesen (CERI) haben wertvolle Forschungs- und Entwicklungsarbeit geleistet, beispielsweise zur Bildungsexpansion, Bildungsplanung, Bildungsverwaltung, Bildungstechnologie und Bildungsreform jeglicher Art. Berühmt wurden die OECD-Länderberichte, die sich kritisch mit der Bildungspolitik der Mitgliedsländer auseinandersetzten. Viele der oben genannten nationalen erziehungswissenschaftlichen Einrichtungen waren an diesen OECD-Arbeiten beteiligt. Allerdings muß berücksichtigt werden, daß die OECD auch Industriestaaten außerhalb Europas wie die USA, Japan und Kanada umfaßt und manche Dinge vielleicht etwas zu stark aus einer amerikanischen Perspektive betrachtet werden.

Die Internationale Arbeitsorganisation (International Labour Organisation)

Diese in Genf ansässige Organisation hat erziehungswissenschaftlich interessante Arbeit geleistet, was die Arbeitsbedingungen und die Stellung der Lehrerschaft angeht.

Der Nordische Ministerrat und das Sekretariat für
Nordische Kulturelle Zusammenarbeit in Kopenhagen

Im Rahmen des Nordischen Rats wurden viele nützliche Arbeiten für die nordischen Länder durchgeführt. Erwähnt sei beispielsweise die nordische Datenbank PEPSY, die bibliographische Daten (z. B. über Zeitschriftenartikel) von bildungspolitischem Interesse speichert.

Internationale nichtstaatliche Organisationen und Einrichtungen

Die Arbeit der internationalen und europäischen zwischenstaatlichen, von Beamten beherrschten Organisationen und Einrichtungen muß durch vielfältige nichtstaatliche Initiativen ergänzt werden, die den Wissenschaftlern eine direkte Zusammenarbeit ohne staatliche Lenkung ermöglichen. Der Europarat hat sich stets bemüht, mit diesen nichtstaatlichen Organisationen und Einrichtungen engen Kontakt zu halten. Einige seien – beispielhaft für viele andere – aufgezählt:

- die Europäische Kulturstiftung in Amsterdam (seit 1954) und ihr Institute of Education and Social Policy in Paris (seit 1975), die maßgebliche Untersuchungen zu Bildungsfragen (z. B. das Projekt „Europa 2000" im Jahre 1966) veröffentlicht haben;
- das Consortium of Institutions for Development and Research in Education in Europe mit Sitz in Schottland, das viele der großen nationalen Einrichtungen der Bildungsforschung vereinigt;
- die European Educational Research Association, ein Zusammenschluß von Erziehungswissenschaftlern;
- die Association Francophone d'Éducation Comparée in Sèvres;
- die European Association for Research on Learning and Instruction;
- die mit Europaratshilfe in den siebziger Jahren gegründete European Association for Research and Development in Higher Education;

- die International Association for the Evaluation of Educational Achievement, die sich um die wissenschaftliche Evaluierung des Unterrichts in verschiedenen Schulfächern in vielen Ländern bemüht;
- die 1975 entstandene International Association for Educational Assessment;
- die auf Anregung des Europarats gegründete Association for Teacher Education in Europe;
- die 1961 gegründete International Association for the Advancement of Educational Research, die Bildungsforschung auf Universitätsebene fördern will;
- die Comparative Education Society in Europe;
- der World Council of Comparative Education Societies (von 1988 bis 1996 mit Professor Mitter als Vorsitzendem);
- das Northern Policy, Review, Research and Advisory Network on Education and Training;
- die Nordic Society for Educational Research (seit 1972);
- die International Reading Association, 1956 entstanden, zwar mit Hauptsitz in den USA, aber mit einem Büro in Paris;
- die European Association for Special Education (für Sonderpädagogik);
- der European Council on High Ability (für Hochbegabtenforschung).

Bewertung des bisher Erreichten

Auf nationaler Ebene

In vielen Ländern, so etwa ganz besonders in Belgien, Deutschland, Frankreich, den Niederlanden, Österreich, Schweden, der Schweiz, Spanien und dem Vereinigten Königreich, hat die Bildungsforschung (einschließlich der Vergleichenden Erziehungswissenschaft) einen gewissen Status erlangt und sich als anerkannte Disziplin etablieren können. In anderen Ländern dagegen, beispielsweise in Osteuropa, steckt sie vielfach noch in den Kinderschuhen, wenn man von der traditionellen, aufs eigene Schulwesen bezogenen pädagogischen Forschung absieht. Andererseits ist die Zeit der großen euphorischen Bildungsreformen einer vom Nullwachstum und Geldmangel geprägten Stagnation gewichen. Die Bildungsforschung hat dadurch wiederum manches an Stellenwert eingebüßt.

Ferner hat sich gezeigt, daß Politiker sich nicht in dem gewünschten Maße von den Ergebnissen der Bildungsforschung beeinflussen lassen, sondern oft der eigenen Intuition, dem Rat der Parteiideologen oder womöglich den gut gemeinten Einflüsterungen ihres Chauffeurs, ihres Friseurs oder ihrer Putzfrau mehr Gewicht beimessen als den oft schwer verständlich vorgetragenen Ergebnissen der Wissenschaftler. Auch scheinen ihnen nicht alle Themen der Bildungsforschung relevant. Die Bildungsforscher ihrerseits sahen sich nicht immer gern in der Rolle des Dieners und Gehilfen der Bildungspolitik und verfolgten ihre eigenen Fragestellungen, ohne sich hinreichend um die Vorbereitung der nötigen bildungspolitischen Entscheidungen zu kümmern. Viele überaus interessante und bedeutsame Forschungsergebnisse wurden von den zuständigen Kultusministern und Beamten und auch der Lehrerschaft nicht zur Kenntnis genommen, weil sie in unverständlicher Fachsprache vorgestellt wurden. Das DIPF und Professor Mitter bilden insoweit eine rühmliche Ausnahme. Die Vor- und Nachteile möglicher alternativer Lösungen wurden oft nicht deutlich aufgezeigt, Forschungsergebnisse manchmal nicht klar von persönlichen Meinungen und nahezulegenden Schlußfolgerungen unterschieden. Es gab auch manche Minister, die lediglich von der Wissenschaft hören wollten, die von ihnen angeordneten Reformen seien in der Tat segensreich gewesen. In manchen Fällen ist es außerdem auch heute noch schwer, auf Anhieb den Stand der Forschung zu einer bestimmten Fragestellung zu ermitteln. Vieles bleibt noch zu tun, um den Dialog zwischen Wissenschaft, Bildungspolitik und Schulpraxis zu verbessern und allen Beteiligten klarzumachen, was die Wissenschaft leisten kann und was nicht. Manche Fragen lassen sich nicht klar mit Ja oder Nein beantworten.

Auf internationaler Ebene

Viel ist getan worden, um Bildungsforschung, Freizügigkeit von Wissenschaftlern, freien Ideenaustausch und gemeinsame Nutzung vorhandener nationaler Ressourcen zu fördern, Bildungspolitiker beim Bemühen um ein besseres Bildungssystem und bei der Vermeidung anderswo gemachter Fehler zu unterstützen sowie den Stand der Forschung zu bestimmten Themen zu ermitteln. Gleichwohl ergaben sich mancherlei Hindernisse und Probleme.

In vielen Ländern waren die Bildungsforscher für großangelegte internationale Zusammenarbeit noch nicht gerüstet:

– Ihre operativen Vorgaben sind in der Regel national, d. h. sie arbeiten in erster Linie in einem regionalen oder nationalen Rahmen und sind deshalb weitgehend auf die Probleme des eigenen Landes fixiert, dessen Bildungspolitik sie zuarbeiten sollen;

- politische Standpunkte spielen mitunter auch eine Rolle;
- Sprachschranken ebenfalls;
- internationale Zusammenarbeit begegnet manchen praktischen Schwierigkeiten, kulturellen Unterschieden, stößt sich an von Land zu Land unterschiedlicher Terminologie und verschiedenen politischen und gesellschaftlichen Gegebenheiten;
- Haushaltskürzungen betreffen internationale Vorhaben oft stärker als nationale;
- die kleineren und mittleren Staaten sind stärker an internationaler Zusammenarbeit interessiert als die großen.

Infolgedessen ist die europäische Bildungsforschungsgemeinschaft noch nicht so weit entwickelt, wie es wünschenswert wäre. Die Vielzahl internationaler und europäischer Organisationen, deren Arbeiten sich oft überlagern und untereinander nicht koordiniert sind, macht die Dinge nicht leichter. Die hauptsächliche Form internationaler Zusammenarbeit ist nach wie vor die Tagung oder der Kongreß: Dort werden Informationen ausgetauscht und Empfehlungen formuliert. Zwei- oder gar mehrseitige Forschungsprojekte sind noch ziemlich selten. Systematische, institutionalisierte Zusammenarbeit auf der Ebene der einzelnen Institute, europäische Ausbildungsprogramme für Erziehungswissenschaftler, eine Europäische Stiftung für Bildungsforschung oder Vergleichende Erziehungswissenschaft: All dies sind Wunschträume geblieben.

Entscheidend ist aber, daß die Notwendigkeit internationaler Zusammenarbeit in der Bildungsforschung weiterhin bejaht wird. Folgende Argumente sprechen auch heute noch dafür:

- In Zeiten knapper Haushaltsmittel kann sich kein Minister mehr leisten, kostspielige Reformen anzuordnen, ohne sie wissenschaftlich vorbereiten, begleiten und auswerten zu lassen und ohne ausländische Erfahrungen einzubeziehen. Hier ist die Vergleichende Erziehungswissenschaft gefordert;
- Wissenschaft ist ihrer Natur nach grenzüberschreitend. Viele ihrer Ergebnisse sind allgemein gültig;
- um der Bildungspolitik gute Dienste leisten zu können, muß die Bildungsforschung gut entwickelt sein. Internationale Kontakte erhöhen das Niveau;
- die meisten Probleme sind vielen Ländern gemeinsam. Forschungsergebnisse aus allen Ländern müssen deshalb auf europäischer oder gar weltweiter Ebene zusammengetragen werden, damit alle von den vorhandenen Erkenntnissen und Erfahrungen profitieren können. EUDISED ist ein Schritt in diese Richtung. Internationale Zusammenarbeit kann somit Kosten sparen;

- internationale Zusammenarbeit erhöht die Bandbreite der zu berücksichtigenden Variabeln;
- Länder ohne ausgeprägte Bildungsforschungstradition können durch ihre Teilnahme an grenzüberschreitenden Projekten von höher entwickelten Ländern lernen.

Anregungen für die Zukunft

Maßnahmen auf nationaler Ebene

Stellenwert der Bildungsforschung. Auch in Zeiten fast leerer Kassen sollten Kultus- und Finanzminister der Bildungsforschung und mit ihr der Vergleichenden Erziehungswissenschaft, was Personal und Geldmittel anlangt, den ihr gebührenden Stellenwert einräumen, wie das beispielsweise in den Niederlanden, in Schweden, im Vereinigten Königreich und in den USA der Fall ist. Denkbar wäre, daß ein fester Prozentsatz der Bildungsausgaben für Forschung angesetzt wird. Auch als Disziplin mit entsprechender Infrastruktur muß die Bildungsforschung einen festen Platz haben, wenn sie der Politik nützlich sein soll.

Auslandskontakte. Die staatlichen Stellen sollten die Beteiligung ihrer Wissenschaftler an internationalen Begegnungen und grenzüberschreitenden Forschungsvorhaben nach Kräften fördern. Dabei sollten sie die Länder wählen, die ihnen als besonders interessante Partner erscheinen. Gerade die Arbeit des DIPF in Richtung Mittel- und Osteuropa hat deutschen Stellen wertvolle Erkenntnisse für ihre Zusammenarbeit mit den dortigen Ländern geliefert.

Dokumentation und Information. Forschungsergebnisse sind nur dann nützlich, wenn sie einem breiten Publikum zugänglich gemacht werden. Alle Institute sollten deshalb dafür sorgen, daß ihre Arbeiten nicht nur über Fachzeitschriften und Bücher, sondern auch über die Einspeicherung in internationale Datenbanken wie z. B. EUDISED bekanntgemacht werden. Zugleich sollten Wissenschaftler sich regelmäßig über anderwärts laufende Arbeiten auf ihrem Fachgebiet informieren, vor allem, wenn sie neue Forschungsarbeiten planen und in Angriff nehmen wollen. Die EUDISED-Datenbank des Europarats wird gegenwärtig viel zu wenig genutzt, weil Wissenschaftler noch weitgehend nicht gewohnt sind, in internationale Datenbanken zu schauen und sich dabei des Europäischen Thesaurus Bildungswesen als Schlagwortkatalogs zu bedienen.

Fremdsprachen. Um auf dem laufenden zu bleiben und mit dem Ausland Kontakt zu halten, sind Fremdsprachenkenntnisse unerläßlich. Titel von Forschungsvorhaben und Abstracts der entsprechenden Arbeiten sollten mindestens ins Englische, aber wenn möglich auch ins Französische oder eine sonstige Fremdsprache übersetzt werden. Durch seine Kenntnisse des Englischen, des Französischen, des Russischen und des Tschechischen hat beispielsweise Professor Mitter seinen internationalen Ruf noch weiter gefestigt.

Zusammenarbeit mit allen Beteiligten. Um durch ihre Arbeit vielen nützen zu können, sollten Bildungsforscher engen Kontakt zu Politikern, Abgeordneten, Beamten der Bildungsverwaltung, den Lehrerbildungseinrichtungen, der Lehrerschaft und auch zur Presse halten. Zutritt zu den Schulen sollte ihnen großzügig gewährt werden.

Einstellung und Fortbildung von Bildungsforschern. Die jeweiligen Einstellungsmodalitäten sind zu überprüfen, etwa in der Hinsicht, daß nicht nur Leute mit einem Hochschulabschluß der Sozialwissenschaften eingestellt werden. Auch Naturwissenschaftler geben gute Bildungsforscher ab. Fortbildungsangebote sollten gemacht werden, etwa im Gebrauch von Fremdsprachen bei der Darstellung und Zusammenfassung von Forschungsergebnissen oder zur Einführung in die Terminologie anderer Länder.

Maßnahmen auf internationaler Ebene

Die folgenden Anregungen richten sich nicht nur an den Europarat, die Europäische Union, die UNESCO, die OECD usw., sondern auch an die oben genannten nichtstaatlichen Organisationen.

Anerkennung der Bedeutung von Bildungsforschung. Auch auf internationaler Ebene bedarf die Bildungsforschung größerer Anerkennung, beispielsweise durch Bildungsforschungsreferate in den internationalen Sekretariaten, Bildungsforschungsausschüsse bei den entsprechenden Gremien und Berücksichtigung von Forschungsergebnissen bei internationalen Arbeiten.

Dokumentation und Information. Internationale und europäische Organisationen sollten weiterhin Forschungsdaten sammeln und weltweit zugänglich machen, dabei aber verstärkt auf die Qualität der gesammelten Daten achten. Nicht jedes weitschweifig im Fachjargon geschriebene Abstract ist von europäischem Interesse. Gerade der Europarat wird sich auch künftig bemühen müssen, Bildungspolitiker zur besseren Nutzung europaweit gesammelter Forschungsergebnisse anzuleiten. Die Vergleichende Erziehungswissenschaft braucht ferner verläßliche, mehrsprachige Informationen zum Schul- und Hochschulsystem der einzelnen Länder, wie sie etwa das EURYDICE-Netz der Europäischen Union oder das Dokumentationszentrum beim Europarat anbieten, desgleichen auch verschiedene fachspezifische Informationsstellen wie beispielsweise das Londoner Centre for Information on Language Teaching and Research oder das Braunschweiger Georg-Eckert-Institut für Internationale Schulbuchforschung. – Auch die Bemühungen um eine einheitliche Terminologie müssen fortgesetzt werden: Der Europäische Thesaurus Bildungswesen mit seinen Ergänzungslisten für Fremdsprachenforschung und Sonderschulwesen muß jährlich fortgeschrieben und möglichst in Einklang mit anderen im Bildungswesen gebräuchlichen Thesauri (z. B. dem UNESCO/IBE-Thesaurus) gebracht werden. – Die EUDISED-Datenbank ist so auszubauen, daß sie tatsächlich für alle Länder Europas die wesentlichen Forschungsarbeiten erfaßt. Derzeit schlüpft noch manches durch die Maschen des Erhebungsverfahrens der Mitgliedsländer des Europarats. – Internationale *Bücher und Zeitschriften* (z. B. das „EUDISED-European Educational Research Yearbook") bleiben auch in Zukunft von Bedeutung.

Bildungsstatistik. Mehr muß getan werden, um statistische Daten zu standardisieren und vergleichbar zu machen.

Förderung der Bildungsforschung. Internationale Zusammenarbeit ist wichtig für die Entwicklung jeglicher Form von Erziehungswissenschaft. Inter- und supranationale Stellen sollten verstärkt Erziehungswissenschaftlern ein Gesprächs- und Austauschforum bieten und Adressen von Forschungsteams und ihren Arbeiten veröffentlichen (z. B. in einem „Who is Who in Educational Research"). EUDISED enthält viele solche Angaben, aber ein gesondertes Adreßbuch wäre nützlich.

Analyse und Synthese. Kritische Analysen und Synthesen von Forschungsergebnissen auf europäischer Ebene, die über sogenannte „Trend Reports" hinausgehen, wären ebenfalls hilfreich. Die Wissenschaftler sollten ihre Ergebnisse gegenseitig begutachten.

Methodologie. Inter- und supranationale Organisationen sollten sich verstärkt um die Entwicklung der Methodologie in der Bildungsforschung bemühen und auf Tagungen die bisher üblichen Methoden und Techniken kritisch durchleuchten.

Nachwuchsförderung und Fortbildung. Auch auf europäischer Ebene sollten Nachwuchsförderung und Wissenschaftlerfortbildung Beachtung finden. Entsprechende Maßnahmen zur Nachwuchsförderung, Studien- und Austauschprogramme und europäische Fortbildungsseminare sollten katalogisiert und begutachtet werden.

Koordinierung und Zusammenarbeit in der Bildungsforschung. Trotz aller Schwierigkeiten sollten die Bemühungen weitergehen, nationale Arbeiten zu koordinieren, etwa nach dem Beispiel der IEA-Studien, knappe Ressourcen gemeinsam zu nutzen und länderübergreifende Zusammenarbeit der einzelnen Institute zu fördern. – Es hat sich gezeigt, daß Fortschritte in dieser Richtung am ehesten in regionalem Rahmen erzielt werden können. Verwiesen sei auf die Zusammenarbeit der Wissenschaftler in den nordischen, den deutschsprachigen, den französischsprachigen und den niederländischsprachigen Ländern.

Organisatorische Beratung. In Mittel- und Osteuropa gilt es außerdem, den Regierungen und Verwaltungen Beratung bei der Reform der Bildungsforschung anzubieten und die insoweit im Westen gemachten Erfahrungen der letzten dreißig Jahre nutzbar zu machen.

Schlußbetrachtung

Viele der aufgezeigten Probleme können überwunden werden, viele der gegebenen Anregungen können verwirklicht werden, wenn die einzelnen Wissenschaftler und ihre Institute sich weiterhin ernsthaft um europäische Zusammenarbeit bemühen. Jahre fruchtbarer Zusammenarbeit zwischen dem DIPF, verkörpert vor allem durch Professor Mitter, und dem Europarat haben gezeigt, was das Engagement eines einzelnen zu bewirken vermag. Persönlichkeiten wie Professor Mitter werden auch aus dem wohlverdienten Ruhestand heraus, für den ihn alle guten Wünsche des Europarats begleiten, im europäischen Geiste weiterhin befruchtend wirken.

Anhang

Erziehungswissenschaftliche Tagungen des Europarats

1. Symposien
- Göteborg (Schweden), 7.-12. 9. 1975: Strategien für Forschung und Entwicklung im Hochschulbereich.
- Granada (Spanien), 4.-7. 10. 1977: Reform und Entwicklung des Hochschulwesens.
- Peebles (Schottland), 26. 2. – 3. 3. 1978: Schule und was nachher? Übergang Schule-Arbeitswelt (mit Prof. Mitter als Referenten).

2. Bildungsforschungskolloquien
- Hamburg (mit dem UNESCO-Institut für Pädagogik), 12.-14. 9. 1978: Chancengleichheit neu gesehen: Werte im Bildungswesen der Zukunft (mit Prof. Mitter als Vorsitzendem).
- Hamburg (mit dem UNESCO-Institut für Pädagogik), 22.-24. 6. 1981: Die sich wandelnde Rolle der Studien- und Berufsberatung in bestimmten Lebensabschnitten.
- Straßburg (Frankreich), 24.-25. 9. 1987: Aktuelle Probleme der Bildungsforschung (mit Prof. Mitter als Vorsitzendem).
- Ericeira (Portugal), 17.-20. 10. 1989: Bildungsforschung zur schulischen Sozialisierung und Erziehung zur Demokratie und Achtung der Menschenrechte.
- San Marino, 9.-13. 9. 1991: Bildungsforschung und Sekundarschule.
- Gent (Belgien), 7.-10. 9. 1993: Wissenschaftliche Untersuchungen zur Studien- und Berufsberatung in der Sekundarschule.

3. Workshops
- Windsor (England), Juni 1976: Messung landeseinheitlich festgesetzter schulischer Leistungsnormen.
- Kiel, Oktober 1976: Bildungsforschung und naturwissenschaftlicher Unterricht in Europa.
- Nijmegen (Niederlande), 29. 11. – 3. 12. 1976: Förderung der sozialen Entwicklung an der Schule – Untersuchungen unter besonderer Berücksichtigung der Altersgruppe 4-12.
- Neusiedl (Österreich), Dezember 1976: Evaluierung von Modellversuchen in der Sekundarstufe I (Gesamtschulproblematik).
- Brügge (Belgien), Juli 1977: Perspektiven der Bildungsforschung im Bereich des Übergangs Schule-Arbeitswelt.
- Saltsjöbaden (Schweden), 26.-30. 9. 1977: Bildungsforschung und Entwicklung des einzelnen Schülers: Studien- und Berufswahl.
- Montreux (Schweiz), 25.-29. 9. 1978: Innovation und Evaluierung im Pflichtschulbereich (Gesamtschulproblematik).
- Sèvres (Frankreich), 20.-24. 11. 1978: Bildungsforschung und neue Entwicklungen im Primarschulbereich.
- Bad Homburg, 11.-15. 12. 1978: Hochschuleingangstests und -interviews (mit Prof. Mitter als Mitveranstalter und Vorsitzendem).
- Dillingen/Bayern, 14.-18. 4. 1980: Schulische Betreuung von Gastarbeiterkindern.
- Straßburg (Frankreich), 20.-23. 10. 1980: Evaluierung von Lehrerfortbildung.
- Hønefoss (Norwegen), 5.-8. 5. 1981: Geschlechtsrollenklischees im Schulunterricht.

- Den Haag (Niederlande), 20.-23. 5. 1981: Sozialwissenschaftliche Forschung und Bildungspolitik.
- Windsor (England), 14.-17. 9. 1982: Schulleiterausbildung.
- Frascati (Italien), 2.-5. 11. 1982: Neue Technologien in der Sekundarschule.
- Puidoux-Chexbres (Schweiz), 1.-4. 5. 1984: Reform des Rechenunterrichts an der Grundschule.
- Edinburgh (Schottland), 3.-6. 9. 1984: Naturwissenschaften und Computer an der Grundschule.
- Madrid (Spanien), 24.-27. 9. 1985: Die Entwicklung des Kindes im Grundschulalter.
- Tilburg (Niederlande), 9.-12. 12. 1986: Lese- und Schreibunterricht an der Grundschule.
- Eindhoven (Niederlande), 3.-6. 6. 1987: Interaktives Lernen und die neuen Technologien.
- North Berwick (Schottland), 22.-25. 11. 1988: Evaluierung von Schulreform: Methoden, Gebrauch und Nutzen.
- Lüttich (Belgien), 12.-15. 9. 1989: Schulische Leistungsbeurteilung: Motivation und Schulerfolg.
- Braunschweig, 11.-14. 9. 1990: Geschichte und Sozialwissenschaften – Methoden der Schulbuchanalyse.
- Nijmegen (Niederlande), 23.-26. 7. 1991: Hochbegabtenförderung in Europa.
- La Valletta (Malta), 6.-9. 10. 1992: Wissenschaftliche Untersuchung zum Lehrplan der Sekundarschule.
- Jyväskylä (Finnland), 15.-18. 6. 1993: Leistungsbewertung an der Sekundarschule und Stellenwert des Abiturs.
- Bautzen, 11.-14. 10. 1994: Schulische Betreuung von Minderheiten (in Zusammenarbeit mit dem DIPF und Prof. Mitter als wissenschaftlichem Berater und Einführungsreferenten).
- Graz (Österreich), 5.-8. 3. 1996: Wirksamkeit von Fremdsprachenunterricht.

4. Gesamteuropäische Konferenzen der Direktoren der Bildungsforschung (zusammen mit der UNESCO)
- Hamburg, 26.-29. 4. 1976: Stand der Bildungsforschung in Europa (mit Prof. Mitter als Teilnehmer).
- Madrid (Spanien), 11.-13. 9. 1979: Das Verhältnis Schule-Arbeitswelt in neuer Sicht (mit Prof. Mitter als Teilnehmer).
- Neusiedl (Österreich), 4.-7. 12. 1983: Bildungsforschung und Grundschule: Was erwarten Staat und Gesellschaft von der Grundschule? (mit Prof. Mitter als Generalberichterstatter).
- Eger (Ungarn), 13.-16. 10. 1986: Neue Herausforderungen für Lehrer und Lehrerbildung (mit Prof. Mitter als Generalberichterstatter).
- Triesenberg (Liechtenstein), 11.-14. 10. 1988: Wirksamkeit von Lehrerfortbildung und Schulleiterfortbildung (mit Prof. Mitter als Generalberichterstatter).
- Bled (Slowenien), 9.-12. 10. 1990: Alphabetisierung und Allgemeinbildung in Europa am Vorabend des 21. Jahrhunderts.
- Nitra (Tschechoslowakei), 27.-30. 10. 1992: Erziehung zum neuen europäischen Staatsbürger: Herausforderungen für die Sekundarschule (mit Prof. Mitter als Teilnehmer).

5. Sonstige erziehungswissenschaftliche Tagungen
- Sofia (Bulgarien), 7.-8. 9. 1992: Stellenwert und Organisationsmuster der Bildungsforschung. Eine Expertenrunde zur Beratung der bulgarischen Regierung (mit Prof. Mitter als einem der Berater).
- Straßburg (Frankreich), 19.-20. 6. 1995: Forschung zum Geschichtsunterricht (insbesondere zur Frage, ob die im Unterricht und in den Geschichtsbüchern verwendeten Termini und Begriffe über die Köpfe der Schüler hinweggehen).

3.

Globale Vergleiche und internationale Aspekte des Bildungswesens
Global Comparisons and International Aspects of Education
Comparaisons globales et aspects internationaux de l'éducation

> *... fixing the word „European" as an attribute to „curriculum" exemplifies a comprehensive trend towards a globalization which is about to grasp more and more areas of our world and our lives: technology and science, economy and ecology, political, social and legal concerns. We speak of „globalizing science" in order to indicate the worldwide range of the scientific spectrum, of „global criminality" and of the need for a „global order". These examples, heterogeneous though they are, show that „Europeanization" is embedded in the trend to „globalization" which has definitely left the realm of aims and expectations; it has reached the level of reality.*
>
> *Wolfgang Mitter, 1996*

Wolfgang Mitter: European Curriculum: Reality or a Dream? In: Winther-Jensen, Thyge (ed.): Challenges to European Education. Cultural Values, National Identities, and Global Responsibilities (= Comparative Studies Series. 6), Frankfurt a. M. et al.: Lang 1996, pp. 295-297 (here: pp. 295-296).

Internationalisierung des Bildungswesens – Eine kritische Perspektive

Birgit Brock-Utne

Einleitung

Ich muß von vorneherein darauf aufmerksam machen, daß ich eine kritische Perspektive bezüglich der zunehmenden Internationalisierung des Bildungswesens vorstellen werde. Ich sehe diese Internationalisierung als etwas an, das die Nationalstaaten – besonders die kleineren oder ärmeren Staaten – in ihren Kulturen und ihrer Vielfalt bedroht. Die große Frage wird sein: Welche Prämissen hat diese Internationalisierung? Wer hat die Macht, seine Schulbücher, seine Curricula, seine Sprache und seine Examenssysteme als „international" zu bezeichnen? Von welchen Nationen lernen wir? Wie sehen die Curricula aus, die unter dem Etikett „international" auf den Markt gebracht werden? Was bedeutet eigentlich „Internationalisierung des Bildungswesens"? Ist der Ausdruck nur ein Euphemismus für „Anglifizierung" oder Kulturimperialismus? Wem dient der internationale Trend des zunehmenden Marktliberalismus, der jetzt auch im Bildungssystem immer deutlicher wird?

Anglifizierung / Amerikanisierung

Als ich nach beinahe fünf Jahren (1987-1992) an der Universität in Daressalam in Tansania auf meine Stelle an der Universität Oslo zurückkehrte, erzählte man mir, daß unsere Universität jetzt dabei sei, mit großer Geschwindigkeit internationalisiert zu werden. Man hätte ein internationales Promotionsprogramm aufgebaut, Wissenschaftler kämen aus der ganzen Welt und einige unserer Studenten hätten angefangen, ihre Doktorarbeiten in Englisch zu schreiben. Ja: das ganze Schulwesen sei inzwischen internationalisiert worden.

Mein jüngster Sohn, der jetzt in das norwegische Schulsystem zurückkehrte und in sein drittletztes Schuljahr vor dem Abitur eintrat, hat uns ein Beispiel der sogenannten „Internationalisierung" gegeben. Als ich vor 35 Jahren mit meinen drei letzten Jahren vor dem Abitur anfing, hatte ich drei Fremdsprachen: Englisch, Deutsch und Französsisch. Wir haben mit Englisch angefangen, und obwohl wir insgesamt mehr Stunden Unterricht in Englisch hatten, haben wir auch Deutsch gut gelernt und ebenso genug Französisch, um die gesprochene Sprache verstehen und Bücher lesen zu können. Mein jüngster Sohn hat heute mehr Stunden Englischunterricht, als ich in der Schule hatte. Das gilt auch für seine Klassenkameraden, die nicht, wie er, eine internationale Schule im Ausland besucht haben. Sie sprechen alle besser Englisch, als wir es im selben Alter gesprochen haben. Neben Englisch konnte er aber nur *eine* andere Fremdsprache wählen. Weil er mit Französisch angefangen hatte, mußte er mit Französisch weitermachen und konnte – beispielsweise – nicht Deutsch wählen. Die sogenannte 'Internationalisierung' ist zu einer 'Anglifizierung' geworden.

Auch das Promotionsprogramm an meinem Institut ist ein Programm, das jetzt zumeist auf Englisch abläuft. Die Gastprofessoren und Dozenten sind meistens Amerikaner. Sie kommen von anerkannten Universitäten aus den USA. Manchmal kommen sie auch aus England, sehr selten aus Deutschland oder Frankreich, aber nie kommen sie aus einem Entwicklungsland. Als ich beispielsweise einige Male vorschlug, einen Gastprofessor aus Afrika einzuladen, hieß es: Wir können für solche Leute kein Geld ausgeben, sie müssen über ein Kooperationsprogramm mit Universitäten in Entwicklungsländern eingeladen werden. Diese Zusammenarbeit hat aber den Charakter von Entwicklungshilfe, bei der wir im Norden sehr viel über die Inhalte bestimmen und die Akademiker aus dem Süden von uns lernen sollen. Sie sollen von *uns* lernen – *wir* lernen von den Amerikanern.

Die zunehmende Anglifizierung läßt sich auch in den früheren englischen Kolonien in Afrika beobachten. In Tansania, wo man nach der Unabhängigkeit plante, Suaheli als Unterrichtssprache nicht nur im Primar-, sondern auch im Sekundar- und Tertiärbereich einzuführen, sind entsprechende Pläne, teilweise infolge des Einflusses des British Council, gescheitert *(Brock-Utne 1993b)*. Erst vor ganz kurzer Zeit, mit der Einführung des Mehrparteiensystems, wurde das Fach „siasa" (politische Wissenschaft), das früher auch im Sekundarbereich auf Suaheli unterrichtet worden ist, umgetauft; es heißt jetzt: „social science". Es wird auf Englisch unterrichtet und mit Lehrbüchern, die aus Großbritannien stammen. Und Namibia hat bei der Unabhängigkeit Englisch als Landessprache gewählt, die auch als die einheitliche Unterrichtssprache nach den drei ersten Klassen der Primarstufe gilt *(Brock-Utne 1995d)*. Die Konsequenzen dieser Entscheidung für die Mehrheit der namibischen Schüler, die afrikanische Sprachen sprechen, scheinen nicht so wichtig zu sein wie die Kommunikation einer kleinen Gruppe Namibier mit dem Ausland *(Phillipson 1992)*.

Die zunehmende Anglifizierung geht Hand in Hand mit einer wachsenden Tendenz zum Marktliberalismus im Bildungsbereich. Wolfgang *Mitter (1996)* hat Recht, wenn er sagt, daß man die Wortführer marktorientierter Bildungsreformen ebenso wie die meisten Initiatoren entsprechender bildungspolitischer Strategien und unmittelbar praxisbezogener Aktivitäten in den Vereinigten Staaten und in Großbritannien findet. In einer Analyse der Politik der freien Schulwahl und der marktorientierten Schulreform in Großbritannien und in den Vereinigten Staaten stellt auch *Boyd (1993)* fest, daß das Marktmodell eigentlich in den USA beheimatet ist.

Die supranationalen Bildungsfachleute

In einem Aufsatz über Bildung und Entwicklung analysiert die britische Professorin Angela *Little (1992)* die Spannungen, die zwischen externen Standards und internen Kulturen existieren. Kulturelle Definitionen optimaler Schulleistungen unterscheiden sich von Land zu Land. Das gilt auch für die Strategien zur Prüfung dieser Schulleistungen. Little hat eine zunehmende Tendenz zur Internationalisierung der Prüfungen von Schulleistungen und Examina festgestellt und fragt:

„Wenn 'internationale Standards' – etwas, das häufig ausländische Standards bedeutet, die im Westen produziert worden sind – allmählich die Oberhand über die nationalen oder regionalen/subnationalen Standards gewinnen: Was bedeutet dies für die national und kulturell bedingten Lehrpläne? Wird eine internationale Technik für die Bewertung des Unterrichts allmählich eine internationalisierte Lehrplanreform hervorrufen? Um wieviel breiter wird die Kluft zwischen der Kultur derjenigen, die die Bildungsleistung bewerten sowie die Prüfungen und Lehrpläne entwickeln (d. h. die 'supranationalen' Bildungsfachleute), und der Kultur des Kindes werden, dessen Lernen das Ziel dieser Bildungsbemühungen ist?" (Little 1992, S. 20)

Vor fünfzehn Jahren, als einige der ostafrikanischen Staaten, wie etwa Tansania, sich darum bemühten, ihr eigenes Bildungswesen auf der Grundlage ihrer eigenen Kulturen aufzubauen, haben sie sich gegen Lehrpläne und Bewertungssysteme des Westens – meistens der früheren Kolonialmächte – gewehrt.

Die Qualität des Unterrichts

In einem Seminar über erziehungswissenschaftliche Forschung in Tansania, das im Jahre 1984 an der Universität von Daressalam veranstaltet wurde, war die Frage der Qualität des Bildungssystems das Hauptproblem *(Ishumi u. a. 1985)*. Die Teilnehmer diskutierten, was „ *'Qualitätsbegriffe' in einem Land bedeuten können, in dem die umfassendere Bedeutung dieses Begriffs in mehr besteht als nur in den schulischen Leistungen"* *(ebd., S. 12)*.

Was den Import des ganzen Apparats amerikanischer Forschung zur Interaktion im Unterricht betrifft, so waren die Forscher sehr skeptisch, insbesondere in bezug auf *„das Messen der tansanischen Schüler mit Hilfe der vielen Tests, die international von Institutionen wie der IEA verwendet worden sind. Diese Ansätze sind in sehr speziellen kulturellen Milieus in den nördliche Industriestaaten entstanden"* *(ebd., S. 13)*.

Die Hilfsorganisationen der nördlichen Länder mögen die besten Absichten haben, wenn sie ein Programm starten, wie das „Basic and Primary Education Program" (BPEP), das 1992 in Nepal in Gang gesetzt wurde. Sie fühlten sich verpflichtet, *„die Qualität der Unterrichtsmethoden zu verbessern und den grundlegenden pädagogischen Bedürfnissen in Nepal gerecht zu werden"* (Conrad 1994, S. 1).

Der Ausdruck „Qualität der Unterrichtsmethoden" ist jedoch ein sehr stark ideologisch geprägter Begriff. „Grundlegende pädagogische Bedürfnisse" umfaßt Strategien für die Verwirklichung der idealen Zielsetzungen, die 1990 von der „Weltkonferenz für Bildung für Alle" in Jomtien in Thailand formuliert wurden. Die Hauptkomponenten des Projekts umfassen Lehrplanentwicklung und Schulbuchproduktion und daneben eine Verbesserung des allgemeinen Prüfungssystems. Man wird sich besonders um die Entwicklung einer effizienten Abschlußprüfung nach dem fünften Schuljahr bemühen, die auf im voraus definierten Kriterien basiert.

Das BPEP ist ein Modellprogramm, das im allgemeinen als ein universal gültiges Programm in bezug auf die Verbesserung der Qualität der Unterrichtsmethoden angesehen wird, wobei man davon ausgeht, daß die charakteristischen kulturellen Bedingungen irgend eines Landes keine Bedeutung haben. Die dänische Wissenschaftlerin Joan Conrad, die gegenüber dem BPEP in Nepal sehr kritisch eingestellt ist, bedauert folgendes: *„Die sehr große Ähnlichkeit solcher Programme ist an sich sehr beunruhigend"* *(ebd., S. 20)*. Ihre Analyse unterstützt die Schlußfolgerung, zu der die dänische Historikerin

Lene *Buchert* in ihrer Analyse der Muster der derzeitigen ausländischen Hilfsprogramme kommt:

„Lehrinhalte sind ein Gebiet, das sehr stark von einer zunehmend von Gebern bestimmten Koordination beeinflußt ist, die auf den Zielen und Prioritäten der 'Education for All'-Strategien basiert. Wie bei strukturellen Anpassungsprogrammen besteht die Gefahr, daß die vom Geber koordinierten Bildungsprogramme über alle Unterschiede in den einzelnen Empfängerländern hinweg und ohne Berücksichtigung der ganzheitlichen Sektorüberlegungen des betroffenen Landes entwickelt werden. In Jomtien wurde viel Gewicht auf Kosten, Effizienz und Effektivität gelegt. Dadurch dürften westliche Lehrpläne noch einmal größere Bedeutung gewinnen als solche, die vor Ort entwickelt werden und auf 'eingeborenen' Kenntnissystemen und Sozialisierungsmethoden sowie einem lokalen Bedarf an speziellen Fertigkeiten basieren. Infolgedessen werden vor Ort entwickelte Erneuerungsexperimente in den Empfängerländern verhindert" (Buchert 1993, S. 10).

Nach einer Analyse der Muster der gegenwärtigen ausländischen Hilfsprogramme und Bildungspolitik für Entwicklungsländer von drei bilateralen Hilfsorganisationen kommt Buchert zu dem Schluß, daß der primäre Ausgangspunkt der drei Organisationen nicht die in den einzelnen Empfängerländern identifizierten Bedürfnisse und eine nachfolgende sorgfältige Lehrplanentwicklung mit dem Ziel, diesen Bedürfnissen nachzukommen, zu sein scheint. Im Gegenteil, die in Jomtien geforderte Qualität der Grundbildung scheint bei ihnen Fuß gefaßt zu haben. Grundbildung scheint mit Grundschulbesuch gleichgesetzt zu werden. Der Wertbegriff „Qualität" wird in diesem Zusammenhang so definiert, wie es die Weltbank tut.

In einem glänzenden Plenarvortrag auf dem 15. Kongreß der Deutschen Gesellschaft für Erziehungswissenschaft vom 11.-13. März 1996 in Halle an der Saale hat *Mitter (1996)* sich mit dem Thema Staat und Markt im internationalen Bildungswesen auseinandergesetzt. Er hat den Schlußfolgerungen von Buchert zugestimmt. Er hat erwähnt, daß er es erstaunlich finde, wie viele Vorschläge zu marktorienterten Bildungsreformen ohne die Berücksichtigung soziokultureller und kulturpsychologischer Faktoren vorgetragen würden.

Der Qualitätsbegriff der Weltbank

Im letzten Jahrzehnt ist die Weltbank für die Entwicklungsländer und besonders für Afrika die wichtigste Institution zur Festlegung der weiteren Entwicklung des formalen Bildungswesens geworden. Was Analysen des Bildungswesens in einzelnen Ländern betrifft, hat die Weltbank inzwischen vollständig die Rolle der UNESCO übernommen. Während die UNESCO eine internationale Organisation ist, in der alle Länder bei Abstimmungen jeweils eine Stimme haben, ist die Weltbank völlig von den westlichen Industriestaaten, insbesondere den USA, dominiert. Während die UNESCO die Kompetenz von Erziehungswissenschaftlern nutzt, ist die Bildungsabteilung der Weltbank völlig von Ökonomen beherrscht. Das bedeutet auch eine Dominanz von „rate of return"- und Kosten-Nutzen-Analysen.

Anfang 1988 hat die Weltbank eine Grundsatzstudie zur Zukunft des Schul- und Hochschulbereichs in Schwarzafrika vorgelegt *(World Bank 1988)*. Auf einer Arbeitstagung der Kommission „Bildungsforschung mit der Dritten Welt" der Deutschen Gesellschaft für Erziehungswissenschaft äußerte ein Erziehungswissenschaftler aus Tansania die Einschätzung, daß diese Studie wahrscheinlich zur *„Bibel afrikanischer Bildungspolitiker"* werden würde *(Bühler / Karcher / Nestvogel 1989, S. 351)*. Mit dieser Einschätzung hat er recht behalten. Die Weltkonferenz „Bildung für Alle" in Jomtien in Thailand vom 5. bis 9. März 1990, die durch eine Zusammenarbeit zwischen der Weltbank, der UNESCO, der UNICEF und dem UNDP zustande gekommen ist, baut auf der Politik der Weltbankstudie von 1988 auf. Das heißt: noch mehr Liberalisierung, Kostenverteilung und Privatisierung des Schulwesens *(Brock-Utne 1995b)*.

Diese Studie signalisiert deutlich, was die Weltbank unter „Bildung" versteht, nämlich die institutionelle Beschulung von Kindern nach europäischem Muster in Primar-, Sekundar-, Berufs- und Hochschulen. In einer Analyse dieser Weltbankstudie zur Bildung in Schwarzafrika stellen *Bühler, Karcher* und *Nestvogel (1989, S. 355)* fest, daß in dieser Studie afrikanische Geschichte und Kultur für die Schulen in Afrika nicht als konstitutiv angesehen werden. Es fehlten Hinweise auf die Curricula: *„Die universale Gültigkeit von Bildungsinhalten, die in Industrieländern üblich sind, wird unhinterfragt unterstellt."*

Man stellt sich nicht die Frage, warum ein Gebäude in einem kleinen afrikanischen Dorf viereckig ist, wenn alle die anderen Gebäude in der Umgebung rund sind *(Odora 1994)*. Man fragt sich nicht, wie die einheimische Bildung und Erziehung, die vor der

Kolonialzeit stattgefunden hat und noch sehr lebendig ist, als Teil des gesamten Bildungssystems gesehen werden kann.

Die Studie signalisiert auch deutlich, was die Weltbank unter dem Wertbegriff „Qualität" im Bildungswesen versteht. In einer Analyse dieser Weltbankstudie, dieser „Bibel afrikanischer Bildungspolitiker", wird der Gebrauch dieses Begriffs von der Weltbank kommentiert und näher analysiert *(Brock-Utne 1993a)*. Die ganze Studie ist voll mit Behauptungen über einen sogenannten „Rückgang der Qualität der Bildung in Afrika". Die Weltbank entscheidet zuerst, was sie unter dem Begriff „Qualität" versteht und dann wird beurteilt, wie es den afrikanischen Ländern gelingt, diese Definition der Weltbank von Qualität zu erfüllen. Die Bank sagt den afrikanischen Ländern auch, was *nicht* hilft, die „Qualität" wiederherzustellen.

Man kommt zu dem Ergebnis, daß die folgenden drei parallelen Maßnahmen nötig seien, um die Qualität wiederherzustellen:

– es muß mehr Lehrbücher und Unterrichtsmaterialien geben;
– es muß eine erneuerte Verpflichtung zu akademischen Standards geben, hauptsächlich durch Verstärkung der Bewertungssysteme;
– es müssen größere Investitionen zur Instandhaltung von Schulgebäuden und deren Einrichtungen vorgenommen werden *(World Bank 1988, S. 131)*.

Diese Art, Bildungsqualität zu definieren, wird in der Studie immer wieder in leicht abgewandeltem Wortlaut wiederholt.

„Die beste Investition in pädagogische Qualität, die man vornehmen kann, ist es, in den meisten Ländern sicherzustellen, daß es ausreichend Lehrbücher und Unterrichtsmaterialien gibt. Lehrbücher und Unterrichtsmaterialien sind effektiv, um Examensresultate zu verbessern, und man hat hier nicht genug investiert im Vergleich zu Investitionen beim Lehrpersonal" (ebd., S. 57).

Hier wird als selbstverständlich angenommen, daß diese höchst umstrittene Behauptung korrekt sei und ebenso die Behauptung der Weltbank, sie wisse, was *nicht* zu einer verbesserten Qualität führe. Ich zitiere:

„Es ist unwahrscheinlich, daß folgende Investitionen eine erkennbare Wirkung auf die pädagogische Qualität der Grundschulbildung haben werden, trotz der potentiell ho-

hen Kosten dieser Maßnahmen: eine Reduktion der Größe der Schulklassen sowie die Ausstattung der Grundschullehrer mit mehr als allgemeiner Bildung auf Sekundarschulniveau und der Lehrer insgesamt mit mehr als einem minimalen Verständnis für pädagogische Theorie" (ebd., S. 57).

Diese Tendenz, künftige Lehrer mit weniger pädagogischer Theorie zu konfrontieren, entstand vor einigen Jahren in der britischen Schulpolitik der Thatcher-Ära *(Editorial 1994; Edwards 1994)*. Auch in Norwegen sind neuerdings die Lehrpläne für die Ausbildung von Grundschullehrern in eben diese Richtung geändert worden. Die künftigen Lehrer erhalten heute mehr Ausbildung in Fachdidaktik als früher, aber viel weniger in pädagogischer Theorie und allgemeiner Didaktik.

Diese „Internationalisierung" ist also ein westliches Phänomen, das die Weltbank nun auch in Schwarzafrika propagiert. An vielen Stellen dieser Weltbankstudie wird gesagt, daß die formelle Ausbildung eines Lehrers verkürzt werden könnte und daß man die Anforderungen für den Lehrerberuf verringern könnte (siehe das Beispiel in *World Bank 1988, S. 135)*. Man argumentiert damit, daß eine solche Taktik eine andere Politik der Weltbank erleichtern würde: nämlich die, die Gehälter der Lehrer zu reduzieren. Man schlägt auch vor, daß Lehrer mehr Stunden pro Tag unterrichten könnten, und man behauptet, eine Klassengröße von 45 Schülern in der Grundschule sei völlig akzeptabel.

Sogar in hoch industrialisierten Ländern gibt es keine professionellen Argumente für die Behauptung, ausreichende und gute Lehrmittel und Schulbücher seien besser als gute Lehrer. Die Weltbank neigt auch dazu, auf der Benutzung von in Europa geschriebenen und veröffentlichten Schulbüchern zu bestehen *(Brock-Utne 1995b)*. Eine Studie, die von der Weltbank selbst bestellt war, aber nicht in der Grundsatzstudie zur Zukunft des Schul- und Hochschulbereichs in Schwarzafrika, „der Bibel afrikanischer Bildungspolitiker", erwähnt wird, zeigt ganz klar, daß gute Lehrer mit einer guten Ausbildung auch in Industrieländern, aber besonders in Entwicklungsländern, sehr viel ausmachen würden *(World Bank 1978, Introduction)*.

Internationalisierung = Liberalisierung und Privatisierung?

Die Frage stellt sich, ob Internationalisierung hauptsächlich Liberalisierung und Privatisierung bedeuten muß. Der britische Bildungsökonom Christopher *Colclough (1995)* hat die Bildungspolitik der Weltbank gegenüber Schwarzafrika analysiert. Er hat auf die

Tatsache hingewiesen, daß die sogenannte „Kostenverteilungspolitik", auf der die Weltbank besteht, zu immer größeren Unterschieden zwischen den Menschen führt. Auch *Mitter (1996, S. 139)* weist auf diese Tatsache hin:

„*Letztendlich arbeiten Märkte gemäß der Logik des Profits nur in gewissen Interessengruppierungen, und sie lassen zu, daß die 'Schwachen' an die Wand gedrückt werden. Sie arbeiten, um eine selbstsüchtige, individualistische Kultur zu produzieren, in welcher der wichtigste moralische Imperativ die Belohnung ist, nicht das gemeinschaftliche Wohl ... Wir befürchten überdies, daß postmoderne Märkte im Bildungswesen neue Formen von Ungerechtigkeit, ..., sowohl erzeugen als auch verbergen. Wir befürchten, daß manche dieser Ungerechtigkeiten sogar noch schwerer zu identifizieren sein werden, weil die globalen Märkte, welche sie erzeugen, außerhalb des Staates stehen und daher außerhalb der normalen Kanäle der Korrektur. In mancher Hinsicht haben wir hier mit einem Teufel zu tun, den wir nicht kennen.*"

Eine empirische Studie in Tansania zeigt diese Tendenz ganz deutlich. Die tansanischen Bildungsforscher Suleman *Sumra* und Naomi *Katunzi (1991*; vgl. auch *Brock-Utne 1995a*) fanden heraus, daß die Wiedereinführung von Schulgebühren in der Sekundarschule stärker Mädchen als Jungen und stärker Schüler der unteren Sozialschichten als der oberen trifft:

Tabelle 1: Schwierigkeiten der Familien, Schulgebühren aufzubringen

	für Mädchen (in Prozent)	für Jungen (in Prozent)
Schüler aus Familien der Mittelschicht	20,6	12,1
Schüler aus Familien der Unterschicht	53	30,3

Wenn die Eltern die Schulgebühren nicht bezahlen können, werden die Schüler nach Hause geschickt und dürfen erst dann zurückkommen, wenn die Eltern wieder in der Lage sind, die Kosten aufzubringen.

Schlußbemerkung

Ganz am Ende möchte ich die Frage stellen: Ist Internationalisierung des Bildungswesens nur etwas Böses? Nein, man kann sich auch darüber freuen, daß die Welt kleiner wird und daß man schnell so viel voneinander lernen kann. Wir sollen aber auch im Westen die Gelegenheit nützen, von anderen Kulturen etwas zu lernen. Der afrikanische Schriftsteller aus Sansibar, Ali *Mazrui (1980, S. 69)*, faßt dies für uns in folgender Weise zusammen:

„*Die westliche Welt muß einen Paradigmenwechsel erleben, einen Wandel hin zu einer kulturellen Demut, zur Bereitschaft, sich von anderen beeinflussen zu lassen, und zur Bereitschaft, eine neue und ausgeglichenere internationale kulturelle Ordnung zu schaffen.*"

Bibliographie

Boyd, William Lowe: Die Politik der freien Schulwahl und marktorientierte Schulreform in Großbritannien und den Vereinigten Staaten. Wie erklären sich die Unterschiede? In: Zeitschrift für Pädagogik, 39 (1993) 1, S. 53-69.

Brock-Utne Birgit: Education Policies for Sub-Saharan Africa as Viewed by the World Bank. A Critical Analysis of a World Bank Report. In: dies.: Education in Africa (= Rapport. 1993, 3), Oslo: Institute for Educational Research 1993a, S. 55-92.

Brock-Utne, Birgit: Language of Instruction in African Schools. A Socio-Cultural Perspective. In: Nordisk Pedagogik, 13 (1993b) 4, S. 225-247.

Brock-Utne, Birgit: Cultural Conditionality and Aid to Education in East Africa. In: International Review of Education, 41 (1995a) 3-4, S. 177-197.

Brock-Utne, Birgit: Educating All for Positive Peace. Education for Positive Peace or Oppression? In: International Journal of Educational Development, 15 (1995b) 3, S. 177-197.

Brock-Utne, Birgit (Hrsg.): States or Markets? Neo-Liberal Solutions in the Educational Policies of Sub-Saharan Africa. Proceedings from a Seminar. Oslo: Institute for Educational Research 1995c. (Rapport. 1995, 3)

Brock-Utne, Birgit: The Teaching of Namibian Languages in the Formal Education System of Namibia. A Study Requested by the Ministry of Basic Education and Culture in Namibia through the National Institute for Educational Development (NIED) and with the Support of the Namibia Association of Norway (NAMAS). Windhoek: NIED 1995d.

Buchert, Lene: Current Foreign Aid Patterns and Policies on Education in Developing Countries. The Case of DANIDA, SIDA and DGIS. Paper presented at the Oxford Conference on The Changing Role of the State in Educational Development, 24-28 September 1993.

Bühler, Hans / Karcher, Wolfgang / Nestvogel, Renate: Die Weltbankstudie zur Bildung in Schwarzafrika. In: Internationales Afrikaforum, 25 (1989) 4, S. 351-356.

Colclough, Christopher: States or Markets? In: Brock-Utne, Birgit (Hrsg.): States or Markets? Neo-Liberal Solutions in the Educational Policies of Sub-Saharan Africa. Proceedings from a Seminar (= Rapport. 1995, 3), Oslo: Institute for Educational Research 1995, S. 39- 79.

Conrad, Joan: A Discussion of the Concept of Quality in Relation to Educational Planning, Taking Nepal as an Example. Paper presented at the NASEDEC Conference on Quality of Education in the Context of Culture in Developing Countries, Tampere, Finland, 13-15 January 1994.

Editorial: Mayday! Mayday! In: Journal of Education for Teaching, 20 (1994) 2, S. 139-141.

Edwards, Tony: The Universities Council for the Education of Teachers. Defending an Interest or Fighting a Cause? In: Journal of Education for Teaching, 20 (1994) 2, S. 143-152.

Ishumi, Abel G. u. a. (Hrsg.): Educational Research in Tanzania. Dar es Salaam: University, Department of Education 1985. (Papers in Education and Development. 1985, 10)

Little, Angela: Education and Development. Macro Relationships and Microcultures. Brighton: University of Sussex, Institute of Development Studies 1992. (Silver Jubilee Paper. 4)

Mazrui, Ali: The African Condition. A Political Diagnosis. London: Heinemann 1980.

Mitter, Wolfgang: Staat und Markt im internationalen Bildungswesen aus historisch-vergleichender Sicht – Gegner, Konkurrenten, Partner? In: Benner, Dietrich u.a. (Hrsg.): Bildung zwischen Staat und Markt. Beiträge zum 15. Kongreß der Deutschen Gesellschaft für Erziehungswissenschaft vom 11.–13. März 1996 in Halle an der Saale (= Zeitschrift für Pädagogik. Beiheft. 35), Weinheim u.a.: Beltz 1996, S. 125-142.

Odora, Catherine: Indigenous Education in East Africa. With Special Reference to the Acholi of Uganda. In: Brock-Utne, Birgit (Hrsg.): Indigenous Forms of Learning in Africa (= Rapport. 1994, 7), Oslo: Institute for Educational Research 1994, S. 61-90.

Phillipson, Robert: Linguistic Imperialism. Oxford: Oxford University Press 1992.

Sumra, Suleman / Katunzi, Naomi: The Struggle for Education. School Fees and Girls Education in Tanzania. Dar es Salaam: University, Department of Education 1991. (WED Report. 1991, 5)

World Bank (Hrsg.): Teacher Training and Student Achievement in Less Developed Countries. Washington, D. C.: World Bank 1978. (Staff Working Paper. 310)

World Bank (Hrsg.): Education Policies for Sub-Saharan Africa. Adjustment, Revitalization and Expansion. Washington, D. C.: World Bank 1988. (Report. 6934)

Berufliche Bildung zwischen Internationalisierung und nationaler Identität

Walter Georg

Berufliche Bildung als „Standortfaktor": Globalisierung als Sachzwang

Die Diskussion über die Zukunft des deutschen „dualen Systems" der Berufsausbildung signalisiert Endzeitstimmung. Der rapide Abbau betrieblicher Ausbildungskapazitäten, beschränkte Beschäftigungsperspektiven für die Absolventen und die Zunahme zirkulärer „Maßnahmenkarrieren" außerhalb regulärer Bildungsgänge und Beschäftigungsverhältnisse sind Krisensymptome, die sich kaum mehr nur als vorübergehende Phänomene eines Konjunktureinbruchs deuten lassen. Zwar begleiten uns die Debatten um die quantitativen und qualitativen Krisen des Ausbildungssystems seit dem Ende der sechziger Jahre. Aber die Reaktionen auf die jüngsten Erosionstendenzen zeigen eine neue Qualität. Die Politik begnügt sich mit hilflosen Appellen an die soziale Verantwortung der Unternehmen, die ordnungspolitischen Forderungen der Gewerkschaften (nach Schaffung eines überbetrieblichen Finanzierungssystems) stoßen angesichts eines generellen Rückzugs des Staates auf wenig Resonanz, und die berufspädagogische Diskussion scheint sich mit den neuen Bedingungen leicht zu arrangieren, attestiert sie dem dualen System mit Verweis auf die weltweiten Globalisierungstendenzen doch seit längerem seine Untauglichkeit als Modernisierungskonzept (vgl. z. B. *Geißler 1996*). Nach dieser Argumentation gilt der spezifisch deutsche Qualifikations- und Arbeitskräftetypus des Facharbeiters als inhaltlich nicht mehr legitimierbar und als ordnungspolitisch nicht mehr begründbar.

Der Beruf als Organisationsmuster von Ausbildung und Arbeit wird gleichermaßen für die strukturellen Diskrepanzen zwischen Bildung und Beschäftigung, für Flexibilitätsdefizite auf den betriebsinternen und -externen Arbeitsmärkten und für Widerstände gegen einen Neuzuschnitt der betrieblichen Arbeitsorganisation verantwortlich gemacht. Die Bemühungen um eine Deregulierung des „Normalarbeitsverhältnisses", um eine Dezentralisierung und Rückverlagerung betrieblichen Lernens an den Arbeitsplatz und um eine Modularisierung beruflicher Ausbildungsgänge zielen auf eine Abkehr beruflicher Bildung von starren Ausbildungsordnungen und letztlich auf eine Erosion des Beruflichkeitsmusters. Die Schlagworte der neuen Erfolgsrezepte heißen Flexibilisierung und Deregulierung, Lean production und Organisationsentwicklung, Gruppenarbeit und Unternehmenskultur. Sie verheißen den Anschluß an die in der Vergangenheit scheinbar so erfolgreichen Organisationsprinzipien japanischer und anderer fernöstlicher Unternehmen, die sich weder am Modell tayloristischer Massenarbeit noch an dem beruflicher Facharbeit orientieren. Der „Sachzwang Japan" *(Wannöffel 1991)* scheint weltweit den Verlauf betrieblicher und industriegesellschaftlicher Umstrukturierung zu diktieren.

Die Internationalisierung der Debatte über Organisationsentwicklung und Personalentwicklung verweist auf weltweit identische volkswirtschaftliche und unternehmenspolitische Problemstellungen und auf eine gemeinsame Suche nach Lösungsmustern, die sich insbesondere an den Strategien erfolgreich erscheinender Industrieländer orientiert. Die Gleichförmigkeit der internationalen Argumentation scheint die Vorstellung zu stützen, daß sich die industriellen Gesellschaften in der Entwicklung ihrer gesellschaftlichen Strukturen immer ähnlicher werden. Da alle Länder denselben ökonomischen Imperativen unterliegen, müssen sie sich in ihren Industrialisierungs- und Modernisierungsstrategien an den Konzepten erfolgreicher Weltmarktkonkurrenten orientieren. Die Übernahme des Erfolgsmodells gilt bei Gefahr des eigenen Untergangs als zwangsläufig. Nach dieser universalistischen Perspektive erscheinen nationale Besonderheiten nur mehr als vorübergehende Phänomene, die auf längere Sicht dem strukturpolitischen Anpassungsdiktat zum Opfer fallen.

Die als Diskussion um die Wettbewerbsfähigkeit der eigenen Nation in Konkurrenz mit dem Ausland geführte Globalisierungsdebatte erinnert nicht selten an eine Art (Wirtschafts-)Kriegsberichterstattung, in der über Siege und Niederlagen an den Fronten der Weltmärkte berichtet und jeder Hinweis auf die inneren Krisen der vermeintlichen Konkurrenten schadenfroh zur Kenntnis genommen wird. Dabei ist die Vorstellung, daß sich Industrienationen im Wettstreit auf den Weltmärkten behaupten müssen, eher absurd. Sie basiert auf einer unzulässigen Analogie zwischen Unternehmen und Nationen *(Krugmann 1994)*. Im Gegensatz zu Unternehmen gehen Industrieländer nicht in Konkurs, die Handelsbilanz eines Landes trägt nur wenig zum Lebensstandard der Bevölkerung bei, und im Unterschied zum Nullsummenspiel zwischen konkurrierenden Unternehmen bedeutet der wirtschaftliche Erfolg eines Landes nicht den Mißerfolg der anderen. Die Konjunkturen und Krisen weltwirtschaftlicher Entwicklungen beweisen eher das Gegenteil. Aber natürlich eignet sich das Argument vom Wettbewerb zwischen den Industrienationen für die politische Auseinandersetzung – etwa um Handelssanktionen und Subventionen, um den Abbau der Sozialausgaben und die Reduktion von Arbeitsrechtsregelungen oder um die Privatisierung bislang staatlicher Aufgaben. Insofern ist die Standortdebatte eher eine interessenpolitische Facette der Auseinandersetzung um Macht und Einfluß als ein hilfreicher Beitrag zur Bewältigung von Zukunftsaufgaben.

Für die nationalen Bildungssysteme bedeutet die Transformation der Arbeitsstrukturen im Rahmen einer „global Japanization" (Elger / Smith 1994) den Verzicht auf und die Auslagerung der Erzeugung beruflicher Qualifikationen aus der staatlichen Verantwortung. Wenn das „schlanke Unternehmen" nur noch „motivierte Generalisten" braucht, dann wird das öffentliche Bildungssystem von der Vergabe berufsbezogener fachlicher Zertifikate und von der Rücksichtnahme auf berufliche Anforderungen entlastet. Umgekehrt wird die betriebliche Rekrutierungspolitik von der Berücksichtigung beruflich definierter Ausbildungszertifikate befreit. Der generelle Anstieg des durchschnittlichen individuellen Bildungsniveaus, die Abnahme der Bedeutung der industriellen Produktionsarbeit zugunsten von Dienstleistungstätigkeiten, der Bedeutungszuwachs von „überfachlichen" Qualifikationen und die Verlagerung arbeitsbezogener Qualifizierungsprozesse von einer der Erwerbsarbeit vorgelagerten beruflichen Erstausbildung zugunsten einer in den Arbeitsprozeß selbst eingebundenen betrieblichen Weiterbildung – all dies kann als empirischer Hinweis auf eine Erosion eigenständiger Berufsbildungssysteme gedeutet werden.

Bildungsexpansion und Marginalisierung der Berufsbildung: Tendenzen der Universalisierung

Die in den sechziger Jahren einsetzenden extremen Zuwachsraten der Bildungsbeteiligung stehen in einem engen, eigentümlich paradoxen Zusammenhang mit weltweit beobachtbaren bildungspolitischen Bemühungen um eine verstärkte „Verberuflichung" nationaler Bildungssysteme. Unter dem Schlagwort „vocationalism" wurde insbesondere seit Beginn der siebziger Jahre der berufsvorbereitende Unterricht in der Pflichtschulphase ausgebaut, in der Sekundarstufe II wurden berufsbezogene Bildungsgänge parallel zu oder in Kombination mit studienbezogenen Bildungsgängen eingerichtet, und auf der tertiären Ebene etablierten sich, überwiegend unterhalb der Universitätsebene, Kurzhochschulen mit dem Anspruch beruflicher Qualifizierung. Die bildungspolitischen Motive dieser Entwicklung und die daran gekoppelten Erwartungen waren ebenso vielfältig wie widersprüchlich. Mit der Diversifizierung der schulischen Curricula und dem Ausbau beruflicher Schulen sollten einerseits die Drop-outs aus den allgemeinen studienbezogenen Bildungsgängen aufgefangen und schulmüden, leistungsschwächeren Schülern und Jugendlichen mit spezifischen Begabungs- und Interessenprofilen Alternativen im öffentlichen Bildungssystem geboten werden. Andererseits diente der „vocationalism" zugleich als bildungspolitischer Hebel zur Umlenkung der Schülerströme in Bildungsgänge unterhalb der Universitätsebene und zur Eindämmung der Expansion akademischer Abschlüsse. Insofern übernahm die Ausweitung der nationalen Bildungssysteme um berufsbezogene Angebote gleichermaßen „warming up"- wie „cooling out"-Funktionen. Die Effekte der von der Verberuflichung selbst mitforcierten Bildungsexpansion sollten durch eben diese Verberuflichung zugleich abgefedert und kanalisiert werden. „Vocationalism" sollte den Übergang der Schulabsolventen in die Arbeitswelt erleichtern und damit das Ausmaß von Jugendarbeitslosigkeit verringern, zur Egalisierung der Chancen beitragen, die Akzeptanz von Arbeitsplätzen in der landwirtschaftlichen und/ oder industriellen Produktion erhöhen, den (vermeintlichen) qualitativen „mismatch" zwischen Arbeitskräftenachfrage und -angebot mildern sowie einen Beitrag zur technologischen und ökonomischen Entwicklung der nationalen Volkswirtschaften leisten.

Der größte Teil dieser Hoffnungen erwies sich schon bald als Illusion. Auf den meisten nationalen Arbeitsmärkten haben sich die Beschäftigungschancen der Absolventen beruflicher Bildungsgänge im Vergleich zu denen mit akademischen Abschlüssen kaum verbessert; das strukturelle Problem der Jugendarbeitslosigkeit hat sich mit dem Angebot berufsbezogener Schulabschlüsse ebensowenig lösen lassen wie das Problem der qualitativen Abstimmung von Arbeitsangebot und -nachfrage. Und auch die Hoffnung auf eine vermeintlich arbeitsmarktgerechte Kanalisierung und Eindämmung der Bildungsexpansion erwies sich als trügerisch. Die Erfahrung der Bildungsteilnehmer, daß die beruflichen Perspektiven mit dem Verbleib im allgemeinen Schul- und Hochschulsystem wachsen, mit der Wahl eines beruflichen Schulzweiges dagegen relativ sinken, hat die Expansion allgemeiner Bildung eher forciert. In seiner kritischen Auseinandersetzung mit der Funktion des „vocationalism" kommt *Grubb (1985, S. 540)* zu dem Ergebnis: *„Since vocational programs prepare students for occupations of lower stature and pay than academic programs, the vocational ethic of schooling has given vocational training the stigma of a second-class education."*

Offenbar unterliegt die Entwicklung der nationalen Bildungssysteme weltweit einer „bildungsmeritokratischen Logik" *(Lutz 1991)*: Die Zuweisung von Positionen und sozialem Status orientiert sich an den Zertifikaten der allgemeinen Bildungsgänge und immer weniger am Nachweis inhaltlich begründeter Fachkompetenzen – mit dem Effekt, daß berufliche Ausbildungsgänge im Wettbewerb um höhere Bildungsabschlüsse unterliegen und auf Dauer marginalisiert werden. Im Zuge der Bildungsexpansion und der Marginalisierung berufsbezogener Schulabschlüsse verlieren die höheren Bildungsabschlüsse aber auch ihren Exklusivitätscharakter. Sie werden wichtiger und wertloser zugleich: Individuell wird es immer notwendiger, sich an diesem Wettbewerb zu beteiligen; zugleich forciert die Expansion der Teilnahme eben diesen Erosionsprozeß der traditionellen Allokationsfunktion von Bildungszertifikaten. Die Flucht in allgemeine weiterführende Bildungsgänge wird zur Vermeidungsstrategie mit dem Ziel, den marginalisierenden und stigmatisierenden Effekten niedrigerer Bildungsabschlüsse zu entgehen. Mit der Zertifikatespirale verlagern sich die Verteilungskämpfe auf die jeweils nächsthöhere Bildungsebene. Diese Entwicklung läßt sich mit der Metapher vom „Rolltreppeneffekt" umschreiben, wonach das ganze System eine Zugkraft nach oben unter Beibehaltung seiner internen Hierarchien entwickelt. Innerhalb dieser Hierarchien übernehmen berufliche Schulformen tendenziell die Funktion eines Auffangbeckens für die im Wettbewerb um den Zugang zu höheren Bildungsabschlüssen Gescheiterten.

Die Enttäuschung der an den „vocationalism" geknüpften Erwartungen hat inzwischen in vielen Industrie- und Entwicklungsländern und bei den internationalen Organisationen eine Wende in der bildungs- und berufsbildungspolitischen Debatte eingeleitet. Vor allem die Weltbank, die in den siebziger Jahren die Diversifizierung schulischer Curricula zugunsten berufsvorbereitender und berufsqualifizierender Angebote intensiv propagiert und gefördert hatte, argumentiert seit Beginn der neunziger Jahre gegen eine Vermischung allgemeiner und beruflicher Bildung im öffentlichen Bildungssystem und für eine Trennung in staatlich getragene Allgemeinbildung einerseits und privat verantwortete, marktkonforme Berufsbildung andererseits *(World Bank 1991)*. Der staatlichen Bildungspolitik empfiehlt die Weltbank die Konzentration auf die Aufgabe einer Stärkung grundlegender und weiterführender allgemeiner Bildungsgänge; der wertvollste Beitrag des Staates zur Förderung der Berufsbildung liege in der Sicherstellung eines breiten Fundaments allgemeiner Bildung, auf dem die privaten Qualifizierungsmaßnahmen aufbauen können. Von einer Deregulierung und Privatisierung beruflicher Qualifizierung erwartet die Weltbank eine Steigerung der Effizienz und eine bessere Abstimmung mit den Qualifikationsanforderungen nationaler Arbeitsmärkte (zur Kritik vgl. *Lauglo 1993; Lenhart 1993; Arnold 1994a)*. Da die Weltbank über ihre Förderungspolitik zu einer der wichtigsten Steuerungsinstanzen nationaler Bildungssysteme vieler Entwicklungsländer geworden ist, dürfte diese konzeptionelle Wende in der Berufsbildungszusammenarbeit die Privatisierung arbeitsmarktbezogener Qualifizierung und den Exodus beruflicher Bildung aus der öffentlichen Bildungspolitik zusätzlich beschleunigen.

Nationale Tradition und berufliche Bildung:
Zum Beharrungsvermögen von Berufsbildungsstrukturen

Versteht man Modernisierung als einen Prozeß kultureller Säkularisierung, d. h. als einen Prozeß, in dessen Verlauf Menschen rationaler, analytischer und erfahrungsorientierter zu entscheiden lernen, dann stehen traditionelle Wert- und Normkomplexe als Inseln der Nichtrationalität der Herausbildung von Modernität im Weg. In den Modernisierungs- und Universalisierungstheorien gelten kulturelle Traditionen als transitorische Residualkategorie oder auch als fest verwurzeltes Hindernis gesellschaftlicher Innovationen: Die Verweigerung von Rationalität wird mit dauerhaftem Entwicklungsrückstand bestraft. Tatsächlich aber kann kein Berufsbildungssystem eines Industrielandes für sich in Anspruch nehmen, seine Strukturen aus den funktionalen Erfordernissen und der Sachlogik industrieller Qualifikationsforderungen entwickelt zu haben. Das ist schon daran erkennbar, daß selbst die hochentwickelten Industrieländer trotz weitgehend identischer volkswirtschaftlicher Zielsetzungen höchst divergente Berufsbildungssysteme und ebenso unterschiedliche Qualifikationstypen und Grundmuster betrieblicher Arbeitsorganisation aufweisen. Die Industrialisierungsprozesse in den europäischen und außereuropäischen Ländern haben bisher keine Entwicklung zu einem „industrietypischen" Berufsbildungsmodell in Gang gesetzt. Ebensowenig ist es der Entwicklungszusammenarbeit gelungen, die Berufsbildungserfahrungen der Industrieländer für die Formulierung eines überzeugenden einheitlichen Modells beruflicher Bildung in Entwicklungsländern fruchtbar zu machen.

Die weltweite Varianz der Regelungsmuster beruflicher Bildung läßt sich also kaum in einen systematischen Zusammenhang mit dem Modernisierungsgrad und den ökonomischen Erfolgen der einzelnen Länder bringen. Traditionell-korporatistische Formen der Lehre, berufliche Vollzeitschulen oder betriebliche Varianten des On-the-job-Trainings finden sich gleichermaßen in Entwicklungs-, Schwellen- und Industrieländern (vgl. z. B. die Übersichten in *Lauterbach u. a. 1995ff.*). Volkswirtschaftliche Entwicklung und betriebswirtschaftliche Erfolge scheinen ebensowenig an bestimmte Qualifizierungsmuster gebunden zu sein wie umgekehrt bestimmte Konfigurationen von Berufsbildung bestimmte ökonomische Effekte auslösen. Dennoch sind solche nationalspezifischen Konfigurationen weder beliebig noch beliebig austauschbar. Versuche einer transnationalen Übertragung von Berufsbildungsmodellen stoßen immer wieder auf Adaptionsbarrieren, die auf die Einbindung von Bildungsstrukturen in den spezifischen historischen, kulturellen und sozialen Kontext eines Landes verweisen. Die Differenzierung und Heterogenisierung der Entwicklungspfade in der Ersten, Zweiten und Dritten

Welt verweisen darauf, daß sich Entwicklung und Modernisierung nicht mehr im Rahmen eines globalen Paradigmas erklären lassen *(Menzel 1992)*.

Kulturen finden ihren Ausdruck in den Strukturen und Funktionen von Organisationen und Institutionen einer Gesellschaft. Die besonderen Ausprägungen von Ausbildungssystem, Arbeitsorganisation, Arbeitsbeziehungen usw. sind das Ergebnis kollektiver und individueller Werthaltungen und Präferenzen und sie sorgen ihrerseits als Sozialisationsagenturen für deren Stabilisierung. Betriebliche Rekrutierungskriterien, Leistungsanforderungen und Sanktionsmechanismen enthalten Mitgliedschaftsentwürfe und Erwartungsmuster, in denen sich kulturspezifische Wertvorstellungen und Teilnahmeregeln widerspiegeln. Diese kulturellen Leitbilder finden sich – wenn auch in unterschiedlicher Varianz – in den organisationsinternen Strukturen und Spielregeln der vorgelagerten Sozialisationsagenturen wieder. Betriebliche Muster der Ausbildungs- und Arbeitsorganisation lassen sich dann als eine Fortsetzung der traditionell verankerten Sozialisations- und Kommunikationsmuster in Familie und Schule interpretieren. In einer Gesellschaft, in der Gruppenorientierung, Harmoniestreben und vertikale Loyalität einen hohen Stellenwert haben, finden sich entsprechende Spielregeln und Strukturen gleichermaßen in Familie, Schule, Betrieb und anderen sozialen Institutionen (vgl. z. B. *Hirata 1991*).

Kulturelle Unterschiede erfordern danach immer auch unterschiedliche Organisationsstrukturen. Organisationen als soziale Gebilde sind eingebunden in eine kulturelle Umwelt, die einer Veränderbarkeit und Manipulierbarkeit von „Organisationskultur" durch ein gezieltes Kulturmanagement enge Grenzen setzt. Die in einer Gesellschaft vorherrschenden Werte, Normen, Einstellungen, Überzeugungen und Ideale können im Rahmen von Organisationskulturen zwar funktionalistisch genutzt, nicht aber unterlaufen oder dauerhaft korrigiert werden. Veränderungen versprechen nur dann Erfolg, wenn sie mit den „mentalen Programmen" der Akteure und der kulturellen und institutionellen Umgebung kompatibel sind *(Hofstede 1993)*. Zentralisierung oder Dezentralisierung von Verantwortung, das Ausmaß der Formalisierung, Standardisierung und Spezialisierung von Arbeitsaufgaben im Rahmen der Ausbildungs- und Arbeitsorganisation, der Zuschnitt von horizontalen und vertikalen Karrieren sind immer auch an Regeln gebunden, die allgemeine gesellschaftliche Anerkennung finden. Diese „relative Absolutheit" (*Stagl 1992*) nationaler Kulturen verpflichtet gleichermaßen zur gegenseitigen Achtung wie auch zur Respektierung kulturimmanenter Regelwerke bei der Variation von Organisationsstrukturen.

Berufliche Bildung zwischen Internationalisierung und nationaler Identität

Studien zum nationalspezifischen Zusammenhang von Arbeit, Technik und Qualifikation zeigen, daß sich nicht nur die Organisationsprinzipien von Ausbildung und Arbeitsgestaltung in den einzelnen Industrieländern unterscheiden, sondern daß auch die Entwicklung und Anwendung von Technik als abhängige Variablen der jeweiligen „Industriekultur" zu verstehen sind (vgl. *Rauner/Ruth 1991; Laske 1995; Rasmussen/Rauner 1996).* Die parallele Existenz unterschiedlicher Entwicklungs- und Anwendungspfade von Technik läßt sich aus deren Einbindung in ein gleichermaßen komplexes wie konsistentes Gefüge gesellschaftlicher Dimensionen erklären, deren Ausprägung und wechselseitige Verflechtungen das Spezifische einer jeden Industriekultur ausmachen. Die Rückkoppelungsmechanismen zwischen Entwicklung und Anwendung von Technik sorgen dafür, daß die Suche nach technischen Funktionslösungen immer auch mitbestimmt wird von den gewachsenen Strukturen von Qualifikation und Arbeitsorganisation auf der Anwenderseite.

Trotz der Internationalisierung technischen Wissens und der Globalisierung der Weltmärkte haben sich die jeweils spezifischen Bedingungen von Technikentwicklung und Technikanwendung und die Organisationsprinzipien von Ausbildung und Arbeit in den Industrieländern in geringerem Maße einander angeglichen, als es die These vom weltweiten ökonomischen, technologischen und sozialpolitischen Imperativ nahelegt. Die Entwicklungen verweisen eher umgekehrt auf eine wachsende Bedeutung nationaler Kulturen und Organisationsstrukturen. Mit der rasanten Verbreitung der Mikroelektronik sind neue Möglichkeiten für eine „flexible Spezialisierung" *(Piore/Sabel 1986)* und damit für die Unternehmen neue strategische Optionen entstanden, die sich gleichermaßen auf die Gestaltbarkeit von Produkten und Produktionsverfahren, Technikeinsatz, Arbeitsorganisation und Qualifizierung beziehen. Die dadurch entstandenen unternehmenspolitischen Handlungsspielräume eröffnen zusätzliche Möglichkeiten des Rückgriffs auf solche Strategien, die mit den institutionellen Strukturen, Konventionen, Normen und Werten der nationalspezifischen Umwelt kompatibel sind.

Soweit sich in den Industrieländern Veränderungen in Arbeitsorganisation und Qualifizierung nachweisen lassen, so folgen diese bisher kaum einer weltweit gültigen Logik industrieller Entwicklung im Sinne eines wie auch immer definierten „one best way", sondern eher einer gesellschafts- und kulturspezifischen Entwicklungslogik, die in unterschiedlichen traditionellen Ordnungen sozialen Handelns und innergesellschaftlicher Funktionalitäten wurzelt. Universalistische Herausforderungen erzeugen zwar Anpassungserfordernisse, aber die kulturellen Tiefenstrukturen und gesellschaftlichen Wechselbeziehungen erzeugen immer wieder nationalspezifische Abweichungen und Sonder-wege. Die Besonderheiten der Auswahl aus einer Vielzahl möglicher Lösungsansätze entstehen dadurch, daß die gesuchten Problemlösungen in den verschiedenen gesellschaftlichen Teilbereichen miteinander in Beziehung stehen und kompatibel sein müssen. Dieses Erfordernis der Kompatibilität und inneren Stimmigkeit bestimmt die besondere Logik gesellschaftsspezifischer Entwicklung *(Stagl 1992)*. Zugleich muß diese Entwicklung immer auch hinreichend offen sein für die Anpassung an neue Problemlagen. Kulturen sind also keine statischen Gebilde, sondern sie sind zur Sicherung ihres eigenen Überlebens angewiesen auf eine partielle Offenheit gegenüber der Verarbeitung „fremder" Kultureindrücke. Erst diese Elastizität sichert die Problemlösungskapazität und Anpassungsfähigkeit sozialer Systeme und damit auch ihre jeweils spezifische „Modernität", die sich aus der Symbiose kultureller Tradition und externer Austauschprozesse ergibt.

Berufliche Bildung in Japan und Deutschland: Kontextspezifische Differenzen

Die jeweilige Interaktion des sozialen Handlungssystems „berufliche Bildung" mit anderen vor-, neben- und nachgelagerten gesellschaftlichen Handlungssystemen und deren funktional-struktureller Zusammenhang erklären erst den kulturspezifischen „Sinn" beruflicher Bildung *(Clement 1996)*. Mit Bezug auf Luhmann definiert *Greinert (1995, S. 31)* ein Berufsbildungssystem als *„Sinnzusammenhang von Handlungen bzw. von Kommunikation, der sich auf ein bestimmtes Problem bzw. spezifische Probleme hin aus anderen Sinnbezügen ausdifferenziert und von seiner Umwelt abgegrenzt hat"*. Von der Konstituierung und Reproduktion eines „Systems" beruflicher Bildung auf der Basis sinnhafter Kommunikation kann also erst dann gesprochen werden, wenn es sich im Zuge der gesellschaftlichen Ausdifferenzierung funktionsspezifischer Teilsysteme als selektiver Kommunikationszusammenhang verselbständigt und dauerhaft etabliert hat. Dazu gehört ein besonderes Maß an selbstreferentieller Geschlossenheit und Abgrenzung gegenüber Einflüssen der innergesellschaftlichen Umwelt *(Schriewer 1987, S. 85)*. Insofern läßt sich mit Recht von einem „deutschen System" der Berufsausbildung *(Greinert 1993)* sprechen: Die soziale Verallgemeinerung des Berufs zum sinnhaften Medium für die Konstitution und Reproduktion von Ausbildungsstrukturen war die historische Voraussetzung für die Ausdifferenzierung eines vom Schulsystem und Betriebssystem (relativ) unabhängigen, selbstbezüglichen Berufsbildungssystems. *„Selbstbezüglichkeit in diesem Sinne heißt, daß der Beruf zur typischen, systemisch immer wieder reproduzierten eigenständigen Perspektive auf soziale und wirtschaftliche Problemlagen wird und* *nicht mehr nur als untergeordneter Bestandteil anderer Systemzusammenhänge vorkommt" (Harney / Storz 1994, S. 355).*

Entsprechende Ausdifferenzierungen eigenständiger „Systeme" beruflicher Bildung mit dem Merkmal der Selbstbezüglichkeit ihrer internen Strukturen und Verarbeitungsmechanismen finden sich im Ausland nur selten. Soweit Berufsausbildung in Schulen stattfindet, sind solche Schulen mehr oder weniger in das allgemeine Schulwesen integriert. Die Mechanismen der schulsysteminternen Strukturierung und Hierarchisierung folgen der Logik der Meritokratie mit den bekannten Effekten einer zunehmenden Marginalisierung fachspezifischer Qualifizierung, wie sie sich auch für die Entwicklung beruflicher Vollzeitschulen in Deutschland nachweisen läßt *(Georg 1984)*. Jedenfalls bleiben solche schulischen Ausbildungsvarianten auf die Logik des allgemeinen Bildungssystems bezogen, also ein untergeordneter, unselbständiger Bestandteil eines „anderen" Systemzusammenhangs. Ein solcher Mangel an Eigenlogik und Selbstbezüglichkeit gilt erst recht für all jene Ausbildungsstrukturen, die in Form betrieblicher Anlernung und Weiterbildung unmittelbar in die Logik betrieblicher Produktions- und Arbeitsorganisation eingebunden sind. Der Sinnzusammenhang von Qualifizierungsmaßnahmen ergibt sich dann nur mehr aus der betriebsspezifischen Reproduktion des Arbeitsvermögens.

Die japanische Variante der Reproduktion des Arbeitsvermögens zeichnet sich durch eine weitgehende Privatisierung und Verbetrieblichung arbeitsbezogener Qualifizierung aus (vgl. *Georg 1993; Demes / Georg 1994)*. Der Beitrag des öffentlichen Bildungssystems zur Entwicklung arbeitsbezogener fachlicher Qualifikationen gilt als marginal. Den Zertifikaten des Schulsystems wird zwar eine entscheidende Allokationsfunktion bezüglich vertikal abgestufter Einstiegs- und Karrierechancen zugeschrieben. Die curriculare Differenzierung des Schul- und Hochschulwesens und die daran geknüpften Titel und Zertifikate haben jedoch nur einen geringen Einfluß auf eine horizontale Differenzierung von Berufslaufbahnen nach Tätigkeitsfeldern. Die an den Besuch bestimmter Bildungseinrichtungen geknüpften Beschäftigungserwartungen richten sich nicht auf bestimmte Inhalte und Bedingungen beruflicher Arbeit, sondern auf den – vor allem nach der Größenordnung und damit der Beschäftigungssicherheit und Karriereperspektive definierten – Unternehmenstypus.

Umgekehrt orientiert sich die betriebliche Personalrekrutierung nicht an der Einbringung beruflich-fachlicher Qualifikationen, sondern eher an den aus der spezifischen Bildungskarriere mitgebrachten Sozialisationseffekten. Die weitgehende Offenheit zukünftiger Arbeitsrollen und die unternehmerische Erwartung an eine mit den Zielen und

Werten der Organisation konforme Einstellung geben den „Charaktereigenschaften" des Bewerbers als einem Rekrutierungskriterium zentrale Relevanz. Bildungsabschlüsse erfüllen als „biographische Signale" die Funktion, den Grad der Lernfähigkeit, der Arbeitsorientierung und der Integrationsbereitschaft des Bewerbers anzuzeigen. Der in Japan zur Kennzeichnung des Zusammenhangs von Bildung und Beschäftigung gebräuchliche Ausdruck *gakureki shakai* (Bildungsgangsgesellschaft) signalisiert, daß die Koppelung von Bildungserfolg und Berufserfolg besonders eng und ausgeprägt ist. Das Maß der in der Bildungskarriere nachgewiesenen Lern-, Leistungs- und Anpassungsfähigkeit liefert noch immer die wichtigste Legitimation für die Übergänge der Absolventen in unterschiedlich attraktive Beschäftigungssegmente wie auch für den dualen Segmentationszuschnitt des Arbeitsmarktes.

Ein Beschäftigungssystem wie das japanische, in dem Qualifikationen zwar einen unternehmensbezogenen Gebrauchswert, kaum aber einen arbeitsmarktbezogenen Tauschwert haben, setzt einen weitgehend abgeschlossenen betriebsinternen Arbeitsmarkt voraus, auf dem soziale Qualifikationskomponenten wie Anpassungsfähigkeit und Einordnungsbereitschaft sowie Kooperationsfähigkeit und Gruppenorientierung einen besonders hohen Stellenwert erhalten. Technisch-funktionale Qualifikationen fallen eher als „Kuppelprodukte" der Arbeitszuweisung und der über wechselnde Arbeitsgruppen gesteuerten betrieblichen Sozialisationsprozesse an. Damit erhält die Gestaltung der betrieblichen Arbeitsorganisation, also die Verteilung der Arbeitsfunktionen und Verantwortlichkeiten auf Arbeitsplätze und Personen, die Ausprägung der Arbeitsbeziehungen untereinander sowie der Grad der Entscheidungsbefugnisse und Gestaltungsmöglichkeiten der Arbeitenden, einen entscheidenden Stellenwert für die Entwicklung und Verwertung von Qualifikationen und für die Reichweite und Schrittfolge „beruflicher" Karrieren. Einerseits definiert die Arbeitsorganisation (wegen des fehlenden überbetrieblichen Berufszuschnitts) die Möglichkeiten und Grenzen des individuellen Qualifikationserwerbs im Betrieb, andererseits eröffnet der fehlende Berufszuschnitt größere arbeitsorganisatorische Gestaltungsspielräume, er macht deren optimale Nutzung zugleich aber auch notwendiger.

Der Integrationsmodus des japanischen „Betriebsclans" *(Deutschmann 1987)* zeichnet sich aus durch eine an die alltägliche Lebenswelt anschließende, diese geradezu vereinnahmende Organisationskultur, die formalisierte Muster der Arbeitsorganisation ebenso erübrigt wie bürokratische Muster von beruflicher Aus- und Weiterbildung. Die Andersartigkeit japanischer Ausbildungs- und Arbeitsorganisation läßt sich deshalb auch weniger an der Besonderheit formaler Strukturen festmachen als vielmehr an der besonderen

Bedeutung informeller Kommunikations- und Kooperationsstrukturen sowie sozialer Bindungen und Beziehungen. Die im japanischen Organisationstypus verankerten Mechanismen der Konformitätssicherung und Verhaltenssteuerung mit dem Effekt einer besonders hohen Einsatz- und Leistungsbereitschaft japanischer Arbeitnehmer sind eng an die Schutzfunktion der Beschäftigungsgarantie und des Senioritätsprinzips für die Kernbelegschaften gebunden. Es sind die strukturspezifischen „Spielregeln" wie Entlohnungssystem, Beförderungsregeln und Karrieremuster, die das Loyalitätsverhalten steuern und die Stammbeschäftigten dauerhaft an das Unternehmen binden.

Im Unterschied zur betriebsbezogenen aufgabenspezifischen Anlernung dient die an Berufen orientierte Ausbildung in Deutschland nicht nur der betriebsspezifischen Reproduktion des Arbeitsvermögens, sondern – und darin liegt der zentrale Unterschied – auch der überbetrieblichen Herstellung beruflich definierter Facharbeitsmärkte. Mit der Existenz eines überbetrieblichen Berufsausbildungssystems und berufsfachlicher Arbeitsmärkte in Deutschland sind notwendigerweise auch andersartige Strukturen des Übergangs in das Beschäftigungssystem, des Arbeitsmarktes, der Arbeitgeber-Arbeitnehmer-Beziehungen, der Arbeitsteilung, der Gratifikationssysteme und der Karriereverläufe verbunden. Selbst wenn den beruflichen Zertifikaten nur eingeschränkte Validität als Indikator für das jeweilige Arbeitsvermögen zukommt, so steuern sie doch die Zugangschancen sowie die Selektions- und Allokationsprozesse auf dem Arbeitsmarkt. Während für Japan eine Zweiteilung des Arbeitsmarktes in ein primäres Segment der Kernbelegschaften mit weitgehend sicheren Arbeitsplätzen und ein sekundäres Segment von Randbelegschaften mit unsicheren, deutlich schlechter entlohnten Arbeitsverhältnissen kennzeichnend ist, gilt für Deutschland das Modell eines dreigeteilten Arbeitsmarktes: Neben einem innerbetrieblichen Teilarbeitsmarkt und einem externen Jedermann-Arbeitsmarkt dominiert der berufsfachliche Teilarbeitsmarkt, auf dem die zwischenbetriebliche Mobilität durch den Nachweis überbetrieblich normierter Ausbildungszertifikate gesichert wird. Die berufliche Prägung der betrieblichen Arbeitsorganisation schließt Arbeitskräfte ohne entsprechend zertifizierte Qualifikationen vom Zugang zu den einschlägigen Arbeitsfeldern aus und macht damit den berufsfachlichen Teilarbeitsmarkt zu einem geschlossenen Segment. Mit der institutionellen Schließung berufszentrierter Teilarbeitsmärkte eröffnen sich innerhalb dieser Märkte zugleich Spielräume für zwischenbetriebliche horizontale Mobilitätsprozesse. Insofern bedeutet die Existenz berufsfachlicher Arbeitsmärkte immer auch eine latente Gefährdung der Stabilität betriebsinterner Arbeitsmärkte *(Georg / Sattel 1995)*.

Beruflichkeit der Ausbildung und der Arbeitsorganisation macht den Aufgabenzuschnitt von der einzelnen Person unabhängig, trägt zur Versachlichung der innerbetrieblichen Sozialbeziehungen bei und verschafft dem Berufsinhaber eine relative Autonomie gegenüber dem einzelnen Betrieb. Der Zugriff des Unternehmens auf die Person des Arbeitenden bleibt beschränkt auf den Rahmen der arbeits- und tarifvertraglichen Arbeitsbedingungen und der vom einzelnen Beruf fixierten Zumutbarkeitsgrenzen. Insofern definiert der Beruf auch das Reproduktionsvermögen der Arbeitskräfte, jene Qualifikationsmomente also, die einen übermäßigen Verschleiß und cine ausschließlich betriebsspezifische Vernutzung von Arbeitskraft verhindern. Berufe bilden den Rahmen für das Ausmaß an Akzeptanz bzw. Kritik betrieblicher Hierarchiestrukturen, Entscheidungsmuster und Arbeitsbelastungen. Vor allem diese Differenz zwischen Berufs- und Betriebszentrismus begründet, weshalb sich japanische Arbeitnehmer dem Zugriff ihres Unternehmens auch außerhalb von Arbeitszeit und Arbeitsrolle weitaus weniger entziehen können als Arbeitnehmer in westlichen Industrieländern.

Nationalspezifische Formen beruflicher Ausbildung stehen also in wechselseitiger Interdependenz mit der charakteristischen Ausprägung anderer organisationsstruktureller Dimensionen. Der gesellschaftsspezifische, industriekulturelle Charakter der Interrelationen liegt in der stabilen Interaktion von Faktorenbündeln, die sich wechselseitig beeinflussen. Die Akteure reproduzieren die Charakteristika in den jeweilgen Dimensionen und Interrelationen auf der Basis spezifischer historischer Ausgangsbedingungen und nach dem Muster der sich daraus ergebenden Handlungs- und Entwicklungslogik.

Stabilität und Wandel: Nationale und internationale Perspektiven

Solange die westlichen Industrieländer noch das weltweite Monopol ökonomischen Erfolgs für sich beanspruchen konnten, galt Modernisierung nach westlichem Muster als ein quasi-naturgesetzlicher Prozeß ökonomischen und gesellschaftlichen Wandels, der sich durch die Steigerung von Rationalität sowie technischer und ökonomischer Effizienz und die Durchsetzung bürokratischer Organisation auszeichnete. Die Erschütterung des traditionellen Überlegenheitsanspruchs des Westens durch die spektakulären Weltmarkterfolge Japans und anderer ostasiatischer Länder hat die Begründungsmuster der bisher für gültig gehaltenen Modernisierungstheorien radikal in Frage gestellt. Rationale Bürokratie und formale Organisation verlieren allmählich ihre Geltung als Ausdrucksformen gesellschaftlicher Modernisierung. Die wirtschaftliche Leistungsfähigkeit Japans und der „newly industrialized countries" (NICs) ist inzwischen derjenigen westlicher Industrieländer vergleichbar, ohne daß sich die Organisationsstrukturen der Berufsbildung und die betrieblichen personalpolitischen Strategien denen der westlichen Gesellschaften angeglichen hätten (vgl. z. B. *Georg 1993; Schoenfeldt 1996).*

Westliche Modernisierungstheorien gingen davon aus, daß sich die weniger entwikelten Länder von ihrer „vormodernen" Vergangenheit nur durch die Übernahme moderner, d. h. westlicher Institutionen befreien könnten. Ihnen lag die Vorstellung von der Möglichkeit und Notwendigkeit einer Wiederholung jenes gesellschaftlichen Transformationsprozesses zugrunde, der die Entwicklung von einer Agrargesellschaft zu einer „modernen" westlichen Industrie- und Dienstleistungsökonomie kennzeichnet. In dieser – eurozentrischen – Perspektive mußte die in den ostasiatischen Industrieländern gelungene Synthese von ökonomischer Modernisierung und Stabilität traditioneller Sozialformen eher als Schizophrenie erscheinen, als unvollständige, verkürzte Übernahme westlicher Zivilisation. Nach einem solchen Modernitätsverständnis weisen die ostasiatischen Varianten der Organisation mit der Betonung informeller Kommunikations- und Kooperationsstrukturen sowie sozialer Bindungen und persönlicher Beziehungen gegenüber der Versachlichung westlicher Organisationsstrukturen deutliche Rückstände auf. Die im Westen lange vorherrschende Überzeugung, daß solche Traditionalismen den rationalen Notwendigkeiten im Wege stünden und den Modernisierungsprozeß eher behinderten, verstellt den Blick auf das vielfältige endogene Entwicklungspotential, das in diesen kulturellen Traditionen steckt.

Die ökonomischen Erfolge Japans und anderer ostasiatischer Länder zwingen zu der Feststellung, daß inzwischen andere moderne Welten entstanden sind, deren kulturelle Besonderheiten nicht nur in marginalen Differenzen zum tradierten Modernitätsbegriff des Westens liegen, sondern die im Zuge ihrer gesellschaftlichen Transformation etwas qualitativ Neues hervorgebracht haben, dessen Phänomene sich unserer bisherigen Vorstellung von Modernität weitgehend entziehen. Im Zuge der weltweiten Internationalisierungs- und Globalisierungstendenzen kommt es zwar zu gegenseitigen Beeinflussungen und Veränderungen innerhalb der einzelnen Gesellschaften und ihrer Teilstrukturen, aber offenbar nicht zu einer Konvergenz im Sinne eines einheitlichen Modernisierungspfades. Kulturen sind zwar keine statischen Gebilde, sondern befinden sich in permanenter Veränderung *(Stagl 1992),* jedoch folgen diese Veränderungen einer kultur- bzw. gesellschaftsspezifischen Entwicklungslogik. Der verbreitete Einsatz neuer Technologien hat in allen Industrieländern Bewegung in die überkommenen arbeitsorganisatorischen und personalpolitischen Strukturen gebracht. Aber diese Veränderungen haben die grundlegenden Organisationsprinzipien von Bildung und Beschäftigung bisher kaum gefährdet.

Dieser Befund bestätigt zum einen eine gewisse Äquivalenz unterschiedlicher sozialer Systeme. Zum anderen verweist er auf die hohe Bedeutung des jeweiligen gesellschaftlichen Gesamtzusammenhanges für die Entwicklung von Unternehmensstrategien. Unternehmen sind nicht nur Organisationen zur Bewältigung technischer und ökonomischer Aufgaben, sondern auch Teil eines kulturellen und sozialen Kontextes, der das unternehmerische Handeln wesentlich mitbestimmt. Modernisierung ist also viel weniger ein ausschließlich zweckrational begründeter Prozeß als häufig angenommen. Traditionelle und affektiv besetzte Wertvorstellungen begründen ihrerseits Funktionalitäten und eine erstaunliche historisch-gesamtgesellschaftliche Kontinuität.

Die weitgehende Unabhängigkeit ökonomischer Erfolge vom (westlich interpretierten) Modernisierungsgrad eines Landes verweist darauf, daß Tradition und Moderne keine Gegensätze sind, sondern daß moderne Gesellschaften traditioneller und traditionelle Gesellschaften moderner sind, als die Modernisierungstheorie glauben macht (*Berger 1996, S. 11*). Moderne und Tradition sind insofern identisch, als es sich immer um eine jeweils spezifische, also traditionsgebundene Moderne handelt. An traditionellen Kulturen lassen sich ebensowenig eindeutig hemmende Faktoren identifizieren, wie sich umgekehrt keine eindeutig modernitätsförderlichen Faktoren in „modernen" Kulturen isolieren lassen. Das damit immer auch verbundene Postulat der Respektierung nationaler Kulturen als Ausgangsbedingungen und integrale Bestandteile eigenständiger Entwicklung ist letztlich das Eingeständnis der Ohnmacht, Entwicklung und Modernisierung im Rahmen eines globalen Paradigmas zu erklären. Diese Einsicht zwingt nicht nur zu einer „neuen Bescheidenheit" des Westens, sondern erinnert auch an die Notwendigkeit, sich der Traditionsgebundenheit der eigenen „modernen" Organisationsstrukturen bewußt zu sein.

Bibliographie

Arnold, Rolf: Neue Akzente der internationalen Berufsbildungs-Debatte – Impulse für eine künftige Entwicklungszusammenarbeit im Bereich der beruflichen Bildung? Ein Literaturreport. In: Biermann, Horst u. a. (Hrsg.): Systementwicklung in der Berufsbildung (= Studien zur vergleichenden Berufspädagogik. 5), Baden-Baden: Nomos-Verlagsgesellschaft 1994a, S. 13-45.

Arnold, Rolf: Unternehmenskulturentwicklung – eine zentrale Aufgabe für Bildungsmanagement. In: Geißler, Harald (Hrsg.): Bildungsmanagement (= Betriebliche Bildung. 5), Frankfurt a. M. u. a.: Lang 1994b, S. 282-297.

Berger, Johannes: Modernisierung und Modernisierungstheorie. In: Leviathan, 24 (1996) 1, S. 8-12.

Clement, Ute: Vom Sinn beruflicher Bildung. Zur Modellbildung in der vergleichenden Berufsbildungsforschung. In: Zeitschrift für Berufs- und Wirtschaftspädagogik, 92 (1996) 6, S. 617-626.

Demes, Helmut / Georg, Walter (Hrsg.): Gelernte Karriere. Bildung und Berufsverlauf in Japan. München: Iudicium-Verlag 1994. (Monographien aus dem Deutschen Institut für Japanstudien der Philipp-Franz-von-Siebold-Stiftung. 9)

Deutschmann, Christoph: Der „Betriebsclan". Der japanische Organisationstypus als Herausforderung an die soziologische Modernisierungstheorie. In: Soziale Welt, 38 (1987) 2, S. 133-147.

Elger, Tony / Smith, Chris (Hrsg.): Global Japanization? The Transnational Transformation of the Labour Process. London u. a.: Routledge 1994.

Geißler, Karlheinz A.: Abschied bei laufendem Betrieb. Die Krise des dualen Systems der industriellen Berufsausbildung. In: Weilnböck-Buck, Ingelore u. a. (Hrsg.): Bildung – Organisation – Qualität. Zum Wandel in den Unternehmen und den Konsequenzen für die Berufsbildung, Bielefeld: Bertelsmann 1996, S. 41-57.

Georg, Walter: Schulberufe und berufliche Schulen. Zum Funktionswandel beruflicher Vollzeitschulen. In: ders. (Hrsg.): Schule und Berufsausbildung, Bielefeld: Bertelsmann 1984, S. 103-126.

Georg, Walter: Berufliche Bildung des Auslands: Japan. Zum Zusammenhang von Qualifizierung und Beschäftigung in Japan im Vergleich zur Bundesrepublik Deutschland. Baden-Baden: Nomos-Verlagsgesellschaft 1993. (Internationale Weiterbildung, Austausch, Entwicklung. 8)

Georg, Walter / Sattel, Ulrike: Arbeitsmarkt, Beschäftigungssystem und Berufsbildung. In: Arnold, Rolf / Lipsmeier, Antonius (Hrsg.): Handbuch der Berufsbildung, Opladen: Leske und Budrich 1995, S. 123-141.

Greinert, Wolf-Dietrich: Das „deutsche System" der Berufsausbildung. Geschichte, Organisation, Perspektiven. Baden-Baden: Nomos-Verlagsgesellschaft 1993. (Studien zur vergleichenden Berufspädagogik. 1)

Greinert, Wolf-Dietrich: Regelungsmuster der beruflichen Bildung. Tradition – Markt – Bürokratie. In: Berufsbildung in Wissenschaft und Praxis, 24 (1995) 5, S. 31-35.

Grubb, W. Norton: The Convergence of Educational Systems and the Role of Vocationalism. In: Comparative Education Review, 29 (1985) 4, S. 526-548.

Harney, Klaus / Storz, Peter: Strukturwandel beruflicher Bildung. In: Müller, Detlef K. (Hrsg.): Pädagogik, Erziehungswissenschaft, Bildung, Köln u. a.: Böhlau 1994, S. 353-381.

Hirata, Helena Sumiko: Brasilien, Frankreich, Japan. Unterschiede und die Suche nach Bedeutung. In: Heidenreich, Martin / Schmidt, Gert (Hrsg.): International vergleichende Organisationsforschung, Opladen: Westdeutscher Verlag 1991, S. 180-189.

Hofstede, Geert: Organisationsentwicklung in verschiedenen Kulturen. In: Fatzer, Gerhard (Hrsg.): Organisationsentwicklung für die Zukunft, Köln: Edition Humanistische Psychologie 1993, S. 327-348.

Krugmann, Paul: Wettlauf der Besessenen. In: Die Zeit, 49 (1994) 18, S. 40-41.

Laske, Gabriele: Eine Musterbranche stürzt ab. Werkzeugmaschinenbau in den USA und in Deutschland. Bremen: Donat 1995. (Schriftenreihe berufliche Bildung)

Lauglo, Jon: Vocational Training. Analysis of Policy and Modes. Paris: UNESCO, International Institute for Educational Planning 1993.

Lauterbach, Uwe u. a. (Hrsg.): Internationales Handbuch der Berufsbildung. Baden-Baden: Nomos-Verlagsgesellschaft 1995ff. (Internationale Weiterbildung, Austausch, Entwicklung. 9) (Loseblattsammlung)

Lenhart, Volker: „Bildung für alle". Zur Bildungskrise in der Dritten Welt. Darmstadt: Wissenschaftliche Buchgesellschaft 1993. (WB-Forum. 77)

Lutz, Burkart: Herausforderungen an eine zukunftsorientierte Berufsbildungspolitik. In: Die Rolle der beruflichen Bildung und Berufsbildungspolitik im internationalen Vergleich, Berlin u. a.: Bundesinstitut für Berufsbildung 1991, S. 27-39.

Menzel, Ulrich: Das Ende der Dritten Welt und das Scheitern der großen Theorie. Frankfurt a. M.: Suhrkamp 1992. (edition suhrkamp. 1718)

Piore, Michael J. / Sabel, Charles F.: Das Ende der Massenproduktion. Studie über die Requalifizierung der Arbeit und die Rückkehr der Ökonomie in der Gesellschaft. Berlin: Wagenbach 1986.

Rasmussen, Lauge / Rauner, Felix (Hrsg.): Industrial Cultures and Production. Understanding Competitiveness. London u. a.: Springer 1996.

Rauner, Felix / Ruth, Klaus: Perspektiven der Forschung zur Industriekultur: In: Hildebrandt, Eckart (Hrsg.): Betriebliche Sozialverfassung unter Veränderungsdruck, Berlin: Edition Sigma 1991, S. 172-203.

Schoenfeldt, Eberhard: Der Edle ist kein Instrument. Bildung und Ausbildung in Korea (Republik). Studien zu einem Land zwischen China und Japan. Kassel: UniversitätGesamthochschule, Fachbereich zwei 1996. (Berufs- und Wirtschaftspädagogik. 22)

Schriewer, Jürgen: Funktionssymbiosen von Überschneidungsbereichen. Systemtheoretische Konstrukte in vergleichender Erziehungsforschung. In: Oelkers, Jürgen / Tenorth, Heinz-Elmar (Hrsg.): Pädagogik, Erziehungswissenschaft und Systemtheorie, Weinheim u. a.: Beltz 1987, S. 76-101.

Schriewer, Jürgen: Internationalisierung der Pädagogik und Vergleichende Erziehungswissenschaft. In: Müller, Detlef K. (Hrsg.): Pädagogik, Erziehungswissenschaft, Bildung, Köln u. a.: Böhlau 1994, S. 427-472.

Stagl, Justin: Eine Widerlegung des kulturellen Relativismus. In: Matthes, Joachim (Hrsg.): Zwischen den Kulturen? Die Sozialwissenschaften vor dem Problem des Kulturvergleichs (= Soziale Welt. Sonderband. 8), Göttingen: Schwartz 1992, S. 145-166.

Wannöffel, Manfred: Sachzwang Japan. Zum arbeitsorganisatorischen Umbruch in der internationalen Automobilindustrie. Münster: Verlag Westfälisches Dampfboot 1991.

World Bank (Hrsg.): Vocational and Technical Education and Training. A World Bank Policy Paper. Washington, D. C.: World Bank 1991.

The „Education Gap"

Torsten Husén

When talking about an „education gap" between Euro-American and Third World countries we can distinguish between three types of gaps:

- *Provisions:* teacher competence, especially subject matter competence, class size, school buildings and classrooms, books per child, and percentage going to school.
- *Throughput:* dropout rate, attempts to use informal or non-formal education to compensate for not attending regular school, retention of literacy during the years when children more or less regularly attend school.
- *Outputs:* level of competence achieved after a certain number of years of formal schooling.

In all three respects there are big differences between affluent, industrialized countries on the one hand and poor, developing countries on the other. The World Bank has regularly mapped out differences in provisions, economic and others. The throughput differences were the focus, for example, at an International Bureau of Education conference in the early 1970s on „wastage" problems in formal education, such as dropout rate and grade repeating. I shall focus here on the third type of gap, outcomes in terms of student competence as measured by cross-nationally valid achievement tests in subjects such as mathematics, science and reading. I shall address this as the „performance gap".

It is important to point out that it is not in the first place the number of years of formal schooling or the amount of instruction in certain subjects that distinguish industrialized and non-industrialized countries. We today find developing countries, for instance in Africa, where a higher percentage of children enter secondary school than was the case in industrialized Western Europe some fifty years ago. In 1976, in my role as chairman of the National Commission on Education in Botswana, I had an interview with the President, Seretse Khama. He told me, almost apologetically, that „only" 20 per cent of the primary-school-leavers entered secondary schools. I could not refrain from asking him why he regarded such a „low" proportion of transfers as a deficiency besetting the educational system in a country with a predominantly subsistence economy and, at that time, a very small modern sector. In my home country Sweden, which by 1930 (when I myself transferred) had an industrial sector employing 45 per cent of the population, only ten per cent went on to secondary school at that time. I felt that my question was the more justified since the quality of primary education in Botswana left much to be desired and needed the resources which were channeled into secondary education.

Formal Schooling and Literacy

We should be aware of the fact that the knowledge and skills, such as the ones in the three *R*s, which we closely associate with formal schooling, do not necessarily have to be acquired in a formal school setting. Those of us in Europe and North America who have grown up in urban areas and gone to school since the 1920s are not usually familiar enough with our own social history to know that before the turn of the century literacy was to a large extent acquired at home. Under the 1686 Swedish Church Law, which regulated the role of the Lutheran State Church, the parish priests were assigned the duty of seeing to it that the parishioners became tolerably able to read passages in the Scriptures. In this task the priests were often assisted by the parish clerks. All adults above the age of 15 were examined once a year by the priest. Those who failed ran the risk of not obtaining a marriage license. Records were kept and in many parishes the examinees were given marks on how well they read aloud and how well they understood what they read. Since these records have recently been transferred onto magnetic tape, we are today able to study not only the development of literacy in the country but also to relate it to the social changes that took place over two centuries. The number of adults who were so to speak given pass marks in the examinations grew slowly in a linear fashion from 1700 to 1900.

Legislation on the provision of mandatory elementary education by the municipalities, passed by the Swedish Parliament in 1842, did not seem to have any accelerating effect on the rise of literacy. Most of the children who entered elementary school had learned the mechanics of reading, for instance to recognize letters, at home. They were expected to have mastered this aspect of reading when they entered school.

This development took place in a country with a highly limited or almost non-existent modern sector. When universal mandatory schooling was legislated more than 80 per cent of the population derived its livelihood from agriculture and related activities. The economy was to a large extent a subsistence one. This historic example is a telling one and is, of course, not irrelevant in a discussion about proper strategies for planning a system of elementary education in developing countries today.

Formal Instruction and Achievement

Another important distinction ought to be made. The amount of formal instruction in terms of years and hours of schooling can by no means be used as a proxy of outcomes in terms of student competence. In other words: the correlation between the number of instructional periods or number of years of schooling and the actual achievement at the end of schooling is far from perfect and, in fact, very modest. Let me illustrate this by citing three examples: one is from the history of elementary education in Scandinavia, the second and third are from the cross-national comparative surveys conducted by the International Association for the Evaluation of Educational Achievement, an organization known under the acronym IEA.

An Example from Sweden

The first example refers to Sweden, where in 1842 legislation was passed making six years of formal schooling mandatory. This meant that the young people were obliged to go to school from the age of seven to the age of 13. It was incumbent upon the parishes to defray the costs, i.e. to make school houses or rooms in other houses available and to employ and pay the teachers. The state took responsibility only for teacher training. But in most parishes children went to school for only a very short period in each consecutive year during the mandatory school period. My father had a total of 540 days of schooling, which meant 90 days or 15 weeks per year. He was, indeed, privileged. In my childhood I met an elderly lady serving as a maid who had gone to school for just one week per year for the six years and thereby complied with what the law required. When I grew up in a small town in a big parish, many children in the periphery of the parish still went to school half-time, every other semester. This was a practical arrangement in making maximum use of the teacher who taught full-time by serving two schools alternately.

The system of half-time schooling was practiced in sparsely populated areas in Northern Scandinavia, where children had a long way to go to school, until the 1950s. A study was undertaken in which children who went to school half-time for seven years were compared with those who went full-time. The results showed that there were no significant differences between the two groups in student achievement in various school subjects at the end of the seven years.

Two Examples from IEA

In the IEA surveys representative national samples at various grade levels were compared across countries. Children, in most industrial countries, enter school at six, but at seven in Scandinavia and Finland. The reason for the delayed entry was, at least in Sweden, that small children should not be subjected to the hardships of trudging a long way through the snow in dark winters to go to school. In Britain they enter schools at five, which is a heritage from the time when infant schools were established and child labour, from the age of seven or eight was still allowed. In the IEA surveys of reading comprehension and science the Swedish 10-year olds on the average performed at the same level as the British ones, in reading even better in spite of having spent at least one and a half years less in school.

The lessons learned from past and more recent empirical evidence are that the amount of formal instruction does not have the crucial importance that for instance teacher unions in affluent countries tend to ascribe to it. The practical implication is that if we want to achieve quality at the expense of quantity – presently it is the other way around in many developing countries – we should consider using teacher-led instruction more wisely by distributing it better over time.

Third world countries have taken over the model of full-time schooling which was developed in Europe and America primarily in urban, industrial areas where there was a need for an institution to take care of the children while parents worked for long hours in factories and other enterprises. The school to some extent served as a baby-sitting institution. In rural areas parents with farming background often were against mandatory school attendance, since the children were needed at home to take over chores such as looking after younger siblings or cattle or working in the fields.

Empirical Evidence about the „Performance Gap"

The real education gap between developed and developing countries has to do with *average performances* in key school subjects and with the *variation in performances* among schools. Until the early 1960s we had very little empirical evidence to allow any judgments on how the two categories of countries differed in these two respects. It was not until an international group of researchers, some of them with a background in testing and measurement and others in comparative education, some 30 years ago, convened and formed the International Association for the Evaluation of Educational Achievement (IEA) that such evidence began to be collected and was made available for analytical purposes. In illustrating the quality or performance gap between industrial and non-industrial countries I shall mainly draw upon the outcomes of various IEA surveys in mathematics, science and reading. The first survey (in mathematics) was conducted in 1964, the next – in six subjects, among them science and reading comprehension – in 1970. A second mathematics survey took place in 1980 and a second science survey in 1984-86. With the exception of the first mathematics survey, an increasing number of developing countries participated in the IEA surveys. In the reading comprehension survey completed in the early 1990s, 36 countries participated, half of them developing countries.

In the rest of my presentation I shall try to highlight summarily some of the major IEA findings which illustrate the performance gap. Finally, still on the basis of the IEA analyses, I shall try to point out some factors which account for the differences in average performance. I shall use the Botswana survey as a typical illustration of the performance level in developing countries. In Botswana I chaired the review of the education sector conducted by the National Commission on Education. I cannot go into details here, therefore I shall limit myself to comparisons between industrial and non-industrial countries which refer to the 10- and 14-year old populations, the age at which the majority of children in most countries are in school. I shall leave out the 18-year olds, as the proportion of this age group in school varies enormously between countries.

If you graphically represent the variation in mean performance between the countries, you find that the two types of country appear as two clusters far apart on a performance scale. I can take the first reading survey *(Thorndike 1973)* as an illustration. Chile, Iran and India participated (cf. table 1). Their mean performance is, in statistical language, about one standard deviation below that of a typical industrial country. Expressed in grade levels this means that children of the former countries are three or four grade levels below the reading level of students in the latter.

Table 1: *Means and Standard Deviations by Country for Reading Comprehension (14-year olds)*

Country	Mean	SD
Chile	14.1	11.1
Iran	7.8	6.7
India	5.2	7.2
Belgium (Flemish)	24.6	9.7
Belgium (French)	27.2	8.7
England	25.3	11.9
Finland	27.1	10.9
Hungary	25.5	9.9
Israel	22.6	12.8
Italy	27.9	9.3
Netherlands	25.2	10.2
New Zealand	29.3	11.0
Scotland	27.0	11.5
Sweden	25.6	10.8
United States	27.3	11.6
Median	25.5	10.8

Source: *Thorndike (1973)*

In this case students took the reading tests in their mother tongue. In the case of Botswana they had to take it in the language used as the medium of instruction, that is to say English. At the end of the 7-year primary school the mean performance was equivalent to that of second or third graders in the United States and Great Britain. Since, at that time, the language used as the medium of instruction switched in grade 3, students became, as I somewhat harshly expressed it, illiterate in two languages.

The same picture emerged from the science survey (cf. table 2). The average 10-year old student in most industrial countries scored 15 to 18 points, whereas students in Chile, India, Iran and Thailand scored between four and nine points. Again, this was at least one standard deviation below the level achieved in the industrial countries. The picture did not change at the 14-year old level.

Table 2: Science Mean Test Scores and Standard Deviations for Population I (10-year olds)

Country	Mean	SD
Maximum	*40*	
Australia	–	–
Belgium (Flemish)	17.9	7.3
Belgium (French)	13.9	7.1
England	15.7	8.5
Germany (Federal Republic)	14.9	7.4
Finland	17.5	8.2
France	–	–
Hungary	16.7	8.0
Italy	16.5	8:6
Japan	21.7	7.7
Netherlands	15.3	7.6
New Zealand	–	–
Scotland	14.0	8.4
Sweden	18.3	7.3
United States	17.7	9.3
Mean	*16.7*	*7.9*
Chile	9.1	8.6
India	8.5	8.3
Iran	4.1	5.4
Thailand	9.9	6.5

Source: *Comber / Keeves (1973)*

Table 3: Sub-Test Comparison Mathematics (13-year olds)

Country	Arithmetic	Country	Algebra	Country	Geometry
Belgium (Flemish)	5	Belgium (Flemish)	3	Belgium (Flemish)	10
Belgium (French)	7	Belgium (French)	6	Belgium (French)	9
Canada (British Columbia)	4	Canada (British Columbia)	7	Canada (British Columbia)	12
Canada (Ontario)	9	Canada (Ontario)	13	Canada (Ontario)	8
England and Wales	13	England and Wales	14	England and Wales	6
Finland	15	Finland	9	Finland	7
France	3	France	2	France	16
Hong Kong	8	Hong Kong	11	Hong Kong	11
Hungary	6	Hungary	5	Hungary	2
Israel	11	Israel	8	Israel	17
Japan	1	Japan	1	Japan	1
Luxembourg	16	Luxembourg	19	Luxembourg	20
Netherlands	2	Netherlands	4	Netherlands	4
New Zealand	14	New Zealand	15	New Zealand	3
Nigeria	19	Nigeria	18	Nigeria	19
Scotland	12	Scotland	10	Scotland	5
Swaziland	20	Swaziland	20	Swaziland	18
Sweden	18	Sweden	17	Sweden	14
Thailand	17	Thailand	16	Thailand	13
United States of America	10	United States of America	12	United States of America	15

Source: *Robitaille / Garden (1989)*

In the second mathematics study other developing countries, namely Nigeria and Swaziland, participated, in addition to Thailand. Table 3 shows the rank order in achievements for 13-year olds. Among the eight-graders the superiority of students from industrial countries was greater in algebra than in arithmetic.

Table 4: Rank Order of Countries for Achievement in Science at Each Level

Country	10-year olds Grade 4/5	14-year olds Grade 8/9	Grade 12/13 Science Students			Grade 12/13 Non-Science Students
			Biology	Chemistry	Physics	
Australia	9	10	9	6	8	4
Canada (English)	6	4	11	12	11	8
England	12	11	2	2	2	2
Finland	3	5	7	13	12	–
Hong Kong	13	16	5	1	1	–
Hungary	5	1	3	5	3	1
Italy	7	11	12	10	13	7
Japan	1	2	10	4	4	3
Korea	1	7	–	–	–	–
Netherlands	–	3	–	–	–	–
Norway	10	9	6	8	6	5
Philippines	15	17	–	–	–	–
Poland	11	7	4	7	7	–
Singapore	13	14	1	3	5	6
Sweden	4	6	8	9	10	–
Thailand	–	14	–	–	–	–
USA	8	14	13	11	9	–
Total number of countries	15	17	13	13	13	8

Source: *Husén / Keeves (1991)*

A report of the second science survey was published by my colleagues T. N. Postlethwaite and John P. Keeves and presented at a Symposium organized by the Royal Swedish Academy of Sciences. Table 4 shows the rank order in achievements for 10-

year olds (grades 4 and 5), 14-year olds (grades 8 and 9) and 17-19-year olds (grades 12 and 13) in 17 countries. The Philippines and Thailand are at the bottom, whereas Japan, Korea and Hungary are at the top. As pointed out earlier, comparisons between mean performances at the upper secondary level are not very meaningful because of the highly varying proportions of the age group in school at that age level.

How Valid and Relevant are Cross-National Comparisons?

The massive volume of empirical data on student achievements in many countries collected by IEA at face value appears to be rather convincing. But how valid is it? Is it possible to conduct cross-national and cross-cultural comparisons which are not only fair but also valid in terms of assessing what we purport to assess? Three objections against such comparisons can easily be advanced.

(1) Is there a common core of curricular objectives large enough to be measured cross-nationally with a satisfactory degree of validity? Expressed in operational terms: can we really devise cross-nationally valid tests and examinations in key school subject areas? The answer to these questions by implication can tell us whether or not we can apply the same standards of quality across nations and cultures.

(2) How much can intervening variables distort cross-national comparisons? I have in mind two types of such variables: genuine cultural differences which have motivational effects not only upon how well students absorb what they are taught in school but also influence test taking itself. The other variable is, of course, the language used as the medium of instruction. This is a major problem in schools in sub-Saharan Africa, where the newly established nations in many cases are outcomes of the colonial era and a rich diversity of tribal languages has for the sake of national unity been replaced by the former colonial language, be it English, French or Portuguese.

(3) Can any *relevance* be ascribed to cross-national comparisons which reveal such big gaps in achievements as IEA and other studies have shown? Can any importance be attached to such differences? Do they play any role on the international scene, for instance do they have any economic and competitive consequences?

As everyone knows, objections have been raised against standardized tests since they began to be used in the schools on both sides of the Atlantic. The objections are of two kinds. In the first place: Is it *technically possible* to measure, for instance, academic achievement in a way that would provide a fair and meaningful rank order between students within the same school and between schools in the same country? Secondly: Can we employ such tests or examinations across countries and cultures so as to yield results with a reasonable degree of meaningful *comparability*?

I shall be brief about the first issue. Space does not allow me to discuss psychometric technicalities. Let me confine myself to mentioning that since the turn of the century we have gained overwhelming experience, both in research and practical applications, that allows us to conclude safely that scholastic competence, defined as both aptitude and achievement, can be assessed with more validity and reliability and, above all, with more comparability by means of a couple of hours of standardized testing than by ratings conducted by teachers on the basis of a year or more of classroom contacts. Achievement tests are convenient instruments in terms of time economy. They are also more effective than the traditional essay type of examinations. Let me illustrate this by means of an experience I had some twenty years ago.

In a country the number of applicants for admission to the universities exceeded the number of places available by a factor of three. The Minister of Education decided that all the applicants should be brought together for essay examinations on the same days in a few places in the country. Thus, thousands of students sat for these examinations at each of these places. More than one hundred university teachers from several universities were hired to mark the *essays* which, of course, was a gigantic task that took several weeks. But worst of all: no common standard of marking the essays could be established, not even between examiners in the same place. Thus, there was no guarantee that the onerous efforts would result in a fair ranking of the applicants and, as a matter of fact, the whole system broke down. Along with some colleagues I advised the Minister to use standardized objective tests which the students answered on separate sheets that could be machine scored. The scores could be transferred directly onto magnetic tape which made the massive selection procedure manageable.

A technical procedure of this kind has been criticized as being too narrow and mechanistic and not taking creativity into account. To be sure, the classical essay examinations do not suffer from such limitations, but they are beset by shortcomings which, when it comes to mass examinations, make them unusable for reasons I have just spelled out.

I have, since the 1940s, been involved in devising standardized achievement tests used by all the Swedish schools. The system was developed to calibrate school marks and to make them comparable all over the country and has been accepted by all involved. It is indispensable if you want to establish a system of marks that forms the basis for selection for post-primary education according to the same standards all over the country and with sufficient validity and reliability.

Over the last 30 years I have also been closely involved in conducting cross-national assessments of student competence in key school subjects. We began back in 1959 with a feasibility study in a dozen industrialized countries with eight different languages. From the outset the enterprise was a genuinely cooperative one with one research institute in each country participating by contributing, for instance, with questions for the tests in reading, mathematics and science. After having tried out most of the proposed items in all the participating countries we arrived at a kind of common core test which was translated into all the eight languages and then translated back independently in order to check the adequacy of the translation.

In addition to items measuring regular school subjects we also included a series of items from so-called culture-free tests consisting to a large extent of non-verbal material which had been devised in order to avoid the verbal handicap that culturally deprived children suffer from. To our surprise we found that the reading comprehension test, where we had to rely entirely on the language and verbal material, showed less between-country variability than the so-called culture-free test: On the whole we found that as far as the industrialized countries with their crystallized school system were concerned we could with sufficient confidence say that it was feasible, possible and meaningful to conduct cross-national comparisons without discriminating against any of the national school populations.

But irrespective of how different the countries under comparison are, from the outset we regarded it as essential to devise tests which took into account differences between countries in curricular objectives and differences in emphasis on the various objectives. When IEA conducted its first mathematics survey in the 1960s, the mathematics curriculum was described in two dimensions: on the one hand the behavior, such as knowledge and information, techniques and skills, comprehension and inventiveness, and on the other hand the content, such as arithmetic, algebra, geometry, calculus, etc. Furthermore, each content area was rated by subject specialists within the country with regard to the emphasis it received in mathematics teaching. In addition all the teachers in the classes in which students were tested were asked to rate each item with regard to the opportunity students had had to learn the material measured by the particular item. The same procedure was used in subsequent IEA surveys.

In certain subject areas, such as mathematics, the common core of objectives and content is rather big, although considerable differences can exist with regard to age level at which a given content area is introduced and the time and emphasis it receives in instruction.

Thus, curricular differences can distort comparisons between countries. But there are also other intervening variables which may have a similar effect. A variable that suggests itself immediately, are, of course, language differences or, even more pertinent, countries where the medium of instruction is a language other than the mother tongue. This is, as you know, the rule rather than the exception in sub-Saharan Africa. Cultures differ with regard to the motivational background of test-taking ability. In some cultures with a competitive orientation and a positive attitude toward going ahead, children desperately try to do their best when faced with any tests and examinations. In other cultures they take it more easily. Anthropologists have gathered quite a lot of evidence about this by studying different ethnic groups within a given nation. We all know, for example, that children of Asian background in California tend to perform much better on tests than Caucasian children with the same socio-economic background.

Over the years, that I have been involved in conducting large-scale cross-national evaluations of educational achievements, I have almost *ad nauseam* been emphasizing that the main purpose of the IEA at least research has *not* been to conduct a kind of „cognitive Olympics" or horse race. The IEA researchers are in the first place interested in conducting analyses which would explain differences between countries and schools in terms of economic and pedagogical resources and practices. We know that a large portion of the inter-country variance is accounted for by differences in parental education, socio-economic status and the like. Another big portion has to do with school resources, in particular with teacher competence and instructional material. IEA has devised sophisticated analytical techniques to study the relative importance of the various background factors: social, economic and pedagogical.

Given all the reservations which I have sketched: Can cross-national comparisons in terms of average performance on international tests developed with the help of the most outstanding expertise available claim any relevance? Is there any point in comparing the standard achieved by children in more affluent countries with educated parents and well-equipped schools with those coming from villages in poor countries with illiterate parents and schools without competent teachers and poor instructional material?

My answer, in spite of all this, is that developing countries would for several reasons stand to gain from such comparisons. In the first place: the economic consequences and the gain in international competitive edge depends to a large extent upon the quality of the products that the schools are turning out. The establishment of a modern sector which turns out products for the world market needs a workforce with a certain level of educational competence. The developing countries are increasingly being compared with the more developed when it comes to international trade and communications. Secondly, there are certain areas of student competence in which comparisons are highly worthwhile. I am thinking of reading comprehension, where a certain level of competence is necessary if the skill in that area is going to be of any use. Let me illustrate this with an example from a country where English is used as the medium of instruction rather early, namely Botswana. I recommended a survey of, among other things, reading at the end of the 7-year primary school. The average level of reading competence in Botswana by 1976, after seven years of schooling, corresponded to that of second grade in the UK or the United States, where English, of course, is the mother tongue. But the objective of reading in Botswana is, after all, to make the children literate in English which justifies a comparison with children in English-speaking nations.

There is, however, a third important reason, namely the monitoring function that surveys with standardized tests can serve. Central agencies in the respective countries need to follow the trends with regard to both the total scores and the scores in the various topical areas over time. Given the tendency in the developing nations to buy quantity at the cost of quality, comparisons with the more affluent countries can provide a perspective for the less developed countries in monitoring the progress made in their schools.

Bibliography

Comber, L. C. / Keeves, John P.: Science Education in Nineteen Countries. New York et al.: Wiley et al. 1973. (International Studies in Education. 1)

Husén, Torsten (ed.): Pupils, Teachers and Schools in Botswana. A National Evaluative Survey of Primary and Secondary Education. Annex to: Education for Kagisano. Report of the National Commission on Education. Vol. 2. Gabarone: Botswana Government Printing Office 1977.

Husén, Torsten / Keeves, John P. (eds.): Issues in Science Education. Science Competence in a Social and Ecological Context. Oxford: Pergamon Press 1991.
Husén, Torsten / Postlethwaite, Thomas Neville: A Brief History of the International Association for the Evaluation of Educational Achievement (IEA). In: Assessment in Education, 3 (1996) 2, pp. 129-141.
Robitaille, David F. / Garden, Robert A. (eds.): The IEA Study of Mathematics. II: Contexts and Outcomes of School Mathematics. Oxford: Pergamon Press 1989.
Thorndike, Robert L.: Reading Comprehension Education in Fifteen Countries. An Empirical Study. New York et al.: Wiley et al. 1973. (International Studies in Education. 3)

From Literacy to Functional Literacy[1]

Joachim H. Knoll

The Problem

In all countries, either developing or industrialized, problems of illiteracy are perceived with great interest and commitment. Especially UNESCO has paid its tribute to the „eradication of illiteracy" and from time to time within the last decades has tried to forecast the solution of the world-wide problem, which is closely linked to solving the problem of socio-political conditions and environment as well *(Schöfthaler 1991-92)*.

To begin the debate on literacy and functional literacy two quotations should be considered. The first is a motto given by François Nourissier in „Letters of Life", an UNESCO publication of 1991: *„The written word is the key to all freedoms. Reading and writing are our second birth. By making them available, we give life twice over"* (Bhola *1994, p. 8).*

Another motto which includes the misery of our cultural environment, looking at it from a global perspective, is given by F. Musgrove and reads: *„No difference could be more fundamental than between peoples who can read and write and those who cannot. The latter have customs but no laws, techniques but no science, religion but no theology"* (ibid.).

Here we get a brief and distinct look at the naive assumption, that 'illiterate societies' are to be seen in contrast to highly differentiated, scientifically and educationally based societies. In any case one should note that in these statements illiteracy is defined by formal cultural techniques such as reading and writing; saying it more precisely in common !!educational terms, these statements just restrict illiteracy to the lack of command of cultural techniques and apparently omit the major issue of social skills, a term which refers to the modern understanding and strategy of literacy which can be circumscribed

---

[1] The following article refers to a series of lectures held by the author at Legon-University, Accra/ Ghana.

as „functional literacy". At present the concept of social skills, which defines the entire strategy of literacy campaigns, will not be discussed; it will be referred to later.

The problem itself becomes more demanding, when figures and tables are compiled to demonstrate, that in spite of all efforts in previous years, we are still far from having solved one of the crucial problems connected with illiteracy, which comes up when contrasting developing countries with countries both prosperous and, as far as the quality of living and economic circumstances are concerned, more or less comfortable. Alan B. Knox, who is one of the leading figures in the academic field of adult education and shows a very practical sense and concern in his scholarly work, presents in his recent publication his view of the present situation which is in fact predominantly characterized by illiteracy. Under the heading of „Basic Education and Literacy" he starts off with the statement: *„A U.S. newspaper-article appearing in May 1991, probably surprised some readers. The article referred to a UNESCO report that during the 1990 International Literacy Year the estimated number of illiterate adults in the world was almost one billion, though the number was a few million less than the 1985 estimate. The current number is more than one-quarter of the total population of adults. Compared with the 1970 estimate of almost 40 per cent illiterates, UNESCO concluded that there had been progress towards its goal of eradicating illiteracy, but it had been painfully slow. The surprising sentence at the end of the article was that the International Literacy Year raised awareness that functional illiteracy in industrialized nations was estimated at between 10 to 20 per cent of the adult population"* (Knox 1993, p. 68). A more precise investigation showed that the last figures are wrong. The average figure of autochthonous illiterates in industrialized countries is rated at between three and five per cent, not including the high number of illiterates in industrialized countries, who have settled there in the process of world-wide migration *(Knoll 1996, p. 145).*

These introductory reflections demonstrate, that besides the overall awareness of the communicative power of educated people, the capability of reading and writing plays an important role in the education policies of both industrialized and developing countries. The number of illiterates was reduced, but the „eradication" of illiteracy is a very slow process and does not allow any definite forecasts. There are various reasons for this slow process which are of personal-individual and social-economic kind.

Literature on the Subject

Academic rigor and scientific seriousness make some brief comments about the literature dealing with illiteracy and literacy campaigns necessary. The general impression is that the flood of literature can no longer be coped with by a researcher. Looking at the access-bibliography of the Library of Congress in Washington shows that even under the very specific sub-heading „Literacy and Basic Adult Education in Ghana" the number of titles mainly stressing the implementation of the Freirean dimension of literacy indicates its evident impact. Besides this general impression the literature shows evidence that especially in recent publications the techniques of evaluation and the specific needs and demands of target groups, such as women or minorities, who try to preserve their language, their cultural and religious tradition and heritage within a new environment, are the main focus of interest. Above all, this indicates that integration is strictly separated from assimilation by guarantees to maintain and retain the heritage of minorities. To my knowledge this problem pertains to Canada and the Federal Republic of Germany. The U.S. assimilation has not turned out to be totally successful due to the separation and segregation of the Hispanics or Latinos *(Internationales Jahrbuch der Erwachsenenbildung 1986)*.

Another observation should be mentioned. To a large extent the literature concentrates on the political and social components of literacy, this means that the literature looks particularly at countries, which launched and carried out *literacy campaigns* under the auspices of a governmental initiative; modes and means of post-literacy-programmes are established and reflect upon the upgrading processes for those having passed literacy programmes.

My personal commitment to the subject and the political strategy stems from my membership in the German Commission of UNESCO and my research on autochthonous minorities and migrants in different countries *(Knoll 1986, 1991-92, 1992)*.

Seen from this perspective, literacy is intensively involved in the economic, social and political development of a country. One example is the Israelian literacy strategy. The literacy project there is conducted under the title „Tehila", which means Glory, and tries to introduce language and religion, cultural heritage and governmental policies to immigrants predominantly coming from the Maghreb countries in Northern Africa. As the state of Israel relies on God's prophecy, that God will gather his „own people" in Israel, literacy means the intellectual and emotional approval of the religious and the para-political dimension of the state *(Knoll 1996, p. 145)*. Therefore literacy programmes try to contribute to the technical side of literacy as well as to the political side of the constitutional framework in which the new citizens are living. Simultaneously citizenship demands the awareness of literacy in order to participate in the further development of communities and the state.

Summarizing this review of the aspects of publications dealing with literacy, one can state that they refer to:

- academic concern in and research on literacy and basic adult education;
- implementation of techniques already tried in countries with similar preconditions for literacy;
- literacy for target groups and for minorities;
- global approaches developed by international and supranational organizations such as UNESCO;
- new tendencies under the perspective of a broader dimension of literacy including social skills.

Later on some of the relevant publications will be mentioned, for now a recent publication by H. S. *Bhola (1994)* is worth notice. Even if the bibliographical notes in this book look rather brief, the content is rich because of its very pragmatic approach and its orientation towards the needs in the field. Bhola, who is a respected expert for the UNESCO and expresses UNESCO's views on Basic Adult Education, works full-time at the Indiana University.

Historical Traces

Looking at the history of literacy one has to admit that a review can not be exhaustive and only indicate some aspects. The German situation is not at all symptomatic for industrialized countries in general, but it gives an impression of how important the commitment of priests and missionaries was for the development of a religious and secular upgrading of people and their communication. Within the Jewish tradition for instance education and religion were closely linked; the services in the synagogues were regarded as a form of lifelong education. The publications of Israelian educationists very often emphasize this aspect of a religious approach to education *(Knoll 1988, p. 3)*. Nevertheless, in my opinion, these foundations of lifelong education are only seldom taken into consideration when lifelong education is on a secular agenda. There are some articles in previous volumes of the International Yearbook of Adult Education dealing with this aspect of the Jewish tradition which is actually extended in the concept of „Tehila" mentioned previously *(Israeli 1984-85)*.

German scholars like to point out in a very naive way that at the beginning of the 19th century German citizens were already participating in the German humanistic-classical dispute. It is assumed that there was widespread knowledge about literature, history and economic science amongst bourgeois people in cities in the era of Schiller, Goethe and Humboldt. But as far as statistics are available, it can be stated in general that at that time only one third of the German adult population can be regarded as literates. There was no compulsory schooling and only nobles were able to send their children to grammar schools, which were highly reputed because of their academic background. With the introduction of compulsory schooling and with the mass enrollment in secondary and higher education after World War II the problem of illiteracy seemed to be solved. But as was demonstrated from time to time in the International Yearbook in the late 1970s there was still a large and even increasing number of illiterates, although there was a large variety of educational facilities *(Knoll 1978)*. The improvement of literacy in the 19th century was guaranteed by churches and sovereigns in areas with a liberal tradition in the southern regions of Germany. But behind the curtain of a bourgeois culture there was a lack of education especially for peasants and people in smaller villages. Our awareness of literacy nowadays started in the late 1970s. When a German representative of voluntary adult education agencies joined the first all-European meeting on Basic Adult Education in St. Andrews, Scotland in 1983 the German contribution appeared very elementary *(European Bureau of Adult Education 1983)*. This has changed tremendously over the past years in many respects.

Looking at developing countries with a colonial tradition one can generally speak of two lines of educational influence. On the one hand there are the priests, who, frankly, not only had educational aims. They intended Christianizing colonial or non-colonial areas in Africa, Latin America and parts of Asia. On the other hand colonial policies tried to implement English, French, Portuguese or Spanish, and in some cases German, mentalities and educational preconditions to areas, where the existing cultures were subjected to something which was strange to them *(Bhola 1994, p. 29)*. In several cases the external influence of culture, language and religion established barriers against redefining and rediscovering the original cultural heritage. As literacy contributes to the process of nation-building to a very high degree, language, writing, reading and traditional customs play an important role. The problem of the language in which people are alphabetized is closely connected with the self-understanding and self-consciousness of newly liberated countries. In conclusion, this does not mean that all facilities which were established under the colonial regime should be abolished.

Taking a look at the history of Basic Adult Education in Ghana we can observe almost the same development as described before. Under the perspective of the development of methodology in literacy *Dorvlo (1993, p. 76)* described the different stages which are important for the growing understanding of a differentiated system of adult literacy: „*Adult literacy work was started in the Gold Coast [now Ghana] by missionaries when establishing their missions in the country ... In the 1940s the Government of the Gold Coast joined the adult literacy exercises with the establishment of a Mass Education Unit which was attached to the Department of Welfare and Housing ... Basically, both the primary education techniques and the Laubach technique have enabled willing illiterate adults 'merely to learn to read and to write'.*"

In the 1970s, it was realized that adult literacy efforts should not merely aim at the teaching „*of reading and writing, but that they should also aim at improving the social, political and economic systems*" *(ibid.)*. Apparently, there is a logical sequence or hierarchy in literacy-methods which starts by giving primary education for children and literacy work for adults, mainly carried out on the basis of a synthetic letter-method, equal status; it is followed by more structured methodological proceedings, for instance by introducing the syllabus method, or the morpheme method in some industrialized countries. The morpheme method is closely connected with the syllabus method, but the adaptation depends on the linguistic structure of the languages used for adult literacy. Finally, all efforts at adult literacy work tend to be based on the conviction that adult literacy work has to start from the introduction of adults into cultural techniques, such as reading, writing and arithmetic, and then proceed to teaching the ability of coping with the demands of the political and economic environment: this means to develop the quality of participating as a citizen with his or her rights and duties. The identification of the elements of what we call social skills and what can be found under the title of basic adult education in a more comprehensive way depends on several factors and can not be explained in general terms. This seems to be a typical argument, but I would like to already take into account at this point of the discussion that the adaptation of the Freirean method is only one way of solving the problem of illiteracy; there might be others, that do not emphasize the socio-economic change of the given system with the impact of literacy work so much.

Definitions and UNESCO's Efforts – Literacy, Functional Literacy, Basic Adult Education

We have already considered some definitions. Here, one has to refer to UNESCO's efforts in adult literacy work in a global approach. Primarily one has to indicate that UNESCO was originally founded on an idealistic and harmonious philosophy of a world-culture. Considering this early phase, UNESCO's assumption was that by means of education conflicts could be avoided *(Knoll 1996, p. 118)*. Thus, the Latin motto was called to mind again: „Si vis pacem para pacem." The phrase world-culture meant – without being used in precise terms – that illiteracy could be eradicated and that in each country a similar education system could be built up in the traditional way: elementary education, primary education, secondary education, higher education and adult education. Until the late 1970s this very simple outline of a harmonious structure of a world-wide system of education was still being propagated outside UNESCO by George Z. F. T. Bereday, who insisted that this system existed world-wide.

The levels of a comprehensive education system and the corresponding age-cohorts are as follows *(Knoll 1996, p. 220)*:

1. Elementary and primary education   0 – 8 years
2. Primary and secondary education   8 – 16 years
3. Secondary and higher education   16 – 24 years
4. Adult education   > 24 years

But looking at this educational framework in detail and adding the age of the cohorts within the different stages to the education system it becomes obvious that this scheme is merely a circumscription of the North-American, highly differentiated education system. Nowadays neither the propaganda of the philosophy of a world-culture nor the proposal of adopting the structural program of the North American system of education is being followed anymore. In the 1950s UNESCO became more and more aware of the necessity of literacy work and realized its efforts by developing a program of literacy as being the transportation of the cultural techniques of reading, writing and arithmetic to illiterate adults. During that time, as can easily be seen, UNESCO included the assumption in its program that primary education for children and adult literacy work could be organized in parallel or could even be organized within the same classroom. Research on the specific ways of adult learning and teaching were not very highly developed at that time.

As far as this early stage is concerned one has to consider three approaches of how adult literacy work may be established and carried out. At first it was felt that due to historical reasons industrialized countries have the responsibility to assist the developing countries in their literacy activities. Some activities of UNESCO were portrayed in World Conferences and Documents (UNESCO World Conferences on Adult Education: 1949 Elsinor, 1960 Montreal, 1972 Tokyo, 1985 Paris, forthcoming 1997 Hamburg; cf. *Faure et al. 1972; UNESCO 1976; Delors et al. 1996).*

The UNESCO World Conference for Adult Education in Montreal in 1960 announced the new philosophy of strengthening adult education as an entity in itself without any harmonizing preconditions; it was said: *„We believe that adult education has become of such importance for men's survival and happiness that a new attitude towards it is needed. Nothing less will suffice, than that the people everywhere should come to accept adult education as normal, and the governments should treat it as necessary part of the educational provision of every country"* (UNESCO 1961, p. 59).

Furthermore, one should read the early definition of literacy very attentively: *„Literacy is the ability to read and to write in the mother tongue"* (Bhola 1994, p. 28). This aspect of these early considerations introduces the problem of language and literacy, the question, in what language and by which linguistic modes of the mother language literacy work should be launched. Primarily this definition indicates that the so-called colonial languages, which were implemented in the administration and education of colonialized countries, cannot automatically be the languages in which literacy work takes place. It has to be considered that there are tribal cultures without a written language. Written characters have to be developed by means of phonetic transcription. As language is a very central component of a nation's identity the selection of the first official language to be integrated into literacy work has to be considered very carefully. But this language selection should not only be based upon aspects of a nation's identity, but also upon the necessity of international communication, which enables a nation to exchange goods and ideas in a broader frame. To illustrate the situation under discussion here: when Sri Lanka, the former Ceylon, was liberated from the British colonial regime the newly established government decided to make Singhala, which is the original native language, the first official language, without accepting any other language of international communication besides it. Due to the fact that there was hardly any language competence in Singhala outside the country the international trade declined tremendously. Bandaranaike – then prime minister of Sri Lanka – changed the policy by promoting a more or less bilingual system, which linguistically relies on the native language and the former colonial language. This is happening in many developing countries.

In 1958, the former UNESCO definition, which I have tried to describe briefly above, was slightly amended, now stating „*that a person is illiterate who cannot* with understanding *both read and write a short, simple statement on* every day life" *(Bhola 1994, p. 29; also UNESCO 1976)*.

The present and accepted definition of literacy by UNESCO originates from the early 1960s and was subsequently integrated in the well-known UNESCO declaration „Recommendation on the Development of Adult Education" which was adopted by the General Assembly in Nairobi in 1976: „*A person is functionally literate who can engage in all those activities in which literacy is required for effective functioning of his group and community and also for enabling him to continue to use reading, writing and calculation for his own and the community's development"* (Bhola 1994, p. 29).

This definition comprises some of the tendencies implied by literacy nowadays: apart from the cultural techniques it includes social skills as necessary elements for the functioning not only within one's profession but also within community life and it includes post literacy activities as well. I do not agree with Bhola in emphasizing a term like critical and that means radical literacy *(ibid., p. 33)*, because the adaptation of the Freirean strategy, for instance, includes the enabling of an emancipative dialogue and competence as well as a perspective on the future development of the socio-political conditions.

The demonstration of the historical dimension of definitions is hardly an academic subject, yet it indicates different approaches to literacy that have existed in different countries until now. There is no agreement on a world-wide strategy for literacy and such an agreement is not even desirable. Literacy as a strategy to create a cultural identity by language, reading and writing and to promote better conditions in the socio-political system depends on regional preconditions. This is actually true for industrialized countries such as the Federal Republic of Germany where a generally agreed-upon strategy in adult literacy does not exist.

The UNESCO World Conference for Adult Education in Paris 1985 brought about and established the term „Basic Adult Education", which had already been used in discussions among literacy experts. Basic adult education as *the* significant term in present expertise is, to a certain extent, an interpretation of the term „functional literacy", in the course of which basic adult education immediately reflects the scheme of lifelong education, opening the field of literacy work to the investigation of the education system in general. In consequence the comprehensive term appears: Basic Adult Education in the framework of lifelong education *(Schöfthaler 1991-92, pp. 6-8; UNESCO 1985)*.

Taking into account the illiteracy not only of adults, an international expert meeting attended by people from UNESCO, UNICEF, UNDP and the World Bank in Jomtien in Thailand in 1990 therefore broadened the term to Basic Education for All. The Declaration of this Conference, which propagated „The Right to Learn", contains some fundamental issues that indicate the new guidelines of functional literacy *(World Conference on Education for All 1990)*:

– Education is a fundamental right of every citizen, men and women.
– Education can contribute to guarantee a safe, sane and flourishing life, education promotes progress, tolerance and international cooperation.
– Education is an indispensable precondition for individual and social development.
– Traditional knowledge and the cultural heritage have a high value and assist and promote further development.
– The present programs of educational institutions show significant deficiencies; the educational programmes must be strongly orientated towards topicality, they have to be qualitatively improved and must be open to everybody.
– A solid basic education serves as a fundament for upgrading educational levels

It seems necessary to convey a broader vision and a new commitment to young generations for basic education so that the young generations can master the demands and the challenges of a complex future world.

Article 1 of the Declaration formulates the aim: learning opportunities for all, or – as the declaration puts it: *„Whether or not expanded educational opportunities will translate into meaningful development – for an individual or for society – depends ultimately on whether people actually learn as a result of those opportunities, i. e. whether they incorporate useful knowledge, reasoning ability, skills and values"* (World Conference on Education for All 1990, p. 5).

In this quotation and in the listing of the major perspectives of education by knowledge, ability and values a new direction of literacy is described and even the formula of social skills is broadened by including a distinctively personal awareness and social responsibility for the learners' own sakes and also for the sake of the society.

The former differentiation between industrialized and developing countries is no longer valid as far as terms of literacy or illiteracy are concerned. The trend seems to indicate that both are getting closer in their confrontation of the three miseries of the 20th century: poverty, discrimination and illiteracy.

The way is now paved from literacy to basic adult education and new decisions by UNESCO as introduced in the third and fourth Medium Term Plan are all looking towards this new dimension *(Neu-Altenheimer 1991-92, pp. 12-15; UNESCO 1990)*.

But even if illiteracy has become a problem for industrialized countries as well, a simple comparison on a large scale is not admissible.

Other Facts and Figures of Illiteracy

The degree of illiteracy in developing countries is still frightening despite all efforts made by UNESCO, World Bank and several national agencies, such as the German Association for Adult Education (Deutscher Volkshochschul-Verband). In this context the problems of industrialized countries appear somewhat marginal despite all the energy put into comprehensive projects like those in Italy, Denmark, the Netherlands or the United Kingdom *(Bundesminister für Bildung und Wissenschaft 1990; Kreft 1991-92)*. We cannot list all the shortcomings which occur, especially in those countries where the entrance to primary education is limited or even restricted, where within the school systems the rate of dropouts is still high and in many cases still increasing, where there is no provision for post-literacy work and where women are still being discriminated under a traditional or religious umbrella. Only a few should be mentioned:

– More than one third of the adult population world-wide has no access to printed material or to the abilities and the knowledge necessary to promote technology and life-quality. These people cannot participate in the process of social and cultural construction or reconstruction.
– More than 100 million children leave school very early; they never pass a complete program of fundamental education.

– In developing countries 134 million young people between the age of 6 and 11 never attend any school-program.
– Compulsory schooling introduced in many developing countries is not strictly monitored and does not guarantee the entrance into the labour market.
– Poverty and the lack of any educational training puts several millions of young people at the fringe of society: the so-called street-kids in Bogota, in Moscow, in New Delhi are on the agenda of international organizations as needing urgent help.

Experts argue that there is a direct interrelationship between illiteracy, poverty, lack of hygiene and high birth-rate, especially amongst women; therefore, the promotion of basic adult education for women is an urgent demand within UNESCO. According to UNESCO statistics there are five countries in which 90% of the adult female population are illiterate. This refers – according to the World Educational Report of 1991 – to the countries South of the Sahara, where until the year 2000 nearly 50% of the adult women should participate in literacy programmes.

UNESCO no longer holds to its forecast that illiteracy can be overcome by the year 2000. The World Declaration of Jomtien assumes that until the year 2000 about 80% of the young people aged 14 should have passed programmes of fundamental education.

Generally speaking UNESCO declares that literacy work is a process of organized learning, knowing, of course, that this vision is not reliable in every case. In many countries neither centralized organizations nor permanent funding is available for literacy activities.

In developing countries literacy work must be linked to rural development. Accordingly, these programmes are generally *„nonformal and may not fit stereotypes based on formal education"* (Knox 1993, p. 336).

Looking at Ghana, it can be stated that there was a shift at the end of the 1980s which made the situation present then quite clear: *„In 1989, the Freirean approach was accepted in a government statement as the one to be used for Ghana's Functional Literacy campaign to eradicate illiteracy among the 5.6 million illiterate adults and about 2.8 million young illiterate adults by the year 2000"* (Dorvlo 1993, p. 11). The *Fischer-Weltalmanach 1994 (1993)* gives the following figures: 40% illiterates in the Republic of Ghana *(p. 422)*, for Niger the statistics mentions 72% *(p. 538)*, for Nigeria 49% *(p. 539)*, for Ivory Coast 46% *(p. 290)*, for Zimbabwe 33% *(p. 614)*, and, to give two Asian examples, for the United Emirates 45% *(p. 667)*, for Sri Lanka just 12% *(p. 623)*.

Up to this point we have not answered the question about the nature of illiteracy. Only in passing we raised arguments for the assumptions

- that poverty and illiteracy,
- that the facilities of the education system and illiteracy,
- that the financing of educational programmes and institutions in general and illiteracy,
- that the lack of motivation and individual enlightenment, awareness and illiteracy are closely interrelated.

Referring to the given literature A. Knox argues reasonably and Solomon-like: *„They (the cited authors) agree that individual performance and societal problems are connected but do not place the main emphasis on individual deficiencies and remediation. They sometimes view such approaches as blaming the victim and suggesting non-participation by undereducated adults reflects their recognition that illiteracy is less a cause than a symptom of powerful socio-economic forces that cause their plight"* (Knox 1993, p. 103-104).

But let me finally remind you of the motto, which I cited at the beginning: *„The written word is the key to all freedoms"* *(Bhola 1994, p. 8)*. This vision and this assumption might not solve the social and individual problems immediately and promptly but by means of literacy, understood as a long lasting process – as lifelong education – we are coming closer to this vision little by little.

Bibliography

Bhola, Harbans S.: Curriculum Development for Functional Literacy and Nonformal Education Programs. Bonn: German Foundation for International Development 1979.
Bhola, Harbans S.: Campaigning for Literacy. Eight National Experiences of the Twentieth Century, with a Memorandum to Decision-Makers. Paris: UNESCO 1984.
Bhola, Harbans S.: World Trends and Issues in Adult Education. London et al.: Kingsley 1988.
Bhola, Harbans S.: Evaluating 'Literacy for Development' Projects, Programs and Campaigns. Evaluation Planning, Design and Implementation, and Utilization of Evaluation Results. Hamburg et al.: Seemann 1990.

Bhola, Harbans S.: A Source Book for Literacy Work. Perspective from the Grassroots. London et al.: Cromwell 1994.
Bhola, Harbans S. / Bhola, Joginder K.: Planning and Organization of Literacy Campaigns, Programs and Projects. Bonn: German Foundation for International Development 1984.
Bundesminister für Bildung und Wissenschaft (ed.): Prävention und Abbau von funktionalem Analphabetismus innerhalb der Europäischen Gemeinschaft. Beitrag der Europäischen Gemeinschaft zum Alphabetisierungsjahr 1990 der UNESCO. Bonn: BMBW 1990.
Delors, Jacques et al.: Learning: The Treasure Within. Report to the UNESCO of the International Commission on Education for the Twenty-First Century. Paris: UNESCO 1996.
Dorvlo, Leonard Kwami Tabernacle: Adult Literacy Teaching in Ghana. Adopting the Freirean Approach and Technique. Accra: Ghana University Press 1993.
European Bureau of Adult Education (ed.): Conference Adult Basic Education. University of St. Andrews, Scotland, June 26 – July 1, 1983. Amsterdam: EBAE 1983.
Faure, Edgar et al.: Learning to Be. The World of Education Today and Tomorrow, UNESCO. Paris: UNESCO 1972.
Der Fischer-Weltalmanach 1994. Frankfurt a. M.: Fischer Taschenbuch-Verlag 1993.
Fuller, Bruce / Habte, Akliku (eds.): Adjusting Educational Policies. Conserving Resources while Raising School Quality. Washington, D. C.: World Bank 1992.
Gage-Brandon, Anastasia J. / Njogu, Wamucii E.: Gender Inequalities and Demographic Behavior: Ghana / Kenya. New York: Population Council 1994.
Glewwe, Paul: Schooling, Skills and the Returns to Government Investment in Education. An Exploration Using Data from Ghana. Washington, D. C.: World Bank 1991.
Glewwe, Paul / Jacoby, Hanan: Estimating the Determinants of Cognitive Achievement in Low-Income Countries. The Case Of Ghana. Washington, D. C.: World Bank 1992.
Gray, William Scott: The Teaching of Reading and Writing. An International Survey. 2. ed. Paris: UNESCO 1969.
Internationales Jahrbuch der Erwachsenenbildung = International Yearbook of Adult Education. Vol. 14 (1986). Köln et al.: Böhlau 1986.
Israeli, Eitan: Lifelong Education in Israel. Continuity and Dilemmas. In: Internationales Jahrbuch der Erwachsenenbildung, 12-13 (1984-85), pp. 11-27.
James, Valentine U. (ed.): Environmental and Economic Dilemmas of Developing Countries. Africa in the Twenty-First Century. Westport, Conn.: Praeger 1994.
Knoll, Joachim H.: Tendenzen der Erwachsenenbildung in Industriestaaten. In: Internationales Jahrbuch der Erwachsenenbildung, 6 (1978), pp. 104-113.
Knoll, Joachim H.: „Multikulturalismus, multikulturelle Bildung und Erwachsenenbildung in Kanada – von außen". In: Internationales Jahrbuch der Erwachsenenbildung, 14 (1986), pp. 79-104.
Knoll, Joachim H.: Erwachsenenbildung vor der 3. industriellen Revolution. Befunde und Zukunftsprogrammatik in Quellen und Dokumenten. Ehingen: Expert-Verlag 1988.
Knoll, Joachim H.: Südöstlich von Berlin – der Spreewald und die sorbische Minderheit – eine erste Näherung. In: Internationales Jahrbuch der Erwachsenenbildung, 19-20 (1991-92), pp. 112-121.
Knoll, Joachim H.: Politik und Bildung für Minderheiten. Ein Exkursionsbericht des Lehrstuhls für Erwachsenenbildung und außerschulische Jugendbildung der Ruhr-Universität Bochum. In: Bildung und Erziehung, 45 (1992) 3, pp. 307-324.

Knoll, Joachim H.: Internationale Weiterbildung und Erwachsenenbildung. Konzepte, Institutionen, Methoden. Darmstadt: Wissenschaftliche Buchgesellschaft 1996.

Knox, Alan B.: Strengthening Adult and Continuing Education. A Global Perspective on Synergistic Leadership. San Francisco: Jossey Bass 1993.

Kreft, Wolfgang: Alphabetisierung in der Europäischen Gemeinschaft. In: Internationales Jahrbuch der Erwachsenenbildung, 19-20 (1991-92), pp. 29-44.

Lavy, Victor: Investment in Human Capital. Schooling Supply Constraints in Rural Ghana. Washington, D. C.: World Bank 1992.

McGivney, Veronica / Murray, Frances: Adult Education in Development. Methods and Approaches from Changing Societies. Leicester: National Institute of Adult Continuing Education 1991.

Neu-Altenheimer, Irmela: Der Beitrag der UNESCO zur Grundbildung. In: Internationales Jahrbuch der Erwachsenenbildung, 19-20 (1991-92), pp. 11-27.

Ouane, Adama / Armengol, Mercy Abreu de / Sharma, D. V.: Handbook on Training for Postliteracy and Basic Education. Hamburg: UNESCO Institute of Education 1990. (UIE Handbooks and Reference Books. 2)

Psacharopoulos, Georges (ed.): Essays on Poverty, Equity and Growth. Oxford: Pergamon Press 1991.

Rosier, Malcolm J. / Keeves, John P. (eds.): The IEA Study of Science. 1. Science, Education and Curricula in Twenty-Three Countries. Oxford: Pergamon Press 1991.

Sallnäs, Ingemar: Comparative Adult Education. A Handbook. Dar es Salaam: Institute of Adult Education 1975.

Schöfthaler, Traugott: Das Internationale Alphabetisierungsjahr 1990 – eine Bilanz aus Sicht der Deutschen UNESCO-Kommission. In: Internationales Jahrbuch der Erwachsenenbildung, 19-20 (1991-92), pp. 1-10.

Singh, Sohan: Learning to Read and Reading to Learn. An Approach to a System of Literacy Instruction. Amersham: Hulton for the International Institute for Adult Literacy Methods 1976.

UNESCO (ed.): UNESCO World Conference 1960, Final Report. Paris: UNESCO 1961.

UNESCO (ed.): Recommendation on the Development of Adult Education, Nairobi 1975. Paris: UNESCO 1976.

UNESCO (ed.): Fourth International Conference on Adult Education. Paris 19-29 March 1985, Final Report. Paris: UNESCO 1985.

UNESCO (ed.): Dritter Mittelfristiger Plan der UNESCO (1990-1995). Bonn: Deutsche UNESCO-Kommission 1990.

Urch, George: Education in Sub-Saharan Africa. A Source Book. New York: Garland 1992. (Reference Books in International Education. 11)

Vélis, Jean-Pierre: Through a Glass. Darkly. Functional Illiteracy in Industrialized Countries. Paris: UNESCO 1990.

Vickers, Jeanne: Women and the World Economic Crisis. London et al.: Zed Books 1991.

World Conference on Education for All, 5-9 March 1990, Jomtien: World Declaration on Education for All and Framework for Action to Meet Basic Learning Needs. Adopted by the Conference on 9 March 1990. New York: Inter-Agency Commission 1990.

Les transformations à l'Est: une leçon pour l'Ouest?[1]

Pierre Laderrière

Introduction

D'une manière générale, les changements intervenus dans les systèmes d'éducation et de formation des pays d'Europe centrale et orientale[2] (PECO) depuis la chute des régimes communistes, a alimenté une littérature consacrée à la valeur et à l'intérêt des modèles occidentaux pour reconstruire les systèmes de ces pays. Compte tenu des événements récents vécus par ces pays et des tâches de reconstruction, on a rarement posé, dans les pays de l'Ouest, la question de l'intérêt que pourrait revêtir, pour eux-mêmes, la nouvelle phase de développement des PECO. Or certains d'entre eux, comme le Groupe de Visegrad,[3] ont pour objectif, après leur admission à l'Organisation de Coopération et de Développement Economiques, de rejoindre l'Union Européenne et donc de rapprocher peu à peu, en quantité et en qualité, leur „production" de ressources humaines de celle des pays de l'Ouest.

Au début de la période de transition, l'intérêt d'un suivi attentif de la mise en œuvre de réformes profondes des systèmes d'éducation n'avait pas échappé à ceux qui escomptaient que la chute du communisme pourrait entraîner, dans certains secteurs-clé, non pas temps une réorientation majeure des politiques et des stratégies, qu'une véritable reconstruction à partir d'une quasi table-rase. D'une certaine façon, les promoteurs de certaines réformes drastiques dans les pays de l'Ouest, qui se heurtent à de très grandes difficultés de mise en œuvre auraient souhaité que les PECO, à l'occasion de la remise à plat de leur système d'éducation et de formation, deviennent une sorte de laboratoire du changement aussi „transparent" que possible. Dans des conditions politiques naturellement plus favorables qu'à l'Ouest, on aurait alors observé avec attention, si ce n'est

---

[1] Les opinions exprimées par l'auteur lui sont personnelles et ne peuvent engager l'Organisation ou les pays Membres.
[2] Albanie, Bulgarie, Estonie, Hongrie, Lettonie, Lithuanie, Macédoine, Moldavie, Pologne, République Slovaque, République Tchèque, Roumanie et Slovénie.
[3] Hongrie, Pologne, République Slovaque et République Tchèque.

concrètement soutenu, un certain type de changement induit par la vague néo-libérale ayant déjà atteint le monde occidental, quelle qu'ait été l'idéologie proclamée des gouvernements en place, et dont les nouveaux dirigeants des PECO souhaitaient s'inspirer. Comme on le sait, ce scénario ne s'est pas exactement déroulé comme leurs auteurs l'auraient souhaité. Il faut essayer d'en comprendre les raisons en analysant les conditions réelles de mise en œuvre des changements dans les PECO. Mais avant d'examiner quelques domaines précis de changement dans ces pays qui mériteraient en tout état de cause, de faire l'objet d'un suivi attentif à l'Ouest, on soulignera quelques difficultés communes aux systèmes des deux groupes de pays.

Le contexte des réformes dans les PECO

Au moment où l'ensemble des autorités responsables des systèmes d'éducation et de formation semblaient légitimer – au moins en paroles – les vues antérieures des experts et de certains organismes internationaux sur l'évolution vers une société du savoir, assise sur un développement systématique des ressources humaines *(Delors et al. 1996)*, on s'attendait à ce que cet axe politique se voit reconnaître une certaine priorité dans les premières mesures de restructuration des PECO. Or, à la surprise de bien des observateurs, ce fut loin d'être le cas. Non seulement aucune priorité ne fût officiellement proclamée au tout début des années 90, mais en outre on découvrait peu à peu une absence quasi totale de vision d'un développement intégré de l'ensemble des institutions susceptibles de contribuer à ce qu'on qualifie dorénavant d'apprentissage à vie *(Organisation de Coopération et de Devéloppement Economiques 1996a)*.

Si face à une opinion publique peu préoccupée par cette question, les partis politiques nouvellement en place n'ont pas volontairement fait „œuvre pédagogique" pour convaincre les citoyens de son importance – et agir en ce sens, c'est en particulier parce que la politique de ressources humaines liée à la logique antérieure de la planification autoritaire, avait également fait faillite aux yeux de la majorité. La plus ou moins ferme direction idéologique antérieure des systèmes d'éducation et de formation étant également rejetée par maints acteurs, ces pays se sont trouvés dans une sorte de vide à la fois conceptuel et organisationnel quant à l'avenir de ce domaine et aux grands axes de sa rénovation. Les restrictions budgétaires drastiques imposées par la période de transition à l'économie de marché à des systèmes ne reposant antérieurement que sur un financement public, ont contraint les divers responsables et partenaires des systèmes, à tous niveaux, à prendre des mesures d'urgence initialement de caractère temporaire, mais souvent appelées à durer plus longtemps que prévu et donc à re-façonner le fonctionnement même des systèmes.

Mais ces facteurs ne sont pas les seuls à retenir pour tenter de brosser un tableau de la situation. Il faut y ajouter ceux intéressant la décentralisation, subie ou voulue, selon les cas et les circonstances, de la gestion des systèmes et de leurs composantes. Cette décentralisation des responsabilités, offertes à des collectivités territoriales et/ou des établissements, s'est accompagnée d'une création (ou re-création dans le cas des écoles religieuses) et d'un développement rapide d'un secteur privé. Ce bourgeonnement d'initiatives diverses de caractère public, para-public et privé, n'a pas été, à de rares exceptions près, guidé par un cadre rénové de pilotage de l'ensemble des systèmes. Même là où subsistait une ossature administrative régionale relativement efficace *(Organisation de Coopération et de Devéloppement Economiques 1996b)*, à cause de l'absence de perspectives à long terme ou autre, couplée au manque de compétences en matière de gestion semi-autonome (si ce n'est quasi-autonome) des établissements de divers types et niveaux à la périphérie, la maîtrise de l'évolution s'est avérée très difficile.

Sur quels éléments d'information et de soutien les responsables les plus dynamiques pouvaient-ils s'appuyer? L'absence de systèmes nationaux d'évaluation tant des élèves et des diplômés que des établissements et de leurs cadres, ne permet pas encore d'avoir un rapport détaillé et pertinent sur l'état des systèmes. D'une manière plus générale, la recherche et le développement en matière d'éducation et de formation est, comme à l'Ouest, soit insuffisamment développée, soit manque de cohérence par négligence de certains domaines-clé, comme l'économie de l'éducation. En outre, la volonté d'alléger les ministères centraux, y compris pour des raisons idéologiques, a entraîné la suppression d'unités de recherche, de développement ou de prospectives en matière d'élaboration de programmes d'études, de méthodes pédagogiques, de cadrage de formation initiale et continue d'enseignants, de relation éducation-emploi etc., sans que de nouvelles unités autonomes ou intégrées aux universités voient réellement le jour ou reçoivent un financement adéquat. Dans ces circonstances, il ne restait plus à ces responsables qu'à considérer deux possibilités:

– soit importer, en les adaptant au mieux aux réalités nationales, des modèles occidentaux;
– soit reconstruire peu à peu les systèmes à partir de la base, en innovant par rapport aux besoins et aux moyens disponibles.

En général, on a suivi ces deux grands axes, l'importance de l'un ou de l'autre pouvant varier au gré des circonstances. Dans un tel contexte, il était clair que la période dite de transition allait se révéler beaucoup plus longue qu'initialement prévue.

Quelques difficultés communes

Du constat ci-dessus, on pourrait conclure que l'intérêt pour les pays de l'Ouest de s'intéresser aux changements dans les PECO et à leur contexte chaotique, apparaît bien limité. Est-ce si sûr? On peut d'abord faire l'hypothèse que peu à peu une société post-industrielle va tenter de se mettre en place dans un nombre de pays toujours plus grand, y compris donc dans ceux de l'ancien empire communiste. Mais ce n'est peut-être pas seulement l'aspiration commune à mettre en place des sociétés post-industrielles, fonctionnant aussi harmonieusement que possible, qui justifie ce point de vue. C'est aussi la difficulté de gérer ce qu'on a appelé „l'ajustement structurel" dans les pays de l'Ouest, avec son cortège de rationalisation du tissu économique et de l'intervention financière de l'État, de réorganisation du travail avec l'émergence d'une société de service, de chômage de plus ou moins longue durée frappant des couches diverses de la population, etc.

Dans ce contexte, le manque évident de volonté politique et de moyens pour bâtir une politique réelle de développement des ressources humaines dans les PECO, évoqué ci-dessus, peut être relativisé quand on compare cette situation à celle qui prévaut dans certains pays de l'Ouest. A de multiples reprises, on y a pu constater une insuffisance, si ce n'est une quasi-absence, de vision cohérente en la matière. L'interministérialité nécessaire au centre, pour coordonner, voire intégrer, de réelles stratégies d'apprentissage à vie, y font encore cruellement défaut. La base de données qualitatives et quantitatives nécessaires à la présentation régulière aux diverses parties prenantes d'un rapport sur l'état de l'enseignement et de la formation n'est pas toujours disponible faute d'appareils de collecte, de méthodes d'analyse et de moyens humains et matériels. La recherche et développement reste éclatée en de multiples lieux, incomplète et ne répondant pas toujours aux véritables questions soulevées par l'évolution nécessaire du développement des ressources humaines dans la société. Beaucoup d'acteurs du monde éducatif de l'Ouest manquent de culture d'évaluation, de développement organisationnel ou de 'leadership' et se méfient du quantitatif et d'une analyse coût/bénéfice de leurs actions. Ils continuent de raisonner comme si les ressources n'étaient pas rares dans la société actuelle et que l'éducation et la formation devraient nécessairement bénéficier d'une priorité absolue et de budgets toujours plus importants, sans réelle responsabilité et contrôle dans l'utilisation des moyens qui leur sont alloués.

Ces tendances, tant à l'Ouest qu'à l'Est, ont de graves conséquences sur la formulation et les conditions de mise en œuvre des politiques:

- en l'absence d'un solide corpus de concepts et de données sophistiquées produits par le système lui-même et s'interrogeant sur son avenir à partir de ses finalités propres, le système pour répondre rapidement à de nouvelles demandes, tend à importer ou à se voir imposer des modèles d'administration et de gestion empruntés à d'autres secteurs d'activité (comme celui de la firme dynamique), artificiellement plaqués sur un milieu plus ou moins hostile ou tout du moins peu préparé à des adaptations pertinentes;
- la crise budgétaire, reflet à la fois de la volonté de désengagement de l'État et de la crise économique rampante, tend à donner le dernier mot aux ministères des finances, toujours mieux placés que les ministères chargés de l'enseignement et de la formation pour prendre des mesures immédiates, mais rarement insérées dans un plan cohérent. Si, au total, l'architecture des systèmes et leur fonctionnement quotidien semblent actuellement mieux assurés dans les pays de l'Ouest que dans les PECO, on peut néanmoins considérer que dans un avenir à long terme et à l'issue d'une période de transition encore incertaine dans sa durée en ce qui concerne l'éducation, il sera intéressant pour les pays de l'Ouest d'examiner comment les PECO auront mis sur pied des modalités nouvelles de formulation et de mise en œuvre de politiques, stratégies et logistiques en ce domaine.

Des transformations à suivre attentivement

Malgré les grandes difficultés rencontrées dans les PECO et évoquées ci-dessus, n'y a-t-il point quelques domaines faisant actuellement l'objet de changements et pouvant offrir des pistes de réflexion, voire d'action, stimulantes pour les pays de l'Ouest? Une question récurrente est celle de l'équilibre entre les divers pouvoirs décisionnels en allant du centre vers la périphérie. Quelle place donner à des structures politico-administratives intermédiaires, au niveau d'une région ou d'un district? Quels pouvoirs leur donner à côté de ceux devant rester au centre et de ceux pouvant et/ou devant être concédés aux autorités locales (municipalités) et aux établissements eux-mêmes? Quel pourrait être le rôle de la déconcentration des pouvoirs centraux à côté du transfert de pouvoir à des collectivités territoriales nouvelles ou renouvelées dans leur fonctions? Faut-il dans le cadre de la décentralisation et/ou de la déconcentration mettre sur pied des services d'éducation et de formation séparés des autres services décentralisés et/ou déconcentrés?

Le partage des pouvoirs et la notion même de partenariat ne concernent pas seulement les divers pouvoirs publics. Alors que beaucoup de pays de l'Ouest continuent de s'interroger sur la place qu'il convient de ménager à des partenaires sociaux aussi essentiels que les divers types d'entreprises et d'administrations, l'évolution à long terme de la situation dans les PECO présente également beaucoup d'intérêt. Bien que l'effondrement des systèmes de formation de type „dual" ou de coopération école-entreprise dans l'enseignement professionnel et technique est un phénomène spécifique et de grande ampleur qui n'a pas son exact équivalent à l'Ouest, on peut néanmoins considérer que les deux groupes de pays en sont plus ou moins au même stade de réflexion sur l'avenir de ce secteur d'enseignement. D'autant plus qu'à l'Ouest, les contraintes de la mondialisation font que dans le cadre d'une compétition plus vive, certaines firmes sont plus hésitantes à investir de larges ressources dans la formation. Il subsiste encore beaucoup trop de formations spécialisées et les innovations sous forme de filières nouvelles de formation par groupe de métiers, doivent maintenant tenir compte de la nécessité d'y inclure des modules plus pluridisciplinaires et de développer des savoirs transférables. Dans les PECO comme dans certains pays de l'Ouest, le pourcentage d'élèves poursuivant des études professionnelles courtes à vocation strictement terminale doit être réduit au profit de filières nouvelles, plus longues, conservant leur vocation professionnelle et d'employabilité, mais préparant aussi, grâce à des programmes d'études rénovés, non seulement à une plus large gamme d'emplois que la transition devrait dégager, mais également à une formation continue ultérieure dans l'enseignement supérieur et d'autres institutions pour adultes. Des filières de ce type sont actuellement testées grâce à l'aide multilatérale et bilatérale *(Organisation de Coopération et de Devéloppement Economiques 1995)* comme en Hongrie et l'évaluation de leur résultats sera très importante pour tous les pays de l'Ouest.

Un troisième élément qui suscite un vif intérêt à l'Ouest est l'émergence, relativement rapide, d'un secteur privé de l'enseignement. Quelle place pourrait ou devrait occuper le secteur privé à l'avenir? A l'instar de certains pays de l'Ouest européen, la croissance exponentielle de certains établissements subventionnés, comme en République Tchèque *(Organisation de Coopération et de Devéloppement Economiques / Commission Européenne 1996)*, a rapidement soulevé un problème de régulation budgétaire, si ce n'est de contrôle de qualité, au nom de l'égalité des chances dans l'enseignement. On a constaté à cette occasion que certains établissements cumulant subventions et droits de scolarité pouvaient disposer de plus de moyens par élève que l'école publique de même catégorie. C'est donc les groupes sociaux élevés, capables de faire face à un coût élevé d'études, qui bénéficient de cette situation, tandis que l'appauvrissement d'autres groupes pendant la période de transition, ne permet pas toujours de supporter le coût croissant des études. Ce phénomène n'a pas seulement concerné des établissements de statut privé, puisque des universités publiques ont pu recruter des étudiants „hors-quotas" en leur faisant payer un droit d'inscription relativement élevé compte tenu de l'état des finances publiques. La fameuse trilogie: „privatisation – droits d'inscription – égalité des chances" continue donc de susciter des interrogations dans les deux groupes de pays.

Si l'on considère le problème des ressources humaines qui sont affectées aux systèmes, on peut également trouver dans la situation des PECO matière à réflexion. Ce qui est apparu le plus intéressant au niveau de la direction des établissements scolaires, dans un contexte de vide juridico-pédagogique et de crise budgétaire, aura été le dynamisme de certains chefs d'établissement. Sans souvent bénéficier d'une formation adéquate, ni de structures de soutien, ces chefs d'établissement ont maintenu en survie leur école, voire les ont hissé à un plus haut degré d'efficacité grâce à la mobilisation de ressources locales, en particulier des parents. Face à l'impossibilité pour le pouvoir central de maintenir le niveau de financement antérieur, les parents et les diverses collectivités locales ont été mises à contribution, révélant en cela des sources additionnelles de financement. Parallèlement à cette action, des chefs d'établissement ont engagé, avec leur personnel, et certains partenaires sociaux, une réflexion et une mise en œuvre de nouveaux programmes d'études mieux adaptés aux besoins des élèves et de la société. Cet effort, soutenu en particulier par des aides multilatérales et bilatérales dans l'enseignement technique et professionnel, apparaît, dans le meilleur des cas, comme une tentative très intéressante de reconstruction de ce type d'enseignement particulièrement sinistré, par la base. Sans négliger l'inspiration que peut offrir les exemples occidentaux, cette stratégie a pour intérêt de mieux ancrer le changement dans le contexte national et local d'évolution des besoins.

On se doit également de souligner, à côté des chefs d'établissement, le dynamisme de certains responsables de l'enseignement, régionaux ou de district, qui, à leur niveau de responsabilité, tentent de mettre en œuvre une approche horizontale des problèmes et de leur solution, grâce à des relations constantes avec tous les acteurs et partenaires sociaux actifs à ce niveau. Enfin, la description des efforts novateurs ne serait pas complète sans la mention des tentatives faites dans certains pays pour récompenser les enseignants les plus dynamiques ou pour proposer un statut rénové du corps enseignant. Même si les moyens disponibles à cet effet sont notoirement insuffisants, c'est un pas en avant, dont une application plus systématique justifierait un suivi particulier, tant cette question de la prise en compte du mérite dans le travail des enseignants reste un sujet de controverse en Europe de l'Ouest.

Conclusion

L'effondrement des régimes totalitaires d'Europe de l'Est a pris tout le monde de court tant à l'Est qu'à l'Ouest. Dans une conjoncture économique et budgétaire difficile des priorités ont été établies dans l'urgence, et le développement des ressources humaines n'en ont pas initialement fait partie. Les premières lois-cadres indispensables à la reconstruction des systèmes d'éducation et de formation soit se sont fait attendre, soit ont été trop succinctes ou ont donné des satisfactions immédiates à certains acteurs au détriment d'une vision à long terme. Néanmoins, grâce à des initiatives individuelles et collectives, dans un contexte de plus grande liberté d'entreprendre, des politiques et des stratégies nouvelles ont été peu à peu mises en œuvre pour répondre à des problèmes fondamentaux partagés par des pays d'Europe de l'Ouest. Ces derniers devraient donc en suivre le développement et en étudier attentivement les résultats.

Bibliographie

Delors, Jacques et al.: L'éducation. Un trésor est caché dedans. Rapport à l'UNESCO de la Commission internationale sur l'éducation pour le vingt et unième siècle. Paris: UNESCO / Jacob 1996. [Version anglaise: Learning: the Treasure within. Report to UNESCO of the International Commission on Education for the Twenty-First Century. Paris: UNESCO 1996]

Organisation de Coopération et de Développement Économiques. Centre pour la Coopération avec les Economies en Transition (ed.): Examens des politiques nationales d'éducation: Hongrie. Paris 1995. (OCDE/GD(95)143)

Organisation de Coopération et de Devéloppement Économiques (ed.): Apprendre à tout âge. Paris: OCDE 1996a.

Organisation de Coopération et de Devéloppement Économiques. Centre pour la Coopération avec les Economies en Transition (ed.): Examens des politiques nationales d'éducation: Pologne. Paris: OCDE 1996b.

Organisation de Coopération et de Devéloppement Économiques / Commission Européenne (eds.): Examens des Politiques nationales d'éducation: République Tchèque. Paris: OCDE 1996.

Relationships of Political Contexts to Democracy in Education

Robert F. Lawson

Introduction

The relationship that I will attempt to describe is that between political assumptions and educational policy – interpreting with special reference to equity provision and its connection to national typologies of democracy.

My laboratories for this analysis are: 1) the former German Democratic republic as a model of theoretical and systematic politicization; 2) Canada as a model of laissez-faire politicization; and 3) apartheid South Africa as a model of culturally-based multi-system politicization. As different as these tentative nations appear to be, they are comparatively useful as models (and have been in my work) because of their derivation from and retention of basic European educational forms in the contexts of Europe itself and in the African and North American colonies.

One way of viewing change is to assume that the usual pattern is one in which the society, as a whole and with minimum disturbance or conflict, steadily reconstructs itself; but that this evolutionary progression may be modified, even to the extent that its form and direction shift, through a sudden political rupture or through the intervention of external „noise" into the social communication system. The elements of conflict do not disappear however. The stuff of the society remains, reorganized but identifiable. The quicker and more drastic the change, the more intact and potential are the values, relationships and „knowledge" of the old society. There is some doubt that education, except in the broadest sense, influences socio-political change or initiates new structuring, and historical evidence for the conservative conspiracy of the education institution is not compelling. Education is simply one of the means by which the present structuring principle is activated. Because of its pervasiveness in and integrity with contemporary culture however, it has immense indicator value for study, and has powerful negative capability *(Lawson 1972)*.

In the societies treated, an evolutionary cultural progression is subject to institutional alteration by specific political events, internally and externally induced. The sources of data for this comparison are essentially from my own work on concrete actions and structural results, but generally instructive works contributing to the interpretation are cited. An interpretation at this macro level must rest on indicators of educational intention, ideological pre-suppositions, planning procedures, system interactions, and social communication which may have heuristic value for a „typology".

The use of comparative method allows the idiosyncratic nature of educational assumptions, decisions, structures, and practices to be determined, and to be set against national claims based on a supposed universal standard of equity. The particular notions of equity, and means of achieving it in education, must then be examined as dimensions of respective concepts of democratic policy. Whether the practice fits the intention in each of these countries, and whether the equity dimension, weak or powerful, overrides other dimensions as a criterion of overall policy are the questions to be addressed.

The criteria for the equity question are system provisions, that is, formal policy and institutionalized measures for accomplishment of equality of access, equality of treatment, and the equality of results (outcome). Latent or informal obstructions, hypocritical policy intentions, mixed messages, and resistance by powerful group actors are equally relevant on the negative side *(Robinsohn et al. 1970)*.

The Socialist Typology of the Former German Democratic Republic

The educational structure established for the German Democratic Republic in 1946 was built of a loosely unified system of recognizable German institutional forms, revised mainly along the lines of historical debate between the left and right in the politics of German education.

Probably the most formidable requirement of a „mobilization system" in education is the reinterpretation of traditional cultural content, language and values to accord with a new political definition. Not only was this done directly, but it was accomplished through bridging concepts such as work, represented by polytechnicization in education, and by collective means. The „politicization of all political life" under central authority, the socialization to East German political life, the very totality of the system – were the basic principles for this translation. All were institutionalized and justified by political

„religion" *(Apter 1963, p. 78)*. One indication of similarity in historically, culturally or organizationally different states is a presumptive „omniscient" leadership perceiving the society as alone, ringed by enemies whose actions are opposed to government interest, and therefore to national interest as guarded by the ruling party. The responsibility then of the leadership is to provide for and secure the people, which requires a continually intense political life, a firm grip on authority, and an effective socialization and communication program. The leaders are fortified by their belief, that the resistance to the destructive tendencies of the modern world is a moral obligation of a people prepared by history to conceive a new order of cultural-political synthesis. The rejection of such presumptions of the state leadership by the people was instrumental in the changes which led finally to the collapse of communist regimes in Eastern Europe *(Mitter 1990)*.

The presumption of the absolute morality of the State demanded *political morality within the established order* of all citizens of the G.D.R. The ideology justified totalitarian authority and permitted exploitation of traditional moral precepts (work, discipline, frugality) in the interest of the economic strategies and political power of the ruling party, say „class". International communication intruded on that internal message. The mode of politicization in the G.D.R. required hierarchical administrative structures and active state socialization. Educational policy was determined from the deliberations of pedagogical congresses which allowed a limited collective role in decision-making, a concentration on means of incorporating new pedagogical information into the curriculum and skills of teachers, and a review of structure and administration according to current party ideology. Both administration and teaching programs operated within a closed system, so there was no possibility that congress decisions would lead to change in administrative style, in institutional behaviors, or, through new information, to essential change in context or epistemology *(Anweiler 1986, 1988)*.

New policy decisions were directives, to be carried by administrators into school operation, where they became collective obligations. Contrary to system rhetoric, collective action was much more functional for implementation than for initiative or decision-making. Decisions were carried directly and overtly into the personal and interpersonal conduct of teachers and students, and into the immediate supervision of curriculum content. In this regard, the exercise of policy complemented the exercise of socialization. That is, actions of administrators and teachers were expected to reflect and to accomplish unquestioning loyalty to the order. This involved a continual rationalization in terms of older and competing values, and an enshrinement of work for both ideological and performance reasons.

The Socialist Unity Party held to old-line communist behaviors. The continuity of hard, unyielding, aging leaders, conditioned by their own struggles through the 1930s and 1940s, created gray, authoritarian, rigid institutional structures which, like themselves, became obsolete while appearing invulnerable – until October 1989.

What was wrong politically in the G.D.R. cannot be applied to equity questions of democratic education. In fact, as the system changes under unification, the sacrifice of gains made in this area may be questioned. The gains included: 1) acceptance and use of equity as a system principle; 2) implementation of the principle through structural and ideological means of achieving equal dignity of all work, through collective responsibilities not only for accomplishing goals but also for building social behaviors and through acceptance of uniformity in those areas where diversity has traditionally meant inequality (e. g., housing, schooling, social services); 3) evaluation of successful implementation in terms of equality of *results* – meeting economic needs, rewarding work, recognizing human status. In regard to social justice, within which equity policy fits, the question is whether the institutionalization of liberal-capitalist ideas will be as sensitive to equity.

Where this broke down has largely to do with the intrusion of other motives or realities. Nonetheless, the reasons are relevant to equity policy. First, the poor quality of life generally occasioned a perception that social equalization means economic loss for *most* of the people, not for a few. Second, the Leninist style of imposing change by a Party authority did not fit easily with the moral dimensions of equalitarian action. Third, the very requirements of national advancement, in the interest of economic and psychological good of all, led to the promotion of excellence (thus status) in international competition, in science, arts and sports particularly. Increasingly, the drawing of talent and performance out of a collective mediocrity signaled inequality of reward, even though the basis departed from the near European past.

Definition of the „national" context is always colored by the interests of the Soviet Union in the history of the G.D.R. and has now submerged into the interest of the new Germany. Outside interests have been influential in Germany since World War II, so the attitude of other powers cannot be ignored in policy decisions on national interest *(Engelbert / Baske 1966)*. The perception of the U.S. and U.S.S.R. and of other European countries, East and West, was for a long time that the post-World War II re-definition of East and West Germany did not and should not serve a German „national" interest, indeed that there was no legitimate national self-interest for Germany. Only with the sequential change in the posture of the U.S. and its former allies and with the dissolution of the former Soviet Union, allowing „space" for German political determination, can institutional provisions for equity be expected to be framed by policies developed independently and consciously in the (West) German national interest. Even so, the regional legacies of „national" policy, because of their substantially opposed ideological histories, are more likely to prolong structural conflict than to result in a consensual pluralism.

In the G.D.R. the party purported to be managing the society for long-term „national" interest, but the perception of the people and of most analysts for some time was that short-term power interest became dominant *(Childs 1985)*. The eruption of opposition once the lid was lifted, after all the years since 1953 if not 1944 (much earlier than the 1962 used in the media) shows the policy itself to have been not sustainable in the long run *(Böhme 1989)*.

Education's role was restricted by its tightness with other institutions in the total system of the G.D.R. The same plans, directives, methods and behaviors were distributed throughout the operations of the unitary state. The very connections which are needed to enliven education in Western liberal societies here limited the dynamism, closed the content, and ideologically channeled interactions. Education was narrowly defined to reproduce a Marxist-Leninist society and economy through direct political infusion.

Given the rigidity of ideas and authority in the last years of the G.D.R., the change of political status makes that education irrelevant, and inapplicable in the eastern provinces now. That does not rule out means and forms developed to serve openness, equality, and social interest, and which could continue to do so as regional or system variants in German or other systems. These means include polytechnical curricula and practice, collective approaches to social responsibility, the serious consideration of philosophy and sociology at school levels, the promotion of new talent in artistic fields, the excellence developed within a physical education program reaching everyone, collaborative research on defined problems of social practice, and the retrieval of excluded aspects of the Western intellectual record.

Since the German school, in elementary, technical, and advanced forms, has had a way of living through political disasters with an intact core, it appears that the formal structures in education need to be targeted for social democratic change. Those informal but formalized processes, such as youth organizations (e. g. Freie Deutsche Jugend) which were used as a part of the state control system are not adaptable to a changed political structure. Interestingly, this may be the reverse of the case in South Africa.

The Cultural Segregationist Typology in South Africa

The first and most obvious observation about white ruled South Africa is: The state was not the people. Second, its rationale was theocratic and meta-colonial. The Christian, familial foundation, identified community as *„part of a national and wider order ... [with] no sharp distinction between the natural universe and the state"* (Apter 1963, p. 72). Belief in divine support and religious justification provided authority for actions of the state and warded off immediate criticism by outside parties. (Such values and beliefs in a society are of course available to opponents as well as those in power.) South Africa, of all African colonies, reproduced the total European state apparatus in an African environment. The attempt was not exclusive to South Africa historically, but its success and endurance were unique. In this form, indigenous people are given the „advantage" of metropolitan culture, but kept caste-differentiated. The colonizers take *also* the identity of the colonized, defining themselves as Africans *(Harrison's, 1982, „white tribe")*. The adaptation of European culture(s) through this identification, symbolically in the language of Afrikaans, meant eventually a total political (but not cultural) separation from parent countries individually, then collectively as in the case of the British Commonwealth, thus completing the formation of the meta-colony.

This identification pertains to what became the ruling Afrikaner ideology. English South Africans were inside and outside the ruling elite: inside because they were, in the „natural order", automatically included and because they had political power when they wished and continue to have economic power; outside because historical conflicts separated them from Afrikaners politically and because they never took collectively the identification which would separate them from European culture and nationality. Characteristics of the meta-colony accommodated the English fantasy of having it both ways.

What this model meant for equity in and through education is well known, as separate structures and hierarchical administration under white control were direct features *(Burman 1986)*. From that institutionalization stemmed inadequate financing, shortage or lack of materials, separate socialization patterns, non-system provisions (e. g. farm schools), and absence of uniform attendance standards.

Reference to the policy evolution of Western countries or to democratic criteria framed in the present period is however ahistorical and reductionist here. American media, later, popular academic involvement never understood or accounted for the nineteenth-century use of „legitimate national interest" on the part of the South African white government to structure a model necessarily recognizing diversity but managing it according to European interests and means. The government claims did not purport to address universal equity, for implicit theocratic and economic reasons, for explicit economic and functional reasons. The government claimed to provide equality through provision of a full ladder of schooling every group separately, a standard curriculum, a European content basis (supposed to be superior by the same reasoning that allows Western academics to expend development assistance funds teaching what they know), through systematic administration, and distribution of wealth (seen to be „white" wealth) to black education in more than equal measure (by racial category, not per capita). In sum, the government provided separate systems of the same institutional scope, affording opportunity for mobility within each racial community, the finances of black communities being augmented by employment and welfare aid. These are characteristics of the model.

Proposed changes stayed within the model, they proposed to increase financial support to black education, partly by levying higher fees on whites. Private school experiments paved the way for voluntary community decision on integrated schooling. Even transitional changes appear to maintain the concept of separation and to define equal opportunity meritocratically. This is conceptually however a far cry from what the leaders of the theocratic state construct. Thus the philosophical infrastructure had already shifted before apartheid was given up. While the old claims were based on equality of treatment within the black population and on opportunity greater than that in other African (comparison-unit) countries, the reform claims were directed toward a competition for higher levels of education on non-racial grounds and toward a fairer distribution of places. The question now is whether to go beyond these criteria for access and treatment, thus jumping to equality of results.

The national interest has never been seen in any unified way by South African groups. Therefore the historical decision of Afrikaner Nationalists to consolidate political power may be seen, not as an alternative to separation, as it would mean in Western politics, but as the only way of guaranteeing (separateness) insularity *(Thompson 1985)*. The reality of group solidarity is recounted in the battles of the Boers against the hostile forces, natural and human. The ideal of totally occupying a large and diverse national environment is a fiction started with some cynicism by Europeans and idealized with some ruthlessness in practice by Americans. Africans accept the inevitable antagonism arising when powerful cultures collide. The Afrikaner solution was thus both African and European, but an improbable synthesis.

The obvious social organization was the necessary inclusion of other groups in the state, but defined and structurally separated. These structures were conditioned by political and racial tones of contemporary periods *(Adam / Moodley 1986)*. The separate opportunities were seen in the 1920s as beneficial and inclusive *in the African context*. In the 1950s, when challenges to racism were brewing internationally, South Africa drew the wagons in a tighter circle with Apartheid policy. In the 1980s international pressure caused the structures to be unlocked in the ways that were used earlier in Western countries. Note however that the countries exerting the greatest pressure are now least comparable. The 'elder members' of the Commonwealth and the United States have faced no overt revolutionary political changes by dismantling racist structures.

It is a Western fantasy to believe a racially constructed state can change under a reformist government to a polity devoid of racial criteria. Politics have become everywhere more rather than less socially-ethnically categorical *(Giroux 1991)*. The inside government interest, reflecting not only white but traditional nationalist views, was not compatible with outside views of South African national interest based on liberal-democratic or socialist models. This put the government in too isolated a position to withstand change, and too late to seek reformist solutions. Since South Africa has been generally more prosperous, stable, environmentally conscious and developmental than other African states however, the change of regime may not serve a broader national interest in the short run and will be dependent on emerging political conditions and specific policies for resolving *African* questions in the long run. Neither the socio-economic outcome for individuals nor the national interest will necessarily be served by equity measures constructed in the ideologies or social contexts of European or other African countries *(Natrass 1983)*.

What can the existent educational institutions contribute to the search for South African equity and real national interest? There is a history of discord everywhere in almost all relationships and schools have been out of tune with their own communities. „Baby-Boomer" generation white adults have largely adopted a rhetoric critical of their traditional culture and institutions without confronting that reality in institutions, therefore leaving the attitudes of youth to just happen. The militancy of black youth is muted generally under the optimism and respect for the new leadership, but urban youth were separated from rural communities during the liberation struggle, and the hostilities among major ethno-linguistic groups is communicated through education and literacy campaigns. With such confusion and disagreement about interests in cultural communication, it is difficult to see the schools as part of a democratic resolution, although students and teachers have certainly participated in the means.

Education is institutionally bound to known structures. It is generally slow to change, closed in content, and conservative in teacher training and role definition. Within these structural constraints however are a new generation of students and liberal teachers who are capable of ensuring another stream of thought and action *(Christie 1985)*. Thus, in a transition period, there are likely to be two irreconcilable streams. Formal education cannot be foreseen to have the capability of instituting strong enough measures fast enough to build a new foundation for national interest. For equity and long-run national interest, consensus for a massive populist, informal education effort appears to be necessary – one including literacy, culture content, vocational direction, if it is reinforced by youth organization, and if it is framed by „comity" and political respect.

The Laissez-faire Typology of Canada

In the spirit of Canadian history, education policy analyses have tended to derive principles from an evolutionary sequence, and to rely heavily on both European (British and/or French) background and North American environment as explanatory factors. While fundamentally useful, such general attribution does not account for the actual policy translations, initiatives, and educational effects in Canadian communities. Although basic cultural influences frame policy process, they are modified significantly through immediately pragmatic approaches to the administration of education, which are in turn conditioned by contemporary knowledge, local characteristics and contests among educational groups seeking influence over education.

Educational policy offering greater educational opportunity and greater individualization of programs has been brought about largely by the removal of some of the constraints that assured traditional socialization, social selection, and cognitive development through the general-education system, with results still favorable to the existing order of society *(Archer 1979)*. The control exercised by traditional elites, either directly through educational selection and occupational recruitment or indirectly through public acceptance of the primacy of certain schools and learnings, has been contested, but the weakening of constraints has not affected the „monopoly" of power in the educational establishment *(Porter 1965)*. On the contrary, it may be reinforced in the areas of uncertainty provided by such a transitional situation. Nevertheless, the cultural monopoly of certain groups in the society has been threatened and the exclusive rights and powers of those persons and institutions in education claiming preferred cultural or political status has been challenged.

The conflict in this situation is now not between social classes or dominant and powerless groups, but between those who see and priorize the social and educational consequences of democratic principles applied to education differently, and secondarily between those who have articulated their intentions and those who have not. It is a conservative portion in an established Western democracy that continued implementation of democratic principles does not require continued substantial institutional change. It is also a naive portion that the structure and rules of democratic educational institutions do not allow, may even promote normative and behavioral changes which contradict some of those principles or render others inoperative. The democratic emphasis on diversity and openness has exposed fundamental problems of economy, feasibility, and the unity of the educational system itself *(Moodley 1989)*. In the absence of creative ideological or structural change, educational policy actors have compromised with the public on substance, and compromised with each other on organizational and technical matters, without disturbing the structure of influence in the policy contest *(Lawson / Woock 1987)*. While this has provided a short term stay against confusion, it is a solution of political means rather than of cultural agreement on educational substance. Although Canada exhibits more than usual policy equivocation, the balancing of disagreement in Western democracies is now more evident than the pursuit of consensus. Societies which are forced to put too much of their effort into the politics of education conserve nothing and change nothing.

In the ostensibly open and liberal social policy environment of Canada, the obstacles to equity take the form of ambiguity, and political pretense not directly aimed at inequity but at power retention which *results* in inequity. The ambiguity shows itself in the many operational compromises made between unbridled capitalist activity in business and banking on the one hand, and the services and attitudes supporting socialization in basic areas of life such as health, welfare and education, on the other. In public or personal relations the ambiguity is between authority and equality (or freedom, whose relationship to either requires a separate discussion). The ambiguity is made manageable by institutionalized separation. The structural and personal level, what you see, is either open or pretends to be. The machinery of the system, what you don't see but do experience, is governed by the rules of authority, which of course become incorporated into social behaviors.

The Canadian Charter of Rights, proclaimed in 1982, brought legal provision for the first time to prevent discrimination on grounds of ethnicity or race by recognizing the equal rights of all citizens. It is relevant to the argument above that a) constitutional rights in regard to schooling are the affirmation of those adopted in 1867 for the „charter groups"; b) protection is guaranteed to individuals; c) neither of the first Canadian minorities, French Canadians in Quebec or aboriginal peoples are satisfied that their collective rights have been adequately addressed; d) although affirmative action programs are enabled, interpretations so far have emphasized the threat to the rights of all which implementation of such actions would entail *(Lawson / Ghosh 1986)*.

In the Canadian model then, equity policies result in acceptance of more categories (women, ethnic minorities, handicapped persons) both officially and in social interaction, but always on some neutralized meritocratic and authoritative terms. This means that gender and racial balance can be affected over time, but any shift is not likely to change the rules, or to affect inequality as a characteristic of the system. That is, inclusion of new social categories reduces discrimination based on *those* categories (e. g. race); it does not alter automatically the inequality inherent in a privilege system.

National definition has developed out of reliance on abundant natural resources, immigration of talent, and regional economic specialization, thus in material terms which though providing unequally for the different regional populations, have been assumed to provide an understood basis of public policy. Internally, where national interest is considered directly, it is in regional terms, or nationally to guard the economic or cultural products which appear essential to Canadian survival. Externally, the indifference with which Canada has been treated by its major referent nations, Britain and the U.S.A., has in recent years turned the government toward the middle powers, toward increased involvement in the Third World, and toward leadership in the Commonwealth. These connections undoubtedly have an effect on equity policies within Canada. How they affect Canada's traditional view of itself is not apparently a primary question, nor is the political relevance of given international connections and positions to Canada's long-term national interest. Short-term interest is considered in *ad-hoc* ways that proceed from decisions made by authorities on shifting criteria of immediate self-interest and protected by continual compromise politics.

In the form of this system, education is loosely related to other institutions. It tends also to function on two levels: a fragmentary, popular top over a traditional base. Although different sectors (subjects, regions, persons, school types) could be shown to carry more or less of each message, that is, of cultural givens or of popular, often imported change, the two levels are discernible generally, in structure, content, and teacher-administrator behaviors. The system is not closed or ideological. It is stubbornly status-quo at the root, and inconsistent at the top.

Education's role in equity provision is mildly favorable, following Canadian political philosophy as that might be inferred from history and external affairs *(Hampson/Maule 1993)*. Rhetoric of intercultural openness, presumed to characterize Canada's social effectiveness if not moral superiority, the actual interest arising out of Canada's well advertised involvement in the third world, and response to pressures and spokespeople from these countries lead to an acceptance of educational change with the appearance of the times. Sensitivity to equity questions can be said to characterize Canadian education, and schools have activated equity values through behavior and content instruction (possibly more for race than gender; more for both than for handicap, personality difference, or poverty).

Because of the relative autonomy of institutions however, education's reciprocal effect in society is weak, and its relationship to national direction generally irrelevant.

Conclusion

The three models generalized here represent approaches to democracy through: forced separation (South Africa); political-economic management, or forced unification (German Democratic Republic); and voluntary manipulation of competitive structures (Canada). In all cases, governments have believed they were addressing equity in ways that fit their historical circumstances and that would minimize social conflict *(Almond/Verba 1963)*. Political leaders rationalized their power not only in terms of national interest but with an historically understood moral purpose *(Leff 1969)*.

Education has been used as an agent of that stabilization process, but appears traditionally to have simultaneously carried messages which worked against the abuse of power and obsolescence of political methods. Thus, while institutionalized education cannot be said to have been a force for social equity, it may have been a necessary prior support. The use of equity politics (gender politics and race politics particularly) by contestants using media, including schools, of cultural communication casts a new light on this kind of analysis. While I have treated these systems as historically rooted twentieth-century reinterpretations of different assumptions about the nature and means of educational opportunity derived from respective political infrastructures. Analyses of the above question requires an equally critical interactive comparison of contemporary political action affecting shifts of power and ideology, thus the meaning of democracy.

What results from this comparison is that equity is less influenced by equity measures than by power – where and by whom it is held formally and informally, its amenability to redistribution, what epistemology governs its legitimacy and exercise, and how it relates to the distribution of social goods and rights. National interest, in any objective sense, is less influenced by management, planning, and direction than by the popular perception of sharing in what can be expected and by outside perception (international, or regional or cultural bloc) that the nation is acting as expected, and therefore pursuit of its own interests can be separated from or combined with the interests of others in understood ways.

Bibliography

Adam, Heribert / Moodley, Kogila: South Africa without Apartheid. Berkeley: University of California Press 1986.
Almond, Gabriel A. / Verba, Sidney: The Civic Culture. Political Attitudes and Democracy in Five Nations. Princeton: Princeton University Press 1963.
Anweiler, Oskar (ed.): Staatliche Steuerung und Eigendynamik in Bildungs- und Erziehungssystemen osteuropäischer Staaten und der DDR. Berlin: Spitz 1986.
Anweiler, Oskar: Schulpolitik und Schulsystem in der DDR. Opladen: Leske und Budrich 1988.
Apter, David: Political Religion in the New Nations. In: Geertz, Clifford (ed.): Old Societies and New States, London: Collier-Macmillan 1963, pp. 57-104.
Archer, Margaret: Social Origins of Educational Systems. London: Sage 1979.
Böhme, Ernst: Die Gelegenheit ist günstig. In: Der Spiegel, 43 (1989-10-30) 44, pp. 20-21.
Burman, Sandra / Reynolds, Pamela (eds.): Growing up in a Divided Society. Johannesburg: Sached/Ravan 1986.
Childs, David (ed.): Honecker's Germany. London: Allen and Unwin 1985.

Christie, Pamela: The Right to Learn. The Struggle for Education in South Africa. Johannesburg: Sached/Ravan 1985.
Engelbert, Martha / Baske, Siegfried (eds.): Zwei Jahrzehnte Bildungspolitik in der Sowjetzone Deutschlands. Vol. 1. 2. Heidelberg: Quelle und Meyer 1966.
Giroux, Henry: Border Crossings: Cultural Workers and the Politics of Education. New York: Routledge 1991.
Hampson, Fen / Maule, Christopher: Canada among Nations 1993-94: Global Jeopardy. Ottawa: Carleton University Press 1993.
Harrison, David: The White Tribe of Africa. London: British Broadcasting System 1982. (Perspectives on South Africa. 31)
Lawson, Robert: Education as Change Agent and Change Object in the Two Germanies. In: Helbig, Louis / Reichmann, Eberhard (eds.): Teaching Postwar Germany in America, Bloomington: Indiana University, Institute of German Studies 1972, pp. 127-144.
Lawson, Robert: Education in Postwar Berlin. A Comparative Laboratory. In: Compare, 18 (1988) 2, pp. 117-126.
Lawson, Robert / Ghosh, Ratna: Canada: Policy Issues in the Education of Minorities. In: Education and Urban Society, 18 (1986), pp. 449-461.
Lawson, Robert / Woock, Roger: Policy and Policy Actors in Canadian Education. In: Ghosh, Ratna / Ray, Douglas (eds.): Social Change and Education in Canada. 3. ed., Toronto: Harcourt, Brace, Jovanovich 1987, pp. 133-142.
Leff, Gordon: History and Social Theory. University: University of Alabama Press 1969.
Lessard, Claude: Equality and Inequality in Canadian Education. In: Ghosh, Ratna / Ray, Douglas (eds.): Social Change and Education in Canada. 3. ed., Toronto: Harcourt, Brace, Jovanovich 1987, pp. 178-195.
Mitter, Wolfgang: Das Bildungswesen in Osteuropa im Umbruch. In: Osteuropa, 40 (1990) 10, pp. 909-924.
Moodley, Kogila: Educational Ideologies and Political Control. State Responses to Cultural Diversity. In: Tomlinson, Sally / Yoger, Abraham (eds.): Affirmative Action and Positive Policies in the Education of Ethnic Minorities (= International Perspectives on Education and Society. 1), Greenwich, Conn.: JAI Press 1989, pp. 17-29.
Natrass, Jill: The Dynamics of Black Rural Poverty in South Africa. Durban: University of Natal Development Studies Unit 1983.
Porter, John: The Vertical Mosaic. An Analysis of Social Class and Power in Canada. Toronto: University of Toronto Press 1965.
Robinsohn, Saul Benjamin et al.: Schulreform im gesellschaftlichen Prozeß. Stuttgart: Klett 1970.
Thompson, Leonard: The Political Mythology of Apartheid. New Haven, Conn.: Yale University Press 1985.

L'éducation à la citoyenneté dans l'Europe multiculturelle: une perspective comparative

Donatella Palomba

L'éducation à la citoyenneté est une question particulièrement actuelle aujourd'hui en Europe, en raison des grands changements de la dernière décennie dûs soit aux transformations politiques qui se sont produites sur le continent (changements de régime, naissance de nouveaux États, agrégations, ré-agrégations et divisions territoriales et nationales, plus ou moins marquées de conflits et de mouvements de population), soit à l'augmentation et au changement de nature du flux migratoire provenant d'autres continents, qui a commencé à s'orienter également vers des pays qui n'en étaient habituellement pas touchés, ou qui, comme l'Italie, étaient au contraire eux-mêmes des pays d'émigration.

Sur le thème de l'immigration, au cours des dernières années le débat s'est largement centré sur l'accueil des étrangers, donnant une place toujours plus grande au droit à l'identité culturelle et donc, sur le plan éducatif, aux thèmes et aux problèmes de l'éducation multi- et interculturelle.

Toutefois, au-delà du moment de l'accueil de l'étranger ou de l'immigré, se dessine progressivement aujourd'hui une société dans laquelle, de plus en plus, ce n'est pas seulement et pas tellement „d'immigrés" que l'on doit parler, mais de citoyens à part entière, qui ont des origines différentes, aux racines souvent hors de l'Europe: ces citoyens sont de plus en plus nombreux, bien qu'on doive remarquer qu'une évaluation quantitative est impossible, puisque, dans un laps de temps relativement court, cette caractéristique „disparaît" des statistiques dans la majeure partie des pays, en raison de l'aspect discriminatoire évident que pourrait revêtir un recensement des citoyens en fonction de leurs origines ethniques.

Le *focus* du problème se déplace donc de la question de l'accueil à celle de la construction d'une citoyenneté commune dans une société où la pluralité des cultures présentes est beaucoup plus ample et plus hétérogène que la pluralité liée aux minorités historiques. Il s'agit donc d'élaborer un modèle de société et d'éducation qui soit en mesure de former un citoyen en respectant les différentes identités, mais aussi l'appartenance commune, dans une entière parité de droits et de devoirs.

C'est dans ce sens que les pays européens affrontent une problématique qui se rapproche, mais sans s'y identifier, de celle qui existe dans les États nés de l'immigration, comme les États-Unis, le Canada, l'Australie, la Nouvelle-Zélande, où justement le débat sur ce sujet a une longue tradition et a connu récemment des développements ultérieurs, avec une attention toute particulière au rôle de l'éducation. Le caractère central de ce rôle est bien prouvé, entre autre, par l'attention que lui dédient non seulement les théoriciens et les praticiens de l'éducation, mais également les spécialistes de divers secteurs – juristes, sociologues, philosophes – qui, à partir de différents points de vue, arrivent à traiter des questions typiquement éducatives.

La problématique en question est particulièrement importante lorsque l'on parle de „citoyenneté européenne". Les pays européens, selon les traditions politiques et culturelles de chacun d'entre eux, ont des politiques différentes sur la citoyenneté, et d'autre part, de nombreux citoyens, auxquels on demande de se sentir européens et de trouver des raisons pour une appartenance commune européenne, sur la base de racines communes, ne sont pas de descendance européenne. C'est ainsi que se pose le problème de „construire" une nouvelle citoyenneté, une nouvelle appartenance à partir de nombreuses diversités; dans ce cadre, l'éducation doit être repensée d'une façon nouvelle par rapport à la tradition de formation à un État national, mais en même temps, elle ne peut pas en faire abstraction.

L'appartenance à une communauté politique *„constitue en réalité le droit d'avoir d'autres droits: les droits individuels n'ont aucune signification dans l'isolement, ni aucune réalité pratique si l'on ne peut légitimement les faire valoir; pour être un citoyen pourvu de droits, le fait d'appartenir à une communauté politique (qui pourrait même être différente et plus ample qu'un État national) semble être une condition nécessaire"* (Albala-Bertrand 1995, pp. 3-4).

L'éducation à la citoyenneté requiert certainement une perspective qui ne se limite pas à celle de l'État national. Dans une société démocratique, il existe certains droits inaliénables qui doivent être garantis à chacun, que l'on soit ou non citoyen à part entière; mais le débat pour définir quels sont ces „droits inaliénables" reste ouvert, et postule, en dernière analyse, une citoyenneté „mondiale", supranationale, qui se projette dans une dimension de dépassement de la réalité nationale. Selon plusieurs spécialistes, on peut déjà remarquer certains éléments de ce dépassement; toutefois, aujourd'hui encore, l'accès à la citoyenneté passe à travers l'appartenance à un État.

La reconnaissance de la citoyenneté européenne passe en particulier à travers la citoyenneté des États membres; les conditions pour la concession/reconnaissance de la citoyenneté varient cependant pour chacun d'entre eux, selon différentes combinaisons de *ius soli* et *ius sanguinis*. Loin d'être une simple question administrative ou bureaucratique, ou même strictement „politique", ces critères reflètent quelque chose de beaucoup plus substantiel, puisqu'ils indiquent en réalité les conditions posées par une société pour que quelqu'un ne soit plus considéré comme „étranger", mais comme l'un de ses membres à part entière.

L'accès à la citoyenneté européenne est donc filtré par des critères qui varient de pays à pays en répondant à différents *„projets sociaux d'ensemble" (Melotti 1995)*; l'éducation à la citoyenneté suit à son tour des approches correspondant à des philosophies qui ne sont pas identiques dans les différents pays; ceci a une incidence sur les différentes politiques d'éducation à l'Europe, tant sur le plan des contenus (curriculum européen) que sur celui des attitudes et des valeurs.

Une première considération concerne donc l'opportunité d'une comparaison entre les „modèles" des différents pays européens, qui, à partir du pluralisme „historique" européen et du nouveau pluralisme de la citoyenneté multiculturelle, examine à fond la diversité des approches, pour identifier des points communs et des différences.[1]

Une telle analyse conduit donc à toucher certains aspects brûlants du rapport entre les anciens et les nouveaux pluralismes. Même dans leurs différenciations, la „citoyenneté démocratique" et „l'éducation à la démocratie" font historiquement partie intégrante du cadre de référence commun européen, au point qu'elles sont souvent indiquées comme les caractères qualifiants d'une véritable „éducation à l'Europe". Dans la période historique actuelle, ceci prend place, dans le contexte de certains États, dans une phase de transition politico-institutionnelle; dans d'autres cas, il s'agit plutôt d'élaborer une conception commune de citoyenneté à partir de différentes cultures.

---

1   Un premier essai se trouve dans *Palomba (1995)*. Pour une réflexion sur la citoyenneté européenne à partir de l'expérience des formateurs, voir aussi *Friebel (1996)*.

Mais lorsqu'on traite le problème de l'éducation à la démocratie, spécialement en présence d'une pluralité de cultures, ce n'est pas seulement la signification que l'on attribue au terme de démocratie qui entre en jeu, mais aussi la légitimité même d'une éducation qui mise sur la tradition démocratique libérale par rapport à des cultures qui n'y appartiennent pas nécessairement. Le débat sur ce sujet, dont nous ne rappelons ici que quelques-uns des aspects marquants, est très vif, et met en lumière les contradictions qui apparaissent et la nécessité de réflexion que cela provoque.

Le point focal est la cohérence de „l'éducation à la démocratie" par rapport à la conception démocratique elle-même.

Comme il a été dit, étant donné que les cultures et les religions ne reconnaissent pas toutes les théories normatives des droits et des obligations des êtres humains sur lesquelles se base la démocratie constitutionnelle, celle-ci risque de devoir affronter un problème qui la place en contradiction avec elle-même: „*l'enseignement transmet inévitablement des valeurs, même lorsqu'il ne traite pas des questions religieuses fondamentales. Jusqu'où une telle transmission à des enfants obligés de fréquenter l'école, mais manquant encore de maturité intellectuelle et émotive, est-elle en accord avec les valeurs de la démocratie constitutionnelle, même si les valeurs transmises sont celles de la démocratie constitutionnelle? C'est-à-dire, la démocratie constitutionnelle est-elle identique aux autres formes de gouvernement, en ce qu'elle essaie de se préserver elle-même par l'endoctrinement des générations futures?*" (Murphy 1994, p. 49).

Murphy arrive à la conclusion que l'éducation à la démocratie se distingue de l'endoctrinement non seulement sur le plan des contenus mais surtout sur le plan de la méthode, puisque, dans la mesure où il s'agit d'une éducation critique, elle provoque chez les élèves une réflexion sur la démocratie elle-même, et donc, elle peut même conduire à son dépassement. Il faut cependant remarquer qu'il reconnaît la légitimité d'un possible dépassement de la démocratie constitutionnelle seulement si celui-ci est encore plus „fondé sur la raison" que la démocratie constitutionnelle elle-même, c'est-à-dire seulement dans une direction qui soit de toute façon située à l'intérieur du même horizon. Mais le plus gros problème réside justement dans la légitimité de soumettre les enfants à la procédure critique, qui est en elle-même culturellement marquée.

On peut convenir, avec Michael *Walzer (1995, p. 186)*, qu'une éducation à la démocratie doive comprendre l'histoire, la philosophie et la pratique de la démocratie. Mais Walzer lui-même nous avertit que ce projet éducatif peut être perçu, – et constituer en fait –

un programme de subordination culturelle s'il s'adresse à des cultures qui n'acceptent ni ne partagent les principes démocratiques libéraux qui constituent en quelque sorte le cœur de toute la réflexion sur l'éducation à la citoyenneté démocratique (en particulier, la valeur de l'autonomie de jugement individuel et la possibilité de se confronter avec, ou tout du moins de connaître des valeurs et des points de vue différents). Les modèles proposés par la culture occidentale ne sont pas ces procédures neutres que l'on voudrait parfois. *„La citoyenneté démocratique n'est pas une idée neutre: elle a sa propre histoire, et elle est orientée vers sa propre culture (politique)"* *(ibid., p. 185).*

D'autre part, l'éducation à la démocratie et la citoyenneté démocratique ne s'identifient pas simplement à des „contenus" spécifiques de l'enseignement. Nous savons combien l'on vise, pour cette éducation, à des approches transdisciplinaires et, surtout, à susciter une participation active et critique des jeunes à la vie scolaire, qui permette d'intérioriser le modèle d'interaction démocratique. Ceci répond à une conception qui voit la démocratie avant tout comme une *way of life,* une façon d'affronter la vie, qui implique la formation de la personnalité toute entière.

„La démocratie est de toute manière et toujours une politique de tension. On gagne et l'on perd, on prend la responsabilité de gouverner sans jamais avoir suffisamment de pouvoir, on vit pendant des années dans l'opposition, on fait des compromis sur ses propres engagements les plus profonds, on cohabite avec des personnes qu'on n'aime pas et en qui on n'a pas confiance ... La politique de la différence est à la fois un produit de la démocratie et un danger pour elle. C'est pour cela que l'éducation est si importante: un apprentissage scolaire (et une expérience pratique) visant à produire la patience, la résistance, la tolérance et la réceptivité sans lesquelles la tension ne peut être ni comprise ni acceptée" *(ibid., p. 188).*

Tel est le modèle de comportement et de valeurs qui est à la base-même de l'éducation à la citoyenneté démocratique, mais qui peut constituer un problème et peut même être totalement inacceptable pour des cultures qui ne partagent pas les principes de base; c'est ce modèle même, d'autre part, qui demande à la démocratie, sous peine qu'elle ne se trahisse toute seule, de laisser de la place à ces autres cultures, de leur donner, justement, un „droit de citoyenneté".

La possibilité de déterminer une forme politique qui soit capable d'être „accueillante envers la différence" sans se trahir elle-même et sans renoncer à défendre ses propres valeurs a été l'objet de contributions désormais nombreuses, avec des positions très différenciées.

En particulier, on a essayé d'opérer une distinction entre diverses acceptions du multiculturalisme, dans le sens „fort" ou dans le sens „faible", et entre divers types de libéralisme, selon que l'on considère la reconnaissance de l'autonomie individuelle comme quelque chose d'irrenonçable pour admettre l'acceptabilité d'une culture, ou que l'on considère comme acceptables des cultures et des sociétés qui ne la reconnaissent pas comme une valeur de fond, pourvu qu'elles soient „raisonnables". La notion de *„société raisonnable"*, introduite par Rawls, est discutée, avec des références spécifiques aux thèmes éducatifs, par Yael *Tamir (1995, p. 167)*, qui signale la distinction possible entre un libéralisme *„basé sur l'autonomie"* et un libéralisme *„basé sur les droits"* (c'est-à-dire qui donne une valeur primordiale aux droits des individus sans pour autant les concevoir comme des droits fondés sur des prérogatives de choix autonome); Tamir fait remarquer que ce dernier type de libéralisme peut exprimer *„non seulement la tolérance, mais aussi le respect pour des cultures non libérales 'décentes' qui, bien qu'elles ne promeuvent pas un idéal d'autonomie personnelle, respectent leurs membres et leur permettent certains moyens de participation et d'influence sociale"* (ibid., p. 168).

Bien sûr, une telle distinction n'est pas unanimement acceptée, puisque pour beaucoup, il est impossible de renoncer à l'autonomie personnelle comme valeur de fond de tout libéralisme et de toute conception acceptable de „démocratie"; c'est ici qu'est fondamentale l'opposition entre ceux qui considèrent que les titulaires de droits sont avant tout les individus, et ceux qui pensent au contraire que les droits, et tout particulièrement les droits culturels, peuvent être attribués à des groupes, même si cela comporte des limitations pour les individus. (Un exemple intéressant du débat à ce sujet se trouve dans *Taylor 1992.*)

Nous n'entendons pas nous attarder ici sur ce débat, qui montre cependant clairement comment le multiculturalisme devient une sorte de „révélateur" de la réflexion démocratique, par rapport à de nombreuses questions primordiales. En ce qui concerne l'éducation en particulier, le multiculturalisme, loin d'être simplement l'un des nombreux problèmes qui se présentent à notre futur, en constitue probablement un point crucial. En effet, toutes les contradictions et les conflits du rapport entre les cultures se reflètent inévitablement et particulièrement dans l'éducation, qui est le lieu destiné à transmettre celles-ci. Il n'est pas seulement nécessaire de trouver des façons d'agir, mais aussi et surtout d'opérer des redéfinissions de concepts, également indispensables pour diriger des actions efficaces. „*Les phénomènes du multiculturalisme invitent à reconsidérer la plupart des concepts utilisés dans la théorie politique: appartenance, frontières, citoyenneté, souveraineté, droits de groupe et droits individuels, pluralisme, tolérance, démocratie, représentation. Aucun de ces concepts ne peut être utilisé de façon traditionnelle. Il faut leur donner à tous une nouvelle forme et une nouvelle justification. Mais le multiculturalisme exige surtout une redéfinition des fins et des moyens de l'éducation"* (Tamir 1995, pp. 171-172).

L'horizon de réflexion et de recherche qui s'ouvre dans cette perspective est certainement très complexe, et peut porter à se demander quelles pistes de recherche l'on peut trouver pour défricher ce terrain si difficile et qui nécessite une remise en question de tant de fondements.

Une place privilégiée peut être donnée dans ce cadre à l'approche comparative. D'une part, des auteurs comme *Taylor (1992)* la considèrent comme essentielle pour l'élaboration d'un modèle „accueillant envers les différences", puisqu'une ouverture à un type d'étude culturelle comparative est supposée être indispensable pour une reconnaissance non superficielle de la valeur des autres cultures.

D'autre part, sur le plan plus strictement inhérent aux questions éducatives, les recherches comparatives sont en mesure de fournir une importante contribution. Au moment où se présente l'exigence de repenser certains concepts de fond, la comparaison permet de vérifier les diverses acceptions et conceptions, pour mettre en évidence leurs ressemblances et leurs différences, voir s'il existe des éléments „forts" communs et analyser quels sont les rapports des différents éléments avec leurs contextes. Ceci est particulièrement vrai en ce qui concerne le concept d'éducation à la citoyenneté démocratique. Même parmi les pays qui se réclament de la démocratie, la signification qui lui est attribuée n'est pas nécessairement identique, et on peut encore moins postuler que les modèles transmis par les systèmes éducatifs soient identiques. La comparaison permet donc d'approfondir la connaissance, tant théorique qu'appliquée, de l'éducation à la citoyenneté démocratique, à travers la connaissance des façons dont elle est conçue et mise en œuvre dans de différents pays et situations.

L'étude comparative des modèles historiquement présents dans les pays de l'Europe occidentale jette, comme nous l'avons remarqué précédemment, une lumière importante sur des approches qui, tout en se situant dans un cadre avec de forts éléments communs, présentent des aspects différents. En perspective, le défi est d'être capable de mieux comprendre les nouveaux problèmes qui se présentent à l'intérieur des sociétés européennes, ainsi que d'élargir l'horizon au-delà des contextes politiques et culturels consolidés, dans la nouvelle situation mondiale.

Prenons deux exemples de l'ampleur des objectifs, mais aussi des difficultés de telles entreprises dans deux recherches comparatives de grande envergure actuellement en cours.

Au début des années quatre vingt dix, l'une des plus importantes associations internationales de recherches comparatives sur les systèmes éducatifs, l'International Association for the Evaluation of Educational Achievement (IEA), a décidé de mener une deuxième enquête sur la *civic education*, après celle qui fut faite au début des années soixante dix, à laquelle avaient participé une dizaine de pays appartenant pour la plupart au monde occidental industrialisé.

L'opportunité de cette seconde enquête est attribuée principalement aux profonds changements de caractère politique et social survenus au niveau international, ainsi qu'aux changements concernant la considération du rôle de l'école (parmi lesquels la reconnaissance de l'importance du curriculum caché). L'une des nouveautés les plus évidentes du projet actuel réside dans la présence, parmi les plus de vingt participants, de nombreux pays de l'Europe orientale et de quelques pays asiatiques, c'est-à-dire de pays dans lesquels le problème de „l'éducation à la démocratie" est perçu comme ayant des caractères d'une urgence et d'une importance particulières.

Le but de l'étude est *„d'identifier et d'examiner dans un contexte comparatif la manière dont les jeunes sont préparés à soutenir leur rôle comme citoyens dans les démocraties et dans les sociétés qui aspirent à la démocratie, ainsi que les aspects d'identité politique qui sont importants pour eux. ... La fin première sera d'obtenir un cadre illustrant comment les jeunes sont initiés aux différents types et niveaux des communautés politiques dont ils sont membres"*. D'autre part, on ne désire identifier „aucune meilleure définition particulière de citoyenneté ni aucune meilleure approche de l'éducation civique"; on se base plutôt sur *„la supposition que ces définitions et ces approches ne peuvent jamais être complètement séparés du contexte d'une société particulière et de sa culture civique" (Torney-Purta 1996, p. 2)*.

La première phase de la recherche prévoit que chacun des pays participants accomplisse une étude de son cas national; cette étude de cas doit discuter les politiques, les pratiques et les problèmes ouverts à propos de la formation pour la citoyenneté, en se référant à des questions-clé, qui sont déterminées d'un commun accord. Les domaines sur lesquels se concentrent principalement l'attention et l'intérêt des pays participants, selon ce qu'on a constaté pendant cette phase, sont la signification de la „démocratie" et des institutions dans lesquelles elle se concrétise; l'identité nationale (même dans ses relations avec les identités sub- et supranationales); les problèmes relatifs aux minorités et aux groupes privés de droits. Ceci était en grande partie prévisible mais confirme cependant combien ces thèmes sont cruciaux dans un grand nombre de pays.

Dans la seconde phase de l'étude (phase qui est à ses débuts) on essaiera donc d'obtenir des connaissances sur ce que les jeunes savent et croient à propos de ces thèmes. Par conséquent, on prévoit l'élaboration de tests et de questionnaires visant à sonder non seulement les connaissances, mais aussi les attitudes, les concepts et les comportements des jeunes par rapport à ces points fondamentaux. Evidemment, cela présente de grandes difficultés en raison de la complexité particulière du domaine en question et de la nécessité d'utiliser des méthodes tant quantitatives que qualitatives, mais l'un des objectifs et des centres d'intérêt de cette recherche est justement la tentative de dépasser l'aspect purement cognitif, en se servant de méthodes rigoureuses. L'enquête sera menée sur des échantillons, qui soient représentatifs sur une base nationale, de jeunes d'âge compris entre 14 et 15 ans, ainsi que (en option) sur un échantillon de jeunes fréquentant la dernière année de l'enseignement secondaire.

Le Bureau International de l'Education (BIE) a également lancé, récemment, un projet de recherche et d'expérimentation, „Quelle éducation pour quelle citoyenneté?", qui se propose de rechercher comment se présente effectivement l'éducation à la citoyenneté et quelle en est la signification dans une pluralité de situations et de cultures différentes. L'enquête, qui porte sur le dernier cycle de l'enseignement secondaire, est effectuée sur des échantillons représentatifs d'élèves, d'enseignants et de parents, dans une quarantaine de pays de toutes les régions du monde.

Le projet du BIE est soutenu par un fort engagement pour l'amélioration de l'éducation à la citoyenneté en fonction du développement de la paix et du respect des droits de l'homme. Le projet a donc l'intention soit de contribuer à l'approfondissement de la connaissance et de la compréhension des pratiques d'éducation à la citoyenneté dans les États participants, soit d'aider à formuler des politiques éducatives en la matière sur la base de résultats de recherche fiables. L'un des objectifs principaux est de divulguer les résultats: avant cela, cependant, une phase expérimentale est prévue, avec une série de projets finalisés pour tester et contrôler dans des situations spécifiques la validité des conclusions obtenues, de façon à éviter des transpositions et des généralisations insuffisamment fondées.

D'autre part, le projet veut examiner s'il est possible de trouver des points communs dans les approches de l'éducation à la citoyenneté qui soient présentes dans des sociétés et des cultures différentes: ceci permettrait d'envisager des pratiques éducatives avec des éléments communs, ce qui pourrait contribuer „*à l'idéal de construire une culture partagée de paix, de démocratie et de droits humains, tout en respectant une variété de cultures diverses*" *(Albala-Bertrand 1995, p. 2).*

En accord avec l'attention consacrée aux possibilités de cohabitation pacifique et démocratique entre les hommes, dans les documents de base on donne une large place à la discussion sur la compatibilité des modèles culturels, avec une référence particulière aux différentes conceptions de citoyenneté et de démocratie, ainsi qu'aux rapports entre individu et collectivité, comme ils se présentent dans les différentes cultures. L'hypothèse de fond qui reste, toutefois, est que la démocratie est encore et toujours le meilleur cadre pour accommoder les différences: „*Il semble probable que la démocratie soit le seul système politique qui puisse fournir un cadre dans lequel un dialogue interculturel peut produire une relation synergique entre l'indépendance personnelle, l'autonomie de la communauté et un sentiment d'appartenance collective. L'éducation à la citoyenneté devrait faire particulièrement attention à renforcer ces orientations sociales et morales, ces messages et ces pratiques qui soutiennent l'appréciation des différences, mais qui soulignent en même temps le sentiment d'appartenance collective*" *(ibid., p. 5).*

A la lumière de l'analyse effectuée plus haut et des contradictions qu'elle met en évidence, ce ton pourrait sembler trop optimiste. On s'attend cependant à ce que les résultats des recherches contribuent à vérifier si ces hypothèses sont valides, et s'il y est possible d'identifier des affinités ou des „traits d'union" entre les différentes conceptions.

Pour ce qui concerne notre continent en particulier, la tradition européenne est basée sur les valeurs universelles et sur les droits fondamentaux de l'homme, dont les droits du citoyen ne peuvent pas faire abstraction. D'autre part, nous savons bien que, s'il est vrai que les droits du citoyen n'ont pas de signification réelle en absence d'une communauté politique de référence, il est également vrai qu'une appartenance politique formelle ne crée pas d'elle-même une véritable „citoyenneté", qui implique l'adhésion a des valeurs partagées.

Pour une formulation de principes qui puissent être partagés à l'intérieur de l'Europe et en même temps échapper autant que possible aux risques de l'eurocentrisme, l'analyse des modèles européens de citoyenneté doit tenir compte tant de l'horizon problématique ouvert par le nouveau multiculturalisme européen, que du cadre international plus vaste dans lequel s'insère l'Europe.

La possibilité d'une interaction entre les différences qui, tout en prenant en compte les inévitables conflits, n'exclue pas un consensus minimum, est évidemment le pari du futur et, bien sûr, il n'est pas facile à gagner. Il est vrai d'autre part que l'éducation ne peut pas se dispenser des responsabilités qui lui incombent dans cette tentative.

La question traitée se rapporte aussi à la possibilité, longuement débattue, d'élaborer un „curriculum européen". Nous avons soutenu ailleurs *(Palomba 1994)* que, dans toute action visant à construire quelque chose de commun, l'éducation doit avoir un rôle actif et créatif, et ne pas être considérée simplement comme un canal de transmission de contenus élaborés en d'autres lieux. Ceci demande l'implication active de tous ceux qui sont engagés dans le monde éducatif: notamment, les enseignants et les élèves. Une si grande participation pourrait sembler utopique, mais en ce moment historique elle peut devenir possible en Europe dans le cadre du renforcement des échanges et des interactions entre institutions scolaires de tous niveaux, qui travaillent à des projets visant non seulement à identifier et confronter des points communs et des différences, mais aussi à construire des programmes éducatifs communs. Il s'agit là d'une procédure permettant de tenir compte concrètement des différences, du moment qu'une action de base est la plus apte à permettre une participation réelle du plus grand nombre de cultures, anciennes et nouvelles, existant en une situation donnée.

Un tel processus a partiellement démarré; mais la position théorique doit se maintenir très solide. Comme le rappelle *Mitter (1996, p. 309), „il y a un nombre croissant d'initiatives transnationales dans lesquelles sont engagés aussi bien des chercheurs que des enseignants. Leurs efforts tendent à concevoir des curriculums européens basés sur les valeurs fondamentales des droits de l'homme, démocratie, paix et tolérance, et de la protection de l'environnement"*. Mitter observe toutefois que tout cela se légitime seulement si l'on évite le *„risque de négliger les différences nationales, ethniques et culturelles";* tandis qu'une perspective correcte, et en même temps concrète, est celle d'un *„rapprochement des curricula, à travers une accentuation des valeurs universelles de fond dans leur relation avec les particularités européennes"* (ibid., p. 311).

Parmi les „particularités européennes", on compte aussi la présence d'héritages très différents par rapport à l'Europe même. Une „citoyenneté européenne" ne serait pas fidèle aux valeurs européennes si elle n'était pas capable de s'y confronter: et en cela l'éducation comparée peut avoir un rôle important à jouer.

Bibliographie

Albala-Bertrand, Luis: What Education for What Citizenship? In: Educational Innovation and Information, (1995) 82, pp. 2-9.
Friebel, Wim (ed.): Education for European Citizenship = Education à la Citoyenneté Européenne. Freiburg i. Br.: Fillibach 1996.
Melotti, Umberto: Immigrazione e culture politiche. In: Prometeo, (1995) 1, pp. 20-29.
Mitter, Wolfgang: European Curriculum: Reality or a Dream. In: Winther-Jensen, Thyge (ed.): Challenges to European Education. Cultural Values, National Identities and Global Responsibilities (= Comparative Studies Series. 6), Frankfurt a. M. et al.: Lang 1996, pp. 295-312.
Murphy, Walter F.: Per creare i cittadini di una democrazia costituzionale. In: Bonazzi, Tiziano / Dunne, Michael (eds.): Cittadinanza e diritti nelle società multiculturali, Bologna: Il Mulino 1994, pp. 15-52.
Palomba, Donatella: Dimension européenne et pluralisme culturel pour l'Europe de demain. Quelques réflexions. In: CESE Newsletter, (1994) 36, pp. 7-12.
Palomba, Donatella: Cittadinanza e educazione. In: Scuola Democratica, 18 (1995) 1-3, pp. 79-88.
Tamir, Yael: Two Concepts of Multiculturalism. In: Journal of Philosophy of Education, 29 (1995) 2, p. 161-172.
Taylor, Charles: Multiculturalism and the „Politics of Recognition". Princeton: Princeton University Press 1992.
Torney-Purta, Judith: Civic Education. Proposal for Phase 2. Vancouver: IEA-CIVICS 1996 (typoscrit polycopié).
Walzer, Michael: Education, Democratic Citizenship and Multiculturalism. In: Journal of Philosophy of Education, 29 (1995) 2, pp. 181-189.

The Crisis in Schools and Solutions to the Problem

Vlastimil Pařizek

Many politicians, economists, educators, and sociologists emphasize the increasing role of education in present and future societies. Education is seen as an essential route to employment, economic competitiveness, social efficiency and more generally the survival of mankind. In addition to education within the family it is the quality of school education in particular which is essential because schools are attended by all young people in developed countries, they offer a system of knowledge, skills and values, and establish a framework for life-long education.

A number of studies and reports, however, have drawn attention to a crisis of education in many countries. The definition of this crisis varies according to the particular continent or country. One reads about the poor performance of school-leavers as being an obstacle to economic development, about students' lack of ability to solve non-standard problems, about weak knowledge of fundamentals, about functional illiteracy and about aggression among children. A large number of politicians, administrators, employers, parents, teachers and students are dissatisfied with the schools. The need to improve schools is the underlying concern of many international conferences as well as the congresses of the World Council of Comparative Education Societies. The task of this paper is to analyze the traits and reasons for the 'crisis' in schools and to give a brief outline of possible solutions.

By the term 'crisis' we understand, in accordance with its original Greek and Latin definitions, 'decision', 'crucial turning point' or 'decisive moment'. There are many reasons for such a turning point in education and society. In spite of the relatively high prestige of education there is also a certain amount of dissatisfaction with educational theories, institutions and with the process of teaching and learning, namely with curricula, methods of teaching and learning, and with textbooks.

The Three Reasons for the Crisis in Schools

First, the discrepancy between what is taught in schools and how it is taught, and what school-leavers really need is the first reason for the crisis. In practical terms this means that school-leavers only apply a small part of what they have learnt at school in their jobs and social lives; that a considerable number of university graduates cannot find jobs in their field or remain unemployed; and that a proportion of students feel bored in the classroom. The ability of students to employ scientific methods when solving even simple problems is often poor; they are unable to communicate in foreign languages and display a low ability to collaborate, learn and work.

The main cause of this discrepancy is the rapid development in the main spheres of society accompanied by rapid growth of scholarship, arts and practical knowledge and at the same time by slow changes in schools.

The second reason for the current crisis in schools is closely linked to the crisis in society: the faults and failures of adult society, drugs, nicotine, alcohol, gambling; the way violence and brutality are presented in films; the decreasing interest of some parents in education as a result of the increasing diversity of education; perhaps both parents having their own careers; or the lack of attention paid by town planners and administrators to the needs of young people are beginning to have an influence on schools. The crisis in education is a reflection of the crisis in society. It is not, however, only a reflection of the negative aspects. Successes in sciences and arts, social welfare, acts of goodwill and good parenting also find repercussions in schools and contribute to social reforms. Schools have often been instrumental in improving society. The current crucial turning point in society needs to be supported by a change in schools.

Third, the teachers, if we are to consider them as 'professionals', are responsible for the quality of teaching and learning, for knowledge, skills and values mastered by their students, just as physicians are responsible for people's health and lawyers for people's awareness and observance of the law. Furthermore teachers, together with other actors in the field of education – politicians and school administrators, parents and the public, employers and students – are able to influence the school system and the conditions in which they work. The low engagement of teachers' organizations in this respect is the third reason for the current crisis in schools.

From what has been said about the reasons for the present state of schools it is possible to conclude that the solutions to the crisis in education are both external and internal. Let us first examine the external relationships operating between education and the main spheres of life. It is possible from an empirical point of view to distinguish and analyze five such fields: work, societal relations, health and environment, concern for the future generation, and leisure.

Education and Work

The economy is a criterion of the usefulness of education from both individual and social points of view, but not directly. Work itself is reciprocally connected with all other spheres of life: it relates to the social structure and has a deep impact upon it, it relates to the health, education and lifestyles of people and is able to improve or adversely affect all these phenomena. Therefore education has a strong impact upon work not only through vocational skills, but also through its influence upon human interaction, health, care of children and lifestyles.

A good relationship between schools and businesses depends on close collaboration between schools, employers, parents, students, and authorities at all levels of school administration. At present in many countries one of the obstacles to an effective solution is a lack of information and flexibility. Edmund *King (1992)* suggests that the participation of 'young adults' in the curriculum-making process could make an effective contribution. Rapid developments in technology and employment structures create uncertainty for both vocational and general education. Education in a constantly changing society should be general enough to cover all developments in the sense of general skills, creativity and general values such as responsibility and willingness and ability to work. It can be concluded that each stage of vocational training should be accompanied by general education because every job is a social phenomenon engaging the whole personality of an employee including his communication skills.

Education is a substantial factor in economic growth and: „*There can be no doubt that education and training, in addition to their fundamental task of promoting the development of the individual and the values of citizenship, have a key role to play in stimulating growth and restoring competitiveness and a socially acceptable level of employment in the Community*" (*Commission of the European Communities 1993, p. 117*).

Education and Human Interaction

It is rather difficult to evaluate the role of education from the viewpoint of societal change because of the controversial ethical values of our society. The values of competition, a career in a hierarchical society, and of social prestige can conflict with the ideas of collaboration, modesty, tolerance, charity, social equality, friendship and brotherhood. The value of hard work conflicts with the value of leisure, the prestige of private property with the cost of a child's education, financial profit with an honest life. Social values are only partly identical with economic ones. The conflicts of many ethical ideas are woven into family education and schools. As far as education is concerned, this means changing the entire system of education, according to Hegel, and of teaching children not the mere rules but the methods of human interaction: to analyze concrete situations, to select values which are good for the child and at the same time for other people, and to choose the best models of behavior through critical analysis of alternatives and their consequences.

Therefore the philosophy of education, the relationships between school, family and community, between teachers and students are the crucial aspects of present educational reform. Three approaches to the moral development of children and young people are most influential – if they are in harmony:

- the intellectual progress of children, their knowledge of nature, society and men;
- humane interaction within the family, schools, clubs, youth organizations, and the church, including the methods of education the child acquires together with the content of the values learnt;
- critical identification with other people, imitation of parents, teachers, classmates, friends.

Education is not the only factor shaping the personality of a person. It is always linked with inherited qualities and with objective social and economic determinants. Each person naturally has freedom of choice and also responsibility for his own actions.

Many primary and secondary schools pay little attention to the class atmosphere, and to the behavior of children, and merely focus on subject matter. Schools stress subjects, the teaching and learning of knowledge and skills. Values, however, remain in the shadow of these prevailing rational aims. Teachers are trained as experts in particular subjects and not in moral education. Moreover the organization of teaching – a secondary school teacher has more than two hundred students a week – reduces the attention paid to the social aspects of life in a classroom.

The role of education in solving social problems is twofold: a direct role, via the acquisition of a system of socially accepted values including socially fair methods of solving social conflicts, and an intermediary role, through social aspirations and social and economic status influenced by education.

Education and Health

The role of education in health care has rapidly changed and increased during the last several decades because of declining physical conditions especially in industrial centers, and because of aspirations toward a longer life and new medical knowledge. The health of young people is threatened by drugs, air pollution, chemicals in water and food.

Education is difficult because of the negative influences of parts of society. Adults who smoke and drink, drug pushers and peers who consume drugs, all have negative influences on children, and conflict with educational aims.

The impact of all these negative influences upon the young generation is not that critical because of family and school education, and because of the freedom to choose from different models of behavior. Unfortunately, many schools are not fully equipped to respond to these demands and consider health to be the domain of medical institutions and the medical education of teachers is limited. Even some biology textbooks, for example, had shortcomings in this respect. On the other hand, there are schools with excellent programmes for health care and environmental protection. Enlightenment has become an increasingly important condition for the survival of each individual because health is at least partly in ones own hands.

Education and Child Care

It is universally accepted that caring for children is a necessary condition for the survival of each social group. Our society accepted the Convention on the Rights of Children *(United Nations 1992)*, it safeguards the financial means for their existence, and offers children medical care and school education. On the other hand the rapidly decreasing number of children in industrially developed countries as well as the population explosion in many poor countries both provide – from different points of view – evidence of the low interest of adults in the welfare of children and consequently in the future of a social group.

Present day society is also controversial in this sphere. The target economy pressure, the claims of professional careers of women with higher education, and social aspirations of both parents, the decreasing sense of responsibility for children expressed in the theory of 'antipedagogics' lead to the conclusion that for rich societies children to some extent are not a priority value.

Caring about children is closely connected with caring about the family and with the prestige of mothers in the society. It is clear that the mother cannot be replaced by any institution and that the absence of a close relationship between mother and child during its first four years can produce a deprived child and that the number of deprived children is increasing. On the other hand it is also clear that investment in a good education of children has a lifelong effect and benefits the whole of society *(Parnes 1986)*.

Education and Leisure

Leisure is of the utmost importance in influencing productivity at work, humane interactions, and the health and education of children. It is an advantage of societies whose members spend their weekends and holidays together with children engaged in cultural, physical, vocational or work activities. An attractive leisure program is the best preventive measure against gambling and drugs among young people. Unfortunately many big cities suffer either from a shortage of facilities or from a lack of organized activities. Towns were built for adults rather than for children or especially teenagers which are sometimes forced to participate in questionable activities.

Some Solutions to the Crisis in Education

Routes out of the labyrinth of schools are lit by a model of society in the 21st century and current trends, and by a model of future mankind. An awareness of social trends is necessary if one is to prepare children to avoid and resist future threats and to support positive tendencies. The traits of education are derived, as Comenius projected in the

17th century, from a program of improvement in human affairs and from the point of view of man in the changing world.

From a historical point of view our society has passed through three main cultural eras: Antiquity, Christianity and the Age of Enlightenment. All of them were built, modified and partly destroyed by men according to the changing needs of the society. We now face a new crucial change of the order expressed in an impetuous criticism of each unity, totality, belief in absolute truth and supremacy of reason in favor of plurality of values and truths. The present trends are expressed in terms of Post-Industrial Society and Post-Modernity which can be understood as the search for a new order adequate to the needs of the reform of the whole society characterized by Globalization, by a European Dimension of Thinking, by each individual's development to their maximum potential.

Schools are slowly moving towards compatibility with the trends in economy, in solutions to social conflicts, in ecology, biology and physiology. On the basis of present discussions and trends we can learn that there are five main strata of education:

- education according to the needs of an individual;
- education in agreement with local needs;
- education directed towards national aims or aims of the state;
- European dimension of education; and
- global education.

Each of these strata could be – and has been – over- or underestimated but essentially all of them are necessary. Everybody grows up as an individual, and at the same time as a member of a social group, of a nation which is a unit of a continent and of the world. Each of these levels of social life has special unavoidable functions for the survival of an individual and for the society. All of them are interrelated.

There is a tension among them: the needs of an individual, of a nation and of mankind are not identical. History offers many examples showing that discrepancy among them has ended in war, but it also offers examples of endeavors for achieving harmony among them. Harmony depends on possibilities for finding agreement in interests at all levels of life and in all spheres, in food, energy, population growth, raw materials, air and water, it means finding a world order satisfying the main needs of most human beings. Today we are still far from achieving this.

The political and economic problems are at the same time problems of educational institutions including families, schools and adult education. Harmony among all these strata is most important for education and education itself can help to strengthen existing positive events.

Conclusion

The solution of the crisis in schools cannot be found in education itself. But in taking into account the external determinants, the educational systems have a large space for their own programmes. Schools are changing in three crucial areas or levels: 1) the doctrines, theories, concepts, ideas; 2) the system of educational institutions; and 3) the process of education, of teaching and learning. All these aspects of education are changing from two main directions: from above, it means by the initiatives of governments and parliaments changing legislation, finance, system of institutions, system of control in states, by the activity of the European Union, UNESCO, World Bank, World Health Organization and other bodies of larger competence, like the World Council of Comparative Education Societies; and secondly from the bottom through the activities of teachers, pupils, parents, employers, local authorities and citizens' organizations. If both these ways proceed in agreement, the transformation of schools can be efficient and education can influence the social development thoroughly. Agreement is necessary especially with regard to the following principles:

- Education should be a locomotive of economic and social development.
- The role of education should increase and therefore one of the main priorities of policy should be to establish sufficient educational opportunities with good teachers as 'professionals'.
- The balance between equality and quality of education is one of the crucial points of school policy. A combination of universal education and a diversity of educational opportunities is a necessity for the school system as well as for society.
- The increasing impact of the market economy upon education may be in conflict with some educational aims and will result in the re-examination of the philosophy of educational institutions.
- Schools are expected to educate students in such a way that they will be able to resist all present and future threats and dangers. There are positive features of our society, but the main attention should be paid to the risks threatening young people and society.

Bibliography

Burrows, Brian / Mayne, Alan / Newbury, Paul: Into the 21st Century. Twickenham: Adamantine Press 1991.
Cerych, Ladislav: Educational Reforms in Central and Eastern Europe. In: European Journal of Education, 30 (1995) 4, pp. 423-435.
Cetron, Marvin / Gayle, Margaret: Educational Renaissance. New York: St. Martin's Press 1991.
Commission of the European Communities (ed.): Growth, Competitiveness, Employment. The Challenges and Ways forward into the 21st Century. Luxembourg: Office for Official Publications of the European Community 1993. (Bulletin of European Communities. Supplement. 1993, 6).
European Commission (ed.): Key Data on Education in the European Union. Brussels: EC 1995.
European Commission (ed.): Youth Policies in the European Union. Structures and Training. Brussels: EC 1995. (Studies. 7)
Ghosh, Ratna / Ray, Douglas: Social Change and Education in Canada. Toronto: Harcourt, Brace, Jovanovich 1991.
Hayhoe, Ruth: An Asian Multiversity? Comparative Reflections on the Transition to Mass Higher Education in East Asia. In: Comparative Education Review, 39 (1995) 3, pp. 299-321.
Hegel, Georg Wilhelm Friedrich: Základy filozofie práva [Grundlinien der Philosophie des Rechts]. Praha: Academia 1992.
King, Edmund James: The Young Adult Frontier and the Perspective of Continuous Change. In: Comparative Education, 28 (1992) 1, pp. 71-82.
Kuhn, Thomas: The Structure of Scientific Revolutions. 2. ed. Chicago: University of Chicago Press 1970.
Mitter, Wolfgang: Education in Eastern Europe and the Former Soviet Union in a Period of Revolutionary Change. An Approach to Comparative Analysis. In: Phillips, David / Kaser, Michael (eds.): Education and Economic Change in Eastern Europe and the Former Soviet Union (= Oxford Studies in Comparative Education. 2), Wallingford: Triangle Books 1992, pp. 15-28.
Mitter, Wolfgang: Educational Adjustment and Perspectives in a United Germany. In: Comparative Education, 28 (1992) 1, pp. 45-52.
Naisbitt, John / Aburdene, Patricia: Megatrends 2000. Zehn Perspektiven für den Weg ins nächste Jahrtausend. Düsseldorf: Econ 1990.
Pařízek, Vlastimil: Human Rights in Education. The Czech and Slovak Experience. In: Ray, Douglas (ed.): Education for Human Rights, Paris: UNESCO 1994, pp. 187-204.
Parnes, Herbert S.: Developing Human Capital. Columbus: Ohio State University 1986.
Suzuki, David T.: Inventing the Future. Twickenham: Adamantine Press 1992.
United Nations: The United Nations Convention on the Rights of the Child (1989). Dordrecht et al.: Nijhoff 1992.
Welsch, Wolfgang: Unsere postmoderne Moderne. 3. durchges. Aufl. Weinheim: VCH, Acta humaniora 1991.

Language Education Policies in Multilingual Settings: Australia and the Philippines

J. J. Smolicz

Despite their differences, Australia and the Philippines have common threads running through their histories, as well as their present circumstances. One of these is the pluralist dilemma which faces their education systems and drives their current language education policies and practices.

In undertaking a comparative study of language education policies in Australia and the Philippines, it is appropriate to heed Wolfgang *Mitter's (1985, p. 4)* advice that, *„it is the international and intercultural dimension and the comparative method which set the framework for investigating the systematic relations between research and practice and for directly tackling educational problem areas of practical relevance".*

The historical dimension provides a convenient starting point for an Australia-Philippines comparison. Both countries were invaded, occupied and had settlements established by leading European powers – Great Britain and Spain respectively. In both instances, the indigenous population was fragmented into small local, rural, pastoral or nomadic communities which could not present viable resistance to the conquerors *(Bourke / Bourke / Edwards 1994; Zialcita 1995)*. Both countries were named by the Europeans and the names given to their inhabitants – Australian and Filipino – were originally reserved for the European settlers. This remains largely true for the present day Australia, where the term Aboriginal, or occasionally Aboriginal-Australian, distinguishes the indigenous people from the settlers and their descendants. In the case of the Philippines, on the other hand, the name Filipinos now denotes the indigenous inhabitants who have very largely absorbed the relatively small number of Spanish settlers, as well as Chinese and other newcomers into their midst.

The numerically small Aboriginal population of Australia (less than 2%) is divided into a number of linguistic groups, with a great number of languages already extinct. Despite current efforts to save those that remain, many are still moving along the path towards extinction *(Fesl 1988)*. In contrast, indigenous languages of the Philippines are thriving, and one of them – renamed Filipino in its „intellectualized" form – has acquired the functions of both official and national language *(Sibayan 1994)*. The two countries also share the impact of an English linguistic heritage, with some 85% of the Australian population in 1991 using English as their home language *(Clyne 1996)*, and some two thirds of the Filipinos declaring an ability to speak English in 1980 *(Gonzales 1996)*.

Despite the dominance of English in all the official spheres of life, both countries are multilingual and have adopted national language policies that take note of this, but in a very significantly different manner. While in Australia the dominance of English is taken for granted, it is not mentioned as either an official or national language in the Constitution, the only historic legislative residue being restrictive laws against „foreign language" education in independent schools that were enacted at the time of xenophobia during World War I, but which have since been repealed in most of the States *(Selleck 1980)*.

In the Philippines, by contrast, national and official languages were first included formally in the 1973 Constitution, with English fulfilling the role of an official language alongside Filipino. The dominance of Spanish ended at the time of the American takeover in 1898, with the number of speakers decreasing to about 3% by 1970, and with Spanish losing its official status in the new Constitution of 1987. The multilingualism of the Philippines is, however, much more complex and deeply embedded in the community than could be inferred from the widely reported rivalry between English and Filipino. The way Tagalog emerged as „Filipino" and the way it was imposed as the only national language to the exclusion of other indigenous languages of the country, is a complex issue which is still not fully resolved. Other Filipino languages (at least outside Manila) are surviving as everyday languages of verbal communication in their particular regions and show no signs of decline – even though they have been virtually eliminated from the school *(Quisumbing 1989; Smolicz / Nical 1997)*.

In this regard, the school and societal settings of multilingualism of Australia and the Philippines are in direct contrast. In Australia, there is at present no prohibition on the teaching of languages other than English (LOTE) and they may be adopted as media of instruction for parts of the curriculum in the State-supported independent schools or, more frequently, taught as school subjects, either in the mainstream or independent schools.

Changing Language Policies in Australia

During the last two decades Australia has made enormous strides away from the post-World War II period, when assimilation was assumed as the norm for all immigrants, while the position of indigenous inhabitants was not even considered *(Bourke / Bourke / Edwards 1994)*. Over the years, the requirement that all inhabitants were to „shed their cultural skins" and become as indistinguishable from Anglo-Australians as possible had proved not only socially and morally unjustifiable, but simply did not work out in a political democracy. Some people refused to assimilate, while others, however desperate to achieve this goal, could not quite manage to obliterate traces of their former heritage, because of their accent or their looks or some other item of their cultural past.

To avoid such predicaments and as a response to the growing political clout of the minorities, there emerged in Australia a pluralist solution, postulating the existence of a state which upholds the principles of both political and cultural democracy *(Smolicz 1995a)*. Changes were rapid after 1967 when Aboriginal-Australians were given the right to vote and to be counted in the census, while the opening of the country to Vietnamese refugees from 1972 tolled the death knell of the White Australia Policy *(Jupp 1988)*.

During the mid-seventies it was possible to observe a new appraisal of Australia's own internal multiculturalism and multilingualism. This was marked by the acceptance of community languages other than English (CLOTEs) as aspects of cultural diversity within the overarching framework of all-Australian values that included English as a lingua franca *(Clyne 1982, 1991)*. This approach recognized the importance of ethnic identity which was underpinned by the language of the group concerned *(Smolicz 1985, 1991; Smolicz / Secombe 1989)*. As a result, several schools introduced CLOTEs, such as Italian and Modern Greek, into their curricula and financial aid was extended to the part-time community-run ethnic schools. This multicultural stance was firmly asserted by some of the State government reports which stressed the essential role of languages in cultural learning, and of language education as a yardstick of the genuineness of the country's multicultural policy *(South Australian Task Force to Investigate Multiculturalism and Education 1984)*.

Australia's achievements in this regard are summarized in the Report of the *Centenary of Federation Advisory Committee (1994, p. 29)* which states:

„*Australia's education and training system has responded to the changing ethnic composition of our population. A system of language training was put into place to provide migrants with access. Community languages were integrated into school curricula and became an important national resource. In 1987 the Federal Government adopted a National Policy on Languages, becoming the first English speaking country to have such a policy and the first in the world to have a multilingual languages policy.*"

The National Policy on Languages *(Lo Bianco 1987)* adopted a dual focus on languages learning, namely the need for speakers of a CLOTE to acquire literacy in their first language, alongside English; and for English background speakers to be given the opportunity to acquire a second language, whatever it might be – geographical, community, trade or one which would combine all those characteristics.

In spite of the continued tension over attempts to give pride of place to foreign Asian languages (such as Thai or Korean), rather than those already widely spoken in the community, the situation has been clarified to the extent that attempts are being made for multicultural and multilingual concerns to be „*incorporated into notions of national interest and become associated with mainstream societal objectives by appropriating the current preoccupation with national reconstruction and economic efficiency*" *(Lo Bianco 1995, p. 27)*. The „resource" significance of languages that were already spoken on a daily basis in Australia was emphasized by the report by the *Advisory Council on Multicultural Affairs (1988, p. 198)* which stated that, „*the economic dimension of multiculturalism means that Australia should be able to make effective use of all the nation's human resources*".

An opposite tendency still persists however, with the recent report *(Rudd 1994)* advocating a dramatic increase in the teaching of four selected Asian languages – Chinese, Indonesian, Korean and Japanese. While Rudd does pay cognizance to the multilingual resources of the country for the achievement of these goals, „*the overwhelming concentration remains on foreign language teaching and learning for economic reasons*", without sufficient acknowledgment of the growing community language status of Chinese *(Lo Bianco 1995, p. 34)*.

Although Australia's multicultural policies have had a positive effect on minority language maintenance in the country as a whole, it is difficult to quantify the extent to which schools have contributed to this phenomenon. According to the 1991 census some 15% of the country's population spoke a language other than English in their homes; Italian was the most frequently used, followed by Greek and Chinese. In some States Chinese has already overtaken Italian as the most frequently spoken CLOTE and it is likely to overtake Greek at the national level by 1996 *(Kipp / Clyne / Pauwels 1995)*.

Languages other than English are now probably more accepted than at any time in the history of the English language domination of Australia. However, although new languages can more easily be added onto a person's existing language repertoire than, say, new religious beliefs, toleration of languages is less firmly entrenched in the Australian ethos than religious pluralism. Minority languages remain therefore vulnerable, even within the current policy of multiculturalism *(Smolicz 1995b)*.

The weakness of Australian bilingualism lies in the fact that despite support from the school system and the great range of languages which are being offered as fully fledged end-of-the-school examination subjects that can count for university entrance, some of these languages have very small enrollments and they are only taught in very few of the schools. Languages remain an unpopular option at senior secondary school level with no more than 10-20% of students presenting LOTE as their matriculation subjects. Furthermore, linguistic erosion at community level (as per 1991 census) is best demonstrated by the shift away from the use of community languages towards only English in the home of the second generation (for Greek Australians the shift is from 4.4% for the first generation to 9.6% for the second generation from an endogamous marriage, to 33.8% from an exogamous one; the corresponding shifts for Dutch-Australians are 57.0%, 88.7% and 97.5%) *(Clyne 1996)*. The differences in the rate of erosion may be partly attributed to the relative significance which the language receives as the core value of the culture concerned within the Australian framework of values *(Smolicz 1981a, 1991; Smolicz / Secombe 1989)*. Despite, therefore, the significant multicultural reforms in Australian schools, the multilingualism of the country for many community languages appears to be transitional, although this to some extent is being counter-balanced by the growing popularity of Asian languages such as Japanese, Chinese and Indonesian and European languages, such as German, which are taught from a foreign language perspective.

Multilingualism and Schooling in the Philippines

The Philippines presents a very contrasting picture to the Australian scene, with our recent studies *(Smolicz / Nical 1997)* confirming a phenomenon to be found in all non-Tagalog regions of the country, namely the vitality of indigenous languages in everyday usage of the population, even in the absence of the teaching of the languages concerned in the school. This demonstrates the importance for language survival of a strong historical community base, especially if it is a territorial one. Local languages (labeled usually as „vernaculars") are maintained through songs, poetry and some prose. All eight major languages belong to the Filipino-Austronesian family and their speakers account for some 85% of the population. Their delayed literary development was initially caused by the dominance of Spanish which, however, was mostly limited to a small elite. The Spanish Catholic clergy used the indigenous languages in their missionary work, which succeeded in making the Philippines one of the most Christian countries of Asia, while helping to preserve the indigenous languages and supply them with their first written records *(Costa 1961)*. While the American policy, which propagated compulsory education for all Filipinos in English, was initially directed mainly against Spanish, it was almost equally hostile to the indigenous languages of the country, with penalties imposed upon pupils using their home languages on the school premises *(Manhit 1980, 1981)*. Although excluded from school and universities and most forms of public life, the indigenous languages survived and gradually a movement arose demanding the recognition of the rights of the Filipinos to their own national language(s).

There was, however, a competition among the major languages, especially between Cebuano, which had the largest number of first language speakers (over a quarter of the population), and Tagalog which was the language of the capital and further developed in the literary and political spheres, as well as being best known to the greater number of Filipinos, for whom it acted as a second language. The situation was not, however, clear-cut, since even in 1960 Tagalog was known only to 44.4% of the population. Under the influence of European models, the Constitution Convention of 1971 assumed that, for the Philippines to be a modern state, it had to apply a nation-state formula that required the adoption of but one national language to the exclusion of all others. It therefore opted for a „synthesis" solution that advocated the emergence of a „multi-based" Filipino language that would be formed through a fusion of all the Filipino languages *(Gonzales / Bautista 1981)*. From the very beginning, the concept of a national language through amalgamation appeared to the advocates of Tagalog as a highly unrealistic proposition *(Gonzales 1974)*. Over the years, the „fusion compromise" proved a useful ploy that enabled the „enriched" Tagalog, under the label of Filipino, to assume the role of the only national language of the country.

Since then, the struggle for linguistic supremacy in the country has come to be perceived almost solely in terms of the rivalry between English and Tagalog/Filipino. This was resolved through the imposition of the Bilingual Education Policy in 1974. The democratic transformation of 1986 preserved this goal, namely „*the achievement of competence, in both Filipino and English at the national level, through the teaching of both languages and their use as media of instruction at all levels*", with Filipino as medium of instruction in social sciences and the humanities and English in science and mathematics *(Department of Education, Culture and Sports 1987)*. The use of regional „vernaculars" was allowed „*as auxiliary to the media of instruction, but only when necessary to facilitate the understanding of concepts being taught in English or Filipino*" *(Quisumbing 1989, p. 311)*.

If one were to rely on census data alone, the Bilingual Education Policy would seem to be meeting its objective by laying foundations for a „bilingual nation", with the number of people aged six and over declaring an ability to speak English rising from 48% to 64.5% by 1980 and those declaring their ability to speak Filipino rising from 55% in 1970 to 77% in 1980 *(Yap 1990; Gonzales 1996)*. Obscured by such data is the question of the state of the non-Tagalog languages of the Philippines, their survival, development and influence upon the educational performance of students from homes and neighborhoods where they remain the usual form of communication.

In the schools in the southern non-Tagalog provinces where almost all the pupils, as well as the majority of teachers, speak their local languages in their homes, schooling often begins in what are virtually two new languages for the children: English and Filipino. The children from the „barrios", rural settlements, frequently remote, can usually speak only a limited form of English, and their knowledge of Tagalog before entry into school is restricted to what they have learned from the television screen, or comics that are often written in a linguistic hybrid known as „Taglish". Even after completing their elementary education and leaving school, the „barrio" children often speak only halting English, or are too shy to speak English at all. For such young people the Filipino language also remains basic and insufficiently internalized. At the same time, they do not become literate in their mother tongue, although they may attempt to write in, say, Cebuano by applying, through their own efforts, the rules of spelling and grammar that they have learned for Filipino. Such efforts may result in a form of semi-literacy and represent a precarious method of acquiring the ability to read and write in their home language. Even teachers themselves are often uncertain of how to write in their native tongue and resort to English in family correspondence. The latter option is, of course, hardly open to most village children, who would find it difficult to compose long texts in English. Unfortunately, they cannot compensate for this deficiency in other ways, since they lack a command of literacy in both Filipino and their native language. Hence there are children who finish school without being fully literate in any language.

According to one of the chief protagonists of the Filipino only policy *Sibayan (1994, p. 80)*, „*If the speakers of the Philippine major languages [other than Tagalog] would like to have their native language as a medium of instruction in the early grades ... they should be willing to provide financial support for the program ... The Filipino who reads and writes in Filipino will have no difficulty in reading and writing in his own language if necessary*". However, in her „Implementing Guidelines for the 1987 Policy on Bilingual Education", the former minister of education, *Quisumbing (1989, p. 314)* herself acknowledged the difference between „*Tagalog-speaking*" students, for whom „*national language education actually starts from childhood and continues throughout life, [with] the school serving to reinforce and refine such language education*", and the non-Tagalog speaking students. At the same time, far from encouraging the latter to become literate in their home languages, she advised them instead that „*compensatory education has been set up for the purpose of equalizing competence in Filipino among Tagalog and non-Tagalog groups through the development of appropriate teaching materials, the offering of special language teachers, the offering of special classes and the establishment of incentives for teachers of Filipino for acquiring minimum standards of language proficiency.*"

The fact that teachers below such minimum standards in Filipino continue to exist after almost three decades of attempts at linguistic homogenization of the whole country to Filipino through the school system, shows inadequacies in the bilingual policy in terms of its own objectives. At the same time, the implication that the students' home languages, if other than Tagalog, are a handicap which must be ameliorated by compensatory programs recalls some of the once fashionable assimilation-driven policies towards migrant children in the USA and Australia *(Clyne 1991; Smolicz 1981b, 1985)*.

The dissatisfaction with the Bilingual Education Policy also appears in relation to one of its other main goals, as witnessed by continued reports in the press on the perceived decline in the standard of English in the school and the failings of the education system in general *(Congressional Commission on Education 1991, p. XII)*. This has been frequently attributed to the greater time allocated to Filipino in the school curriculum and its influence upon the structure of the students' English, causing difficulties particularly in the study of Mathematics and Science, which continue to be taught in English from Grade one.

The non-Tagalog Filipino groups' placid acquiescence to the virtual elimination of their tongues from education, may need an explanation when compared with demands for the recognition of linguistic rights by minorities in many other parts of the world. One explanation is that among the more influential sections of the population in all the regions of the country, English is often used at home, so that children have a background knowledge of that language when they start school at six, or even earlier, when they have their formal introduction to English in a fee-paying pre-school. Private schools have often been able to increase the time allocated to English without incurring too much trouble with Filipino language directives of the Bilingual Education Policy.

Another interpretation for the lack of teaching of vernaculars was provided by student respondents who explained that it was due to their insufficient confidence in the maturity of their home tongue as a literary language and their sense of its inadequacy in the learning situation *(Smolicz / Nical 1997)*. Such diffidence among speakers of the various Filipino vernaculars is quite understandable, especially in view of over three centuries of subordination to the Spanish language in public administration and subsequent imposition of English as the literary language of the country. The present policy of achieving „filipinisation" through Filipino/Tagalog as the only national language and excluding other Filipino languages from the school has the effect of further strengthening this diffidence.

The example of Europe suggests, however, that such a lack of confidence in the maturity of their native tongue may not last forever. If the Philippines' authorities feel impelled to follow the less than fortunate European tradition that presumes that each state should possess a single and exclusive national language, it may be only a matter of time before similar notions are adopted by the non-Tagalog provinces of the Philippines. This has already occurred in the Islamic part of the Southern Philippines where the population, with its quite distinct culture and religion, has been in long standing rebellion against the current government authorities and has already been successful in winning a special status for Arabic, as well as a degree of local autonomy. This rebelliousness has not been, and is most unlikely to be extended to the Christian parts of the country. It is, therefore, possible that in time the Philippines could follow the pattern of Spain, where even the prolonged imposition of Castilian as the single national language of the country has to a large extent been reversed by democratic and peaceful means in accord with the demands of the historic regions to have their native languages formally reinstated as core values of their cultures. In this way, these languages have proved to be a most effective rallying call for greater regional autonomy.

Our empirical studies of Filipino students from non-Tagalog backgrounds who have succeeded in breaking through the double linguistic barrier of English and Filipino shows that the on-going use and positive evaluation of the vernaculars does not conflict with gaining a mastery of English and Filipino *(Smolicz/Nical 1997)*. It can be argued that the political and social stability of the country, as well as an equitable distribution of education opportunities, favors the principle that it is possible for Filipinos to be literate in their mother tongue and still be fluent in Filipino, as the national language of the country, with English continuing in its present role as the international language.

From a comparative perspective the achievement of Australia lies in the way it has been able to reshape itself as a multicultural country. It has demonstrated that tolerance of diversity and gradually emerging pluralist policies in languages education are a better guarantee of stability than forced assimilation to one dominant language and culture.

Bibliography

Advisory Council on Multicultural Affairs (ed.): Towards a National Agenda for a Multicultural Australia – A Discussion Paper. Canberra: Australian Government Publishing Services 1988.
Bourke, Colin / Bourke, Eleanor / Edwards, Bill (eds.): Aboriginal Australia. St. Lucia: University of Queensland Press 1994.
Centenary of Federation Advisory Committee: 2001. A Report to the Council of Australian Governments. Canberra: Australian Government Publishing Service 1994.
Clyne, Michael: Multilingual Australia. Melbourne: River Seine 1982.
Clyne, Michael: Community Languages. The Australian Experience. Cambridge: Cambridge University Press 1991.
Clyne, Michael / Kipp, Sandra: Language Maintenance and Language Shift in Australia, 1991. In: Australian Review of Applied Linguistics, 19 (1996) 1, pp. 1-9.
Congressional Commission on Education: Making Education Work. Manila et al.: Congress of the Republic of the Philippines 1991.
Costa, Horacio de la: The Jesuits of the Philippines, 1581-1768. Cambridge: Harvard University Press 1961.
Department of Education, Culture and Sports: The 1987 Policy on Bilingual Education. DECS order No. 52, s. 1987. In: Sutaria, Minda C. et al. (eds.): Philippine Education. Vision and Perspectives, Manila: National Book Store 1989, pp. 353-355.
Fesl, Eve D.: Language Death Among Australian Languages. In: Australian Review of Applied Linguistics, 10 (1988) 2, pp. 12- 23.
Gonzales, Andrew: The 1973 Constitution and the Bilingual Education Policy of the Department of Education and Culture. In: Philippine Studies, 22 (1974) 4, pp. 22-31.

Gonzales, Andrew: Bilingual Communities. National/Regional Profiles and Verbal Repertoires. In: Bautista, Maria Lourdes S. (ed.): Readings in Philippine Sociolinguistics, Manila: De la Salle University Press 1996, pp. 38-62.

Gonzales, Andrew / Bautista, Maria Lourdes S.: Aspects of Language Planning and Development in the Philippines. Manila: Linguistic Society of the Philippines 1981.

Jupp, James (ed.): The Australian People. An Encyclopedia of the Nation, Its People and Their Origins. Australia 1788-1988. North Ryde et al.: Angus and Robertson 1988.

Kipp, Sandra / Clyne, Michael / Pauwels, Anne: Immigration and Australia's Language Resources. Canberra: Australian Government Publishing Services 1995.

Lo Bianco, Joseph: National Policy on Languages. Canberra: Commonwealth Department of Education et al. 1987.

Lo Bianco, Joseph: Australian Experiences. Multiculturalism, Language Policy and National Ethos. In: The European Journal of Intercultural Studies, 5 (1995) 3, pp. 26-43.

Manhit, Basilissa J.: The Case for Reading. A Socio-Political Perspective. In: Education Quarterly, 26 (1980) 4, pp. 32-41.

Manhit, Basilissa J.: Alternatives for Functional Literacy. A Socio-Psychophilosophical Perspective. In: Education Quarterly, 27 (1981) 4, pp. 1-25.

Mitter, Wolfgang: Education and the Diversity of Cultures. Some Introductory Remarks. In: ibid. / Swift, James (eds.): Education and the Diversity of Culture. Vol. 1 (= Bildung und Erziehung. Beiheft. 2, 1), Köln et al.: Böhlau 1985, pp. 3-14.

Quisumbing, Lourdes: The DECS Bilingual Education Policy. In: Sutaria, Minda C. et al. (eds.): Philippine Education. Vision and Perspectives, Manila: National Book Store 1989, pp. 309-315.

Rudd, K. M. (ed.): Asian Languages and Australia's Economic Future. A Report Prepared for the Council of Australian Governments on a Proposed Asian Languages/Studies Strategy for Australian Schools. Brisbane: Queensland Government Printer 1994.

Selleck, Richard Joseph Wheeler: The Trouble with My Looking Glass. A Study of the Attitude of Australians to Germans during the Great War. In: Journal of Australian Studies, 6 (1980) 1, pp. 1-25.

Sibayan, Bonifacio P.: Philippine Language Problems. In: Acuña, Jasmin Espíritu (ed.): The Language Issue in Education, Manila: Congressional Oversight Committee in Education, Congress of the Republic of Philippines 1994, pp. 47-86.

Smolicz, J. J.: Core Values and Cultural Identity. In: Ethnic and Racial Studies, 4 (1981a) 1, pp. 75-90.

Smolicz, J. J.: Culture, Ethnicity and Education. Multiculturalism in a Plural Society. In: World Year Book of Education, (1981b), pp. 17-36.

Smolicz, J. J.: Multiculturalism and an Overarching Framework of Values. In: Mitter, Wolfgang / Swift, James (eds.): Education and the Diversity of Cultures. Vol. 1 (= Bildung und Erziehung. Beiheft. 2, 1), Köln et al.: Böhlau 1985, pp. 245-268.

Smolicz, J. J.: Language Core Values in a Multicultural Setting. In: International Review of Education, 37 (1991) 1, pp. 35-52.

Smolicz, J. J.: The Emergence of Australia as a Multicultural Nation. An International Perspective. In: Journal of Intercultural Studies, 16 (1995a) 1-2, pp. 3-23.

Smolicz, J. J.: Language – a Bridge or a Barrier? Languages and Education in Australia from an Intercultural Perspective. In: Multilingua, 14 (1995b) 2, pp. 151-182.

Smolicz, J. J. / Nical, Illuminado: Languages of the Philippines. A Study of the Usage of English, Filipino and the „Vernaculars" in Three Linguistic Communities. In: Wölck, Wolfgang et al. (eds.): Recent Studies in Contact Linguistics, Brussels: Research Centre for Multilingualism 1997 (forthcoming).

Smolicz, J. J. / Secombe, Margaret Jones: Types of Language Activation and Evaluation in an Ethnically Plural Society. In: Ammon, Ulrich (ed.): Status and Function of Languages and Language Varieties, Berlin et al.: de Gruyter 1989, pp. 478-514.

South Australian Task Force to Investigate Multiculturalism and Education (ed.): Education for a Cultural Democracy. Adelaide: South Australian Government Printers 1984.

Yap, Fe Aldave: A Comparative Study of the Philippine Lexicons. Manila: Institute of Philippine Languages, Department of Education, Culture and Sports 1990.

Zialcita, Fernando N.: State Formation, Colonialism and National Identity in Vietnam and the Philippines. In: Philippine Quarterly of Culture and Society, 23 (1995), pp. 77-117.

Lehrer und Gesellschaft – Ein internationaler Vergleich

Werner Stephan

Braucht die postindustrielle Gesellschaft noch Lehrer im herkömmlichen Sinne? Diese Frage scheint nicht unberechtigt zu sein: Viele Dienstleistungen werden zunehmend von Computern übernommen, und globale Informationsdienste wie auch Massenmedien erheben den Anspruch, den Wissensbedarf des 'modernen' Menschen schnell und zuverlässig befriedigen zu können. Hinzu kommt, daß fast alle Länder öffentliche Haushaltsdefizite aufweisen und das Bildungswesen als eines der kostspieligsten Sozialprogramme von finanziellen Einschränkungen nicht verschont geblieben ist.

Die nachfolgenden Ausführungen stellen die Zusammenfassung einer umfassenden Untersuchung der Arbeitsbedingungen von Lehrern in sechs Ländern dar, die über einen Zeitraum von sieben Jahren durchgeführt wurde. Da dieses Projekt mit Eigenmitteln finanziert wurde, mußten bestimmte Regionen dieser Länder ausgewählt werden, die ähnliche Merkmale wie relative Bevölkerungsdichte und Sozial- und Wirtschaftsstruktur aufweisen. Somit konzentrierte sich die Untersuchung auf den Bezirk Lublin in Polen, die Länder Sachsen-Anhalt und Niedersachsen in Deutschland, die Grafschaft Northamptonshire in England, den Staat South Dakota in den Vereinigten Staaten und die Provinz Saskatchewan in Kanada. Insgesamt wurden mehr als 200 Lehrer, Eltern, Verwaltungsbeamte und Hochschullehrer befragt; jedes Interview dauerte etwa 45 Minuten. Diese Informationen wurden durch schriftliche Materialien wie amtliche Dokumente, Fachzeitschriften, Zeitungsmeldungen und Schulzeitungen ergänzt, um ein möglichst umfassendes Bild herzustellen, das auch auf nationale Tendenzen hinweist.

Was die Auswahl dieser Länder anbetrifft, so sind Polen und die frühere DDR als ehemalige Mitglieder des sozialistischen Blocks Übergangsgesellschaften von einer sozialistischen zu einer liberal-demokratischen Gesellschaftsordnung, wohingegen die alte Bundesrepublik und England als traditionelle westliche Demokratien während der letzten Jahrzehnte keine radikalen sozialen oder politischen Umwälzungen erlebt haben. Als die wichtigsten Vertreter der 'Neuen Welt' haben die Vereinigten Staaten und Kanada in gewisser Hinsicht Varianten europäischer Erziehungstraditionen herausgebildet und weisen inzwischen ihre eigene kulturelle, soziale, wirtschaftliche und politische Dynamik auf.

Die nachfolgende Diskussion beschränkt sich aus Raummangel auf die wesentlichen Teilaspekte der Arbeitsbedingungen der Lehrer. Es sei an dieser Stelle darauf hingewiesen, daß Verallgemeinerungen nur im beschränkten Umfang möglich sind, da die untersuchten Regionen nicht unbedingt für die entsprechenden nationalen Bildungssysteme repräsentativ sind.

Lublin / Polen

Die sozialen und politischen Spannungen, die den Wechsel von einer stark zentralisierten und kontrollierten Gesellschaftsstruktur zu einer liberalen Demokratie mit Betonung auf Individualität und sozialer Mobilität charakterisieren, spiegeln sich auch im gegenwärtigen Bildungssystem wider. Lehrer erleben diesen Übergang als Unsicherheit hinsichtlich ihrer materiellen Arbeitsbedingungen und ihrer persönlichen Lebensumstände. Der tägliche Unterrichtsablauf war früher durch klare Richtlinien vorgezeichnet, doch plötzlich sind die alten Maßstäbe nicht mehr gültig, und wo Schulen und Lehrer zuvor von der Regierung mit den notdürftigsten Unterrichtsmaterialien versorgt wurden, bestimmt nun die freie Marktwirtschaft den Umfang materieller und finanzieller Zuwendungen.

In seiner Beurteilung der Reformen und ihrer Auswirkungen auf das Bildungssystem bemerkt *Rust (1992, S. 88)*: *„Zusätzlich zu den programmatischen und strukturellen Veränderungen machen sich gleichzeitig Veränderungen auf emotionaler und psychologischer Ebene bemerkbar. Die Schule benötigt eine gewisse Stabilität und Routine, um produktiv zu sein, aber auch ein Minimum an Wertübereinstimmung, um als gesundes Ganzes zu funktionieren. Die Lehrerschaft braucht ein bestimmtes Maß an Vertrauen und Respekt, um erfolgreich unterrichten zu können. In den letzten beiden Jahren ist all das hinweggefegt worden."* Diese „programmatischen und strukturellen Veränderungen" hatten bereits in den späten achtziger Jahren eingesetzt, aber statt den Lehrern ein Gefühl von Stabilität und klarer Richtung zu vermitteln, haben die fortwährenden politischen und wirtschaftlichen Veränderungen neue Probleme im Sozialbereich geschaffen, und das Ergebnis ist eine beträchtliche Skepsis gegenüber der neuen sozialpolitischen Ordnung.

Die Befragung deutet jedoch darauf hin, daß polnische Lehrer unter diesen schwierigen Umständen weiterhin versuchen, ihr Bestes zu leisten. Obwohl sie insgesamt gesehen mit ihren Arbeits- und Lebensbedingungen unzufrieden sind – besonders was die überfüllten Klassenräume, den Mangel an Unterrichtsmitteln und die niedrigen Gehälter anbelangt – zeigen sie eine erstaunliche berufliche Integrität und sogar eine Spur von Optimismus hinsichtlich der Zukunft des polnischen Bildungssystems.

Als Beispiel der gegenwärtigen Spannungen weist *Pszczolkowski (1992)* darauf hin, daß während des kommunistischen Regimes die Bildungsbehörden von den Lehrern erwarteten, daß sie den wissenschaftlichen Marxismus zur Grundlage ihres Unterrichts machten. Doch unter dem wachsenden Einfluß der Kirche wird *„die Arbeit der Lehrer nun vornehmlich durch das Prisma christlicher Werte beurteilt. Darüber hinaus schafft die Diskrepanz zwischen den gepredigten Werten und dem tatsächlichen Verhalten sicherlich nicht die erwünschte gesellschaftliche Einstellung in der jungen Generation"* (S. 230). Die Lehrer stehen den Versuchen der Kirche, ihre sozialen und erzieherischen Dogmen durchzusetzen, abwartend gegenüber, und während sie in ländlichen Gegenden die Zusammenarbeit mit der Kirche oft befürworten, ist in den Städten ihre Einstellung eher kritisch und ablehnend.

Wie in den meisten Industrieländern ist auch in Polen der Sozialstatus der Lehrer gesunken. Die Lehrer empfinden es als paradox, daß in dem autoritären sozialistischen Bildungssystem die Lehrer als die Erzieher der jungen Generation generell respektiert wurden, während jetzt, da sie in ihrem Urteil weitgehend unabhängig sind und die Freiheit haben, ihre Schüler nach bestem Wissen und Gewissen zu erziehen, die Öffentlichkeit gegenüber der Lehrerschaft kritischer und vielleicht sogar zynischer ist. Es bleibt dahingestellt, ob selbst Verbesserungen der Arbeits- und Lebensbedingungen, einschließlich der Besoldung, in der Lage sein werden, das Sozialprestige der Lehrer zu verbessern.

Sachsen-Anhalt / Deutschland

Wie auch in den anderen Gebieten der ehemaligen DDR sind in Sachsen-Anhalt die tiefgreifenden Veränderungen nach der 'Wende' nicht immer von den Lehrern begrüßt worden, und Gefühle der Unsicherheit, Entfremdung und sogar Opposition haben sich nach der anfänglichen Euphorie vor allem in jenen Teilen der Bevölkerung ausgebreitet, die sich aus den verschiedensten Gründen benachteiligt fühlen. Hierzu meint Wolfgang *Mitter (1992, S. 53f.): „Die 'Unterstützung', die von den westdeutschen Behörden gelei-*

stet wurde, vor allem in bezug auf die Schaffung effizienter Verwaltungseinheiten in Ostdeutschland, wurde zum großen Teil als eine Form von 'Dominanz', zumindest aber 'Einmischung' wahrgenommen. Natürlich hat sich dies als nicht hilfreich erwiesen, insofern als die konkreten Bedürfnisse der 'Hilfsempfänger' oft ignoriert wurden. Das Bildungswesen kann als schlagendes Beispiel dafür angesehen werden."

Die meisten der befragten Lehrer gehörten zumindest in den ersten Jahren nach der Wende zu diesen Bevölkerungsgruppen, da sie weder den politischen noch den wirtschaftlichen Einfluß hatten, ihre beruflichen und persönlichen Interessen mit Nachdruck zu vertreten. Als Angehörige des öffentlichen Dienstes sind sie sehr stark vom guten Willen der Öffentlichkeit und, was viel wichtiger ist, der Politiker und Regierungsbehörden abhängig.

Die Befragungen zeigten deutlich, daß viele von ihnen hinsichtlich ihrer beruflichen Stellung innerhalb des neuen Schulsystems unzufrieden und frustriert sind. Hier ist es vor allem die Unsicherheit des Arbeitsplatzes, geschürt von der langwierigen Untersuchung der politischen Vergangenheit einzelner Lehrer, und darüber hinaus die ungleiche Einstufung erfahrener Lehrer und damit die geringere Besoldung (und Altersversorgung) im Vergleich mit ihren westdeutschen Kollegen. Diese politische Überprüfung wird besonders dann als Strafaktion empfunden, wenn Lehrer ihre Situation mit der von ehemaligen hohen Parteifunktionären und Staatsbeamten vergleichen, die bereits wieder in Amt und Würden sind.

Andererseits bestätigten die Lehrer, daß sich ihre Lebensbedingungen grundlegend verbessert haben, und sie sind zögernd optimistisch, daß auch Verbesserungen ihrer materiellen Arbeitsbedingungen folgen werden. Trotz aller Bedenken und Beschwerden, die während der Befragung vorgebracht wurden, wurde immer wieder mit Genugtuung hervorgehoben, daß die Lehrer nicht mehr unter strenger Kontrolle stehen und keine politischen Repressalien mehr befürchten müssen. Allerdings ist der politische Druck auf die Lehrer in vieler Hinsicht noch immer vorhanden, wenngleich er nun aus einer anderen Richtung kommt.

Wie ein Schulrat betonte, hatten die Lehrer sich in der Vergangenheit ständig von den Schulpolitikern bevormundet gefühlt, wohingegen sie jetzt in der Lage sind, neue Wissensgebiete zu erforschen und neue Methoden zu erproben und anzuwenden. Die meisten von ihnen sind mit der neuesten Fachliteratur vertraut, zeigen ein gesundes Selbstbewußtsein als Erzieher und sind sich ihrer pädagogischen Fähigkeiten und ihrer Verantwortung durchaus bewußt. Dennoch gibt es nach seiner Meinung auch viele Lehrer, die sich völlig an die strikten pädagogischen Vorschriften und die starren Lehrpläne gewöhnt hatten und es als fast unmöglich ansehen, eigene Ideen zu entwickeln und ihrem eigenen Denken zu folgen.

Niedersachsen / Deutschland

Die Kontroverse über die Einführung der Gesamtschule als Alternative zum dreigliedrigen Schulsystem ist kennzeichnend für den ideologischen Streit, der in Niedersachsen (und ähnlich in anderen Bundesländern) das Bild der Schulpolitik bestimmt. Viele Lehrer an den traditionellen Sekundarschulen, unterstützt von weiten Kreisen der CDU, den Industrie- und Handelskammern, den Arbeitgeberverbänden und vielen Elternbeiräten, plädieren für den Erhalt des gegenwärtigen Schulsystems, wohingegen die SPD, mit Unterstützung der Grünen und der Lehrergewerkschaft (GEW), die Gesamtschule befürwortet. Eingebettet in diesen Schulstreit ist die Zukunft der Orientierungsstufe. Es sind wiederum die 'konservativen' Stimmen, lautstark unterstützt von Handel und Gewerbe *(Wirtschaft fordert 1992),* welche die Abschaffung der Orientierungsstufe fordern und die Reformen der siebziger Jahre rückgängig machen wollen. Anstatt ihre fehlgeleitete Schulpolitik weiter zu verfolgen, solle die Regierung dafür sorgen, daß die Lehrerstellen an allen Schulen voll besetzt seien. Demgegenüber argumentieren die 'Reformer', die Abschaffung der Orientierungsstufe werde die sozial schwachen Bevölkerungsgruppen weiter benachteiligen, und anstelle von Gleichheit der Bildungschancen werde die Betonung schulischer Höchstleistung (gleichbedeutend mit erhöhter Produktivität) zur Grundlage der Bildungspolitik werden. Die Lehrer sehen sich hier in einem Zwiespalt, weil sie sich einerseits verpflichtet fühlen, ihre Schüler maximal zu fördern, andererseits aber nicht in der Lage sind, die zahlreichen sozialen und kulturellen Barrieren zu beseitigen, die vielen Kindern den Weg zum Schulerfolg versperren.

Aus vielfachen Gründen wird die Einführung von Computern als Lehr- und Lernmittel mit Argwohn betrachtet. Besonders Grundschullehrer betonen die Wichtigkeit des persönlichen Kontaktes im Erziehungsprozeß, und Computer stellen in dieser Hinsicht eine gewisse Gefahr für die Persönlichkeitsentwicklung dar. Darüber hinaus wird die Befürwortung von Computern auch als Versuch angesehen, die Zahl der Lehrer zu verringern. So argumentierte ein Professor der Erziehungswissenschaften, rund 25 Prozent der Unterrichtszeit von Lehrern könnten durch den Einsatz von Computern eingespart werden, ohne den Lernerfolg zu beeinträchtigen. Zwar seien die Kosten für eine derartige Umstellung gegenwärtig noch zu hoch, doch sei die Investition in Hinblick auf die erhöhte Effektivität der Schulen vertretbar *(Weniger Lehrer durch Computer 1992)*.

Die Erneuerung der Lehrerschaft wird von vielen Lehrern und Schulbehörden als vorrangiges Problem angesehen. Der Druck auf die Lehrer, sich schulisch und gesellschaftlich stärker zu engagieren, hat besonders unter älteren Lehrern Verschleißerscheinungen zur Folge, und verringerte Widerstandskraft, Mangel an Energie beim Lösen schulischer Konfliktsituationen sowie physische und psychosomatische Beschwerden sind der Preis für die Entscheidung der Regierung, die Klassenstärken zu erhöhen, statt neue Lehrer einzustellen *(Schwarting 1991)*. Hinzu kommt, daß offensichtlich weder für die Lehrer eine Verpflichtung besteht, sich regelmäßig fortzubilden, noch genügend Mittel bereitgestellt werden, um den Lehrern zentrale Fortbildungsmöglichkeiten anzubieten. Zwar hat die örtliche Lehrerfortbildung gewisse Vorteile, doch wäre ein besser organisiertes (und veröffentlichtes) Programm sicherlich in der Lage, das berufliche Ansehen der Lehrer zu verbessern.

Die meisten Lehrer vertraten den Standpunkt, daß außerschulische Arbeitsgemeinschaften Kindern und Jugendlichen sehr in ihrer sozialen und emotionalen Entwicklung helfen würden. Ihrer Meinung nach hat der soziale Wandel der letzten Jahrzehnte – vor allem Veränderungen in der Familienstruktur – oft zu Entfremdung und Vereinsamung, aber auch zu Perspektivlosigkeit, Straffälligkeit und Drogensucht geführt. Für viele Schulpflichtige scheint die Schule der einzige Ort zu sein, an dem sie Hilfe und Verständnis – von den Lehrern – erhalten.

Northamptonshire / England

Die Animosität der achtziger Jahre zwischen Regierung und Lehrern hat bis heute kaum abgenommen. Im Zentrum der Unzufriedenheit vieler Lehrer stehen die verschiedenen Regierungserlasse und Direktiven, die zum Beispiel als nationale Lehrpläne, als regelmäßige und umfangreiche Überprüfung der Schulleistungen und als die zahlreichen Rechenschaftsberichte Kontrollmechanismen darstellen, welche die berufliche Autonomie der Lehrer stark einschränken. *Broadfoot (1994, S. 11)* bemerkt dazu: „*Für einige dieser Lehrer schwand die Befriedigung, die ihnen das Unterrichten gebracht hatte, langsam dahin, während die Frustration zunahm. Hinsichtlich der Werte, die ihrer Aufgabe als Lehrer zugrunde lagen, wurden Lehrer in die Entfremdung oder zum bloßen instrumentalen Funktionieren getrieben, im Gegensatz zu der demonstrierten moralischen Verpflich-*

tung, die sie bisher als Erzieher gezeigt hatten." Ähnlich bezieht sich *Neave (1992)* auf die vorgenannten Regierungsmaßnahmen als weitere Schritte auf dem Wege zur beruflichen Entmündigung und damit zur Proletarisierung des Lehrerstandes.

Die Betonung der Eigenverwaltung der Schulen (*local management of schools*) hinterläßt in der Öffentlichkeit den Eindruck, daß die Schulverwaltungsräte (*boards of governors*), bestehend aus Schulleitern, Eltern, Geschäftsleuten und anderen Interessenvertretern, die schulischen Belange in Eigenregie bestimmten. Die Lehrer finden sich in einer ambivalenten Situation wieder: Sie sind Angestellte der lokalen Bildungsbehörde (*Local Education Authority*), die allerdings kaum einen Einfluß auf die schulischen Arbeitsbedingungen hat, während sie gleichzeitig vom Schulverwaltungsrat ihrer Schule abhängig sind, der über alle Aspekte der Arbeitsbedingungen entscheidet. Dem Schulverwaltungsrat sind andererseits die Hände gebunden, da die Regierung die Höhe der finanziellen Zuwendungen festlegt, und davon sind wiederum die Gehälter, die Zahl der beschäftigten Lehrer und die generellen Arbeitsbedingungen stark betroffen.

Angesichts der bevorstehenden allgemeinen Wahlen waren die befragten Lehrer skeptisch, ob sich – selbst bei einem Regierungswechsel – die Bildungspolitik wesentlich ändern würde. Nach ihrer Meinung lasse die wirtschaftliche Situation des Landes der Regierung nur wenig Spielraum für Verbesserungen. Hinzu komme, daß unter aufeinanderfolgenden konservativen Regierungen die Grundlagen des Sozialstaates neu definiert worden seien, mit dem Ergebnis, daß Mittel für Sozialprogramme, einschließlich solcher im Bildungswesen, drastisch gekürzt wurden.

Begrüßt wurden die Bildungsreformen allerdings von Unternehmern, von vielen Elterngruppen und von bestimmten Teilen der Lehrerschaft, die am meisten von der teilweisen Privatisierung des Schulwesens profitieren werden. Zusammenfassend entsteht der Eindruck, daß Schulen von nun an wesentliche Bestandteile der freien Marktwirtschaft sind und auch entsprechend konzipiert werden: Die Schulleitung bildet die Managementgruppe, die Lehrer sind die Arbeiter, die für ihre Klassen verantwortlich sind, und die Schüler stellen die Produkte des Erziehungsprozesses dar und werden als solche durch ständige Qualitätskontrollen – wie umfangreiche Beurteilungen und Testprogramme – auf ihre Eignung für die Teilnahme an der Gesamtwirtschaft überprüft. Damit hat das industrielle Bildungsmodell, das zuerst in den sechziger Jahren von Bildungsökonomen antizipiert wurde, in England seinen sichtbarsten Ausdruck gefunden.

South Dakota / USA

Die politischen Veränderungen, die seit Jahren das Bild Amerikas tiefgreifend verändert haben, sind auch an den Schulen und ihren Lehrern nicht spurlos vorübergegangen. Entsprechend der neo-konservativen Ideologie wurde das Prinzip der Gleichheit der Bildungschancen als Hindernis für Amerikas wirtschaftliche Wettbewerbsfähigkeit im internationalen Rahmen erachtet, und das Motto der Bildungsreformen ist von nun an: „Verbesserung der Bildungsqualität". Die Autoren der Studie „A Nation at Risk: The Imperative for Educational Reform" aus dem Jahre 1983 sahen als Ursache für die Bildungsmisere das damalige Schulwesen an, in dem nicht nur finanzielle Ressourcen, sondern auch das menschliche Potential Amerikas von den Lehrern verschwendet würden. Damit war die Lehrerschaft aufgefordert, sich neuen Zielsetzungen und Anforderungen anzupassen. Dazu bemerkte eine Gruppe von Akademikern, die *Holmes Group (1986)*, daß sowohl die gegenwärtige Schulstruktur als auch die Arbeitsbedingungen und das Autoritätsverhältnis zwischen Lehrern und Schulverwaltung nicht den Voraussetzungen eines neuen Berufsbildes entsprächen: *„Wenn die Herstellung eines Lehrerstandes, der seinen Namen verdient, erfolgreich sein soll, dann müssen sich die Schulen ändern" (S. 67).* Das Ziel war, die Lehrerausbildung stärker zu steuern und alle Lehrer einem rigorosen Eignungstest zu unterwerfen. Hierzu meint *McKenna (1988, S. 263):*

„Die Verschmelzung der Schule mit der neuen kapitalistischen Ordnung kann nirgends deutlicher werden als in der Logik einer Schulreform, die, angetrieben vom nationalen Hunger auf technologische und kommerzielle Vorherrschaft, versucht, die industriellen, wissenschaftlichen und wirtschaftlichen Hochöfen der Vereinigten Staaten erneut anzuheizen. Schulreform wird mit wirtschaftlicher Erneuerung gleichgesetzt, da der wirtschaftliche Niedergang als Ergebnis des schlechten Schulsystems erklärt wird. Die Verteufelung der Schulen seitens der Wissenschaftler, der Wirtschaftskapitäne, der Politiker und der Autoren der Reformliteratur sowie die Reformvorschläge selbst stellen ein spießbürgerliches Bildungskonzept dar, das auf den Arbeitsmarkt ausgerichtet ist. In der Meinung der Kritiker sind Bildung und Arbeitswelt aufs engste miteinander verbunden; Qualität wird an Kosten und Ergebnissen gemessen, und akademische Leistung und Profitorientierung sind identisch."

Wie die befragten Lehrer erklärten, wurden einige wichtige Faktoren bei diesen Veränderungen allerdings außer acht gelassen: Geldmittel für Schulen waren gekürzt worden, die sozialen Unterschiede zwischen Arm und Reich hatten sich verschärft, und die Wirtschaftswelt hatte sich zunehmend als Partner bei der Definition von Bildungs- und

Erziehungszielen etabliert. Obwohl die meisten der Lehrer sich ihrem Beruf gegenüber verpflichtet fühlten, war jedoch vor allem die Höhe ihrer Besoldung wie auch die Altersversorgung ein Problembereich ersten Ranges. Offensichtlich hatte sich ihr Sozialstatus in den letzten Jahren stark verschlechtert, und da ihre Gehälter zunehmend aus Gemeindesteuern bezahlt werden, sind Aufbesserungen ihrer Einkommen kaum zu erwarten.

Saskatchewan / Kanada

Gewissermaßen als Antwort auf die Vorschläge, welche die OECD im Jahre 1976 den kanadischen Bildungspolitikern unterbreitet hatte, skizzierte *Livingstone (1987)* folgende Alternative für die Ausrichtung zukünftiger Bildungsreformen: Konservative Kreise befürworten Kürzungen der Ausgaben für Schulen und Universitäten, eine Rationalisierung der Verwaltung mit dem Ziel, den wachsenden Umfang und die Breite des Unterrichtsangebotes einzuschränken, die Reduzierung der Lehrpläne auf die wesentlichsten Bildungsziele sowie die Einführung eines ausgedehnten Systems von Bildungswegen und Examina, das den Zugang zu tertiären Bildungsinstitutionen einengt und gleichzeitig junge Menschen in eine paralleles Berufsausbildungssystem, das sie auf nur einfache Arbeiten in Industrie und Wirtschaft vorbereitet, umleitet. Gleichzeitig empfehlen sie die Abzweigung von Geldern für öffentliche Schulen zur Entwicklung von Privatschulen und von kommerziell produzierten Lehr- und Lernsystemen, die es den Schülern, die diese kaufen müssen, ermöglichen sollen, sich selbst zu unterrichten. Die humanistische Alternative würde *„die polytechnische Richtung betonen, mit dem Ziel, die allseitige Entwicklung der Schüler zu erleichtern"* (Livingstone 1987, S. 57).

Regierungsnahe Organisationen und Interessengruppen, wie der Wirtschaftsrat (*Economic Council of Canada*), verlangen die Entwicklung eines nationalen Bildungsprogramms. Wie einige Schulvertreter bemerkten, werden den Schulen Ziele und Prinzipien der freien Marktwirtschaft ohne öffentliche Debatte oder Konsultation aufgedrängt. Unter dem starken Einfluß der Massenmedien hat sich inzwischen der *Canadian Council of Ministers of Education*, die kanadische Kultusministerkonferenz, dem „intensiven politischen Druck" gebeugt und zunächst einmal ein nationales Prüfungsprogramm in den akademischen Grundfächern für alle Schüler des öffentlichen Schulwesens im Alter von 16 bis 18 Jahren eingeführt. Als nächster Schritt der bundesweiten Bildungsinitiative kann die Erstellung von einheitlichen Lehrplänen und Beurteilungskriterien erwartet werden.

Bei diesen Reformen dürfte der verstärkte Einsatz von Computern eine Rolle spielen, da unterschwellig die weitere Reduzierung der Bildungsausgaben angestrebt wird. Kritische Beobachter stellten allerdings fest:

„Zentralisierung, Vereinheitlichung und größerer Nachdruck auf Kontrolle mögen Kosten senken, Wirtschaftsinteressen dienen und Regierungen politische Vorteile bringen, solche Maßnahmen bedeuten jedoch keinerlei Verbesserungen für Schüler und Lehrer zu einem Zeitpunkt, da man in den Klassenzimmern verzweifelt auf Hilfe wartet" (Kunkel 1995, S. 2).

Ähnlich wie in den Vereinigten Staaten werden Bildungsausgaben für Schulen, einschließlich der Lehrergehälter, vornehmlich durch lokale Vermögenssteuern finanziert. Das Ergebnis ist, daß Steuerzahler, besonders wenn sie keine schulpflichtigen Kinder haben, allen Erhöhungen der Schulabgaben ablehnend gegenüberstehen. Davon sind besonders finanzschwache Provinzen wie Saskatchewan betroffen, und die Schließung der Schulen während der Sommermonate bringt es mit sich, daß die Lehrer (und anderes Schulpersonal) nur für zehn Monate bezahlt werden. Gleichzeitig aber erwarten die Eltern zunehmend von den Lehrern, daß sie mehr außerschulische Aufgaben vor 9 Uhr und nach 15.30 Uhr übernehmen. Auch wenn diese zusätzliche (und unbezahlte) Arbeit offiziell freiwillig erfolgt, so sind die Schulbehörden entschlossen, dem Wunsch der Eltern nachzukommen und achten bei der Einstellung von Junglehrern darauf, daß sie sich freiwillig zu diesen Arbeiten bereit erklären. Infolgedessen ist die Arbeitsmoral in vielen Lehrerkollegien sehr niedrig und das Mißtrauen gegenüber den Schulbehörden sehr stark.

Vergleichende Zusammenfassung

Die Arbeitswelt der Lehrer hat sich in den letzten zwei Jahrzehnten erheblich verändert. In Polen und in der früheren DDR sind grundlegende Verbesserungen vor allem in den materiellen Lebens- und Arbeitsbedingungen zu erkennen, wohingegen die Übernahme westlicher Prinzipien wie Individualismus und Konkurrenzkampf das frühere Gemeinschaftsgefühl verdrängt haben und das soziale Bewußtsein von Eltern und Schülern negativ beeinflussen.

Reformen besonders in den drei angelsächsischen Ländern haben generell zu Nachteilen für die Lehrer geführt. Hier argumentieren Politiker und Wirtschaftsführer, daß internationale Leistungsvergleiche auf ein deutliches Versagen der Schulen hinwiesen, was zu Schwächen im internationalen Wirtschaftswettbewerb geführt habe. Um den Rückstand wieder aufzuholen, müßten die Lehrer stärker kontrolliert werden. Die Mittel dieser Kontrolle sind eine verschärfte Auslese der Lehrer vor und nach ihrem Eintritt in den Beruf, verbindliche nationale Lehrpläne, ein umfangreiches nationales Prüfungsprogramm zur Messung von Schulleistungen und ein größeres Mitspracherecht der Öffentlichkeit, vor allem der Eltern und der Wirtschaft. Die Folge ist eine erhebliche Einschränkung der Eigenverantwortlichkeit der Lehrer.

In allen untersuchten Ländern werden Haushaltsdefizite als Rechtfertigung für Kürzungen der Bildungsausgaben angeführt, mit dem Erfolg, daß sich die Ausstattung der Schulen mit Lehr- und Lernmitteln verschlechtert, die Lehrergehälter stagnieren, die Klassenstärken erhöht werden und, besonders in Kanada, die Lehrer aufgefordert werden, zumeist unbezahlte außerschulische Pflichten zu übernehmen. Während einerseits an das Berufsethos der Lehrer appelliert wird, werden andererseits gewisse Privilegien, wie Ferien und die vergleichsweise wenigen Unterrichtsstunden, als Argumente für höhere Anforderungen an die Lehrerschaft in die Debatte eingeführt. Die Verschärfung sozialer Probleme wie Arbeitslosigkeit, Armut, Kriminalität, Drogenmißbrauch, Familienkonflikte und Rassismus hat dazu geführt, daß Politiker und Schulbehörden von Schulen und Lehrern erwarten, daß sie sich zusätzlich zu ihrem Bildungsauftrag auch um die Lösung dieser Probleme kümmern und viele der Aufgaben übernehmen, die früher in den Verantwortungsbereich der Familie fielen. Was die Lehrer fast einstimmig beklagen, ist die Tatsache, daß Eltern in zunehmendem Maße ihre Pflichten als Partner in der Erziehung ihrer Kinder vernachlässigten, gleichzeitig aber mehr Einflußnahme auf die Arbeit der Lehrer forderten.

Als Ergebnis dieser stärkeren Belastung nehmen Verschleißerscheinungen unter der Lehrerschaft zu. Ironischerweise ist dieses Problem besonders akut in Deutschland, wo die vergleichsweise besseren Lebens- und Arbeitsbedingungen der Lehrer vielfach zu einer Überalterung der Lehrerschaft geführt haben und jungen Lehrern der Zugang zum Lehrerberuf versperrt wird.

Die anfänglich gestellte Frage kann nun teilweise beantwortet werden. Aktuelle Tendenzen weisen auf eine zunehmende professionelle Entmündigung der Lehrer hin. Gleichzeitig sind aber auch sie den politischen, technologischen und administrativen Zwängen ausgesetzt, die bereits andere Angehörige des öffentlichen Dienstes erfahren haben. Es sollte die Aufgabe der Lehrerverbände sein, sich diesen Tendenzen entgegenzustellen und sich aktiv an der Erarbeitung eines neuen Berufsbildes des Lehrers zu beteiligen. Falls diese Aufgabe allein den Politikern und den Wirtschaftsunternehmen überlassen bleibt, scheint der Proletarisierung des Lehrerberufs nichts mehr im Wege zu stehen.

Bibliographie

Broadfoot, Patricia: Teachers and Educational Reforms. Teachers' Response to Policy Changes in England and France. Paper presented at the Annual Meeting of the British Educational Research Association, Oxford, September 1994.
Holmes Group: Tomorrow's Teachers. Lansing: The Holmes Group 1988.
Kunkel, Audrey: Herron Slams National Agenda. In: Saskatchewan Bulletin, 61 (1995) 12, S. 2.
Livingstone, D. W.: Crisis, Classes and Educational Reform in Advanced Capitalism. In: Wotherspoon, Terry (Hrsg.): The Political Economy of Canadian Schooling, Toronto: Methuen 1987, S. 57-67.
McKenna, Francis: Privatization: The Reform Agenda for American Secondary Schools. In: Lawson, Robert (Hrsg.): Changing Patterns of Secondary Education: An International Comparison, Calgary: The University of Calgary Press 1988, S. 261-267.
Mitter, Wolfgang: Education in Present-Day Germany. Some Considerations as Mirrored by Comparative Education (July 1991). In: Compare, 22 (1992) 1, S. 53-67.
Neave, Guy: The Teaching Nation. Prospects for Teachers in the European Community. Oxford: Pergamon Press 1992.
Pszczolkowski, Tadeusz: Basic Assumptions and Dilemmas of the Polish Educational System. In: Educational Media International, 29 (1992) 4, S. 229-234.
Rust, Val: Educational Responses to Reforms in East Germany, Czechoslovakia, and Poland. In: Human Development, 35 (1992) 1, S. 86-91.
Schwarting, Knut: Oma und Opa unterrichten die Jugend. In: Schulverwaltung. Ausgabe Brandenburg, Mecklenburg-Vorpommern, Sachsen, Sachsen-Anhalt, Thüringen und Berlin, 1 (1991) 2, S. 44-45.
Weniger Lehrer durch Computer. In: Elbe-Jetzel-Zeitung vom 25. Januar 1992.
Wirtschaft fordert: Orientierungsstufe abschaffen. In: Elbe-Jetzel-Zeitung vom 30. Januar 1992.

Looking Back, Looking Forward: Education in Central-Eastern Europe on the Eve of the XXIst Century

Janusz Tomiak

The long and impressive list of publications which have come during the course of the last four decades from the German Institute for International Educational Research in Frankfurt am Main is a very convincing proof that this great European centre of intensive academic activity has consistently paid great attention to the educational developments in the Central-Eastern European countries. These may be said to include three Slavonic countries: Poland, the Czech Republic and Slovakia and also Hungary. Most prominent role in this process has for many years been played by Professor Wolfgang Mitter, whose academic career has embraced several important functions. He has been a keen and punctilious observer of educational developments in all the four countries; a very reliable and unceasing rapporteur on what has been going on there; a frequent visitor to practically all important educational establishments in these lands; an active participant in numerous conferences, meetings and congresses which have been taking place there from the early 1960s onward; a scholar who has consistently promoted all kinds of co-operative efforts concerning educational growth and closer contacts between the two parts of Europe, divided for much too long by the tragic aftermath of the Second World War. And, above all, in all the four countries he has invariably been seen not only as an educator of great repute but also as a friend who can be trusted to say openly what he judges to be the case, to offer criticism when it is required and the words of advice when it is necessary; and, perhaps most importantly, as a scholar who, while combining the high qualities of an academic assessor and analyst, is at the same time a determined and constant promoter of international understanding and co-operation through education. One can travel to Warsaw, Prague, Bratislava or Budapest and easily find that the name of Wolfgang Mitter is quite well known to the wider ranks of pedagogues and educators at all levels. And more than this. One can visit any major city in any of the four countries and discover that his books and articles, translated into many other languages have been widely read and discussed and have sometimes served as a basis for formulating new ideas and even policy measures of greater importance.

It is, therefore, quite appropriate that on the occasion marking Professor Mitter's seventieth birthday we give some attention to a short, but synthetic overview of the educational developments in Central-Eastern European countries in the recent past and at the present moment and explore, though necessarily rather briefly, two important dimensions in comparative studies: continuity and comparability. These, I believe, are important dimensions for the following reasons. Continuity clearly demonstrates the key significance of the educational process in any national setting, despite discontinuities of all kinds in the parallel processes of political, social, economic and even religious developments in a country. Comparability offers an opportunity to identify what is uniquely characteristic of a particular country and its educational system through juxtaposition and a critical evaluation of the evidence available.

Yet, this exercise should not be seen as passing a judgement upon a particular system and arriving at a set of final conclusions. It is more appropriate to see it as a part of a continuous debate concerning educational developments, where the imaginative insights and constructive thinking of a particular investigator can be confronted with alternative viewpoints and lead to the emergence of new perspectives and new forms of interpretation of educational phenomena examined in a longer perspective of time in more than just one single country.

The Significance of Continuity in the Study of Educational Change

Perhaps one should begin by stating the obvious. In all countries educational systems evolve and respond over time to different kinds of challenge and different kinds of pressure from outside: political, social, economic and, sometimes, even religious. At the same time, all educational systems possess an inertia of their own. Educational provision, educational personnel and the general facilities available for educational purposes cannot be radically changed in the short run. One must also necessarily be aware of the fact that changes in what the educators ought to aim at, in what they teach and in how they teach what they teach, quite often are more formally apparent than real. That is why the studies of what really is the case often reveal a substantial gap between what ought to be the case and what manifestly is taking place.

Moreover, the relevance and the impact of the past upon the present day developments is, generally, inversely proportional to the length of time separating the presence from the events and experiences of the days gone by. Only the most traumatic and consequential events and developments retain their significance over a longer span of time, though that, no doubt, sometimes, may be the case. Normally, one should think in terms of years, decades at the most, and no longer, in considering what is directly relevant to the current form and substance of educational developments in any given country.

Naturally, the past never unilaterally predetermines the present and the future course of events in any field of human endeavour. Yet, one ought not to ignore it but consider it very carefully and use it to illuminate the unique course of development which is characteristic of any particular country in order to help to explain the contrasts between different countries which can be observed, but not necessarily easily explained without reference to the collective experiences of a given nation. Therefore, by selecting and identifying recent elements, politically, socially, economically and culturally most significant elements and occurrences much light, I believe, can be thrown upon the subsequent developments, particular tensions, difficulties and conflicts which make up the existing patterns and forms of educational evolution in each country.

The Comparative Perspective in the Study of Educational Change

Demonstrably, there is a place for both, analytical as well as synthetic studies in comparative education and the approaching turn of the century provides an opportunity for an attempt to summarise the essential features of educational development in the different countries over the last two or three decades in order to identify the most pressing problems of today and to assess the prospects for the future. In doing this, I want to argue, there is no need for yet another attempt to list all the educational laws, rules and regulations or to present statistical tables of various kinds dealing with the age cohorts or the quantitative growth at the different levels of education. That has been done admirably in several studies and reports dealing with all the countries on many occasions. What is important in this case is a broad, but clear delineation of the principal lines of educational evolution, pointing out the main influences shaping the national systems of education, revealing what the researcher in question believes to be the real forces significantly influencing the character and nature of educational endeavours in some countries over a period of time. The emphasis, therefore, must be placed upon the selection and scrutiny of what one believes to be the most potent and lasting influences over education in the countries with which one is more intimately familiar. That familiarity can only come through a long involvement in comparative analysis, frequent visits to the countries in question and a determined effort to keep up with the changing educational scene there.

Many of the countries in Western Europe have been given considerable attention in this respect through the writings of very competent and able scholars, though the final synthesis can only be attempted after the sorting out of different views and opinions has been accomplished through comparison, juxtaposition and a critical evaluation of the evidence that has been provided and a careful scrutiny of the conclusions which have been reached by the different investigators. In the case of many other countries the position is rather different.

Education in the Central-Eastern European Countries: The Background

The educational developments in the countries of Central-Eastern Europe have in the recent years been given attention by some scholars in the West and particular aspects of these developments have been analysed in, for instance, special studies of the changing school structures and curriculum change, published by the German Institute for International Educational Research in Frankfurt. However, the books by the Eastern-European writers on education in their own countries published in the 1950s, 1960s, 1970s and even in the 1980s were generally lacking scientific objectivity, tended to serve political imperatives of the day and have been based upon an *a priori* accepted system of values and politically conditioned social and economic theories. For this reason, they have often been considered biased and unduly adulatory. The nature of the difficulty should, nevertheless, not be too easily glossed over in an exercise of this kind. Full objectivity, value-free judgements and universally acceptable conclusions simply are not attainable even in the best of academic exercises coming from honest and experienced scholars, aiming at a detached, scientific analysis. While this consideration should always be kept in mind, this cannot be the reason for not examining important educational developments in the different parts of the world.

The four Central-Eastern European countries possess certain common denominators such as geographical proximity, similar cultural roots and levels of cultural development, but they have different languages, significantly different literary and cultural histories, social structures and economic potentials. All the four should be considered to be important countries at the present stage of the historical evolution of Europe. They now aspire to the fullest possible political, cultural and economic integration with the countries of Western, Northern and Southern Europe which already possess common political, economic and military structures and enjoy a very considerable degree of political and economic cohesion. The integration of Poland, the Czech Republic, Hungary and Slovakia should be greatly facilitated by a sounder knowledge of the principal features of cultural and educational developments in these four countries and a proper understanding of the problems encountering them in these respects today and likely to face them at the beginning of the twenty-first century.

In analysing the full range of educational phenomena it is advisable to deal separately with a) the aims of education, b) the principles of control, finance and administration of the educational systems, c) the structure of the educational systems, d) the contents and methods of education. This mode of analysis is particularly useful in all cases when, following a major political and social upheaval reaching the very core of the existing set-up, most fundamental changes have to be expected as a result of a radical alteration of the policies pursued so far, requiring a total break with the past and complete remodelling of the system. Transition from the old to the new is often difficult and creates problems and friction, because the existing institutional set-up in any sector of the social framework tends to resist all far-reaching changes and particularly those which affect vested interests and well established procedures. One must, therefore, proceed carefully in sorting out the difficulties which have to be encountered in the educational field, following a rapid transition from well entrenched communism to fully developed free-market liberalism, as that transition affects the very foundations of the educational process in every country in Central-Eastern Europe.

Concerning the Aims of Education

One can assume that a quick transition from one generally accepted and internalised system of values to another, quite different in character, is bound to create widespread disorientation and even resistance in a country. In fact, one can argue, that this cannot really take place in the short-run and at the very best result in anomie – to use Emile Durkheim's sociological concept of great practical significance – and bring about not only general confusion, but also result in cynicism and a natural tendency to consider all value systems fraudulent and deceptive by the citizens. The forthcoming evidence, covering the last five years or so, suggests that this is exactly what has been happening in Eastern Europe recently. It could hardly be otherwise, if one recalls that in the case of the Central European countries the communist system of values was a facade propped up by empty rhetoric coming from a small section of the political vanguard remaining in power which pretended to propagate it among – and sometimes to force it upon – the population at large, with little success. Here, one must stress the difference between Central-Eastern Europe and the former Soviet Russia and most of the Soviet Union. Historically, Central-Eastern Europe tended to shape its political culture upon a fundamental respect for human life, rational choice and personal responsibility for individual action, even if from time to time there were clear and undeniable departures from such an orientation. In this area communist domination following the Second World War, never degenerated into ruthless and primitive forms of persecution of religious believers and a total elimination of the opposition en masse was not acceptable. A return to a liberal outlook and an open society represents, therefore, in these countries a return to the old socio-political pattern and it is not tantamount with the establishment of a value system which is unknown and inexperienced. This must not, however, be taken to mean that there are no problems in this aspect of change. One problem is rooted in the disdain in which the members of the previous political elite are held, following their sudden and, indeed, enthusiastic conversion to unbridled capitalism. Another is that the ideological vacuum created by the complete disappearance of the previous normative framework has opened the field to a suspect effort by other secular or religious institutions to fill the existing gap and enforce other value systems. Such a development creates a new challenge for the developing democratic order in Central-Eastern Europe.

Orienting all education towards the ideals of liberalisation, democratisation, humanisation and differentiation which could ensure the fullest possible opportunity for individual choice and self-fulfilment, unhindered development of all talent and a willing acceptance of civic responsibility by all should, therefore, be seen as a natural process, facilitated by earlier historical developments associated with the growth of pluralism, political and cultural in this part of Europe, but requiring time and determination.

Concerning Control, Finance and Administration of Education

The principles concerning control, finance and administration of education in post-communist societies are posing problems particularly noticeable to a keen observer from outside. One cannot help noticing that gradually, yet quite perceptibly, a dual system of schools is creeping in. One part of it constitutes the sector of private and fee-charging schools (including a whole variety of new schools which have now come to operate outside the state sector in response to social demand) with very significant advantages such as favourable staff-pupil-ratios, highly competent and enthusiastic teachers, excellent facilities, numerous optional study courses, etc. The other sector consists of state schools, controlled by the Ministries of Education, increasingly financially supported by impoverished local authorities, staffed by poorly paid and disgruntled teachers and manifestly experiencing all kinds of problems. The contrast between the two sectors seems to be growing all the time and it is specially noticeable at the level of upper secondary and specialist higher education, with the old boys' networks gradually reasserting themselves in many fields of social, cultural and economic development which ultimately leads to social divisiveness and marked differentials in subsequent income and social prestige. That must be viewed as a less acceptable development, though it could be acceptable if the quality of education in the provided sector was not inferior to that in the private sector. There is, however, no evidence that this is the case anywhere. Rather to the contrary, the contrasts between the two sectors are growing with the flow of time. The problem is that balancing the state budgets (which is an economic imperative) allows for no major increases in social expenditure in the four countries under consideration. The growth in national incomes may enable the respective governments to increase their spending on education and this is not an impossibility, but the demands of similar kind from the other services, such as health, old age pensions and social welfare must also be taken into account. It will require a real commitment to education of the future governments in the Central-Eastern European countries to the cause of education of the people and ensuring that the more substantial inequalities in access, retention and performance in respect of individual pupils are eliminated in the long run and that they do not undermine social and political stability in each country.

Concerning the Structure of the Systems of Education

The structure of the systems of education inherited from the communist regimes in the Central-Eastern European countries was not dissimilar to the one prevailing in some of the West European countries in the sense that the common school for all children aged 5/6/7 to 15/16 resembled the comprehensive primary/secondary school pattern. Early selection, important in the West and of great significance in the South of Europe, is proving a tempting proposition in the Central-Eastern European countries in their schools outside – and even within the provided sector. This tends to result everywhere in the growing controversies concerning the supposed advantages and drawbacks of early selection at 10, 11 or 12. An open debate on this issue is, of course, quite in order, though the arguments for or against early (and, as a rule, irrevocable) selection must be properly elaborated and presented for consideration and scrutiny.

Diversification at the level of upper secondary education into academically, technically and vocationally oriented forms of study is an economic necessity and it must correspond to the prospects for employment for the school leavers. There is, however, a real challenge to ensure that the vocational courses of different kind do in fact relate directly to the changing pattern of production and employment. Under the former system, educational planning, rooted in and closely associated with economic planning more or less guaranteed a job for everybody finishing a given form of specialised professional or vocational training. But the pattern of production in the four Central-Eastern European countries was rigidly predetermined by the COMECON rationalisation and regional specialisation serving the requirements of the communist bloc as a whole. Its collapse brought about a complete breakdown of industrial integration of the area. A new productive pattern, requiring substantial investment in new branches of industry and fundamentally restructuring the old units of production is gradually being forged, but it is a long drawn process, dependent on the fluctuations in foreign trade. Foreign capital is, however, moving into Central-Eastern Europe on an increasingly significant scale and new employment opportunities in all the four countries are bound by their very nature to impose a system of vocational training suiting the new situation. Hence, structural unemployment, so visible today in many regions in Central-Eastern Europe will decline, though not necessarily very rapidly and, alas, not everywhere. Quite considerable unemployment has, after all, now become also a feature in all countries of the European Union.

Concerning the Content and Methods of Education

Reforming the content of learning has ostensibly proceeded quickly in Central-Eastern Europe, but this has often been more apparent than real. Removing some subjects from the official curricula and introducing new ones or fundamentally changing the content of the syllabuses requires much more than just administrative measures. It is, for example, very naive to suppose that the former professors and lecturers in Marxist dialectics can suddenly turn into effective teachers of philosophy as it is known and taught in the West. It is equally unrealistic to assume that the teachers of Russian can overnight become experts in teaching a Western language. Bringing in the teaching of religion causes often major administrative and financial difficulties and in some cases outright opposition. Most difficult is proving ensuring a proper preparation for effective democratic citizenship, the education of honest individuals, capable of fully exercising their rights and dutifully meeting their civic obligations, instilling in the young a firm faith in the lasting advantages of trusting the democratic process and defending it against corrupt practices and manipulation by unscrupulous individuals and, also, against cynicism which brings inaction and resignation. It is here, more than anywhere else, that meaningful Western help is required. Regular meetings and conferences with educators and teachers from a whole range of countries taking part, are necessary. So are multilateral arrangements to share useful experiences in this area. The Council of Europe has been conducting periodical conferences on civic education. These now also involve educators from Central-Eastern Europe, but this is not enough. If progress is to be made, many more international organisations, institutions of higher learning, teacher training establishments and professional bodies involved in the teaching of civics and social studies must actively co-operate. Only this can ensure that democracy and democratic procedures, with all that they involve and require of the citizens at all levels of civic participation, are firmly rooted in the Central-Eastern European soil.

Similar considerations can be said to arise with respect to teaching and learning methods. Obsolete methods, placing stress upon memorisation and passive learning, demanding little imaginative thinking and academic rigour and lacking drive and continuous forms of regular assessment of individual progress in studies cannot be tolerated. Here is a real challenge for school inspectors, teacher training experts, authors of textbooks and modern learning materials. Above all this requires that the top personnel in the Ministries of Education, exercising overall control of the educational systems, are individuals with wide and varied experience, extensive international contacts, speaking Western languages, who well understand what modern education is about and what it must involve and not bureaucrats accustomed to issuing endless directives and fond of empty rhetoric. Only when, as a result of the joint efforts, every lesson creates in the learner a genuine thirst for knowledge and purposeful action, provides a challenge corresponding to the interests and abilities of all pupils and students and brings personal satisfaction to each one of them, a satisfactory situation will be reached.

There is at least one additional point. Research and development in education must be given a higher preference on the scale of national priorities. International reports indicate that the central governments' budgetary allocations devoted to this end in the Central-Eastern European countries are inadequate. This is a serious drawback which will delay further growth in the effectiveness of learning. Considering the highly competitive character of modern production as well as the commercial and financial sectors of the economy, this impediment must be removed as soon as possible. Only wisely chosen educational initiatives and carefully considered policy measures, supported by adequate resources can ensure that Central-Eastern European countries will become real partners in united Europe at the dawn of the twenty-first century.

Bibliography

Baske, Siegfried / Beneš, Milan / Riedel, Rainer: Der Übergang von der marxistisch-leninistischen zu einer freiheitlich-demokratischen Bildungspolitik in Polen, in der Tschechoslowakei und in Ungarn. Darstellung und Dokumentation. Wiesbaden: Harrassowitz 1991. (Osteuropa-Institut der Freien Universität Berlin: Erziehungswissenschaftliche Veröffentlichungen. 20)

Lewowicki, Tadeusz / Mieszalski, Stefan / Szymański, Mirosław: Szkoła i pedagogika w dobie przełomu. Warszawa: Żak 1995.

Mitter, Wolfgang / Kopp, Botho von (eds.): Die Zeitdimension in der Schule als Gegenstand des Bildungsvergleichs. Köln et al.: Böhlau 1994. (Studien und Dokumentationen zur vergleichenden Bildungsforschung. 61)

Mitter, Wolfgang / Schäfer, Ulrich (eds.): Upheaval and Change in Education. Papers presented by members of the German Institute at the VIIIth World Congress of Comparative Education, „Education, Democracy and Development", Prague, July 8-14, 1992. Frankfurt a. M.: German Institute for International Educational Research 1993.

Mitter, Wolfgang / Weiss, Manfred / Schaefer, Ulrich (eds.): Recent Trends in Eastern European Education. Proceedings of the UNESCO Workshop held at the German Institute for International Educational Research, Frankfurt am Main, 5-7 June 1991. Frankfurt a. M.: German Institute for International Educational Research 1992.

Muszyński, Heliodor / Walterowa, Eliška: Curricula in der Schule: Polen. Tschechische Republik. Köln et al.: Böhlau 1995. (Studien und Dokumentationen zur vergleichenden Bildungsforschung. 58, 2)

Open Society Institute (ed.): Building Open Societies. New York: Soros Foundation 1995.

Organisation for Economic Co-operation and Development (ed.): Science and Technology Statistics in the Partners in Transition Countries and the Russian Federation. Paris: OECD 1996. (Working Papers Series. 4, 19)

Perdue, William Dan: Modernization Crisis. The Transformation of Poland. Westport, Conn. et al.: Praeger 1995.

Rust, Val / Knost, Peter / Wichmann, Jürgen (eds.): Education and the Values Crisis in Central and Eastern Europe. Frankfurt a. M. et al.: Lang 1994. (Comparative Studies Series. 4)

Tjeldvoll, Arild (ed.): Education in East/Central Europe 1991. Report form the Educational Leadership International Seminar in Oslo, November 28-30, 1991. Oslo: University of Oslo 1992.

Tomiak, Janusz: Educational Change in Central Eastern Europe. A View from London. In: East/West Education, 13 (1992) 1, pp. 1-10.

Tomiak, Janusz: Implications of Political Change in Eastern Europe for Educational Policy Development. In: Journal of Education Finance, 17 (1992) 3, pp. 19-34.
Tomiak, Janusz: Culture, National Identity and Schooling in Eastern Europe. In: Thomas, Elwyn (ed.): International Perspectives on Culture and Schooling. A Symposium Proceedings, London: Institute of Education, University of London 1994, pp. 415-427.
Tomiak, Janusz: Education, Work and Restructuring of Central-Eastern and Eastern Europe. In: World Yearbook of Education, (1995), pp. 49-61.

The German Dual System of Vocational Education and Training: A Comparative Study of Influence upon Educational Policy and Practice in Other Countries

David N. Wilson

Introduction

As a Comparative and International Educator specializing in the study of technical-vocational education and training (TVET), I have been informed during my international work in nations as diverse as Israel, Singapore and Sri Lanka that they are 'adopting' the German dual system as a 'model' for their TVET system reform. Moreover, in many studies of TVET system reform, including those undertaken in Canada and the U.S.A., the dual system 'model' is cited as worthy of adoption. Yet, after hearing these claims and reading these recommendations I am left with the idea that the German dual system 'model' is either not well understood, or completely misunderstood, by many who view the 'model' as the *cure* for their nations' TVET problems.

One of my post-graduate students *(Lehmann 1995, p. 3)* that „*recommendations of the German system as a possible solution to training problems in North America should be approached with some hesitation*". Lehmann also noted that „*citations of the dual system seem to be based on rather superficial observations and facts*". He noted further that the „*intricate framework of legislation and voluntary co-operation on national, individual state* (Länder) *and local levels are ignored*", as well as „*the cultural and historical basis on which the system functions in Germany*". These comments reinforced my own international observations and are likely to have significantly influenced the idea for this study.

I chose to take this opportunity to honor my good friend and colleague, Wolfgang Mitter, by examining German contributions to policy and practice in technical-vocational education and training. His anecdotal commentary upon the Czech and Slovak educational systems, during evenings while attending the VIIIth World Congress of Comparative Education in Prague, proved to be an invaluable briefing for my subsequent participation in a European Community Labour Market Restructuring Project to reform TVET in these two nations. Those efforts to restore the systems to their pre-Russification state exemplify many of the ideals with which Wolfgang Mitter advocated as a comparative and international educator.

The Dual System

The dual education/training system in Germany is *„grounded in over 500 years of craft and trade apprenticeship, which has instilled a 'training culture' in the mind-set of all Germans"* (Wilson 1992, p. 33). The dual system is a *„combination of practical and theoretical vocational training at two places of learning with different legal and structural characteristics: in-plant and in-school training"* (ibid.). Although craft training has its roots in the guilds and trades of the Middle Ages, *Lehmann (1995 p. 24)* pointed out that *„the term 'dual system' is relatively new"*, having been *„coined in 1964 by the Commission for Education"*. Castro / Alfthan (1992, p. 3) characterized the dual system as the *„most sophisticated"* apprenticeship system in the world because *„it has become very complex and structured"*.

This *quadra-partite* (business, government, labour union, and education) system trains apprentices in 378 occupations (consolidated from about 700 in 1980) which are established by legislation. Legislation governing the Chambers of Commerce and Industry, which control the in-plant component *(Berufsbildungsgesetz*, Vocational Education Law), was promulgated at the federal level in 1959. In contrast, legislation governing the in-school component has been promulgated at the *Land* (i.e. the state, plural: *Länder*) level. Education in Germany has been the exclusive responsibility of *Länder* governments since 1947, when the allied powers de-centralized the former nazi unitary educational system. In 1986, there were approximately 786.000 registered *Meisters*, or trainers, in German industry, compared to only 60.000 teachers in *Länder* schools complementing the in-plant vocational training *(Berufsschulen)* and full-time upper secondary vocational schools *(Berufsfachschulen)* (Wilson 1992, p. 35).

Lehmann (1995, p. 13) indicates that the dual system *„relies on the heavily streamed secondary school system ... to attract qualified young people to participate in apprenticeship training programs"*. Following the attainment of employment and the signing of a formal apprenticeship *(Lehrstelle)* contract, these apprentices attend *Länder* schools *(Berufsschulen)* for one or two days per week (normally between 8 and 16 hours) where they receive theoretical instruction. The apprenticeships are of three to three and a half years, with three or four days per week in on-the-job training and one or two days in vocational and specialized schools. The training period culminates with a final examination *(Wilson 1993a, p. 35)*.

Table 1 depicts the legislative, governance, organizational and functional components of the dual system.

Table 1: Components of The German Dual System

Vocational Training Components	Dual System Components	
Location of Training/Education	Enterprise/Institution	Vocational School
Learner	Trainee (Apprentice)	Vocational School Student
Teacher/Trainer	Trainer (Regulation on the Competence of Trainers)	Vocational School Teacher (Study and Examination Regulations)
Constitutional Authority	Federal Government	Länder
Organization	Industry	Länder
Funding	Individual Enterprises	Länder
General Training Plan	Training Regulations	Framework Curriculum
Supervision	Chambers of Industry and Commerce	Länder
Primary Didactic Principle	Labour Process Orientation (practice)	Job-related and General Knowledge (theory)
Target	Occupational Skills Sectors	for the Public and Private

Source: *Gilardi / Schulz (1989)*.

One possible reason for misunderstanding of the dual system in North America, and elsewhere, was provided by Weidman, who noted that „*secondary schooling in ... Germany is highly differentiated*" with the *Hauptschule, Realschule,* and *Gymnasium* at the lower-secondary school level and an equally-differentiated variety of upper secondary academic *(Gymnasium* upper level) and TVET institutions. This highly differentiated system is quite different from the U.S. where „*there is only one secondary level, the high school, in which differentiation takes place in terms of curriculum, rather than in terms of different institutions" (Weidman 1987, p. 176).* It is also noted that the German *„secondary school and vocational training system for adolescents is more highly differentiated, linked to employers and formally organized under state control in ... Germany than in the United States" (ibid., p. 177.).* Therefore, these *„fundamental differences"* between the systems appear likely to constitute a source of confusion about the nature and function of the dual system in nations with unitary lower and upper secondary educational institutions.

Influence upon Policy and Practice

As noted in the introduction, many nations have considered the adoption – and adaptation – of the German dual system as a 'model' for their reform of TVET. Some writers have described this fascination with the 'model' and provided their perceptions of why the 'model' is considered to be attractive and/or appropriate to their nation's TVET system. Glover exemplifies these authors, noting that, *„the German apprenticeship system has attracted the attention of many American policy-makers because it has demonstrated the ability to produce high skills in a majority of German school leavers, while conferring recognition and status to a wide variety of occupations not requiring university training" (Glover 1994, p. 5).*

Exactly what attributes of the dual system are considered to be attractive and/or appropriate by authors like Glover? The first factor is that *„two-thirds of all young people completing full-time secondary education in Germany enter apprenticeships in the dual system".* Secondly, *„about 90 percent ... will complete and pass their comprehensive examination".* Third, the dual system includes *„assessment and certification procedures"* for apprentices, in addition to *„curriculum guides and outlines" (ibid.)* for the *Berufsschulen* (for part-time study) and *Berufsfachschulen* (for full-time, non-apprenticeship, study).

The fourth factor is that *„industry does not simply set the standards and let the schools implement them ... industry stays involved by conducting the assessments of apprentices on a continuous basis"* by means of the *„competent bodies"* so that *„the certifying agent [is] not the school".* This *„continuous involvement in assessment keeps industry close to the process and provides a direct communication link between schools and industry on the effectiveness of the training".* Fifth, the collapsing and consolidation *of „apprenticeable occupations into fewer occupations",* plus the re-design of training *„so that several spe-*

cialties branch from a common stem" *(ibid.)* is viewed as an exemplary attribute; particularly, one which appears to have built flexibility to adapt to change into the system.

The sixth factor is because *„training outlines and skill standards are so explicit, [this] provides ... a genuine advantage"*. Seventh, the connection between the Occupational Information Centres, operated by the Federal Employment Service *(Arbeitsamt)*, and Chambers of Industry and Commerce, Chambers of Agriculture, Chambers of Professions, and/or Chambers of Handicrafts is indicative of the level and degree of viable public-private sector partnerships achieved in Germany. Finally, Germans *„recognize that developing skill standards is as much a political process as it is a technical process and, thus, they attempt to maximize the participation and input of all stakeholders into the process in order to facilitate consensus"* *(ibid.)*.

Castro and Alfthan indicate that the dual system is quite similar in Austria, Germany and Switzerland. Since these three nations are *„essentially the German-speaking nations of Europe"* *(Castro / Alfthan 1992, p. 8)*, this suggests that cultural factors are extremely important for the adoption and adaptation of the 'model' in other nations. They caution that *„it remains a system that is particularly difficult to reproduce in other cultures [and] requires that society attaches a high prestige to manual occupations – which is not at all the case in less industrialized societies where manual occupations are disdained"* *(ibid.)*.

Examples of the Reproduction of the Dual System

From an international and comparative perspective, I have been informed by postgraduate students from Sri Lanka that their TVET policies had been modeled upon the German dual system. In 1995, I had an opportunity to visit TVET institutions in Sri Lanka, while evaluating one Canadian assistance program, and found that disruptions caused by civil conflict had rendered these institutions almost ineffectual.

While undertaking a study of TVET policy-formulation in Israel, I found that historically *„the Israeli educational system was patterned on 'a European' model of differentiated secondary schooling"* with *„the European models adopted – and adapted – by Israel were those of both Britain and Germany, with the 'academic' secondary schools following British trends and the vocational secondary schools – particularly those under the aegis of the Ministry of Labour – patterned on German trends"* *(Wilson 1990, p. 2)*. However, I concluded that *„in spite of the maintenance of strong linkages between the [Israel]*

Ministry of Labour and the Ministry of Education of the Federal Republic of Germany, the MoL system appears to resemble North American models more than the German dual system" (ibid., p. 34).

In my comparative study of the effectiveness of National Training Boards, I examined the structure and function of the the Federal Institute for Vocational Training (*Bundesinstitut für Berufsbildung* or *BiBB*) and found that „*the German ... philosophy that all youth should be provided with initial occupational training ... appears to be gaining favor with many other developed, and some developing, nations*" (Wilson 1993a, p. 2). The reasons for this favorable perception of the German approach were, *inter alia*, that „*initial training is not merely technical ... but also attitudinal*" and those „*employees who have acquired a 'solid' initial training are more easily re-trained than those without initial training*" (ibid.).

In addition, it was noted that „*an important feature*" of the *Berufsbildungsgesetz* is its „*delegation of administrative autonomy to BiBB*" (ibid., p. 11). The BiBB 'model' of shared decision-making „*with relevant government ministries to decide which occupations will be regulated within the apprenticeship system, and the content and length of training for each occupation*", is also considered to be of importance to those nations desiring to adopt, and adapt, the German 'model' *(ibid., p. 13)*. The BiBB guidelines enabled „*committees of regional Chambers of Commerce and Industry [to] decide which employers may offer apprenticeship training, and establish examination content*" (ibid.). The hierarchical structure of BiBB „*from the level of the individual enterprise to the federal level*" was also noted to be a valuable attribute of the system *(ibid., p. 19)*.

The integration which seemed to have been built into the German 'model' was noted to be admirable. For example, it was noted that „*training committees at the individual enterprise level are rare, but worthy of examination*". The absence of involvement at the enterprise level was considered to be one possible reason why many training initiatives failed to attain their stated objectives. The Works Councils component of the dual system was noted to have been

„*statutorily mandated since 1969 for all firms with more than ten employees (although Works Councils had been in existence since after World War I). These councils are elected by workers and have the right to participate in establishing and implementing training policy at the level of the individual enterprise*" (ibid.). „*The Works Councils also enable worker participation in curriculum development for the dual system*" *(ibid., p. 31).*

One lesser known aspect of the dual system which was of interest to the Israel Ministry of Labour was the mechanism for pilot-testing research developed by the German Federal Ministry of Education and Science (BMBW), to which BiBB reports *(Glover 1994)*. Dehnbostel informed the Israelis that between 1971 and 1989 about 500 pilot projects were conducted in industry, for which about 25 million DM (matched by funds from *Länder* Ministries of Education and Culture) had been allocated annually, and that these pilot projects *„rapidly developed into efficient tools of innovation" (Dehnbostel 1989, p. 69)*. BMBW provides these funds to BiBB for disbursement. Industry pilot projects are assessed by BiBB and BMBW while school-based pilot projects are evaluated by the joint Federal-State-Commission on Educational Planning and Research Funding *(Bund-Länder-Kommission für Bildungsplanung und Forschungsförderung* or *BLK) (ibid., p. 39)*. He also noted that, *„experimental pilot projects are an important instrument of the state's vocational training policy whose aim it is to increase the efficiency of the vocational training system" (ibid., p. 20)*.

This approach was even more attractive, since he also indicated that:

„A constituent element of the experimental pilot project is that 'practitioners' (teaching staff in companies and in vocational training establishments) and 'theoreticians' (researchers and scientists from universities and other research establishments involved in the scientific monitoring) actively participate and play a key role in any such project. This will help in developing solutions that meet real practical needs ... and increase the acceptance of pilot project results by practitioners at a later stage ... since the 'grass roots' level ... [was involved] in such processes" (ibid., p. 23).

These research-based innovations appear to have been of interest to the Israelis, since although Israel does have *„an Apprenticeship law which requires that each employer who employs an apprentice under the age of 18 must see to it that his right to study in some school for at least one day a week is assured" (Niv-Kovetz 1989, p. 116)*, the apprenticeship system is considered to need modernization.

The interest of Singapore in the dual system was documented by *Pillay (1992, p. 26)*, who noted that:

„In 1991, the Vocational and Industrial Training Board (VITB) introduced new and improved provisions modeled towards achieving a 'dual system' as practiced in Germany,

to create job entry skills training for the majority of school leavers not proceeding to post-secondary or tertiary institutions."

The Singaporean adaptation of the dual system 'model' comprises industry-based training and apprenticeship in the service sector with VITB (now re-named The Institute of Technical Education) institution-based training, leading to certification. Singapore introduced its version of the dual system for two major reasons:

"First, it is being adopted in very specific areas. These are areas where pre-employment training is not enough, is not in place (like most service areas) or is not cost-effective (as in the hotel business), given the relatively small number of trainees and the very high cost of training facilities. In this sense, it is an alternative mechanism which contributes to increasing the reach and the flexibility of the existing training system. But there is also another, very important reason: the dual system is being introduced as an alternative training mechanism for those already engaged in the workforce or for youngsters who start working before they finish a technical education program. In other words, it is part of the governmental effort to upgrade the level of the entire workforce" (Oliveira / Pillay 1992, p. 4).

The Singaporean adaptation appears to have replicated the degree of *integration* of system elements evident in Germany and also shows evidence of similar *dedication* and/or *sense of purpose* and *discipline;* attributes which have made the dual system effective in Austria, Germany, and Switzerland. It is also likely that the presence of German aid personnel in Singapore from the early 1970s, at the German-Singapore Training Institute for precision optics, provided a good introduction to the dual system model *(Wilson 1981, p. 93).*

Therefore, from both the structural and functional perspectives, and the perspective of being a fully integrated system, the German 'model' was perceived as offering important lessons to nations interested in establishing national training boards to support effective TVET systems.

Conclusion

This brief examination of *factors* and *forces* which play upon the perceptions of the German dual system of occupational education/training and some examples of international efforts to adopt and adapt the system was intended to illustrate the *complexity* of the model and the difficulties associated with its replication in other nations. A deliberate decision was made not to describe the German educational system in its totality, or to fully situate the dual system within the German system, because this would have been analogous to „carrying coals to Newcastle". Rather, sufficient descriptive and explanatory information was provided to set the stage for the intended discussion. It is hoped that these efforts have proven successful and that policy-makers in nations which have not understood the dual system well, or completely misunderstood the system, might be better informed about the transfer of such a system from one cultural milieu to another and the implications of its replication in their nations as a *cure* for their TVET problems.

To conclude this study, a summary of these factors and forces is provided. This approach is deemed useful for those policy-makers desirous of the adoption and adaptation of the 'model' to their TVET systems. It is hoped that the superficiality of previous descriptions of the dual system can be avoided.

The dual system is grounded in 500 years of craft and trade apprenticeship history which has become part of the 'culture' in Germany (and similar in Austria and Switzerland). The *hierarchical* framework of legislation and co-operating institutions ranges from the Federal Institute for Vocational Training to the regional Chambers of Commerce and Industry, Agriculture, Professions and Handicrafts to Works Councils at individual enterprises. This complex structure facilitates communication and co-operation at all levels of TVET in these countries. The *quadra-partite* involvement of representatives of government, business, labour unions and education/training institutions along his hierarchy validates such co-operation and communication.

The dual system relies upon the differentiated secondary school system to provide youth to participate in training programmes. The onus is upon these youth to secure employment, arrange the *Lehrstelle*, or apprenticeship contract, and then the employer is required to place the apprentices for part-time upper secondary studies in *Berufsschulen*. A parallel 'career path' has evolved through attendance at *Berufsfachschulen* for full-time studies with practical experience obtained in common workshops operated by the *Arbeitsamt*, or Federal Employment Service.

Countries with undifferentiated lower and upper secondary educational systems, or with less differentiation than is present in Germany, should understand that the dual system may not be compatible with a unitary educational infrastructure.

The dual system is favored by many policy-makers and policy-analysts because it:

- has demonstrated the ability to produce high skills in a majority of school leavers;
- provides initial *attitudinal* training in addition to technical skills;
- is a comprehensive and integrated system with shared decision-making;
- confers recognition and status to a wide variety of occupations;
- provides occupational training to between two-thirds and three-quarters of graduates from full-time secondary education who enter apprenticeships;
- includes explicit skill standards and training outlines;
- includes assessment and certification procedures;
- involves industries in the planning, governing and assessment, which keeps industry involved in the process and provides a direct communication linkage between schools and industry;
- undertakes certification by competent bodies, rather by the school;
- includes a research and pilot-testing component that builds in flexibility and innovation;
- maximizes the participation and input of all stakeholders in the *hierarchy* from the Federal, and *Länder,* governments to enterprises, education and training institutions and Workers Councils, in order to facilitate consensus.

Finally, the brief descriptions of efforts to adopt the dual system in Israel, Singapore and Sri Lanka suggest that while the adoption – and adaptation – of the system in Singapore appears successful, it is questionable how much impact and/or change has taken place within the Israeli system. Further, it is quite evident that the system has made no impact in Sri Lanka, but some of this lack of impact can be explained by the dislocations suffered as a result of civil conflict.

One attribute of the Israeli and Singaporean educational systems which may render them more favorable for the successful adoption of the dual system is their enrollment mix. Israel has developed a technological education infrastructure with 47 percent of secondary enrollment in technical courses. Singapore currently enrolls 25 percent of its 34.000 secondary school graduates in programmes at its four Polytechnics and Economic Development Board Institutes. These enrollment patterns more closely resemble those of Germany than many other nations and may well constitute yet another factor likely to contribute to the successful transfer of the dual system *(Wilson 1996, p. 12).*

In closing, I trust that this brief comparative exercise has accomplished its stated purposes. I could think of no better way to honor my friend and colleague, Wolfgang Mitter, than by describing and explaining the contributions which I believe the German dual system of occupational training has made to international educational development and its potential future contributions.

Bibliography

Castro, Claudio de Moura / Alfthan, Torkel: Five Training Models. Geneva: International Labour Organisation 1992. (Training Occasional Paper. 9)

Dehnbostel, Peter: Pilot Projects on the Introduction of New Technologies in In-Company Vocational Training. In: Proceedings of The Eleventh Joint Israeli-German Seminar on Planning, Implementation and Evaluation of Experimental Projects in the Field of Vocational Training, Jerusalem: Ministry of Labour 1989, pp. 69-74.

Gilardi, Rüdiger von / Schulz, Winfried: In-Firm Trainers of Young People in the Framework of the Dual Vocational Training System of the Federal Republic of Germany. Edited by the European Centre for the Development of Vocational Education. Luxembourg: Office for Official Publications of the European Communities 1989.

Glover, Robert W.: Issues for Designing a System of Skill Standards and Certification for the American Workforce. On What Basis Should Occupational/Skill/Industry Clusters Be Organized? Austin: University of Texas, Center for the Study of Human Resources 1994.

Lehmann, Wolfgang L.: The dual system of Vocational Training in Germany. Its Organisation, Structure, Context and Current Debate. Toronto, University of Toronto, M. A. Thesis 1995.

Niv-Kovetz, Netta: The Hebrew University Apprenticeship Programme. In: Proceedings of The Eleventh Joint Israeli-German Seminar on Planning, Implementation and Evaluation of Experimental Projects in the Field of Vocational Training, Jerusalem: Ministry of Labour 1989, pp. 116-121.

Oliveira, João / Pillay, Gerald F.: Training for New Technologies in Singapore. Geneva: International Labour Organisation 1992. (Training Policy Paper. 96)

Pillay, Gerald F.: Training of Middle Level Workers in Singapore. Geneva: International Labour Organisation 1992. (Training Policy Paper. 94)

Weidman, John C.: Problems in the Transition from School to Work for Adolescents in West Germany and the United States. In: Journal of Adolescent Research, 2 (1987) 2, pp. 175-182.

Wilson, David N.: Education and Occupational Training in Singapore and Malaysia. Toronto: Ontario Institute for Studies in Education 1981. (Sabbatical Monograph)

Wilson, David N.: Exploratory Study of Technical-Vocational Education Policy-Making. Jerusalem: Hebrew University, Programme of Canadian Studies 1990. (Occasional Paper. 10)

Wilson, David N.: An International Perspective on Trainer Competencies, Standards and Certification. Toronto: Ontario Training Corporation 1992.

Wilson, David N.: The Effectiveness of National Training Boards. Geneva: International Labour Organisation 1993a. (Training Policy Paper. 110)

Wilson, David N.: Reforming Technical and Technological Education. In: The Vocational Aspect of Education, 45 (1993b) 3, pp. 265-284.

Wilson, David N.: Development of Post-Secondary Occupational Training in Developing Nations. A Comparative Perspective. Paper read at the 1996 Annual Conference of the Comparative and International Education Society, Williamsburg, Virginia, U.S.A.

Vergleichende Erziehungswissenschaft
Herausforderung – Vermittlung – Praxis

Festschrift für Wolfgang Mitter zum 70. Geburtstag

Comparative Education
Challenges – Intermediation – Practice

Essays in honour of Wolfgang Mitter on the occasion of his 70th birthday

Éducation Comparée
Défis – Médiations – Pratiques

Mélanges offerts à Wolfgang Mitter pour son 70ᵉ anniversaire

Herausgegeben von / Edited by / Edité par

Christoph Kodron, Botho von Kopp, Uwe Lauterbach,
Ulrich Schäfer, Gerlind Schmidt

Band 2 / Volume 2 / Tome 2

Böhlau Verlag 1997

Die Deutsche Bibliothek - CIP-Einheitsaufnahme

Vergleichende Erziehungswissenschaft : Herausforderung - Vermittlung - Praxis ; Festschrift für Wolfgang Mitter zum 70. Geburtstag = Comparative education / hrsg. von Christoph Kodron ... - Köln : Böhlau.
ISBN 3-412-06597-8

Bd. 2. - (1997)

Copyright © 1997 by Deutsches Institut für Internationale Pädagogische Forschung, Frankfurt am Main

Ohne schriftliche Genehmigung des Verlages ist es nicht gestattet, das Werk unter Verwendung mechanischer, elektronischer und anderer Systeme in irgendeiner Weise zu verarbeiten und zu verbreiten. Insbesondere vorbehalten sind die Rechte der Vervielfältigung – auch von Teilen des Werkes – auf photomechanischem oder ähnlichem Wege, der tontechnischen Wiedergabe, des Vortrags, der Funk- und Fernsehsendung, der Speicherung in Datenverarbeitungsanlagen, der Übersetzung und der literarischen oder anderweitigen Bearbeitung. Ausgenommen von diesem Vorbehalt sind die Zusammenfassungen der Aufsätze in Deutsch, Englisch und Französisch auf den Seiten 763 bis 824. Diese dürfen in Datenbanken übernommen werden.

Druck und buchbinderische Verarbeitung:
Deutsches Institut für Internationale Pädagogische Forschung
Frankfurt am Main

Printed in Germany
ISBN 3-412-06597-8

INHALT / CONTENTS / SOMMAIRE

Band 2 / Volume 2 / Tome 2

4. Länderstudien
Country and Area Studies
Études par pays

Christel Adick 451
Formale und nonformale Grundbildung in Afrika –
Komplementarität oder Konkurrenz?

Cesar Bîrzea 468
The Use and Abuse of Educational Research:
The Case of a Political Manipulation in Romania

Günter Brinkmann 477
Lehrerrolle und Lehrerausbildung in den Niederlanden

Harold Herman 490
Education and Political Change in the New South Africa

Vitalij Grigor'evič Kostomarov 502
Das Bildungswesen in den Nachfolgestaaten der Sowjetunion
und die russische Sprache

Nikolaj Dmitrievič Nikandrov 512
Die Werteproblematik in Gesellschaft und Bildungswesen
der Russischen Föderation

Ioannis Pirgiotakis 524
Greek Education: Myths and Realities

Jan Průcha 538
Private versus State Schools: A Comparison of Their Quality
in the Czech Republic

Bernhard Schiff 550
Das Orthodoxe Klassische Gymnasium in Moskau

Witold Tulasiewicz 559
Education for Sale: Recent Developments in the United Kingdom

Makoto Yûki 572
Die rechtliche Struktur der Bildungsverwaltung in Japan

5.
Historische Dimension
Historical Dimension
La dimension historique

Siegfried Baske 583
Die neuhumanistische Phase des Jenkauer Conradinums
im Urteil der deutschen und polnischen Bildungsgeschichte

Wilhelm Ebert 593
Magna Carta for the Status of Teachers: Thirty Years of
the UNESCO-Recommendation for the Status of Teachers

Yaacov Iram 610
The Status of the Humanities in Education

Victor Karady 621
Schulbildung und Religion – Zu den ethnisch-konfessionellen
Strukturmerkmalen der ungarischen Intelligenz in der Zwischenkriegszeit

Michael Kelpanides 642
Universitätsstudium für jedermann? Die Politisierung der
Sozialwissenschaften als bleibendes Erbe der Bildungsexpansion

Marianne Krüger-Potratz 656
Ein Blick in die Geschichte ausländischer Schüler
und Schülerinnen in deutschen Schulen

David Phillips 673
Prolegomena to a History of British Interest in Education in Germany

Hermann Röhrs 688
Gründung und Gestaltung der „Deutschen Sektion" des „Weltbunds für
Erneuerung der Erziehung" (1921 bis 1931) – Ein bildungspolitisch
bedeutsames Kapitel der internationalen Reformpädagogik

Leo Roth 707
Die Reformation als Zäsur in der deutschen Universitätsentwicklung –
Von der Universalität zur Regionalisierung

Mirosław S. Szymański 725
Erziehung zur Demokratie durch die Schülerselbstregierung
in der Zweiten Polnischen Republik (1918 bis 1939)

Heinz-Elmar Tenorth 740
Pädagogik und Soziologie

Verzeichnis der Autoren / List of authors / Liste des auteurs 757

Zusammenfassungen 763

Abstracts 785

Résumés 804

Band 1 / Volume 1 / Tome 1

Oskar Anweiler 1
Vergleichende Erziehungswissenschaft und international vergleichende
Bildungsforschung als Herausforderung und Aufgabe

1.
Theoretische und methodische Aspekte der Vergleichenden Erziehungswissenschaft
Theoretical and Methodological Aspects of Comparative Education
Aspects théoriques et méthodologiques de l'éducation comparée

Philip G. Altbach 15
Research on Higher Education: Global Perspectives

Erwin H. Epstein 32
Filtering Democracy through Schools:
The Ignored Paradox of Compulsory Education

Mark B. Ginsburg 46
The Limitations and Possibilities of Comparative
Analysis of Education in Global Context

Detlef Glowka 52
Überlegungen zu einer „Einführung in die
Vergleichende Erziehungswissenschaft"

Wolfgang Hörner 65
„Europa" als Herausforderung für die Vergleichende Erziehungswissenschaft –
Reflexionen über die politische Funktion einer pädagogischen Disziplin

Edmund King 81
A Turning-Point in Comparative Education: Retrospect and Prospect

Richard Koch 91
Gesellschaftliche Steuerung von Berufsbildungssystemen –
Ein Analysekonzept für politikorientierte internationale Vergleiche

Mauro Laeng 105
From Yesterday to Tomorrow: Developments in Comparative Education

Jean-Michel Leclercq 117
Comment envisager et prendre en compte la culture d'un système éducatif?

Vandra L. Masemann 127
Recent Directions in Comparative Education

Heliodor Muszyński 135
Die Pädagogische Studienreise als Instrument
der wissenschaftlichen Erkenntnis

Shin'ichi Suzuki 143
Shifts in Political Regimes and the Geopolitical Reorganization
of Educational Space: Implications for Comparative Education

Juan Carlos Tedesco 152
Le renouveau de l'éducation comparée

Ulrich Teichler 161
Vergleichende Hochschulforschung – Probleme und Perspektiven

Henk Van daele 173
Éducation comparée et éducation internationale: problèmes linguistiques

Anthony R. Welch 182
Things Fall Apart: Dis-Integration, Universities, and the Decline of
Discipline(s). Problematising Comparative Education in an Uncertain Age

Christoph Wulf 192
Mimesis des Anderen – Annäherungen an das Fremde

2.
Bildungspolitik und Vergleichende Erziehungswissenschaft
Educational Policy and Comparative Education
Politique éducative et éducation comparée

Candido Alberto Gomes 209
Comparative Education and Public Policies: A View from the South

Stephen P. Heyneman 219
Educational Cooperation between Nations in the 21st Century

Georg Knauss 234
Von 1988 bis 1996 – Wege zur Weiterentwicklung der gymnasialen Oberstufe

Hermann Müller-Solger 245
Anerkennung, Akkreditierung, Transparenz – Notwendige
Begriffsklärungen für die Europäische Union

Raymond Ryba 262
Developing the European Dimension of Education in Practice:
The Contribution of the Council of Europe's European Dimension
Pedagogical Materials Programme

Rita Süssmuth 272
Politik und Vergleichende Erziehungswissenschaft in gemeinsamer
Verantwortung für eine humane Lerngesellschaft

Michael Vorbeck 282
Bildungsforschung und besonders Vergleichende Erziehungswissenschaft
in Europa – für Europa

3.
Globale Vergleiche und internationale Aspekte des Bildungswesens
Global Comparisons and International Aspects of Education
Comparaisons globales et aspects internationaux de l'éducation

Birgit Brock-Utne 301
Internationalisierung des Bildungswesens – Eine kritische Perspektive

Walter Georg 312
Berufliche Bildung zwischen Internationalisierung und nationaler Identität

Torsten Husén 329
The „Education Gap"

Joachim H. Knoll 344
From Literacy to Functional Literacy

Pierre Laderrière 359
Les transformations à l'Est: une leçon pour l'Ouest?

Robert F. Lawson 367
Relationships of Political Contexts to Democracy in Education

Donatella Palomba 381
L'éducation à la citoyenneté dans l'Europe multiculturelle:
une perspective comparative

Vlastimil Pařizek 393
The Crisis in Schools and Solutions to the Problem

J. J. Smolicz 402
Language Education Policies in Multilingual Settings:
Australia and the Philippines

Werner Stephan 414
Lehrer und Gesellschaft – Ein internationaler Vergleich

Janusz Tomiak 426
Looking Back, Looking Forward: Education in Central-
Eastern Europe on the Eve of the XXIst Century

David N. Wilson 437
The German Dual System of Vocational Education and Training:
A Comparative Study of Influence upon Educational Policy and
Practice in Other Countries

4.

Länderstudien
Country and Area Studies
Études par pays

Länderstudien haben in der Gegenwart ihren Wert nicht nur als Informationsquelle beibehalten, sondern bilden darüber hinaus eine unverzichtbare Grundlage für den Komparatisten zur Identifizierung und Formulierung von Hypothesen für vergleichende Untersuchungen, die nur aus der Kenntnis der Grunddaten und Rahmenbedingungen der Vergleichsobjekte heraus sinnvoll sein kann. Dies gilt insbesondere für Bildungssysteme, die dem Interpreten „fern" sind. „Fern" hat in dieser Überlegung insofern nicht nur eine geographische, sondern auch eine kognitive Komponente, als damit Bildung und Erziehung von anderen Ländern gemeint sein können, die im eigenen Sprach- und Forschungsraum bislang nicht oder nur unzulänglich behandelt worden sind.

Wolfgang Mitter, 1984

Wolfgang Mitter: Vorwort des Herausgebers. In: Stephan, Werner: Das kanadische Bildungswesen. Grundlagen – Tendenzen – Probleme (= Studien und Dokumentationen zur vergleichenden Bildungsforschung. 30), Köln u. a.: Böhlau 1984, S. V.

Formale und nonformale Grundbildung in Afrika –
Komplementarität oder Konkurrenz?

Christel Adick

Begrifflichkeit und Fragestellungen zur Grundbildung

Unter Grundbildung wird im folgenden in Anlehnung an die Diskussionen der Weltbildungskonferenz in Jomtien in Thailand im Jahre 1990 die Aneignung *„grundlegender Kenntnisse, Fertigkeiten, Werte und Haltungen"* verstanden, die jeder Mensch, ob Kind, Jugendlicher oder Erwachsener, *„für sein Überleben, die volle Entfaltung seiner Fähigkeiten, für ein menschenwürdiges Leben und menschenwürdige Arbeitsbedingungen, seine uneingeschränkte Beteiligung an der Entwicklung sowie die Fortsetzung des Lernens"* benötigt; hierzu zählen z. B.: *„Lesen, Schreiben, mündlicher Ausdruck, Rechnen und das Lösen von Problemen"* (Weltdeklaration 'Bildung für Alle' 1990, Art. 1).

In der internationalen Diskussion wird ferner unterschieden zwischen formaler und nonformaler Bildung: Der Begriff 'formale Bildung' ist dabei weitgehend deckungsgleich mit schulischer Erziehung und Bildung in nationalen Schulsystemen, die sich aufgrund der Internationalisierungstendenzen inzwischen weltweit weitgehend strukturell und inhaltlich ähnlich gestalten *(Adick 1992)*. Unter 'nonformaler Bildung' werden dagegen organisierte Erziehungs- und Bildungsaktivitäten außerhalb der nationalen Schulsysteme verstanden. Wenngleich aus analytischen Gründen sinnvoll und internationalen Gepflogenheiten entsprechend, bleiben jedoch Fragen der Zuordnung ganzer Bildungssektoren offen, z. B. die Einordnung der beruflichen Bildung. Obwohl die Unterscheidung in Allgemeinbildung und berufliche (Aus-)bildung internationalen Konventionen entspricht (im Englischen: education and training, im Französischen: éducation et formation) und die Arbeitsteilung internationaler Organisationen widerspiegelt (UNESCO: education; International Labour Organisation: training), *„wird das Verhältnis beider Bereiche besonders bei der Frage relevant, inwieweit grundlegende berufliche Kenntnisse und Fertigkeiten zur 'Grundbildung' (basic education) gehören"* (Lenhart 1993, S. 3).

Ein weiterer Einwand ist grundsätzlicherer Natur: So international gebräuchlich die Begrifflichkeit auch sein mag, so muß ihr dennoch ein kultureller Bias, ein Eurozentrismusverdacht angelastet werden. Formale Schulsysteme nicht-westlicher Art, z. B. die Koranschulen in arabischen, etlichen asiatischen und afrikanischen Gesellschaften, werden – sofern sie nicht strukturell in ein nationales Bildungssystem eingegliedert sind – trotz ihres Formalisierungsgrades gemeinhin nicht der Kategorie 'formale Bildung' zugerechnet; andererseits ergeben sich auch Schwierigkeiten, sie der Kategorie 'nonformale Bildung' zuzuordnen. Eingedenk dieser Einwände bei der Verwendung der Kategorien 'formale' und 'nonformale' Bildung soll aus Gründen des Anschlusses an internationale Diskussionen im folgenden mit ihnen gearbeitet werden.

Anhand des Länderbeispiels Senegal wird Einblick in die Praxis formaler und nonformaler Grundbildung gegeben. Nach einem Blick auf die allgemeine Bildungssituation des Senegal werden die Beispiele einer ländlichen staatlichen Primarschule, der islamischen Bildungsstätten und einer städtischen Alphabetisierungsinitiative vorgestellt. Für die Ausführungen zur allgemeinen Bildungssituation im heutigen Senegal stütze ich mich besonders auf die Arbeiten von Ben *Asdonk (1994, 1995)*, Ulrike *Wiegelmann (1994a, 1994a)* und *Wiegelmann / Naumann / Faye (1997)*. Für die Praxisberichte greife ich auf Interviews und Beobachtungen zurück, die ich während mehrerer Besuche im Senegal in den Jahren 1995 und 1996 durchführen konnte.[1] Anschließend wird vergleichend gefragt, welchen spezifischen Beitrag die typologisch verschiedenen Ausschnitte aus der gesamten Erziehungswirklichkeit des Senegal zur 'Grundbildung' leisten, operationalisiert in der Fragestellung, ob sich diese eher gegenseitig ergänzen oder miteinander konkurrieren.

Zur Bildungssituation des Senegal

Mit der Unabhängigkeit im Jahre 1960 übernahm die senegalesische Regierung ein frankophones Schulsystem, wie es die Kolonialmacht Frankreich nach diversen missions- und kolonialpädagogischen Aktivitäten in früheren Jahrhunderten praktisch erst seit 1903 als einheitliches, laizistisch geprägtes Bildungswesen in ganz Französisch-Westafrika etabliert hatte. Dieses koloniale Schulwesen koexistierte mit den im Zuge der Islamisierung Westafrikas ins Land gekommenen Koranschulen (zur Bildungsgeschichte Französisch-Westafrikas vgl. *Bouche 1975*). Die bei der Unabhängigkeit des Senegal

---

1 Ich danke all meinen Gesprächspartnern herzlich, die ich hier leider nicht alle namentlich aufführen kann. Mein besonderer Dank gilt meinen Kollegen Jens Naumann und Ulrike Wiegelmann (Universität Münster) sowie Samba Ndiaye (Schulleiter der Primarschule in Ngohé/Region Diourbel) und Moussa Camara (Bildungszentrum „Dioko Xalaat" in Dakar).

nur äußerst geringe Einschulungsquote (1960: 16%) stieg in den folgenden Jahrzehnten rapide an, so daß heute etwa die Hälfte (1992: 48%) aller Kinder (Mädchen in geringerem Ausmaß als Jungen) die öffentliche Primarschule besuchen *(Wiegelmann 1994a, S. 804)*. Strukturell wurde das französische Bildungssystem im wesentlichen beibehalten: mit einer sechsjährigen Primarschule (école primaire bzw. école élémentaire), einer vierjährigen unteren Sekundarstufe (enseignement moyen) und einem darauf aufbauenden dreijährigen höheren Sekundarschulzyklus (enseignement secondaire), der zum Abitur (baccalauréat) führt.

Nach ersten Reformüberlegungen in den siebziger Jahren kam es in den achtziger Jahren zur Ausformulierung einer neuen Bildungspolitik, die jedoch noch nicht flächendeckend umgesetzt worden ist: 1984 wurde eine 'neue Schule' proklamiert, eine 'école nationale, démocratique et populaire', die durch eine bessere Ausnutzung der knappen Ressourcen (jahrgangsübergreifende Klassen, Schichtunterricht) gekennzeichnet sein sollte, durch die fakultative Einführung eines Religionsunterrichts in das ansonsten laizistisch gebliebene staatliche Schulwesen sowie durch neue, an die senegalesischen Verhältnisse angepaßte berufs- und lebenspraktische Lerninhalte, die in Schulgärten, Kleintierhaltung, handwerklichen Werkstätten usw. vermittelt werden sollen. Umgesetzt wurden seit 1986 bestenfalls Teile dieser Ideen in einigen Versuchsschulen ('écoles-pilotes') bzw. in einzelnen Versuchsklassen ('classes-pilotes') der weiterhin bestehenden gängigen Primarschulen: Im Schuljahr 1990/91 arbeiteten, ersten Evaluationsstudien zufolge *(Institut National d'Étude et d'Action pour le Développement de l'Éducation 1991, S. 9f.)*, erst 24 Primarschulen als Pilotschulen mit insgesamt 264 Schulklassen sowie 146 Schulklassen experimentellen Charakters innerhalb der 'traditionellen' Primarschulen.

Auf die Reformierung des französisch geprägten senegalesischen Schulsystems zielt auch die proklamierte Förderung der Nationalsprachen im Bildungswesen und damit die Abkehr vom Französischen als alleiniger Unterrichtssprache sowie die Aufwertung nonformaler Bildungsbemühungen durch die Schaffung einer eigenen Bildungsbehörde, die sich auch um staatlich geförderte Alphabetisierungsprogramme kümmert. Hierzu wurde eigens ein Ministerium für Alphabetisierung und Nationalsprachen geschaffen.

Staatliche Grundbildung im Senegal am Beispiel einer ländlichen Primarschule

Ngohé besteht aus elf kleineren, jeweils bis einen Kilometer auseinander liegenden Ansiedlungen, deren Gesamteinwohnerzahl vor einigen Jahren auf 3 000 geschätzt wurde *(Bracklo 1989)*. Seine Bevölkerung scheint fast nur aus Frauen, Kindern und älteren Leuten zu bestehen; denn die meisten Männer im erwerbsfähigen Alter halten sich unter der Woche oder sogar monatelang auf der Suche nach Arbeit in der nächsten Stadt oder in der Hauptstadt Dakar auf. Als der jetzige Schulleiter, Samba Ndiaye, 1989 an die Schule kam, hatte die Schule vier Klassenräume. Zwei Jahre später kamen zwei Klassen mit neuen Räumlichkeiten hinzu. Bis auf einen Klassenraum, der mit Mitteln des Europäischen Entwicklungsfonds gebaut wurde, hat die Bevölkerung die Schule praktisch mit eigenen Mitteln aufgebaut. Die Schule verfügt ferner über ein Magazin zur Lagerung und zum Verkauf von Schulmaterialien, womit bescheidene eigene Einkünfte erzielt werden.

Zwar gab es in Ngohé eine Zeitlang ein abnehmendes Interesse an Schulbildung, weil die Eltern sahen oder befürchteten, daß der Schulbesuch die Tendenz zur Landflucht ihrer Kinder fördern würde. Derzeit aber liegen wieder mehr Einschulungsgesuche vor als die Schule verkraften kann. Im März 1995 hatte die Schule insgesamt 323 Schülerinnen und Schüler. Von insgesamt 110 Aufnahmegesuchen wurden 75 Kinder in die Anfangsklasse aufgenommen. Ab 80 Kindern müßte nämlich Schichtunterricht eingeführt werden, was der Schulleiter angesichts seines Lehrpersonals als pädagogisch nicht durchführbar ansieht. Die Frage, was er den Eltern der abgewiesenen Kinder empfehle, beantwortete er mit dem Hinweis auf die private katholische Primarschule, die arabische Schule und die Koranschulen. Da etliche Kinder ihren Schulbesuch erst im Alter von sieben oder acht Jahren beginnen, bevorzugt der Schulleiter deshalb oftmals zuvor abgewiesene Kinder im nächstfolgenden Jahr, wenn diese zwischenzeitlich z. B. eine Koranschule besucht haben. Das Problem sei aber, daß seine Schule öffentlich und kostenlos sei, wohingegen die Eltern z. B. in der arabischen Schule 2 000 CFA-Francs (ca. 6 DM) pro Kind und Jahr für die Bezahlung des Lehrers aufwenden müßten und andere Schulen offiziell nicht anerkannt seien.

Die Besonderheit dieser Schule besteht einerseits darin, daß sie seit Jahren mit dem Landesverband Berlin der Deutschen Gesellschaft für die Vereinten Nationen kooperiert. Hierdurch kommen regelmäßig deutsche Lehrerinnen und Lehrer und Studierende nach Ngohé, und einige der senegalesischen Partner, so auch der Schulleiter, haben inzwischen ihrerseits Deutschland besucht. Weiter gehört sie zum Kreis der Pilotschulen der oben angesprochenen Bildungsreform. 1992 waren im Kreis Diourbel zwei Schulen in das Versuchsprogramm aufgenommen worden: eine in der Stadt Diourbel und eine ländliche, die in Ngohé. Auf die Frage nach der Umsetzung der Reformideen antwortete der Schulleiter mit Hinweis auf den gerade entstehenden Schulgarten und auf praktische

Landwirtschaft auf einigen Feldern während der Regenzeit und wöchentlich zweimal Kochunterricht. Geplant seien ferner Kleintierzucht und handwerkliche Werkstätten, einstweilen würden aber einfache handwerkliche Kenntnisse je nach Möglichkeit vermittelt, z. B. die Herstellung eines Tisches mit einfachen Mitteln. Da die Lehrer für diese Ausbildungsleistungen nicht vorgebildet sind, werden hierfür eigens lokale Fachleute eingeladen, z. B. jemand, der sich mit tiermedizinischen Problemen auskennt. Oder die Lehrer gehen zu den Bauern und Handwerkern des Dorfes und beschaffen sich so die nötigen Kenntnisse zunächst einmal selbst.

Die Ngohé-Schule befindet sich zur Zeit des Interviews noch in der drei Jahre dauernden Experimentierphase, die durch eine Evaluation abgeschlossen werden soll. Der Schulleiter begrüßt die Reformziele der 'école nouvelle'. Schon in den achtziger Jahren hätten gewerkschaftlich orientierte Lehrer die Grundlinien der Reform akzeptiert, aber diese seien eben immer noch nicht landesweit durchgesetzt worden. Alles hänge am Institut National d'Etude et d'Action pour le Développement de l'Éducation in Dakar. Vor allem fehle es an Finanzmitteln. So gebe es z. B. keine kostenlosen Unterrichtsmaterialien mehr, und dies erzeuge besondere Probleme für die Eltern, obwohl die Akzeptanz der Reform bei den Eltern und bei der Bevölkerung eine Voraussetzung für ihren Erfolg sei. In der Primarschule in Ngohé werden als Ausweg aus dem Mißstand fehlender Unterrichtsmittel inzwischen die Schulbücher gegen eine Gebühr von 100 CFA-Francs (ca. 0,30 DM) pro Buch und Jahr ausgeliehen.

Für die meisten Schüler in Ngohé bedeutet der Abschluß der Primarschule, wenn sie diese nicht, wie dies in Afrika häufig der Fall ist, schon vorher wieder verlassen haben, das Ende ihrer Bildungslaufbahn. Die Schüler können nach Beendigung der sechsten Primarschulklasse das „Certificat d'Etudes Primaires Elémentaires" (CEPE) erlangen und an der Aufnahmeprüfung zum Besuch einer Sekundarschule teilnehmen. Die Kosten für diese landesweite Prüfung (concours national) betragen 250 CFA-Francs (ca. 0,75 DM); aber nicht alle Eltern der Schüler der Abschlußklasse können sich diese Gebühren ein- oder mehrmals leisten. Die nächste Sekundarschule befindet sich in der circa zehn Kilometer entfernten Regionalhauptstadt Diourbel. Die Übergangsrate von Ngohé dorthin ist sehr gering. Bei ungenügenden Leistungen können die Schüler die Abschlußklasse wiederholen – landesweit ist dies immerhin eine Wiederholerquote von 35% in der Klasse CM2 (Cours Moyen 2), der Abschlußklasse der Primarschule *(Wiegelmann 1994a, S. 805)* –, oder sie können ihren Schulbesuch ohne formalen Schulabschluß beenden.

Die Geschlechterverteilung und die Kompetenzen der Schülerinnen und Schüler der Abschlußklasse in Ngohé in Französisch, das zwar Unterrichtssprache ist, aber nicht die Muttersprache der Schüler, kommen in Schüleraufsätzen zum Ausdruck, die im März 1995 zum Thema „Mon avenir" (Meine Zukunft) in der Abschlußklasse CM2 der Schule geschrieben wurden: Ohne auf die Inhalte hier eingehen zu können, fällt auf, daß von den 41 Aufsätzen einer vollkommen unleserlich ist (und ohne Angabe von Alter und Geschlecht), und daß nur sieben von Mädchen geschrieben wurden. Die Mehrzahl der Schüler ist 12 oder 13 Jahre alt (29 von 40). Bemerkenswert ist hierbei wiederum, daß die wenigen Mädchen alle 12 oder 13 Jahre alt sind, wohingegen neun von 33 Jungen 14 Jahre oder älter sind. Der Schulleiter erklärte diese Unterrepräsentation der Mädchen, gerade auch in den höheren Klassenstufen so: Die Mädchen müssen ihren Müttern helfen, da diese wegen der vielfachen Abwesenheit ihrer Ehemänner ohnehin sehr in Anspruch genommen sind durch Ackerbau, Wasser und Holz holen, Hirse stampfen usw. Auch wenn die Mädchen zur Schule gehen, wird von ihnen erwartet, daß sie solche Arbeiten, teils frühmorgens vor der Schule, erledigen, so daß sie schon erschöpft zur Schule kommen und ihnen das Lernen deswegen schwerer fällt. Während es Jungen durchaus zugestanden wird, bei mangelnden Leistungen eine Klasse zu wiederholen, nimmt man ein Mädchen in einem solchen Fall einfach von der Schule. Außerdem werden viele Mädchen immer noch in sehr jungem Alter verheiratet und verlassen dann die Schule ohne Abschluß. Oder sie gehen als Dienstmädchen in fremde Haushalte, um ihre Familien finanziell zu unterstützen. All diese Faktoren führen dazu, daß weniger Mädchen als Jungen die Primarschule in Ngohé besuchen und noch weniger diese auch erfolgreich abschließen.

Es fällt ferner die große Spanne der schriftsprachlichen Kompetenzen auf: Einige Aufsätze sind äußerst kurz, semantisch schwer verständlich und weisen enorm viele Rechtschreibfehler auf. Andere dagegen, anteilmäßig ist das jedoch nicht die Mehrzahl, sind äußerst elaboriert und nahezu fehlerfrei geschrieben. Nach sechs Jahren Primarschulunterricht in der Unterrichtssprache Französisch, so muß gefolgert werden, ist nur ein Bruchteil der Kinder (zumindest in einer ländlichen Primarschule wie der in Ngohé) wirklich hinreichend in dieser Sprache alphabetisiert. Meine Unterrichtsbeobachtungen in der Abschlußklasse unterstreichen diesen Eindruck: Im Mathematikunterricht beispielsweise (Flächenberechnungen zum rechtwinkligen Dreieck) hatten viele Schülerinnen und Schüler erhebliche Schwierigkeiten, ein alltagsweltliches Beispiel korrekt in französischsprachige Geometrie umzusetzen. Die mangelnden Kompetenzen in der Unterrichtssprache haben Folgen für die Leistungen in den anderen Fächern, wenn tendenziell der Unterrichtsstoff sprachlich nicht verstanden wird. Vor diesem Hintergrund wäre es zu begrüßen, wenn im Senegal die offiziell proklamierte Alphabetisierung in den Nationalsprachen auch tatsächlich umgesetzt würde.

Islamische Bildungseinrichtungen im Senegal

Schon vor Ankunft der Europäer gab es infolge der Islamisierung Westafrikas Koranschulen im Senegal, die vor allem von Jungen etwa im Alter von 6 bis 16 Jahren aus islamisierten Bevölkerungsschichten besucht wurden. Während der französischen Kolonialherrschaft wurde im Anschluß an den Aufbau eines laizistischen Bildungswesens ab 1903 zunächst versucht, die Zahl und Bedeutung der Koranschulen zu reduzieren oder doch wenigstens zu begrenzen *(Bouche 1975, S. 704ff.)*. Dies gelang jedoch nicht, so daß man schließlich zu einer Politik der stillschweigenden Duldung oder Kooperation mit den islamischen Bruderschaften und ihren Würdenträgern überging, auf deren Kooperationsbereitschaft man für den Aufbau einer profitablen Erdnußproduktion im Senegal angewiesen war. Das islamische Bildungswesen im Senegal weist heute eine große Vielfalt auf: Zu ihm zählen die 'daaras', einfache traditionelle Koranschulen, wie auch weiter ausgebaute arabische, französisch-arabische und islamische Schulen und Institute *(Wiegelmann 1994a, 1994b, Wiegelmann / Naumann / Faye 1997)*.

Die traditionelle Form der Koranschule im Senegal ist die ländliche oder städtische 'daara', in der grundlegende Kenntnisse des Korans in Arabisch vermittelt werden. Sie dient primär der religiösen Unterweisung; eine Alphabetisierung und eine gewisse Grundbildung sind gleichsam Nebeneffekte der primär religiösen Bildung dieser Institutionen. Der Unterricht findet unter den einfachsten Bedingungen statt, z. B. im Freien, in einer mit Stroh oder Wellblech gedeckten Hütte oder im Gehöft des 'marabout', d. h. des Lehrers oder Mentors. Dieser wird für seine Dienste von den Eltern in Naturalien oder kleinen Geldbeträgen entlohnt. Auf dem Lande war und ist es auch üblich, daß die Schüler auf den Feldern des 'marabout' mitarbeiten, vor allem, wenn die Koranschule als Internat genutzt wird. In der Stadt leben die Koranschüler überwiegend in überaus beengten Räumlichkeiten, wobei nicht selten ein einziger notdürftig hergerichteter Raum für zwanzig, dreißig oder noch mehr Kinder als Lernort und Schlafstätte zugleich dient.

In der Stadt hat die Verpflichtung, zum eigenen wie zum Lebensunterhalt des Lehrers beizutragen, dazu geführt, daß viele Koranschüler um Nahrung und Almosen bettelnd in ihrem jeweiligen Wohnviertel umherziehen (vgl. zum folgenden besonders *Wiegelmann / Naumann / Faye 1997*). Obwohl diese 'talibés mendiants' (bettelnde Koranschüler) in der senegalesischen Gesellschaft grundsätzlich als soziale Institution akzeptiert sind und in das islamische Gebot des Almosengebens passen, haben sie und ihre vielfach unzuträglichen Lebensverhältnisse inzwischen ein Ausmaß erreicht, das zu gesellschaftlichen Reaktionen Anlaß gab. Wirtschaftskrisen, Strukturanpassungsprogramme, Landflucht und die Krisensituation im öffentlichen Bildungssystem haben im Senegal dazu geführt, daß immer mehr Eltern in Sorge um eine religiöse Bildung wie auch aus Ermangelung anderer Alternativen ihre Kinder den 'marabouts' städtischer 'daaras' anvertrauen. Die daraus hervorgegangene heutige Praxis der kulturellen Tradition des Bettelnschickens grenzt inzwischen vielerorts an krasse Kinderausbeutung und Vernachlässigung der Schutzbefohlenen durch unverantwortliche und wenig vorgebildete 'marabouts'. Aus den 'talibés mendiants', die den unerträglichen Situationen ihrer 'daaras' zu entfliehen versuchen, rekrutieren sich daher nicht wenige der sogenannten 'Straßenkinder' im heutigen Senegal. Die Lebenssituation der bettelnden Koranschüler sowie ihre Ernährung und Gesundheit sind angesichts des Erbettelns von Nahrungsresten und unzureichender hygienischer Verhältnisse nicht immer sichergestellt. Krankheiten, körperliche Strafen, Fehlernährung, mangelnde Aufsicht und unzureichende Grundbildung sind vielfach die Folge. Neueren Untersuchungen zufolge verbringen die 'talibés mendiants' oft mehr als drei Stunden täglich mit Betteln bei einer durchschnittlichen Unterrichtszeit von 4,5 bis 5,5 Stunden. Nur ein Teil von ihnen ist nach einigen Jahren in diesen 'daaras' tatsächlich alphabetisiert, geschweige denn lebens- und berufspraktisch vorgebildet.

Trotz einer Tendenz zur Tabuisierung des Problems ist im Senegal eine öffentliche Diskussion um die 'talibés mendiants' und die 'daaras' entstanden: Im Zusammenhang mit der Ratifizierung der UN-Kinderrechtskonvention, im Zusammenwirken mit reformwilligen islamischen Kreisen und mit Unterstützung von UNICEF sollen in einem Fünfjahresplan (1992-1996) gezielte Maßnahmen zur Verbesserung der Lebens- und Unterrichtsbedingungen in den Koranschulen ergriffen werden mit dem Ziel, mindestens 50% der Schüler zu alphabetisieren. In etlichen 'daaras' haben inzwischen mit Billigung reformbereiter 'marabouts' tatsächlich Veränderungen stattgefunden: So erteilen beispielsweise gering entlohnte Alphabetisierer nicht-staatlicher Hilfsorganisationen Unterricht in Französisch, Geographie oder Mathematik in Ergänzung zur religiösen Bildung. Anderseits ist ein Widerstand gegen eine derartige vermeintlich 'westliche' Überfremdung der traditionellen Koranschulerziehung weiterhin vorhanden.

Neben den 'daaras' hat sich inzwischen im Senegal eine Vielzahl anders strukturierter islamischer Bildungsstätten etabliert, deren gemeinsames Merkmal aber weiterhin ist, daß sie in der Regel nicht in das formale staatliche Schulwesen integriert sind: écoles arabes, écoles franco-arabes und Instituts Islamiques (arabische Schulen, französisch-arabische Schulen und Islamische Institute). Ziel dieser Schulen ist es, das Curriculum und die Unterrichtsziele und -methoden über das reine Auswendiglernen des Korans hinaus zu erweitern. Auf diese Weise werden z. B. eine Alphabetisierung in Arabisch und einige grundlegende Kenntnisse in Rechnen und Geschichte und teilweise auch Französischunterricht angeboten. Die didaktischen Materialien stammen häufig aus Nordafrika oder arabischen Ländern. Manchmal führt der Schulabschluß auch dazu, daß anschließend weiterführende Bildungsanstalten in arabischen Ländern besucht werden.

Die sogenannten 'Instituts Islamiques' und die 'écoles franco-arabes' sind am weitesten ausgebaut und systematisiert. In den häufig von arabischen Staaten unterstützten und mit Schulgeldern finanzierten 'Instituts Islamiques' werden mittlere und höhere Sekundarschulzyklen angeboten, die nach 12 Jahren zum arabischen Abitur führen. In den 'écoles franco-arabes' werden Arabisch und Französisch gleichberechtigt als Fächer und als Unterrichtssprachen verwendet, und die Schüler können neben den arabischen auch die offiziellen französischen Schulabschlüsse erwerben. Im Unterschied zu den einfachen Koranschulen finden sich in den islamischen und in den französisch-arabischen Schulen Strukturmerkmale wie ausdifferenzierte Schulstufen, ein kodifiziertes Fächerangebot, formalisierte Schulabschlüsse usw., die als funktionale Äquivalente der 'modernen' Schule angesehen werden können (zu universalen Strukturmerkmalen moderner Schulen vgl. *Adick 1992, S. 177*). Ein Merkmal jedoch fehlt bzw. ist unzureichend ausgebaut: die staatlich kontrollierte, öffentlich-rechtlich reglementierte Schulpraxis in diesen Schulen. Da genau steckt das Problem des islamischen Bildungswesens im Senegal: Das laizistische koloniale Erbe erschwert die Integration explizit religiös akzentuierter, d. h. partikularer Bildungsinstitutionen in eine kohärente nationale Bildungspolitik.

Nonformale Grundbildung im Senegal am Beispiel eines stadtteilbezogenen Bildungszentrums

Im Schuljahr 1992/93 schlossen sich 37 Mädchen und junge Frauen aus dem Stadtviertel Rebeuss in Dakar zu einer Gruppe zusammen, und zwar aus den Reihen der 'petites bonnes', (junge, oft vom Lande kommende Dienstmädchen in städtischen Haushalten)[2] und 'filles désœuvrées', was in heutiger umgangssprachlicher Terminologie am

---

2 Über die 'petites bonnes' ist eine empirische Untersuchung durchgeführt worden, die ihre derzeitige Lebenssituation beschreibt (Les MBINDAAN SANS MBINDOU 1994).

ehesten mit 'Mädchen, die einfach nur so herumhängen' übersetzt werden könnte. Ziel der Gruppe war es, Lesen, Schreiben, Rechnen und weitere Kenntnisse zu erwerben, d. h. ihren Anspruch und ihre Vorstellungen von Grundbildung in die Tat umzusetzen *(Coulibaly/Faye 1995)*. Man stellte ihnen zunächst die Benutzung der Örtlichkeiten einer Sekundarschule zur Verfügung, und die Organisation ENDA Jeunesse Action[3] erklärte sich bereit, die Initiative mit didaktischem Material und einem pädagogischen Berater zu unterstützen. Da eine herkömmliche Alphabetisierung, z. B. mit Grundschullehrbüchern, weder altersgemäß (Alter etwa 15 bis 22 Jahre) noch auf die betreffende Lebenssituation zugeschnitten wäre, wurde eingedenk des von ENDA favorisierten partizipativen Entwicklungsmodells die Methodologie einer sogenannten 'recherche-action' zur Erstellung eines Aktions- und Bildungsprogramms angewendet. Diese Methode ist aus der Praxis entstanden und inzwischen in einem Bericht, der mehrere Beispiele aus Afrika umfaßt, dargelegt und erläutert worden *(Enfants en Recherche et en Action 1995)*.

Auch wenn nirgends im Text darauf hingewiesen wird, kann man sich des Eindrucks nicht erwehren, daß Paulo Freires Konzept der Bewußtwerdung in zirkulären Aktions-Reflexionsprozessen bei der Ausarbeitung der Methodologie Pate stand: Das beginnt schon bei der ersten Aussage des Buches zur Methodologie: „*La terminologie n'est jamais neutre*" (Die Begrifflichkeit ist nie neutral. *Ebd., S. 40*) und setzt sich fort in den methodologischen Anleitungen zur Erkundung des Terrains und der Bedürfnisse der Betroffenen sowie in den Ausführungen zur Rolle der pädagogischen Mitarbeiter. Das methodologische Konzept dient neben der Erstellung von Bildungsprogrammen auch zur Schulung des diversen pädagogischen Personals im nonformalen Bildungssektor mit Bezeichnungen wie: animateur, moniteur, alphabetiseur, facilitateur, für die es bisher noch kaum deutsche fachterminologische Entsprechungen gibt, geschweige denn formale professionsspezifische Definitionskriterien wie Ausbildungsgänge, Qualifikationsmerkmale, fest umrissene Tätigkeitsmerkmale, arbeitsrechtliche Einordnung o. ä.

Die Mädchen und jungen Frauen des Stadtviertels machten sich unter Mitarbeit eines pädagogischen Beraters auf die Suche nach ihren spezifischen Lernbedürfnissen und -möglichkeiten, die über eine bloß funktionale Alphabetisierung hinausgingen. Die Ausgangsfragen konzentrierten sich auf die Infrastruktur und die Bevölkerung sowie die Le-

---

3 ENvironment Development Action – eine internationale Nichtregierungsorganisation mit Hauptsitz in Dakar – hat mehrere Unterabteilungen, u. a. „Jeunesse Action", die sich um basisnahe pädagogische und soziale Arbeit mit Kindern und Jugendlichen kümmert.

bensprobleme im Stadtteil Rebeuss. Sie teilten sich in drei Untergruppen auf und gingen von Haus zu Haus. Die Ergebnisse dieser Erhebung wurden im Dezember 1993 zusammengetragen und diskutiert. Als Hauptprobleme wurden folgende – in der Terminologie Freires gesprochen – 'generative Themen' ermittelt: Arbeitslosigkeit, Abwässer, Prostitution, Alkohol, Müßiggang (désœuvrement), Mangel an gesundheitlicher Aufklärung und mangelnde Ausbildung der Jugendlichen *(Coulibaly / Faye 1995)*. Als Schlüsselproblem wurde „Désœuvrement des filles", der Müßiggang der Mädchen, ausgewählt. Dieses Schlüsselproblem wurde in einzelne Verursachungsfaktoren zerlegt: fehlende Ausbildungsstrukturen und Lernmöglichkeiten, Armut der Eltern, Faulheit/Trägheit, die Kontrolle der Eltern und fehlende finanzielle Unterstützung. Da der Hauptansatzpunkt in den fehlenden Bildungs- und Ausbildungsmöglichkeiten für Mädchen gesehen wurde, einigte sich die Gruppe darauf, ein stadtteilbezogenes Bildungszentrum zu planen. Zur Realisierung der Idee erfolgten nun weitere Aktions-Reflexions-Etappen, in denen sich die Betroffenen über die zu vermittelnden Bildungsinhalte einigten, pädagogisches Personal rekrutierten, didaktisches Material sichteten oder erstellten und Finanzierungsmöglichkeiten erkunden mußten. Die Gruppe gab sich eine vereinsrechtliche Struktur, führte Spendenaktionen durch und mietete schließlich ein altes Kino für monatlich 100 000 CFA-Francs (etwa 300 DM) als Sitz ihres Bildungszentrums *Dioko Xalaat*, was soviel bedeutet wie „Meinungs- oder Erfahrungsaustausch". Es wurden die ersten Kurse für Dienstmädchen, arbeitende 'Straßenkinder' und andere durchgeführt und eine Basketballgruppe eingerichtet. Die Bildungsinhalte beziehen sich auf die Bereiche Alphabetisierung, Nähen, Stricken, Sticken und Gesundheit. Ferner dient das Zentrum als regelmäßiger Treffpunkt. Das Bildungszentrum wurde im November 1994 offiziell eröffnet; sein Aufbau ist jedoch noch nicht abgeschlossen.

**Verschiedene Praxisformen von Grundbildung:
Komplementarität oder Konkurrenz?**

Wie wird in den drei Beispielen 'Grundbildung' in der anfangs genannten Definition betrieben und in welchem komplementären oder konkurrierenden Verhältnis stehen die drei Bereiche zueinander?

In der Primarschule von Ngohé wird per definitionem Grundbildung betrieben. Das Besondere dieser Grundbildung sind folgende Momente: Die Alphabetisierung erfolgt in Französisch, einer Sprache, die nicht die Muttersprache der Schüler ist. Das Lernen ist vor allem auf den Erwerb formaler Abschlüsse und Ausleseverfahren ausgerichtet.

Der weiterführende Besuch der Sekundarschule ist in der Logik dieser Schulbildung implizit mitgedacht. Trotz Pilotschulcharakter bleibt in der Praxis der lebenspraktisch und beruflich orientierte Wissenstransfer nur gering. Auf diese Weise werden zwar einige grundlegende Kulturtechniken erlernt, besonders defizitär bleiben jedoch die Beherrschung der (Mutter-)Sprache in Wort und Schrift und das Problemlöseverhalten.

In den islamischen Bildungsstätten, vor allem in den einfachen Koranschulen, wird eine religiöse Grundbildung vermittelt. Auswendiglernen, Gehorsam und moralische Erziehung bilden den Kern der Unterweisung. Staatliche Reglementierungen sind so gut wie nicht vorhanden. Die Schulabschlüsse sind entweder gar nicht (im Falle der 'daaras') oder erst in Ansätzen (z. B. in den 'écoles franco-arabes') auf das offizielle schulische Berechtigungssystem bezogen. Die Schulen finanzieren sich durch Eigenbeteiligung der Eltern – im Falle der 'daaras' auch durch die (bettelnden) Kinder – oder durch Zuwendungen arabischer Staaten. Säkulare Bildung ist im Falle der 'daaras' entweder absolut nachgeordnet oder erscheint in einem religiös vermittelten Sinne. Nur die weiter ausgebauten islamischen Bildungsgänge in den 'écoles franco-arabes' und den 'Instituts Islamiques' sind in ihren Unterrichtsgegenständen und Intentionen in gewisser Weise kompatibel zum staatlichen Bildungssektor, wenngleich (noch?) nicht in diesen integriert.

Im selbstorganisierten Bildungszentrum *Dioko Xalaat* wird auch Grundbildung betrieben; allerdings entspricht diese Grundbildung nicht dem offiziellen Primarschullehrplan des Landes, aber auch nicht der religiös geprägten Bildung der Islamischen Institute. Die in *Dioko Xalaat* praktizierte Bildung basiert auf einem eigenverantwortlichen, im Freireschen Sinne 'bewußtseinsbildenden' Arrangement dessen, was 'Grundbildung' für eine spezifische Lerngruppe bedeutet. Sie enthält neben der Alphabetisierungsarbeit lebens- und berufspraktische Bildungsanteile (Stricken, Sticken usw.) dieser spezifischen Gruppe. Eine solche Grundbildung ist stadtteil- und klientelspezifisch orientiert, d. h. in diesem Fall auf die Bedürfnisse der 'petites bonnes et filles désœuvrées' in Rebeuss zugeschnitten. Trotz dieser sehr spezifischen, sehr engen Anfangsorientierung zeigt *Dioko Xalaat* inzwischen über den ersten Ansatz hinausweisende Bildungsangebote für andere soziokulturelle, pädagogische 'Problemgruppen', wie z. B. (männliche) 'Straßenkinder', arbeitende Kinder und Jugendliche.

Ergänzen sich die verschiedenen Arrangements von Grundbildung, oder machen sie sich gegenseitig Konkurrenz? In den Konzeptionen nonformaler Bildung wird *„zwischen komplementärer (sich auf die Schüler im formalen Bildungssystem beziehender und*

Schulbildung ergänzender), supplementärer (an Schulbildung zu einem späteren Zeitpunkt anknüpfender und sie durch neue Kenntnisse und Fähigkeiten erweiternder) und substitutiver (an die Stelle formaler Bildung tretender) nonformaler Bildung unterschieden" (Lenhart 1993, S. 2).

Dieser Differenzierung zufolge sind weder die diversen islamischen Bildungsstätten noch Grundbildungsangebote wie die in Rebeuss wirklich 'komplementär' zur staatlichen Primarschule. Ein Teil der Koranschüler geht zwar zeitgleich oder zu einem späteren Zeitpunkt auch in öffentliche Primarschulen, ein Umstand, der vielleicht für ihre Komplementarität sprechen könnte. Einer solchen Interpretation steht jedoch entgegen, daß die Koranschulen und noch weniger die anderen, weiter ausgebauten, islamischen Bildungsangebote ihre Legitimation mitnichten aus einem intentionalen Bezug auf das öffentliche Schulwesen beziehen. Auch die in Rebeuss angebotene Grundbildung bezieht sich nicht auf Schüler im formalen Bildungsbereich und ergänzt nicht die schulische Bildung, sondern rekrutiert vielmehr gerade solche, die aus dem formalen Bildungsbereich herausgefallen sind.

Ist die in den islamischen Bildungsstätten und den nonformalen Bildungszentren angebotene Grundbildung dann vielleicht 'supplementär', d. h. knüpft sie an Schulbildung an und erweitert diese durch neue Kenntnisse und Fähigkeiten? Auch das ist nicht der Fall. Die Koranschulen beziehen sich nicht auf die öffentliche Schule, und die Lernenden in Rebeuss haben mehrheitlich nie eine Schulbildung genossen, an die man (falls überhaupt gewünscht) anknüpfen könnte.

Die dritte Differenzierung nonformaler Bildung wurde als 'substitutiv' definiert: Nonformale Bildung tritt an die Stelle formaler Bildung. Diese Charakterisierung trifft nun sowohl auf die islamischen Bildungsstätten wie auch auf Grundbildungsangebote nach der Art von *Dioko Xalaat* zu. Wer z. B. in eine 'école arabe' geht, besucht eben nicht die staatliche Primarschule; wer andererseits die staatliche Primarschule absolviert hat, benötigt keine Alphabetisierung in einem Bildungszentrum wie dem in Rebeuss. Es mag zwar Schülerinnen und Schüler geben, die de facto zwischen den verschiedenen Bildungssektoren wechseln, deren Bildungserwerb in diesem Sinne also 'supplementär' ist, aber die raison d'être der geschilderten Grundbildungsinstitutionen ist und bleibt eine eigenständige Konzeption von Grundbildung, die 'substitutiv' an die Stelle der staatlichen Primarschule tritt. Welche Qualität nimmt diese Substitution an?

Angesichts einer uneingelösten flächendeckenden Verwirklichung von Schulpflicht bzw. dem Recht auf Bildung im staatlichen Schulsektor treten sowohl die islamischen wie auch die nonformalen Alphabetisierungsmaßnahmen an die Stelle fehlender formaler Schulbildung, wobei es fraglich bleibt, ob sie die staatliche Primarschule wirklich ersetzen, d. h. funktionale Äquivalente zu dieser konstituieren. *Dioko Xalaat* zeigt, wie junge Menschen mit fehlenden formalen Bildungsmöglichkeiten eine weitgehend selbstbestimmte Grundbildung bewerkstelligen. Ein Ersatz für Grundschulbildung ist das jedoch kaum, da z. B. die Abschlußqualifikationen nicht kodifiziert und kompatibel sind. Am ehesten stellen einige der elaborierteren islamischen Bildungsinstitutionen einen Ersatz der staatlichen Primarschule dar, wenn sie einen hohen Formalisierungs- und Systematisierungsgrad aufweisen.

Beim Faktor 'Substitution' ist allerdings die implizite normative Bezugsgröße kritisch mitzureflektieren: Nonformale Grundbildung substituiert die formale und nicht etwa umgekehrt; d. h. die Vergleichsmaßstäbe setzt das universale Modell von Schule. Die Konkurrenz zwischen den verschiedenen Zugängen zu Grundbildung scheint also weitgehend vorentschieden zugunsten der abschlußbezogenen, staatlichen Grundschulbildung. Dennoch sollte nicht verkannt werden, daß die außerhalb des öffentlichen Bildungsangebots angesiedelten Grundbildungsmaßnahmen eine je eigene Dynamik entfalten können, die andere oder neue Vorstellungen vom Lernen sowie von angemessenen Unterrichtsinhalten und Bildungszielen enthalten. Diese können tatsächlich oder potentiell mit dem relativ unflexiblen und reformträgen staatlichen Bildungswesen in Konkurrenz treten. Im Senegal ist dies insbesondere in bezug auf die religiöse islamische Bildung der Fall, wohingegen nicht bekannt ist, daß die Schule sich bisher z. B. durch eine partizipatorisch-bewußtseinsbildende Curriculumentwicklung, wie sie in *Dioko Xalaat* und anderswo betrieben wird, hätte herausfordern lassen. Daß das islamische Bildungswesen im Senegal tatsächlich in Konkurrenz zum öffentlichen getreten ist, wird auch daran sichtbar, daß sich die Bildungsreformpolitik offenbar dazu genötigt sah, islamischen Religionsunterricht in der Schule vorzusehen und damit eine Abkehr vom Laizismus im Bildungswesen zu vollziehen (vgl. *Asdonk 1994, 1995*). Angesichts fehlender Vergleichsuntersuchungen kann jedoch noch nichts darüber ausgesagt werden, welche Variante von 'Grundbildung' in welcher Hinsicht überlegen oder unterlegen ist: Ist die Alphabetisierung in einer herkömmlichen Primarschule effektiver oder nachhaltiger als die in einem selbstverwalteten Bildungszentrum oder in einer Koranschule erworbene? Können Kinder und Jugendliche, die eine staatliche Primarschule besucht haben, besser oder schlechter Probleme lösen und ihren Alltag bewältigen, als die Absolventinnen und

Absolventen der Kurse eines nonformalen Bildungszentrums oder als die Schüler eines 'Institut Islamique'?[4]

Vorsichtig formuliert wage ich folgende These: Formale Grundbildung wird mit allen Vorzügen und Mängeln weitgehend das bleiben, was sie ist; hierfür wäre auf die Universalisierung und das Beharrungspotential dieser Form von Grundbildung als Allgemeinbildung hinzuweisen. Nonformale Grundbildung wird in Richtung dieses universalen Schulmodells gehen. Es gibt zwar möglicherweise einige Konkurrenz zwischen dem formalen Schulsystem und nonformalen Grundbildungskonzeptionen, da im nonformalen Bereich angesichts fehlender staatlicher Reglementierungen ein größeres Reform- und Innovationspotential vorhanden ist. Trotzdem bleibt festzuhalten, daß die Kompensation fehlender formaler Bildungschancen die Haupttriebkraft für die Existenz nonformaler Grundbildung darstellt und daß die öffentliche Pflichtschule weiterhin das herrschende Modell bildet. Der islamische Bildungssektor im Senegal stellt allerdings einen Sonderfall von 'nonformaler' Grundbildung dar. Wie gezeigt wurde, ist dieser Sektor sowohl bereits eher als 'formale' Bildung zu klassifizieren denn als 'nonformale', als auch tatsächlich eine Herausforderung für die staatliche Bildungspolitik; er ist daher wohl treffender als Alternative zur staatlichen Schule zu kennzeichnen *(Wiegelmann 1994a)*. Damit stellt sich allerdings schulgeschichtlich für den Senegal die auch in anderen Ländern anzutreffende Problematik der Segmentation des Bildungswesens in Form 'dualer' *(Colclough 1976, S. 54)*, 'zweigleisiger' *(Nestvogel 1980, S. 278)* oder 'paralleler' *(Hanf 1980, S. 278)* Bildungsformationen. Mit welchem Terminus auch immer bezeichnet, ist damit das Nebeneinander von zwei verschiedenen Schulsystemen in einem Staat bezeichnet, wobei das eine akademische, an internationalen Standards ausgerichtete Bildung anbietet und das zweite ein irgendwie alternatives Modell von Schule. Da die Bevölkerung des Senegal weit überwiegend islamischen Glaubens ist und angesichts der auch in Regierungskreisen eingestandenen Notwendigkeit, die französisch geprägte öffentliche Schule an die soziokulturellen Gegebenheiten anzupassen, würde ein Ausbau der islamisch geprägten Bildungsgänge bei einem gleichzeitig zu erbringenden Beweis deren gleicher oder sogar besserer Leistungsfähigkeit das krisengeschüttelte staatliche Schulsystem tatsächlich in Bedrängnis bringen.

---

4 Diese Fragestellungen werden zum Teil von Jens Naumann und Ulrike Wiegelmann in einem laufenden, von der Deutschen Forschungsgemeinschaft geförderten Forschungsprojekt empirisch untersucht.

Bibliographie

Adick, Christel: Die Universalisierung der modernen Schule. Eine theoretische Problemskizze zur Erklärung der weltweiten Verbreitung der modernen Schule in den letzten 200 Jahren mit Fallstudien zu Westafrika. Paderborn u. a.: Schöningh 1992. (Internationale Gegenwart. 9)

Asdonk, Ben: Zum Verhältnis von Religion und moderner Schule – Das Beispiel aktueller Diskussionen im Senegal. Münster, Universität, Schriftliche Hausarbeit im Rahmen der Ersten Staatsprüfung für das Lehramt Sekundarstufe II 1994.

Asdonk, Ben: Säkularer Staat und öffentlicher Religionsunterricht – die senegalesische Variante eines globalen Problems. In: Zeitschrift für Internationale Bildungsforschung und Entwicklungspädagogik, 18 (1995) 4, S. 13-20.

Bouche, Denise: L'enseignement dans les Territoires Français de l'Afrique occidentale de 1817 á 1920. Mission civilisatrice ou formation d'une élite? Bd. 1. 2. Paris u. a.: Champion u. a. 1975.

Bracklo, Hilde: Dorfprofil Ngohé. In: Fünf Dörfer – unsere Partner im Senegal, Berlin: Deutsche Gesellschaft für die Vereinten Nationen, Landesverband Berlin 1989, S. 34-41.

Colclough, Christopher: 1976: Basic Education. Samson or Delilah? In: Convergence, 9 (1976) 2, S. 48-63.

Coulibaly, Pierre Marie / Faye, Alassane: Les petites bonnes et filles désœuvrées de Rebeuss. In: Enfants en recherche et en action. Une alternative africaine d'animation urbaine, Dakar: ENDA-Jeunesse Action 1995, S. 193-201.

Enfants en recherche et en action. Une alternative africaine d'animation urbaine. Ouvrage collectif. Dakar: ENDA-Jeunesse Action 1995.

Freire, Paulo: Pädagogik der Unterdrückten. Reinbek: Rowohlt Taschenbuch-Verlag 1983. [1. Aufl.: 1970]

Hanf, Theodor: Die Schule der Staatsoligarchie. Zur Reformunfähigkeit des Bildungswesens in der Dritten Welt. In: Bildung und Erziehung, 33 (1980) 5, S. 406-432.

Institut National d'Étude et d'Action pour le Développement de l'Éducation (Hrsg.): Etude de l'expérience des écoles-pilotes en relation avec l'implantation de la réforme dans l'enseignement élémentaire. Dakar: Ministère de l'Éducation Nationale 1991.

Lenhart, Volker: „Bildung für alle". Zur Bildungskrise in der Dritten Welt. Darmstadt: Wissenschaftliche Buchgesellschaft 1993. (WB-Forum. 77)

Les Mbindaan sans Mbindou. Les Petites Bonnes à Dakar. Dakar: ENDA u. a. 1994.

Nestvogel, Renate: Bildungspolitik in Afrika: Mittel zur Produktivkraftentwicklung oder Instrument der Herrschaftskonsolidierung? In: Hanisch, Rolf / Tetzlaff, Rainer (Hrsg.): Historische Konstitutionsbedingungen des Staates in Entwicklungsländern (= Darstellungen zur internationalen Politik und Entwicklungspolitik. 5), Frankfurt a. M.: Metzner 1980, S. 241-281.

Weltdeklaration über 'Bildung für alle' und Aktionsrahmen zur Befriedigung der grundlegenden Lebensbedürfnisse. Dokumente der Weltkonferenz Jomtien / Thailand 5. – 9. 3. 1990. Berlin: Sekretariat der UNESCO-Kommission der DDR in Zusammenarbeit mit der Deutschen UNESCO-Kommission 1990.

Wiegelmann, Ulrike: Die Koranschule – eine Alternative zur öffentlichen Primarschule in einem laizistischen Staat? Ein Fallbeispiel: Die Republik Senegal. In: Zeitschrift für Pädagogik, 40 (1994a) 5, S. 803-820.

Wiegelmann, Ulrike: Von 'Daaras', arabischen Schulen, der 'Ecole Nouvelle' und anderen Aspekten der senegalesischen Bildungswirklichkeit. In: Fünf Dörfer – unsere Partner im Senegal, Berlin: Deutsche Gesellschaft für die Vereinten Nationen, Landesverband Berlin 1994b, S. 48-55.

Wiegelmann, Ulrike / Naumann, Craig / Faye, Alassane: Zwischen Ausbildung und Ausbeutung: Die talibés mendiants im Senegal. In: Adick, Christel (Hrsg.): Straßenkinder und arbeitende Kinder. Sozialisationstheoretische, historische und kulturvergleichende Studien, Frankfurt a. M.: Verlag für Interkulturelle Kommunikation 1997, S. 273-292.

The Use and Abuse of Educational Research: The Case of a Political Manipulation in Romania

Cesar Bîrzea

There is nothing new in affirming that within the framework of any educational reform the *contribution of educational research* is essential. What is special about the conditions prevailing in Romanian educational research is its status as an *indicator* of *political change*. This status can not be found anywhere else in any country of Central and Eastern Europe. In fact, in all post-communist countries educational research detached itself from ideology, became more pragmatic and was directly connected to the reform projects. Unlike other countries that restructured or closed the old institutions of educational research (Bulgaria, Poland, Russia) or preserved the old ones (Hungary, Slovenia) or created new ones connected with the new national identities (Ukraine, Moldavia, the Baltic states), in Romania educational research benefits from a privileged status owing to the *guilt complex* of the political authorities. Unlike other Eastern European countries, where educational research played a modest part among the ideological disciplines as a whole, in Romania it had „the privilege" of being at the centre of attention from the authorities in a political frame-up at a national level, we can say. This is *a unique example of political power using educational research*.

In a more systematic way, we can identify the following stages in the evolution of educational research in Romania.

The Period before 1945

Educational research was developed in parallel with other efforts to modernize Romanian society in the inter-war period. It was developed in universities and their affiliated structures:

– the Experimental Pedagogy and Psychology Laboratory at the University of Cluj, founded by Ghidionescu in 1925;

- the Romanian Pedagogical Institute, founded within the University of Bucharest by G. G. Antonescu in 1926;
- the Forum for Experimental Pedagogical Studies at the University of Bucharest, founded by Brandza, Muster, and Sulea-Firu in 1932;
- the National Institute of Pedagogy and Education, founded by Onisifor Ghibu at Sibiu in 1943.

The Period 1945 to 1965

As soon as communism was installed, educational research was suspended for a period of almost ten years. It was resumed in 1952 when the Institute of Pedagogical Sciences was created under the Ministry of Education. As mentioned in the resolution to establish the institute, it had „to implement the experience of the Soviet pedagogical school, the most progressive in the world". The specialists trained in the USSR who formed the majority of the personnel strictly strove to meet those provisions leading to expected results. Educational research, traditionally developed in universities, concentrated on a powerful ideological core controlled directly by the governing party.

The Period 1965 to 1971

This was the short period of Romanian „Perestroika" when Ceausescu (in office since 1965) moved closer to the Western countries in order to consolidate his independence from Moscow.

The new regime encouraged research in social and human sciences that were asked to legitimate the new political trend (for example, history became one of the key factors in the nationalist movement of the new political leadership). The best teachers and researchers who had been imprisoned at the end of 1940s were released and transferred directly to the psychological and educational research institutes: Margineanu, Nestor, Herseni, Bontila, Neamtzu, Krasnaseschi. New specialized centers were created to run in parallel with the Institute of Pedagogical Sciences:

- the Laboratory of Educational Analysis and Prognosis;
- the Laboratory of Experimental Didactics;
- the Laboratory for Educational Planning;
- the Research Centre for Vocational Training.

The Period 1971 to 1982

After a visit to China Ceausescu was so impressed with the cultural revolution in that country that in June 1971 he started his own ideological-cultural revolution. Consequently, a large campaign of ideological purification of institutions, school textbooks and political structures was started. Educational research was directly affected by this new trend in politics. The small specialized centers were closed, the pro-Western direction of the late 1960s was halted and educational research once again became an enterprise of ideological inculcation. Meanwhile, the professionals trained in Western universities were isolated and replaced with „professional revolutionaries". On his way to building an „original democracy", Ceausescu rejected any possible form of deviation from national communism. Beginning in 1977 and in order to control this important activity, education was declared an ideological sector and was directly controlled by Elena Ceausescu.

Because they could possibly compete with the official ideology, the social sciences were practically suppressed. The chairs for psychology, sociology and education were closed and training in these fields was replaced by a polyvalent political training called „philosophy". The research field was gradually limited by reducing personnel or institutional fusion. The Institute of Pedagogical Sciences merged first with the Institute of Psychology, becoming the Institute for Educational and Psychological Research (1975), then with the Central Institute of Teacher Training (1977). Educational publications vanished as well as the importation of Western documentation.

The Period 1982 to 1989

But Ceausescu was not content with this marginalization process and ideological perversion of educational research. An advocate of preventive measures against the background of the „Solidarność Syndrome" (that led to the dangerous alliance of intellectuals and workers in Poland), Ceausescu organized a political framework having its epicenter at the Institute for Educational and Psychological Research. Based on some commonplace experimentation influenced by Oriental psychotherapy, researchers were accused of membership in a universal religious sect that undermined public order. This led to the closure of the Institute for Educational and Psychological Research in June 1982. For their ideological purification the researchers were employed as unskilled workers in big communist plants.

A campaign against intellectuals followed that affected all areas of culture. Under the pretext of the „Transcendental Meditation Gate" intellectuals were compromised, and ridiculed, and marginalized: they were dabbling in esoteric extravagances while workers bore the country's hardship. As a climax of this paranoia the words „psychology" and „education" were forbidden in the official language.

The Period after 1990

The political changes initiated after Ceausescu's fall in December 1989 led to a *revival of educational research* in Romania. Not only was educational research rehabilitated but it also received a *privileged status*.

On the one hand, the abolition of activities in this field in the 1980s and the ambitious program of reform launched after 1990 increased *the need for expertise and educational information*. As a consequence, one of the first measures taken by the new political authorities was the setting up of the Institute of Education Sciences in January 1990. In March 1990 the Institute of Psychology was also established, and in September 1990 the chairs in psychology, pedagogy and sociology were re-opened. The importation of educational documentation was re-established and training abroad in these fields was encouraged. Specialized centers and laboratories were set up alongside the main Romanian universities. Against the background of this new social need for expertise and information, educational research is encouraged and solicited in decision-making while its practitioners began to enjoy greater social prestige and more of the necessary resources.

On the other hand, this special attention to educational research in Romania could also be the result of *a guilt complex* on the part of the political authorities. After almost a decade of irrational attitudes, hate and the exclusion of experts, of burning specialist books, educational research has become a *symbol of communist victimization*. That is why re-launching educational research was considered one of the first signs of normalizing the political situation in Romania.

Against the background of the Ministry of Education's preoccupation with decentralization, most of the tasks concerning the design, experimentation and evaluation of reform programmes have been taken over by the Institute of Education Sciences (IES). Although it was created as a compensatory measure against communist abuses, IES did not re-employ personnel and resume projects of the institute that was dissolved in 1982.

Young specialists working in universities or schools were employed after they passed a competitive national examination. In the absence of specialists in these fields (the first graduates of psychology, educational sciences and sociology faculties re-created in 1990 were available in the summer of 1995) specialists were employed from all educational domains: linguistics, economics, mathematics, computer science, biology (hence the syntagm „education sciences" used to name this institute).

The Institute of Education Sciences has its headquarters in Bucharest (and as a climax of irony it is situated in an ex-office of the „Securitate", which organized the „Transcendental Meditation Gate") and has offices in the main university centers – Cluj, Iasi, and Timisoara.

For many decades the Central and Eastern European people waited for communism to fall. They hoped that the suppression of the three strands of totalitarianism (ideology of the one-party system, political police and state dictatorship) would automatically lead to another social order, similar to that of Western Europe.

Unfortunately, experiences during the seven *years of transition* indicate that communism cannot disappear as suddenly as it was established. Even though during these years constitutional, political and economic reforms have been accomplished, what may be called *residual communism* still persists. This is particularly apparent in the field of social behavior, mentalities and attitudes.

As a paradox, democracy proves to be a favorable framework in which all options are possible, including those for residual communism. Taking advantage of the discontentment created by the transition difficulties, lack of political culture on the part of the population and the permissive mechanisms of democracy, the crypto-communist parties (under the mask of socialist or socialdemocratic titles or coalitions) could have access to power again by democratic elections.

The effects of the *struggle for power* that characterize the post-communist transition are felt in *education* too. In this sense, starting with the case of Romania, our study reveals three specific problems:

– stability/breaking off and continuity/change dilemmas;
– role of ideology in evolving educational policies;

- relationship between experts and the decision-making process (especially the relationship between educational research and educational changes).

These three aspects seem to characterize the present evolution of the Central and Eastern European countries. Our analysis refers mainly to the case of Romania, especially viewed in terms of three issues: *breaking-off/continuity, ideological opportunism, and the dramatic need for investment in human resources*.

Considering some of the links we have tried to emphasize, the conclusions of this analysis may also be valid for other countries in transition.

Transition Dilemmas

One of the external analysts' errors has been to consider „the Eastern block" as a compact, homogeneous entity. In reality, this term covered a large variety of peoples, cultures, languages, religions, traditions and historic experiences. This variety explains the great diversity of models and problems to be solved following the changes of 1989. Some countries had attempted economic reforms during the 1970s within the communist regime while others passed directly from classical Stalinism to political democracy.

For this reason the problem of *continuity* and *stability* on the one hand, and *breaking-off* and *change* on the other hand, has different significances from one country to another. The countries that tried a limited liberalization within the communist system had to face the problem of continuity and finalization of the „semi-reforms" (Anweiler 1992) of the 1970s. The elimination of ideological control over curricula was most marked in Hungary after 1978 and in 1985 educational administration was decentralized. In Hungary they spoke of change, transformation or modernization but not reform. In other countries, such as Poland, the reforms proposed in the 1980s by „Solidarność" are only just being put into practice under favorable political conditions. In other countries, such as Romania, where rigid and ultra-nationalist totalitarianism was a feature of the 1980s, the year 1989 marked the first stage in a spectacular break with the old regime, followed by a slowing down of educational reforms and even the development of a *counter-reform movement* on the part of the neo-communist, populist and nationalist parties. Finally, during the seven years of post-communist transition there have been moments of denouncing and rejecting the reforms started. This is the case of Bulgaria and the Russian

Federation where they speak of „*a reform of reforms*", of reforms to correct the initial reforms.

The Role of Ideology

The communist model of education is relatively simple. It is based upon the equation: *one* party = *one* ideology = *one* nation = *one* educational system = *one* curriculum = *one* textbook = *new man*.

After the fall of communism the official prohibition of Marxism-Leninism left an *ideological void* which was filled by a multitude of political movements and groups (for example, in Bulgaria there are over 100 political parties). In the new countries created after breaking with communist federations, *nationalism* has become a state ideology. In others anti-war traditions and doctrines were reactivated, explained by the nostalgic feeling of „lost paradise" (*neo-traditionalism, orthodoxism, Magyarism, pan-Slavism, etc.*). In other countries the negation of Marxism determined a sudden switch to the opposite pole of the political spectrum and the adoption of *neo-liberalism* as official doctrine. For instance, after some years, the 1988 Thatcherist reform began to be contested in Great Britain, but it has been taken as an inspiration in some countries of Central Europe. Finally, especially in the countries of Eastern Europe where the role of the state and social protection prevail, they speak mainly of *social democracy*. Even though the word „socialism" is avoided, simple reference to the „Swedish model", the „Spanish model", or „the social market economy" is not convincing. These are only verbal labels that cover a confused and contradictory situation in which many of the old regime's practices still persist (for example, state propriety over the big bankrupt enterprises).

The case of Romania provides us with a good opportunity to draw interesting conclusions regarding *the role of ideology in the new educational policies*. On the one hand, the governing ideology is social democracy, at least as this word is understood and applied in Central and Eastern Europe. On the other hand, under the pressure of the International Monetary Fund and the World Bank, different innovations have been adopted starting from a neo-liberal ideology and market economy principle. Finally, regardless of the ideological correctness of these measures, educational reform in Romania will be imposed from top to bottom, with the essential contribution of the state and centralized structures.

Experts' Contribution

Acknowledging the need for expertise and the indispensable role of the „intelligentsia" is one of the most important acquisitions of the post-communist transition. Before 1989 intellectuals were regarded with suspicion and even hostility. Their ability for autonomous thinking and their possible influence over workers had made intellectuals uncertain partners who had to be permanently supervised, manipulated and intimidated.

„The Transcendental Meditation Gate" in Romania to which we referred in our study, is a typical example of intellectual repression and *negative use of educational research*. It may be a unique case in the global history of education that a power used educational research as a scapegoat and pretext for a vast political diversion. As a victim of „witch hunting" that justified the „cultural revolution" of the 1980s, educational research in Ceausescu's Romania was subjected to some unprecedented repression: experts were sent in to forced labour and employed as unskilled workers, educational papers were destroyed, experts' access to schools was forbidden (not to contaminate the teaching staff ideologically), trials for the public conviction of the heretics were framed, even the words „psychology" and „education" were forbidden in the official language. Obviously, it was an extreme case. But it shows us how vulnerable the experts' status is in a totalitarian regime and how selfish power can be in its relation to intellectuals.

The case of Romania in the 1980s shows that, especially in countries where the Law is deficient, educational research needs the *protection and guarantee of autonomy*.

Maybe, if international organizations had been more efficient and had had better protection mechanisms for intellectual work, the dramatic case of the „Transcendental Meditation" and other „cultural revolutions" would not have occurred. Unfortunately, international organizations as well as professional associations did not react to the barbaric treatment that a dictatorship applied to its own educational research.

In the absence of some more efficient mechanisms and by indulging in sterile approaches the international community tolerates such situations. Under such conditions even if the situation is radically changed in the Central and Eastern European countries, the anomalous case mentioned above may reoccur at any time, in any of the numerous dictatorships that still are in power in other regions of the world.

Bibliography

Anweiler, Oskar: Some Historical Aspects of Educational Change in the Former Soviet Union and Eastern Europe. In: Phillips, David / Kaser, Michael (eds.): Education and Economic Change in Eastern Europe and the Former Soviet Union (= Oxford Studies in Comparative Education. 2), Wallingford: Triangle Books 1992, pp. 29-39.

Bîrzea, Cesar: Educational Policies of the Countries in Transition. Strasbourg: Council of Europe Press 1994.

Bîrzea, Cesar: Educational Reform in Romania. Conditions, Strategy and Implementation. In: East/West Education, 15 (1994) 1, pp. 37-42.

Bîrzea, Cesar: Educational Research in Romania. In: Calderhead, James (ed.): Educational Research in Europe, Clevedon et al.: Multilingual Matters 1994, pp. 41-44.

Bîrzea, Cesar: Educational Research in the Countries of Central and Eastern Europe. Problems and Future Prospects. In: Edwards, Lynne et al. (eds.): Education for Democratic Citizenship in Europe. New Challenges for Secondary Education, Lisse: Swets and Zeitlinger 1994, pp. 25-29.

Cerych, Ladislav: Renewal of Central European Higher Education. Issues and Challenges. In: European Journal of Education, 25 (1990) 4, pp. 351-359.

Gilberg, Trond: Nationalism and Communism in Romania. The Rise and Fall of Ceausescu's Personal Dictatorship. Boulder, Colo.: Westview Press 1990.

Kopp, Botho von: Global Changes and the Context of Education, Democracy and Development in Eastern Europe. In: Mitter, Wolfgang / Schäfer, Ulrich (eds.): Upheaval and Change in Education, Frankfurt a. M.: German Institute for International Educational Research 1993, pp. 85-98.

Mitter, Wolfgang: Education in Eastern Europe and the Soviet Union in a Period of Revolutionary Change. In: idem / Schäfer, Ulrich (eds.): Upheaval and Change in Education, Frankfurt a. M.: German Institute for International Educational Research 1993, pp. 121-136.

Sadlak, Jan: Higher Education Reform in Romania. Challenges and Responses. In: Hüfner, Klaus (ed.): Higher Education Reform Processes in Central and Eastern Europe, Frankfurt a. M. et al.: Lang 1995, pp. 217-233.

Lehrerrolle und Lehrerausbildung in den Niederlanden

Günter Brinkmann

Einleitung

Ein wissenschaftlicher Beitrag für eine Festschrift sollte original, originär und auf einem Forschungsfeld verfaßt sein, auf dem der Autor ausgewiesen ist. Ein Festschriftbeitrag für Wolfgang Mitter, dem weltweit renommierten Komparatisten, hat sich zudem am methodologischen Anspruch des Jubilars zu orientieren. Es ist deshalb zu begründen, warum sich dieser Artikel auf eine auslandspädagogische Analyse beschränkt, obwohl der Autor gerade ein Forschungsprojekt zur Lehrerausbildung in Europa bearbeitet. Die Wahl fiel auf ein auslandspädagogisches Thema, weil das umfassende Projekt zur Lehrerbildung in Europa in einem notwendigerweise eng begrenzten Einzelbeitrag nicht so dargestellt werden kann, daß ein sachkundiger Leser aus der Lektüre neue Erkenntnisse gewinnen würde. Deshalb beschränken wir uns hier auf neuere Entwicklungen in der niederländischen Lehrerausbildung, die international bisher wenig beachtet worden sind. Über den impliziten Vergleich mit anderen Lehrerausbildungssystemen hinaus sollen diese Entwicklungen und Tendenzen in Bezug gebracht werden zu einem Verständnis der Lehrerrolle, das sich in unseren modernen demokratischen Gemeinwesen weitgehend durchgesetzt hat. Diese Vorstellung von der Rolle des Lehrers kann im Anschluß an den Bericht „The Teacher Today" (*Organisation for Economic Co-operation and Development 1990*) als die eines „Professionals" bezeichnet werden. Dieser versteht sich nicht mehr als weisungsgebundener Arbeitnehmer im Sinne des Top-down-Modells, der die auf zentraler Ebene getroffenen didaktischen Entscheidungen auf eine größtenteils vorgeschriebene Art und Weise im Schulalltag umsetzt. Er versteht sich vielmehr als der pädagogische Fachmann, der im Gespräch mit allen am Unterricht Betroffenen entscheidet, wie die Bedürfnisse der Schüler auf möglichst effektive Weise in praktisches Handeln umgesetzt werden. Das setzt u. a. voraus, daß dem Lehrer in seiner Ausbildung die Kompetenz vermittelt wird, sein eigenes Handeln und dessen Ergebnisse zu reflektieren, selbstkritisch zu sein und die Lernbedürfnisse und -probleme von Schülern analysieren und adäquat darauf reagieren zu können.

Schulstruktur und Lehrerausbildung in den Niederlanden

In den Niederlanden gibt es keine Trennung zwischen Vorschule und Grundschule. Am 1. August 1985 trat ein neues Primarschulgesetz in Kraft, das die bisherigen Vorschulen für Kinder von vier bis sechs Jahren und die sechsjährigen Grundschulen für Kinder von sechs bis zwölf Jahren zu einer achtjährigen Primarschule *(basisschool)* zusammenfaßte. Dieser Innovationsprozeß ist heute abgeschlossen.

Auf dieser neuen Primarschule baut der allgemeinbildende Sekundarunterricht auf. Er ist für Schüler im Alter von zwölf bis achtzehn Jahren bestimmt. Seine gesetzliche Grundlage ist bis heute das am 1. August 1968 in Kraft getretene Gesetz über den Sekundarunterricht, das sogenannte „Mammutgesetz". Der allgemeinbildende Sekundarunterricht gliedert sich seither in den Vorbereitenden Wissenschaftlichen Unterricht *(VWO, Voorbereidend Wetenschappelijk Onderwijs)*, den Allgemeinbildenden Sekundarunterricht auf Höherem Niveau *(HAVO, Hoger Algemeen Voortgezet Onderwijs)* und den Allgemeinbildenden Sekundarunterricht auf Mittlerem Niveau *(MAVO, Middelbaar Algemeen Voortgezet Onderwijs)*. Im VWO gibt es drei Schultypen, in denen die Schüler in einer sechsjährigen Schulzeit auf das Studium an Universitäten und Hochschulen vorbereitet werden: *Atheneum, Gymnasium* und *Lyceum*.

Das System dieser nebeneinander bestehenden Sekundarschulen mit unterschiedlichem Anspruchsniveau, unterschiedlichem curricularem Angebot und verschiedenartigen Abschlußqualifikationen wird immer wieder kritisiert. Deshalb erfreuen sich die Schulgemeinschaften zunehmender Beliebtheit. Die Schulgemeinschaft wurde als eine gesamtschulähnliche Schulform additiver Art durch das „Mammutgesetz" eingeführt, um die Durchlässigkeit zwischen den verschiedenen Schultypen zu erhöhen und zur Vereinheitlichung des Sekundarschulwesens beizutragen. Sie hat sich seit Ende der sechziger Jahre zahlenmäßig stark entwickelt und erlebt in den neunziger Jahren einen erneuten Aufwärtstrend.

Wie werden nun die Lehrer für diese verschiedenen Schulstufen und Schulformen ausgebildet?

In den Niederlanden gibt es drei völlig unterschiedliche Lehrerausbildungsgänge. Voraussetzung zur Aufnahme des Grundschullehrerstudiums ist nicht der dem deutschen Abitur vergleichbare VWO-Abschluß, sondern der HAVO-Abschluß. Die Ausbildung erfolgt an derzeit 40 kleineren Pädagogischen Hochschulen *(PABO, Pedagogische Aca-*

demie Basis-Onderwijs), die Teil des berufsbildenden Tertiärbereichs sind. Sie umfaßt vier Jahre, von denen das erste Jahr propädeutischen Charakter hat. Die Studierenden erwerben eine breite Lehrbefugnis. Sie müssen nach dem Examen in der Lage sein, alle an der achtjährigen *basisschool* gelehrten Fächer zu unterrichten.

Auch die Ausbildung zum Lehrer an der Sekundarstufe I *(tweedegraads lerarenopleiding,* Lehrer zweiten Grades) findet nicht an der Universität statt, sondern an elf der Pädagogischen Hochschulen. Diese werden ebenfalls dem berufsbildenden Tertiärbereich zugerechnet. Nach dem ersten propädeutischen Jahr konzentrieren sich die Studierenden in den folgenden drei Jahren auf das Studium nur eines Faches. Dabei steht die fachwissenschaftliche Ausbildung im Vordergrund. Sie macht ca. 75% der Studienzeit aus. Auf die fachdidaktische und schulpraktische Ausbildung entfallen dagegen nur ca. 25% der Zeit. Die Studienpläne der Pädagogischen Hochschulen sind nicht vereinheitlicht. So beginnt beispielsweise die schulpraktische Ausbildung je nach Institut im zweiten oder dritten Studienjahr.

Die universitäre Lehrerausbildung führt zum sogenannten Lehrer ersten Grades *(leraar voortgezet onderwijs eerstegraads)* für die Sekundarstufe II. Sie konzentriert sich seit September 1994 auf die sechs Universitäten in Groningen, Leiden, Utrecht, Nijmegen, Amsterdam und die Freie Universität Amsterdam sowie auf die Universität Twente in Eindhoven. Es handelt sich dabei nicht um ein grundständiges Lehramtsstudium, sondern um eine einjährige sogenannte „postdoktorale", d. h. auf das vierjährige Fachstudium aufbauende Berufsausbildung für ein Fach. Im Laufe des vorausgehenden vierjährigen Fachstudiums findet nur eine zweimonatige Orientierungsphase auf den Lehrerberuf statt. In dem postdoktoralen Ausbildungsjahr wird die Hälfte der Zeit der Theorie und praxisorientierter Ausbildung in der Universität gewidmet. Die übrige Zeit steht für Übungen in der Berufspraxis zur Verfügung. Die universitäre Ausbildung liegt in Händen von Pädagogen und Fachdidaktikern (die fachwissenschaftliche Ausbildung erfolgte in dem vorgeschalteten vierjährigen Fachstudium). Die Verantwortung für die schulpraktische Ausbildung übernehmen allein die Mentoren in den verschiedenen Schulen.

Der Lehrer – ein Beruf mit Perspektive?

Schule und Lehrerausbildung sind in den Niederlanden in den letzten Jahren ins Zentrum des öffentlichen Interesses getreten. Nachdem in den achtziger Jahren in der pädagogischen Öffentlichkeit vielfach Beschwerde über den Lehrerberuf, über die Qualität des Unterrichts sowie über die Qualität der Lehrerausbildung geführt wurde, reagierte die niederländische Bildungspolitik Ende der achtziger Jahre darauf zunächst dadurch, daß sie ein nationales System der Qualitätsvorsorge in Form von Unterrichtsvisitationen einrichtete. Diese Visitationen führen zu Evaluationsstudien, die vom Ministerium für Bildung und Wissenschaften in Auftrag gegeben und von Expertenkommissionen ausgearbeitet werden. Die Experten haben die Aufgabe, die Unterrichtsqualität zu beurteilen und Vorschläge zu deren Verbesserung zu machen. Auf diese Weise sind in den letzten Jahren alle Schulstufen und die zuvor dargestellten verschiedenen Formen der Lehrerausbildung (neben anderen universitären Studiengängen) durchleuchtet worden. Die Fülle der Einzelergebnisse kann hier nicht wiedergegeben werden. Es ist gegenwärtig auch noch nicht abzuschätzen, ob die zahlreichen Verbesserungsvorschläge auf den jeweiligen Bildungsstufen zu Veränderungen in deren Praxis führen, da dieser Prozeß gerade erst begonnen hat bzw. noch in der Diskussionsphase ist. Klar ist dagegen die Forderung nach einer systematischen permanenten Qualitätskontrolle, der sich Schulen und Hochschulen und damit auch die Lehrerausbildung in Zukunft zu stellen haben.

Die gewachsene Bedeutung von Schule und Lehrerbildung in der niederländischen Gesellschaft geht aber auch daraus hervor, daß das Ministerium für Bildung und Wissenschaften zeitlich parallel zu den Unterrichtsvisitationen weitere Kommissionen eingerichtet hat, die den Auftrag erhalten haben, spezielle Empfehlungen vorzulegen. So hat die 1991 eingerichtete „Zukunftskommission Lehrerschaft" mit ihrem 1993 vorgelegten Bericht „Een beroep met perspectief" [Ein Beruf mit Perspektive] (*Commissie Toekomst Leraarschap 1993a*) ungewöhnlich große Beachtung gefunden. Es gibt sicherlich mehrere Gründe für die große Resonanz eines Fachberichtes einer externen Beratungskommission des Ministeriums: Dazu gehört neben der Aktualität des Untersuchungsgegenstandes die Persönlichkeit der Vorsitzenden, die Zusammensetzung der Kommission, ihre Arbeitsweise und die Präsentation der Ergebnisse. Zur Vorsitzenden hat Staatssekretär Wallage die populäre Parlamentarierin Andrée van Es ernannt. Der Kommission gehörten neben Bildungsexperten auch Fachleute auf den Gebieten Arbeitsmarktanalyse, Personalführung und Rechtsfragen an. Die Kommission hat neben der Aufarbeitung der umfangreichen Fachliteratur gezielt Auftragsarbeiten an Forschungsinstitute vergeben – z. B. über die Mobilität von Lehrern –, die wesentlich zur Aktualität des Berichts beigetragen haben. Schließlich hat sie gleichzeitig mit der Vorlage ihres Originalberichtes im März 1993 eine publikumswirksame zweite Version des Berichtes für die breite Öffentlichkeit vorgelegt: „Het gedroomde koninkrijk. De toekomst van het leraarschap" [Das geträumte Königreich. Die Zukunft der Lehrerschaft].

Die „Zukunftskommission Lehrerschaft" hatte am 8. November 1991 von Staatssekretär Wallage den Auftrag erhalten, eine grundsätzliche Empfehlung zur Rolle, Position und Wertschätzung der Lehrerschaft zu erarbeiten und sich mit den damit zusammenhängenden Fragen der Lehrerausbildung und der Berufsanforderungen zu befassen. Diesen Auftrag entsprechend analysierte die Kommission in ihrem am 30. März 1993 vorgelegten Bericht „Ein Beruf mit Perspektive" zunächst die durch Untersuchungen bekannten Fakten über den Lehrerberuf. Diese faßt sie wie folgt zusammen:

- *Professionalisierung:* Die Personalführung steckt noch in den Kinderschuhen ... Lehrerfortbildung gibt es nur in geringem Ausmaß, und die Ausbildung des Personals ist die Ausnahme. Dadurch bleibt die Professionalisierung zurück.
- *Mobilität:* Die interne und externe Arbeitsmobilität im Schulwesen ist sehr gering. Die Folge davon ist, daß die Lehrer das Gefühl haben, in einer Reuse zu sitzen. Außer dem Mangel an Möglichkeiten, die Laufbahn zu verändern, hat sich infolge der die Aufgabenverteilungen betreffenden gewachsenen Tradition eine sehr begrenzte Diversität an Funktionen herausgebildet.
- *Vergreisung:* Es ist die Rede von Vergreisung des Personalbestandes infolge des Mangels an Arbeitsplätzen ...
- *Arbeitsbelastung und Krankheitsausfall:* Der Krankheitsausfall ist hoch und viele Lehrer empfinden ihren Beruf als Belastung.
- *Arbeitsunfähigkeit:* Die meisten Lehrer erreichen das 55. Lebensjahr im Schuldienst nicht. Die Alterskategorie von 55 Jahren und älter ist klein ... Die permanente Arbeitsunfähigkeit hat in den vergangenen zehn Jahren stark zugenommen, vor allem in der Altersgruppe der 30- bis 40jährigen.
- *Ausbildung:* Die Qualität einiger Ausbildungsgänge könnte besser sein. Der Wirkungsgrad ist unterschiedlich, der Zustrom von Studenten reicht nicht überall aus und liefert keine Garantie dafür, daß die Studenten eine Lehrtätigkeit im Schulwesen aufnehmen. Der Übergang zwischen Ausbildung und Praxis läßt zu wünschen übrig.
- *Gehalt:* Das Gehalt ist niedriger als in anderen Sektoren ...: bei vergleichbarem Ausbildungs- und Erfahrungsniveau bis zu 10%.
- *Status:* Der Status des Lehrerberufs ist von großem Interesse und ist Gegenstand der Diskussion. Es gibt keine empirischen Belege dafür, daß der Status niedriger geworden ist, man könnte sogar von einer leichten Verbesserung sprechen.
- *Befähigung/Qualifikation:* ... Mehr als die Hälfte der Schuldirektoren finden, daß die Anforderungen für die Lehrbefähigung keine Garantie für Lehrqualifikationen sind *(Commissie Toekomst Leraarschap 1993a, S. 42-43).*

Nach Ansicht der Kommission verdeutlichen diese Fakten, daß viele Aspekte des Berufsbildes des Lehrers verändert werden müssen, um den Beruf attraktiver zu machen. Voraussetzung hierfür sei die Schaffung einer professionellen Arbeitsorganisation, in der u. a. Platz wäre für eine eigenständige Unterrichts- und Personalentwicklung auf der Ebene der einzelnen – autonomen – Schule. Die Kommission schlägt vor allen eine neue Laufbahnentwicklung für Lehrer mit vertikaler und horizontaler Durchlässigkeit vor. Vertikale Durchlässigkeit bedeutet eine Beförderung nach einer höheren Funktion. Horizontale Durchlässigkeit bezieht sich auf eine Funktion mit anderem Inhalt auf demselben Gehaltsniveau: so könnte ein Lehrer beispielsweise statt zu unterrichten curriculare Entwicklungsarbeit leisten. Die verschiedenen Funktionen könnten in kurzen Perioden wahrgenommen werden, damit die Tätigkeit in der Schule insgesamt abwechslungsreicher, flexibler und damit attraktiver wird. Dem soll auch die Einführung von verschiedenen Funktionstypen von Lehrern dienen. Gedacht ist an ein neues System mit fünf Funktionsniveaus: 'Lehrer in der Ausbildung, Junior-Lehrer, Lehrer, Senior-Lehrer und Außerordentlicher Lehrer'. Die neue Funktion des 'Lehrers in der Ausbildung' ist eine Übergangsfunktion zwischen Lehrerausbildung und Schulpraxis. Dazu könnte das letzte Jahr der heutigen Lehrerausbildung auf zwei Jahre ausgedehnt werden und gleichzeitig der letzten Phase der Ausbildung und dem Einstieg in die Unterrichtstätigkeit dienen. Der Übergang würde somit fließend gestaltet. Der Junior-Lehrer oder Ko-Lehrer ist nicht mehr in der Ausbildung, wird aber noch systematisch durch einen Senior-Lehrer zu größerer Professionalität geführt, die ihm als Lehrer und später als Senior-Lehrer zugute kommt.

Die Zukunftskommission befaßt sich in ihrem Bericht weiterhin schwerpunktmäßig mit Schulautonomie und Unterrichtsqualität, mit der neuen Rolle des Staates im Schulwesen und mit der Rolle des Schulmanagements, aber auch mit der Lehrerausbildung. Sie fordert eine Verbesserung der Qualität der Lehrerausbildungsgänge, die in enger Abstimmung mit den Anforderungen der Schulpraxis zu erfolgen habe. Sie spricht sogar von der *„Produktion eines Modell-Lehrers für Schulen"* (Commissie Toekomst Leraarschap 1993a, S. 90). Außerdem fordert sie eine Integration der bestehenden drei Lehrerausbildungsgänge in „Edukative Fakultäten" *(vgl. ebd., Kap. 4)* unter Einbeziehung eines modularen Systems von Lehrerfort- und Weiterbildungsaktivitäten.

Der Bericht „Ein Beruf mit Perspektive" hat nicht nur große Beachtung in der Öffentlichkeit gefunden, sondern auch das Ministerium für Unterricht und Wissenschaften veranlaßt, darauf ungewöhnlich schnell schriftlich zu reagieren. Bereits im September 1993 veröffentlichte das Ministerium die Broschüre „Vitaal leraarschap" [Vitale Lehrerschaft]

(Ministerie van Onderwijs en Wetenschappen 1993), nachdem sich das niederländische Kabinett mit den Vorschlägen der Zukunftskommission befaßt hatte. Kabinett und Ministerium unterstützen im wesentlichen die Forderungen der Zukunftskommission, vertreten aber in zwei Punkten andere Positionen. Sie sehen den Lehrer deutlicher in der Rolle des Unterrichtenden, der dabei neue gesellschaftliche Entwicklungen – wie die zunehmende multikulturelle Zusammensetzung der Bevölkerung oder den Trend zur Individualisierung – beachten muß. Außerdem plädieren sie für ein Gleichgewicht bei der Aufteilung von Verantwortlichkeiten zwischen Staat und Schule. Während die Zukunftskommission sich auf die Verantwortlichkeiten der einzelnen Schule konzentriert hat, machen sie deutlich, daß die Verantwortung des Staates für das Unterrichtsniveau, die Qualität der Lehrer und für die Finanzierung des Schulwesens bestehen bleiben muß. Diese beiden divergenten Positionen sind ein Beispiel dafür, daß die einzelnen Interessengruppen natürlich auch in den Niederlanden bei der Lösung konkreter Probleme unterschiedlicher Meinung sein können. Charakteristisch für das niederländische System ist, daß die verschiedenen Positionen immer wieder neu verhandelt werden und nur auf Zeit zu Kompromissen führen, die von allen beachtet und befolgt werden. Auf der anderen Seite gibt es eindeutige Trends, denen sich im Grundsatz alle anschließen.

Zu diesen Trends zählt die Entwicklung einer professionellen Schulorganisation. Diese Anregungen aus dem Bericht der Zukunftskommission wird vom Kabinett voll unterstützt und auf folgenden sechs Gebieten konkretisiert:

1. *Der primäre Prozeß:* Die selbständigen Schulen sollen innerhalb des gesetzlich festgelegten Rahmens, zu dem auch neu zu formulierende zentrale End- und Kernziele gehören, größere Freiheit erhalten, die Unterrichtsprozesse auf verschiedene Weise zu gestalten. Die Schulen sollen sogar stimuliert werden, die Möglichkeiten zu einer nicht-traditionellen Unterrichtsorganisation zu nutzen. Die Reglementierung soll verringert werden.
2. *Arbeitsbedingungen:* Die Deregulierung des Bildungswesens soll auf die Arbeitsbedingungen der Lehrer ausgedehnt werden. Angestrebt wird, den Schulen zu gestatten, eigene Tarifvereinbarungen zu treffen.
3. *Aufgaben- und Funktionsdifferenzierung:* Das dritte Kennzeichen einer professionellen Schulorganisation ist die eigenständige Personalpolitik, in der Platz ist für Aufgaben- und Funktionsdifferenzierung. Diese Differenzierung, beispielsweise durch Einführung der verschiedenen Funktionstypen von Lehrern, kann Besoldungsunterschiede nach sich ziehen. Das Schulmanagement soll dafür geschult werden, die Personalbeurteilung selbst vorzunehmen.

4. *Mobilität von Lehrern:* Die neu zu treffenden Maßnahmen sollen zu einer größeren Mobilität der Lehrer führen. Dazu sollen auch die Lehrerausbildungsgänge flexibilisiert werden, damit eine einmal getroffene Wahl nicht notwendigerweise eine Sackgasse für die Laufbahn des Lehrers bedeutet.
5. *Schulmanagement:* Eine Voraussetzung für Veränderungsprozesse in Schulen ist ein modernes professionelles Schulmanagement. Die Schulleitung und die Bewerber für Posten in der Schulleitung sollen durch Fortbildung entsprechend geschult werden.
6. *Der finanzielle Rahmen:* Im Rahmen eines Schulprofilbudgets werden die finanziellen Möglichkeiten geschaffen für Qualitätsverbesserung, Innovationen und eigenständige Personalpolitik an den Schulen.

Der Bericht „Vitale Lehrerschaft" beschäftigt sich außerdem mit der Qualifikation von Lehrern und mit der Lehrerausbildung. Eine zentrale Frage einer professionellen Schulorganisation lautet: *„Wen darf die Schule als Lehrer anstellen?" (Ministerie van Onderwijs en Wetenschappen 1993, S. 7).* Es wird vorgeschlagen, auch Lehrer anzustellen, die keine Lehrerausbildung durchlaufen haben, aber bestimmte Befähigungserfordernisse erfüllen. Dazu muß ein neues Beurteilungssystem auf der Basis von Berufsprofilen entwickelt werden.

Im Bereich der Lehrerausbildung unterstreicht das Kabinett zunächst die Ansicht der Zukunftskommission, daß die Lehramtsstudiengänge stärker auf die Schulpraxis bezogen sein müssen und daß ein flexibles Angebot an Ausbildungswegen entwickelt werden muß. Sodann bezieht es sich auf ein Ergebnis der ersten drei Visitationskommissionen, die die Lehramtsstudiengänge untersucht haben, nach dem den Lehramtsstudiengängen ein inhaltlicher Ausbildungsrahmen fehlt, der auf dem Berufsbild des modernen Lehrers beruht. Zur Verbesserung der Lehramtsstudiengänge werden vier Vorschläge unterbreitet *(ebd., S. 8, 34-39):*

1. *Entwicklung von Berufsprofilen und Befähigungsanforderungen:* Auf der Basis von noch zu formulierenden Befähigungsanforderungen sollen neue Ausbildungsprogramme entwickelt werden. Neu eingeführt werden soll eine Überwachung des Studienfortschritts mit Hilfe eines objektiven Beurteilungssystems.
2. *Der Lehrer in Ausbildung:* Durch die Einführung des 'Lehrers in Ausbildung' soll im letzten Jahr der Lehrerausbildung eine Dualisierung von Studieren und Arbeiten stattfinden. Dadurch soll der Praxisschock junger Lehrer vermieden und ein strukturelles Feedback der Schulen auf die Ausbildungsprogramme in der Lehrerbildung ermöglicht werden.

3. *Zusammenarbeit zwischen den Einrichtungen:* Nach Art und Inhalt unterschiedliche Kooperationsverbände (Edukative Fakultäten) sollen zur Verbesserung von Qualität und Flexibilisierung der Ausbildungsgänge führen.
4. *Spezifische Absprachen:* Das Kabinett will unverzüglich mit allen an der Lehrerausbildung interessierten Organisationen zu Absprachen darüber kommen, welche Maßnahmen aufgrund der spezifischen Signale der Visitationskommissionen zu ergreifen sind.

Aktuelle Entwicklungen in der Lehrerausbildung

Nachdem in enger Verschränkung mit den Problemen der Schulpraxis die Forderung nach einer verbesserten Lehrerausbildung untermauert worden war, wurden Mitte der neunziger Jahre die konzeptionellen Arbeiten für diese Neuorientierung verstärkt. Erstes und wichtigstes Ergebnis ist wiederum eine Publikation des Ministeriums (das inzwischen in Ministerium für Bildung, Kultur und Wissenschaften umbenannt wurde). Im Mai 1995 gab es die Broschüre „Vitale lerarenopleidingen voor de school van de toekomst" [Vitale Lehrerausbildungsgänge für die Schule der Zukunft] *(Ministerie van Onderwijs, Cultuur en Wetenschappen 1995)* heraus, die als amtliche Grundlage für die aktuellen Entwicklungen in der Lehrerausbildung einzustufen ist. Darin räumt das Ministerium der Erneuerung der Lehrerausbildung in der laufenden Kabinettsperiode hohe Priorität ein. Die wichtigsten Vorschläge beziehen sich auf die Entwicklung von gemeinsamen Curricula, auf die Bildung von Kooperationsverbänden für die einzelnen Studiengänge sowie auf die Verstärkung der Personalpolitik innerhalb der Institutionen.

Curriculumentwicklung

Für die verschiedenen Lehramtsstudiengänge sollen landesweit einheitliche Curricula entwickelt werden. Dadurch verspricht man sich nicht nur eine bessere inhaltliche Abstimmung der Ausbildungsprogramme, sondern auch eine größere Effizienz in diesem komplexen und arbeitsintensiven Prozeß. Das einheitliche und für alle Institutionen verpflichtende Curriculum bezieht sich auf 70% aller Abschlüsse. Hierfür wird der Begriff Kernqualifikation eingeführt. Die restlichen 30% bleiben den jeweiligen Ausbildungsstätten überlassen. In diesem Bereich haben sie die Möglichkeit, eigenständige Profile zu bilden.

Ausgangspunkt der gemeinsamen Curriculumentwicklung sind die zuvor angesprochenen Berufsprofile und Befähigungsanforderungen. Alle Studiengänge sollen in Zukunft regelmäßig durch Experten daraufhin überprüft werden, inwieweit sie diesen Anforderungen gerecht werden. Bei der Entwicklung und Implementation der gemeinsamen Curricula sollen die Kooperationsverbände eine wichtige Rolle spielen.

Bildung von Kooperationsverbänden

Im Jahre 1992 wurden in den Niederlanden erstmals acht 'Edukative Fakultäten' eingerichtet, 1993 kam eine neunte hinzu. Staatssekretär Wallage definierte diese 'Edukativen Fakultäten' wie folgt: *„Es geht um die Bündelung von Aktivitäten, wobei Ausbildung, Fortbildung und Unterstützung der Unterrichtenden, der Schulleitung und der Schule als ganzer auf zusammenhängende Weise Gestalt erhalten"* (Ministerie van Onderwijs en Wetenschappen 1994, S. 5). Die mit der Evaluation der 'Edukativen Fakultäten' beauftragte Unterrichtsinspektion hat hieraus folgende Merkmale abgeleitet:

„1. Die Fortbildungsaktivitäten müssen inhaltlich in das Projekt der Bildungsentwicklung und Schulerneuerung integriert sein. Dazu bedarf es einer zentralen Steuerungsagentur ...
2. Die Errungenschaften aus der Phase nach dem Grundstudium werden zur Qualitätsverbesserung der Grundausbildung genutzt.
3. Es wird eine feste Beziehung zwischen den verschiedenen Lehrerausbildungsgängen etabliert" (ebd., S. 6).

Aus den Evaluationsstudien geht hervor, daß die 'Edukativen Fakultäten' in einigen Fällen zur Erneuerung und Verbesserung des Angebotes in der Lehrerfortbildung geführt haben. Dagegen haben sie den einzelnen Lehramtsstudiengängen keine neuen Impulse geben können. Dies veranlaßte das Ministerium, in der Broschüre „Vitale Lehrerausbildungsgänge" eine veränderte Strategie vorzuschlagen. Priorität soll nun die Verbesserung der Lehramtsstudiengänge haben. Erst nach dieser Qualitätsverbesserung seien die verschiedenen Institutionen und Einrichtungen, die jede für sich betrachtet qualitativ stark sein müßten, in der Lage, erfolgreich in 'Edukativen Fakultäten' zusammenzuarbeiten. Damit wird nach offizieller Version das innovative Projekt der 'Edukativen Fakultäten' keineswegs aufgegeben, sondern für eine Übergangszeit mit einem veränderten Anspruch weitergeführt. Es kann aber nicht ausgeschlossen werden, daß die

'Edukativen Fakultäten' infolge der neuen Prioritätensetzung nur noch geringe Entwicklungschancen haben.

Dagegen setzt das Ministerium im Innovationsprozeß neuerdings auf nationale Lösungen und auf Kooperationsverbände zwischen Lehrerausbildungsinstitutionen derselben Art. So sollen beispielsweise für die Grundschullehrerausbildung sieben regionale Kooperationsverbände gebildet werden. Diese haben folgende Aufgaben zu erfüllen:

– die Entwicklung des auf landesweiter Ebene vereinbarten nicht vorgeschriebenen Teils der Curricula (etwa 30%);
– die Herbeiführung von Absprachen über eine Aufgabenverteilung für bestimmte Spezialisierungen;
– strukturelle Beratungen mit dem Schulsektor sowie mit relevanten Informationsagenturen und gesellschaftlichen Einrichtungen;
– das Entwerfen und Ausführen einer gemeinsamen Initiative in der Personalpolitik (Förderung von Fachleuten, Mobilität der Dozenten, kollegiales Feedback) *(Ministerie van Onderwijs, Cultuur en Wetenschappen 1995, S. 23).*

Der zuletzt genannte Aspekt verweist bereits auf den dritten Vorschlag des Ministeriums.

Professionelle Organisation und Personalpolitik

Das Studium, das der zukünftige Lehrer absolviert, soll bezüglich der Professionalität ein Modell sein für die Art und Weise, in der dieser seinen Beruf einmal ausüben wird. Deshalb ist eine weitere Professionalisierung der Führungskräfte und ein verbessertes Management in den Lehrerausbildungsgängen erforderlich. Das Ministerium denkt zu diesem Zweck an einen obligatorischen Schulungskurs für alle Dozenten.

Auf dem Gebiet der Personalpolitik wird an die Möglichkeit zum Wechsel des Personals zwischen Lehrerausbildung und Schulen sowie an in kürzeren Zeitabständen wiederkehrende Praxisperioden für die Dozenten gedacht. Außerdem muß Platz geschaffen werden, um jüngere Dozenten anzustellen. Dabei sollte auch an Teilzeitanstellungen gedacht werden. Das Ministerium stellt in Aussicht, zeitlich begrenzt besondere Finanzmittel bereitzustellen, falls solche Maßnahmen ergriffen werden.

Neben diesen drei Hauptvorschlägen der Ministeriumsbroschüre „Vitale Lehrerausbildungsgänge" wird ein zukunftsweisender Aspekt angesprochen, der in den letzten Monaten zunehmend in den Vordergrund getreten ist: die Einführung moderner Informationstechnik in Hochschule und Schule, damit die Kinder *„nicht die Analphabeten des kommenden Jahrhunderts" (ebd., S. 4)* werden. Deshalb sollen die vorgesehenen Kooperationsverbände zu Innovationszentren auf dem Gebiet der Informationstechnik ausgebaut werden, um – so wörtlich – *„den Sprung ins 21. Jahrhundert zu machen"*. Diese Zentren sollen speziell die Kenntnisse auf dem Gebiet der Informatik sammeln und entwickeln, beispielsweise den Einsatz von neuen Medien und von computerunterstütztem Unterricht. Für die Planung einer entsprechenden Lernumgebung der Zukunft kündigte der Minister im Mai 1995 die Bildung einer Gruppe von in- und ausländischen Experten aus den Bereichen Informatik und Curriculumentwicklung an.

Diese Expertengruppe zur Beratung des Ministers wurde noch im Jahre 1995 eingerichtet. Sie geht davon aus, daß die Nutzung der Informations- und Kommunikationstechnik im Bildungswesen in drei verschiedenen Formen erfolgt: als Objekt, als Aspekt und als Medium. Als Objekt bezieht es sich auf Kurse in Computerbenutzung oder über Informatik, die weitgehend schon Bestandteile der Curricula an Schulen sind. Ziel ist die Vermeidung von Computeranalphabetismus. Als Aspekt bezieht es sich u. a. auf die computergestützte Gestaltung von Arbeitsprozessen. Ziel ist die Berufsvorbereitung. Als Medium für Lehren und Lernen bezieht es sich auf Simulationen, Tutorien, individuelle Lernsysteme, pädagogische Netzwochen usw. Obwohl zunehmendes Interesse an diesen Aspekten besteht, wird in der Lehrerbildung bisher wenig Gebrauch davon gemacht.

Die Entschlossenheit von Kabinett und Ministerium, große Anstrengungen zu unternehmen, um der Informations- und Kommunikationstechnik im gesamten Bildungswesen zum Durchbruch zu verhelfen, geht schließlich auch aus einem bislang noch nicht veröffentlichten Positionspapier des Ministeriums für Unterricht, Kultur und Wissenschaften vom 10. Juni 1996, das dem Autor vorgelegen hat, hervor. Darin gesteht das Ministerium zu, daß in den letzten Jahren große Anstrengungen unternommen worden sind, um die Informations- und Kommunikationstechnik im Bildungswesen zu fördern. Die entsprechende Hardware ist angeschafft, die Software ist entwickelt und die Lehrer sind entsprechend fortgebildet worden. Trotzdem muß der Staat sich weiter um die Optimierung der Nutzung dieser neuen Technik bemühen, da dieser Prozeß – wie alle Erfahrungen zeigen – sich nicht von selbst trägt. Zu den größten Defiziten zählt die Tatsache, daß neue Lehr- und Unterrichtsmethoden und neue Medien noch keinen Eingang in die Lehrerausbildung gefunden haben. Deshalb denkt das Ministerium darüber nach, die

Zielsetzungen des Innovationsprozesses neu zu fassen und 'Aktionsbahnen' vorzugeben. Dazu zählen die Entwicklung von Software, die Beschaffung von Hardware, die Digitalisierung amtlicher Informationsströme und die Einrichtung nationaler Expertise-, Innovations- und Steuerungsfunktionen. Hierfür sollen folgende Prinzipien gelten: ein integrierter Ansatz, eine nicht von vorneherein festgelegte Dauer, ein offenes Ende bezüglich der Inhalte sowie das Einverständnis der Betroffenen. Es kann mit Spannung verfolgt werden, ob Kabinett und Ministerium alle Betroffenen von der Notwendigkeit dieser Innovationen überzeugen können. Andernfalls könnte es zu einer neuen bildungspolitischen Kontroverse zwischen der Regierung und den auf ihre traditionelle Unterrichtsfreiheit pochenden, mit großer Autonomie ausgestatteten Schulen und Hochschulen kommen.

Bibliographie

Commissie Toekomst Leraarschap: Een beroep met perspectief. De toekomst van het leraarschap. Amsterdam u. a.: CTL 1993a.

Commissie Toekomst Leraarschap: Het gedroomde koninkrijk. De toekomst van het leraarschap. Amsterdam u. a.: CTL 1993b.

Ministerie van Onderwijs, Cultuur en Wetenschappen (Hrsg.): Vitale lerarenopleidingen voor de school van de toekomst. Zoetermeer u. a.: Ministerie u. a. 1995.

Ministerie van Onderwijs en Wetenschappen (Hrsg.): Vitaal leraarschap. Beleidsreactie naar aanleiding van het rapport „Een beroep met perspectief" van de Commissie Toekomst Leraarschap. Zoetermeer u. a.: Ministerie u. a. 1993.

Ministerie van Onderwijs en Wetenschappen (Hrsg.): Educatieve faculteiten. Twede tussenrapportage. Zoetermeer u. a.: Ministerie u. a. 1994.

Ministerium für Unterricht und Wissenschaften (Hrsg.): Informationsdossiers über die Struktur der Bildungssysteme in der Europäischen Gemeinschaft: Niederlande. Zoetermeer: Ministerium 1993.

Ministerium für Unterricht und Wissenschaften (Hrsg.): Das Bildungswesen in den Niederlanden. Zoetermeer: Ministerium 1994.

Organisation for Economic Co-operation and Development (Hrsg.): The Teacher Today. Paris: OECD 1990.

Education and Political Change in the New South Africa

Harold Herman

South Africa is seen by many political and economic analysts as one of the giants of Africa and the gateway to the development of Southern Africa. The stumbling block to the fulfillment of these goals was the highly undesirable policy of apartheid and its undemocratic state. Since the release of Nelson Mandela in 1990 there has been a period of rapid and fundamental political change in South Africa. Centuries of apartheid and white minority rule have since 1990 been replaced by a new political order with a democratically elected government of national unity. The achievement of a political settlement based on universal suffrage and democratic values, without a violent revolution, has been quite remarkable. An interim constitution was approved by consensus between the major political parties, and is soon to be replaced by a final constitution within the five year term of the current democratically elected parliament. Unlike in many other countries where education has tended to assist in maintaining the status quo, education has been a key site of the liberation struggle in South Africa. The new political dispensation envisages fundamental changes in the system of schooling as part of the process of democratization and social reconstruction.

South Africa as a Democratic State

Prior to 1990 a key international concern about South Africa was its undemocratic apartheid regime which denied the black majority of citizens basic human rights, freedom and justice. As the era of democracy dawns in the country, there is intense speculation as to whether the new, democratic constitution will in fact lead to a stable democracy which will meet the aspirations of the vast majority of people in the country.

Attempts to establish democratic rule since independence in post-colonial Africa have had limited success. South Africa is one of the most highly developed countries in Africa and in terms of economic development and infra-structure has the capacity to sustain democratic structures within a liberal democracy. However, given the devastations, inequality, disparities and the breakdown of social structures caused by oligarchic rule during centuries of apartheid, there is some reason to doubt whether a liberal democracy is sustainable in the country.

Before I discuss education's role in democratization, I wish to make one brief argument about the kind of democracy I think is possible in South Africa. I am optimistic that democracy will continue developing in South Africa but that it will take a form different from the liberal Western democracies which tend to be seen as the model to follow. I agree with C. B. MacPherson's distinction in the 1960s between three kinds of democracy, the Western liberal democracy, the communist variant of non-liberal democracy and the underdevelopment variant of non-liberal democracy *(MacPherson 1966)*. The latter has emerged strongly in post-colonial Africa and one is inclined to link South Africa to this category.

This kind of democracy, although adopted more recently, seems to go directly back to the old notion of democracy which pre-dates Marx and pre-dates the liberal state, the notion of democracy as rule by and for oppressed people. Unlike the Western liberal democracies, the underdevelopment variant of non-liberal democracies in newly independent underdeveloped countries traditionally tended to rate equality and community more highly than individual freedom. It makes the criterion of democracy the achievement of ends which the mass of the people share and which are put ahead of separate individual ends. This pre-liberal notion of democracy with strong echoes of Rousseau, is found in many of the statements made by leaders of underdeveloped countries. They find the source of their social ills, of moral depravity, of dehumanization and loss of freedom, in equality. Dignity, freedom and humanity are to be achieved by re-establishing the equality that had been so fundamentally (during the colonial period) taken from them *(MacPherson 1966, p. 29)*.

Liberal democracies have a direct link with capitalist industrial economic systems. Since the underdeveloped nations had on the whole simpler cultures than those who had dominated them in the colonial era, it is not surprising that they resorted to a concept of democracy that goes back to a simpler pre-industrial society.

Democracies in underdeveloped states have in the post-independence phase tended to reject the competitive market society as it was something imposed on them from outside and above. In Africa they tended to opt for single party systems of government foreign to the liberal notion of democracy. South Africa differs from democracies of the underdeveloped variant in that capitalist economic relations are firmly entrenched and the free market operates, albeit predominantly in favor of a privileged sector. A capitalist consciousness is firmly entrenched, even among the black working class who aspire to the goods which racial capitalism has denied them. Peter *Berger (1992)* sees a clear link between liberal democracies and capitalism. He drew heavy criticism from the Marxist left on his views on liberal democracy and its link with capitalism, also his skepticism about democratic socialism.

In a nutshell, South Africa has every chance of sustaining its fledging multi-party democracy, different from the communist variant or underdeveloped variant. However, it will probably not be a epitome of the liberal Western variant, but will share many characteristics. There are significant reasons for difference from the first two variants. The strong capitalist base of the economy, the strong notions of freedom of the press, the avowed pledge of the new government not to lapse into a suppression of basic freedoms perpetuated by its predecessors, and the demonstrated political commitment to a Bill of Rights and transparent government, augur well for sustained democratic practices. The world tide against communism and socialism, the failure of socialist policies in Tanzania, Zambia and Zimbabwe, also the failure of Mozambique and Angola to develop stable socialist societies, mitigate against a socialist future, with at most a social market economy being a prediction for South Africa. Even committed Marxist-Leninists of the South African Communist Party have now accepted the idea of the market, a mixed economy, minimum if any nationalization, and a multi-party electoral system. The pervasiveness of world capitalism and the strong resurgence of agencies such as the World Bank and the International Monetary Fund as influences in South Africa, have strongly impacted on the debates about a future economy and democratic state.

There are however, other reasons why South Africa may not easily become a typical liberal democracy. In terms of the distribution of resources South Africa is one of the most unequal societies in the world at present. The Gini Coefficient measuring the inequality between a country's rich and poor, is 0,66 for South Africa, the highest of the 57 countries in the world for which statistics existed in 1978. Poverty and unemployment are widespread, with the proportion of the total population living below subsistence (measured as the urban minimum level) estimated to be above 50%. Here lies one of the biggest challenges for the newly democratically elected government, the redistribution of resources and wealth under the pressure of rising popular expectations. It faces the classical dilemma of many Third World societies in transition, of fostering social justice and equity without causing a drop in economic growth. It is estimated that the South African economy will have to grow by at least 5% per annum (at present less than 3%

per annum) to accommodate the 350.000 or more people who will enter the labour market annually during the nineties if it is to stem the tide of large-scale unemployment *(Terblanche 1989)*.

Underdevelopment has been a big factor eroding democratic structures in post-independence African states. South Africa has a unique First/Third World dichotomy with an advanced economy, agricultural, social and communication structures on the one hand, and highly underdeveloped urban ghettos and rural sector on the other. The adult functional literacy rate is only 50%. The education profile of the working population is typical of a developing country – 30% have no schooling, 36% have primary schooling, 31% have secondary schooling and only 3% have degrees and diplomas. Yet the white sector of the population has one of the highest rates of access to higher education per school-leaving cohort in the world. The biggest challenge to democracy in the future is fundamentally dependent upon addressing the disparities within education and society at large, the upliftment of the oppressed through policies fostering equity, redress, and redistribution of wealth and land which is to a large extent at present in the hands of the white minority. Samuel Huntingdon saw the world as experiencing its third wave of democratization since 1974 in Portugal, Spain, Greece and Latin America. These countries have become democracies after undergoing a transition process which has often been painful, even traumatic, but which ultimately succeeded in bringing about a democratic system. South Africa is seen to be in a similar situation, in the throes of a process that displays remarkable similarities with those that Spain and Brazil experienced on the way to democracy *(Giliomee 1992, p. 20)*. I think that South Africa will sustain its growth in democracy despite the current economic unevenness and low-level of violence in its society.

Democratization in Education since the April 1994 Elections

Throughout the history of South African education during this century, there has been considerable centralized control over all education which enabled the state to keep a tight grip on educational policy and practice. The racially exclusive education departments, the provinces and the Bantu homelands have resulted in an excessive fragmentation of South African education. Prior to 1990 there were 19 education departments, eleven in African education which produced administrative chaos and prevented the implementation of a single national policy *(Selfe 1990)*. Because of the deliberate fragmentation of apartheid education to the advantage of the white minority, the popular cry of the black majority has been for one ministry of education.

This has now been achieved. There is a national Ministry of Education controlling overall education policy, financial provision and higher education. Control of primary and secondary education has been devolved to the nine new provinces in the country, each with a provincial ministry. The control of education is now firmly in the hands of the black majority population in South Africa.

Margaret *Archer (1979)* contends that the degree and nature of centralization is the most crucial structural issue in education systems. The need to implement far-reaching educational reforms which any new democratically elected government will have to initiate in order to earn legitimacy, will also drive any new state towards centralization of control. Hans *Weiler (1990)* argues that the large-scale decentralization of power is largely incompatible with the manifest interests of a modern state in maintaining effective control. The most significant motivation for decentralization, according to Weiler, is the use of decentralization to defuse and disperse conflict and reinforce the legitimacy of the state. According to Hofmeyer and Buckland all these processes are evident in the South African situation. On the one side there is the demand for centralization to enable policy changes for a democratic, equitable, unfragmented post-apartheid system of schooling, and on the other side a call for decentralized control from oppressed groups seeking greater democratic input into the policy process *(Hofmeyer / Buckland 1992, p. 46)*.

The new government has centralized educational control to establish its power-base and effectively implement policies of redress and equity in the current racially unequal system of schooling. To be democratic this has to be balanced against the need to pass more power to communities and the private sector if they are to be meaningfully involved and contribute to the costs of education. Throughout the years of struggle for democracy in education, civil society structures and community involvement have been mooted as essentials for real democratic participation by the people. It was against this background that the 'People's Education for People's Power' movement was launched after the establishment of the National Education Coordinating Committee in 1986 *(Kruss 1988)*. Civil society structures were to be created to allow meaningful participation in education by all citizens. Central to the success of People's Education is the organization of all sectors of the people to take control of their lives and education. Students, teachers and parents need to build democratic organizations, as well as establish strong working alliances and mutual understanding. It must instill democratic values such as cooperative work and active participation, in opposition to authoritarian and individualistic values dominant in schools during the apartheid era. Civil society structures such as the regional branches of the National Education Coordinating Committee (NECC) and Parent-Teacher-Student-Associations (PTSA's) at schools were created alongside the state structures to ensure the involvement of all people in education.

The former racially-based education departments have been integrated into the provincial, regional education departments. In practice this means the integration of the former White, Colored, Asian, African and homeland departments into one education department per province/region. Implicit in this is deracialization and regionalization of staff and resources in a primary and secondary education structure which will be less bureaucratic, more legitimate and closer to communities it serves, democracy on the ground.

Democratic Values and Principles in the White Paper on Education

In February 1995 the Department of Education of the new National Ministry of Education published its first White Paper entitled 'Education and Training in a Democratic South Africa'. A draft was released for public comment five months prior to the publishing of the final White Paper. The Education White Paper was linked to an earlier government White Paper formulating a Reconstruction and Development Program (R.D.P.) which is a government strategy for fundamental transformation of government and renewal of society. It formulates a policy to address the role of government, the public service and other stakeholders in socio-economic development, transforming government and reconstructing society; also, the strategy of the government for efficient, transparent and accountable management of public resources, long-term strategic planning, capacity and consensus building. It outlines the strategy for meeting the basic needs and creating an environment for a growing and stable economy *(Reconstruction and Development Program 1994)*. President Mandela said the following about the R.D.P. in his Inaugural address in Parliament on 24 May, 1994:

> „*My Government's commitment to create a people-centered society of liberty binds us to the pursuit of the goals of freedom from want, freedom from hunger, freedom from deprivation, freedom from ignorance, freedom from suppression and freedom from fear. These freedoms are fundamental to the guarantee of human dignity. They will therefore*

constitute part of the centerpiece of what this Government will seek to achieve, the focal point on which our attention will be continuously focused. The things we have said constitute the true meaning, the justification and the purpose of the Reconstruction and Development Program, without which it would lose all legitimacy" (Reconstruction and Development Program 1994).

The Education White Paper seeks to enhance democratic values and principles in educational policy and practice such as the following:

1. Education and training are basic human rights. The state has an obligation to advance these rights, so that all citizens irrespective of race, class, gender, creed or age, have the opportunity to develop their capacities and potential, and make their full contribution to society.
2. Parents have an unalienable right to choose the form of education which is best for their children, these rights to include the choice of language, cultural or religious basis of the child's education.
3. The state has an obligation to address the needs of the countless South African families who have suffered under apartheid. It has an obligation to provide advice and counseling on education services and render or support appropriate care and educational services for parents, especially mothers and young children within the community.
4. The over-arching goal of policy must be to enable all individuals to value, have access to, and succeed in lifelong education and training of good quality.
5. The system must increasingly open access to education and training opportunity of good quality, to all children, youth and adults, and provide the means for learners to move easily from one learning context to another. The Constitution guarantees equal access to basic education for all.
6. In achieving this goal, there must be special emphasis on the redress of educational inequalities among those sectors of the people who have suffered particular disadvantages, or who are vulnerable, including street children, out-of-school youth, the disabled and citizens with special educational needs, illiterate women, rural communities, squatter communities, and communities damaged by violence.
7. The state's resources must be deployed according to the principle of equity, so that they are used to provide essentially the same quality of learning opportunities for all citizens. The improvement of quality of education and training services is essential. The rehabilitation of the schools and colleges must go hand in hand with the restora-

tion of ownership of these institutions to their communities through the establishment and empowerment of legitimate, representative governance bodies.
8. The principle of democratic governance should increasingly be reflected in every level of the system, by the involvement in consultation and appropriate forms of decision-making of elected representatives of the main stakeholders, interest groups and role-players.
9. The realization of democracy, liberty, quality, justice and peace are necessary conditions for the full pursuit and enjoyment of lifelong learning.
10. The curriculum, teaching methods and textbooks at all levels should encourage independent and critical thought, the capacity to question, inquire, reason, weigh evidence and form judgments and achieve understanding. Curriculum choice, particularly in the post-compulsory period, must be diversified in order to prepare increasing numbers of young people and adults with the education and skills required by the economy and for future learning and career development, with special attention to science, mathematics and technology education.

Analysis of the Education White Paper clearly indicates that the Ministry is committed to democratic values and principles for the new educational dispensation.

Education and Training in the New Constitution

There is no doubt that the tone and substance of the Education White Paper is such that it supports democracy in education. Yet a situation may arise where the actions of the Ministry of Education may be challenged by educators, parents, students and other societal foundations. The preamble to the 1993 Constitution declares the *„need to create a new order in which all South Africans shall be entitled to a common South African citizenship in a sovereign and democratic constitutional state in which there is equality between men and women and people of all races so that all citizens shall be able to exercise their fundamental rights and freedoms"*.

The government is in the process of examining all relevant international human rights conventions with a view to signing them and, where necessary, amending South African laws which contravene them. These international instruments include a number of conventions which deal partly or wholly with rights to education and the rights of the child. It includes the UNESCO's „Convention Against Discrimination in Education" (1960), the United Nations' „International Covenant on Economic, Social and Cultural Rights"

(1966), it's „Convention on the Rights of the Child" (1989) and also international documents such as the „World Declaration on Education for All" (1990), the Organisation of African Unity's „Charter on the Rights and Welfare of the African Child" (1992). The „South African Children's Charter" (1992) falls in the same category and government has decided in conjunction with UNICEF to draw up a National Program of Action for Children in South Africa, with the Department of Education actively participating in the process.

Chapter Three of the Constitution has clauses which protect individual, group and constitutional rights and freedoms which bear directly and indirectly on education. Section 32 expresses the right of every person to:

1. Basic education and to equal access to educational institutions.
2. Instruction in the language of his or her choice where this is reasonably practicable.
3. Establish educational institutions based on common culture, language or religion, provided that there shall be no discrimination on the grounds of race.

The constitution also makes special provision for the rights of children including the right not to be subject to exploitive labour practices. The White Paper commits the Ministry to an Action Plan for Human Rights in Education and a Gender Equity Unit. The constitutionality of any law or executive act of the government, and the meaning of any constitutional provisions, may be tested in a competent court and ultimately be determined by the newly instituted Constitutional Court. The educational rights of the individual are impressively spelt out in the Education White Paper and this augers well for the future of democracy.

Civil Society Structures in Democratization in Education

The political rhetoric and action programs of the liberation movements during the anti-apartheid struggles emphasized the important role of civil society structures in education. The manifestos and policy documents of the African National Congress, the Pan Africanist Congress and the Azanian People's Organization clearly state the rights of parents, students and the community at large to be active participants in educational structures and decision-making. These determinations are perhaps best captured in the policy documents of the People's Education for People's Power movement of the late 1980s. So for example the rights of Parent-Teacher-Student-Associations (PTSA's) and

Teachers Unions are clearly articulated as instruments to secure participation of educational stakeholders on the ground in educational policy making and practice. These agencies played a very important role in re-establishing educational democracy during the liberation struggle.

However, as the new educational dispensation unfolds, teachers unions and PTSA's are showing signs of not as effectively as in the past, participating in the reconstruction program in education. So for example, the PTSA's in many working class black areas are struggling to fulfill their stated role. The low educational levels, inadequate management skills and the fragile infrastructure of schools hinder the effective functioning of PTSA's beyond the previous levels of the politics of protest. The administrative structures of the new education system at provincial level is not yet effectively in place, and this is hindering the ability of the school management and civil society structures to exercise their key roles in restoring the culture of learning, teaching and sound management in schools.

Constraints in the Advancement of Democratization in Education

This paper has indicated that the constitutional structures, laws and broad educational plans are firmly in place to allow democracy in education to flourish. The structures of democracy are necessary, but not sufficient in themselves. Beyond a democratic constitution, the rule of law and the mechanism of universal suffrage, there must be an acceptance by the people of South Africa of the values and the culture of democracy. In the end, democracy is a way of thinking and behaving, a way of working and interacting with others in society. Critical to its survival is the exercise of tolerance, the right of independent judgment, the right of dissent, the capacity to discuss and negotiate, the use of rational argument rather than rhetoric, slogans and intimidation.

Education has a key role to play in fostering these democratic values in a country where the vast majority of the population (50% adult functional illiteracy and 30% of children with no schooling) have been historically disadvantaged. Democracy and the democratic spirit can flourish only where there is an educated and informed citizenry, and where education itself is democratic in spirit and practice. The challenge is to create this informed citizenry by utilizing the substantial existing, albeit racially skewed, educational infrastructure to the benefit and upliftment of all children and adults who have been denied educational opportunity in the past. All the educational actors should direct their energy, intellect, imagination and will to practical planning of an education system consistent with a democratic, unitary, non-racial, just South Africa. It will be comparatively easy to create the structures that will be necessary, but to create 'new' teachers, 'new' bureaucrats, 'new' democratic citizens and to transform their values, attitudes and behavior, to step up quality and relevance in the classroom will be more difficult and demanding *(Hartshorne 1992, p. 13)*.

Life in the urban ghettos and in the poor rural areas where a large sector of the disadvantaged black population live, is a struggle for survival. South Africans of all social classes have always had great faith in education as a vehicle for social upliftment. However, the ravages of apartheid, the huge disparities in provision of education in the past, will create obstacles for the new educational plan for equity, redress and upliftment of the poor.

Another constraint in the development of a stable school system is the continued militancy of the black youth whose contributions during the liberation struggle was important in the fall of apartheid. It has been difficult for young people to move forward from the campaigns of class boycotts, protest marches and direct confrontation with Bantu education to an era of reconstruction and restoration of the culture of learning. The number of educated unemployed has exacerbated the problem of youth lawlessness and intolerance. The calls of youth for change overnight, the phenomenon of 'immediatism' has put the government and educational system under increasing pressure. The culture of violence as is often seen in the power struggle between the Zulu Inkatha group and the supporters of the African National Congress, has added to the concerns about tolerance and reconciliation.

In conclusion, the legislative structures, goals and policies for an equitable, democratic educational system in South Africa are now in place. The success and quality of schooling, as well as its contribution to society, is however dependent upon the vision, skills and commitment of educators, students, parents and administrators, in a growing economy which can make realization of educational goals possible.

Bibliography

Archer, Margaret Scotford: Social Origins of Education Systems. London et al.: Sage 1979.
Berger, Peter: Democracy and Capitalism. In: Development and Democracy, Johannesburg: Urban Foundation 1992, pp. 1-8.
Giliomee, Herman: Towards Democracy. In: Journal of the Institute for Multi-Party Democracy, 1 (1992), pp. 20-23.
Hartshorne, Ken: Foreword: In: McGregor, Robin / McGregor, Anne (eds.): McGregor's Education Alternatives, Kenwyn: Juta 1992, pp. 1-14.
Hofmeyer, Jane / Buckland, Peter: Education System Change in South Africa. In: McGregor, Robin / McGregor, Anne (eds.): McGregor's Education Alternatives, Kenwyn: Juta 1992, pp. 15-60.
Kruss, Glenda: People's Education – an Examination of the Concept. Cape Town: Centre for Adult and Continuing Education, University of the Western Cape 1988.
MacPherson, C. B.: The Real World of Democracy. Oxford: Clarendon Press 1966. (The Massey Lectures. 1965)
Reconstruction and Development Program (R.D.P.). South African Government White Paper. Pretoria: Government Printer 1994.
Selfe, James: The Present Surplus and the Dynamics Arising and Constraining Change. Current Flashpoints. Cape Town: Urban Foundation 1990 (mimeographed).
Terblanche, Sampie: Democracy in Action. In: IDASA Journal, (1989) April, p. 17.
Weiler, Hans N.: Comparative Perspectives on Educational Decentralization. An Exercise in Contradiction? In: Educational Evaluation and Policy Analysis, 12 (1990) 4, pp. 433-448.

*Das Bildungswesen in den Nachfolgestaaten der Sowjetunion
und die russische Sprache*[1]

Vitalij Grigor'evič Kostomarov

Die Nachfolgestaaten der UdSSR gehören nicht zum Staatsverband der Russischen Föderation, dennoch gelten ihnen weiterhin die Sorge und Aufmerksamkeit Rußlands. Die geographische Nähe, die jahrhundertealte Lebensgemeinschaft, begleitet von einer beträchtlichen Vermischung der Ethnien, die gewachsene Aufteilung von Arbeit und Produktion, deren ökonomische Vorteile für Industrie, Landwirtschaft, Energieversorgung, Transport und Handel sowie die daraus erwachsenen Traditionen, die Probleme der Landesverteidigung – das alles sind Gründe dafür, auch unter den neuen Bedingungen enge Beziehungen und ständige Kontakte aufrecht zu erhalten. Hierzu gehören auch die gemeinsame Geschichte mit ihren Freuden und Leiden, die Leistungen von Wissenschaft und Bildungswesen sowie die wechselseitige Durchdringung der Kulturen. Die russische Sprache ist für die Bevölkerung der Gemeinschaft Unabhängiger Staaten sowie der Länder des Baltikums das gemeinsame Kommunikationsmedium, das bereits seit Jahrhunderten die Grundlage für ihr gemeinsames Leben und ihre Zusammenarbeit bildet.

Auf die Entwicklung der russischen Sprache fiel jedoch auf einmal ein dunkler Schatten, der seinen Niederschlag in der Einstellung ihr gegenüber fand. Diese Situation bestimmt in vielerlei Hinsicht seit dem Putschversuch von 1991 die Beziehungen der zwölf neuen Staaten und der Länder des Baltikums untereinander und besonders ihre Beziehungen zur Russischen Föderation. In der Tat stehen alle an einem Scheideweg. Die Menschen, die früher Staatsangehörige einer Supermacht, sogenannte Sowjetbürger waren, haben bei aller Euphorie über die errungene nationale Souveränität noch nicht ganz begriffen, was es bedeutet, daß sie nun Staatsbürger einzelner Länder sind – das heißt Armenier, Georgier, Ukrainer und sogar Bürger eines solch riesigen Staates wie Rußland. Hier ist eine hypothetisch formulierte Analogie einflußreicher amerikanischer Schriftsteller nicht von der Hand zu weisen *(Choate / Davidson 1995, S. 2)*: Was wäre,

---

[1] Aus dem Russischen übersetzt von Heike Wehner und Gerlind Schmidt.

wenn jeder einzelne der Vereinigten Staaten unabhängig würde? Wieviel Zeit würde es sogar das mächtige Kalifornien kosten, selbständig zu werden, wenn es Wasser vom „ausländischen" Arizona importieren müßte, Öl aus der „ausländischen" Republik Texas und Autos aus dem fernen, „fremden" Michigan? Wie sollte die Bevölkerung damit fertig werden, wenn äußere Umstände dieser Art über sie hereinbrächen, die langjährigen, natürlichen Beziehungen abrissen und dadurch selbstverständlich auch der Lebensstandard stark sinken würde! Überhaupt wäre es alles andere als leicht zu vergessen, daß die Bewohner dann keine Amerikaner mehr wären, sondern Untertanen der nunmehr eigenständig gewordenen Staaten Iowa, Oregon oder Georgia, in denen dazu noch ganz unterschiedliche Staatssprachen gesprochen würden und gegenüber dem früher gemeinsamen Englisch nun eine offizielle Abneigung existierte!

Die gegenwärtigen Lebensumstände, die sich in mehreren Jahrhunderten und über viele Generationen hinweg entwickelt haben, lassen sich nicht einfach wie durch Zauberhand verändern. Durch die Zentralisierung der Macht in der Sowjetära, ja zuvor auch schon im Zarenreich, haben sich einheitliche, dauerhafte Charakterzüge herausgebildet, wenn auch zum Nachteil der nicht-russischen Kulturen und Sprachen. Die Widersprüche zwischen der Bewertung und Wahrnehmung ethnischer Identität in der Sowjetzeit und der weiter zurückliegenden Vergangenheit sowie in den gegenwärtigen Prozessen ethnischer Wiedergeburt sind unübersehbar. Obwohl sich in den mittelasiatischen Republiken das asiatische Erbe, der Islam sowie die Muttersprachen zunehmend ausbreiten, stehen deren Bewohner der Bevölkerung Rußlands innerlich näher als der Afghanistans oder des Iran. Es gibt kein Gleichgewicht zwischen den echten Interessen des Volkes, den Zukunftsperspektiven und dem, was die Zeitungen als sogenannte „Paraden der Souveränitäten"[2] ins Kreuzfeuer nehmen.

Während sich die neuen Staaten ihrer gerade erst gewonnenen nationalen Würde rühmen – mitunter auf eine schizophrene Weise sogar ihrer Überlegenheit – und sich eine eigene Staatlichkeit und Armee sowie ein eigenes Bildungssystem schaffen, berufen sie sich doch eher auf ihre gemeinsame Ausgangssituation, statt auf ihre alten Traditionen

---

2   Anm. d. Übers.: Mit diesen Worten wird auf unterschiedliche zeitliche Abfolgen politischer Selbständigkeitsbestrebungen innerhalb des Territoriums der Sowjetunion und Rußlands angespielt. Bereits im Jahre 1990 erklärten alle Unionsrepubliken der UdSSR ihre Souveränität. Zum Zerfall der Union in der zweiten Hälfte des Jahres 1991 führten die jeweiligen Unabhängigkeitserklärungen der postsowjetischen Staaten. Eine weitere „Parade der Souveränitäten" ist die in den vergangenen Jahren erfolgte Erklärung der inneren Souveränität einer wachsenden Zahl von Nationalen Republiken innerhalb der Russischen Föderation (z. B. Tatarstan).

zu pochen, aus denen sie, wie es scheint, lediglich die Namen, die Symbolik und die Formen der politischen Rhetorik übernommen haben. So gibt es nun anstelle des früher überall gültigen sowjetischen Rubels in Aserbaidschan den Manat, in Armenien den Dram, in Kasachstan den Tenge, in Kirgistan den Som, in Lettland den Lat, in Moldawien den Lei, in der Ukraine die Grivna und in Estland die Krone. Entscheidend ist der Übergang vom dem polit-ökonomischen Konzept der Planwirtschaft zu dem der freien Marktwirtschaft. Die Suche nach einem spezifischen Weg und Tempo der Reformprozesse um jeden Preis führt zum Verlust von Zeit und Kraft, zu unnötigen Kosten und sogar zu Konflikten.

In keinem der neuen Staaten ist eine Sprachenpolitik formuliert worden, die den Anforderungen des marktwirtschaftlichen Handelsverkehrs entspricht, in dem unkomplizierte Beziehungen noch unerläßlicher sind als in Wissenschaft, Bildung und Tourismus (*Michal'čenko 1994*). Alle Länder erklärten die Sprache der jeweiligen Titularnation – jener Ethnie, die dem Land seinen Namen gegeben hatte – zur Staatssprache und begannen, auf die eine oder andere Art und Weise das Russische und die anderen Sprachen zurückzudrängen. Fast wie eine Ausnahme erscheint die Anerkennung des Russischen als zweite Staatssprache bzw. „Amtssprache" und ebenso auch die Akzeptierung der Rechte der anderen Sprachen in Belarus, Kasachstan und Kirgistan. Demgegenüber wurde in Lettland und Estland der Kurs einer sprachlichen Assimilation der andersprachigen Bevölkerung eingeschlagen. Die Gesetzgebung verlangt dort, daß man zur Erlangung der Staatsbürgerschaft eine Prüfung ablegen muß. Dies gilt auch bei Stellenbewerbungen, beispielsweise für Beamte und Mediziner, ja sogar Verkäufer oder Kellner. Allmählich gewinnt allerdings der gesunde Menschenverstand die Oberhand, und sowohl die persönliche Voreingenommenheit als auch die Einstellung in der Öffentlichkeit verändern sich. Hierzu ein ironisch-wohlmeinender Beleg. Seitdem Estland ein souveräner Staat ist, verstehen plötzlich alle wieder Einwohner Russisch, *„die bis zum oben erwähnten Ereignis in der sogenannten 'Besatzersprache' nicht einmal das Wort 'Mama' verstanden. ... Selbst wenn man Sie nicht sofort versteht, lächelt man trotzdem; man hilft und 'souffliert' Ihnen sogar. Sie sind nun in diesem Land kein Okkupant mehr, sondern ein Tourist. Das hört sich zwar gut an, bedeutet jedoch in jeder Sprache ungefähr das gleiche: Sie stellen eine gute Einnahmequelle für die einheimische Bevölkerung dar"* (*Jašina 1996*).

In der Tat ist es so, daß man ohne Fremdsprachenkenntnisse zwar einkaufen, nicht aber verkaufen kann. Aufschlußreich ist das von amerikanischen Fremdsprachendidaktikern entworfene Modell zur Analyse des Sprachbedarfs, das sich auf eine Untersuchung der „Marktkräfte" gründet und zur Bestimmung des Bedarfs an russischen Sprachkenntnissen in den USA erfolgreich genutzt wurde *(Brecht 1995, Kap. 1 und 6)*. Dieses Modell stellt Gesetzmäßigkeiten von Handel, Wirtschaft und Produktion, außerdem internationale und innere Interessen eines Landes in den Mittelpunkt (also Interessen im Bereich von Politik, Militär, Sozialwesen, Wissenschaft, Kultur usw.) und erhebt hiermit Anspruch auf Universalität. Es kann herangezogen werden, wenn es darum geht, in einem Land ein Gleichgewicht von Angebot und Nachfrage für die jeweilige Sprache zu bestimmen. Das heißt, es dient einer wissenschaftlich begründeten Planung der Sprachentwicklung, einer klar umrissenen „Sprachenpolitik". Das Modell berücksichtigt nicht nur die gegenwärtige Nachfrage, sondern auch zukünftige Perspektiven der nationalen Entwicklung und verweist, über die utilitaristische Bedeutung der Sprache als Mittel der Kommunikation hinaus, auf deren ästhetische und poetische Funktion sowie auf ihre Rolle innerhalb des interkulturellen Austauschs. Die Autoren gehen vom amerikanischen Bedarf an russischen Sprachkenntnissen aus (auch was das benötigte Lehrpersonal und die Lehrbücher angeht, die man nur für eine längere Zeitspanne bereitstellen kann). Deshalb haben die praktischen Schlußfolgerungen und Empfehlungen große Bedeutung, ungeachtet der sich schnell ändernden, scheinbar nicht vorhersagbaren Situation in Rußland und der konjunkturell schwankenden Launen amerikanischer Schüler und Studenten.

In der Gemeinschaft Unabhängiger Staaten und innerhalb der baltischen Republiken ist die politische Instabilität für ein solches Vorgehen hinderlich. Oft trifft man auch auf romantisch-naive Vorstellungen über die Wege einer eigenständigen Entwicklung *(Neroznak 1995, S. 107f., Kap. „Ethnopädagogik")*. Der Sachverhalt verkompliziert sich noch durch die Existenz von Personen, die sich nicht im Verband ihrer ethnischen Gruppe aufhalten. Dies war auf dem Gebiet eines geschlossenen Herrschaftsbereichs bedeutungslos. Es kann hingegen innerhalb des Staates einer anderen Nation äußerst schmerzhaft sein, wo bereits die Anwesenheit dieser Menschen ungute Emotionen hervorruft, die im Konfliktfall das Faß zum Überlaufen bringen. Daran erinnern zur Genüge Brennpunkte wie Nagornyj Karabach. In Usbekistan zum Beispiel leben eine Million Tadschiken und in Tadschikistan 1,2 Millionen Usbeken. Zahlreiche Diasporen bilden die 25 Millionen ethnischer Russen, die zusammen mit anderen „Russischsprachigen" (das heißt, Menschen unterschiedlicher Nationalitäten, die aber als Muttersprache Russisch sprechen) außerhalb der heutigen Grenzen Rußlands leben. Die Entscheidung für eine Wiedereinbürgerung in Rußland wird dadurch beeinträchtigt, daß viele in den Ländern außerhalb der Russischen Föderation geboren sind und sich eine Zukunft in einem anderen Land nicht vorstellen können. Im übrigen versiegt der Flüchtlingsstrom bislang nicht.

Ganze Generationen z. B. der Kasachen und Kirgisen wurden auf Russisch unterrichtet und gebrauchten diese Sprache an ihrem Arbeitsplatz und oft auch innerhalb der Familie. Früher störte dies ihre Eltern, weil sie nur die Muttersprache kannten. Jetzt ist es umgekehrt: Die Kinder wollen nicht mehr Russisch lernen, sondern oft nur noch ihre Muttersprache, weil diese in ihren Augen globale Bedeutung gewonnen hat. Es war tragisch, als Familien auf einmal in sich zerrissen (waren doch Mischehen während der Sowjetzeit gefördert worden) und dadurch sogar die allernächsten Verwandten wie Ausländer erschienen. Plötzlich mußte auf die natürlichen Alltagsbeziehungen verzichtet werden. Sogar die Wege zur gegenseitigen Hilfe wurden wegen der Paß- und Visavorschriften sowie der Umtauschbestimmungen problematisch.

Unter diesen Umständen, die von den Erfordernissen der Marktwirtschaft hervorgerufen und durch die Tatsache verstärkt wurden, daß eine isolierte Entwicklung unmöglich ist, bleibt die russische Sprache zumindest als eine „Lingua franca" erhalten – trotz des verbalen Kampfes gegen sie. Es änderte sich im Grunde genommen nur der in Losungen gekleidete, ideologische Gehalt: Früher war sie die „zweite Muttersprache", ohne die es nicht möglich war, die Schüler zu vollwertigen Persönlichkeiten zu erziehen. Jetzt ist sie nicht einmal mehr die Fremdsprache mit dem höchsten Prestige (man spricht inzwischen sogar schon nicht mehr von „Russisch und anderen Fremdsprachen", sondern von „Fremdsprachen, darunter Russisch"). Bedauerlicherweise zieht das die Zerstörung des gesamten Systems des Sprachunterrichts nach sich, was zur Folge hat, daß die Beherrschung der russischen Sprache im ganzen an Niveau verliert.

Angesichts des psychologischen Drucks, der von extremen patriotischen Politikern, der schöpferischen Intelligenz und den Massenmedien hervorgerufen wird, wählen immer weniger Schüler die russische Sprache. Die sinkende Schülerzahl führt zu einer Reduzierung des Bestandes an Lehrern und beschränkt die Möglichkeiten für Praktika in Rußland sowie die Fortbildung auf ein Minimum. Wenn früher die Unterrichtsinhalte an allen Schulen einheitlich waren, so hängt mittlerweile sogar der Fächerkanon von der einzelnen Schulleitung ab, die, je nach Laune, die Anzahl der Unterrichtsstunden für die russische Sprache kürzen bzw. ganz streichen kann. Weil sich die Finanzierung der Wissenschaft und des Bildungswesens überall in einer Krise befindet, kommt die Herausgabe von Wörterbüchern, Lehrbüchern und didaktischer Literatur zum Erliegen – ja sogar der Austausch von Büchern generell. Das betrifft auch die Übermittlung von Informationen in russischer Sprache – von den Zeitungen und Zeitschriften über Fernseh- und Radiosendungen bis hin zur wissenschaftlichen und schöngeistigen Literatur. Die Ausbildung des Lehrer- und Wissenschaftlernachwuchses, der die Versorgung des jeweiligen

Landes mit Fachleuten, die gute Russischkenntnisse besitzen, garantiert, gerät in eine gefährliche Abhängigkeit von den sich schnell ändernden Einstellungen der Menschen, die sich aufgrund der erlangten Unabhängigkeit und Freiheit in einem nur allzu verständlichen Rauschzustand befinden.

Man macht sich aber bisher wenig Gedanken darüber, daß die Muttersprache nicht ausreicht, um auf den Weltmarkt zu gelangen und die aus historischen Gründen unbedingt notwendigen Beziehungen untereinander, zu Rußland sowie zur gesamten Außenwelt aufrechtzuerhalten. Ebensowenig werden die notwendigen Schritte unternommen, um die russische Sprache durch eine andere verbreitete Sprache zu ersetzen, beispielsweise durch Englisch oder Türkisch; letzteres wird in den turksprachig-islamischen Staaten jedoch im mündlichen Gebrauch als von Vorteil akzeptiert.

Paradoxerweise wird ein solches Erfordernis bislang noch nicht wahrgenommen, weil russische Sprachkenntnisse auf der persönlichen Ebene noch ausreichend vorhanden sind. Im Grunde bestehen immer noch die gleichen Funktionsmechanismen wie früher. Ausgenommen ist wohl nur die offizielle öffentliche Kommunikation, in der die russische Sprache aufgrund der schon beschriebenen Politik gemieden wird. Die Auswertung der Umfrageergebnisse, die bei Feldstudien von Mitarbeitern des Vinogradov-Instituts für die Russische Sprache in Moskau erhoben wurden, überzeugt insofern, als eindeutige Funktionseinschränkungen für die russische Sprache nicht feststellbar sind: *„Obwohl Russisch weiterhin die wichtige Rolle der allgemeinen Verkehrssprache im gesamten postkommunistischen Raum spielt, wird dieser Tatsache von den neuen Staaten keine Aufmerksamkeit geschenkt. Die Anwendung der russischen Sprache wird nicht gefördert und noch dazu in solchen Fällen mißbilligt, in denen die negative Einstellung gegenüber der Sprache nur auf Russisch artikuliert werden kann"* (Grigorjan 1996, S. 46).

Die negativen Folgen, die mit dem unwiderruflichen Rückgang der Zahl von Menschen mit guten Russischkenntnissen in nicht allzu ferner Zukunft verbunden sind, werden aus den Augen verloren. Zu einem solchen Rückgang führt aber die Situation im Bildungswesen. Diese Entwicklung wird sich auch in Zukunft durch den Verlust einer Reihe von geeigneten Faktoren fortsetzen, die zur Verbreitung des Russischen beigetragen haben: die Massenmigration, die Mischehen, die „Großprojekte" des Kommunismus, der Armeedienst, das ungehinderte und preiswerte Reisen durch den gesamten weiten Raum vom Baltikum bis zum stillen Ozean (durch elf Zeitzonen!), die Pflege zwischennationaler Maßnahmen und Aktivitäten sowie andere Elemente der Lebenswirklichkeit in der UdSSR. Selbst wenn uns eine Reintegration der neuen Länder beschieden sein sollte – die einmalige Situation der russischen Sprache kann nicht wiederhergestellt werden. Denn sie spiegelte eine ungerechte, in vielem heuchlerische Gesellschaftsordnung wider und war für die anderen Sprachen und sogar das Russische selbst von Nachteil.

Die Gesetzmäßigkeiten der modernen Welt legen eine interkulturelle Perspektive nahe, in der das wechselseitige Zusammenwirken der Kulturen organisch mit einer Festigung der Identität verbunden ist und gleichzeitig von ihr genährt wird (übrigens sind deshalb die Termini „interkulturell" und „cross-cultural" gegenüber „pluri"- oder „multikulturell" vorzuziehen). Beim Versuch, die wachsende ethnische Intoleranz zu überwinden, geht man von einem vielschichtigen, individualisierenden Ansatz der Sprachenpolitik aus. Man erkennt eine große Vielfalt von Sprachsituationen als naturgegeben an, die sich nicht mit Begriffen wie Muttersprache, zweite Muttersprache, Fremdsprache oder auch Staatssprache, Amtssprache, Minderheitensprache, Sprache der Diaspora usw. in einen starren Rahmen pressen lassen. Wissenschaftler und Didaktiker *(Batley 1993, S. 8, 20-22, 46-48)*, die als anerkannte Autoritäten gelten, bestehen bei der Planung von Sprachsituationen auf einem holistischen Ansatz zur Analyse der Motive sowie der Bedürfnisse von Individuen und ethnischen Gruppen, wobei eine krampfhafte Reduktion auf die Muttersprache und die Sprache der internationalen Verständigung – die Lingua franca – vermieden wird.

Mit Ausnahme der eng begrenzten wissenschaftlichen und fachbezogenen Kommunikation (z. B. der Verwendung des Englischen im internationalen Luftverkehr) ist es unnatürlich, wenn Menschen untereinander eine Sprache benutzen, die für keinen der Beteiligten die Muttersprache ist. Von daher wird insbesondere die Idee einer einheitlichen Weltsprache verworfen. Als ein wichtiger Faktor bei der Ausarbeitung von Modellen für die Einmaligkeit zwei- und mehrsprachiger Situationen treten staatenübergreifende sprachliche Gemeinsamkeiten hervor. Wollen sie diese nutzen, so stehen die Bürger dieser Staaten vor der Aufgabe, von der gewöhnlich negativen Einstellung der Regierungen solchen Bestrebungen gegenüber Abstand zu gewinnen. Neben der Erhöhung der Vielfalt im Fremdsprachenangebot müssen auch Vorstellungen und Ansätze weiterentwickelt werden, die darauf abzielen, die Ziele und Anwendungsbereiche sowie die Niveaus der Sprachbeherrschung in der einen oder anderen konkreten Situation zu diversifizieren. So wird berücksichtigt, daß in vielen Fällen in der konkreten Situation eine der Sprachen von „ihrer" Kultur bereits losgelöst ist, daß sie überhaupt nur die Variante eines Prototyps („Emigrantensprache") ist oder nur in bestimmten eingegrenzten Bereichen benutzt wird („Sprache in der Familie", „Sprache der Zuwanderer aus ..." usw., die nur untereinander gesprochen wird, manchmal sogar heimlich). Als ein grober Mangel der Lingua franca erscheint gerade ihr Code-Charakter, das heißt ihre ethnisch-kulturelle Neutralität und somit die Tatsache, daß sie nichts und niemandem zugehörig ist.

Diese Überlegungen stehen im Einklang mit dem beobachtbaren Wandel der Einstellungen zur russischen Sprache und ihrer Funktionen, die die Analyse der bereits oben erwähnten Umfrage zutage gebracht hat: Das vorherrschende Motiv ist jetzt nicht mehr die Heranführung an kulturelle Werte und der Erwerb von Bildung (obwohl auch das ein wichtiger Motivationsgesichtspunkt ist), sondern der Zugang zu kaufmännischen und unternehmerischen Tätigkeiten. Infolgedessen verliert die russische Sprache an Prestige und büßt ihre Funktion als vorrangige Sprache ein. Das Niveau der Sprachbeherrschung sinkt. Russisch frei sprechen zu können wird jedoch als lebenswichtig angesehen. Diese Überzeugung wird von Menschen immer breiterer sozialer Kreise zum Ausdruck gebracht *(Grigorjan 1996, S. 42-44).*

Die konkrete Sprachsituation ist in der Gemeinschaft Unabhängiger Staaten und in den baltischen Ländern zweifellos sehr unterschiedlich. Gemeinsam ist lediglich die Auffassung, daß ein Bedarf an russischen Sprachkenntnissen besteht. Die Dringlichkeit dieses Bedarfs und die Aktivitäten bei der Suche nach neuen Formen der Bildung verhalten sich direkt proportional zueinander. In Kirgistan gibt es bereits seit einigen Jahren eine Slawische Universität in kirgisisch-russischer Trägerschaft. Studenten aller Fakultäten lernen hier intensiv Russisch, erhalten in dieser Sprache eine Berufsausbildung und verbringen ein bis zwei Semester an Universitäten in Rußland. Die Frage, ob es ähnliche Universitäten in Armenien und Usbekistan geben wird, wird sich sicher nicht so rasch lösen lassen. Die russischen Schulen, die beim Austritt der einzelnen Länder aus der Sowjetunion schließen mußten, werden, oft als Privatschulen, zu neuem Leben erweckt – natürlich auf anderer Grundlage und mit neuen Lehrplänen. Dies geschieht auf Wunsch nicht nur der russischen, sondern auch anderer ortsansässiger Eltern. Langsam wird auch die unterbrochene berufliche Kommunikation der Russisten wieder aufgenommen. Diese wenden sich jetzt an den Internationalen Verband der Lehrkräfte der Russischen Sprache und Literatur (MAPRJAL) und nicht nur direkt an russische Einrichtungen.

Es ist vor allem die Verpflichtung Rußlands, die russische Sprache in den Nachfolgestaaten der UdSSR zu erhalten und für deren Fortleben im Alltag zu sorgen. Die Lösung dieser Aufgabe ist auch Voraussetzung für die Entwicklung eines einheitlichen Marktes sowie eines einheitlichen Wissenschafts- und Bildungsraumes. Es waren auch Empfehlungen aus dem neuen Ausland, die den russischen Präsidenten dazu veranlaßten, einen eigenen Rat für die russische Sprache zu schaffen. Inzwischen wurde ein Föderales Programm zur Unterstützung der russischen Sprache für die Jahre 1996 bis 2000 bestätigt, das von diesem Rat vorgeschlagen worden ist. Mit der vollen Finanzierung soll im Januar 1997 begonnen werden. Das Programm zielt auf die Ausarbeitung einer wissenschaftlich fundierten und offensiven Sprachenpolitik ab, die der derzeitigen Situation entspricht.

Neben den dafür notwendigen wissenschaftlichen Forschungsarbeiten (dem Studium der Bedarfsanalyse in bezug auf die russische Sprache, der Analyse von ethnolinguistischen Prozessen und Problemen der Mehrsprachigkeit, der Erarbeitung funktional orientierter Lehrbücher usw.) sieht das Programm konkrete Maßnahmen für die kulturelle und sprachliche Förderung derjenigen Russen vor, die im Ausland leben und für Ausländer, die Russisch lernen – besonders durch Rundfunk, Fernsehen und andere moderne Medien. Das Wichtigste an diesem Programm ist vermutlich die zugrundeliegende Erkenntnis, daß sich die Strukturen und Systeme der Volksbildung sowie die Möglichkeiten der Zusammenarbeit bei der Planung und der Behauptung des Russischen innerhalb konkreter Sprachsituationen im Wandel befinden. Es gibt Vorschläge, das System der Fortbildung für Russisten als Lehrer und Dozenten wiedererstehen zu lassen und gemeinsam mit ihnen eine neue Generation von Lehrmaterialien für Schulen und Hochschulen in den verschiedenen Ländern der GUS zu entwickeln. Es sollen, in Absprache mit jedem einzelnen Staat, von Rußland unterhaltene Sprachzentren für die russische Sprache, Fachräume für den Sprachunterricht und Bibliotheken eingerichtet werden – und ebenso Lehranstalten auf russischem Boden. Große Aufmerksamkeit wird der Ausarbeitung von Tests und Zeugnissen zuteil, die einer internationalen Zertifizierung unterschiedlicher Grade der Beherrschung der russischen Sprache dienen sollen.

Bibliographie

Batley, Edward u. a.: Language Policies for the World of the Twenty-First Century. Paris: Unesco 1993.
Brecht, Richard / Caemmerer, John / Walton, Ronald: Russian in the United States. A Case Study of America's Language Needs and Capacities. Washington, D. C.: National Foreign Language Center at the Johns Hopkins University 1995.
Choate, Liza / Davidson, Dan: Cultural Handbook to the New Independent States. Washington, D. C.: American Council of Teachers of Russian 1995.
Grigorjan, Éduard: Dinamika sovremennych jazykovych situacij [Die Dynamik der aktuellen Sprachsituation]. In: Russkaja Reč', (1996) 2, S. 40-48.

Jašina, Jana: Uezžaja v gorod Tallin [Reise in die Stadt Tallin]. In: Argumenty i Fakty, (1996) 33, S. 7.

Michal'čenko, Vida: Jazykovye problemy Sodružestva Nezavisimych Gosudarstv [Sprachprobleme in der Gemeinschaft Unabhängiger Staaten]. In: Solncev, Vadim / dies. (Hrsg.): Jazyk v kontekste obščestvennogo razvitija [Sprache im Kontext der gesellschaftlichen Entwicklung], Moskva: Nauka 1994, S. 9-28.

Neroznak, Vladimir (Hrsg.): Etničeskoe i jazykovoe samosoznanie [Ethnisches und sprachliches Selbstbewußtsein]. Moskva: Nauka 1995.

Die Werteproblematik in Gesellschaft und Bildungswesen der Russischen Föderation[1]

Nikolaj Dmitrievič Nikandrov

Anfang des Jahres 1996 setzte der russische Präsident, Boris Jelzin, die Aufgabe auf die Tagesordnung, für Rußland eine nationale Idee zu formulieren. Als ich davon zum ersten Mal erfuhr, empfand ich gleichzeitig Freude und Verdruß. Meinem ersten Empfinden nach war es gut, daß ein solcher Gedanke endlich ausgesprochen wurde. Denn das bedeutete vom Standpunkt des Präsidenten aus, daß wir eine Ideologie brauchen, die nicht um der Vorherrschaft allein politischer Ideen willen notwendig ist, welche den Maßstab für alles andere setzen; vielmehr wird diese Ideologie als ein System grundlegender Prinzipien benötigt, die unser Verhalten untereinander sowie gegenüber anderen Ländern und anderen Kulturen leiten. Andererseits bedeutete die Aufgabenstellung zu diesem Zeitpunkt das Eingeständnis, daß die russischen Reformen, die vielerlei Zerstörungen und Verluste mit sich gebracht haben und keineswegs nur Neues schufen – ich beziehe mich dabei nur auf die Zeit nach der Selbständigkeit des Landes seit 1991 –, ohne klare Zielsetzung eingeführt wurden; ja wir selbst wußten nicht einmal, was wir da gestalteten.

Heute ist häufig zu hören, jede Reform im Bildungswesen stoße letzten Endes auf das Problem, daß neue Lehrer gebraucht würden. Skeptiker behaupten sogar, Reformen seien so lange nicht möglich, bis eine neue Lehrergeneration herangewachsen sei. Wie unschön das auch klingen mag, im Kern kommt es der Feststellung gleich, daß die Reformen erst dann greifen werden, wenn die jetzige Lehrergeneration nicht mehr da ist – wenn auch noch unter den Lebenden, so doch nicht mehr in der Schule. Mir erscheint eine solche Ansicht nicht nur allzu pessimistisch, sondern schlichtweg falsch. Denn es ist doch leicht einzusehen, daß die Schule, die zu den stabilsten Institutionen der menschlichen Gesellschaft gehört, ihre Arbeit nicht einfach unterbrechen und auf bessere Zeiten warten kann. Aber das angesprochene Problem ist tatsächlich vorhanden, und mir scheint es im allmählichen Wandel der Werte und Wertorientierungen zu liegen, darunter

---

1 Aus dem Russischen übersetzt von Gerlind Schmidt.

auch der Wertvorstellungen in der Lehrerschaft. Der Wertewandel findet in einem schrittweisen Prozeß statt, weil Revolutionen in diesem Bereich auf der persönlichen Ebene sehr häufig wie ein Zusammenbruch der Welt wahrgenommen werden. Selbstverständlich ist dabei nicht die Rede von einem Wandel des gesamten Wertsystems. So kann zum Beispiel vieles aus dem methodischen Instrumentarium des Lehrers durchaus überdauern, wie gekränkt sich auch die Neuerer unter den Unterrichtsmethodikern durch eine solche Feststellung fühlen mögen. Aber gerade die Tatsache, daß sich in unserem Leben so vieles so stark verändert hat, zum Guten wie zum Schlechten gewendet hat, läßt ernsthafte Schwierigkeiten im Bereich der Erziehung entstehen. Wir können nicht wissen, was für eine Art von Gesellschaft wir errichten werden, wenn wir nicht für solche reichlich vieldeutigen Begriffe, wie Demokratie, Bürgergesellschaft und Rechtsstaat sowie ein lebenswertes Leben für alle, zufriedenstellende Lösungen finden.

Das bedeutet aber, daß auch nicht klar ist, wohin unsere Erziehung zielt, auf was für ein Leben sich die jungen Menschen mit unserer Hilfe vorbereiten sollen. Und ein Stillstand in der sittlichen und moralischen Erziehung ist in der Tat gefährlich. Das vorhandene Vakuum füllt sich sehr schnell. Man betrachte nur als ein einzelnes, aber erschreckendes Beispiel die Art, wie die kriminelle Welt einen „würdigen" Nachwuchs unter den jungen Menschen anwirbt. Im gegenwärtigen Rußland läßt sich mit dem normalen Menschenverstand, aber auch anhand von theoretischen Überlegungen ein spürbares Sinken der Moral in der Bevölkerung erkennen. Zum Nachweis werden gewöhnlich die ständig steigenden Kriminalitätszahlen, besonders unter den Jugendlichen, aber auch die Bereitschaft vieler Menschen angeführt, für ihren materiellen Wohlstand im Grenzbereich zwischen gesetzestreuem Verhalten und Rechtsbruch zu agieren. Aber auch, was völlig mit den Gesetzen in Übereinstimmung steht (präziser: was nicht dem Buchstaben des Strafrechts widerspricht, weil der Begriff des sittlichen Handelns viel weiter gefaßt ist), stößt nicht immer auf Begeisterung. Nehmen wir als Beispiel das Streben vieler, ausschließlich auf dem Wertpapiermarkt zu spekulieren, ohne einer weiteren Beschäftigung nachzugehen, sowie die verbreitete Neigung, Handel zu treiben, während gleichzeitig die Produktion immer mehr zurückgeht. Das kann doch im Endeffekt wohl kaum dazu führen, daß ein in sittlicher und moralischer Hinsicht gesundes Rußland entsteht. Aber was als Verfall von Moral und Sittlichkeit charakterisiert wird, bedeutet seinem Wesen nach einen Wandel der Wertorientierungen unter dem Einfluß unterschiedlicher Umstände auf die Menschen – darunter auch der schlechten ökonomischen Versorgung.

Ein Hauptinstrument der Erziehung – darunter der Erziehung zu Sittlichkeit und Moral – ist das Bildungssystem und innerhalb desselben wiederum vor allem die Schule. In

Vergangenheit und Gegenwart jedoch stand und steht die Schule in ihrem Handeln gezwungenermaßen in einem Widerspruch zwischen den deklarierten Wertvorstellungen (den Erziehungszielen) und jenen Werten, die das Leben selbst den Heranwachsenden im Sozialisationsprozeß vermittelt. Unter diesen Bedingungen erweist sich die Sozialisation gegenüber der organisierten Erziehung in der Regel als der stärkere Einflußfaktor. So lehrt man beispielsweise in keiner Schule das Stehlen; wenn aber das Leben vorführt, daß Diebstahl rasch zu materiellem Wohlstand führt und oft ungestraft bleibt, so sind die Folgen nur zu verständlich. Hier hält auch der Erwachsene nicht immer stand, und was die Kinder betrifft, so ergibt sich für sie häufig nicht einmal ein Problem: Schließlich machen es doch „alle" so, obwohl natürlich bei weitem nicht alle, tatsächlich aber viele – also ist es völlig normal.

Wofür also soll man in einer so komplizierten Situation die Menschen überhaupt noch bilden? Ein moralischer Rigorismus oder Maximalismus ist unter diesen Umständen kaum möglich. Eher muß man sich schon an einem gewissen ideellen Minimalkanon orientieren, den die Gesellschaft insgesamt und die Mehrzahl ihrer Mitglieder als unumgängliche „Spielregeln" akzeptieren können. Aber selbst dieses Minimum festzulegen, ist eine ziemlich komplizierte Angelegenheit. In der pädagogischen Literatur unseres Landes gibt es nicht wenige Arbeiten für die Vorbereitung der Lehrer auf die Wahrnehmung von Erziehungsaufgaben – sowohl allgemein als auch zu einzelnen Aspekten der Erziehungstätigkeit. Die Ergebnisse dieser Untersuchungen haben weitgehend ihre Bedeutung behalten. Durch die Veränderungen in den wenigen Jahren nach der Perestroika ist es zugleich dringend notwendig geworden, das Wertsystem theoretisch zu überdenken und in diesem Zusammenhang die Erziehungsziele der Schule und der Ausbildung von Lehrern in der Hochschule pädagogisch neu zu definieren.

Heutzutage wird der Begriff der „allgemeinmenschlichen Werte" immer häufiger gebraucht. Eine allgemein anerkannte Begriffsbestimmung und, wichtiger noch, einen mehr oder weniger einhellig akzeptierten Kanon von Werten gibt es jedoch nicht. Außerdem schließen die allgemeinmenschlichen Werte die Existenz nationaler und „lokaler" Werte nicht aus, sondern sie bedingen sie geradezu; nur innerhalb eines derartigen Wertsystems kann sich der Mensch entwickeln. Denn in der Tat: „Womit beginnt die Heimat", wenn man sich an die Worte des bekannten, heute allerdings nicht mehr so modernen Liedes erinnert? Sie beginnt bei den allereinfachsten Dingen in der nächsten Umgebung des kleinen Kindes. Und selbst wenn man die Erziehung von frühester Kindheit an politisiert – wie das in noch nicht allzu ferner Vergangenheit der Fall war –, so ist dennoch das Bild des „jetzigen" Führers und, sagen wir, das von „Väterchen Lenin" erst später in die Seele des Kindes eingedrungen. Die Lebensweise der Eltern und Altersgefährten hingegen übt einen beständigen Einfluß aus. Meiner Auffassung nach kann die Herausarbeitung allgemeinmenschlicher Werte nur dadurch erfolgen, daß man sich den großen (historischen) Religionen der Menschheit zuwendet. Diese Möglichkeit besteht keineswegs nur für die religiöse Erziehung. Vielmehr vermute ich, daß dieser Weg sowohl gläubigen als auch nichtreligiösen Menschen, ja sogar „streitbaren Atheisten" offensteht. Von den zuletzt Genannten gibt es freilich nicht mehr so viele. Dies gilt natürlich nicht im physischen Sinne: Vielmehr haben sie sich rasch und geschickt umgestellt.

Die Analyse der Hauptreligionen bringt zwei wichtige Tatsachen zum Vorschein. Erstens liegen die Kataloge positiver Werte (Gebote) und Verbote nicht weit auseinander; zweitens machen nur den geringeren Teil spezifisch religiöse Werte aus, den weitaus größeren aber die dem Alltagsverständnis nach allgemeinmenschlichen Werte. Aber sofort stellt sich eine Frage: Wenn wir durch die Hinwendung zur Religion im Prinzip zu denselben Schlußfolgerungen gelangen wie auf außerreligiösem Wege, brauchen wir dann überhaupt eine solche Hinwendung zur Religion? Dem Gläubigen stellt sich natürlich eine solche Frage nicht. Für den nichtreligiösen Menschen aber ist offensichtlich eine Antwort allein aus pragmatischen Erwägungen durchaus möglich. Ich will versuchen zu zeigen, daß ein solcher Ansatz gemeinhin denkbar ist, wenn er mir auch nicht naheliegt. Die Wertorientierungen, die das Erscheinungsbild des Menschen ausmachen, verändern sich in ihrer Gesamtheit nur sehr langsam. Dies gilt für deren Gesamtheit als ein bestimmtes System, weil in einzelnen Teilbereichen – sogar bei wesentlichen Details – rasche Veränderungen möglich sind. Rufen wir uns nochmals ins Gedächtnis, wie binnen weniger Jahre für halb Rußland eine Psychologie des „Kaufe und verkaufe" akzeptabel wurde; dabei ist es unwichtig, ob es sich um den Verkauf von Millionen Tonnen „heimischer" Rohstoffe ins Ausland oder um den Weiterverkauf eines Päckchens Zigaretten in der Metrostation handelt. Aber der Handel ist ja nicht durch religiöse Gebote untersagt, auch wenn Jesus die Händler aus dem Tempel vertrieben hat.

Das wichtigste – wenn man noch einmal auf diese Gebote schaut – ist zuzugeben, daß Eltern und Erzieher ihnen beipflichten als dem bedeutsamsten Bestandteil eines „Muster-Erziehungsplans für Schüler", auch außerhalb der Schule. Übrigens ist das Buch „Muster-Erziehungsplan für die Schule" *(Mar'enko 1976)* mehr als einmal, besonders in der Zeit vor der Perestroika, wegen seines Formalismus und seiner Rezepthaftigkeit kritisiert worden. Und doch schließen seine Grundsätze in anderer verbaler „Verpackung" Grundwerte der Bibel ein. Diese lassen sich als eine Art verallgemeinerte „Leitlinien der Erziehungsarbeit" in bezug auf die sittliche Erziehung interpretieren. Und das sind Inhalte, Leitlinien, die sich – wenn man die großen Religionen der Menschheit betrachtet – nicht nur über Jahrhunderte, sondern gar über Jahrtausende gefestigt haben. Oft wurden sie bekämpft, hat man versucht, sie durch andere zu ersetzen, aber sie waren bereits ein so fester Bestandteil des kollektiven Gedächtnisses der Menschheit geworden, daß sich dies als ein äußerst schwieriges Unterfangen erwies. Oder aber, selbst wenn ein teilweiser Austausch stattfand, bewahrten die Ideologen dennoch die allgemeinmenschlichen Werte. So schloß der Moralkodex für die Erbauer des Kommunismus viele jüdisch-christliche Werte ein, wenn auch dieser Humanismus natürlich „sozialistisch" und nicht „abstrakter" Art war *(Kommunističeskaja Partija Sovetskogo Sojuza 1962)*.

Etwas früher in unserer Geschichte hatte es auch Versuche gegeben, alles von Grund auf auszutauschen. Genauer gesagt, nicht eigentlich auszutauschen, sondern neu zu überdenken. So analysierte A. B. *Zalkind (1925)* die zehn Gebote des Christentums und machte sich Gedanken, wie die moderne Jugend (d. h. die Jugend der zwanziger Jahre) sich ihnen gegenüber verhalten sollte. Beispielsweise stellte der Autor solche Gebote wie „Du sollst nicht töten" oder „Du sollst Vater und Mutter ehren" in Frage. Man müßte, so meinte er, vom Klassenstandpunkt aus sachlich an die Lösung entsprechender Fragen herangehen. Und daher sei die Ermordung eines unverbesserlichen Feindes der Revolution ethisch gerechtfertigt. Und ehren solle man nur den Vater, der den Standpunkt der Revolution und des Proletariats vertritt. Was einige Aspekte der Sexualmoral angeht, verneint der Autor natürlich, was in der Heiligen Schrift dazu gesagt ist. Die Auswahl des Sexualpartners müsse von der Klassenzugehörigkeit bestimmt sein. Und für Eifersucht beispielsweise dürfe es keinen Raum geben, wenn der Sieger im Werben um die Aufmerksamkeit einer Frau (bzw. eines Mannes) im Sinne der Klasse der nützlichere Mensch sei.[2] Über all dies könnte man lachen, wenn es nicht so traurig wäre. Immerhin ließen sich diese Argumentationen doch als eine moralische und sogar pädagogische Rechtfertigung auch von Massenmorden heranziehen. Aber stellen wir trotzdem die Frage, ob es denn vollständig gelungen ist, die Weltanschauung, das Wertsystem des Volkes zu verändern? Nein, die allgemeinmenschlichen Werte, die jahrhundertelang geheiligten Traditionen blieben erhalten. Zwar kam es aus menschlicher Schwäche oder Angst zu Verstößen gegen diese, sie wurden jedoch vom Volk bewahrt und harrten der Zeit ihrer Wiederkehr – und sie kehrten wieder!

---

2 In einer grundlegenden und erst kürzlich verfaßten Arbeit *(Ravkin 1995)* wurde eine genauere und tiefere Analyse der dramatischen Umbrüche im Wandel der Werte vom neunzehnten zum zwanzigsten Jahrhundert vorgelegt.

Selbstverständlich geht die Zeit dahin, und die äußeren Formen der Anwendung und Erfüllung der alten Gebote verändern sich. So konnte nach dem Buchstaben des alten Gesetzes die Mißachtung der Eltern, die heute niemand mehr beachten würde (der Form nach wohl, nicht aber was den Inhalt anbelangt), streng bestraft werden. Wir wollen dies alles doch lieber zu den Details zählen, die am Grundsätzlichen nichts ändern, nämlich daran, daß die Gebote einen in Jahrtausenden und von vielen Geschlechtern und Völkern erprobten allgemeinmenschlichen sittlichen Sinn haben. Einen absoluten Wert besaßen diese über Generationen tradierten Motive natürlich nicht. Es hat immer Handlungen, Taten und Verbrechen gegeben, die von der Gesellschaft nicht gebilligt wurden. Aber kaum jemand wird abstreiten, daß es für sehr, sehr viele Menschen hinreichend zuverlässige sittliche Handlungsregulative waren, die von entsprechenden moralischen Normen untermauert wurden. Auch gegenwärtig, da es an solchen Regulativen mangelt, kann die Hinwendung zur Religion als einer die allgemeinmenschlichen Werte bewahrenden Kraft dem Erziehungsanliegen nur dienlich sein. So ist zum Beispiel aufgrund allseits bekannter Ereignisse die Autorität der politischen Macht gegenwärtig sehr gesunken, und die Einstellung zur Armee, die vom russischen Volke stets geehrt und geliebt wurde, hat sich spürbar gewandelt. Diese Veränderungen hätten nie solche Ausmaße erreicht, wenn die Erzieher – wie es viele Jahrhunderte hindurch üblich war – sich auf die Autorität der Kirche gestützt hätten, unter der bei jedem Gottesdienst für die „Obrigkeit" und das „ruhmreiche russische Heer" Gebete gesprochen wurden.

Wenn ich der Wertfrage seitens der Religion eine so große Bedeutung beimesse, so soll damit nicht das Gewicht auch anderer Ansätze geschmälert werden, darunter solcher, die vom Standpunkt der Alltagsvernunft oder der pädagogischen Erfahrung ausgehen. So zählt V. A. *Karakovskij (1993, S. 106-113)* zu Recht zu seinem Kanon allgemeinmenschlicher Werte den Menschen, die Familie, die Arbeit, das Wissen, das Vaterland, den Planeten Erde und den Frieden (die öffentliche Ruhe und Eintracht). Zwar läßt sich über die Reihenfolge dieser Kategorien streiten, wenn damit eine relative Gewichtung der Werte zum Ausdruck gebracht werden soll. Wichtiger ist aber festzuhalten, daß der Kanon zu einem Teil mit den oben angeführten Werten zusammenfällt, zum anderen Teil aber einfach eine andere „Ebene" von Werten betrifft, die nur im Rahmen des zugehörigen Wertsystems für das Menschenbild bestimmend sind. Hinsichtlich des Lehrers und jeder anderen beruflichen Tätigkeit muß auch noch eine weitere Ebene einbezogen werden – die professionelle, die sich in einem Berufsbild, einem Ehrenkodex, einem Berufseid usw. widerspiegelt. Im Ausland haben übrigens viele Firmen ihren eigenen Ehrenkodex, und die Verletzung desselben wird streng bestraft *(Richardson / White 1993)*. Zur Berufsethik des Lehrers, die unmittelbar mit dem Wertsystem des Pädagogenberufs verbunden ist, gibt es in der pädagogischen Literatur Rußlands nicht wenige Arbeiten, auf die hier aber nicht weiter eingegangen werden soll.

Eine direkte Vermittlung von Werten durch Unterricht verfehlt in der Regel ihr Ziel. Ein solches Vorgehen wird als Moralpredigt empfunden, die nur dann Wirkung erzielt, wenn die moralische Autorität des „Predigers", zum Beispiel des Lehrers oder Erziehers, unzweifelhaft ist. Wenn man auf eine solche unbedingte Autorität nicht zählen kann – was in der Regel der Fall ist – so bedeutet die direkte Unterweisung, ein Informieren (einschließlich des Überzeugens) nur den ersten Arbeitsschritt. Gleichzeitig ist die Information – namentlich der künftigen Lehrer – ebenfalls bedeutsam, da ja die Tradition unterbrochen war. Nicht nur der Jugend, sondern auch den Menschen mittleren Alters fehlen systematische religiöse Kenntnisse, jedenfalls was moderne Vorstellungen anbetrifft. Dabei muß festgehalten werden, daß der Grund für den Traditionsbruch ein ideologisches Monopol war. Genauso zweifelhaft ist aber die Entideologisierung, wenn man darunter eine Absage an jegliche Form von Ideologie, an einen systematischen Kanon weltanschaulicher Grundideen versteht.

Und dennoch bedeutet die Informationsvermittlung eine Einwirkung auf Denken und Urteil, ja möglicherweise mittelbar sogar auf das Verhalten. Sie kann das Wertsystem, die inneren Überzeugungen des Menschen beeinflussen oder auch nicht – sogar im Gegensatz zur eigentlichen Absicht. Alles hängt von der Autorität des Sprechenden und den bereits vorhandenen Einstellungen des Zuhörenden ab, von der Art und Weise, wie unter den gegebenen Umständen gewöhnlich Druck ausgeübt wird. Beispielsweise wird gegenwärtig von allen Seiten die politische Führung für die zügellose Kriminalität verantwortlich gemacht, und in bestimmtem Sinne wird stets der Obrigkeit die Schuld gegeben, wenn im Lande, der Universität oder der Schule, in der Brigade oder Werkstatt usw. etwas nicht zum besten steht. Genauso wahr ist aber auch, daß die relativ niedrige Kriminalitätsrate der Vergangenheit weithin auf Angst und auf strengen Zwangsmaßnahmen beruhte, die sich nur schwerlich mit Demokratie und Freiheit vereinbaren lassen.

Meiner Meinung nach verfügen wir gegenwärtig über ausreichende Grundlagen, die Werte zu bestimmen, die das ethische Rüstzeug der Gesellschaft bilden sollen oder – weniger pointiert – von denen wir gern hätten, daß sie dazugehörten. Im Unterschied zu den vergangenen Jahren werden wir dieses Wertsystem aber schwerlich in kurzer Zeit dauerhaft in die Köpfe „pressen" können. Das traditionelle Instrumentarium (Gewöhnung, Information, Überzeugung, Einbeziehung in die lebendige Situation) büßt seine

Bedeutung so rasch nicht ein und wird natürlich weiter genutzt. Allerdings darf man keine große Effizienz erwarten, wenn das Instrumentarium, was häufig vorkommt, mit dem System von Anreizen und Bestrafungen der weiteren sozialen Umwelt in Konflikt gerät. Tagtäglich läßt sich im Unterricht die Überzeugung verbreiten, daß der Mensch selbst den höchsten Wert darstellt. Dieser Appell wird sein Ziel nicht erreichen, wenn in der Umgebung Verbrechen und Gewalt um sich greifen, die natürliche Umwelt zerstört wird, die medizinische Betreuung ineffizient ist, die Produktion zurückgeht und die Gehälter niedrig sind.

Da hilft es auch nicht mehr, sich auf den Ausspruch des Protagoras „Der Mensch ist das Maß aller Dinge" zu berufen, insbesondere, wenn man all das bedenkt, was der Philosoph dabei im Sinn hatte. Wir sind schon so sehr gewohnt „verkürzt" und aus dem Zusammenhang gerissen zu zitieren, daß wir manchmal den wahren Sinn eines Zitats vergessen. So verhielt es sich zum Beispiel mit dem Marxschen Satz „Der Erzieher muß selbst erzogen werden", in trivialem Verständnis: „Der Erzieher muß ein gut erzogener Mensch sein!" Denken wir auch an den wahren Sinn des berühmten Ausspruchs von Protagoras aus dem fünften Jahrhundert vor unserer Zeitrechnung, wozu wir den ersten Satz seines Traktats „Die Wahrheit" vollständig lesen wollen: „Der Mensch ist das Maß aller Dinge, der seienden, daß sie sind, der nichtseienden, daß sie nicht sind." Das heißt, alle Wahrheiten und Werte sind relativ, sie hängen von dem Menschen ab, der sie bewertet. Obwohl man dies offensichtlich auch so verstehen kann, daß alles in der Welt in seiner Bedeutsamkeit hinter dem Menschen zurückstehen muß. So wollen auch wir diese Aussage nicht im wörtlichen, sondern in ihrem humanistischen Sinn verstehen. Damit jedoch erkennen wir auch etwas anderes an: Nur nach Maßgabe des Wandels unserer Lebensordnung, wenn in der Tat Gutes belohnt und Böses bestraft wird, wird auch die sittliche Erziehung, die Werteerziehung erfolgreich sein. Der Weg dorthin ist freilich weit. Sehen wir uns zunächst an, wie es gegenwärtig um die Werte in Rußland bestellt ist.

Ausführlicher habe ich darüber in einem Buch mit gleichem Titel wie dieser Aufsatz geschrieben *(Nikandrov 1996)*. Seine Kapitel entsprechen bestimmten Gruppen von Werten: Leben und Natur; Liebe und Familie, Erotik und Sexualität; Kultur und Bildung, Freizeit; Arbeit, Karriere, Eigentum, Reichtum; Ideologie, Politik, Freiheit, Macht. Betrachtet man diese Gruppen von Werten unter der Perspektive, wie einzelne Russen und die Gesellschaft insgesamt auf der Ebene von Umfragen und des realen Verhaltens dazu stehen, dann gelangt man zu dem Schluß, daß sich die Gesellschaft unter diesem Aspekt in einer Krisensituation befindet. Es handelt sich um eine Krisensituation im ursprünglichen Wortsinn, d. h. die Gesellschaft ist sich der Notwendigkeit tiefgreifender Veränderungen bewußt, sie erkennt, daß man nicht mehr dieselbe Richtung beibehalten kann.

So unterliegt der Wert des Lebens augenscheinlich keinem Zweifel – das spiegelt sich auch in öffentlichen Meinungsumfragen wider. Doch muß man die erschreckende Statistik über den Anstieg der Kriminalität im Auge behalten, von der die russischen Zeitungen – sowohl die zentrale als auch die lokale Presse – voll sind. Fügen wir noch die sich ständig verschlechternde ökologische Situation hinzu, ferner das Problem der Ernährung (ihrer suboptimalen Zusammensetzung und – freilich seltener – schlichtweg der Unterernährung) die Preise, die zu den Gehältern der Mehrheit der Bürger Rußlands in keinerlei Verhältnis stehen, den nachlassenden Gesundheitszustand und die in den letzten fünf Jahren deutlich zurückgehende Lebenserwartung und Erhöhung der Sterblichkeitsrate. All dies spiegelt sich wider in den volkstümlichen Maximen „Die Preise sind astronomisch, und die Gehälter stehen in den Sternen" oder: „In der Rubelzone hat das Leben gerade noch den Wert einer Kopeke". Die beschriebene Situation manifestiert sich auch in Massenprotesten der Beschäftigten, die in den aus dem Staatshaushalt finanzierten Wirtschaftsbereichen tätig sind.

Und es ist nur folgerichtig, daß die aus subjektiver Sicht höchste Bewertung des Lebens als eines natürlichen Menschenrechts in den Umfragen nicht mit der tatsächlich gesunkenen Einstellung der Gesellschaft zum Wert des Lebens korrespondiert. Einen gewissen Optimismus erweckt jedoch die Einstellung einer Gruppe von Werten gegenüber, die mit der Familie und der Sexualität verbunden sind. Die Familie ist immer noch wie früher der wichtigste Wert des Menschen, und auch die Liebe gilt weiterhin als natürliches Fundament der Familiengründung. Bedauerlicherweise führt die schlechte materielle Lage der Russen auch hier zur Relativierung. Die Zahl der Scheidungen steigt (in den Großstädten kommt auf jede Eheschließung eine Scheidung, in einigen Städten ist die Lage noch schlechter). Die Familie mit einem Kind wird zur Hauptform der Familie, oder die jungen Paare ziehen es vor, zunächst für längere Zeit überhaupt keine Kinder in die Welt zu setzen. Wie überall auf der Welt ist die Sexualmoral in Rußland ziemlich freizügig geworden. Und in der Tat breitet sich auch die Prostitution immer weiter aus.

Die Einstellung zur Bildung verändert sich; zwar wird die Bedeutung einer guten Bildung nicht geleugnet, in öffentlichen Meinungsumfragen erscheint sie aber nur auf den Plätzen elf bis dreizehn der Werteskala. Und das ist verständlich: Priorität vor der Bildung haben persönliche Sicherheit, Ernährung und Kleidung, Wohnung, Umwelt, Arbeit und Einkommen – Bildung und Ausbildung dagegen werden im realen Leben wenig belohnt. Wenn ein Junge beim Autowaschen am Ufer der Moskva wesentlich mehr Geld verdient als ein Universitätsprofessor durch seine Arbeit, so wird ihn das kaum motivieren, seinen Bildungsweg fortzusetzen. Wenn die junge Generation dennoch zum Weiterlernen tendiert, so wird dies nicht in erster Linie von den Interessen und Neigungen, sondern von der Einträglichkeit der künftigen Arbeit diktiert. Die Kommerzialisierung der Kultur hat sich einschneidend und vor allem negativ auf die Zugänglichkeit von Kulturmustern für die Mehrheit der russischen Bevölkerung ausgewirkt. Was noch erreichbar ist, erweist sich nicht selten als billige Nachahmung, als Kitsch. Wertvolle Kulturgüter Rußlands und der Welt werden für die Russen immer schwerer erreichbar.

Veränderungen unterliegt auch die Einstellung zu Arbeit und Eigentum. Bei der Wahl des Berufsweges wird der Zwang immer größer, auf das materielle Auskommen abzustellen und weniger den persönlichen Neigungen zu folgen. Das bringen öffentliche Meinungsumfragen unter Jugendlichen unzweideutig zum Ausdruck. Ein weiteres, für das heutige Rußland charakteristisches Moment stellt der Kult des Reichtums dar, der faktisch von den Regierenden ebenso wie von den Massenmedien propagiert wird. Natürlich ist Reichtum an sich nichts Schlechtes. Aber angesichts der massenhaften Verarmung der Bevölkerung, niedriger Einkommen und des Rückgangs der Produktion ist es zumeist nur auf kriminellem und halbkriminellem Weg möglich, schnell reich zu werden; die Bereitschaft, um des Reichtums willen solche Wege zu beschreiten, gibt in anonymen Umfragen mehr als die Hälfte der Jugend zu. Was ehrliche, ausdauernde Arbeit angeht, so ist sie, einstmals – ebenfalls anonym – als natürliche Grundlage des Lebens genannt, heute „nicht in Mode".

Ideologie, Politik, Freiheit und Macht – das ist die letzte Gruppe von Werten, über die noch zu reden ist. Heute hat sich erneut die Erkenntnis durchgesetzt, daß eine Ideologie als ein System von weltanschaulichen Leitprinzipien gebraucht wird, über die sich die Mehrheit des Volkes einig ist. Die Schwierigkeit besteht freilich darin, daß einer jeden Ideologie inspirierende Ideen zugrundeliegen müssen. Solche Ideen lassen sich aber nicht im Rahmen eines Wettbewerbs zu einem vorausbestimmten Termin erarbeiten.[3] Nachdem der kommunistischen Ideologie abgeschworen wurde, ohne daß dafür irgendein Ersatz angeboten wurde, befanden sich die führenden Kräfte des Landes und das ganze Volk in einem gewissen geistigen Vakuum. Dadurch wird der Zwiespalt in der Ge-

---

3 Anm. d. Übers.: Der Autor spielt hier auf den von Präsident Jelzin ausgeschriebenen Wettbewerb für die Ausarbeitung einer „russischen Idee" an.

sellschaft noch verstärkt, der das Ergebnis vor allem einer bislang ungekannten scharfen Differenzierung der Besitzverhältnisse ist. Zusätzlich wird hierdurch noch die Mißachtung gegenüber der Macht und den Machtausübenden sowie die Überzeugung vieler Menschen genährt, daß die Machthaber insgesamt korrumpiert seien.

Der Patriotismus stellt in jeder nationalen Ideologie einen wichtigen Wert dar. Vor noch nicht allzu langer Zeit war dieser Begriff bei uns beinahe ein Schimpfwort. Die ungehemmte Lobhudelei für alles, was aus anderen Ländern kam, der Import ausländischer Kulturmuster bei gleichzeitiger Diskriminierung der eigenen Kultur, die Zerstörung der russischen Wirtschaft durch Importe – dies alles trägt nicht dazu bei, die jungen Menschen zu Patrioten zu erziehen, die natürlich auch die ausländische Kultur, Wissenschaft und Industrie schätzen sollten. Gegenwärtig aber wird der Patriotismus, wie die Ideologie überhaupt, schrittweise wieder in seine Rechte eingesetzt – für immer, wie es scheint.

Was die Freiheit angeht, so gilt es, zwei Momente zu unterscheiden. Vor allem gab es in Rußland in der Tat niemals zuvor solche Freiheiten – besonders in den Bereichen von Politik und Kultur – wie jetzt, und den Anstoß dazu hat unbestritten Michail S. Gorbatschow mit seiner Perestroika gegeben. Andererseits wird der bekannte Ausspruch des russischen vorrevolutionären Politikers P. N. Stolypin immer verständlicher: „Armut ist schlimmer als Sklaverei." In Anbetracht dessen, daß drei Prozent der Bevölkerung zur Kategorie der Reichen gehören, etwa zwanzig Prozent erträglich leben und die übrigen sich kaum oder überhaupt nicht mehr das Notwendigste zum Leben leisten können, erscheinen die zahlreichen Möglichkeiten der freien Wahl als bloße Abstraktion.

Letztlich aber soll dieser Beitrag mit einer optimistischen Note schließen: Die Notwendigkeit von Veränderungen wird in Rußland anerkannt; auch ist die Einsicht vorhanden, daß die Werteproblematik bearbeitet und nationale Ziele formuliert werden müssen. Man möchte meinen, daß dies der gesamten Bevölkerung Rußlands, vor allem aber der Jugend helfen wird.

Bibliographie

Karakovskij, Vladimir Abramovič: Orientirovanie škol'nikov na obščečelovečeskie cennosti [Die Orientierung der Schüler auf allgemeinmenschliche Werte]. In: Teorija i praktika vospitatel'nych sistem [Theorie und Praxis der Erziehungssysteme]. T. 2, Moskva: Institut Teorii Pedagogiki i Meždunarodnych Issledovanij v Obrazovanii Rossijskoj Akademii Obrazovanija [Institut für Pädagogische Theorie und Internationale Bildungsforschung der Russischen Akademie für Bildung] 1993, S. 106-114.

Kommunističeskaja Partija Sovetskogo Sojuza: Programma Kommunističeskoj Partii Sovetskogo Sojuza [Programm der Kommunistischen Partei der Sowjetunion]. Moskva: Gospolitizdat 1962.

Mar'enko, Ivan Sergeevič (Hrsg.): Primernoe soderžanie vospitanija škol'nikov. Rekomendacii po organizacii sistemy vospitatel'noj raboty obščeobrazovatel'noj školy [Muster-Erziehungsplan für die Schule. Empfehlungen für die Organisation des Systems der Erziehungsarbeit in der allgemeinbildenden Schule.]. 2. vyd. Moskva: Prosveščenie 1976.

Nikandrov, Nikolaj Dmitrievič: Vospitanie cennostej. Rossijskij variant [Werteerziehung. Die russische Variante]. Mosvka: Magistr 1996.

Ravkin, Zachar Il'ič (Hrsg.): Obrazovanie: idealy i cennosti. Istoriko-teoretičeskij analiz [Bildung: Ideale und Wertorientierungen. Eine historisch-theoretische Analyse]. Moskva: Institut Teorii Obrazovanija i Pedagogiki Rossijskoj Akademii Obrazovanija [Institut für Bildungstheorie und Pädagogik der Russischen Akademie für Bildung] 1995.

Richardson, Michael L. / White, Karen K. (Hrsg.): Ethics Applied. New York: McGraw-Hill 1993.

Zalkind, Aaron Borisovič: Revoljucija i molodež' [Revolution und Jugend]. Moskva: Izdatel'stvo Kommunističeskogo Universiteta Imeni Ja. M. Sverdlova 1925.

Greek Education: Myths and Realities

Ioannis Pirgiotakis

Introduction

Educational debates in Greece are usually highlighted at general elections, while no attempt is made to locate and analyse the educational crisis or to examine its elements and define its problems. After having studied systematically the educational theories and practices of the members of the so-called 'Pedagogic Demoticism' movement at the turn of the century, who mainly dealt with the internal functions of the school and its ineffectiveness, we feel that the only serious and consistent endeavour to assess the Greek educational crisis remains that of the „Educational Committee" in 1957. However, even this was limited to the mere registration of the operational weaknesses of schools as well as to pointing out a number of educational problems; its criteria were inadequately defined and failed to place the Greek educational situation into an international frame of reference.

The present paper will analyse Greek educational policies and practices in the light of 1) the expansion of education in relation to the concept of the human capital theory *(Schultz 1960, 1972; Edding 1963; Picht 1964; Kazamias 1983; Pesmatzoglou 1987; Glampedakis 1990)*, 2) equality of educational opportunity, a concept that originates in the philosophy of enlightenment and was prominent in international educational debates from the 1950s to the 1970s *(Dahrendorf 1965; Jencks 1972; Organisation for Economic Co-operation and Development 1975; Pirgiotakis 1988b)*. In this framework the educational level of the Greeks as well as the extent to which Greek education favoured equality of educational opportunity is explored. Given that educational systems do not operate in a vacuum, but are in continuous interaction with other systems of modern society, the Greek system of education is examined with regards to the occupational structure of the country. In conclusion, an attempt is made to answer the question of whether Greek education faces a crisis or not, i. e. whether this imminent predicament is real or not.

It seems necessary to refer to the distinction between the terms 'problem' and 'crisis' as applied here. A 'problem' refers to a specific condition that influences the function of a particular sub-system and upsets its compatibility with the general system in which it exists. However, the accumulation of such 'problems' might threaten the system as a whole and bring about a 'crisis'. In this respect a 'crisis' is much broader than a 'problem' and it incorporates the latter. The confrontation with and the elimination of one or more of the problems might not necessarily lead to the improvement and reinstating of a satisfactory and efficient system of operation.

Greek Education: Anatomy of Aims and Choices

Functionalist Emphasis until 1960

An analysis of the functions of the school seems necessary for the satisfactory examination of Greek education and the systematic assessment of its aims and choices. And in spite of the divergence of opinions that characterises the work of educationalists and sociologists of education, it is possible to discern four basic functions of education, in accordance with the structural-functionalist paradigm: provision of qualifications and specialisation; social selection; social legitimation and social interpretation *(Fend 1981, p. 13; Lenhart 1987, p. 204)*.

As far as Greek educational reality is concerned, it is necessary to refer to the exaggeration of a well-pronounced ideological-cultural function at the expense of the function of providing qualifications and specialisation. It has to be admitted that the modern Greek school from an early stage onward was marked by a powerful theoretical orientation and was cut-off from occupational reality. This was moreover accentuated by the influence of German Neo-Humanism and the foreign intellectuals who visited Greece, attracted by the ancient Greek monuments. Greek education was, thus, not connected to the realities of everyday life and failed to serve the needs of the society.[1]

---

1 It is underlined that Ioannis Kapodistrias, the first Governor of Greece, influenced by the theories of Pestalozzi and von Fellenberg, whom he knew personally, was interested in connecting education and productivity. However, after his assassination, and the establishment of the Bavarian Dynasty, Bavarian educational patterns were consolidated in Greece and education received a deeply theoretical character and orientation.

This deeply theoretical orientation in the education system of the Greek state of 1830 was not coincidental. It can be shown that ideological processes are prominent in newly established states, or states in transition, that seek a socio-political identity *(Pirgiotakis 1990)*. It might be said that in circumstances such as the above, the school serves the needs of various ideological and political groups that wish to consolidate and legitimise their domination in society by propagandising their beliefs, values and attitudes *(Gramsci 1972)*. The vigorous debates on educational reform that occurred in Greece as a consequence of the establishment of certain socio-political ideologies – the main educational trends were: the conservative, the liberal and the radical – must be interpreted within the above context.

Thus, the practical side of education was overlooked and its links to the socio-political needs of the country were only circumstantial. The efforts of the 'Pedagogic Demoticism' to free the educational system from its barren theoretical orientation and to direct it towards the practical needs of modern society had but a marginal effect *(Terzis 1983, 1988)*. Moreover, the members of the „Educational Society", mainly on account of the language issue, found themselves at the centre of a complex and vague ideological struggle, that failed to tackle practical educational problems and overlooked the occupational task of education. This functional weakness of the Greek educational system has, in our opinion, been the main cause of the current crisis that has, until recently, marked the system.

Furthermore, the idiosyncratic character of the Greek economy must also be connected to these problems of the school. Since the premiership of Trikoupis in the last quarter of the 19th century, a distorted economic course has led, on the one hand, to an oversized tertiary sector, and on the other, to an underdeveloped secondary sector *(Tsoukalas 1988, p. 212)*. The effort to modernise the country without any, or weak industrial development, has left its negative imprint on Greek educational principles and values. Yet, the school has contributed significantly to the consolidation of this particular economic development, for it has failed to produce able individuals, who would have facilitated the application of new methods and techniques promoting badly needed economic development. The particular educational process must be considered responsible for the poor development of farming and livestock units, the development of which could, to an extent, have compensated for the absence of industrial development.[2]

---

2   The perpetuation of the traditional modes of farming posed an obstacle to the expansion of schooling, since this demanded working hands, and children had to leave the school in order to work in the fields.

In this context, the school not only failed to connect itself with the process of production but was also provided as a service for those with no occupational concerns, who wished to expand their education and culture.[3] This is also well manifested by the particularly late establishment of a network of technical education *(Kassotakis 1986)*. And the fact, that the major part of technical education was virtually left to the private sector, underlines the refusal of the Greek state to accept technical training as a form of education and to include it in the public education system *(Ministry of Education 1971, p. 67)*.

Any attempts to accomplish this aim were strongly resisted by the adherents of the humanities who saw it as a means to expand technical education at the expense of classical education *(Papanoutsos 1965b)* and the cultural-ideological process. According to *Kalliafas (1945, p. 81)*, „*technical learning may not be called education, since it educates professionals, not men*". The well pronounced distinction between disciplines, i. e. the overestimation of some of them, and the underestimation of others, is well manifested in this statement.

The entire 19th century as well as the first decades of the 20th were dominated by a tendency to restricting instead of developing educational provision. This is also evident in the small number of academic secondary schools established and the even smaller number of tertiary institutions as well as the complicated system of examinations *(Mylonas 1989, p. 5)*. This certainly did not favour equality of educational opportunity; in this respect another comment of *Kalliafas (1945, p. 89)* should be mentioned: „*It is wrong to believe that all clever children of the working class can enter higher education.*"

Transition of Society and Changing Priorities

At the end of the 1950s, the prospective membership of the country in the European Economic Community began to cause Greek governments' concern, since it was apparent that it would presuppose groundwork and modernisation. Moreover, Greece entered a period of socio-economic transition. This was accompanied by a gradual decrease of the primary sector of production, the share of which fell from 53.8% in 1961 to 30.7% in 1981 *(Stavrou 1985, p. 19)*. Furthermore, a relative increase of the secondary and tertiary sectors of the economy was observed. The above conditions favoured gradual demo-

---

3 A number of children did not work in the fields; they aimed at gaining the secondary school certificate, in order to seek employment in the public sector.

graphic changes that involved mainly a migration from urban and semi-urban regions to cities, by persons seeking employment in the main industrial plants.

It is thus understandable that education had to cope with the newly emerging needs of a society that was in transition, abandoning its traditional elements and adopting new ones. Schools had to cover the above needs and equip the adolescents with new qualifications and skills that were impossible to obtain from the family. All these circumstances made educational reform a matter of utmost necessity for the country.

In 1959, Xenophon *Zolotas (1959)*, clearly influenced by the human capital theory, underlined in an article the vital significance of technical-vocational education for the economic development of Greece. Two years earlier, Konstantinos Karamanlis, the then Prime Minister, had established the „Educational Committee" with the objective to study the country's educational problems and to focus on the founding of state technical-vocational education *(Ministry of Education 1958, p. 7)*.

As was mentioned in the introduction, the educational issues were, for the first time, examined and analysed systematically and consistently. However, it was regrettable that the reform of 1958 that followed[4] shattered the hopes of the committee members, since no drastic measures were taken and the situation remained largely unchanged. As Greece entered the 1960s, educational issues were once again prioritised. Stefanos *Pesmazoglou (1987, p. 77)*, a deputy of the Centre Union Party, referring to educational expenditure, reported that „*the percentage of the educational expenditure in the country's budget was 3.4% in 1948 and 4.8% in 1950; in 1955 it reached the figure of 10.6%, while stabilising around 13 to 15% during the years 1960-1964. Educational expenditure particularly increased from 1960 to 1966, when it reached its highest level of 16.2%*".

At this point, it must be emphasised, that the reform of 1964 was very important to the modernisation of Greek education *(Kazamias 1983, p. 436)*.[5] The reform was initiated by the government of Georgios Papandreou, who saw education as a common good that

---

[4] The main figure of this reform was Niki Dendrinou-Antonakaki. It was the first time, that, through the establishment of technical state schools, it was attempted to link education with production. Yet, the objectives of the reform were never implemented.

[5] There were significant differences between the reform of 1964 and that of 1976. The former was marked by enthusiasm and commitment to educational growth and equality of educational opportunity, while the latter was geared towards the restriction of the educational community and especially that of tertiary education.

had to be enjoyed by all citizens. Papandreou's politics led to an impressive increase in the number of students both at secondary and tertiary level, while the rate of illiteracy decreased sharply: from 14.6% in 1961 to 11.6% in 1971, and to 7.3% in 1981. Moreover, from 1961 to 1981 the number of graduates of secondary schools more than doubled, although, what was particularly impressive, was the number of higher education graduates, which was 124.068 in 1961, and nearly doubled, reaching 210.104 in 1971 and 329.489 in 1981. The 'openness' of the educational system can also be observed in the ratio of higher education students to citizens. In the beginning of the 1960s there were 3.4 students for every 1.000 citizens. This ratio increased to 11:1000 in the 1970s and, despite a decrease in the following years, reached 11.9:1000 in the years 1988-89.[6]

It is highly likely that the policies, that led to the above educational booms owed much to human capital investment theories. The architect of the educational reforms of Papandreou's government, Evagelos Papanoutsos, stated at a conference of UNESCO, that investment in education had the largest and the most secure returns. Georgios Papandreou, the Prime Minister, declared in Parliament that the educational reform laid the foundations for the revival of Greece *(Kazamias 1983, p. 436)*. At a symposium on the newly introduced educational reform, minister Spiros *Papaspiliopoulos (1966)* in his address to the participants highlighted the economic aspect of the educational reform and referred repeatedly to the human capital theory, and especially to Theodore Schultz himself. A few years later, *Schultz's* book was translated into Greek under the title: „The Economic Value of Education" *(1972)*.

The above educational reform was, even at a theoretical level, an earnest attempt to emancipate the educational system from the political-ideological monologue and to establish the badly needed element of specialisation, i. e. to provide for specific knowledge and skills, responding to the occupational needs of the participants. And despite the fact that the opponents of the reform put forward endless political-ideological debates and managed to drag the reformers into them, the reform had some effect in the end and the links of the school with the occupational structure were maintained.

The open character of the educational system as well as the principle of the equality of educational opportunities were also at the centre of the reform, described above. The then Minister of Education Evangelos *Papanoutsos (1965b, p. 280)* stated clearly that,

---

[6] Revised data from the Greek Statistical Service.

„*in real democracy every route must be free and open to all citizens, provided of course that they wish and are able to accept the challenge. It is inconceivable to let in only those that come from influential families, having a title or possessing wealth*". It was probably the first time that the concept of equal opportunity was expressed in the Greek language, and this was put into effect, by means of removing entry examinations at the first level of the secondary school, the establishment of secondary schools in rural areas and institutions of higher education outside the capital[7] *(ibid., p. 367)*.

However, as far as the equality of opportunity is concerned, it must be underlined that the educational reform of 1964, by means of establishing a large number of schools throughout the country, was limited to the abolishment of economic barriers in education. Yet, the leaders of the reform, including Papanoutsos himself, failed to grasp the significance of socio-economic barriers. Papanoutsos may have spoken about schools open to all, 'without walls and roof', as he put it metaphorically, but he did not support the establishment of a uniform type of school common for all *(Papanoutsos 1965a, p. 99)*.

The educational system was seen by the reformers as an unbiased meritocratic mechanism, open only to the able. The ability and intelligence necessary to succeed in education were not considered problematic issues, a fact that is manifested in a widely accepted 'biological determinism' that was taken for granted. The significance of the influence of social factors was presumably neglected as well as the means to implement positive discrimination. Still, the 1964 reform produced results and, in spite of its inadequacies, it would be unfair to ignore its success in ameliorating educational inequalities.

Nonetheless it can be argued, that educational equality in Greece seemed to gain ground remarkably from 1961 to 1981 *(Pirgiotakis / Kanakis 1991, p. 190)*.[8] Specifically, it can be seen that in 1961 the group of scientists and related professionals (physicians, lawyers, etc.) comprised 3.4% of the economically active population and represented 13.5% of the population in higher education; in 1971, the figures were 5.7 and 11.1%, while in 1981 they reached 9.6 and 15.6% respectively. As far as the group of farming

---

7 The Universities of Ioannina and Patras were established and the establishment of the Universities of Thrace, Crete and Attica was planned.
8 Revised data from the Statistical Service of Greece. It has to be mentioned that the statistical reports of 1961 did not include the category „technicians, workers, transport workers", which appeared in the reports of the following years. Instead there were the three different categories: mining workers, workers of transport and technicians, which were later examined as one without question.

and related workers is concerned, rates are not as impressive; farming and related workers comprised to 53.7% of the economically active population in 1961 and represented 25.8% of those in higher education; these figures changed to 28.3 and 16.4% respectively in 1981 *(ibid.)*.

The above mentioned improvement was also underlined by a OECD report that examined the access to education of individuals from various social strata, classified in five groups according to profession. The report showed that the chances of children from families of the 'upper' strata to enter university in 1960 were eight times higher (8:1) than those of children from families of the lower strata, while in 1970 the above ratio changed to 3:1 *(ibid., p. 188)*.

However, it has to be emphasised that the Greek education system continued to restrict educational access for the children of the lower social strata. This can be shown by examining the higher education population in accordance with the educational background of the parents, in particular that of the father. While higher education graduates comprise only 2.6% of the population, their children represent 14.4% in the higher education population; in contrast, the group of illiterates is significantly under-represented with a ratio of parents to students of 12.6 to 1.6 *(ibid., p. 192)*. It is thus clearly evident, that the father's educational level is a very important factor in determining the educational level of the children, while there is a well-pronounced gap between the children of university educated parents and children of illiterate parents.

Women and Greek Education

The education of women in Greece has to be given special attention. What is remarkable in this respect is the steady increase in the number of female higher education graduates over the past decades: thus in 1961 the percentage of women with a university degree was 22.6%. In 1971 it changed to 28.7%, while in 1981 30.5% of the Greek women graduated from higher education institutions. Moreover, there was an impressive growth in the participation rates of female students: in 1961 the percentage of women in the Greek higher education population was a meagre 25.4%, it reached 31.9% in 1971 and 42.4% in 1981. In 1989 the percentage of female students reached the figure of 53% which is particularly impressive.

Yet, the high participation of Greek women in higher education cannot be taken as an indication that gender bias has been eliminated in modern Greek society. This can be seen, if the distribution of female students in the different university departments is examined.[9] Thus, women seem to be over-represented in the departments of literature, in which they reach 85.3%. They are also well represented in the humanities (66.5%), the fine arts (59%) and in law (58.3%). In contrast, women are heavily under-represented in science disciplines, which are supposed to be typically 'male', with participation varying from 25 to 35%. The above patterns seem to be changing, however, bearing in mind that women have currently been entering typically 'male' domains, such as the medical or polytechnic schools, where women's participation (40.8 to 46.3%) tends to equal that of men.

The Relationship between Education and Occupation

An analysis of the relationship between education and the occupational structure goes beyond the objectives of this paper. And although the possibilities of finding a job increase in accordance with the level of education, this does not seem to apply, as far as Greek women are concerned. Thus, the rate of unemployment of women rose despite the increasing number of women graduates *(Stavrou 1989, p. 42)*. It is apparent that the issue has to be examined in greater detail, cross-relating unemployment and the educational level of the unemployed individuals. Yet, it is likely that the role of education in women's employment will be marginal.

At this point we have to emphasise that both equality of educational opportunity and the expansion of education occurred autonomously and independently of the occupational structure. This led to the creation of specific problems with regards to searching for jobs. This has also been manifested in research by the author *(Pirgiotakis 1991)* examining the later decision of a considerable number of young people to become primary-school teachers. The decision to pursue a teaching qualification must be attributed to the difficulty of finding employment by means of their initial degree.

The majority (71.9%) of the group under consideration, come from the lower strata of society, while only 16.1 and 12% are from the middle and upper strata respectively. It might be argued that this type of graduates traditionally used to enter teacher training

---

9   Revised data from the Greek Statistical Service.

colleges in order to follow the teaching profession. But the increased 'openness' of the educational system let these young people acquire university degrees. However, the overproduction of graduates and the increased competition in the occupational structure forces these graduates to go back to teaching, because they are not able to overcome socio-economic obstacles in order to take up remunerative and influential professions. Thus, it can be argued that the large number of graduates has upset the relationship between the system of education and the occupational structure at the expense of the candidates from the lower strata *(ibid.)*.

It is felt that the Greek case can be adequately interpreted through the structural-functionalist model. The social transformation of the Greek society, i. e. the transition from an agrarian society to a modern but relatively underdeveloped one, which began after the 1950s, led to the urbanisation of a large part of the population and the establishment of a diverse system of social roles. This modernisation was also connected to the rationalisation of the organisation of production and the establishment of new values, conditions that required specialisation and division of labour in the society. In this context, the school acquired special significance as the main provider of qualifications and specialisation; its expansion thus becoming a matter of utmost importance.

The socio-economic transformation demanded the establishment of an extensive bureaucratic system with a large number of public servants and other related employees, which had to recruit young people originating from the lower strata, since the offspring of the upper strata could only fill a small number of the newly created vacancies. And in spite of the fact of the expansion of the system of education, that occurred independently of the occupational system, the posts in the bureaucratic system offered employment to the large number of graduates, thus preserving the critical balance between the two systems. Yet, this 'modus operandi' was temporary, and bearing in mind that the public sector has been replete for a long time, Greek society is facing an continually increasing number of unemployed graduates today, an 'academic proletariat'.

Educational Crisis: Myth or Reality?

After the examination of Greek educational policies and their manifestations in the occupational structure, we cannot avoid the question of whether there is really a crisis in the country's educational system or not. It has to be admitted that, considering the issues of educational expansion and equality of educational opportunity, it would be difficult to determine some kind of crisis in Greek education. The rates of increase in schooling and the impressively improved situation regarding educational inequality not only rules out the existence of a crisis but also promises very beneficial developments. In this respect, the designers of Greek educational policies must be given some credit, bearing in mind the very impressive Greek educational record in the European context.

Thus, arguments referring to a drop in the cultural level, despite the increased educational participation, cannot be readily accepted. To start with, assertions about the poor vocabulary of the young people and 'credential inflation' have not been supported by empirical evidence. Moreover, the romantic recourse to the past and the comparison of incomplete and biased data of those schools with today's is an unsatisfactory and misleading way of coming to conclusions. It is likely, that the current system of education can be adequately assessed after twenty or thirty years, when the present pupils and students will be in the position to judge, as we are today.

Even if it one accepts that the expansion of educational provision and the increase of the educational indices might lead to a drop in the quality of the education offered, it is difficult to answer a number of questions: Is an educational system in a state of crisis when it assists a few to attain high objectives, or when is it accessible to the majority with more mediocre targets? What are the criteria of choosing the most appropriate educational strategy? What is academic attainment and what can be used as criteria for its assessment? As long as these questions are debatable, the positive educational indices are a palpable, optimistic element in Greek education and in this respect we cannot accept the existence of an alleged crisis.

And as far as the two basic educational functions are concerned, i. e. the political-ideological and the specialisation function of the Greek school, a well-pronounced bias in favour of the former should be emphasised, leading to the absence of co-ordination between education and economy. Modern Greek education at its initial stages neglected the real needs of the newly established Greek state and due to its classical orientation failed to provide the latter with the necessary equipment to contribute to the economic development of the country by promoting modern production methods in the farming and manufacturing sectors. On the contrary, the system of education emphasised the ideological orientation toward the ancient classical past. By the time education adopted modern methods and principles of providing specialisation and specific qualifications, the training of specialised personnel had begun, without prior co-operation and co-ordination with the occupational sector, leading to discrepancies between graduates and availability of job positions.

The above mentioned conditions brought about another form of inequality, established in the occupational structure, since a direct relationship between the degree holders and the job vacancies cannot be found. As stressed earlier, this condition has basically undermined the lower social strata, since the school, as a basic means of social advancement, loses its social dynamics and gradually becomes unreliable. This, in our judgement, has been the real crisis that currently threatens the educational edifice.

This paper set out to outline the loci, in which the myths and realities of the Greek educational crisis must be sought. Other elements of Greek education have to be the focus of scientific research as well: the curricula, the teaching methods, and generally the dark side of the educational crisis of the country. The unfounded and only theoretical educational dialogue that appears at times when the political parties in government change, portrays education on the edge, ready to collapse, only to be saved by the *deus ex machina* – the new Minister of Education – and assists the confrontation of the crisis. These cases underline a deeper crisis in the conscience of those politicians, who instead of delving into the real educational problems and increasing the educational expenditure, do not hesitate to condemn it to the fate of Sisyphus, sacrificing the school on the altar of their patronage system policies.

Bibliography

Anweiler, Oskar et al.: Vergleich von Bildung und Erziehung in der Bundesrepublik Deutschland und in der Deutschen Demokratischen Republik. Bonn: Verlag Wissenschaft und Politik 1990.

Dahrendorf, Ralf: Bildung ist Bürgerrecht. Plädoyer für eine aktive Bildungspolitik. Hamburg: Nannen 1965.

Edding, Friedrich: Ökonomie des Bildungswesens. Lehren und Lernen als Haushalt und Investition. Freiburg i. Br.: Rombach 1963.

Fend, Helmut: Theorie der Schule. 2. ed. München: Urban und Schwarzenberg 1981.

Fragoudaki, Anna: Technical Education: Difficulties and Prospects. In: Bulletin of the Society for the Study of the Neo-Hellenic Culture and General Education, (1982) 5a, pp. 16-22 (in Greek).

Fragoudaki, Anna: Sociology of Education. Social Inequalities in the School. Athens: Papazissis 1985 (in Greek).

Glampedakis, Michael: Economy and Education. Athens: Ion 1990 (in Greek).

Gramsci, Antonio: The Intellectuals. Athens: Stochastis 1972 (in Greek).

Jencks, Christopher (ed.): Inequality. A Reassessment of the Effect of Family and Schooling in America. New York et al.: Basic Books 1972.

Kalliafas, Spiridion Michael: Reorganisation of Education. A Sociological Essay on the Development of Capable Citizens and Social Leaders. Athens: University of Athens Press 1945 (in Greek).

Kassotakis, Michael: The Failure of Development of Technical-Vocational Education in the Period 1950-1980. An Explanatory Attempt. In: Kazamias, Andreas / idem (eds.): Educational Reforms in Greece, Athens: Grigoris 1986, pp. 21-54 (in Greek).

Kazamias, Andreas: The Greek Educational Crisis and its Contradictions. A Comparative/Historical Study. In: Academy of Athens Abstracts, (1983) 58, pp. 415-465 (in Greek).

Lenhart, Volker: Die Evolution erzieherischen Handelns. Frankfurt a. M. et al.: Lang 1987. (Studien zur Erziehungswissenschaft. 23)

Maier, Hans: Bildungsreformen in Ost und West – eine Bilanz. In: Allgemeiner Schulanzeiger, 17 (1983) 4, pp. 99-104.

Ministry of Education (ed.): Proceedings of the Educational Committee. Athens: The Ministry 1958 (in Greek).

Ministry of Education (ed.): Information Bulletin of the Proceedings of the Educational Committee. Athens: The Ministry 1971 (in Greek).

Mylonas, Theodoros: The Greek Educationists and Their Social Constraints. In: Pedagogical Journal, (1989) 10, pp. 5-38 (in Greek).

Organisation for Economic Co-operation and Development (ed.): Education, Inequality and Life Chances. Vol. 1. 2. Paris: OECD 1975.

Papanoutsos, Evangelos P.: Memoirs. Athens: Filipotis 1965a (in Greek).

Papanoutsos, Evangelos P.: Struggles and Agony for Education. Athens: Ikaros 1965b (in Greek).

Papaspiliopoulos, Spiros: The Economic Aspects of the Educational Reform. Athens: Technological Institute Publications 1966 (in Greek).

Pesmatzoglou, Stephanos: Education and Development in Greece. 1948-1985. The Incompatibility of a Relationship. Athens: Themelio 1987 (in Greek).

Picht, Georg: Die Deutsche Bildungskatastrophe. Analyse und Dokumentation. Olten et al.: Walter-Verlag 1964.

Pirgiotakis, Ioannis: Socio-Historical Course of the Teacher's Profession. The Odyssey of the Professional Teacher in Greece. Athens: Kyriakidis 1972 (in Greek).

Pirgiotakis, Ioannis: I. Kapodistrias and Greek Education. In: Synantisi, (1984) 4, pp. 26-34 (in Greek).

Pirgiotakis, Ioannis: Schulreformen in Griechenland. Köln et al.: Böhlau 1988a. (Studien und Dokumentationen zur vergleichenden Bildungsforschung. 39)

Pirgiotakis, Ioannis: Socialisation and Educational Inequalities. 3. ed. Athens: Grigoris 1988b (in Greek).

Pirgiotakis, Ioannis: Das griechische Bildungswesen im Spannungsfeld von Gesellschaft und Politik. Paper presented at the Conference of the Osteuropagesellschaft, Berlin 1990.

Pirgiotakis, Ioannis: The Odyssey of Teaching. Thessaloniki: Kyriakidis 1991 (in Greek).

Pirgiotakis, Ioannis / Kanakis, Ioannis (eds.): Educational Crisis in the World. Athens: Grigoris 1991 (in Greek).

Psacharopoulos, George / Kazamias, Andreas: Education and Growth in Greece. A Social and Economic Study of Tertiary Education. Athens: Ekke Athinas 1985 (in Greek).

Schultz, Theodore William: Capital Formation by Education. In: Journal of Political Economy, 68 (1960) 6, pp. 571-583.

Schultz, Theodore: The Economic Value of Education. Athens: Papazissis 1972 (in Greek).

Stavrou, Stavros: Das Berufsschulwesen in Griechenland. Berlin: Europäisches Zentrum für die Förderung der Berufsbildung 1985.

Stavrou, Stavros: Adult Education as a Means for the Confrontation of Long-Term Unemployment. In: Adult Education and Training in the Periphery, Symi: Educational Society of Smirni 1989, pp. 18-32 (in Greek).

Teichler, Ulrich: Hochschule und Beschäftigungssystem. In: Huber, Ludwig (Hrsg.): Ausbildung und Sozialisation in der Hochschule (= Enzyklopädie Erziehungswissenschaft. 10), Stuttgart: Klett-Cotta 1983, pp. 59-77.

Terzis, Nikolaos: The Pedagogy of A. Delmouzos. Thessaloniki: Kyriakidis 1983 (in Greek).

Terzis, Nikolaos: Educational Policy and Educational Reform. Thessaloniki: Kyriakidis 1988 (in Greek).

Tsoukalas, Konstantinos: Dependency and Reproduction. Athens: Themelio 1988 (in Greek).

Zolotas, Xenophon: Economic Development and Technical Education. Athens: Bank of Greece 1959. (Archive of Studies and Lectures. 4) (in Greek).

Private versus State Schools:
A Comparison of Their Quality in the Czech Republic

Jan Průcha

Introduction

I would like to begin this contribution with a personal retrospective: I am pleased that since the late seventies I know Professor Wolfgang Mitter as an eminent scholar in comparative education – with his studies concerning also education in pre-war Czechoslovakia, the country where he was born. However, it pleases me even more that I met Professor Mitter on several occasions at which I could perceive the charming impact of his personality. Some of them took place in Prague – the city where I live and work and which he loves (as he often declared) and, therefore, visited year by year.

At the beginning of 1990, just shortly after the 'Velvet Revolution' which has restored democracy in Czechoslovakia, Professor Mitter was the first 'Western' scholar to visit the free meeting-seminar of educationists in Prague. As an organizer of his presentation (and an interpreter of his speech into Czech) I was lucky enough to have Professor Mitter there – a brilliant speaker with a deep understanding of the problems which Czech educational science faced in its development during the totalitarian regime. Thus, he did not try to 'instruct' us on how underdeveloped we were, compared with the standard of science in Western Europe (though we were convinced we were), but rather he tried to discover some positive sides of our education that we were tending to neglect (as a consequence of the post-revolutionary criticism of our past). In some respect, he was a better *Kenner* of the educational problems in our country than some of the Czech educationists. He helped us much – by encouraging our hopes and intentions for necessary changes.

The other occasion, when I experienced Professor Mitter's help, was the VIIIth World Congress of Comparative Education held in Prague in 1992. As I was responsible for organizing the scientific program of the congress, I had (together with several Czech colleagues) a lot of discussions in Prague or in Frankfurt with Wolfgang Mitter, who at that time was President of the World Council of Comparative Education Societies. Both before and during the congress this active and energetic man affected us, the Czech organizers who were sometimes loosing their nerves when having to guarantee such a big enterprise, much – by his considerate and helpful suggestions and recommendations.

Thus, I am pleased not only to read Mitter's scientific works, published with his inexhaustible energy, but also to know from my own experience that this author is a generous, friendly man.

In this contribution I will focus on two points:

- I will describe a new phenomenon in the Czech educational system, i. e. private schools emerging rapidly since 1990.
- I will discuss some findings of empirical comparisons of the outcomes of private versus state schools in the Czech Republic that were conducted in the years 1995 and 1996.

Both parts concern the topic that *Mitter (1992)* once labeled as „*the role of educational research in school reforms*". Sharing Mitter's opinion, I am convinced that educational research can and must be in the service of not only preparing and implementing school reforms but also of evaluating their results, i. e. immediate outputs as well as long-term effects. I can also agree with Mitter's *(ibid., p. 18)* 'warning' that the question of how and to what extent educational research can support school reform is influenced very much by the interrelations between policy-makers and researchers.

This fits in to the present situation in the Czech Republic perfectly. After 1990 great, substantial changes have been made in education (they have been described, for an international audience, in some papers by *Průcha 1993, 1994* among others). However, the assistance of research (i. e. empirical and experimental) for purposes of conducting this transformation of education was, unfortunately, very limited. This was mainly due to the chaotic state of Czech educational research as a result of changes in its infrastructure, limited resources, etc.

Only in the last couple of years some activities of Czech educational research focusing on educational evaluation were developed, i. e. measuring the qualities of educational programs and instructional materials, processes and products *(Průcha 1996c)*. Among them, a comparative evaluation of achievements produced by private versus state schools has been conducted. And this is what I will be discussing in the following.

Private Schools in the Czech Educational System: The Present Situation

Before 1990 there were no private schools in the Czech educational system. Some private schools existed in the pre-war Czechoslovak Republic but they all had to be closed when communists came in power in 1948. Thus, during four decades (1948-1989) the educational system in Czechoslovakia consisted of state schools only. Immediately after the Velvet Revolution some efforts to establish private schools and schools run by churches appeared. At the beginning of the school year 1990/91 the first private schools started their activities. At present (as illustrated below by some statistical data) they represent a rather important sector at some levels of schooling in the Czech Republic.

What Does the Concept 'Private School' Actually Mean?

In Czech educational theory and school-policy there is a common agreement to differentiate between three types of schools according to the founder and/or owner of the school:

- *state schools*, i. e. schools managed by public authorities such as the ministry of education, school authorities in districts and municipalities;
- *private schools*, i. e. schools founded and owned by private persons, stock-holders, private companies, cooperative societies, etc.;
- *church schools*, i. e. schools founded and owned by the Catholic or the Protestant church (since 1997 also by the Jewish community).

On the other hand, in educational theory another concept is used at an angle to this differentiation – and this is 'alternative school'. The concept has been defined *(Průcha 1996a)* not on the basis of who the founder and/or owner of the school is but on the basis of criteria of pedagogical and didactic nature:

Alternative schools are those schools that use curricula and/or methods of instruction which are more or less different from those used in standard schools. Thus, alternative schools are not only private or church schools but also some state schools that offer non-standard educational programs (i. e. more hours for teaching foreign languages, or a more flexible time-table, etc.). In fact, practically all non-state schools are supposed to be alternative (e. g. Waldorf or Montessori Schools) because their educational programs and/or ways of learning and teaching are different from most of the state schools. On the other hand, state schools are supposed to fit a common standard – which is not correct because some of them are highly innovative.

In the Czech educational environment the problems of alternative (and private) schools have been described in two books that appeared under the same title, „Alternativní skoly": the first one *(Průcha 1996a)* focuses mainly on theoretical and comparative aspects of alternative education, the second *(Svobodová / Juva 1996)* to a large extent deals with history and practical aspects of alternative education.

The Development of Private Schools up to the Present

Starting in 1990 the legislative provisions (issued by the Czech Ministry of Education) have enabled the establishment of private schools. It was above all the decree, „Vyhláška ministerstva školství, mládeže a tělovýchovy České republiky ze dne 22. července 1991 o soukromých školách (Sbírka zákonů č. 353/1991, částka 68)", that determined who can found a private school and what the criteria for accepting a new private school as part of the network of the Czech educational system are. In fact, the official requirement for establishing a private educational enterprise are very liberal (following the *too liberal* spirit of Czech legislation after the Velvet Revolution). Unfortunately, there is no precisely defined criterion for evaluating the quality of private schools: The ministerial decree declares – in a rather vague way – that private schools which are accepted into the national network of schools must provide „an education equivalent" to the one provided by parallel state schools.

Public opinion among the Czech population after 1990 also supported the idea of establishing private schools as 'better' than state schools. This idea was strongly promoted by the mass media, in which some journalists described state schools as harmful for the development of young people, as providing traditional and conservative education, etc. whereas private schools were celebrated as the best way for making the Czech educational system healthy and overcoming an old-fashioned way of instruction.

Thus, the survey of a representative sample of 1.216 Czech parents *(Postoje české veřejnosti ke vzdělání a ke Školství 1991)* showed that they had predominantly positive attitudes toward private schools: Most parents were convinced that private schools are an instrument for improving the quality of Czech education, so e. g.:

- 88% of the parents responded that „private schools create a necessary competition for state schools"
- 87% of the parents proclaimed that „private schools probably provide, or will provide in future, a higher quality of education than state schools", etc.

In this atmosphere of parents, the media and even some of the educationists sharing the admiration for and uncritical expectations about private schools, it is not surprising that their numbers increased rapidly since 1990, when the first private schools appeared, till now, when several hundreds of them exist. The dynamics of this development is illustrated by statistical data (cf. table 1 and 2).[1]

The data indicate some specific features of private schools in the Czech educational system:

(1) Though the number of private schools has increased rapidly during the last few years (and this tendency is still continuing) the total number of all pupils attending private schools is relatively low: A total of 95.450 pupils now attend various levels of private schools which corresponds to only 4.3% of the total population (N = 2.211.251 pupils) in the formal school system (without higher education where there are no private establishments).

In this respect the Czech Republic probably faces a situation similar to that of some countries of the European Union. According to the *European Commission (1995, p. 52)*, state schools predominate in most member countries, i. e. over 70% of schools belong to the public sector. The data about the proportions of students in private schools are not available in the source mentioned but there are data published by particular countries.

For example, in Germany (in the former western part of FRG) there were about 4.000 private schools in 1986, attended by about 400.000 pupils *(Führ 1989)*. This, however, represents a relatively low proportion of the total number of all pupils in the formal school system: about 5.8% of pupils in general-education schools and 6.7% in vocational schools. Thus, the situation has been appropriately described by a group of researcher of the Max Planck Institute for Human Development and Education with the following words:

---

[1] All quantitative data in this table and in the following ones have been taken from official statistical surveys published in annual reports by the „Ústav pro Informace ve Vzdělávání (Institute for Information on Education) in Prague.

Table 1: General Survey of Private Schools in the Czech Republic

school-year	number of private schools	increase in number of private schools per year
1990/91	16	16
1991/92	111	95
1992/93	270	159
1993/94	496	226
1994/95	689	193

Table 2: Number of Pupils in Particular Levels of Private Schools[2]

level of private school	number of pupils (1995)	proportion (%) of the total number of pupils at the given level
kindergarten	5.371	1.5
elementary schools	2.471	0.2
elementary schools of art	5.976	2.7
gymnasiums	9.412	7.4
upper secondary vocational schools	42.225	20.1
apprentice-training schools	25.006	13.1
special schools (for handicapped children)	2.006	2.7

„Es ist keine Frage, die Schule der Bundesrepublik ist die Staatsschule ... Insgesamt spricht wenig dafür, im wachsenden Privatschulbesuch Vorzeichen eines grundlegenden Wandels im Schulsystem der Bundesrepublik zu sehen. Vielmehr scheint der zunehmende relative Anteil von Privatschülern nur den Differenzierungsprozeß sichtbar zu machen, der auch im öffentlichen Schulwesen – wenn auch unter der Decke formeller Gleichartigkeit – längst am Werke ist" (Max-Planck-Institut für Bildungsforschung. Arbeitsgruppe Bildungsbericht 1990, p. 140, 143).

---

[2] The Czech *gymnasium* is an upper-secondary school preparing students mainly for higher education.

(2) This evaluation fits the Czech situation perfectly too, with regards to the number of private schools. There is, however, one special feature in the development of the private sector in the Czech educational system. The data in Tables 1 and 2 clearly indicate that the quantitative increase is very dissimilar at particular levels of the educational system.

On the one hand, the greatest number of private schools and their pupils is at the upper secondary vocational-education level in which about one fifth of all students of that level are involved. On the other hand, private basic schools and special schools involve a very small proportion of pupils, i. e. 0.2% and 2.7%, respectively.

There are two possible explanations for this unbalanced development of private schools in the Czech Republic: one reason for the rapid increase of the number of private vocational schools is that they provide those educational programs that have not been offered sufficiently by state schools. It concerns, first of all, private schools that prepare specialists for business and commercial administration, management, insurance industry, banking, tourism, etc. that predominate among private secondary schools.

The other reason is a financial one: the owners of private secondary schools can obtain (besides the regular financial allocations from state resources) relatively large funds from fees paid by students. As *Smolka (1993)* argues, it is not as profitable for founders of private schools to develop their activities at the level of elementary education because there parents are not willing to pay high fees and prefer their children to attend state schools that are free of charge; in contrast, in secondary vocational education parents are much more interested in choosing those schools for their children that offer training for attractive professions (such as computer specialists or hotel managers) and, therefore, are even willing to pay even very high fees for private schooling.

Everything that has been described till now concerns the quantitative increase of private schools in the Czech educational system. However, what about the *quality* of private schools? Are the private schools really 'better' than state schools as parents and some educationists expected?

Quality of Private versus State Schools

The problem called „quality of education / quality of schools" has been raised frequently during the last years among educationists and school-policy makers. The problem has also started to be analyzed at the level of cross-national comparisons as it is apparent from recent publications by the *Organisation for Economic Co-operation and Development* (e. g. *1995*). As yet, no clear-cut definition of the concept „quality of education" exists in educational theory. For practical purposes we have formulated a general definition of the concept as follows *(Průcha 1996b)*:

„*Die Qualität (von Bildungsprozessen, Bildungsinstitutionen und Bildungssystemen, u. a.) bedeutet ein erwünschtes (optimales) Niveau des Funktionierens und/oder der Produktion dieser Prozesse oder Institutionen. Dieses Niveau kann mittels bestimmter Anforderungen oder Normen (z. B. Bildungsstandards) vorgeschrieben werden, und läßt sich daher objektiv messen und bewerten.*"

This approach presupposes that the quality of schools should be evaluated as measured through indicators at four levels (the respective theory and methods have been described in *Průcha 1996c*):

– input determinants, i. e. indicators reflecting characteristics of pupils, teachers, curricular materials, etc.;
– process determinants, i. e. indicators of classroom learning and instruction, characteristics of teacher-pupils communication, characteristics of classroom psychosocial climate, etc.;
– outputs of education, i. e. indicators of what the learners have actually learned in terms of cognitive and affective competencies (knowledge, skills, attitudes, values, etc.);
– effects of education, i. e. indicators of long-term consequences of the results of education in terms of professional qualification, consumer behavior, political attitudes, etc. of the graduates in different types of formal education.

It follows that if one wants to evaluate the quality of private versus state schools (or alternative versus standard schools) a complex procedure has to be applied. This, however, is very rare in educational research and the quality of schools has been measured mainly through their outputs, i. e. students' achievement. Among the various attempts to compare private versus state schools in a complex way, there is, above all, the large-scale investigation conducted in the U.S. by *Coleman / Hoffer / Kilgore (1982)*.

In the Czech Republic, the prevailing opinion was, as mentioned above, that private schools are better than state schools simply because they are different. Many people believed that otherness automatically leads to higher quality and that pupils in all alternative schools produce better achievements than those in standard schools. However, there was no exact evidence about this. It was necessary to collect some data in order to prove or disapprove this opinion.

At present, some empirical studies are available that compare private and state secondary schools in the Czech Republic. We will describe one of them briefly with regard to its methods and results.

Students' Achievement in Private and State Gymnasiums

In Spring 1995 the Czech School Inspectorate (Česká Školní Inspekce) organized and conducted a comparative evaluation called „A Comparative Analysis of Results of Education in State and Non-State Gymnasiums" *(Hradecký / Byčkovský 1995)*. It was a soundly prepared research study with the following characteristics:

The sample consisted of 29 state *gymnasiums* and 18 private *gymnasiums*. The schools were selected from different localities so that all types of socio-economic areas of the republic were represented in the sample. A total of 1.100 students in the final grade (i. e. around the age of 18 years) were studied in the research.

Students' achievements were evaluated by means of written tests that were constructed for mathematics, mother tongue (Czech language), literature, history, civics, and physics. In addition a special questionnaire was completed by students to ascertain some characteristics of the psycho-social climate in classrooms and the style of teaching in both kinds of school.

The results of the analysis were quite surprising:

- The achievement of students in private schools was lower than that of those in state schools. The differences in the students' achievement were found in *all* six areas of testing but most significantly in mathematics and physics.

- The overall achievement (i. e. an indicator summarizing all tests) was significantly higher in state schools than in private schools. For example, among the first ten *gymnasiums* with the highest scores there were nine state schools and only one private school. On the other hand, among the schools with lowest results there were predominantly private *gymnasiums*.

This research can be taken as evidence for the differences in quality between Czech private schools and state schools – at least differences concerning students' knowledge gained in the *gymnasium*. In this respect, state schools have better quality than private schools as documented by *objective* testing. On the other hand, however, the *subjective* assessment of the social climate made by the students themselves as measured by the questionnaire offers another view: students in private schools assess their classroom climate as more agreeable, open and non-authoritarian than students in state schools.

Thus, the results lead to a conclusion that is quite important for evaluating the quality of learning and instruction in private versus state schools:

In state schools mainly classical didactic procedures are utilized with the aim to develop solid knowledge in students. The learning environment in such schools is highly demanding and, therefore, some students perceive it as authoritarian. In private schools, in contrast, teachers use 'progressive' methods of teaching trying to develop, first of all, the personality of students, to encourage their self-esteem, the ability to express their opinions openly, etc. However, such a learning environment is less demanding with regard to students' knowledge – which is then reflected in their academic achievement and, maybe, as long-term effect influencing their professional careers.

Czech Private Schools in International Perspective

Are the differences between private schools and state schools as measured by the above mentioned indicators of quality peculiar to the Czech educational system only, or are they a universal characteristic also existing in other countries?

This question is difficult to answer because comparative analyses (cross-national) of state versus private schools have not been conducted. Besides, private schools have quite different positions in particular countries, depending also on their number and importance in the national education system. For example, as „Key Data on Education in the

European Union" *(European Commission 1995)* shows, the private sector provides for 68% of the schools in the Netherlands, but only 2% in Ireland or 15% in Denmark, etc.

There are, however, empirical studies that present some findings about the nature and effects of the psycho-social climate in certain private schools. In the Czech Republic it is believed (and seemingly supported by subjective perceptions of students as reflected in their answers to the questionnaires) that classroom climate in private schools is „less stressing", „more stimulating to individual development", „creating democratic relations between students and teachers", and so on. Of course, this matter is probably not as unambiguous as some educationists conclude from opinions expressed by students.

Namely, some empirical evidence has been published that indicates that the 'ideology' which dominates in private schools can have some negative consequences. Among others, *Everhart (1985)*, in California, has conducted a comparative study of some state and private schools. They were observed for a relatively long period (a whole school-year) with the aim to evaluate, how particular schools stimulate the psychological and social development of the students. Everhart describes an interesting phenomenon which he calls „possessive individualism". It is, briefly put, the attitude developed in young people that all that they have learned is a result of their own abilities and efforts and, therefore, all the subject knowledge, skills, etc. are in their own possession. With respect to classroom instruction this ideology leads teachers in private schools to create a very liberal environment for students, not demanding from them too much with regards to academic achievements but focusing rather on encouraging students' self-esteem.

Everhart and others maintain that this ideology of some private schools, with high degrees of 'freedom' in student – teacher relations can result in some negative consequences, e. g. losing the feeling for authority necessary for the functioning of any organization, i. e. of school as well.

Thus, we can conclude this paper with the statement that the results and effects of private schools are not quite clear, and probably not only in Czech education. It means that the problem of quality of private versus state schools has not been solved as yet. As Wolfgang Mitter states in one of his papers, we now live in a revolutionary period of educational changes in which not only curricula but also the 'ethos' of schools must be innovated. Comparative studies on private versus state schools – or alternative versus standard schools – represent a field in which educational research has to analyze and evaluate the changes brought about.

Bibliography

Coleman, James S. / Hoffer, Thomas / Kilgore, Sally: High School Achievement. Public, Catholic, and Private Schools Compared. New York: Basic Books 1982.
European Commission (ed.): Key Data on Education in the European Union. Brussels: EC 1995.
Everhart, Robert B.: On Feeling Good about Oneself. Practical Ideology in Schools of Choice. In: Sociology of Education, 58 (1985) 4, pp. 251-260.
Führ, Christoph: Schulen und Hochschulen in der Bundesrepublik Deutschland. Bildungspolitik und Bildungssystem – Ein Überblick. Köln et al.: Böhlau 1989. (Studien und Dokumentationen zur deutschen Bildungsgeschichte. 39)
Hradecký, Václav / Byčkovský, Petr: Srovnávací analýza výsledků vzdělávání na státních a nestátních gymnáziích [A Comparative Analysis of Results of Education in State and Non-State Gymnasiums]. Praha: Česká Školní Inspekce 1995.
Max-Planck-Institut für Bildungsforschung. Arbeitsgruppe Bildungsbericht: Das Bildungswesen in der Bundesrepublik Deutschland. Strukturen und Entwicklungen im Überblick. Reinbek: Rowohlt Taschenbuch-Verlag 1990.
Mitter, Wolfgang: Unity and Diversity. A Basic Issue of European History and its Impact on Education. In: idem / Weiss, Manfred / Schaefer, Ulrich (eds.): Recent Trends in Eastern European Education, Frankfurt a. M.: German Institute for International Educational Research 1992, pp. 17-26.
Organisation for Economic Co-operation and Development (ed.): Measuring the Quality of Schools. Paris: OECD 1995.
Postoje české veřejnosti ke vzdělání a ke školství [Attitudes of the Czech Public towards Education and Schools]. Praha: AISA 1991.
Průcha, Jan: Transformation of Education in the Czech Republic. Urgent Requirements for Educational Research. In: Benner, Dietrich / Schriewer, Jürgen / Tenorth, Heinz-Elmar (eds.): Strukturwandel deutscher Bildungswirklichkeit (= Arbeitstexte. 1), Berlin: Humboldt-Universität, Institut für Allgemeine Pädagogik 1993, pp. 141-153.
Průcha, Jan: School Reform in the Czech Republic. The Problem of National Standards. In: Rust, Val D. et al. (eds.): Education and the Values Crisis in Central and Eastern Europe (= Comparative Studies Series. 4), Frankfurt a. M. et al.: Lang 1994, pp. 107-118.
Průcha, Jan: Alternativní školy [Alternative Schools]. Praha: Portál 1996a.
Průcha, Jan: Evaluation der Qualität der Schulen aus der Sicht der Forschung. Vortrag auf der Konferenz „Autonome Entwicklung der Schulen – Suche nach neuen Perspektiven", Brno, 25.-27. November 1996b.
Průcha, Jan: Pedagogická evaluace [Educational Evaluation]. Brno: Masarykova Univerzita 1996c.
Smolka, Radovan: Soukromé školy – iluze a skutečnost [Private Schools – Illusions and Reality of the Contemporary School System]. In: Průcha, Jan et al. (eds.): Pedagogický výzkum a transformace české školy, Praha: Česka Asociace Pedagogického Vyzkumu 1993, pp. 178-182.
Svobodová, Jarmila / Juva, Vladimir: Alternativní školy [Alternative Schools]. Brno: Paido 1996.

Das Orthodoxe Klassische Gymnasium in Moskau

Bernhard Schiff

Der Zusammenbruch des sowjetkommunistischen Systems hat eine Reihe von Reformen im Bildungswesen der ehemaligen Sowjetunion ausgelöst. Die russische Schule – und auf diese bleiben die nachfolgenden Ausführungen bezogen – befindet sich seit der Auflösung der Sowjetunion in einem fortwährenden Wandel. Diese Entwicklung ist gekennzeichnet durch eine zunehmende Demokratisierung der Schule, die ihren Ausdruck in der Verlagerung der Kompetenzen von der zentralen auf die regionale und lokale Ebene der Bildungsverwaltung findet. In der Schule selbst werden Lehrern und Eltern immer mehr Mitspracherechte bei der Regelung der Schulangelegenheiten eingeräumt, bis hin zur Mitbestimmung der Lehrplaninhalte. Ein weiteres Merkmal dieses Demokratisierungsprozesses ist die Entstehung neuer Schulformen und -typen, zu denen auch Privatschulen mit unterschiedlichen Bildungsschwerpunkten gehören.

Diese Entwicklung bietet eine einmalige Chance, das als Erbe der Vergangenheit übernommene erstarrte Schulsystem der untergegangenen Sowjetunion durch ein flexibles, den differenzierten Bedürfnissen einer freien Gesellschaft angemessenes Schulwesen abzulösen, das der Bildungsnachfrage unterschiedlicher gesellschaftlicher Gruppierungen Rechnung trägt. Dieser hoffnungsvollen Situation steht jedoch die Tatsache gegenüber, daß nach der Beseitigung des Monopols der kommunistischen Partei auf die Bestimmung der Bildungs- und Erziehungsziele der Jugend ein Vakuum entstanden ist, das nunmehr mit neuen Wertvorstellungen gefüllt werden muß, die eine Neuorientierung der schulischen Bildung und Erziehung ermöglichen.

Ungeachtet aller Verwirrung und Unsicherheit, die der Zusammenbruch der alten Ordnung mit sich gebracht hat, sind in der russischen Gesellschaft Ordnungskräfte und Orientierungsmuster vorhanden, die dem einzelnen Halt und Zukunftsorientierung bei seiner Lebensgestaltung zu geben vermögen. Hier ist an erster Stelle die russisch-orthodoxe Kirche zu nennen, die trotz ihres an Verfolgungen reichen wechselvollen Schicksals das Weltbild der russischen Orthodoxie und die christlich-orthodoxe Ethik bewahrt und überliefert hat. Trotz ihrer traditionellen politischen Abstinenz beginnt die russische Kirche, eine neue und wichtige Rolle als moralische Instanz in der postsowjetischen Gesellschaft zu spielen. In diesem Zusammenhang ist zu fragen, welchen Beitrag das russisch-orthodoxe Christentum zur Neuorientierung der russischen Schule zu leisten vermag. Eine Antwort auf diese Frage zu geben, versucht das Orthodoxe Klassische Gymnasium, das 1990 in Moskau gegründet wurde.

Im folgenden soll über diese Schule berichtet werden.[1] Der vorliegende Beitrag versteht sich dabei als ein Kurzbericht und erhebt keinen Anspruch darauf, eine wissenschaftliche Analyse zu sein.

Das Orthodoxe Klassische Gymnasium wurde im September 1990 im Moskauer Stadtbezirk Jassenevo eröffnet. Gründer und Kurator der Schule ist die Gesellschaft „Radonež", eine orthodoxe Laienvereinigung, die sich der Unterstützung und Verbreitung des orthodoxen Glaubens widmet und deren besondere Verehrung dem heiligen Sergius von Radonež (1314?-1392), dem Gründer zahlreicher Klöster im Norden von Moskau, gilt.

Im Gründungsjahr 1990 wurde das Gymnasium von 1 100 Schülern besucht, die außer im zentralen Gebäude in Jassenevo in drei Zweigstellen in den Stadtteilen Saburovo, Botaničeskij Sad und Krylantkoe unterrichtet wurden. Das Gymnasium nimmt Schüler unabhängig von ihrer Zugehörigkeit zum orthodoxen Glauben auf, informiert jedoch deren Eltern ausführlich über die Grundlagen der angestrebten Bildung und verlangt von ihnen das Einverständnis mit dem Unterricht nach den vom Gymnasium entwickelten Lehrplänen.

Das Gymnasium hat den Status einer Privatschule und ist als solche bei der Schulbehörde registriert. Die Finanzierung erfolgte im Jahr der Gründung durch Spenden und Schulgelder. Finanzielle Unterstützung von staatlicher Seite wurde abgelehnt.

Das Gymnasium umfaßt die Schuljahre 1 bis 11 und ist in zwei Stufen gegliedert: zu der ersten gehören die Klassen 1 bis 5, zu der zweiten die Klassen 6 bis 11.

---

1 Der Bericht über das Orthodoxe Klassische Gymnasium in Moskau stützt sich auf folgende Quellen: 1. Informationsmaterialien der Gesellschaft „Radonež"; 2. Video-Mitschnitte der Interviews mit dem Direktor und den Lehrern des Orthodoxen Klassischen Gymnasiums über die Ziele des Unterrichts; 3. Videoaufnahmen des Unterrichts und außerunterrichtlicher Aktivitäten im Gymnasium; 4. Gespräche mit Eltern, deren Kinder das Orthodoxe Klassische Gymnasium besucht haben.

Die Schulgründer mußten sich bei der Auswahl der ersten Lehrer zunächst auf ihren unmittelbaren Eindruck verlassen. Inzwischen wurden von der Gesellschaft „Radonež" gemeinsam mit der Interrepublikanischen Orthodoxen Pädagogischen Gesellschaft und mit Beteiligung des Orthodoxen Klassischen Gymnasiums Lehrerfortbildungskurse eingerichtet, die Lehrer auf den Unterricht im Orthodoxen Klassischen Gymnasium vorbereiten sollen.

Die Lehrziele des Gymnasiums werden von der Gesellschaft „Radonež" wie folgt beschrieben:

„The teaching in the Gymnasium has the goal to give to the students a comprehensive humanitarian education based on the Christian system of ethics. The main discipline in the Gymnasium are the 'Foundations of Orthodox Culture'. Thus the Orthodox Classical Gymnasium suggests to the students a special humanitarian education oriented to the admission to humanitarian higher educational institutions. Its essential aim is the moral education and the spiritual promotion of the student's personality as well as the formation of their civic and patriotic self-consciousness. Those main pedagogical tasks are realised through the acquaintance of students with systems of Christian philosophy and morality accumulating the best achievements of the universal human culture" (Orthodox Classical Gymnasium, S. 1).

Eine besondere Rolle spielt dabei der Kurs „Grundlagen der orthodoxen Kultur", der zusammen mit den Kursen für Literatur, antike Kultur und die geistliche Musik des christlichen Europa einen Kernbereich im Unterricht bildet. Der Unterricht in alten Sprachen (Griechisch ab Klasse 5, Latein ab Klasse 8) und die Studien der antiken Kultur weisen die Schule als klassisches Gymnasium aus. Mit der ersten modernen Fremdsprache (Englisch) beginnt man bereits in der Grundschule.

Die Gründer des Gymnasiums betonen zwar den weltlichen Charakter des Unterrichts, andererseits aber wird die Nähe zum orthodoxen Christentum nicht nur in den Unterrichtsinhalten, sondern auch im Schulleben selbst angestrebt:

„The Orthodox Classical Gymnasium does not introduce doctrinal disciplines, but permits to the students to make their own world-conceptual choice, and this is the most important. ... The secular character of education does not hamper the possibility for the students to learn and love the masterpieces of the national Orthodox art. The design of class-rooms gives a chance to the students to appreciate the beauty and more purity of

the monuments of national iconography. The students from Orthodox families may express externally (through a short prayer) their religious affiliation (or visit the Church on great religious feasts). But of course no student can be obliged to perform religious rites, or reject them with an offence to the faithful consciousness" (Orthodox Classical Gymnasium, S. 1).

Der Unterricht in der ersten Stufe (Klassen 1 bis 5) beinhaltet neben den üblichen Grundschulfächern und einer modernen Fremdsprache (Englisch) auch die ersten „Grundlagen der orthodoxen Kultur": *„Besides the subjects of general education, we introduce rudiments of Orthodox culture (Catechism), the church singing together with liturgics (we attach much attention to this subject, because it helps churching the children), ..."* (Avdeenko, S. 2).

Ein besonderes Merkmal der Lehrstoffanordnung ist das jährliche Schwerpunktthema, dem sich die Inhalte einzelner Unterrichtsfächer zuordnen:

- Das dominierende Thema des 6. Schuljahres beispielsweise ist die antike Welt. Das Curriculum weist dazu aus: Geschichte der antiken Welt; die Kunst der Griechen und Römer; die Geschichte des Alten Testaments. Zwei neue Fächer kommen in der 6. Klasse hinzu, die von nun an bis zur 11. Klasse durchgehend unterrichtet werden: Altgriechisch und „Kultur der antiken Welt".
- Das Schwerpunktthema des 7. Schuljahres ist die Geschichte Rußlands bis zum 16. Jahrhundert, eingeschlossen sind das westliche Mittelalter und die byzantinische religiöse Kultur.
- Im 8. Schuljahr dominiert die Hinwendung Rußlands zum Westen. Hier erfolgt die Einführung in die westeuropäische Kunst und Literatur, im Religionsunterricht werden vergleichende Religionsstudien angeregt. *„A prominent place in grade 8 is to be given to physics, as a powerful symbol of West-European culture, and the Latin language is introduced"* (Avdeenko, S. 2).
- Das 9. Schuljahr steht unter dem Motto „Dialog der Kulturen" und wird von der Geschichte Rußlands und des Westens im 19. Jahrhundert dominiert. Im Literaturunterricht liegt der Schwerpunkt auf der russischen klassischen Literatur des 19. Jahrhunderts.
- Im 10. Schuljahr erfolgt die Auseinandersetzung mit der jüngsten Geschichte und den Problemen des 20. Jahrhunderts. Drei Themenkreise bilden dabei die Schwerpunkte: *„.... the Communist ideology, known to us by experience; the idea of the nationalist state of the fascist type and the view, holding that the progress of technology and*

the development of democracy ensure the growth of humanism and improve the moral state of the society" (ebd.).
- Das letzte, das 11. Schuljahr dient der Analyse und Zusammenfassung des erarbeiteten Wissens und der Vorbereitung auf den Eintritt in die Hochschule. Die orthodoxe Kirche als Phänomen der Kultur steht im Mittelpunkt der Beschäftigung mit der Antike. Insgesamt bildet die Kirche den thematischen Schwerpunkt des 11. Schuljahres: *„In short, the Holy Church in its mystic, historical, and cultural dimensions, is the 'dominant' of the 11th grade" (ebd., S. 3).*

Das vorgestellte Bildungsprogramm des Orthodoxen Klassischen Gymnasiums zeigt deutlich seine Orientierung an den Grundwerten des orthodoxen Christentums und an der Institution Kirche als deren Trägerin. In diesem Zusammenhang drängt sich die Frage auf, ob es in der vorrevolutionären Geschichte der russischen Schule, in der die orthodoxe Kirche zeitweilig eine bedeutende Rolle gespielt hat, Bildungskonzeptionen gegeben hat, die dem Orthodoxen Klassischen Gymnasium als Vorbilder dienen könnten.

Das Gymnasium der Zarenzeit, dessen Ursprünge bis ins 18. Jahrhundert zurückreichen, war anfänglich als eine Schule konzipiert, die den Schülern eine höhere Allgemeinbildung ohne besondere Zweckbestimmung vermitteln sollte. Erst im 19. Jahrhundert wurde die Vorbereitung auf das Universitätsstudium zu seiner fast ausschließlichen Aufgabe. In seinen Grundzügen – wie Unterrichtsziele und Lehrplanstruktur – orientierte es sich an den westlichen Vorbildern, wobei der deutsche und französische Einfluß überwogen. Die Schulfächer wurden isoliert nebeneinander unterrichtet, der Religionsunterricht war mit zwei Wochenstunden im Stundenplan vertreten. Das Gymnasium war seit der Regierungszeit Alexanders I. (1801-1825) dem Ministerium für das Bildungswesen unterstellt, und der Einfluß der Kirche auf seine Bildungsinhalte reichte nicht über die Möglichkeiten des Religionsunterrichts hinaus. Als weltliche Schule konzipiert und verwaltet, bot das Gymnasium keine Möglichkeit, die Ziele des Unterrichts vorrangig an den Grundwerten des orthodoxen Christentums zu orientieren, so daß das vorrevolutionäre Gymnasium wie auch die übrigen in der zweiten Hälfte des 19. Jahrhunderts entstandenen Sekundarschultypen (Progymnasien und Realschulen) kein Vorbild für das Orthodoxe Klassische Gymnasium sein konnten.

Die russisch-orthodoxe Kirche besaß – anders als im Fall des Gymnasiums – im Bereich des Elementarschulwesens relativ große Einflußmöglichkeiten.² Das galt besonders für die ihr unterstellten kirchlichen Elementarschulen (cerkovno-prichodskie školy). Im Unterschied zum Sekundarschulwesen, das im Verlauf des 19. Jahrhunderts parallel zur Gründung der Universitäten einen kontinuierlichen Aufschwung nahm, kam das Elementarschulwesen erst im letzten Viertel des 19. Jahrhunderts zur Entfaltung. Der Anstoß dazu war die Überstellung der Dorfschulen in die Zuständigkeit der ländlichen Selbstverwaltungen (zemstva), die 1864 im Zuge der Reformen Alexanders II. (Regierungszeit: 1855-1881) eingeführt wurden und sich mit viel Engagement dem Aufbau des Dorfschulwesens widmeten. Als Gegengewicht dazu gründete die Kirche, die sich um ihren Einfluß sorgte, zahlreiche kirchliche Elementarschulen auf der Grundlage der von Zar Alexander III. am 13. Juli 1884 erlassenen „Regeln für die kirchlichen Elementarschulen in Kirchspielen".³ Diese Schulen hatten die Aufgabe: „... *die orthodoxe Glaubenslehre und christliche Sittlichkeit im Volke zu festigen und nützliche Anfangskenntnisse zu vermitteln" (Miljukov 1931, S. 832)*. Der Unterricht sollte durch Geistliche, Diakone und „besondere" von der Kirchenverwaltung ausgewählte und von Geistlichen beaufsichtigte Personen erteilt werden.

Begünstigt wurde diese Entwicklung durch die äußerst konservative Kulturpolitik, die unter der Herrschaft Alexanders III. (1881-1894) und im ersten Jahrzehnt der Regierungszeit Nikolaus' II. (1894-1917) betrieben wurde. Der Schöpfer und Wortführer dieser Politik war der Erzieher und einflußreiche Berater Alexanders III., Konstantin Petrovič Pobedonoscev, der zudem noch Oberprokurator des Heiligen Synod (der obersten Kirchenbehörde Rußlands) war und seinen Einfluß in maßgeblichen Kirchenkreisen geltend machen konnte.

Pobedonoscev war überzeugt, daß die Volksfrömmigkeit eine der tragenden Säulen der russischen Kultur war, und strebte danach, den Einfluß der Kirche auf die Schule zu verstärken.⁴ Auf sein Drängen hin erließ der Zar die oben zitierten „Regeln" für die Ein-

---

2 Für die russischen Elementarschulen wurden vor der Revolution die Bezeichnungen „načal'naja škola" (Grundschule) und „narodnaja škola" (Volksschule) fast synonym verwendet. Diese Schulen waren auf dem Lande in der Regel einklassig; die Schuldauer betrug 2 bis 3 Jahre.

3 „Pravila o cerkovno-prichodskich školach". Der Zar vermerkte eigenhändig auf dem Original: „*Ich hoffe, daß die Kirchspiel-Geistlichkeit sich der hohen Berufung zu dieser wichtigen Sache würdig erweist" (Miljukov 1931, S. 832).*

4 Nach Čiževskij *(1961, S. 103)* war Pobedonoscev der „*... einzige bedeutende Ideologe der Reaktion, der dazu noch fast fünfundzwanzig Jahre lang (1881-1904) einen beinahe uneingeschränkten Einfluß auf die beiden Kaiser Alexander III. und Nikolaus II. (1894-1917) ausübte". – „Pobedonoscev versuchte, die Volksschule in die Hände der Geistlichkeit zu bringen" (ebd., S. 107).*

richtung der kirchlichen Elementarschulen. Als Vorbild für diese Schulen diente Pobedonoscev ein ganz bestimmtes Schulmodell: die vom ehemaligen Biologieprofessor und Gutsbesitzer S. A. Račinskij geleitete Elementarschule in seinem Gutsdorf Tatevo im Gouvernement Smolensk. Pobedonoscev wurde nicht müde, Račinskij und dessen pädagogisches Werk lobend zu erwähnen *(S. A. Račinskij i ego škola 1956, S. 81-84).*[5]

Das Besondere an der Schule Račinskijs war ihre enge Verbundenheit mit der Kirche und Kirchengemeinde. Kirchliche Feste und Gottesdienste bestimmten den Rhythmus des Schullebens. Der Schule war ein Internat für auswärtige Schüler angegliedert, und Račinskij wohnte dort zusammen mit den Schülern. Gebete und das Singen geistlicher Lieder gehörten zum Schulalltag. Ausgiebig wurde der Kirchengesang geübt, um den Schülern Gelegenheit zu geben, zur liturgischen Ausgestaltung der Gottesdienste beizutragen. Račinskij ergriff jede Gelegenheit, um Verbindungen zwischen der Schule und dem religiösen Leben des Volkes herzustellen. Selbst eine mehrtägige Fußwanderung, die er mit seinen Zöglingen unternahm, wurde als Wallfahrt zu einer nahe gelegenen heiligen Stätte durchgeführt.

Einen besonderen Wert legte Račinskij auf den Unterricht in der kirchenslawischen Sprache, der Sprache der russischen Bibel und anderer heiliger Schriften der russisch-orthodoxen Kirche.[6] Der Unterricht im Kirchenslawischen begann bereits im ersten Schuljahr noch vor dem Erlernen des Schreibens und Lesens in der Muttersprache. Sein Ziel war *„volles Verständnis der Sprache des kirchenslawischen Neuen Testaments"*, der Weg dahin führte über das wiederholte Lesen des Neuen Testaments *„mit geduldigem Verweilen bei jeder Redewendung, die Anlaß zum Mißverständnis hätte geben können"* (*S. A. Račinskij i ego škola 1956, S. 21*). Über das Neue Testament hinaus sollten nach seiner Ansicht auch das Buch der Psalmen und das Stundenbuch im Unterricht gelesen werden. Die besondere Stellung des Kirchenslawischen im Unterricht seiner Schule hing mit der Überzeugung Račinskijs zusammen, daß *„das erste der ... Bedürfnisse des russischen Volkes ... der Umgang mit der Gottheit ist"*, und der *„russische Bauer sich auf der Suche nach Kunst nicht zum Theater und zur Zeitung, sondern zur Kirche und zum*

---

5 Sergej Aleksandrovič Račinskij (1836-1902) leitete die Schule in Tatevo von 1875 bis 1902. Der Liberale russische Historiker Pavel *Miljukov (1931, S. 832)*, ein Zeitgenosse Račinskijs, bezeichnete ihn als den „Ideologen" der kirchlichen Elementarschule.

6 Die kirchenslawische Sprache wird bereits in der 1864 erlassenen „Ordnung für die Grund- und Volksschulen" (Položenie o načal'nych narodnych učiliščach) zum obligatorischen Unterrichtsfach. Der Unterricht in kirchenslawischer Sprache strebte allein die Lesefähigkeit an und begann in der Regel im zweiten Schuljahr.

Buch Gottes hingezogen fühlt" (zitiert nach *Miljukov 1931, S. 833).* Die gesamte russische Literatur nach Puškin war nach Meinung Račinskijs für die Schüler „absolut unverdaulich".

In der Geschichte der vorrevolutionären russischen Schule und Pädagogik entspricht die an der russischen Orthodoxie und der Kirche orientierte Pädagogik Račinskijs am ehesten den Intentionen des Orthodoxen Klassischen Gymnasiums in Moskau, sieht man einmal von den Unterschieden zwischen den historischen Situationen der beiden Schulen ab.

Auf die pädagogischen Experimente und die Versuchsschule des großen russischen Schriftstellers Lev Tolstoj kann im Zusammenhang dieses Beitrages nicht eingegangen werden. Zwar war seine Konzeption der Freien Erziehung von *seinem* Verständnis des Christentums mit beeinflußt, doch lehnte er die Orthodoxe Kirche und die von ihr vertretene Auslegung der Bibel konsequent ab, wofür er bekanntlich 1901 vom Heiligen Synod exkommuniziert wurde.

Der unternommene vergleichende Rückblick auf die russische Schulgeschichte zeigt, daß zwischen dem Orthodoxen Klassischen Gymnasium und der Schule Račinskijs Ähnlichkeiten in den pädagogischen Konzeptionen bestehen, denn beide versuchen, ihre Bildungsziele an den Grundwerten des orthodoxen Christentums russischer Prägung zu orientieren. Zwischen den beiden besteht jedoch über die Vergleichbarkeit dieses Ansatzes hinaus auch ein fundamentaler Unterschied:

Račinskij versucht, das kulturelle Bewußtsein seiner Schüler ausschließlich auf die heiligen Schriften und die Traditionen der russisch-orthodoxen Kirche zu gründen und westliche Einflüsse von den Schülern fernzuhalten, bis hin zu seiner Ablehnung der russischen Literatur des 19. Jahrhunderts, in der sich westliche Ideen widerspiegeln und die er als für die Schüler „unverdaulich" bezeichnet.

Das Orthodoxe Klassische Gymnasium vertritt dagegen – unbeschadet der zentralen Stellung des orthodoxen Christentums in seinem Bildungskanon – ein offenes Konzept des geistigen Dialogs mit der westlichen Kultur. Dies wird deutlich, wenn man die Religionsvergleiche und den großen Anteil der Studien zur politischen und geistigen Geschichte Westeuropas am Unterricht bedenkt. Bei der pädagogischen Konzeption des Orthodoxen Klassischen Gymnasiums haben wir es mit einer originären Kreation zu tun, die einen Beitrag zur Neubegründung der kulturellen Identität Rußlands zu leisten vermag.

Bibliographie

1. Monographien

Čiževskij, Dmitrij: Zwischen Ost und West. Russische Geistesgeschichte. Von Dimitrij Tschischewskij. Bd. 2. Reinbek bei Hamburg: Rowohlt Taschenbuch-Verlag 1961.
Miljukov, Pavel Nikolaevič: Očerki po istorii russkoj kul'tury. Tom 2. Vera, tvorčestvo, obrazovanie. Čast 2. Iskusstvo, škola, prosveščenie [Abriß der Geschichte der russischen Kultur. Bd. 2. Glaube, Schöpfertum, Bildung. T. 2. Kunst, Schule, Bildungswesen]. Paris: Editions des „Annales contemporaines" 1931.
S. A. Račinskij i ego škola. Sbornik statej [S. A. Račinskij und seine Schule. Eine Aufsatzsammlung]. Jordanville, N. Y.: Holy Trinity Monastery 1956.

2. Materialien der Gesellschaft „Radonež". (o. J.):

Avdeenko, E. A.[7]: Religious Education in the Secondary School.
Orthodox Classical Gymnasium.

---

7 Avdeenko ist der Direktor der Kurse für die Fortbildung orthodoxer Lehrer.

Education for Sale: Recent Developments in the United Kingdom

Witold Tulasiewicz

Introduction

Ten years ago in the Festschrift celebrating Wolfgang Mitter's sixtieth birthday I quoted the words used by the then education junior minister in the Thatcher government to describe the new direction of Conservative education policy as „*away from ... a knee jerk reaction to the policies of other parties*" to „*policies that any subsequent non-conservative government could not undo*" *(Tulasiewicz 1987, p. 189)*. Ten years and a score or more of education acts and measures later this promise can confidently be said to have been kept. Judging from newspaper and party political briefing accounts, it can be said that the Labour opposition once elected to form a government will retain most of the controversial education measures passed, such as the publication of pupil performance in school league tables, the grant maintained status for schools which had opted out of local education authority control and the increased selection by individual schools of pupils according to ability and the respectability of their parents. Less than a couple of years ago it was assumed that all such measures would be rescinded immediately Labour took office. In the event, only the most extreme measures such as the assisted places scheme which allows taxpayers' money to be spent on buying expensive places in prestigious fee paying independent schools for gifted but impoverished children, will disappear.

Whatever the educational merits of the measures introduced, and a detailed discussion of them is not attempted in this paper, there is no doubt that they have had an impact on public opinion, in particular by invoking the popularly endorsed principle of choice. However, the question practitioners of education did ask themselves at the time of the first Thatcher administration was: What was the moving force behind the changes inflicted on education in Britain overtly given out as intended to produce an overall improvement in the quality of education provision? In other words: What was the ideology which prompted the changes?

Education in the Free Market

Several of the major educational measures which started being introduced more than ten years ago could indeed be described as capable of bringing about the improvements announced. Such were the National Curriculum to ensure that a compulsory educational minimum was available to all pupils, and the introduction of a wider representation of parents on school governing bodies to remind them of their co-responsibility for their children's education. The need for these two measures had been anticipated by the previous Labour government and had been made the subject of committees and legislation introduced earlier. Whether curtailing the powers of local education authorities, which included the abolition of the Inner London Education Authority in 1990, depriving one of the largest conurbation in the world of its own voice in education, could merit the name of improvement was more difficult to substantiate. But then terms like 'improvement' are well nigh impossible to define with precision. This particular act, however, was one which could begin to be used to provide the answer to the ideological question posed earlier: the changes introduced at great speed added up to what are known as 'free market' policies, an ideology in which the then prime minister was assiduously coached by Sir Keith Joseph, education secretary and one of the staunchest advocates of the free market.

In contrast to the benevolent, caring and responsible one world (albeit an unequal one) of Tory policies, delivered by previous Conservative prime ministers, the new Conservative Party became identified with an ideology, surprising since ideology is widely assumed to be the prerogative of left wing politicians and Marxist thinkers *(Gilmour 1992)*.

Against the accumulating problems of the second phase of post-World War Two developments which included the oil crisis with its accompanying inflation, unemployment and balance of payments difficulties, it became the accepted view that the post war achievement of the welfare state which since 1945 had served Britain well for thirty five years with its generous subsidy of public services including education, could no longer be afforded *(Roche 1993)*. Though this view is certainly not confined to Britain, the road travelled since the mid-seventies in the United Kingdom has taken this country farther along free market consumerism than those taken by other industrial nations in Europe. The noun 'Thatcherism' began to be used to describe conservative social as well as economic policies and applied to educational measures around that time also *(Ahier / Flude 1983)*. The realities of the free market, the consumer and customer, the provider, quality standards and choice left a mark on all spheres of public life including the provision of education. This rhetoric was summed up by Adams and Tulasiewicz contrasting the terms 'teacher-' and 'teaching-quality' *(Adams / Tulasiewicz 1995, pp. 25-32).*

The areas most affected by the revolutionary and controversial changes were those of welfare: health and education, the two buzzwords 'payment' and 'competition' as loudly proclaimed by the proponents of the market as they were stifled by its opponents. The question asked by *Grace (1989)* whether education is a good which society dispenses as an entitlement or a commodity which citizens can purchase, could by the end of the eighties be answered by affirming the second part: education had become a commodity which like all other market commodities would have to be assessed for its quality, tested, chosen and paid for before being taken into ownership.

Putting education on the market is accompanied by setting up stalls and ensuring that interest in it remains strong enough to attract purchasers and bidders. A commodity clearly belongs on the market if it has to be paid for, although in the case of education, when often a direct act of purchase is not made, its place on the market is ensured by its being made a differentiated commodity which can be chosen or rejected according to the satisfaction it does or does not give. It is this which has led to the advertising rhetoric and the efforts made to attach the label commodity to as many educational services as possible. Among these I identify the availability of a choice of school for one's children which, apart from what is broadly perceived as 'good value', includes the choice of an education policy manifested in such matters as pupil selection and school government. The choice of good quality demonstrated by league tables accepted as proving the superiority of one school over another, is a development which further ensured that education remains firmly accepted as a commodity.

Education as a Commodity

The important caveat is that education is not a marketable commodity in the strictest sense of the word. Education, or compulsory education at least, does not generate money, while genuine curriculum choice can only be found on a minor scale in a relatively small number of schools which teach to particular philosophies, such as anthroposophy. In England such schools have made less of an impact than the 'public' schools whose philosophies rarely aspire to cater for the more esoteric tastes and most of which teach the National Curriculum though not obliged to do so. Even so, although this may only mean that in practice they are in a position to offer a richer portion of the same curriculum, there is a modicum of choice of how, when and by whom the public school curriculum is delivered. This enables a distinction between different types of schools and an assessment of their quality which fits in with the criteria of the market. On the other hand, the ultimate choice, breaking down the schools into self-contained units – in terms of financial management or the extent to which they allocate a place to a moral or ethics education which is completely different to the rest of the system – is hardly an option. This is proved by the curriculum conditions laid upon so-called 'voluntary aided' schools which cater for the requirements of a religious denomination. While the process and manner of delivery of education rather than its contents can therefore be said to constitute choice of a marketable commodity, this is because state intervention in the curriculum precludes the full extent of a free market to develop.

The above innovatory changes, the result of educational measures passed long after the War, were of course additions to the classical example of educational choice which exists in the form of fee paying independent schools. In that sense, all the new measures did was to widen the spectrum of choice by the introduction of the grant maintained schools or the colleges of technology which, in respect of pupil intake and standards of delivery, may indeed be closer to independent schools. It is necessary to point out the different socio-political and educational climate existing in Scotland. To England's total of nearly 1.200 opted out grant maintained schools there is only one in the whole of Scotland! Even so, the unequal character of schools, their state of repair and standard of teaching present sufficient differences to consider education as a commodity. While the National Curriculum is the main guarantee of the quality of the commodity it is the individual school which ensures that it is delivered preventing any uniformity of procedures in this respect. The personal interest this is bound to generate, the opportunity for choice with the opening to public scrutiny of school performance by inspections of the Office for Standards in Education, the efficiency of its government, assisted by involving the discerning consumer (the parent?) through good public relations strengthened by the position of the educational services advisor, demonstrate the most important market ingredient which is that of popular choice.

This incomplete list must reiterate the important fact that education recognised as a part of the market can be divided into the sector of services which can be bought directly and processes of education which though they are not available separately are 'associated' with the purchase made of the service. This can be shown in the example of a parent paying his son's independent school fees in return for the education provided or obtaining a voucher which can be redeemed for education received or not used at all. This is possible in the case of nursery education which is not a statutory requirement in England, so that vouchers are an extra which the market makes available in an educational establishment, a nursery school, or in the form of financing an alternative provision, such as employing more teachers in primary schools. These differences further confirm the existence of choice, albeit a limited one, which the voucher can advertise as a market commodity.

The devolution of school management to individual schools which, as suggested, promotes difference to attract a particular buyer, is another 'associated' measure which can help to stimulate the market. A school largely in control of its own budget with the funds received in capitation moneys either directly as a grant maintained entitlement or through the local education authority may be able to advertise its own variety of statutory teaching services for its pupils reinforced recently by the regulation allowing the selection of up to 15 percent of pupils and more according to criteria it has set. This is despite the fact that in name the bulk of British maintained schools remain comprehensive, making no selection of pupils according to ability. The variety of services has been described by *Downes (1994)*.

By drawing attention to the variety and different emphasis given to them the 'associated' measures lend themselves best to advertising such items as aspects of the curriculum on offer, a wider choice of subjects, distinctive pupil care facilities or indeed the fact that the school is high in the league tables. Encouraging such practices leads to problems of supply and demand. While excellent schools are oversubscribed others fail because declining numbers involve a fallback on 'difficult' pupils whose ability and discipline are responsible for the poor school image. It is significant that the English league tables in true market style are set out in simple ranking order reflecting the raw points acquired for examination passes with no allowance made for the socio-economic conditions in the school, the character of its pupil population and its location. It is no wonder that it makes choice easy! In the latest November 1996 tables some schools scored 0 in the column for passes, because the special needs schools did not have any non-disabled pupils on roll who could take the points scoring examinations. The excessive involvement of public opinion through using this strategy gives it a say in education which had been taken away from professionals, and is a perfect example of what has been called 'associate measures' designed to keep the provision received in the market.

An account of the role of the market in education would be incomplete without an examination of the morality of the application of market policies to education. Unlike problems such as those arising from the geographical situation of a 'poor' school in an inner city area morality addresses the entire purpose and nature of education and upbringing which not only is accepted as a necessity like food, but unlike adequate feeding, is everywhere compulsory. That truancy or not sending one's child to a school is a more easily identifiable offence, whereas with respect to ill treatment of a minor more proof is required for the guilty party to be punished, exemplifies the different levels touched by education and upbringing. They leave unanswered the question about the advantages of certain types of education over others and the entitlement to them. These even the best of school inspection systems can resolve only in part since it reinforces the easily visible marketable features of education which in themselves are not answerable for the morality of the market and only skim the surface of the ability to read its trends.

Some Critiques of the Marketing of Education

In the following eight sections an attempt is made to assess the compatibility of free market education with some basic human qualities (morality), the impact of the consumer's market on some educational procedures (partnerships and collaboration) and its efficiency with respect to contributing to new developments and sound management of resources. Since it is beyond the scope of this paper to present education in the alternative setting of a directed economy no attempt will be made to define education as a public good, to cost its financing or suggest the machinery required to delimit its scope. The polarised format of setting out the arguments is intended to convey a clear evaluation of the situation.

(1) The morality of a market education has been strongly argued and condemned as much by critics of the economic system itself as by philosophers and sociologists of education, notably *Wringe (1986)* and *Grace (1995)*. I tend to agree with their arguments that education is incapable of being regarded as a market commodity, which means that it is an entitlement. Since receiving it is also a requirement of compulsory schooling control agencies are necessary to define its scope and to appoint the providers. In that case where are the limits to be set against expansion and diversity and who is to decide their extent? Over the years various agencies have attempted alternatively to encourage and to impede access to education and its products. The financial contribution made for receiving an education cannot avoid an examination of resources available and a deci-

sion made about priorities. A convincing argument is the most zealously guarded freedom of choice, a scenario in which the quality of the goods often plays only a second role. Inequality of access and provision has been condemned on all fronts, both as purchase and availability of education. Since there are already many natural causes for educational inequality, such as talent and resourcefulness, is it morally defensible to complicate this further by societal manipulations? General considerations of this kind are incapable of immediate resolution and application, although *Grace (1989, p. 214)* argues persuasively in the somewhat grand terms of „*education provides the basic conditions for making democracy possible ...*" How undemocratic then is the use of educational choice?

(2) The actual discovery of conditions of inequality in education especially in terms of provision which for long had been accepted as inherent, is the result of checks carried out for the market. The context of debates on inequality of provision and the application of league tables has focused attention to ways of attracting pupils to a school which involve overt or covert ways of discouraging them from attending a competitor. Although this may promote far-reaching debates on deeper differences in the educational philosophies of schools and the way in which they may affect the quality of the product on offer, including an assessment of the value of courses in the psycho-sociology of education, the main market argument has concentrated on simple inequality and diversity of provision. In such a context the price of the product is more likely to be taken into account than the attendant morality of its use. The admissibility of advertising the standard of educational facilities has always figured more prominently in popular debate than the criteria used to define the standard.

(3) A comprehensive debate of children's needs and abilities and the conditions in which they receive their education – which includes a serious examination of the merits and demerits of such different methods as child- and school-subject-centred education – has been hindered by the dominance of values more easily accommodated in a market economy. Descriptions and evaluations expressed in such terms as excellence and quality tend to find less room to take account of the child as learner and the recipient of the education on offer. In recent British discussions of educational reforms the child's persona has been given less attention than the teaching subject, while concern with teachers' teaching styles has concentrated more on discipline than the academic and social progress of pupils. Economic considerations have encouraged placing the child as a statistic as demonstrated by the league tables. The likely prognosis is that market conditions will continue to push out further any demand for a discussion of the socio-psychological conditions affecting children's behaviour and their role in the learning process.

(4) Education does not fully fit into the context of a market economy. State interest in the provision of a mono-cultural education linked to the requirements of the nation state has made necessary an intervention on a scale not found in other sectors. The use of instruments to control and monitor progress in the form of state curricula and national systems of inspections and examinations has prevented the emergence of real alternatives in the content of provision and style of delivery. The only potential for alternative provision which stops the purely linear development of education becomes manifest when used to eliminate approaches regarded as less appropriate in the free market, for example child-centred teaching styles when believed to affect progress made in the study of approved school subjects. The arrival of some alternatives tends to hasten the consolidation of an approved monolithic system of education. Thus, the development of administration and teaching practices associated with the 1988 Educational Reform Act has been criticised by market-independent observers for its endorsement of priorities considered incompatible with the guarantee of absolute standards openly presented.

(5) A description of education in a market economy is incomplete without noting the emergence of new agents to help manage and control the much diversified system. Analogous to the tier of administrators of other public services, such as the National Health Service 'Education for sale' has also contributed to the rapid growth in the numbers of agents other than the providers of the teaching. School governors involved in the day-to-day running of schools, curriculum designers to draw up the new curricula, producers of teaching aids and education brokers who advertise the service, statisticians who measure the achievements, and particularly inspectors who control the entire system, when taken together may begin to outnumber the providers. It is characteristic of the system that apart from the planners and advisors all the agents involved have come out into the open to be scrutinised which makes it easier to identify and repair mistakes which are essential to the maintenance of the market system.

The involvement of new agents appointed to ensure the existence of desirable choice has resulted in a reduction of the influence wielded by professionals. Among the most influential now are the parents, both as customers and administrators, whose roles have proliferated in the market. Their acceptance of the role of critic and chooser has brought out their frequently ill informed judgements, and indeed their bias based on their own experience in which the personal element plays an important part. By encouraging, in the name of choice, attempts to transfer such individual and local experiences onto a wider area the market may in fact inhibit the development of innovations incompatible with popular choice. Particularly affected would be examining the adverse effects of competition. Since more than two thirds of school governors are complete laymen in matters of education the combined effect of their choice of priorities, such as economies of provision, on de-professionalising the service is bound to be considerable.

The involvement of public opinion in determining the choice of priorities as part of the market is at the same time a practical demonstration of democracy in action. It is well to remember this considering that the choice of a particular kind of education also affects the availability of employment, a sector better qualified to assess the needs of applied and vocational preparation. The link between industry and education may get lost in arguments about the public good of a general education.

(6) The educational diversity for the creation of which the competing mechanism of the market is responsible has alerted the recipients or indeed their guardians to the need for monitoring the quality of the output. Here standards compete with costs and both are assessed by persons often more conversant with the economy than with the substance of the educational product received. In such cases the government is frequently aligned on the side of public opinion and its interpretation of choice. There is the real danger of a drop in output particularly of a loss of inventiveness and innovation which may be believed to be necessary to avoid wastage through repetition and duplication. Depending on the market there may be more or less opportunity for the introduction of some approaches. The dogmatic espousal of market policies by a public easily impressed by visible, albeit untried, results exemplifies the situation with education having to fall back on outmoded but cheaper traditional procedures. The diversity which makes competitive differences wasteful of resources demonstrates the quasi-market position of education which depends on higher market considerations for its funding priorities *(Glatter 1995)*. A national monopoly in education exacerbates the situation in the absence of comparison with other models.

As done early in this chapter it may be helpful also in this case to reduce the argument to determine who is or should be entitled to choose, the extent and costs of the diversity of provision and the profitable investment of education, however, attempts to identify those to and on whom the choice should fall are not entirely democratic.

(7) The change caused by market forces in educational practices marked by a re-alignment of such procedures as competition, collaboration and partnership which constitute the way in which teaching in the context of educational institutions is conducted has been addressed by looking whether partnership is still an option when schools compete

with one another. There cannot be a total isolation of the producer, with each school completely on its own, in view of the operation of the principle of state control. Deregulation is followed by regulation which re-imports some uniformity but is compensated by savings which happen in the case of joint purchasing of services or materials, an important consideration when education does not generate money. *Aitchinson (1995)* is confident that partnerships will continue to develop since competition alone will not suffice to address sophisticated future new initiatives. According to *Gallacher (1995)* the market economy which forges links with employment also encourages the formation of new school-industry or business partnerships in which there is no competition. This forgets that the overall aim of good business links to improve the position of the school involves competition with other schools. The phenomenon is also evident when secondary schools compete in order to attract primary school pupils. It is a feature of the economy that further developments generating regulations will prevent schools from becoming completely isolated to face the competition of the market ensuring that practices such as modified partnerships and consultation will continue.

(8) Though restricted by the system of control the competitive climate of educational choice is inherent in the presence of alternative provision claiming to provide a valid service which can be resolved in two ways: the more objective way is the application of tests for grading, the more subjective – the use of free choice, with a significant grey area linking the consumerist and the quality criteria. This situation can be encountered in local, national and international contests supported by comparisons, the results of which are then found in league tables. It is with respect to what to do with the education received, the product of the market economy, that education finds its strongest support in business and political circles likely to exhort groups and individuals to outperform using the services of the country initiating the competition to 'beat' the competitor after reference to such evidence as the international mathematical and science league tables. The competitive drive in education is especially strong in Britain with more emphasis given to competitive sports than elsewhere. A very recent proposal is to introduce boxing in schools on a wide scale. In the education systems of a number of other European countries the competitive spirit is either absent or tempered by appeals to 'adjust' to other practices approximating to the level of performance to be found in other European Union member states. Although the market economy has made an appearance elsewhere current British policies tend to emphasise it more. There is no evidence of a widespread use made of the international league tables to ensure higher output. As mentioned above a distinction, often forgotten, must be made between general and vocational education in respect of delivery styles used.

Summary

Has the market improved the service? Diversity, choice and customer satisfaction are a desirable outcome although the cost at which these are achieved must be taken into account when making comparisons with practices found elsewhere. The cost is both financial, probably relatively easy to meet in a free market, and social which it is impossible to measure and to meet. The victims are the reduction in the general level of an education which some cannot afford to pay for, and the concomitant alienation of those sections of society affected by it. The pursuit of market policies, which include education, has to some extent neglected their impact on social conditions. The relative neglect of the socio-psychological education of children in favour of subject learning is a part of this trend. The control required is a good outcome, though in this respect too it is necessary to distinguish between educational and market commodity control and the personnel entrusted with administering it. There is no doubt that the buyer has secured a strong position in current market conditions, especially, if not exclusively, in Britain to comment on the quality by using his purse. The quasi-commodity illustration proves that education depends on market forces since the allocation of priority funding has to take account of 'higher' priorities which may lie in another sector of services altogether. An example is the recent (October 1996) ministerial decision to transfer funds from the further education account to finance schools. Advice assumed to be an integral part of the market tends to favour the more consumerist wishes perceived as easier to satisfy than the exclusively educational ones. The market in education has attracted wide criticism from those who do not agree that 'commodity' has a place in the service sector which includes education.

Conclusion

A neat scenario with reference to marketable education has been proposed by Michael Barber quoted by *Brighouse (1995)* which operates with the four markers: equality/inequality, diversity/uniformity, of which the socially most desired outcome is diversity with equality. This philosophical scenario takes no account of the socio-political system which would have to be built around it, although it is theoretically possible to provide an education blueprint for it.

Examining the various possibilities within a political system reveals that a directed compulsory system of identical (equal) education is theoretically possible. However, apart from the directional approach which has been criticised the political dictatorship necessary to support it would be resisted. Moreover the detailed system of education would have to evolve first, a development which is either utopian or arrived at by coercion. While an identical system is not likely, neither is an unlimited diversity arising out of a complete absence of control. To reconcile diversity with equality requires some adjustment in both, in other words there are restrictions on both the equality and the diversity.

The dynamic nature of any system has to acknowledge that it will be subject to change. There is no agreement on who will be in a position to decide since in all such cases there is more than one candidate. It is good that the profession does not speak with one voice, which brings in the question of who makes the decision? A solution which ensures as much equality as possible while encouraging diversity so as not to foreclose new developments must allow for a wide circle of participant choosers, which prevents any single interest from being too closely identified with possession, as well as monitors not identified with a single party. The market has to be watched so as not to be in a position to decide in matters where the individual cannot. *Criticism must be free to criticise which requires a system of balances, to which Education for Sale must inevitably submit.*

Bibliography

Adams, Anthony / Tulasiewicz, Witold: The Crisis in Teacher Education. A European Concern. London et al.: Falmer Press 1995.
Ahier, John / Flude, Michael (eds.): Contemporary Education Policy. London: Croom Helm 1983.
Aitchinson, James: School Management in the Market Place. A Secondary School Perspective. In: Macbeth, Alastair et al. (eds.): Collaborate or Compete? London et al.: Falmer Press 1995, pp. 85-86.
Brighouse, Tim: Competition, Devolution, Choice and Accountability. An Education Authority View of the Need for Diversity and Equality. In: Macbeth, Alastair et al. (eds.): Collaborate or Compete? London et al.: Falmer Press 1995, pp. 36-42.
Downes, Peter: Local Management of Schools. An English Case Study. In: Tulasiewicz, Witold / Strowbridge, Gerald (eds.): Education and the Law, London et al.: Routledge 1994, pp. 211-223.
Gallacher, Nisbet: Partnership in Education. In: Macbeth, Alastair et al. (eds.): Collaborate or Compete? London et al.: Falmer Press 1995, pp. 19-23.
Gilmour, Ian: Dancing with Dogma. London: Simon and Schuster 1992.
Glatter, Ron: Partnership in the Market Model: Is it Dying? In: Macbeth, Alastair et al. (eds.): Collaborate or Compete? London et al.: Falmer Press 1995, pp. 32-33.
Grace, Gerald: Education: Commodity or Public Good? In: British Journal of Educational Studies, 37 (1989) 3, pp. 207-221.

Grace, Gerald: Urban Education, Democracy and the Culture of Contentment. In: Gordon, Peter (ed.): The Study of Education. Vol. 4, London: Woburn Press 1995, pp. 224-231.
Roche, Maurice: Rethinking Citizenship. Welfare, Ideology and Change in Modern Society. Cambridge: Polity Press 1993.
Tulasiewicz, Witold: The Development of the Education System in England and Wales under the Conservative Administration of Mrs. Thatcher. In: Döbrich, Peter / Kopp, Botho von (eds.): Vergleichende Bildungsforschung. Festschrift für Wolfgang Mitter zum 60. Geburtstag (= Zeitschrift für Internationale Erziehungs- und Sozialwissenschaftliche Forschung. Sonderheft. 1987), Köln et al.: Böhlau 1987, pp. 189-219.
Wringe, Colin: The Human Right to Education. In: Educational Philosophy and Theory, 18 (1986) 2, pp. 31-35.

Die rechtliche Struktur der Bildungsverwaltung in Japan[1]

Makoto Yûki

Überblick über das Schulsystem

Das japanische Schulsystem ist ein sogenanntes „eingliedriges", d. h. im Grundsatz folgen auf die sechs Jahre Grundschule drei Jahre weiterführende Mittelschule (erste Phase der Sekundarstufe),[2] drei Jahre an einer Oberschule (zweite Phase der Sekundarstufe) und vier Jahre an der Universität (tertiärer Bildungssektor). Dieses System entstand durch die Reformen der Nachkriegszeit, welche ab 1947 das bisherige „vielgliedrige Schulsystem" veränderten. Die Grundstruktur blieb bis auf kleinere Korrekturen – so z. B. 1962 die Einrichtung der auf fünf Jahre begrenzten Fachhochschulen (*senmon gakkô*) – bis zum heutigen Tage erhalten.

Vom Gesetz her sind neun verschiedene reguläre Schultypen festgelegt: Kindergärten, Grundschulen, Mittelschulen, Oberschulen, Fachhochschulen, Universitäten (einschließlich der Kurzzeituniversitäten und des Graduierten-Bereichs) Blindenschulen, Gehörlosenschulen sowie Schulen für andere Behinderte. Die ersten sechs Typen gehören zu den allgemeinbildenden Schulen, die letzten drei Formen gehören zum Sonderschulwesen. Die Zielsetzung eines jeden Schultyps ist im Schulbildungsgesetz von 1947 festgelegt, z. B. gilt für die Grundschule: „Das Ziel ist eine allgemeine Grundbildung gemäß dem Fortschreiten der körperlichen und geistigen Entwicklung."

Neben diesen oben aufgeführten regulären Schulen gibt es noch Fachoberschulen (*senshûgakkô*, seit 1975), sowie weitere „verschiedenartige" Schulen (*kaku shu gakkô*) als Einrichtungen der schulischen Bildung. Weiterhin gibt es nicht dem Bildungsministerium zugeordnete Einrichtungen auf besonderer gesetzlicher Grundlage (so die Verteidigungshochschule der Verteidigungsbehörde, die Selbstverwaltungshochschule des Selbstverwaltungsministeriums sowie die Berufsbildungsschulen des Arbeitsministeri-

---

1 Aus dem Japanischen übersetzt von Peter Enderlein.
2 Die Schulpflicht in Japan beträgt 9 Jahre (Grund- und Mittelschulen sind Pflichtschulen), allerdings besuchen etwa 95% der Mittelschulabgänger weiterführende Schulen (Anm. d. Übers.)

ums). Die Möglichkeit zur Gründung einer Schule ist prinzipiell auf drei Organe oder (juristische) Personen beschränkt: den Staat, die regionalen und kommunalen Selbstverwaltungen oder einen privaten Schulträger, d. h. es gibt staatliche (*kokuritsu*), öffentliche (*kôritsu*) oder private (*shiritsu*) Schulen.

Tabelle 1: Anzahl der Schulen nach Schultyp im Jahre 1995

Kindergärten	14 856
Grundschulen	24 548
Mittelschulen	11 274
Oberschulen	5 501
Blindenschulen	70
Gehörlosenschulen	107
Schulen für andere Behinderte	790
Fachhochschulen	62
Kurzzeituniversitäten	596
Universitäten	565

Quelle: Statistical Abstract of Education, Science and Culture. Tôkyô: Ministry of Education, Science and Culture 1995.

Als auffälligste Besonderheit des japanischen Schulwesens läßt sich der außergewöhnlich hohe Anteil privater Schulen ansehen. In der vorschulischen Erziehung und im tertiären Bildungssektor ist diese Tendenz am bedeutsamsten. Betrachtet man die Zahlen der Bildungseinrichtungen, so besuchten 1995 80% der Kindergartenkinder, 73% der Universitätsstudenten und 92% der Studenten an Kurzzeituniversitäten eine private Institution.

Organisation und Struktur der Bildungsverwaltung

Besonderheiten der Bildungsverwaltung unter der japanischen Vorkriegsverfassung

Zentralstaatlich geregelte Bildungsverwaltung

Unter der japanischen Vorkriegsverfassung (Verfassung des Großjapanischen Kaiserreiches von 1889) wurde schulische Bildung grundsätzlich und konsequent als Aufgabe des Staates angesehen, d. h. unter dem Prinzip „Subjekt der schulischen Bildung ist der Staat" wurde das staatliche Schulmonopol als materielles Recht durchgesetzt. Außerdem war die schulische Bildung nichts geringeres als eine staatliche Machtausübung, der Schulbesuch gehörte neben der Wehr- und Steuerpflicht zu den drei großen Pflichten des Untertans (Bildung als Pflicht).

Dem Charakter einer solchen schulischen Bildung entsprechend war die Bildungsverwaltung wesentlich zentralstaatlich organisiert und darüber hinaus der allgemeinen Verwaltung untergeordnet. Unter Weisung des Kultusministers waren die Präfekten[3] als obere Schulaufsichtsbehörde eingesetzt, diese wiederum setzten die lokale Schulaufsicht ein. Die Schulverwaltungsabteilungen der Präfekturen verfügten über die Schulinspektoren und die Schulinspektionen und übten so machtvoll Weisung und Aufsicht gegenüber den Schulen aus. Ebenso unterstanden Bürgermeister und Ortsvorsteher der Weisung und Aufsicht des Kultusministers und der Präfekten.

In Bildungsfragen wurde klar zwischen inneren und äußeren Schulangelegenheiten unterschieden: Bildungsziele, Bildungsinhalte und Lehrmethoden zählten zu den ersteren, Bildungsfinanzen und Bau von Bildungseinrichtungen zu den letzteren. Daß der Staat die inneren Schulangelegenheiten selbst vollständig in die Hand nahm und die mit finanziellen Lasten verbundenen äußeren Schulangelegenheiten an die regionalen und lokalen Verwaltungen delegierte, gehörte zu den großen Besonderheiten der Vorkriegsbildungsverwaltung.

Grundsatz der Bildungsgesetzgebung durch Kaiserliche Erlasse

Unter der Vorkriegsverfassung unterlagen wichtige Belange der schulischen Bildung sowie der Bildungsverwaltung dem kaiserlichen Prärogativ und wurden durch Erlaß (*chokurei*) festgelegt, was als „Grundsatz der Bildungsgesetzgebung durch Kaiserlichen Erlaß" bekannt war. Dieser Grundsatz sollte zwar das Prinzip einer „neutralen Erziehung" gewährleisten, jedoch wurde so die Bildung dem Parlament und den Staatsbürgern aus der Hand genommen und lud zu allen Mißbräuchen einer nur durch die Administration bestimmten Bildungsverwaltung ein. Außerdem trog das Bild einer neutralen

---

3 Im Zuge der Neugliederung Japans nach westlichem Vorbild wurden als mittlere Stufe der Regionalverwaltung Präfekturen (städtisch: *fu* oder ländlich: *ken*) eingeführt, an deren Spitze ein durch die Regierung eingesetzter Präfekt der Verwaltung vorstand. In den Reformen der Nachkriegszeit wurde die Präfektur als Verwaltungseinheit beibehalten (heutige Anzahl 47, neben die Bezeichnungen *fu* und *ken* traten *to* für die Hauptstadt Tôkyô und *dô* für die Insel Hokkaidô), jedoch werden Präfekt (*chiji*) und Präfekturparlament heute von der Bevölkerung gewählt. (Anm. d. Übers.)

Erziehung, die schulische Bildung war in bedeutendem Ausmaß politisch und religiös eingefärbt.

Reformen der Nachkriegszeit und die Grundleitlinien der Bildungsverwaltung

Die mit Annahme der Potsdamer Erklärung eingeleiteten Bildungsreformen stellten einen prinzipiellen Wandel der oben geschilderten Vorkriegs-Bildungsadministration dar. Im wesentlichen folgte man dabei den Vorschlägen der ersten US-Delegation zu Bildungsfragen, die im März 1946 nach Japan kam. Die Nachkriegsreformen, die auch die Grundprinzipien der heutigen Bildungsverwaltung bestimmen, sind durch folgende drei Leitsätze definiert:

Bildungsrecht durch Gesetzgebungsverfahren

Alle wichtigen Belange der Bildung werden durch das Parlament als repräsentatives Organ des Volkes mittels Gesetzgebung festgelegt, infolgedessen müssen alle Maßnahmen der Bildungsverwaltung prinzipiell auf gesetzlicher Grundlage durchgeführt werden. Dies bedeutet die Anerkennung der Volkssouveränität in Bildungsfragen, wie sie in Artikel 26 der Verfassung festgelegt ist.

Regionale Selbstbestimmung in der Bildungsverwaltung

Die von der Verfassung garantierten Rechte der Regionen gelten auch konkret bei der Bildung. Dadurch löste sich der Staat von der einheitlichen und zentral bestimmten Bildungsverwaltung und beschränkte seine bildungsbezogenen Aufgaben und die Autorität des Kultusministeriums in hohem Maß. Die Bildungsverwaltung ist als Bildungsselbstverwaltung eingerichtet, und die Möglichkeit zu einer der regionalen Situation entsprechenden Bildungsselbstverwaltung ist hierbei der entscheidende Punkt.

Unabhängigkeit der Bildungsverwaltung von der allgemeinen Verwaltung

Dies gilt als Prinzip, um die politische und administrative Neutralität der Bildungsverwaltung zu wahren. Zur systematischen Garantie dieses Prinzips wurden in allen Städten und Kommunen Bildungsausschüsse eingerichtet, die als verantwortliche Organe der

Bildungsverwaltung alle bildungsbezogenen Aufgaben vollziehen. Dies fußt auf den Lehren der Geschichte, denn durch die Unterordnung der Bildungsverwaltung unter die allgemeine innerstaatliche Verwaltung war der Neutralität der Bildung schwerer Schaden zugefügt worden.

Struktur der Bildungsverwaltung unter der heutigen japanischen Verfassung

Die zentrale Bildungsverwaltung

In Artikel 65 der Verfassung ist festgelegt: „Die Exekutivgewalt ruht beim Kabinett." Daher ist das Kabinett auch höchstes Organ der Bildungsverwaltung. Das Kabinett tagt unter der Leitung des Premierministers, übt so seine Autorität aus und trägt gegenüber dem Parlament die gemeinsame Verantwortung. Die Befugnisse des Kabinetts bezüglich der Bildungsverwaltung erstrecken sich auf Gesetzesinitiativen und Haushaltsvorschläge gegenüber dem Parlament, den Erlaß von Verordnungen und die Verabschiedung von Kabinettsbeschlüssen zu wichtigen Bildungsangelegenheiten. Das staatliche Organ, welches unter Aufsicht des Kabinetts die Verwaltungsaufgaben im Bildungsbereich direkt wahrnimmt, ist das Kultusministerium (*monbushô*). Das Kultusministerium wurde durch das „Gesetz über die Organisation der staatlichen Verwaltung" (*kokka gyôsei soshiki hô*) und das „Gesetz über die Einrichtung eines Kultusministeriums" (*monbushô setchi hô*) für die „Planung der Förderung und Verbreitung schulischer und gesellschaftlicher Bildung sowie von Wissenschaft und Kultur" geschaffen (§4 des „Gesetzes über die Einrichtung eines Kulturministeriums"). Als einer Regierungsbehörde steht ihm der Kultusminister vor, es verfügt über sechs Ministerialabteilungen (*naibu bukyoku*), wie Ministerialsekretariat (*daijin kanbô*), Abteilung für Primar- und Sekundarschulbildung (*shôtô chûtô kyoku*) usw. Nachgeordnete Behörden sind u. a. das Kulturamt (*bunkachô*), und nachgeordnete Einrichtungen sind staatliche Schulen sowie alle Arten von Forschungseinrichtungen und beratenden Organen.

Mit den Nachkriegsreformen der Bildungsverwaltung wandelte sich auch der Charakter des Kultusministeriums stark. Das Vorkriegs-Kultusministerium hatte die direkte Verantwortung für das gesamte Bildungswesen und war bis zu den entlegensten Bildungsorganen aufsichts- und weisungsberechtigt, während es heute im Grunde hauptsächlich fachliche Maßnahmen vorschlägt und als zentrales Organ gegenüber regionalen Behörden und Bildungsorganen Leitung und Rat (*shidô jogen*) zur Verfügung stellt.

Abgesehen davon, daß das „Gesetz über die Einrichtung eines Kultusministeriums" als wesentliche Befugnis Leitung (*shidô*), Rat (*jogen*) und Empfehlungen (*kankoku*) gegenüber Bildungsorganen und Bildungsausschüssen vorgibt, ist folgendes deutlich aufgeführt: „Das Kultusministerium ist nicht befugt, außer in durch Gesetz ... besonders bestimmten Fällen, in Verwaltung und Betrieb eine Aufsicht auszuüben" (§6, Abs.2). Das Leitungs- und Beratungsrecht wurde nach dem Krieg aufgrund amerikanischen Einflusses in Japan als Gegenmodell zum Aufsichts- und Weisungsrecht eingeführt. Als Besonderheit gilt daher, daß es auf Gebieten hoher fachlicher Eigenständigkeit keine Rechtsverbindlichkeit besitzt. Im heutigen Bildungsrechtssystem ist von einem solchen Leitungs- und Beratungsrecht zu erwarten, daß die Bildungsverwaltung reibungslos und effektiv funktioniert.

Regionale Bildungsverwaltung

Daß die heutige Verfassung (Abschnitt 8) die regionale Selbstverwaltung garantiert und durch die Nachkriegsreformen der Bildungsverwaltung das Prinzip der „regionalen Selbstverwaltung in der Bildungsadministration" eingeführt wurde, ist bereits erwähnt worden. Die heutige regionale Bildungsadministration wird nämlich von den Gebietskörperschaften,[4] die den Status unabhängiger juristischer Personen haben, als Selbstverwaltung ausgeübt. Die jeweiligen bildungsbezogenen Aufgaben der Körperschaften sind im Gesetz über die regionale Selbstverwaltung geregelt. Zu den wichtigsten gehört die Errichtung, Verwaltung und Unterhaltung von Schulen sowie Einrichtungen der gesellschaftlichen Bildung. Dabei ist die Aufgabe der Errichtung aller Arten von Pflichtschulen den Städten und Gemeinden übertragen.

Bei öffentlichen Schulen und anderen Bildungseinrichtungen tragen die errichtenden Gebietskörperschaften grundsätzlich die Betriebskosten. Man spricht hier von der „Kostenlast des Errichters", aber es gibt anerkannte Ausnahmen davon, z. B. die Kostenübernahme durch den Staat bei der Pflichtschulbildung.

In den Gebietskörperschaften sind die für Bildungsaufgaben zuständigen Organe die Bildungsausschüsse und die Leiter der jeweiligen Körperschaften.[5] In die Amtsbefugnis

---

4 Als Gebietskörperschaften gelten die schon erwähnten Präfekturen (*to*, *dô*, *fu* und *ken*) sowie die Kommunen bzw. Kreise (Stadt: *shi*, Kleinstadt: *chô*, ländlicher Kreis: *son*). (Anm. d. Übers.)
5 Präfekten, Bürgermeister usw. (Anm. d. Übers.)

letzterer gehören Bildungsangelegenheiten, z. B. bezüglich der öffentlichen Universitäten und Privatschulen sowie Fragen der Bildungsfinanzierung. Dagegen nehmen die Bildungsausschüsse eine wichtige Stellung in der regionalen Bildungsverwaltung ein und spielen dort eine große Rolle.

Das System wurde 1948 als notwendiger Bestandteil der Nachkriegsreformen im regionalen Bildungswesen eingeführt, gemäß dem berechtigten Wunsch der Bevölkerung nach einer den lokalen Bedürfnissen entsprechenden Bildungsverwaltung. 1956 wurde das System durch eine Reform des Gesetzes über die regionale Bildungsverwaltung weitgehend abgeändert und ist so bis heute in Kraft.

Die Bildungsausschüsse sind die Organe der Bildungsverwaltung in den Gebietskörperschaften und besitzen den Charakter von Verwaltungsausschüssen, d. h. sie sind als Kollegien tätig, und die Unabhängigkeit vom Leiter einer Gebietskörperschaft in der Ausübung ihrer Amtsbefugnisse ist garantiert. Bezüglich den Arten von Ausschüssen gibt es, je nach aufstellender Körperschaft, drei Formen: Präfekturausschüsse, Ausschüsse einer Kommune oder eines besonderen Stadtbezirks sowie Ausschüsse für mehrere kooperierende Kommunen. Im Jahre 1994 betrug die Anzahl aller Ausschüsse 3 418.

Ein Bildungsausschuß setzt sich prinzipiell aus fünf Mitgliedern zusammen, die den Ausschuß im engeren Sinne bilden. Im weiteren Sinne werden darunter auch der Leiter des Bildungswesens (*kyôikuchô*) und die Verwaltung (*jimukyôku*) als gesamte Organisation verstanden. Die Mitglieder der Bildungsausschüsse werden vom jeweiligen regionalen oder lokalen Parlament in Übereinstimmung mit dem jeweiligen Präfekten oder Bürgermeister ernannt. Die Mitglieder müssen nicht notwendigerweise Spezialisten der Bildungsverwaltung sein. Die Befugnisse des Ausschusses werden durch das Kollegium der Mitglieder ausgeübt. Die Sitzungen leitet der von den Mitgliedern aus ihrem Kreis gewählte Ausschußvorsitzende, der den Ausschuß auch nach außen vertritt. Die Zuständigkeit des Ausschusses ist weit, sie umfaßt alle Bildungsaufgaben einer Gebietskörperschaft außer denen, die dem Präfekten oder Bürgermeister vorbehalten sind. Die konkreten Aufgaben der Bildungsausschüsse sind in 19 Punkten des Gesetzes über die regionale Bildungsverwaltung festgelegt. Man kann gut sagen, daß alle wichtigen Bildungsaufgaben hier enthalten sind. Außerdem können die zu den Befugnissen des Ausschusses gehörenden Aufgaben durch ihn in Regeln festgelegt werden.

Der Leiter des Bildungswesens ist ein regulärer Kommunal- oder Präfekturbeamter und er wird vom Bildungsausschuß ernannt, allerdings muß auf Präfekturebene die Zustimmung des Kultusministers eingeholt werden, bzw. auf kommunaler Ebene die Zustimmung des präfekturalen Bildungsausschusses. Der Leiter des Bildungswesens führt die den Bildungsausschüssen obliegenden Aufgaben konkret durch und hat so weitgehende Amtsbefugnisse. Unterteilt man diese dem Charakter des Amtes entsprechend, ergibt sich in etwa folgende Gliederung der Befugnisse des Leiters des Bildungswesens:

1. Die Befugnis als fachlicher Berater des Bildungsausschusses.
2. Die Befugnis als leitender, (dem Ausschuß) assistierender Vollzugsbeamter.
3. Die Befugnis als Handlungsbevollmächtigter des Ausschusses.
4. Die Befugnis als Leiter der Verwaltungsabteilung (*jimukyoku*).

Die Bildungsausschüsse und die Schulen

Öffentliche Schulen sind durch eine Gebietskörperschaft gegründete „öffentliche Einrichtungen" und daher hat, nach dem Prinzip der „Verwalterschaft durch den Einrichter", die gründende Körperschaft auch das Recht der Verwaltung. Daß als Exekutivorgan für die Bildungsangelegenheiten einer Gebietskörperschaft die Bildungsausschüsse eingerichtet sind, ist bereits erwähnt worden. Die Bildungsausschüsse sind aber auch das die öffentlichen Schulen direkt verwaltende Schulverwaltungsorgan.

Über die Qualität des Schulverwaltungsrechts der Bildungsausschüsse gehen die Ansichten auseinander. Mit anderen Worten, es besteht das Problem, in welchem Bereich und welchem Maß die Bildungsausschüsse befugt sind, die Schulen zu verwalten und zu lenken.

Hierzu gibt es für die Interpretation der Verwaltung die Theorie eines besonderen Gewaltverhältnisses im öffentlichen Recht. Danach ist die Verwaltungsbeziehung zu den öffentlichen Schulen solcherart, daß in ihr das Gewaltverhältnis besonders stark ist, also eben ein besonderes Gewaltverhältnis des öffentlichen Rechtes darstellt, wonach die Bildungsausschüsse den Schulen gegenüber das umfassende Weisungsrecht besitzen.

Der Verwaltungsinterpretation vollkommen entgegengesetzt ist die Theorie der Bildungsselbstverwaltung. Hierunter verstehen man, daß es der Logik von Bildung entspricht, Schulen (oder dem Lehrerkollegium) in bezug auf die Bildung ein Selbstverwaltungsrecht zu gewähren, was bedeutet, daß in den sogenannten inneren Schulangelegenheiten und besonders bei der Steuerung des Bildungsprozesses das Entscheidungsrecht bei der Schule (oder beim Lehrerkollegium) liegt und der Bildungsausschuß in diesen Angelegenheiten keine Weisungsrechte haben sollte.

Der Bildungsausschuß muß zu den grundlegenden Punkten der Lenkung und Verwaltung der Schulen Bildungsausschußvorschriften festlegen. Diese werden allgemein Schulverwaltungsregeln genannt. Das Ziel der Schulverwaltungsregeln ist es, die Leitung der Schulen und die Beziehung zwischen Schule und Bildungsausschuß klarzustellen.

Der in den Schulverwaltungsvorschriften festgelegte Inhalt besteht nach dem Gesetz über die regionalen Bildungsverwaltung aus „grundlegenden Punkten bezüglich Institution, Ausstattung, organisatorischer Zusammenstellung, Bildungsprozeß, Gebrauch der Lehrmaterialien und ... der Schulleitung und Schulverwaltung". Das Problem besteht also darin, wie die Verteilung der Befugnisse bezüglich dieser Punkte zwischen Schule und Bildungsausschuß konkret festgelegt wird. Als allgemeine Tendenz läßt sich feststellen, daß Leitungs- und Verwaltungsangelegenheiten an Schulen in die Befugnisse des Schulleiters fallen und Aufsichtsbefugnisse den Bildungsausschüssen zugerechnet werden. Weiterhin müssen sich die Schulverwaltungsregeln der kommunalen Bildungsausschüsse an den durch die Präfekturausschüsse aufgestellten Standards orientieren.

5.

Historische Dimension
Historical Dimension
La dimension historique

Chaque fois que le principe d'„education pour tous" est formulé, le problème du contenu et de l'extension du concept d'„éducation" se pose. La controverse concernant le sens du terme remonte à des temps très anciens. On peut en trouver des exemples „classiques" dans la conception grecque de la paideia ainsi que dans d'autres cultures. Selon Confucius, ce concept peut être considéré comme la transmission d'un patrimoine culturel de base tout au long des 2000 années d'histoire chinoise. Les grandes religions du monde voient aussi dans l'„éducation" une chose dont l'homme fait usage de son propre chef, en l'occurrence une clef pour le développement de sa personnalité.

Wolfgang Mitter, 1984

Wolfgang Mitter: L'éducation pour tous. Paris: UNESCO 1984. (Annuaire international de l'éducation. 36) (Ici: p. 45).

Die neuhumanistische Phase des Jenkauer Conradinums im Urteil der deutschen und polnischen Bildungsgeschichte

Siegfried Baske

Obwohl das 1801 in Jenkau bei Danzig gegründete Conradinum eine wechselvolle Entwicklung durchlaufen hat, blieben sein vom Stifter Carl Friedrich von Conradi (1742-1798) hergeleiteter Name und die Funktion als Sekundarschule bis heute erhalten. Die zahlreichen Veränderungen betrafen vor allem die Organisationsformen, die Bildungsinhalte, die staatlichen Rahmenbedingungen (preußisch, deutsch, freistädtisch, polnisch), den Standort (1900 Verlagerung nach Langfuhr) und schließlich auch die Unterrichtssprache. Der tiefe Einschnitt im Jahre 1945 schloß den Wechsel zur berufsbildenden (auf den Schiffbau orientierten) Schule ein. Erst 1991 wurde wieder ein allgemeinbildender Zweig eingerichtet.

Von Anfang an fand das Conradinum überregionale Beachtung. Schon 1798, als das Stiftungstestament öffentlich bekannt wurde, äußerten der preußische König und der Chef des Oberschulkollegiums ihre lebhafte und große Freude. Ein Jahrzehnt später, während der zeitweiligen staatlichen Trennung (1807-1814), veranlaßte Wilhelm von Humboldt als Leiter der Sektion des Öffentlichen Unterrichts eine das Conradinum betreffende – den Zugang für preußische Schüler sichernde – Konvention *(Geheimes Staatsarchiv, Nr. 236)*. Zur frühen Publizität trugen ebenfalls die weitgespannten Aktivitäten des ersten Direktors Reinhold Bernhard Jachmann bei, so seine 1804 erschienene, noch heute anerkannte Biographie Immanuel Kants, auf deren Titelblatt er sich als „Königlicher Direktor" des Conradinums auswies, und auch sein 1806 gemeinsam mit Johann Wilhelm Süvern ausgearbeiteter Plan für ein westpreußisches Bildungssystem, der im Oberschulkollegium zwar gelobt, aber als zu anspruchsvoll beiseite gelegt wurde *(Geheimes Staatsarchiv, Nr. 289a)*.

Die 1810/11 von Jachmann gemeinsam mit dem zweiten Direktor, Franz Passow, in Jenkau entworfene und sogleich praktizierte neuhumanistische Bildungskonzeption hat ein nachhaltiges, bis heute reichendes Echo gefunden. Die überzeitlichen – allerdings von unterschiedlichen Wertungen getragenen – Reaktionen gründeten sich weniger auf die nur kurzzeitige Praxis, sondern vor allem auf zwei in Berlin verlegte Publikationen:

die 1811 von Jachmann veröffentlichte Abhandlung „Über das Verhältnis der Schule zur Welt" und das 1812 von beiden Direktoren herausgegebene „Archiv Deutscher Nationalbildung".

Schon die zeitgenössischen Stellungnahmen wichen stark voneinander ab. Am positivsten urteilte der damalige Hanauer Gymnasialdirektor Johannes Schulze, der von 1818 an im preußischen Kultusministerium als Nachfolger Süverns fungierte. Er würdigte die Konzeption der Jenkauer als ein kühnes, geistvolles und anregendes Reformprojekt. Sein Lob kulminierte in der Feststellung, daß *„das Ganze preiswürdig"* sei *(Schulze 1812, S. 143).* Dagegen äußerte sich Johann Wolfgang von Goethe in einem Brief an Franz Passow im Oktober 1811 skeptisch: er glaubte, dem *„Unternehmen wenig Glück weissagen zu können" (Goethe 1965).* Von den Universitätspädagogen nahm seinerzeit als einziger Hermann Niemeyer, und zwar positiv, Stellung. Ob der damals im nahen Königsberg lehrende Johann Friedrich Herbart aus Unkenntnis, grundsätzlichen Erwägungen oder aus Verärgerung darüber schwieg, daß kurz zuvor seine „Allgemeine Pädagogik" von *Jachmann (1811a)* überaus scharf rezensiert worden war, ist eine offene Frage. Die einzige entschieden negative Stellungnahme gab – allerdings erst am Ende des Jahrhunderts – Friedrich Paulsen ab, als er die Konzeption der Jenkauer als *„das Ausschweifendste jener an ausschweifenden Erziehungstheorien nicht armen Zeit"* kennzeichnete *(Paulsen 1885, S. 236).*

Die bissige Kritik Paulsens erstickte jedoch keineswegs das Interesse an der Konzeption der Jenkauer und verhinderte nicht weitere, überwiegend positive Reaktionen. Das Interesse nahm sogar im 20. Jahrhundert zu und erreichte in den sechziger und siebziger Jahren einen Höhepunkt.

In der ersten Hälfte des 20. Jahrhunderts gab es indes neben ausschließlich deskriptiven Ausführungen im Rahmen bildungsgeschichtlicher Darstellungen nur zwei wertende Stellungnahmen zu der nun schon über hundert Jahre zurückliegenden Konzeption. Die erste stammte von Eduard Spranger, der 1932 in einer Untersuchung über den Anteil des Neuhumanismus an der Entstehung des deutschen Nationalbewußtseins darlegte, daß dieses *„weder aus realpolitischer Wurzel, noch aus einem überhitzten Selbstgefühl des Volkes, sondern aus geistigen, ja teilweise schöngeistigen Zusammenhängen"*, aus dem an den Griechen orientierten Neuhumanismus hervorgegangen sei. Ausgehend von Lessing und Herder und über viele namhafte Repräsentanten des Neuhumanismus wie Fichte, Schiller, Jacobs und Wilhelm von Humboldt, bei denen *„Nationalerziehung und Erziehung zum Griechentum zu einer untrennbaren Einheit verschmolz"*, schlug er den

Bogen zu Jachmann und Passow und stellte in Bezug auf das von ihnen herausgegebene „Archiv Deutscher Nationalbildung" fest: *„Hier vollendet sich die vergessene, umfangreiche Literatur über Nationalerziehung aus dem 18. Jahrhundert ... Erziehung zum reinen Menschentum im Staate der Humanität ist nun die Losung ... 'Die höhere Geisteskultur' der Griechen [bleibt] der letzte Menschheitspol, an dem man sich orientiert, um das Ideal einer vollkommenen Nation zu erreichen"* (Spranger 1932, S. 45).

Auf ein anderes Strukturelement der Jenkauer Konzeption machte in den zwanziger Jahren Karl-Ernst Schellhammer aufmerksam. Er sah darin vor allem einen „Höhepunkt in der Entwicklung der Einheitsschulidee", die insofern mit den graecophilen Tendenzen zusammenhing, als sie aus der Forderung resultierte, allen Jugendlichen bis zum 18. Lebensjahr in einer einheitlichen Nationalschule Griechischunterricht zu erteilen. Obwohl Jachmann die Möglichkeit eines früheren Schulabgangs eingeräumt hatte, kritisierte *Schellhammer (1925, S. 65) „die Verstiegenheit des Theoretikers, der bei seinem Ideenflug den Boden unter den Füßen verloren und auf die praktische Durchführbarkeit seiner Pläne verzichtet hat".*

Unvergleichlich vielfältiger nahmen sich die Reaktionen in der zweiten Hälfte des 20. Jahrhunderts aus. Grundlegend war zunächst die Neuauflage der Originalquellen. So wurde Jachmanns Schrift „Über das Verhältnis der Schule zur Welt" seit 1951 in die von Rudolf *Joerden (1962)* bearbeitete, wiederholt aufgelegte, vor allem für die Ausbildung von Pädagogen konzipierte Textsammlung „Dokumente des Neuhumanismus" aufgenommen, und in den sechziger Jahren besorgte der Frankfurter Bildungshistoriker Heinz-Joachim Heydorn, nachdem vorher schon Auszüge publiziert worden waren, einen (inzwischen wieder vergriffenen) Faksimile-Neudruck des über 500 Seiten starken „Archivs Deutscher Nationalbildung". Ebenso begann in den fünfziger Jahren dieses Jahrhunderts eine neue Welle von deskriptiven und wertenden Darstellungen, und zwar in beiden Teilen des geteilten Deutschlands.

In der DDR konzentrierte sich das Interesse fast ausschließlich auf die Schriften Jachmanns. In der 1954 publizierten Arbeit „Deutsche Nationalerziehungspläne aus der Zeit des Befreiungskrieges" untersuchte Helmut *König (1954, S. 16-23, 49-148)* Abhandlungen, in denen Jachmann 1812 seine Ideen über Nationalbildung und Nationalschule entwickelt hatte. Noch ausführlicher behandelte er diese 1972/73 in seiner zweibändigen Arbeit „Zur Geschichte der bürgerlichen Nationalerziehung in Deutschland zwischen 1807 und 1815" *(König 1972/73)*. Welchen beachtlichen Stellenwert DDR-Pädagogen Jachmann einräumten, zeigte sich nicht zuletzt darin, daß er in allen 16 Auflagen der von einem vielköpfigen Kollektiv herausgegebenen „Geschichte der Erziehung" als Neuhumanist und Bildungsreformer gewürdigt wurde *(Günther u. a. 1957–1988).*

In der alten Bundesrepublik Deutschland waren die Publikationen, die sich mit der neuhumanistischen Phase des Conradinums beschäftigten, nicht nur zahlreicher, sondern auch thematisch vielfältiger, vor allem schlossen sie gleichermaßen Franz Passow ein, dessen pädagogisches Wirken sogar Gegenstand einer speziellen Dissertation wurde *(Quanz 1970).* Die Forschungen in der DDR, die sich schwerpunktmäßig auf die politischen und bildungspolitischen Bestrebungen Jachmanns, insbesondere auf die egalitären und Einheitsschultendenzen, konzentrierten, wurden in der Bundesrepublik durch umfassendere, aspektreichere Interpretationen zugleich wesentlich ergänzt und modifiziert. Dies geschah jedoch weniger in den Darstellungen, die jeweils die gesamte Entwicklung des Conradinums – wie etwa Erich *Hoffmann (1968)* – zu fassen versuchten, sondern fast ausschließlich in Arbeiten, die spezielle Problemkomplexe wie die neuhumanistische Bildung, die Entwicklung der Gymnasien, die preußischen Reformen sowie Repräsentanten der Geistesgeschichte am Anfang des 19. Jahrhunderts untersuchten. Bemerkenswert sind aber auch die Aussagen, die in dem seit 1987 erscheinenden „Handbuch der deutschen Bildungsgeschichte" über Jachmann, Passow und das Conradinum zu finden sind. So heißt es bei der Bewertung von neuhumanistischen Reformversuchen: *„Sie sind großenteils gescheitert, nur in Internaten – dem Conradinum in Jenkau, der Cauerschen Anstalt in Berlin – konnte das Griechische in enger Verbindung mit dem Deutschen dem Sprachunterricht zugrunde gelegt werden; offenbar mit solchem Erfolg, daß noch nicht elfjährige Kinder 'außer einer guten Zahl Homerischer Gesänge, auch bereits mehrere Bücher des Herodot und die platonischen Gespräche Kriton und die Apologie des Sokrates gelesen und vollkommen verstanden hatten'" (Jeismann / Lundgren 1987, S. 194).*

Im Sinne einer generellen Charakterisierung wurde das Conradinum als *„das am energischsten experimentierende Organ des Neuhumanismus" (Joerden 1962, S. 9)* und das „Archiv Deutscher Nationalbildung" als ein *„Höhepunkt in der Geschichte der deutschen Pädagogik" (Heydorn 1969, S. V)* bezeichnet sowie den beiden Autoren bescheinigt, daß sie pädagogische Grundfragen artikuliert und *„mit der Reform des Conradinums ein Stück nachwirkender Wirklichkeit" (Sochatzy 1973, S. 147)* geschaffen hatten. DDR-Pädagogen zählten Jachmanns Nationalerziehungsplan *„zu dem progressiven Erbe, das uns der Neuhumanismus hinterlassen hat" (König 1972, S. 261)* und zu jenen progressiven Traditionen, *„die auch zum Fundament des ersten deutschen Arbeiter-und-Bauern-Staates und seines sozialistischen Bildungssystems gehören" (König 1973, S. 280).*

Im Unterschied zu der einseitigen Interpretation in der DDR fußten die Urteile der bundesrepublikanischen Bildungshistoriker jeweils auf der Bewertung mehrerer Strukturelemente der in Jenkau entworfenen Konzeption. Am häufigsten wurden hervorgehoben:

1. Die Art, in der Schule definiert wurde, nicht als Erfahrungs-, sondern als Vernunftbegriff, *„a priori aus dem höchsten Zweck der Menschheit"* abgeleitet, so daß die Schule ein *„präordiniertes"* Verhältnis zur Welt gewinnt *(Jachmann 1811b in Joerden 1962, S. 91)*.

2. Die curriculare Orientierung am hellenistischen Altertum, vornehmlich begründet mit dem Bildungswert der griechischen Sprache, wobei nicht an einen Rückzug in die Vergangenheit gedacht war, sondern daran, über die Erkenntnis des „Wahren, Guten und Schönen" zur Bestimmung des Menschseins und von daher zur Lösung aktueller Aufgaben zu gelangen.

3. Die dem platten Nützlichkeitsstreben der Aufklärung gegenübergestellte „rein menschliche Bildung".

4. Die vielfältigen gesellschaftspolitischen Intentionen, die mit einer der Politik vorgeordneten Pädagogik nach einer *„vollkommenen Umwälzung aller bestehenden gesellschaftlichen Verhältnisse" (Heydorn 1969, S. XXXVIII)* strebten. So sollten *„die erzieherischen Postulate als politische Ziele erscheinen"* und die wahre Bildung *„zugleich Mittel nicht nur einer neuhumanistischen Schulverbesserung, sondern einer gesellschaftlichen und politischen Reform"* sein *(Jeismann 1974, S. 250-251)* und *„eine frei geordnete Gesellschaft – ohne konkrete Machtstruktur – anstreben" (Quanz 1970, S. 126)*. Hinzu kam *„die Auffassung von der prinzipiellen Gleichheit aller Menschen, die in der gleichen Vernunft ihren Grund hatte" (Lassahn / Stach 1979, S. 40)*, und die daraus resultierende Forderung nach einer einheitlichen Bildung.

5. Das klare Rangverhältnis von Humanität vor Nationalität und von National- vor Staatserziehung. Diesbezügliche Ausführungen von Bildungshistorikern zeigen volle Übereinstimmung: *„In der Nationalität sehen die Jenkauer den leitenden Begriff ihrer Pädagogik, die als Nationalbildung aber eine, wenn auch modifizierte Menschenbildung bleibt und ihren Gegenstand in der inneren Natur einer Nation findet. Sie setzen sich damit von einer Staatspädagogik ab und erklären Nation und Staat für nicht identisch" (Quanz 1970, S. 169)*. „Humanität, Nationalität und Individualität offenbaren ein Rangverhält-

nis, in dem die Bildung zur Humanität vorangeht ... Die Erziehung der Nation bleibt dem Ideal 'vollkommener Menschheit oder Humanität' untergeordnet" (Heydorn 1969, S. XXIX-XXX). *„Der Begriff der Menschheit ist mit allen seinen Merkmalen im Begriff der Nation, dieser wieder im Begriff des Individuums enthalten"* (Lassahn 1970, S. 156). *„Radikal lehnte Jachmann den Begriff einer 'preußischen Nationalerziehung' und damit alle älteren Nationalerziehungsvorstellungen ab als eines Widerspruchs in sich ... Die erzieherische Idee überflog hier nicht nur die Standes- und Berufsschranken, sondern auch die Grenzen des Territorialstaates"* (Jeismann 1974, S. 255). Helmut *König (1972, S. 258)* erklärte die Haltung Jachmanns gegen die *„preußische Nationalerziehung"* damit, daß er *„in ihr ein Mittel zur Germanisierung und Verpreußung anderer Nationen sah"*.

Die Beschäftigung mit der neuhumanistischen Bildungskonzeption Jachmanns und Passows hat auch in der zweiten Hälfte des 20. Jahrhunderts nicht nur zu positiven Urteilen geführt. Kritisiert wurden drei Punkte:

Der erste betraf die Übersteigerung des pädagogischen Anspruchs, die vor allem in der Forderung gesehen wurde, daß ausnahmslos alle Kinder über viele Jahre Griechisch und Latein lernen sollten. Rudolf *Joerden (1962, S. 10)* sprach angesichts des Versuches, *„den Gedanken der alle Deutschen umfassenden Nationalbildung mit der am klassischen Altertum gebildeten Geisteskultur zu vereinigen"* und der daraus abgeleiteten Forderung, *„daß jeder Deutsche, wes Standes er sei, die alten Sprachen lernen müsse"*, von einer *„grotesken Konsequenz"*.

Der zweite Einwand galt der prioritären Bedeutung von Bildung und Schule und richtete sich dagegen, daß Jachmann und Passow darauf aus waren, *„die scheinbare Trennung von Bildung und Gesellschaft dadurch aufzuheben, daß sie die Welt zur Schule zu machen versuchten ... Diese reinmenschliche Bildung war eine allzu reinmenschliche Bildung, als daß sie verwirklichbar gewesen wäre"* (Sochatzy 1973, S. 34).

Als drittes wurde kritisiert, daß die Konzeption Jachmanns und Passows überwiegend, wenn nicht gar ausschließlich nur formale Bildung intendiere: *„Letztlich klaffen bei dieser Art der Bildung immer die zu entwickelnde Kraft und die Welt auseinander. Sie wieder zusammenzubringen wird dann ein besonderes Problem der Pädagogik"* (Lassahn 1970, S. 149). *„Es ist eigentümlich, daß in dieser Zeit die am revolutionärsten argumentierenden Neuhumanisten den formalen Bildungswert am stärksten betonten. Natürlich ist zu fragen, ob sie sich damit nicht selbst den pädagogischen Weg zum politischen Ziel verbau-*

ten und dazu beitrugen, den künftig Gebildeten sowohl vom 'Volk' wie auch vom politischen Inhalt der alten Literatur zu isolieren" (Jeismann 1974, S. 252).

Aus der marxistischen Sicht der DDR-Pädagogen war es selbstverständlich eine „*utopische Vorstellung, daß eine 'Erneuerung der Nation' allein durch Erziehung und Reformen zu erreichen sei" (Günther u. a. 15. Aufl. 1987, S. 221).*

Schließlich ist zu fragen, ob Jachmann und Passow in ihrem neuhumanistischen Denken von Zeitgenossen beeinflußt wurden und deren Ideen rezipiert haben. Abgesehen von den „Studien zur Wirkungsgeschichte Fichtes als Pädagoge" von Rudolf *Lassahn*, der in einem von drei Kapiteln *(1970, S. 140-169)* ausschließlich den Einfluß Fichtes auf die Jenkauer untersuchte, wurde diese Frage bislang weder ausführlich noch detailliert behandelt. Sonst wurden nur knappe Hinweise auf einzelne Personen gegeben. Insgesamt läßt sich das Resultat dahingehend zusammenfassen, daß Anregungen von vielen Seiten angenommen oder auch Prägungen – bei Jachmann durch Immanuel Kant und bei Passow durch die Altphilologen Friedrich Jacobs und Gottfried Hermann – aufgezeigt wurden, daß aber die Konzipierung der neuhumanistischen Schulverfassung des Conradinums doch als eine eigene kreative Leistung beider Direktoren beurteilt wurde. So sah *Heydorn* in Jachmann zwar einen „*strengen Schüler Kants"*, der dessen „*pädagogischen Auftrag vollstreckte: 'Kinder sollen nicht dem gegenwärtigen, sondern dem zukünftig bessern Zustande des menschlichen Geschlechts, das ist: der Idee der Menschheit, und deren ganzer Bestimmung angemessen, erzogen werden'"* (1969, S. LIII), dann aber konstatierte er: „*Der Kantische Gedanke bildet den Ausgangspunkt, das 'Conradinum' die empirische Basis, die die Modalitäten der Verwirklichung stets wieder neu zu durchdenken zwang"* (ebd., S. XXVIII). Ähnlich resümierte *Heydorn* (ebd., S. XL-XLI) über Passow: „*Humboldt und Niethammer müssen hier vorausgesetzt werden, aber es besteht kein Zweifel, daß Passow den veränderten Bildungsinhalt des Conradinum entscheidend selbst im Sinne eines philologisch geschulten Neuhumanismus bestimmt hat."* Auch Wilhelm von Humboldts Einfluß wurde im generellen Anstoß durch seine vor der Jenkauer Konzeption publizierte Schrift über die griechischen Altertumsstudien, auf keinen Fall aber in seinen erst später veröffentlichten Schulplänen gesehen. Dementsprechend folgerte *Quanz (1970, S. 235)*, bezogen auf Passow: „*Was sich als erstes anbietet, nämlich Bezüge zur Humboldtschen Bildungs- und Sprachtheorie zu verfolgen, verbietet sich auch gleich wieder. Denn weder läßt sich philologisch eine Abhängigkeit Passows von Humboldt nachweisen, da dessen entscheidende Werke entweder nach Passows pädagogischen Arbeiten liegen oder aber erst viel später veröffentlicht werden, noch scheint es angemessen, Passows praktische, nie lange im theoretischen Bereich verweilende Art mit der subtilen*

Reflexion Humboldts in direkte Beziehung zu bringen." Auch die gründliche Untersuchung Lassahns über die Wirkung Fichtes auf Jachmann und Passow zeigte, daß die Jenkauer viele Gedanken Fichtes aufgenommen haben, daß man aber *„mit Fichte kaum mehr gemeinsam"* hatte *„als die vielen anderen Gymnasien des 19. Jahrhunderts, die eine neuhumanistische Konzeption verfolgten und in ihren Schulprogrammen Fichte verherrlichten" (Lassahn 1970, S. 169).* In einer besonders wichtigen Frage, nämlich in der Auffassung von Staat und Nation, stellte er fest, daß die Ansätze weit auseinanderklafften.

In Polen hat die Beschäftigung mit der Geschichte des Conradinums erst nach dem Zweiten Weltkrieg begonnen und sich bisher nur in zwei Publikationen niedergeschlagen. Die erste ist die zweibändige, von Ludwik *Kurdybacha (1968)* herausgegebene „Geschichte der Erziehung". In ihr wird nach Fichte und Harnisch und vor Wilhelm von Humboldt kurz auf Reinhold Bernhard Jachmann als Repräsentant demokratischer pädagogischer Ideen eingegangen. Als deutlichster Ausdruck seines Schaffens wird der auch in deutschen Publikationen am meisten zitierte Ausruf vorgetragen: *„Hinweg also mit den verschiedenartigen Schulen für Stände und Berufsgeschäfte, die in einem Volk den Geist der Zwietracht nähren! Hinweg mit den sogenannten gelehrten und ungelehrten Schulen, mit den Gymnasien, höhern und niedern Bürgerschulen und wie sonst ihr Name sein mag! Es ist nur Eine Menschheit! Es ist nur Eine deutsche Nation! Es muß auch nur Eine Nationalschule sein" (Kurdybacha 1968, Bd. 2, S. 95).*

Die zweite Publikation ist die zum 200. Jahrestag der Stiftung von Aleksander Henke verfaßte, ausschließlich dem Conradinum gewidmete Schrift. Darin bezeichnet er das Conradinum während der neuhumanistischen Phase – wie schon Erich *Hoffmann (1968)* – als *„szkoła uczonych pierwszej rangi"* („gelehrte Schule ersten Ranges") *(Henke 1994, S. 18)* und zieht das Resümee: *„Jene an schöpferischen Ideen reichen Jahre des jungen Instituts waren die interessanteste Periode (najciekawszym okresem) in der langjährigen Geschichte der Schule" (ebd., S. 22).* Im Unterschied zu Kurdybacha, aber in Übereinstimmung mit Erich Hoffmann betont er die Rolle Passows stärker als die Jachmanns und schenkt Passows Engagement für die Leibesübungen große Aufmerksamkeit.

Da sich die polnischen Darstellungen in Quantität und Intensität erheblich von den deutschen Abhandlungen unterscheiden, erlauben sie keinen detaillierten, exakten Vergleich. Aber es läßt sich sagen, daß die wenigen Urteile eindeutig eine tendenzielle Übereinstimmung mit denen der deutschen Bildungsgeschichte zeigen: die 1811 und 1812 von Jachmann und Passow publizierten Schriften und die damit verbundene neuhumanistische Phase des Conradinums haben bis in die Gegenwart hinein nicht an Attraktivität verloren.

Bibliographie

Goethe, Johann Wolfgang von: Brief an Franz Passow. In: Goethes Briefe. Hrsg. von Bodo Morawe. Bd. 3. Briefe der Jahre 1805-1821, Hamburg: Wegener 1965, S. 168.
Günther, Karl-Heinz u. a.: Geschichte der Erziehung. 1. bis 16. Aufl. Berlin: Volk und Wissen 1957 – 1988.
Henke, Aleksander: Conradinum. W 200 rocznicze fundacji [Conradinum. Zum 200. Jahrestag der Stiftung]. Gdańsk 1994.
Heydorn Hans-Joachim: Einleitung. In: Jachmann, Reinhold Bernhard / Passow, Franz (Hrsg.): Archiv Deutscher Nationalbildung. Unveränd. Neudr., Frankfurt a. M.: Sauer und Auvermann 1969, S. V-LIX.
Hoffmann, Erich: Das Conradinum. Geschichte einer Danziger Schule im Abriß. Remagen: Selbstverlag 1968.
Jachmann, Reinhold Bernhard: Recension der Herbart'schen „Allgemeinen Pädagogik". In: Jenaische Allgemeine Literaturzeitung, (1811a) 234-237, Sp. 81-110.
Jachmann, Reinhold Bernhard: Über das Verhältnis der Schule zur Welt. Berlin: Maurer 1811b. [Wiederabdruck in: Joerden, Rudolf (Hrsg.): Dokumente des Neuhumanismus. Bd. 1. 2. Aufl., Weinheim: Beltz 1962, S. 88-110]
Jachmann, Reinhold Bernhard / Passow, Franz (Hrsg.): Archiv Deutscher Nationalbildung. Berlin: Maurer 1812. [Unveränd. Neudruck: Frankfurt a. M.: Sauer und Auvermann 1969]
Jeismann, Karl-Ernst: Das preußische Gymnasium in Staat und Gesellschaft. Stuttgart: Klett 1974.
Jeismann, Karl-Ernst / Lundgren, Peter (Hrsg.): Handbuch der deutschen Bildungsgeschichte. Bd. 3. 1800-1870. München: Beck 1987.
Joerden, Rudolf (Hrsg.): Dokumente des Neuhumanismus. Bd. 1. 2. Aufl. Weinheim: Beltz 1962. (Kleine pädagogische Texte. 17)
König, Helmut: Deutsche Nationalerziehungspläne aus der Zeit des Befreiungskrieges. Berlin: Volk und Wissen 1954.
König, Helmut: Zur Geschichte der bürgerlichen Nationalerziehung in Deutschland zwischen 1807 und 1815. T. 1. 2. Berlin: Volk und Wissen 1972. 1973. (= Monumenta paedagogica. A. 12-13)
Kurdybacha, Ludwik (Hrsg.): Historia wychowania [Geschichte der Erziehung]. 1. 2. Warszawa: Państwowe Wydawnictwo Naukowe 1968.
Lassahn, Rudolf: Studien zur Wirkungsgeschichte Fichtes als Pädagoge. Heidelberg: Quelle und Meyer 1970.
Lassahn, Rudolf / Stach, Reinhard: Geschichte der Schulversuche. Theorie und Praxis. Heidelberg: Quelle und Meyer 1979.
Paulsen, Friedrich: Geschichte des gelehrten Unterrichts auf den deutschen Schulen und Universitäten vom Ausgang des Mittelalters bis zur Gegenwart. Bd. 2. Leipzig: Veit 1885.
Quanz, Dietrich Reiner: Nationalität und Humanität. Studien zur Pädagogik Franz Passows (1786-1833). Köln, Univ., Diss., 1970.

Schellhammer, Karl-Ernst: Geschichte der Einheitsschulidee. Oppeln: Raabe 1925.
Schulze, Johannes: Rezension zu „Ueber das Verhältniß der Schule zur Welt". In: Jachmann, Reinhold Bernhard / Passow, Franz (Hrsg.): Archiv Deutscher Nationalbildung, Berlin: Maurer 1812, S. 142-143.
Sochatzy, Klaus: Das Neuhumanistische Gymnasium und die reinmenschliche Bildung. Göttingen: Vandenhoeck und Ruprecht 1973.
Spranger, Eduard: Volk, Staat, Erziehung. Leipzig: Quelle und Meyer 1932.

Ungedruckte Quellen

Geheimes Staatsarchiv Berlin: Rep. 76 alt I Nr. 236, vol. I. Rep. 76 alt I Nr. 289a, vol. I.

Magna Carta for the Status of Teachers: Thirty Years of the UNESCO-Recommendation for the Status of Teachers

Wilhelm Ebert

Introduction

Thirty years ago representatives of some 75 nations met in the Palais of the UNESCO in Paris, from the 21st of September to the 5th of October 1966. This special intergovernmental conference adopted an international document on the 5th of October which influenced educational politics and the status of teachers in various countries directly and indirectly. The adopted „International Recommendation for the Status of Teachers" on one hand stopped intensive long-standing discussions between teachers and teachers' associations, between politicians and governments, and on the other hand it articulated such widespread goals for educational policies and the status of teachers that no end to the discussions is in sight.

In autumn 1996, UNESCO and ILO[1] took the 30 years of the Magna Carta for the Teaching Profession as a reason to convene the 45th International Education Conference from the 3rd to the 6th of October in Geneva under the theme „Strengthening of the Role of Teachers" and to celebrate the International Day of the Teacher exactly on the 5th of October. In times when regional, national and international problems of education and educational politics are overshadowed by other themes and other political arenas it is necessary to remember the pros and cons of the status document, which is already considered „historical". It is time that educational politicians and members of teachers' associations remind themselves of the content and the development of a document that has promoted the status of teachers over many years. The facts stated in this document are still valid today, but there is not one country in which the demands adopted because of educational concerns are realised entirely. The adoption of the charter, however, has brought about various changes in the education system and in the status of teachers.

---

1 At the end of the text there is a list explaining the abbreviations used.

The 70th birthday of Professor Wolfgang Mitter gives me the welcome opportunity to report on the birth of this Magna Carta for the teaching profession. Over many years Professor Mitter has gained merit as Director of the German Institute for International Educational Research. He is a well-known personality in the field of comparative educational science and a member of the German UNESCO Commission. Recently he actively participated in the above mentioned UNESCO conference on the role of teachers.

As Permanent Representative of WCOTP at UNESCO I had the honour of attending actively all substantial conferences and congresses which led to the adoption of the Charter of Teachers in 1966. Over many years I was linked with most of the founders of this charter in collegial relationships or even in unique friendships. The latter concern mostly the three great teacher leaders, without whom neither the birth of the charter with this content nor the „Special Intergovernmental Conference" would have been thinkable or possible. I refer to the American William G. Carr, the Briton Sir Ronald Gould and the Indian Shri Natarajan, of course.

As highly regarded pedagogues, successfully involved in international politics, all three practised exemplary ethically oriented leadership.[2] William G. Carr was the last surviving member of this triumvirate. After his death on the 1st of March 1996 (he was by then 94 years old) I am one of the few living witnesses of the thrilling international educational politics of that time.

UNO, UNESCO and the Status of Teachers

The 25th anniversary of the „Magna Carta for the Status of Teachers" was celebrated during the 26th General Conference of UNESCO in October 1991 in Paris. ILO Deputy Director-General Heribert Maier and the French Minister of State and National Education, Lionel Jospin, amongst others, spoke at the conference. Federico Mayor, UNESCO Director-General, remembered the radical changes which have swept through the education system and the teaching profession since the 1960s. Quantitatively the number of teachers had increased from 16 million in 1966 to some 44 million in 1991. Overcrowded and under-equipped classrooms were the rule in many countries, especially in

---

2 Sir Ronald Gould was President of WCOTP from 1952 to 1970, Dr. William G. Carr was General Secretary from 1952 to 1970 and President of the WCOTP from 1970 to 1972, Shri Natarajan was Vice-President of WCOTP from 1956 to 1971.

developing countries. Ironically enough, Mayor said, this alarming situation can be seen at a time when all countries have begun to realise the importance of having an educated population. He stressed that by „educated" he does not mean knowing only how to read, write and express one's thoughts, but also possessing knowledge about the principles of tolerance, respect and understanding of others, which he considers to be the foundations of peace and co-operation among nations. He was worried that the status of teachers is far from satisfactory in many parts of the world. Therefore the importance of the „Magna Carta for the Teaching Profession" as an international standard-setting measure cannot be underestimated. The 146 provisions still provide useful guidelines in all countries, both for national legislation and for collective bargaining.

At the end of his speech at the conference, attended by ministers, diplomats and members of teachers' associations, Federico Mayor welcomed the guest of honour of this festive meeting, one of the founders of UNESCO and General Secretary of WCOTP for many years, Mr. William Carr, with whom many internationally active pedagogues in Germany have felt closely linked for years. As early as 1946 he had pointed out that UNESCO's central task should be to promote the improvement of and the right to education. This, however, could not be achieved without the participation of teachers. He became the advocate of an international charter that would be acceptable to all countries, and, 20 years later in 1966, he served as rapporteur at the Special Intergovernmental Conference on the Status of Teachers.

William G. Carr replied to this welcoming introduction in a long speech. First he remembered the general mood after World War II. Its aftermath included not only the usual post-war longing for enduring peace, but also an uneasy awareness that this war had arisen to a large extent as a result of the neglect and misuse of the immense power of education. The United Nations Charter responded primarily to these almost universal feelings. In 1919 the draftsmen of the League of Nations Covenant had firmly rejected all proposals for co-operation in education. „In contrast", Carr said, „at the 1945 Conference on International Organisation, we inserted education at nine points in the United Nations text.[3] Signed by the delegates at the San Francisco Opera House in June 1945,

---

3   On May the 7th, the document of the unconditioned surrender of Germany was signed at Karlshorst. At this time the United Nations Charter had already been in the making in San Francisco. On the 16th of May 1945 the breakthrough for education became visible in San Francisco. The *San Francisco Chronicle* declared that the role of education had become a crucial issue at the United Nations Conference. The *San Francisco News* predicted that a United Nations Conference would be held within the next few months. The *New York Times* said that the discussion about education was one of the most significant developments of the Conference.

the UNO Charter became effective on October 24." One week later, Prime Minister Clement Attlee opened the founding conference of UNESCO. „He urged us to construct the defences of peace in the minds of men because there, he said, is where wars begin. The delegates promptly applied his advice in the famous UNESCO Preamble[4] and added that ignorance and prejudice, hostile to the dignity and equality of mankind, had made the recent war possible."[5]

William Carr, who, as Secretary General of the UNESCO founding conference, had contributed actively to formulating the UNESCO Charter, also illuminated during his speech the 1950s and 1960s. The UNESCO had wisely supplemented its lofty public pronouncements on education by enlisting the energies of professional organisations of teachers. However, despite unprecedented expressions of public concern about education, the general status of the teaching profession remained unchanged. Governments that eloquently proclaimed their devotion to education remained unable or unwilling to draw enough gifted young people into teaching or to compensate those already in the profession adequately. After some attempts and drafts the Intergovernmental Conference of 1966 reviewed all the previous work and adopted the amended text unanimously.

At the end of his speech in October 1991, William Carr concluded that history has revealed UNESCO as a necessary instrument for some of the highest purposes of the United Nations, and that a corps of competent, dedicated teachers would be required to achieve the goals of UNESCO.

History of the Development of the Magna Carta for the Teaching Profession

Already the second General Conference of the UNESCO (Mexico City, 1947) and the third (Beirut, 1948) demanded that the General Director together with the international teachers' associations and the IBE collect some material so that a „Carta of Teachers" could be developed. Therefore UNESCO and IBE published some comparative reports about education and status of teachers in various countries. After the founding of WCOTP in 1952 in Copenhagen work on an international survey about the situation and

---

4 „Since wars begin in the minds of men, it is in the minds of men that the defence of peace must be constructed."
5 45 of the 51 UN-member countries participated at this founding Conference of UNESCO in London. The only large, powerful and eligible country absent was the Soviet Union. This absence was considered as the beginning of „the Cold Peace".

the demands of teachers was started in 1953. The Delegates' Assembly of WCOTP in 1954 in Istanbul had as it's main theme „The Status of Teachers". A report about 33 countries and a resolution with eleven statements and demands was adopted and published. In the ILO the „Advisory Committee on Salaried Employees and Professional Workers" decided to include the teachers' group in 1952 and 1954. In October 1958 the ILO held its first „Experts Meeting" on the economic and social conditions of teachers. This meeting was chaired by WCOTP President Sir Ronald Gould and took place in Geneva. At this week-long congress Karl Bungardt, experienced editor of the Allgemeine Deutsche Lehrerzeitung,[6] participated for Germany. He was a liberal man with experience in education and educational politics.

Some days before the General Conference of UNESCO in Paris in November 1958 I had started work as Director of the Paris Office and „Permanent Representative of WCOTP at UNESCO". There was no time to get used to the situation or to decide on an orientation for my work. At once I was confronted with the problems of the status of teachers. I used all opportunities to stress the professional role of teachers for education and the importance of teachers' participation in the political discussions. Some proposals were adopted by the General Conference in 1960.

The WCOTP expanded to include some new member organisations. An individual programme commission was developed for Africa, Asia and Latin America.

UNESCO, ILO and WCOTP

In spring 1961 the Assistant Director of the Department of Education of the UNESCO, Leo Fernig, asked WCOTP some questions concerning the criteria for appraising the status of teachers, the methods which could bring about improvements and the part UNESCO could play. He was looking for an international and comparative point of view and conclusions derived from previous studies. Mr. S. H. M. Jones, President of the Teachers' Association of Gambia, was at that time discussing a plan of a WCOTP study about the teachers' status in African Countries with me. His report, published in 1962 was based on travels to and studies in 26 African countries and served as a pilot

---

[6] This General German Teachers' Journal was the official organ of the German Teachers' Federation (AGDL). In the Executive Committee of the AGDL Bungardt reported in detail on the course of the meeting and the leading role of Sir Ronald Gould.

study for reports about the teachers' status in Asia (published in 1963) and of North, Middle and South America (published in 1964). These studies answered Leo Fernig's main questions raised in May 1961 thoroughly.

But then the question of a more effective co-ordination of the work of UNESCO and ILO arose, if two independent documents were to be avoided. UNESCO was working on the professional status of teachers and ILO stressed the working conditions of teachers. Through friends who were members in the Executive Board of UNESCO I brought these questions about the status of teachers to the attention of this council very often, which was – after the General Conference – the highest decision-making organ of UNESCO. A few members of this council mentioned to me: „We are not here to deal with the salary and the well-being of teachers, we have other problems, there is, at least, the ILO for problems like that." In the discussion, however, they only made vague remarks or kept silent. The General Conference in 1962, however, adopted a resolution, which was presented by France and co-sponsored by nine other countries (Columbia, Ecuador, Finland, Italy, Morocco, Niger, Senegal, Vietnam and Yugoslavia). Because of the great importance of this resolution I quote the main content:

> „Considering that the development and improvement of education are possible only as a result of the limitless devotion of teachers;
> Recognising the difficulties that most countries experience in providing a sufficient number of fully qualified teachers for the schools;
> Convinced that the progress of education throughout the world requires that teachers everywhere should enjoy a moral and material status worthy of their lofty mission;
> Authorises the Director-General to undertake, in consultation with Member States and appropriate international organisations, both governmental and non-governmental, a study of the various aspects of the question of teachers' status, and to submit to the General Conference the conclusions of this study, accompanied by proposals for appropriate action in this field."

Encouragement

With this resolution development went into the decisive phase. If I had not been aware about it beforehand, I was now told by international confidants that I now held a key-position, being responsible not only for the further development of the document concerning thematic questions, but also for the methodological and tactical ways to push it through. From now on I took a lot of time to talk with the responsible people in UNESCO – from the „lowest" advisors up to the General Director, but also with diplomats of any grade. There were not many doors which stayed shut for an official, half-official or entirely private exchange of ideas. Very often over „a cup of tea" in the UNESCO house or during a dinner somewhere else, I reached new insights or achieved some substantial agreement with my interlocutor. During such opportunities I noticed to what an extent this task had taken hold of me. Being a gourmet under normal circumstances, I did not even notice during these exquisite dinners what kind of food was being served. A lot of UNESCO people became friends. Some of them became chief of a mission, ambassador, minister, professor or even president of the Club of Rome. I want to mention just three of them: first of all Leo Fernig, a benevolent, experienced counsellor from the beginning, then the always helpful pedagogue and Quaker Herbert Abraham and from ILO the cosmopolitan Karl Grünberg, who, in working together with me for the same goal, untiringly, became a close friend.

„How", I asked myself and some competent personalities, „can I take advantage of all my opportunities to influence the further development in the true interest of the teachers and the WCOTP?" Four themes for consequent action crystallised:

- I had to keep myself informed as much as possible about the next steps and the further goals and plans of all people involved;
- I had to become influential in choosing the people who had the task of developing the document concretely, step by step;
- I had to help to place these personalities, who seemed right to me, into an optimal, functional position for this work;
- I had to convince as many participants as possible of the rightness of our – possibly mutual – point of view.

Knowing about the different opinions in WCOTP concerning some questions I was well aware of the difficulties of producing a document that would not only take into account the interests of WCOTP and very different international, national and regional teachers' associations, but also of governments of the various member states of UNESCO. It turned out that there were more helpers and personalities with mutual interests and so the work began encouragingly well.

Meeting of Experts in Geneva and Paris

From the 21st of October to the 1st of November 1963, a Committee of Experts of ILO met in Geneva. Heinrich Rodenstein, an expert from the Federal Republic of Germany and Vice-President of the AGDL, was actively involved in the negotiations.[7] WCOTP Vice-President, Srinavasa Natarajan, a sharp-witted and wise Indian, was chairing this meeting at which social and economic problems of the teachers were discussed thoroughly. The results were phrased carefully in 129 paragraphs and were adopted unanimously. The committee of experts was in favour of a Charter of Teachers, compiled jointly by UNESCO and ILO. A draft for a resolution for the World Teacher's Day, however, which had been prepared by the Labour Office was voted down after a long discussion about the pros and cons (10 to 7 votes, with 6 abstentions).

Due to Natarajan's diplomacy a full consent could be achieved in the sometimes difficult negotiations about various social and economic problems. The discussions, which took place in the evenings in the hotel and were held between either two partners or whole groups, helped on the road to success as well. Considering the political, ideological, geographical and economical differences in the backgrounds and life-experiences of these experts this first round of discussions could be celebrated as a complete success.

But how should the further negotiations continue, if educational politics were to be stressed even more than ever before? Positions and answers to questions were required in areas where decision-making was totally usurped by single national and regional governments, parliaments or school boards that considered themselves to be autonomous. Especially in these areas standards were involved which influenced the status of teachers directly and indirectly. In this aspect no problems were seen in the relationship between UNESCO and ILO. Which central questions should be put before an UNESCO expert committee? In the end a consensus was reached on four central tasks:

– to elaborate principles and criteria in the light of which it would be possible for the Secretariat of UNESCO, in close liaison with ILO, to formulate international standards for a) teacher preparation, b) education policy affecting the teaching staff;
– to make such observations and comments as the committee deemed appropriate to

---

7 Heinrich Rodenstein was a very active man with various interests. After the Second World War he contributed considerably through the AGDL to the enhancement of the German teaching profession in foreign countries.

complement the Report of the Meeting of ILO experts on social and economic conditions of teachers (Geneva, 1963);
- to give advice on scope, structure and content of an international document on teachers' professional, economic and social problems;
- to make suggestions on UNESCO's immediate or long-term action designed to assist teachers in the discharge of their growing professional responsibilities.

It was difficult to choose suitable experts for this task, as the different ideologies, political and economic systems and the differing interests and opinions from members of governments, school boards, teachers' education and teachers' associations had to be considered. A committee consisting of eleven experts was chosen carefully. Some of them already had rich experiences in international educational politics. One of them was the Indian educationist Shri Natarajan mentioned before, another the French general school-inspector and former General-Director of the UNESCO, Jean Thomas and, last but not least the former Executive Secretary of the National Education Association of the United States and General-Secretary of the WCOTP, William Carr, who was unanimously elected chairman of the important committee meeting which took place in Paris from the 4th to the 15th of May 1964.

Here I cannot mention all details, different opinions and various controversies. But I want to stress the constructive spirit of the meeting, which was exemplary, because four of these eleven experts came from teaching, four from school boards and three from teachers' education. From the latter sector Mrs. Z. Malkova from the Academy of Educational Science of Moscow has to be specially mentioned, because she participated in the discussions so matter-of-factly in that period of the cold war. The work of this committee, which worked for eleven days on the four central tasks, resulted in a report which included the conclusions of the ILO experts' committee of 1963. This report included the complete content of a status document, from teachers' education over tasks, security, rights and duties of the profession. Even questions concerning holidays and pensions were considered in the total of 203 paragraphs with various under-paragraphs. In the appendix the first entire draft for a possible international document concerning the status of teachers was added. The impressive volume of this report and the fact that it was agreed upon unanimously by the experts' committee was a decisive step on the way to the Magna Carta for the Teaching Profession.

It was a happy coincidence that two years before it had been decided that the Delegates' Assembly of the WCOTP should be held in the UNESCO building in Paris in the beginning of August 1964 that is only ten weeks after this experts' meeting. The Assembly gave the WCOTP as well as the General-Director of the UNESCO and other personalities the chance to stress the importance of education and the Carta of Teachers in this context.

The UNESCO General Conference in November 1964 gave the education system high priority, and I once again had the chance to stress – with general consent – the importance of the contribution of teachers and their organisations in realisation of UNESCO programmes.

„Diplomatic Conference"

UNESCO and ILO decided to proceed in four steps:

- both Offices would compile a (second) joint draft which would include the two previous experts' reports (ILO 1963, UNESCO 1964);
- this draft would be send to the international teachers' associations and to all member states of UNESCO and ILO for additional comments;
- a representative committee would formulate a new text, including all additional comments;
- this final draft would be presented for adoption at a „diplomatic conference", summoned by both the UNESCO and ILO.

The General-Secretary of the Teachers' Association of British Columbia (Canada), Charles D. Ovans, came to visit me in my Paris Office. We discussed the content of the Charter of Teachers and how to proceed further. Ovans was on his way to Geneva, where he started work on the status document as a consultant of ILO. On the 15th of April 1965 the draft which had been composed by both Offices (ILO and UNESCO), was sent to all member states for additional comments.

At all former meetings concerning the teachers' charter the WCOTP had been represented by well-informed and committed colleagues (myself included). Now the next step had to be planned very carefully. Knowing that Carr, Natarajan, Ovans and other members and friends of WCOTP (like Jean Thomas) belonged to the expert commission of UNESCO and ILO, WCOTP nominated a delegation of observers, consisting of eight well-informed leaders of teachers' organisations, who should vet the procedures for WCOTP under my leadership.

By the 15th of September 1965, 46 member states had answered the (second) joint draft by UNESCO/ILO and until the 6th of December eleven more followed. The development led to the penultimate important round – with regards to the content.

The Final Draft

From the 17th to the 28th of January UNESCO-ILO-experts from 29 countries were discussing the final text of the draft in Geneva. Shri Natarajan was again voted chairman and William G. Carr head of the drafting committee. The WCOTP observers' delegation met our „official experts" nearly every evening to judge the outcome of the day and to plan the course of the discussion for the next days, with regard to positions on the contents and following arguments, proposals and votes. Many later arguments (such as the question of taking influence in school politics, the education of teachers at universities and the question of strikes) were already hotly disputed at these meetings.

The issue at the centre of the school policy controversy was, if and to what extent teachers and their organisations should be involved in decision-making in educational politics. Both vocal and reserved participants were angry because some (not all) communist experts promoted a total involvement of the teachers' organisations in the above. I was silently amused about that, because in the „socialist" countries government, employers and unions were always united in one opinion – which was fixed „from above". This became even more transparent, as some were arguing for an extremely broad interpretation of the right to strike. Sometimes I asked these people in a conference break why there was never a strike in their country. The answer was very easy: „Where workers (and that included teachers) had the power in government, they would have to strike against themselves." The right of teachers to strike was one of the hottest themes at the conference. In the WCOTP this topic, too, was repeatedly discussed. One evening especially was marked by fierce and intense disputes. With a delicately phrased formulation a compromise was reached.[8]

---

8   *„Appropriate joint machinery should be set up to deal with the settlement of disputes between the teachers and their employers arising out of terms and conditions of employment. If the means and procedures established for these purposes should be exhausted or if there should be a breakdown in negotiations between the parties, teachers' organisations should have the right to take such other*

The question of teachers' education was also argued in a controversial manner but rationally. An important preliminary decision had already been taken at the Experts' Meeting in Paris. The need for a university education of teachers, which I stressed again and again, was met with lack of understanding by the experts from developing countries (including Natarajan). In many of these countries the education of teachers did not even entail a solid secondary education. Here the differences between the first and the third world crystallized clearly. An optimal compromise was realised through the formulation.[9]

These „quasi-meetings" of WCOTP under my leadership are some of the most exhilarating and successful events in my professional life. Naturally a close relationship of trust developed between myself and the experts and members of the WCOTP delegation, but also with personalities outside the sphere of influence of WCOTP until then. Relationships developed which influenced my future work in a positive way and enriched me personally as well, especially the relations with the personalities actively involved in one or other experts' committees. An appreciation of the work involved can not only be gained from the many heated and controversial discussions, but also from the consideration of the complexity and quantity. Therefore I quote some numbers.

A total of 29 experts were examining the draft of about 170 paragraphs. The main themes (if I dare to classify them at all) were salary and social security, conditions for successful learning, rights and duties and the education and further education of teachers. In addition to this draft from **UNESCO** and **ILO** the committee had statements from about 60 member states that consisted of about 150 pages. Furthermore, there were about 100 statements from international teacher organisations concerning various paragraphs. The experts themselves supplied about 173 oral proposals and about 200 written for changes. To complicate the proceedings even more every result had to be translated in English, French, Spanish and Russian. People were waiting for the report of the chairman of the editorial committee at the end of the congress with high expectations.

---

steps as are normally open to other organisations in the defence of their legitimate interests" (VIII., 84).

[9] *„All teachers should be prepared in general, special and pedagogical subjects in universities, or in institutions on a level comparable to universities, or else in special institutions for the preparation of teachers" (V., 21.1.).*

William Carr was pleased that the drafting committee was able to present a text which was completely supported by all ten members. After lively discussions for eleven days the proposed text (with a few minor alterations) was agreed upon unanimously.

Shifts in Emphasis Endanger Success

Some days after this conference in Geneva the WCOTP informed all member organisations of the result and stressed the importance of the „Diplomatic Conference" which was to take place in September or October. We succeeded in convincing UNESCO to ask the member states in the invitation to include people who had experience with teacher organisations in their delegations. Everyone in Geneva was sure that nothing could stop the „Diplomatic Conference". But history took an unexpected turn. Surprisingly, one month after the meeting in Geneva the ILO decided to leave the invitations to the „Diplomatic Conference" to UNESCO alone. The reason given by ILO was that without any doubt the member states would send more delegates from the ministries of education than from the ministries of employment. But it had never been questioned that ILO would participate with an adequate delegation which would protect their interests. In May there were heated discussions in the Executive Committee of UNESCO on whether a „Diplomatic Conference" was legal. The argument against this was the fact that without any doubt not all members would have a diplomatic status. In the end the Executive Committee decided to stick to the date, but to call the „Diplomatic Conference" the „Special Intergovernmental Conference" from then on. Without further difficulties the conference took place from the 21st of September to the 5th of October.

The International Special Intergovernmental Conference

178 people from 75 countries represented their governments as voting delegates at the conference. Added to these were 15 non-voting members of the ILO and 21 additional non-governmental organisations (NGOs).[10]

Jean Thomas (France) was voted chairman and William G. Carr (USA) Rapporteur General of the Conference. After the festive opening an encouraging mutual consent about the main principles could be recognised. But some paragraphs led to controversy

---

10 The NGOs included four important teachers' organisations: WCOTP, WFTU, IFFTU and ISL.

and alterations. On the whole the main draft was not endangered by phrasing the text in a different way. The main argument centred on the question of whether teachers and their organisations should take part in decision-making and educational politics. Some delegates tried to water down the rights of the teachers as they were written down in the proposed text. With an impressive speech for the rights of teachers the British delegate Carmichael changed the atmosphere. With the help of the USA and the USSR the phrase was agreed upon in a vote.[11]

A Historical Document – Standards of the Profession

All in all it took 18 years during which UNESCO, ILO, national and international teachers' associations as well as important personalities had advocated the case of education for this document to come into being.

It honours all participants that in the time of the „Cold War" and the ideological and military clashes there were no feelings of secret or open enmity or hostility in the discussions. The talks were conducted as serious arguments between experienced personalities and led to the development of a document which improved the status of teachers all over the world.

For the first time the international community of states recognised the immense importance of the status of teachers for education in the modern world. The community of states described and set up principles and standards of the teaching profession and their relationship to and participation in society.

Adaptation to New Developments

Although this Carta of Teachers, in the form of a recommendation, did not put any legal pressure on the member states, its moral force is still alive. In the past 30 years a joint ILO-UNESCO-committee dealt with complaints from teachers' associations, proved and judged their content. Very important were the questionnaires which were sent to the member states from time to time, concerning individual standards regulated

---

[11] For details concerning special German aspects cf.: Ebert, Wilhelm: Magna Charta des Lehrerberufes. Dreißig Jahre UNESCO-Empfehlung zum Status der Lehrer. In: Forum E, 49 (1996) 9, pp. 4-12.

in the document. The answers were always published in a carefully worked-upon report. Now is the time to check the approach to the realisation of the document as well as the content once again and to make changes – if necessary – to adapt the document to new goals and conditions in our world which is changing in many sectors of the education system. Professional training, universities, public and private institutions, the influence of family and society on the pupil, technological media- and communication-systems in and for education, all are a challenge for the teachers. Their participation and the methods of their involvement in the decisive processes concerning working conditions and educational politics are to a large extent no longer up-to-date.

Today there are about 55 million teachers. The break-down of the former communist Eastern Bloc and the merging of two strong international teachers' associations have led to the creation of a new international teachers' organisation (EI) which has a lot of power. Now it is important that the power of this „International Education Force" is used to reach the high goals which have to be attained for the further evolution of mankind.

List of Acronyms and Abbreviations

AGDL	Arbeitsgemeinschaft Deutscher Lehrerverbände (German Teachers' Federation – consisting of GEW and BLLV)
BLLV	Bayerischer Lehrer- und Lehrerinnenverband (Bavarian Teachers' Association)
EI	Education International
GEW	Gewerkschaft Erziehung und Wissenschaft (German Union for Education and Science)
IBE	International Bureau of Education
IFFTU	International Federation of Free Teachers' Unions
ILO	International Labour Organisation (also: International Labour Office)
ISL	International Section of Teachers in the International Federation of Christian Trade Unions of Employees in Public Services and PTT
NGO	Non-Governmental Organisation
UNESCO	United Nations Educational, Scientific and Cultural Organisation
UNO	United Nations Organisation
WCOTP	World Confederation of Organisations of the Teaching Profession
WFTU	World Federation of Teachers' Unions

Annex

The main chapters of the „Recommendation concerning the Status of Teachers, adopted by the Special Intergovernmental Conference on the Status of Teachers, Paris, 5 October 1966 (Magna Carta for the Status of Teachers)". In: Status of Teachers, Paris: UNESCO 1967, pp. 9-20.

I. Definitions
II. Scope
III. Guiding principles
IV. Educational objectives and policies
V. Preparation for the profession
   Selection
   Teacher-preparation programmes
   Teacher-preparation institutions
VI. Further education for teachers
VII. Employment and career
   Entry into the teaching profession
   Advancement and promotion
   Security of tenure
   Disciplinary procedures related to breaches of professional conduct
   Medical examinations
   Women teachers with family responsibilities
   Part-time service
VIII. The rights and responsibilities of teachers
   Professional freedom
   Responsibilities of teachers
   Relations between teachers and the education service as a whole
   Rights of teachers
IX. Conditions for effective teaching and learning
   Class size
   Ancillary staff
   Teaching aids
   Hours of work
   Annual holidays with pay
   Study leave
   Special leave

Sick leave and maternity leave
Teacher exchange
School buildings
Special provisions for teachers in rural or remote areas
X. Teachers' salaries
XI. Social security
General provisions
Medical care
Sickness benefit
Employment injure benefit
Old-age benefit
Invalidity benefit
Survivors' benefit
Means of providing social security for teachers
XII. The teacher shortage
XIII. Final provision

The Status of the Humanities in Education

Yaacov Iram

Introduction: Humanities – Humanistic Education

The Latin source of the term „humanities" is „humanitas" and „humanus". The term „humanitas" relates to all the human attributes which are unique to mankind and distinguish man from animals. Yet, in spite of the historical roots of the idea in the Greek „paideia", in order to clarify its modern significance, we must turn to the universities of the Middle Ages. These universities included three faculties: Theology, Medicine and Law. The fourth faculty was that of Liberal Arts. The role of this faculty was to provide its students with a general education in preparation for one of the „higher" faculties, Theology, Medicine and Law, mainly by teaching languages, especially Latin, and the basics of mathematics, astronomy and music. The university of the Middle Ages was controlled by the Faculty of Theology. That is why there were frequent disputes between the theologians and the liberal arts teachers, who sought to preserve the Greek and Roman heritage of „paideia" and „humanitas". Every discussion concerning mankind took place within a theological framework, while philosophy was considered to be the „handmaiden" of the queen of sciences – theology. It was Francis Bacon, the English philosopher of the 16th century, who claimed that it was necessary to distinguish between religious philosophy and the philosophy of nature or humanity, which emphasizes the study of mankind and human attributes. Thus, Bacon laid the foundations for the secular study of man's nature *(Bell 1966; Rothblatt 1976; Kimball 1986)*. A parallel development also took place in the universities in France in the 16th century. However, it was only in the 19th century that the term „humanities" was accepted into the English language and, at the same time, it almost disappeared from the French language and was replaced with the expression „lettres et philosophie", while the term „sciences humaines" was applied to the social sciences. In the German language, the term „humanities" does not exist and the closest equivalent to it is „Geisteswissenschaften", literally „mental sciences", as distinct from „Naturwissenschaften", natural sciences. The social sciences had not yet found their place in the universities of the 19th century.

The term „humanistic education" relates to three wider terms, namely: „Liberal Education", „General Education" and „Paideia" in classical Greece *(Roth 1961; Adar 1963)*. It is possible to follow the changes in this idea continuously from the days of the Greek Sophists in the 5th century BCE, via Rome, the universities of the Middle Ages and the Renaissance, up to its recent transformation in the guise of the „Paideia Program" in the 1980s *(Adler 1982, 1983, 1984)*. The common element in the different uses of this term, through all its various transformations in the course of history and up to our time is education which aims to free the intellect and to develop the human mind. The aim of a humanistic education is preparation for life in its wider sense and not the provision of specific vocational training for earning a living. That is to say, such education is intended to satisfy the spiritual needs of the person and not the instrumental-practical ones. In this spirit, the Encyclopedia Britannica also defines the „humanities" as *„Those branches of knowledge that concern themselves with man and his culture or with analytical and critical methods of inquiry derived from an appreçiation of human values and the unique ability of the human spirit to express itself" (Humanities 1986, p. 138)*. Such an education was supposed to prepare the young generation to take an active part in the life of the Polis, the Greek city-state, to serve as the basis for the education of an Orator in Roman society, and to train the intellectual and political elite from the Middle Ages to the modern era. Whereas in our era a humanistic education is supposed to be imparted to every human being.

Erosion of the Status of Humanistic Education

In recent years, the fields of humanistic knowledge and their expression as curricular subjects taught at school have been faced with a situation in which they have to justify their existence. In many countries in the Western world, whether small like Israel and Finland, or big like Britain, the U.S.A. and Germany, pressures are intensifying to enlarge the share of the scientific and technological subjects and „scientific thinking" in the curriculum, and to increase the resources available to it *(Iram / Mitter / Raivola / Yogev / Ayalon 1995)*.

Such pressures exist not only at the national level, but also at the personal level. A growing practical approach to studies is developing; this regards them as a means to acquire a profession or occupation which is expected to yield a high income. Such an attitude gives priority to the study of scientific and technological subjects, at the expense of the humanities. To these „practical" considerations one should add the objective factor of the „information explosion" which also confronts the system of education with a quantitative challenge in the allocation of study hours to the various fields of knowledge. There is also the psychological factor associated with intensive exposure to mass media entertainment, and especially with its orientation towards and with its emphasis on materialistic consumption, on the one hand, and simple amusement, on the other hand.

These factors caused the humanistic subjects to be moved from their central position in the curriculum, to the margins, and to be replaced by more „practical" subjects thus bringing about *„the closing of the mind"* *(Bloom 1987)*, for which the school is held responsible. Such developments have intensified the phenomenon of a widening lacuna between the *„two cultures"* *(Snow 1964)*, the humanistic and the scientific-technological. Realizing the negative results of these developments many Western countries considered possible ways to narrow the gap between the „two cultures". These measures aim to reduce the harm resulting from the conflict between them, to bring the „two cultures" into a state of coexistence and to regard „cultural literacy" as the basis for professional training and higher education in general *(Hirsch 1988)*.

The Humanistic Components in the Curriculum

The humanistic subjects provide a foundation for investigating cultural phenomena in order to clarify their significance, that is to say, the beliefs and values which lie behind them. Thus, all subjects should be taught from a humanistic perspective, namely, regarding them all as containing elements of social-political, cultural and moral values, which have to be revealed, discussed and understood.

We will not discuss here the complex question of the interactions among „humanistic education", „liberal education" and „general education". It will suffice merely to note that „humanistic education" is not identical with „liberal education" or with „general education", which also includes the foundations of the exact sciences and mathematics. However, it forms the part which includes the cultural components, i. e. languages, literature, history, philosophy and the fine arts. That is to say, a humanistic education is identified with what is recognized today as the disciplines of the humanities in the universities, following the German model.

In the following, we will briefly survey the „traditional" components of the contents of the humanities.

Language

Following Aristotle, it is common to characterize the human being as a thinking creature (logos); and thinking as being manifested in the ability to talk (the „Rambam", i. e. Maimonides, defined the unique character of a human being as „a locutor"). For this reason, language, which is used as more than a tool for the transfer of information, is the core of the humanities. In fact, language was the most important subject in the „trivium" of the universities of the Middle Ages. It comprised grammar, rhetoric and dialectic, which formed the linguistic components of the intellect. During the Renaissance period, language, especially the ancient languages, Greek, Latin and Hebrew, continued to occupy a central position in humanistic studies. Thus arose the term „philology", in its strict meaning of „love of language – wisdom". The „international" role of language was carried over into the modern era. In fact, all national movements assigned a central role to the national language in their struggle for self-determination.

Literature

Classical literature, and also contemporary literature give aesthetic and ethical expression to the human spirit and its achievements. Also, literature affects the development of individuals and the values of those who read and study it. It was literature, in its diverse forms – prose, poetry and essays – which marked the rebirth of nations, and often even guided it. Throughout history, literature has reflected the main turning points in the ideological, religious, social and aesthetic changes of nations *(Yaoz / Iram 1987)*.

Literature has the power to exert influence, both through the nature of its contents and through its aesthetic form. Therefore, an appropriate balance must be struck, at each and every stage of education, between the „content" – the human and national-social message of the literature – and the „form" – the aesthetic expression which is the heart of literature as an art. Although „textual analysis" is important, it is also important to make sure that it does not kill the spirit of the literary work, so that this will kindle the creative imagination of the reader through his participation in reconstructing the experience described in the work *(Knights 1975)*.

Arts

The plastic arts (painting and sculpture) and the performing arts (music, dance, theater and cinema) are an expression of the human imagination. Apart from literary studies, the study of the arts is usually relegated to the margin and generally appears in the curriculum in the form of the history of art. Creative art remains a subject in the lower classes of elementary schools, but aesthetics as a subject is unknown at any stage of elementary or secondary school, and only rarely receives a mention in philosophy lessons. Artistic expression, which is an innate need of humanity, as expressed by the child's spontaneous expressions in the early developmental stages, steadily loses its place as the pupil progresses up the educational ladder, from the kindergarten to secondary school.

It is worth emphasizing that it is the duty of the educational system to consider the two aspects of artistic education: the active, creative, in which a person can give expression to his artistic powers; and the passive, receptive aspect, namely the role of the person, as a „consumer" of cultural works in literature or of the plastic and performing arts. All of these have the power both to enrich the individual's spirit and to extend the bounds and limits of human existence in place and time. Furthermore, at the pedagogic level, Dewey and others emphasized that art also plays a role in the cognitive development of the learner *(Dewey 1934; Langer 1976)*, and that aesthetic awareness is one of the characteristics of knowledge *(Eisner 1985)*.

History

Reconstruction of the past, history, is a distinct part of the humanistic field of knowledge. Study of the past, regarding it as a process which extends its influence into the present time, is an important part of the fields of knowledge which are taught to pupils in schools. It seems impossible to overemphasize the importance of teaching national history, whether in parallel with or integrated into the general historical processes, as factors which formed and transformed national and international realities in the past and which continue to influence them in the present. Beyond the cultural-content aspect that the learning of history may contribute to the student, it also has a methodological value in its ways of recalling the reality and tracing the truth of history, namely, the question of objectivity and point of view.

The teaching of history at the different stages of education may emphasize different perspectives, starting from the value of literary narratives and progressing to the analytical-critical point of view. The aim in each of these stages is to provide students with a broad perspective of reality in time and space. Historiography at school should also reflect the trend of historical research, to move closer towards the social sciences, both in its methods and subjects, including the use of quantitative methods involving the computer. Such an approach may transform the teaching of history into a bridge between the humanities and the social sciences – political, social and economic history – alongside the history of ideas and cultures, and individual and collective biography (prosopography).

Indeed: „*There is no other subject as eclectic as historiography: It has proved its readiness to absorb ideas, ways of thinking and analysis from all the social science fields, starting from political and social philosophies and continuing to statistics*" *(Shapira 1993, p. 226)*. One of the many answers to the question „why history" is that it is „*only by reflection on completed experience that we can interpret in depth the human experience in the making, which is the present*" *(Reeves 1975, p. 117)*.

Philosophy

Philosophy as a distinct and independent field of study in school has been relegated to the fringes of the curriculum to a greater extent than any other subject among the humanities, for both objective and subjective reasons alike. On the one hand, philosophy, in its primary meaning of „love of wisdom", is linked to the foundations of all the sciences: natural sciences, life sciences and social sciences. From this perspective, it is not, in itself, a separate and independent field of knowledge or subject matter. It is always „philosophy of ..." (science, medicine, mathematics, morality, etc.). From this point of view, it is worthwhile for it to be studied, not as a separate subject but in conjunction with the relevant fields of knowledge. The classical fields of philosophy – ethics or moral philosophy – were devalued in the period of moral relativism and suspicion of indoctrination in a pluralistic society.

It is important to strengthen the methodological component of philosophy, which is worth addressing in the context of the relevant fields of knowledge. It is also worthwhile that philosophy should be incorporated into the curriculum and should retrieve its original meaning of „love of wisdom" both in its material-content and methodological-rational context.

An Alternative Approach to Humanistic Studies

There are two approaches to teaching the humanities. First, the traditional one regards them as a group of subjects in defined fields of knowledge. The second, the integrative approach sees the humanistic subjects as accumulations of knowledge and a way of investigating aspects of human activities and conditions. According to the integrative approach, the question is not what is included in the humanistic subjects, but rather what questions are to be asked about each subject of study in the humanities, social sciences, natural sciences and in technology, alike. Following this approach, the choice is not between teaching the humanities or the sciences, but between two different approaches to the teaching of the respective fields of knowledge. The humanistic integrative perspective has the power to impart „cultural literacy", the components of which are cultural communication between the individual and his society, cultural loyalty in accepting and evaluating norms, and development of the individual, in the sense of developing in him an independent attitude towards the culture.

The problem of the humanistic subjects is not only the small proportion of the curriculum allocated to them, at least not at the elementary and lower-secondary school stages, but also their poor image in the eyes of the public, parents and pupils. This manifests itself in the negative selection of pupils for the humanistic subjects in secondary schools, teacher training colleges and university courses. The main explanation for the decline in status of the study of the humanities, which becomes more evident with the progression of students up the steps of the educational ladder, lies in their being less practical and less useful to the students in their future professional careers. Nevertheless, part of the „blame" must also be attributed to the way in which the humanities are taught. We shall discuss this issue in the following. It should be pointed out that such a claim was presented in the U.S.A. in the „Report on the Humanities in Higher Education" *(Bennet et al. 1984)*. The authors of the report attributed the steady decline in the number of students in the humanities courses to the failure of their teachers *„to bring the humanities to life"*, in addition to the students' concern to train themselves for *„good-paying jobs"* *(ibid., pp. 6, 10)*.

It has already been mentioned that it is possible to address the humanities as separate subjects of study, albeit with certain characteristics in common, or to regard them integrally, in their relation to certain aspects of human activity, as an holistic approach to culture. The latter is the approach advocated here, for reasons of both principle and pragmatism alike. The concept „perspective" is used here, as: „*A relatively organized way of grasping (recording, perhaps also interpreting, explaining) some aspects of 'experience'*" *(Black 1975, p. 83)*. It is possible to distinguish between two kinds of perspectives: the personal perspective and the group perspective. The personal perspective is that by which the individual attempts to understand reality and to express his attitudes, feelings, intentions and ambitions. The personal perspective intersects the group perspectives because of shared social experiences of human life and because of the social nature of language and other kinds of expression, by means of which individuals construct and express their own personal perspectives. The overlapping of the personal and the group perspectives forms the human perspective. Whereas science attempts to neutralize the differences between the two perspectives in its striving towards scientific objectivity, the humanities are concerned with the clarification of the human perspective. Thus, the overall role of the humanities is the interpretation and criticism of the activities of the human individual and of his society.

These three perspectives parallel the three possibilities open to the person in his aspiration to explore reality: that of the sciences, that of the creative arts and that of the humanities. Indeed, the humanistic perspective elucidates culture. If the general definition of the curriculum is „a selection of culture" and the role of education is „cultural socialization", then the role of the humanistic perspective is to clarify the basic value assumptions of the culture: Culture, in the sense of systems of meaning, which give form, order and direction to our lives, and not separate fields of knowledge (subject matter). Teaching following the humanistic-perspective approach would be the teaching of cultural phenomena in order to clarify their meanings, i. e. the beliefs and values on which they are based. These meanings are to be found in the manifestations of the culture, so that the humanities will not restrict this clarification to one cultural system but extend it to all of them. For that, the humanities must broaden their fields of knowledge to include the social sciences and also aspects of the exact sciences, in an holistic approach. Thus, scientific research and the study of its findings are not identical with learning how a scientific concept influenced and was, at the same time, influenced by social beliefs and religious faith, that is to say, the understanding of science as part of the culture. This is indeed the uniqueness and role of the humanistic approach.

The teacher's role is not only analyzing the culture but also transmitting it from generation to generation. Thus, culture will also fulfill an associative role, i. e. it will provide the individual with logical, linguistic and creative means in the context of his activities and his thinking, equally. The humanities provide the individual with the content and methods of thinking shared by him and his society: a common language. However, we are not concerned here only with a passive acceptance of culture but with an intergenerational dialogue, which includes transmitting, receiving and adding to culture.

Conclusions: Educational Implications

Following our survey of the contents of humanistic knowledge, i. e. culture in its broad sense, and the integrative approach to teaching them, it is worth briefly discussing their educational promise. We will focus here on two fields of education, moral and political. A humanistic education focuses on man and his way of life within the context of culture and time. Through the student's encounters with diverse ideas and values, his perspective is widened and he becomes more aware of the variety of attitudes and values of various societies in various periods. This awareness provides him with a perspective to reflect on himself and on his society. In this way, humanistic education helps the individual in autonomous development instead of uncritical acceptance of the society and culture within which he was born. This autonomy includes freedom of choice and responsibility for his choice, which is a major component of moral perception and behavior. At each and every stage of education, a humanistic education must confront the pupil with a variety of controversial questions in the culture of his society. The student's confrontation with such questions will develop his capacity for critical thinking, and power of expression and argument, and in this way will help his moral development, as indicated by moral thinking which is also connected with the empathetic understanding of others *(Kohlberg 1984)*.

The view of humanistic studies as presented here is based on human activities in the broadest sense of the concept. Their aim is to develop understanding of and respect for the variations in the way of life of the individual and society in their continuity through time and place. The humanities are concerned with culture in its scientific, economic, technological, artistic, social and ideological aspects. Strengthening of the humanistic components of the education system is a necessity if we are to prevent the danger of widening the gap between an expanding technology and a shrinking morality in our society.

The long-term aims of all education are to impart knowledge, skills, norms and values and to transmit them from generation to generation in order to imbue the young generation with the spiritual and material culture of its time and place, in the light of the heritage from the past. An education worthy of the name will not be satisfied with the passive reception of this heritage but will aim at active participation in it and its development by those who are receiving it. The civilization in which we are living is becoming more complex than anything known to earlier generations. The characteristics of this complexity are expressed in the improvement of technological capabilities and in social, political and economic implications. These improvements in the capabilities of civilization enlarge the possibilities of improving the material well-being of individuals, societies and humanity in general, but, at the same time, they also intensify the fears of potential hazards: ecological dangers; weapons of mass destruction; and also prejudices, economic injustices, and political conflicts which flare up into wars from time to time, sometimes threatening the quality of human existence and sometimes endangering that very existence, itself. A humanistic education is also defined as the imparting and the acquisition of knowledge relating to man and his culture by means of analytical and critical thinking. The point of departure for such an education is respect for human values, as well as the free expression of the human spirit. These may strengthen trends towards mutual understanding, tolerance and cooperation between individuals and societies, in order to further the advancement of humanity, society and individuals towards contentment and self-fulfillment.

Bibliography

Adar, Zvi: What is Education? Jerusalem: Magnes Press 1963 (in Hebrew).
Adler, Mortimer Jerome: The Paideia Proposal. An Educational Manifesto. New York: Macmillan 1982.
Adler, Mortimer Jerome: Paideia Problems and Possibilities. New York: Macmillan 1983.
Adler, Mortimer Jerome: The Paideia Program. An Educational Syllabus. New York: Macmillan 1984.
Bell, Daniel: The Reforming of General Education. New York: Columbia University Press 1966.
Bennet, William John et al.: To Reclaim a Legacy. A Report on the Humanities in Higher Education. Washington, D.C.: National Endowment for the Humanities 1984.
Black, Max: Some Tasks for 'the Humanities'. In: Niblett, William Roy (ed.): The Sciences, the Humanities, and the Technological Threat, London: University of London Press 1975, pp. 79-89.
Bloom, Allan David: The Closing of the American Mind. New York: Simon and Schuster 1987.
Dewey, John: Art as Experience. New York: Minton, Balch 1934.

Eisner, Elliot W.: Aesthetic Modes of Knowing. In: idem. (ed.): Learning and Teaching the Ways of Knowing (= Yearbook of the National Society for the Study of Education. 84, 2), Chicago: University of Chicago Press 1985, pp. 23-36.

Hirsch, Eric Donald: Cultural Literacy. New York: Random House 1988.

Humanities. In: The New Encyclopedia Britannica. 15. ed. Vol. 6, Chicago: Encyclopedia Britannica 1986, pp. 138-139.

Iram, Yaacov / Mitter, Wolfgang / Raivola, Reijo / Yogev, Abraham / Ayalon, Hanna: Panel on The Status of the Humanities as a Global Issue, presented at the 39th Annual Conference of the Comparative and International Education Society, Boston, Mass., 1995.

Kimball, Bruce A.: Orators and Philosophers. A History of the Idea of Liberal Education. New York: Teachers College Press 1986.

Knights, Lionel Charles: Literature and the Teaching of Literature. In: Niblett, William Roy (ed.) The Sciences, the Humanities, and the Technological Threat, London: University of London Press 1975, pp. 127-138.

Kohlberg, Lawrence: The Psychology of Moral Development. San Francisco: Harper and Row 1984.

Langer, Susanne Katherine: Problems of Art. New York: Scribner 1976.

Reeves, Marjorie: Why History? In: Niblett, William Roy (ed.): The Sciences, the Humanities, and the Technological Threat, London: University of London Press 1975, pp. 116-126.

Roth, Leon: Education and Human Values. Tel-Aviv: Dvir 1961 (in Hebrew).

Rothblatt, Sheldon: Tradition and Change in English Liberal Education. An Essay in History and Culture. London: Faber and Faber 1976.

Shapira, Anita: Secrets of Biography. In: Two Thousand, 8 (1993), pp. 225-239 (in Hebrew).

Snow, Charles Percy: The Two Cultures and a Second Look. An Expanded Version of 'The Two Cultures and the Scientific Revolution'. New York: The New American Library 1964.

Yaoz, Hanna / Iram, Yaacov: Transformations in the Hebrew Literature Curriculum. A Comparative Study. In: Studies in Education, (1987) 46-47, pp. 157-170 (in Hebrew).

Schulbildung und Religion – Zu den ethnisch-konfessionellen
Strukturmerkmalen der ungarischen Intelligenz in der Zwischenkriegszeit

Victor Karady

Die ungarische Intelligenz im modernen Sinne ist vor allem ein Produkt des nationalen Gymnasial- und Universitätswesens, das im Rahmen des staatlich gesteuerten Entwicklungsprozesses der liberalen Epoche (vom österreichisch-ungarischen Ausgleich im Jahre 1867 bis zum Zusammenbruch der Doppelmonarchie 1918) ausgebaut beziehungsweise modernisiert worden war. Nach dem damals gültigen schulischen Berechtigungswesen stellte das Abitur die Eintrittsbedingung zur – wie es in der offiziellen statistischen Benennung hieß – 'intelligenten Klasse' dar, die durch eine Anzahl von objektivierten Privilegien, auf dem Arbeitsmarkt (Zugang zum privaten oder öffentlichen Beamtenstand), im Wertesystem der Gesellschaftseliten (Satisfaktions- und 'Salon'fähigkeit) und in der Symbolik und Praxis der militärischen Hierarchie ('freiwilliger' Militärdienst, Recht zum Schwerttragen und zur Aufnahme ins Offizierskorps), ihre gesellschaftliche Absicherung fand. Zu den Eigentümlichkeiten dieses Schulsystems gehörte seine Größe und Dezentralisierung, seine relative Billigkeit für seine Benutzer und daher seine relativ breite, bis in die untere Schichten der Mittelklasse (Kleinbürgertum, besitzendes Bauerntum) reichende Zugänglichkeit, seine weitgehende (wenn nicht vollkommene) konfessionelle Neutralität oder Offenheit und sein ausgeprägt ungarischer Charakter: weniger als 10% der Sekundarschulen waren Schulen mit deutscher oder ausnahmsweise rumänischer oder serbischer Unterrichtssprache. Elitebildung wurde – mit Ausnahme der Siebenbürger Sachsen – für potentiell ethnisch nicht-ungarische Bevölkerungsgruppen nur auf Ungarisch angeboten.

Dadurch hat das ungarische Schulsystem den, größtenteils aus der damals noch fremdsprachigen Bevölkerungsmehrheit[1] stammenden, aufkommenden neuen Mittelschichten gegenüber eine starke symbolische Gewalt ausgeübt, weil es sie unter assimilatorischen Druck setzte. Es hat sogar dazu beigetragen, daß die durch das klassische

---

1 Nach Angaben der Volkszählung von 1910, gegen Ende des langen Assimilationsprozesses während des Ausbaus des Nationalstaates, betrug der Anteil der Ungarischsprachigen an der Bevölkerung im Königreich Ungarn (ohne Kroatien) nur etwa 54%.

Gymnasium und die Fachausbildung vermittelten Chancen zum wirtschaftlich-beruflichen Aufstieg und zur Integration in die vom ungarischen Adel beherrschte Gesellschaftselite und Staatsstrukturen eine mit starkem nationalen Bildungsgut und Bildungsansprüchen ausgestattete Mittelklasse mit mehrheitlich nicht-ungarischem Hintergrund ins Leben gerufen hat. Noch um 1900 machten nicht-ungarische, d. h. deutsche oder slawische, Namen tragende sowie die Studenten jüdischen Bekenntnisses zwischen zwei Dritteln und drei Vierteln der Budapester Studentenschaft aus *(Karady 1989, S. 292-294).* Am Ende der zwanziger Jahre dieses Jahrhunderts findet man in manchen Sektoren des hohen Staatsdienstes eine beträchtliche Anzahl, manchmal eine Mehrzahl von Beamten mit fremden (vor allem deutschen) Namen,[2] obwohl die noch im Vormärz begonnene und seit dem Ausgleich (vor allem seit dem Milleniumsjahr 1896) beschleunigte Bewegung der Madjarisierung der Namen einerseits und das Zusammenschrumpfen des altungarischen Vielvölkerstaates zu einem ethnisch im wesentlichen homogenen Rumpfstaat andererseits das Vorhandensein von Beamten mit nicht-ungarischen Namen wesentlich seltener hat werden lassen.[3]

Der Anspruch an die 'gesinnungsmäßige' nationale Einheit der gebildeten Mittelklassen und an die durch ihre Wirkung im mitteleuropäischen Raum auszuübende 'ungarische kulturelle Überlegenheit' *(kulturfölény)* – wie es in der Propaganda des neuen autoritären politischen Kurses hieß – wurde besonders nach der Verstümmelung des historischen Nationalstaates im Friedensvertrag von Trianon von der revanchehungrigen neokonservativen Führungsschicht auf die Tagesordnung gesetzt. Das Problem wurde unter zweierlei Vorzeichen thematisiert: einmal bezüglich der durch die Anwesenheit von als 'assimilationswidrig' und 'zur Dominierung eingestellt' angesehenen, vor allem jüdischen (aber gelegentlich auch deutschen), Bruchteilen der Mittelschichten hervorgerufenen 'Gefahr', und zweitens bezüglich der Ungleichheit zwischen der in der Provinz und in der Hauptstadt – nach dem Ausdruck des Regenten Horthy im 'sündhaften Budapest' – ansässigen Intelligenz.

Im folgenden wird der Versuch unternommen, eine Reihe von soziologischen Indikatoren zu analysieren, die die infolge der angehäuften Summe von Bildungsgütern und deren unterschiedlicher beruflicher Nutzung erstandenen inneren Spaltungen der gebil-

---

[2] Nach dem zeitgenössischen Sozialstatistiker Alajos *Kovács (1930)* gab es um 1930 herum im höheren Staatsdienst (vor allem in den Ministerien) noch immer zwischen 20 und 30% Bedienstete mit deutschen und zwischen 10 und 20% mit slawischen (vor allem slowakischen) Namen.

[3] Nach dem Zensus von 1920 gab es nur rund 10% Fremdsprachige in der Bevölkerung des neuen Kleinstaates (davon 6,7% Deutschsprachige).

deten Schichten Ungarns unter dem Gesichtspunkt der regionalen und konfessionellen Verteilung verdeutlichen. Damit wird angestrebt, die gesellschaftlichen Grundlagen und objektiv erfaßbaren Kriterien der in der Zwischenkriegszeit tobenden antisemitischen und oft allgemein xenophoben und 'anti-urbanistischen'[4] Polemik zu beleuchten.

Tabelle 1 bietet eine genaue Übersicht über die konfessionsspezifische Streuung des Bildungsniveaus der Männer unterschiedlicher Altersgruppen im Ungarischen Reich (1910) verglichen mit der Situation im Rumpfstaat 1930. Die daraus ableitbaren Schlüsse können in wenigen Punkten zusammengefaßt werden.

Zuerst muß man auf teilweise bemerkenswert enge Parallelitäten, aber auch auf Verschiebungen zwischen den auf die Vor- und Nachkriegszeit bezogenen Zahlen hinweisen. Obwohl die Angaben innerhalb von zwanzig Jahren für jede Gruppe eine sprunghafte Entwicklung aufzeigen, darf dies selbstverständlich nur teilweise der tatsächlichen Verbesserung der Bildungschancen zugerechnet werden, da sie zum großen Teil der Umwandlung der gesellschaftlichen Basis der Messung entspricht. Rumpfungarn hatte bekanntlich die in jedem Sinne am meisten entwickelten Regionen des historischen Staates, damit auch diejenigen, die die relativ größte Dichte der gebildeten Klassen aufwiesen, behalten. Zur weiteren Konzentration der Intelligenz in Restungarn haben auch Zehntausende von aus den verlorenen Gebieten hereinströmenden Vertriebenen und Flüchtlingen beigetragen. Eine ähnliche Wirkung hat die in der jungen Nachkriegsgeneration aus verschiedenen Gründen (Arbeitslosigkeit, Kompensation der in den Schützengräben verlorengegangenen Jahre, Suche nach verstärkten Berechtigungen im sich verschärfenden Konkurrenzkampf am Arbeitsmarkt usw.) sich ausbreitende konjunkturelle Bewegung zum Besuch höherer akademischer Institutionen ausgeübt. Diese Entwicklung konnte sich natürlicherweise auf die größere Schuldichte des im Rumpfstaat verbliebenen zentralen Gebietes stützen. Daher die Komplexität der Variabeln, die in den von Zahlen vermittelten Ereignissen eine Rolle spielten. Dennoch wird damit die Tatsache nicht völlig relativiert, daß Kleinungarn in relativen Zahlen über fast doppelt so viele Diplomierte verfügte wie das frühere Reich, und daß der Anteil seiner des Lesens und Schreibens unkundigen Bevölkerung, verglichen mit der Vorkriegszeit, nur einen Bruchteil ausmachte.

---

4 Seit den dreißiger Jahren dieses Jahrhunderts ist es zur Gewohnheit geworden, unter der progressiv eingestellten Intelligenz Ungarns zwischen der 'populistischen' und der 'urbanistischen' Gruppe zu unterscheiden und sie einander gegenüber zu stellen. Die 'Populisten' sollen bäuerlicher Abstammung sein, weil die 'Urbanisten' durch ihren städtischen, bürgerlichen und oft jüdischen Ursprung so bezeichnet werden *(Borbándi 1976)*.

Wenn man die diesbezüglichen Angaben zu den religiösen Bekenntnisgruppen betrachtet, stellt sich heraus, daß die Rangordnung des Vorhandenseins von Bildungsgütern von der Vor- bis zur Nachkriegszeit gar keine Veränderung erfahren hat und das proportionale Verhältnis zwischen den Gruppen sehr ähnlich geblieben ist: Die jüdische Überlegenheit behauptet sich 1930 ebenso stark wie früher mit einem Prozentsatz der Abiturientenzahlen, der dem Drei- bis Sechsfachen gegenüber den Nichtjuden entspricht. Die Lutheraner sind nach wie vor zweite auf der Stufenleiter, vom Leistungsniveau der Juden allerdings mit großem Abstand entfernt. Die kleine unitarische Splittergruppe zeigt ein vergleichbares Niveau auf; Römisch-Katholische und Kalvinisten halten sich in der Mitte der Bildungshierarchie, während die orthodoxen und die griechisch-katholischen Griechen in jeder Hinsicht die untersten Plätze einnehmen. Diese interessanten Ergebnisse können mit dem Hinweis auf die wirtschaftlich-berufliche Klassenstruktur und den sprachlichen Assimilationsgrad bzw. die erwiesene Ungarischsprachigkeit der Bekenntnisgruppen gedeutet werden.

Die Bildungselite ist die auf dem Wege der Verbürgerlichung am stärksten fortgeschrittene und am entschiedensten assimilierte Gruppe, was durch vorzügliche Beispiele historisch zuerst vom Judentum und – weniger markant – vom Luthertum belegt ist. Beide stellten in Ungarn ursprünglich überwiegend fremdsprachige (deutsche oder jiddisch-deutsche, bei Lutheranern auch slowakische) und seit dem Anfang des Modernisierungsprozesses mehr (Juden) oder weniger (Deutschlutheraner) zur Verbürgerlichung neigende Bevölkerungsgruppen dar.[5] Bei beiden kann man in der Tendenz zur relativen – bei Juden auch klassenspezifisch bemerkenswerten – 'Überschulung'[6] kompensatorische Bestrebungen von in der Gesamtgesellschaft dominierten Minderheiten wahrnehmen. Das gilt besonders für die in Kleinungarn ansässigen Teile dieser Konfessionsgruppen. (Die Siebenbürger Sachsen, als in dieser Hinsicht einzigartig privilegierte Schicht, verfügten vor 1919 über ein eigenes deutschsprachiges Gymnasialnetz, das ihre Widerstandsfähigkeit gegen jeglichen Assimilationsdruck wesentlich erhöhte.) Am anderen Ende der Rangordnung findet man die Christen griechischen Bekenntnisses. Diese weisen eine Anzahl von negativ wirkenden Merkmalen der beruflich und geographisch im-

---

5   Im Jahre 1910 waren die ungarischen Lutheraner zu 32% deutschsprachig, zu 35% slowakischsprachig und nur zu 32% ungarischsprachig. Bei den Juden war der Assimilationsprozeß schon so weit fortgeschritten, daß sie sich beim Zensus schon zu 77% als ungarische Muttersprachler bezeichneten *(Karady 1990, S. 12)*.
6   Tendenzen zur jüdischen Überschulung findet man während des Modernisierungsprozesses überall in der Habsburger Monarchie (und auch sonst in Europa). Siehe dazu: Der *Fall der Jüdischen Überqualifizierung (1990)*.

mobilen, politisch dominierten und auch daher assimilationswidrig eingestellten oder zur Teilnahme am Assimilationsprozeß unfähigen, massiv fremdartigen und ideologisch durch ethnisch verwandte Nationalstaaten (Serbien, Ukraine, Rumänien) beeinflußten Minderheitengruppen auf.

Es lohnt sich, die nach Bildungsstufen unterschiedlichen Resultate von Tabelle 1 miteinander zu vergleichen. Die Rangordnung der Konfessionen ist nämlich nicht ganz gleichartig, wenn man sie den Indizes der Mittel- oder Hochschulfrequenz und des Analphabetentums gegenüberstellt. Im Bereich der letzteren sind erstens die Abweichungen geringer, da das Vorkommen von Schreibunkundigkeit für jede Gruppe (ausgenommen die griechischen Bekenntnisse) schon Anfang des 20. Jahrhundert zu einem im schnellen Verschwinden begriffenen Randphänomen geworden war. Doch sollte man hervorheben, daß die Protestanten in dieser Hinsicht die mehrheitliche römisch-katholische Gruppe in allen Kategorien weit überholten. Damit erfaßt man wahrscheinlich den besonderen Ausdruck einer durch religiöse Erfordernisse bedingte Neigung zur Lese- und Schreibkundigkeit, die nur bei zur unmittelbaren Kenntnis der Heiligen Schrift angeregten Gruppen (neben den Protestanten natürlich auch die Juden) regelmäßig vorkommt.

Wie auch immer, das diesbezüglich auffallendste Ergebnis von Tabelle 1 ist die nachhaltig ausgeprägte jüdische Vorrangstellung in den gebildeten Klassen. Während in den christlichen Milieus der Prozentsatz der abgeschlossenen (aber selbst nur der mit vier Mittelschulklassen begonnenen) Gymnasialbildung nur selten 10% erreicht, hat fast die Hälfte der jüdischen Männer gegen 1930 ein Gymnasium besucht. Das bedeutet, daß die Sozialpyramide aller christlichen Gruppen eine nur schmale Bildungselite innehatte. Dahingegen schloß diese beim Judentum schon fast ein Drittel der Bevölkerungsgruppe ein – und trotzte so dem in den ungarischen Hochschulen seit Herbst 1920 eingeführten antisemitischen Numerus clausus *(Karady/Kemény 1980)*. Die Zielscheibe der antijüdischen Propaganda war also eine mit Bildungsgütern außerordentlich stark ausgestattete Gruppe. Daher sollte man unter den Motiven des protofaschistischen Antisemitismus in Ungarn das Element der Klassenkonkurrenz zwischen jüdischen und nichtjüdischen Bildungseliten nicht unterschätzen.

Tabelle 2 legt eine Reihe von mit den bisherigen nicht streng vergleichbaren Beobachtungen über die regionalen Ungleichheiten der konfessionell ausgeprägten Bildungschancen um 1930 vor. Die auf die vier zahlenmäßig wichtigsten Bekenntnisgruppen beschränkten Angaben wurden nach fünf (die Hauptstadt und das zentrale Komitat um Budapest eingeschlossen) Regionen und dazu innerhalb der drei peripheren Provinzen nach größeren (administrativ selbständigen) Städten und anderen Gebieten aufgeteilt. Das Bildungsniveau jeder Gruppe erweist sich am markantesten in Budapest, dann in den anderen Städten und drittens fast überall im die Hauptstadt umgebenden Komitat Pest als das höchste. Daneben erscheinen die regionalen Abweichungen im geographischen Sinne ziemlich gering. Die oft behauptete historische Überentwicklung des Westens von Ungarn gegenüber den östlichen Landesteilen dürfte aber namentlich anhand dieser Zahlen kaum bestätigt werden. Die transdanubischen Prozentsätze der höher Beschulten (mit Abitur oder Gymnasialbesuch) liegen nur für Juden wesentlich über dem Provinzdurchschnitt, während sie zum Beispiel für die mehrheitlichen Katholiken eher im Durchschnitt bleiben. Beim Judentum drücken also diese Angaben einen in der Zwischenkriegszeit noch immer bedeutenden Unterschied zwischen dem westlichen (ursprünglich meistens aus dem Nordwesten stammenden und deutschsprachigen) und östlichen Judentum (mit jiddischsprachigem, galizischem Hintergrund) aus. Für Nichtjuden bemerkt man vergleichbare Abweichungen eher zugunsten der Regionen außerhalb der östlichen Tiefebene (also zugunsten des Nordens und des Westens). Diese regionalen Gegensätze erscheinen besonders beim Index der Schreib- und Lesekundigkeit ausgeprägt und zeichnen die Konturen eines historisch sehr alten Kontrastes zwischen einerseits den in der frühen Neuzeit unter osmanischer Herrschaft stehenden und südöstlichen, und andererseits den die Kontinuität der mittelalterlichen, städtischen Kultur beibehaltenden nordöstlichen Regionen. Die seit dem 18. Jahrhundert beginnende und im 19. Jahrhundert beschleunigte Entwicklung vor allem der Wanderbewegung der neuen Bildungseliten und der planmäßige Ausbau des Gymnasialwesens haben aber diese traditionellen Unterschiede des höheren Bildungsniveaus vollauf nivelliert. Der relativ große Prozentsatz von Analphabeten in der Tiefebene legt also Zeugnis über ein historisch weitgehend überholtes Restphänomen ab.

Den vom Verstädterungsgrad abhängigen Unterschieden dürfte vielleicht eine gewichtigere Bedeutung zukommen. Aus den zwei letzten Zahlenspalten ersieht man die wesentlich überdurchschnittliche jüdische Urbanisationsfrequenz – mit der Mehrheit der jüdischen Bevölkerung in den Großstädten gegenüber nur einem Sechstel bei den anderen Bekenntnisgruppen. Aber diese unterschiedliche städtische Konzentration hat sehr verschiedenartige Folgen für das Bildungsniveau bei beiden miteinander verglichenen Bevölkerungsgruppen. Obwohl das städtische Judentum mit seinem Bildungsgrad das Niveau des Landjudentums – teilweise deutlich – übertrifft, bleibt diese regionale Streuung der investierten Bildungsgüter doch in der Nähe des hohen jüdischen Durchschnitts. Bei allen christlichen Gruppen erscheinen dagegen die vergleichbaren Differenzen viel drastischer. In Budapest und in den Städten findet sich eine viel stärkere relative Konzentration der gebildeten christlichen Mittelschichten, als dies beim Judentum der Fall ist. Das Niveau der Lutheraner von Budapest oder Miskolz zum Beispiel ist hinter dem Niveau der dortigen Juden gar nicht wesentlich zurückgeblieben. Das bedeutet unter anderem, daß die in den Städten ansässigen Christen und Juden im Spannungsfeld der intellektuellen Arbeitsmärkte miteinander in viel engerem Kontakt und, gelegentlich, auch in einem engeren Konkurrenzverhältnis standen als auf dem Lande, wo die überwiegende Mehrheit der Christen in vom Judentum weit entfernten beruflich-gesellschaftlichen Geltungsfeldern (überwiegend in der Landwirtschaft) tätig war. Diese Tatsache dürfte möglicherweise zur Steigerung des in der städtischen Bevölkerung in viel höherem Maße als auf dem Lande beobachteten Potentials antisemitischer Einstellungen erheblich beigetragen haben. Wenn der politische Antisemitismus in Ungarn weitgehend ein städtisches Phänomen blieb, so dürfte dies als strukturelle Grundbedingung mit der außerordentlichen Überkonzentration des gesamten Judentums und des gebildeten Christentums in den Städten, vor allem in der Hauptstadt, zusammenhängen.

Tabelle 3 gibt direkte Auskunft über den religionsspezifischen Anteil der Angehörigen intellektueller Berufe in den verschiedenen regionalen Einheiten Ungarns. Die wichtigsten Unterschiede für das ganze Land erscheinen in den drei letzten Zeilen. Sie verstärken die oben besprochenen Kontraste zwischen Juden mit breiter und Christen (besonders Nichtlutheraner) mit schmaler Basis gebildeter Mittelklasseschichten. Andererseits veranschaulichen sie die ungleiche interne Verteilung dieser Gruppen zwischen Privatbeamten und anderen (d. h. öffentlichen Beamten und Freiberuflern). Die beobachteten Ungleichheiten sind auffallend genug, so daß sie trotz der durch die Zusammenfassung der freien Berufe mit den Staatsbeamten gegebenen Grobheit der statistischen Erfassung interpretierbar bleiben: Wenn man nämlich 'bürgerlich' und 'nichtbürgerlich' gesinnte Gruppen würde miteiander vergleichen wollen, dann müßte man die auf offenen, von den Behörden nicht oder nur wenig kontrollierten Märkten tätigen freien Berufe mit den Privatbeamten zusammenfassen, was nach den hier benutzten statistischen Quellen sich aber als unmöglich erwies. (Einige diesbezügliche gruppenspezifischen Eigenschaften werden bei der Erörterung von Tabelle 5 erläutert).

Bleiben also hier zwei wesentliche Beobachtungen zu machen. Erstens müssen die sehr beträchtlichen – nach Größenordnung von 1 zu 4 skalierten – Unterschiede zwischen Juden und Nichtjuden erwähnt werden, die zwischen ihren Anteilen an denjenigen Gesellschaftsschichten bestehen, die überhaupt Bildungskapital beruflich benötigen und nutzen: diese Anteile machen bei Juden fast ein Drittel der aktiven Bevölkerung aus gegenüber weniger als einem Zehntel bei den anderen Bevölkerungsgruppen (und nur 7,3% bei den Katholiken). Wichtig erscheint dabei die Tatsache, daß diese gebildete, aktive Bevölkerung innerhalb des Judentums auf dem Lande fast so dicht konzentriert ist wie in den Städten, ohne eigentlich entscheidende regionale Abweichungen aufzuzeigen, während bei Christen die Konzentration dieser Schichten in der Hauptstadt und in den anderen Städten auffallend ausgeprägt bleibt. Die jüdischen Bildungseliten sind also viel harmonischer in die ländliche Gesellschaftsstruktur (und den regionalen Beschäftigungsmarkt) der betroffenen Bevölkerung eingefügt als ihre christlichen Äquivalente. Auch in den von der traditionsgebundenen Orthodoxie dominierten nördlichen und südöstlichen Regionen gehört ein Fünftel bis ein Viertel der aktiven jüdischen Männer dieser gebildeten Mittelschicht an. Bei den Christen erreichen die vergleichbaren Prozentsätze kaum 5 bis 10%. In Budapest sind die diesbezüglichen Zahlen der Christen die günstigsten mit einem Viertel bis zu einem Drittel (gegenüber allerdings zwei Fünfteln bei den Juden). Die städtische und besonders hauptstädtische Konzentration der gebildeten christlichen Berufsgruppen ist also die Quelle einer wichtigen Gleichgewichtsstörung innerhalb der ohnedies schon verhältnismäßig schmalen nichtjüdischen Mittelschicht.

Zweitens sind die meisten Juden dieser gebildeten Schichten (fast drei Viertel von ihnen) in privatbeamteten Stellen aktiv, während bei den Christen die Mehrheit (in einem Verhältnis von 2 oder 3 zu 1) im öffentlichen Dienst und in den freien Berufen tätig ist. Diese Ungleichheit in der inneren Struktur der die Fachbildung nutzenden Schichten – was das relative jüdische Übergewicht auf den offenen Märkten begünstigt – würde noch viel krasser ausfallen, wenn die freien Berufe mit ihrer hohen, oftmals fast die Mehrheit erreichenden jüdischen Beteiligung[7] von der Kategorie 'öffentlicher Dienst' getrennt registriert worden wären. Mit der allgemeinen Wirtschaftsstruktur Ungarns – einem relativen Mangel an großen Industriebetrieben, Verkehrsknotenpunkten und Großhandelseinrichtungen – hängt es zusammen, daß der Anteil des Privatbeamtentums in den ländlichen Gruppen viel schwächer ausgeprägt ist als in den Städten, besonders in Budapest. Die diesbezüglichen ziemlich starken Unterschiede nach Landesteilen dürften auch den regionalen Ungleichheiten der Wirtschaftsentwicklung zuzuschreiben sein. Dabei erscheinen aber nur bei den Juden die verhältnismäßig hohen Prozentsätze der Privatbe-

---

7   Nach dem Zensus von 1910 waren im ganzen Lande 45% der Rechtsanwälte, 48% der Mediziner, 42% der Journalisten und 37% der Privatingenieure jüdischen Glaubens. Die Prozentsätze wären nennenswert höher, wenn man die betroffenen Angehörigen dieser Berufsgruppen jüdischer Herkunft – d. h. die zum Christentum übergetretenen – mit einbezöge.

amten im Westen und im Zentrum (Komitat Pest) als auffallend. Dieses Phänomen hat bestimmt auch mit der inneren Teilung des ungarischen Judentums in zwei, im Hinblick auf den Prozeß der Verbürgerlichung und, mit dieser zusammenhängend, der kulturellen Assimilation, wesentlich entgegengesetzte Gruppen 'westjüdischer' und 'ostjüdischer' Richtung zu tun.

Tabelle 4 verdeutlicht die spezifischen wirtschaftlichen (nach Tätigkeitssektoren) und regionalen Struktureigenschaften des unterschiedlichen Bekenntnisgruppen angehörenden Privatbeamtentums. Auch hier zeichnen sich die wichtigsten Varianzen zwischen Juden und Christen ab.

Die Mehrheit – nahezu zwei Drittel – der jüdischen Privatbeamten sind im Handel und im Bankwesen, also in diesen historisch bedingten und traditionell als 'jüdischen' angesehenen Tätigkeiten aktiv, dagegen sind dies nur etwas mehr als ein Drittel in der christlichen Vergleichsgruppe. Die Industrie erscheint, mit ganz ähnlichen Prozentsätzen, als der zweitgrößte Berufszweig für alle Gruppen. Landwirtschaft und Verkehr stellen jedoch für die Bekenntnisgruppen sehr unterschiedlich erreichbare Möglichkeiten wirtschaftlichen Erfolgs dar. Wegen ihrer starken Repräsentation in der im global unterentwickelten Ungarn ursprünglich völlig dominierenden Landwirtschaft (als adelige Grundbesitzer oder besitzende Bauern) sind Christen auch in der Intelligenz dieser Branche überdurchschnittlich häufig vertreten, obwohl die Landwirtschaft dieser Periode noch mit relativ geringem Bedarf an Fachbildungskapital auskommt. Das bedeutet aber keineswegs, daß Juden auch im landwirtschaftlichen Beamtentum keine wichtigen Positionen eingenommen hätten. Im Gegenteil, wenn Juden statistisch auf Landesebene hier selten aktiv sind, so erscheint ihr Anteil in mehreren Regionen (im Norden oder in der südöstlichen Tiefebene) dem entsprechenden Anteil der in der Landwirtschaft beschäftigten christlichen Intelligenz nahestehend. Der Transportbereich mobilisierte intellektuelle Arbeitskräfte besonders im öffentlichen Sektor. Das Eisenbahnnetz stand schon damals unter staatlicher Kontrolle und auch die meisten städtischen Verkehrsmittel waren diesem öffentlichen Sektor angeschlossen. Daher ist hier auch eine sehr bedeutende christliche Überrepräsentation zu finden. Weil die jüdischen gebildeten Schichten nur selten im Verkehrswesen tätig sind, beschäftigt dieser Wirtschaftszweig zwischen einem Viertel und einem Fünftel der christlichen Hochschulqualifizierten. In den Städten außerhalb Budapests, in denen die Industrie wenig entwickelt und die jüdische Konkurrenz in Handel und Bankwesen mächtig war, blieb für diese Gruppen der Verkehrszweig das zweitgrößte industrielle Beschäftigungsfeld. Das jüdische Defizit unter den Beschäftigten des Verkehrswesens muß also eigentlich dem im wesentlichen nicht-privaten Charakter dieses Zweiges zugeschrieben werden.

Tabelle 5 erlaubt eine nähere Beobachtung der Differenzen zwischen Juden und Nichtjuden (hier Katholiken) im Bezug auf die innere Struktur der komplexen statistischen Kategorie 'öffentliche Beamte und freie Berufe'. Wegen der großen Spannbreite der Kategorie 'andere' (Pensionierte, untere Angestellte usw.) konnten hier nur die wichtigsten Berufszweige betrachtet werden. An sich lassen sich die Unterschiede im Bestand der zur Kategorie 'andere' zählbaren Beschäftigten (mit einem viel geringeren Anteil von Juden gegenüber einen mehrheitlichen Anteil bei den Katholiken) so interpretieren, daß die Juden in diesen Gruppen mit höheren Prozentsätzen als die Katholiken in den relativ mehr Prestige tragenden, höheren oder durch Pensionsalter weniger begrenzten beruflichen Stellungen vertreten waren.

Die wichtigsten durch Tabelle 5 vermittelten Resultate betreffen aber nochmals die tiefe Dualität der Verteilung der jüdischen und katholischen Gruppen dieser Kategorie. Während die überwiegende Mehrheit der hierher gehörenden Juden auf freien Märkten tätig sind (die freien Berufe allein repräsentieren 41 von den insgesamt 53% der angeführten Berufsgruppen), macht die entsprechende Gruppe der Katholiken nur einen Bruchteil ihrer Gesamtzahl aus (weniger als 7 der insgesamt 44% der hier identifizierten Berufsgruppen). Katholiken sind natürlich im öffentlichen Dienst in allen seinen Spielarten mit hohem Gewicht vertreten. Mehr als ein Drittel unter ihnen befindet sich in der Staatsverwaltung selbst, ein anderes Drittel im Lehrerberuf. Die in Tabelle 3 durchgeführte zweifache Aufteilung der ungarischen Intelligenz nach Regionen und nach religiösem Hintergrund gewinnt hier eine weitere Bestätigung. Regionale Verschiebungen, obwohl sie oft beträchtlich sind, besitzen im Hinblick auf die vorliegende Fragestellung keine grundlegende Bedeutung: sie sind in der Regel wirtschaftlichen oder institutionell-strukturellen Bedingungen zuzuschreiben. Das Personal in der Staatsverwaltung findet man bei Katholiken zum Beispiel in viel größeren Proportionen in Budapest und in den Städten – wo die staatlichen und komitatlichen Zentralbehörden untergebracht sind – als auf dem Lande. Das gleiche gilt für die Gymnasiallehrer und die Bediensteten der Landesgerichte.

Die angeführten Angaben und die Kommentare dazu verdeutlichen die tiefe Spaltung der ungarischen Intelligenz in den Krisenjahren der Zwischenkriegszeit. Der ungarische Soziologe Ferenc Erdei hat dies die 'Doppelstruktur' der Mittelklassen genannt, deren emblematischer Ausdruck in den unterschiedlichen Marktchancen von Juden und Nichtjuden (aber im weiteren Sinne auch von bürgerlichen und nichtbürgerlichen, das heißt, dem Lebensmodell des Adels folgenden, Gruppen und Individuen) zu finden ist. Was sich dabei als das wichtigste Ergebnis herauskristallisiert, ist die Allgemeinheit ähnlicher 'Doppelstrukturen' im Modernisierungsprozeß der meisten mitteleuropäischen Länder, wobei unter dem Einfluß bestimmter historischer Konjunkturen des 20. Jahrhunderts die sich ethnisch definierende Mehrheit unterschiedliche (meistens nicht nur jüdische) Minderheitengruppen aus den 'geschützten' staatlichen Arbeitsmärkten der Intelligenz ausschließt. Diese 'Doppelstruktur' hat etliche ideologisch-politisch zugespitzte Konfliktsituationen ausgelöst,[8] die in den meisten Ländern auf direkte oder indirekte Weise stark zur Krisenlage unter dem Faschismus und/oder der Naziherrschaft beigetragen haben.

Bibliographie

Borbándi, Gyula: Der ungarische Populismus. Mainz: Von Hase und Köhler 1976. (Studia hungarica. 7)

Der Fall der jüdischen Überqualifizierung. (Themenschwerpunkt). In: Karady, Victor / Mitter, Wolfgang (Hrsg.): Bildungswesen und Sozialstruktur in Mitteleuropa im 19. und 20. Jahrhundert (= Studien und Dokumentationen zur vergleichenden Bildungsforschung. 42), Köln u. a.: Böhlau 1990, S. 141-246.

Karady, Victor / Kemény, István: Antisémitisme universitaire et concurrence de classe: la loi de numerus clausus en Hongrie entre les deux guerres. In: Actes de la Recherche en Sciences Sociales, 34 (1980) 9, S. 67-96.

Karady, Victor: Assimilation and Schooling. National and Denominational Minorities in the Universities of Budapest around 1900. In: Ránki, György (ed.): Hungary and European Civilization (= Indiana University Studies on Hungary. 3), Bloomington: Indiana University Press 1989, S. 285-319.

Karady, Victor: Egyenlötlen elmagyarosodás [Ungleiche Madjarisierung]. In: Századvég, (1990) 2, S. 5-37.

Kopp, Botho von: Schooling and the Antagonism between Czechs and Germans in the Czechoslovak Republic 1918-1938. In: Karady, Victor / Mitter, Wolfgang (Hrsg.): Bildungswesen und Sozialstruktur in Mitteleuropa im 19. und 20. Jahrhundert (= Studien und Dokumentationen zur vergleichenden Bildungsforschung. 42), Köln u. a.: Böhlau 1990, S. 85-103.

Kovács, Alajos: A nevek és névváltoztatások statisztikája [Statistik der Namen und Namensänderungen]. In: Magyar Statisztikai Szemle, 3 (1930), S. 228-240.

Mitter, Wolfgang: Civic Education in German Schools in Czechoslovakia (1918-1938) in the Mirror of Loyalty Conflict. In: Karady, Victor / ders. (Hrsg.): Bildungswesen und Sozialstruktur in Mitteleuropa im 19. und 20. Jahrhundert (= Studien und Dokumentationen zur vergleichenden Bildungsforschung. 42), Köln u. a.: Böhlau 1990, S. 71-83.

---

8 Zum Sonderfall der Tschechoslowakei siehe *Mitter (1990)* und von *Kopp (1990)*.

TABELLENANHANG

Tabelle 1: Das Bildungsniveau der Männer in Ungarn nach religiösem Bekenntnis (1910-1930) (Zahlenangaben in 1 000)

Bekenntnis-gruppen	Jahr	Bevölke-rung über 5 Jahre Anzahl	davon Schreibkundige Anzahl	davon Schreibkundige in %	Bevöl-kerung über 10 Jahre Anzahl	davon mit 4 oder mehr Mittelschulklassen Anzahl	davon mit 4 oder mehr Mittelschulklassen in %	Bevöl-kerung über 19 Jahre Anzahl	mit Matura oder Hochschulbildung Anzahl	mit Matura oder Hochschulbildung in %
Juden	1910	387,8	38,4	9,9	295,2	98,3	33,3	250,4	45,5	18,2
	1930	197,2	2.788	1,4	173,2	78	45	155,8	47,3	30,4
Röm.-Kath.	1910	3.715,5	795	20,8	2.791	190,9	6,8	2.653	98,6	3,7
	1930	2.381,9	203	8,5	1.932	196,9	10,2	1.657	109,8	6,6
Lutheraner	1910	551,9	61	11,1	423,8	36,6	8,6	363	20,1	5,6
	1930	233,5	8,8	3,8	194,3	22,4	11,5	169,6	16,3	9,6
Reformierte	1910	1.116,1	183	16,5	867,7	54,7	6,3	742,4	29,2	3,9
	1930	786,9	39,6	5	650,3	54,1	8,3	566,4	33,8	6,0
Griech.-Kath.	1910	833,2	508	61	624,4	14,1	2,2	520,5	8.249	1,6
	1930	83,7	14	16,7	65,3	4.668	7,1	55,8	2.540	4,5
Griech.-Orth.	1910*	1.009	502	49,7	796,7	16,5	2,1	683,4	8.211	1,2
Unitarier	1910*	32.313	6.435	19,9	25.473	2.636	10,3	21.949	1.634	7,4

* Nach 1919 ist der Bestand des in Ungarn gebliebenen Bruchteils dieser Gruppen statistisch unbedeutend geworden.

Quelle: Für die Bevölkerung nach Alter im Jahre 1910: Magyar statisztikai közlemények 61, S. 32f.; für 1930: ibid. 96, S. 284f.; für Schulbesuch 1910: ibid. 61, S. 527f.; für 1930: ibid. 96, S. 314f.

Tabelle 2: Regionale Verteilung der über fünf Jahre alten männlichen Einwohner Ungarns nach Bildungsniveau und religiösem Bekenntnis (1930) (in ganzen Zahlen und in Prozent)

		Hochschulabschluß (in %)	Mittelschulabschluß (in %)	mit 4 Mittelschulklassen (in %)*	Schreibunkundige (in %)	männliche Bevölkerung** (ganze Zahlen)	männliche Bevölkerung** nach Regionen (in %)
JUDEN							
Transdanubien (West)	Städte	7,6	18,7	50,4	1,2	6.162	3,1
	Komitate	4,0	13,3	40,0	1,3	20.452	10,8
Südöstliche	Städte	7,9	18,8	51,3	1,3	8.799	4,4
Tiefebene	Komitate	4,1	8,4	26,4	3,0	27.745	14,7
Norden	Miskolc	5,2	13,9	40,0	1,5	4.848	2,5
	Komitate	4,1	8,8	29,5	2,4	16.207	8,6
Komitat Pest		4,3	12,4	41,7	1,3	19.460	9,9
Budapest		8,1	23,5	56,5	0,8	93.547	46,1
Ganz Ungarn		6,4	17,5	45,7	1,4	197.220	100,0
RÖMISCH-KATHOLISCHE							
Transdanubien (West)	Städte	4,1	6,1	21,8	3,7	61.568	2,5
	Komitate	0,9	1,5	5,5	7,3	853.328	36,0
Südöstliche	Städte	2,5	4,1	14,4	8,9	104.391	4,3
Tiefebene	Komitate	0,9	1,5	5,7	13,4	370.622	15,8

		Hochschulabschluß (in %)	Mittelschulabschluß (in %)	mit 4 Mittelschulklassen (in %)*	Schreibunkundige (in %)	männliche Bevölkerung** (ganze Zahlen)	männliche Bevölkerung** nach Regionen (in %)
Norden	Miscolc	4,4	6,9	26,1	4,8	11.471	0,5
	Komitate	0,8	1,5	5,3	11,4	315.627	13,5
Komitat Pest		1,1	2,5	10,1	8,4	414.867	17,5
Budapest		6,9	10,6	31,9	2,2	250.074	9,8
Ganz Ungarn		1,7	2,9	10,0	8,5	2.381.948	100,0
LUTHERANER							
Transdanubien (West)	Städte	5,5	7,2	22,3	1,7	7.698	3,3
	Komitate	1,5	2,1	6,6	3,4	77.611	33,3
Südöstliche Tiefebene	Städte	8,2	10,5	31,8	2,6	3.571	1,5
	Komitate	1,1	1,7	6,6	4,7	69.074	30,0
Norden	Miscolc	11,3	13,3	43,0	1,7	1.075	0,4
	Komitate	2,9	3,9	12,1	4,2	13.348	5,7
Komitat Pest		1,8	3,4	11,4	5,1	38.842	16,9
Budapest		13,6	16,8	45,8	1,1	22.249	8,9
Ganz Ungarn		2,9	4,1	12,5	3,8	233.468	100,0

		Hoch-schulab-schluß (in %)	Mittelschul-abschluß (in %)	mit 4 Mittel-schulklassen (in %)*	Schreib-unkundi-ge (in %)	männliche Be-völkerung** (ganze Zahlen)	männliche Be-völkerung** nach Regionen (in %)
REFORMIERTE							
Transdanubien	Städte	7,0	7,4	27,6	2,7	5.241	0,6
(West)	Komitate	1,2	1,7	5,7	4,9	126.999	15,8
Südöstliche	Städte	2,9	4,0	14,4	6,8	59.288	7,4
Tiefebene	Komitate	0,8	1,2	4,5	10,4	343.565	44,6
Norden	Miscolc	4,1	5,5	21,2	4,2	7.290	0,9
	Komitate	1,2	1,8	5,8	7,7	85.172	11,0
Komitat Pest		1,4	2,7	10,8	5,4	104.850	13,2
Budapest		8,8	10,5	32,8	1,4	54.464	6,5
Ganz Ungarn		1,8	2,5	8,6	7,5	786.869	100,0

* Diese Zahl schließt auch diejenigen ein, die weniger als 4 Gymnasialklassen absolviert haben. Der Prozentsatz der-jenigen, die 4 Mittelschulklassen oder mehr absolviert haben, schließt auch die ehemaligen Studenten oder Diplo-mierten mit 4, 6 oder 8 Sekundarklassen oder mit Hochschulbildung ein. Es scheint, daß Studenten, die ein Niveau zwischen diesen Klassen erreicht haben, der unmittelbar niedrigeren Kategorie zugewiesen wurden (das heißt zum Beispiel, daß ehemalige Studenten der 5. Klassen in die Kategorie „4 Klassen" eingeteilt wurden).

** männliche Bevölkerung über 5 Jahre.

Quelle: Magyar statisztikai közlemények 96, S. 314-325 (für Angaben über das Bildungsniveau) und ibid., S. 284f. (für Angaben über die Bevölkerung).

Tabelle 3: Regionale Prozentsätze der intellektuellen Berufstätigen nach größeren Bekenntnisgruppen unter Männern von 20 bis 69 Jahren in Ungarn (1930)

	Katholiken		Reformierte		Lutheraner		Juden	
	Privat-beamte	freie Berufe / Öffentlicher Dienst	Privat-beamte	freie Berufe / Öffentlicher Dienst	Privat-beamte	freie Berufe / Öffentlicher Dienst	Privat-beamte	freie Berufe / Öffentlicher Dienst
Transdanubien (West)	1,3	3,8	1,1	4,1	1,9	4,7	16,0	8,6
Komitat Pest Mitte	2,7	4,7	2,4	5,9	3,4	5,0	17,8	7,2
Budapest	9,8	12,9	9,8	16,7	16,2	16,7	30,4	8,0
Südöstliche Tiefebene*	1,8	4,6	1,0	4,2	1,5	4,3	14,7	9,8
Norden**	1,4	3,6	1,2	4,6	3,7	7,0	11,8	9,4
Ungarn	2,6	5,2	1,9	5,4	3,7	6,0	23,2	9,0
Komitate	1,5	3,6	1,1	4,0	1,9	4,1	13,3	8,7
Städte (ohne Budapest)	3,6	9,4	2,7	8,0	6,0	13,3	22,4	9,9

* Die gesamte Tiefebene ohne Budapest, das Komitat Pest und den Norden.
** Komitate Abauj Torna, Borsod, Gömör, Heves, Nográd Hont und Zemplén.

Quelle: Angaben der Volkszählung von 1930. Siehe für den Bestand der Altersgruppen: Magyar statisztikai közlamények 96, S. 284-295; für den Bestand der Berufsgruppen: ibid, S. 78ff.

Tabelle 4: Regionale Verteilung von männlichen Privatbeamten in Ungarn nach Bekenntnis und Wirtschaftssektor (1930) (in Prozent)

	Transdanubien (West)	Komitat Pest	Budapest	Südöstliche Tiefebene*	Norden**	Ungarn	Komitate (alle)	Städte (ohne Budapest)
KATHOLIKEN								
Landwirtschaft	12,6	4,2	1,1	13,7	13,0	6,9	13,6	3,0
Industrie	27,9	41,2	43,5	24,1	30,5	37,0	32,0	30,2
Handel und Banken	29,4	29,3	35,9	36,1	28,2	38,0	30,2	32,3
Verkehr	26,1	25,3	19,6	26,1	28,3	23,2	24,2	34,4
zusammen	100,0	100,0	100,0	100,0	100,0	100,0	100,0	100,0
N =	7.988	77.220	18.541	4.773	2.822	41.294	18.503	4.250
REFORMIERTE								
Landwirtschaft	20,2	6,7	1,4	9,9	13,0	7,4	13,1	3,7
Industrie	19,2	30,8	35,2	24,9	24,8	29,5	24,5	29,6
Handel und Banken	29,6	33,1	43,5	42,4	33,8	39,3	36,4	37,0
Verkehr	31,0	29,4	19,9	22,8	28,3	24,0	25,8	29,8
zusammen	100,0	100,0	100,0	100,0	100,0	100,0	100,0	100,0
N =	977	1.736	3.949	2.531	706	9.898	4.627	1.323
LUTHERANER								
Landwirtschaft	20,1	4,2	1,5	3,9	11,4	7,1	14,3	3,1
Industrie	25,4	46,1	44,3	40,7	42,1	38,2	32,8	30,5

	Transdanubien (West)	Komitat Pest	Budapest	Südöstliche Tiefebene*	Norden**	Ungarn	Komitate (alle)	Städte (ohne Budapest)
Handel und Banken	30,0	29,1	39,5	37,7	23,4	35,5	32,1	35,6
Verkehr	24,4	20,4	15,7	17,7	23,1	19,2	20,9	30,7
zusammen	100,0	100,0	100,0	100,0	100,0	100,0	100,0	100,0
N =	392	892	2.855	742	368	5.839	2.473	511
JUDEN								
Landwirtschaft	8,4	1,5	0,2	9,8	11,0	2,6	10,0	3,1
Industrie	25,8	38,0	36,8	19,8	21,0	32,6	26,7	24,1
Handel und Banken	60,3	54,3	63,0	67,8	64,2	61,6	60,4	67,6
Verkehr	5,5	4,1	3,0	2,5	3,7	3,2	3,4	5,1
zusammen	100,0	100,0	100,0	100,0	100,0	100,0	100,0	100,0
N =	1.640	1.021	6.620	2.436	1.354	13.071	5.052	1.399

*   Die gesamte Tiefebene ohne Budapest, das Komitat Pest und den Norden.
**   Komitate Abauj Torna, Borsod, Gömör, Heves, Nográd Hont und Zemplén.
Quelle: Angaben der Volkszählung von 1930: Magyar statisztikai közlemények 96, S. 100ff.

Tabelle 5: Regionale Verteilung der ungarischen Arbeitnehmer im öffentlichen Dienst und in den freien und intellektuellen Berufen (Männer und Frauen) nach Bekenntnisgruppen (nur Katholiken und Juden) und Tätigkeitszweigen (1930)

	Transda-nubien	Komitat Pest	Budapest	Südöstliche Tiefebene	Norden	Ungarn	Komitate	Städte (außer Budapest)
KATHOLIKEN								
Öffentlicher Dienst	11,4	14,1	19,8	7,2	11,7	15,0	11,4	19,1
Gericht	2,7	2,7	2,9	1,9	3,2	3,0	3,0	4,3
Lehrer	4,6	12,6	5,0	6,5	16,9	10,9	15,9	6,4
Gymnasialprofessoren	3,4	3,2	4,2	1,6	3,0	3,5	3,0	4,5
Kirchlicher Dienst	7,7	3,0	2,8	2,5	5,6	4,8	5,8	6,0
Anwaltschaft	1,4	1,3	2,3	1,2	1,2	1,9	1,5	2,3
Gesundheitsdienst	4,2	3,6	4,6	2,5	3,7	4,3	4,3	3,7
Ingenieure	0,2	0,4	0,8	0,1	0,3	0,5	0,3	0,2
andere*	54,4	59,1	57,6	76,5	54,4	56,1	54,8	53,5
zusammen	100,0	100,0	100,0	100,0	100,0	100,0	100,0	100,0
N =	32.721	18.700	40.362	39.254	10.548	122.892	65.852	15.367
JUDEN								
Öffentlicher Dienst	2,9	5,1	2,9	2,7	3,3	3,1	2,0	4,4
Gericht	0,8	0,9	0,5	0,9	0,6	0,6	0,8	1,0
Lehrer	4,2	5,6	2,6	5,6	5,6	3,8	5,5	4,4

	Transda-nubien	Komitat Pest	Budapest	Südöstliche Tiefebene	Norden	Ungarn	Komitate	Städte (außer Budapest)
Gymnasialprofessoren	1,5	0,6	2,7	1,7	1,3	2,1	0,7	3,7
Kirchlicher Dienst	3,5	2,5	0,5	4,4	5,6	2,1	4,7	2,1
Anwaltschaft	19,8	16,6	18,5	18,9	13,1	18,5	17,0	23,8
Gesundheitsdienst	26,2	24,7	17,9	23,4	19,8	20,5	24,4	21,1
Ingenieure	1,2	1,5	2,9	0,7	0,5	2,1	0,9	1,2
andere*	39,9	42,5	51,5	41,7	45,2	47,3	43,1	38,3
zusammen	100,0	100,0	100,0	100,0	100,0	100,0	100,0	100,0
N =	2.006	1.256	9.612	2.876	1.604	17.354	5.968	1.774

* Der hohe Prozentsatz dieser Kategorie erklärt sich durch die hier nicht angeführten, statistisch aber hierher gehörenden Berufsgruppen und die große Anzahl von ebenso zu diesen Tätigkeitszweigen gezählten Pensionisten, Dienstboten und sämtlichen unteren Angestellten.

Quelle: Angaben der Volkszählung von 1930: Magyar statisztikai közlemények 96, S. 79 und 132ff.

Universitätsstudium für jedermann?
Die Politisierung der Sozialwissenschaften
als bleibendes Erbe der Bildungsexpansion

Michael Kelpanides

In Systemen mit komplexer Interdependenz ihrer Elemente wie Organismen und Gesellschaften haben massive Wandlungen in einem Bereich Auswirkungen in mehreren anderen Bereichen, die um so schwieriger zu identifizieren und ihren tatsächlichen Ursachen zuzurechnen sind, je größer die räumliche und zeitliche Distanz ist, in welcher sich die ursprünglichen Wandlungen auswirken.

Über die unmittelbaren Auswirkungen der Bildungsexpansion, durch die sich von Ende der fünfziger bis Anfang der siebziger Jahre, in weniger als zwanzig Jahren, die Studentenzahlen an den Universitäten der westlichen Welt verdrei- bis vervierfacht haben, ist viel geschrieben worden. Die Änderungen in der sozialen Zusammensetzung der Studentenschaft, ihre breiter gefächerten Interessen und Studienmotivationen, ihre unterschiedliche didaktische Ansprechbarkeit und Leistungsbereitschaft waren bevorzugte Untersuchungsgegenstände pädagogischer und bildungssoziologischer Abhandlungen. Auch über die zu geringe Angleichung der relativen Bildungsbeteiligung sozialer Schichten während der expansiven Bildungsreformen, durch welche – so Kritiker – die Chancengleichheit im Kapitalismus sich erneut als Illusion erwiesen hat, bietet der Büchermarkt reichlich Auskunft.

In welche Richtung sich jedoch mit der Bildungsexpansion die zentralen Funktionen der Universität verschoben und ihr Charakter gewandelt hat, darüber gibt es im einschlägigen sozialwissenschaftlichen Schrifttum keinen Konsens. War die Universität in ihrer jahrhundertelangen Tradition der Ort der von Handlungszwängen befreiten Reflexion und Wahrheitssuche einer Gemeinschaft von Lehrenden und Lernenden, so wurde dieser Zustand durch die seit der Bildungsexpansion stattgefundene, tiefgreifende und dauerhafte *Politisierung der Universität und der Inhalte der universitären Bildung* – zumindest in den Sozial- und Geisteswissenschaften – von Grund auf geändert.

Unter den bekenntnishaften Ideologien, die seit der Bildungsexpansion sich der universitären Sozialwissenschaft erfolgreich zu bemächtigen versuchten, nimmt der Neomarxismus den dominanten Platz ein. Er beherrscht heute bei weitem die westliche Sozialwissenschaft, die Soziologie, die Politikwissenschaft und nicht zuletzt die Pädagogik. Gerade in der deutschen Pädagogik hätte eigentlich eine Reihe komparativer Studien über die Bildungssysteme sozialistischer Länder, unter welchen an hervorgehobener Stelle die Arbeiten von Wolfgang Mitter und seinen Mitarbeitern *(Mitter / Novikov 1976)* zu nennen sind, für Aufklärung und Desillusionierung sorgen können.

Obwohl der universitäre Neomarxismus mit der intendierten begrifflichen Vagheit seiner Immunisierungsstrategien das Verhältnis seiner gesellschaftstheoretischen Annahmen zu den Tatsachen der Wirklichkeit in einen kunstvoll gewebten Schleier von Unklarheit hüllt, kann er nicht darüber hinwegtäuschen, daß er im Grunde genauso dogmatisch wie der orthodoxe Marxismus ist, was das Festhalten an zentralen Marxschen Annahmen betrifft. Dazu gehört die Basisannahme, daß der Kapitalismus wegen des vermeintlich nicht aufhebbaren „Widerspruchs von Kapital und Arbeit" prinzipiell nicht reformierbar, sondern nur abschaffbar sei.

Das Festhalten an dieser empirisch falschen Annahme ist für den Neomarxismus unvermeidlich, denn sie macht gerade seinen Unterschied und zugleich seine spezifische Identität und „Neuheit" als intellektuelle Strömung in der – ganz entgegen den Marxschen Annahmen im Osten wie im Westen entwickelten – Nachkriegsgesellschaft aus: es ist der Standpunkt der totalen Negation des Kapitalismus. Würde der Neomarxismus diese und die mit ihr logisch zusammenhängenden Grundannahmen von Marx fallenlassen, so würde er sich vom sozial engagierten, aber nicht dogmatischen, sondern theoretisch offenen Bernsteinschen Revisionismus nicht unterscheiden. Dies käme dann dem ehrlichen Eingeständnis gleich, daß das, was an der Idee des Sozialismus im Unterschied zur geschichtsmetaphysischen Spekulation wirklich Substanz besitzt, von der realreformerischen, systemimmanenten Sozialdemokratie zum Wohl des arbeitenden Menschen schon längst verwirklicht wurde.

Zu einem solchen ehrlichen Eingeständnis des Scheiterns und zur damit verbundenen und nötigen Selbstaufhebung ist es beim Neomarxismus bis heute nicht gekommen, obwohl nicht erst seit 1989 einleuchtet, daß die vom Neomarxismus vorausgesagten Krisen und der Zusammenbruch des Kapitalismus nicht stattgefunden haben, sondern – umgekehrt – das Gesellschaftssystem des marxistischen Sozialismus kläglich untergegangen ist, das seit 1917 – trotz seiner eingeräumten realen Unvollkommenheiten – von den östlichen wie den westlichen Marxisten als der historische Triumph der Marxschen Theorie und der Beginn der Geschichte gefeiert wurde.

Wenn in der Tat alle Versuche, die Marxsche Theorie in die Wirklichkeit umzusetzen, gescheitert sind, dann ergibt sich die Frage, wie die massive Konversion der westlichen Sozialwissenschaften unter der unumstrittenen Führung der Soziologie seit den sechziger Jahren zur Marxschen Theorie zu erklären ist, deren Annahmen offenbar so realitätswidrig sind, daß ihre sämtlichen empirischen Aussagen eindeutig falsifiziert wurden. Obwohl die Einsicht in das empirische Scheitern der Theorie nicht erst seit dem Zusammenbruch des Sozialismus im Osten gekommen, sondern aus einer jahrzehntelangen Kumulierung negativer Erfahrungen hervorgegangen ist, stieg der Marxismus in der westlichen Sozialwissenschaft zur beherrschenden Richtung auf und wurde in weiten Bereichen der soziologischen Forschung und Lehre als das leitende theoretische Paradigma zur Analyse und Erklärung der gesellschaftlichen Prozesse etabliert.

Die Neomarxisten haben lange Zeit versucht, die empirischen und prognostischen Mißerfolge der Theorie mit artifiziellen *Ex-post*-Erklärungen zu rechtfertigen, um die Marxsche Theorie vor ihrer Falsifikation zu retten. An Texten wie die Einleitung von Narr und Offe zu dem von ihnen herausgegebenen Band „Wohlfahrtsstaat und Massenloyalität" *(Narr / Offe 1975, S. 9-46)* kommt die durch Neologismen und geschraubte Syntax nicht zu verhüllende theoretische Ratlosigkeit neomarxistischer Theoretiker zum Vorschein, die entgegen allen nicht mehr zu leugnenden Tatsachen das theoretische Modell der krisenerzeugenden Widersprüchlichkeit des Kapitalismus zu verteidigen versuchen. Auf der einen Seite stellen sie die Diagnose auf, daß *„die fortgeschrittenen kapitalistischen Systeme das Potential kategorial erschöpft haben, das ihnen zur Verfügung steht, um die Folgen ihrer Selbstwidersprüchlichkeit zu kompensieren ..."* (ebd., S. 19). Daraus folgt, daß die kapitalistischen Systeme wachsender Krisenhaftigkeit und dem dadurch wahrscheinlich werdenden Untergang entgegensteuern.

Auf derselben Seite, etwas weiter unten, müssen sie jedoch das *Gegenteil* einräumen, daß nämlich die entwickelten kapitalistischen Systeme ihr adaptives Problemlösungspotential keineswegs erschöpft haben, denn sie sind immer noch fähig, ihre Grenzen hinauszuschieben und zu überleben, anstatt zusammenzubrechen, wie sie es nach der Theorie sollten. Das zwingt nun die Theorie, so die genannten Theoretiker, davon Abstand zu nehmen, *„die Frage nach dem Zusammenbruch des Kapitalismus in naiver Weise zu stellen ... Wo in früheren Phasen der kapitalistischen Entwicklung die Frage nach den Gren-*

zen des Systems gestellt wurde, ergibt sich heute die zusätzliche Frage nach den Möglichkeiten des Systems, seine Grenzen selbstadaptiv hinauszuschieben" (ebd.).

Da es nun weder Narr noch Offe noch irgendeinem anderen neomarxistischen Theoretiker geglückt ist, *vorauszusagen*, wie weit denn das systemische Adaptionspotential der „fortgeschrittenen kapitalistischen Systeme" reicht und vor allem welche qualitativen Systemwandlungen dieses Potential beinhaltet, denn das ist die eigentlich theoretisch interessante Frage, bleibt ihnen nichts anderes übrig als jedesmal *im Nachhinein*, nach jedem erhofften, aber nicht eingetroffenen Zusammenbruch des Kapitalismus festzustellen, daß sein Adaptionspotential offensichtlich doch noch weiter reicht als die Theoretiker gedacht hatten.

Während Marx zumindest kühne Prognosen aufstellte, die jedoch fehlschlugen, ist der Neomarxismus auf den Stand eines degenerierenden theoretischen Paradigmas herabgesunken, das nicht nur keine neuen Erkenntnisse ermöglicht, sondern seine begrifflichen Mittel mühsam dafür einsetzen muß, plausibel erscheinende Rechtfertigungen für seine prognostischen Mißerfolge *ex post* zu formulieren. Lakatos resümiert diesen Sachverhalt wie folgt: „*... the early predictions of Marxism were bold and stunning but they failed. Marxists explained all their failures: they explained the rising living standards of the working class by devising a theory of imperialism; they even explained why the first socialist revolution occurred in industrially backward Russia. They 'explained' Berlin 1953, Budapest 1956, Prague 1968. They 'explained' the Russian-Chinese conflict. But their auxiliary hypotheses were all cooked up after the event to protect Marxian theory from the facts. The Newtonian programme led to novel facts; the Marxian lagged behind the facts and has been running fast to catch up with them*" (Lakatos 1984, S. 6).

Da der oben zitierte Text von Offe und Narr 1975 geschrieben wurde, sind mit der seitdem gewachsenen negativen empirischen Evidenz gegen den Neomarxismus die *Expost*-Scheinrechtfertigungen für die Mißerfolge der marxistischen Theorie immer unrealistischer und unglaubwürdiger geworden. Folglich mußte die Marxsche Gesellschaftskritik, wenn sie den marxistischen Intellektuellen als Waffe gegen den Kapitalismus erhalten werden sollte, von allen ihren empirisch faßbaren Implikationen „bereinigt" werden, denn sie alle waren bereits so gut wie endgültig falsifiziert.

Zur Rettung des Marxismus als „reine Kritik", ohne alle seine empirischen Gesetzesaussagen über Konzentration des Kapitals, Proletarisierung, Zusammenbruch des Kapitalismus usw., die nicht eingetroffen sind und auf die man sich daher nicht mehr beziehen kann, wurde die Legende von den „Zwei Marxismen" verbreitet: dem westlichen kritisch-humanistischen Marxismus und dem deterministisch-mechanistischen, östlichen Marxismus. *Gouldner (1980)* widmete dem Thema sein gleichnamiges Buch „The Two Marxisms". Als Urheber des zur Herrschaftsideologie im Osten erstarrten deterministisch-mechanistischen Marxismus gilt in dieser zeitgenössischen Legende Engels – was jedoch Gouldner mit gutem Recht bestreitet. Marx selbst wird der, von allen empirisch präzisen, daher falsifikationsbedrohten, nomologischen Aussagen befreite, „originäre" westliche Marxismus zugeschrieben. Dieser – man ist hier versucht zu sagen: „gute" – Marxismus trägt keine, weder ursächliche noch moralische Verantwortung für die sowjetische Entwicklung, für welche, nach der üblichen Strategie, *ex post* die besonderen historischen Umstände des kapitalistisch unterentwickelten Zarenreiches oder die Machtgelüste von Personen (,Stalinismus") verantwortlich gemacht werden. Da hier aus Platzgründen nicht möglich ist, auf diese zu kurz greifenden Argumente einzugehen, muß ich auf die vorletztes Jahr erschienene Arbeit von *Walicki (1995)* verweisen, die sich gründlich mit dieser Thematik auseinandersetzt.

Mit Verweis auf die späteren Engelsschen Schriften, wie die „Dialektik der Natur" *(Engels 1961)*, den „Anti-Dühring" *(Engels 1960)* und „Die Entwicklung des Sozialismus von der Utopie zur Wissenschaft" *(Engels 1966)* wird der sogenannte „deterministische" oder „wissenschaftliche" Marxismus auf den vermeintlich mechanistischen Denkstil von Engels zurückgeführt. Das ist nicht gerechtfertigt. Bei Marx ist die anti-utopische, wissenschaftliche Tendenz seiner Argumentation nirgendwo zu verkennen, von ganz frühen und zumeist unveröffentlichten Schriften abgesehen. Man vergleiche z. B. seine scharfen Angriffe auf alle Spielarten des utopischen Sozialismus im „Kommunistischen Manifest" *(Marx / Engels 1966)*.

Der Grund für die „Belastung" von Engels mit dieser Anklage liegt darin, daß er als Nachlaßverwalter – im juristischen wie im theoretischen Sinne – des Marxschen Erbes in dem Maße zu theoretisch komplexen Fragen und Aporien Stellung nehmen und kohärente Antworten geben mußte, wie die Marxsche Theorie an Bekanntheit gewann. Dazu mußte Engels in dem enormen Feld der Gesamtgeschichte und Gesellschaft, in welchem sich Marx bewegt hatte, und zu darin enthaltenen Themen, die Marx nur angerissen oder bestenfalls skizzenhaft behandelt hatte, systematische und mit anderen Marxschen Aussagen konsistente Darstellungen und Antworten entwerfen. Mit anderen Worten: Engels hatte gegenüber einer an Marx interessierten intellektuellen Öffentlichkeit, an welcher sich zunehmend auch Exponenten der akademischen Sozialwissenschaft beteiligten, für Lücken und Schwächen der Marxschen Argumentation geradezustehen. Von zentraler

Bedeutung ist hierbei, daß das Interesse dieser Öffentlichkeit nicht rein theoretisch war, denn der Aufstieg der – zu dieser Zeit noch ganz marxistischen und klassenkämpferischen – SPD hatte weite Kreise der Öffentlichkeit in bezug auf die Ziele, das Programm und die Gesellschaftstheorie dieser umstürzlerischen Partei sensibilisiert.

Die größere oder geringere Überzeugungskraft der Engelsschen Antworten auf die Fragen der interessierten Öffentlichkeit in Bezug auf die Marxsche Theorie hatte somit nicht nur akademische sondern auch unmittelbar politische Folgen, da die Gültigkeit einer Gesellschaftstheorie in Frage stand, auf deren Basis eine revolutionäre Massenarbeiterpartei für den Umsturz des Gesellschaftssystems agitierte. Lückenlos nachzuweisen, daß der Zusammenbruch des Kapitalismus von der Marxschen Theorie wissenschaftlich einwandfrei bewiesen und daher unvermeidlich sei, wäre das stärkste Argument, das die politischen Energien der Anhänger aktivieren und diejenigen der Opponenten lahmlegen würde.

Aus eben denselben Gründen basierte auch die theoretische Argumentation des Gothaer und noch mehr des Erfurter Programms der SPD ganz eindeutig auf den ökonomischen Annahmen der materialistischen Geschichtsauffassung und des „Kapitals" *(Marx 1966)* und machte weitreichenden argumentativen Gebrauch von Marx' Aussagen über die unerbittlichen Bewegungsgesetze des Kapitalismus. Denn es ging um die theoretische Legitimation des Revolutionsprogramms und darum, ob der in ihm als notwendig vorgezeichnete Gang der Geschichte zu vermeiden war oder nicht. Das sind die wirklichen Gründe, warum die Marxsche Kapitalismuskritik mit der Gültigkeit des in seiner Theorie enthaltenen nomologischen Aussagenfundaments steht und fällt.

Denn jede Kritik, wenn sie belangvoll ist und mächtige Interessen oder tiefverwurzelte Überzeugungen angreift, setzt sich dem Angriff der Gegenkritik aus. Kann sie ihre Gültigkeit mit Rekurs auf objektive und bindende Prinzipien nicht begründen, so gilt sie soviel – oder sowenig – wie ihre Gegenkritik. In Hegelscher Ausdrucksweise: Ein besonderer Standpunkt steht gegen einen anderen besonderen Standpunkt und keiner ist mehr berechtigt als der andere. Die Quintessenz des Marxschen Denkens ist aber, daß der Standpunkt des Proletariats kein besonderer, sondern der *allgemeine* und der *historisch absolute* ist. Um diese zentrale Annahme zu begründen, braucht Marx das nomologische Fundament der materialistischen Geschichtsauffassung.

Marx teilte den Drang der radikalen europäischen Linken zur revolutionären Aktion, aber er verfügte zugleich über die intellektuellen Ressourcen, die blindes, aus der bloßen

Empörung erwachsendes Handeln als naiv erscheinen ließen. Seine Energie floß in die Formulierung derjenigen Theorie, die – im Unterschied zu der politisch impotenten „kritischen Kritik" der junghegelianischen Philosophen und Literaten – die tatsächlich wirkenden geschichtlichen und gesellschaftlichen Kräfte aufzudecken versuchte. Die in der „Deutschen Ideologie" *(Marx / Engels 1962)* schon ziemlich früh dargestellte materialistische Geschichtsauffassung reduzierte die gesellschaftliche Wirklichkeit auf die realen Wirkungsparameter, deren historische Änderungen die geschichtlichen Epochen einleiten. Erst auf dieser noch skizzenhaften theoretischen Basis wurde revolutionäres Handeln möglich, das nicht als blinder Aktionismus erfolgen, sondern aus der *rational begriffenen* Notwendigkeit der geschichtlichen Umwälzungen hervorgehen würde. So basiert das Revolutionsprogramm des „Kommunistischen Manifests", knappe zwei Jahre nach der „Deutschen Ideologie" verfaßt, bis in seine Formulierungen hinein ganz auf den Erkenntnissen der materialistischen Geschichtsauffassung.

Daraus folgt, daß Marx *wegen* – und nicht *trotz* – des Primats des Praktischen, das heißt, wegen des Primats der radikalen politischen Praxis, der er sich verschrieb, die deterministische Theorie, nämlich seine materialistische Geschichtsauffassung und die spätere Spezifizierung ihrer universalhistorischen Annahmen für die kapitalistische Produktionsweise im „Kapital" brauchte, um, angesichts der Komplexität gesellschaftlicher Prozesse und der objektiven Unsicherheit, ihren Ausgang vorauszusagen, und nicht nur blind einen globalen Angriff auf das gesamte System zu starten und damit ein totales Scheitern zu riskieren.

Wenn unter objektiver Unbestimmtheit des künftigen Ausgangs von Ereignissen, die von eigenen, fremden und auch von gegnerischen Handlungen beeinflußt werden, von den Akteuren ein hoher Einsatz zu riskieren ist, dann können Menschen zu einem solchen Handeln nur mobilisiert werden, wenn ihnen eine die Unbestimmtheit reduzierende, unbezweifelbare Einsicht geboten wird, daß das risikoreiche Handeln – zumindest langfristig – zum Erfolg führen wird. Eine solche Garantie kann nur eine deterministische bzw. quasi-deterministische Theorie geben, deren Annahmen nomologischen Charakter haben. Marx formulierte in der Tat eine solche Theorie, aber sie scheiterte total an der Wirklichkeit.

Die Frage, die zum eigentlichen Thema unserer Arbeit zurückführt, lautet: Wie läßt sich die Hinwendung der westlichen Sozialwissenschaften zum Marxismus erklären, der trotz der totalen Falsifikation seiner nomologischen Annahmen zum leitenden theoretischen Paradigma in Soziologie, Politikwissenschaft und Pädagogik aufstieg?

Die institutionelle Etablierung der Soziologie und der Sozialwissenschaften als neue wissenschaftliche Disziplinen fällt, international betrachtet, in die Nachkriegszeit. Da die neuen Lehrstühle in der Regel an philosophischen Fakultäten eingerichtet wurden, dominierte unter den vorherrschenden Orientierungen die textexegetische, sprachzentrierte, mathematik- und empirieferne geisteswissenschaftliche Tradition und verhinderte lange Zeit den Einzug und den effektiven Einsatz des Instrumentariums der empirischen Methoden in den neuen Disziplinen. Der historisierende Zugang zum Gegenstand und die sozialgeschichtliche Ausrichtung der Forschung blieben dominant. Ein Ausnahme davon bildeten die an wirtschaftswissenschaftlichen Fakultäten (später Fachbereichen) eingerichteten soziologischen Lehrstühle.

Ebenso unterschiedlich war auch die Rekrutierung des Hochschulpersonals je nach Vorherrschen der geistes- oder wirtschaftswissenschaftlichen Orientierung. In der ersten überwog der Typus des philosophisch und historisch gebildeten Intellektuellen aus dem Bereich der Kulturwissenschaften, der in der Regel der mathematischen Denkweise fern stand. In der zweiten schrieb der wirtschaftswissenschaftliche Hintergrund eine viel enger definierte Kompetenz in empirischen, statistischen und ökonometrischen Methoden vor.

Am folgenreichsten für die weitere Entwicklung der neuen Disziplinen erwies sich die Heterogenität der methodisch-erkenntnistheoretischen Positionen. Bei gemeinsamer methodologischer Basis können, sobald die Datenlage es erlaubt, Entscheidungen über die Richtigkeit oder Falschheit von inhaltlichen Hypothesen gefällt werden, die von allen Forschern akzeptiert werden. Hingegen stellt Dissens über methodologische und erkenntnistheoretische Fragen ein ganz andersartiges und im Grunde kaum zu lösendes Problem dar, weil es in diesem Fall keine gemeinsame Basis mehr gibt, auf welcher die Forscher über diese Fragen miteinander kommunizieren können. Besteht ein erkenntnistheoretischer Konsens nicht einmal darüber, ob kausale Erklärungen – seien es deterministische oder statistische – in den Sozialwissenschaften möglich sind, dann gibt es in der Tat keine (Meta-)Ebene mehr, auf der man sich über das eigene Tun als Forscher, das in Wirklichkeit kein *gemeinsames* Tun ist, verständigen kann.

Wie das lange Nachwirken des Positivismusstreits in der deutschen Soziologie zeigt, wurden zwei miteinander im Grunde inkompatible methodologisch-erkenntnistheoretische Positionen in der soziologischen Forschung und Lehre als gleichberechtigt etabliert. An dieser desolaten Situation der institutionell erzwungenen „friedlichen Koexistenz" hat sich eigentlich bis zur Gegenwart nichts geändert, selbst wenn inzwischen die

Fronten äußerlich aufgeweicht und beide Orientierungen durchaus an denselben Fachbereichen vertreten sind.

Zwar ist die Ablehnung der empirisch-mathematischen Methodologie seitens der Frankfurter Schule in der Praxis nicht allgemein durchgehalten worden; aber die Kritik ihrer jüngeren Vertreter am Logischen Empirismus und am Kritischen Rationalismus Poppers auf *philosophisch-erkenntnistheoretischer* Ebene hat auch auf *methodologischer* Ebene weite Spielräume eröffnet, von den Regeln der empirisch-mathematischen Methodologie, bedingt durch die, wie es heißt, nur qualitativ und „verstehend" zu erschließenden „Sinnhorizonte" der Subjekte, abzuweichen oder diese Regeln unter Umständen sogar ganz zu suspendieren.

Teilweise bedingt dadurch, daß von den Nationalsozialisten vertriebene Wissenschaftler in den ersten Nachkriegsjahren auf sozialwissenschaftliche Lehrstühle wiederberufen wurden, ergab sich, daß viele unter diesen Intellektuellen dem Marxismus nahestanden. Ihre gesellschaftstheoretischen Orientierungen waren in den krisenerschütterten Jahrzehnten zwischen den beiden Weltkriegen entscheidend geprägt worden und sie neigten zum Teil dazu, ihre Deutungen der vergangenen gesellschaftlichen Realität auf die gewandelte westliche Gesellschaft der Nachkriegszeit zu übertragen. Während in der Gesellschaft der Appell des Kommunismus und die Stärke der kommunistischen Parteien überall zurückgingen, trug dieser Umstand dazu bei, daß im von der übrigen Gesellschaft relativ abgehobenen Hochschulbereich die Voraussetzungen für ein intellektuelles Klima geschaffen wurden, das marxistische Ideen und Gesellschaftskritik begünstigte.

Im politischen Klima der ersten Nachkriegsjahrzehnte, das Kommunismus und Marxismus nicht begünstigte, blieben die Appelle der akademischen Marxisten zunächst ohne Echo. Kritik an der Marktwirtschaft und an der liberalen Gesellschaftsordnung erwuchs jedoch, für die universitären Marxisten ganz unverhofft, aus dem ideologischen Kontext der zumeist durch sozialdemokratische Parteien initiierten, großangelegten Gesellschaftsreformen der sechziger Jahre, die eine öffentliche Kritik an der Markwirtschaft begünstigten, um mehr Staatseingriffe und staatliche Planung gesellschaftlicher Bereiche zu legitimieren.

Mit der raschen Bildungsexpansion der sechziger Jahre ballte sich in den Universitäten ein neues Massenpublikum von jungen, sozial unerfahrenen, die Schule und ihre Herkunftsfamilie gerade verlassenden, politisch noch nicht sozialisierten und noch stark von den Spannungen des postadoleszenten Statusübergangs betroffenen Studenten zusammen. In dieser als „institutionelle Verlängerung der Pubertät" bezeichneten Lebenssituation und bedingt zugleich durch die relative Isolation der universitären Umwelt von der übrigen Gesellschaft und der Arbeitswelt, war das neue Studentenpublikum geradezu prädestiniert, die Botschaften der radikalen Gesellschaftskritik aufzunehmen und zu versuchen, sie in die Tat umzusetzen.

Zugleich rückte der Massencharakter der Universität die Ereignisse auf dem Campus viel stärker in den Mittelpunkt der öffentlichen Aufmerksamkeit als es in der kleinen Eliteuniversität der Vergangenheit der Fall gewesen war *(Trow 1974)*. Um so mehr eröffneten die Medien dann, als die massenhaften Studentenproteste ausbrachen, den akademischen Mentoren, die die Ziele, „um die es den Studenten ging", öffentlich artikulierten, ein weites Forum, vor welchem diese sich als unerbittliche Ankläger der kapitalistischen Gesellschaft profilieren konnten. Dadurch wurde es möglich, daß ausgerechnet in einer Zeit der politischen und sozialen Konsolidierung der westlichen Demokratien in einem empfindlichen und exponierten gesellschaftlichen Funktionsbereich, dem Hochschulsystem, ein *totaler*, ohne jede Reformabsicht formulierter, vielmehr auf den Umsturz des gesellschaftlichen Systems abzielender Angriff – ganz abgesehen von seiner politischen Irrealität – begann und in diesem von der übrigen Gesellschaft isolierten Bereich sich eine Massenbasis schuf.

Über den temporären studentischen Radikalismus hinaus gibt es jedoch nachhaltige und permanente Effekte der Hochschulexpansion. Mit der Verbreitung von Massenhochschulbildung ist innerhalb und – mit entsprechender Zeitverschiebung – auch außerhalb der Universität ein neues massenhaftes Publikum der intellektuellen Presse und derjenigen Medien entstanden, die sich auf politische und gesellschaftliche Thematiken spezialisieren. Damit hat sich insbesondere die Klientel des politischen Fachjournalismus vervielfacht, dessen Kompetenz auf den genannten Themengebieten liegt. Die neuen Medienbenutzer, aus welchen sich dieses Publikum zusammensetzt, sind wegen des Charakters ihrer allgemeinen Hochschulbildung, die weder eine technische noch eine spezialisierte Kompetenz im engeren Sinne beinhaltet, und zugleich wegen ihres hauptsächlich konsumptiven Verhaltens gegenüber den Kulturprodukten am ehesten als „intellektuelle Laien" zu bezeichnen.

Die Konkurrenz der Medien am Markt der kritischen Information bedingt, daß die einzelnen Medienunternehmen permanent auf der Suche nach tragfähigen kritischen Konzepten sein müssen, um den Konkurrenten voraus zu sein. Die Arbeiten derjenigen Exponenten der universitären Intelligenz, die in und außerhalb der Universität sich in der Rolle des kritisch-engagierten Intellektuellen einen Namen gemacht haben oder machen, dienen dem politischen Journalismus, dessen eigene professionelle Herkunft die Universität ist, als Quelle tragfähiger kritischer Themen bei seiner kontinuierlichen Suche nach sozialen Problemen, unterprivilegierten Gruppen und Mißbrauch politischer Macht. Erleichtert wird dieser Austausch akademischer gegen massenmediale Ressourcen – anders gesagt: wissenschaftlich fundierter Kritikkonzepte gegen massenmediale Wirkung in der Öffentlichkeit – dadurch, daß die Redakteure der Fachressorts der politischen Nachrichtenmagazine, die in ihrer aktuellen Funktion kritische Ideen von der universitären Intelligenz erwarten, um ihnen Gehör in der Öffentlichkeit zu verschaffen, zuvor in den meisten Fällen die engagierten Studenten eben derselben Hochschullehrer gewesen sind.

Aus den obigen Ausführungen ergibt sich, daß unter den genannten Bedingungen eines expandierten, aus intellektuellen Laien bestehenden Massenpublikums und einer starken Medienkonkurrenz diejenigen Erzeugnisse der Sozialwissenschaft Verbreitung finden, die sich mit kritischen Themen befassen, die aus der Sicht der Öffentlichkeit als „Probleme" definiert sind. Damit steigt zwangsläufig die Bekanntheit und das Prestige eben derjenigen universitären Exponenten der Sozialwissenschaft, die sich auf die *Rolle der kritischen Intellektuellen* spezialisieren.

In den theoretisch wenig entwickelten Sozialwissenschaften ist die Fachöffentlichkeit weniger scharf von der allgemeinen Öffentlichkeit abgegrenzt als dies bei den theoretisch avancierten Wissenschaften der Fall ist, in welchen das Tempo der neuen Wissensproduktion, die Fachterminologie und die mathematische Formulierung ihrer Theorien für Laien unüberwindbare Zugangsbarrieren darstellen. Je weniger scharf die Fachöffentlichkeit einer Disziplin von der allgemeinen Öffentlichkeit abgegrenzt ist, desto eher wird die in der allgemeinen Öffentlichkeit durch die Rolle des „kritischen Intellektuellen" erlangte allgemeine Bekanntheit in *fachliches Prestige* in der fachinternen Öffentlichkeit umgemünzt.

Unter den hier umrissenen Bedingungen *ist es seit den sechziger Jahren in der Soziologie und ihren Nachbarwissenschaften zu einer Überproduktion von Gesellschaftskritik und zu einer damit untrennbar zusammenhängenden Hypertrophie der „kritischen Intelligenz" an den Universitäten gekommen.* Die kritischen Intellektuellen, denen in säkularen Gesellschaften die Funktion der Realitätsdeutung zugefallen ist, welche in theokratischen Gesellschaften Priestern und Theologen zukam, entwerfen unter Verwendung der ihnen jeweils verfügbaren kognitiven Ressourcen handlungsrelevante Deutungen der gesellschaftlichen Realität, die über das spezialisierte Wissen der Einzelwissenschaften hinausgehen. Da ihre Tätigkeit – zwar nicht ausschließlich aber auch – *kognitiver* Art ist, ist die institutionelle Basis der kritischen Intelligenz, trotz der Unterschiede und des Spannungsverhältnisses zwischen ihren Realitätsdeutungen und den spezialisierten Erkenntnissen der Einzelwissenschaften, die Universität. Die Universität hat somit mehrere, über den Fortschritt der Erkenntnis und die Ausbildung von Forschern hinausgehende Funktionen, die in einen theoretisch konsistenten Rahmen eingeordnet werden müssen.

In Talcott Parsons' und Gerald Platts Arbeit „Die amerikanische Universität" *(Parsons / Platt 1990)* wird der Aufbau eines solchen theoretischen Bezugssystems unternommen, in welchem die moderne Universität vier zentrale Funktionen erfüllt:

1. die Produktion neuer Erkenntnis in ihrem kognitiven Kernsubsystem der Forschung;
2. die Sozialisations- und Allgemeinbildungsfunktion im College;
3. die Ausbildung für die Professionen und
4. die Produktion von Realitätsdeutungen, zu welcher Kritik wie Legitimation von Herrschaftsansprüchen gehören.

Alternative Legitimationen und Realitätsdeutungen, die von konkurrierenden Eliten formuliert werden, gehen aus unterschiedlichen gesellschaftlichen Interessen hervor, die es in jedem differenzierten Gesellschaftssystem mit zumindest minimalem Pluralismus gibt. In der säkularen modernen Gesellschaft hat der Ort der Austragung der Konflikte über Realitätsdeutungen und Herrschaftslegitimationen von der Theologie auf die Wissenschaft übergewechselt. Damit fielen die Funktionen der Realitätsdeutung und Legitimation nun der Wissenschaft zu. Rivalisierende Eliten sowie den Elitenstatus anstrebende Gruppen suchen somit Zugang zum institutionellen Zentrum der modernen Wissenschaft, zur Universität, um jeweils ihre eigene, mit anderen konkurrierende Legitimation und Deutung der Wirklichkeit als diejenige darzustellen, die allein auf die rationalen Argumente der Wissenschaft begründet sei. Konflikte über Realitätsdeutungen können der Ausdruck von konfligierenden Überzeugungen über die „letzten Dinge", aber auch von konkurrierenden Interessen und Machtpositionen sein. Für ihre intellektuellen Urheber, deren Basis die Universität ist, haben jedoch diese Deutungen objektiv Vorrang vor allen anderen Rücksichten und damit auch vor kognitiver Rationalität.

Kognitive Rationalität – wir dürfen diesen Parsonsschen Terminus mit dem gesamten Komplex des wissenschaftslogischen Instrumentariums für die Überprüfung von Theorien und die Produktion neuer Erkenntnis wohl gleichsetzen – hat nach Parsons und Platt absolute Priorität nur im Kernbereich der Universität, im Subsystem der Forschung. In den anderen Subsystemen haben die jeweiligen Funktionsimperative relativen Vorrang vor kognitiver Rationalität. In ihnen haben, mit anderen Worten, die *Anwendungen* des Wissens zur Erreichung der jeweiligen Ziele der Subsystene relative Priorität. Damit ist die Möglichkeit von Konflikten theoretisch eingeräumt. So gehen in die Konstruktion von Realitätsdeutungen zwar die verfügbaren kognitiven Ressourcen ein, aber die intellektuellen Urheber dieser Deutungen haben eine von derjenigen des Forschers unterschiedliche Funktion, die bedingt, daß sie nicht *dasselbe Interesse* an der Produktion neuen Wissens haben. Auf der anderen Seite kann dieser Unterschied unter normalen Bedingungen nicht so weit gehen, daß die von Intellektuellen produzierten Realitätsdeutungen auf längst falsifizierten Theorien basieren – um ein berühmtes Beispiel aufzugreifen – etwa auf der Ptolemäischen Theorie.

Die westlichen Linksintellektuellen verdanken ihren massiven Aufstieg insbesondere seit den sechziger Jahren in Elitepositionen im Hochschulsystem der Nachfrage nach Gesellschaftskritik, die von dem neuen Massenpublikum der intellektuellen Laien ausging, die selbst das Produkt der Massenhochschulbildung sind. Begünstigt wurde ihr Aufstieg zugleich auch von dem marktkritischen Klima der Staatsexpansions- und Reformphase, wie bereits oben ausgeführt. Die Vermassung der Universität zerstörte das Gleichgewicht zwischen den Funktionen der Universität und gab der Funktion der „kritischen Intellektuellen" in den Sozialwissenschaften ein enormes Übergewicht über die Funktion der Forscher. Begünstigt wurde diese Entwicklung vom Stand der mangelnden theoretischen Konsolidierung der Sozialwissenschaften, der sich als ein Faktor von erheblicher Wirkung in diese Richtung erwies.

Der Schaden für die Sozialwissenschaften ist groß. Es wird lange dauern bis ein kumulatives Wachstum der Erkenntnis in diesen Wissenschaften möglich sein wird. Und es wird nicht möglich sein, solange sie sich nicht entscheiden können, dem Beispiel der Psychologie zu folgen, das heißt, die gegenwärtig vertretenen inkompatiblen methodologischen Positionen, zwischen welchen in Wirklichkeit *keine Kommunikation stattfindet*, auch institutionell zu trennen. Im Klartext: Die Anerkennung und praktische Anwendung der experimentellen bzw. empirisch-mathematischen Methodologie sollte als Beitrittsbedingung zu den Fachvereinigungen für jedes künftige Mitglied obligatorisch sein.

Bibliographie

Engels, Friedrich: Herrn Eugen Dührings Umwälzung der Wissenschaft. 13. Aufl. Berlin: Dietz 1960.
Engels, Friedrich: Dialektik der Natur. 5. Aufl. Berlin: Dietz 1961. (Bücherei des Marxismus-Leninismus. 18)
Engels, Friedrich: Die Entwicklung des Sozialismus von der Utopie zur Wissenschaft. In: Marx, Karl / ders.: Ausgewählte Schriften in zwei Bänden. Bd. 2. 16. Aufl., Berlin: Dietz 1966, S. 80-140.
Gouldner, Alvin: The Two Marxisms. New York: Seabury Press 1980.
Lakatos, Imre: The Methodology of Scientific Research Programmes. Vol. 1. 3. ed. Cambridge: Cambridge University Press 1984.
Marx, Karl: Das Kapital. Bd. 1-3. Berlin: Dietz 1966. (MEW. 23-25)
Marx, Karl / Engels, Friedrich: Die deutsche Ideologie. Berlin: Dietz 1962. (MEW. 3)
Marx, Karl / Engels, Friedrich: Manifest der Kommunistischen Partei. In: dies: Ausgewählte Schriften in zwei Bänden. Bd. 1. 16. Aufl., Berlin: Dietz 1966, S. 17-57.
Mitter, Wolfgang / Novikov, Leonid: Sekundarabschlüsse mit Hochschulreife im internationalen Vergleich. Weinheim u. a.: Beltz 1976. (Studien und Dokumentationen zur vergleichenden Bildungsforschung. 1, 5)
Narr, Wolf-Dieter / Offe, Claus: Einleitung. In: dies. (Hrsg.): Wohlfahrtstaat und Massenloyalität, Köln: Kiepenheuer und Witsch 1975, S. 9-46.
Parsons, Talcott / Platt, Gerald: Die amerikanische Universität. Ein Beitrag zur Soziologie der Erkenntnis. Frankfurt a. M.: Suhrkamp 1990.
Trow, Martin: Problems in the Transition from Elite to Mass Higher Education. Paris: OECD 1974.
Walicki, Andrzej: Marxism and the Leap to the Kingdom of Freedom. The Rise and Fall of the Communist Utopia. Stanford, Calif.: Stanford University Press 1995.

Ein Blick in die Geschichte ausländischer Schüler und Schülerinnen in deutschen Schulen

Marianne Krüger-Potratz

„... Kein Staat kann ein Interesse daran haben, Ausländer zu verpflichten, ihr Wissen im Inlande zu vervollkommnen ..."[1]

Zur Einführung

Die Frage nach den Bedingungen, unter denen im Deutschen Reich nicht-staatsangehörige Kinder im schulpflichtigen Alter, auch Kinder von Wanderarbeitern, die staatliche Pflichtschule in Deutschland besuchen konnten, ist bisher weder von der Schulgeschichtsforschung noch von der interessierten interkulturellen Bildungsforschung systematisch aufgegriffen worden.[2] Daß die staatliche Pflichtschule für die Bildung der 'eigenen Landeskinder' etabliert worden ist, ist aus der Geschichte der Schule hinreichend bekannt. Der mit dem Ausschluß der 'fremden' Kinder einhergehende Grundsatz, daß *„kein Staat ein Interesse daran haben [könne], Ausländer zu verpflichten, ihr Wissen im Inlande zu vervollkommnen" (ZBl. 1924, S. 323),* hat hingegen keine Beachtung gefunden. Ob und wie diese für das nationalstaatlich verfaßte Bildungswesen grundlegende

---

1 ZBl. 1924, S. 323. (Eine Liste der aufgelösten Abkürzungen findet sich am Ende des Textes.)
2 Wenige Hinweise finden sich z. B. zu russischen Schülern, meist Emigranten (vgl. *Basler 1983; Wiese 1988).* Beiträge zur Kinder-Wanderarbeit und Schule in Deutschland bei *Kasberger (1991)* und *Uhlig (1984)* sowie, bezogen auf Italiener vor dem Ersten Weltkrieg, eine Passage bei *DelFabbro (1996).* Eine systematische Dokumentation der schulrechtlichen Vorschriften für nicht-staatsangehörige Kinder und Kinder der „fremdsprachigen Volksteile" ist im Projekt: „Bildung und Erziehung ethnischer Minderheiten im Deutschen Reich: Die Minderheitenschulfrage in der Weimarer Republik" (DFG-Schwerpunktprogramm „Folgen der Arbeitsmigration für Bildung und Erziehung" – FABER) erarbeitet worden. Die in der Weimarer Republik in Preußen ergangenen Vorschriften werden in zwei kommentierten Quellensammlungen für den Druck vorbereitet (*Krüger-Potratz 1996),* eine weitere für die Zeit zwischen 1871 und 1918 ist geplant. Weitere Ergebnisse vgl. *Reich / Bender-Szymanski (1997, S. 75-88).* Die Entwicklung in der Bundesrepublik Deutschland (BRD) wird im Projekt „Schulbildung für Migrantenkinder und Kinder autochthoner Minderheiten in der BRD – eine Bestandsaufnahme" (I. Gogolin, U. Neumann, L.-R. Reuter, Universität Hamburg) erarbeitet.

Ein Blick in die Geschichte ausländischer Schüler und Schülerinnen in deutschen Schulen

Denkfigur bis heute weiterwirkt, ist nicht gefragt worden. Als in den sechziger Jahren unseres Jahrhunderts nach und nach in allen Bundesländern die nicht-staatsangehörigen Kinder in die Schulpflicht einbezogen wurden,[3] ist dies nicht als Bruch mit jenem Grundsatz wahrgenommen worden, sondern eher wie eine quasi-natürliche Entwicklung: als Anpassung an neue, durch die internationale Arbeitsmigration geschaffene Gegebenheiten einerseits und als – längst fällige – Umsetzung internationaler Resolutionen und Beschlüsse gegen die Diskriminierung im Unterrichtswesen und für die Durchsetzung des Menschenrechts auf Bildung andererseits.[4]

Auch als ab Ende der siebziger Jahre die für die Kinder der Arbeitsmigranten eingeführten bildungspolitischen Maßnahmen in die Kritik gerieten, wurde die Frage nach dem Verhältnis von Staatsangehörigkeit und Bildung nicht aufgenommen. Insofern überhaupt nach der Tradition der Beschulung 'fremder' Kinder gefragt wird, gilt das Interesse dem Umgang mit den Kindern der autochthonen sprachlichen und ethnischen Minderheiten. Daß diese Kinder ihrer Staatsangehörigkeit nach Inländer waren, wird zwar angemerkt, aber – im Unterschied zur Frage der sprachlichen und kulturellen 'Fremdheit' – scheint dies ohne Bedeutung.[5]

Hiermit wird ein erster Versuch unternommen, das angesprochene Forschungsdesiderat zu bearbeiten. Gegenstand sind die Gesetze und Erlasse, in denen die Bedingungen fixiert waren, unter denen nicht-staatsangehörige Kinder im schulpflichtigen Alter staatliche bzw. staatlich anerkannte Schulen in Deutschland besuchen konnten. Aufgenommen wird die Frage schwerpunktmäßig für die Zeit der Weimarer Republik und für Preußen. Für die politisch-geographische Eingrenzung spricht, daß in Preußen zwei Drittel der bei der Volkszählung von 1925 im Deutschen Reich gezählten Reichsauslän-

---

3 Voraussetzung ist ein „gesicherter Aufenthalt".
4 International: z. B. „Allgemeine Erklärung der Menschenrechte der Vereinten Nationen" vom 10. Dezember 1946 (Art. 26); „Übereinkommen der Vereinten Nationen gegen die Diskriminierung im Unterrichtswesen" vom 15. Dezember 1960 (Art. 3); „Erklärung der Rechte des Kindes" vom 20. November 1959 (Grundsatz 7); „Richtlinie über die schulische Betreuung der Wanderarbeiter" (77/486/EWG vom 25. Juli 1997). National: „Gesetz zu dem Übereinkommen vom 15. Dezember gegen Diskriminierung im Unterrichtswesen" *(BGBl. 1968, S. 385-401, insbes. Art. 3e)*; Empfehlungen und Beschlüsse der KMK seit Anfang der fünfziger Jahre, denen die Länder der BRD (unterschiedlich) in den sechziger Jahren folgten.
5 Vgl. die Arbeiten von *Hansen (1979, 1983)*, angegeben in *Hansen (1986)* und das in Anm. 2 genannte Projekt. Erst im Verlauf der Forschung wurde deutlich, daß bei der Beschulung ausländischer Schüler zwei Traditionen zu beachten sind: die Beschulung der reichsausländischen Kinder einerseits und die reichsinländischen Kinder der „fremdsprachigen Volksteile" (*Art. 113 RV*) andererseits.

der lebten. Die zeitliche Eingrenzung auf die Periode der Weimarer Republik bietet sich an, weil mit der Reichsverfassung (RV) von 1919 die Schulbesuchspflicht in der Verfassung verankert worden ist; ihre Umsetzung in Landesrecht erfolgte in Preußen 1927. Mit der neuen politischen Lage nach dem Ersten Weltkrieg und der für alle reichsinländischen Kinder in Preußen vorgeschriebenen achtjährigen Schulbesuchspflicht in einer deutschen Schule stand auch die Frage der Ausländerbeschulung erneut zur Regelung an.

In einem ersten Teil der Darstellung werden sehr knapp Informationen über die in Preußen nach dem Ersten Weltkrieg lebenden Reichsausländer, über die äußerst komplexe Problematik der Staats- und Reichsangehörigkeit und über die mit der Einführung der Schulbesuchspflicht verbundenen Folgen gegeben. Auf diesem Hintergrund werden im zweiten Teil die Erlaßlage für die verschiedenen Gruppen reichsausländischer Schüler und Schülerinnen vorgestellt und die sie bestimmenden Problemdefinitionen diskutiert. Zum Abschluß wird die Frage nach den Traditionslinien, die die Situation der ausländischen (und ausgesiedelten) Kinder bis heute bestimmen, kurz wieder aufgenommen.

Teil I

Reichsausländer in Preußen nach dem Ersten Weltkrieg

Bei der Volkszählung vom 16. Juni 1925, der zeitgenössisch umfangreichsten, aber keineswegs vollständigen Datensammlung über Reichsausländer im Deutschen Reich, wurden 957 096 Personen ohne deutsche Staatsangehörigkeit gezählt: 921 000 Personen mit einer bestimmten fremden Staatsangehörigkeit, 25 227 Staatenlose und 9 969 Personen, deren Staatsangehörigkeit nicht festgestellt werden konnte. 94,7 Prozent der Reichsausländer stammten aus europäischen, vier Fünftel aus den an das Reich angrenzenden Staaten. Polen, Russen und Tschechen bildeten die drei größten Gruppen im Reich wie in Preußen. Doch auch die in Preußen – z. B. in der Rheinprovinz, in Westfalen und in Berlin – lebenden Niederländer und Österreicher bildeten zahlenmäßig nicht unbedeutende Gruppen *(Volks-, Berufs- und Betriebszählung 1930, S. 623f., 632)*.

Nach dem verlorenen Krieg war die Politik angesichts der schwierigen politischen und wirtschaftlichen Situation und den im Versailler Vertrag fixierten Friedensbedingungen auf eine Verringerung des Ausländeranteils und vor allem der Ausländerbeschäftigung gerichtet. Doch in der Landwirtschaft blieb die Zahl der Wanderarbeiter weiterhin bedeutend. Zum einen gab es eine nicht kleine Zahl von illegal Beschäftigten und zum anderen eine ihrer Größe nach ebenfalls beachtenswerte Gruppe von – auch polnischen – Wanderarbeitern, die aufgrund der Dauer ihres Aufenthalts das Recht auf eine unbefristete Aufenthalts- und Arbeitserlaubnis hatten *(Herbert 1986, S. 118; Woydt 1987, S. 52; Wenning 1996, S. 101-105)*. Daten, die Aufschluß über Anzahl und Nationalität der im Deutschen Reich bzw. in Preußen lebenden reichsausländischen Kinder im schulpflichtigen Alter geben könnten, sind jedoch weder im Rahmen der Volkszählung von 1925 noch zu anderen Gelegenheiten erhoben bzw. veröffentlicht worden. Aus verstreut aufzufindenden Angaben für einzelne Orte und/oder Gruppen läßt sich kein Gesamtbild ermitteln. Allerdings lassen sich, mit aller gebotenen Vorsicht, aus Einzelhinweisen und Volkszählungsergebnissen zwei wichtige Schlußfolgerungen ziehen: Es gab reichsausländische Schüler in allen Schulformen und die Zahl derjenigen, die keine Kenntnisse der deutschen Sprache hatten, scheint relativ klein gewesen zu sein. Nach den im Rahmen der Volkszählung von 1925 erhobenen Angaben zur Muttersprache der Reichsausländer haben sich 358 729 in Preußen lebende Reichsausländer als deutschsprachig, 71 562 als doppelsprachig und 171 438 als nur fremdsprachig eintragen lassen. Über die Hälfte der fremd- und doppelsprachigen Ausländer – so heißt es im Kommentar zur Volkszählung – seien polnische Staatsangehörige, die mehrheitlich als landwirtschaftliche Wanderarbeiter in den östlichen preußischen Provinzen arbeiteten; die zweitgrößte Gruppe rein fremdsprachiger Ausländer bildeten die Niederländer, gefolgt von den Russen *(Volks-, Berufs- und Betriebszählung 1930, S. 634, 637)*. Bei der – naheliegenden – Schlußfolgerung, daß ein Großteil der reichsausländischen Kinder mit ständigem Wohnsitz im Deutschen Reich ohne größere Probleme dem deutschsprachigen Unterricht folgen konnte, darf nicht übersehen werden, daß die Angabe über Deutschkenntnisse noch nichts über die Sprachkompetenz der Kinder aussagt.

Staats- und Reichsangehörigkeit nach 1918

Bis zur Schaffung einer primären *deutschen* Staatsangehörigkeit durch die Verordnung vom 5. Februar 1934 galt die im Reichs- und Staatsangehörigkeitsgesetz von 1913 getroffene Unterscheidung zwischen der primären Staatsangehörigkeit, die es nur im Rahmen des Einzelstaates gab, und der erst aus ihr sekundär abgeleiteten Reichsangehörigkeit. Diese 1919 durch Artikel 110 der RV bestätigte Teilung war darin begründet, daß auch nach 1919 das Reichsgebiet staatsrechtlich „aus den Gebieten der deutschen Länder" bestand, wie es im Vorspruch zur RV festgehalten war.

Die Frage der Staats- und Reichsangehörigkeit war nach dem Ersten Weltkrieg in vielfacher Weise schwierig *(Schätzel 1927)*. Die Experten klagten, daß die im Versailler Vertrag getroffenen Bestimmungen hinsichtlich der Staatsangehörigkeit für Personen aus den besetzten und aus den abgetretenen Gebieten nicht immer eindeutig und vor allem äußerst uneinheitlich seien. Selbst die mit einer Reihe von Ländern zu Staatsangehörigkeitsfragen abgeschlossenen Verträge seien nicht geeignet, alle strittigen Fragen zu lösen. So gab es z. B. Personen, die ihre (deutsche) Staats- und Reichsangehörigkeit sozusagen automatisch verloren hatten, weil sie vor einem bestimmten Stichtag an einem Ort in einem der nun abgetretenen Gebiete geboren waren, auch wenn sie selbst schon seit langem in einem anderen, nach 1919 weiterhin zum Reich gehörenden Gebiet lebten. Nur in einigen Fällen hatten die Betroffenen das Recht zur Option. Andere fanden sich als Staatenlose wieder *(ebd.)*. Die Konsequenzen dieser völker- und staatsrechtlichen Situation waren weitreichend: So z. B. wenn Ehepartner bzw. Eltern und Kinder 'plötzlich', ohne eigenes Zutun, Angehörige verschiedener Staaten waren, oder wenn die Ausübung der Berufstätigkeit an die Staatsangehörigkeit gebunden war, wie z. B. bei Lehrkräften, und somit die Entlassung drohte,[6] oder wenn Kinder – als dann reichsausländische – in ihren Bildungsmöglichkeiten eingeschränkt wurden.

Ein anderer, politisch wie juristisch interessanter Fragenkomplex steht in Zusammenhang mit den nach 1919 gegebenen Einbürgerungserleichterungen für einzelne, als deutschstämmig definierte Gruppen von Reichsausländern, die sich in Deutschland niedergelassen hatten, so z. B. für Österreicher oder für Danziger. Ihre Einbürgerung war an zwei Voraussetzungen geknüpft: an die Anerkennung als „deutschstämmig" und an die, auch durch den anderen Staat zu gebende Verbürgung der Gegenseitigkeit. Mit der letztgenannten Bedingung sollte verhindert werden, daß das Recht auf eine erleichterte Einbürgerung grundsätzlich allen deutschstämmigen Ausländern gewährt werden mußte, insofern *„die Verbürgung der Gegenseitigkeit anderwärts nicht zu erreichen sein und die völkische Zugehörigkeit und politische Zuverlässigkeit zu häufig besonderer Prüfung bedürfen wird"* (Schwalb 1931, Sp. 1110).

---

6 Belegt sind Entlassungen (einschließlich Verweigerung einer Abfindung) von im Deutschen Reich geborenen und ausgebildeten, aber mit einem Ausländer verheirateten Lehrerinnen, da die Ehefrau automatisch die Staatsbürgerschaft des Ehemanns erhielt und somit Reichsausländerin wurde *(Pastenaci/Ewers 1927, S. 525);* ferner Bestimmungen, die Ehefrauen die doppelte Staatsangehörigkeit erlaubte, z. B. mit Deutschen verheiratete Belgierinnen *(FMINBl. 1923, S. 458)*.

Von der Bildungspflicht zur Schulbesuchspflicht

Mit den Schulartikeln der RV war ein Programm für die Gestalt einer Schule in der Demokratie vorgegeben, das – trotz aller Kompromisse und nicht realisierten Vorgaben – einschneidende Veränderungen mit sich brachte: neben der staatlichen Schulaufsicht *(RV Art. 144)* und der Ausrichtung des Unterrichts auf *„sittliche Bildung, staatsbürgerliche Gesinnung, persönliche und berufliche Tüchtigkeit im Geiste des deutschen Volkstums und der Völkerversöhnung"* *(RV Art. 148),* insbesondere die Durchsetzung der Schulbesuchspflicht anstelle der Bildungspflicht *(RV Art. 145).* Das einzige reichsweit ergangene Schulgesetz war das 1920 verabschiedete Grundschulgesetz.[7] Alle weiteren gesetzlichen Bestimmungen in Ausführung der Schulartikel sind auf Landesebene verabschiedet worden, so auch das preußische Schulpflichtgesetz, das einschließlich der Ausführungsbestimmungen am 15. Dezember 1927 ergangen ist.

Schulbesuchspflicht in Preußen bedeutete, daß im Anschluß an die staatliche vierjährige Grundschule entweder die vier oberen Klassen der staatlichen Volksschule oder eine andere „als ausreichend anerkannte Unterrichtsform" zu besuchen waren. Im Unterschied zum Kaiserreich galt dies sowohl für alle staatsangehörigen – preußischen – Kinder wie auch reichsweit für *„diejenigen anderen reichsangehörigen Kinder, die sich dauernd in Preußen"* aufhielten, und somit auch für Schüler *„aus denjenigen deutschen Ländern, die an den früheren Vereinbarungen der preußischen Regierung mit mehreren deutschen Bundesstaaten über die gegenseitige Durchführung der Schulpflicht ... nicht beteiligt waren" (ZBl. 1928, S. 95).*[8] Zugleich verpflichtete sich Preußen anzuerkennen, daß preußische Schüler ihre Schulpflicht in jeder außerpreußischen deutschen Schule im Reich ableisten konnten, auch wenn die vorgesehene Schulpflichtzeit, wie z. B. in Bayern, kürzer oder, wie in der Provinz Schleswig-Holstein, länger war *(Vorbrodt / Herrmann 1930, S. 605).* Jede von diesen Grundsätzen abweichende Praxis, so auch die Zulassung anderer nicht-staatsangehöriger Kinder zum Besuch einer deutschen staatlichen Schule wie der Besuch einer Schule außerhalb der Grenzen des Deutschen Reichs[9] durch reichsinländische Schülerinnen und Schüler in der Schulpflichtzeit, bedurfte der Ausnahmeerlaubnis. Der entsprechende Passus in den Ausführungsbestimmungen zum

---

7   Zur Problematik der (nicht zustande gekommenen) Reichsschulgesetze vgl. *Führ (1972).*
8   Bis dahin galten spezielle Vereinbarungen zwischen den deutschen Ländern zur Anerkennung der Bildungspflicht bzw. der Bildungsabschlüsse.
9   Dies hieß auch – zumindest in der Regel – in einer der deutschen Auslandsschulen.

Schulpflichtgesetz endet mit dem Satz: „*Andere nicht reichsangehörige Kinder sind in Preußen nicht schulpflichtig*" *(ZBl. 1928, S. 95)*.

Teil II

Deutschstämmige Schüler und Schülerinnen in der Pflichtschule

Die Formulierung „andere nicht reichsangehörige Kinder" macht auf ein politisches Spezifikum aufmerksam. Sie bezieht sich auf die österreichischen Schüler, die als einzige reichsausländische Gruppe im preußischen Schulpflichtgesetz den reichsinländischen Kindern gleichgestellt worden war. Die Grundlage für diese – 1922 schon per Erlaß erfolgte – Gleichstellung war der 1925 abgeschlossene und 1926 durch Gesetz genehmigte Staatsvertrag zwischen Österreich und Preußen. In ihm verpflichteten sich beide Vertragspartner, „*hinsichtlich des Besuchs der Pflichtschulen jeglicher Art, der Bestrafung der Schulversäumnisse, der Schulunterhaltung und der Zahlung von Schulgeld die in Preußen sich aufhaltenden österreichischen Bundesbürger den preußischen Staatsangehörigen und die in Österreich sich aufhaltenden preußischen Staatsangehörigen den österreichischen Bundesbürgern*" gleichzustellen *(ZBl. 1926, S. 178)*. Österreich bekam, so könnte man sagen, den Status eines deutschen Landes außerhalb des Reiches. Die politische Vorgabe findet sich in Artikel 61, Abs.2 der RV von 1919, in dem – Österreichs Anschluß an das Deutsche Reich in naher Zukunft voraussetzend – den Vertretern Österreichs schon eine der Größe ihrer Bevölkerung entsprechende Anzahl von Sitzen und eine beratende Stimme im Reichsrat eingeräumt worden waren. Zwar mußte das Deutsche Reich mit Änderungsprotokoll vom 22. September 1919 diesen Absatz für ungültig erklären, weil er den in Art. 80 des Versailler Vertrags festgehaltenen Bestimmungen widersprach *(Kraus 1920, S. 304)*, aber die Tendenz, Österreich als eigentlich zum Deutschen Reich zugehörig zu betrachten, wird in vielen weiteren, auch bildungspolitisch relevanten Entscheidungen und Argumentationen der Zeit erkennbar.

Im gleichen Erlaß, mit dem im September 1922 „*Deutsch-Österreicher... den inländischen Schülern (Schülerinnen)*" hinsichtlich aller für den Schulbesuch zu entrichtenden Gebühren gleichgestellt worden waren, sind noch drei weitere, ebenfalls wie Reichsinländer zu behandelnde Gruppen aufgeführt: „*Deutsch-Balten, Reichsausländer deutscher Abstammung und Muttersprache, die in abgetretenen Gebieten oder in der Diaspora beheimatet sind [und] Schüler (Schülerinnen), deren Eltern die deutsche Staatsange-*

hörigkeit zwar nicht haben, aber bereits längere Zeit im Inlande ansässig sind[10] *und ihr Einkommen wesentlich aus dem Inlande beziehen" (ZBl. 1923, S. 78).* Ebenfalls als reichsinländisch – so ein weiterer Erlaß – seien die Kinder von ehemals deutschen Reichsangehörigen einzustufen, die durch die Nachkriegsregelungen zwar polnische Staatsangehörige geworden, aber zur Option zwischen Deutschland und Polen berechtigt seien *(PrVA 1921, S. 264).* Damit reichte die Gruppe der in Preußen schulbesuchspflichtigen deutschen Schüler und Schülerinnen wie auch das Gebiet, in dem als reichsinländisch definierte Kinder ihre Schulpflichtzeit absolvieren konnten, nicht nur über die Grenzen Preußens, sondern auch über die des Deutschen Reichs hinaus.[11] In bestimmten Fällen war auch der Besuch einer deutschen Schule im Ausland möglich, nicht aber der einer anderen ausländischen Schule *(Vorbrodt / Herrmann 1930, S. 606f.).* Für letzteres bedurfte es einer Ausnahmegenehmigung. Ignorierten Eltern diese Vorschrift, so machten sie sich der „strafbaren Nichterfüllung der Schulpflicht" schuldig. Daß sie auch tatsächlich vor Gericht zitiert und bestraft wurden, zeigen verschiedene, in der Deutschen Juristen-Zeitschrift veröffentlichte Gerichtsurteile *(DJZ 1927, Sp. 752; ZBl. 1927, S. 307f.).*

Andere reichsausländische Schüler in der preußischen Pflichtschule

Über den Ausschluß „anderer nicht reichsangehöriger" Kinder aus der Schulpflicht bestand Konsens quer durch alle Parteien, mit Ausnahme der KPD.[12] Begründet wurde dies mit der Plazierung der Schulartikel im zweiten Hauptteil der Reichsverfassung über die „Grundrechte und Grundpflichten der Deutschen", mit dem in Artikel 148 der RV verankerten Auftrag, die Schüler „im Geiste des deutschen Volkstums" zu erziehen, und mit dem Hinweis auf die finanziellen Folgen und (pädagogischen) Aufgaben, die die

---

10 Zur Interpretation von „längere Zeit" vgl. ZBl. 1923, S. 78: „*deren Eltern schon im Juli 1914 in Deutschland ansässig waren und noch ansässig sind*".
11 In diese „Anerkennungslinie" gehören weitere Erlasse, mit geringen Regelungsgegenständen, z. B. die Vereinbarung zwischen Preußen und Memel über die gegenseitige Anerkennung von Reifezeugnissen und Lehramtsprüfungen *(ZBl. 1921, S. 253)*, der Erlaß vom 6. Mai *(ZBl. 1927, S. 169)*, der darauf hinwies, daß zu den Reichsausländern deutscher Abstammung in den abgetretenen Gebieten, die beim Besuch einer höheren Lehranstalt nur das Inländerschulgeld zu entrichten haben, auch Kinder aus Danzig zu zählen seien. Zu Einbürgerungserleichterungen für „Deutschstämmige" vgl. *Gosewinkel (1995, S. 368f.).*
12 Vgl. den von der KPD 1929 im Preußischen Landtag eingebrachten Entschließungsantrag zur Änderung des Schulpflichtgesetzes, in dem u. a. gefordert wurde, daß „*die Schulpflicht in Preußen ... auch auf alle nicht staats- und nicht reichsangehörigen Kinder für die Dauer ihres Aufenthalts in Preußen Anwendung*" finden solle *(Preußischer Landtag, Drucksachen, Bd. 3, S. 1489).*

Einbeziehung reichausländischer Kinder in die Schulpflicht bedeuten würden – Folgen und Aufgaben, für die die verantwortlichen Behörden sich nicht zuständig fühlten, da *„kein Staat ein Interesse daran haben [könne], Ausländer zu verpflichten, ihr Wissen im Inland zu vervollkommnen" (ZBl. 1924, S. 323).*

Die Betonung liegt auf verpflichten, denn den Schulbesuch gewähren konnte der Staat und hat es in der Mehrzahl der Fälle auch getan. Nach einer Übergangsphase in den ersten Nachkriegsjahren sind fast alle anderen reichsausländischen Kinder auf der Grundlage von zwischenstaatlichen Abkommen mit Gegenseitigkeitsverbürgung den reichsinländischen hinsichtlich des Zugangs zur (Pflicht-)Schule gleichgestellt worden. Der entscheidende Unterschied, daß sie nicht schulpflichtig waren, war damit jedoch nicht aufgehoben. Mit welchen Staaten Preußen im Laufe der zwanziger Jahre entsprechende Verträge zu welchen Regelungsgegenständen abgeschlossen hatte, wurde in der Regel jeweils per Erlaß mitgeteilt (insbesondere *ZBl. 1924, S. 285; 1928, S. 271; PrVA 1930, S. 79).*[13]

Für die allgemeinbildende Schule sind zwei Erlaßgruppen zu unterscheiden: eine, die sich auf den Besuch der höheren Schulen bezieht und deren erste Vorschriften vom Anfang der zwanziger Jahre nach Aufhebung der zu Beginn des Ersten Weltkriegs erlassenen Sperrvorschrift stammen *(ZBl. 1921, S. 287),* und eine zur Pflicht(volks)schule, zu der die ersten Regelungen nach Inkrafttreten des preußischen Schulpflichtgesetzes ergangen sind. Gegenstand der ersten Erlaßgruppe ist das Schulgeld für den Besuch staatlicher sowie staatlich anerkannter höherer Lehranstalten. Während 1923 der „Ausländerschulgeldsatz" das Fünffache und 1924 das Doppelte der Summe betrug, die Eltern reichsinländischer Schüler und Schülerinnen aufbringen mußten *(ZBl. 1923, S. 77f.; 1924, S. 53),* durfte mit Wirkung vom 1. Oktober 1924 von *„Kindern solcher Ausländer, welche als Botschafter, Gesandte, Sekretäre, Berufskonsuln und als Mitglieder der Ententekommission von ihren Regierungen in Preußen beglaubigt sind ... nur noch das Inländerschulgeld"* erhoben werden, sofern *„von den Kindern der deutschen Diplomaten und Berufskonsuln in dem betreffenden Auslande kein erhöhtes Schulgeld gefordert wird" (ZBl. 1924, S. 285).* Nach Auskunft des Kultusministers erfüllten zu diesem Zeitpunkt 44 Staaten diese Bedingungen; weitere Staaten werden in Anschlußerlassen bekanntgegeben und mit Erlaß vom 25. Februar 1925 wurde die Beschränkung auf die Berufsgruppe

---

13 Weitere Erlasse in: *ZBl. 1925, S. 14, 54; 1926, S. 390,* in: *Schulrecht, Beilage zur Preußischen Lehrerzeitung 1925, S. 44* sowie im *ZBl. 1928, S. 271.*

der Diplomaten aufgehoben *(ZBl. 1925, S. 14, 44; 1926, S. 390;* vgl. auch *PrGS 1930, S. 203).*

In den Erlassen der zweiten Gruppe geht es um die Gleichstellung reichsausländischer Kinder in der Frage der (Volks-)Schulpflicht bzw. des Besuchs der unentgeltlichen Grund- und Volksschule. Auch hier war die erste Voraussetzung, daß zwischen Preußen und den Herkunftsstaaten Verträge mit Gegenseitigkeitsverbürgung bestanden. Der erste dieser Erlasse stammt vom Mai 1928; im August und November 1928 sowie im März 1929 folgten weitere. 29 Staaten werden genannt, für deren Kinder nun auch die Volksschulen, die dafür eine Genehmigung hatten, kein Fremdenschulgeld mehr erheben durften. Mit den meisten dieser Länder bestanden auch schon Abkommen über die Gleichstellung in der Frage des Schulgeldes für höhere Lehranstalten. In der Praxis bedeuteten die Erlasse von 1928 und 1929 für die preußische Seite, daß für Kinder aus diesen Staaten (a) von der Reichsangehörigkeit zur Anerkennung der Schulpflichtigkeit abzusehen und daß (b) *„hinsichtlich der Berechnung der Mehrstellen und des Beschulungsgeldes"* wie bei inländischen Kindern zu verfahren war *(ZBl. 1928, S. 271).*

Ein entscheidender Unterschied zwischen den reichsinländischen und den als reichsinländisch definierten Schülern und Schülerinnen einerseits und den ihnen gleichgestellten „anderen reichsausländischen" bestand darin, daß für letztere kein Schulbesuchszwang gegeben war. Sie konnten – ohne bei den preußischen Behörden eine Ausnahmeerlaubnis beantragen zu müssen – auch private Schulen (einschließlich privater Grundschulen) oder Schulen im Ausland besuchen. Denn – anders als im Staatsvertrag mit Österreich – war die Frage der Bestrafung bei Schulversäumnissen nicht Gegenstand dieser Abkommen. Zugleich bedeutete dies, daß die Schulen der Vertragspartnerstaaten weiterhin als ausländische Schulen galten, für deren Besuch die Eltern preußischer Kinder eine Ausnahmeerlaubnis beantragen mußten. Ein anderer Unterschied war, daß (andere) reichsausländische Kinder bei den jährlich einzureichenden Nachweisungen über die Zahl der Schulstellen und Schulkinder an den öffentlichen Volksschulen nicht mitzuzählen waren *(ZBl. 1927, S. 64).* Sie stellten somit in finanzieller Hinsicht eine Belastung für die Schulen dar. Für die preußischen Schulen ergab sich aus den Verträgen, daß sie nicht gezwungen waren darauf zu achten, daß „andere reichsausländische" Kinder in jedem Fall den Unterricht besuchten. Sie waren allerdings aufgefordert, Schüler aus den Vertragsstaaten aufzunehmen, damit diese nicht ohne Unterricht blieben. Bei der hierfür herangezogenen Begründung ging es zwar auch um die Erfüllung der Verträge, vor allem aber sollten diese Schüler nicht ohne Unterricht bleiben, *„weil die eine Schule nicht* *besuchenden Kinder ein schlechtes Beispiel für die einheimischen Kinder geben"* (PrVA 1929, S. 252).

Diese Regelungen bezogen sich ausschließlich auf die (Pflicht-)Schulen des Schulverbandes, innerhalb dessen die Erziehungs- oder Sorgeberechtigten der reichsausländischen Kinder ihren Wohnsitz hatten. Bevorzugten sie hingegen eine Schule in einem anderen Schulverband, so konnte von ihnen, wie von den reichsinländischen Kindern auch, Fremdenschulgeld verlangt werden. Außerdem konnte der fremde Schulverband die Aufnahme ablehnen, *„wenn er dadurch zur Beschaffung weiterer Sch[ul]Räume oder zur Vermehrung der Lehrkräfte genötigt"* wurde *(Vorbrodt / Herrmann 1930, S. 186; PrVA 1929, S. 82; 1933, S. 61-63).*

Die Verträge mit Verbürgung der Gegenseitigkeit sind weniger aus allgemein humanitären Überlegungen heraus abgeschlossen worden,[14] als vornehmlich aufgrund des Interesses der Staaten, die Bildung ihrer im Ausland lebenden staatsangehörigen Kinder zu sichern, auch dort wo die Einrichtung von Auslandsschulen nicht möglich war. Daß auch ordnungspolitische Überlegungen eine Rolle gespielt haben, läßt die oben zitierte Befürchtung erkennen, der zufolge Kinder, die die Schule nicht besuchten, ein schlechtes Beispiel für die dem Schulzwang unterworfenen abgeben könnten. Aus den zwischenstaatlichen Verträgen ließ sich über den gleichberechtigten Zugang zur (Pflicht-) Schule hinaus für „andere reichsausländische" Kinder und Jugendliche kein weiteres Anrecht auf Bildung in einer öffentlichen, staatlichen Schule ableiten. Weder die Herkunftsstaaten noch die Eltern konnten besondere Integrationsmaßnahmen erwarten oder gar einfordern. Von der Schule bereitzustellende zusätzliche Hilfen zum Erlernen der deutschen Sprache oder die Rücksichtnahme auf sprachliche Schwierigkeiten aufgrund (noch) nicht ausreichender Kenntnisse der deutschen Sprache waren mit dieser Rechtslage ebenso wenig zu begründen, wie Maßnahmen zum Erhalt der nicht-deutschen Muttersprache und der 'fremden Kultur'. Auf dem Weg der Einzelfallregelung sind allerdings gewisse Zugeständnisse gemacht worden. So war es z. B. türkischen Schülern an höheren Lehranstalten für die männliche Jugend bei Reife- oder Schlußprüfungen er-

---

14 Ein internationales Abkommen über das Recht jedes Kindes auf Bildung gab es noch nicht. Erst die vom Völkerbund 1925 verabschiedete „Erklärung der Kinderrechte" legte den Anspruch eines jeden Kinder auf „normale körperliche und geistige Entwicklung" fest, doch fehlten rechtsverbindliche Umsetzungen. Auf den internationalen (Kinderschutz-)Konferenzen von Washington (1919) und Genf (1921) wurde ein Arbeitsverbot für Kinder unter 14 Jahren proklamiert, was *Hessen (1928, S. 422)* als indirekte Aussage für den obligatorischen Schulbesuch bis zum 14. Lebensjahr wertet.

laubt, Türkisch anstelle des Englischen oder Französischen zu wählen *(ZBl. 1918, S. 744).*[15]

Schüler dänischer und polnischer Staatsangehörigkeit in den Minderheitsvolksschulen

Eine Ausnahme unter den anderen reichsausländischen Schülern und Schülerinnen stellten die in den Grenzgebieten lebenden Kinder dänischer[16] und polnischer Staatsangehörigkeit dar. Sie waren den reichsinländischen Kindern nicht nur über die von Preußen mit Dänemark und Polen abgeschlossenen Verträge mit Gegenseitigkeitsverbürgung in der Frage des Schulgeldes und des Zugangs zur Pflichtschule gleichgestellt, sondern darüber hinaus auch den preußischen Schülern der polnischen und dänischen Minderheit. Sie waren die einzigen anderen reichsausländischen Schüler und Schülerinnen, die – zumindest der Erlaßlage nach – den Zugang zu einer (Pflicht-)Schule in ihrer Muttersprache (bzw. in der „Sprache ihres Vaterlandes") als Unterrichtssprache hatten.[17]

Entsprechende Bestimmungen finden sich für die Kinder polnischer Staatsangehörigkeit in Art. 101 der Genfer Konvention über Oberschlesien vom Mai 1922[18] und in der Verordnung des Preußischen Staatsministeriums zur Regelung des Schulwesens für die polnische Minderheit vom Dezember 1928 *(ZBl. 1929, S. 39f.)*, für die reichsdänischen Kinder im Minderheitsschulerlaß für Südschleswig von 1926, 1928 abgelöst durch die – ebenfalls im Dezember 1928 ergangene – Ordnung für die dänische Minderheit.[19] Bemerkenswert ist, daß im Oberschlesienabkommen, wie auch in den Erlassen für die dä-

---

15 Die alle schulpflichtigen Kinder einbeziehenden Gegenseitigkeitsverbürgungen bezogen sich ausschließlich auf die achtjährige Pflichtschulzeit und auf den Besuch höherer Schulen, nicht aber auf den der Fortbildungsschule. Zu den daraus folgenden Problemen vgl. *Sachse (1931, S. 456f.)* und *Koehne (1924, Sp. 917)*.
16 Reichsdänische Schüler ist der offizielle Terminus.
17 Im Unterschied zu allen anderen reichsinländischen Kindern konnten sie dem Schulpflichtgesetz auch „*durch den ordnungsgemäßen Besuch einer privaten Minderheitsvolksschule*" genügen *(ZBl. 1929, S. 39; 41)*.
18 Genaue Angabe: Titel II, Kap. IV, Abschnitt I, Art. 101. Das Oberschlesienabkommen *(RGBl. 1922, Teil II, S. 237-304)* galt ausschließlich für den beim Deutschen Reich verbliebenen Teil des Abstimmungsgebietes. Im Oberschlesienabkommen waren nur die privaten Minderheitsschulen den reichsausländischen polnischen Kindern geöffnet; im Abschnitt II über die öffentlichen Volksschulen findet sich keine entsprechende Regelung.
19 PAAA, Nr. R 63320, Anlage 1 zum Schreiben des Ministers für Wissenschaft, Kunst und Volksbildung (Berlin) an den Preußischen Ministerpräsidenten und die Staatsminister vom 1. Februar 1926; der Erlaß von 1928 in *ZBl. 1929, S. 41*.

nische Minderheit ausschließlich die Staatsangehörigkeit als Voraussetzung für die Zulassung aufgeführt wird, während in der Ordnung für die polnische Minderheit von 1928 als zusätzliche Bedingung von den „nichtreichsdeutschen Kindern" der Nachweis „*ihre[r] Zugehörigkeit zum polnischen Volkstum nach Abstammung oder Sprache*" verlangt wird *(ZBl. 1930, S. 39)*.

Doch auch die mit den Oberschlesienabkommen von 1922 und den Ordnungen von 1928 erfolgte Gleichstellung der Kinder polnischer, respektive dänischer Staatsangehörigkeit mit den reichsinländischen Kindern der polnischen, respektive dänischen Minderheit tangierte in keiner Weise den Grundsatz, daß „*kein Staat ein Interesse daran haben [könne], Ausländer zu verpflichten, ihr Wissen im Inland zu vervollkommnen*" *(ZBl. 1924, S. 323)*. Denn auch hier folgte aus der Gleichstellung im Hinblick auf den Zugang zu den Minderheits(volks)schulen in polnischer bzw. dänischer Sprache kein weiteres Recht. Weder gab es für reichsdänische oder polnisch-staatsangehörige Kinder staatliche Beihilfen, noch durften sie mitgezählt werden, wenn es darum ging, die für die Genehmigung einer Minderheitsschule notwendige Zahl von (berechtigten) Kindern nachzuweisen. Minderheitsrechte – so der Grundsatz – waren ausschließlich Reichsinländern vorbehalten.[20]

Wanderarbeiterkinder in der preußischen Pflichtschule

Eine gesondert zu betrachtende Gruppe sind die reichsausländischen Kinder von Wanderarbeitern, d. h. Kinder im schulpflichtigen Alter, die – statt in ihrem Herkunftsland die Schule zu besuchen – aus Gründen wirtschaftlicher Not der Familien zur Saisonarbeit nach Preußen wanderten, zusammen mit einem der Elternteile, älteren Geschwistern oder aber auch allein. Der Volkszählung von 1925 wie auch anderen Texten ist lediglich zu entnehmen, daß nach dem Ersten Weltkrieg die Mehrzahl der Wanderarbeiter in Preußen aus Polen kam und – abgesehen von einer nicht bekannten Zahl illegal arbeitender – nicht wenige von ihnen über einen Befreiungsschein und damit über eine unbefristete Aufenthalts- und Arbeitserlaubnis verfügten *(Wenning 1996, S. 103)*. Daß gerade in der letzten Gruppe auch schulpflichtige Kinder waren, ist anzunehmen. Ihre Zahl ist unbekannt, ebenso ist unbekannt, ob darunter – trotz Schulpflicht und Kinder-

---

20 Unmißverständlich z. B. Art. 130 des Oberschlesienabkommens: „*Für die Berechnung der Unterstützung kommen nur die staatsangehörigen [i. e. reichsinländischen] Kinder, die in der Gemeinde oder in dem Kommunalverband wohnen, in Betracht.*"

schutz – auch Kinder unter 14 Jahre waren, die, statt die Schule zu besuchen, gearbeitet haben.

In der Diskussion über Schulpflicht und Staatsangehörigkeit nach 1919 wird die Gruppe der reichsausländischen Wanderarbeiterkinder nicht gesondert beachtet. Spezielle Vorschriften sind für sie weder im „Zentralblatt für die gesamte Unterrichts-Verwaltung in Preußen" noch in den verschiedenen Sammlungen schulrechtlicher Bestimmungen aus der Weimarer Republik zu finden. Daß die Frage der Beschulung dieser Gruppe das Kultusministerium beschäftigt hat, läßt sich jedoch aus einem Erlaß vom Dezember 1929 ablesen. Hier wurden die Gemeinden aufgefordert, auf Antrag grundsätzlich „*Kinder von Ausländern, die sich nur vorübergehend in Preußen aufhalten, namentlich ... Kindern von ausländischen Wanderarbeitern*" aufzunehmen, soweit es die Raumverhältnisse gestatteten, und die „*unterrichtliche Versorgung der deutschen Kinder*" nicht beeinträchtigt würde. Vor allem werden sie aufgefordert, „*bei der Aufnahme der Kinder deutschstämmiger ausländischer Wanderarbeiter ... besonders entgegenkommend zu verfahren*" (PrVA 1927, S. 252).

Aus dem Fehlen einer besonderen Erlaßlage kann jedoch nicht auf ein mangelndes Problembewußtsein der Verantwortlichen geschlossen werden. Denn für die Kinder der ausländischen Wanderarbeiter galt zunächst einmal die gleiche Erlaßlage, wie für die anderen reichsausländischen Kinder auch. Probleme dürften sich allerdings immer dann ergeben haben, wenn es zu klären galt, ob bestimmte Kinder das Kriterium des „dauernden Aufenthalts" erfüllten. Die Erläuterung in den Ausführungsbestimmungen zum Schulpflichtgesetz von 1927 ließen den Behörden einen breiten Ermessensspielraum, denn dort heißt es lediglich: „*Wann die Voraussetzung des dauernden Aufenthalts gegeben ist, ist nach Lage der tatsächlichen Verhältnisse zu entscheiden*" (ZBl. 1928, S. 95). Wie die jeweiligen Schulen sich tatsächlich verhalten haben, und zwar insbesondere dann, wenn es sich nicht um einzelne, sondern um eine größere Zahl solcher Kinder mit zudem mangelhaften Kenntnissen der deutschen Sprache handelte, und von daher ein mehr oder weniger 'reibungsloses' Einfügen in den Unterrichtsalltag erschwert war, muß hier offen bleiben.

Schlußbemerkung

Mit der hier grob skizzierten Gesetzes- und Erlaßlage und dem sie bestimmenden Grundsatz, daß „*kein Staat ein Interesse daran haben [könne], Ausländer zu verpflichten, ihr Wissen im Inland zu vervollkommnen"* (*ZBl. 1924, S. 323*) ist – was die rechtliche Seite angeht – in den sechziger Jahren gebrochen worden. Doch die Frage, ob die nationale (deutsche) Schule – so wie sie sich seit der Wende vom 18. zum 19. Jahrhundert als eine der zentralen Institutionen des (entstehenden) Nationalstaats herausgebildet und entwickelt hat, überhaupt geeignet ist, 'fremde' Kinder in ihrer 'fremden' Nationalität und Sprache zu fördern bzw. welche Konsequenzen die Internationalisierung bzw. Europäisierung der nationalen Schule heute für alle Kinder hat, konnte hier nicht behandelt werden. Unter Vernachlässigung der Staatsangehörigkeitsfrage und fixiert auf das Problem der sprachlichen und kulturellen Differenz konzentrierte sich das Interesse der historischen Forschung bislang auf die bildungspolitischen und pädagogischen Maßnahmen, die vor 1945 – speziell im Kaiserreich und in der Weimarer Republik – zur Beschulung der Kinder der polnischen, dänischen und sorbischen Minderheiten etabliert worden sind. Damit folgte die Forschung – gewissermaßen blind – der in den sechziger Jahren zunächst von der Kultusministerkonferenz und später von den Kultusministerien der Länder vollzogenen Problemverschiebung: „ausländisch" wurde weniger als Hinweis auf die fremde Staatsangehörigkeit, sondern vorrangig als Synonym für sprachliche und kulturelle Differenz verstanden.

In Konsequenz dieser Problemdefinition wurden – wie unbewußt auch immer – Maßnahmen wieder installiert, die ursprünglich für die Kinder der autochthonen Minderheit im Kaiserreich und vor allem in der Weimarer Republik entwickelt worden sind. Daß diese Maßnahmen sowohl der Eingliederung der ausländischen Kinder in die deutsche Schule wie auch dem Erhalt der 'fremden' Sprache und Kultur dienten, wurde unterstellt. Seit den achtziger Jahren sind die bildungspolitischen und pädagogischen Maßnahmen und die mit ihnen verbundenen Denkmuster in die Kritik geraten und – wie die nordrhein-westfälische Denkschrift „Zukunft der Bildung – Schule der Zukunft" (*Bildungskommission NRW 1995*) zeigt, hat diese Kritik Eingang in bildungspolitische Entwürfe gefunden. Doch die Frage nach den Traditionslinien, in denen die Bildungspolitik für ausländische Kinder einerseits und für inländische bzw. als inländisch definierte Kinder andererseits steht, und wieweit diese bis heute wirksam sind und den Bemühungen um ein *„reflektierte[s] Zusammenleben in einer multikulturellen Schule und insgesamt in einer dauerhaft multikulturellen Gesellschaft"* (*ebd., S. 117*) entgegenstehen, ist noch unzureichend geklärt. Es bedarf weiterer Untersuchungen, um die 'Logiken' zutage zu fördern, die nicht nur die schulrechtlichen Vorschriften zur Beschulung ausländischer, ausgesiedelter und auch einheimischer Kinder kennzeichnen, sondern auch die Strukturen der Schule bis hinein in die Sichtweisen, die die inhaltliche und pädagogische Arbeit bestimmen. Ein notwendiger Schritt hierzu ist die Aufklärung über die rechtlichen Traditionen, denen die bildungspolitischen Entscheidungen für ausländische und ausgesiedelte Kinder bis heute – unaufgeklärt – verpflichtet sind.

Abkürzungen

Abs.	Absatz
Art.	Artikel
BGBl.	Bundesgesetzblatt
DJZ	Deutsche Juristen-Zeitung
FINMBl.	Finanz-Ministerialblatt
PAAA	Politisches Archiv des Auswärtigen Amtes, Bonn
PrGS	Preußische Gesetzessammlung
PrVA	Preußisches Volksschularchiv
RV	Reichsverfassung von 1919
ZBl.	Zentralblatt für die gesamte Unterrichts-Verwaltung in Preußen

Bibliographie

Basler, Franz: Die Deutsch-Russische Schule in Berlin, 1931-1945. Geschichte und Auftrag. Wiesbaden: Harrassowitz 1983. (Veröffentlichungen der Abteilung für slawische Sprachen und Literaturen des Osteuropa Instituts (Slawisches Seminar) an der Freien Universität Berlin. 54)

Bildungskommission NRW: Zukunft der Bildung – Schule der Zukunft. Denkschrift der Kommission „Zukunft der Bildung – Schule der Zukunft" beim Ministerpräsident des Landes Nordrhein-Westfalen. Neuwied u. a.: Luchterhand 1995.

DelFabbro, René: Transalpini. Italienische Arbeitswanderung nach Süddeutschland im Kaiserreich, 1870-1918. Osnabrück: Rasch 1996. (Studien zur historischen Migrationsforschung. 2)

Führ, Christoph: Zur Schulpolitik der Weimarer Republik. Die Zusammenarbeit von Reich und Ländern im Reichsschulausschuß (1919-1923) und im Ausschuß für das Unterrichtswesen (1924-1933). Darstellung und Quellen. 2., durchges. Aufl. Weinheim: Beltz 1972.

Gosewinkel, Dieter: Die Staatsangehörigkeit als Institution des Nationalstaats. Zur Entstehung des Reichs- und Staatsangehörigkeitsgesetzes von 1913. In: Grawert, Rolf u. a. (Hrsg.): Offene Staatlichkeit. Festschrift für Ernst-Wolfgang Böckenförde zum 65. Geburtstag, Berlin: Duncker und Humblot 1995, S. 359-378.

Hansen, Georg: Diskriminiert. Über den Umgang der Schule mit Minderheiten. Weinheim u. a.: Beltz 1986.

Herbert, Ulrich: Geschichte der Ausländerbeschäftigung in Deutschland 1880-1980. Saisonarbeiter, Zwangsarbeiter, Gastarbeiter. Berlin u. a.: Dietz 1986. (Dietz-Taschenbücher. 19)

Hessen, Sergius: Kritische Vergleichung des Schulwesens der anderen Kulturstaaten. In: Nohl, Herman / Pallat, Ludwig (Hrsg.): Handbuch der Pädagogik. Bd. 4: Die Theorie der Schule und der Schulaufbau, Langensalza: Beltz 1928, S. 421-510.

Kasberger, Erich: Von Sonnenaufgang bis Sonnenuntergang. Das Leben jugendlicher Gastarbeiter in Süddeutschland um 1900. In: Süddeutsche Zeitung vom 16./17. November 1991.

Koehne, ...: Mitteilungen, 3. Strafsachen. In: Deutsche Juristen-Zeitung, 29 (1924) 21-22, Sp. 916-917.

Kraus, Herbert: Der Friedensvertrag von Versailles. In: Jahrbuch des Öffentlichen Rechts, 10 (1920), S. 292-318.

Kraus, Herbert: Das Recht der Minderheiten. Materialien zur Einführung in das Verständnis des modernen Minderheitenproblems. Berlin: Stilke 1927. (Stilke's Rechtsbibliothek. 57)

Krüger-Potratz, Marianne: Schulpolitik für Kinder der „fremdsprachigen Volksteile" und Reichsausländer in der Weimarer Republik – ein Beitrag zur Geschichte der Interkulturellen Pädagogik. Projektskizze und ausgewählte Texte aus der Laufzeit des Projekts: „Bildung und Erziehung ethnischer Minderheiten im Deutschen Reich: Die Minderheitenschulfrage in der Weimarer Republik". Münster 1996 (unveröffentlichtes Typoskript).

Pastenaci, Theodor / Ewers, Georg (Hrsg.): Schulrecht enthaltend Gesetze, Erlasse und gerichtliche Entscheidungen über das den Preußischen Regierungen unterstellte Schulwesen nebst den grundlegenden Bestimmungen über die Jugendpflege, Jugendfürsorge und die ländlichen Berufsschulen. Wiesbaden: Selbstverlag 1927.

Reich, Hans H. / Bender-Szymanski, Dorothea (Hrsg.): Folgen der Arbeitsmigration für Bildung und Erziehung. Ein Schwerpunktprogramm der Deutschen Forschungsgemeinschaft. Kommentierte bibliographische Informationen. 3., veränd. Aufl. Frankfurt a. M.: Deutsches Institut für Internationale Pädagogische Forschung 1997.

Sachse, Arnold: Schulpflicht. In: Schwartz, Hermann (Hrsg.): Pädagogisches Lexikon. Bd. 4, Bielefeld u. a.: Velhagen und Klasing 1931, Sp. 454-457.

Schätzel, Walter: Zur Reform des Staatsangehörigkeitsgesetzes. In: Deutsche Juristen-Zeitung, 32 (1927), Sp. 1577-1580.

Schwalb, ...: Empfiehlt es sich, das Reichs- und Staatsangehörigkeitsgesetz in seinen grundsätzlichen Bestimmungen abzuändern? In: Deutsche Juristen-Zeitung, 36 (1931), Sp. 1107-1110.

Uhlig, Otto: Die 'Schwabenkinder'. Kinder wanderten zur Arbeit ins Ausland. In: Bade, Klaus J. (Hrsg.): Auswanderer – Wanderarbeiter – Gastarbeiter. Bevölkerung, Arbeitsmarkt und Wandlung in Deutschland seit Mitte des 19. Jahrhunderts. Bd. 2, Ostfildern: Scripta-Mercaturae-Verlag 1984, S. 794-798.

Volks-, Berufs- und Betriebszählung vom 16. Juni 1925: Volkszählung. T. 2. Textliche Darstellung der Ergebnisse. Berlin: Hobbing 1930. (Statistik des Deutschen Reiches. 401)

Vorbrodt, Walter / Herrmann, Kurt: Handwörterbuch des gesamten Schulrechts und der Schul- und Unterrichtsverwaltung in Preußen. Leipzig: Quelle und Meyer 1930.

Wenning, Norbert: Migration in Deutschland. Ein Überblick. Münster u. a.: Waxmann 1996.

Wiese, Klaus: Von den Schulen russischer Emigranten zur nationalsozialistischen „Ostschule". Zur Geschichte der russischen Emigranten-Gymnasien und der deutsch-russischen Schulen in Berlin, 1920-1945. In: Mitteilungen und Materialien der Arbeitsgruppe Pädagogisches Museum, (1988) 26, S. 5-69.

Woydt, Johann: Ausländische Arbeitskräfte in Deutschland. Vom Kaiserreich bis zur Bundesrepublik. Heilbronn: Distel 1987.

Zentralblatt für die gesamte Unterrichts-Verwaltung in Preußen. [Ab 1918 hrsg. vom Ministerium für Wissenschaft, Kunst und Volksbildung.] Berlin 1 (1859) – 75 (1933).

Prolegomena to a History of British Interest in Education in Germany

David Phillips

The question of what I have called „cross-national attraction" in education *(Phillips 1989a)* is of enduring interest to comparativists. What is it that causes educational policy makers and other informed observers in a particular country at a particular time to focus their attention on aspects of education in another country? The reasons for such interest range from earnest academic („scientific") examination of discrete features of successful educational practice „elsewhere", through more or less serious general consideration of, or casual curiosity about, how other countries organise their education systems, to the cheap political expediency of governments and opposition parties anxious for a range of dubious reasons to demonstrate that education in their country is either under- or over-performing in comparison to other nations.

A historical analysis of the long-standing interest in England shown towards all particulars of educational provision in Germany would reveal aspects of the whole spectrum of reasons suggested above. Analyses have been undertaken in the past, particularly by W. H. G. *Armytage (1969)* in a brief and flawed account and Friedrich *Schneider (1943)* in a lengthy and more scholarly study not limited to England. The purpose of the present paper is to describe – in a highly selective fashion – some aspects of English interest in education in Germany since the late eighteenth century and in particular to consider, using the material with which I am – idiosyncratically – familiar, some of the sources that inform our understanding of that interest. In this latter regard what follows is something of a bibliographical trawl through some favourite writings germane to our subject.

Travellers' Tales

Throughout the nineteenth century information on German life and letters became increasingly accessible to the non German-speaking British reading public through English translations of German works. *Morgan* in his „Critical Bibliography of German Literature in English Translation" *(1965, p. 8)* charts the number of translated works and demonstrates an increase in such publications from 1800 to the peak decade of 1880-90 of the order of some 300 per cent. There was then much material available in English translation for those with sufficient interest to seek it out; in addition, considerable effort was expended by academics and others on learning German, though this proved in many cases a very difficult, sometimes an impossible, task *(Phillips 1989b)*.

As the century progressed, and as travelling (particularly as a result of the growth of the railroads) became much easier, so the number of accounts of continental travels increased. Germany had often been visited by British travellers – usually gentlemen of leisure – in the eighteenth century; from the turn of the century it became an extraordinarily popular destination for British travellers of all kinds. Though most of them headed for the Rhine – often on their way to Switzerland – other parts of Germany were not neglected.

The German universities in particular were a focus of attention for those writing accounts of their travels, and many books recorded at least a few facts and figures; the condition of education for the poor was also often commented upon, Britain lagging far behind Germany in its approach to free and compulsory schooling; and there was interest too in the way children were brought up in the home.

Thomas *Nugent (1768, Vol. 1, pp. 203-204)* – to take one early example from among many – reports briefly and positively on the University of Rostock, „*reckoned one of the best in Germany ... Many of the first princes of the empire have thought it an honour to be rectors of this great academy*"; and John *Moore (1786, Vol. 2, p. 58)* takes pride in recording that the University of Göttingen „*founded here by George the Second [of England] has a considerable reputation*". Of the military academy at Brunswick he notes *(pp. 70-71)* that „*students now resort to this academy from many parts of Germany; and there are generally some young gentlemen from Britain, who are sent to be educated here*"; „*Every branch of science is taught by masters of known abilities*". Thomas *Raffles (1819, p. 307)* speaks favourably of free schooling for children of the poor in Koblenz: „*The people here are catholics. Education is general. The schools are obliged to educate the children of the poor, gratis; so that there are very few who cannot read and write*".[1] Samuel *Pratt (1797, Vol. 3, pp. 209-210)* reports that:

---

1 Richard *Bright (1818, p. 82)* reports similarly on the „*most formidable nature*" of education in Vienna, where he found sixty schools instructing the poor in reading, writing and arithmetic for three florins a year.

„The Germans bring up their children with great tenderness, but in a manner to prevent the effects of effeminacy, or the ordinary ailments proceeding therefrom. I have seen the sons and daughters of gentlemen run through the dews of the morning without shoes, stockings, or any under garments, but shirts and shifts ... but they all look as healthy as if they were educated in the way of England. The mothers of Great Britain will shudder at this relation; yet ... it might deserve adoption. Colds and coughs ... are rarely heard of along the continent of Germany."

Such brief coverage of educational topics in these early and typical accounts concerned with all aspects of life in particular parts of Germany gives some insight into those features which the writers in question considered significant enough to report to their home audience. They can of course be criticised for highlighting – and most probably exaggerating – supposedly bizarre or quaint or sensational features of educational provision which might appeal to the imagination of a readership of 'armchair travellers'.

In the case of descriptions of German university life in the nineteenth century this was certainly so, supporting the view of *Noah* and *Eckstein (1969, p. 9)* that the reports of most travellers *„were subjective and unsystematic, the colourfulness of their descriptions alone redeeming their lack of objectivity"*. The anonymous author of *An Autumn Near the Rhine (1818)*, for example, describes students as *„a crew of noisy grotesque looking figures"*, instantly recognisable: *„You never fail to distinguish them by their strange costume and looks, and riotous behaviour"*. Later *(pp. 329-345)* he provides some detailed analysis of the main distinguishing features of German universities, drawing sharp contrasts with their English counterparts (then only Oxford and Cambridge), fearing that *„the unbounded licence of the [German] University can only produce unqualified mischief"* *(p. 342)*, and regarding reform as improbable.

Joseph Moyle *Sherer (1826, p. 85)*, while critical of the students of Oxford, speaks favourably of German students:

„No man can pass an hour in a room with German students without discovering that they are worshippers of knowledge, and lovers of their father-land. This love of fatherland does indeed give them heated and vague notions, the warmth of which does never, I hope, entirely die away, while the vagueness settles down into something defined and valuable in permanent principles of life."

He forgives their more picturesque qualities: *"Their costume, when clean, I am far from disliking, and their sins of smoking and singing appear to me venial offences; even the drinking of beer where they cannot get wine I forgive"* (ibid., p. 83).

Henry *Mayhew (1865)*, well known for his work on the poor of London, devotes some 55 pages in his study of German life and manners to schools, but some 118 pages to a range of university topics of often sensational nature: „Student Life at Jena", „On the Beer-Drinking Customs at Jena", „Drinking-Bouts of the Jena Students", „Of the Duels at Jena", and „Three Fights in Jena". William *Howitt (1842)*, a prolific mid-century writer on Germany, wrote a whole book on student life. Duels, singing and drinking figure prominently in his exhaustive account of the current state of university life in Germany. Henry *Vizetelly* in his account of life in Berlin *„under the new Empire" (1872)* likewise emphasises smoking, drinking and singing in his chapter on the students of the University of Berlin, despite admitting that *„no other German city can offer such an advanced scientific education as Berlin, the advantages derived from which are surely more worthy of commemoration than the follies of a student's life in a provincial town"* (Vol. 2, p. 107).

Frances Trollope, a prolific writer of accounts of her travels (and mother of the novelist Anthony Trollope) wrote an entertaining account of „Belgium and Western Germany" in 1833. In it she extols the advantages of state provision of education: *„This system, already so prolific of the happiest of results, has attracted the attention of all Europe; and England, among the rest, is said to be taking a lesson on this most important branch of government, from the benignant absolutism of Prussia"* (Trollope 1834, Vol. 2, p. 170). Later she puzzles over the paradox that *„the idea ... of the relaxed discipline of the German Universities accords so ill with the equally general belief that the scholars they send out stand pre-eminently high"* (ibid., p. 225).

In such accounts as these the more colourful aspects of the German universities tend to come to the fore, but there is an underlying respect for the serious scholarship which characterised them as they developed over the century. And it was advanced scholarship and a particular „idea" of what a university should be like (*Lehr- und Lernfreiheit*; combination of research and teaching) that informed much commentary on the German university by serious academic observers.

Academic and Literary Observers

As the number of travellers' accounts increased, so, gradually, did the more objective analyses of serious social observers and visiting scholars. A good example of early nineteenth-century commentary from a serious writer/traveller of literary disposition is to be found in the diary of Henry Crabb *Robinson (1872)*, who counted his studies at the University of Jena (1802-05) as *„one of the happiest periods of my life" (Vol. 1, p. 67)* and who, on leaving the University, felt it his good fortune *„to come to Jena while the ancient spirit was still alive and active, and I saw the last not altogether insignificant remains of a knot of public teachers who have seldom been surpassed in any university" (ibid., p. 115)*. Robinson, together with better known literary figures and men of letters like Samuel Taylor Coleridge, Thomas Carlyle and George Henry Lewes (biographer of Goethe) and the novelist George Eliot, did much to promote familiarity in England with the literary and philosophical scene in Germany *(Ashton 1980)*. The seeds of his enthusiasm for the German university were sown long before the founding of the University of Berlin and marked an early stage in the considerable interest in higher education in Germany that was to develop throughout the century.

Mme de *Staël*'s work „De l'Allemagne", banned in France, was published in English translation (my 'new' edition is of *1814*) and contained a serious chapter on the German universities and another on education generally. By the middle decades of the century there were available serious studies of a socio-historical nature like *Hawkins*'s „Germany" *(1838), Laing*'s „Notes" *(1842)*, and his „Observations on Europe" *(1850)*, as well as translated sources such as the four volumes of *Menzel*'s „German Literature" *(1840)*, all of which have sections dealing fully with education in Germany.

At the same time the publications of German educators and general information on the state of pedagogy in Germany were being disseminated. Friedrich Wilhelm Schubert's Memoir of Bernard Overberg, for example, appeared in English translation in 1838, with an account (by the unnamed translator) of the *„system of national education"* in Prussia *(Schubert 1838)*. The translator, intrigued by the notion of a „national" system, cautiously reserved judgement as far as lessons for his own country were concerned: *„Should any national plan be adopted in England, we must recollect that we are only sowing the seeds for a harvest when we have passed on" (p. XXVII)*. Contrast this view with that of Frances Trollope quoted above.

Later, the distinguished American educationist Henry *Barnard (1876)* published an important and exhaustively thorough collection of translated papers on „German Pedagogy", which was made widely available to a British audience through a London educational depository. Herbart's work in particular was of course widely discussed and much translated. Available also were detailed introductory accounts such as those of *Perry (1887)* on elementary schools and training colleges and *Russell (1899)* on German „higher schools".

The Growth of „Official" Interest in Education in Germany

At the same time interest in German education in England was boosted by the considerable enthusiasm of Matthew *Arnold (1868, 1874)*. Arnold combined fame as a poet with being an inspector of schools, and in that latter capacity he produced some very thorough accounts of the educational scene in Germany. It is to Arnold that we owe the dictum „*the French university has no liberty and the English universities have no science; the German universities have both*" *(Arnold 1868, p. 232)*. Arnold gave, as it were, official imprimatur to interest in the public education system of Germany. And that interest was later to be developed to great effect by another official, the renowned comparativist Michael Sadler, who was Director of Special Inquiries and Reports at the Board of Education and under whose aegis in the early years of the century a remarkable series of studies of aspects of education in other countries – Germany prominent among them – appeared. Volume 9 of the series *(Board of Education 1902)* is entirely devoted to Germany and covers a very wide range of subjects.[2] The emphasis in these studies was on topics from which lessons might be learnt.

Sadler was a prolific writer of journal and newspaper articles, and spoke often at public meetings on the subject of education in Germany *(Sadler 1979)*. Even during the War he could write a piece for *The Times* entitled „Need we imitate German education?", in which he makes a point that still concerns policy-makers in England today: German education „*makes good use of all second-grade ability, which in England is far too much of a waste product*". The achievements of the German system are summarised thus:

„*Whatever we may feel about its capital defect – its idol-worship of the State and its subordination of conscience to system and success – German education has high*

---

2 Volume 3 of the series (1898) contains eleven papers on Germany (out of fourteen).

merits. ... [It] has made the nation alert to science. It has made systematic cooperation a habit. It has taught patriotic duty. It has kept a whole people industrious. Combined with military training, it has given them the strength of discipline. It has made profitable use of second rate intelligence. It has not neglected the mind" (Sadler 1916).*

There was still considerable interest in aspects of educational provision in Germany, despite the conflict. Representative of the interest in the teaching of particular subjects, for example, is Ethel *Davies's (1917)* account of modern language teaching in German schools.

Sadler was ousted from his post at the Board of Education in 1903, but his work had helped to raise awareness – at a level beyond that of popular writing – of the progress of education in Germany at a time when industrial and commercial competition between the two countries was a matter of increasing concern in Britain. Much reporting on education in Germany was becoming negative as political tensions mounted,[3] but the respect for what the Germans had achieved in education was still conceded.

Numerous sources could be cited which draw attention to the competitive edge which Germany had gained through education and training. Percy Gardner, in a book proposing reform in Oxford, praises educational achievement in Germany:

„Into whatever seas of fact one may sail, one is almost sure to find that the German investigator is there already with his telescope and his microscope, with his tables of statistics and his infallible indexes. And the result of this pursuit of fact, this cultus of realities, has been beyond all denial an immense success, at least in many directions. It is this which has made Germany prominent in science, in applied knowledge, in arms" (Gardner 1903, p. 5).

In 1910 one commentator could declare that *„Germany is the land of schools, and she is rapidly taking a leading place in the world" (Berry 1910, p. 73)*. The great eleventh edition of the „Encyclopedia Britannica" devotes much space to education in Germany, judging that *„in point of educational culture Germany ranks high among all the civilised*

---

3   Friedel's „Pédagogie de Guerre Allemande" was translated into English as „The German School as a War Nursery", with an introduction by Michael Sadler *(Friedel 1918).*

great nations of the world" (Encyclopedia Britannica 1910, Vol. 11, p. 822).[4] Begrudgingly, another commentator would write, during the War, that

> *„it has been very truly said that Germany is the world's schoolmaster, and like many another of that profession, the Fatherland has fallen into the error of believing that the rod – in this case the mailed fist – is an end in itself. Nevertheless, the world owes a great debt to our Teutonic cousins for a long list of great pedagogues, as well as for the system of schools which have been models for the rest of the world"* (Smith 1916, p. 17 – in a chapter headed „German Schools – Intellectual Barracks").

Writing at about the same time, an American author (whose views can serve for many)[5] could make the same kind of judgement:

> *„Germany cannot be understood at all by one who knows nothing of its system of education. There is no subject, not even that of the national defences, to which the German has devoted more careful attention. There is no institution of the state upon which he is more willing to spend money and labour than upon the system of schools, lower and higher. It is education that has made Germany what it is, and Germany knows it"* (Fullerton 1915, p. 60).

The link between educational provision, particularly of the higher technical kind, and industrial efficiency was often made, here typically in a short introductory book on Germany published at about the end of the War:

> *„It is the smooth working of the more delicate parts of the German industrial machine which is one of its most prominent characteristics, and this may be due to some extent to the fact that the parts are ready for adjustment when they are delivered from the technical high school"* (Tower 1914, p. 150).

The President of the Board of Education at the end of the war was H. A. L. Fisher, who had studied in Göttingen and who held a high opinion of German scholarship:

---

[4] The interested reader had many other informed sources available, in particular translations of Friedrich *Paulsen*'s important writings *(1906, 1908)* and the work of W. *Lexis (1904)*.
[5] See also *Farrington (1914)*.

„During the last two decades of the nineteenth century the German universities enjoyed a wide reputation for freedom, courage, and learning. To sit at the feet of some great German Professor, absorbing his publications, listening to his lectures, working in his seminary, was regarded as a valuable, perhaps as a necessary passport to the highest kind of academic career" *(Fisher 1940, p. 79).*

Fisher was the architect of the important 1918 Education Act, which drew explicitly on the example of Germany. Its espousal of the notion of „continuation schools" and some form of compulsory education up to the age of 18, came directly from the experience of Germany and was not well received in some quarters. A commentator on the Act describes fears that the creation of continuation schools would introduce into Britain *„the German socialism of the Bismarckian welfare state"* *(Andrews 1976, p. 48).*

But despite such criticism there was recognition – still with us today – that the Germans had got it right when they extended part-time compulsory education way beyond the 'normal' school-leaving age. The 1944 Education Act laid down provision for „county colleges" for those not in full-time attendance at school, but this provision was never implemented.

The Modern Period

During the inter-war years there was much interest in the German *Reformpädagogik*. A. S. *Neill (1923)*, for example, wrote an entertaining book based on ideas in education in Germany. But as the political situation again worsened there was increasing suspicion of the German educational scene, and accounts began to be written of the transformation of educational provision under the Nazis. Many published in England were written by Germans, chief among them Erika *Mann*, whose „School for Barbarians" appeared in *1939* with an introduction by Thomas Mann. Peter *Wiener*'s „German With Tears" appeared in *1942*; Abraham *Wolf*'s „Higher Education in Nazi Germany" came out in *1944*. Widely available were publications from the American perspective like Gregor Ziemer's „Education for Death" *(1942)* and Howard *Becker*'s „German Youth: Bond or Free?" *(1946)*.

Following the Second World War the Allies were anxious to pay particular attention to education in Germany. Numerous documents address what needed to be done, while expressing the hope that the traditional strengths of the German system could be built upon. The catchphrase „On from Weimar!" to some extent sums up what happened, with the Western Allies happy to see stability restored in a general return to the post-war structures. The „German Miracle" that followed in the wake of reconstruction of course attracted the attention of the world. Education – and there is a certain historical inevitability in this – came again to be recognised as the lynchpin of success in the industrial and commercial sphere. In particular the German „Dual System" of provision in vocational education became widely admired.

It was not surprising that in the period leading up to the Education Reform Act of 1988, the most far-reaching educational legislation in England and Wales since the famous 1944 Act, there was much mention of education in Germany.[6] Her Majesty's Inspectors of Schools chose the Federal Republic as the object of the first of their investigative studies to be published in series form since the days of Michael Sadler. Their report *(Department of Education and Science 1986)* was the first of a series on Germany now numbering seven *(Department of Education and Science 1991, 1992; Department for Education 1993a, 1993b; Office for Standards in Education 1993, 1994)*. In it we can isolate some of the features of educational provision that provide evidence of its attractiveness to those working in the mid 1980s towards the new arrangements formalised in the 1988 Act:

- *„The most important fact to bear in mind about the Federal Republic's system of assessment generally and about the Abitur in particular is that for the Federal Republic it works. ... Ultimately [it] works because virtually everybody involved seems determined that it should do so. ... It is, as much as anything else, an article of faith. This wide agreement about education and its assessment is in itself an important message for English education where such agreement, undertaking and trust are lacking.*
- *The curriculum is in the lead and has public confidence and clarity; teacher training in all its practical aspects ... is well-tried and effective.*
- *The educational system in the Federal Republic is efficient at achieving quickly a broad consensus about which subjects to teach, in which years and for how many pupils.*
- *There can ... be a greater confidence that pupils' work in each year and ability group bears a clear relationship to subsequent work than is often the case in England.*
- *There is a degree of openness and general accountability about the assessment system*

---

6   The remaining part of this section is adapted from the Introduction to „Education in Germany: Tradition and Reform in Historical Context" *(Phillips 1995, pp. 6-9)*.

in the Federal Republic which would be much appreciated by pupils, parents and employers in England" (Department of Education and Science 1986, pp. 34-37).

I have expressed the main attraction of German educational provision in the years before the legislation of 1988 in these terms, which would be unsurprising in any German context:

„*The Germans have decided what it is their school system offers; it is clearly stated and known to all who have a part in the system. For better or worse this incontestably clear approach does mean that parents know what precisely they can expect for their children from a particular school and they are able, through well established procedures, to make sure that it is provided*" *(Phillips 1987, p. 215).*

Writing in 1989 Detlef Glowka summarised in five categories those aspects of the German education system which had been singled out for particular attention by Her Majesty's Inspectors and others. They were:

- the continuous assessment of pupil performance;
- the compulsory nature and breadth of the curriculum;
- the wide distribution of school-leaving qualifications and the systematic correlation between them;
- the developed and systematic paths towards accredited vocational education;
- the regulating force of central guiding and controlling authorities *(Glowka 1989, p. 321).*

„*It appears,*" Glowka says, „*that in these five areas something could be learnt from the Germans*"; and he notes that they constituted central features of the 1988 Education Reform Act.

At the same time attention was being given to an important research report from the National Institute of Economic and Social Research in London. The study in question, by *Prais* and *Wagner (1985),* examined schooling standards in England and Germany and made comparisons „*bearing on economic performance*". It has since been widely quoted in support of moves in the United Kingdom towards greater curricular control along German lines. Its authors were concerned principally with the attainment of pupils in the middle and lower half of the ability range, especially in mathematics. Among their findings we can quote three as being of most significance in the context of the UK policy debate:

- over half of all German pupils, compared with only just over a quarter of the pupils in England, attain a standard above or equivalent to a broadly-based set of O-level passes;
- the German system provides a broader curriculum combined with significantly higher levels of attainment in core subjects, for a greater proportion of pupils than does the English system;
- attainments in mathematics by those in the lower half of the ability-range in England appear to lag by the equivalent of about two years' schooling behind the corresponding section of pupils in Germany *(Prais / Wagner 1985)*.

This latter finding in particular has been given great prominence by commentators at all levels. If it is legitimate, it reinforces the view of Michael Sadler some seventy years earlier that Germany was profiting from its attention to the education of those not aspiring to the highest levels of academic attainment; it certainly reinforced the tendency of the then Department of Education and Science in London to support its arguments about policy with reference to developments in other leading industrialised countries.

Concluding Remarks

The main perceived advantages of the German education system, as now seen from England, are closely allied to the general thrust of reforms in England and Wales under successive Conservative governments since 1979. Those advantages have to do largely with accountability at all levels, with greater centralised control coupled with responsible, regulated autonomy, with government-controlled authority in the curriculum and in assessment, with high standards, and with increased respect for education generally. These, and related matters, are deserving of continuing investigation by historians and others interested in exploring the interest shown in England in the educational scene in Germany.[7]

---

7 A recent historical study of the German influence on education in the United States is that edited by *Geitz, Heideking* and *Herbst (1995)*. A useful account of Anglo-German relations in adult education is to be found in a study by Stuart *Marriott (1995)*.

It is of course clear that there is much in educational provision in the Federal Republic that would not be uncritically welcomed in England, but the general coherence of education in Germany, its acceptability to most of those involved with it, and its demonstrably high standards, have continued to provide a challenge to British policy makers since the early years of the last century. Learning from Germany is likely to remain on the educational agenda for some considerable time yet.

Bibliography

[Note: The editions cited are those in the author's possession. They are not always the earliest.]

Andrews, Lawrence: The Education Act, 1918. London: Routledge and Kegan Paul 1976.
Armytage, W[alter] H[arry] G[reen]: The German Influence on English Education. London: Routledge and Kegan Paul 1969.
Arnold, Matthew: Schools and Universities on the Continent. London: Macmillan 1868.
Arnold, Matthew: Higher Schools and Universities in Germany. London: Macmillan 1874.
Ashton, Rosemary: The German Idea. Four English Writers and the Reception of German Thought, 1800-1860. Cambridge: Cambridge University Press 1980.
An Autumn Near the Rhine. London: Longman, Hurst, Rees, Orme and Brown 1818.
Barnard, Henry: German Pedagogy. Education, the School, and the Teacher, in German Literature. 2. ed. Hartford: Brown and Gross 1876.
Becker. Howard: German Youth. Bond or Free? London: Kegan Paul, Trench, Trubner 1946.
Berry, Robert M.: Germany of the Germans. London: Pitman 1910.
Board of Education (ed.): Special Reports on Educational Subjects. Vol. 9. Education in Germany. London: HMSO 1902.
Bright, Richard: Travels from Vienna through Lower Hungary; with Some Remarks on the State of Vienna During the Congress in the Year 1814. Edinburgh: Constable 1818.
Davies, Ethel: Modern Language Teaching in German Secondary Schools. Oxford: Oxford University Press 1917.
Department for Education (ed.): Aspects of Full-Time Vocational Education in the Federal Republic of Germany. London: HMSO 1993a.
Department for Education (ed.): Aspects of Higher Education in Germany. Design, Technology and Engineering, 14-19. London: HMSO 1993b.
Department of Education and Science (ed.): Education in the Federal Republic of Germany. Aspects of Curriculum and Assessment. London: HMSO 1986.
Department of Education and Science (ed.): Aspects of Vocational Education and Training in the Federal Republic of Germany. London: HMSO 1991.
Department of Education and Science (ed.): Aspects of Higher Education in the Federal Republic of Germany. The Fachhochschulen. London: HMSO 1992.
Diehl, Carl: Americans and German Scholarship, 1770-1870. New Haven et al.: Yale University Press 1978.

Education Act, 1944. Ch. 31. London: HMSO 1944.

Encyclopaedia Britannica. A Dictionary of Arts, Sciences, Literature and General Information. 11. ed. Cambridge: Cambridge University Press 1910. [Entries on „Education", „Germany" and „Universities"]

Farrington, Frederic Ernest: Commercial Education in Germany. New York: Macmillan 1914.

Fisher, H[erbert] A[lbert] L[aurens]: An Unfinished Autobiography. London: Oxford University Press 1940.

Friedel, V. H.: The German School as a War Nursery [with an Introduction by M. E. Sadler]. London: Melrose n. d. [1918].

Fullerton: Germany of To-Day. Indianapolis, Ind.: Bobbs-Merrill 1915.

Gardner, Percy: Oxford at the Cross Roads. London: Black 1903.

Geitz, Henry / Heideking, Jürgen / Herbst, Jürgen (eds.): German Influences on Education in the United States to 1917. Washington, D. C.: German Historical Institute and Cambridge University Press 1995.

Glowka, Detlef: Anglo-German Perceptions of Education. In: Comparative Education, 25 (1989) 3, pp. 319-332.

Hawkins, Francis Bisset: Germany. The Spirit of her History, Literature, Social Condition, and National Economy. London: Parker 1838.

Howitt, William: The Student-Life of Germany. Philadelphia: Carey and Hart 1842.

Laing, Samuel: Notes of a Traveller, on the Social and Political State of France, Prussia, Switzerland, Italy and Other Parts of Europe, during the Present Century. London: Longman, Brown, Green, and Longmans 1842.

Laing, Samuel: Observations on the Social and Political State of the European People in 1848 and 1849. London: Longman, Brown, Green and Longmans 1850.

Lexis, Wilhelm: A General View of the History and Organisation of Public Education in the German Empire. Berlin: Asher 1904.

Mann, Erika: School for Barbarians. London: Drummond 1939.

Marriott, Stuart: English-German Relations in Adult Education 1875-1955. A Commentary and Select Bibliography. Leeds: University of Leeds 1995.

Mayhew, Henry: German Life and Manners, as Seen in Saxony at the Present Day. London: Allen 1865.

Menzel, Wolfgang: German Literature. Oxford: Talboys 1840.

Moore, John: A View of Society and Manners in France, Switzerland and Germany. With Anecdotes Relating to Some Eminent Characters. Vol. 1. 2. London: Strahan and Cadell 1786.

Morgan, B[ayard] Q[uincy]: A Critical Bibliography of German Literature in English Translation, 1481-1927. New York et al.: Scarecrow Press 1965.

Neill, A[lexander] S[utherland]: A Dominie Abroad. London: Jenkins n. d. [1923].

Noah, Harold J. / Eckstein, Max A.: Toward a Science of Comparative Education. London: Macmillan 1969.

Nugent, Thomas: Travels Through Germany. Vol. 1. 2. London: Dilly 1768.

Office for Standards in Education (ed.): The Initial Training of Teachers in Two German Länder: Hessen and Rheinland-Pfalz. London: HMSO 1993.

Office for Standards in Education (ed.): The Development of Double Qualification Courses in Secondary Schools in North Rhine Westphalia. London: HMSO 1994.

Paulsen, Friedrich: The German Universities and University Study. London: Longmans, Green 1906.

Paulsen, Friedrich: German Education. Past and Present. London: Unwin 1908.
Perry, Charles Copland: Reports on German Elementary Schools and Training Colleges. London: Rivington 1887.
Phillips, David: The German Universities – Citadels of Freedom or Bastions of Reaction? In: Comparative Education, 17 (1981) 3, pp. 343-352.
Phillips, David: Lessons from Germany? The Case of German Secondary Schools. In: British Journal of Educational Studies, 35 (1987) 3, pp. 211-232.
Phillips, David: Neither a Borrower nor a Lender Be? The Problems of Cross-National Attraction in Education. In: Comparative Education, 25 (1989a) 3, pp. 267-274.
Phillips, David: Problems with an Alien Tongue. The Nineteenth-Century Traveller in Germany. In: Modern Languages, 70 (1989b) 2, pp. 104-110.
Phillips, David: Introduction. In: ibid. (ed.): Education in Germany. Tradition and Reform in Historical Context, London et al.: Routledge 1995, pp. 1-11.
Prais, S[igbert] J[on] / Wagner, Karin: Schooling Standards in England and Germany. Some Summary Comparisons Bearing on Economic Performance. In: National Institute Economic Review, 112 (1985) May, pp. 53-76 [reprinted in *Phillips 1995, pp. 95-134*].
Pratt, Samuel Jackson: Gleanings Through Wales, Holland and Westphalia. With Views of Peace and War at Home and Abroad. Vol. 1-3. 4. ed. London: Longman 1797.
Raffles, Thomas: Letters During a Tour through some Parts of France, Savoy, Switzerland, Germany and The Netherlands in the Summer of 1817. 2. ed. Liverpool: Taylor 1819.
Robinson, Henry Crabb: Diary, Reminiscences, and Correspondence of Henry Crabb Robinson. Ed. by Thomas Sadler. Vol. 1. 2. London et al.: Macmillan 1872.
Robinson, Henry Crabb: Henry Crabb Robinson in Germany, 1800-1805. Extracts from his Correspondence. Ed. by Edith J. Morley. London: Oxford University Press 1929.
Russell, James Earl: German Higher Schools. The History, Organization, and Methods of Secondary Education in Germany. New York et al.: Longmans, Green 1899.
Sadler, Michael: Need we Imitate German education? In: The Times, 14 January 1916.
Sadler, Michael: Selections from Michael Sadler. Studies in World Citizenship. Compiled by J. H. Higginson. Liverpool: Dejall and Meyorre 1979.
Schneider, Friedrich: Geltung und Einfluß der deutschen Pädagogik im Ausland. München et al.: Oldenbourg 1943.
Schubert, Friedrich Wilhelm: A Memoir of Baron Overberg, with a Short Account of the System of National Education in Prussia, from the German of Professor Schubert. London: Seeley 1838.
[Sherer, Joseph Moyle]: Notes and Reflections During a Ramble in Germany. London: Longman, Rees, Orme, Brown, and Green 1826.
Smith, Thomas F. A.: The Soul of Germany. London: Hutchinson 1916.
Staël, Anne-Louise-Germaine Necker: Germany. London: Murray 1814.
Tower, Charles: Germany of To-day. London: Williams and Norgate n. d. [1914].
Trollope, Frances: Belgium and Western Germany in 1833. Vol. 1. 2. London: Murray 1834.
Vizetelly, Henry: Berlin under the New Empire. Vol. 1. 2. London: Tinsley 1879.
Wiener, Peter F.: German With Tears. London: The Cresset Press 1942.
Wolf, A[braham]: Higher Education in Nazi Germany, or Education for World-Conquest. London: Methuen 1944.
Ziemer, Gregor: Education for Death. London: Constable 1942.

Gründung und Gestaltung der „Deutschen Sektion" des „Weltbunds für Erneuerung der Erziehung" (1921 bis 1931) – Ein bildungspolitisch bedeutsames Kapitel der internationalen Reformpädagogik

Hermann Röhrs

Die Anfänge

Die Gründung der deutschen Sektion des „Weltbundes für Erneuerung der Erziehung", wie die deutsche Gruppe der „New Education Fellowship" sich nennt, wird in mehreren Schritten vollzogen; sie erstreckt sich über ein volles Jahrzehnt von 1921 bis 1931. Es handelt sich um eine schöpferische Epoche, die eine pädagogische Neubesinnung mit der Planung und Konzeptualisierung verbindet. Die Reformpädagogik hatte ihre Probe aufs Exempel seit 1890 in vielen verheißungsvollen Ansätzen bestanden, und die geweckten Hoffnungen schienen nicht unberechtigt, daß die pädagogische Praxis und Reflexion in produktiver Wechselwirkung ein tragfähiges Fundament für die zukünftige Entwicklung sichern könnten. Namen wie John Dewey, Michael Sadler, Maria Montessori, Adolphe Ferrière, Paul Geheeb und viele andere weckten im pädagogischen Raum die Zuversicht, daß die Neue Erziehung auch eine sozial gerechtere Welt erwirken könnte. Daß alle diese Pädagogen der „New Education Fellowship" als dem neuen Forum zur Markierung eines Wendepunkts entscheidend verbunden waren, stärkte die Überzeugung, daß mit dem „Weltbund" eine neue Ära beginne, die darum bedeutsam werden könne, weil sie über die Ländergrenzen hinweg international eingeleitet worden war.

Ein erster vorbereitender Schritt hinsichtlich der Gründung einer deutschen Sektion erfolgte während der Konferenz in Calais; sie fand im August 1921 auf Grund einer Initiative der englischen „New Education Fellowship" unter Beatrice Ensor – unterstützt durch die „World Association for Adult Education" und das „Institut Jean-Jacques Rousseau" in Genf – statt. Das Thema der Konferenz lautete „The Creative Self-Expression of the Child". In Calais wurde in Erweiterung der „Fellowship" der „Internationale Arbeitskreis für Erneuerung der Erziehung" (Ligue Internationale pour l'Éducation Nouvelle) gegründet; Elisabeth Rotten wurde gebeten, die „Deutsche Mittelstelle" dieses Arbeitskreises aufzubauen *(Rotten 1930a)*. Wenn seither wiederholt von der deutschen Sektion gesprochen wird, so ist dies eine informelle Sprachregelung; bis zu ihrer offiziellen Konstituierung war es noch ein beschwerlicher Weg.

Unterstützt wurde dieser Prozeß durch die Gründung der Zeitschrift „Das Werdende Zeitalter", deren Herausgeber Elisabeth Rotten und Karl Wilker sind. Der internationale Charakter der Zeitschrift kommt darin zum Ausdruck, daß auf dem Titelbild zugleich die englische Ausgabe mit den Herausgebern Beatrice Ensor und A. S. Neill sowie die französische Ausgabe mit Adolphe Ferrière angegeben werden (seit Jahrgang 1, 1922). Die Zeitschrift war zunächst dem Organ „Die Neue Erziehung" – herausgegeben von Paul Oestreich und Siegfried Kawerau – beigeheftet, was wegen der verwandten Zielsetzung konfliktfrei möglich war. Sie schließt aber bereits an die Tradition der „Internationalen Erziehungsrundschau" an, die der Abteilung der „Deutschen Liga für den Völkerbund" diente, einem speziellen Aufgabenfeld von Elisabeth *Rotten (1922, S. 6).*

In Calais wurde beschlossen, die drei „Schwesterzeitschriften" – „Das Werdende Zeitalter", „The New Era", „Pour l'Ère Nouvelle" – so kooperativ zu gestalten, daß die Redaktionen in London, Berlin und Genf eine gemeinsame Strategie verfolgen, die zum Austausch bzw. zur Übersetzung des einen oder anderen Beitrags führen kann. Als Ergebnis zeigt sich eine gewisse Verwandtschaft der Organe in Anlage und Gestaltung im Dienste der internationalen Reformpädagogik. Wer das breite Spektrum neu erscheinender pädagogischer Zeitschriften analysiert, der wird feststellen, daß sie in der Thematik und inhaltlichen Darstellung auf die Fragen der Bildungsreform mit den flankierenden Themen einer Humanisierung der Schule, Gestaltung der Friedenserziehung und Stärkung der Soziabilität so streng ausgerichtet sind wie nie zuvor und auch später nicht wieder. Diese Feststellung gilt in erster Linie von den Zeitschriften des Weltbundes.

Die treibende Kraft während des gesamten Jahrzehnts der Entfaltung einer deutschen Sektion ist Rotten; sie vertritt die pädagogischen Interessen der deutschen Seite, sie aktiviert und motiviert mögliche Mitstreiter und sie stellt die internationalen Kontakte her; darin wird sie von Wilker unterstützt, der seit der ersten Stunde ein Vertreter der Neuen Erziehung ist; bereits seit Erscheinen der „Neuen Erziehung" 1919 publiziert er über sein Spezialgebiet „Pädagogik der geistig und sittlich Abnormen" *(Wilker 1919).*

Die Vorbereitung einer formellen Gründung der deutschen Sektion des „Weltbundes" beschäftigt seit Calais die Konferenzen der deutschen Gruppe. Ein Meilenstein auf diesem Wege ist die Konferenz 1925 in Heidelberg unter der Thematik „Die Befreiung der schöpferischen Kräfte im Kinde". Sie zeigt zum ersten Mal das pädagogische Profil der deutschen Gruppe um Martin Buber, einem ihrer geistigen Gründungsväter. Die Rede Bubers in Heidelberg „Über das Erzieherische" hat wegweisend für die weitere Arbeit gewirkt. Einen wichtigen Zwischenschritt im Hinblick auf eine Lösung bildet die internationale Konferenz in Helsingör 1930. Erich Weniger, der seit 1929 im Weltbund mitwirkt, hat in Helsingör das Referat „Philosophie der Neuen Erziehung" gehalten, um das er von Rotten und anderen Mitgliedern nachdrücklich gebeten wurde. Gerade die rationalere Argumentationsweise Wenigers wirkte klärend und war geeignet, einen weiteren Kreis anzusprechen. Die Kommunikation wurde seit den in Helsingör vermittelten Impulsen lebhafter. Damals wurde von William Lottig der Begriff der „spezifischen Weltbundgeistigkeit" geprägt, auf den man sich seither gern berief. Aber es entstanden auch die ersten ernsthaften Konflikte – insbesondere zwischen Fritz Karsen und Rotten.

Wer die Protokolle – und vor allem den Briefwechsel der Sprecher der Neuen Erziehung – liest, dem kann nicht entgehen, daß seit der Ausweitung des Kreises eine vorsichtig kaschierte Tendenz spürbar wird, die Kompetenzen von Rotten zu reduzieren und sie von den Entscheidungsgremien fernzuhalten. Dafür gibt es mehrere Gründe. Einmal ist Rotten, trotz ihrer freundlich entgegenkommenden Art, ein gewisser autokratischer Stil eigen. Als ein Beispiel mag die 1928 aus verwandten Gründen erfolgte Aufkündigung der Mitarbeit durch Paul und Edith Geheeb, den überaus treuen Gefolgsleuten des Weltbunds und Rottens, angeführt werden. Nach einem Hinweis auf den autokratischen Stil Rottens sowie deren „Unsachlichkeit" folgt die Entscheidung: *„Hiermit hätte ich im Grunde das Wesentliche gesagt, was meine Frau und mich hindert, weiterhin mit Ihnen zu gehen, obgleich die Sache der New Education Fellowship wohl immer die wichtigste Angelegenheit auf der Welt bleiben wird"* (Brief an Elisabeth Rotten vom 3. März 1931, *Geheeb 1970, S. 136*).

Elisabeth Rotten hat schwer an den Konflikten und insbesondere an dem Bruch mit den Geheebs getragen. Nicht zuletzt unter dem Eindruck dieser Erfahrungen entsteht 1930 ein (gemeinsam mit Wilker geschriebener) Aufsatz: „Weltanschauung oder nicht?". Darin wird die durch die Auseinandersetzungen wichtig gewordene Frage aufgeworfen, ob das Wirken im Rahmen der „New Education Fellowship" an eine besondere Weltanschauung gebunden sei. Nach einer Verneinung der Frage folgt das weltbündische Bekenntnis: *„Glauben wir an die schöpferische Kraft, die in der letzten Treue und Hingabe an die Aufgabe liegt!"* (Rotten/Wilker 1930, S. 7) Hinsichtlich des Stellenwerts dieser Anschauung wird auf die „kleine Tagung in Heppenheim im Frühjahr 1919" hingewiesen, die – unabhängig von der Gründung der „New Education Fellowship" – als die frühe Geburtsstunde dieser Auffassung bezeichnet werden kann. Das Konzept eines internationalen Gremiums und sein spezifischer Geist der Erneuerung des Menschen und der menschlichen Bezüge durch eine Neue Erziehung geht demnach auf die deutsche Gruppe um Rotten und Geheeb zurück; sie wäre somit älter als die „Fellowship" selber.

Diese zunächst als unbedeutsam erscheinende Anmerkung Rottens führt bei genauer Sichtung der Archivmaterialien auf einen Pädagogenkreis, der seit 1919 regelmäßig tagte und dessen Ziele in innerer Verwandtschaft mit denjenigen des Weltbunds auf eine Erneuerung des Erziehungswesens gerichtet sind. Dem in Heppenheim 1919 zusammenkommenden Kreis gehören 60 Teilnehmer an; darunter u. a. die folgenden Persönlichkeiten: Martin Buber, Paul Geheeb, Paul Natorp, Adolf Reichwein, Robert von Erdberg, Alfons Paquet, Johannes Langermann, Richard Benz, Otto Erdmann, Dr. Schultz-Hencke, Hermann Herrigel, Dr. Spira, Dr. Strecker.

Das Ziel der Heppenheimer Tagung, die durch weitere (u. a. 1920 in Wetzlar) fortgeführt wurde, ist die Gestaltung der Weltgemeinschaft durch eine Neue Erziehung. *„Damit dieser Weltgemeinschaftsgedanke wirklich verstanden und gepflegt wird, dazu bedarf es einer grundsätzlichen Erneuerung der Menschheit selbst wie sie die Erziehung im weitesten Sinne uns erreichen kann. Man kann, wie uns die Heppenheimer Tagung zeigte"* *(Koch 1920)*. Nochmals: Es zeigt sich eine übernationale Bündigkeit der Idee einer Erneuerung des Lebens und der Weltgemeinschaft durch Erziehung – insbesondere durch Friedenserziehung – bereits vor der Gründung der „Fellowship".

Die „Grundsätze"

Der Weltbund wurde 1921 auf Grund einer Initiative von Beatrice Ensor, einer Schulinspektorin und Leiterin der Freien Schule „Frensham Heights" in England, als „Fraternity in Education" – einer Erziehungsbruderschaft auf der Grundlage der Quäker-Philosophie in reformpädagogischer und zivilisationskritischer Absicht – gegründet. Der Weltbund konnte also 1996 auf eine 75jährige Geschichte zurückblicken. Er dürfte damit als internationale pädagogische Organisation eine der ältesten, wenn nicht gar die älteste pädagogische Vereinigung mit einem weltweit wirksamen Programm sein.

Das Grundmotiv der Fellowship „Entfaltung der schöpferischen Kräfte im Kinde" wirkte wie ein pädagogischer Aufruf und löste bei allen einen pädagogischen Missionierungswillen aus. Das Kind als potentieller Neubeginn des Lebens, das daher jederzeit eine Erneuerung von Lebensziel und -inhalt eröffnet, war die Substanz der Botschaft; sie vermochte eine weltumgreifende Bewegung in Gang zu setzen. Sie wurde wie so oft in der Bildungsgeschichte vielfältig ergänzt durch flankierende Bestrebungen – etwa die Entfaltung einer Kinder- und Entwicklungspsychologie.

Die offene Gründungssituation in der „New Education Fellowship", der die pädagogische Wirksamkeit und Kooperation wichtiger war als formelle Regularien, führte bald zur Mitarbeit deutscher Repräsentanten. So gehörte Rotten bereits früh zu den Gesprächspartnern des Londoner Kreises. Seit der internationalen Konferenz von Calais 1921 nahm eine deutsche Gruppe teil, die lebhaft Inhalt und Methode der Konferenz zu diskutieren begann. Der Zusammenhang blieb informell; es sollte ein „äußerst elastisches Band" zwischen Weltbund und Mitgliedern sowie darüber hinaus zu den internationalen Gruppierungen geschaffen werden. Eine sozialpolitische Toleranz nach innen und außen ist kennzeichnend für den Geist der Fellowship.

Das Ziel wurde jedoch bald die Gründung einer deutschen Sektion, die aus der Sicht der spezifisch deutschen Bildungsproblematik einen Beitrag zu den internationalen Konferenzen zu formulieren vermöchte. Dazu wurden seit 1922 die „Grundsätze" formuliert. Sie wurden regelmäßig zur Information und Werbung in der Zeitschrift „Das Werdende Zeitalter" publiziert. Diese „Grundsätze" repräsentieren weitgehend den Geist der Reformpädagogik, wie er sich nach den ersten beiden Entwicklungsphasen im begonnenen internationalen Gespräch zu manifestieren begann. Unter diesem Aspekt seien die „Grundsätze" vorgestellt:

1. Grundsatz: *„Das wesentliche Ziel aller Erziehung sollte sein, das Kind bereit zu machen, die Überlegenheit des Geistes über das Stoffliche zu erkennen und der Verwirklichung dieses Geistes im täglichen Leben zu dienen. Daher muß die Erneuerung der Erziehung – welche Gesichtspunkte der Erzieher im übrigen haben möge – nur bestrebt sein, die geistige Kraft im Kinde zu wahren – und zu erhöhen."*

Die geistige Kraft als die orientierende Mitte für die kindliche Entfaltung zu deklarieren, mag als zentraler Programmpunkt des „Weltbunds", dem gern ein emotional bestimmter Internationalismus und eine ideologisch verbrämte Kinderphilosophie unterstellt wird, allseitig Erstaunen auszulösen. Hinsichtlich des speziellen Falles ist zu sagen, daß der sich bildende Arbeitskreis, in dem viele Repräsentanten der Hamburger Versuchsschularbeit vertreten waren, trotz aller Passionsbereitschaft und -fähigkeit in seiner pädagogischen Grundeinstellung erstaunlich rational argumentierte. Darüber hinaus ist festzustellen, daß die Formulierung von der Wahrung und Erhöhung der „geistigen Kraft im Kinde" auch eine vorsichtige Ausgrenzung aus der Kindesmythologie im begonnenen „Jahrhundert des Kindes" bedeutet. Die Förderung der geistigen Kräfte geschieht nicht nur kognitiv durch den Unterricht, sondern ebenbürtig durch das gestaltende Schaffen, das neben dem Werken auch das kreative Gestalten im Medium künstlerischer Aktivitäten einschließt. Der „Urhebertrieb", wie ihn Buber in seiner großen Rede auf dem Heidelberger Kongreß 1925 gedeutet hat, umfaßt daher Geist, Schaffen und künstlerisches Gestalten in einem erzieherischen Prozeß, wobei die geistige Grundkraft als das spezifische Humanum die ordnende Mitte verkörpert. Buber hat übrigens dem Weltbund und insbesondere dem Hamburger Gesprächskreis stets nahegestanden; er gehörte neben Paul Geheeb von Anbeginn zu dem Mitarbeiterkeis der Zeitschrift „Das Werdende Zeitalter".

2. Grundsatz: *„Dies ist besonders wichtig für die Frage der Disziplin. Der Erzieher muß sich ehrfürchtig in die Eigenart des Kindes einleben und eingedenk sein, daß seine besonderen Kräfte sich nur entfalten können unter einer von innen nach außen wirkenden Disziplin, die den geistig-seelischen Fähigkeiten des Kindes vollen Spielraum läßt."*

Wer die Weckung und Förderung der geistigen Grundkräfte als ersten pädagogischen Grundsatz befürwortet, der kann nur auf die *innere* Disziplin bauen. Innere Disziplin reift im sozialen Miteinander unter der Prägekraft des freie Nachfolge erwartenden Vorbildes. Sie ist primär Erziehung (und nicht Dressur), wie auch der zu Erziehende von Geburt an vom Geist geleiteter Mensch ist – trotz vieler zunächst vorherrschender Reflexe und Triebe.

3. Grundsatz: *„Alle Erziehung in Schulen von diesem neuen Typus sollte den in der Kinderseele erwachenden Interessen gerecht werden. Dies gilt für die Bildung von Charakter und Gefühlsleben so gut, wie von der Übermittlung von Kenntnissen. Der Lehrplan sollte allen diesen Interessen ein Betätigungsfeld bieten, sei es, daß einzelne Arbeitsgebiete den intellektuellen oder künstlerischen, sozialen oder anderen Impulsen besonders entgegenkommen, sei es, daß eine Synthese etwa in einer organisch eingegliederten handwerklichen Ausbildung gefunden wird."*

Angestrebt wird eine lehrplantheoretische Synthese, die eine schöpferische Einheit zwischen Kenntnisvermittlung sowie künstlerischen und sozialen Bewährungsfeldern anstrebt. Ziel ist eine lebendige Schule, die aus dem Miteinander heraus die Initiativen für das Lernen in intellektueller sowie sozial-emotionaler Hinsicht freisetzt. Darin zeigt sich das Profil einer reformpädagogischen Institution, die das spezifisch „Schulische" durch ein klassenübergreifendes Gemeinschaftsleben zu ersetzen versucht.

4. Grundsatz: *„Die Schulgemeinde als ein Ganzes sollte gemeinsam von den Kindern und Erwachsenen gebildet und verwaltet werden. Die Selbstverwaltung und die Selbstzucht, in der jedes Kind gestärkt werde, müssen das klare Ziel haben, durch freie Einordnung in das Lebensganze eine auf äußere Mittel gestützte Autorität überflüssig zu machen."*

Das Konzept der Schulgemeinde als Kooperationsfeld zwischen Schülern, Lehrern, Eltern und Mitgliedern der politischen Gemeinde ist das Ziel einer lebendigen Schule. Verwirklicht ist sie einmal in Deweys Idee der Schule als „embryonic community life", die einen überzeugenden Ausdruck in den Experimentierschulen fand, die von John und Evelyn Dewey in „Schools of Tomorrow" 1915 dargestellt werden, und zum anderen in den Hamburger Versuchsschulen, die die Mitglieder des Weltbunds lebendig vor Augen haben. Das Konzept der Schulgemeinde gewährleistet die wechselseitige Durchdringung von geistig-sittlicher und künstlerisch-sozialer Arbeit in einem für alle gestaltbaren Bewährungsfeld. Sie wird zu einem Exempel für die Wirksamkeit, der inneren Autorität, die jedem seinem reifenden Urteilsvermögen und seiner fachlichen Kompetenz entsprechend Selbsttätigkeit und Freiheit einräumt.

5. Grundsatz: *„Der neue Geist der Erziehung wirkt sich vor allem darin aus, daß er selbstsüchtigem Wettbewerb keinen Raum gibt und daß beim Kinde an seine Stelle der Sinn für gemeinsames Schaffen tritt, aus dem heraus es lernt, sich freiwillig einzuordnen in den Dienst der Gemeinschaft."*

Der „neue Geist der Erziehung" ist geprägt von dem reformpädagogischen Erfahrungsschatz, wie er im Rahmen der weltweiten Reformbewegung als pädagogische Essenz gewonnen und im internationalen Gespräch seine weitere Klärung findet. Trotz aller differenzierenden Abwägung des pädagogisch Notwendigen hinsichtlich der besonders begabten Kinder und den aus den verschiedensten Gründen speziell förderungsbedürftigen Menschen hat dem Weltbund stets eine Gemeinschaftserziehung vorgeschwebt, deren Legitimität sich aus der pädagogischen Verantwortbarkeit herleitet. Die Achtung vor dem Humanum in jeder Gestalt bleibt das Grundgebot. „Learning by living" ist dazu das Leitmotiv, das in nahezu allen internationalen Konferenzen anklingt; es kennzeichnet zugleich die Richtung, die hier pädagogisch intendiert wird.

6. Grundsatz: *„Der Weltbund tritt im vollen Umfange für Gemeinschaftserziehung im eigentlichen Sinne des Wortes ein, also auch für das Miteinander der Geschlechter, sowohl außerhalb als innerhalb der Klasse, wobei beide Geschlechter vollauf ihre Eigenart entfalten und wohltätigen und ergänzenden Einfluß aufeinander ausüben können."*

Koedukation und Koinstruktion sind das Ziel, das indessen weniger von einem emanzipatorischen Geist als von gegenseitiger Achtung vor der Eigenform des anderen Geschlechts bestimmt ist. Das Bei- und Miteinander soll daher weniger von Wetteifer und einer Sucht nach Selbstbestätigung zeugen als von dem steten Erleben einer natürlichen Gemeinschaft, die erst im Respekt vor dem Verschiedenen das Gemeinsame erfahren läßt.

7. Grundsatz: *„Eine in diesem Sinne erneuernde und verwirklichende Erziehung wird im Kinde nicht nur den künftigen Gemeindebürger, Volksgenossen und Weltbürger bilden, der seinen Dienst für den Nächsten, für sein Volk und die Menschheit erfüllt; er wird auch den Menschen in ihm befreien, der, seines eigenen Menschentums bewußt, dieses in jedem anderen ehrt."*

Die 'global vision' – eingebunden in eine pädagogische Verantwortbarkeit hinsichtlich der internationalen Entwicklung – ist die (alle weiteren Maximen) übergreifende Einstellung des Weltbundes geblieben. Die Ermöglichung der internationalen Begegnung und des lebendigen Erfahrungsaustausches soll gewährleisten, daß die internationale Verständigung im pädagogischen Rahmen angesichts der realen Aufgabenstellung beispielhaft wird und die Möglichkeit zur Kooperation eröffnet.

Erich Weniger, der erste Vorsitzende der konstituierten Deutschen Sektion

Die lange Gründungssituation mußte zu Konflikten führen. Äußerlich schien der Auslöser die Dualität der Gremien – Mittelstelle und Deutsche Sektion – zu sein, die eine hinhaltende Wirkung ausübte. Faktisch wurde sie häufig als ein taktisches Instrumentarium von Elisabeth Rotten genutzt. Objektiv steht dahinter die Sorge, daß die ursprüngliche Konzeption des Weltbunds eine Verfremdung durch den Einbezug zu vieler Repräsentanten der offiziellen Pädagogik erfahren könnte.

Da der Führungsstil nicht völlig unabhängig von dem Erfolg der Sektionsbildung ist, soll noch ein letztes Wort darüber geäußert werden. Die Kritik ist auch von anderen Seiten geübt worden. Bei dem sanften „Paulus" (Geheeb) ist sie nicht sonderlich vorsichtig gegenüber mehreren Personen zum Ausdruck gekommen. So nennt er in Briefen die „Mittelstelle" um Rotten distanzierend wiederholt die „Clique"; so noch 1931 in einem Brief an Carl H. Becker mit dem kritischen Hinweis: *„gegen den Autokratismus jener Frau komme ich nicht an"* (Brief vom 2. März 1931. *Nachlaß Carl H. Becker*). An Mrs. B. Ensor, in deren Freier Schule „Frensham Heights" er 1928 mehrere Wochen weilte, während sie die Odenwaldschule später ebenfalls besuchte, schreibt Geheeb 1928 nach Abwägung mehrerer Möglichkeiten, um Rotten und Wilker zum Rücktritt zu bewegen: *„Much better would I think it if you, who are above all trifles and who know the development of the organisation in all Countries, would correspond with them about the necessity of their resigning."* Als geeigneten Kandidaten nennt er Becker, den Preußischen Kultusminister, der vermutlich aufgrund politischer Schwierigkeiten zum Rücktritt veranlaßt werden könnte: *„I shall try at once to win him for a leading post in the German Section"* (Brief an Beatrice Ensor vom 21. Dezember 1928, *Geheeb 1970, S. 128-129*).

Übersehen werden darf darüber jedoch nicht das große historisch bleibende Verdienst dieser Frau in einer Welt der Männer, in der während der Nachkriegszeit immer noch die autoritären Entscheidungsstrukturen vorherrschten; sie hat eine breite Bewegung im Dienste der Neuen Erziehung sowie der pädagogischen Friedenssicherung ohne ein besonderes politisches Mandat geschaffen.

Offenkundig wird der Gegensatz durch einen Rundbrief von J. M. Mack – einem verdienstvollen Schulmann, der viele Jahre im Stuttgarter Raum wirkte und in Senat in Holstein in einem Schloß ein Erziehungsheim aufbaute – vom 18. Februar 1932, in dem er kritisiert, daß die neuere Entwicklung zu einer Einschränkung des Einflusses von Rotten führe. Rotten wiederum nimmt diesen Brief 1930 zum Anlaß zu einer offenen Aussprache in einem Rundschreiben. Darin versteht sie – trotz der sehr persönlichen Form und der Parteinahme in dem Mack-Brief –, den sachlichen Kern herauszuheben: *„Mit der Sache meinte ich und meinte wohl auch Mack etwa das, was William Lottig kürzlich in einem Privatbrief an mich als die spezifische Weltbundgeistigkeit bezeichnete"* (Rotten 1930b). Damit ist die ursprüngliche pädagogische Passion gemeint, die in einem durchaus originären Anschluß an die Reformpädagogik eine Erneuerung des Bildungswesens im Geiste der Internationalität und der Friedensliebe anstrebt. Die offizielle Erziehungswissenschaft war an diesem Prozeß durchaus beteiligt, jedoch als wissenschaftlicher Sicherungsfaktor und keineswegs in einer Führungsrolle. Die Befürchtung richtet sich gegen die Brechung des pädagogischen Elans durch eine mögliche Szientifizierung der Bewegung mit dem Effekt einer Formalisierung, die wiederum zu einem Verlust des Spezifikums des Weltbundgeistes führen kann.

Daß es sich jedoch um die Frage einer klugen Einstimmung der neuen Gruppierung unter dem Aspekt der Kooperationsbereitschaft und -fähigkeit handelt, die nur durch Fortführung des Gesprächs erreicht werden kann, wird aus der abschließenden Stellungnahme Wenigers zum Rundbrief Macks und zur Affäre um Fritz Karsen ersichtlich. Der Weniger-Brief vom März/April 1930 soll in einer geschlossenen Partie zur Sprache kommen, weil er die Unterschiedlichkeit – nicht Gegensätzlichkeit – der Denk- und Argumentationsweise der Positionen einsichtig werden läßt: *"Ich möchte scheiden zwischen der formellen und sachlichen Seite des Streites. Zum Formalen ist die Lage, daß das Verhalten der Mittelstelle doch nicht ganz einwandfrei war und daß dabei Herr Karsen und ich mit verschiedenem Maß gemessen sind. Ich sagte ja schon in der Versammlung [in Helsingör], daß ich es nicht für richtig ansehen könnte, wenn man Kritiker, die zufällig in einer zufälligen Versammlung das Wort ergreifen, dann gleich in einen Ausschuß hineinwählt, der so zentrale Angelegenheiten zu behandeln hat. Das bewog mich damals abzulehnen. Darauf wurden wir beide gebeten, als Gäste an den Sitzungen teilzunehmen. Daß Herr Karsen dann zu der ersten Sitzung nicht erschien, konnte doch nicht ohne weiteres gegen ihn ausgelegt werden und erst in einer ganz offiziellen Sitzung hätte entschieden werden können, ob die deutsche Sektion uns weiter zu den Beratungen hinzuziehen wollte. Dagegen war es falsch, die Kompetenz der Versammlung zu dieser Wahl anzuzweifeln, mich aber dabei zu lassen. Die großen sachlichen Meinungsverschiedenheiten würden ja zweifellos bei der ersten offiziellen Sitzung herausgekommen sein und man hätte dann im Frieden auseinander gehen können"* (Brief nachträglich datiert März/April 1930, Weniger-Briefe).

Aus dem Brief spricht eine rational bestimmte Humanität, die auf Transparenz der Vorgehensweisen, selbst in Fällen scheinbarer Formverletzungen, dringt. In dieser Einstellung geht Weniger auf die Kritik Macks ein, indem er darauf hinweist, daß er seine Tätigkeit im Rahmen der Deutschen Gruppe erst nach langen zaudernden Überlegungen auf weiteres Bitten angenommen hatte, was auch von weiteren Mitgliedern gelte. Nach dieser Klarstellung stellt er ausdrücklich seinen *"Auftrag zur Mitarbeit wieder zur Verfügung"*.

Trotz dieser (aus der Sicht Wenigers) nicht unberechtigten Bedenken nimmt er nach weiteren Verständigungsbemühungen seine Arbeit als Mitglied der Deutschen Gruppe wieder auf, weil er die große Bedeutung des vom Weltbund geschaffenen Forums zur

Darstellung der deutschen pädagogischen Lage im Rahmen der internationalen Entwicklung richtig einschätzt.

In Helsingör war vorgeschlagen worden, einen „Freundesrat" mit dem Ziel zu bilden, das pädagogische Gespräch im Sinne der Sektionsbildung kontinuierlich zu führen. Als ein Ergebnis wurde am 4. März 1930 eine Bezirksgruppe unter dem Namen: „Weltbund für Erneuerung der Erziehung. Deutsche Sektion. Bezirksgruppe Norden. Sitz Hamburg" gegründet. In der Satzung wird als Zweck der Vereinigung angegeben, *„... für die Erziehungsbewegung der Gegenwart einzutreten, insbesondere für die deutsche pädagogische Bewegung und ihr Zusammenwirken mit der Weltbewegung, wie sie der 'Weltbund für Erneuerung der Erziehung' zu erfassen sucht."* Zum Vorsitzenden wurde Otto Wommelsdorf und zum Geschäftsführer Julius Gebhard gewählt *(Gebhard 1930)*.

Ein ganz entscheidender Erfolg war der Beitritt des Hamburger Lehrervereins – der traditionsreichen „Gesellschaft der Freunde des Vaterländischen Unterrichts- und Erziehungswesens" – am 5. Mai 1930 zur Deutschen Gruppe als körperschaftliches Mitglied. Während einer weiteren Sitzung im Januar 1931 kam es zur Gründung einer regionalen Gruppe mit Sitz in Hamburg. Dem vorbereitenden Ausschuß gehörten die folgenden Persönlichkeiten an: Martha Muchow, Julius Gebhard und Otto Wommelsdorf sowie Wilhelm Flitner, Erich Weniger, Kurt Zeidler, Paula Grau, William Lottig, Heinrich Sahrhage und Dr. Herz. Die Gründung der regionalen Gruppe mit Sitz Hamburg hat aufgrund einer ersten Konzentration der Kräfte die eigentliche Sektionsgründung entscheidend vorbereitet.

Diese Entwicklung wurde durch zwei Umstände indirekt erleichtert. Einmal bildeten die Hamburger Versuchsschulen für den internationalen Kreis der Mitglieder der „New Education Fellowship" einen wichtigen reformpädagogischen Orientierungsrahmen. Wer sich über den Entwicklungsstand der Bildungsreform – insbesondere im staatlichen Sektor – informieren wollte, der setzte sich mit den Hamburger Versuchsschulen auseinander. Die Repräsentanten dieser Schulen waren gern gesehene Redner auf den Konferenzen der „New Education Fellowship": so z. B. William Lottig, Senator Krause und Wilhelm Paulsen 1927 in Locarno, letzterer auch 1929 in Helsingör. Heinrich *Landahl (1932)* konnte noch einen Artikel über die Lichtwark-Schule in der „New Era" publizieren. Daher ist es naheliegend, daß Hamburg zu einem Sammelpunkt auf dem Entwicklungsgang zu einer deutschen Sektion des Weltbundes wurde. Da Weniger während dieser Jahre Direktor der Pädagogischen Akademie in Altona war, gehörte er zu diesem Kreise.

Der zweite entscheidende Schritt zur Gründung einer „Deutschen Sektion" wird 1931 während einer Konferenz in Dortmund unter dem Thema „Die Lebenswelt des Kindes unserer Zeit" vollzogen. Den öffentlichen Vortrag hielt Leo Weismantel. Besonders große Resonanz fand der Beitrag von Martha Muchow, die es verstand, auf dem Hintergrund ihrer eigenen Forschungen und unter Berücksichtigung der Probleme des industriellen Umfeldes in Dortmund das bedrängende Problem des Verhältnisses von „Kind und Umwelt" in erzieherischer Hinsicht zu behandeln.

Während der Mitgliederversammlung in Dortmund wurde am 3. Oktober 1931 die deutsche Sektion des „Weltbundes für Erneuerung der Erziehung" formell gegründet. Der von der Hamburger Gruppe formulierte Entwurf einer Satzung wurde angenommen. Als Mitglieder des Vorstands wurden die folgenden Persönlichkeiten gewählt: Carl Heinrich Becker (Berlin), Julius Gebhard (Hamburg), Friedrich Schieker (Stuttgart), Kurt Sonntag (Wandsbek bei Hamburg), Robert Ulich (Dresden), Leo Weismantel (Marktbreit am Main), Erich Weniger (Altona). Zum erweiterten Vorstand gehörten u. a. Elisabeth Rotten (Dresden-Hellerau) und Martha Muchow (Hamburg). Zum ersten Vorsitzenden wurde Weniger und zum Geschäftsführer Gebhard gewählt *(Gebhard 1931)*.

Eine weitere wichtige Aufgabe des in Helsingör gebildeten Ausschusses war die Kontaktaufnahme mit bereits bestehenden Kreisen – so beispielsweise mit dem Hohenrodter Bund. Der Plan wurde aufgegriffen, nachdem Weniger während eines Treffens im Januar 1930 in Hamburg nochmals daran erinnert hatte. Die großen Vorbehalte – insbesondere von Seiten Theodor Bäuerles – gegen eine derartige Kooperation gehen aus dem Briefwechsel hervor, den Weniger, aber auch Becker, der wiederholt nachdrücklich um Mitwirkung gebeten wurde, geführt haben. Die grundsätzlichen Absichten hat Weniger in einem Brief vom 19. Juli 1930 an Bäuerle beschrieben: *„Der Kreis hat Nohl, Flitner und mir die entscheidenden Stellen in seinem Rat angeboten und hofft, auf diese Weise eine breitere und politisch neutralere Basis zu gewinnen und ein Gesicht, das der wirklichen Lage in Deutschland besser entspricht. Für uns ist nun die schwere Frage, ob die Sache es wert ist, daß sie von unseren Händen getragen wird. Und zwar ist das vor allen Dingen eine Frage der innerdeutschen Kulturpolitik."* Und er fügt hoffnungsvoll und vielleicht auch ermutigend hinzu: *„Vom Nohl-Kreis werden jedenfalls Nohl, Flitner und ich mitmachen"* *(Weniger-Briefe)*.

Wie stark die Gegensätze dennoch zwischen den Positionen sind, zeigt ein langer und grundsätzlicher Brief von Weismantel 1930 an Staatsminister Becker; der Brief läßt, trotz der emsigen Verständigungsversuche, die immanenten Vorbehalte deutlich werden.

Da es sich um ein überzeitlich bedeutsames Problem handelt, soll die Aussage geschlossen angeführt werden: *„Es wird sehr gut sein, wenn die akademischen Theoretiker auf diesem Weltkongress erscheinen, aber was echt und gut an ihnen ist, wird auf diesen Kongressen von der gewaltigen pädagogischen Not, die da ist, erst einmal zusammenbrechen müssen. Die kristallklare Theorie, die uns so blendend von den Kathedern zukommt, kann hier nur ihre Unverbundenheit mit den wirklichen Lebensnöten erfahren. Dann wird sich zeigen, wer von ihnen in der Lage ist, die unnütze gelehrte Philosophie ü b e r die Erziehung – eine Philosophie, die doch der ganze Stolz unserer Gelehrten ist – fahren zu lassen und sich in die Reihe der von der Not Befallenen einzufügen. Der Führer und Retter steigt aus dem Volk der Not, er kommt nicht vom Katheder. Der Weg, den wir anzustreben haben, ist der umgekehrte; von dort her zum Katheder. ... Uns Pädagogen der Praxis kann kein Theoretiker erlösen. Aber das staatliche Bildungswesen ist in der Hand der Theoretiker überall in aller Welt. So geht der Kampf darum, daß entweder Theoretiker und Praktiker einander vollständig ablehnen oder aber sie erfahren an einander eine Veränderung. Hier fallen die kulturpolitischen Schicksalsentscheidungen der Völker und auch die Schicksalsentscheidungen innerhalb unseres eigenen Volkes. So halte ich es für begrüßenswert und für ein Glück, daß diese beiden Gruppen sich aufeinander bewegen, sich an den gleichen Tisch setzen, einander anhören. Und gelänge es Ihnen, sehr verehrter Herr Staatsminister, diese Bewegung der Kräfte dadurch zu einer dauernden zu machen, daß Sie den Vorsitz in diesem Kreis der Geister übernehmen, so wäre dies ein großer Gewinn"* (Weniger-Briefe).

Auf diese vermeintliche Gegensätzlichkeit der Positionen geht Weniger in einem Brief vom 19. Mai 1931 an Ministerialrat Becker, der der Deutschen Mittelstelle nahesteht, klärend ein, indem er die Auffassung der Theoretiker (aus seiner Sicht) präzisiert und das Verhältnis Theorie – Praxis relativiert: *„Es ist von uns nicht beabsichtigt, eine Diktatur für die deutsche Abteilung des Weltbundes zu errichten oder den Weltbund an uns zu reißen oder sonst etwas Schönes zu machen. Sondern in einer bestimmten Schwierigkeit der Deutschen Sektion haben wir auf wiederholtes Drängen und nach langem Zaudern unsere guten Dienste angeboten ... Noch weniger ist die Rede davon, eine Herrschaft der theoretischen Pädagogik oder einer ihrer Richtungen zu begründen. Die Antithese: schöne Theorie – notleidende Praxis, die Weismantel aufstellte, ist völlig falsch"* (Weniger-Briefe).

Nach eingehenden Bemühungen kam es schließlich zu einer Konferenz am 7. und 8. März 1930 in Marktbreit in der Schule der Volkschaft unter dem Vorsitz Wolfgang Pfleiderers. Die Diskussion im Kreise der 17 Teilnehmer wurde durch ein Referat Wenigers eingeleitet. Die (von Friedrich Paulsen übernommene) These des Referats besagt, daß die Erziehungsbewegung der Kulturbewegung erst in erheblichem Abstand folgt. Den bildungsreformerischen Bestrebungen ist es nach Weniger jedoch gelungen, die Distanz weitgehend aufzuheben, so daß der Reformbewegung unter diesem Aspekt eine große volkspädagogische Bedeutung zukommt. Dieses Argument schien eine gemeinsame Basis aufzuzeigen, und die Erörterung des Begriffs der pädagogischen Autonomie machte darüber hinaus bewußt, daß eine Kooperation zwar Gemeinsamkeit voraussetze, die jedoch keine Preisgabe der eigenen Position bedeute. Es wurde beschlossen, einen Rat zu bilden, der die internationalen Konferenzen und insbesondere Nizza eingehend vorbereiten sollte. Minister a. D. Becker wurde gebeten, dessen Vorsitz zu übernehmen.

Dem Rat gehörten die folgenden Persönlichkeiten an; sie wurden während einer Sitzung am 20. Juni 1931 in Berlin gewählt: Vorsitzender: Carl Heinrich Becker, stellvertretender Vorsitzender: Robert Ulich, Schriftführer: Ministerialrat Becker, Gertrud Bäumer, Aloys Fischer, Georg Kerschensteiner, Ernst Müller, Herman Nohl, Martha Schmidt, Friedrich Schneider, Pater S. J. Schröteler, Eduard Spranger[1], Heinrich Weinstock, Erich Weniger, Otto Wommelsdorff. (An der Sitzung nahmen nicht teil: Nohl, der sich entschuldigt hatte, ferner Kerschensteiner und Schneider, die erst auf der Sitzung hinzugewählt wurden). Ferner waren als Vertreter der Deutschen Sektion und der Deutschen Mittelstelle des Weltbundes für Erneuerung der Erziehung anwesend: Julius Gebhard, Martha Muchow, Elisabeth Rotten, Karl Wilker.

Erstaunlich an dieser Vorgeschichte ist das unverzagte Vorgehen Wenigers, der sich in dieser Haltung durch Carl H. Becker, ohne großartige Verständigungsversuche, gestärkt sah. Er schätzte Becker als eine gradlinige, aufrechte Persönlichkeit, der es um die Verbindung beider Seiten im Dienste einer wichtigen internationalen Aufgabe ging, die die pädagogische Entwicklung in Deutschland vielfältig zu fördern vermochte. Die immer noch offenkundigen pädagogischen Vorbehalte versuchte er durch einen Vortrag vor dem „Weltbund für Erneuerung der Erziehung" (Bezirksgruppe Norden) über „Aufbau einer positiven Pädagogik der Nothilfe" am 20. November 1931 in der von ihm geleiteten Pädagogischen Akademie in Altona zu überwinden bzw. zu mindern.

---

1 Eduard Spranger wird in der Liste zunächst nicht angeführt, da Bedenken geäußert wurden. Erst nach einem Einspruch Beckers, der aus der Optik des Auslands den Verzicht als nicht verantwortbar betrachtete, stimmte Spranger auf Anfrage Beckers zu *(Becker 1931)*.

Staatsminister a. D. Carl Heinrich Becker
als Repräsentant der Deutschen Sektion

Somit war der Kongreß in Nizza von der deutschen Sektion denkbar gründlich vorbereitet. Als Redner waren neben dem Grundsatzreferat von Becker zur Konferenzthematik „Education and Changing Society" u. a. Kerschensteiner, Fischer, Bäumer, Schneider, Ulich, Flitner, Martin Keilhacker, Karsen vorgesehen. Die 6. Weltkonferenz stand unter der Präsidentschaft von Paul Langevin (Collège de France), Vizepräsidenten waren Becker und Sir Percy Nunn (Universität London); der Letztere konnte wegen Krankheit nicht anwesend sein. Muchow gehörte weiterhin dem „International Organising Committee" an.

Die Überzeugung, daß ein „elastisches Band" den Weltbund am wirksamsten prägen werde, führte seit der Gründung dazu, daß auch Nichtmitglieder zu Kongreßvorträgen eingeladen wurden und daß verdienstvolle Repräsentanten der Reformpädagogik zu Präsidenten ernannt werden konnten, wie beispielsweise Sir Michael Sadler 1927 in England. Darin besteht gerade das lebendig Zukunftsweisende der Vereinigung. Fern einer unbeweglichen Organisation konnte ein überzeugendes Forum für jene entstehen, die aufgrund ihrer Pionierarbeit zu wegweisenden Sprechern der Reformbewegung geworden sind. Darin erblickt auch Friedrich Schneider in seinem grundsätzlichen Bericht über den Weltkongreß in Nizza 1932 die Bedeutung des Weltbunds, daß er nicht zu einer „erstarrten Organisation" wurde, sondern ein pädagogisch fruchtbarer Treffpunkt der Agenten der Reformbewegung blieb. Er faßt seine Erfahrungen in der generellen Aussage zusammen, daß die Nizzaer Konferenz als Ganzes genommen ein Erfolg war. Diese allgemeine Feststellung kommentiert er durch eine direkte Ansprache des Lesers: „*Und er überlege doch einmal, was das bedeutet: Viele hundert Pädagogen aus aller Welt sind vierzehn Tage lang in einer einheitlichen Atmosphäre zusammen, um sich mit brennenden pädagogischen Problemen zu beschäftigen. Viele unter ihnen haben die weite Reise und den 14tägigen Aufenthalt nur unter großen Opfern möglich gemacht. Bewundernswert waren Fleiß, Ausdauer und Interessiertheit der Teilnehmerscharen. Mochte die Wunderwelt der Riviera und in der tropischen Hitze der Badestrand locken, nur sehr wenige erlagen der Versuchung. Und selbst außerordentliche Ereignisse der Nizzaer Sommersaison, wie ein internationales Autorennen oder ein Festzug 'der Nacht in Weiß', störten die Konferenzveranstaltungen nicht*" (Schneider 1932-33, S. 305).

Der Kongreß in Nizza war kurz vor der Machtübernahme durch die Nationalsozialisten noch einmal eine internationale Sternstunde der deutschen Pädagogik – so haben es viele ausländische Kollegen empfunden, wie einige mir nach dem Kriege als letzte lebende Zeugen spontan mitteilten. Was ist daraus geworden? Becker mußte aus Krankheitsgründen vorzeitig von Nizza abreisen; er ist bereits am 10. Februar 1933 allzu früh in einer Zeit gestorben, die sich gegen sein pädagogisches Werk stellte. Die bedeutenden Ansätze zur Reform des Bildungswesens und der Lehrerbildung in Preußen wurden rückgängig gemacht. Ulich emigrierte nach Amerika und wurde ein hoch angesehener Hochschullehrer für Erziehungswissenschaft in Harvard, der weit über seinen breiten Schülerkreis hinaus 'Praeceptor Americae' genannt wurde. Erst im hohen Alter kehrte er 1976 nach Deutschland zurück, um hier zu sterben. Unmittelbar nach seiner Heimkehr ernannten wir ihn zum Ehrenmitglied der Deutschen Sektion. Darüber hat er sich sehr gefreut, weil ein Lebenskreis sich zu seiner Genugtuung schloß *(Röhrs 1995, S. 45)*. „Das Werdende Zeitalter", das zentrale Organ der „Deutschen Sektion" des Weltbunds, stellte bereits im Juli 1932 sein Erscheinen ein, weil die Schwierigkeiten wirtschaftlicher und politischer Art zunahmen. Elisabeth Rotten ging in die Schweiz. Martha Muchow, die Mitarbeiterin von William Stern, dem Vertreter der Psychologie an der Universität Hamburg, der dem Freundeskreis der „Deutschen Sektion" angehörte, verübte Selbstmord angesichts der unüberwindbaren Schwierigkeiten, die ihrem Lehrer und ihr bereitet wurden *(Röhrs 1990, S. 41)*. In der Anklageschrift der Universitätsbehörde spielte die Mitwirkung im Weltbund, der von den Nationalsozialisten als pazifistisch und sozialistisch verurteilt wurde, eine erhebliche Rolle. Somit hat der politische Bannstrahl des Nationalsozialismus die „Deutsche Sektion" weitgehend ausgelöscht.

Dennoch hat die Mitwirkung der „Deutschen Sektion" in Nizza bleibende Spuren hinterlassen. So konnten Becker und Ulich ihre pädagogischen Grundanschauungen 1932 im Oktoberheft der „New Era" vorstellen. Es ist vielfältig aufschlußreich, was Becker am Vorabend des von vielen – und sicherlich auch von ihm – befürchteten Machtwechsels als bildungspolitische Zielsetzung (auch im Sinne des Weltbunds) in dieser schwierigen Stunde im Ausland nannte. Eingangs beschreibt er die übernationale Struktur der europäischen Population: *„The Common basis of the European and American World is of Latino-Germanic origin with a strong Hebrew infiltration, and it possesses a development based on Christianity and on the civilization of the ancients. The Mohammedan world shares with us the Semitics strain, and also the heritage of Greece and Rome, and that is why it is nearer to us than the Indian and Chinese world."* Und nach einer Charakteristik der spezifischen Wertwelt der Nationen folgert er vorsichtig: *„Summarizing therefore I say that the nations are different, and that this diversity should be maintained. Just as we educate our children to be both individuals and good citizens, so the nations should re-*

main individual retaining as much of their peculiar talent as they can, in order to contribute to a collaborating community of human beings" (Becker 1932).

Diesem Ansatz entsprechend differenziert er die Kongreßthematik in seinem Vortrag „Der soziale Wandel und die Erziehung unter dem Gesichtspunkt der Verschiedenheit der Völker". Im Mittelpunkt steht die Erörterung der Frage: „Gibt es nun wirklich eine einheitliche Menschheit?"[2]

Schließlich sollen noch einige Worte aus dem „Gedenkartikel" von van der Leeuw im Namen der „Fellowship" anläßlich des Todes von Becker festgehalten werden: *„To all of us who attended the Nice Conference it came as a great shock to hear of the death of Dr. Becker, whose presence and work at that gathering has meant so much. To me, personally, it does not only mean the death of one for whose character and work I had a profound admiration, but it means the loss of a friend, who in the short time I knew him, became very dear to me ... Dr. Becker's death coincided with the history of the Nazi movement in Germany. Unfortunately, the educational activity of the government has, so far, been distinctly reactionary and nationalistic in the narrow sense ... Our next Educational Congress will miss his presence, but I am sure all of us will be aware of his memory when we meet again to continue the work for which he lived so nobly"* (van der *Leeuw 1933).*[3]

Diese Würdigung eines bedeutenden Mannes, der sich nicht scheute, über die ministerielle Ära hinaus sich in den mühevollen Dienst des Weltbundes sowie der verantwortungsvollen Vorbereitung und Gestaltung einer internationalen Konferenz zu stellen, läßt auch ein wenig Licht auf die „Deutsche Sektion" fallen. Daß alles am Beginn einer Weltkatastrophe geschah, die die „Deutsche Sektion" besonders hart traf, ist ein weiterer Grund für die Darstellung ihrer Geschichte. Eine besondere Tragik besteht darin, daß die vielen Bemühungen um eine Förderung und Vertiefung der Weltbundarbeit im Sinne einer internationalen Verständigung nicht zur Reife kommen konnten, weil die „Machtübernahme" durch die Nationalsozialisten am 30. Januar 1933 alles jäh zunichte machte und ins Gegenteil verkehrte.

---

2 Die Rede wurde, wie auch diejenigen aller anderen deutschen Redner, in deutscher Sprache gehalten (*Nachlaß Carl H. Becker*).
3 J. J. van der Leeuw ist drei Monate später nach einem Vortrag in Johannesburg als Vertreter der „New Education Fellowship" mit einem selbstgesteuerten Flugzeug über Südafrika tödlich abgestürzt. Beatrice Ensor schreibt in ihrem Nachruf: *„I lose a splendid colleague and an old and deeply valued friend"* (*Ensor 1934*).

Bibliographie

Becker, Carl Heinrich: The Changing Social Structure. In: The New Era in Home and School, 13 (1932) 5, S. 283-284.
Boyd, William (Hrsg.): Towards a New Education. London u. a.: Knopf 1930.
Boyd, William / Rawson, Wyatt: The Story of the New Education. London: Heinemann 1965.
Ensor, Beatrice: Dr. J. J. van der Leeuw. In: The New Era in Home and School, 15 (1934) 5, S. 165.
Gebhard, Julius: Weltbund für Erneuerung der Erziehung. Deutsche Sektion. Bezirksgruppe Norden. Sitz Hamburg. In: Das Werdende Zeitalter, 9 (1930), S. 196.
Gebhard, Julius: Weltbund für Erneuerung der Erziehung. Deutsche Sektion. Das deutsche Zwischentreffen in Dortmund. In: Das Werdende Zeitalter, 10 (1931), S. 552.
Geheeb, Paul: Briefe. Mensch und Idee in Selbstzeugnissen. Hrsg. von Walter Schäfer. Stuttgart: Klett 1970.
Landahl, Heinrich: The Lichtwark School – Hamburg. In: The New Era in Home and School, 13 (1932) 6, S. 176-178.
Leeuw, J. J. van der: Dr. C. H. Becker. An Appreciation. In: The New Era in Home and School, 14 (1933) 3, S. 100.
Röhrs, Hermann: Nationalsozialismus, Krieg, Neubeginn. Eine autobiographische Vergegenwärtigung aus pädagogischer Sicht. Frankfurt a. M. u. a.: Lang 1990.
Röhrs, Hermann: Der Weltbund für Erneuerung der Erziehung. Wirkungsgeschichte und Zukunftsperspektiven. 2. Aufl. Weinheim: Deutscher Studien-Verlag 1995. (Schriftenreihe des Weltbundes für Erneuerung der Erziehung. 1)
Röhrs, Hermann: Erinnerungen und Erfahrungen – Perspektiven für die Zukunft. Weinheim: Deutscher Studien-Verlag 1997. (Gesammelte Schriften. 9)
Röhrs, Hermann: Die Reformpädagogik. Ursprung und Verlauf unter internationalem Aspekt. 5. Aufl. Weinheim: Deutscher Studien-Verlag 1997.
Rotten, Elisabeth: Der internationale Arbeitskreis für Erneuerung der Erziehung. In: Das Werdende Zeitalter, 1 (1922) 1, S. 5-17.
Rotten, Elisabeth / Wilker, Karl: Weltanschauung oder nicht? Eine Betrachtung nach zehn Jahren internationaler pädagogischer Zusammenarbeit. In: Das Werdende Zeitalter, 9 (1930) 1, S. 3-7.
Schneider, Friedrich: Bericht über den 6. Weltkongreß der New Education Fellowship in Nizza vom 29. Juli bis 11. August 1932. In: Internationale Zeitschrift für Erziehungswissenschaft, 2 (1932-33) 2, S. 300-307.
Wilker, Karl: Pädagogik der geistig und sittlich Abnormen. In: Die Neue Erziehung, 1 (1919) 25, S. 833-838.

Ungedruckte Quellen

Becker, Carl H.: Rundschreiben vom 1. August 1931 „An die Mitglieder des Rates für die Vorbereitung des nächstjährigen Kongresses der New Education Fellowship" [Becker-Briefe. Geheimes Staatsarchiv Berlin.]
Koch, Walter: Bericht [über die Tagung in Heppenheim 1919]. 1920. [Archiv der École de l'Humanitée Goldern.]

Nachlaß Carl H. Becker. Geheimes Staatsarchiv Berlin.
Rotten, Elisabeth: Geschichte der Deutschen Mittelstelle des Weltbundes für Erneuerung der Erziehung. April 1930a. [Weniger-Briefe. Niedersächsische Staats- und Universitätsbibliothek Göttingen.]
Rotten, Elisabeth: Rundschreiben. 1930b. [Weniger-Briefe. Niedersächsische Staats- und Universitätsbibliothek Göttingen.]
Weniger-Briefe. Niedersächsische Staats- und Universitätsbibliothek Göttingen.

Danksagung

Dank sei folgenden Personen und Institutionen für die Bereitstellung der Archivmaterialien ausgesprochen:

- Wolfgang Harder, Odenwaldschule, Ober-Hambach
- Armin Lüthi, École de l'Humanité, Goldern
- Bibliothek des Deutschen Instituts für Internationale Pädagogische Forschung, Frankfurt am Main
- Bibliothek für Bildungsgeschichtliche Forschung des Deutschen Instituts für Internationale Pädagogische Forschung, Berlin
- Geheimes Staatsarchiv, Berlin
- Niedersächsische Staats- und Universitätsbibliothek, Abteilung für Handschriften und seltene Drucke, Göttingen

Die Reformation als Zäsur in der deutschen Universitätsentwicklung – Von der Universalität zur Regionalisierung

Leo Roth

Die Entwicklung der Universitäten

Im Jahre 1495 soll Kaiser Maximilian I. alle Fürsten auf dem Reichstag zu Worms aufgerufen haben, in jedem einzelnen Staat eine eigene Universität zu gründen. Universitäten müssen sich bis zu dieser Zeit als Bildungsstätten und Legitimations- bzw. Machtfaktoren durchgesetzt haben, so daß ihre Vermehrung insgesamt wie auch ihre Streuung über die Regionen des Deutschen Reiches als nützlich erschien.[1] Zum Zeitpunkt des Reichstages gab es im Deutschen Reich bereits 15 Universitäten (einschließlich Basel 1460). Doch diese Vermehrung (vgl. Schaubild 1) hatte mit Maximilians Aufruf im Grunde nichts zu tun, sondern war durch die Reformation beeinflußt, wie noch deutlich werden wird. Der territorialstaatliche Gedanke realisierte sich dabei auch, aber in einem anderen Sinne als Maximilian es gemeint haben mag. Ohne den Einfluß der Reformation ist die Herausbildung der Universitäten in den Territorialstaaten nicht zu erklären.

In den einhundert Jahren vor 1495 waren es immerhin zehn universitäre Neugründungen gewesen. Bereits ab der Mitte des 14. Jahrhunderts bis zum 15. Jahrhundert waren die sechs ältesten deutschen Universitäten entstanden. Insgesamt sind es Gründungen von Fürsten und Städten nach dem Muster von Italien und Frankreich (vgl. Schaubild 1). Im 13. Jahrhundert waren in Italien, Frankreich, England und Spanien immerhin über 30 Universitäten entstanden – alle ohne einen Stiftungsbrief von Papst oder Kaiser *(Kaufmann 1896, Bd. 2, S. 4)*. Nach *Verger (1993, S. 70)*, der aber nicht immer präzise ist, waren es 24 Universitäten.

---

1 Auf die Sozialgeschichte kann hier allerdings nicht eingegangen werden. Vgl. dazu beispielsweise *Prahl (1978, 1991)* und vor allem *Rüegg (1993)*.

Schaubild 1: Entwicklung deutscher Universitäten

			Gründungsjahr(e)	
↑ 4 Univ.	1350	Prag	1348/1365	
	1380	Heidelberg	1385	
		Köln	1388	
		Erfurt	1392	
	1400			Würzburg 1402/1410
		Leipzig	1409	
		Rostock	1419	
	1420			
↑ 8 Universitäten	1440			
		Greifswald	1456	
		Freiburg i. Br.	1456	
	1460			(Basel 1460)
		Ingolstadt	1472	
		Trier	1454/1473	
		Mainz	1476	
		Tübingen	1477	
	1480			
				1495 Reichstag in Worms: Aufruf Maximilians I., in jedem Land eine Universität zu gründen
↓	1500	Wittenberg	1502	
		Frankfurt / O.	1498/1506	
				Reformation
↑ 8 Universitäten	1520	Marburg	1527	
	1540	Königsberg	1544/1560	
		Dillingen	1549/1554	
		Jena	1558	
	1560			
		Helmstedt	1574/1576	
		Altdorf	1578/1623	
	1580			
	1600	Gießen	1607	
		Paderborn	1615	
↓	1620			
		Rinteln	1621	
		Straßburg	1621	
		Salzburg	1623	
		Osnabrück	1630	
		Breslau	1638/1702	
		Bamberg	1648/1773	
		Kiel	1665	

Für diese frühen Gründungen ist charakteristisch, daß sich z. B. die italienischen Stadtuniversitäten wenig um Stiftungsurkunden von Päpsten oder Kaisern scherten.[2] Weiterhin ist charakteristisch, daß nach der Lehrfreiheit des 12. Jahrhunderts, die *„unerträgliche Zustände geschaffen"* *(Kaufmann 1888, Bd. 1, S. 352)* hatte, auch nach der Käuflichkeit akademischer Grade – entsprachen sie doch Adels- und Ehrenprädikaten –, die Erwerbung der akademischen Grade in Stufen formalisiert und die Lehrbefugnis ebenfalls in Stufen festgelegt wurde, bis das volle Lizentiat erworben werden konnte. Diese zunehmend erreichte Gleichwertigkeit der akademischen Grade hing verständlicherweise mit der Gleichartigkeit der an den Universitäten gelehrten Inhalte zusammen.

Die Inhalte und ihre Wissenschaft

Die Scholastik

Die dominierende Wissenschaftsmethode der frühen Universitäten das gesamte Mittelalter hindurch ist die Scholastik. Sie ist im historischen Rückblick besonders aufgrund der Angriffe durch den Humanismus negativ akzentuiert worden. Ihr wesentliches Verdienst wurde dabei häufig ignoriert: Sie hat neben Staat und Kirche eine dritte Macht installiert – die Wissenschaft. Zwar entwickelte sich die Wissenschaft als zweite geistige Gewalt in enger Anlehnung und Auseinandersetzung mit der Kirche und deren Inhalten, aber sie erreichte durchaus ihre Eigenständigkeit. War im frühen Mittelalter die Wissenschaft von der Kirche gefördert worden, um Waffen zum Kampf gegen die Ketzer *(Kaufmann 1888, Bd. 1, S. 2)* zur Verfügung zu stellen, so wurde sie seit dem 10. Jahrhundert mit dem Höhepunkt im 12., 13. und 14. Jahrhundert zu einer eigenständigen Macht, die ihr Urteil in weltlichen und geistlichen Streitigkeiten abgab. Ein wesentliches Verdienst der Scholastik war die Tradierung antiker (römischer) Autoren, nicht um ihrer Inhalte, sondern um der Form willen. Der Satz des Augustinus, daß man die goldenen Gefäße

---

2 Anders ist es bei den deutschen Universitäten. Hier wurde auf Stiftungsbriefe beider Universalmächte Wert gelegt, obwohl Universitäten auch eingerichtet wurden, bevor der päpstliche Stiftungsbrief eintraf (z. B. Wien) oder nach Eintreffen des päpstlichen Stiftungsbriefes (z. B. Heidelberg) oder auch nach Eintreffen des kaiserlichen Stiftungsbriefes überhaupt nicht errichtet wurden (z. B. Lüneburg). Bis in die Mitte des 15. Jahrhunderts sind in Deutschland nur päpstliche, nie kaiserliche Stiftungsbriefe erbeten worden (Prag, Wien, Erfurt, Heidelberg, Kulm, Köln, Würzburg, Leipzig, Rostock). In gleicher Zeit (1355-69) aber erteilt Kaiser Karl IV. acht Stiftungsbriefe für Burgund und Italien. Die ersten kaiserlichen Stiftungsbriefe in Deutschland gibt Friedrich III. für Freiburg 1456, Lüneburg 1471, Tübingen 1484. Diese Stiftungsbriefe wurden von Landesfürsten, Bischöfen oder städtischen Behörden erbeten.

der Ägypter nehmen und sie für die neuen (christlichen) Inhalte nutzen solle, markiert hier die Position der Antikenrezeption.

Wenn auch die Scholastik im Laufe der Jahrhunderte durch ihren Methodendogmatismus verkam und sich in abstrusen Spitzfindigkeiten erging,[3] gegen die die Humanisten – nicht zuletzt Erasmus – schärfste Kritik anmeldeten, so bleibt doch festzuhalten: Die Einheit der Wahrheit war um der Eigenständigkeit der Wissenschaft (vorübergehend) aufgegeben worden. Es konnte nach der Lehre der Wissenschaft etwas wahr sein, was nach der unbestrittenen Lehre der Kirche als falsch galt – und umgekehrt.

Der Renaissance-Humanismus

Über ihn sind zahllose Bücher geschrieben worden, die Bibliotheken füllen. Es ist auch die Frage gestellt worden, ob es ihn überhaupt gab. Eine andere These lautet, daß er nicht so grundlegend neu gewesen sei, wenn man die karolingische und ottonische Renaissance berücksichtige. *Niethammer (1808)* hat ihn als eine pädagogische Richtung bezeichnet, *Hagen (1841)* benutzte ihn als Kennwort für eine Geistesbewegung, *Voigt (1859)* wählte den Begriff für die Bezeichnung einer Epoche. Diese umfaßt in gegenwärtigen Publikationen etwa die Zeit von 1300 bis 1600. Der Renaissance-Humanismus kam nicht über Nacht. Seiner Entstehung und Entwicklung nachzugehen, ist hier nicht Aufgabe. Für die Universitäten hatte er erhebliche Konsequenzen, die wesentlich die Lehrinhalte, weniger die Struktur betrafen.

Vier Hauptmerkmale deuten bereits den Gegensatz zur Scholastik an:

– *Antikenverehrung:* Die Verehrung vor allem der römischen Antike und ihrer Autoren um ihrer selbst willen wie um ihrer Bedeutung für das eigene in dieser Welt zu gestaltende Leben;

---

[3] Man darf dabei die unerhörte Leistung der Scholastik über Jahrhunderte nicht unbeachtet lassen, die versucht hatte, antikes Wissen und christliche Offenbarungsreligion kompatibel zu machen. Hohe Leistungen erbrachte sie auf den Gebieten der Naturwissenschaft und Medizin. Ihre Negativbewertung folgt auch gegenwärtig häufig noch der kämpferischen Kritik der Humanisten. Für eine positive Würdigung vgl. etwa *Piltz (1982)*. Man erinnere sich auch an den höchst anspruchsvollen Versuch der Scholastik, über das Konstrukt der modi essendi, modi cogitandi und modi significandi zu klären, wie u. a. Sprache sich zur bezeichneten Wirklichkeit verhalte, wobei die Humanisten die modi significandi als die übelste Verkommenheit der Scholastik bezeichneten und selbst, weniger anspruchsvoll, die Persönlichkeit durch (klassische) Literatur bilden wollten.

- *editorische Leistung:* die Edition der Schriften römischer und griechischer Autoren;
- *Text- und Quellenkritik:* durch Vergleich vorliegender Quellen erfolgte die Entwicklung philologischer und sprachwissenschaftlicher Fähigkeiten (obwohl bereits seit Bernald von Konstanz, gestorben 1100, Gratian, gestorben ca. 1160, und Abélard, gestorben 1142, in Ansätzen angewendet);
- *„Rationalismus":* Versuch, die Phänomene in Gesellschaft und Natur, die Wirklichkeit rational zu verstehen und die Prinzipien der Erklärung in der Wirklichkeit selbst zu suchen.

Aus solcher Charakterisierung kann man auch folgern: *„Der Klerus wurde als Träger der Ideologie und damit auch als Garant gelehrter Bildung in Frage gestellt" (Fläschendräger u. a. 1981, S. 35).* Landfester *(1972, S. 19)* charakterisiert den Humanismus als geistige Bewegung, *„die in produktiver Auseinandersetzung mit der antiken Überlieferung bei gleichzeitiger kritischer Wendung gegen die fortschrittshemmenden Schranken der mittelalterlichen Weltanschauung erstmals den geistigen Idealen und kulturellen Lebensformen der Moderne zum Durchbruch verholfen hat".* Die Vertreter dieser Bewegung bieten also ein recht modernes geschichtliches Weltbild an, eine neue Auffassung von Mensch, Wissenschaft und Staat, ein von Theologie und Metaphysik weitgehend befreites Denken. Trotz der zunehmenden Säkularisierung sind die Humanisten der christlichen Lehre verbunden – mehr oder weniger. Unter pädagogischem Aspekt kann man diese Positionen als „educazione cristiana" und als „educazione morale civile" beschreiben *(Müller 1969).* Zu letzteren läßt sich Alberti (1404-1472) zählen, der schreibt: *„Wenn Du aber die Ursachen des Übels vermeidest, brauchst Du niemals die Götter zu bitten, sie möchten Dich davon erlösen; und wenn Du meinst, die Menschen schadeten einander, brauchst Du nicht die Götter um Hilfe zu rufen, sondern was not tut ist, auf die Menschen besänftigend einzuwirken. Sollten aber die Götter selbst unser Leid verursachen, so möchte ich Dir sagen: mit Deinen Gebeten wirst Du sie keineswegs von ihrer alten Gewohnheit abbringen"* (nach *Müller 1969, S. 275).*

Hier wird eindeutig die Moralphilosophie christlicher Dogmatik vorgezogen. Dieser neue Geist zieht in die Universitäten ein. Alles erscheint machbar, der Mensch wird als Maß aller Dinge wiederentdeckt – ein Satz des Protagoras, der in dieser Zeit häufig zitiert wird, besonders von Alberti. Das ist eine auf Praxis des Diesseits angelegte Wissenschaft, die auch ökonomischen und politischen Bedürfnissen entgegenkommt. Die neue Wissenschaft wird nicht nur von der weltlichen Macht geschätzt, sondern auch von der geistlichen.

Schaubild 2   Entwicklung der Studentenzahlen 1358 bis 1560 nach fünfjährigen Durchschnitten an deutschen Universitäten

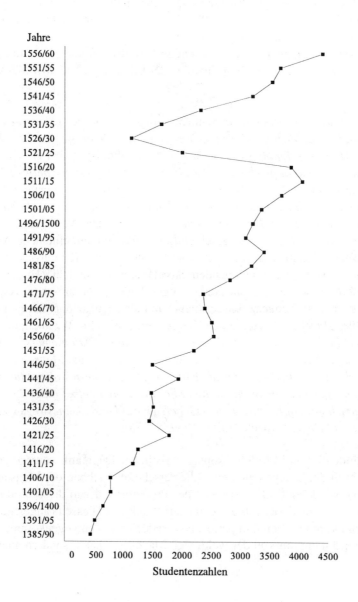

Der Einfluß der Reformation

Der quantitative Aspekt: Die Entwicklung der Studentenzahlen

Es waren zweifellos nicht nur die interessanten Inhalte, sondern auch die nützliche Verwendung der Absolventen in der Praxis, die die Zahl der Studenten seit dem Mittelalter gewaltig anwachsen ließ. Nach fünfjährigen Durchschnitten berechnet studierten 1391/1395 an den drei deutschen Universitäten Heidelberg, Köln und Erfurt 515 Studenten (Zahlen: *Eulenburg 1904, S. 54-55, 102-105*; neuere und sehr differenzierte Frequenzanalysen für die Zeit von 1385-1505 finden sich bei *Schwinges 1986*). Die Zahl stieg kontinuierlich an und erreichte 1511/1515, also in 120 Jahren, 4 041 an nun immerhin elf Universitäten, von denen Greifswald mit 77 Studenten die kleinste und Leipzig mit 819 Studenten die größte Universität ist, gefolgt von Köln mit 581 (für Trier und Mainz liegen keine Zahlen vor). Die Gesamtzahl der Studenten mag heute bescheiden anmuten. Doch ist zu berücksichtigen, daß das prozentuale Wachstum in diesen 120 Jahren bei etwa 800 Prozent liegt. Für die nächsten einhundert Jahre (bis 1601/1605) ist die Gesamtstudentenzahl auf 6 824 gestiegen (keine Zahlen für Trier), was eine Zunahme um nur etwa 60 Prozent bedeutet.[4] Dazwischen gab es erhebliche Schwankungen, worauf noch einzugehen sein wird (siehe Schaubild 2).

Ein Anstieg der Studentenzahlen um fast 800 Prozent in 120 Jahren ist erst wieder erreicht, wenn man ab 1910 (52 766 Studenten) zurückrechnet und sich auf die Zahlen von 1790 (6 635 Studenten) bezieht. Erst unser gegenwärtiges Bildungssystem kennt dann wieder gewaltige prozentuale Steigerungen in relativ kurzen Intervallen. Vergegenwärtigen wir uns nochmals die Studentenzahlen für 1511/1515 von 4 041 im Fünfjahresdurchschnitt und vergleichen sie mit den darauf folgenden Jahren, so finden wir einen rapiden Rückgang, der 1516/1520 zwar noch 3 850 Studenten ausweist, für 1521/1525 um 50 Prozent auf 1 949 zurückgeht, seinen Tiefpunkt in den Jahren 1526/1530 mit 1 135 erreicht und erst danach langsam ansteigt. Das bedeutet, daß von 1510/1515 bis 1526/1530, also in 15 Jahren, die Studentenzahl von 4 041 auf 1 135 im Fünfjahresdurchschnitt sinkt; relativ ist es ein Rückgang um über 74 Prozent. Anders gewendet: 1510/1515 studierten 250 Prozent mehr als 15 Jahre später. Noch eindeutiger ist das Absinken ab 1516/1520 bis 1526/1530. Solche Einbrüche sind in der deutschen Bildungs-

---

[4] Selbstverständlich wurden nicht alle graduiert. *Verger (1993, S. 141)* schätzt, daß weniger als zehn Prozent den Magistergrad erreichten. Das gilt für die etwa 200 000 deutschen Universitätsbesucher zwischen 1348 und 1505, wobei vor 1380 nur wenige tausend Personen die Universitäten besuchten *(Moraw 1993, S. 248)*.

geschichte bis in die Gegenwart nicht bekannt. Selbst der Dreißigjährige Krieg reduziert die Zahlen der Jahre 1616/1620 bis 1636/1640 von 7 740 nur auf 4 298, also nicht einmal um 40 Prozent, wobei man berücksichtigen muß, daß in dieser Zeit die Bevölkerung erheblich dezimiert war.[5] Will man einen Vergleich ziehen, so wird man wahrscheinlich auf die Kulturrevolution in China bis 1976 zielen müssen. Der Rückgang der Studentenzahlen ab 1516/1520 ist regional spezifisch, im Norden stärker, im Süden geringer, allerdings auch örtlich unterschiedlich. Darauf wird noch einzugehen sein.

Der qualitative Aspekt: Die Wissenschaftsfeindlichkeit der Anfänge

Der deutsche Humanismus wurde *„von der Reformation hinweggefegt"*, schreibt *Heller (1982, S. 8)* in ihrem Buch „Der Mensch der Renaissance". Das trifft zweifellos für die Anfänge der Reformationszeit zu, aber sicherlich nicht aus den Gründen, die Heller anführt, wenn sie meint, daß z. B. in Deutschland die Renaissance nicht als *„gesamtgesellschaftliches Phänomen"* bestanden hätte, sondern der Humanismus als *„Projektion einiger Aspekte der Renaissance"* nur *„höchstens in den oberen Gesellschaftsschichten, im Kreis der politischen oder geistigen Aristokratie Fuß zu fassen"* vermochte, *„wo er jedoch alsbald ein isoliertes Dasein führte"*. Die Renaissance sei in Deutschland also kein „gesamtgesellschaftlicher Prozeß" gewesen. Nun, das war sie selbst in Italien nur in Grenzen. In Deutschland erhält der Humanismus seine eindeutige politische Dimension durch die Reformation. Darauf hat *Böhme (1986, S. 291)* nachdrücklich aufmerksam gemacht: *„In dem Maße, in dem die Reformation zu einem politischen Kampf der weltlichen Mächte wird, zwingt sie auch den Humanismus zu politischen Entscheidungen. Manche Humanisten vertreten viel eher einen politischen als einen gelehrten Humanismus. ... Das religiöse Bekenntnis wird auch zum politischen Bekenntnis."* Doch das gilt nur sehr eingeschränkt für die Anfänge der Reformation. Daß der Humanismus in Deutschland durch die Reformation „hinweggefegt" wurde, hatte zunächst mehr einen irrationalen Grund als den von Heller indizierten politisch-ökonomischen. Dieser Grund ist zweifel-

---

5 Bevölkerungszahl und Immatrikulationsfrequenz zeigen allerdings häufig einen antizyklischen Zusammenhang, wie z. B. die Pestwellen zwischen 1348 und 1450 belegen. Aber auch die *„Agrarpreiszyklen" (Schwinges 1993, S. 179)* bieten keine Erklärung für den Rückgang der Studentenzahlen zwischen 1521 und 1530. Allerdings erklärt für diese Zeit ein anderer sozioökonomischer Faktor einen Teil der abnehmenden Studentenzahlen: Aus Klöstern und Domkapiteln kam der große Teil der Studenten des Mittelalters, von diesen finanziell unterstützt. Durch Auflösung eines großen Teils dieser Institutionen in der Reformationszeit wurde potentiellen Studenten die Existenzgrundlage entzogen.

los in der Person Luthers zu sehen; hier machte in der Tat zunächst der Mann Geschichte.

Man wird Luther nicht als Humanisten bezeichnen können, doch hat er in regem Kontakt mit den bekanntesten Humanisten gestanden. Schon vor Veröffentlichung seiner 95 Thesen im Jahre 1517 hatte er mit Mutius, der in Erfurt lehrte, korrespondiert (1516), danach mit Reuchlin (1518) und Erasmus (1520). Luther, 1512 zum Doktor promoviert, lehrte in Wittenberg, *„vom Rand der Zivilisation her" (Bornkamm 1983, S. 41)* als Professor für Heilige Schrift. Seine Kritik an Lehre und Praxis der Kirche war zunächst nicht außergewöhnlich, das gehörte gewissermaßen zum guten Ton. Die literarische Kritik eines Boccaccio, die ironische Kritik eines Erasmus sind viel schneidender. Luther hatte sich durch theologische Kritik am 'Mönchsgezänk' beteiligt; mehr schien es anfangs nicht zu sein. Luther, dieser zutiefst religiöse und zutiefst abergläubische Mensch, ist allerdings kein Wissenschaftler humanistischer Provenienz: Der Blitz hatte ihm seinen Weg gewiesen, auf der Wartburg hatte er den Teufel gesehen.

Ein Teufel ist ihm auch der Papst, der Antichrist in Person. Auch mit dieser Ansicht steht Luther nicht allein. Er kennt viele weitere Teufel, unter anderem Aristoteles. Dieser ist zur Grundlage des Studiums an den Universitäten geworden, *„und allein der blinde heidnische Meister Aristoteles regiert, auch weiter denn Christus"* (Luther: An den christlichen Adel deutscher Nation. 1520, zitiert nach: *Luther 1889, Bd. 1, S. 274*). Dieser *„verdammte, hochmütige, schalkhafte Heide mit seinen falschen Worten"* lehre doch, *„daß die Seele mit dem Körper sterblich sei" (ebd.)*. Logik, Poetik und Rhetorik als einzige Schriften des Aristoteles könnten bleiben; auch diese ohne Kommentare und Quästionen. In gekürzter Form akzeptiert Luther, daß sie *„nützlich gelesen würden, junge Leute zu üben, wohl zu reden und zu predigen" (ebd., S. 275)*. Ist so der Artistenfakultät ihre Grundlage entzogen, so macht Luther auch vor den anderen Fakultäten nicht halt. Zusammenfassend ist sein Urteil: *„Ich habe große Sorge, die hohen Schulen sind große Pforten der Hölle, so sie nicht emsiglich die Heilige Schrift üben und in das junge Volk treiben" (ebd. S. 280)*. Auch in späteren Schriften sieht Luther die Universitäten als die *„eigentlichen Burgen des Teufels auf Erden"* (nach *Paulsen 1921, Bd. 1, S. 191*). Bedeutete den Humanisten die Antike das Ideal, so war sie für die Reformatoren zunächst das Heidentum per se.

Doch Luther ist nicht alleine der Kritiker. Sein Freund Melanchthon, auch er fürchtet täglich, ihm könne irgendwo der Teufel begegnen, Melanchthon also, dieser ausgewiesene und bekannte Humanist, steht Luther zu dieser Zeit keineswegs nach. Im Februar

1521 schreibt er in der Verteidigung Luthers gegen Emser ein vernichtendes Urteil über die aristotelische Philosophie. Und dann erst über die Universitäten: „*Nie sei etwas Verderblicheres, Gottloseres erfunden worden, nicht die Päpste, der Teufel selbst sei ihr Urheber; Wiclef zuerst habe es gesehen, daß die Universitäten des Teufels Schulen seien: konnte er etwas Frömmeres oder Weiseres sagen?*" (nach *Paulsen 1921, Bd. 1, S. 193*). Daß die Juden ihre Jünglinge dem Moloch opferten, sei Beispiel für unsere Universitäten geworden, wo die Jünglinge heidnischen Götzenbildern geopfert würden. Hier ist von dem 'praeceptor Germaniae', wie er später, noch zu seinen Lebzeiten, genannt werden wird, nichts zu ahnen. Drei Jahre vorher hatte es bei Melanchthon noch ganz anders geklungen. Als Großneffe Reuchlins, von diesem empfohlen, von Tübingen nach Wittenberg gekommen, trat der 21jährige hier vier Tage nach seiner Ankunft mit einer Rede zur Universitätsreform auf (29. August 1518). Er verlangt das Studium der griechischen Sprache, ohne die man Aristoteles nicht verstehen könne. Allerdings ist das nicht im Gegensatz zu seinem religiösen Engagement zu sehen *(Stempel 1979, S. 28)*. Ende 1520 besucht Spalatin die Universität Wittenberg. Er berichtet an den Kurfürsten, daß er bei Melanchthon 500 bis 600 Hörer gesehen habe – bei Luther 400 *(Muther 1866, S. 429)*. Die echte aristotelische Philosophie herzustellen, hatte Melanchthon sich 1518 zur Aufgabe gesetzt. Und ein Jahr nach Spalatins Besuch (1520) dieses! Wieder ein Jahr später (1522) spricht Melanchthon allerdings eine andere Sprache – zu spät?

Diese zentrale Kritik, diese Wissenschaftsfeindlichkeit der reformatorischen Anfänge – mag sie vom protestantischen Ansatz her auch verständlich sein, waren doch die Universitäten stark dem kirchlichen Einfluß ausgesetzt –, traf die Universitäten entscheidend; sie traf vor allem – wenn auch so nicht beabsichtigt – die humanistischen, die „schönen Wissenschaften". Innerhalb von 10 bis 15 Jahren schien der Humanismus in Deutschland sich durchzusetzen – und unterzugehen. Zeitzeugen haben es miterlebt. Die Klagen sind bekannt. Noch 1516 hatte Erasmus in einem Brief an Capito gewünscht, etwas jünger zu sein, um das Wiederaufleben der schönen Wissenschaften und ihre glänzendere Entfaltung zu erleben. 1528 schreibt Erasmus an Pirckheimer: „*Wo immer das Luthertum herrscht, da sind die Wissenschaften zugrunde gegangen*" (nach *Paulsen 1921, Bd. 1, S. 202*).

Die lutherische Lehre brauchte keine Theoretiker, sie war auf Praxis gegründet. Zwischen dem Individuum und Gott brauchte es keinen professionellen Mittler; der Theologenstand schien überflüssig. Dessen Nachwuchs allerdings hatte bisher die Universitäten besucht. Das gleiche galt für das kirchliche und weltliche Recht. Worauf sollten letztlich die drei oberen Fakultäten überhaupt aufbauen, wenn der Artistenfakultät mit

Aristoteles die Grundlage entzogen wurde? Es gab aus früher protestantischer Sicht keine Verwendung für eine Universitätsqualifikation; es gab auch keine ausformulierte Bildungstheorie. Man wußte, was man nicht wollte; was man wollte, wußte man um 1520 allerdings nicht.

Die Universität Wittenberg, Luthers Wirkungsstätte, hatte ab 1505 eine relativ gleichbleibende jährliche Immatrikulationszahl[6] von etwa 200. Durch Luthers und Melanchthons Attraktivität stieg die Zahl von 1517 (242 Studenten) bis 1520 (579 Studenten), also in drei Jahren, um über 150 Prozent sprunghaft an.[7] Damit war sie die größte im deutschen Reich vor Leipzig, das immer schon mehr als das Doppelte bzw. Dreifache von Wittenberg an Zahl hatte. Im Jahre 1527, also nur sieben Jahre später, hat Wittenberg noch 73 Studenten.[8] Erfurt schrumpft von 345 im Jahre 1518 auf 14 im Jahre 1526.[9] In Rostock gehen die Zahlen seit 1523 zurück, 1529 wurde kein Student mehr immatrikuliert (*Paulsen 1921, Bd. 1, S. 198*). Aber selbst die Universität Köln, die entschiedene Kämpferin gegen das Luthertum, deren Studentenzahlen früher bei 300 lagen, zeigt ab 1522 eine kontinuierliche Abnahme der Immatrikulationszahlen bis auf 54 im Jahre 1534. Auch die Universität Wien – 1501 hatte Maximilian zusätzlich eine eigene humanistische Fakultät errichtet, an der um 1515 jährlich um 600 Studenten immatrikuliert wurden – begann ab 1522 schnell zu schrumpfen; in den Jahren 1527/1528 wurden zusammen nur zwischen 20 und 30 Studenten immatrikuliert.[10] 1530 gab es insgesamt nur noch 30 Studenten, so daß der Betrieb eingestellt wurde (*Paulsen a. a. O., S. 199*). Die Universität Greifswald schloß ihre Tore zwischen 1525 und 1540, in Heidelberg gab es mehr Professoren als Studenten. Basel schloß seine Universität, als die Stadt sich 1529 der Reformation anschloß; Erasmus ging im gleichen Jahr nach Freiburg. Freiburg, Tübingen und Ingolstadt waren – nach kurzer Rezession in den Bauernkriegen – die einzigen Universitäten, deren Zahlen unverändert bzw. ansteigend blieben. Erst ab 1531 nimmt die Zahl der Studenten an den deutschen Universitäten wieder allmählich zu, erreicht den Stand von 1516/1520 aber erst um 1556/1560, also 50 Jahre später (vgl. Schaubild 2).

---

6 Wir wählen hier die Immatrikulationszahlen nach *Paulsen (1921, Bd. 1, S. 629)* anstelle der Frequenzberechnungen nach fünfjährigen Durchschnittswerten, wie *Eulenberg (1904)* und *Prahl (1978)* sie benutzen. Die Immatrikulationszahlen bilden verständlicherweise einen wesentlich konkreteren Indikator für die studentische Nachfrage, weil sie jährlich kontinuierlich die Zu- bzw. Abnahme zeigen, während die Durchschnittszahlen stark über den Mittelwert relativieren.
7 Das bedeutet: 1520 studierten ca. 300 Prozent mehr in Wittenberg als sieben Jahre davor.
8 Das bedeutet: 1520 studierten etwa 700 Prozent mehr Studenten in Wittenberg als 7 Jahre später.
9 Das bedeutet: 1518 studierten 2 100 Prozent mehr in Erfurt als acht Jahre danach.
10 Das bedeutet: 1520 wurden in Wien ca. 3 000 Prozent Studenten weniger immatrikuliert als um 1515.

Die Reformation braucht die Wissenschaft

Im Grunde hatten weniger als fünf Jahre gereicht, um die Universitäten zu zerschlagen. Der Wiederaufbau dauerte wesentlich länger. Er wurde von seiten der Reformatoren mit Melanchthons Sinneswandel 1522 eingeleitet. Es mögen die Bilderstürmer gewesen sein, die Schuster, Schmiede, Schneider, die aufgrund innerer Erleuchtung Gottes Wort in Wittenberg predigten und die Wissenschaft verachteten, die diesen Sinneswandel bewirkten. Bereits ein Jahr nach seiner Verdammung der Universität, also ab 1522, beginnen Melanchthons Klagen über das Ende der schönen Wissenschaften. Diese Klagen dauern fort. Im Jahre 1524 hören bei ihm nur noch vier Studenten die Vorlesung über Demosthenes *(Melanchthon 1842, S. 193)*. Melanchthon ist nicht Autorität genug, um eine Wende herbeizuführen. Luther muß her, die geistliche Autorität, die Melanchthon von der Wartburg herbeiruft. Die Lage ist in der Tat desolat. Im Jahre 1530 wird Luther feststellen, daß allein in Sachsen wohl an die 4 000 gelehrte Personen (Pfarrer, Juristen, Ärzte, Lehrer, Küster) fehlen würden. Beim Niedergang der Studentenzahlen läßt sich 1524 die weitere Entwicklung bereits abschätzen. Luther verfaßt 1524 die programmatische Schrift „An die Ratsherren aller Städte deutschen Landes, daß sie christliche Schulen aufrichten und halten sollen." Er skizziert die Lage, *„wie man allenthalben die Schulen zergehen läßt. Die hohen Schulen werden schwach, die Klöster nehmen ab ..."* *(Luther 1889, Bd. 3, S. 7)*. Der Teufel als *„Gott der Welt"* (ebd., S. 8) wird dafür verantwortlich gemacht. Schließlich kommt Luther mit seiner Begründung für den gelehrten Unterricht, besonders die Sprachen: *„Niemand hat gewußt, warum Gott die Sprachen hervor ließ kommen, bis daß man nun allererst sieht, daß es um des Evangelii willen geschehen ist ..." (ebd., S. 16f.). „Und laßt nur das gesagt sein, daß wir das Evangelium nicht wohl werden erhalten ohne die Sprachen. Die Sprachen sind die Scheiden, darin dies Messer des Geistes steckt"* (ebd., S. 17). Er wird noch drastischer: Ohne die alten Sprachen würde auch die *„deutsche Sprache zerstört, Christentum, Bildung"* und die *„natürliche Vernunft"* (ebd., S. 18) gingen verloren. Das alles mag dahingestellt bleiben. Luther formuliert zweifellos überspitzt. Aber eines ist deutlich gesehen: ohne Wissenschaft kann sich die Reformation auf intellektueller Ebene nicht durchsetzen. Die Berufung auf das richtig verstandene Wort Gottes mußte eine Auseinandersetzung mit den Vertretern des Wortes Gottes in der römischen Kirche wissenschaftlich, d. h. philologisch führen. Das galt für die Theologen. Aber Luther begründet darin auch den Wert der Bildung für den weltlichen Stand wie ihren Nutzen für die Kommunen.

Das Verfassungsmoment ist von Bedeutung: Die weltliche Obrigkeit hat für Schulen und Hochschulen zu sorgen. In einem Brief an den Markgrafen Georg von Brandenburg

(1529) empfiehlt er, ein oder zwei hohe Schulen zu gründen, *„da man nicht allein die heilige Schrift, sondern auch die Rechte und allerlei Künste lehret" (Luther 1887, S. 119)*. Nicht nur das: die Obrigkeit habe ihre Untertanen zu zwingen, *„die Kinder zur Schule, d. h. zum Studium zu schicken" (nach Paulsen 1921, Bd. 1, S. 209)*. Das könne die Obrigkeit leisten, denn letztlich zwinge sie ihre Untertanen ja auch zum Krieg. Dieser Krieg nun aber wäre gegen den Teufel zu führen *(Luther 1887, S. 116)*, *„daß Prediger, Juristen, Pfarrer, Schreiber, Ärzte, Schulmeister und dergleichen bleiben, denn man kann ihrer nicht entbehren"* (nach *Paulsen, Bd. 1, S. 209*). Die Not ist tatsächlich groß. Die Pfarrstellen verwaisen durch Tod oder Vertreibung. Die aus den Klöstern ausgetretenen Mönche reichen als Nachfolger nicht aus. Seit 1537 werden dann in Wittenberg Männer ordiniert, die kein Studium absolviert haben. Es sind Drucker, Tuchmacher, Schneider, Schreiber, Schuster, Leineweber, Bauern. Erst ab 1544 bessert sich die Situation.

Nach der Zerschlagung der internationalen Universität und damit ihrer Universalität war aus notwendigem Bedarf an akademisch Gebildeten jetzt erst die Zeit gekommen, die Forderung Maximilians von 1495 in die Tat umzusetzen. Jeder Landesherr war auf loyale geistliche und weltliche Führungskräfte angewiesen. Loyal, und daher nur nützlich verwendbar, konnten sie sein, wenn sie an Schulen ausgebildet wurden, die von dem jeweiligen Landesfürsten kontrolliert waren. So setzte zunächst eine Reorganisation der bestehenden Universitäten entsprechend der jeweiligen Konfession ein. In kleinen Ländern wurden Gymnasien zu Universitäten aufgewertet. In protestantischen Territorien wurden zu protestantischen Universitäten umgewandelt: Wittenberg, Frankfurt an der Oder. Als neue protestantische Universitäten entstanden: Marburg (1527), Königsberg (1544), Jena (1558), Helmstedt (1576), Gießen (1607), Altdorf (1578/1622), Rinteln (1621); nach dem Dreißigjährigen Krieg wurden gegründet: Duisburg (1655), Kiel (1665). Die katholischen Landesherren vollzogen ebenfalls Neugründungen: Dillingen (1549), Würzburg (1582), Paderborn (1615), Osnabrück (1630), Bamberg (1648). Auf katholischer Seite kamen noch die Gründungen des Hauses Habsburg hinzu: Olmütz (1581), Graz (1586), Linz (1636), Innsbruck (1672), Breslau (1702). Manche dieser Universitäten erhielten einen großen Zulauf (Helmstedt, wo man sich um die Überwindung der Konfessionen bemühte,[11] Duisburg, Dillingen). Es gab auf beiden Seiten eine Fülle erweiterter Gymnasien, die zeitweise als Hochschulen galten, aber den Status einer Universität nie erreichten. Manche Universität, personell und finanziell schlecht ausgestattet, schloß bald wieder – für gewisse Zeit oder für immer.

---

11 Ob dieses auch daran lag, daß Kanzler der Universität der Erbprinz von Braunschweig war, der gleichzeitig designierter Bischof von Halberstadt war, ist nicht zu belegen.

Hatte die Reformation zu Anfang die Universitäten zerschlagen, so brachte sie sie ab 1527 auch direkt oder indirekt hervor. Direkt zur Ausbildung ihrer Pastoren und Lehrer wie zur Systematisierung der Lehre, indirekt, indem sie katholische 'Gegengründungen' hervorrief.[12]

Die Wissenschaft, wie sie nur an der spezifischen Institution Universität denkbar schien, war zu einer geistigen und politischen Macht geworden, ohne die Kirche und Staat nicht mehr auskommen zu können glaubten. Und da Kirche und Staat nicht nur – wie vor der Reformation – religiös miteinander verbunden waren, wobei die Beziehung zwischen den Universalmächten Kaiser und Papst alles andere als konfliktfrei gewesen war, sondern nun konfessionell ineinandergebunden wurden, was besonders für die protestantischen Territorien bis zur Personalunion führte, kamen territorialpolitische Interessen zum Zuge, die außer der Konfessionalisierung eine staatsbezogene Partikularisierung der Wissenschaft und ihrer Institution, der Universität, nach sich zogen.

So wichtig die qualitative Veränderung und die quantitative Ausweitung der Universitäten auch war, sie war für die nachfolgenden Jahrhunderte nicht das entscheidende Merkmal für die deutsche Universität. Wesentlich und überaus konsequenzenreich war die grundlegende Strukturveränderung.

Von der Universalität zur Regionalität

Im Mittelalter war die Universität ein relativ autonomer Zusammenschluß der Magister- und Scholarenkorporationen. Sie wurde durch die Städte oder die beiden Universalmächte garantiert.

Es hatte bereits einmal eine erste Regionalisierung der Universitäten durch das Schisma (1378 bis 1417) gegeben, als Studenten und Magister nicht an Universitäten studieren sollten, die in Territorien lagen, deren Herrscher den jeweiligen Gegenpapst aner-

---

12 Man muß hier den Einfluß des Jesuitenordens besonders berücksichtigen. Zwischen 1553 und 1564 entstanden neben den fünf protestantischen Universitäten Helmstedt, Gießen, Rinteln, Straßburg und Altdorf ebenso viele deutsche Jesuitenuniversitäten: Dillingen, Paderborn, Molsheim (Elsaß), Osnabrück und Bamberg. Dazu kamen noch Olmütz und Graz. Daneben gibt es noch an elf deutschen Universitäten einschließlich Prag (Klemenskolleg) und Wien Jesuitenfakultäten oder -lehrstühle. Um den wachsenden Einfluß der protestantischen Universität Königsberg zurückzudrängen, wird das 1569 von Jesuiten gegründete Kolleg 1579 zur Universität Vilnius (nur Theologie, 44 Jesuiten als Lehrende).

kannten. Das hatte knapp 40 Jahre gedauert, und danach war die Universität über 100 Jahre universal und übernational.[13] Im 16. Jahrhundert dagegen dehnt die jeweilige landesherrliche Regierung „*ihre Verordnungsgewalt immer mehr aus; sie gibt Statuten und Ordnungen für die Universität und die Fakultäten, für die äußeren Verhältnisse und den Unterrichtsbetrieb. Die Professoren werden Staatsbeamte, die im Auftrag und unter Aufsicht der Landesregierung lehren. Die Aufsicht wird durch Visitationen geübt, zu denen landesherrliche Kommissarien erscheinen mit dem Auftrag, Leben und Lehre der Professoren und Studenten zu erforschen. Es ist der Polizeistaat, der sich hier ankündigt ... Auch die Studierenden unterliegen der Aufsicht; sie werden als künftige Diener des Landesherrn, im weltlichen oder im geistlichen Amt, angesehen ... Regelmäßig findet bei der Anstellung die eidliche Verpflichtung auf die landeskirchlichen Bekenntnisschriften statt; auch bei der Promotion ist die Verpflichtung auf Schrift und Symbole gewöhnlich ... Auch das Studieren auf fremden Universitäten, wenigstens auf den in der Lehre nicht reinen, wurde den Landeskindern vielfach untersagt, bei Verlust der Anstellungsfähigkeit*" (*Paulsen 1921, Bd. 1, S. 257f.*). Die Vorteile waren: Verbreiterung der finanziellen und administrativen Basis der Universitäten, regelmäßige Besoldung der Professoren als Staatsbeamte, Sicherung der Kontinuität in der Lehre. Die Nachteile lagen auf der Hand; sie wirkten sich besonders auf die Berufung von Professoren aus, wobei der Vereidigung auf das jeweilige Bekenntnis häufig ein 'examen doctrinae', die Prüfung des Glaubensbekenntnisses vorausging. Kriecherei, Denunziation, Intrigantentum waren die Folge.

Man muß in diesem Zusammenhang auch beachten, daß die uns heute kaum vorstellbare Autonomie und Selbstverwaltung der Universitäten, wie sie im 14. und 15. Jahrhundert bestanden hatte, sehr stark eingeschränkt wurde. Entscheidend ist allerdings, daß die Ubiquität der scholastischen und der humanistischen Lehrer und Schüler beendet war. Einst war die gesamte abendländische Christenheit das Universitätsgebiet. Die Universitäten hatten internationalen Charakter. Wie nun die Einheit der Kirche durch die Reformation ihr Ende fand, so auch die Einheit des europäischen Humanismus *(Böhme 1986, S. 331)* und der Wissenschaft.

---

13 Vgl. *Westphalen (1979, S. 45)*: „*Die Verbindung von französischem Königtum und avignonerischem Papsttum versperrte ... den deutschen Magistern – sofern sie aus Territorien römischer Obödienz stammten – die Teilnahme an der Pfründensupplik der Pariser Universität bzw. den Zugang zu kirchlichen Ämtern in ihrer Heimat. Mit dem Schisma verlor der akademische Titel seine Bedeutung als selbstverständliche und universale Eingangsvoraussetzung zu kirchlichen Ämtern qua akademischer Ausbildung.*"

Die Reformation zerschlug die Universalität der Universität und führte zur Territorialisierung, ja zur Regionalität, bzw. brachte sie erst hervor. Diese Territorialität betraf nicht nur die Universitäten, die man nun nach katholischen und protestantischen unterschied, sondern die gesamte Wissenschaft und das politische und geistige Leben selbst – auf einzelnen Gebieten bis weit in unser Jahrhundert. Die konfessionelle Lehrerausbildung an spezifischen Hochschulen endete z. B. erst in den sechziger Jahren unseres Jahrhunderts.

Bibliographie

Böhme, Günther: Bildungsgeschichte des europäischen Humanismus. Darmstadt: Wissenschaftliche Buchgesellschaft 1986.
Bornkamm, Heinrich: Das Jahrhundert der Reformation. Frankfurt a. M.: Insel-Verlag 1983. (Insel-Taschenbuch. 713)
Burger, Heinz Otto: Renaissance, Humanismus, Reformation. Deutsche Literatur im europäischen Kontext. Bad Homburg u. a.: Gehlen 1969. (Frankfurter Beiträge zur Germanistik. 7)
Classen, Peter: Studium und Gesellschaft im Mittelalter. Hrsg. von Johannes Fried. Stuttgart: Hiersemann 1983. (Schriften der Monumenta Germaniae historica. 29)
Cobban, Alan Balfour: The Medieval English Universities. Oxford and Cambridge to c.1500. Aldershot: Scholar Press 1988.
Ellwein, Thomas: Die deutsche Universität. Vom Mittelalter bis zur Gegenwart. Königstein, Ts.: Athenäum-Verlag 1985.
Esch, Arnold: Die Anfänge der Universität im Mittelalter. Bern: Haupt 1985. (Berner Rektoratsreden. 1985)
Eulenburg, Franz: Die Frequenz der deutschen Universitäten von ihrer Gründung bis zur Gegenwart. Leipzig: Teubner 1904. (Abhandlungen der Königlich Sächsischen Gesellschaft der Wissenschaften. Philosophisch-historische Klasse. 24,2)
Fläschendräger, Werner u. a.: Magister und Scholaren. Professoren und Studenten. Geschichte deutscher Universitäten und Hochschulen im Überblick. Leipzig u. a.: Urania-Verlag 1981.
Fried, Johannes (Hrsg.): Schulen und Studium im sozialen Wandel des hohen und späten Mittelalters. Sigmaringen: Thorbecke 1986. (Vorträge und Forschungen. 3)
Garin, Eugenio: La cultura filosofica del Rinascimento italiano. Firenze: Bompiani 1994. (Saggi tascabili. 34)
Hagen, Karl: Deutschlands literarische und religiöse Verhältnisse im Reformationsalter. Mit besonderer Berücksichtigung auf Wilibald Pirckheimer. Erlangen: Palm 1841.
Heller, Agnes: Der Mensch der Renaissance. Köln: Hohenheim 1982.
Ijswijn, Jozef / Paquet, Jacques (Hrsg.): The Universities in the Late Middle Ages. Leuven: University Press 1978. (Mediaevalia lovanensia. 6)
Janssen, Johannes: Geschichte des deutschen Volkes seit dem Ausgang des Mittelalters. 13., verb. u. 14. Aufl. Bd. 1. 6. Freiburg i. Br. u. a.: Herder 1887-1893.
Kaufmann, Georg: Geschichte der deutschen Universitäten. Bd. 1. 2. Stuttgart: Cotta 1888-1896.

Landfester, Rüdiger: Historia magistra vitae. Untersuchungen zur humanistischen Geschichtstheorie des 14. bis 16. Jahrhunderts. Genève: Droz 1972. (Travaux d'humanisme et renaissance. 123)

Le Goff, Jacques: Les intellectuels au moyen âge. Paris: Editions du Seuil 1957. (Le temps qui court. 3)

Lundberg, Mabel: Jesuitische Anthropologie und Erziehungslehre in der Frühzeit des Ordens (ca. 1540-1650). Uppsala: Almqvist och Wiksell 1966. (Studia doctrinae christianae Upsalensis. 6)

Luther, Martin: Tischreden oder Colloquia. Eisleben: Gaubisch 1566.

Luther, Martin: Luther als Pädagog. Hrsg. von Ernst Wagner. Langensalza: Schulbuchverlag 1887. (Die Klassiker der Pädagogik. 2)

Luther, Martin: Werke für das christliche Haus. Hrsg. von Georg Buchwald u. a. Bd. 1-3. Braunschweig: Schwetzschke 1889.

Melanchthon, Philipp: Opera, quae supersunt, omnia. Hrsg. von Karl Gottlieb Bretschneider und Heinrich Ernst Bindseil. Bd. 10. Halle a. S.: Schwetschke 1842. (Corpus Reformatorum. 10)

Miclescu, Maria: Die spanische Universität in Geschichte und Gegenwart. Köln u. a.: Böhlau 1985. (Studien und Dokumentationen zur vergleichenden Bildungsforschung. 33)

Moraw, Peter: Der Lebensweg der Studenten. In: Rüegg, Walter (Hrsg.): Geschichte der Universität in Europa. Bd. 1: Mittelalter, München: Beck 1993, S. 227-254.

Müller, Gregor: Bildung und Erziehung im Humanismus der italienischen Renaissance. Grundlagen, Motive, Quellen. Wiesbaden: Steiner 1969.

Müller, Rainer A.: Geschichte der Universität. Von der mittelalterlichen Universitas zur deutschen Hochschule. München: Callwey 1990.

Muther, Theodor: Aus dem Universitäts- und Gelehrtenleben im Zeitalter der Reformation. Erlangen: Deichert 1866.

Niethammer, Friedrich Immanuel: Der Streit des Philanthropismus und Humanismus. Jena: Frommann 1808.

Paulsen, Friedrich: Geschichte des gelehrten Unterrichts auf den deutschen Schulen und Universitäten vom Ausgang des Mittelalters bis zur Gegenwart. 3., erw. Aufl. Bd. 1. 2. Berlin u. a.: de Gruyter 1921.

Piltz, Anders: Die gelehrte Welt des Mittelalters. Köln u. a.: Böhlau 1982.

Prahl, Hans-Werner: Sozialgeschichte des Hochschulwesens. München: Kösel 1978.

Prahl, Hans-Werner: Hochschule und Universität. In: Roth, Leo (Hrsg.): Pädagogik. Handbuch für Studium und Praxis, München: Ehrenwirth 1991, S. 507-517.

Prahl, Hans-Werner / Schmidt-Harzbach, Ingrid: Die Universität. Eine Kultur- und Sozialgeschichte. München u. a.: Bucher 1981.

Roth, Leo: Der Erziehungstheoretiker Erasmus von Rotterdam. In: Duwe, Gert / ders. (Hrsg.): Kunst und Humanismus in den Niederlanden des 15. bis 17. Jahrhunderts, Frankfurt a. M. u. a.: Lang 1995, S. 153-176.

Roth, Leo: Universalität und Regionalisierung der deutschen Universität im 15. bis 17. Jahrhundert. In: Duwe, Gert / ders. (Hrsg.): Kunst und Humanismus in den Niederlanden des 15. bis 17. Jahrhunderts, Frankfurt a. M. u. a.: Lang 1995, S. 85-109.

Rückert, Hans: Die Stellung der Reformation zur mittelalterlichen Universität. In: ders.: Vorträge und Aufsätze zur historischen Theologie, Tübingen: Mohr 1972, S. 71-95.

Rüegg, Walter (Hrsg.): Geschichte der Universität in Europa. Bd. 1: Mittelalter. München: Beck 1993.

Schwinges, Rainer Christoph: Deutsche Universitätsbesucher im 14. und 15. Jahrhundert. Studien zur Sozialgeschichte des Alten Reichs. Stuttgart: Steiner 1986. (Beiträge zur Verfassungsgeschichte des alten Reichs. 6)

Schwinges, Rainer Christoph: Die Zulassung zur Universität. In: Rüegg, Walter (Hrsg.): Geschichte der Universität in Europa. Bd. 1: Mittelalter, München: Beck 1993, S. 161-180.

Stempel, Hermann-Adolf: Melanchthons pädagogisches Wirken. Bielefeld: Luther-Verlag 1979. (Untersuchungen zur Kirchengeschichte. 11)

Verger, Jacques: Die Universitätslehrer. In: Rüegg, Walter (Hrsg.): Geschichte der Universität in Europa. Bd. 1: Mittelalter, München: Beck 1993, S. 139-157.

Voigt, Georg: Die Wiederbelebung des classischen Alterthums oder das erste Jahrhundert des Humanismus. Berlin: Reimer 1859.

Westphalen, Raban von: Akademisches Privileg und demokratischer Staat. Ein Beitrag zur Geschichte und bildungspolitischen Problematik des Laufbahnwesens in Deutschland. Stuttgart: Klett-Cotta 1979.

Erziehung zur Demokratie durch die Schülerselbstregierung in der Zweiten Polnischen Republik (1918 bis 1939)

Mirosław S. Szymański

„Die Interdependenz zwischen Erziehung, Demokratie und Entwicklung ist keine Entdeckung der Gegenwart ... Glücklicherweise lenkt die Erfahrung unsere Aufmerksamkeit auch auf Erziehungstheoretiker und Erziehungspraktiker, welche ihr Engagement darin entfalten, Entwicklung und Demokratie auf der Grundlage menschlicher Grundwerte zu erfassen und behandeln. Es ist diese Erfahrung, welche meiner Meinung nach unsere Anstrengungen rechtfertigt, die Interdependenz zwischen Entwicklung, Demokratie und Erziehung zu erforschen und zu erörtern."

(Wolfgang Mitter 1992)

Bei der Entstehung und Entwicklung von Theorie und Praxis der Schülerselbstregierung[1] in der Zweiten Polnischen Republik haben zwei Werke von weltweiter Wirkung die größte Rolle gespielt.

Das erste war „Schule und Charakter", dessen heute nahezu vergessener Verfasser Friedrich Wilhelm Foerster – aufgrund seines bedingungslosen Kampfes gegen den Nationalismus, Chauvinismus und Militarismus in Deutschland das „Gewissen einer Generation" (z. B. *Antz / Pöggeler 1955*) genannt – im Zwischenkriegspolen hoch geachtet und geschätzt war. Er war zweifellos der meist gelesene ausländische pädagogische Schriftsteller. Davon zeugt allein schon die Tatsache, daß bis zum Ausbruch des Zweiten Weltkrieges 19(!) Buchveröffentlichungen von ihm ins Polnische übertragen wurden. Ähnlich wie in Deutschland galt er als führender Reformpädagoge auf moralpädagogi-

---

1   Der englische Terminus „self-government", von Foerster wie von Kerschensteiner wörtlich mit „Selbstregierung" übersetzt, wurde im hierarchisch-monarchischen Deutschland sehr bald durch den bis heute verwendeten Terminus „Selbstverwaltung" ersetzt. Dies wird folgendermaßen erklärt: *„Im Kaiserreich war man sich der monarchiegefährdenden und damit staatsgefährdenden Eigenschaft von Selbst-Regierung des Volkes wohl bewußt. Selbst-Verwaltung dagegen ist nicht unbedingt eine demokratische Errungenschaft. Verwalten kann auch der Untertan, sogar der Häftling ..."* (Kamp 1995, S. 34f.). Zu Beginn des 20. Jahrhunderts wurde in der polnischen Sprache meistens auch nicht der Begriff „samorząd" – also „Selbstregierung" –, sondern „gmina szkolna" also „Schulgemeinde" verwendet: So wurde der amerikanische Begriff „school city" übersetzt, der

schem Gebiet sowie als einflußreicher katholischer Moralpädagoge. Die Tatsache, daß er sich im katholischen Polen so großer Popularität erfreute, läßt sich wohl in erster Linie damit erklären, daß er in seinem Erziehungssystem die Verwirklichung traditioneller katholischer Erziehungsziele mit Hilfe moderner Erziehungsmethoden empfahl, unter denen kein Platz war für eine „Prügelpädagogik" und mündliche Belehrungen nur unter besonderen Bedingungen zugelassen waren.

Einen Abriß seines Erziehungssystems stellte Foerster in seinem Hauptwerk „Schule und Charakter" dar, in dem er aus katholischer Sicht Stellung nahm zu wesentlichen pädagogischen Problemen, unter anderem zu: Ursachen der Disziplinlosigkeit in den Schulen, Gehorsam und Freiheit, Sexualerziehung und Schülerselbstmorde, Koedukation und Elitenbildung. Vor allem aber machte er durch dieses mehrfach ergänzte und immer wieder überarbeitete Buch die Schülerselbstregierung in Deutschland bekannt und populär; er wurde – neben Georg Kerschensteiner, den man in Polen ebenfalls gut kannte – zum einflußreichsten deutschsprachigen Theoretiker der Selbstregierung und spielte eine führende Rolle bei der Einführung dieser Erziehungsmethode in die Schulen, erlebte doch dieses Werk in der Originalsprache 15 Auflagen: die erste 1907, die letzte 1953. Ins Polnische wurde es bereits im Jahre 1909 übersetzt und erlebte insgesamt sechs Auflagen: die letzte im Jahre 1934.

Die Hauptaufgabe der Schulerziehung besteht laut *Foerster (1930, S. 18)* in der Formung eines starken Charakters bei den Schülern, „... *1. um das Menschentum des Schülers vor den Gefahren einseitiger Verstandesbildung zu bewahren; 2. um die durch die Schule geweckten und entwickelten Fähigkeiten und Fertigkeiten von vornherein einem höherem Zwecke und Gesetz zu unterwerfen; 3. um der Schularbeit und der Schulordnung die tieferen Kräfte der Seele zuzuführen; 4. um die vielen Gelegenheiten, die das Schulleben selber für die Übung der Charakterkräfte und für die Klärung des sittlichen Urteils bietet, planvoll auszunutzen ...*". Die Charakterbildung ist die gezielte Erziehung zu den „ewigen" Werten, zu einer Einfügung in das „größere Ganze", zu einer stark katholisch geprägten Moral und Sittlichkeit, zur Selbstgesetzgebung, zum freiwilligen Gehorsam, zur Verantwortlichkeit, zur Selbstbeschränkung, zur Selbstkontrolle usw. Durch die

---

1897 von dem einflußreichen Theoretiker und Praktiker des self-government in den Schulen, W. L. Gill, eingeführt worden war. Erst nach dem Niedergang der drei Monarchien und der Wiedergeburt Polens in Form einer Republik hat sich der Begriff „Selbstregierung" durchgesetzt und behauptet. Es war keine bloße terminologische Änderung, sondern durchaus ein Programm, denn zum Regierungssystem gehören alle drei politischen Gewalten: die Selbstregierung, die Selbstgesetzgebung und die Selbstrechtsprechung.

Charakterbildung soll die schlechte menschliche Natur durch eine anerzogene gute Kultur unterdrückt und überlagert werden. Zwei Methoden der erzieherischen Einwirkungen stehen dem Lehrer hier zur Verfügung: die individualpädagogische Methode und die sozialpädagogische Methode. Die letztere besteht wesentlich darin, *„... daß man das jugendliche Bandenwesen sozusagen legalisiert, ihm positive Aufgaben der Ordnung, der Fürsoge und der Verwaltung anvertraut ..."* *(ebd., S. 100)*. Die sozialpädagogische Methode ist daher nichts anderes, als die Methode der Schülerselbstregierung. Die Schülerselbstregierung – auch Schülerselbstverwaltung genannt – sei die beste Methode sowohl für die Einhaltung der Schuldisziplin als auch für eine echte Charakterbildung der Kinder und Jugendlichen in der Schule.

In seinem Buch „Schule und Charakter" beschrieb Foerster einige meist wenig radikale Experimente mit der Schülerselbstregierung in der Schweiz, in Österreich und in Deutschland. Die größte Aufmerksamkeit schenkte er der amerikanischen *school city* und der englischen *public school*, um auf dieser Grundlage sehr konkrete Vorschläge für die Einführung und Organisation der Schülerselbstregierung zu formulieren. *„Ihre Aufgabe sieht er in großer Breite, angefangen von den kleinen Ämtern für das Fensteröffnen, die Betreuung von Sammlungen, der Sorge für die Sauberkeit, bis zu der Tätigkeit umfassenderer Schülerausschüsse, die bei der Beurteilung von Straffällen mit zu Wort kommen. Mit dem Problem des Schülergerichts setzt er sich eingehend auseinander, er entwickelt dessen Möglichkeiten und ist sich auch der Grenzen bewußt"* (Scheibe 1959, S. 9). Darüber hinaus empfiehlt er – wie es sich für einen Anhänger der monarchistischen Regierungsform geziemt – den Lehrern, sie sollten sich vor *„verhängnisvollen gefährlichen Übertreibungen"* hüten, die Nachahmung der parlamentarisch-demokratischen Regierungsform vermeiden, sich dem *„Amerikanismus"* widersetzen, der *„die pädagogische Bedeutung der absoluten Autorität des Lehrers"* ignoriere. Letztendlich ist die Selbstregierung in seinem Erziehungssystem nur eine schulische Einrichtung, *„... die die Autorität gegeben hat, um die Übung in neuen Pflichten zu ermöglichen"* (Foerster 1930, S. 273).

Ein letzter Sinn der Schülerselbstregierung erfüllt sich in der staatsbürgerlichen Erziehung. Und staatsbürgerliche Erziehung zum Verantwortungsgefühl für das „größere Ganze" – das Volk und/oder den Staat – war ja in Polen eine der Hauptaufgaben des wiedergeborenen Staates. Hier dürfte die zweite Ursache für die große Popularität liegen, die Foersters Bücher in der Zweiten Polnischen Republik genossen haben.

Das zweite Werk, das die Praxis und Theorie der Schülerselbstregierung in Polen maßgeblich bestimmte, ist das – in deutscher Fassung nicht vorliegende – Buch „L'autonomie des écoliers". Ins Polnische übersetzt wurde es zwar erst 1933 *(Ferrière 1933)*, doch war es aufgrund zahlreicher Besprechungen sowie im Original (1920 erschien die erste französische Auflage) in Polen bereits seit den frühen zwanziger Jahren bekannt. Der Autor des Buches ist der namhafte Schweizer Reformpädagoge Adolphe Ferrière: Mitarbeiter von Hermann Lietz in den deutschen Landerziehungsheimen in Ilsenburg im Harz und in Haubinda; Mitbegründer des ersten Landerziehungsheimes der Schweiz in Glarisegg; Professor des „Institut Jean-Jacques Rousseau" in Genf; Mitbegründer der „New Education Fellowship", die sich in Deutschland „Weltbund für Erneuerung der Erziehung" nannte; Mitbegründer eines Internationalen Erziehungsbüros, das als „Bureau International d'Éducation" in der Welt berühmt wurde; Autor von über 40 Büchern und Hunderter von Aufsätzen; Hauptvertreter und unermüdlicher Befürworter der „école active", der „Schule der Tat" *(Hilker 1960; Grunder 1987)*.

In den zwanziger Jahren führten ihn Vortragsreisen in viele Länder der Welt. 1929 besuchte er auch Polen, wo er viele Schulen besichtigte und sich mit der polnischen Pädagogik bekannt machte. Der Aufenthalt resultierte einerseits in Aufsätzen über die polnischen „Neuen Schulen", die Ferrière in französischsprachigen pädagogischen Fachzeitschriften veröffentlichte, und andererseits in polnischen Übersetzungen seiner Hauptwerke: Auszüge aus dem Buch „L'école active" *(Ferrière 1930)* sowie des oben genannten Buches „L'autonomie des écoliers".

Die „Schule der Tat" definiert Ferrière als eine: *„Gegenbewegung gegen alles, was es noch an Mittelalterlichem im gegenwärtigen Schulbetrieb gibt: gegen allen Formalismus; gegen die Gewohnheit, der Schule eine nebengeordnete Stelle im Leben einzuräumen; gegen die völlige Verständnislosigkeit für das, was das Wesentliche und Grundlegende in der Natur des Kindes ist"* (nach *Hilker 1960, S. 453*). Er befürwortet eine kindzentrierte Schule, deren Hauptaufgabe es sei, ein gesundes Milieu zu schaffen, aus dem der Schüler die Kräfte zur Entwicklung schöpfen könne. Es handelt sich um eine „Befreiung" des Schülers von hemmenden Faktoren, die der Entfaltung seines Wesens, seiner natürlichen Anlagen im Wege stehen, und damit um eine Förderung der schöpferischen Aktivität, der inneren produktiven Kräfte, des Interesses, der freien Tätigkeit. Die natürlichen Antriebe des Schülers müßten aber mit den objektiven Anforderungen des Lebens verbunden werden. Ein vorzügliches Mittel dafür sei in erster Linie die Schülerselbstregierung.

Das Buch „L'autonomie des écoliers" gibt einen umfassenden Überblick über viele Versuche der schulischen Selbstregierung in den Vereinigten Staaten und in westeuropäischen Ländern, wobei allerdings auch radikalere Selbstregierungsmodelle mit berücksichtigt wurden, wie etwa Gustav Wynekens „Freie Schulgemeinde" in Wickersdorf, Paul Geheebs Odenwaldschule in Ober-Hambach oder Stanislav T. Šackijs Kolonie „Munteres Leben" in Rußland. Aufgrund der vorgenommenen Übersicht wurde die Schülerselbstregierung als Erziehungsmethode definiert, und „*... erziehen bedeutet von Inkompetenz zu Kompetenz, von Unbeholfenheit zu Fähigkeit, von Unwissen zu Wissen, von mangelnder Voraussicht zu Umsicht zu führen" (Ferrière 1933, S. 170)*. Vor die Schülerselbstregierung stellt Ferrière die doppelte Aufgabe: Einerseits soll sie die Befriedigung und freie Entfaltung der guten natürlichen Antriebe und Bedürfnisse der Schüler ermöglichen, andererseits soll sie den Schülern einen Versuchsraum bieten, in dem solche staatsbürgerlichen Tugenden wie Wahrhaftigkeit, Verantwortungsgefühl, Selbständigkeit, Nächstenliebe geweckt und gepflegt werden. Abgeschlossen wird das Buch mit der Aufzählung zahlreicher Vorteile, die sich aus der Anwendung der Methode der Schülerselbstregierung ergeben, sowie mit der Formulierung allgemeiner Richtlinien für ihre Einführung in die Schule. Durch die Selbstregierung „*... lernt die Mehrheit unserer Kinder drei grundlegende Dinge: Initiative für den Fortschritt der Menschengemeinschaft, kritischen Sinn auf rationaler Grundlage sowie den Geist gegenseitiger Hilfe auf der Basis der Gerechtigkeit" (ebd., S. 225)*.

Unter den zahlreichen polnischen Veröffentlichungen über die Theorie und Praxis der Schülerselbstregierung findet sich keine einzige zur vergleichenden Analyse der pädagogischen Ansichten von Foerster und Ferrière. Obwohl beide Pädagogen allgemein zitiert und ihre Empfehlungen bei der Erziehungsarbeit in der Schule befolgt wurden, war man sich in der Regel nicht bewußt, von welch unterschiedlichen anthropologischen Voraussetzungen sie ausgingen, wenn sie ein und derselben Erziehungsmethode das Wort redeten.

Dem Autor von „Schule und Charakter" nach sei der *Mensch* „*... nun doch einmal ein zügelloses Wesen, das keine Grenzen und keine Selbsteinschätzung kennt" (Foerster 1930, S. 278)*; der Mensch sei von Natur aus schlecht. Durch die Erziehung soll daher die menschliche Natur unterdrückt und überwunden werden. Nur auf diese Art und Weise könne der pflichtorientierte, moralische, selbstbeherrschte, gewissensstarke und dem Staat gehorsame und dienende Charakter ausgebildet werden. Dem Autor von „L'autonomie des écoliers" nach muß dagegen „*... die menschliche Natur eine große Dosis gesunden Verstands enthalten, einen angeborenen Widerstand gegen das Böse, eine Kraft,* *die ihn dem Lichte zuwendet ... " (Ferrière 1933, S. 8):* der Mensch sei von Natur aus gut. Die Hauptaufgabe der Erziehung sei denn der Schutz und die Pflege der menschlichen Natur. Erziehung zielt hier auf die Unterstützung und Hilfe zur Befriedigung der natürlichen Bedürfnisse und auf die Entfaltung der inneren Kräfte in sozial akzeptablen Formen. Nur auf diese Art und Weise kann der sich seiner Rechte und Pflichten bewußte, über seine eigenen Handlungen entscheidende und am Leben der Gemeinschaft teilnehmende Staatsbürger ausgebildet werden: zwei verschiedene Auffassungen von der Natur des Menschen – zwei schulische Selbstregierungsmodelle. Das erste versuchte man in Polen als „monarchistisch", das andere dagegen als „demokratisch" zu benennen. Beide fanden ihren Niederschlag in der erzieherischen Praxis.

In der polnischen pädagogischen Fachliteratur wurde eine Unterscheidung von zwei Phasen in der geschichtlichen Entwicklung von Idee und Praxis der Schülerselbstregierung eingeführt: eine *„sehr lange intuitive Entwicklungsphase"*, gefolgt von einer *„sehr kurzen und bei weitem noch unvollkommenen rationalen Phase" (Mirski 1933, S. 72).* Im Sinne dieser Unterscheidung dauerte die „intuitive" Phase von der Reformationszeit an, als Trotzendorf (im Jahre 1531) in Goldberg in Schlesien einen Schulstaat gegründet hatte, der nach dem Muster der römischen Republik des Altertums organisiert war – bis zur Wende zum 20. Jahrhundert, der Zeit der dynamischen Entwicklung psychologischer, pädagogischer und soziologischer Forschung, als man daran ging, das bei den bisherigen Versuchen mit der Schülerselbstregierung angesammelte Wissen zu verallgemeinern und zu synthetisieren. Eben zu diesem Zeitpunkt, in der Epoche der Reformpädagogik, soll die „rationale" Phase in der weltweiten Geschichte der Selbstregierung eingesetzt haben. Diese Unterscheidung läßt sich auf die Entwicklung der Bewegung der Schülerselbstregierung im Zwischenkriegspolen sinnvoll anwenden, wobei als Zäsur das Jahr 1930 angesetzt werden kann.

Das Hauptkennzeichen der ersten „intuitiven Phase" besteht darin, daß einzelne Schulleiter oder Lehrer voneinander unabhängige und nicht aufeinander abgestimmte Versuche unternommen haben, auf eigene Faust und eigenes Risiko die Methode der Selbstregierung in ihre Schulen einzuführen. Gegen Ende dieser Phase erschienen zahlreiche gedruckte Berichte über die Erfahrungen, die mit dieser Erziehungsmethode gemacht wurden.

Auf welche Art und Weise wurde die Schülerselbstregierung eingeführt? Vor welche Aufgaben wurde sie gestellt? Welche Organisationsform nahm sie an? Welchen Umfang hatte ihre Praxis?

Verallgemeinernde Antworten auf die obigen Fragen erteilt ein bündiger, sehr informativer Aufsatz *(Majkowska 1930)*, der im Jahre 1930 – mit Rücksicht auf ausländische Leser – für die „polnische Nummer" der Zeitschrift „The New Era", des offiziellen Publikationsorgans der „New Education Fellowship", geschrieben wurde. Aus diesem Aufsatz geht das folgende synthetische oder idealtypische Bild der polnischen Schülerselbstregierung hervor.

Die Schülerselbstregierung entstand auf verschiedene Art und Weise. Nur selten entstand sie sofort als besondere Organisationsform; in der Regel entwickelte sie sich organisch von einer geringeren Organisationseinheit (etwa Arbeits- und Interessengemeinschaft oder Schulorganisation des Roten Kreuzes), die allmählich ihren Tätigkeitsumfang erweiterte. Am häufigsten – insbesondere in Lehrerseminaren – war die Schülergenossenschaft der Kristallisationspunkt der Selbstregierung, ihr schlossen sich verschiedene Arbeits- und Interessengemeinschaften an: für Sport, Hygiene, Selbstbildung, Bibliotheksarbeit und andere, die sich mit der Zeit zu einer Einheit mit dem Namen „Schülerselbstregierung" zusammenschlossen.

Die folgenden Zwecke der Schülerselbstregierung wurden am häufigsten genannt: alle Schüler der Klasse oder Schule zu einer einheitlichen und disziplinierten Gemeinschaft zu vereinigen, sie Solidarität und Kameradschaft zu lehren, ihr sittliches Niveau zu heben, ihr Verantwortungsgefühl zu formen sowie ihren Unternehmungsgeist und ihre schöpferischen Möglichkeiten zu entwickeln.

Die Schülerselbstregierung umfaßte entweder die Schüler einer Klasse oder der ganzen Schule. Im ersten Fall wählten die Schüler einer Klasse einen „Schülerausschuß" oder „Schülerrat", der sich zumeist aus drei Personen, nämlich dem Klassensprecher, dem Klassensekretär und dem Klassenkassenwart, zusammensetzte; er trug die Verantwortung für die Tätigkeit der gesamten Klasse gegenüber dem Klassenlehrer und vertrat sie nach außen. Durch ihn kamen die Klassen miteinander in Verbindung und zur Zusammenarbeit. Im zweiten Fall wählten die Mitglieder aller Schülerräte der Klassen unter sich selbst einen Schülerrat der Schule; er trug die Verantwortung für die Tätigkeit der gesamten Schülerschaft der Schule gegenüber dem Schulleiter und vertrat sie nach außen. Das oberste Organ der Selbstregierung war die Vollversammlung einer Schule.

Der Tätigkeitsradius der Schülerselbstregierung war sehr umfangreich und konnte solche Aufgabenbereiche umfassen wie: gegenseitige Selbsthilfe materieller (Speisung, Kleidung, ärztliche Behandlung, Anleihekasse), fachlicher (gegenseitige Lernhilfe) und sittlicher Art (Betreuung von unangepaßten Mitschülern); Kameradschaftsgericht; Schülerladen, verwaltet nach den Grundsätzen des Genossenschaftswesens; Herausgabe von Schülerzeitung, Schuljahrbuch, Schulchronik; Betreuung von Schulbibliothek und -lesesaal (unter Anleitung des Lehrers); Aufrechterhaltung von Ordnung und Sauberkeit in der Schule – über Wirtschafts- und Ordnungsausschüsse; Pflege der Selbsthygiene – über Hygieneausschüsse; Organisation von Sportveranstaltungen – über Kunst- und Unterhaltungausschüsse; Zusammenarbeit mit den verschiedensten öffentlichen Organisationen. Selbstverständlich wurde der Tätigkeitsumfang der einzelnen Schülerselbstregierungen jeweils durch die Initiative und das Engagement der Schüler bestimmt.

Dank der Methode der Schülerselbstregierung sollte die junge Generation lernen, „... *für den [polnischen] Staat einzustehen und ihn zum Erblühen zu führen, im Wettbewerb mit anderen Staaten, deren politische Existenz nie unterbrochen war"* (Majkowska 1930, S. 221).

Zur grundlegenden Informationsquelle über Umfang und Ergebnisse der Praxis der Selbstregierung in den polnischen Schulen wurde ein umfangreicher Aufsatz, der von dem bei Wilhelm Windelband promovierten Philosophen, Theoretiker der Moralerziehung und herausragenden Übersetzer Adam *Zieleńczyk (1932)* veröffentlicht wurde. Der Aufsatz präsentiert und analysiert die Ergebnisse einer in Polen durchgeführten Umfrage, die das Bureau International d'Éducation in Genf an alle Länder der Welt gesandt hatte, in denen in den Schulen die Methode der Selbstregierung praktiziert wurde. Die polnische Bildungsbehörde verschickte ihrerseits die Umfrage an 400 Lehrer im ganzen Land, wobei nur diejenigen Schulen angesprochen wurden, in denen die Methode „interessante Ergebnisse" – seien es positive oder negative – erbrachte.

Die äußerst detaillierte Umfrage umfaßte drei Rubriken: Entstehung und Geschichte der Versuche mit der Schülerselbstregierung, ihre Organisationsformen und ihre Ergebnisse im Bereich der sittlichen, intellektuellen und gesellschaftlichen Erziehung. Die Antworten der Lehrer ergeben selbstverständlich ein recht buntes Bild, sie lassen jedoch gewisse Verallgemeinerungen zu.

Als eigentliche Ursachen der Einführung der Selbstregierung in die Schule genannt wurden sowohl die von Foerster hervorgehobenen Motive („mangelnde Achtung vor der Staatsmacht und dem Recht", „mangelnde Liebe zu Ordnung und Sauberkeit", „Nachlässigkeit in der Pflichterfüllung") wie auch jene von Ferrière („den natürlichen Bestrebungen der Jugend freien Lauf zu lassen", „Rücksicht auf die Individualität des Schülers", „Bekämpfung der Untätigkeit und des Mangels an Initiative"). Nur sieben Lehrer hatten in ihrer Schule eine bereits funktionierende Selbstregierung vorgefunden, fast alle haben sie von Grund auf selbst aufgebaut, und zwar allmählich, Schritt für Schritt, über die „Vermehrung der Funktionen" oder die „Erweiterung der Kompetenzen". Anregungen suchten sie zumeist in einem Büchlein *(Przanowski / Szczawińska / Wójcik 1928)*, das drei Beispiele für die Verwirklichung der Methode der Selbstregierung in den Schulen anführte; unter diesen Beispielen befand sich ein gelungener Versuch, nämlich der, Janusz *Korczaks (1989)* Selbstregierungssystem aus „Unser Haus" in die Volksschule zu verpflanzen.

Was die Organisationsformen der Schülerselbstregierung angeht, so gab es – im Sinne von Ferrière – 223 „demokratische" und 99 „monarchistische" Selbstregierungen. Allerdings gab es auch viele Übergangsformen. Dabei änderte sich die Form beziehungsweise die „politische Verfassung" ein und derselben Selbstregierung je nach ihrer Entwicklungsphase – Ausgangspunkt war in der Regel eine „Monarchie", die sich dann in Richtung der „vollen Demokratie" veränderte; Unterschiede bestanden auch je nach Umstand und Angelegenheit – beispielsweise galten in der Rechtsprechung demokratische Grundsätze, während in anderen Tätigkeitsbereichen das monarchistische Muster bestimmend und die Autorität des Lehrers die letzte Instanz war. Vielfach läßt sich ein deutlicher Zusammenhang zwischen der Form der Schülerselbstregierung und der Staatsform feststellen; nicht wenige Lehrer begriffen die Selbstregierung einfach als ein Modell des polnischen Staates, d. h. als einen Staat im Kleinen. Die Selbstregierungen spiegelten ganz deutlich das politische Klima im Lande sowie die nationalen Sitten und die vorherrschende Geisteshaltung wieder.

Was schließlich die Ergebnisse der Praxis der Schülerselbstregierung angeht, so beurteilten die Lehrer ihre Rolle bei der sittlichen („sie formt das Verantwortungsgefühl"), intellektuellen („sie erweitert die geistigen Horizonte") und sozialen Erziehung („sie entwickelt die Fähigkeiten zu Zusammenleben und Zusammenarbeit") recht positiv.

In der polnischen pädagogischen Fachliteratur der zwanziger Jahre lassen sich viele praktische Hinweise, aber auch allgemeine Überlegungen zur Einführung der Methode der Selbstregierung in den Schulen wiederfinden. Selbstverständlich gab es hierbei Meinungsverschiedenheiten und Kontroversen, die sich in der Regel allerdings auf Einzelfragen bezogen. Die Selbstregierung an sich und ihre Erziehungsvorzüge wurden nicht in Frage gestellt, selbst wenn Beschränkungen, Schwierigkeiten und Gefahren im Zusammenhang mit der Anwendung dieser Erziehungsmethode nicht übersehen wurden.

Zur Debatte standen viele Einzelfragen (vgl. *Sobczak 1979, Bereźnicki 1984, Koźmian 1991*). Im folgenden beschränken wir uns darauf, vier der wohl am häufigsten erörterte Problemkreise zu benennen.

Worin liegt das Wesen der Schülerselbstregierung begründet? Bei der Beantwortung der obigen Frage wurde die Auseinandersetzung zwischen Ferrière und Foerster auf polnischen Boden verpflanzt. Für die einen nämlich bestand das Wesen dieser Bewegung in der Erziehungsarbeit nach dem Motto: *„Vaterland, Bildung, Tugend... Insbesondere geht es darum ..., a) äußere wie innere Ordnung zu wahren; b) die geistige, sittliche und körperliche Entwicklung der Bürger zu fördern; c) sie reifen zu lassen und auf ein Leben zum Nutzen des Vaterlandes vorzubereiten"* (Bykowski 1921). Für die anderen dagegen bestand das Wesentliche – wie der Titel einer vielgelesenen Broschüre sagt – in der *„Erziehung der Generation im Geiste der demokratischen Idee der Kooperation"* (Patkowski 1922).

Dürfen fremde Muster in polnischen Schulen ganz einfach übernommen werden? In dieser Frage galt die vorherrschende Meinung, man dürfe und solle ausländische Erfahrungen nutzen, dabei *„... sollte die Schülerselbstregierung nicht eine tropische Pflanze sein, die unter einen völlig fremden Himmel verpflanzt wird. Lebendig ist sie erst dann, wenn sie den Bedürfnissen der Jugend nicht nur eines bestimmten Landes, sondern sogar einer konkreten Schule entspringt ..."* (Nawroczyński 1928, S. 8).

Sollten Schülergerichte eingeführt werden? Obwohl dieses Organ der Selbstregierung in vielen Schulen existierte, stand man ihm meist kritisch gegenüber. Der Standpunkt Korczaks, der ein entschiedener Befürworter des Schülergerichts als Methode der sittlichen Erziehung war, blieb ein Einzelfall. Repräsentativ dürfte die folgende Meinung sein: *„Nach einigen Jahren sind ... wir zu dem Schluß gekommen, daß diese Institution entbehrlich, wenn nicht sogar schädlich ist. Wo Richter sind, da muß es auch Streitfälle geben, da die Richter, um ihren Eifer zu beweisen, 'nach Arbeit Ausschau halten'..."* (Przanowski / Szczawińska / Wójcik 1928, S. 40).

Womit sollte man die Organisation der Schülerselbstregierung beginnen? Mit der Gründung einer Schülergenossenschaft, und ist sie einmal da – mit der allmählichen Erweiterung ihres Tätigkeitsumfangs: so war die häufigste Antwort auf diese Frage *(Dąbrowski 1925, Mittek 1936)*. Hierzu ist zu bemerken, daß die Genossenschaftsidee sich in den polnischen Schulen wie in der gesamten Gesellschaft einer ungeheuren Popularität sowie der offiziellen Unterstützung der Bildungsbehörde erfreute. 1935 schätzte man die

Zahl der Schülergenossenschaften auf mehr als 6 700 *(Thogutt 1939, S. 459)*, die meisten davon in den Volksschulen; 1933 gab es in knapp 61% der Schulen Schülergenossenschaften *(Koźmian 1988, S. 438)*. Sie waren den Genossenschaftsorganisationen (in erster Linie den Konsumgenossenschaften) nachgebildet, die von Erwachsenen gegründet wurden. Die oberste Macht gehörte der Vollversammlung aller Mitglieder, die die Satzung verabschiedete und den Vorstand wählte. Ihre Tätigkeit begannen die Schülergenossenschaften in der Regel mit der Kapitalsammlung und der Gründung eines Schulladens. Der Lehrer, der die Gründung einer Schülergenossenschaft anregte und sie dann betreute, ließ sich nicht so sehr von wirtschaftlichen Motiven leiten – schließlich konnten die Gewinne aus dem Verkauf von Schulutensilien nicht allzu groß sein –, ausschlaggebend waren vielmehr erzieherische und gesellschaftliche Erwägungen. Es ging um Erziehung zu Selbständigkeit und Solidarität sowie um Erziehung *zu* Demokratie *durch* Demokratie; es ging um die Verwirklichung der beiden Hauptgrundsätze des Genossenschaftswesens: gegenseitige Hilfe und freiwillige Arbeit für das Allgemeinwohl. Die Schülergenossenschaft war weit mehr als der Schulladen. Sehr oft entwickelten die Schülergenossenschaften weit darüber hinausgehende Tätigkeiten: Produktions-, Dienstleistungs-, kulturelle und Bildungs- sowie Selbstbildungsaktivitäten; durch sie entstanden massenweise Schulsparkassen. Bereits auf dem dritten Internationalen Kongreß für Moralische Erziehung im Jahre 1922 wurden die Schülergenossenschaften – die ja auch in anderen Ländern, vor allem in Frankreich, sehr populär waren – als das „polnische Spezifikum" bezeichnet (nach *Dąbrowski 1924, S. 105*).

Ende der zwanziger Jahre „... *hat sich bei uns dank den Schriften Foersters, Ferrières ... [und] denen polnischer Autoren die Grundeinstellung eingebürgert, daß eine gut geführte Selbstregierung der Jugend zu einem wirksamen Erziehungsmittel werden kann"* (*Nawroczyński 1928, S. 7*). Allerdings schlug diese Grundeinstellung nicht so sehr in breiten Lehrerkreisen, als vielmehr bei Vertretern der Bildungsbehörde Wurzeln. Die Schülerselbstregierung wird nicht mehr als pädagogische Neuigkeit oder Erziehungsexperiment betrachtet, sondern vielmehr für eines der wirksamsten Mittel bei der Realisierung der staatlichen Bildungspolitik gehalten. Damit geht die „intuitive" Entwicklungsphase der Schülerselbstregierungbewegung zu Ende, und es setzt deren „rationale Phase" ein.

Nach dem „Mai-Putsch" von 1926 wurde die „Staatserziehung" *(wychowanie państwowe)* zum obersten Leitspruch der polnischen Bildungspolitik erhoben. Ziel einer solchen Erziehung war es, die junge Generation „auf ein Leben *im* Staat" und „auf ein Leben *für den* Staat" statt auf „ein Leben *vom* Staat" vorzubereiten. Auch wenn die Durchsetzung des Programms der Staatserziehung die Abkehr von den Grundsätzen der parlamentarisch-demokratischen Ordnung im gesellschaftlichen Leben bedeutete, wurde der Schülerselbstregierung in Foersters „monarchistischer" Form eine besondere Rolle zugewiesen. Nunmehr sollte die Selbstregierung vor allem – wenn nicht gar ausschließlich – die junge Generation auf die „romantische Tat" und die „positive Arbeit" für die Stärkung des polnischen Staates vorbereiten, d. h. den Schülern die Bürgertugenden einprägen.

Die Arbeit an der Schaffung der Grundlagen des Systems der „Staatserziehung" ging im März 1932 zu Ende, was sich in dem vom Parlament verabschiedeten neuen Schulgesetz niederschlug, das tiefgreifende, sowohl strukturell-organisatorische als auch inhaltlich-curriculare Reformen des ganzen Bildungswesens einleitete. Bereits vor diesem Zeitpunkt hielt die Bildungsbehörde die Lehrer der Höheren Schulen und Volksschulen an, die Schülerselbstregierung allmählich und vorsichtig einzuführen. Zu diesem Zweck erließ das Bildungsministerium entsprechende Verordnungen und Empfehlungen, beschickte die Schulen mit Mustersatzungen für eine Selbstregierung, organisierte Methodiktagungen für die Lehrer sowie Tagungen für die Schulleiter der einzelnen Schulbezirke. Diese Maßnahmen wurden von den Lehrerorganisationen gefördert.

Unter den zahlreichen Maßnahmen, die Idee der Selbstregierung als einer Methode der „Staatserziehung" bei der Lehrerschaft populär zu machen, seien die Sitzungen der Schulleiter des Schulbezirks Łódz genannt, die im Schuljahr 1930/31 stattfanden *(Z zagadnien wychowawczych 1931)*. In einer dieser Sitzungen hielt der Philosoph und Jurist Rudolf Taubenschlag ein Referat, dem umfangreiche einschlägige ausländische und polnische Fachliteratur sowie die Ergebnisse einer Umfrage zugrundelagen, die im Jahre 1929 unter 1 790 Schülerinnen und Schülern der höheren Klassen in 14 Höheren Schulen von Łódz und Umgebung durchgeführt wurde. Unter anderem brachte Taubenschlag in seinem Beitrag Argumente für und wider die Einführung der Selbstregierung in den Schulen vor, referierte verschiedene Auffassungen von ihren Wesenszügen, unter Berücksichtigung historischer wie vergleichender Aspekte, und bestimmte die Ziele und Organisationsformen der Schülerselbstregierung; schließlich definierte er die Grenzen, innerhalb derer sie tätig werden sollten. Die in diesem Beitrag dargestellten Betrachtungen wurden vom Verfasser zu einem Buch erweitert und ergänzt, das aufgrund seines Umfangs und der vielseitigen Problematik sowie scharfsinnigen Analysen als das bedeutendste polnische Werk zur Frage der Schülerselbstregierung galt *(Taubenszlag 1932)*.

„Die Leser dieses Buches finden hier keine fertigen Satzungen, Regelungen, Schemata, Muster, Empfehlungen im Sinne von universellen Mitteln zur Erreichung des erwünschten Zieles" (ebd., S. 134), wobei das erwünschte Ziel „... *nicht in der Förderung herausragender, führender Persönlichkeiten, ... sondern in der Aktivierung eines jeden Zöglings ...* " bestehen sollte. „*Gerade um jene Namenlosen, die für die Gesellschaft wirken, ist es uns zu tun – ihre Zahl ist Legion, die ins Gewicht fallende Legion kleiner Leute, die es wachzurütteln, anzuspornen, zu mobilisieren gilt"* (ebd., S. 40f.).

Dieses Ziel zu erreichen, ist jedoch der Bildungsbehörde nicht gelungen. Die Hals über Kopf massenhaft in den Schulen eingeführte Methode der Selbstregierung auf dem Wege von oben kommender Verordnungen und Empfehlungen, meist ohne die Bedingungen vor Ort und die Qualifikation der Lehrer zu berücksichtigen, führte zur Entartung der Idee der Schülerdemokratie. Staatlichen Institutionen nachgebildet, aufgebauschte Satzungen und Regelungen annehmend, wurden die Schülerselbstregierungen zu Fassadenorganisationen, bei denen die Form den Inhalt verdrängte. Infolgedessen geriet die Bewegung der Schülerselbstregierung Mitte der dreißiger Jahre in eine tiefe Krise. So kann auch auf Taubenschlags Werk der bekannte Aphorismus Hegels angewandt werden, daß die Eule der Minerva erst in der Dämmerung fliegt.

Kurz nach der Novemberrevolution vom Jahre 1918 und der Errichtung der Weimarer Republik hatte man versucht, auch in Deutschland die Idee der Schülerselbstverwaltung fruchtbar zu machen. Dies kann man beispielsweise den Jahrgängen 1919 und 1920 solcher Zeitschriften wie „Die Neue Erziehung" oder „Monatschrift für Höhere Schulen" entnehmen. Nicht zu vergessen seien hier der „Aufruf vom 27. November 1918", erlassen vom preußischen Ministerium für Wissenschaft, Kunst und Volksbildung in Berlin, sowie die „Bekanntmachung vom 9. Dezember 1918", erlassen vom bayerischen Staatsministerium für Unterricht und Kultus in München (vgl. *Scheibe 1959, S. 127-131*). Durch diese beiden Erlasse über die Einsetzung von Schülerausschüssen und Schülerräten versuchte man, den Geist der Demokratie in die Höheren Schulen einzuführen. Die Versuche stießen aber bei Lehrern, Schülern und Eltern auf Widerstand und wurden von Pädagogen erbittert kritisiert. Die Erlasse mußten bald zurückgenommen werden. Allgemein betrachtet „*.... muß gesagt werden, daß bis 1933 die Schülerselbstverwaltung in der Breite des öffentlichen Schulwesens über geringe Ansätze nicht hinausgekommen ist"* (ebd., S. 12).

Von der Zweiten Polnischen Republik läßt sich das nicht sagen. Will man dem Vorwurf der Parteilichkeit entgehen, so läßt man am besten einen Ausländer sprechen. Im

„Vorwort" zur polnischen Ausgabe seines Buches „L'autonomie des écoliers" schrieb Adolphe *Ferrière (1933, S. 3): „Polen ist, so viel ich weiß, das Land, das als erstes das System der Schülerselbstregierung übernommen, vollkommen verstanden und eingesetzt hat ... Bereits auf dem dritten Internationalen Kongreß für Moralische Erziehung ... im Jahre 1922, als ich mich mit dem Bericht aus Polen bekannt machte, bewunderte ich, mit welch tiefem Verständnis die Idee der Schülerselbstregierung begriffen und auf welch vorbildliche Weise sie in vielen polnischen Schulen verwirklicht wurde."*

Bibliographie

Antz, Joseph / Pöggeler, Franz (Hrsg.): Friedrich Wilhelm Foerster und seine Bedeutung für die Pädagogik der Gegenwart. Ratingen: Henn 1955.
Bereźnicki, Franciszek: Innowacje pedagogiczne w Polsce (1918-1939). Szczecin: Wydawnictwa Wyższej Szkoły Pedagogicznej 1984.
Bykowski, Ludwik: Samorząd w szkołach polskich. In: Rocznik Pedagogiczny, 1 (1921), S. 151-161.
Dąbrowski, Franciszek: Kooperatywa uczniowska jako warsztat pracy społecznej. In: Rocznik Pedagogiczny, 2 (1924), S. 105-110.
Dąbrowski, Franciszek: Spółdzielnie uczniowskie. Podręcznik praktyczny z ilustracjami i wzorami. Warszawa: Wydawnictwo Związku Polskich Stowarzyszeń Spożywców 1925.
Ferrière, Adolphe: O szkole aktywnej. In: Ruch Pedagogiczny, 17 (1930) 1, S. 1-4; 2, S. 49-53.
Ferrière, Adolphe: Samorząd uczniowski. Sztuka kształtowania obywateli dla narodu i ludzkości. Przełożył K. Sosnicki. Lwów-Warszawa: Książnica-Atlas 1933.
Foerster, Friedrich Wilhelm: Schule und Charakter (1907). Moralpädagogische Probleme des Schullebens. 14. Aufl. Zürich: Schultheß 1930.
Grunder, Hans-Ulrich: Die Ecole Nouvelle in der französischsprechenden Schweiz. Schulkritik und Schulreform zu Beginn des 20. Jahrhunderts. In: Pädagogische Rundschau, 41 (1987) 6, S. 721-745.
Hilker, Franz: Adolphe Ferrière zum Gedächtnis. In: Bildung und Erziehung, 13 (1960) 8, S. 449-456.
Kamp, Johannes-Maria: Kinderrepubliken. Geschichte, Praxis und Theorie radikaler Selbstregierung in Kinder- und Jugendheimen. Opladen: Leske und Budrich 1995.
Korczak, Janusz: Wie man ein Kind lieben soll (1919/20). Hrsg. von Elisabeth Heimpel und Hans Ross. 9. Aufl. Göttingen: Vandenhoeck und Ruprecht 1989.
Koźmian, Danuta: Spółdzielnie uczniowskie w szkolnictwie polskim okresu miedzywojennego 1918-1939. In: Chowanna, 32 (1988) 4, S. 430-446.
Koźmian, Danuta: Samorząd uczniowski w polskiej pedagogice Drugiej Rzeczypospolitej (1918-1939). Szczecin: Wydawnictwa Naukowe Uniwersytetu Szczecinskiego 1991.
Majkowska, Marja: Samorząd uczniowski. In: Oświata i Wychowanie, 2 (1930) 3, S. 220-227.
Mirski, Jozef: Współzdalanie młodzieży w pracy wychowawczej szkoły. Lwów-Warszawa: Książnica-Atlas 1933.
Mittek, Franciszek: Idea współdzialania w szkole nowoczesnej (1928). 2. Aufl. Włocławek: Nakładem Spółdzielczej Księgarni Szkolnej 1936.

Mitter, Wolfgang: Erziehung, Demokratie und Entwicklung in einer Periode revolutionären Wandels. Vortrag zur Eröffnung des VIII. Weltkongresses für Vergleichende Erziehungswissenschaft. In: Bildung und Erziehung, 45 (1992) 4, S. 477-487.
Nawroczyński, Bogdan: Przedmowa. In: Przanowski, Władysław / Szczawińska, Marja / Wójcik, Józef: Samorząd w szkole powszechnej (przykłady realizacji), Warszawa: Nakładem „Naszej Księgarni" Spółki Akc. Związku Pol. Nauczycielstwa Szkół Powszechnych 1928, S. 5-9.
Patkowski, Aleksander: Wychowanie pokolenia w duchu demokratycznej idei spółdziałania. Warszawa: Nakładem Spółki Akcyjnej „Nasza Ksiegarnia" 1922.
Przanowski, Władysław / Szczawińska, Marja / Wójcik, Józef: Samorząd w szkole powszechnej (przykłady realizacji). Warszawa: Nakładem „Naszej Księgarni" Społki Akc. Związku Pol. Nauczycielstwa Szkół Powszechnych 1928.
Scheibe, Wolfgang: Schülermitverantwortung. Ihr pädagogischer Sinn und ihre Verwirklichung. Berlin-Spandau u. a.: Luchterhand 1959.
Sobczak, Jędrzej: Recepcja idei „nowego wychowania" w polskiej pedagogice okresu miedzy wojnami. Bydgoszcz: Wyzsża Szkoła Pedagogiczna w Bydgoszczy 1979.
Taubenszlag, Rudolf: Samorząd uczniowski jako czynnik wychowania społecznego. Teorja-praktyka. Zalety-wady. Wskazania. Warszawa: Skład Głowny w Domu Książki Polskiej 1932.
Thogutt, Stanisław: Spółdzielczość w szkole. In: Encyklopedia wychowania. Bd. 3, Warszawa: Wydawnictwo „Naszej Księgarni" Zw. Nauczycielstawa Polskiego 1939, S. 458-467.
Z zagadnień wychowawczych. Referaty wygłoszone na zjazdach dyrektorow Okręgu Szkolnego łódzkiego w roku szkolnym 1930/31. Łódz: Nakładem Kuratorjum Okręgu Szkolnego Lódzkiego 1931.
Zieleńczyk, Adam: Samorząd uczniowski w Polsce. In: Oświata i Wychowanie, 4 (1932) 4, S. 324-365; 5, S. 429-455; 6, S. 501- 545.

Pädagogik und Soziologie

Heinz-Elmar Tenorth

Disziplinrelationen als Forschungsproblem

Disziplinrelationen und -differenzen sind unter aufgeklärten Sozialwissenschaftlern – und andere gibt es ja bekanntlich nicht – an sich kein Thema mehr. An der Front der wissenschaftlichen Erforschung von Mensch und Gesellschaft regiert die einheitliche Bezeichnung der „Human-" oder „Kulturwissenschaften"; in der interessierten Öffentlichkeit wird die schöne Unterstellung der Interdisziplinarität der Sozialwissenschaften genährt, und gegenüber dem – ja nicht vollständig verschwundenen – Autonomieanspruch von Disziplinen bedarf das Verdikt des traditionellen und überholten Denkens kaum mehr einer Begründung.

Auch in der wissenschaftlichen Pädagogik, deren Status als Wissenschaft innen wie außen kontrovers war (und vielleicht heute noch ist), hat sich die fortschrittlich-szientifische Fraktion längst auf die Rede von der Erziehungswissenschaft als einer Sozialwissenschaft verständigt.[1] Die Disziplin setzt sich von philosophischen und geisteswissenschaftlichen Denkformen inzwischen nahezu radikal oder mit nachsichtiger Toleranz ab und reklamiert Normalität. Die Erziehungswissenschaft nutzt dann die Begriffe – von Lernen und Interaktion, von System und Sozialisation – die auch in anderen Sozialwissenschaften geläufig sind; sie behandelt Fragen von Bildung und gesellschaftlicher Ungleichheit, die auch andere Disziplinen kennen und erforschen, und sie benutzt Methoden, die als Handwerkszeug der empirischen Sozialforschung keine disziplinäre Zurechnung mehr erlauben.

Andererseits: In Beobachtungen aus der Distanz, aber auch in der internen Selbstbeschreibung der Erziehungswissenschaft wird rasch sichtbar, daß der Umgang mit Theorien und Methoden doch noch Disziplindifferenzen stiftet, die in der lauten Propaganda

---

1 Sammelbände zur Bilanzierung der Erziehungswissenschaft, unter anderem im Umfeld des Bielefelder Kongresses der Deutschen Gesellschaft für Erziehungswissenschaft von 1990, sind ebenso Beleg wie neue Texte, u. a *Krüger / Helsper (1995)* sowie *Krüger / Rauschenbach (1995)*.

der Normalität bedeutungslos zu sein scheinen: *Lautmann / Meuser (1986)* haben am Beispiel von Jurisprudenz und Pädagogik gezeigt, wie diese Disziplinen in der Rezeption sozialwissenschaftlichen Wissens Eigentümlichkeiten entwickeln, die sie als differente Fächer unterscheidbar sein lassen. An den von ihnen beobachteten Mechanismen der Moralisierung, Dogmatisierung und pragmatischen Transformation sozialwissenschaftlicher Theorien ist unschwer zu erkennen, daß alte Selbstbeschreibungen dieser „pragmatischen Disziplinen" vielleicht doch noch Sinn machen. In eigenen Untersuchungen über ihre Praxis (eine Übersicht bietet *Tenorth 1996*) hat die Erziehungswissenschaft selbst entdecken müssen, daß sie einerseits zwar zu einer Sozialwissenschaft wie alle anderen wurde, im Prozeß der Normalisierung zugleich aber in ihren Begriffen, Untersuchungsmethoden und praktischen Ambitionen eine Fülle an Merkmalen bewahrt hat, die eindeutig auf einen disziplinären Sonderweg verweisen.

Die hier skizzierten Beobachtungen sollen die Ausgangsthese begründen, daß die Frage nach der Relation und Differenz von Disziplinen selbst in einem Revier noch sinnvoll ist, in dem programmatisch Einheitsformeln und wissenschaftspraktisch eine universale Methodik alle Unterschiede verwischt zu haben scheinen. Im folgenden sollen daher einige dieser Besonderheiten ausdrücklich gemacht werden, und zwar auf dem Wege vergleichend-historischer Überlegungen zur Genese und zum Status der Erziehungswissenschaft.

Dabei ist – historisch – die Annahme leitend, daß die Erziehungswissenschaft als Disziplin sich einer kontingenten theoretischen Konstruktion und Fügung von Problemen verdankt,[2] sowie – vergleichend –, daß sich an der Relation von Erziehungswissenschaft und Soziologie zeigen läßt, wie aus gemeinsamen Themen unterschiedliche Disziplinen entstehen. Die Relation von Pädagogik und Soziologie führt zugleich zu der Frage, ob die Unterscheidung von Disziplinen und die Behauptung theoretischer Autonomieansprüche noch sinnvoll ist, und zugleich, ob die wechselseitige Wahrnehmung als anders und fremd erklärt werden kann.

Am Beginn der Überlegungen stehen historische Bemerkungen und Hinweise auf Konstruktion und Abgrenzungsmechanismen; dann folgen Analysen aktueller theoretischer und metatheoretischer Relationen, bevor abschließend ein systematisches Fazit

---

2 Damit wird in systematischer Weise selbstverständlich der Disziplinbegriff nur bestätigt, den schon Karl Popper vorgeschlagen hat.

und eine Prognose über die Disziplinbeziehungen – jenseits des überlieferten Mißverhältnisses – riskiert wird.

Distanz und Kooperation – historisch

Die Geschichte des Verhältnisses von Soziologie und Pädagogik läßt sich am Beispiel der Universität Halle schildern, und zwar in zwei Etappen der Disziplingeschichte: im ausgehenden 18. und am Beginn des 20. Jahrhunderts.

Für die erste Periode wird jeder stolze Erziehungswissenschaftler immer an Ernst Christian Trapp erinnern und an seine frühe Berufung auf ein Ordinariat für Philosophie und Pädagogik; ich folge dem Brauch auch insofern, als ich vom schmählich raschen Ende dieser Tätigkeit hier vornehm schweige – Auskünfte dazu gibt *Fuchs (1984)*. Sicherlich, Trapps Hauptaugenmerk gilt der Anthropologie und Psychologie, der Erfahrungsseelenkunde und der Methode der Beobachtung der Erziehung; aber eines seiner Hauptprobleme ist die Tatsache, daß Erziehung in der Moderne sowohl gesellschaftlich wie in der Interaktionssituation ein eigenes, neues und zudem leider ungelöstes Problem aufwirft, gesamtgesellschaftlich und in der Interaktion. Für die Relation von Pädagogik und Soziologie ist Trapp deshalb interessant, weil er „pädagogisch-soziologisches Denken" zwar als Thema kennt, aber noch im prä-disziplinären und prä-theoretischen Status formuliert.

Die Analyse der gesellschaftlichen Seite der Erziehung führt Trapp zunächst und relativ bald zur radikal-liberalen Kritik des Obrigkeitsstaates (anonym im letzten Band des Revisionswerkes, vgl. die Analyse bei *Urban 1980*). Die Konsequenzen der modernen Gesellschaft nimmt er insofern zwar wahr, aber primär doch politisch und professionell, als liberaler Bürger und als reformorientierter Pädagoge, noch nicht aus der theoretischen Distanz einer erziehungswissenschaftlichen Analyse.

Trapp bemerkt andererseits, und für die Probleme der pädagogischen Interaktion, daß es hier ebenfalls „soziologische" Probleme gibt. Trapp sieht nämlich, wie mühsam und folgenreich es – für Lehrer und Schüler – ist, daß der Lernende primär als *„großer Haufen"* (Trapp 1787, S. 208), d. h. in ungeordneter Menge, in Schulen gegenwärtig ist; denn das drängt den Lehrer in eine belastende Rolle. Der Unterricht wird schwierig, *„besonders ... bei einem Haufen Kinder, deren Anlagen, Fähigkeiten, Fertigkeiten, Neigungen,*

Bestimmungen verschieden sind, die aber doch in einer und derselben Stunde von dir erzogen werden sollen" (Trapp 1780, S. 25).

Die spezifische Gesellschaftlichkeit, die der modernen Erziehung in der Interaktion eigen ist, erschwert die Arbeit auch noch aus einem weiteren Grunde; denn „*was die Erziehung noch schwerer macht, ist, daß sich der Erzieher in der Notwendigkeit befindet, sich zu den Kindern herabzulassen. Das ist dem gebildeten Geist höchst unangenehm, besonders wenn es mehrere Stunden hintereinander dauert...*" *(ebd., S. 23)*. Trapp kennt dafür keine theoretische Lösung, sondern nur den Appell an das Ethos des Pädagogen – und das bleibt lange Zeit so, wenn das Problem der spezifischen Gesellungsform des Pädagogischen überhaupt eingestanden wird.

Im Wissen der Pädagogen ist für dieses Thema zwar der Begriff der Gesellschaft, gar der der Soziologie, noch zur Mitte des 19. Jahrhunderts keineswegs selbstverständlich, aber man findet von „Gesellschaft" aus doch – und charakteristisch – den Verweis auf „*Umgang*" *(Schmid 1860, S. 849)*. Dort wird ausgiebig – und im Verweis auf den Freiherrn Knigge *(Palmer 1873)* – erörtert, wie Umgang als ein „dauerndes Wechselverhältnis", in dem das Kind lebt, für den Pädagogen von Bedeutung ist, welche Realität zwischen Familie, Geschwistern und Umwelt der Umgang für das heranwachsende Kind hat, und welche „*Umgangsregeln*" *(ebd., S. 528)* für den Lehrer bedeutsam sind (und auf die Artikel „Anstand" sowie „Geselligkeitstrieb" wird von Palmer zurückverwiesen). Aber im Kern reicht die Analyse jetzt nur bis zur Mahnung an den Lehrer, den „*Privatverkehr*" mit dem Schüler nicht zu weit zu treiben, und den „*Widerspruchsgeist*" nicht zu fördern *(ebd., S. 525, 527)*. Weder die Probleme des „Haufens", die Trapp umtrieben, noch die Fragen der „Socialforschung", die – bereits in den siebziger Jahren des 19. Jahrhunderts – bei anderen Theoretikern – von Lorenz von Stein bis Otto Willman – eine Rolle spielen, nimmt das pädagogische Professionswissen aber aktiv und theoretisch produktiv auf.

In den zwanziger Jahren unseres Jahrhunderts kann man dagegen – auch jetzt sehr schön in Halle – die Relation von Pädagogik und Soziologie bereits als disziplinär geformtes Thema[3] erkennen, und sowohl institutionell wie theoretisch in seinen Konsequenzen für die Konstitution der Erziehungswissenschaft beobachten.

---

3 Im Lehrerwissen ist diese Differenz ebenfalls schon eindeutig präsent, allerdings reduziert auf die gesellschaftliche Seite, ohne den Sinn für die Interaktion, vgl. *Barth (1908)* mit den schönen Thesen: „*Die Soziologie ist identisch mit der Philosophie der Geschichte*" und „*Was jetzt Soziologie, hieß ursprünglich 'Politik'*". Im übrigen, „Umgang" verweist jetzt auf „Geselligkeit".

Zunächst zur institutionellen Seite: Als der damalige Inhaber der Professur für Pädagogik, Max Frischeisen-Köhler, ein Dilthey-Schüler, eingefleischter Geisteswissenschaftler, scharfsinnig-folgenreicher Kritiker der empirischen Psychologie und Jugendkunde, intensiv engagiert in der linken Lehrerbewegung der Stadt, am 22. Oktober 1923 in Halle starb,[4] wurde als einer seiner möglichen Nachfolger auch der Berliner Ministerialbeamte Paul Ziertmann in Erwägung gezogen. In der Entscheidung über diesen Vorschlag wird zugleich darüber disponiert, in welchem Umfang soziologische Fragestellungen Eingang in die Erziehungswissenschaft finden.

Paul Ziertmann war zwar ebenfalls ein Dilthey-Schüler, hatte allerdings schon 1914 gefordert, die Pädagogik als „Gesellschaftswissenschaft" theoretisch zu verstehen und als forschende Disziplin an den Universitäten institutionell zu verankern *(Ziertmann 1914)*. Nach 1918 arbeitete Ziertmann im preußischen Ministerium für Handel und Gewerbe, begründete die Ausbildung der Lehrer an beruflichen Schulen und begann, sich durch Vorträge über die gesellschaftliche Funktion des Berechtigungswesens hervorzutun, und zwar mit einer eminent soziologischen Argumentation.

Ziertmann interpretierte das Berechtigungswesen nämlich – gegen die vor allem bei Pädagogen herrschende Topik der Klage über Zertifikate und ihre sozialen Konsequenzen – als *„einen geradezu meisterhaft konstruierten soziologischen Apparat, auf den stolz zu sein eigentlich alle Veranlassung vorläge"*; denn – so seine These – diesem „*Apparat*" gelinge es, „*das Problem der Korrelation von Schule, Gesellschaft und objektiven Kulturgütern organisatorisch in nahezu vollkommener Weise [zu] lösen"*.[5] Diese Funktion – in der man unschwer die nüchterne Fassung des emphatisch artikulierten Bildungsproblems der Zeit erkennt – sei im übrigen unabhängig von ideologischen Differenzen in allen Gesellschaften zu erbringen, der Blick des Theoretikers müsse deshalb auch ein „*rein sachliches Verhalten der Wirklichkeit gegenüber*" entwickeln, jedenfalls von „*allen unseren Wertungen ... absehen*" und „*verfahren wie der Ingenieur*" *(Ziertmann 1922, S. 490)*.

In einem Vorschlag der Universität wird dieser Ziertmann, erstaunlich genug, zunächst im März 1923, dann im Sommer 1924 dem Kultusministerium in Berlin für den

---

4 Zu seinen theoretischen Positionen vgl. u. a *Frischeisen-Köhler (1933)*, zu seiner Biographie u. a. *Lehmann (1933)*.

5 Eine ausführliche Darstellung der Leistung von Paul Ziertmann findet sich in *Tenorth (1990, bes. S. 62)*; die Zitate stammen aus *Ziertmann (1922, S. 501)*.

Lehrstuhl in Halle benannt. Zunächst mit der Begründung, er habe sich „*mit pädagogischen und soziologischen Problemen beschäftigt*" *(Akten Bd. 7, Bl. 18)*, das Interesse der Lehrer und Studenten sei groß, später allerdings nur noch mit dem Hinweis, daß er nicht nur seine „*Lebensarbeit hauptsächlich dieser Wissenschaft [der Pädagogik] gewidmet hat*", sondern auch „*praktische Erfahrung im Erzieherberuf besitzt*" *(Akten Bd. 6, Bl. 395)*. Bei genauerem Hinsehen und nach Rückfrage des Ministeriums wird freilich klar, daß mit Ziertmann nicht der gesuchte Theoretiker einer soziologischen Perspektive in der Erziehungswissenschaft, sondern anscheinend der bequeme Kompromißkandidat benannt worden war. Wie der Kurator dem Minister im Frühjahr 1925 erläutert: „*In dem scharfen Gegensatze, in dem die beiden hiesigen Vertreter der Philosophie zueinander stehen, ist Ziertmann der einzige geblieben, auf den sie sich einigen konnten*" *(ebd., Bl. 424)*, aber „*sehr wohl ist ihnen hierbei nicht mehr zu Mut*" *(Akten Bd. 7, Bl. 20v)*.

Die folgende Kontroverse zwischen dem Ministerium in Berlin und der Universität kann hier nicht weiter interessieren; denn sie zeigt zunächst nur, daß sich Fakultät und Ministerium weder über die Besetzungskriterien noch über die geforderten Kompetenzen einig sind. Konsequenz ist jedenfalls, daß der soziologisch interessierte Erziehungswissenschaftler Ziertmann in Halle ohne Chance bleibt. Den zweiten philosophischen Lehrstuhl erhält der Ästhetiktheoretiker Emil Utitz, die Pädagogik vertritt weiterhin einer der philosophischen Streithähne, der Kantianer Paul Menzer (und 1927 hält er eine Rede zum Verfassungstag, die wegen ihrer eindeutig antidemokratischen Tendenz einen öffentlichen Eklat erzeugt). Auch dem örtlichen Lehrerverein gelingt es nicht, die Professur für die „pädagogische Wissenschaft" zu retten, trotz der Traditionen von Franke und Trapp und der guten Erfahrungen mit Frischeisen-Köhler.

Die Pädagogik erleidet also in Halle im kleinen ein Schicksal, das den reformorientierten modernen Disziplinen nach 1918, und dann der Pädagogik genauso wie der Soziologie, sowohl theoretisch wie institutionell im großen widerfährt: sie werden zum Opfer der etablierten Disziplinen. Theoretisch sind dennoch schon die Jahre der Weimarer Republik eine Phase, in der beide Disziplinen nicht nur – in Preußen – als Exponenten der Hochschulreform politisch gefördert werden, sie treten auch erstmals deutlich als autonome Fächer auf und sind eindeutig unterscheidbar geworden. Die Weimarer Republik wird auch eine Zeit, in der beide Fächer – das scheint das Schicksal engagierter Newcomer – in ihren Ambitionen von den Etablierten mißtrauisch beäugt werden.

Der Romanist Ernst Robert Curtius jedenfalls kritisiert – in der Auseinandersetzung mit Karl Mannheims Wissenssoziologie – den „Imperialismus der Einzelwissenschaften" und den jüngst erhobenen Anspruch der Soziologie mit dem Hinweis, daß sie in einen altbekannten Fehler verfalle, den er „neuerdings" auch an der Pädagogik erlebt habe. Curtius lehnt solche Gelüste scharf ab und er wünscht statt dessen, daß (Pädagogik wie) Soziologie das werden möge, was er ihr zugesteht zu sein: *„eine ehrliche Spezialdisziplin" (Curtius 1929, S. 417)*. Mehr sei auch kaum möglich, denn schon die Pädagogik habe ihre Versuchung zur Universalwissenschaft *„mit unzureichenden Mitteln unternommen"*. Die historische Konstruktion der Disziplin vollzieht sich also nicht allein in Besetzungsverfahren, sie ist auch Produkt theoretisch verstandener Grenzziehungen.

Für die Pädagogik war der Streit über die „Grenzen" von Erziehung und Erziehungswissenschaft schon drei Jahre vor Mannheim und Curtius abgelaufen, und die herrschende philosophische Pädagogik hatte dabei vergleichbare Empfehlungen gehört.[6] Pädagogik möge doch endlich „Tatsachengesinnung" entwickeln, hatte Siegfried Bernfeld ihr empfohlen, und geraten, sich *„zu einer psychologisch und soziologisch fundierten Erziehungswissenschaft"* auszubauen, zu einer Disziplin, so Bernfeld, *„die in ihrem Gegensatz zur, nach wie vor allein anerkannten, geisteswissenschaftlichen Pädagogik als naturwissenschaftliche, im Gegensatz zu der idealistischen Gesinnung der heute noch gültigen Pädagogik als materialistische bezeichnet werden müßte"* (Bernfeld 1971). Bernfeld legt dabei den Finger auf die wunden Punkte, die verhindern, was er fordert, einen Kontakt zwischen Pädagogik und Soziologie; denn er würde die Disziplin zwingen, ihre soziale Funktion und ihren methodischen Status gegen das idealistische Modell pädagogischen Handelns zu formulieren.

An vergleichbaren Modernisierungsabsichten waren aber nicht nur Außenseiter wie Bernfeld, sondern auch schon Insider der Disziplin gescheitert: Auf die gesellschaftliche Tatsache der Erziehung war die Pädagogik in den zwanziger Jahren ja auch schon von anderen verwiesen worden (wenn auch nicht mit der scharfen These, daß sie ohne Rücksicht auf Soziologie *„diesen höchst häßlichen Vorgang [daß 'die herrschende Klasse nach ihren Machtzielen' die Erziehung bestimmt – Bernfeld] mit einem schönen Gespinst von Idealen [verschleiert]"*). Es war der hoch angesehene Münchener Ordinarius der Pädagogik Aloys *Fischer (1928)*, der gegen die von ihm kritisierte Sehnsucht der Pädagogik, Philosophie zu sein, in immer neuer und entschiedener Argumentation versuchte, das professionelle Selbstbild der Disziplin zu ändern und ihr eine soziologische Denkweise nahezulegen – weitgehend vergeblich. Fischer hatte dabei in feinsinnigen

---

6 Die philosophische Pädagogik wiederum hatte in diesen „Grenzen"-Diskursen die reformorientierten Praktiker der Pädagogischen Bewegung an das „Handwerk" erinnert, vgl. *Litt (1926)*.

Unterscheidungen von „Soziologischer Pädagogik" und „Pädagogischer Soziologie" den Versuch unternommen, eine systematisch begründete Relation zwischen diesen Humanwissenschaften zu stiften, ohne die spezifische Theorieperspektive der Erziehungswissenschaft aufzugeben. Man kann nicht behaupten, daß er mit diesen kunstvollen Unterscheidungen erfolgreich geblieben wäre. Er – und andere Mitstreiter[7] – blieben letztlich doch in einer Randstellung.

Dieses kontinuierliche Scheitern hatte mehrere Gründe, sowohl theoretische als auch politische:

– Im Kontext der dominierenden Geisteswissenschaftler und ihrer jugendbewegten Auffassung von „Individuum und Gemeinschaft" war das „bloß Gesellschaftliche", wie Wilhelm Flitner sagte, gegenüber der Emphase der Bünde und der Gemeinschaft nicht legitimierbar.[8]
– Dieses Scheitern hatte aber auch professionspolitische Gründe, weil erst mit dem Autonomieanspruch der Erziehungswissenschaft der soziale Status der Erziehung und ihrer Disziplin gegenüber Politik und Theologie zu behaupten war. Eine Annäherung an andere Disziplinen, z. B. die Soziologie, war dafür nicht hilfreich.
– Das Scheitern der Anstrengungen von Fischer und die Konzentration auf philosophische Reflexion hatten schließlich auch wissenschaftstheoretische Gründe; denn die Abgrenzungsversuche im Kontext der geisteswissenschaftlichen Selbstbegrenzung waren letztlich erfolgreich, auch wenn sie heute in ihrer Begründung immer quälend und im Ertrag nur dann akzeptabel sind, wenn man bereit bleibt, dem objektiven Geist gegenüber den sozialen Tatsachen Kredit einzuräumen.[9]

Dabei darf man – wie wenigstens am Rande erwähnt sein soll – durchaus fragen, ob nicht der Gegensatz zwischen geisteswissenschaftlicher und soziologischer Fragestellung schon historisch falsch plaziert war: Theodor Litt wird, von außen (z. B. *Freund 1979*), aber noch bis in die Gegenwart, nämlich als Soziologe wahrgenommen, Georg

---

7 Eine Übersicht über diese Anstrengungen gibt *Brinkmann (1986)*, besonders für Paul Barth (der früh von Herbert Spencer inspiriert war), Carl Weiß (der vergeblich versuchte, Soziologie und Kulturkritik theoretisch zu versöhnen), Rudolf Lochner (dessen deskriptive Pädagogik zwischen Soziologie und Phänomenologie unentschieden schwankte) und Karl Mannheim (der die Pädagogik als Disziplin erst ernst nahm, nachdem er nach London emigriert war).
8 In programmatischer Wendung findet sich dies bei *Flitner (1933)*; für die politische Dimension vgl. *Tenorth (1988)*.
9 Eine erschöpfende Übersicht über das wissenschaftstheoretische Verhältnis gibt *Stieglitz (1970)*.

Simmel muß, in Straßburg endlich zum Ordinariat gekommen, zwar eine Vorlesung über Schulpädagogik halten, aber er ist deshalb doch nicht Pädagoge. Der leitende theoretische Begriff der Geisteswissenschaftlichen Pädagogik ist ein Strukturbegriff, der das pädagogische Verhältnis in einer Weise bestimmt, die gar nicht so fern von Durkheimschen Gedanken ist, wie man vielleicht vermutet; aber wenn man mit Herman *Nohl (1978, S. 119)* z. B. unterstellt, daß diese Struktur – *„das Kultursystem Erziehung"* wie das pädagogische Verhältnis – nicht nur *„relativ selbständig"* ist, sondern auch eigenlogisch arbeitet, *„unabhängig von den einzelnen Subjekten, die in ihm tätig sind"*, dann ist Geisteswissenschaftliche Pädagogik soziologischer als sie sich, aus ethischen Gründen, eingesteht.

Dennoch, in der Forschungspraxis über Erziehung fehlt zwar das soziologische Argument nicht, es bleibt aber doch randständig, belastet mit exotischen Einsprengseln, sieht man, daß z. B. Ernst *Krieck (1922)*, der spätere Nazi-Konvertit, die soziale Funktion der Erziehung in den zwanziger Jahren als „Urfunktion der Gesellschaft" stark macht. Aber man findet nach 1920 auch schöne Studien, die noch erkennen lassen, daß selbst Trapps Gesellungsproblem der Interaktion nicht übersehen wird: 1928 erscheint z. B. eine „Soziologie der Volksschulklasse" *(Schröder 1928)*,[10] und damit bleibt die weitgehend reformpädagogisch und praktisch inspirierte Literatur über das „Schulleben" ebensowenig ohne theoretische Fundierung wie die Analysen von „Milieu" und „Lebensraum" der Jugendlichen, die ja schon vor 1933 theoretisch entschieden untersucht wurden.[11] Von hier aus konnten sich auch, im linken Lager der Reformpädagogik, Konzepte der Pädagogik entwickeln, die theoretische Orientierung an der Soziologie mit praktischem Engagement zu verbinden wußten, z. B. bei Siegfried *Kawerau (1924)*. Aber man darf auch nicht übersehen, daß ein am Phänomen der Gruppe ansetzender Theoretiker wie Peter Petersen deshalb des „Soziologismus" beschuldigt wurde.[12]

---

10 Schröders akademischer Lehrer ist freilich Eduard Spranger, so daß man auch hier die nicht eingestandene Nähe zu soziologischen Denkweisen erkennt; vgl. parallel – aus einer Vielzahl thematisch und konzeptionell ähnlicher Titel – *Döring (1930)*.
11 *Schwerdt (1930)* sowie Arbeiten von Alfred Busemann oder Martha Muchow.
12 Der Vorwurf gegen Petersen findet sich bei *Flitner (1933)*, Petersens 'soziologische' Denkweise spiegelt selbst der „Kleine Jena-Plan".

Relation und Distanz – systematisch

Noch 1960 aber war unübersehbar, daß mit der herrschenden Tradition eher Distanz als Nähe das Verhältnis von Soziologie und Pädagogik bestimmten. Die Distanz aber schlug ohne Zweifel nicht zum Nutzen der Pädagogik aus. Auch das könnte man vielleicht noch von Halle aus historisch rekonstruieren, aber nicht mehr allein; jedenfalls wäre auch der Ost-West-Vergleich wichtig und z. B. die erstaunliche Tatsache, daß nach 1945 in der Sowjetischen Besatzungszone in ernsthaften Diskussionen über Ernst Krieck das Recht der soziologischen Denkform in der Pädagogik und die Differenz zu einem (partei-)politischen Standpunkt erörtert wurden *(Rang 1982, bes. S. 23ff.)*. An dieser Stelle kann diese historische Rekonstruktion nicht geleistet werden, aber man kann heute schon systematisch argumentieren und von drei Aspekten aus, wissenschaftstheoretisch, theoretisch und pragmatisch, die Relation der Disziplinen betrachten.

Die dominierende Betrachtungsweise wird sicherlich die wissenschaftstheoretische; denn hier lassen sich alle Fragen bündeln – die grundbegriffliche Orientierung, die methodische Kontrolle des Wissenserwerbs und die Relation zur Praxis: Als in der Mitte der sechziger Jahre die tradierte Pädagogik, zugleich selbstkritisch und von außen angestoßen,[13] ihre Erneuerung begann, da mußte sie feststellen, daß sie nicht einmal mit ihrem Kernbegriff, dem der Bildung, zu empirisch und gesellschaftsgeschichtlich akzeptablen und für die Aufklärung pädagogischer Praxis geeigneten Einsichten gekommen war; zu schweigen von der Tatsache, daß ihre Methode der Auslegung der Erziehungswirklichkeit nicht einmal geeignet war, zwischen überlieferten, aber ideologisch korrumpierten Traditionsbeständen und der gesellschaftlichen Funktion von Bildung angemessen zu unterscheiden *(Roeder 1964, 1969)*.

Die Soziologie war dann – neben der (Pädagogischen) Psychologie – in jeder Beziehung ein naheliegender Anknüpfungspunkt für eine Erneuerung. Heute kann man sehen, daß diese Verbindung nützlich und notwendig, aber letztlich nicht hinreichend war, und das gilt in einem zweifachen Sinne: zum einen, weil die Pädagogik, wenn sie Soziologie wurde, dabei ohne Identität blieb,[14] zum anderen, weil die Soziologie in der Vielfalt widerstreitender Angebote nicht Orientierung stiftete, sondern Beliebigkeit förderte.

---

13 Vor allem die Arbeit des Deutschen Instituts für Internationale Pädagogische Forschung in Frankfurt am Main, allen voran Eugen Lemberg und Heinrich Roth, dann die Tagungen des Comenius-Instituts in Münster sorgten für diesen kritischen Außenanstoß.

14 Eine sehr schöne kritische Diagnose findet sich dann bei *Rauschenberger (1971, S. 399): „Hat die Pädagogik die Krise des Autonomiestrebens, in der sie 'verzweifelt sie selbst sein' wollte, überwun-*

Am Beispiel der wissenschaftstheoretischen Kontroversen in der deutschen Erziehungswissenschaft ist das sehr klar zu erkennen, weil beide Lager – auch hier als 'Positivisten' und 'kritische Erziehungswissenschaft' codiert und simplifiziert – in gleicher Weise an Soziologie anschlossen. Für Wolfgang Brezinka, der bis heute (und fälschlich) den positivistischen Part spielen muß, mag das überraschen, aber es scheint mir unbezweifelbar: Brezinka sucht die grundbegriffliche Orientierung für den Begriff der Erziehung ausgehend von Max Webers Begriff des „sozialen Handelns", seine frühen Arbeiten zur theoretischen und forschungsmethodischen Verbesserung der Pädagogik gehen aus vom Begriff der Sozialisation, und zwar schon in den fünfziger Jahren,[15] er beansprucht positiv für sich und gegen die geisteswissenschaftliche Tradition nicht zuletzt die Argumente von Siegfried Bernfeld, und gemeinsam mit Rudolf Lochner u. a. konzipiert er die Erziehungswissenschaft als Subdisziplin einer soziologischen Theorie (*Brezinka 1971, S. 1* bereits als Motto seiner Einleitung).

Seine Gegner könne alle diese Gemeinsamkeiten und potentiellen Anknüpfungspunkte bald ignorieren, weil sie sich aus anderen soziologischen Quellen bedienen, in Frankfurt vor allem, und dann eine Front aufbauen, die den verqueren Kontroversen der Soziologie selbst entspricht. Produktiv wurde das alles metatheoretisch nicht, schon weil die Brezinka-Gegner, z. B. Klaus Mollenhauer, bald selbst entdeckten, daß Gesellschaft zwar eigenes Thema der Pädagogik sein muß,[16] daß aber die Argumentationspraxis, z. B. seiner eigenen Assistenten, dieses Verhältnis in Politik hinein aufzulösen drohte und dann weder wissenschaftstheoretisch noch theoretisch produktiv blieb.[17] *Mollenhauer (1983)* geht auf die Suche nach „Vergessenen Zusammenhängen" und entdeckt die schönen Künste; Wissenschaftstheorie oder gar die Kontroverslinien der späten sechziger und frühen siebziger Jahre sind jedenfalls weder für ihn noch für andere aktuell von großer Bedeutung.

Dazu mag auch die theoretische Enttäuschung über die Soziologie beigetragen haben, die man exemplarisch am Begriff der Sozialisation studieren kann. Für die theoretische

---

den, so scheint jetzt das Pendel in die umgekehrte Richtung auszuschlagen: die Pädagogik will 'verzweifelt nicht sie selbst sein', indem sie die Soziologie imitiert."

15 Vgl. z. B. *Brezinka (1959)* sowie die zahlreichen sozialwissenschaftlich-empirisch orientierten Beiträge, die von ihm in den fünfziger Jahren in der Zeitschrift „Die Sammlung" erschienen sind.
16 *Mollenhauer (1964)* schreibt das einschlägige Stichwort im Fischer-Lexikon Pädagogik (das im übrigen noch ein weiteres Stichwort „Soziologie der Erziehung" – von Peter M. Roeder – enthält, der 1968 mit seiner Arbeit über Lorenz von Stein die disziplin- und dogmenhistorischen Relationen von Pädagogik und Gesellschaftstheorie im 19. Jahrhundert aufklärt).
17 Dafür stand die Vorrede zu *Mollenhauer (1972)*.

Relation von Pädagogik und Soziologie und für die Erneuerung der Erziehungswissenschaft war dieser Begriff ja zunächst überwältigend und anscheinend faszinierend. Seine Konjunktur war dabei nicht nur Indiz für den allfällig notwendigen Theorieimport, über den sich die Erziehungswissenschaft modernisierte, sondern auch für die Tatsache, daß die Pädagogik gegenüber der Soziologie eine „negative Importbilanz" verzeichnete. Das Fundament des neuen sozialwissenschaftlichen Selbstverständnisses war geborgt.

Wir wissen heute, daß es eine Schwundstufe soziologischen Denkens war, von der sich die Pädagogen faszinieren ließen, denn es war nur die These von der „schichtenspezifischen Sozialisation", die sie rezipierten, und „manche", nicht allein im „pädagogischen Milieu", wie Ulrich Oevermann (1979, S. 145) suggeriert, „haben hinter dem Schlagwort gar eine Theorie vermutet". Aber dennoch hat dieses Thema, samt dem Begriff, aufklärerisch, zu Recht verstörend und innovativ gewirkt, nicht allein auf die Theorie, auch auf bildungspolitische Anstrengungen.[18]

Die Erfahrung, zunächst der Pädagogen, dann der Erziehungswissenschaft (und, eher als Affekt, ganz früh schon, die Distanz der Erziehungsphilosophen), hat aber gelehrt, daß Sozialisation kein Grundbegriff der Erziehungswissenschaft ist und sein kann (aber selbstverständlich ein Thema ist, dem sich erziehungswissenschaftliche Forschung relationieren muß). Nutzt man erneut die Themenreferenzen, die anscheinend seit dem ausgehenden 18. Jahrhundert die Relation unserer Disziplinen bestimmen, dann haben die aus der Soziologie rezipierten Begriffe – von Sozialisation bis Interaktion oder Kommunikation, auch: Klasse und Schicht – zwar aufklärerische Kraft und erhellende Empirie, aber unverkennbar auch erziehungswissenschaftliche Leerstellen: Bezogen auf die gesamtgesellschaftliche Problematik zeigt das die Debatte über Bildungsreform, in der niemand mehr glaubt, daß sich die Strukturen der Gesellschaft über die Veränderung von Schulstrukturen aufbrechen lassen (und niemand ist auch mehr so optimistisch, Parsons folgend, in der sozialen Logik der Schulklasse allein das Medium der Demokratisierung und Modernisierung der Gesellschaft zu entdecken). Pierre Bourdieu wird von entgeisterten Pädagogen gefragt, ob er es denn wirklich so deterministisch meine, wie es

---

18 *Mollenhauer (1969)* hat die Fragestellung in die theoretische 'Bibel' der Bildungsreform eingeführt; der Kongreß der Deutschen Gesellschaft für Erziehungswissenschaft von 1974 (in Salzburg, vgl. *Pädagogische Institutionen und Sozialisation 1974*) macht ihn zum zentralen Gegenstand, 1976 wurde – über „Interaktion und Organisation in pädagogischen Feldern" – das Anschlußthema noch einmal behandelt, bevor 1978 (in Tübingen, u. a. in Beiträgen über Theorie und Praxis der Pädagogik) die eigenen Fragen der Pädagogik wieder zur Geltung kamen. In der Publizistik spiegelt sich die Re-Autonomisierung dann schon Anfang der achtziger Jahre, vgl. *Tenorth (1981)*.

die „Illusion der Chancengleichheit" beschreibt (typisch dafür ist *Schwibs / Bourdieu 1985*), und gegen die kühlen Analysen der Strukturen und Grenzen pädagogischer Professionalität setzen die Pädagogen – systematisch gesehen zwar selbstdestruktiv, aber handlungsoptimistisch wie in reformpädagogischen Zeiten – das Pathos der Persönlichkeit, weil ihnen ihr Handeln sonst unverständlich bleibt (ein typisches Beispiel, auch für die unterschiedlichen Referenzen von Theorie und Praxis, geben *Ehrhardt-Kramer / Hoppe 1986*).

Die Logik der Sozialisation, das haben wir dabei gelernt, ist nicht identisch mit der Logik der pädagogischen Aktion. Aber uns fehlt noch die Theorie, in der vermittelt wird, was wir inzwischen als different kennen: Soziale Struktur und pädagogische Aktion (aber auf soziologische Theorien der Vermittlung lassen wir uns schon deshalb nicht ein, weil die zum Problem gehören, dessen Folgen Pädagogen heute spüren).

Pragmatisch machen sich deshalb heute vor allem die Folgeprobleme der Strukturen von Import und Export bemerkbar: Die Erziehungswissenschaft scheint sich in eine unfruchtbare Dichotomie zu verrennen, zwischen einer methodisch abgeklärten, den Sozialwissenschaften nahen und im Standard vergleichbaren Forschung, die zugleich das Handlungsproblem aus dem Blick verliert, und der Erneuerung moralisch-praktischer Emphase, als die sich erneut die Pädagogik versteht. Viele Arbeiten der „New Sociology of Education" scheinen, auch in der deutschen Rezeption, diesem Dilemma zu entsprechen: Wir wissen inzwischen sehr viel über die kulturelle Willkür, die sich in Lehrplänen manifestiert, über die Strukturen von Ungleichheit, die trotz der Bildungsreform reproduziert werden, über die palliative Funktion der Sozialen Arbeit, die von der gesellschaftlichen Entwicklung und der kapitalistischen Ökonomie erzwungen und geprägt wird,[19] aber den Graben zwischen klugen Analysen und pädagogischer Aktion macht das eher tiefer: Lehrplandiskussionen bleiben dem Mechanismus der Politik überlassen, Bildungsreformen den Ökonomen, den Marktgesetzen oder der Verwaltung, und die Jugendhilfe den hilflosen Praktikern, die von soziologisch aufgeklärten Forschern beobachtet, aber allein gelassen werden.

Soziologen können anscheinend nicht einmal mehr in der früher so bekannten Klarheit sagen, wem wir denn zuzurechnen haben, was wir als Beschwernis erleben. Da kann dann auch die Pädagogik wieder selbstbewußter denken; denn sie hat ihre eigene Generalthese: Im Begriff der Bildsamkeit ist als pädagogische Prämisse erziehungswis-

---

19 Exemplarisch dafür scheint mir ein Band wie der von *Sünker / Timmermann / Kolbe (1994)*.

senschaftlicher Analyse festgehalten, daß es die Menschen selbst sind, gelegentlich mit Hilfe organisierter Erziehung, die sich entwerfen und ihre Geschichte machen. Das geschieht nicht immer aus freien Stücken, wie der Soziologe einzuwenden liebt, aber wie es geschieht, das weiß man erst, wenn man den Prozeß der Bildung erforscht und sich nicht in seinem Umfeld verliert.

Programmatische und selbstkritische Schlußbemerkung

Die Konsequenz meiner Analyse und eine vielleicht als Empfehlung formulierbare Schlußfolgerung geht zunächst in Richtung Distanz, sie mündet in ein Plädoyer für Disziplinrelation nach je autonomen Kriterien. Produktiv sind dann auch eher Beziehungen, die sich zufällig ergeben, nicht intendiert, aber vielleicht folgenreicher. Selbstverständlich redet dann ein jeder von seinen eigenen Lernprozessen. Bei Bernfeld ist insofern ein Leitbegriff für Erziehung (als Summe der Reaktionen einer Gesellschaft auf die Entwicklungstatsache) zu finden, der die Gesellschaftsgeschichte in pädagogischer Absicht inspirieren kann; bei Niklas Luhmann kann die Disziplin erkennen, daß ihre Denkform und ihr Status gegenüber der Praxis nicht allein von Forschung aus definiert sein kann, sondern nur zweifach und gebrochen: im Status der Beobachtung von Paradoxien theoretisch und d. h. als Erziehungswissenschaft, im Modus reflektierender Reflexion pragmatisch und d. h. als Pädagogik. Und sicherlich gilt auch, daß Import- und Exportverhältnisse heute auch in andere Richtungen als zur Soziologie produktiv sein können, wenn man sich nur nicht überwältigen läßt. Für die Aufklärung der pädagogischen Formen, Codes und Rituale kann man sich z. B. in die Ethnologie begeben, weil sie auch dem tradierten kulturbegrifflichen Denken der Pädagogik gegenwärtig theoretische Weite und komparativ-methodische Raffinesse geben kann.

Muß die Erziehungswissenschaft deswegen wieder zur „pragmatischen Disziplin" mutieren, vom Konsens mit Erziehungsgemeinschaften ausgehen und die Ethik zum Zentrum ihrer Argumentation machen? Alle Ratschläge, „Moralwissenschaft" zu werden – die ja gegenwärtig auch die Soziologie erreichen[20] – dürften eigentümliche Folgeprobleme erzeugen. Riskant wird vor allem eine Ethisierung des Diskurses über Erziehung, die disziplinäre Argumente ununterscheidbar werden läßt von parteilich-ideologischen Positionen. Man braucht nicht Soziologe zu sein, um das als Irrweg zu kennen.

---

20 Von außen, durch den ehemaligen CDU-Politiker *Dettling (1996)*, gefolgt von einschlägigen Abwehrbewegungen der Soziologen (vgl. *Käsler 1996*).

Bibliographie

Akten des preußischen Kultusministeriums, GHSTA Rep. 76 Va, Sekt 8, Tit. IV, No. 48, Bd. 6. 7.
Barth, Paul: Soziologie und Pädagogik. In: Rein, Wilhelm (Hrsg.): Enzyklopädisches Handbuch der Pädagogik. 2. Aufl. Bd. 8, Langensalza: Beyer 1908, S. 682-691.
Bernfeld, Siegfried: Sisyphos oder die Grenzen der Erziehung. Vorwort zur zweiten Auflage (1928). In: ders.: Antiautoritäre Erziehung und Psychoanalyse. Ausgewählte Schriften. Bd. 2 (= März-Archiv. 1), Frankfurt a. M.: März-Verlag 1971, S. 469.
Brezinka, Wolfgang: Die Pädagogik und die erzieherische Wirklichkeit. In: Zeitschrift für Pädagogik, 5 (1959) 1, S. 1-34.
Brezinka, Wolfgang: Von der Pädagogik zur Erziehungswissenschaft. Weinheim u. a.: Beltz 1971.
Brinkmann, Wilhelm: Zur Geschichte der pädagogischen Soziologie in Deutschland. Würzburg: Königshausen und Neumann 1986. (Internationale Pädagogik. 12)
Curtius, Ernst Robert: Soziologie – und ihre Grenzen (1929). In: Meja, Volker / Stehr, Nico (Hrsg.): Der Streit um die Wissenssoziologie, Bd. 2 (= Suhrkamp-Taschenbuch Wissenschaft. 361), Frankfurt a. M.: Suhrkamp 1982, S. 417-426.
Dettling, Warnfried: Fach ohne Boden. Brauchen wir überhaupt Soziologen? Eine Polemik. In: Die Zeit, 51 (1996) 2, S. 23.
Döring, Woldemar Oskar: Psychologie der Schulklasse. 2.-3. Aufl. Osterwieck a. H.: Zickfeldt 1930. (Handbücher der neueren Erziehungswissenschaft. 4)
Ehrhardt-Kramer, Angelika / Hoppe, Jörg Reiner (Hrsg.): Persönlichkeitsförderung als Ausbildungsauftrag. Frankfurt a. M.: Deutscher Verein für Öffentliche und Private Fürsorge 1986. (Materialien zur sozialpädagogischen Praxis. 13)
Erler, ...: Unterrichtszeit. In: Schmid, Karl Adolf (Hrsg.): Encyklopädie des gesamten Erziehungs- und Unterrichtswesens. Bd. 9, Gotha: Besser 1873, S. 599-612.
Fischer, Aloys: Die pädagogische Wissenschaft in Deutschland. In: Die neuzeitliche deutsche Volksschule, Berlin: Comenius-Verlag 1928, S. 76-93.
Flitner, Wilhelm: Systematische Pädagogik. Breslau: Hirt 1933.
Flitner, Wilhelm: Das Selbstverständnis der Erziehungswissenschaft in der Gegenwart. Heidelberg: Quelle und Meyer 1958. (Pädagogische Forschungen. 1)
Freund, Julien: German Sociology in the Time of Max Weber. In: Bottomore, Tom / Nisbet, Robert (Hrsg.): A History of Sociological Analysis, London: Heinemann Educational 1979, S. 149-186.
Frischeisen-Köhler, Max: Philosophie und Pädagogik. Berlin u. a.: Beltz 1933. (Kleine pädagogische Forschungen. 20)
Fuchs, Max: Das Scheitern des Philanthropen Ernst Christian Trapp. Eine Untersuchung zur sozialen Genese der Erziehungswissenschaft im achtzehnten Jahrhundert. Weinheim u. a.: Beltz 1984.
Käsler, Dirk: Suche nach der guten Gesellschaft. Schrankenlose Individualisierung ist eine bildungsbürgerliche Illusion. Der Kult des Individuums kann die Utopien nicht ersetzten. In: Die Zeit, 51 (1996) 4, S. 43.
Kawerau, Siegfried: Soziologische Pädagogik (1921). 2. Aufl. Leipzig: Quelle und Meyer 1924.
Krieck, Ernst: Philosophie der Erziehung. Jena: Diederichs 1922.
Krüger, Heinz-Herrmann / Helsper, Werner (Hrsg.): Einführung in Grundbegriffe und Grundfragen der Erziehungswissenschaft. Opladen: Leske und Budrich 1995. (Einführungskurs Erziehungswissenschaft. 1)

Krüger, Heinz-Herrmann / Rauschenbach, Thomas (Hrsg.): Einführung in die Arbeitsfelder der Erziehungswissenschaft. Opladen: Leske und Budrich 1995. (Einführungskurs Erziehungswissenschaft. 4)

Lautmann, Rüdiger / Meuser, Michael: Verwendung der Soziologie in Handlungswissenschaften am Beispiel von Pädagogik und Jurisprudenz. In: Kölner Zeitschrift für Soziologie und Sozialpsychologie, 38 (1986) 4, S. 685-708.

Lehmann, Rudolf: Max Frischeisen-Köhler (1878-1923). In: Frischeisen-Köhler, Max: Philosophie und Pädagogik (= Kleine pädagogische Forschungen. 20), Berlin u. a.: Beltz 1933, S. 8-19.

Litt, Theodor: Möglichkeiten und Grenzen der Pädagogik. 2. Aufl. Berlin u. a.: Teubner 1926.

Mollenhauer, Klaus: Gesellschaft in pädagogischer Sicht. In: Groothoff, Hans Hermann (Hrsg.): Pädagogik (= Das Fischer-Lexikon. 36), Frankfurt a. M.: Fischer-Bücherei 1964, S. 102-112.

Mollenhauer, Klaus: Sozialisation und Schulerfolg. In: Roth, Heinrich (Hrsg.): Begabung und Lernen (= Gutachten und Studien der Bildungskommission. 4), Stuttgart: Klett 1969, S. 269-296.

Mollenhauer, Klaus: Theorien zum Erziehungsprozeß. München: Juventa-Verlag 1972. (Grundfragen der Erziehungswissenschaft. 1)

Mollenhauer, Klaus: Vergessene Zusammenhänge. Über Kultur und Erziehung. München: Juventa-Verlag 1983.

Nohl, Herman: Die pädagogische Bewegung in Deutschland und ihre Theorie (1933). 8. Aufl. Frankfurt a. M.: Schulte-Bulmke 1978.

Oevermann, Ulrich: Sozialisationstheorie. In: Lüschen, Günther (Hrsg.): Deutsche Soziologie seit 1945 (= Kölner Zeitschrift für Soziologie und Sozialpsychologie. Sonderheft. 21), Opladen: Westdeutscher Verlag 1979, S. 143-168.

Pädagogische Institutionen und Sozialisation. (Themenheft). In: Neue Sammlung, 14 (1974) 4, S. 317-426.

Palmer, Ch.: Umgang. In: Schmid, Karl Adolf (Hrsg.): Encyklopädie des gesamten Erziehungs- und Unterrichtswesens. Bd. 9, Gotha: Besser 1873, S. 522-528.

Rang, Brita: Pädagogische Geschichtsschreibung in der DDR. Frankfurt a. M.: Campus-Verlag 1982. (Campus Forschung. 252)

Rauschenberger, Hans: Zum Verhältnis von Pädagogik und Soziologie. In: Ellwein, Thomas u. a. (Hrsg.): Erziehungswissenschaftliches Handbuch. Bd. 3. 2, Berlin: Rembrandt-Verlag 1971, S. 390-400.

Roeder, Peter Martin: Soziologie der Erziehung. In: Groothoff, Hans Hermann (Hrsg.): Pädagogik (= Das Fischer-Lexikon. 36), Frankfurt a. M.: Fischer-Bücherei 1964, S. 314-323.

Roeder, Peter Martin: Bildung und Bildungsbegriff: Sozialwissenschaftliche Ansätze der Kritik. In: Goldschmidt, Dietrich u. a.: Erziehungswissenschaft als Gesellschaftswissenschaft (= Gesellschaft und Erziehung. 1), Heidelberg: Quelle und Meyer 1969, S 45-67.

Schmid, Karl Adolf (Hrsg.): Encyklopädie des gesamten Erziehungs- und Unterrichtswesens. Bd. 2. Gotha: Besser 1860.

Schröder, Hugo: Soziologie der Volksschulklasse. Vom Gemeinschaftsleben der Volksschulkinder. Halle: Niemeyer 1928.

Schwerdt, Theodor: Die Schule als Lebensform. Über die Wirkensweise schulpraktischen Handelns und erzieherischen Geschehens. Paderborn: Schöningh 1930.

Schwibs, Bernd / Bourdieu, Pierre: „Vernunft ist eine historische Errungenschaft, wie die Sozialversicherung". In: Neue Sammlung, 25 (1985) 3, S. 376-394.

Stieglitz, Heinrich: Soziologie und Erziehungswissenschaft. Wissenschaftstheoretische Grundzüge ihrer Erkenntnisstruktur und Zusammenarbeit. Stuttgart: Enke 1970.

Sünker, Heinz / Timmermann, Dieter / Kolbe, Fritz-Ulrich (Hrsg.): Bildung, Gesellschaft, Soziale Ungleichheit. Frankfurt a. M.: Suhrkamp 1994. (Suhrkamp-Taschenbuch Wissenschaft. 1085)

Tenorth, Heinz-Elmar: Über die Identität der Erziehungswissenschaft. In: Zeitschrift für Pädagogik, 27 (1981) 1, S. 85-103.

Tenorth, Heinz-Elmar: Einfügung und Formierung, Bildung und Erziehung – Positionelle Differenzen in pädagogischen Argumentationen um 1933. In: Herrmann, Ulrich / Oelkers, Jürgen (Hrsg.): Pädagogik und Nationalsozialismus (= Zeitschrift für Pädagogik. Beiheft. 22), Weinheim u. a.: Beltz 1988, S. 259-279.

Tenorth, Heinz-Elmar: Paul Ziertmann – oder: Verwaltungs-Reflexion aus Distanz. In: Harney, Klaus / Pätzold, Günter (Hrsg.): Arbeit und Ausbildung, Wissenschaft und Politik. Frankfurt a. M.: Gesellschaft zur Förderung Arbeitsorientierter Forschung und Bildung 1990, S. 57-69.

Tenorth, Heinz-Elmar: Normalisierung und Sonderweg. In: Borelli, Michele / Ruhloff, Jörg (Hrsg.): Deutsche Gegenwartspädagogik. Bd. 2, Baltmannsweiler: Schneider-Verlag Hohengehren 1996, S. 170-182.

Trapp, Ernst Christian: Versuch einer Pädagogik. Berlin: Nicolai 1780. [Unveränderter Neudruck: Paderborn: Schöningh 1977]

Trapp, Ernst Christian: Vom Unterricht überhaupt. In: Campe, Joachim Heinrich (Hrsg.): Allgemeine Revision des gesamten Schul- und Erziehungswesens, von einer Gesellschaft praktischer Erzieher. Bd. 8, Hamburg u. a.: Schulbuchhandlung 1787, S. 1-210.

Urban, Gert-H.: Vom Bürger zum Menschen, von der Staats- zur öffentlichen Schule, ein Wandel in den Auffassungen der Philanthropisten. Tübingen, Universität, Diss., 1980.

Ziertmann, Paul: Pädagogik als Wissenschaft und Professuren der Pädagogik. Berlin: Weidmann 1914. (Schriften der Wheelergesellschaft zur Erörterung von Fragen des deutschen und ausländischen Bildungswesens. 2)

Ziertmann, Paul: Das Berechtigungswesen. In: Kühne, Alfred (Hrsg.): Handbuch für das Berufs- und Fachschulwesen, Leipzig: Quelle und Meyer 1922, S. 485-518.

Verzeichnis der Autoren / List of authors / Liste des auteurs

Professorin Dr. Christel Adick, Ruhr-Universität, Institut für Pädagogik, Universitätsstraße 150, D-44801 Bochum

Professor Philip G. Altbach, Boston College, School of Education, 211 Campion Hall, USA-Chestnut Hill, Mass. 02167

Professor em. Dr. Oskar Anweiler, Ruhr-Universität, Institut für Pädagogik, Arbeitsstelle für Vergleichende Bildungsforschung, Universitätsstraße 150, D-44801 Bochum

Professor em. Dr. Siegfried Baske, Im Dol 2-6, D-14195 Berlin

Dr. Cesar Bîrzea, Institutul de Ştiinţe ale Educaţiei (Director), Strada Ştirbei Vodă 37, RO-Bucureşti 70732

Professor Dr. Günter Brinkmann, Pädagogische Hochschule, Fachbereich I, Abteilung Schulpädagogik, Kunzenweg 21, D-79117 Freiburg im Breisgau

Professor Dr. Birgit Brock-Utne, Universitetet i Oslo, Pedagogisk Forskningsinstitutt, Postboks 1092, Blindern, N-0317 Oslo

Dr. Wilhelm Ebert, Ehrenpräsident des Bayerischen Lehrer- und Lehrerinnenverbandes, Bavariaring 37, D-80336 München

Professor Erwin H. Epstein, Ohio State University, School of Educational Policy and Leadership, 145 Ramseyer Hall, 29 West Woodruff Avenue, USA-Columbus, Ohio 43210-1177

Professor Dr. Walter Georg, Fernuniversität Hagen, Fachbereich Erziehungs-, Sozial- und Geisteswissenschaften, Lehrgebiet Berufs- und Wirtschaftspädagogik, Fleyer Straße 203, D-58097 Hagen

Professor Mark B. Ginsburg, University of Pittsburgh, School of Education, Institute for International Studies in Education, 230 South Bouquet Street, USA-Pittsburgh, Pa. 15260

Die Autoren — The authors — Les auteurs

Professor Dr. Detlef Glowka, Westfälische Wilhelms-Universität, Institut für Allgemeine und Historische Erziehungswissenschaft, Abteilung Vergleichende Erziehungswissenschaft, Georgskommende 26, D-48143 Münster

Professor Dr. Candido Alberto Gomes, Senado Federal, Consultoria Legislativa, Praça dos Três Poderes, BR-70165-900 Brasília

Professor Harold Herman, University of the Western Cape, Faculty of Education, Department of Comparative Education, ZA-7537 Belville

Dr. Stephen P. Heyneman, The World Bank, Human Resources and Social Policy Division, Technical Department, Europe, Central Asia/Middle East and North Africa Regions (Chief), 1818 H Street N.W., USA-Washington D.C. 20433

Professor Dr. Wolfgang Hörner, Universität Leipzig, Erziehungswissenschaftliche Fakultät – Vergleichende Pädagogik –, Karl-Heine-Straße 22b, D-04229 Leipzig

Professor em. Dr. Torsten Husén, Stockholms Universitet, Institutionen för Internationell Pedagogik, S-10691 Stockholm

Professor Dr. Yaacov Iram, Universitat Bar-Ilan, Beit ha-Sefer le-Chinuk, IL-52900 Ramat-Gan

Professeur Dr. Victor Karady, Centre de Sociologie de l'Éducation et de la Culture, 54 Boulevard Raspail, F-75006 Paris

Professor Dr. Michael Kelpanides, Aristotelio Panepistimio, Tmima Philosophias ke Pedagogikis, Pontou 5, GR-54006 Thessaloniki

Emeritus Professor Edmund King, 40 Alexandra Road, GB-Epsom, Surrey KT17 4BT

Ministerialdirigent a. D. Georg Knauss, Mühlbaurstraße 14, D-81677 München

Professor Dr. Joachim H. Knoll, Ruhr-Universität, Institut für Pädagogik, Universitätsstraße 150, D-44801 Bochum

Dr. Richard Koch, Bundesinstitut für Berufsbildung, Abteilung Internationaler Vergleich Beruflicher Bildung, Fehrbelliner Platz 3, D-10707 Berlin

Die Autoren – The authors – Les auteurs

Professor Dr. Vitalij Grigor'evič Kostomarov, Institut Russkogo Jazyka Imeni A. S. Puškina (Direktor), Ulica Volgina 6, RUS-117485 Moskva

Professorin Dr. Marianne Krüger-Potratz, Westfälische Wilhelms-Universität, Institut für Allgemeine Erziehungswissenschaft, Arbeitsstelle für Interkulturelle Studien, Georgskommende 33, D-48143 Münster

Pierre Laderrière, Organisation de Coopération et de Développement Économiques, Programme sur la Gestion des Établissements d'Enseignement Supérieur (Chef), 2 rue André Pascal, F-75775 Paris Cedex 16

Professore emèrito Dr. Mauro Laeng, Terza Università degli Studi di Roma, Dipartimento di Scienze dell'Educazione, Via del Castro Pretorio 20, I-00185 Roma

Professor Robert F. Lawson, Ohio State University, College of Education, Department of Educational Policy and Leadership, 29 West Woodruff Avenue, USA-Columbus, Ohio 43210-1177

Dr. Jean-Michel Leclercq, Président de l'Association Francophone d'Éducation Comparée, c/o Centre International d'Ètudes Pédagogiques, 1 avenue Léon Journault, F-92311 Sèvres Cedex

Dr. Vandra L. Masemann, Florida State University, College of Education, Department of Educational Foundations and Policy Studies, 306 Stone Building, USA-Tallahassee, Fla. 32303-4070

Ministerialrat Dr. Hermann Müller-Solger, Bundesministerium für Bildung, Wissenschaft, Forschung und Technologie, Heinemannstraße 2, D-53175 Bonn

Professor Dr. Heliodor Muszyński, Uniwersytet imienia Adama Mickiewicza, Instytut Pedagogiki, Ul. Szamarzewskiego 89, PL-60569 Poznan

Professor Dr. Nikolaj Dmitrievič Nikandrov, Rossijskaja Akademija Obrazovanija (Vice-Prezident), Pogodinskaja ulica 8, RUS-119905 Moskva

Professoressa Dr. Donatella Palomba, Università degli Studi di Roma Tor Vergata, Dipartimento di Ricerche Filosofiche, Cattedra di Pedagogia, Via Bernardino Alimena, I-00173 Roma

Die Autoren – The authors – Les auteurs

Professor em Dr. Vlastimil Pařizek, Univerzita Karlova, Pedagogická Fakulta, M. Rettigové 4, CZ-11639 Praha

Dr. David Phillips, University of Oxford, Department of Educational Studies, Centre for Comparative Studies in Education, 15 Norham Gardens, GB-Oxford OX2 6PY

Professor Dr. Ioannis Pirgiotakis, Panepistimio tis Kritis, Tmima Pedagogikis, Dimitriakou 17, GR-74100 Rethymnon

Professor em. Dr. Jan Průcha, Varnsdorfská 333, CZ-19000 Praha

Professor em. Dr. Hermann Röhrs, Bergstraße 58, D-69259 Wilhelmsfeld

Professor Dr. Leo Roth, Universität Bremen, Fachbereich Erziehungs- und Gesellschaftswissenschaften, Bibliotheksstraße, D-28359 Bremen

Professor Raymond Ryba, University of Manchester, School of Education, GB-Manchester M13 9PL

Professor em. Dr. Bernhard Schiff, Hollige 46, D-29664 Walsrode

Professor J. J. Smolicz, University of Adelaide, Centre for Intercultural Studies and Multicultural Education (Director), G.P.O. Box 498, AUS-Adelaide, SA 5005

Emeritus Professor Werner Stephan, University of Saskatchewan, College of Education, Department of Educational Foundations and Indian Northern Education Programme, CDN-Saskatoon, Sask. S7N 0W0

Professorin Dr. Rita Süssmuth, Präsidentin des Deutschen Bundestags, Bundeshaus, D-53113 Bonn

Professor Dr. Shin'ichi Suzuki, Waseda-Daigaku, Kyôikugakubu, 6-1 Nishiwaseda, 1-chome, Shinjuku-ku, J-Tôkyô 169

Professor Dr. Mirosław S. Szymański, Uniwersytet Warszawski, Wydział Pedagogiczny, Ul. Mokotowska 16/20, PL-00561 Warszawa

Dr. Juan Carlos Tedesco, Bureau International d'Éducation (Directeur), 15 route des Morillons, CH-1218 Grand-Saconnex

Die Autoren — The authors — Les auteurs

Professor Dr. Ulrich Teichler, UniversitätGesamthochschule Kassel, Wissenschaftliches Zentrum für Berufs- und Hochschulforschung (Leiter), Henschelstraße 4, D-34109 Kassel

Professor Dr. Heinz-Elmar Tenorth, Humboldt-Universität zu Berlin, Institut für Allgemeine Pädagogik, Geschwister-Scholl-Straße 6, D-10099 Berlin

Emeritus Professor Janusz Tomiak, 15 Radbourne Road, GB-London SW12 0EA

Professor Witold Tulasiewicz, University of Cambridge, Department of Education, 17 Trumpington Street, GB-Cambridge CB2 1QA

Professor em. Dr. Henk Van daele, Vrije Universiteit Brussel, Faculteit voor Psychologie en Opvoedkunde, Afdeling Vergelijkende en Internationale Pedagogiek, Pleinlaan 2, B-1050 Brussel

Ministerialrat Dr. Michael Vorbeck, Europarat, Unterabteilung Hochschule und Forschung, B.P. 431 R6, F-67075 Strasbourg Cedex

Dr. Anthony R. Welch, University of Sydney, School of Social and Policy Studies, Building A 35, AUS-Sydney, NSW 2006

Professor David N. Wilson — President of the World Council of Comparative Education Societies —, Ontario Institute for Studies in Education, Comparative, International, and Development Education Centre, 252 Bloor Street West, CDN-Toronto, Ont. M5S 1V6

Professor Dr. Christoph Wulf, Freie Universität Berlin, Institut für Allgemeine Pädagogik, Arnimallee 11, D-14195 Berlin

Professor Dr. Makoto Yûki, Kokuritsu-Kyôiku-Kenkyûsho, 5-22 Shimomeguro, 6-chome, Meguro-ku, J-Tôkyô 153

Zusammenfassungen[1]

Adick, Christel: *Formale und nonformale Grundbildung in Afrika – Komplementarität oder Konkurrenz? (S. 451-467)*
Die Weltkonferenz zum Thema „Bildung für Alle" in Jomtien in Thailand im Jahre 1990 erklärte Bildung zu einem allgemeinen Menschenrecht. Bis zum Ende des Jahrtausends soll sich die Aufmerksamkeit der nationalen Bildungspolitiken sowie von Bildungsforschern und Praktikern der internationalen Zusammenarbeit verstärkt auf die Verwirklichung des Rechts auf Bildung für alle Menschen konzentrieren. Die Konferenz traf jedoch keine Entscheidung darüber, ob der Anspruch auf eine zumindest grundlegende Bildung eher in verstärkter schulischer Grundbildung oder besser in Bildungskonzepten nonformaler Art umgesetzt werden soll. Am Beispiel des Senegal werden verschiedene Praktiken formaler und nonformaler Grundbildung vorgestellt: staatliche Primarbildung, islamische Bildung und das Grundbildungsangebot freier Bildungszentren. Weiter wird vergleichend diskutiert, welche Spezifika diese verschiedenen Bildungszugänge aufweisen und in welchem eher komplementären oder konkurrierenden Verhältnis sie zueinander stehen.

Altbach, Philip G.: *Hochschulforschung in weltweiter Sicht (in Englisch) (S. 15-31)*
Mit dem Näherrücken des 21. Jahrhunderts sehen sich die Universitäten einer Vielzahl von Herausforderungen gegenüber. Daher besteht ein großer Bedarf an Expertenwissen und Daten zum Hochschulwesen. Dieser Aufsatz stellt die bisherige, die gegenwärtige und die zukünftige Hochschulforschung in internationaler Perspektive dar; so soll dem Leser ermöglicht werden, das komplexe Geflecht des Forschungsfeldes zu verstehen. Der Autor beleuchtet die Gründe für den Mangel an Daten und Analysen, z. B. den weitverbreiteten Brauch, Forschungsergebnisse in Form von grauer Literatur zu veröffentlichen oder als „vertraulich" zu behandeln. Die Ausweitung und das Wachstum einer Infrastruktur der Hochschulforschung werden ebenso behandelt wie die Informations-Infrastruktur des Hochschulwesens, insbesondere Sammelbände zum „state of the art", Lexika, Fachzeitschriften und Datenbanken. Der Autor wirft außerdem einen Blick auf die Geschichte und die geographische Ausdehnung des Forschungsfeldes. Mögliche zu-

---

1 Die Zusammenfassungen dürfen in Datenbanken übernommen werden.

künftige Tendenzen werden behandelt wie auch die für die Weiterentwicklung des Forschungsfeldes notwendigen Maßnahmen.

Anweiler, Oskar: *Vergleichende Erziehungswissenschaft und international vergleichende Bildungsforschung als Herausforderung und Aufgabe (S. 1-12)*
Der einleitende Überblick versucht, auf der Grundlage der in der Festschrift enthaltenen Aufsätze einige allgemeine Fragestellungen und Richtungen auf dem durch Wolfgang Mitter repräsentierten Arbeits- und Forschungsgebiet vorzustellen. Dabei geht es um historische Rückblicke auf die Disziplin der Vergleichenden Erziehungswissenschaft, um begriffliche Klärungen und methodische Ansätze, um die Bedeutung kultureller, nationaler und regionaler Differenzierungen sowie um globale und universelle Perspektiven. Die international vergleichende Bildungsforschung und die Vergleichende Erziehungswissenschaft müssen sich kritisch und produktiv mit den durch Globalisierung einerseits, Fragmentierung und Partikularismen andererseits bestimmten neuen Herausforderungen auseinandersetzen.

Baske, Siegfried: *Die neuhumanistische Phase des Jenkauer Conradinums im Urteil der deutschen und polnischen Bildungsgeschichte (S. 583-592)*
In der deutschen und der polnischen Bildungsgeschichte wird der neuhumanistischen Phase des Jenkauer Conradinums bis heute herausragende Bedeutung zugemessen. Im Zentrum des Interesses stehen zwei Publikationen, in denen 1811 und 1812 die beiden Direktoren Jachmann und Passow ihre Konzeption vorgetragen haben. Schule wird dabei nicht als Erfahrungs-, sondern als Vernunftbegriff definiert und in ein „präordiniertes" Verhältnis zur Welt gesetzt.

Bîrzea, Cesar: *Gebrauch und Mißbrauch erziehungswissenschaftlicher Forschung – Das Beispiel einer politischen Manipulation in Rumänien (in Englisch) (S. 468-476)*
In diesem Artikel dient die Entwicklung der erziehungswissenschaftlichen Forschung als Indikator für politischen Wandel. Nach der näheren Betrachtung dieser Forschung in Rumänien, insbesondere in den achtziger Jahren, wird ein berühmter, ohne Zweifel einzigartiger Fall in der Geschichte der Erziehungswissenschaft, eine regelrechte „Hexenjagd" mitten im zwanzigsten Jahrhundert, beschrieben. Abschließend wird allgemeiner auf die Transformationsproblematik eingegangen. Tatsächlich benutzte das rumänische kommunistische Regime die erziehungswissenschaftliche Forschung nicht, um seine Entscheidungen für das Bildungswesen darauf zu stützen, sondern um eine politische Manipulation auf nationaler Ebene zu begründen. Es handelt sich um die Affäre, die als „Tor der Transzendentalen Meditation" bekannt wurde. Ceaucescu benutzte diese Affäre

1982 als vorbeugende Maßnahme gegen das Eindringen des „Solidarność-Syndroms" nach Rumänien. Es handelt sich um einen einmaligen Mißbrauch erziehungswissenschaftlicher Forschung durch die politische Macht.

Brinkmann, Günter: *Lehrerrolle und Lehrerausbildung in den Niederlanden (S. 477-489)*
Schule und Lehrerausbildung sind in den Niederlanden in den letzten Jahren ins Zentrum des öffentlichen Interesses gerückt. Seit Ende der achtziger Jahre hat man ein nationales System der Qualitätsvorsorge in Form von Unterrichtsvisitationen eingerichtet. Diese Visitationen führten zu Evaluationsstudien. Daneben wurden Empfehlungen zur Verbesserung von Schule und Lehrerausbildung vorgelegt: von der Zukunftskommission Lehrerschaft der Bericht „Ein Beruf mit Perspektive", vom Bildungsministerium die Broschüren „Vitale Lehrerschaft" und „Vitale Lehrerausbildungsgänge". Diese Dokumente werden ebenso analysiert wie die jüngste Tendenz, moderne Informationstechnologien in Hochschule und Schule einzuführen.

Brock-Utne, Birgit: *Internationalisierung des Bildungswesens – Eine kritische Perspektive (S. 301-311)*
Dieser Artikel beschäftigt sich mit der Frage, was „Internationalisierung des Bildungswesens" heißt. Bedeutet diese „Internationalisierung" eigentlich nur eine Anglifizierung bzw. Amerikanisierung oder – was die afrikanischen Länder betrifft – eine erneute Kolonisation? Wer sind die „supranationalen Bildungsfachleute", die über die globalen Curricula und die internationalen Maßstäbe für die Prüfungen der Schulleistungen bestimmen? Der Artikel analysiert die Spannungen, die zwischen externen Standards und internen Kulturen existieren und nimmt den Bildungsqualitätsbegriff der Weltbank unter die Lupe. Weiterhin wird folgende Frage gestellt und analysiert: Wem dient der internationale Trend des zunehmenden Marktliberalismus, der jetzt auch im Bildungssystem immer deutlicher zutage tritt?

Ebert, Wilhelm: *Magna Charta des Lehrerberufs – Dreißig Jahre UNESCO-Empfehlung zum Status der Lehrer (in Englisch) (S. 593-609)*
Seit ihrer Gründung 1946 bis gegen Ende der siebziger Jahre war die UNESCO nach der UNO die bedeutendste internationale Organisation. Alle anderen Politikbereiche wurden in ihrem Verhältnis zu Bildung, Wissenschaft und Kultur definiert, und umgekehrt war man sich bewußt, daß man auch mit einer internationalen Politik wesentlich die Richtung und Mächtigkeit von Bildung, Wissenschaft und Kultur mitbestimmte. Da sich als wichtigster Faktor für die Qualität von Schulen immer wieder die Lehrerschaft her-

auskristallisiert hatte, beschloß die UNESCO zusammen mit der ILO 1966 eine internationale Empfehlung zum Lehrerstatus. Der nachfolgende Beitrag versucht, den Weg nachzuzeichnen, der zu diesem internationalen Dokument zum Status der Lehrer führte.

Epstein, Erwin H.: Wie die Demokratie durch die Schule gefiltert wird – Ein übersehenes Paradoxon der Schulpflicht (in Englisch) (S. 32-45)
Man erwartet von der Schule einerseits, daß sie, um die Ziele der Demokratie zu erfüllen, objektives Wissen objektiv vermittelt, andererseits aber auch, daß sie nationale Mythen lehrt, die zwar die Realität vernebeln, aber aus den Schülern loyale Bürger machen, und all dies mittels der undemokratischen Maßnahme des verpflichtenden Schulbesuchs. „Demokratische Erziehung" ist infolgedessen ein Oxymoron bei der Beschreibung der Schulbildung insbesondere in denjenigen Staaten, die sich im gesellschaftlichen Übergang befinden, und ganz besonders in den ehemals sozialistischen Staaten, die darum ringen, sich zu Demokratien zu entwickeln. Die Inanspruchnahme der Schule als eines Mediums zur Filterung des „richtigen" Wissens für die Schüler macht aus der „demokratischen" Erziehung eine „undemokratische", insbesondere für Gruppen, die außerhalb der vorherrschenden Kultur, an der Peripherie stehen, wo die Kinder und ihre Eltern besonders anfällig für Mystifizierungen sind. Das Paradoxon wird noch einmal gesteigert durch die Vision der westlichen Demokratien, die, im Namen der Demokratie, ihre eigene Form des Zwangslernens „liefern". Dieser Beitrag untersucht die Instrumentalisierung der Schule als ein bislang bitter vernachlässigtes Kapitel der Demokratieforschung.

Georg, Walter: Berufliche Bildung zwischen Internationalisierung und nationaler Identität (S. 312-328)
Der Autor untersucht die arbeits-, berufs- und bildungsrelevanten Implikationen der Globalisierungsthese und des daraus abgeleiteten Universalisierungszwanges. Soweit sich entsprechende Tendenzen nachweisen lassen, betreffen sie vor allem einen globalen Trend zur Expansion der weiterführenden „allgemeinen" Bildung und die damit verbundene Marginalisierung der staatlich verantworteten, überbetrieblichen Berufsbildung. Jenseits dieses Trends sind die nationalspezifischen Strukturen und Institutionen beruflicher Qualifizierung weitgehend stabil geblieben. Trotz eines generellen Modernisierungsdrucks lassen sich die Systemveränderungen weder zu einem universellen Entwicklungspfad bündeln, noch läßt sich die Varianz der nationalspezifischen Muster von Berufsbildung in einen systematischen Zusammenhang mit dem Modernisierungsgrad und Wirtschaftserfolg der einzelnen Länder bringen. Eine Gegenüberstellung von Merkmalen des „Systems" der beruflichen Bildung in Deutschland und Japan verweist auf die

Relevanz der jeweiligen Industriekultur, die jedem Versuch einer sich als universalistisch verstehenden Berufsbildungspolitik enge Grenzen setzt.

Ginsburg, Mark B.*: Grenzen und Möglichkeiten der vergleichenden Analyse in der Erziehungswissenschaft im weltweiten Kontext (in Englisch) (S. 46-51)*
Eine vergleichende Analyse in der Erziehungswissenschaft ist aus folgenden Gründen problematisch aber auch lohnend: 1. identifizierte Spezifika und Unterschiede zwischen Erscheinungen sind an die Subjektivität sowohl der Forscher als auch der Gegenstände der Forschung gebunden; 2. zwischen verschiedenen Nationen – ebenso wie zwischen sub- bzw. supranationalen Einheiten – bestehen im Weltsystem Konvergenzen und Divergenzen; 3. zu den Zielen der Analyse können die Anleitung kollektiver Aktionen von Pädagogen ebenso wie die Schaffung eines wachsenden Verständnisses und die Einschätzung alternativer Optionen von Politik und Praxis gehören.

Glowka, Detlef*: Überlegungen zu einer „Einführung in die Vergleichende Erziehungswissenschaft" (S. 52-64)*
Die vorliegenden Betrachtungen wurden angeregt durch das Projekt einer ERASMUS-Gruppe, gemeinschaftlich einen Kurs „Einführungen in die Vergleichende Erziehungswissenschaft" zu entwickeln, zu erproben und zu veröffentlichen. Ein in die Gruppe eingebrachter Entwurf fand rasch allgemeine Zustimmung und wurde als Gerüst für den Einführungskurs akzeptiert. Im Sommersemester 1996 versuchten wir an der Universität Münster, dieses Gerüst in ein Seminar umzusetzen. Es wird über die während dieses Prozesses gewonnenen Einsichten und Erfahrungen berichtet. Um das Ergebnis vorwegzunehmen: Die Struktur der Vergleichenden Erziehungswissenschaft als einer wissenschaftlichen Disziplin und der Stand ihrer „Didaktik" ließen den Entwurf eines Einführungskurses zu einem ebenso schwierigen wie stimulierenden Unternehmen werden.

Gomes, Candido Alberto*: Vergleichende Erziehungswissenschaft und Politik aus der Sicht des Südens (in Englisch) (S. 209-218)*
Der Schwerpunkt des ersten Teils dieses Textes liegt zum einen auf den Spannungen zwischen der Universalität der Wissenschaft und den besonderen Umständen der Länder auf der südlichen Halbkugel, und zum anderen auf denjenigen Charakteristika der Vergleichenden Erziehungswissenschaft, die für den Süden von Bedeutung sind. Im zweiten Teil beschreibt der Verfasser seine Erfahrungen als Parlamentsberater und schildert, wie ihm die Vergleichende Erziehungswissenschaft bei dieser beruflichen Tätigkeit geholfen hat.

Zusammenfassungen

Herman, Harold: *Bildung und politischer Wandel in Südafrika (in Englisch) (S. 490-501)*
Seit dem Ende der Apartheid, den ersten demokratischen Wahlen und der Einsetzung einer Regierung der nationalen Einheit im Jahre 1994 sieht sich Südafrika einer großen Zahl von Problemen des Übergangs zur Demokratie und der Entwicklung sozialer Gleichheit gegenüber. Analysiert wird die Möglichkeit, daß Südafrika ein demokratischer Staat wird, und ebenso die Art von Demokratie, die sich in einem Land herausbilden kann, das durch eine Geschichte der Rassentrennung, ein starkes kapitalistisches Wirtschaftssystem und extreme gesellschaftliche Ungleichheit geprägt ist. Seit 1994 wurden wichtige Gesetze verabschiedet und politische Maßnahmen zur Förderung der Demokratisierung im Bildungswesen in Angriff genommen. Dieser Beitrag analysiert die Stärkung demokratischer Prinzipien und Werte durch das „White Paper on Education" des Nationalen Bildungsministerium vom Februar 1995. Zum Abschluß wird die Rolle, welche das Bildungswesen zum Gelingen einer zukünftigen Demokratie in Südafrika beisteuern kann, analysiert.

Heyneman, Stephen P.: *Die Zusammenarbeit im Bildungswesen zwischen den Nationen im 21. Jahrhundert (in Englisch) (S. 219-233)*
Wie werden die Beziehungen auf dem Gebiet des Bildungswesens zwischen souveränen Staaten in der Zukunft aussehen? Viele mögliche Themen bieten sich hier an: Lehr-/Lernprozesse, Lehrerausbildung und -entlohnung, Lebenslanges Lernen, Bildungsstandards usw. Natürlich sind alle diese Themen interessant, aber: Welche davon sind so interessant, daß die Nationen dazu motiviert sein werden, auf einem dieser Gebiete zusammenzuarbeiten? Werden sich die Motivationen verändern, oder werden sie gleichbleiben? Wenn sich die Motivationen verändern: Wie werden diese Veränderungen die Zusammenarbeit verändern, welchen Einfluß werden sie auf die im Bildungsbereich tätigen internationalen Organisationen sowie auf deren personelle Ausstattung und die Inhalte ihrer Programme haben? Meiner Meinung nach wird die Motivation für die internationale Zusammenarbeit in der Zukunft völlig anders sein. Ich stelle hier in Kürze die Gründe für meine Überzeugung dar und verliere dann einige Worte über die Auswirkungen auf die nationalen und internationalen Einrichtungen sowie ihre Beschäftigten und die Inhalte ihrer Programme.

Hörner, Wolfgang: „Europa" als Herausforderung für die Vergleichende Erziehungswissenschaft – Reflexionen über die politische Funktion einer pädagogischen Disziplin (S. 65-80)

Ausgehend von einer Analyse der Disziplinbezeichnungen der Vergleichenden Erziehungswissenschaft in verschiedenen europäischen Sprachen und der Beschreibung ihrer möglichen Funktionen in Forschung und Lehre wird der mögliche Beitrag der Vergleichenden Erziehungswissenschaft zum europäischen Integrationsprozeß erörtert. Es zeigt sich, daß die Disziplin gerade in dieser Hinsicht eine wichtige politische Funktion wahrnehmen kann.

Husén, Torsten: Die „Bildungslücke" (in Englisch) (S. 329-343)

Die hier behandelte „Bildungslücke" bezieht sich auf die erheblichen Unterschiede bei den Schülerleistungen, die nach einer bestimmten Anzahl von Jahren des Schulbesuchs in Entwicklungsländern erworben wurden im Gegensatz zu solchen in Industrieländern, die eine lange Geschichte des Schulbesuchs sowohl im Primar- als auch im Sekundarbereich aufweisen. Diese Unterschiede werden als „Leistungslücke" bezeichnet. Die Daten entstammen Erhebungen, die von der „Internationalen Vereinigung für Schulleistungsbewertung" (International Association for the Evaluation of Educational Achievement – IEA) durchgeführt wurden, sowie den Erfahrungen, die der Autor Mitte der siebziger Jahre in Botsuana gewonnen hat, als er Vorsitzender der Nationalen Bildungskommission war, deren Aufgabe damals in der Planung des Bildungswesens bis in die neunziger Jahre bestand. Die hier angesprochenen Untersuchungen lassen sich für die Dauerbeobachtung der in einem bestimmten Land gebotenen Bildungsqualität einsetzen. Im Falle Botsuanas dienten sie außerdem zur Bewertung der Auswirkungen der Verwendung des Englischen als Unterrichtssprache nach mehreren Jahren des Besuchs der Elementarschule.

Iram, Yaacov: Die Stellung der Humanwissenschaften in Bildung und Erziehung (in Englisch) (S. 610-620)

Dieser Beitrag behandelt den Niedergang des Status der humanistischen Bildung und analysiert Gründe und Auswirkungen ihrer schwächer gewordenen Position. Der Autor schlägt die Einführung eines „integrativen Ansatzes" für die humanistische Bildung vor. Nur durch die Einbeziehung eines humanistischen Ansatzes auf allen Gebieten des Wissens, d. h. durch die Unterrichtung der kulturellen Phänomene zum Zwecke der Klärung ihrer Bedeutungen, kann die humanistische Perspektive ihre zentrale Rolle wiedergewinnen. Diese Rolle besteht nicht allein in der Weitergabe von wertvollem Wissen – „kulturelle Alphabetisierung" –, sondern auch in der Stärkung von Tendenzen hin zu wechselseitigem Verstehen, zum Akzeptieren des je Anderen und zur Kooperation zwischen Individuen und Gesellschaften mit dem Ziel der Selbstverwirklichung.

Karady, Victor: *Schulbildung und Religion – Zu den ethnisch-konfessionellen Strukturmerkmalen der ungarischen Intelligenz in der Zwischenkriegszeit (S. 621-641)*
Der Autor untersucht auf der Grundlage von umfangreichem statistischen Quellenmaterial das Verhältnis von Bildungsstand und Beschäftigung in bezug auf die ethnische bzw. konfessionelle Zugehörigkeit im nach dem ersten Weltkrieg unabhängig gewordenen ungarischen Staat bis hin zum Beginn der dreißiger Jahre unter besonderer Berücksichtigung der Schichten mit hohem Bildungsniveau. Er stellt historische Vergleiche zur Zeit vor 1918 an und analysiert regionale Unterschiede (insbesondere das Verhältnis von Stadt und Land) sowie die Verteilung auf bestimmte Sektoren der Volkswirtschaft. Besondere Bedeutung kommt dabei dem Verhältnis von jüdischen und nicht-jüdischen Teilen der gebildeten Schichten zu. Die angeführten Angaben verdeutlichen eine tiefe Spaltung der ungarischen Intelligenz in den Krisenjahren der Zwischenkriegszeit. Als wichtigstes Ergebnis läßt sich die Allgemeinheit von ähnlichen „Doppelstrukturen" im Modernisierungsprozeß der meisten mitteleuropäischen Länder und ihrer ideologisch-politischen Auswirkungen festhalten.

Kelpanides, Michael: *Universitätsstudium für jedermann? Die Politisierung der Sozialwissenschaften als bleibendes Erbe der Bildungsexpansion (S. 642-655)*
Thema des Beitrags ist die seit der Bildungsexpansion der sechziger Jahre erfolgte Politisierung und Ideologisierung der Sozialwissenschaften, in welchen, primär von der Soziologie ausgehend, der Neomarxismus – trotz der weitgehenden Falsifikation der zentralen Annahmen der Marxschen Theorie – als das dominante theoretische Paradigma der Sozialwissenschaften in Lehre und Forschung etabliert wurde. Diese Entwicklung wird mit der Störung des Gleichgewichts zwischen den Funktionen der Universität und der Hypertrophie der „kritischen Intelligenz" an den Universitäten erklärt.

King, Edmund: *Ein Wendepunkt in der Vergleichenden Erziehungswissenschaft – Rückblick und Ausblick (in Englisch) (S. 81-90)*
Die Vergleichende Erziehungswissenschaft hat sich inzwischen weit über ihre früheren Aufgaben – historische Erklärungen, Definition von Bezeichnungen, Theoriebildung und „Prophezeiungen" – hinaus entwickelt. Heute kann sie sich auf ein ständig wachsendes Netz von Partnerschaften stützen, erhält Rückmeldungen von Forschern in vielen Wahrnehmungs- und Entscheidungspositionen und muß sich auf einen weltweiten Horizont von neuen Ungewißheiten vorbereiten. Wolfgang Mitters Präsidentschaft der Com-

parative Education Society in Europe – und später des World Council of Comparative Education Societies – setzt bis heute ein Zeichen für seine Offenheit gegenüber dieser gewandelten Ausrichtung und Zusammenarbeit.

Knauss, Georg: *Von 1988 bis 1996 – Wege zur Weiterentwicklung der gymnasialen Oberstufe (S. 234-244)*
Seit dem Ende des Zweiten Weltkriegs sind in Deutschland Ziele, Inhalte und Struktur des Gymnasiums als der zur allgemeinen Hochschulreife führenden Schulart in immer neuen Reformwellen diskutiert und verändert worden. Nach 1960, 1972 und 1988 stand eine neue Reform bevor, die sowohl eine Festigung zentraler Fächer und Inhalte als auch eine Öffnung für neue Anforderungen bewirken soll. Der Beitrag schildert die komplizierten Beratungs- und Entscheidungsvorgänge im Rahmen der Kultusministerkonferenz.

Knoll, Joachim H.: *Von der Alphabetisierung zur funktionalen Alphabetisierung (in Englisch) (S. 344-358)*
Das Phänomen des Analphabetismus ist schon seit langem nicht nur in den Entwicklungsländern, sondern auch in den Industriestaaten als Problem erkannt worden. Der Beseitigung des Analphabetismus hat sich die UNESCO in vielfältigen Zusammenhängen angenommen, wobei unterschiedliche Ansätze konzipiert wurden. Zunächst zeichnet der Aufsatz die Entwicklung der Alphabetisierungsbemühungen nach und hebt dabei besonders die Diskussion unterschiedlicher Ansätze hervor. Sodann werden Definitionen und aktuelle Tendenzen aus einschlägigen Dokumenten, wie der „Recommendation on the Development of Adult Education" oder der „World Declaration on Education for All", entnommen. Abschließend dienen einige Fakten und Zahlen zur Illustration der momentanen Situation in Ghana.

Koch, Richard: *Gesellschaftliche Steuerung von Berufsbildungssystemen – Ein Analysekonzept für politikorientierte internationale Vergleiche (S. 91-104)*
Die international vergleichende Berufsbildungsforschung bietet ein von der Berufsbildungspolitik nutzbares Erkenntnispotential, das bislang in Deutschland nur begrenzt ausgeschöpft wurde. Zur Bearbeitung bildungspolitisch relevanter Fragestellungen sind komplexe Forschungskonzepte erforderlich, die eine konkrete Analyse von institutionellen Ausgestaltungen und Handlungsfeldern ermöglichen. Das hier skizzierte Konzept der gesellschaftlichen Steuerung von Berufsbildungssystemen stellt das für die Berufsbildungspolitik zentrale Problem der Wechselbeziehungen zwischen institutionellen Systemstrukturen, öffentlichen Interventionen und dem Handeln sozialer Akteure in das

Zentrum der Analyse. Dieses Forschungskonzept läßt sich auf den internationalen Vergleich der verschiedensten Funktionsprobleme von Berufsbildungssystemen beziehen. Die Erfolge und Mißerfolge des Auslands bei der Lösung vergleichbarer Probleme der Systemsteuerung können wertvolle Anregungen für die nationale Berufsbildungspolitik geben.

Kostomarov, Vitalij Grigor'evič: *Das Bildungswesen in den Nachfolgestaaten der Sowjetunion und die russische Sprache (S. 502-511)*
Nach dem Zusammenbruch der UdSSR begannen sich in allen neu entstandenen Staaten nationale Bildungssysteme zu entwickeln, wobei höchster Wert auf die einheimischen Sprachen, Kulturen und Religionen gelegt wurde. Seither muß kein Schüler oder Student mehr Russisch lernen. Auch wenn diese Sprache nicht länger als ein unentbehrliches Instrument (zumindest als Lingua franca) angesehen wird, hat sie nach wie vor die meisten ihrer früheren Funktionen behalten und wird diese – aus vielerlei Gründen – in absehbarer Zukunft auch weiterhin haben. Ein langfristiger Sprachplanungsprozeß mit dem Ziel, den strategischen Bedürfnisse der einheimischen und fremden Sprachen insgesamt gerecht zu werden, erfordert die Verbreitung des Russischen, auch wenn die Zahl der Schüler und Studenten, die diese Sprache erlernen, zurückgeht. In Rußland wurde ein föderales Programm ausgearbeitet, dessen Umsetzung zur Zeit mit allem Nachdruck verfolgt wird.

Krüger-Potratz, Marianne: *Ein Blick in die Geschichte ausländischer Schüler und Schülerinnen in deutschen Schulen (S. 656-672)*
In welcher Tradition stehen die heutigen Maßnahmen, die für die Kinder und Jugendlichen aus Einwandererfamilien und aus Aussiedlerfamilien ergriffen worden sind? Wie wirken diese Traditionen weiter, obwohl auf rechtlicher Ebene vor rund dreißig Jahren mit dem bis dahin geltenden Grundsatz, daß ausländische Kinder nicht schulpflichtig seien, gebrochen wurde? Bis dahin wurde ihnen in der Regel der Zugang zu Schulen zwar nicht verwehrt, doch war entscheidend, daß aus ihrer Aufnahme in die Schulen dem Staat keine weiteren Verpflichtungen entstanden. Im nachstehenden Beitrag werden die rechtlichen Bestimmungen, die zur Regelung des Schulbesuchs nicht reichsdeutscher Kinder in der Weimarer Republik ergangen sind, dargestellt und unter interkultureller Perspektive diskutiert.

Laderrière, Pierre: Die Transformation im Osten – Eine Lehre für den Westen? (in Französisch) (S. 359-366)
Für die westlichen Länder könnte es von Nutzen sein, vom Wiederaufbau der Bildungssysteme in Osteuropa zu lernen. Sieht man vom schwierigem Start der Reformen in diesen Ländern ab, so gibt es in der Tat einen gemeinsamen, sich entwickelnden Zusammenhang einer sich auf Wissen gründenden postindustriellen Gesellschaft, wodurch sich die westlichen Länder aufgefordert fühlen sollten, den Lösungen aufmerksam zu folgen, mit deren Verwirklichung man in Osteuropa bereits begonnen hat.

Laeng, Mauro: Vom Gestern zum Heute – Entwicklungen in der Vergleichenden Erziehungswissenschaft (in Englisch) (S. 105-116)
Der Artikel umreißt die Entwicklung der Vergleichenden Erziehungswissenschaft, anhand von Beispielen überwiegend aus Europa und Italien, über drei Phasen hinweg, die durch unterschiedliche Blickwinkel gekennzeichnet sind: 1. eine philosophische und geschichtliche Perspektive, die den Geist der Völker verstehen will; 2. eine strukturelle und statistische Dokumentation der verschiedenen Schulsysteme; 3. eine angemessene bildungspolitische Planung durch Ausrichtung an ökonomischen Entwicklungen. Heute eröffnen die neuen Perspektiven der elektronischen Information Möglichkeiten und Gelegenheiten zu neuen Beziehungen und Dialogen.

Lawson, Robert F.: Der Zusammenhang zwischen politischem Kontext und Demokratie im Bildungswesen (in Englisch) (S. 367-380)
Der hier untersuchte Zusammenhang ist derjenige zwischen den politischen Annahmen, die der institutionellen Organisation immanent sind, und einer auf Chancengleichheit ausgerichteten Bildungspolitik. Folgende Länder wurden hierfür herangezogen: die DDR als ein Modell der auf einer Theorie basierenden systematischen Politisierung; Südafrika als ein Modell der auf Kultur basierenden multisystemischen Politisierung und Kanada als ein Modell der Laissez-faire-Politisierung; diese Modelle werden als Phänomene der Zeitgeschichte abgehandelt sowie als Typologien, die für die Analyse nach wie vor von Bedeutung sind, auch wenn die politischen Inhalte durch Konflikte und Veränderungen beeinflußt wurden. Die Anwendung der vergleichenden Methode erlaubt es, die idiosynkratischen Werte der Annahmen, Entscheidungen, Strukturen und Handlungen im Bildungswesen zu ermitteln und sie politischen Ansprüchen gegenüberzustellen, die auf einem vermuteten universellen Gleichheitsstandard beruhen.

Leclercq, Jean-Michel: *Wie läßt sich die Kultur eines Bildungssystems sehen und berücksichtigen? (in Französisch) (S. 117-126)*
Kultur ist untrennbar mit Bildung und Erziehung verbunden. Besonders die Vergleichende Erziehungswissenschaft unterstreicht immer diese enge Beziehung. Dennoch ist die Kultur des Bildungssystems nicht einfach die Spiegelung der Kultur der Gesellschaft. Deshalb wäre es um so notwendiger zu versuchen, das je Besondere zu erfassen, welches die Kultur der verschiedenen Systeme auszeichnet. Die Globalisierung hat eine Relativierung dieser Besonderheiten zur Folge und zwingt dazu, sie formal eher durch den Grad ihrer Kohärenz oder ihrer Entwicklungsmöglichkeit zu bestimmen als aufgrund ihrer Besonderheiten.

Masemann, Vandra L.: *Neuere Richtungen in der Vergleichenden Erziehungswissenschaft (in Englisch) (S. 127-134)*
Dieser Artikel bietet einen Rückblick auf die wichtigsten Entwicklungen in der Vergleichenden Erziehungswissenschaft in den Jahren 1990 bis 1996: die verschiedenen Tagungen des World Council of Comparative Education Societies und dessen angegliederter Verbände; einflußträchtige politische Begebenheiten; die Rolle der UNESCO; die Entwicklung und das Wachstum des World Council; Veröffentlichungen, Forschernetzwerke und Einsatz elektronischer Medien sowie die Hauptthemen der jüngsten Tagungen des World Council.

Müller-Solger, Hermann: *Anerkennung, Akkreditierung, Transparenz – Notwendige Begriffsklärungen für die Europäische Union (S. 245-261)*
Eine der zentralen Aufgaben der Europäischen Union im Bildungsbereich ist die Erleichterung der Anerkennung von Abschlüssen oder Studienleistungen der verschiedenen Bildungswege. Es werden zunächst zehn zentrale Begriffe der Diskussion definiert und erläutert. Anschließend wird die Rolle des Prüfungswesens im Bildungssystem beleuchtet, und eine neue Initiative der Europäischen Kommission zum Nachweis und zur Anerkennung von Qualifikationen wird vorgestellt und problematisiert. Nach Auffassung des Autors sind Transparenz und Dezentralisierung notwendige Bedingungen für deren Gelingen. Abschließend werden vier Aufgaben skizziert, auf die sich die gemeinschaftliche und gemeinsame Politik im Bildungsbereich in den kommenden Jahren konzentrieren sollte.

Muszyński, Heliodor: Die Pädagogische Studienreise als Instrument der wissenschaftlichen Erkenntnis (S. 135-142)
Studienreisen, die seit der Begründung der Vergleichenden Erziehungswissenschaft zu einem der fruchtbarsten Forschungsansätze dieser Disziplin zählten, waren für einige Zeit in der Forschergemeinschaft „in Ungnade gefallen". Der Autor geht den Gründen dafür nach, die er vor allem in der Entwicklung einer positivistischen Methodologie sieht, der nur solche Forschung als „richtige" Wissenschaft galt, deren Ergebnisse quantitativ erfaßbar waren und auf deren Grundlage man zu Verallgemeinerungen gelangen konnte. Der damit einhergehende Verlust, nämlich die Möglichkeit der Identifizierung von Individualität und Einzigartigkeit nationaler Bildungssysteme, führte zu einer Renaissance qualitativer Ansätze auch in der Bildungsforschung. Was diese leisten können, wird am Beispiel einer Reihe von Forschungsreisen, die der Autor seit 1989 zusammen mit Wolfgang Mitter in Polen unternommen hat, verdeutlicht, wobei insbesondere der spezifische Nutzen der „verstehenden Erkenntnis" herausgearbeitet wird.

Nikandrov, Nikolaj Dmitrievič: Die Werteproblematik in Gesellschaft und Bildungswesen der Russischen Föderation (S. 512-523)
Der Autor geht von der These aus, daß Rußland auch nach dem Zusammenbruch des Kommunismus keineswegs auf eine Ideologie verzichten kann, die als ein System von Prinzipien und grundlegenden Werten die Maßstäbe setzt für das Verhalten der Bürger untereinander sowie gegenüber anderen Ländern und Kulturen. In diesem Zusammenhang geht er vor allem auf die Lehrerschaft ein wie auch auf die Erziehungsziele für eine Jugend, die in einer Gesellschaft ohne feste Wertorientierungen aufwächst – es sei denn das Ziel, ohne jegliche Rücksichtnahme auf die Mitmenschen schnell reich zu werden. Als ein mögliches Referenzsystem für einen neuen Wertekanon der russischen Gesellschaft sieht er die Religion(en) an und arbeitet die darin enthaltenen „allgemeinmenschlichen" Werte heraus, d. h. solche, die von allen Bürgern unabhängig davon, ob sie „gläubig" sind oder nicht, akzeptiert werden können. Er diskutiert auch die Unergiebigkeit einer direkten Vermittlung von Werten durch Unterricht, solange Lehrer und Schüler in der Gesellschaft kein konsistentes Wertesystem vorfinden.

Palomba, Donatella: Politische Bildung zum Bürger im multikulturellen Europa – Eine vergleichende Übersicht (in Französisch) (S. 381-392)
Politische Bildung für eine Bürgerschaft (citoyenneté) in Europa gründet auf einer Konzeption demokratischer Bürgerschaft, die jedoch je nach Land und Bezug geschichtlich unterschiedlich ist. Wenn man die Bürger bezüglich ihrer gemeinsamen Zugehörigkeit zu Europa befragt, stellt man sehr unterschiedliche Überlieferungen fest. Dies erfordert

Überlegungen nicht nur zum Verhältnis zwischen verschiedenen politischen und kulturellen Traditionen, sondern auch zur Rolle einer Erziehung, die auf einer liberal-demokratischen Tradition beruht, im Hinblick auf Kulturen, die dieser Tradition nicht unbedingt verhaftet sind. Eine vergleichende Sicht drängt sich auf, um bessere Kenntnisse von Konzepten und Praktiken zu gewinnen, die der demokratischen politischen Bildung in den unterschiedlichen Zusammenhängen zugrundeliegen, wie auch zur Ausarbeitung eines Modells, das die „Verschiedenheiten" aufnimmt.

Pařizek, Vlastimil: *Die Krise der Schule und Wege zu ihrer Überwindung (in Englisch) (S. 393-401)*
In vielen Büchern und auf vielen Konferenzen liest und hört man von der Unzufriedenheit mit dem Stand der Familien- und Schulerziehung und von ihrer „Krise". Für diese werden drei Ursachen verantwortlich gemacht: 1. die Diskrepanz zwischen Kenntnissen, Fertigkeiten und Werten, welche die Schüler in der Schule erwerben, und dem, was sie im Leben brauchen; 2. eine Krise der Gesellschaft insgesamt; 3. die schwache öffentliche Aktivität der Lehrer und ihrer Organisationen. Der Autor analysiert folgende fünf Bereiche, die für eine Überwindung der Krise entscheidend sind, in ihrem Zusammenhang mit der Bildung: Arbeitswelt, Sozialbeziehungen, Gesundheit und Umwelt, Sorge für zukünftige Generationen sowie Freizeit. Abschließend werden einige Vorschläge dazu unterbreitet, wie das Bildungswesen selbst zur Überwindung der Krise beitragen kann.

Phillips, David: *Prolegomena zu einer Geschichte des Interesses für das deutsche Bildungswesen in Großbritannien (in Englisch) (S. 673-687)*
In diesem Aufsatz wird eine Reihe von veröffentlichten Quellen erörtert, die für ein Studium des weitgefächerten Interesses am deutschen Bildungswesen in Großbritannien seit dem Beginn des 19. Jahrhunderts in Frage kommen können. Insofern handelt es sich um einen Beitrag zur Untersuchung der wechselseitigen Anziehungskraft zwischen den Völkern in bezug auf die Bildung, da die Gründe für das Interesse am deutschen Bildungswesen in Großbritannien zu bestimmten Zeiten angesprochen werden.

Pirgiotakis, Ioannis: *Das Bildungswesen in Griechenland – Mythos und Wirklichkeit (in Englisch) (S. 524-537)*
Während der Wahlkämpfe finden in Griechenland immer wieder Debatten über die „Krise" des Bildungswesens statt. Der Autor fragt, ob es eine solche Krise überhaupt gibt. Zur Beantwortung der Frage untersucht er – nach einem Rückblick auf die Bildungsgeschichte des neuzeitlichen Griechenland – die Bildungsreformen seit den fünfzi-

ger Jahren unter Bezugnahme auf zwei internationale Tendenzen: 1. die Expansion des Bildungswesens im Zusammenhang mit dem Konzept der Humankapital-Theorie; 2. die Förderung von Chancengleichheit. Besonderes Augenmerk richtet er auf die Bildung von Frauen und das Verhältnis von Bildung (insbesondere Hochschulbildung) und Beschäftigung. In bezug auf die Ausweitung der Bildungsbeteiligung und die Chancengleichheit kann keineswegs von einer Krise gesprochen werden; es muß aber festgestellt werden, daß dadurch, daß die Reformen des Bildungswesens ohne entsprechende Reformen im Beschäftigungssystem durchgeführt wurden, die Arbeitslosigkeit von Akademikern zur Entstehung eines „akademischen Proletariats" geführt hat. Nur insofern kann man von einer Krise des Bildungswesens sprechen.

Průcha, Jan: Privatschulen und öffentliche Schulen – Ein Vergleich ihrer Qualität in der Tschechischen Republik (in Englisch) (S. 538-549)
Der Aufsatz behandelt ein neues Phänomen in der Tschechischen Republik: das Aufkommen von Privatschulen nach 1989. Zur Zeit gibt es auf allen Ebenen des Schulsystems – jedoch nicht auf Hochschulebene – private Bildungseinrichtungen. Die Anzahl der Privatschulen hat von Jahr zu Jahr erheblich zugenommen; so besuchen beispielsweise heute 20% der Schüler von beruflichen Schulen der Sekundarstufe II eine private Bildungseinrichtung. Allerdings ist nach wie vor nicht klar, welche Qualität von Bildung die neuen Privatschulen vermitteln. Es werden die Ergebnisse einer ersten Vergleichsuntersuchung der Schülerleistungen in öffentlichen und privaten (Oberstufen-)Gymnasien präsentiert. Erstaunlicherweise erzielten die öffentlichen Gymnasien bessere Resultate als die privaten. Der Autor geht den Gründen für diese Unterschiede nach; dabei werden die Ergebnisse von empirischen Untersuchungen in anderen Ländern, in denen die Qualität von Privatschulen bewertet wurde, einbezogen.

Röhrs, Hermann: Gründung und Gestaltung der „Deutschen Sektion" des „Weltbunds für Erneuerung der Erziehung" (1921 bis 1931) – Ein bildungspolitisch bedeutsames Kapitel der internationalen Reformpädagogik (S. 688-706)
Die Studie deutet die wechselvolle Gründungsgeschichte der deutschen Sektion als ein bildungspolitisch hochinteressantes Kapitel. Nach jahrelanger Kooperation mit der „New Education Fellowship" gelang die offizielle Gründung erst 1931 unter dem Vorsitz von Erich Weniger, mit der Unterstützung durch Robert Ulich. Die internationale Repräsentanz wurde von Carl Heinrich Becker, dem ehemaligen preußischen Kultusminister, wahrgenommen.

Roth, Leo: *Die Reformation als Zäsur in der deutschen Universitätsentwicklung – Von der Universalität zur Regionalisierung (S. 707-724)*
An der deutschen Universitätsgeschichte wird der Weg von der Universalität zur Regionalisierung durch die Reformation vergleichend dargestellt. Die qualitativen und quantitativen Analysen zeigen im Inter- und Intrasystemvergleich den Einfluß geistesgeschichtlicher Auseinandersetzungen auf die Institution Universität mit Konsequenzen nicht nur für diese, sondern für die gesamte Wissenschaft und das politische und geistige Leben bis in die Gegenwart.

Ryba, Raymond: *Zur Entwicklung der Europäischen Dimension von Bildung und Erziehung in der Praxis – Der Beitrag des Programms „Didaktische Materialien zur Europäischen Dimension" des Europarats (in Englisch) (S. 262-271)*
Dieser Beitrag legt Konzeption, Umsetzung und Ergebnis eines großen europäischen Curriculumentwicklungs-Programms (European Dimension Pedagogical Materials Programme) dar, das vom Autor für den Europarat als Teil des kürzlich abgeschlossenen Projekts „Sekundarbildung für Europa" (Secondary Education for Europe Project) durchgeführt wurde.

Schiff, Bernhard: *Das Orthodoxe Klassische Gymnasium in Moskau (S. 550-558)*
Mit dem Zusammenbruch der Sowjetunion haben die sowjetkommunistischen Erziehungsziele ihre Gültigkeit verloren. Einen Versuch, die Schulerziehung an neuen Werten auszurichten, stellt die Gründung des Orthodoxen Klassischen Gymnasiums (im September 1990) in Moskau dar. Gründer und Träger dieser Schule ist die christliche Laienvereinigung „Radonež". Das neue Gymnasium versteht sich als eine weltliche Schule, deren Unterrichtsziele sich an der Weltanschauung und Ethik des russisch-orthodoxen Christentums orientieren. Ähnliche Versuche hat es im vorrevolutionären Rußland nur im Elementarschulwesen gegeben.

Smolicz, J. J.: *Sprachenpolitik im Bildungswesen in einem vielsprachigen Umfeld – Australien und die Philippinen (in Englisch) (S. 402-413)*
Am Beispiel von Australien und den Philippinen werden die Veränderungen in der Sprachenpolitik im Bildungswesen hinsichtlich der ethnischen Vielfalt der Bevölkerung und deren sich veränderndem politischen Status seit dem Zweiten Weltkrieg untersucht. Australien hat die Politik der einseitigen Assimilation an das Englische aufgegeben zugunsten einer Multikulturalität, die es den Minderheiten ermöglicht, die zu Hause gesprochene Sprache auch in der Schule zu lernen. Analysiert wird weiterhin die gegenläufige Entwicklung auf den Philippinen, wo die Entscheidung, eine einzige Sprache zur Natio-

nalsprache zu erklären, in einem vielsprachigen Land dazu geführt hat, daß alle anderen autochthonen Sprachen aus den Lehrplänen verschwunden sind. Es wird jedoch deutlich, daß das Vorhandensein von regionalen Sprachgemeinschaften auf den Philippinen dazu beigetragen hat, die Vielfalt der gesprochenen „Verkehrssprachen" zu bewahren, während in Australien die Zersplitterung der sprachlichen Minderheiten und das Nichtvorhandensein territorialer Gemeinschaften die Anstrengung der Bildungspolitik, andere Sprachen außer dem Englischen zu bewahren, konterkariert hat.

Stephan, Werner: *Lehrer und Gesellschaft – Ein internationaler Vergleich (S. 414-425)*
Dieser Beitrag skizziert die Arbeitsbedingungen von Lehrern in Polen, Deutschland, England, den Vereinigten Staaten und Kanada. Unter dem Druck politischer und wirtschaftlicher Interessen hat sich ihr Lebensstandard verschlechtert und ist das soziale Ansehen des Lehrerstandes gesunken. Die Tendenz zur professionellen Entmündigung der Lehrer ist in den angelsächsischen Ländern sehr stark und führt potentiell zu einer Proletarisierung des Lehrerstandes.

Süssmuth, Rita: *Politik und Vergleichende Erziehungswissenschaft in gemeinsamer Verantwortung für eine humane Lerngesellschaft (S. 272-281)*
Politik und Wissenschaft stehen in der gemeinsamen Verantwortung bei der Bewältigung globaler Herausforderungen. Bildung ist beim Übergang in eine Wissensgesellschaft der Schlüssel zum Erfolg. Die Vergleichende Erziehungswissenschaft kann den politischen Paradigmenwechsel zu transnationaler Kooperationsarbeit unterstützen. Im folgenden Beitrag wird dies exemplarisch für die Frauen-, Medien- und Persönlichkeitsbildung aufgezeigt.

Suzuki, Shin'ichi: *Politischer Systemwechsel und die geopolitische Neuordnung des Bildungsraums – Konsequenzen für die Vergleichende Erziehungswissenschaft (in Englisch) (S. 143-151)*
Seit dem Fall der Berliner Mauer im Jahre 1989 sind die Völker in nahezu allen Regionen des Erdballs Zeugen eines gewaltigen Anwachsens des Nationalismus. Vor dem Hintergrund einer Mixtur von religiösem Eifer und der Wahrnehmung von kulturellen und ethnischen Unterschieden haben neue Formen von „Staatszentriertheit" vielerorts zu Bürgerkriegen, politischer Gewalt und terroristischen Aktionen in den vom Wandel betroffenen Gesellschaften geführt, was ein Symptom für das Fehlen von Leitprinzipien für den gesellschaftlich-politischen Wiederaufbau sein dürfte. Auf der Folie des Ringens um die Überwindung von politischen Wirren und gesellschaftlicher Instabilität unternimmt der Autor eine Klärung der verborgenen Zusammenhänge von „Problemen im

Bildungswesen" aus der Perspektive sich wandelnder geopolitischer Dimensionen des gesellschaftlichen Lebens; näher behandelt werden Veränderungen durch die neuen Medien und Probleme, die aus der Zentrum-Peripherie-Kluft resultieren. Abschließend wird die Verwendbarkeit des „Profilansatzes" bei Vergleichsuntersuchungen analysiert.

Szymański, Mirosław S.: Erziehung zur Demokratie durch die Schülerselbstregierung in der Zweiten Polnischen Republik (1918 bis 1939) (S. 725-739)
Ausgangspunkt ist die These, daß bei der Entstehung und Entwicklung von Theorie und Praxis der Schülerselbstregierung in der Zweiten Polnischen Republik (1918-1939) zwei Werke von weltweiter Wirkung eine entscheidende Rolle gespielt haben: Friedrich Wilhelm Foersters „Schule und Charakter" und Adolphe Ferrières „L'autonomie des écoliers". Vor dem Hintergrund der Beschreibung der zwei sich gegenüberstehenden und miteinander wetteifernden Modelle der Schülerselbstregierung – des „monarchistischen" und des „demokratischen" Modells – werden dann zwei Phasen der geschichtlichen Entwicklung von Theorie und Praxis der Selbstregierung an den Schulen dargestellt. Der Beitrag versucht darüber hinaus die polnische Schülerselbstregierung „idealtypisch" zu schildern, indem er u. a. folgende Fragen beantwortet: Auf welche Weise wurde die Selbstregierung in den Schulen eingeführt? Vor welche Aufgaben wurde sie gestellt? Welche Organisationsformen nahm sie an? Wie umfangreich war ihre Praxis?

Tedesco, Juan Carlos: Die Erneuerung der Vergleichenden Erziehungswissenschaft (in Französisch) (S. 152-160)
Gegenwärtige sozioökonomische, kulturelle und politische Veränderungen verlangen nach einer Revision der Forschungsprogramme und -methoden auf dem Gebiet der Vergleichenden Erziehungswissenschaft. Die neuen Themen lassen sich in drei Hauptkategorien einteilen: Sozialisationsprozeß, kognitive Entwicklung und Diskussion über die Ziele von Bildung und Erziehung. Zur Verwirklichung dieser neuen Programmatik müssen Methoden eingesetzt werden, welche die Analyse der drei genannten Kategorien unter Verwendung eines interdisziplinären Ansatzes ermöglichen.

Teichler, Ulrich: Vergleichende Hochschulforschung – Probleme und Perspektiven (S. 161-172)
Vergleichende Hochschulforschung gewinnt in Europa an Interesse – insbesondere aufgrund der zunehmenden internationalen Kooperation. Theoretisch klar strukturierte Projekte vernachlässigen allerdings oft die Komplexität des Gegenstands. Ausreichende Finanzen stehen meist nur für allzu praktische Fragen bereit. Hinderlich sind Sprachbarrieren, begrenzte Feldkenntnisse sowie heterogene Lehrmeinungen und Arbeitsstile in

internationalen Forschungsteams. Außergewöhnliche Erträge werden nur mit halbstrukturierten Forschungsdesigns erzielt, die es erlauben, vielfältige Phänomene einzuordnen und zugleich überraschende Erfahrungen durch konzeptionelle Restrukturierung zu verarbeiten.

Tenorth, Heinz-Elmar: Pädagogik und Soziologie (S. 740-756)
Wissenschaftliche Pädagogik und Soziologie sind heute selbständige Disziplinen, nach ihren Theorien unterscheidbar, in ihren Methoden relationierbar. Der Beitrag diskutiert exemplarisch, wie sich diese Differenz von gemeinsamen Themen aus entwickelt. Dafür werden sowohl thematische Indikatoren der Theorieentwicklung, ausgehend vom Problem der Lerngruppe, als auch institutionelle Mechanismen, vor allem der Besetzung von Lehrstühlen in der Weimarer Republik, historisch behandelt und systematisch ausgewertet.

Tomiak, Janusz: Rückblicke, Vorausblicke – Das Bildungswesen in Ostmitteleuropa am Vorabend des 21. Jahrhunderts (in Englisch) (S. 426-436)
Die Bildungssysteme in Ostmitteleuropa sind zur Zeit einem fundamentalen Wandel unterworfen. Sie bewegen sich weg von einem durchgehend gesteuerten, zentral geplanten und uniformen Modell hin zu einem offenen, liberalen und differenzierten Muster. Dies läßt sich nicht auf kurze Sicht erreichen. Die Demokratisierung und Modernisierung des Bildungswesens dort kann schneller vorankommen, wenn westliche Hilfe ohne Verzögerungen und auf effektive Weise zur Verfügung gestellt wird. Gleichermaßen wichtig ist, daß sich die Regierungen der Länder Ostmitteleuropas bewußt sind, daß Bildung eine grundlegende Investition darstellt, und dem Bildungswesen daher einen höheren Stellenwert in der Rangordnung der nationalen Prioritäten einräumen.

Tulasiewicz, Witold: Bildung als Ware – Jüngste Entwicklungen in Großbritannien (in Englisch) (S. 559-571)
Dieser Beitrag stellt eine Fortsetzung der Analyse der bildungspolitischen Entwicklungen in Großbritannien seit der Regierungsübernahme durch die Konservativen im Jahre 1979 durch den Autor dar, von der bereits zwei frühere Folgen in der „Zeitschrift für Internationale Erziehungs- und Sozialwissenschaftliche Forschung" erschienen sind. Die enthusiastische Aufnahme der Wirtschaftspolitik und der Praktiken des freien Marktes durch die Verwaltung wurde auch auf das Angebot von Dienstleistungen im Bildungssektor übertragen. Der Aufsatz diskutiert die Verdienste und Nachteile dieser Politik und ihre Angemessenheit für die Bereitstellung einer öffentlichen Dienstleistung; es werden

Beispiele aus der jüngeren Gesetzgebung herangezogen, um die aus dieser Politik resultierenden erheblichen Veränderungen in der Praxis aufzuzeigen.

Van daele, Henk: *Vergleichende Erziehungswissenschaft und Internationale Erziehung – Einige Probleme sprachlicher Natur (in Französisch) (S. 173-181)*
Die Vergleichende Erziehungswissenschaft ist ein schwieriges Forschungsfeld, nicht zuletzt aufgrund der unzähligen sprachlichen Probleme. Drei Voraussetzungen müssen daher erfüllt sein: 1. Die Spezialisten auf dem Gebiet der Vergleichenden Erziehungswissenschaft müssen mehrsprachig sein; 2. die Bezeichnungen für Bildungseinrichtungen, Abschlüsse usw. sind äußerst schwierig zu übersetzen und sollten deshalb als Eigennamen behandelt werden, die niemals übersetzt werden dürfen; 3. in Europa ist ein eindeutiges Glossar für Begriffe aus Bildung und Erziehung dringend erforderlich.

Vorbeck, Michael: *Bildungsforschung und besonders Vergleichende Erziehungswissenschaft in Europa – für Europa (S. 282-297)*
Der Beitrag gibt einen Überblick über die Entwicklung der Bildungsforschung und der Vergleichenden Erziehungswissenschaft in Europa seit den sechziger Jahren: das Entstehen der maßgeblichen Forschungsinstitute in den einzelnen Staaten und parallel hierzu das besondere Engagement des Europarats in diesem Bereich. Daneben werden die Aktivitäten anderer internationaler Organisationen (UNESCO, OECD, Europäische Union u. a.) beleuchtet. Auf das Engagement Wolfgang Mitters und des Deutschen Instituts für Internationale Pädagogische Forschung wird dabei jeweils verwiesen. An die Darstellung schließt sich eine Bewertung des bisher Erreichten (und Nicht-Erreichten) an, und abschließend werden Forderungen nach notwendigen Aktivitäten auf nationaler wie auf internationaler Ebene aufgestellt.

Welch, Anthony R.: *Die Dinge fallen auseinander: Die Desintegration, die Universitäten und der Niedergang der Disziplin(en). Eine Problematisierung der Vergleichenden Erziehungswissenschaft in einer Zeit voller Ungewißheit (in Englisch) (S. 182-191)*
In diesem Aufsatz werden die gegenwärtige Situation und die Aussichten der Vergleichenden Erziehungswissenschaft im Lichte des gesellschaftlichen, ökonomischen und geistigen Klimas des ausgehenden Jahrhunderts analysiert. Der von Zuversicht geprägte Positivismus der Vergleichenden Erziehungswissenschaft in der Nachkriegszeit ist inzwischen Ungewißheiten in den Bereichen der Wirtschaft, der Pädagogik und des Geisteslebens gewichen. Will sie überleben, so muß die Vergleichende Erziehungswissenschaft lernen, auf diese Ungewißheiten eine Antwort zu finden, und – unter Bedingun-

gen erheblich geringerer Finanzmittel – unter Beweis stellen, daß sie weiterhin von Bedeutung ist.

***Wilson, David N.**: Das deutsche duale System der Berufsausbildung – Eine vergleichende Untersuchung seines Einflusses auf Bildungspolitik und Bildungspraxis in anderen Ländern (in Englisch) (S. 437-448)*
In diesem Beitrag wird das deutsche duale System im Hinblick auf andere Länder untersucht, die an einer Übernahme dieses „Modells" und dessen Anpassung an ihre Verhältnisse interessiert sind. Da das System als eine mögliche Lösung für die Ausbildungsprobleme sowohl in entwickelten als auch in Entwicklungsländern angesehen wird, wird hier untersucht, welche Realitäten, Mythen und Mißverständnisse in der Literatur und den Bildungssystemen jener Länder zu finden sind, die behaupten, sie hätten dieses Modell übernommen. Die legislativen, bildungspolitischen, organisatorischen und funktionellen Komponenten des Systems werden erörtert und in Bezug zur deutschen Wirklichkeit gesetzt. Die Auffassungen mehrerer Autoren, welche die Übernahme des „Modells" befürworten, werden daraufhin befragt, warum das „Modell" so attraktiv und/oder angemessen für das Berufsbildungssystem ihres Landes zu sein scheint. Die erfolgreiche Übernahme des dualen Systems in Singapur wird dargestellt und analysiert ebenso wie das Interesse an dem „Modell" in Israel. Schließlich werden die Gründe dafür, daß es in Sri Lanka keinen Erfolg hatte, herausgearbeitet.

***Wulf, Christoph:** Mimesis des Anderen – Annäherung an das Fremde (S. 192-206)*
In Erziehungs- und Bildungsfragen spielt der Andere eine zentrale Rolle. Insofern Bildung und Erziehung es mit der Annäherung und Verarbeitung zunächst fremder Gegenstände, Zusammenhänge und Personen zu tun haben, ist die Auseinandersetzung mit dem Anderen hier unerläßlich. Infolge der Globalisierung der Lebenszusammenhänge und der durch die Entstehung der Europäischen Union notwendigen politischen, ökonomischen und kulturellen Anforderungen sind Bildung und Erziehung zu einer interkulturellen Aufgabe geworden. Um dieser gerecht zu werden, ist die Begegnung und die Auseinandersetzung mit dem Anderen eine Herausforderung für die Bewahrung und Transformation der eigenen Kultur.

***Yûki, Makoto:** Die rechtliche Struktur der Bildungsverwaltung in Japan (S. 572-580)*
Das japanische Bildungssystem hat nach 1945 entscheidende Wandlungen durchgemacht: Von einer zentral gesteuerten und unter kaiserlicher Prärogative stehenden Bildungsverwaltung wurde der Schritt zu einem von parlamentarisch beschlossenen Gesetzen bestimmten System vollzogen, in dem auch die regionalen Interessen gewahrt blei-

ben. Hauptmerkmale dieser neuen Bildungsverwaltung im Vergleich zur Vorkriegszeit sind: wesentlich geringere Befugnisse des Kultusministeriums als Zentralorgan sowie auf regionaler Ebene gewählte Bildungsausschüsse, die von der allgemeinen Verwaltung unabhängig sind.

Abstracts[1]

Adick, Christel: *Formal and Non-Formal Basic Education in Africa: Complementarity or Rivalry? (in German) (pp. 451-467)*
The World Conference „Education for All" in Jomtien in Thailand in 1990 declared education a universal human right. Therefore, national educational policies, educational research, and the practice of international educational co-operation are expected to devote more of their work towards the realization of this right for all mankind until the turn of the millennium. However, the Conference did not predetermine, if the access to at least basic education should best be realized by expanding formal primary schooling, or by devoting more efforts to institutions offering nonformal education. The practice of various forms of formal and nonformal basic education programs in Senegal is described: national primary schools, Islamic institutions, and basic education in non-governmental community education centers. These different concepts of basic education with their specific characteristics and the relationship between them, being either more of a complementary kind or rather competitive in nature, are discussed.

Altbach, Philip G.: *Research on Higher Education: Global Perspectives (pp. 15-31)*
As the 21st century approaches, universities face a variety of challenges. Therefore, there is a great need for expert knowledge and data about all aspects of higher education. This essay looks at the past, present and future of research on higher education. It adopts an international perspective and seeks to help the reader understand the complex web of the research field. The author considers the reasons for the scarcity of data and analysis, e. g. the widespread custom to publish research results in „gray literature" or keeping them „confidential". The expansion and growth of a higher education research infrastructure are dealt with as well as the information infrastructure in higher education, especially information sources such as „state of the art" compilations, encyclopedias, specialized periodicals and databases. Also the history and geographical spread of the field are looked at. Future trends are suggested and needs that have to be addressed if the field is to develop further are listed.

---

1 The abstracts may be included in data bases.

Anweiler, Oskar: Comparative Education and International Comparative Education as Challenge and Task (in German) (pp. 1-12)
On the basis of the essays in this *Festschrift* the introductory overview attempts to present some general issues and directions in the work and research field represented by Wolfgang Mitter: historical reviews of the discipline of comparative education; a clarification of concepts and methodological approaches; the relevance of cultural, national und regional differentiations; global and universal perspectives. International comparative education and comparative education must tackle the challenges of globalisation on the one hand and fragmentation and particularisms on the other in a critical and productive way.

Baske, Siegfried: The Neo-Humanistic Stage of the Jenkau Conradinum from the Perspective of German and Polish Educational History (in German) (pp. 583-592)
In German and Polish history of education the Neo-Humanistic stage of the Jenkau Conradinum has been credited with outstanding significance until today. Of central interest are two publications of 1811 and 1812 in which in the two headmasters, Jachmann and Passow, presented their conception. They conceived school in terms of reason rather than experience and placed it in a „pre-ordinated" relationship to the world.

Bîrzea, Cesar: The Use and Abuse of Educational Research: The Case of a Political Manipulation in Romania (pp. 468-476)
In the article the development of educational research is used as an indicator of political change. After a closer examination of the research conducted during the eighties in Romania, a specific, undoubtedly unique case in the history of educational research, a veritable „witchhunt" in the middle of the twentieth century, is described. In conclusion problems encountered in the transitional period are discussed in general. The Romanian Communist regime did not use educational research to legitimate its decisions regarding educational policies. In fact it used the results for political manipulations at a national level. The affair referred to, because known as the „transcendental mediations doorway". Ceaucesu used this affair in 1982 as a preventative measure against the invasion of the „Solidarność Syndrome" into Romania. It is a unique example of the abuse of educational research by political powers.

Brinkmann, Günter: The Role of the Teacher and Teacher Education and Training in the Netherlands (in German) (pp. 477-489)
In recent years schools and teacher training have become the focus of public attention in the Netherlands. Since the end of the eighties a national system of quality provision in

form of teaching inspections has been established. These inspections led to evaluation studies. Besides that recommendations for improving schools and teacher training were presented: „A Profession with Perspective" by the Future Commission for Teaching Staff, the brochures „Vital Teaching Staff" and „Vital Teacher Training Courses" by the Ministry of Education. These documents as well as the latest tendencies to introduce modern information technologies in universities and schools are analysed.

Brock-Utne, Birgit: *Internationalisation of Education: A Critical Perspective (in German) (pp. 301-311)*
This article deals with the question of what internationalisation of education means. Does „internationalisation" only mean Anglification/Americanisation or – in the case of the African countries – re-colonisation? Who are the „supranational educators", who make decisions on global curricula and set international examination standards? The article analyses the tensions that exist between external standards and internal cultures and scrutinises the way the World Bank uses the term quality in education. In addition the article analyses the question: Who profits from the international trend of greater reliance on market forces within education?

Ebert, Wilhelm: *Magna Carta for the Status of Teachers: Thirty Years of the UNESCO Recommendation for the Status of Teachers (pp. 593-609)*
Since its foundation in 1946 and until the end of the seventies, the UNESCO was – after the UNO – one of the most important international organisations of the world. At that time all political areas were defined in relation to education, science and culture, and vice versa one was conscious of the fact that international politics also determined the direction and power of education, science and culture, and conversely one was conscious of the fact that international politics determined the direction and power of education, science and culture. Because teachers have – again and again – been acknowledged to be the most important factor in schooling, the UNESCO – in agreement with the ILO – adopted an international recommendation on the status of teachers in 1966. The following essay attempts to show how this international document on the status of teachers came into being.

Epstein, Erwin H.: *Filtering Democracy through Schools: The Ignored Paradox of Compulsory Education (pp. 32-45)*
Schools are expected to convey objective knowledge objectively to satisfy the aims of democracy, yet also to teach national myths that obscure reality but make citizens loyal, and to do so through the undemocratic measure of compulsory attendance. „Democratic

education" is therefore an oxymoron when used to describe schooling especially in transitional states, and most especially in formerly socialist countries struggling to be democratic. The imposition of schools as vehicles by which to filter „correct" knowledge to children makes „democratic" education undemocratic, most notably among populations outside the cultural mainstream, at the periphery where children and their parents are the most vulnerable to mystification. The paradox is magnified by the specter of Western democracies purveying their own forms of compelled learning in the name of democracy. This essay explores the instrumentality of schools as a sorely missing chapter in scholarship about democracy.

Georg, Walter: Vocational Education between Internationalization and National Identity (in German) (pp. 312-328)
The article examines the implications of the globalization thesis for the workplace, occupations and education, and the universalization dictate derived from it. When trends can be identified they predominantly show a global move towards the expansion of secondary „general" education linked with a corresponding marginalization of public, non-company-based vocational education. Apart from this trend specific national structures and institutions of vocational qualification have remained stable. Despite the general modernization pressure, system changes can neither be integrated into a global developmental path nor is it possible to systematically relate the variance of specific national patterns of vocational education to the degree of modernization and economic success of a specific country. Contrasting the characteristics of the „systems" of vocational education in Germany and Japan indicates the relevance of the respective industrial cultures that limit any attempt to consider vocational-education policy as universally applicable.

Ginsburg, Mark B.: The Limitations and Possibilities of Comparative Analysis of Education in Global Context (pp. 46-51)
Comparative analysis in education is problematic but worthwhile because: 1) identified singularities and differences among phenomena are tied to the subjectivity of researchers and the researched; 2) convergencies and divergencies of nations (and sub- and supra-national units) exist within the world system; 3) its goals may include informing educators' collective action as well as increasing understanding and assessing alternative policy/practice options.

Abstracts

Glowka, Detlef: *Reflections on an „Introduction to Comparative Education" (in German) (pp. 52-64)*
The observations presented here were suggested by the project of an ERASMUS-group to jointly develop a course „Introduction to Comparative Education", to put it to the test and finally to publish it. An outline that was presented in this group soon found agreement and was accepted as a framework for the introductory course. In the summer semester of 1996 we attempted to implement the course in a seminar at the University of Münster. Here we want to report the insights and experiences that we gained during this process. To come straight to the result: the enterprise of designing an introductory course was as difficult as it was stimulating because of the structure of comparative education as a scientific discipline and the state of its „didactics".

Gomes, Candido Alberto: *Comparative Education and Public Policies: A View from the South (pp. 209-218)*
In the first part of this text the focus is on the tensions between the universality of science and the particular circumstances of countries located on the southern hemisphere as well as on the characteristics of comparative education that are of interest to the South. In the second part the author describes his experiences as a parliamentary adviser and discusses how comparative education helped him with his professional role.

Herman, Harold: *Education and Political Change in the New South Africa (pp. 490-501)*
Since the demise of apartheid, the first democratic national elections and the establishment of a government of national unity in 1994, South Africa is facing numerous issues of transition to democracy and equalization of social development. The possibility of South Africa becoming a truly democratic state is analyzed, also the kind of democracy which could develop in a country with a history of racial segregation, a strong capitalist economy and extreme social inequalities. Since 1994 there has been significant legislation passed and policies implemented to foster democratization in education. This article illustrates how democratic principles and values are enhanced by the White Paper on Education released by the new National Ministry of Education in February 1995. It concludes with an analysis of the role education can play in a future successful democracy in South Africa.

Heyneman, Stephen P.: Educational Cooperation between Nations in the 21st Century *(pp. 219-233)*
What will be the future relationship among sovereign states in the field of education? There are many potential issues: teaching processes, teacher preparation and remuneration, lifelong learning, educational standards, etc. All are important, but what will actually motivate nations to cooperate on these issues? Will motivations change or will they remain the same? If motivations change, how will the changes influence the nature of cooperation, the international agencies charged with educational responsibilities, the staffing of these agencies, and the content of their programs? I believe the motivations for international cooperation will be different in the future. Briefly, I will summarize why I believe this, and then say a few words about the implications for international and national agencies, their staff, and the content of their programs.

Hörner, Wolfgang: „Europe" as a Challenge for Comparative Education: Reflections on the Political Function of a Field of Education (in German) *(pp. 65-80)*
Beginning with the examination of the term „comparative education" in different European languages, the article explains the different functions of the discipline both in research and in university teaching, in order to show its possible contribution to the process of European integration. Evidence is given that comparative education is able to fulfil an important political function in this respect.

Husén, Torsten: The „Education Gap" *(pp. 329-343)*
The kind of „education gap" dealt with here refers to the enormous difference in student competence achieved after a given number of years of formal schooling in developing countries in contrast to industrialized countries, which have a long history of both primary and secondary schooling. It is referred to as „the performance gap". The data presented stem from the surveys conducted by the „International Association for the Evaluation of Educational Achievement (IEA)" and the particular experience the author gained in Botswana when he chaired the National Commission on Education in the mid-1970s with the task of planning education up to the 1990s. Surveys of the kind referred to in the article can be of use in monitoring the quality of education provided in a given country. In the case of Botswana they were also useful in evaluating the effects of using English as the medium of instruction after several years of elementary schooling.

Iram, Yaacov: The Status of the Humanities in Education *(pp. 610-620)*
This article describes the declining status of humanistic education and analyses the reasons and effects of its diminishing role in education. The author suggests the adoption of

an „integrative approach" to humanistic education. Only by incorporating the humanistic perspective into all fields of knowledge, i. e. by teaching of cultural phenomena in order to clarify their meanings, the humanities can reclaim their central role. This role not only comprises imparting of valuable knowledge – „cultural literacy" – but also strengthening the trends towards mutual understanding, acceptance and co-operation between individuals and societies with the aim of achieving self-fulfillment.

Karady, Victor: Schooling and Religion: Ethnic and Denominational Patterns of the Hungarian Intelligentsia in the Years between World War I and II (in German) (pp. 621-641)
On the basis of extensive statistical material the author examines the relationship between the level of education and occupation on the one hand, and the ethnic or denominational membership on the other, in the newly independent state of Hungary from the end of World War I to the early 1930s, laying special emphasis on the classes with a higher educational level. He compares the situation with the period before 1918 and analyses regional differences (especially between urban and rural areas) as well as the distribution of ethnic or denominational membership among special sectors of the national economy. In this respect the relation of Jewish and non-Jewish sections of the educated classes is of particular importance. The facts and figures presented show a wide gap within the Hungarian intelligentsia during those years of crisis. An important finding is the general similarity of „dual structures" in the process of modernization of most Central European countries and the ideological and political implications of these structures.

Kelpanides, Michael: University Education for Everyone? Politicisation of the Social Sciences as a Lasting Legacy of Educational Expansion (in German) (pp. 642-655)
Since the enormous expansion of higher education in the 1960s the social sciences became more political and ideological with sociology taking the leading part in this development. Neo-Marxism became established as the dominant paradigm in research and teaching despite the almost complete falsification of the central assumptions of Marxist theory. This development is explained as resulting from the disturbance of the equilibrium between the function of the university and the hypertrophy of the „critical intelligence" at universities.

King, Edmund: A Turning-Point in Comparative Education: Retrospect and Prospect (pp. 81-90)
Comparative Education has moved on from its former tasks of historical explanations, definition of terms, theories and „predictions". Now it relies on expanding partnerships,

with feedback from researchers at many points of perception and decision, in preparation for a world-wide horizon of evolving uncertainties. Wolfgang Mitter's presidency of the Comparative Education Society in Europe, and later of the World Council of Comparative Education Societies, has been marked by his welcome for that change of orientation and co-operation.

Knauss, Georg: *From 1988 to 1996: Approaches to the Further Development of the Upper Level of the Academic Secondary School (in German) (pp. 234-244)*
Since the end of World War II, there have been several attempts to reform the German „Gymnasium". Its school-leaving certificate entitles students to enrol at any kind of higher education institution. After the reforms of 1960, 1972 and 1988 a new reform was undertaken with the purpose of strengthening general education as well as opening up avenues to accommodate new requirements. The article describes and discusses the complicated processes of consultation and decision-making in the context of the German federal education system.

Knoll, Joachim H.: *From Literacy to Functional Literacy (pp. 344-358)*
Illiteracy is recognised as a problem that concerns both developing and industrialised countries. Consequently UNESCO has taken up the issue and attempts to eradicate illiteracy. The article outlines the development of literacy with particular emphasis on the discussion of different approaches. Definitions and present trends are mentioned, taken from relevant documents such as the „Recommendation on the Development of Adult Education" or the „World Declaration on Education for All". Finally some facts and figures are presented to illustrate the current situation in Ghana.

Koch, Richard: *Societal Control of Vocational-Education Systems: An Analytical Framework for Policy-Oriented International Comparisons (in German) (pp. 91-104)*
International comparative research in the field of vocational education presents a potential knowledge base for public policy which has not been utilized in Germany to its full extent. Complex research designs which allow concrete analyses of both institutional configurations and fields of action are necessary for the study of policy-relevant issues. The problem of the reciprocal relationships between the institutional structures of the system, public interventions and the actions of societal agencies, central to vocational-education policy, is the analytical core of the societal control approach of vocational-education systems, as presented here. This research framework can be applied to the international comparison of various functional problems of vocational-education systems.

Success and failure in trying to solve similar problems of systems control abroad can provide valuable impulses for national vocational-education policies.

Kostomarov, Vitalij Grigor'evič: *Education in the Successor States of the Soviet Union and the Russian Language (in German) (pp. 502-511)*
After the collapse of the USSR all of the newly independent states began to develop national education systems setting great store on native language, culture and religion. Students are no longer required to study Russian. Even though this language is no longer perceived as an indispensable instrument (at least as lingua franca), it retains most of its former functions, and will – for many reasons – do so in the foreseeable future. A longterm language planning process, aimed at addressing the strategic needs of indigenous and foreign languages in general, demands the spread of Russian, despite the decline in enrolments of students in its courses in schools and universities. In Russia, a federal programme has been elaborated and its implementation is now being pursued vigorously.

Krüger-Potratz, Marianne: *A Look into the History of Foreign Pupils in German Schools (in German) (pp. 656-672)*
On what traditions are the current measures taken with regard to children of immigrant families and of German resettlers (Aussiedler) based? How do these traditions continue to influence policies although the principle of non-compulsory schooling for foreign children was broken thirty years ago at the legal level? As a rule until then the children were not prevented from attending school, however, it was critical that the state would not incur any further obligations through their enrolment in schools. In the following article the legal provisions that were issued to regulate the school attendance of non-German children in the Republic of Weimar are described and discussed form an intercultural perspective.

Laderrière, Pierre: *Transformation in the East: A Lesson for the West? (in French) (pp. 359-366)*
It could be useful for Western countries to draw lessons from the reconstruction of the educational systems in Eastern Europe. In spite of the difficult start to the reforms in these countries, there is indeed a common developmental context of a knowledge based post-industrial society which calls for a close Western follow-up of the solutions which begin to be implemented in Eastern Europe.

Laeng, Mauro: *From Yesterday to Tomorrow: Developments in Comparative Education (pp. 105-116)*
The article outlines the developments of comparative education, referring mainly to Europe and Italy, through three phases characterized by different perspectives: 1) a philosophical and historical overview of the outstanding features of each culture; 2) a structural and statistical documentation of several school systems; 3) planning educational policies adequately by aligning them to economical developments. Today, the new perspectives of electronic information offer opportunities and facilities for new contacts and dialogues.

Lawson, Robert F.: *Relationships of Political Contexts to Democracy in Education (pp. 367-380)*
The relationship investigated is that between political assumptions built into institutional organization and educational policy affecting equity. The countries selected: the German Democratic Republic as a model of theoretically-based systematic politicization; South Africa as a model of culturally-based multi-system politicization; and Canada as a model of laissez-faire politicization are treated as phenomena of contemporary history, as typologies which continue to exist analytically even through their policy content has been affected by conflict and change. The use of the comparative method allows the idiosyncratic value of educational assumptions, decisions, structures and practices to be identified and set against political claims based on a supposed universal standard of equity.

Leclercq, Jean-Michel: *How Can the Culture of an Educational System be Viewed and Taken into Account? (in French) (pp. 117-126)*
Culture is inseparably connected with education. Comparative education always underlines their close relationship. Nevertheless, the culture of the educational system is not simply a reflection of the culture of the society. For this reason it would be even more necessary to try to grasp the distinctive features that characterize the culture of different systems. Globalization has resulted in the relativization of these distinctive features. It forces one to define these through the degree of their coherence or their developmental capacities rather than in terms of their uniqueness.

Masemann, Vandra L.: *Recent Directions in Comparative Education (pp. 127-134)*
This paper presents a review of the major developments in comparative education in the years 1990-1996: the conferences of the World Council of Comparative Education Societies and its member societies; influential political events; the role of UNESCO; the

growth of the World Council; publications, scholarly networks, and electronic communication; and the major themes of recent congresses.

Müller-Solger, Hermann: *Recognition, Accreditation, and Transparency: A Necessary Clarification of Concepts for the European Union (in German) (pp. 245-261)*
One of the central tasks of the European Union in the field of education is to facilitate the recognition of diplomas or certificates of different courses of study. To begin with, ten central concepts used in the discussion are defined and examined. Following this, the role played by examinations and testing in education is illustrated and a recent initiative of the European Commission for the certification and recognition of qualifications is presented and problematic aspects discussed. The author thinks that transparency and decentralisation are necessary preconditions for the success of this initiative. The article concludes by outlining four tasks that community and common policies in education should concentrate on in the forthcoming years.

Muszyński, Heliodor: *Visiting a Foreign Country as Means of Gaining Insight into its System of Education (in German) (pp. 135-142)*
Visits of the kind referred to in this essay have been one of the most prolific research approaches of the discipline from the early times of comparative education. Unfortunately they had „fallen into disgrace" in the scientific community for some years. The author traces the origin of the reasons for this attitude back to the development of the positivist methodology which only accepted research as „scientific" if it produced results which could on the one hand be quantified and on the other serve as a basis for generalisations. The concomitant deprivation, i. e. not being able to recognise the individuality and singularity of an education system, resulted in a renaissance of qualitative approaches in educational research too. What such approaches can achieve is illustrated by a number of expeditions the author undertook together with Wolfgang Mitter in Poland from 1989 onward. The report particularly elucidates the specific usefulness of „hermeneutic insights".

Nikandrov, Nikolaj Dmitrievič: *Value Problems in the Russian Federation's Society and Education (in German) (pp. 512-523)*
The thesis the article begins with is that even today, after the collapse of communism, Russia still needs an ideology which, as a system of principles and basic values, sets the standards of the citizens' behaviour towards one another and towards other countries and cultures. In this respect the article particularly deals with the role and function of teachers as well as with the educational aims of a younger generation growing up in a

society without any stable value orientations – except perhaps the aim of becoming rich as quickly as possible without any regard for ones fellow beings. The author sees religion(s) as a possible reference system for a new code of values for the Russian society and extracts the inherent „universal human" values, i. e. values that all citizens, whether believers or not, can accept. He also states that imparting values directly by teaching can not be fruitful as long as teachers and pupils do not find a consistent value system in society.

Palomba, Donatella: *Education for European Citizenship in a Multicultural Europe: A Comparative Survey (in French) (pp. 381-392)*
Education for citizenship in a multicultural Europe is based on the concept of democratic citizenship, which differs, however, depending on the country and the historical point of reference involved. When one asks today's citizens about their sense of belonging to the community of Europe, then one notices the presence of very diverse heritages. This indicates the need to reflect not only on the relationship between different political and cultural traditions, but also on the role of education in cultures based on liberal democratic traditions as compared to those that do not necessarily subscribe to this tradition. One has to take a comparative view if one wishes to gain a better understanding of the concepts and practices on which democratic political education in various contexts is based and to develop a model that takes the differences into account.

Pařizek, Vlastimil: *The Crisis in Schools and Solutions to the Problem (pp. 393-401)*
Discontent with the state of education in families and schools is voiced again and again in many publications and at conferences. Three factors are held responsible for this crisis: 1) the discrepancy between the knowledge, skills and values pupils learn in school and what they need in their lives; 2) a general crisis of society; 3) the low level of public activity by teachers and their organizations. The article analyzes five fields decisive for overcoming the crisis with respect to their relationship to education: work, societal relations, health and environment, concern for the future generation, and leisure. In conclusion some proposals are made on how education itself can contribute to the solution of the problem.

Phillips, David: *Prolegomena to a History of British Interest in Education in Germany (pp. 673-687)*
This paper considers some of the published sources that might be used in a study of the broad sweep of British interest in education in Germany since the beginning of the nineteenth century. As such it is a contribution to the study of cross-national attraction in

education, touching as it does on the reasons for British interest in education in Germany at particular times.

Pirgiotakis, Ioannis: *Greek Education: Myths and Realities (pp. 524-537)*
In Greece debates about a crisis in education usually occur during general elections. The author asks whether such a crisis really exists. To answer this question he examines – after a retrospective look at the educational history of modern Greece – the reforms in Greek education since the 1950s within the conceptual framework of two international trends: 1) the expansion of education in relation to the concept of the human capital theory; 2) measures to foster equality of educational opportunity. Special emphasis is placed on the education of women and the links of education (especially of higher education) and employment. As far as the expansion of education and equality are concerned the existence of an educational crisis cannot be detected. However, the reforms of the education system occurred without corresponding reforms in the employment sector. As a result of the unemployment among academics an „academic proletariat" was created. Only in this respect an educational crisis exists.

Průcha, Jan: *Private versus State Schools: A Comparison of Their Quality in the Czech Republic (pp. 538-549)*
The paper describes a new phenomenon in Czech education, namely the emergence of private schools after 1989. At present private schools operate at all levels of the educational system with the exception of higher education. The number of private schools has increased enormously year by year so that e. g. private upper-secondary vocational schools are attended by about 20% of all students enrolled at that level. However, the quality of the outcomes of private schools remains unclear. The paper informs about the findings of the first comparative evaluation of students' achievements in state versus private *gymnasiums* (upper-secondary academic schools). It was found, surprisingly, that state *gymnasiums* produce better results than their private counterparts. The author discusses the causes of this difference, also with respect to some empirical findings gained by evaluations of private schools in other countries.

Röhrs, Hermann: *Foundation and Organisation of the „German Section" of the „New Education Fellowship" (1921 to 1931): A Significant Chapter of the Educational History of Progressive Education (in German) (pp. 688-706)*
This study interprets the eventful history of the foundation of the German section as an highly interesting chapter of educational policy. Under the chairmanship of Erich Weniger and with the support of Robert Ulich the official foundation was achieved in

1931, only after years of co-operation with the „New Education Fellowship". The international representative of the German section was Carl Heinrich Becker, the former Minister of Education and Culture of Prussia.

Roth, Leo: *The Reformation as a Turning Point in the Development of German Universities: From Universality to Regionalisation (in German) (pp. 707-724)*
On the basis of the history of German universities the development from universalism to regionalism because of the Reformation is described. Qualitative and quantitative analyses of inter- and intra-systemic comparisons show the influence that conflicts in the history of ideas have on the universities, with consequences not only for this institution but also for science in general as well as the political and spiritual life up to present times.

Ryba, Raymond: *Developing the European Dimension of Education in Practice: The Contribution of the Council of Europe's European Dimension Pedagogical Materials Programme (pp. 262-271)*
This paper offers an account of the conception, implementation and outcomes of the European Dimension Pedagogical Materials Programme, a major curriculum development programme carried out by the author on behalf of the Council of Europe as part of its recently completed „Secondary Education for Europe Project".

Schiff, Bernhard: *The Orthodox Classical Grammar School in Moscow (in German) (pp. 550-558)*
With the collapse of the Soviet Union the educational goals of Soviet Communism have lost their validity. The founding of the Orthodox Classical Grammar School in Moscow (in September 1990) represents an attempt to orient school education towards new values. The founder and sponsor of the school is the Christian lay association „Radonež". The new grammar school considers itself to be a secular institution whose educational goals are based on the world-view and ethical principles of Russian Orthodox Christianity. Similar experiments can only be found in pre-Communist Russia, exclusively in the area of elementary education.

Smolicz, J. J.: *Language Education Policies in Multilingual Settings: Australia and the Philippines (pp. 402-413)*
The paper examines how language education policies in Australia and the Philippines have changed since World War II in response to the ethnic plurality of their populations and their changing political status. The analysis reveals Australia's abandonment of the

policy of unidirectional linguistic assimilation into English, in favor of multiculturalism, which provides opportunities for minorities to study their home languages within the school setting. It also shows the contrasting development in the Philippines, where the adoption of a single national language in a multilingual country led its educational system to eliminate all other indigenous languages from the school curriculum. The findings demonstrate that the existence of regionally-based language communities has helped to preserve Filipino linguistic pluralism as spoken „vernaculars", in contrast to the situation in Australia, where the fragmentation of minority language groups and the absence of a territorial community base have counteracted educational efforts to ensure effective perpetuation of languages other than English.

Stephan, Werner: *Teacher and Society: An International Comparison (in German) (pp. 414-425)*
Outlining teachers' working conditions in Poland, Germany, England, the United States and Canada, the paper concludes that the impact of political and economic forces on education has generally led to a deterioration of teachers' lives and to a decline in their social status. This situation is particularly true for the three anglophone countries and potentially results in the proletarization of the teaching profession.

Süssmuth, Rita: *The Joint Responsibility of Policy and Comparative Education for a Humane Learning Society (in German) (pp. 272-281)*
Policy and science share a joint responsibility for mastering global challenges. Education is the key to success in the process of transition to a knowledge society. Comparative education can support the political paradigm-shift to transnational co-operation. How this can be done is shown in this paper for women's education, media education and personality formation.

Suzuki, Shin'ichi: *Shifts in Political Regimes and the Geopolitical Reorganization of Educational Space: Implications for Comparative Education (pp. 143-151)*
Since the collapse of the Berlin Wall in 1989 people have been witnessing a vast growth of nationalism in almost all regions of the globe. As religious zeal is very often mixed with a sense of cultural and ethnic differences, new types of statecentrism cause a rather high frequency of civil wars or political violence and terrorism in changing societies. This can be taken as a symptom of the absence of leading principles to guide the socio-political reconstruction in the societies concerned. Against the background of the struggle towards solutions of political disorders and social instability the author intends to clarify the hidden contexts of „problems in education" from the viewpoint of the shift-

ing geopolitical dimensions of social life. Shifts resulting from new media and problems as a result of the centre-periphery division are dealt with in detail. Finally the feasibility of the profile approach in comparative studies is analyzed.

Szymański, Mirosław S.: *Learning Democratic Values through Pupil Self-Government in the Second Republic of Poland (1918 to 1939) (in German) (pp. 725-739)*
The starting point is the proposition that two publications were of importance for establishing and developing the theory and practice of pupil self-government in the Second Republic of Poland: „Schule und Charakter" by Friedrich Wilhelm Foerster and „L'autonomie des écoliers" by Adolphe Ferrière. Against the background of two opposing models of pupil self-government – the „monarchic" and the „democratic" model – two stages in the historical development of pupil self-government are described. The article also attempts to portray Polish pupils self-government as an „ideal type" by answering among other things the following questions: How was pupil self-government introduced to schools? What tasks did it have to accomplish? How was it organised? What was the scope of its activities?

Tedesco, Juan Carlos: *Renewal of Comparative Education (in French) (pp. 152-160)*
Present socio-economic, cultural and political changes are provoking a revision of the research agenda and methods in comparative education. The new themes can be classified in three main categories: the process of socialisation, cognitive development and the discussion about the goals of education. This new programme implies adopting methods that permit the analysis of these new dimensions by means of an interdisciplinary approach.

Teichler, Ulrich: *Comparative Research on Higher Education: Problems and Perspectives (in German) (pp. 161-172)*
Interest in comparative research on higher education has increased in Europe – in particular due to growing international co-operation. However, theoretically well-structured projects often disregard the complexity of the issues under scrutiny. Funds are often only available for narrow practical research questions. Language barriers, lack of field knowledge as well as heterogeneous schools of thoughts and work styles are impediments. Comparative higher education is most promising if projects are semi-structured thus allowing researchers to cope with the wealth of phenomena encountered and to restructure initial conceptions in response to surprising information obtained.

Tenorth, Heinz-Elmar: *Education and Sociology (in German) (pp. 740-756)*
Nowadays science of education and sociology are two independent disciplines, distinguishable by their theories, but related in their methods. This contribution discusses how the differences developed out of common themes. To this end both thematic indices of theory development, starting with the problem of learning groups (Lerngruppe), and institutional mechanisms, particularly the appointment of professorships in the Weimar Republic, are analysed historically and evaluated systematically.

Tomiak, Janusz: *Looking Back, Looking Forward: Education in Central-Eastern Europe on the Eve of the XXIst Century (pp. 426-436)*
The educational systems in Central-Eastern Europe are in the process of undergoing more fundamental change. They are moving away from a rigidly controlled, centrally planned and uniform model towards an open, liberal and more diversified system. This cannot be achieved within a short time. Democratisation and modernisation of education can be achieved more speedily in Central-Eastern Europe, if Western advice and help are made more readily available and effective. It is equally important that the Central-Eastern European governments realise that education is an essential investment and accord it a higher position on the agenda of national priorities.

Tulasiewicz, Witold: *Education for Sale: Recent Developments in the United Kingdom (pp. 559-571)*
This paper continues the writer's analysis of educational developments in the United Kingdom after the Conservative take over in 1979, two earlier instalments of which have been published in the „Zeitschrift für Internationale Erziehungs- und Sozialwissenschaftliche Forschung". The enthusiastic acceptance of the economic policies and practices of the free market by the administration has been applied to the provision of education services. The paper argues the merits and demerits of this policy and its suitability in the provision of a public service using examples of recent legislation to record the significant changes in practice which have resulted from it.

Van daele, Henk: *Comparative Education and International Education: Some Language Problems (in French) (pp. 173-181)*
Comparative education is a difficult field of study because of, inter alia, the many language problems. Three conditions should be fulfilled: 1) comparative educationists should be really multilingual; 2) names of schools, degrees, etc., are very difficult to translate; they should be considered as proper nouns and therefore never be translated; 3) in Europe, there is a need for a univocal multilingual glossary of educational terms.

Abstracts

Vorbeck, Michael: *Educational Research and Comparative Education in Particular – In Europe and for Europe (in German) (pp. 282-297)*
The paper sums up developments in educational research and comparative education in Europe since the 1960s: the establishment of major national research institutes in individual states, and at the same time the special commitment of the Council of Europe in educational research. In addition the activities of other international organisations (UNESCO, OECD, the European Union, etc.) are illustrated. The commitment of Wolfgang Mitter and the German Institute for International Educational Research are highlighted. The achievements (and shortcomings) are assessed and necessary future activities at national and international level are formulated.

Welch, Anthony R.: *Things Fall Apart: Dis-Integration, Universities, and the Decline of Discipline(s). Problematising Comparative Education in an Uncertain Age (pp. 182-191)*
This essay analyses the situation and prospects for comparative education, in light of the *fin de siècle's* social, economic and intellectual climate. The confident positivism of post war comparative education has now been replaced by economic, pedagogical and intellectual uncertainties, to which comparative education must learn to respond if it is to survive, and stand the test of relevance, in much more stringent environments.

Wilson, David N.: *The German Dual System of Vocational Education and Training: A Comparative Study of Influence upon Educational Policy and Practice in Other Countries (pp. 437-448)*
This study examines the German dual system from the perspective of other nations interested in the adoption – and adaptation – of this „model". Since the system is advocated as a potential solution to training problems in both developed and developing nations, the study examines the realities, myths and misunderstandings found in some literature and in educational systems which purport to have adopted the „model". The legislative, governance, organizational and functional components of the system are examined and related to conditions in Germany. The perceptions of several authors favoring adoption of the „model" are examined to determine why the „model" is considered to be attractive and/or appropriate to their nations technical-vocational education and training system. The successful adoption of the dual system in Singapore is examined and analyzed, and also the interest of Israel in the „model"; furthermore the failure of the „model" to make any significant impact in Sri Lanka.

Abstracts

Wulf, Christoph: *Mimesis of the Other: Approaching the Alien (in German)*
(pp. 192-206)
The Other plays a central role in issues of education. Insofar as education concerns approaching and processing unknown objects, relations and persons examining the role of „others" is indispensable in questions of education. As a result of the globalisation of life contexts and the necessary political, economic and cultural requirements that developed as a consequence of the European Union education has become an intercultural task. To live up to this task encountering and confronting „others" is a challenge that needs to be met for conserving and transforming one's own culture.

Yûki, Makoto: *The Legal Structure of Educational Administration in Japan (in German)*
(pp. 572-580)
The Japanese educational system changed decisively after 1945: from central control and imperial prerogative in the educational administration to a system guided by parliamentary laws and protecting the regional interests. Compared to the pre-war system the main characteristics of this new educational administration are: a considerably reduced authority of the Ministry of Education as a central body and the existence of elected regional boards of education, which are independent of the general administration.

Résumés[1]

Adick, Christel: *Formation de base formelle et non formelle en Afrique: complémentarité ou concurrence? (en allemand) (pp. 451-467)*
La conférence mondiale sur l'Éducation pour Tous de Jomtien en Thaïlande en 1990 a déclaré l'éducation droit universel de l'homme. C'est pour cela que l'attention des politiques d'éducation nationales, des chercheurs en éducation et des praticiens de la coopération internationale doit se porter encore plus sur la réalisation de ce droit pour tous. La conférence a laissé ouverte la question de décider si l'exigence d'une éducation élémentaire devait se traduire plutôt par un renforcement d'une éducation de base scolaire ou s'il valait mieux la réaliser sous forme de conceptions éducatives non formelles. Les différentes pratiques d'éducation formelle et non formelle au Sénégal sont présenté: éducation primaire publique, éducation islamique, et offre de formation de base des centres éducatifs libres. Les spécificités de ces différents modes d'accès à l'éducation et des rapports complémentaires ou plutôt concurrentiels qui existent entre formations de base formelle et non formelle sont comparées.

Altbach, Philip G.: *Recherche sur l'enseignement supérieur d'un point de vue global (en anglais) (pp. 15-31)*
A l'approche du XXIe siècle les universités doivent faire face à nombre de défis. En conséquence les besoins en matière de compétences et de données sont importants. L'article présente la recherche sur l'enseignement supérieur passée, actuelle et à venir d'un point de vue international afin de permettre au lecteur de saisir l'écheveau complexe de ce champ de recherche. L'auteur met en évidence les raisons qui expliquent le manque de données et d'analyses, par exemple l'usage largement répandu qui veut que les résultats des recherches ne soient publiés que de façon inofficielle ou traités comme documents „confidentiels". L'élargissement et l'essor d'une infrastructure de la recherche sur l'enseignement supérieur sont traités de la même façon que l'infrastructure de l'information de l'enseignement supérieur lui-même, en particulier les recueils tels que „state of the art", les compilations, les encyclopédies, les revues spécialisées et les bases de données. On prend ici aussi en considération l'élargissement historique et géographique de

---

[1] Les résumés peuvent être repris dans les banques de données.

ce domaine de recherche. Il en va de même pour les tendances futures et les mesures nécessaires à l'évolution ultérieure des recherches.

Anweiler, Oskar: *Les sciences de l'éducation comparées: défis et tâches (en allemand) (pp. 1-12)*
La vue d'ensemble en introduction tente de présenter sur la base des articles contenus dans les mélanges quelques-unes des problématiques et des directions générales du domaine de travail et de recherche représenté par Wolfgang Mitter. Il s'agit en cela de regards rétrospectifs sur la discipline de l'éducation comparée, de clarifications conceptuelles et méthodologiques, de la signification des différenciations culturelles, nationales et régionales ainsi que de perspectives globales et universelles. La recherche internationale en éducation et l'éducation comparée se doivent de débattre de façon critique et productive des nouveaux défis qui découlent, d'une part, de la mondialisation et, d'autre part, des particularismes.

Baske, Siegfried: *La phase néohumaniste du Conradinum de Jenkau au travers des jugements de l'histoire de l'éducation allemande et polonaise (en allemand) (pp. 583-592)*
Tant dans l'histoire de l'éducation allemande que polonaise on accorde une signification de premier plan à la phase néohumaniste du Conradinum de Jenkau jusqu'à aujourd'hui. Deux publications dans lesquelles les deux directeurs, Jachmann et Passow ont présenté leur conception en 1811 et 1812 occupent une place centrale. L'école y est définie non comme un concept pragmatique mais comme un concept rationnel et mis en relation „préordonnée" au monde.

Bîrzea, Cesar: *Du bon et du mauvais usage de la recherche pédagogique: le cas d'une manipulation politique en Roumanie (en anglais) (pp. 468-476)*
L'article révèle une hypostase moins habituelle de la recherche pédagogique, celle-ci étant envisagée comme un indicateur des changements politiques. En examinant de près l'état de la recherche pédagogique en Roumanie, dans les années 80, l'auteur s'attache à explorer un cas célèbre, sans doute unique dans l'histoire de la pédagogie universelle, une véritable „chasse aux sorcières" en plein vingtième siècle. A la fin, la problématique générale de transition est traité. En effet, le régime communiste en Roumanie a utilisé la recherche pédagogique non pas pour fonder ses décisions en matière d'éducation. Il s'en est servi plutôt pour légitimer une manipulation politique à l'échelle nationale. Il s'agit de l'affaire dite de „La Porte de la Méditation Transcendentale". En 1982, Ceaucescu a utilisé cette affaire comme une mesure préventive contre la pénétration du „syndrome

Solidarność" en Roumanie. C'est un cas unique d'utilisation négative de la recherche pédagogique par le pouvoir politique.

Brinkmann, Günter: *Les enseignants au Pays-Bas: rôle et formation (en allemand) (pp. 477-489)*
Ces dernières années, les écoles et la formation des professeurs sont au centre des préoccupations de la population des Pays-Bas. Depuis la fin des années 80, il a été établi un système de prévoyance de la qualité sous forme de visites de classes. Ces visites permirent de réaliser des études d'évaluation. En outre, il fut présenté des recommandations concernant une amélioration des écoles et de la formation des professeurs, de la part de la Commission des Enseignants Responsables des Recherches pour l'Avenir, le rapport „Une profession avec des perspectives", et du Ministère de l'Éducation les brochures „Enseignants dynamiques" et „Formation des enseignants". Ces documents seront aussi bien analysés que la tendance actuelle d'introduire des technologies modernes d'informatique dans les universités et les écoles.

Brock-Utne, Birgit: *L'internationalisation en éducation: une approche critique (en allemand) (pp. 301-311)*
Le présent article se penche sur la notion d'„internationalisation du système éducatif". Celle-ci signifie-t-elle en fait tout simplement une anglicisation ou une américanisation ou bien, dans le cas des pays africains, une nouvelle colonisation? Qui sont ces „experts en éducation supranationaux" qui décident des curricula globaux et des normes internationales pour l'évaluation des connaissances scolaires? Ce texte analyse les tensions existant entre les contraintes externes et les cultures internes et questionne d'un point de vue critique la notion de qualité éducative de la Banque Mondiale. Au-delà, il entend poser la question suivante: à qui sert la tendance internationale de libéralisation croissante du marché qui se dégage actuellement de plus en plus nettement dans les systèmes éducatifs.

Ebert, Wilhelm: *Magna Charta des enseignants: troisième ans de la recommandation de l'UNESCO à propos du statut des enseignants (en anglais) (pp. 593-609)*
Depuis sa fondation en 1946 jusqu'à la fin des années soixante-dix l'UNESCO a été, après l'ONU, la plus importante organisation internationale. Tous les domaines de la politique ont été envisagés dans leurs rapports avec l'éducation, les sciences et la culture. Inversement on était conscient qu'une politique internationale contribuait de façon importante à fixer l'orientation et le pouvoir de l'éducation, des sciences et de la culture. L'enseignant réapparaissant constamment comme facteur décisif de la qualité de l'école,

l'UNESCO, en liaison avec l'Organisation Internationale du Travail, a décidé de formuler une recommandation à propos du statut des enseignants. L'article essaie de retracer le chemin qui a mené à ce document international concernant le statut des enseignants.

Epstein, Erwin H.*: Le filtrage de la démocratie par l'école: un paradoxe ignoré de l'école obligatoire (en anglais) (pp. 32-45)*
On attend de l'école, d'une part, qu'elle transmette un savoir objectif pour permettre d'atteindre les objectifs de la démocratie, mais d'autre part aussi, qu'elle enseigne des mythes nationaux, le tout par le biais d'une mesure dépourvue de démocratie qui est l'obligation de fréquenter l'école. „L'éducation à la démocratie" représente en conséquence un oxymoron dans la description de l'enseignement, en particulier dans les états en cours de transition, et tout particulièrement dans les anciens états socialistes qui luttent pour leur accès à la démocratie. Le fait d'imposer l'école comme véhicule pour filtrer du „bon" savoir à destination des élèves transforme l'éducation „démocratique" en éducation non démocratique, tout particulièrement pour les groupes en marge de la culture dominante, à la périphérie où les enfants et leurs parents sont particulièrement touchés par les mystifications. Ce paradoxe se trouve encore renforcé par la vision des démocraties occidentales qui „livrent" leurs propres formes d'enseignement imposé au nom de cette même démocratie. La présente contribution analyse l'instrumentalisation de l'école, chapitre jusqu'à maintenant gravement négligé des recherches sur la démocratie.

Georg, Walter*: La formation professionnelle entre l'internationalisation et l'identité nationale (en allemand) (pp. 312-328)*
Le présent article examine les implications des thèses sur la mondialisation et les contraintes de l'universalisation qui en découlent sur le travail, sur la formation professionnelle et sur l'enseignement. Pour autant que les tendances correspondantes puissent être démontrées, elles concernent surtout une tendance globale à l'expansion de l'enseignement „général", avec pour conséquence une marginalisation de la formation professionnelle dans des centres de formation régionaux non liés aux entreprises et dont l'État a la responsabilité. Au-delà de cette tendance, les structures spécifiques aux états nationaux et les organismes chargés de la qualification professionnelle sont restés stables dans l'ensemble. En dépit d'une pression générale très forte à la modernisation, les modifications structurelles ne peuvent être regroupées sous forme d'une évolution universelle non plus que les variations des modèles nationaux spécifiques ne peuvent être mis en relation directe avec le degré de modernisation et la réussite économique des différents pays. Une comparaison des traits caractéristiques du „système" de la formation

professionnelle en Allemagne et au Japon renvoie à la pertinence de chacune des cultures industrielles qui montre les limites de toute tentative d'une politique de la formation professionnelle qui se prétendrait universelle.

Ginsburg, Mark B.*: Les limites et possibilités de l'analyse comparative en sciences de l'éducation dans un contexte de mondialisation (en anglais) (pp. 46-51)*
Une analyse comparative en sciences de l'éducation est problématique mais aussi productive du fait que: 1. les spécifités et les différences entre les phénomènes relevées par les chercheurs sont liées à leur subjectivité et aussi à celle de leur objet; 2. les convergences et les divergences constatées entre les nations (et les entités régionales et supranationales) font partie d'un système mondial; 3. ses objectifs peuvent inclure la formation d'actions collectives des pédagogues tout autant que l'approfondissement de la compréhension et l'évaluation d'autres choix politiques et pratiques.

Glowka, Detlef: *Quelques réflexions à propos d'„Une introduction à l'éducation comparée" (en allemand) (pp. 52-64)*
Les considérations ici exposées sont inspirées du projet d'un groupe ERASMUS qui avait pour objectif d'élaborer en commun un cours d'„initiation aux sciences de l'éducation comparées", de l'expérimenter et de le publier. Une esquisse présentée au groupe a fait très vite l'unanimité et a servi de base au cours d'initiation. Nous avons ensuite tenté à Münster, lors du semestre d'été 1996, d'en faire un séminaire. On trouvera ici un compte-rendu des réflexions et des expériences acquises au cours de celui-ci. Disons dès maintenant pour anticiper sur les conclusions que la structure des sciences de l'éducation comparées en tant que discipline scientifique et l'état actuel de sa „didactique" ont fait de l'ébauche d'une initiation à celle-ci une entreprise tout à la fois ardue et stimulante.

Gomes, Candido Alberto: *Éducation comparée et politique publique vue du Sud (en anglais) (pp. 209-218)*
Ce travail traite, d'une part, des tensions entre l'universalité de la science et les circonstances particulières des pays de l'hémisphère sud, d'autre part, des caractéristiques de l'éducation comparée qui intéressent ces pays. Ensuite l'auteur décrit ses expériences en tant que conseiller parlementaire dans ses effort pour bâtir des ponts entre la recherche et les politiques publiques. Il expose en quoi l'éducation comparée a pu l'aider dans l'exercice de sa fonction.

Herman, Harold: Éducation et changement politique en Afrique du Sud (en anglais) (pp. 490-501)
Depuis la fin de l'apartheid, les premières élections démocratiques et la mise en place d'un gouvernement d'union nationale en 1994 l'Afrique du Sud se trouve confrontée à un grand nombre de problèmes liés à la transition et au développement de l'égalité sociale. On analysera ici la possibilité de voir l'Afrique du Sud devenir un état démocratique ainsi que le type de démocratie qui peut naître dans un pays marqué par un passé de discrimination raciale, un système économique capitaliste fort et une société fortement inégalitaire. Depuis 1994 des lois importantes ont été votées et des mesures en faveur d'une démocratisation du système éducatif mises en place. La présente contribution analyse le renforcement des principes et des valeurs démocratiques grâce au „White Paper on Education" du Ministère National de l'Éducation de février 1995. En conclusion se trouve une analyse du rôle que peut jouer le système éducatif dans la réussite d'une future démocratie en Afrique du Sud.

Heyneman, Stephen P.: La coopération éducative entre les nations au XXIe siècle (en anglais) (pp. 219-233)
A quoi ressembleront les futures relations entre les états souverains dans le domaine de l'éducation? Diverses questions se posent: les processus éducatifs, la formation des enseignants, leur rémunération, l'apprentissage tout au long de la vie, les standards éducatifs, etc. Tout cela est important, mais qu'est-ce qui incitera les nations à coopérer entre elles pour aborder ces questions? Les motivations changeront-elles ou resteront-elles les mêmes? Si celles-ci sont amenées à changer, en quoi les changements influenceront-ils la nature de la coopération, les organismes internationaux chargés de responsabilité en matière éducative, leur équipement en personnel et le contenu de leurs programmes? Je pense que les motivations en faveur de la coopération internationale seront différentes à l'avenir. En conclusion je résumerai les raisons qui fondent ma conviction et je dirai quelques mots à propos de l'implication que cela aura sur les organismes internationaux et nationaux, sur leurs personnels et sur le contenu de leurs programmes.

Hörner, Wolfgang: L'Europe: un défi pour l'éducation comparée. Réflexions à propos de la fonction politique d'une discipline pédagogique (en allemand) (pp. 65-80)
Partant d'une analyse des dénominations de „l'éducation comparée" dans différentes langues européennes et de la description de ses éventuelles fonctions aussi bien pour la recherche que pour l'enseignement universitaire, l'article soumet au débat la contribution possible de l'éducation comparée à l'intégration européenne. Il fait apparaître que cette discipline peut remplir à cet égard une fonction politique non négligeable.

Husén, Torsten: *La „lacune éducative" (en anglais) (pp. 329-343)*
La „lacune éducative" dont il est question ici se réfère à l'énorme différence entre les résultats obtenus par les élèves au terme d'un certain nombre d'années d'éducation formelle dans les pays en voie de développement par opposition aux pays industrialisés qui ont une longue tradition d'enseignement primaire et secondaire. C'est ce qu'on entendra ici par „lacune éducative". Les données présentées proviennent des enquêtes réalisées par l'„International Association for the Evaluation of Educational Achievement (IEA)" et l'expérience particulière de l'auteur recueillie au Botswana, alors qu'il assurait la direction de la Commission Nationale de l'Enseignement au milieu des années soixante-dix dont la tâche était de planifier l'enseignement jusqu'aux années quatre-vingt-dix. Les enquêtes de ce type dont il est question dans le présent article peuvent se révéler utiles pour juger de la qualité de l'éducation dans un pays donné. Dans le cas du Botswana elles sont apparues aussi utiles pour évaluer les effets de l'usage de l'anglais comme support de l'enseignement au bout de plusieurs années de scolarisation dans le primaire.

Iram, Yaacov: *Le statut des sciences humaines en éducation (en anglais) (pp. 610-620)*
Le présent article décrit le déclin du statut de l'éducation humaniste et analyse les raisons et les effets liées à l'affaiblissement de son rôle dans les humanités en éducation. L'auteur suggère d'adopter une „approche intégrative" dans une éducation humaniste. Seule l'intégration d'une perspective humaniste dans tous les domaines de la connaissance, et donc l'enseignement des phénomènes culturels permettant de rendre compte de leur signification, sera en mesure de permettre à une perspective humaniste de recouvrer son rôle central. Ce rôle ne consiste pas seulement à transmettre un savoir précieux – „alphabétisation culturelle" – mais aussi à renforcer les tendances en faveur d'une meilleure compréhension mutuelle, de l'acceptation de l'autre et de la coopération entre les individus et les sociétés afin de leur permettre de se réaliser pleinement.

Karady, Victor: *Enseignement scolaire et religion: des caractéristiques ethno-confessionnelles de l'intelligentsia hongroise dans l'entre-deux guerres (en allemand) (pp. 621-641)*
Sur la base de sources statistiques très abondantes, l'auteur analyse les rapports entre niveau d'instruction et emploi en relation avec l'appartenance ethnique et confessionnelle dans l'État hongrois devenu indépendant après la première guerre mondiale jusqu'au début des années trente, en prenant particulièrement en compte les couches très instruites. Il procède à des comparaisons historiques avec l'époque d'avant 1918 et analyse les disparités régionales (en particulier les rapports ville-campagne) ainsi que la distribution dans certains secteurs de l'économie. Dans ce contexte, les rapports entre les parties

juives et non-juives des couches instruites ont une signification particulière. Les informations présentées montrent une profonde division de l'intelligentsia hongroise dans les années de crise de l'entre-deux guerres. Le résultat le plus important réside dans le caractère général de „doubles structures" semblables dans la modernisation de la plupart des pays d'Europe Centrale et dans leurs effets politiques et idéologiques.

Kelpanides, Michael: Éducation universitaire pour tous? La politisation des sciences sociales, un héritage durable de l'expansion de l'éducation (en allemand) (pp. 642-655)
La présente contribution porte sur la politisation et l'idéologisation des sciences sociales qui a eu lieu depuis l'expansion éducative des années soixante. Impulsé en premier lieu par la sociologie, le néo-marxisme s'est établi en tant que paradigme dominant dans l'enseignement et dans la recherche, en dépit de l'interprétation erronée de ses thèses centrales. On expliquera cette évolution à partir du bouleversement de l'équilibre entre les fonctions de l'université et l'hypertrophié de „l'intelligence critique" des universités.

King, Edmund: Un changement crucial en éducation comparée: rétrospective et prospective (en anglais) (pp. 81-90)
Les sciences de l'éducation comparées ont largement dépassé dans l'intervalle ce qui était ses objets initiaux: les interprétations historiques, la définition de concepts, l'élaboration théorique et les „prophéties". Elle est en mesure actuellement de s'appuyer sur un réseau toujours plus étendu de partenariats, bénéficie des critiques en retour des chercheurs sur de nombreuses questions de perception et de décision tout en se préparant à l'émergence d'un horizon mondial de nouvelles incertitudes. La présidence de Wolfgang Mitter à la tête de l'Association d'Éducation Comparée en Europe puis du Conseil Mondial des Sociétés d'Éducation Comparée a marqué jusqu'à aujourd'hui, par son ouverture face aux changements d'orientation et de coopération.

Knauss, Georg: De 1988 à 1996: pistes pour le développement de l'enseignement secondaire deuxième degré (en allemand) (pp. 234-244)
Depuis la fin de la seconde guerre mondiale, les objectifs, les contenus et la structure du „Gymnasium", en tant que type d'établissement donnant accès aux études supérieures, ont été débattus et modifiés au cours des réformes qui se sont succédées. Faisant suite à celles de 1960, de 1982 et de 1988, une nouvelle réforme s'annonce, destinée à renforcer les matières et les contenus principaux et à permettre une ouverture vers de nouvelles qualifications. Le présent article décrit les processus complexes de consultation et de décision de la Conférence Permanente des Ministres de l'Éducation.

Résumés

Knoll, Joachim H.: *De l'alphabétisme à la littératie (en anglais) (pp. 344-358)*
L'illetrisme est connu depuis longtemps en tant que phénomène qui concerne tout aussi bien les pays en voie de développement que les pays industrialisés. En conséquence, l'UNESCO apporte son concours en tentant de lutter contre l'illettrisme. Le présent article esquisse le développement de l'alphabétisation en insistant particulièrement sur le débat à propos des différentes approches. Des définitions et des tendances sont fournies empruntées aux documents qui font autorité en la matière: „Recommandation sur le Développement de l'Éducation des Adultes" ou la „Déclaration Mondial sur l'Éducation pour Tous". En conclusion, on présentera quelques faits et quelques chiffres pour illustrer la situation actuelle au Ghana.

Koch, Richard: *Le contrôle sociétal des systèmes de formation professionnelle: une proposition d'approche pour les comparaisons internationales à usage politique (en allemand) (pp. 91-104)*
Les recherches internationales comparatives sur la formation professionnelle constituent un potentiel de réflexion et de connaissance pour la politique de la formation utilisé de façon limitée jusqu'à maintenant en Allemagne. Pour aborder les problématiques pertinentes en matière de formation on a besoin de projets complexes qui permettent une analyse concrète des formes institutionnelles et des champs d'action. La conception d'un contrôle sociétal des systèmes de formation professionnelle ici exposée pose la question vitale pour la politique en matière de formation professionnelle de l'interrelation entre les structures institutionnelles, les interventions des pouvoirs publics et l'action des acteurs sociaux. Cette conception de la recherche s'applique à la comparaison internationale des problèmes de fonctionnalité des systèmes de formation professionnelle. Les réussites et les échecs de l'étranger dans la résolution de problèmes comparables dans le contrôle du système peuvent constituer autant d'incitations positives en matière de politique nationale de formation.

Kostomarov, Vitalij Grigor'evič: *Le système éducatif dans les états qui ont succédé à l'URSS et la langue russe (en allemand) (pp. 502-511)*
A la suite de l'effondrement de l'URSS, des systèmes éducatifs nationaux ont commencé à se développer dans les états nouvellement créés tout en accordant la plus grande importance aux langues, aux cultures et aux religions. Dorénavant aucun élève ou étudiant n'est plus obligé d'apprendre le russe. Bien que cette langue ne soit plus considérée comme un outil de communication indispensable, elle a toutefois conservé la plupart de ses fonctions et continuera à les conserver pour toutes sortes de raisons dans un avenir proche. La diffusion du russe est nécessaire à un processus de planification linguistique

à long terme visant à prendre en compte globalement les besoins stratégiques des langues autochtones et étrangères, même si le nombre de ceux qui apprennent cette langue tend à diminuer. Un programme fédéral a été élaboré en Russie dont la réalisation prioritaire se poursuit actuellement.

Krüger-Potratz, Marianne: *Aperçu de l'histoire des élèves étrangers dans les écoles allemandes (en allemand) (pp. 656-672)*
Dans quelles traditions s'inscrivent les mesures actuelles prises en Allemagne en matière de scolarisation des enfants de immigrants et des enfants de ressortissants de souche allemande (Aussiedler)? Comment celles-ci perdurent-elles alors que, juridiquement parlant, on a depuis une trentaine d'années rompu avec le principe de la non-scolarisation des enfants étrangers? Jusqu'à cette époque on ne leur refusait en général pas la scolarisation. Il était toutefois décisif que cette prise en charge scolaire n'ait pour l'État pas valeur de contrainte par la suite. Le présent article se propose de présenter et de soumettre à la discussion les dispositions visant à réglementer la scolarisation des enfants étrangers à l'Empire allemand pendant la République de Weimar.

Laderrière, Pierre: *Les transformations à l'Est: une leçon pour l'Ouest? (pp. 359-366)*
Il peut être utile aux pays de l'Ouest de tirer des leçons de la reconstruction des systèmes d'éducation dans l'Europe de l'Est. En effet, malgré un démarrage difficile des réformes dans ces pays, il existe un contexte commun de développement d'une société postindustrielle assise sur le savoir qui plaide en faveur d'un suivi attentif à l'Ouest des solutions qui commencent à être mises en œuvre dans l'Europe de l'Est.

Laeng, Mauro: *D'hier à aujourd'hui: les développements de l'éducation comparée (en anglais) (pp. 105-116)*
L'article essaie d'esquisser l'évolution de l'éducation comparée, avec des exemples surtout de l'Europe et de l'Italie, à travers trois phases principales caractérisées par une différence de perspectives: 1) une vision philosophique et historique des caractères essentiels des civilisations de peuples différents; 2) une documentation statistique et documentaire des différents systèmes éducatifs; 3) une planification adaptée de la politique d'éducation en liaison avec le développement économique. Aujourd'hui, les nouvelles perspectives liées à l'informatique fournissent des occasions et facilitent de nouveaux contacts et de nouveaux dialogues.

Lawson, Robert F.: *Les rapports entre contextes politiques et démocratie en éducation (en anglais) (pp. 367-380)*
Les rapports étudiés ici sont ceux qui existent entre les présupposés politiques liés à l'organisation institutionnelle et la politique éducative concernant l'égalité. Les pays suivants ont été retenus: la R.D.A. en tant que modèle de politisation systématique se référant à une théorie globale, l'Afrique du Sud en tant que modèle de politisation multisystémique fondée sur la culture et le Canada, enfin, comme exemple de politisation sous forme de laissez-faire. Les trois exemples sont traités comme des phénomènes de l'histoire contemporaine tout autant que comme des typologies qui continuent à rester valables dans les analyses, même si leur contenu politique est affecté par des conflits et des changements. L'utilisation d'une approche comparative permet d'identifier la valeur idiosyncratique des présupposés éducatifs, des décisions, des structures et des pratiques et de les opposer aux revendications politiques censées reposer sur une conception universelle de l'égalité.

Leclercq, Jean-Michel: *Comment envisager et prendre en compte la culture d'un système éducatif? (pp. 117-126)*
La culture est indissociable de l'éducation. L'éducation comparée souligne du reste toujours leur étroite relation. Pourtant la culture de l'éducation n'est pas seulement le reflet de celle de la société. Il faudrait donc davantage se préoccuper de saisir la spécificité que présente la culture des différents systèmes éducatifs. Mais la mondialisation a pour conséquence de rendre cette spécificité relative et d'obliger à la définir formellement par son degré de cohérence ou sa capacité d'évolution plus qu'en termes de contenus originaux.

Masemann, Vandra L.: *Les évolutions récentes en éducation comparée (en anglais) (pp. 127-134)*
L'article présente un panorama des évolutions majeures de l'éducation comparée des années 1990 à 1996: les conférences du Conseil Mondial des Sociétés d'Éducation Comparée et des sociétés-membres; les événements politiques qui ont exercé une influence pendant cette période; l'extension du Conseil Mondial; les publications, les réseaux de chercheurs et l'utilisation de la communication informatique et, enfin, les thèmes majeurs des récents congrès.

Müller-Solger, Hermann: Reconnaissance, accréditation, transparence: les nécessaires clarifications conceptuelles pour l'Union Européenne (en allemand) (pp. 245-261)
L'une des tâches majeures de l'Union Européenne dans le domaine éducatif réside dans la facilitation de la reconnaissance des diplômes et des études des différents cursus de formation. On procédera ici d'abord à la définition et à l'élucidation de dix notions essentielles utilisées dans le débat. Ensuite on mettra en évidence le rôle des examens dans le système éducatif et on présentera une récente initiative de la Commission Européenne pour l'attestation et la reconnaissance des qualifications tout en la problématisant. L'auteur est d'avis que la transparence et la décentralisation sont des conditions nécessaires à sa réussite. On conclura en esquissant quatre tâches auxquelles la politique communautaire et la politique commune en matière d'éducation devraient s'atteler en priorité dans les années qui viennent.

Muszyński, Heliodor: Le voyage d'études pédagogique en tant qu'instrument d'investigation scientifique (en allemand) (pp. 135-142)
Les voyages d'études qui comptaient parmi les approches scientifiques les plus fructueuses depuis la création de l'éducation comparée, étaient tombés „en disgrâce" au sein de la communauté des chercheurs. L'auteur en cherche les raisons qu'il voit pour l'essentiel dans le développement d'une méthodologie positiviste, pour laquelle seule une recherche ne mérite le nom de „véritablement" scientifique que si elle produit des résultats quantitatifs et permet des généralisations. La déperdition qui y était liée, en l'occurrence la possibilité d'identifier ce qu'il peut y avoir d'individuel et de singulier dans les systèmes éducatifs nationaux a fini par déclencher une sorte de renaissance des approches qualitatives dans les recherches en éducation. On verra mieux ce à quoi elles peuvent mener à partir d'une série de voyages d'études que l'auteur a entrepris en compagnie de Wolfgang Mitter en Pologne depuis 1989; on essaie aussi d'y mettre particulièrement en valeur une telle „heuristique".

Nikandrov, Nikolaj Dmitrievič: La problématique des valeurs dans la société et le système éducatif de la Fédération Russe (en allemand) (pp. 512-523)
L'auteur se fonde sur l'hypothèse que la Russie, même après l'effondrement du communisme, ne peut en aucun cas renoncer à une idéologie qui, en tant que système de principes et de valeurs fondamentales, est censée définir les limites du comportement des citoyens entre eux ainsi que par rapport à des pays ou des cultures tiers. Dans ce contexte, il se penche surtout sur les enseignants et les objectifs éducatifs assignés à une jeunesse qui grandit dans une société sans repères définis, ou à considérer comme un tel objectif le fait de vouloir s'enrichir le plus vite possible sans se soucier de ses concitoyens. Il

considère la religion comme l'un des systèmes de références possibles à même de fournir un ensemble de valeurs à la société russe et essaie d'en dégager ce qu'elle contient de valeurs „universelles", c'est-à-dire de valeurs que tous les citoyens peuvent accepter, indépendamment du fait qu'ils soient croyants ou pas. Il débat aussi de ce qu'il y a de vain à vouloir transmettre directement des valeurs par l'enseignement aussi longtemps qu'enseignants et élèves ne trouvent pas de systèmes de valeurs consistants dans la société.

Palomba, Donatella: *L'éducation à la citoyenneté dans l'Europe multiculturelle: une perspective comparative (pp. 381-392)*
L'éducation à la citoyenneté en Europe se fonde sur une conception de la „citoyenneté démocratique" qui varie selon les pays et les traditions historiques. Si on interroge aujourd'hui des citoyens sur leur appartenance européenne commune, on constate la présence d'héritages très différents. Cela implique une réflexion non seulement sur les rapports entre des traditions politiques et culturelles différentes, mais aussi sur le rôle d'une éducation qui mise sur la tradition démocratique libérale par rapport à des cultures qui n'y appartiennent pas nécessairement. Une approche comparative s'impose, tant pour fournir une meilleure connaissance des concepts et des pratiques qui sous-tendent l'éducation à la citoyenneté démocratique dans différents contextes que pour l'élaboration d'un modèle „accueillant envers les différences".

Pařizek, Vlastimil: *La crise de l'école et les solutions (en anglais) (pp. 393-401)*
De nombreuses publications et de nombreuses conférences se font l'écho d'un profond mécontentement à propos de l'éducation familiale et scolaire. Trois facteurs en sont rendus responsables: 1. le décalage qui existe entre les connaissances, les habiletés et les valeurs acquises et ce dont ils auront besoin dans leur vie future; 2. une crise générale de la société; 3. le manque d'engagement dans le débat public de la part des enseignants et de leurs organisations. Le présent article analyse les cinq champs, décisifs pour sortir de la crise, et les met en relation avec l'éducation. Il s'agit du travail, des rapports sociaux, de la santé et de l'environnement, de la prise en compte des générations futures et des loisirs. En conclusion quelques propositions sont énoncées sur la façon dont l'éducation peut contribuer à la résolution du problème.

Phillips, David: *Prolégomènes à une histoire de l'intérêt porté en Grande-Bretagne au système éducatif allemand (en anglais) (pp. 673-687)*
Le présent article reprend quelques-unes des sources publiées utilisables dans une étude sur le large éventail de l'intérêt porté en Grande-Bretagne au système éducatif allemand depuis le début du XIXe siècle. En tant que tel, il constitue une contribution à l'étude de

l'attirance mutuelle des différents pays en matière d'éducation en abordant les raisons de cet intérêt à des moments particuliers.

Pirgiotakis, Ioannis: *Le système éducatif en Grèce: mythes et réalités (en anglais) (pp. 524-537)*
En Grèce les débats sur la crise du système éducatif ont en général lieu pendant les campagnes électorales. L'auteur pose la question de savoir si une telle crise existe réellement. Pour ce faire il examine, après une rétrospective de l'histoire de l'éducation dans la Grèce moderne, les réformes éducatives depuis les années cinquante en relation avec le cadre conceptuel défini par deux tendances lourdes sur le plan international: 1. le développement éducatif lié à la théorie du capital humain; 2. les mesures en faveur de l'égalité des chances. Une attention particulière est accordée à l'éducation des femmes et aux relations entre l'enseignement (en particulier l'enseignement supérieur) et l'emploi. Pour ce qui est du développement de l'éducation et de l'égalité il ne peut être question de crise. Toutefois les réformes éducatives ont lieu sans avoir d'équivalent dans le secteur de l'emploi. A la suite du chômage de nombreux diplômés du supérieur on assiste à la création d'un „prolétariat académique". Il n'y a que de ce point de vue qu'on peut parler de crise éducative.

Průcha, Jan: *Écoles privées ou écoles publiques: une comparaison sur leur qualité en République Tchèque (en anglais) (pp. 538-549)*
Le présent article décrit un phénomène nouveau dans l'enseignement tchèque, à savoir l'émergence d'écoles privées depuis 1989. Actuellement les écoles privées opèrent à tous les niveaux du système éducatif à l'exception de l'enseignement supérieur. Le nombre des établissements a progressé énormément d'année en année à tel point que les écoles privées d'enseignement professionnel du second cycle accueillent environ 20% de l'ensemble des élèves de ce niveau. Néanmoins la qualité de l'enseignement transmis dans ces établissements privés reste incertaine. L'article présente les résultats de la première évaluation comparative des performances des élèves entre les lycées publics et les lycées privés. A notre grande surprise il est apparu que les établissements publics produisent de meilleurs résultats que leurs équivalents du secteur privé. L'auteur débat des raisons de cette différence en tenant compte aussi de quelques résultats empiriques obtenus dans l'évaluation d'établissements privés d'autres pays.

Résumés

Röhrs, Hermann: *Fondation et organisation de la „Section Allemande" de la „Ligue Internationale pour l'Éducation Nouvelle" (de 1921 à 1931): un chapitre important du mouvement de l'éducation nouvelle international (en allemand) (pp. 688-706)*
La présente étude interprète la riche histoire de la fondation de la section allemande comme un chapitre éminemment important du point de vue de la politique éducative. Faisant suite à une longue collaboration avec le „Ligue Internationale pour l'Éducation Nouvelle", ce n'est qu'en 1931 que réussit la création officielle de celle-ci sous la présidence de Erich Weniger, avec le soutien de Robert Ulrich. Quant à la représentation internationale elle fut assurée par l'ancien Ministre de l'Éducation de la Prusse, Carl Heinrich Becker.

Roth, Leo: *La Réforme comme moment de rupture dans l'évolution des universités allemandes: de l'universalité à la régionalisation (en allemand) (pp. 707-724)*
A l'exemple de l'histoire de l'université allemande on met en évidence que la Réforme a conduit de l'universalité à la régionalisation. Une étude comparative des analyses qualitatives et quantitatives des inter- et des intrasystémes démontre l'influence qu'a exercée l'histoire des idées sur l'institution et les conséquences qu'elle a eues, non seulement sur celle-ci, mais aussi sur les sciences et sur la vie politique et intellectuelle jusqu'à nos jours.

Ryba, Raymond: *Elaboration pratique de la Dimension Européenne en Éducation: la contribution du programme du Conseil de l'Europe (en anglais) (pp. 262-271)*
Cette contribution expose la conception, la mise en œuvre et le résultat du „Programme de ressources pédagogiques pour la dimension européenne", un grand programme européen d'élaboration curriculaire que l'auteur a mené pour le Conseil de l'Europe, faisant partie du programme „Un enseignement secondaire pour l'Europe" et qui s'est achevé récemment.

Schiff, Bernhard: *Le Lycée Classique Orthodoxe de Moscou (en allemand) (pp. 550-558)*
A la suite de l'effondrement de l'Union Soviétique, les objectifs éducatifs communistes ont perdu toute valeur. La création du Lycée Classique Orthodoxe de Moscou en septembre 1990 constitue une tentative de fonder l'enseignement scolaire sur de nouvelles valeurs. L'association laïque „Radonež" en est le fondateur et le soutien financier. Ce nouveau lycée se veut un établissement laïc dont les objectifs se réfèrent à la philosophie et à l'éthique du christianisme russe orthodoxe. De telles tentatives n'ont existé dans la Russie prérévolutionnaire qu'au niveau de l'enseignement primaire.

Smolicz, J. J.: Politique d'éducation linguistique dans des contextes plurilingues: l'Australie et les Philippines (en anglais) (pp. 402-413)
L'évolution de la politique d'éducation linguistique depuis la Seconde Guerre Mondiale est examinée en Australie et aux Philippines, en réponse à la diversité ethnique de leurs populations et du changement de statut politique de celle-ci. L'analyse révèle que l'Australie a abandonné sa politique unidirectionnelle d'assimilation linguistique en donnant aux minorités l'occasion d'étudier leur langue dans le cadre scolaire. Le développement opposé aux Philippines montre que l'adoption d'une langue nationale unique dans un pays plurilingue a conduit à éliminer toutes les langues indigènes du curriculum scolaire. Les résultats démontrent toutefois que l'existence de communautés linguistiques à base régionale a permis de préserver le pluralisme linguistique philippin sous forme de langues orales vernaculaires en opposition à la situation australienne où la dispersion des groupes linguistiques minoritaires et l'absence de communautés territoriales a contrecarré les efforts éducatifs destinés à assurer l'établissement effectif de langues autres que l'anglais.

Stephan, Werner: Enseignants et société: une comparaison internationale (en allemand) (pp. 414-425)
La présente contribution esquisse les conditions de travail des enseignants en Pologne, en Allemagne, en Angleterre, aux Etats-Unis et au Canada. Sous la pression d'intérêts politiques et économiques leur niveau de vie s'est détérioré et le prestige des enseignants a diminué. La tendance à la dévalorisation professionnelle des enseignants est particulièrement nette dans les pays anglo-saxons et mène en germe à une prolétarisation de la fonction enseignante.

Süssmuth, Rita: La responsabilité conjointe de la politique et des sciences de l'éducation comparées face à une société de l'éducation à visage humain (en allemand) (pp. 272-281)
La politique et les sciences assument une responsabilité commune face aux défis globaux. L'éducation et la formation sont les clés du succès dans l'accès à une société cognitive. Les sciences de l'éducation comparées peuvent soutenir l'émergence d'un nouveau paradigme politique de la coopération transnationale. Dans la présente contribution on cherchera à l'illustrer dans le domaine de l'éducation des femmes, de l'éducation aux média et dans celui de la formation de la personnalité.

Suzuki, Shin'ichi: *Les changements dans les systèmes politiques et dans la réorganisation géopolitique de l'espace éducatif et leurs implications pour l'éducation comparée (en anglais) (pp. 143-151)*
Depuis la chute du mur de Berlin en 1989 les peuples ont assisté dans presque toutes les régions du globe à une recrudescence du nationalisme. Sur fond d'engouement religieux mêlé à une sensibilité accrue aux différences culturelles et ethnique, un nouveau type de recentrage sur l'état-nation a causé en de nombreux endroits des guerres civiles, de la violence politique et du terrorisme dans des sociétés en changement. On peut y voir un symptôme de l'absence de principes guidant la reconstruction sociopolitique des sociétés en question. Sur la toile de fond de ces luttes pour surmonter les désordres politiques, l'auteur entreprend de clarifier les contextes cachés des „problèmes éducatifs" en se plaçant du point de vue des changements géopolitiques dans la vie sociale. Il se penchera sur les changements liés aux nouveaux médias et sur les problèmes liés aux relations entre centre et périphérie. En conclusion il analysera la faisabilité d'une approche de profil dans les études comparatives.

Szymański, Mirosław S.: *L'éducation à la démocratie dans le gouvernement autonome des élèves de la Deuxième République Polonaise (de 1918 à 1939) (en allemand) (pp. 725-739)*
On partira de l'hypothèse que deux œuvres de portée mondiale – le „Schule und Charakter" (École et caractère) de Friedrich Wilhelm Foerster et „L'autonomie des écoliers" d'Adolphe Ferrières – ont joué un rôle-clé dans la naissance et l'élaboration d'une théorie et d'une pratique de gouvernement autonome des élèves au cours de la Deuxième République Polonaise entre 1918 et 1939. En se référant aux deux modèles concurrents de l'autogestion des élèves – le „monarchiste", d'une part, et le „démocratique", d'autre part – on présentera ensuite les deux phases de l'évolution historique de la théorie et de la pratique de l'autogestion scolaire. Au-delà, la présente contribution tente de faire une présentation idéalisée et typique en répondant aux questions suivantes: comment l'autogestion a-t-elle été introduite dans les écoles? A quelles tâches a-t-elle dû faire face? Quelles formes d'organisation a-t-elle pris? Quelle importance quantitative a-t-elle eu?

Tedesco, Juan Carlos: *Le renouveau de l'éducation comparée (pp. 152-160)*
Les changements socio-économiques, culturels et politiques actuels provoquent une révision du programme de recherche et des méthodes en matière d'éducation comparée. Les nouveaux thèmes peuvent se classer en trois catégories principales: le processus de socialisation, le développement cognitif et le débat sur les finalités de l'éducation. Ce

nouveau programme implique l'adoption de méthodes qui permettent l'analyse de ces nouvelles dimensions, selon une approche interdisciplinaire.

Teichler, Ulrich: *Les recherches comparatives sur l'enseignement supérieur (en allemand) (pp. 161-172)*
Les recherches comparatives sur l'enseignement supérieur connaissent un regain d'intérêt en Europe en particulier du fait d'une coopération internationale en plein essor. Les projets qui sont clairement structurés sur le plan théorique négligent toutefois souvent la complexité de l'objet abordé. Les moyens financiers suffisants ne sont le plus souvent consacrés qu'aux questions trop pratiques. Les barrières linguistiques sont un obstacle tout autant que le manque de connaissance du terrain, que des conceptions et des habitudes de travail divergentes dans les équipes internationales. Des résultats intéressants ne peuvent être obtenus qu'à condition de formuler des projets ouverts capables d'intégrer des phénomènes multiples et de procéder en même temps à des reformulations en cas de surprises et d'expériences inattendues.

Tenorth, Heinz-Elmar: *Science de l'éducation et sociologie (en allemand) (pp. 740-756)*
La science de l'éducation et la sociologie constituent aujourd'hui des disciplines autonomes, distinctes entre elles grâce à leurs théories tout en étant comparables au plan de leurs méthodes. Le présent article propose à titre exemplaire de soumettre à la discussion la constitution de cette différence à partir de thèmes communs. Pour ce faire on traitera de façon historique et on s'appuiera de manière critique tout aussi bien sur des indicateurs thématiques dans l'élaboration théorique, en partant du problème du groupe d'apprentissage, que surtout sur l'attribution des chaires d'enseignement pendant la République de Weimar.

Tomiak, Janusz: *Rétrospective et prospective: le système éducatif dans l'Europe du Centre-Est à la veille du XXIe siècle (en anglais) (pp. 426-436)*
Les systèmes éducatifs de l'Europe du Centre-Est sont soumis actuellement à des bouleversements fondamentaux. Ils sont en train de passer d'un modèle de contrôle rigide, de planification centrale et d'uniformité à un système ouvert, libéral et plus diversifié. Cela ne peut se faire en peu de temps. La démocratisation et la modernisation éducative peuvent s'accomplir plus rapidement en Europe du Centre-Est si l'aide occidentale est disponible sans atermoiements et de façon efficace. Il est tout aussi important que les gouvernements concernés prennent conscience que l'éducation est un investissement essentiel et lui accordent en conséquence une plus grande importance dans les priorités nationales.

Tulasiewicz, Witold: *L'éducation mise en vente: les récents développements au Royaume-Uni (en anglais) (pp. 559-571)*
Le présent article fait suite à l'analyse que l'auteur a faite de l'évolution du système éducatif du Royaume-Uni à la suite de la prise du pouvoir par les Conservateurs en 1979 et dont deux écrits antérieurs ont déjà été publiés dans le „Zeitschrift für internationale erziehungs- und sozialwissenschaftliche Forschung". L'accueil enthousiaste réservé à la politique économique du libre marché par l'administration a été transféré aux prestations de service dans le secteur éducatif. On débattra ici des avantages et des inconvénients de cette politique et de son adéquation pour les services publics en faisant référence à des exemples tirés de la législation récente pour montrer les modifications importantes de la pratique qui en découlent.

Van daele, Henk: *Éducation comparée et éducation internationale: problèmes linguistiques (pp. 173-181)*
L'éducation comparée est un champ d'étude difficile entre autres à cause des problèmes linguistiques qui s'y présentent. Trois considérations s'imposent: 1. les spécialistes en éducation comparée doivent être multilingues; 2. les noms des écoles, des diplômes, etc., sont difficiles à traduire; il faut les considérer comme des noms propres dont la traduction est proscrite; 3. en Europe, on a besoin d'un glossaire multilingue univoque pour la terminologie de l'éducation et de la formation.

Vorbeck, Michael: *La recherche en éducation et notamment l'éducation comparée en Europe – pour l'Europe (en allemand) (pp. 282-297)*
La présente contribution donne une vue d'ensemble de l'évolution de la recherche en éducation et de l'éducation comparée en Europe depuis les années soixante: la naissance des grands instituts de recherche dans les différents états et, parallèlement à cela, l'engagement tout particulier du Conseil de l'Europe dans ce domaine. Par ailleurs, on mettra en lumière les activités d'autres organismes internationaux (UNESCO, OCDE, Union Européenne, etc.). Dans ce contexte, on fera référence dans les cas en question à l'engagement de Wolfgang Mitter et de l'Institut Allemand de Recherche Pédagogique Internationale. Une évaluation de ce qui a été réalisé, mais aussi de ce qui ne l'a pas été, fera suite à cette présentation et on terminera en énonçant des revendications en faveur des activités nécessaires sur le plan national et international.

Welch, Anthony R.*: Les choses se décomposent: la désintégration, les universités et le déclin des disciplines. Une problématisation de l'éducation comparée à une époque incertaine (en anglais) (pp. 182-191)*
Dans le présent article on analysera la situation actuelle et les perspectives de l'éducation comparée à la lumière du climat de fin de siècle qui règne sur le plan social, économique et intellectuel. Le positivisme confiant de l'éducation comparée de l'après-guerre a cédé la place à des incertitudes économiques, pédagogiques et intellectuelles auxquelles celle-ci se doit de répondre si elle veut survivre et prouver son utilité dans un contexte de restrictions budgétaires.

Wilson, David N.*: Le système d'alternance allemand de formation professionnelle: une étude comparative de l'influence sur la politique et la pratique de formation dans d'autres pays (en anglais) (pp. 437-448)*
La présente étude examine le système d'alternance allemand du point de vue des autres nations intéressées par l'adoption et l'adaptation de ce „modèle". Etant donné que celui-ci fait figure de solution éventuelle aux problèmes de formation dans les pays développés et ceux en voie de développement, l'étude examine les réalités, les mythes et les malentendus qu'on peut trouver dans la littérature à ce sujet et dans les systèmes de formation qui prétendent avoir adopté ce „modèle". On se penchera sur les composantes législatives, gouvernementales, organisationnelles et fonctionnelles du système et on les reliera aux conditions présentes en Allemagne. On étudiera la perception de différents auteurs favorables à l'adoption de ce „modèle" afin de déterminer en quoi on peut considérer ce „modèle" comme attrayant et adéquat pour la formation technique et professionnelle de ces nations. On analysera l'adoption réussie du système d'alternance à Singapour et aussi l'intérêt d'Israël. Enfin, on mettra en évidence les raisons de l'échec de ce „modèle" à Sri Lanka.

Wulf, Christoph*: Mimesis de l'autre: approches de l'altérité (en allemand) (pp. 192-206)*
L'autre joue un rôle fondamental dans les questions éducatives. Dès lors que l'éducation touche à l'approche et au traitement d'objets, à des contextes et à des personnes étrangers dans un premier temps, le questionnement de l'autre dans les questions éducatives est incontournable. A la suite de la globalisation des contextes de vie et des exigences politiques, économiques et culturelles nécessaires liées à l'avènement de l'Union Européenne, l'éducation est devenue une tâche interculturelle. Pour être à la hauteur de celle-ci, la rencontre et le débat avec l'autre s'imposent comme un défi nécessaire au maintien et à la transformation de notre propre culture.

Yûki, Makoto: La structure juridique de l'administration scolaire au Japon (en allemand) (pp. 572-580)

Le système éducatif japonais a connu de profonds bouleversements après 1945 en passant d'un système administratif centralisé, lié aux prérogatives de l'Empereur, à un système défini par des lois votés par un parlement et au sein duquel les intérêts régionaux restent pris en compte. Les caractéristiques principales de la nouvelle administration scolaire sont les suivantes: des compétences nettement plus limitées du Ministère de l'Éducation en tant qu'organe central ainsi que des commissions scolaires régionales indépendantes par rapport à l'administration générale.